A Panoramic View of the Song Dynasty Through the Lens of Shipbuilding Industry

Chunyan Huang

A Panoramic View of the Song Dynasty Through the Lens of Shipbuilding Industry

上海人民出版社

Springer

Chunyan Huang
East China Normal University
Shanghai, China

Translated by
Wenghui Zhang
Jiangsu Normal University
Xuzhou, Jiangsu, China

Jiaoyao Zhang
Freelancer
Xuzhou, Jiangsu, China

Xiaohong Shen
Jiangsu Normal University
Xuzhou, Jiangsu, China

Translation Proofreader
Patrick Thomas
University of Central Arkansas
Conway, USA

ISBN 978-981-97-6127-2 ISBN 978-981-97-6128-9 (eBook)
https://doi.org/10.1007/978-981-97-6128-9

Jointly published with Shanghai People's Publishing House
The print edition is not for sale in China (Mainland). Customers from China (Mainland) please order the print book from: Shanghai People's Publishing House.
ISBN of the Co-Publisher's edition: 978-7-208-14319-7

This project is sponsored by Chinese Fund for the Humanities and Social Sciences. (Project No. 21WZSB030)

This Springer imprint is published by the registered company Springer Nature Singapore Pte Ltd.
The registered company address is: 152 Beach Road, #21-01/04 Gateway East, Singapore 189721, Singapore

Preface

This study focuses on the shipbuilding industry, one of the pillar "heavy industries" in China before modern times (B. Li 2010:174–210),[1] which developed unprecedentedly during the Song Dynasty and had significant effects on social operation and development. It offers a comprehensive analysis of how shipbuilding interacted with technology, economy, social structures, and military development from a historical perspective. In ancient China, agriculture served as the foundation of the country, while the handicraft industry played a secondary role in social and economic growth. However, certain important technologies and industries played a crucial role in social, economic, and civilizational progress. A prime example is the invention and application of paper-making and printing technology, which revolutionized knowledge production, preservation, and dissemination, greatly advancing Chinese civilization.

As the primary mode of transportation in ancient China, the use of ships had profound effects on the economy, transportation, military affairs, beliefs, and social life during the Song Dynasty, and its impact continued beyond that era. Therefore, gaining a comprehensive understanding of these impacts requires studying from multiple perspectives, rather than focusing solely on technological, economic, social, or military history.

Several factors contributed to the booming shipbuilding industry in the Song Dynasty. First, the development of the commodity economy reached its second peak in ancient China, leading to further market prosperity and opening up. Additionally, the Song Dynasty's economic center shifted southward, resulting in unprecedented economic development in the lower reaches of the Yangtze River. Third, the introduction of more policies for overseas trade and flourishing maritime trade contributed to the industry's growth. Fourth, the defense of the Yangtze River and coastal areas played a vital role in frontier security and even the survival of the Southern Song Dynasty. Given the transportation conditions of ancient times, ships

[1] Li Bozhong holds that shipbuilding industry was one of the most important sectors in the heavy industry before modern times, and in the Ming and Qing Dynasties, shipbuilding industry was the largest department with the most advanced technology and the most concentrated capital, standing outing of all the sectors of heavy industries.

were the largest and most economical means of transportation. Domestic trade, official grain transportation, official and private travel, and maritime trade in the Song Dynasty heavily relied on ships. In such circumstances, both the scale and core technologies of shipbuilding greatly advanced. Particularly, the Southern Song Dynasty, having lost its coal and iron production bases in the north, saw only the shipbuilding industry continue to grow among the heavy industry sectors focusing on manufacturing means of production, while other sectors declined (J. Ge 2012: 238). In the Song Dynasty, 20,000 warships participated in battles on the Yangtze River. The coastal prefectures of Mingzhou, Wenzhou, and Taizhou in Liangzhe East Province alone had nearly 20,000 registered civilian ships, although this number was smaller than that of Fujian Province. The Song Dynasty implemented technologies such as watertight compartments and pedal wheel shipbuilding, marking unprecedented changes in the industry.

The comprehensive and profound influence of the shipbuilding industry on the society of the Song Dynasty is incomparable to that of previous dynasties. While the capital of the Northern Song Dynasty was Kaifeng, a northern city, its development relied heavily on southeast grain transportation. The Southern Song Dynasty could be aptly described as "a nation on ships." In terms of military affairs, the pivotal role played by water transportation was crucial to the rise and fall of the Song Dynasty, given its impact on national security. Economically, thriving commercial logistics and official grain transportation heavily relied on ships. In terms of social life, ships served as important means of travel and livelihood for people in the lower reaches of the Yangtze River. Compared to previous dynasties, a significantly larger population lived on ships during the Song Dynasty, giving rise to new social dynamics. The importance of ships as a mode of transportation in the society of the Song Dynasty cannot be overstated. They played a vital role equivalent to the functions of automobiles, trains, and airplanes in modern times. A life without ships in the Song Dynasty would be akin to today's world without automobiles, trains, and airplanes—a concept that is unfathomable to us today.

Whether conducting a comprehensive study on the significant influence of ships on the Song Dynasty society or examining the development of the shipbuilding industry, it is imperative to consider the Song Dynasty's economy, society, and military. To thoroughly analyze the development of shipbuilding in the Song Dynasty and its societal impact, research must be undertaken from the perspectives of technological history, economic history, social history, and military history. Pedal wheel ships serve as an illustrative example. During the Southern Song Dynasty, they were widely utilized for military purposes and became major warships in inland water battles. Scholars laud the application of this technology as a groundbreaking invention that preceded Europe by approximately 400 years, labeling it a technological revolution (Needham 1986: 262; F. Xi 2000:131; S. Wu 1960).

When we examine the craftsmanship history, the extensive use of pedal wheel propulsion and its originality in shipbuilding are apparent. However, the core technology of pedal wheel ships, while innovative to some extent, was limited to military applications and did not find widespread use in other sectors of social economy, nor did it bring about fundamental changes to shipbuilding technology in the Song

Dynasty. Furthermore, the military application of pedal wheel ships dwindled over time, posing a thought-provoking problem that is challenging to address solely from the perspective of technological history.

In the field of institutional history research, scholars have recognized that the study of institutions cannot solely rely on textual sources, but must also incorporate investigations into existing systems' history. Consequently, research focus should be placed on the background and implementation of these systems. Similarly, when studying the history of technology, it is essential to move beyond a narrow technological lens and consider the social context and practical applications. This critique extends to previous studies on handicraft industries, including the shipbuilding industry, which have often overlooked these aspects.

The existing research on the shipbuilding industry in the Song Dynasty has mainly focused on technological history and economic history, but these perspectives have been approached separately, lacking integration. Technological history-based research has always been the central focus of shipbuilding studies. In the paper "Previous Studies about Traditional Ships in China (1962–2008)," Xi Longfei provides a review of previous research on traditional Chinese ships both domestically and internationally, primarily summarizing the academic progress in shipbuilding studies based on technological history and its research findings (F. Xi 2009). The research on technological history extensively examines ship types, structures, technical performance, manufacturing processes, raw materials for shipbuilding, accessory equipment, and so on (F. Xi 2000; F. Xi 2004; Needham 1986; X. Zhang 1991; Editorial Committee of Excavation Report of the Quanzhou Bay Song Dynasty Shipwreck Excavation 1975; Quanzhou Bay Song Dynasty Shipwreck Restoration Group and Fujian Quanzhou Shipyard 1975; *Quanzhouwan Songdai Haichuan Fajue Yu Yanjiu* 1987; W. Zhuang and J. Zhuang 1977; L. Xi and G. He 1978; Y. Yang 1982; L.Xi 1981; Tianjin Municipal Office of Cultural Relics 1983; W. Ni 1979). Scholars studying the history of technology have two clear advantages when examining the shipbuilding industry in the Song Dynasty. Firstly, they can establish the status of the Song's shipbuilding industry based on their long-term research into the development history of ancient Chinese shipbuilding, revealing the inheritance and innovation of the Song Dynasty's shipbuilding technology. Secondly, they possess expertise in using archaeological data, extensive experience in physical research, a strong understanding of ship structures and process technology, and have conducted detailed studies on the Song's ships excavated in Quanzhou, Ningbo, Tianjin, and other locations. However, current studies based on technological history have two shortcomings. Firstly, there has been insufficient comprehensive exploration of the relationship between the shipbuilding industry and the Song Dynasty's economy, society, and military, as well as the broader social background of the Song Dynasty. Secondly, existing research is limited to a few historical records within typical data sets, which are not comprehensive enough, resulting in a small and restricted number of cited historical records. These two shortcomings are interconnected.

Scholars in the field of dynastic history studies have primarily focused on the shipbuilding industry of the Song Dynasty from an economic history perspective, particularly emphasizing its grain transportation system. The studies on shipbuilding have mainly discussed the distribution patterns and management systems of shipyards, as well as various types of ships. They have also briefly touched upon topics such as raw materials, financing, and the sources of craftsmen (H. Feng 1957; Z. Wang 1975; Y. Shiba 1985; D. Xu 2006; X. Chen 1990; J. Wu 1999; Y. Tang 2008). Research on the relationship between ships and economic growth has primarily revolved around grain transportation. Scholars have conducted in-depth investigations into the grain transportation system, batch transportation personnel, ferries, and transit during the Song Dynasty (F. Chen 1991; F. Chen 1997; Y. Shiba 1997; J. Cao 2002; Y. Wang 2010). Additionally, their studies on *Riverside Scene at Qingming Festival* also focus on the boats on the Bianhe River and grain transportation (B. Zhou 1997; S. Chen 1997). However, these single-perspective studies still require systematic re-examination and exploration from multiple perspectives. The same applies to studies on the relationship between ships and the military, with a particular emphasis on pedal wheel ships (H. Feng 1957; Z. Wang 2006; D. Wang 1963; T. Qi 1987; J. Wang 1983; L. Lin 1982; S. Lin 1979), while other warships were briefly mentioned and indirectly linked to the study of naval forces and warfare in the Song Dynasty (G. Wang 2000; Z. Wang 1983; S. Sogabe 1993; B. Zhu 1994; Q. Wang 2004; D. Huang 2007). Overall, the studies in dynastic history have delved deeply into specific issues, but they lack a comprehensive exploration of the relationship between the shipbuilding industry and various aspects of Song Dynasty society. Furthermore, there is a need for research from the perspective of technological history.

This book is not dedicated to writing a history of shipbuilding but intends to examine the impact of shipbuilding on the economy, society, military, daily life, and religious beliefs of the Song Dynasty from a comprehensive perspective. It combines technological history, economic history, social history, and military history to provide a holistic understanding. In terms of the problems to be discussed, this book is based on fundamental aspects such as hydrological conditions of inland rivers, navigation modes, management regulations, public–private interaction, types of warships, methods of battles on rivers and the sea, defense systems on the Yangtze River and the sea, fleet personnel composition, the daily life of Southern Song people, and their beliefs.

As for the main topics to be discussed, this book does not focus on shipbuilding technology and the grain transportation system of the Song Dynasty, as these have already been extensively studied. Instead, it targets topics that have received little attention in previous researches. Regarding the research methods, the book examines how the shipbuilding industry influenced the life, economy, military, national defense, and even the rise and fall of the Song Dynasty from multiple perspectives. By scrutinizing the reasons for the development and delay of certain shipbuilding technologies in the Song Dynasty from a comprehensive perspective, it aims to contribute to the study of the history of ancient Chinese technology and the handicraft industry.

Shanghai, China Chunyan Huang

References

Cao, Jiaqi 曹家齐. 2002. *Songdai Jiaotong Guanli Zhidu Yanjiu* 宋代交通管理制度研究 [A Study on Traffic Management System in the Song Dynasty]. Kaifeng: Henan University Press.

Chen, Feng 陈峰. 1991. "Beisong Dongnan Caoyun Zhidu De Yanbian Jiqi Xingxian 北宋东南漕运制度的演变及其影响 [The Development of the Grain Transportation Law and its Influences in the Southeastern Region of the Northern Song]". *Hebei Academic Journal* 2.

Chen, Feng 陈峰. 1997. "Songdai Caoyun Yagang Renyuan Kaoshu 宋代漕运押纲人员考述 [Studies on the Grain Transportation Escorts in the Song Dynasty]". *Journal of Chinese Historical Studies* 1.

Chen, Xu 陈叙. 1990. "Songdai Zhejiang De Zaochuanye 宋代浙江的造船业 [Shipbuilding of Zhejiang in the Song Dynasty]". *Journal of Hangzhou Teachers College* 4.

Editorial Committee of Excavation Report of the Quanzhou Bay Song Dynasty Shipwreck Excavation 泉州湾宋代海船发掘报告编写组. 1975. "Quanzhouwan Songdai Haichuan Fajue Jianbao 泉州湾宋代海船发掘简报 [Report of the Quanzhou Bay Song Dynasty Shipwrecks]". *Cultural Relics* 10.

Feng, Hanyong 冯汉镛. 1957. "Chechuan Kao 车船考 [Studies on Pedal Wheel Ships]". *Journal of Literature, History and Philosophy* 9.

Feng, Hanyong 冯汉镛. 1957. "Tang Song Shidai De Zaochuanye 唐宋时代的造船业 [Shipbuilding Industry in the Tang and Song Dynasties]". *History Teaching* 10.

Ge, Jinfang 葛金芳. 2012. *Shehui Jingji Yu Duiwai Maoyi (Juan Xia)* 社会经济与对外贸易 (卷下) [Social Economy and Foreign Trade (Vol. 2)]. Collected in The Complete History of the Southern Song Dynasty 6. Shanghai: Shanghai Chinese Classics Publishing House.

Huang, Dehui 黄德辉. 2007. "Song Meng (Yuan) Zhanzheng Beijingxia De Nansong Shuijun 宋蒙 (元) 战争背景下的南宋水军 [A Study on the Navy of South Song Dynasty under the Background of Song-Mongolia (Yuan) War]". Master's diss., Sichuan University.

Joseph Needham 李约瑟. 1986. *Liyuese Wenji* 李约瑟文集 [A Collection of Joseph Needham's Essays]. Translated by Pan Jixing. Shenyang: Liaoning Science and Technology Publishing House.

Li, Bozhong 李伯重. 2000. Jiangnan De Zaoqi Gongyehua 江南的早期工业化 [Early Industrialization in the South of the Yangtze River]. Beijing: Social Sciences Academic Press (CHINA).

Lin, Lin 林琳. 1982. "Chechuan Daodi Shi Shui Faming De "车船"到底是谁发明的 [Who invented 'Pedal Wheel Ships']". *Academic Forum* 2.

Lin, Sheng 林声. 1979. "Zhongguo Gudai De 'Chechuan': Zhongguo Gudai Zaochuan Shiliao Huikao Zhiyi 中国古代的"车船":(中国古代造船史料汇考)之一 ["Pedal Wheel Ships"of Ancient China: One of the Collections of Historical Materials About Ancient Chinese Shipbuilding]". *Journal of Zhengzhou University* 1.

Ni, Wenjun 倪文俊. 1979. "Jiading Fengbang Songchuan Fajue Jianbao 嘉定封浜宋船发掘简报 [A Briefing on the Excavation of the Song Boat in the Fengbang River of Jiading County]". *Cultural Relics* 12.

Qi, Tao 齐涛. 1987. "Chechuan Bingfei Shiyu Yangyao 车船并非始于杨么 [Pedal Wheel Ships were Initially not Built by Yang Yao]". *Historical Research in Anhui* 4.

Quanzhou Bay Song Dynasty Shipwreck Restoration Group 泉州湾宋代海船复原小组, and Fujian Quanzhou Shipyard 福建泉州造船厂. 1975. "Quanzhouwan Songdai Haichuan Fuyuan Chutan 泉州湾宋代海船复原初探 [A Preliminary Study on Restoration of the Song Dynasty's Shipwreck Found in Quanzhou Bay]". *Cultural Relics* 10.

Quanzhouwan Songdai Haichuan Fajue Yu Yanjiu 泉州湾宋代海船发掘与研究 [Excavation and Studies on the Song Ships in the Quanzhou Bay]. Edited by Quanzhou Maritime Museum Fujian. 1987. Beijing: China Ocean Press.

Sogabe Shizuo 曾我部静雄. 1993. "Nansong De Shuijun 南宋的水军 [Southern Song Water Forces]". *Riben Xuezhe Yanjiu Zhonggushi Lun* 日本学者研究中国史论著选译 [Selected

Translation of the Essays on Chinese History of Japanese Scholars] 5. Beijing: Zhonghua Book Company.

Tang, Yong 唐勇, et al. 2008. "Songdai Ningbo Diqu De Zaochuanye 宋代宁波地区的造船业 [Shipbuilding of Ningbo Area in the Song Dynasty]". *Journal of Ningbo Institute of Education* 1.

Tianjin Municipal Office of Cultural Relics 天津市文物管理处. 1983. "Tianjin Jinghai Yuanmengkou Songchuan De Fajue 天津静海元蒙口宋船的发掘 [The Excavation of the Song Ship at Yuanmengkou Village, Jinghai County, Tianjin]". *Cultural Relics* 7.

Wang Qingsong 王青松. 2004. "Nansong De Haijun 南宋的海军 [The Navy of the Southern Song Dynasty]". Master's diss., Hebei University.

Wang, Guanzhuo 王冠倬. 2000. *Zhongguo Gudai Chuanpu* 中国古船图谱 [A Pictorial History of Ancient Chinese Boats]. Beijing: SDX Joint Publishing Company.

Wang, Jieyun 王界云. 1983. "Chechuan Zhizao Kaolue 车船制造考略 [Studies on the Making of Pedal Wheel Ships]". *Academic Monthly* 11.

Wang, Yunshang 王云裳. 2010. "Jianshu Songdai Caoyun Yu Wuzhi Yagang Duiwu Ji Zhouzu 简论宋代漕运与武职押纲队伍及舟卒 [Water Transport and Custody Staff of Military Officers and Soldiers]". *Journal of Shaoxing University* 1.

Wang, Zengyu 王曾瑜. 1975. "Tan Songdai De Zaochuanye 谈宋代的造船业 [On Shipbuilding in the Song Dynasty]". *Cultural Relics* 10.

Wang, Zengyu 王曾瑜. 1983. *Songchao Bingzhi Chutan* 宋朝兵制初探 [The Studies on the Military System of the Song Dynasty]. Beijing: Zhonghua Book Company.

Wang, Zengyu 王曾瑜. 2006. "Zhonggu gudai De Chechuan 中国古代的车船 [Pedal Wheel Ships in Ancient China]". "*Zizhu Bian* 锱铢编 [A Collection of *Wang Zengyu's Essays*]. Baoding: Hebei University Press."

Wu, Jingshan 吴景山. 1999. "Song Jin Yuan Shiqi Xibei De Zaochuanye Ji Hangyun Guanli 宋金元时期西北的造船业及航运管理 [Boat making and water transport System in the Northwest Area During the Song, Jin and Yuan Dynasties]". *Journal of Lanzhou University* 1.

Wu, Shimo 吴示模. 1960. "Shilun Zhongxiang Yangyao Qiyi Zai Lishishang De Zuoyong 试论钟相杨么起义在历史上的作用 [On the Historical Role of the Uprising of Zhong Xiang and Yang Yao]". *Journal of Historical Science* 3.

Xi, Longfei 席龙飞, et al. 1981. "Dui Ninbo Guchuan De Yanjiu 对宁波古船的研究 [A Study on Ningbo Junk of Song Dynasty]". *Journal of Wuhan University of Water Transportation Engineering* 2.

Xi, Longfei 席龙飞. 2000. *Zhongguo Zaochuanshi* 中国造船史 [A History of China Shipbuilding]. Wuhan: Hubei Education Press.

Xi, Longfei 席龙飞. 2004. *Zhongguo Kexue Jishushi (Jiaotong Juan)* 中国科学技术史 (交通卷) [The History of Science and Technology in China (Traffic Volume)]. Beijing: Science Press.

Xi, Longfei 席龙飞. 2009. "Zhongguo Chuantong Chuanbo Yanjiu Xianzhuang (1962–2008 Nian) 中国传统船舶研究现状 (1962–2008年) [Research Status of Traditional Chinese Ships (1962–2008)]". *The Chinese Journal for the History of Science and Technology* 3.

Xi, Longfei 席龙飞 and He Guowei 何国卫. 1978. "Quanzhouwan Chutu De Songdai Haichuan Jiqi Fuyuan Chidu De Tantan 对泉州湾出土的宋代海船及其复原尺度的探讨 [A Study on the Junk of Song Dynasty Excavated in Quanzhou Bay and its Original Dimensions to be Restored]". *Journal of Wuhan University of Technology* 2.

Xu, Dongsheng 徐东升. 2006. "Songdai Guanying Zaochuanchang De Yunzuo 宋代官营造船场的运作 [Operation of Government-Running Shipyards in the Song Dynasty]". *Journal of Southwest China Normal University*, No.5, 2006

Yang, You 杨槱. 1982. "Dui Quanzhouwan Songdai Haichuan Fuyuan De Jidian Kanfa 对泉州湾宋代海船复原的几点看法 [My Observations on the Restoration of Song Dynasty Sea Vessels in Quanzhou Bay]". *Journal of Maritime History Studies* 4.

Yoshinobu Shiba 斯波义信. 1985. "Song Yuan Shidai De Chuanbo 宋元时代的船舶 [Vessels in the Song and Yuan Dynasties]". Translated by Jing Hui. *Marine History Studies* 1.

Yoshinobu Shiba 斯波义信. 1997. *Songdai Shangyeshi Yanjiu* 宋代商业史研究 [A Study on the Business History of the Song Dynasty]. Translated by Zhuang Jinghui. Daoxiang Press.

Zhang, Xun 章巽. 1991. *Zhongguo Hanghai Kejishi* 中国航海科技史 [A History of Chinese Maritime Science and Technology]. Beijing: China Ocean Press.
Zhou, Baozhu 周宝珠. 1997. *Qingmingshanghetu Yu Qingmingshanghexue* 〈清明上河图〉与清明上河学 [Riverside Scene at Qingming Festival and the Studies on the Scroll]. Kaifeng: Henan University Press.
Zhu, Baoshu 朱保书. 1994. "Song Jin Chenjiadao Dahaizhan 宋金陈家岛大海战 [The Naval Warfare between Song and Jin on Chenjia Island]". *Journal of Kaifeng University* 1.
Zhuang, Weiji 庄为玑, and Zhuang Jinghui 庄景辉. 1977. "Quanzhou Songchuan Jiegou Fenxi 泉州宋船结构的历史分析 [An Analysis on the Structure of the Song Boat Unearthed in Quanzhou]". *Journal of Xiamen University* 4.

Contents

1 Shipbuilding Industry in the Song Dynasty 1
- 1.1 Geographical Distribution of Official Makers in the Song Dynasty 1
  - 1.1.1 The Official Shipbuilding in the Provinces of Jiangnan East and Jiangnan West 2
  - 1.1.2 The Official Shipyards in Liangzhe East and West Provinces and Jinghu South and North Provinces 6
  - 1.1.3 Official Shipyards in the Provinces of Fujian, Guangnan East and West, Huainan, Sichuan and the Provinces of North China 10
  - 1.1.4 Summary 15
- 1.2 Raw Materials and Costs for Shipbuilding in the Song Dynasty 16
  - 1.2.1 Major Raw Materials and Their Distribution 17
  - 1.2.2 The Auxiliary Materials for Shipbuilding and Their Sources 24
  - 1.2.3 The Costs of Ships in the Song Dynasty 28
  - 1.2.4 Summary 33
- 1.3 Load Capacities and Shapes and Sizes of Ships in the Song Dynasty 33
  - 1.3.1 Discussions on Lisheng (Deadweight Tonnage) and Liao (Load Capacity) 34
  - 1.3.2 The Deadweight Tonnage of Boats and Their Shapes and Structures in the Canals in the Song Dynasty 39
  - 1.3.3 The Deadweight Tonnage and Their Shapes and Structures of Inland River Boats 44
  - 1.3.4 The Deadweight Tonnage, Shapes and Structures of the Seagoing Boats in the Song Dynasty 49
  - 1.3.5 Summary 53

1.4 Estimated Number of Ships in the Song Dynasty ... 54
1.4.1 The Number of Cargo Transportation Ships in the Song Dynasty ... 55
1.4.2 The Number of Inland River Warships ... 59
1.4.3 The Number of the Seagoing Ships in the Song Dynasty ... 61
1.4.4 Summary ... 64
References ... 64

2 Hydrological Conditions and Navigation of Inland Rivers in the Song Dynasty ... 71
2.1 Navigation Modes and the System of Ports Along the Yangtze River in the Song Dynasty ... 71
2.1.1 Sails and Boat Trackers in the Yangtze River Navigation ... 71
2.1.2 Sailing Near the Bank or Going Through River Forks or Artificial Waterways ... 78
2.1.3 The Port System of the Yangtze River Navigation ... 85
2.1.4 Summary ... 96
2.2 Hydrological Conditions and Navigation of Canals in the Song Dynasty ... 97
2.2.1 An Overlook of the Canals in the Song Dynasty ... 97
2.2.2 The Weirs and Gates of Canals During the Song Dynasty ... 108
2.2.3 The Sails Lifting and Boats Towing ... 123
2.2.4 Summary ... 129
2.3 The Navigation Methods of Other Inland Rivers ... 130
2.3.1 Punt-Poles, Oars, Yulohs and Sails in Inland River Navigation ... 131
2.3.2 Boat Trackers and Towpaths in the Inland River Navigation ... 136
2.3.3 Summary ... 142
2.4 The Regulations on the Transportation of Horses in the Southern Song Dynasty—Discussions on the Costs of Water Transportation ... 143
2.4.1 The Methods and Routes of Horse Batch Transportation in Sichuan and Guangnan West Provinces ... 144
2.4.2 The Supportive Policies on the Composition and Assessment of Convoys of Horse Batch Transportation ... 148
2.4.3 Cost Sharing and Efficiency Guarantee of the Batch Horse Transportation ... 156
2.4.4 Summary ... 167
References ... 169

3 Seagoing Vessels and Voyages in the Song Dynasty 175
3.1 Crew Composition and Modes of Navigation 175
3.1.1 Crew Composition 175
3.1.2 Ocean Shipping Routes and Navigation Modes 181
3.1.3 Summary 191
3.2 An Examination of Offshore Routes in the Song Dynasty 192
3.2.1 The Offshore Routes North of Mingzhou 193
3.2.2 The Offshore Routes South of Mingzhou 200
3.2.3 Connections Among Offshore Routes, Oceangoing Routes, and Inland Waterways 206
3.2.4 Summary 214
3.3 Offshore Trade in the Song Dynasty 215
3.3.1 The Commodity Mix of Offshore Trade 215
3.3.2 Offshore Traders 226
3.3.3 The Policies on Offshore Trade Administration in the Song Dynasty 232
3.3.4 Summary 239
3.4 Shipwrecks and Salvation in the Song Dynasty 240
3.4.1 Historical Records About Shipwrecks in the Song Dynasty 241
3.4.2 Official Aid in Response to Shipwrecks 248
3.4.3 Summary 254
3.5 Ocean Knowledge and Imagery in the Song Dynasty 256
3.5.1 Sources and Dissemination of Ocean Sciences in the Song Dynasty 256
3.5.2 Construction of Oceanic Imagery in the Song Dynasty 264
3.5.3 Summary 275
References 276

4 Warships and Defense on the Yangtze River and the Sea in the Song Dynasty 283
4.1 Types of Warships and Ways of Battles on the Rivers and the Sea in the Song Dynasty 283
4.1.1 Shape, Structure and Function of Warships 284
4.1.2 Power Systems of Warships in the Song Dynasty 289
4.1.3 The Function and Deployment of the Song Warships 293
4.1.4 The Fighting Methods of the Navy in the Song Dynasty 301
4.1.5 Summary 306
4.2 The Pedal Wheel Ships in the Southern Song Dynasty and Their Historical Fate 307
4.2.1 The Debut of Pedal Wheel Boats and the Connotation of "Wheel" 307
4.2.2 The Entailment of "Pedal Wheel" 310

4.2.3 The Application and Evolution of Pedal Wheel Ships in the Southern Song Dynasty 315
4.2.4 Summary 324
4.3 Composition and Functions of the Defense System on the Yangtze River in the Southern Song Dynasty 325
4.3.1 The Situation of the River Defense in the Southern Song Dynasty 326
4.3.2 The Navy Deployment and Fortress Layout in the River Defense of the Southern Song Dynasty 332
4.3.3 The Piracy on the Yangtze River and the River Defense in the Southern Song Dynasty 339
4.3.4 Summary 344
4.4 The Composition and Functions of Coastal Defense System in the Southern Song Dynasty 345
4.4.1 Stations and Characteristics of the Northern Song's Coastal Defense 346
4.4.2 The Construction of River and Coastal Defense System in the Southern Song Dynasty 350
4.4.3 Functions of the Southern Song Dynasty's Coastal Defense 367
4.4.4 Summary 374
4.5 Piracy and Measures for Eradicating Pirates in the Southern Song Dynasty 375
4.5.1 Distribution and Composition of the Pirates in the Song Dynasty 376
4.5.2 Suppression of Pirates and Offering Amnesty and Enlistment to Pirates in the Southern Song Dynasty 387
4.5.3 Household Registration and Social Control of Coastal Residents 391
4.6 The Great Convenience of Water Transportation and the Rise and Fall of the Southern Song—A Study from the Perspective of Military History 395
4.6.1 The Standoff Between the Song Navy and the Jin Cavalry Forces 395
4.6.2 The Rising Water Forces of the Yuan Dynasty and the Collapse of the Southern Song Dynasty 403
4.6.3 Summary 411
References 412

5 Shipbuilding Industry and Social Life in the Song Dynasty 419
5.1 The Composition and Livelihood of Inland River Boatmen in the Song Dynasty with a Focus on Grain Transportation 419
5.1.1 The Quantity of Boatmen in the Song Dynasty 420
5.1.2 The Sources of Boatmen in the Song Dynasty 427

5.1.3 The Strata and Composition of Boatmen in the Song Dynasty 432
5.1.4 Boatmen's Work and Benefits in the Song Dynasty 438
5.1.5 Summary 444
5.2 Boats and the Daily Livelihood of Southerners in the Song Dynasty 445
5.2.1 The People Who Lived on Boats in the Song Dynasty 446
5.2.2 Boats and Fishing of the Southerners 450
5.2.3 Boats and the Trade and Entertainment of the Southerners 453
5.2.4 Summary 457
5.3 Water Travel in the Song Dynasty—From the Perspective of Officials' Business Journeys 458
5.3.1 Comparison on Speed of Travelling by Boat and by Land 458
5.3.2 The Choice of Travelling by Boat During the Whole Journey or Travelling by Both Water and Land 462
5.3.3 The Ways to Go on Boats 467
5.3.4 Activities on the Journey 471
5.3.5 Summary 481
5.4 Sacrificing Ceremonies of the Song People for Smooth Sailing 482
5.4.1 The Risks of Navigation in the Song Dynasty 482
5.4.2 Belief in Gods in Inland River Navigation 486
5.4.3 Deity Beliefs in Seafaring Activities in the Song Dynasty 497
5.5 The System of the Water Deities and Gods and Their Evolution in the Song Dynasty 503
5.5.1 The Constitution of the Song's Water Deities System 503
5.5.2 New Changes to the Original Beliefs in Water Deities in the Song Dynasty 509
5.5.3 Newly Created Deities to Protect Navigation in the Song Dynasty 520
5.5.4 Summary 525
5.6 The Ferry Operation and Management in the Song Dynasty 525
5.6.1 Establishment and Management of the Public Ferry 526
5.6.2 The Privately Contracted Public Ferry and the Management of Private Ferry 534
5.6.3 Charges of Ferry Boats 538
5.6.4 Summary 544
5.7 Management, Requisition and Recruitment of the Civilian Boats 546
5.7.1 Registration of the Civilian Boats 546
5.7.2 The Taxation System on Civilian Boats 550

5.7.3 Requisition and Recruitment of Civilian Boats 556
5.7.4 Summary 562
References 563

Postscript 573

Bibliography 575

Chapter 1
Shipbuilding Industry in the Song Dynasty

1.1 Geographical Distribution of Official Makers in the Song Dynasty

In the Song Dynasty, the great convenience of water transportation and its wide application ushered in a booming age of shipbuilding, evidenced by numerous shipbuilding yards, both official and private, scattered in the south and north regions of China. The development of the shipbuilding industry was limited by the accessibility of raw materials, the navigability of various bodies of water, and other natural conditions, such as the local availability of lumber. Previous studies discuss the geographical features of the shipbuilding industry and official shipyards. Zhang Jiaju broke the shipbuilding industry map into five regions: the northern region, and the regions of Huaizhe, Jingjiang, Min'guang and Xichuan, listing the official shipyards together with some examples (J. Zhang 2010: 337–42). Yoshinobu Shiba also listed the prefectures and military prefectures of shipbuilding in the Song Dynasty (Y. Shiba 1985). Xu Dongsheng and Ge Jinfang made further studies on the distribution features of official shipyards and the regulatory mechanisms and operation methods in the Song Dynasty (D. Xu 2006; J. Ge 2006: 154–69). Wu Jingshan and Tang Yong studied shipbuilding in Northwest China and Mingzhou in the Song Dynasty (J. Wu 1999; Y. Tang et al. 2008). Wang Zengyu discussed the shift from boats to warships for transporting grain in the Song Dynasty (Z. Wang 1975). Although the above mentioned studies roughly outline the geographical distribution of shipbuilding, they are too brief to provide sufficient details of the evolution of shipbuilding across the country. Expanding on these previous studies, this section discusses the distribution of official shipyards in greater detail.

C. Huang, *A Panoramic View of the Song Dynasty Through the Lens of Shipbuilding Industry*, https://doi.org/10.1007/978-981-97-6128-9_1

1.1.1 The Official Shipbuilding in the Provinces of Jiangnan East and Jiangnan West

In the Northern Song Dynasty, Jiangnan West Province was assigned the biggest task of building ships among all the official shipyards. In the late Tianxi Reign, the shipyards were scattered across the country with quotas for shipbuilding, which include Qianzhou (605 ships), Jizhou (525 ships) of Jiangnan West Province, Mingzhou (177 ships), Wenzhou (125 ships), Wuzhou (105 ships), Taizhou (126 ships) of Liangzhe East Province, Tanzhou (280 ships), Dingzhou (241 ships) of Jinghu South and North provinces, Chuzhou (87 ships) of Huainan East Province, Yegu of Fengxiang Municipality (600 ships) of Shaanxi Province, and Jiazhou (45 ships) of Sichuan Province (Z. Wang 1975).[1] In the annual total of 2916 ships, the production of Jiangnan West Province accounted for 39%, Shaanxi Province 20.5%, Liangzhe East Province 18.1%, Jinghu South and North provinces 17.9%, Huainan East Province 3%, and Sichuan 1.5%. Obviously, Jiangnan West Province dominated the manufacturing of ships, and Liangzhe East Province was the second important producer. The output of ships in Shaanxi Province went down with less demand for grain transportation vessels along the Yellow River. "In the fourth year of the Jiayou Reign, 300 ships were pulled out of use for the abolition of grain transportation via the Yellow River course" (Toqta 1977: 4252). The smaller number of Sichuan-made ships was due to a smaller demand for grain transportation along the Yangtze River, but as a matter of fact, the abundant timber supply allowed Sichuan to build more ships than Huainan provinces. Such is the general situation in shipbuilding of grain vessels in the early Song Dynasty, indicating the deployment of official manufacturers. In terms of grain vessel building, the most important manufacturers were located in the provinces of Jiangnan West, Liangzhe and Hu'nan. It was the same with the Southern Song Dynasty.

In the Northern Song Dynasty, Jiangnan West Province placed its major shipyards in Qianzhou, Jizhou and Hongzhou. In the first year of the Tianxi Reign (AD 1017), the chief of royal shipping division mentioned the fact of "dispatching newly-built ships from Hongzhou, Qianzhou and Jizhou to the state capital" (T. Li 2004: 2082). It was the same with the Southern Song Dynasty, as suggested by the description that "the official posts in charge of shipbuilding and shipyards were still kept there since the period of Emperor Taizu's Reign" (X. Li 2013:1824). Vessels for official grain transportation were routinely adapted from passenger ships in the counties of the eastern regions of the Yangtze River. Jiangnan West Province established shipyards in Hongzhou, Jizhou and Ganzhou. In the Shaoxing Reign of Emperor Gaozong, the above-mentioned three shipyards "managed to finish building a ship each day as a normal practice" (S. Xu et al. 2014, 6991). In the first year of the Qiandao Reign (AD 1165), "the official shipyard was moved to Longxing Municipality from Jizhou" and

[1] The *Anthology of Laws and Regulations of the Song Dynasty* incorrectly recorded Qianzhou as Chuzhou, and recorded the number of boats built in Dingzhou is 240. *A Full-Scale Textual Criticism on Ancient Systems and Regulations* incorrectly recorded the number of boat built in Wuzhou as 103. If these two sources are put together, the total number is consistent with the total of 2916 boats.

"later it was moved back." But Ganzhou and Jizhou still kept their shipyards (S. Xu et al. 2014: 7132, 7135). In the fifth year of the Chunxi Reign (AD 1178), it was suggested by some to stop building ships since grain vessels made a smaller margin than passenger ships, and to instead replace the once profitable shipbuilding industry with the spinning industry. Thus, the profits earned from spinning could be used for ship rentals (B. Zhou 1990). However, this measure could not last long. Later, in the 10th year of the Chunxi Reign (AD 1183), the governor of Jiangnan West Province submitted his proposal to the emperor "for cutting one hundred ships in production and was approved to implement the imperial decree since September 27th of the fifth year of the Qiandao Reign. And the two prefectures were ordered to build 400 ships only" (S. Xu et al. 2014: 7136). In the 10th year of the Chunxi Reign (AD 1183), shipyards resumed their production in Ganzhou and Jizhou municipalities. Apart from the above mentioned three municipalities, the military prefectures also undertook the tasks of shipbuilding. For example, Zheng Siyong, the mayor of Xunzhou, once mentioned that "following the practice of county-chief to supervise the counties in shipbuilding, they could ensure the service of passengers sailing on the rivers or lakes" (X. Li 2013: 3186). Fuzhou once was ordered by the imperial court "to build 22 warships within five months" and "20 pedal-driven ships by copying the court's authorized models." Moreover, the tailored shipbuilding was not restricted to Fuzhou Prefecture. "More prefectures got engaged in such tailored ships" (Z. Wang, n.d.). In the sixth year of the Chunxin Reign (AD 1179) the emperor decreed that "Jiangnan West military prefectures should build 100 horse-carrying ships by copying the authorized model at the section of rivers where lumber is good and available for ships" (S. Xu et al. 2014: 7136).

The shipyards in Jiangnan West Province built both grain vessels and war ships. The tasks of building vessels for transporting grains were mainly designated to six provinces in the southern region of Yangtze River. In the fourth year of the Zhenghe Reign (AD 1114), Emperor Huizong issued an imperial decree to Liangzhe provinces to build 300 ships with a load capacity of 9000 kg by each shipyard; while each shipyard in Jiangnan East and West provinces, as well as those in Jinghu South and North provinces, was required to build 300 ships with a load capacity of 15,000 kg (S. Xu et al. 2014: 7124). Jiangnan West Province was the major producer of grain vessels. The threefold State Finance Commission in charge of salt, iron, and taxation ordered that "ships made in Qianzhou and Hongzhou were taken over to transport grains, currency and silk" (S. Xu et al. 2014: 7122). The Southern Song Dynasty followed the same pattern of shipbuilding and its application. In the second year of the Jianyan Reign (AD 1128), Jiangnan East and West, and Jinghu South and North provinces were ordered to build 1000 ships for transporting grains. These tasks were designated to Tanzhou, Hengzhou, Qianzhou and Jizhou (S. Xu et al. 2014: 7125). In the 10th year of the Chunxi Reign (AD 1183), Mr. Li Changtu, Minister of Ministry of Works, said that "the ships for transporting grains were built in the seven prefectures of Liangzhe, Hu'nan, Jiangnan West provinces" (S. Xu et al. 2014: 7136). To be specific, they included Wenzhou and Mingzhou of Liangzhe Province, Tanzhou and Hengzou of Hunan Province, Qianzhou, Jizhou and Hongzhou of Jiangnan West Province. They were the major producers of grain vessels. In the Southern Song Dynasty, the central government "spent the sacrifices of grains of 27 million kilograms and the annual taxation of one million strings of copper coins on building ships in Ganzhou and Jizhou" (B. Zhou 1990).

In the Northern Song Dynasty, Jinming Lake was used to exercise sailors, but was restored to be a public garden for entertainment after pacifying the rebellion in the south, where the dragon boats were built in Jizhou's shipyard. In the first year of the Dazhongxiangfu Reign (AD 1008), ten dragon boats were made there "to exercise sailors to safeguard the state capital" (T. Li 2004). In the Southern Song Dynasty, Jiangnan West Province was the major producer of war ships. In order to pacify Yang Yao Rebellion, the pedal-driven ships built for this purpose, and the looted boats, were sent to Jiangnan West Province for refurbishment. However, the famous poet Ye Mengde believed that it was not necessary to mend all the looted boats "as there were enough built by the shipyards in Qianzhou and Jizhou" (M. Ye 2002). After conquering Yang Yao Rebellion, the building of pedal-driven ships reached a new high. Jiangnan West Province was the major manufacturer of such ships. In the fifth year of the Shaoxing Reign (AD 1135), Wu Shen reported and narrated to the emperor the demerits of making warships. He said, "the boats built today in Nanchang followed Yang Yao's model", and "the model adopted in other prefectures followed the craftsmanship in Nanchang." (S. Yang et al. 1990) The best practice of building pedal-driven ships in Jiangnan West Province secured the province as a vital maker of warships. Fuzhou was ordered to build warships and 20 pedal-driven ships. Moreover, the military prefectures along the river courses undertook the task of building ships for carrying horses for battle, benefiting from the rich timbers in Jiangnan West Province.

The above-mentioned vessels for grains in Jiangnan East Province were mainly rented from commercial ships as the province was not a base for building such vessels. However, Jiangnan East Province also undertook some of these tasks. For example, in the fourth year of the Shaoxing Reign (AD 1134), "Liangzhe, Jiangnan East and Jiangnan West provinces were also required to build 200 ships each for transporting grains" (S. Xu et al. 2014:7129). In the Southern Song Dynasty, as municipalities in the South Region of the Yangtze River evolved into vital towns for defense, they began to build war ships. Jiankang Municipality was one of them, so it set up a post in charge of garrison sailors along the Yangtze River and founded the Longwan Shipyard (Y. Zhou 1990: 1698). In the third year of the Chunxi Reign (AD 1176), Guo Gang, Marshall of Jiankang Municipality's navy, petitioned to the emperor that a new model of multiple-paddle ships should be built to make compensation for the pedal-driven ships and warships which were ruined or damaged in battles. Emperor Xiaozong required navy commanders to mend the damaged pedal-driven ships right away rather than replacing them with multiple-paddle ships, and he furthermore ordered the construction of over 100 multiple-paddle ships for later use (S. Xu et al. 2014: 7135). In the tenth year of the Chunxi Reign (AD 1183), the administrator of Jiankang Municipality "managed to build 90 pedal-driven ships and warships" (S. Xu et al. 2014: 7137). Between the ninth year of the Chunyou Reign (AD 1249) and the first year of the Xianchun Reign (AD 1265), speedboats, multiple-paddle ships, four-oar boats, seagoing vessels and boats for carrying horses were built and put into use in the Jiankang Municipality navy, with various warships totaling 2287 (Y. Zhou 1990 1982–83).

However, the timbers for ships in Jiankang Municipality were mostly purchased from other places, or Jiangnan West Province was entrusted to build ships. In the fourth year of the Qiandao Reign (AD 1168), 100 thousand strings of copper coins were granted to "the military prefectures in Jiankang Municipality navy for purchasing planks. Then shipyards established by Jiankang Municipality built many 12-paddle warships with a load capacity of 12,000 kg each" (Y. Zhou 1990: 1734). In the fourth year of the Jiatai Reign (AD 1204), the marshal of all generals in Jiankang Municipality, "asked his under institutions to buy large logs for building ships in the upper range of the Yangtze River with money" (S. Xu et al. 2014: 7139). In the third year of the Baoyou Reign (AD 1255), Ma Guangzu served as the governor of military prefectures along the Yangtze River, and "granted large sum of money and ordered Guo Jun, his under navy officer, to purchase timbers and co-built ships in Jizhou's shipyard. Later, they produced 50 four-oar seagoing vessels with a load capacity of 9000 kg, and 50 four-oar Picket ships with a capacity of 7500 kg (known as Fuyang Boats)". This project was supervised by Jizhou administrators. In the first year of the Xianheng Reign (AD 1265), Ma Guangzu ordered his officials to buy timbers in Jiangnan West Province for the third time and built 300 Picket boats for carrying horses. In the following year, he issued the fourth decree to build 21 Fuyang Boats with a load capacity of 9000 kg, together with 21 swift warships. In the third year of the Xianchun Reign (AD 1267), for the fifth time, Jin Quan, "the local administrator, was entrusted to build 100 Fuyang Boats with a capacity of 6000 kg, together with 100 pedal-driven boats and 100 Picket boats" (Y. Zhou 1990: 1983, 1985).

Apart from Jiankang Municipality, warships were also built in Chizhou, Jiangzhou and Taipingzhou prefectures. In the 32nd year of the Shaoxing Reign (AD 1162), the emperor laid a decree to military prefectures for building warships. The imperial edict required that "in building warships, Jiankang Municipality should spend 40 thousand strings of 1000 coins, Zhenjiang Municipality 30 thousand strings, Jiangyin, Taiping, Chizhou, Jiangzhou, Ezhou, Jingnan municipalities 20 thousand strings each". "Local governors, navy marshals, and military generals, together with craftsmen to build warships" (S. Xu et al. 2014: 7131). In the fifteenth year of the Chunxi Reign (AD 1188), Li Sixiao, vice marshal of the palace garrison in Chizhou, got promoted for his contribution in building 27 magnificent warships. In the third year of the Jiatai Reign (AD 1203), Qin Shifu became known for building swift iron-clad warships and plated boats. The emperor issued an imperial decree "to increase the production of Chizhou model" and promoted such warships to all the navies along the Yangtze River (S. Xu et al. 2014: 7137–38).

1.1.2 The Official Shipyards in Liangzhe East and West Provinces and Jinghu South and North Provinces

In the later years of the Tianxi Reign, the central government made a list of shipbuilding tasks for official shipyards, situated in Mingzhou (177 ships), Wenzhou (125 ships), Wuzhou (105 ships) and Taizhou (126 ships). *The Record of Military* in the seventh volume of *Baoqing Period Chronicles of Siming* mentioned, "the municipalities of Hangzhou, Mingzhou, Wenzhou and Taizhou were authorized to recruit soldiers for shipyards." This is evidence for the existence of the Hangzhou shipyard. Apart from the above-mentioned municipalities, others also built ships. When Zhang Jing acted as the mayor of Chuzhou Municipality, "he attempted to build large boats and his underlings didn't know how to do so. In order to solve this problem, they enlarged the parameters of a small boat by tenfold times" (Toqta 1977: 11,696). Such methods were also adopted by the shipyards of Mingzhou and Wenzhou, whose shipyards had undergone ups and downs. In the *County Journal (Vol. 3)* of *Baoqing Period Chronicles of Siming (Vol. 3)*, a paper described the evolution of shipyards in Mingzhou and Wenzhou. It said that "in the middle of the Huangyou Reign, shipyards did exist in Wenzhou and Mingzhou. In the second year of the Daguan Reign, the manufacturing operations were merged into Mingzhou shipyard; and the timber purchasing was charged by Wenzhou. That explains why there were two officials in charge of manufacturing in Mingzhou and two officials in charge of timber purchasing in Wenzhou". In the first year of the Zhenghe Reign (AD 1112), Mingzhou resumed shipbuilding and timber purchasing, with two officials in charge of such businesses. In the seventh year of the Zhenghe Reign (AD 1117), Mayor Lou Yi of Mingzhou asked "to move shipyards to Mingzhou for the convenience of craftsmen in building ambassadorial ships to visit the three tribes of ancient Korea. Later, the shipyards were moved back to Wenzhou again. In the seventh year of the Xuanhe Reign, shortly after the merging of shipyards in Liangzhe Province into Mingzhou and Wenzhou, they were further moved to Tonghui Town of Huizhou". In the fifth year of the Shaoxing Reign (AD 1135), ministers pointed out that "the administrative pattern and officials in charge of shipyards in the municipalities of Wenzhou, Mingzhou, Qianzhou and Jizhou, were well kept from their origin onward." (X. Li 2013: 1824)

Mingzhou and Wenzhou in the Liangzhe East Province had long been undertaking the tasks of building grain vessels for sailing in the inland rivers. In the late Tianxi Reign, the above-mentioned two provinces were assigned the tasks of building 177 and 125 ships respectively. In the fourth year of the Zhenghe Reign (AD 1114), Liangzhe East Province was ordered to build 300 flat-bottomed vessels with a capacity of 18,000 kg, which were used for transporting grains (S. Xu et al. 2014: 7124). In the Southern Song Dynasty, Wenzhou also undertook such tasks of building grain vessels. Wang Zhiwang mentioned "the outbreak of a big fire ruined four uncompleted grain ships in the Southern Town Shipyard." (Z. Wang 1990a, b, c) In the first year of the Shaoxing Reign (AD 1131), shipyards in Wenzhou "had the quota of building 340 cargo boats exclusively for its own province" (S. Xu et al. 2014: 7124). Lou Yao said, "in the Southern Song Dynasty, shipyards in Wenzhou built 100 grain vessels each year". In the first year of the Chunxi Reign (AD 1174), shipbuilding cuts were made to set quotas separately for Liangzhe provinces. The initial quota for Wenzhou was 120 vessels, and was reduced to 50. The quota for Wenzhou's grain ships was reduced to below 100. In the middle and late Southern Song Dynasty, "the reduction in timber and passengers caused a drastic decline in shipbuilding to only ten vessels a year" (S. Xu et al. 2014: 7135; Y. Lou 1990).

As the shipbuilding bases, Mingzhou and Wenzhou undertook the tasks of "building ambassadorial ships to Goryeo (ancient Korea)" under Emperor Shenzong's imperial edict in the Yuanfeng Reign of the Song Dynasty (T. Li 2004: 7023). Such ships to Goryeo were famous for two vessels, named "Marvelous Ship for Great Expectation" and "Marvelous Ship for Smooth Sailing". In the Xuanhe Reign, Emperor Huizong ordered Mingzhou to build two more of the same model, but in larger size. They were called "Marvelous Ship for Reform and Expeditions", and "Marvelous Ship for Long Voyage and Great Experience" (J. Xu 2006: 129). As the importance of coastal defense grew in the Southern Song Dynasty, Mingzhou and Wenzhou undertook the tasks of building warships by imperial edicts. Emperor Gaozong of the Song Dynasty "issued 60 imperial edicts to official candidates to build seagoing vessels in Wenzhou and Fuzhou", "adopting the model of patrol boats made by Pumenzhai of Pingyang County, which were 28 feet wide." (X. Li 2013: 3703) In the first year of the Xinglong Reign of Emperor Xiaozong (AD 1163), 10 flat-bottomed ships were made by Mingzhou and Wenzhou each by imperial decrees. In the fifth year of the Qiandao Reign (AD 1169), 50 multiple-oar warships were made by Mingzhou, and 100 seagoing ships by Wenzhou in the seventh year of the Chunxi Reign (AD 1180) (S. Xu et al. 2014: 7131, 7133). In the fourteenth year of the Jiading Reign (AD 1221), "the coastal military office sent two blueprints of ships to Wenzhou, and required it to build 25 boats of each model by setting an official to supervise timber purchasing and shipbuilding, which were to be taken over by Huaiyin County" (S. Xu et al. 2014: 7139).

In the Northern Song Dynasty, the central government set posts to supervise shipbuilding in Hangzhou, Zhenjiang of Liangzhe West Province, and Changzhou, Xiuzhou and Pingjiang municipalities. Apart from Hangzhou and Zhenjiang, other municipalities of Liangzhe West Province had commissioned officials to operate shipyards, and such affairs in Changzhou, Xiuzhou, Huzhou and Pingjiang municipalities were undertaken by a military officer, with the administration of grain transportation included. Since the implementation of direct transportation by the imperial central government, "at least 32 groups of grain vessels were deployed to carry grains each year. As such affairs increased, each municipality had to add one more official in charge of ports arrangement, with transportation affairs included" (S. Xu et al. 2014:3697). Not late than the Southern Song Dynasty, quite a few counties of Liangzhe West Province founded shipyards. Hangzhou set up the office of civil, legal and fiscal affairs, and the office of fiscal and cargo transfer affairs in Liangzhe West Province, both in charge of shipyards. The shipyards administered by the office of civil, legal and fiscal affairs were located beyond Dongqing Gate, and the shipyards administrated by the office of fiscal and cargo transfer affairs were situated beyond the Jiangqiao Gate (S. Qian 1990: 3697). In the sixth year of the Shaoxing Reign

(AD 1136), "the shipyard established in Huating County of Xiuzhou made 120 boats each year" (X. Li 2013: 1918). In the first year of the Chunxi Reign (AD 1174), the emperor gave an imperial edict that "money, cargo and craftsmen could not be embezzled, transferred or enslaved" (S. Xu et al. 2014: 7135). In the first year of the Longxing Reign (AD1163), Shen Zuoyi was again head of Zhenjiang Shipyard (S. Xu et al. 2014: 3336). This provides proof of established shipyards in Zhenjiang and Xiuzhou, as well as in Huzhou. Changshu's shipyard was placed away from the Yingqiu Gate. Dantu County also set up a shipyard of its own in the lower reaches of the Yangtze River (X. Lu 1990: 2410; Y. Tan 1990: 4724; Y. Zhu 1990: 3003).

Shipbuilding tasks had been placed on Liangzhe West Province from the Northern and Southern Song dynasties. The reason for setting up a shipyard in Huating County in the sixth year of the Shaoxing Reign (AD 1136) was "its urgent need for grain vessels, especially the lack of official boats", and it needed to take over all the transportation affairs and the grain vessels for future use. The feudal government "sold load capacity to the rich families to make up for the less official transportation capacity (X. Li 2013: 1918). Then Mingzhou and Huating built ships for transportation" (Y. Lou 1990). In the first year of the Qiandao Reign (AD 1165), an imperial ordinance said that "Wenzhou, Mingzhou, Xiuzhou, Ganzhou and Jizhou had their own quotas of grain vessel building" (S. Xu et al. 2014: 7617). From this, building grain vessels in Xiuzhou was supported with a historical record.

Meanwhile, Liangzhe West Province was an important base for sea and river defense. The coastal defense sites were dotted in Zhenjiang, Jiangyin and Xupu for garrisoning sailors, as well as for building and mending ships. In the fifth year of Shaoxing Reign (AD 1135), "the military prefectures of Jiangnan and Liangzhe provinces built 9-pedal or 13-pedal warships, and each province should follow the patterns of 5-pedal, 10-oar ships made in Hu'nan". People could build boats by copying and following the blueprints. Liangzhe East and West provinces were required "to build 14 ships in each province, Jiangnan East Province 12, and Jiangnan West Province 16" (S. Xu et al. 2014: 7130). In the 32nd year of the Shaoxing Reign (AD 1162), the decree for building warships issued to Jiangzhou Military Prefecture was to support Zhenjiang Municipality 30 thousand strings of 1000 coins, and Jiangyin Military Prefecture 20 thousand strings of 1000 coins. Moreover, "Zhenjiang Municipality was summoned to take the lead in building 24 vessels for carrying horses" (S. Xu et al. 2014: 7131). In the sixth year of the Chunxi Reign (AD 1179), Zhenjiang Municipality was ordered to build 30 vessels for carrying horses (S. Xu et al. 2014: 7136). And in the 15th year of the Chunxi Reign (AD 1188), the Pingjiang Prefecture allowed Pushui Military prefecture "to mend three ships made in the south and 8 multiple-oar boats" (S. Xu et al. 2014: 7137).

In the Jinghu South and North provinces, boats built in the South outnumbered those built in the North. The major producers of Jinghu South Province were based in Tanzhou and Hengzhou. In the later part of the Tianxi Reign, official shipyards in Tanzhou were assigned to build 280 ships. The Hengzhou shipyard was put into use in the third year of the Yuanfeng Reign (AD 1080). In this year, Emperor Shenzong issued an imperial edict that Chaling County of Hengzhou submit taxation in the form of timbers for shipbuilding, but the transportation from Chaling County to

Tanzhou's shipyard cost too much to both the local governments and the general public. After the imperial edict, timbers for 200 ships to be built in the county were transported by the Office of Transportation and Fiscal Revenues giving some subsidies for transportation" (S. Xu et al. 2014: 7123). Originally, Hengzhou was expected to provide timber to shipyards in Tanzhou, but started building ships instead. Ever since then, the authority set quotas for the two sub-prefectures. In the second year of the Jianyan Reign (AD 1128), the deputy governor of the Office of Marine and Landmass Transportation said, "within two years, Tanzhou, Hengzhou, Qianzhou and Jizhou had 839 ships in arrears;" "And this year's quotas for the four prefectures are 723 ships in total," (S. Xu et al. 2014: 7125–26) among which the quotas were set based on the quotas in the tenth year of Chunxi Reign (AD 1183), 168 ships in total. In that year, the governor of Jinghu South Province presented a memorandum to the emperor, "It is our hope that the 168 grain vessels made of pine timbers could be reduced to 100." (S. Xu et al. 2014: 7136)

As Hubei Province had an abundance of wood, Hou Jin, the navy commander in the Southern Song Dynasty was dispatched "to buy timbers there with the official allocation of 50 thousand strings of 1000 coins" (S. Hong, n.d.). Dingzhou was an important ship producer in Jinghu North Province in the Northern Song Dynasty, which had a quota of 241 ships in the late years of the Tianxie Reign. As Jingzhou was an important base of shipbuilding, Zhang Yong once said that "taxation on this industry was levied to Jingzhou and Langzhou for shipbuilding" (Y. Zhang 1990). The Jingmen Military Prefecture undertook the task of "felling trees for shipbuilding by transporting to Jingnan" (Toqta 1977: 10,619) each year. Ezhou was also an official shipbuilding base. In the 15th year of the Jiading Reign (AD 1222), the General Commander of Ezhou Military Prefecture "built 30 salvation ships for carrying horses later" (S. Xu et al. 2014: 7139–40).

The above-mentioned quotas are mainly restricted to grain vessels. Emperor Taizu of the Song Dynasty launched a punitive expedition to the Kingdom of Southern Tang, and his warships were built in Jinghu provinces. "An official was sent to Jinghu South Province to supervise craftsmen working on Imperial Yellow Dragon Boat in the shipyard of Jinghu South Province. They broke bamboos into timbers used as cables" (W. Shi 1990). Thousands of warships sailed southward from Jinghu South Province along the river. Catering to the war to conquer Yang Yao's rebellion, Jinghu South Province witnessed a climax of warship building financially. In the third year of the Shaoxing Reign (AD 1133), according the blueprints of large warships with miniatures to copy and sizes of length and width in traditional length measures, an imperial edict was laid down to "the governments of Jiangnan East and West provinces, and Jinghu South and North provinces to build ships by following the models." In the fourth year of Shaoxing Reign (AD 1134), Cheng Changyu, Governor of Dingzhou "made pedal-driven ships which were about 100 m or over 66 m long" (S. Xu et al. 2014: 7128–29). Later, he went to Chenzhou, Ruanzhou and Jingzhou sub-prefectures to plan the timber purchasing. In the same year, "the royal court sold permits of taxation exemption to make up for the military expenditures, at the value of 60,000 strings of 1000 coins, which were used to cover the costs of building warships in Tanzhou and Dingzhou. General Zhang Xun once spent gold of 15 kg on shipbuilding" (X. Li 2013: 1391). Hubei Province still kept the shipbuilding industry in the period of Emperor Xiaozong's Reign. During his tenure as military marshal of Jinge Military Prefecture, Guo Jun had planned to build ten 8-pedal-driven ships, but only five were finished. The reason was that "they were overwhelmed by the huge expenditures". In the eighth year of the Chunxi Reign (AD 1181), Yue Jianshou took over Guo Jun's post. Emperor Xiaozong "asked the unfinished five ships to be built in the models of five, six and seven-pedal-driven ships" (S. Xu et al. 2014: 7136). During this period, the pedal-driven warships emerged and became the dominant warships in the rivers of the Southern Song Dynasty. In the previous discussions, the duplicate giant pedal-driven ships were made in Jiangnan West Province, and techniques were transmitted to other provinces along the Yangtze River. Meanwhile, the hybrid model of pedal-driven or oar-driven boats was also promoted during this period. This explains the fact that in the fifth year of the Shaoxing Reign (AD 1135), the duplicated Hu'nan model of five-pedal (ten-oar driven) boats was ordered to be made in other provinces.

1.1.3 Official Shipyards in the Provinces of Fujian, Guangnan East and West, Huainan, Sichuan and the Provinces of North China

Fujian is the most important base for building seagoing ships. In the previous discussions, Zhang Jiaju pointed out that Quanzhou was a base of shipbuilding, and he left Fuzhou unmentioned, which was really the most important shipyard at that time. In the Northern Song Dynasty, a shipyard was established, whose existence is supported by the historic record on regulation and governance in the Qingli Reign, saying "the shipyard was situated to the east of the old salt storage of Nantai." "The map of Zhiping Administration in the Northern Song Dynasty suggested that the oldest shipyard was founded beyond the Well Tower in the north-east of Fuzhou. The shipyard gate suggested its existence in ancient times. The official shipyards were founded at the river outlet, close to the Temple of Miller" (K. Lang 1990: 7855). In Fujian Province, the most productive producer is Fuzhou. For example, in the tenth year of the Shaoxing Reign (AD 1140), the governor of disaster relief of Fujian Province once recruited 200 oar boats and paddle boats, among which 104 were recruited in Fuzhou. In the five counties of Fuzhou, Fuqing County contributed the most. For example, in the sixth year of the Shaoxing Reign (AD 1136), Fuzhou made 90 boats, among which Fuqing built 26 boats. The next county is Houguan (20 boats), then comes Minxian County (19 boats), Huaian (15 boats) and Changle (10 boats) (K. Lang 1990: 7900).

In the Southern Song Dnyasty, Fujian Province undertook the tasks of "making warships and delivering them" (S. Zhang 1990). After the third year of the Jianyan Reign (AD 1129), the work of requisition of ships began, and Lin Zhiping, in charge of sea defense, sent administrators to recruit seagoing ships in Quanzhou and Fuzhou.

"Over 200 large ships were procured from Fujian" (X. Li 2013: 685). Moreover, the yard for them to recruit ships is 12 feet between girders, meeting the criterion of 10 feet between girders. This gives evidence for the high quality and capacity of shipbuilding in Fujian. In the fifth year of Shaoxing Reign (AD 1135), Li Bing submitted his petition to Emperor Gaozong that the tasks of "building 700 ships assigned on Fujian would be completed in due time" (X. Li 2013: 1684), which proved the productivity of shipbuilding in Fujian.

Ships made in Fujian were of a strikingly high quality, and there was a common view in the Song Dynasty that "in terms of producers of seagoing ships, Fujian is the best, while the next is Guangnan East and West provinces, followed by Changming" (Y. Lü 1990). Also noteworthy was the large quantity of ships built in Fujian. Take the numbers of ships made in the nineteenth year of Shaoxing Reign (AD 1149) as an example. "2434 ships by the measurement of 12 feet between girders were purchased from Fuqing County" (K. Lang 1990: 7901). From the criterion of 12 feet width between girders, it is not difficult to understand its strong capacity of building large ships. 2434 ships were those above the criterion, let alone the number of smaller boats in that county. Also relevant was the fact that the water courses were more suitable for large ships in Fujian than in Mingzhou. "The surrounding sea is shallow with little waves in Mingzhou, but the sea water channels for ships are much larger than those in Mingzhou's shallow sea". Thus the herring swift warships in the water channels of Mingzhou were comparatively smaller than those in Fujian's broader channels. The Left-wing Navy of Fujian was equipped with sharp bottomed ships, twice larger than the herring swift warships. "Its top was 30 feet wide and its bottom 3 feet wide, and its load capacity was 120,000 kg." (S. Xu et al. 2014: 7130) Such ships were very popular in Fujian's navy, different from the ambassadorial ships sent to ancient Korea in the periods of Emperor Shenzong's Reign and Emperor Huizong's Reign in Mingzhou.

Guangnan West Province has its geographical features in shipbuilding. *The Land Beyond the Passes* once recorded the technique of rattan shipbuilding in Guangnan West Province. Because of a smaller supply of iron nails and China wood oil, rattan was used to bind the planks. In order to solve the problem of leakage, dry Rubia-like grass was crammed into the cracks of boats. It would be swollen when wet so as to stop the leaks. "As such ships were bulky and heavy loaded, they naturally became merchants' favorite vessels for ocean shipping." Canoes were also seen in the water channels of Guangnan West Province, which were made by hollowing the middle of large logs. As the logs were usually six to seven feet broad, no nails were needed and no decoration was made when a large log was used to make a canoe. Such canoe building facilitated by the abundance of large trees in Guangnan West Province, and many of their logs are "larger than two people's hugs" (Q. Zhou 1999: 216). In the 32nd year of the Shaoxing Reign (AD 1162), navy troops were founded respectively in Qiongzhou, Leizhou, Huazhou, Qinzhou and Lianzhou of Guangxi. For the navy, the 15-foot-wide assault boats and 24-foot-wide large warships were in urgent need (S. Xu et al. 2014: 9625) No record showed whether they were made by adopting the technique of Robia water-proofing.

In addition to having the geographical advantage of being well-connected with rivers and oceans, Guangnan East Province was also endowed with fine shipbuilding. In the Northern Song Dynasty, Guangnan provinces were garrisoned by three thousand soldiers and sailors together with 500 workers in the shipyard (T. Li 2004: 8398). When Guangzhou was besieged by Nong Zhigao at night (G. Sima 2003:174), the County Chief of Dongguan ordered Huang Gu "to recruit several thousand jobless young men, and they boarded more than one hundred ships to rush to Guangzhou by trending down the river". This is a story about recruiting ships temporarily for war affairs in Dongguan. In the first year of the Chunxi Reign (AD 1174), Emperor Xiaozong "issued an imperial edict to halt the shipyards in Guangnan East and Fujian provinces" (S. Xu et al. 2014: 7135). This shows that similar to Fujian, Guangdong also undertook the shipbuilding tasks.

The Huainan Canal running through Huainan Province served a major channel for grain shipping. Additionally, the coastal areas of Chuzhou and Taizhou were the origin of Huaiyan Salt. This bordering region with the Jin Kingdom was also an important site for sea defense, as well as a busy waterway. In the third year of the Yuanfeng Reign (AD 1080), the emperor ordered the construction of "three hundred shallow grain vessels by Zhenzhou, Chuzhou and Sizhou" to carry bulk cargoes on the Bianhe River (S. Xu et al. 2014: 7123). Such a task of shipbuilding was also required by the court in the fifth year of the Yuanyou Reign (AD 1090). Zhenzhou, Chuzhou and Sizhou undertook the tasks of building one thousand three hundred ships with a load capacity of 18,000 kg (T. Li 2004: 10,525), among which they were asked to make 100 official boats, 200 shallow boats, and 1000 mixed-ownership boats (S. Xu et al. 2014: 7124). As an important sea defense fortress, Chuzhou was authorized to build warships. In the third year of the Shaoxi (AD 1192), Huangpu Bin of Chuzhou was required to build 100 two-mast ships whose head was 12 or 13 feet wide (S. Xu et al. 2014: 7138). It seems that building warships in private shipyards was prohibited. Zhou Bida, the then chancellor-in-chief, once mentioned the fact that Zhang Chong, Mayor of Chuzhou, investigated the non-official households' crimes of privately building warships and military utensils for commercial affairs in Yancheng. As Zhang Chong was the militia chief, whose servicemen existed as both farmers in agricultural production for the year round and soldiers only for emergent military operations, he was caught for this reason. The reason was that "militia chief was greatly linked to frontier defense, and thus, his soldiers were prohibited from building warships and military supplies". Otherwise they would break the law (B. Zhou 1990). This evidence proves that the general public was prohibited from building seagoing vessels. Such a special policy may be developed from the adjacency of Huainan Province to the Jin Kingdom.

In the upper Yangtze River, Sichuan was economically developed in the Song Dynasty, and it was well connected to the middle and lower reaches of the Yangtze River for water course transportation. As battles were conducted in some areas of Sichuan and Shaanxi in the Southern Song Dynasty, Sichuan provided an important water course for grain vessels and other water transportation along the Yangtze River. *The Land Beyond the Passes* recorded the craftsmanship of shipbuilding in Sichuan that three-bristle cudrania was cut into wedges for building boats to replace iron nails" (Q. Zhou 1999: 216). The reason may be due to the numerous rocks lying on the riverbeds in Sichuan. This is one type of ship built in Sichuan. Few records were made about the official shipbuilding there in the Northern Song Dynasty. In the first year of Yuanfeng Reign (AD 1078), the Department of Tea Trade and Tax of Sichuan Province built 30 ships with a load capacity of 6000 kg for carrying tea to the coastal areas officially (T. Li 2004: 7078). This may not be a great reflection of the flourishing shipbuilding industry of Sichuan in the Northern Song Dynasty, but great progress was made in shipbuilding in the Southern Song Dynasty. Sichuan "was besieged by ranges of mountains, and violent rivers ran through mountains. Big trees would block roads which formed difficulties for cargo transportation". The reason for this is that deforestation was banned in the early Northern Song Dynasty onward. However, when it came to the Southern Song Dynasty, "the great movement of deforestation for grain vessels caused the lush forest to drastically decline" (X. Li 2013: 1903). This shows the great consumption of wood for shipbuilding at that time. In the sixth year of the Shaoxing Reign (AD 1136), in order to meet the great official demand of water transportation, "Luzhou, Xuzhou, Jiazhou, Qianzhou and other sub-prefectures had to hook timbers afloat in rivers and cut trees from official forests for shipbuilding" (X. Li 2013: 2001). One of Fan Chengda's tasks as the mayor of Xuzhou was to oversee shipbuilding in Sichuan. In Emperor Xiaozong's Reign, the court summoned Wu Lin, a famous general, "to raise funds for transporting staple commodities by over 30 horse-carrying boats. As horse-carrying boats were not strong and solid enough, they need to be replaced by new ones each year." (S. Wang 2012: 635) In later years, when water transportation came to a halt, Sichuan kept building such boats as usual. In the sixth year of the Qiandao Reign (AD 1170), "a marshal of the garrison in Jiangzhou and Chizhou was appointed to supervise the shipbuilding of 117 horse-carrying boats in Luzhou, Xuzhou, Jiazhou and Meizhou." (S. Xu et al. 2014: 7133)

In the Northern Song Dynasty, the Yegu Shipyard in Fengxiang of Shaanxi Province was an important base. In the late period of the Tianxi Reign, the shipyard undertook the tasks of building 600 ships each year, second to Qianzhou of Jiangxi Province at the annual quota of 605 ships (S. Xu et al. 2014; D. Ma 2011: 7029 743–44).[2] Later, with the decline of grain transportation, only 9000 tons of beans were to be transported each year, as the grain transportation via the river course was given up when, "in the fourth year of the Jiayou Reign, 300 grain vessels were cut from its quotas" (Toqta 1977: 4252). Then, some of the productivity was laid idle in Shaanxi Province. "People were levied taxes in the form of wood for building ships in Qinlong Yegu Valley Shipyard" (Toqta 1977: 10,316). In the first year of the Tiansheng Reign (AD 1023), as wood purchasing for shipbuilding would disrupt people's lives, the royal court "cut the annual quotas of Fengxiang Municipality" (T. Li 2004: 2334). Bao Zheng, the chancellor-in-chief pointed out that the task of "building 600 vessels with a load capacity of 18,000 kg was set for Fengxiang

[2] The number of ships being built is verified by the following two sources: *The Anthology of Laws and Regulations of the Song Dynasty* and *A Full-Scale Textual Criticism on Ancient Systems and Regulations*. The first one took Xuzhou for Chuzhou.

Municipality". Timbers for these ships were bought from Qinlong and Fengxiang. In addition, Fengxiang was also given the task of building 44 pedal-driven boats (Z. Bao 1999: 108).

Apart from the shipyards in Yegu Valley, the Baibo Transportation Department of Sanmen also established a shipyard. In the sixth year of Yuanfeng Reign (AD 1083), this shipyard could "build large ships with a load capacity of 18,000 kg" (T. Li 2004: 8162). In the ninth year of the Xi'ning Reign (AD 1076), Emperor Shenzong "gave an imperial edict to Zhongtao Military Prefecture for building ships." Then it recruited 500 sailors and solders for safeguarding the city (T. Li 2004: 5811). Another shipyard was founded in Yangping to meet the demands. Zhang Ping, served as the director-general of Yangping District at the imperial court of Emperor Taizong's Reign in charge of taxation, timber purchasing and shipbuilding (Toqta 1977: 9405). In the fourth year of the Yuanfeng Reign (AD 1081), Emperor Taizong made an imperial edict that "a shipyard project should be launched by the upper reaches of the Taoshui River, which was a branch of the Yellow River. And wood from Mount Mobang could be exploited for building ships." And "the weapon craftsmen could be selected from the Shipyard Department of Fengxiang Municipality" (T. Li 2004: 7603). The central government then had planned to build a shipyard in Lanzhou, and the tasks of "building 500 ships with a load of 9000 kg and 500 ships with a load of 15,000 kg, were assigned to the Taxation Transmission Department of Xihe Province". The warships were planned to sail along the Yellow River to capture Xingzhou sub-prefecture. However, there was only one craftsman available there. Summoning and hiring craftsmen from other provinces such as Jiangnan provinces, Liangzhe provinces, or Jinghu South and North provinces would not have been an easy matter. Due to this, as well as the high costs of raw materials and iron nails from other provinces, the imperial administrators had to give up this idea (F. Li 1990).

In the Northern Song Dynasty, the official shipyards in Hebei Province were the major suppliers for vessels patrolling moats of the capital city, transporting staple commodities, dredging and deepening riverbeds of the Yellow River and patrolling on the boundary rivers. There was a shipyard in Beijing (then called Daming Municipality) directly under the jurisdiction of the central government. Those 300 grain vessels for the imperial court needed to be made in Beijing's shipyard. "But the big timbers needed for shipbuilding were in smaller demand". "Then workers were sent to Mount Xishan in the boundary region of Daming Municipality for deforestation, and the logs were transported to Beijing's shipyard on large rafts" (Z. Bao 1999: 50). Ouyang Xiu once mentioned that only over 300 of the 1800 grain ships were left. The rest could not be found, and were probably sold in broken lots by soldiers. In order to avoid losses of ships, Guangxin Military Prefecture "deployed craftsmen from Jiangnan Province to build locks for securing ships by locking their girders." With this practice, the number of missing boats was greatly reduced. The standard for a grain vessel was set at the load capacity of 9000 kg, and the record of dates and batch number of grain transportation, together with the official seal, was carved on the front top of the girders. The name and number of planks used in a standard grain vessel were carved into an iron plate. "If any boats were missing, boatmen are responsible for reporting the facts". "If the ships did not come to the end of life, they should not be phased out; or intentional damages to the in-service ships or fake declarations about their status retreated for sundries were prohibited" (X. Ouyang 2001: 1809–11, 1802–03), which suggested that the imperial court attached a high priority to grain transportation vessels at that time.

The ships built in Huaizhou and Weizhou were mostly used for dredging and deepening water courses of the Yellow River. Fan Ziyuan said that "Lush forests could be found along the Yellow River in the bordering areas of Huaizhou and Weizhou sub-prefectures, which might be used for building 200 riverbed-clearing ships with a load capacity of 16,000 kg each (T. Li 2004: 6642). A shipyard had been established in Xiangzhou, evidenced by the fact that in the fourth year of the Jingyou Reign (AD 1037) it was decreed that, "the shipyard authority should be moved from Xiangzhou to Tianxiong Military Prefecture" (T. Li 2004: 2836). In the early Song Dynasty, shipyards were founded at the sea mouths of Nigu and Zhangkou to keep alert on the military operations of the Liao Kingdom, but later they were abolished. "In the fifth year of the Xianping Reign (AD 1002), the shipyard was resumed", but later it was abolished again (Toqta 1977: 2365). Chanzhou also set its own shipyard. The Chanzhou Pontoon Bridge was built in Wenzhou on 49 ships, with twenty components included, such as burrocks and dikes. It took some three years to transport to Chanzhou. In the sixth year of the Tiansheng Reign (AD 1028), "the production procedure was changed that pine timbers purchased from Qinzhou, Longzhou, Tongzhou, iron nails and limestone from Cizhou, Xiangzhou were carried to Chanzhou for shipbuilding" (S. Xu et al. 2014: 9544).

In the Northern Song Dynasty, Kaifeng Municipality established a shipyard and was a supplier of raw materials. In the seventh year of the Tiansheng Reign (AD 1029), the shipyard authority mentioned that "craftsmen in the western shipyards whose shipyards were abolished, were accepted to the processing plant of raw materials; and they were asked to jointly build the familiar ships with local craftsmen. If light boats were built, the shipyard authority would allocate raw materials as previous practices" (S. Xu et al. 2014: 7245–46). There was a shipyard in Hedong Province. Wang Sui said that "when a ban was imposed on salt business in Xiechi, which was famous for salt production, the local government began to cut woods for shipbuilding (Toqta 1977: 4416). This provides proof of the established official shipyard in Hedong Province.

1.1.4 Summary

Obviously, the most developed shipbuilding was in Jiangnan West Province in the Song Dynasty, then Liangzhe East Province, followed by Jinghu South Province. The Yegu Shipyard of Shaanxi Province was also a leading producer in shipbuilding across the country. With a decrease in the demand of grain vessels, the output of ships was greatly reduced. The official shipyards were the main producers of grain vessels and warships. Thus, it is not difficult for us to understand the construction of grain vessels as a primary task in the Northern Song Dynasty. But in the Southern

Song Dynasty, the priority was shifted to national defense, which brought an urgent demand of warship building. The distribution of official shipyards was decided by grain vessel shipping and military patterns, with the next decisive factor being raw materials. As the six provinces served as centers of grain vessels shipping as well as financial centers in the Northern Song Dynasty, Hu'nan, Jiangnan West and Fujian provinces were home to official shipyards for their rich resources of wood, while the great demand for river and sea defense turned Hu'nan, Jiangnan West, Liangzhe East and Fujian provinces into major producers of war ships.

As discussed above, the record of official shipyards indicates their geographical distribution in the Song Dynasty. The flourishing businesses along the inland rivers and in coastal cities fueled the development of private shipbuilding for people's urgent needs in daily life in the southern regions of the Yangtze River. This conclusion can be drawn from the existing historical records; however, these records could not provide enough details to reveal distribution of private shipyards. The most detailed information was about official shipyards, grain vessels in particular. The less detailed information was about warship manufacturing, and details were lacking in the narration about seagoing ships. Therefore, it is difficult to ascertain a complete picture of shipbuilding in the Song Dynasty.

1.2 Raw Materials and Costs for Shipbuilding in the Song Dynasty

The majority of wood for building ships came from pine trees and China firs in the Song Dynasty. These two kinds of wood, China fir in particular, originated from the south. Although pine trees did grow in the north, some were ruined by battle fires and over-deforestation year after year. While Qinlong of Shaanxi was blessed with an abundant supply of timber, other places in North China lacked wood. Jiangnan West, Hu'nan, Hubei, Liangzhe East, Fujian and other provinces boasted the richest forest resources. This explains why the most productive shipyards were based in these provinces. The cost of ships was highly variable, depending on shape and structure. The most expensive large ships in the Song Dynasty were pedal-driven ships and official passenger ships, which might cost 10–20 thousand strings of 1000 coins. Generally speaking, the medium and large ships were valued two to four thousand strings of 1000 coins, most of which were valued less than one thousand strings of 1000 coins. Previous studies do not discuss the distribution of raw materials. Only Ge Jinfang listed costs of seven types of ships and the fund-raising sources in the Song Dynasty (J. Ge 2008:158–159). The following section provides a comprehensive account of the distribution of raw materials and their prices.

1.2.1 Major Raw Materials and Their Distribution

Summary of River Flood Prevention Work discusses records of "building a small boat with a load capacity of 6000 kg whose length was 40 feet, with a facial width of 12 feet, a bottom width of 8.5 feet, and slanting width of 3 feet". To build such a medium-sized boat, 474 wooden planks were needed in total. The following are needed for shipbuilding: 242 boards, 24 bottom planks, 4 long planks, 22 side planks, 8 cover plates, 2 head plates, 1 flat plank, 1 side thick plank, 1 stump plate, 2 facing water plates, 2 linking plates, 2 pooling plates, 2 front planks, 2 rear planks, 12 blockup plates, 12 waist-supporting plates, 20 terrestrial poles, 24 pilasters, 26 wrought columns, 2 girders, 1 boat-mouth plate, 2 main beams, 36 padding boards, 1 pole, 4 axis, 10 thin boards, 1 tooth-like plate, 1 spinning pole, 6 mechanical poles for lifting water, 2 long oars, 1 short wooden stake, 7282 iron nails, 3685 nails for sealing cracks, 2497 N-shaped nails, 20 J-shaped nails, 221 6-inch-head nails, 643 4-inch-head nails, 184 3-inch-head nails, 46 nails for connecting beams, 6 nails for connecting girders, 18 plat-head nails, and another 8 nails for connecting girders. Other materials needed for building a ship include oil of some 27 kg, and limestone of about 82 kg (e.g. 1.5 kg of limestone mixed with 0.5 kg of oil). Further materials include smashed flax of 4 kg. 19 ropes include 1 cable, 9 big or small flax ropes, 1 upturned cable, 8 towlines, 1 slim cable, 6 thick ropes. 1 tent and about 0.5 kg of thread for connecting curtains. In addition, other auxiliary materials were required, such as warm rings, bamboo shoots, bamboo poles, straws, decorative ornaments, bamboos and sanders, and so on. The above objects clearly listed the length, width, thickness, sizes and heights of the materials.[3]

From the above narration, the major raw materials for shipbuilding at that time included timber, bamboo, iron nails, limestone, and wood oil. An official in the Song Dynasty once summarized that "the raw materials for the shipyards in Mingzhou, including timbers, bamboos, iron, limestone and others, were levied from merchants' taxation by real objects in Wenzhou, and no subsidies needed to be paid by the prefectural government" (S. Xu et al. 2014: 7124). "But they had to pay the expenditures on iron, charcoal, limestone and wood oil" (Y. Lou 1990). Wood was the staple material as it was used to make keels, shells, masts, cabins, oars, and other auxiliary implements. Bamboo was used to make sails, punt-poles and coverings of ships. Iron was used to build nails and anchors. Limestone and wood oil were the raw materials for stopping leaks, and crop fibers and bamboo shavings were used too.

The historical records and unearthed objects suggest that pine trees and firs were the most frequently used wood for shipbuilding in the Song Dynasty. The tight and pliant texture and high availability of pine make it an ideal material for shipbuilding. Firs are light and pliable, resistant to corrosion, and grow quickly. Thus, they were planted widely in South China. For these reasons, pine and fir trees were heavily consumed by shipyards across China. In 1974, the major keel and tail keel extracted

---

[3] Shakeshi states in the preface to *Summary of River Flood Prevention Works* that the book is a copy of *National Academy*. There is another copy recorded in *The History of Song Dynasty*. Re-editing of the two versions is helpful to reflect the basic information about the ships built the Song Dynasty.

from the sea at the site of a shipwreck in Quanzhou Gulf were made of pine timbers. Its shell planks used Cryptomeria fortunei, and its dummy plates of the cabin were constructed from fir, but camphorwood and pine also contributed a small share. In November of 1979, a Song Dynasty ship was discovered in Ningbo, which was found to have pine keels, and a shell made from fir timber. In February, a Song Dynasty ship was unearthed in Jiading, Shanghai. Fir was mostly used for building this ship, with the exception of its masts and hatchways, which were made of mulberry. In June of 1978, a wooden boat built in the Song Dynasty was found in Mengyuankou Village of Tianjin's Jinghai District, whose bottom was made of fir timbers (Editorial Committee of Excavation Report of the Quanzhou Bay Song Dynasty Shipwreck Excavation 1975; L. Xi 1981; W. Ni 1979; S. Ji 1987; Tianjin Municipal Office of Cultural Relics 1983).

In the Song Dynasty, the important bases for shipbuilding were situated in the areas which were rich in pine or fir trees. As the most important manufacturer of inland river ships, Jiangnan West Province was blessed with rich timber resources in the Ganjiang River drainage basin. When Fan Chengda toured in Jiangnan West Province, "he saw lush trees and wild jungles in his way" (C. Fan 2012a, b, c: 41). Timbers for shipyards in Jiangnan West Province were purchased by merchants from the Ganjiang River and its tributaries. Timber transactions were popular in every county along the river. Yongxin and Longquan counties bought large trees for making boats, as did Nan'an Military Prefecture (S. Xu et al. 2014: 7122). The official registrar of Xinfeng County in Qianzhou once mentioned of the shipbuilding affairs, that "the timbers for shipbuilding had to be apportioned to the grass-root people if those sub-prefectures or counties could not manage to provide for themselves enough wood. This is because wood does not come from the heavens." (S. Yang et al. 1990) "The biggest warship made in Fuzhou was 220 feet long. To build such a big ship, 40-foot long timbers were needed, which could only be found in desolate remote mountainous areas" (Z. Wang, n.d.). The imperial court of the Song Dynasty made Jiangnan West Province its most important shipbuilding base, especially for the maintenance and manufacturing of large pedal-driven ships. One of the reasons for selecting Jiangnan West Province as such an important producer lies in its rich and high-quality wood resources. Moreover, Jiangnan West Province also sold its timber to other provinces. This attracted merchants or officials from Jiankang Municipality of Jiangdong Province to purchase wood or even simply sent craftsmen to build ships in Jiangxi, as evidenced by Ma Guangzu's operation of building ships discussed in the previous section. When he was in charge of Jiankang Military Prefecture, he sent craftsmen to purchase wood and build ships in Jiangnan West five times (Y. Zhou 1990: 1984–85).

Jiankang Municipality's shipbuilding in Jiangnan West Province outside its own border could not deny the existence of its lush pine trees and firs. Evidence for this can be found in the poet Yang Wanli's poem, which says "Mount Zhongshan situated in a mountainous area, to pray at Dinglin Temple you have to walk through lush forests. Through pine and fir trees, on zigzagged rocky path, finally you will be greeted by a small but steep mount in the wandering white cloud." (W. Yang 2007: 1607) As Jiankang Municipality was an important military base, a large number of ships were needed, and thus the local wood alone could not meet the great demand for shipbuilding. The mountainous areas of Jiangnan East Province were rich with pine and fir timbers. Huizhou had a sufficient supply of pine, catalpa, sandalwood and fir trees. Each year, the logs carried along the Yangtze River were probably made of pine and fir. Seizing the opportunity to excel in the timber business, merchants local to Xiuning became rich. Afterwards, a new custom developed in Xiuning. When a girl was born, the family would plant fir trees for good luck. By the time she was old enough to marry, those firs would have grown into tall trees for different usages (Y. Luo 1990: 7604, 7619) Fan Chengda mentioned the custom of planting firs in Xiuning of Huizhou. "As the mountainous areas provide favorable conditions for firs, the locals earned their living by planting firs rather than farming. So its affluent fir supplies were brought about by the easy growing of firs". Additionally, Yushan County of Xinzhou was rich in wood, as evidenced by Fan's words, "from Changshan County to this place, it impressed me with lush arbors, thick forests, clear brooks, white sand, which is short in Liangzhe West Province." (C. FanC. Fan 2012a, b, c: 35)

Taizhou of Liangzhe East Province was a producer of sciadopitys, pine, fir (including thorny firs, slim firs and metasequoia), camphor and sandalwood trees (Q. Chen 1990: 7565) As Wenzhou and Chuzhou were producers of wood, good timber there brought flourishing business to local people. "The timbers produced by Wenzhou were used for making seagoing ships". Timbers for the shipyard in Wenzhou were levied as taxation in real objects from wood merchants in the Southern Song Dynasty. As the shipyard was founded, a regulation was imposed for taxation in the form of wood, which brought affluent timbers for shipbuilding. Such staffs could be used for building 100 ships each year to carry grains. The shipyards in Mingzhou and Huating also imported wood from Wenzhou. However, due to deforestation in the mountainous areas of Chuzhou and Wenzhou in the Southern Song Dynasty, "tall trees became scarce. As a result, wood merchants visited less and they could afford only 10 ships in wood supply" (Y. Lou 1990). Changguo County of Mingzhou was also a producer of pine, fir and camphor trees (F. Feng et al. 1990: 6091). Moreover, there were pine planks imported from Japan, "which could be categorized into the top class with fine figures and sparking surfaces". Mingzhou also imported cedar planks and Robin boards from Japan (J. Luo et al. 1990: 5057).

Liangzhe West Province was rich in the resources of pine trees, firs and other shipbuilding materials. Hangzhou was home to pine trees, firs and camphor trees (C. Zhou 1990: 3230). Ganshui (now Ganpu Town of Haiyan County) also produced pine trees, firs, wingceltis, phoebe zhennan and other trees (T. Chang 1990: 4667). Suzhou was a supplier of pine, Chinese catalpa, phoebe zhennan, fir and other trees (C. Zhu 1990: 643). The trees in this region could satisfy the local shipbuilding needs, with its abundant supply of wood. In addition, Huzhou was also a supplier of pine, fir, phoebe zhennan and other trees. *The Jiatai Period Chronicles of Wuxing* mentioned a quotation from *the Annals of Yudi Geography* which states that, "in the surrounding areas of Shushan Mountain ranging 7.5 square kilometers, only green pine trees were planted. The pines covering path extends several kilometers before it reaches Fahua Temple, and pine-tree surrounding villages can be found here and there in the mountainous areas of Changxing County (Y. Tan 1990: 4864). Changshu was a provider of pine, fir, Chinese catalpa, wingceltis, phoebe zhennan (Y. Zhu 1990: 3065). Zhenjiang produced pine, fir and phoebe zhennan and other trees, but pine trees account for the biggest share, "which were growing in the mountainous areas. And the original inhabitants rely on the mountain to offer them firewood." (X. Yu 1990: 2668) Danyang was described by two lines of a poem, which says, "pine trees before the river banks, at the end of forest passers-by could be seen (W. Yang 2007: 1386). As an economically developed region, Liangzhe West Province was in urgent need of wood for shipbuilding and houses. Thus, it was the biggest importer of wood. Based on the previously mentioned facts, we know Huating County imported wood from Wenzhou. The wood was mostly exported to Liangzhe West Province from Jiangnan East and West, and Hubei, provinces. The export volume of firs from Huizhou to Liangzhe West Province was so large in quantity that no one would neglect firs imported from Shexian County as a taxation object (C. Fan 2012a, b, c: 34). "Additionally, merchants in Xuanzhou and Xizhou shipped wood for rafts to Liangzhe East and West provinces." (E. Shan 1990) The above passage mentioned the fact that Hou Jin, the general of Zhenjiang Navy, went to Hubei for wood purchasing with the official fund of 50 thousand strings of 1000 coins, giving some evidence of the exports of wood from Hubei Province to Liangzhe West Province. In the first year of the Shaoxing Reign (AD 1131), the royal shipping division "submitted a proposal to the emperor requesting 50% of the taxation (bamboo and wood, in real term) levied from Liangzhou Province to be used for iron-head wooden ships by the shipping division" (S. Xu et al. 2014: 7127). This shows the importance of the timber industry in the Liangzhe provinces.

Aside from this, Jinghu North Province also produced pine, fir and other trees for shipbuilding. Yang Yao, the peasant rebellion leader in the Southern Song Dynasty, cut some 10 thousand pine and fir trees in Deshan Mountain of Dingzhou Prefecture for his shipbuilding. Apart from those trees, he also went to Qinshan Mountian, Yaoshan Mountain and Jiashan Mountain in Lizhou to cut down another 10 thousand trees for shipbuilding, including pine, fir, camphor, and phoebe zhennan trees. We also noticed that some merchants of Qianzhou traveled to the mountainous area of Jingzhou to purchase fir planks, shipping them to Taoyuan County via Ruanshui River (K. Yue 1989: 1568). On the way from Jiangnan West Province to Tanzhou in Hu'nan Province, pine trees were welcoming passengers on both banks of the Yangtze River. In the region of Dongting Lake and Xiangjiang River, the tall and straight pine trunks were very suitable for shipbuilding. However, the pine trees in the region of Suzhou Prefecture had curling trunks, which were not as good as those in Hu'nan Province (C. Fan 2012a, b, c: 42). Hengzhou was abounded with pine trees, however, out of people's expectations, the merchants of Chaling County peddled local pine trees to the shipbuilding yard in Jizhou of Jiangnan West Province, which was rich in such trees (S. Xu et al. 2014: 7122).

The fact that Fujian Province was the most important ship-maker in the coastal regions was partly fostered by its affluent pine resources (when Cai Xiang served as the mayor of Fuzhou, he ordered to plant pine trees by the roadside in Fuzhou, Quanzhou, and Zhangzhou, which were called guests-welcoming pine trees). Others, like fir, phoebe zhennan and camphor trees, were good for making large boats (K. Lang 1990: 8259). Xianxi County of Fujian Province was teeming with pine, maple and fir trees (Y. Huang 1990: 8279). The rich families in Zhangzhou stored Keteleaxia for later use, which was much better than other wood (Toqta 1977: 1449). When Song Jinzhi served as the assistant magistrate of Changxi County, he supervised the wood-cutting affairs in person as the deadline for shipbuilding set by the royal court approached. He, in person, selected and checked the trees to ensure high-quality wood for shipbuilding. The purpose for doing so was based on his consideration for reducing the effort required for building ships. The pine trees he chose were called "Mr. Song's Favorite Pine Trees" (Y. Lou 1990). The wood for shipbuilding benefited from Fujian's rich resources. Guangnan East and West provinces also produced pine and fir trees. The necessary wood for shipbuilding came from camphor trees, phoebe zhennan, fir, and pine trees in Guangzhou region (D. Chen 1990: 8427). Fushui Prefecture of Guangnan West Province was famous for its narrow, steep roads, deep valleys (Toqta 1977: 14,207), and lush firs. Wang Can, the chief of minority ethnic groups in Luzhou "transported thousands of fir trees in the water course for commercial purposes." (Toqta 1977: 12,269)

The reason why Yegu Shipyard of Shaanxi Province got the biggest quota in shipbuilding in the Northern Song Dynasty lies in its rich forest in the Qinlong region. The main raw materials transported from Guanzhong to Guandong were bamboo and trees. Although the establishment of Baibo Batch Shipping Department was designated to supervise grain shipping, it was said that only bamboo and trees were transported, rather than grains (S. Su 2003: 278). Qinshan Mountain was blessed with tall trees (Toqta 1977: 11,051), which could be transported eastward in the Weishui River. The Yegu Shipyard of Fengxiang Prefecture was ordered to make 600 ships with a load capacity of 18,000 kg each year. "The purchasing and supply of wood lumps were mainly assigned to Qinzhou and Longzhou, and Fengxiang Municipality." In three consecutive years of the Qingli Reign (AD 1046–1048), Bao Zheng, the then prime minister used 190,000 timbers to build ships in Kaifeng (Z. Bao 1999: 108), which was dependent on the import of timber from Qinzhou and Longzhou. In the second year of the Chunhua Reign (AD 991), Wen Zhongshu, the mayor of Qinzhou Municipality, ordered the soldiers to cut trees to meet the need of the royal court in Kaifeng every year (Toqta 1977: 9182). "During Emperor Taizong's Reign, Zhang Ping undertook the task of supervising the markets of wood in Qinzhou and Longzhou. "They made two huge rafts in spring and autumn to carry wood to the capital city Kaifeng from Weihe River passing by Dizhu Mountain. Finally, these quality logs were piled like small hills at Kaifeng port within a year." (Toqta 1977: 9405) In the reign of Emperor Shenzong, Xihe Province set up an independent bureau to supervise wood procurement affairs. Only in the fourth year of the Yuanfeng Reign (AD 1081), the royal court allocated 2 million strings of coins as expenditures on purchasing and transporting wood (T. Li 2004: 7543). Over 93,000 large logs were transported to Kaifeng, "which were cut down in Qinzhou of Shaanxi Province." (Z. Bao 1999: 109) Some officials were put into prison for embezzlement in trading bamboo and wood imported from Qinzhou and Longzhou, including Shi Baoji, Zhao Yanpu, Zhang Yongde, Zhao Pu, Shen Lun, Cheng Dexuan and Liu Zhixin and others (Toqta 1977: 8812, 8899, 8917, 8933, 9113, 10,156, 13,543). In the Northern Song Dynasty, not only were bamboo and wood cut and transported eastward, but wood trading markets were also set up in some counties along the river, resulting in a great increase of tree-cutting in Guanzhong region for eastward shipping. This resulted in "those officials governing batches of goods shipping in Shaanxi Province going bankrupt and being punished." (Y. Wen 1990) The abundant wood resources in Qinzhou and Longzhou could not only meet the needs of shipbuilding yards in Shaanxi Province, but also could supply the capital city. However, due to rampant deforestation in Guanzhong in the Northern Song Dynasty, the wood resources dropped sharply. In the Xi'ning Reign, the fashion of magnificent building resulted in almost all tall trees being cut down, including the tall trees in the graveyard of the royal Zhaoling Tomb (Toqta 1977: 10,912). Thus, in this period, the arboreal resources were greatly reduced.

As the broad areas of Hebei and Jingdong provinces were mostly plains, the long-term deforestation resulted in fewer pine trees available for shipbuilding. In the early years of the Northern Song Dynasty, the wood consumption in Hebei Province was mostly from Xishan Mountain. When Li Yunze served as the mayor of Yingzhou Prefecture, he ordered his soldiers to cut trees from Xishan (Toqta 1977: 10,480). Zhang Wenzhi was transferred to Hebei Province. At that time, the bordering prefectures sent soldiers to cut trees on Xishan Mountain, but Zhang warned them not to cut trees in the territory of Qidan Kingdom (Toqta 1977: 10,033). In the period of Emperor Shenzong, Li Xian was given an imperial edict to administrate fiscal affairs, "to transport huge trees to the capital city for building and repair projects" (Toqta 1977: 13,639). However, at that time, many of the tall trees were gone due to the years of deforestation. In the period of the Xi'ning Reign, the repair project of Zhanghe River needed over 100 thousand elm and willow trees to be cut on the banks of Zhanghe River within its administrative area". "As no firewood could be found in the wilderness, farmers had to burn wheat straws in their kitchens." (S. Yang et al. 1990) During Emperor Shenzong's reign, not only Hebei Province was in urgent need of wood, but the prefectures of Tanghe, Dengzhou, Xiangyang, Ruzhou were also poor in forest resources. "Since the Xi'ning Reign, people flocked there and began to claim farmlands, which were well-cultivated croplands reaching out several thousand kilometers in all directions" (S. Xu et al. 2014: 8113). The enlarged farms caused a decrease in the supply of wood. When Han Zongyan garrisoned Yingzhou, "encountering river floods, he had to lead 500 soldiers to cut trees nearby so as to consolidate the dams. Even the trees in the graveyards were cut to contain flooding" (Toqta 1977: 10,311). This provides evidence for the comparative lack of wood at that time. In Emperor Huizong's Reign, the royal high official Lin Lü, was sent to chair the administration of Hebei Province. "His suggestion was to halt deforestation in Xishan region." (Toqta 1977: 11,110) In the previous section, Shen Kuo has been quoted by his words, "the forests in Qi Kingdom and Lu Kingdom were almost cut down, and Taihang Mountain, Jingxi Province and Jiangnan East and West provinces also suffered from less forest coverage, and Songshan was almost bare without any forests." (K. Shen 2006: 177)

The populous elms, willows and other trees growing in the plain of Hebei Province were not suitable for shipbuilding. Wu Qian once said that "the vast plains of North China produce little wood like pine and fir trees. People had to use willows to build boats" (Q. Wu 2002). When Li Yunze served as the mayor of Yingzhou Prefecture, he ordered that elm trees should be planted in all the empty land throughout the whole region." (Toqta 1977: 10,481) In the fifth year of the Shaoxing Reign (AD 1135), the Jin Kingdom wanted to build seagoing boats in Huzhou, and had "to dispatch 400,000 river workers from Youzhou and Yunzhou. They cut trees on Jiaoya Mountain in Weizhou so as to build rafts, and dug river courses to Huzhou for wood transportation." (X. Li 2013: 1843) The location of the tree-cutting areas proved that the plains of Hebei Province could not produce enough wood for shipbuilding. In the thirty-first year of the Shaoxing Reign (AD 1161), the large flat-bottom boats built by the Jin Kingdom in Binzhou could not be used for seagoing transportation as they were made of pine (X. Li 2013: 3727). Such wood was probably transported to the coastal shipyard. In the first year of the Shaoding Reign (AD 1228), Li Quan, the chief of peasant rebels in the Jin Kingdom had an envious eye on the Song Dynasty. "To offset the advantages of the navy in the southeast region of the Song Dynasty, he ordered his soldiers to conduct military exercises on the sea and built more large boats in Shandong and Huainan provinces. As there was a smaller supply of China wood oil and firs, Li Quan dispatched soldiers and officials to buy China wood oil and fir rafts, and recruited craftsmen from the south to build ships." As there was a rule banning China wood oil and fir rafts from being transported into domestic rivers, Li Quan had to replace the firs with elm planks for shipbuilding. The ships built in this way easily became stranded in the shallow waters as the elm planks were too heavy." When Li Quan and his soldiers could not find enough fir planks and China wood oil, they would dig tombs to collect fir planks, and melt iron coins to make nails and cramps for shipbuilding, and refine fat for making putty (Toqta 1977: 13,840)". As was pointed out by Lu Yihao, the prime minister of the Southern Song Dynasty, "wood produced in the north was not suitable to be put in sea water as the corrosive salt was prone to damage the wooden structures of boats. Thus, the boats could not endure long voyages in the sea, as they were not strong enough to contend with violent waves, and were prone to sinking" (X. Li 2013: 1676). Therefore, elm and similar trees were not suitable for shipbuilding. The north shipyards had to patch different kinds of local timbers together to make boats although there were fewer pine and fir trees. For example, one ship built in the Song Dynasty was discovered in Mengyuankou Village, Jinghai County of Tianjin, in June, 1978, which was patched with different kinds of wood. Its breast board was made of Chinese catalpa, phoebe zhennan and locust, its bottom plates were made of fir, and the ship ribs were made of jujube and sandalwood trees (Tianjin Municipal Office of Cultural Relics 1983).

1.2.2 The Auxiliary Materials for Shipbuilding and Their Sources

As a hard and precious wood, Phoebe zhennan was usually used to build passenger boats and other luxury boats. For example, the tower boat in Jinming Lake for navy exercises in the capital city Kaifeng "used only yellow nanmu and Phoebe zhennan". For this boat, workers were ordered to cut huge trees, and had to spend two years carrying the precious wood to the capital city, whose transportation expenditures reached several million strings of coins (C. Liu 1990). For another example, the royal boat on the West Lake of Hangzhou, then the capital city of the Southern Song Dynasty, "adopted fragrant nanmu for shipbuilding" (Z. Wu 1980: 111). "In the Lizong Reign, they built a boat embedded with gold patterns by completely adopting fragrant nanmu." (Sishuiqianfu 1981: 39) In the late Southern Song Dynasty, the extravagant Zhao Meishi "once built a black-japan painted passenger boat for officials, whose decks were made of fragrant nanmu with ornamental engravings." (M. Zhou 1988: 197) The passenger boat built by Yang Yao in Yizhou was probably made of Phoebe zhennan. In March 1960, a wooden boat discovered at Shiqiao Town of Yangzhou City was made of Phoebe zhennan, which, as discussed, was both rare and precious (Jiangsu Heritage Working Team 1961). As such precious wood was mainly produced in the south, it is easy for us to find the records about the wood used for ships in Taizhou, Hangzhou, Suzhou, Changshu, Yizhou, Fuzhou and Guangzhou in south China. The seagoing vessel in Quanzhou Bay had its ribs, head masts, center mast bases and cabin base made of camphor wood, and its main body of cabin partition was made of Chinese firs, with several camphor wood planks. The south region was home to camphor wood. The above-mentioned prefectures all produced camphor wood, including Taizhou, Mingzhou, Hangzhou, Huzhou, Zhenjiang, Yizhou, Fuzhou and Guangzhou. Besides, there were several hundred camphor trees whose trunk circumference needed to be measured by several hugs in the islets of Qingcaozhou Islet close to Dongting Lake (S. Zhang 1990).

In addition, other kinds of wood were used for boat parts. For example, lichi chinensis was used to make large oars. Emperor Gaozong once pointed out that "the different geographical conditions resulted in different features of wood. For example, large boats' oars were made of lichi chinensis, but in the north it is another case. The carts were usually made of elm, but in the south such practice could not be seen (X. Li 2013: 3593). Wulanmu Wood was used to make rudders. Qinzhou's Wulanmu Wood "was once used to make quality rudders for large boats. That's perfect usage." Rudders built in other places were only 10 m long each, just meeting the basic requirement of 300,000 kg. However, these rudders were not suitable for larger seagoing boats sailing in 200-m-deep sea for fear their hardness could not survive in the huge waves. Only those made in Qinzhou could meet the harsh requirements of seagoing voyages. The rudders produced in Qinzhou were almost 15 m long, densely textured and with enough strength to survive in the furious wind. They functioned like a tiny silk which could hold a large amount of weight. The rudders were really a treasure for sailing boats in the sea." If they were transported to Guangzhou,

Wenzhou, or other southern cities, their prices could increase tenfold (Q. Zhou 1999: 219, 220). *The Notes of the Kuixin Reign* also mentioned Wulan Wood, noting that "the rudders were made of Mesua ferrea or Wulan Wood, and originated in Qinzhou. Every 100 kg of this wood was worth 500 units of silver currency. An iron anchor weighs several hundred kilograms each. If the boat happened to sail in a strong wind, it had to lay down its pegs to secure the boat. Sometimes, the gusts were so terrible that they could break four claws of the anchor, resulting in a ruined boat." (M. Zhou 1988: 157)

Tung oil, lime, and wood are necessities for shipbuilding. Ye Mengde once mentioned the fact that the shipyards in Huainan provinces and Jiangnan East Province had no putty to apply in the shipbuilding during the cold winters, forcing them to temporarily suspend their shipbuilding operations (M. Ye 2002). Wei Guofeng and other scholars discussed the function of Tung oil mortar material in shipbuilding and architecture in ancient times. They pointed out that mortar for shipbuilding was made out of a mixture of slaked lime wrought Tung oil, which had stronger compressible strength and shear strength than common lime mortar by 72% and 245% respectively. Its absorption coefficient was only 1/620 of common lime slurry, so its freezing and thawing cycle was greatly enhanced. Such features of Tung oil originated from its fossilization, and the chemical changes between Tung oil and slaked lime. Therefore, the Tung oil mortar had a strong waterproofing and gluing function. It was widely used to waterproof materials in the ancient shipbuilding industry, and to seal in ancient buildings to help keep them free of unwanted moisture. It was also used in wood structures for its anti-corrosive properties. Tung oil lime was used in the plaster joints of ancient ships. The resulting increase in the strength of the adhesive bonds in the ships' joints, as well as the relative impermeability, strongly helped to prevent ships from sinking (G. Wei 2013).

Tung oil was a popular product in Jinghu South and North provinces, Jiangnan East Province, Liangzhe East Province, and Fujian Province in the Song Dynasty. "People used Tung oil to light their lamps in Jiangzhou and Huzhou, rather than using flax." (C. Zhuang 2008: 36) Records show that the Jinghu South and North provinces and Jiangnan East and West provinces were rich in Tung oil. At the age of twenty, Zhu Ang, later the deputy minister of industries, would go to Hengshan Academy, where he and his classmates usually stayed up late at night to read books. What they were consuming in their lamps was Tung oil." (Z. Zhang 1990) This suggests Hengshan is the origin of Tung oil. "Hu Jingchun, the famous ink-making craftsman, used Tung oil to burn charcoal for making a kind of ink stick, which was called Tonghuayan (Tung oil black ink stick)." (Y. He 2008: 270) When Yang Wanli passed by Leping County of Raozhou in Jiangnan East Province, he let out an exclamation in a poem. "As spring is passing by, nobody bid farewell to it by drinking liquor aside, only Tung flowers see it off when the late spring flies" (W. Yang 2007: 1777). These lines show that Jiangnan East Province was a noteworthy producer of Tung oil. *Essays on Mountain Huts* provides an anecdote wherein a father and son retreat to the mountains after the Song Dynasty was invaded by the Yuan Dynasty, earning their living by pounding Tung seeds for oil with a pestle (Z. Tao 1990). This suggests that Tung oil was also produced in Shaoxing Prefecture of Liangzhe East

Province. The Tung trees can be classified into three categories: Chinese parasol, princess tree and gangtung tree (K. Lang 1990: 8260). According to *The Testament of Herbal Plants*, "the material for squeezing out Tung oil by the Han ethnic group was Tung trees instead of other two kinds." (S. Tang 1990) Thus, Tung oil must be squeezed out of gangtung seeds. They are the right kind of tree for refining Tung oil. Zhen Dexiu, the official of the Southern Song Dynasty, once pointed out that Jinjiang County released a notice to buy farmers' Tung oil and red vines for building official ships before the deadline. If local officials refused to pay for Tung oil, they would be exiled to desolate mountains or remote border regions (D. Zhen 1990). This provides further evidence for Tung oil as a product of Fujian Province.

The sunken ships of the Song Dynasty that have been discovered used Tung oil, lime, bamboo shavings, and hemp threads as gap filling materials (Editorial Committee of Excavation Report of the Quanzhou Bay Song Dynasty Shipwreck Excavation 1975; L. Xi 1981; W. Ni 1979; S. Ji 1987; Tianjin Municipal Office of Cultural Relics 1983). Sometimes, fish oil was also used in seagoing ships. The dead whales encountered by boatmen were often towed to shore, and their fat was refined into oil and used as a coating for ships (K. Lang 1990: 8266). However, Tung oil was comparatively low in price, and it was not practical to replace Tung oil with fish oil. Therefore, its use in shipbuilding was standard. "And sesame oil was expensive and black, which was not suitable for shipbuilding, but Tung oil was transparent and cheap. So the competitive price of Tung oil made it dominant in shipbuilding rather than other oils." (M. Ye 2013: 236)

The Land Beyond the Passes once mentioned the fact that no nails were used in building "the Vine-Connected Boats" and "the Boats made in Sichuan", but most ships used nails to connect planks, evidenced by newly discovered Song Dynasty boats. The nailing technique was observed in various shipwrecks, including the ship in Quanzhou Bay, the wooden ship in Fengbang of Jiading County in Shanghai, the ship in Dazhi River of Nanhui in Shanghai, and the ship at Mengyuankou Village of Jinghai County in Tianjin. The last one is a 14.62-m long wooden ship, and its widest mouth is 4.05 m. 600 nails were used in its right and left starboards (Tianjin Municipal Office of Cultural Relics 1983). This large quantity of nails used in shipbuilding is attested in historical records. When Huang Zhen was the mayor of Fuzhou Prefecture, he issued an order to ban racing boats. The result of this order was that 1300 boats were burned, and their nails were melted for the need of 500 garrison rooms. Racing boats refer to dragon boats, a kind of mini boat. However the quantity of nails used in 1300 boats could be used for the nails in building 500 rooms of military camps. There are multiple records discussing the consumption of nails used for shipbuilding. One record says that, due to many officials wishing to be promoted to higher posts, they lied to the court, saying that 200 kg of nails would be consumed in building a ship with a load capacity of 21,000 kg. Zeng Chushan, the provincial fiscal commissioner, found a ruined boat and asked his underlings to burn it. 100 kg of nails were procured from this boat. At first, nobody knew his intention of burning the boat. Afterwards, this was reported to the court, who set up a norm that building a boat with a load capacity of 21,000 kg needs nails weighing only 100 kg rather than 200 kg. This standard was put into effect after Zeng Chushan's report"

(Y. Shi 2008: 185). Another record says that "when Xu Yuan acted as deputy supply commissioner, he worried about lower officials exaggerating statements regarding the quantity of nails, as the nails were hammered into the boats and the boats were submerged in water, so there was no way to determine the actual consumption of nails. One day, Xu Yuan went into a shipyard and asked his soldiers to burn a newly built boat, and then he scaled the weight of nails used in it. He found out that the weight of nails was only one tenth of the claimed quantity. Then Xu Yuan made a standard of nail consumption for building a boat." (S. Jiang 1990) However, we could not figure out the real proportion of nail quantity to load capacity. Nevertheless, it is apparent that false reports were made regarding the quantity of nails used for building boats.

Iron anchors were used on boats during the Song Dynasty. Some ships "loaded anchors of several hundred kilograms each in seagoing voyage. One day when a strong wind began to toss the boat violently, the boatmen hurriedly threw such an anchor into the sea to stable the boat, but contrary to their expectations, its four claws were broken." (M. Zhou 1988:157) Iron anchors were also used to collect corals from the sea, "which were winched up by the five claws of the iron anchor connected with a rope on the windlass." (R. Zhao 1996:200)

As quite a few accessories on board were made of bamboo, the necessary raw materials must include wood, bamboo, iron, charcoal and so on (S. Xu et al. 2014: 7124). These materials were transported from Jingmen Military Prefecture to Jingnan Prefecture every year, for use in Mingzhou's shipyards (Toqta 1977: 10,618–19). As Chen Fuliang said in *On Boats,* "bamboo mats could be made into sails, bamboo split could be woven into cables. What's more, bamboo could be made into barge poles, and boat mats could be made of cattail leaves". (F. Chen 1990) Bamboo was used for making sails, cables, and barge poles. Some boats installed their mat roofing made of cattail leaves, and some others were made of bamboo. But it was quite often to use bamboo for shipbuilders to make sails. Huang Tingjian, the famous poet, asked "as the boatmen were busy with making bamboo ropes, how could they have time to think about lifting sails?", "The lifted sails in strong winds would serve a strong engine as if a good crossbow could reach remote targets when the bow was pulled to its fullest" (T. Huang 2011: 1014, 1008). Thus, the bamboo mats on the boat were actually used as sails. In the Southern Song Dynasty, Guo Ning pointed that "the roofing of bamboo mats was convenient for making full use of wind power during sea voyages," (X. Li 2013: 224) corroborating the fact that some seagoing ships also adopted bamboo sails to gather wind power.

Apart from making sails, bamboo was also used for other purpose S. Xu et al. Jing once mentioned "the coverage over the passenger boat was made of bamboo". "They were piled up in sunny days, but they would be laid closely on the roof of the boat in the rainy days." On both sides of the boat, big bamboo poles were tied and laid down from the roof so as to offset the strong winds. The suitable load capacity for a boat was judged by the horizontal bamboo poles (J. Xu 2006: 130), which were used as plimsoll lines. Barge poles were also usually made from bamboo. "Travelling southeastward along the river, the equipment and materials on the official boats were found different from other places, as their barge poles were made of bamboo with an iron drill at the end." (Y. Zhao 2013: 203) The construction of hawsers also required a large quantity of bamboo. In the early years of the Song Dynasty, the court built several thousand Yellow Dragon Boats, whose hawsers "were made of bamboo cut and transported from Jingnan Province." (W. Shi 1990) In order to supply the need of Yegu Shipyard of Fengxiang in Shaanxi Province, about 1,503,820 bamboos were cut in Tanzhou and Hezhong Prefecture (Z. Bao 1999: 109). The long boat towing ropes used as hawsers in Jinghu and Sichuan provinces were made of bamboo skin. "The bamboo skins originating in the Dongting Lake and the Xiangjiang River were connected as long hawsers for towing boats, which was dabbed the Baizhang Towing Ropes. Such ropes were widely used in sailing boats along the Yangtze River in the gorges." (Y. Sun 1990a, b)

1.2.3 The Costs of Ships in the Song Dynasty

The expenditures of ships include costs relating to both production and maintenance. If properly maintained, private boats could be used for up to twenty years. However, most warships were not properly preserved. In actuality, "they could be kept and used in good condition for only ten years at most, with some lasting only three years." As the military defense infrastructure along the Yangtze River in Jiankang Prefecture was good, the warships there were maintained in good condition. As an important garrison place, the warehouses for warship maintenance were built and put into use, "where 250 houses were installed with water gates being easily operated when necessary" (Y. Zhou 1990: 1985). For the dragon boats of Jinming Lake, the navy exercise venue, a large bay was dug to build docks for warships in the period of the Xi'ning Reign. Huge houses were built to cover the docks, which served as a repair workshop as well as a shelter for boats (K. Shen 2006: 236–237). Such facilities could extend the life of the boats. Usually, however, most warships "needed to be repaired for some minor repairs every three years, and heavy repair every five years." Otherwise, "within two or three years, most boats would be decayed." (D. Zhen, n.d.) Horse-carrying boats were especially prone to damage, and needed to be repaired each year (S. Wang 2012: 635).

Although the total cost of repairing and maintaining such a number of ships could not be calculated, it is certain that such expenditures would be tremendous. It has been attested that some boats were quite expensive to repair. For example, the Supervisory Commission of Huainan West Province in the Southern Song Dynasty had to "spend four hundred strings of 1000 coins to repair each paddle wheel warship" once owned by Yang Yao, the rebel chief. In some instances, even this quantity of money "could not cover the costs in repairing one boat." (M. Ye 2002) Repairing the dragon boats used in the navy exercises in Jinming Lake was even more expensive. In the third year of the Shaosheng Reign (AD 1096), money allocated for the repair of boats was given to Yang Yan, the vice commissioner of military supplies. This took the form of 15 tax exemption certificates for monks, valued at 200 strings of 1000 coins for each certificate (S. Yang et al. 1990). In the tenth year of the Chunxi Reign (AD 1183), the royal court summoned the coastal manufacturing commissions and assigned them the tasks of repairing the seagoing vessels at the cost of twenty thousand strings of 1000 coins in a frugal way (S. Xu et al. 2014: 7136). And in the fifth year of the Chunxi Reign (AD 1194), a fund of 31,655 strings of 1000 coins to repair 15 warships was allocated to the coastal manufacturing commission (S. Xu et al. 2014: 7138). The average expenditures for repairing one boat reached 2110 strings of 1000 coins.

The costs for building ships included raw materials and labor. Fan Zhongyan once mentioned the total expenditures on grain shipping and wages for soldiers and boatmen reached 5–7 million strings of 1000 coins each year (T. Li 2004: 2624). In the 15th year of the Jiading Reign (AD 1222), the royal central government allocated 29,973 strings and 545 coins, as well as 45,730 workers to the Ezhou Branch Commander of Garrison Forces, for building five boats with a load capacity of 45,000 kg, five with a load capacity of 30,000 kg, five with a load capacity of 9000 kg, and fifteen swift paddle-driven boats with a load capacity of 2100 kg (S. Xu et al. 2014: 7140). In the first three consecutive years of the Xianchun Reign (AD 1265–1267), the central government respectively allocated Jiankang Prefecture 150,000 strings, 142,293 strings and 520,000 strings to build ships on the basis of the 18th group of currencies issued by the Southern Song Dynasty, and ordered it to build small swift battleships, Fuyang-made ships, pedal-driven ships, and others (Y. Zhou 1990: 1984). These figures are based on historical records, and were calculated by adding together the expenditures of various institutions from different counties. However, the amounts spent on shipbuilding by the country as a whole remains unknown.

We classify boats into three categories on the basis of their functions: cargo transportation ships, battleships, and passenger boats, in addition to studying the cost of their construction. *Summary of River Flood Prevention Works* recorded the costs of boats with a load capacity of 3000 kg, referred to as the Yellow River cargo transportation ships. The amount of labor required for constructing these boats was recorded as follows: "including 106 man-days of a shipwright, 106 man-days of a sawyer, and 106 man-days of a short axe carpenter, altogether 318 man-days. The odd-jobs done by other workers were not included." (Shakeshi 1990) However, this book did not mention the pay standards of different craftsmen or prices of the raw materials. Therefore, we could not ascertain the full construction cost of a Yellow River cargo transportation Ship. However, the cost of raw materials does not go up with deadweight tonnage at the same proportion accordingly. The cost of constructing cargo transportation vessels varied based on their intended purpose, a fact which was rarely discussed in existing historical documents. In the third year of the Xuanhe Reign (AD 1121), the Western Urban Grain Administration Station attached to Yanfu Palace mentioned the fact that "Two procurement boats cost 600 strings of 1000 coins each, to carry grains on the Bianhe River." (S. Xu et al. 2014: 3110) 10 grain vessels made in Wenzhou in the Southern Song Dynasty were built on the revenues by payment in kind, "which were levied from the ships to and from on Bianhe River, together with some official subsidies." That is to say, the large timbers for building ships were acquired by means of taxation from the boats on the river, and official funds were mainly used to cover the wages of shipyard supervisors, craftsman's food and clothes, expenditures on iron, charcoal and paint oil. "The annual expenditures of over 3600 strings of 1000 coins and 21,000 kg of rice would be paid to cover shipbuilders' salaries and soldiers' wages, food and clothes, but the spending on supervisors' costumes and higher military officers' hospitality were not included in the list." (Y. Lou 1990) Thus, it is likely that these were the total expenditures necessary to build a ship. If the revenues levied on a boat simply passing by were included, the cost of one boat would be a much higher figure.

During the Qiandao Reign, Wu Lin, the famous general of the Southern Song Dynasty, ordered his soldiers to build horse-carrying boats. Zhang Zhen estimated that each would cost them 800 strings of 1000 coins (X. Li 2000: 429). In fact, at that time, they were building two kinds of horse-carrying boats with a load capacity of 21,000 or 15,000 kg. "And the spending of 75 thousand strings of currencies issued by the Song Dynasty which was funded to shipyards by general supply commission, could only cover the costs of 200 horse-carrying boats." The salaries for helmsmen and sailors were probably not included in the expenditures of 370 strings of 1000 coins for building one boat. "If all the costs of raw materials, labor, and food were covered, the total could reach 440 strings of 1000 coins for each boat." (S. Xu et al. 2014: 9106) Generally speaking, the load capacity of horse-carrying boats planned by Wu Lin was probably larger than that of a canal boat.

There are more historical records detailing the costs of warships. Large pedal-wheeled ships sailing in domestic rivers were usually more expensive than others. Before undertaking the task of conquering the rebel Yang Yao and his men, Cheng Changyu, the governor of Dingzhou Prefecture, "wished to build six 60-m-long paddle-wheeled ships, each of which may cost 20 thousand strings of 1000 coins by putting labor, timber and other raw materials together". If the officially supplied timbers were adopted, each boat may have cost only 10 thousand strings of 1000 coins, totaling 60 thousand strings for all of the boats (S. Xu et al. 2014: 7129). In the fifth year of the Shaoxing Reign (AD 1135), Jiangnan West Province planned to build several 60-m-long paddle-wheeled boats, but because the officials did not know the total expenditures for such boats, they guessed that a single boat may cost scores of thousand strings of 1000 coins (S. Yang et al. 1990). In the same year, Emperor Gaozong laid an edict to Jiangnan East, Jiangnan West, Liangzhe East, and Liangzhe West provinces to build fifty 5-wheel and 10-oar small boats. The local governments had to subsidize 50 thousand strings of 1000 coins for these vessels (X. Li 2013: 1715). The average cost of such small boats was one thousand strings of 1000 coins. This, however, was only the cost of a small paddle-wheeled boat. In comparison, it was generally the case that over a thousand strings of 1000 coins would be spent in the construction of an inland river boat. For example, in the fifth year of the Qiandao Reign (AD 1169), Feng Zhan, the general of the navy, asked his craftsmen to build a multiple-oar boat with a load capacity of 24 tons at the price of 1607 thousand strings of 1000 coins each (S. Xu et al. 2014: 7133). Others cost only over three hundred strings. For example, two hundred battle boats and one hundred grain boats were built at the cost of three hundred strings of 1000 coins in the early years of the Shaoxing Reign. The total cost of these boats was over 100,000 strings (S. Yang et al. 1990), with the average cost of each boat only some 300 strings.

Warships varied in cost depending on their size and type. Li Gang, the Prime Minister of the Southern Song Dynasty, once ordered 700 warships to be built, "at the cost of 2000 strings each. The total expenditures for 700 boats reached 1.4 million strings of 1000 coins" (G. Li 2004: 1170). However, their sizes and types were not clear from the historical records. In the first year of the Jianyan Reign (AD 1127), the coastal patrol agency employed fishing boats, as well as sharp-bottomed boats, which could carry 50 people. These boats were 4 m wide and 15 m long. Calculated by the private craftsmen, the labor and materials for building such a boat would cost 400 strings of 1000 coins (S. Xu et al. 2014: 7125; X. Li 2013: 203). In the third year of the Shaoxi Reign (AD 1192), the government of Chuzhou Prefecture built 200 "two-mast boats driven by multiple oars, and their costs were just over 100 million strings of 1000 coins, whose head beam was about 4 m long." (S. Xu et al. 2014: 7138) So the average cost for building such a boat was five hundred strings of 1000 coins, which is roughly equivalent to the cost of a boat in the first year of the Jianyan Reign (AD 1127) if we adjust for inflation. In the third year of the Jianyan Reign (AD 1129), "The eight-oar battleship with a load capacity of 12,000 kg built by the Pingjiang Municipality costed 1159 strings of 1000 coins. The eight-oar boat was 24 m long. But the four-oar battleship was about 15 m long, and it would cost 329 strings of 1000 coins." (S. Xu et al. 2014: 7126) The cost of a 15-m-long four-oar boat was almost the same as the Saury-shaped boat which was 4 m wide and 15 m long, if we calculate the cost on the proportion of a seagoing vessel. Thus, the cost of raw materials for building a Saury-shaped boat which was 4 m wide would be less than that of a 24-m-long eight-oar battleship. Such a boat could not be counted as a large seagoing vessel. In the twenty-ninth year of the Shaoxing Reign (AD 1159), the eight coastal counties of Fuzhou built 60 sharp-bottomed battleships with the investment of 50 thousand strings of 1000 coins, at the average cost of 833 strings of 1000 coins (K. Lang 1990: 7901). Based on the cost to build such a ship, it is likely that its load capacity was less than 12,000 kg.

In the seventh year of the Chunxi Reign (AD 1180), "Wenzhou built 100 seagoing vessels at the cost of 100 thousand strings of 1000 coins in total" (S. Xu et al. 2014: 4982), at the average cost of 1000 strings of 1000 coins. In the tenth year of the Chunxi Reign (AD 1183), warships were built in Zhangzhou and Quanzhou. "The allocation cost of each ship was 500 strings of 1000 coins, which was not enough and the gap needed to be filled by the local government" (S. Xu et al. 2014: 7136–37) In the fourteenth year of the Jiading Reign (AD 1221), before Wenzhou built 25 seagoing boats, the local government asked for 50 certificates of tax exemption from the central government. However, only 30 certificates were allocated to the municipal government, who sold the certificates at the price of 800 strings each. If we calculate by the standard of Wenzhou Municipality, each boat likely cost 1600 strings. If we calculate by the allocation of royal certificates of tax exemption, each may have cost 960 strings (S. Xu et al. 2014: 7139), which might be the cost of small battleships.

In the fifth year of the Qiandao Reign (AD 1169), Feng Zhan, the navy general, built multiple-oar boats to sail in the Yangtze, Huaihe, and Yellow Rivers. These were larger and more expensive than the 26-m-long 8-oar boats with a load capacity of 12,000 kg built by Pingjiang Municipality. Feng Zhan's boats were 27 m long and 6.6 m wide, with a load capacity of 24,000 kg, with 42 paddles and 200 sailors on board. "The total expenditures for each boat would be 1670 strings and seven hundred coins on average (S. Xu et al. 2014: 7133). Zhao Shankuo remarked that the expenditures for building a boat "at the cost of 10,000 kg of gold, was equivalent to 200 strings of 1000 coins" (S. Zhao 1990). However, building even larger boats required greater expenditures. Zhen Dexiu mentioned three large battleships built in Fujian which totaled 120 thousand strings of 1000 coins, at the average of 4 thousand strings for each boat. Besides, Fujian Province provided 5000 strings of 1000 coins to build another two large boats, with each boat costing 2500 strings (D. Zhen, n.d.). In the second year of the Longxing Reign (AD 1164), Mingzhou and Wenzhou municipalities built ten flat-bottomed seagoing vessels. "As the central government sponsored the two municipalities by levying additional taxes of 30 thousand strings to build 10 boats, they must be large ones." (S. Xu et al. 2014: 7131) Thus, we can conclude that these boats built in Fujian Province must have been quite large.

Passenger boats would cost much more than other kinds as they employed fine wood and exquisite techniques. The most luxurious passenger boat would be the dragon boat in Jingming Lake in the capital city of Kaifeng in the Northern Song Dynasty. As the dragon boats were made with nanmu wood, they undoubtedly cost more than 10 thousand strings of 1000 coins, as described by an official in charge of their construction. While the exact figure was not mentioned, it must have been very expensive, "as 90 thousand kilograms of iron were consumed on this boat. Other costs of raw materials might be equivalent to the costs of iron" (C. Chen 1990a, b; T. Cai 2008: 213). Jin Nai, the rich tycoon, once built a seagoing boat as a bribe for Wang Jixian, the treacherous court official in the southeast region, "which costed 10 thousand strings of 1000 coins, with all kinds of precious goods stored in the cabin." (X. Li 2013: 3663) This passenger boat was used for personal entertainment rather than for military affairs or transportation of goods. In the first year of the Chunxi Reign (AD 1265), Jiankang Municipality sent officials to build detailed drawings of passenger boats in Jiangnan West Province at the price of 10 thousand strings of 1000 coins (Y. Zhou 1990: 1984). However, the costs were less for building the passenger boats for lower officials. Cai Xiang, the prime minister of the Northern Song Dynasty, once mentioned the fact that sacked officials from Jiangnan East, Jiangnan West, Liangzhe East, and Liangzhe West provinces, or even those in Xiangtan could travel to and from the capital city of Kaifeng on such boats, either in a small group of 10–20 passengers, or scores of passengers. The costs of building these ships were either 500 strings for a small boat, or 700 strings for a larger one (X. Cai 1996: 388). The average costs of such passenger boats were higher than grain boats.

1.2.4 Summary

Some of the most important raw materials in the Song Dynasty included timber, bamboo, iron nails, lime, tung oil and others. Most of the widely used timbers were pines and Chinese firs. Firs were widely planted in south China, and the fir planting was commercialized in Huizhou. Pine trees could be planted in both south and north China, but in the north, only Hexi and Longyou regions were rich in pine trees. Due to devastating deforestation, the North China Plain produce less pine trees. Other trees, such as willows and elms there, were not suitable for building ships. South China, however, was rich in pine trees, including Jiangnan West Province, Jianghu South Province and Liangzhe East and West provinces, whose abundant resources turned them into major shipbuilders. In addition, the nanmu for making dragon boats and advanced passenger boats was taken from south China's Jianghu South Province.

As equally important raw materials, Tung oil and lime, together with bamboo shavings and hemp thread, were mixed to make padding for cracks. Jinghu South and North provinces, Jiangnan East Province, Liangzhe East Province, and Fujian Province produced tung oil, which was comparatively inexpensive in these provinces compared to other locales. Apart from Vine Boats made in Guangnan East and West provinces and Sichuan-made Boats, boats built in other places adopted iron nails to connect parts of boats. Iron was also widely used in the shipbuilding industry of the Song Dynasty to make iron anchors on seagoing vessels. Bamboo was used to make sails, barge poles, towlines and hawsers.

As the number of boats in use in the Song Dynasty was great, the construction and maintenance expenditures must have also been tremendous. The repair expenditures on a large paddle-wheeled ship reached 400 strings of 1000 coins, and it would cost even more to repair the dragon boat in Jinming Lake, the navy exercise venue. As a large number of grain boats and warships were put in use, their maintenance fees would also be great in number. Generally speaking, the repair expenditures of a grain boat was over 1000 strings of 1000 coins, or at least several hundred strings. However, the warships and seagoing vessels with the same load capacity would cost much more in maintenance. Some large paddle-wheeled ships costed 10–20 thousand strings of 1000 coins each. The passenger boats were more expensive than ordinary boats like grain vessels due to their expensive raw materials and top techniques.

1.3 Load Capacities and Shapes and Sizes of Ships in the Song Dynasty

The shipbuilding industry and marine navigation flourished in the Song Dynasty like never before. Were there any differences in the structures of boats sailing in different waters? The previous studies provide a simple classification of the boats in the Song Dynasty rather than studying them in a holistic way. The shape, structure, and sizes of various boats must be studied as well. People in the Song Dynasty adopted the concepts of load capacity and size to measure the shape and structure of boats. The total deadweight tonnage was called lisheng (load capacity), measured in traditional Chinese units of weight such as the Liao, Dan, or Hu. Sizes are described in terms of length, width and depth. However, different scholars have different ideas about deadweight tonnage and load capacity, and the relations among Chinese weight units like Dan, Hu and Liao, which deserves additional discussion. Unfortunately, errors and misunderstandings about these facts abound in previous studies. In this section, the classification of boats is made based on their deadweight tonnages, shapes and structures.

1.3.1 Discussions on Lisheng (Deadweight Tonnage) and Liao (Load Capacity)

Deadweight tonnage refers to the load capacity of a boat. But what do shape and structure refer to: weight or volume in the Song Dynasty? In his discussions on deadweight tonnage, Yoshinobu Shiba believed that it was a term for sizes of different ships, measured by Chinese weight units of Dan or Liao. This means deadweight tonnage is neither total weight of the ship nor its net load capacity. It does not refer to water discharge, either. "It must be the load capacity of goods on board." (Y. Shiba 1997: 504) Chen Xiyu held the same idea that the deadweight tonnage refers to the load capacity of a boat (X. Chen 1991: 55). In fact, the deadweight tonnage has two meanings in the Song Dynasty: 1. it refers to the payload of a boat, or the total tonnages of the loaded cargoes; 2. it refers to net tonnage of a boat, namely, the effective cubage of a boat. The authorities in the Song Dynasty levied taxes on the deadweight tonnage, which was calculated by the load capacity of a boat (S. Xu et al. 2014: 6381). That is to say, the taxes were to be levied by the real load capacity of a boat. Whether the load capacity was calculated by weight or by volume depends upon the categories of goods on board. In the Northern Song Dynasty, "the empty official grain boats going upstream to Jianghu Province in the military prefectures of the Yangtze River reaches were issued certificates of tax exemption." (S. Xu et al. 2014: 6355) The deadweight tonnage of empty boats can only be calculated by the real volume of a boat. Therefore, the deadweight tonnage of a boat obviously refers to the total load capacity.

As for deadweight tonnage designating the shapes and structures of boats must be the real load capacity, or net tonnage, not the weight of load capacity mentioned by Yoshinobu Shiba and Chen Xiyu. In *the General Record of Military Affairs*, they described "the load capacity of warships put into use to be calculated by the rice cubage of two Dans for carrying a soldier on board." (G. Zeng 1990) It does not refer to the weight of a soldier as being equivalent to two Dans of rice, but refers to the cubage occupied by a soldier equivalent to that of two Dans of rice. In the Song Dynasty, one Dan of rice weighed 92.5 Song Jin, equivalent to 59.2 kg. Two Dans are

118.4 kg (K. Shen 2006: 19; Z. Guo 1993: 180),[4] which is heavier that the weight of an ordinary soldier. This has also been attested by Li Hongqi (H. Li 2013: 455). Thus, the deadweight tonnage refers to the real volume of a boat, not the weight or load capacity of a boat. As rice was the most common good to be transported, the volume of rice (Dan) was used as a unit of load capacity. In the third year of the Tiansheng Reign (AD 1025), a royal edict mentioned the fact that "the grain volumetric vessels used in the transfer warehouses adopted the 50 Dan (1000 L)as a taxation standard of a boat. But for some boats shipping top-class grains, 40 Dan (800 L) was adopted as a taxation standard of a boat." (S. Xu et al. 2014: 7037) Here, the deadweight tonnage was measured by Dan (20 L), which must be a unit of volume for load capacity. In the third year of the Zhenghe Reign (AD 1113), the Transfer Agency of Taxation in Liangzhe East and West provinces submitted a memorandum to the emperor saying that 20% of load capacity should be allowed to carry private goods or grains for personal use on the 300 Liao (18,000 kg) of cargo transportation boats. That is to say, apart from 240 Liao (4800 L) of grains, about 60 Liao should be used for carrying private goods or personal grains (S. Xu et al. 2014: 7013). In the fourth year of the Jianyan Reign (AD 1130), Song Hui, the vice supply commissioner, submitted his proposal to the imperial court that the cargo transportation boats from Zhenzhou to Kaifeng, the capital city, should be allowed to leave 20% space for private goods for the boats with the load capacity of five-hundred-Liao (30,000 kg) as a standard. 400 Dan (26,800 L) was used to carry official grains, and 100 Dan (6700 L) was used to carry private goods. 40 Dan (2680 L) of loaded goods was used to cover sailors' wages and food. The prior standard of paying sailors' wages and food was 20 Dan (1340 L) of grains (S. Xu et al. 2014: 7062). Thus, about 20 percent of load capacity was used for labor costs (S. Xu et al. 2014: 7061). From the above two memoranda to the throne, we could reach a conclusion in three points: 1. 80% of the load capacity was used to carry grains, and 20% of the load capacity was used to carry private goods, which make the whole load capacity of a boat (either 300 Liao or 500 Liao). 2. The deadweight tonnage of 300 Liao or 500 Liao refers to the net load capacity, which refers to the cubage of total deadweight minus the share of the load capacity which was not used to carry official grains. 3. 1 Liao is equivalent to 1 Dan, and either unit of measurement can replace the other in describing the volume of a boat.

From the above discussion, we know that deadweight tonnage refers to the net load capacity of a boat. Apart from the accounts about the proposals made by the commissioner of the transfer agency of taxation in Liangzhe East and West provinces, and made by Song Hui in the fourth year of Jianyan Reign (AD1130), Liu Zhuo's narration in the ninth year of the Qiandao Reign (AD 1173) also verifies our idea. Liu pointed out that "370,000 Dan (24,790,000 L) of grain was carried by six hundred boats with a load capacity of 500 Liao (27,500 kg) each." (S. Xu et al. 2014: 7135) Here, 500 Liao must be the net tonnage of a boat. When Xu Jing led a delegation to

---

[4] *Shen Kuo states that in Mengxi Bitan (Dream Pool Essays)* one Hu of polished round-grained rice is one Dan, and that one dan is 92.5 Jin is a standard/has been standardized. In addition, based on Guo Zhengzhong statement in his book *The weights and measures in China Between 3rd and 14th Centuries*, one song jin is equal to 640 g today, that is, present-day 1.28 Jin.

Goryeo, they boarded on a passenger boat with a load capacity of 2000 Hu, which was 30 m long, about 8 m wide and 10 m high, which could carry 2000 Hu (30,000 L) of grains (J. Xu 2006: 129). Here the load capacity refers to net tonnage of the boat. In The General Summary of River-flood Prevention Work, the calculation method of raw materials for building a boat with a load capacity of 300 Liao (20,100 L) pointed directly to the net tonnage of a boat. To be specific, if a boat of 300 Liao (20,100 L) was used to ship goods, it could afford room for carrying 150 stones and 18 sailors and boatmen on the boat, which was 15 m long and 3.3 m wide. Apart from the watertight compartments on both ends of the boat occupying about 5 m of the body length (about one third of the boat length), the rest of the 10-m-long body was left for carrying goods. Every 33 cm length of the space was designated to carry 10 Liao (550 kg) if each Liao was counted as 30 kg (Shakeshi 1990).[5] This shows the calculation standard of load capacity, meaning the net tonnage on the boat minus the unusable cubage of the boat.

Liao was a core concept for measuring deadweight tonnage and shape and structure of a boat, which has been widely discussed without consensus. Yoshinobu Shiba believed that Hu and Liao were in fact the same unit to measure the load capacity of a boat (Y. Shiba 1997: 59, 503). Chen Xiuyu held that Liao was a unit of volume rather than of weight, and that Liao was used to describe the length of boat's keel, width and depth of cabin (X. Chen 1991: 54, 55). Li Hongqi shared the opinion of Chen Xiyu, and thought that one Liao could contain the cubage of one Dan literally (H. Li 2013: 447). Here two questions were raised: whether Liao means weight or volume, and the relationship between the Liao, Dan, and Hu units. It is certain, however, than in the Song Dynasty, the Hu was a unit of volume. One full Hu equals one full Dan in terms of volume, which was unified by Wensiyuan, the Bureau of Weights and Measures in the Song Dynasty. Hu and Dan were the same measures of cubage in the Northern Song and Southern Song dynasties (Z. Guo 1993: 304, 316). Moreover, Dan itself was a cubage unit. One full Dan equals 10 full Dou, 100 full Chinese liters (or 67 metric liters) and 1000 full He (or 1000 Chinese milliliters). So, used as units of volume, Dan and Shuo are equivalent. The weight of one Dan of rice was comparatively stable, and one Dan of polished round-grained rice weighed 46.25 kg, as described by Shen Kuo, the ancient scientist in the Song Dynasty (K. Shen 2006: 19). Thus, the weight of rice, cereal, wheat and millet, and even the weight of salt, soil and stones were all measured by Dan. As different substances weigh differently due to their varying densities, the Dan must have been used as a unit of volume in the Song Dynasty. As the volume of a boat was measured by Liao in the Song Dynasty, when Liao was used to describe deadweight tonnage, they could be interchangeable. Thus, when people described deadweight tonnage, they used "Dan" or "Hu" to replace the units of "Liao". For example, they used expressions of "100-Hu Boat", "200-Hu Boat", "300-Hu Boat", "10,000-Hu Boat", "2500-Hu Large Boat", "400-Dan Boat", "10,000-Dan Boat" and others (Toqta 1977: 2342: T. Li 2004: 11,337; Z. Wang 1990a, b, c; S. Yang 1990; T. Huang 2011: 1018; Y. Lun

[5] ThE foregoing passage points out that Shakeshi's *Summary of River Flood Prevention Works* can reflect the basic information about the ships built in the Song Dynasty.

2012: 204; K. Shen 2006; S. Zhang 1990). From this fact, we know that when they were used to describe deadweight tonnage, Liao, Dan, Shuo and Hu are synonymous.

No record was left about how to measure Liao in the Song Dynasty. In the previous discussions, a quotation about 300-Liao Boat on the Yellow River, describes the boat as being "about 10 m long and 3.3 m wide. Apart from the watertight compartments covering 5 m of the l5-meter-long keel, the cabin of each foot could carry 10 Liao of goods." This is only one method of calculating the deadweight tonnage of 300-Liao boats sailing in the Yellow River. The effective shipping space was measured by every foot of the cabin's length, which was designated to carry 10 Liao. This was not the universal measure for all the boats' Liao, as different depths and widths of boats could carry different volumes of goods. Han Zhenhua made this method universal, claiming that "the feet of the length times the feet of width can be used to figure out the cubage of the boat, with the average load capacity of 10 Liao carried on each foot of the cabin." He also pointed out the differences in measuring the load capacity of boats built by official authorities and those built in the private sector. Where the official authorities measured the length and width of the bottom, boats built in the private sector were measured based on the length of waterline and width of the surface. Therefore, the official load capacity of a boat is only half of the private sector's cubage. On the basis of standardization, he determined the deadweight tonnage of the Haihu Warship made by Qin Shifu in the Song Dynasty as "an iron-covered-cabin Haihu Warship with a load capacity of 1000 Liao (55,000 kg), which was 33 m long, 6 m wide, and could carry 108 soldiers and 42 sailors and helmsmen. Such a boat had 11 watertight compartments and applied 5 oars on both sides. It was estimated that a 400-Liao warship was 33 m long, its waterline was 23 m long, its bottom was 16.5 m long, its surface was 6 m wide, and its bottom was 4.16 m wide. The waterline (23 m) times surface width (6 m) equals 126 square feet (138 square meters). Or judging by 10 Liao for each square foot, 120 times 10 Liao, we get 1200 Liao. Using integers only, we can get 1000 Liao as the load capacity of a boat. This was result determined by using calculation methods of the private sector." (Z. Han 1988: 201)[6] One of the two mistakes made by Han is that he took the iron-covered-cabin Haihu Warship for the flat-bottom Haihu Warship (S. Xu et al. 2014: 7138), when in fact, they are quite different in load capacity and shape. Yang took the 1000-Liao Haihu Warship and the 400-Liao iron-covered-cabin Haihu Warship to have the load capacity judged by the official authorities and the private sector's standard. As mentioned, however, these are different ships with different load capacities, and as such, Yang's calculations were incorrect. The other mistake made by Yang was that the 70-foot-long waterline times 18-foot-wide surface should be 1260 square feet (138 square meters) rather than 126 square feet. Moreover, *The General Summary of River-flood Prevention Works* only mentioned that the length of each foot in the cabin could carry 10 Liao,

[6] Han Zhenhua pointed out that the proportion between the boat bottom length, the waterline length, the hull length and the total length is 1:1.4 times respectively. But he didn't offer the evidence of how to reach the conclusion of the relation between these length and of the official load capacity of a boat is only half of the private sector's cubage. The official calculation rules of the load capacity of a boat and the private ones have not been found out in the historical records of the Song Dynasty by the author this book, Dr. Huang Chunyan.

rather than giving the figure as a square foot. The above passage also mentioned that this could not be used as measuring standard, and the discrepancies were great in their shapes and structures.

Chen Xiyu and He Feng adopted Han Zhenhua's calculation method. They believed the length, width and depth of boats could be figured out in a converse way, and then the tonnage could also be determined. However, Chen Xiyu made some adaptations to the method of calculation, as he believed that Liao (load capacity) could be figured out by length times width times depth. He claimed that the proportions of length, width and depth of three keels and surface width should be 5:4:3:1, and that the depth of the cabin must be about 10–13% of the keels. This was considered to be a universal formula to calculate the volume of a boat. Chen also figured out the load capacity of the Haihu Warship built by Qin Shifu, whose keel was determined to be 70 feet long, as inferred from the boat's length of 100 feet. "So, 70 feet (keel length) times 18 feet (surface width) times 8.5 feet (depth) equals 1070 cubic feet (Liao). Using only whole integers, then it must be 1000 Liao (F. He 2005: 28; X. Chen 1991: 54). In this article, Mr. Han reached a conclusion that the load capacity was 10,700 cubic feet. Obviously, Han's quotation from *The General Summary of River-flood Prevention Works* was completely against the facts, and as such, its conclusion was groundless. We noticed the appropriateness in universally applying formula to calculate the proportion of length and width. The above mentioned three scholars' ideas were wrong in calculating the load capacity of the boats built in the Song Dynasty.

When discussing the volume of boats in the Song Dynasty, Li Hongqi was pessimistic to say that we could not find such a formula, nor could we have any expectations on such a formula from the existing historical records (H. Li 2013: 453). After surveying the historical records about the Song Dynasty, I hold the same opinion. In terms of different water conditions of seagoing, canal and river shipping, there were a number of varieties of boats with different shapes and structures. Also, there were no detailed records about the boats' dimensions. Today, the formulas of calculating a boat's load capacity are targeted at existing boats. Based on limited data in the historical records, we could not get a universal formula for cubage calculation. Even if we can measure the shipwrecked "South Sea 1" in Quanzhou of Fujian Province, we still could not get a universal formula which could be used to describe various ships built in the Song Dynasty.

Next, we discuss the relations between Liao and the load capacity of a boat. In fact, this depends on the objects to be carried on a boat, which could not be summarized using a universal formula. According to the article about the weight of goods on the boat from *The General Summary of River-flood Prevention Works* (Vol. II), the average of upriver load and downriver load was used to calculate the weight of wood on board. The average weight of wood was 18.5 kg each Liao. He believed that a volume of 300 Liao can only carry 100 Dan of rice (about 4,662.5, or 8125 kg) (H. Li 2013: 448, 457).[7] This means that people wrongly consider wood and rice to have the same density. If we look into the load capacity of each Liao from their sizes and

[7] According to the record of *Summary of River Flood Prevention Works*, the upriver load and downriver load of a volume of 300-Liao boat are about 4,662.5, or 8,125 kg respectively.

shapes, we need to consider their maximum load capacities when goods were loaded on the boat. The maximum load capacity of boats in the Yellow River from 300 to 800 Liao were respectively 8125, 10,825, 13,750, 16,225, 18,725, and 21,625 kg. Apart from the boats of 500 Liao and 700 Liao (with a load capacity of 27.5 and 26.75 kg respectively), the average load capacity of the remainder of the boats was 27 kg.

The load capacity on board may vary due to objects of different densities. Each type of boat would be installed with a different number of sailors, ranging from 15 to 30 people based on the standard of raw materials in building ships. To test the relationship between volume and weight of 300-Liao boats, "150 stones and 18 sailors were placed on the boat. And the cubage of one Liao was equivalent to 30 kg." "Each stone was 1.5 feet long, and its width and thickness was 1 foot, and its weight was 60 kg." 150 stones times 60 kg equals 9000 kg, which means 300 Liao times 30 kg (Shakeshi 1990). As the density of stones is greater than that of wood, the 300-Liao boat could carry the same weight of wood plus 3 people. If we consider the total weight of 300-Liao stones and people on the boat to be the load capacity of 300-Liao Boat, and assuming the average person weighs 70 kg, then the total weight of people and stones must be 998.45 kg in total. If we put an equal weight of rice on the boat, the load capacity must be 216 Dan. So, we cannot say that the 300-Liao boat could carry only 216 Dan of rice, let alone the load capacity of 100 Dan of rice. In fact, in his memorandum to the throne, Song Hui, the commissioner of Transfer Agency, mentioned the boats with load capacity of 300 Liao and 500 Liao used in the third year of the Zhenghe Reign (AD 1113) and in the fourth year of the Jianyan Reign (AD 1130) were batch goods vessels, whose full loads were 300 Liao or 500 Liao. At the standard of 46 kg each Liao, the 300-Liao boat could carry 13,875 kg, which was bigger than that of boats sailing in the Yellow River. The different load capacity lies in the fact that different objects have different densities.

So the maximum cubage of a boat is different from its maximum load weight. The maximum cubage is decided by the real load space of the boat, but the maximum load weight is decided by the displacement of water. Due to the different parameters of boats in shapes and structures, different length, width and depth of plimsoll marks, and different block coefficient, we could get different displacement of water at each Liao. So, when we calculate the load capacity of a boat, we need to consider the following parameters of density of objects, shapes and structures of boats.

1.3.2 The Deadweight Tonnage of Boats and Their Shapes and Structures in the Canals in the Song Dynasty

In the Song Dynasty, boats were categorized into quite a few classes, which were described by Yoshinobu Shiba, who identified dozens of types of boats according to their places of production, functions and shapes (Y. Shiba 1997: 58). This listing could not provide details of boats, and the need for additional research remains. To facilitate sailing in waters whose depth, flow speed and waves were different, the boats needed to adopt different shapes and structures, with deadweight tonnages set for different functions. Of course, even in the same river, the shapes and structures of boats may vary for different purposes. For example, the warship must be made suitable for battles, and passenger boats must be elegant in appearance and comfortable for passengers. In general, the various shapes and structures of boats must be suitable to sail in different waters. From this aspect, we classify boats into three categories: canal boats, domestic boats and seagoing boats.

In the Northern Song Dynasty, the major routes for inland river transportation included the canals in the Bianhe River, the canals in Huainan East and West provinces, and those in Zhejiang West and East provinces. Moreover, the Yuhe River and Lingqu Channel also played a role in water transportation. However, in the Southern Song Dynasty, the Bianhe and Yuhe Rivers had been included in the territory of the Jin Kingdom. The natural conditions for sailing were different in different sections of the river. Among all the rivers, the Bianhe River was relatively conducive to easy sailing as it was suitable for full navigation without the application of weirs and sluices. However, the Bianhe River was only 1–1.7 m deep. "As the section of Bianhe River was only 1–1.7 m deep (Toqta 1977: 2324), the river surface went up and down occasionally, or even became dried in Summer, only leaving one or two feet of water in the shallow riverbed." (S. Xu et al. 2014: 9590) The grain vessels in the Bianhe River were crowded with 400 or 500-Liao Boats (S. Xu et al. 2014: 7060). Every 30 boats formed a batch of grain transportation ships with a serial number." (S. Xu et al. 2014: 7038) Such boats were often seen sailing in this river. The 4-foot-deep water could also carry the heavier boats with a load capacity of 600 Liao (S. Xu et al. 2014: 9596). In the early years of the Yuanfeng Reign, someone recorded the fact that "the heavy boats could sail in the water at less than 4 feet below plimsoll mark. When the river was 5 feet deep, large grain vessels could sail safely." (S. Xu et al. 2014: 9593) When the Bianhe River was at its high level, 600-Liao grain vessels could sail smoothly in it.

When the grain vessels were fully loaded, they were very heavy. As commercial boats and passenger boats were comparatively lighter than grain vessels, even 1000-Liao passenger boats could still sail in the Bianhe River. One scholar studied the boats sailing in the Bianhe River after examining the famous painting "Riverside Scene at Qingming Festival" painted by artist Zhang Zeduan, and estimated the load capacity of cargo ships to be 1000 Liao (F. Xi 2000: 147). Such larger and heavier boats were more likely to become stranded during the dry season. "The convoy leader of the grain shipping agency had to buy an official passenger boat by himself to follow the batch grain vessels. Such a passenger boat usually had a load capacity of 1000 Liao." "When such boats were approaching the capital city Bianliang, most of them got stranded in the shallow water." (S. Xu et al. 2014: 7060) This record shows that such grain boats with a load capacity of several thousand Liao or even ten thousand Liao were unable to sail in the Bianhe River. For another example, "Yang Yao's battleships, including Wangsanzhou-made boats, big or small Deshan-made boats and others, could not sail unless the water was 3 m deep." Big Deshan-made boats were installed with 22-group-wheel Pedal-driving Ships and could carry 300 soldiers. If we adopt the proportion of soldiers, high-ranking officers, and helmsmen proposed by She Yanzhi, the total number of people would be some 420 on board the large Deshan-made paddle-driving boat (K. Yue, n.d., 1574, 1600; S. Xu et al. 2014: 8813).[8] Based on the calculation method described in *the General Record of Military Affairs*, the deadweight tonnage of one person was two Dan (G. Zeng 1990). Thus, the deadweight tonnage of a big Deshan-made boat must be 840 Liao. Generally speaking, a warship needed to carry arrows and stones for military use, and if we adopt the proportion of people to objects as one to three (S. Xu et al. 2014: 9537),[9] a large Deshan-made boat had a volume of 2500 Liao, far less than the load capacity of a 10-thousand-Dan boat. Furthermore, judging from the draught marks of a boat in the Bianhe River, we know that such a boat was not a 10-thousand-Dan boat (Jojin 2009: 275). So, "the argument that there were 10-thousand-Dan boats sailing in the Bianhe River," (B. Zhou 1997: 58) made by Zhou Baozhu was groundless, due to the poor water conditions in the Bianhe River compared to other rivers.

The water was four or five feet deep in the canals in Huainan East and West provinces, and in Liangzhe East and West provinces, which were less advantageous than the Bianhe River. Later, in the Southern Song Dynasty, the dredging and deepening project at the south end made it 8 feet deep, but its whole water course could not still be compared to the Bianhe River. "As the banks between Zhenzhou in the south and Chuzhou in the north were used to build weirs for reserving water, no heavy boats could sail through such sections." (Toqta 1977: 4258) As the bottom of the canal was flat and its depth was not sufficient, the dredging and deepening project needed to be done frequently so as to meet the 5-foot depth requirement for sailing (S. Xu et al. 2014: 7044). The frequency at which this work needed to be done suggests that it was not easy to keep the river 5 feet deep. Thus, the most suitable vessels for the canals were the 200–300 Liao boat (S. Hong, n.d.; S. Xu et al. 2014: 7066).[10] The boats with a load capacity of 2000 Liao could not sail in the canals in Huainan East and West provinces. The goods on each boat had to be allocated to several boats with a load capacity of 200 or 300 Liao, which was called Panjian (load redistribution).

Another factor restricting shipping capacity was the widely applied weirs and sluices used for water control. Apart from the whole water course of the Bianhe River, almost all the goods on the large boats into the canal sections in Huainan East, Huainan West, Liangzhe East, and Liangzhe West provinces had to be redistributed

---

[8] She Yanzhi states that pedal wheel ships can hold 250 soldiers, 100 high-ranking officers and helmsmen, on the basis of this proportion, Big Deshan-made boats can carry 300 soldiers and 120 high-ranking officers and helmsmen.

[9] According to the record of *The Anthology of Laws and Regulations of the Song Dynasty*, the Song government made the rules that the 300-Liao boat can hold 100 people with no luggage, the 200-Liao 60 people, the 100-Liao 30 people, and the number of the approved load capacity of the boast under 100 Liao decreases progressively.

[10] Based on the records of *Panzhou Anthology* and *The Anthology of Laws and Regulations of the Song Dynasty,* the boats with the load capacity from 200 and 300 Liao only served as transporting the taxes paid in kind by local governments of Liangzhe East and West provinces to the imperial court. The standard is that a transporting fleet consists of 30 boats.

to smaller boats to pass through the weirs and sluices as the universal width of sluices was only 2.8 m wide. For example, a historical book recorded the events surrounding Emperor Gaozong's mother returning from the Jin Kingdom and Emperor Huizong's coffin sent from the Jin Kingdom. "As the royal boat was 2.8 m wide, wider than the old one, anywhere when it passed, the weirs were probably damaged by its sailing." (S. Wang 2012: 657–658) From this description, we know that the lock gate would be no wider than 2.8 m. In the Yuan Dynasty, the limit of boat width was set as 2.8 m. "The head of shipbuilding craftsmen claimed that the boat's beam must be 2.8 m wide and the boat must be 21.5 m long in total." (L. Song 1976: 1613)[11] This record described the size of boats required for passing the sluices. In the Song Dynasty, the biggest sluice gate in Zhenzhou was 4.95 m wide in beam and 1.65 m deep in the entry." (S. Xu et al. 2014: 9618) Due to the width limit of the sluice gate, it was difficult to sail two boats in parallel. In the Northern Song Dynasty, "when the cargo transportation vessels went through Guazhou Sluices, the empty boats from the north and the heavy cargo transportation boats meeting in the sluices, would disrupt each other." In the fourth year of the Zhenghe Reign (AD 1114), the empty cargo transportation boats from the north were required to sail out of Guazhou Sluices at the exit, and heavy cargo transportation boats from the south were required to enter the sluices at the entry (S. Xu et al. 2014: 7053–54). This prevented two boats from encountering and potentially disrupting one another in the sluices. The basic conditions defined the shapes and structures of the boats, that is to say, grain boats in the canals in Huainan East and West provinces were probably small boats with a load capacity of 200 or 300 Liao each, smaller than the 400 or 500-Liao boats, or even 600-Liao boats sailing in the Bianhe River.

The navigation conditions in Liangzhe West Province were much better than in Huainan East and West provinces. However, weirs and sluices were also installed in the canal in Liangzhe West Province, which likely increased the possibility that boats would become stranded. "The load capacity of boats sailing in the canal in Liangzhe East and West provinces was no more than 500 Dan, and the river was about 2 m deep, which was enough to sail boats with a load capacity of 500 Dan" (E. Shan 1990). Thus, the 5-m-deep water and the 500-Dan load capacity were established facts in the navigation of canals. However, the canal in Liangzhe West Province "had dry seasons in spring and winter." (X. Li 2013: 3531) In the sixth year of the Qiandao Reign (AD 1179), when Lu You passed Benniu Sluices, he remarked that "turbulent water was running down noisily." This is in contrast to the account of Su Shi, who passed by Benniu Sluices during the dry season, noting that "people had to raise their heads towing boats and let out sighs over the dry river bed in June." (Y. Lu 2012a, b: 163; Y. Lu 2011: 497) The navigation conditions of the canal in Liangzhe East Province were even poorer than in Liangzhe West Province. The section between

[11] The width of the lock gate allows only the boats whose maximum beam is below 2.8 m in length to pass through. It is certain that the middle beam width of a boat is its maximum width. The Song and Yuan calculation rules must be the same. "The width of the surface", "width" and "maximum beam width " in the quotations of this section all refer to the width of the boat's middle beam, which is the maximum width of a boat. In addition, "length" "the total length" in the quotations refer to the full length of a boat.

Shanyin County and Xiaoshan County in the west could support the navigation of 500-Dan boats, but the section between Xiaoshan and Lin'an in the west could only allow 200-Dan boats to sail safely. Likewise, the section between Shangyu County and Kuaiji County in the west could also only allow 200-Dan boats to sail (S. Shi et al. 1990: 6925, 6933, 6938). As the section between Xixing Sluices and Qianqing Weir was often choked with silt, the river was only about one meter deep (H. Zhang 1990: 7135). Thus, this river could only support 200-Dan or 300-Dan boats to sail safely.

The Southern Song authorities laid a few decrees to Liangzhe provinces to build boats with a load capacity of 200 or 300 Dan for batch shipping. In the first year of the Shaoxing Reign (AD 1131), an imperial edict required that the transportation agency of Liangzhe East and West provinces should build 35 cargo transportation boats with a load capacity of 250 Liao (S. Xu et al. 2014: 7127). In the fifth year of the Shaoxing Reign (AD 1135), Emperor Gaozong issued an edict that Liangzhe East and West provinces should "buy 200-Liao to 300-Liao boats to transport grains and coins which were to be distributed back to their own provinces." (S. Xu et al. 2014: 7066) In the eighth year of the Qiandao Reign (AD 1172), the provinces from Liangzhe West Province downward were required to raise funds for building 350-Liao boats to meet the need of grain transportation." (S. Xu et al. 2014: 7134) The Taxation Transfer Agency of Liangzhe East and West provinces mentioned the fact that "the cargo transportation boats under the supervision of the provincial taxation transfer agency had the load capacity of 300-Liao each." (S. Xu et al. 2014: 7110) This description reveals the facts of grain shipping in the two provinces. Jojin, the famous Japanese monk, in his canal voyage in Lingzhe East Province, took a large boat "which was 33 m long, 2.6 m high at the cabin roof, and 3.9 m wide." When they travelled through Qianqing Weir, they had to "make use of eight buffaloes to tow the boat to cross the weir," but they struggled to reach Xiaoshan, and the shallow water stranded the boat completely. They had to request the Xiaoshan County to lend them six smaller boats and reloaded the people and goods on them (Jojin 2009: 199).

As the canals were usually shallow, the boats in them had to be flat-bottomed. For example, in the third year of the Yuanfeng Reign (AD 1180), "an imperial edict required 10 batches of boats for shipping in Zhenzhou, Chuzhou, and Sizhou prefectures to build 100 flat-bottomed boats in each prefecture to transport goods to the capital city Bianliang." (T. Li 2004: 7432) Such flat-bottomed boats could sail in the canal sections of Huainan East and West provinces and in the Bianhe River. In the sixth year of the Yuanfeng Reign (AD 1083), Sanmen Shipping Department requested to borrow 300 flat-bottomed boats with a load capacity of 400 Liao from the Shipping Ministry (T. Li 2004: 8016). These flat-bottomed boats were designated for canal shipping. In the seventh year of the Yuanfeng Reign (AD 1084), Emperor Shenzong planned to transport grains as food relief to the central Shanxi Plain, "but the shallow water from the west gate of the capital to Luokou forced them to adopt flat-bottomed shallow boats." (S. Xu et al. 2004: 6964) Another example was that in the fourth year of the Zhenghe Reign (AD 1114), Emperor Huizong laid an imperial edict to the Transfer Agency of Taxation in Liangzhe East and West provinces to build 300 flat-bottomed boats with a load capacity of 300 Liao, while Jiangnan East,

Jiangnan West, Jinghu South, and Jinghu North provinces were to build 300 boats with a load capacity of 500 Liao. These boats were for the capital city's use (S. Xu et al. 2004: 7124). As these were shallow draft boats with resistance against waves, they could sail safely in the torrential rivers. In the sixth year of the Xi'ning Reign (AD 1073), the imperial court ordered the Bianchuan boats to sail in the Yangtze River. "In winter these boats were driven by the north wind to carry salt as cargo transportation tasks to Hubei Province, and in spring they could carry grains as tributes back to the capital city driven by the south wind. As a result, over five hundred boats were damaged by strong winds." "The numbers of drowned people and ruined ships were growing as the Bianchuan boats went to sail in the Yangtze River." (T. Li 2004: 5992) This serves a piece of evidence that Bianchuan boats were not suitable to sail in the torrential Yangtze River.

Although no records were found regarding the proportion of length and width of the canal boats, considering the limits of weirs and sluices, these proportions must have been greater than that of domestic river boats, in order to ensure their load capacity. One scholar calculated the proportion of length and width of cargo ships in the Bianhe River to be 4.8:1 (24 m long and 5 m wide) (L. Xi 2000: 147). No width limit for boats sailing in the Bianhe River was required when they passed through sluices, but in other rivers, this was not the case. Therefore, the boats traversing the Bianhe River were broader than those in the canals of Huainan East and West provinces and Zhejiang East and West provinces. As discussed in the previous sections, the boats passing through water gates in Zhenzhou in the Yuan Dynasty could be regarded as the shapes and structures of boats sailing in the canal of Huainan East and West provinces, with a proportion of 7.6:1 (21.5 m long and 2.8 m wide). The load capacity of grain vessels sailing in the canal of Huainan East and West provinces would be 200–300 Liao. Based on the maximum width of the sluices, the load capacity of grain boats in the Yuan Dynasty must be 300 Liao. The proportion of length and width of the grain boats in the Yellow River with a load capacity of 300 Liao must be 4.5:1 (14.9 m long and 3.3 m wide) (see the following discussions). Thus, the proportion of length and width of the boats in the Yellow River was much smaller than that of grain boats in Huainan East and West provinces. Due to the limit of width of weirs and sluices, boats in the canal had to be reduced in width and increased in length. This increase in the proportion of length and width helps to facilitate safe sailing. Generally speaking, the proportion of length and width would be larger than other similar domestic river boats with the same load capacity.

1.3.3 The Deadweight Tonnage and Their Shapes and Structures of Inland River Boats

The term "inland river boat" is used to refer to boats sailing in all rivers other than canals. This chapter restricts the focus of its study to ships sailing in the Yangtze River. Du Fu, the famous poet in the Tang Dynasty, once mentioned the fact that "the rich could afford a big spacious ship for their voyage, but the poor had to board on a small barge." Southerners used the word "Ge" to refer to a large ship, while a small barge was referred to as "Die" (Z. Wu 2012: 137). The sizes of canal boats were restricted by the various factors affecting the different rivers. The boats could be very large or small based on the natural conditions of the river. Yang Wanli pointed out that "in terms of boat size, they may be as large as a 10,000-Dan ship or as small as a small barge driven by an oar." (S. Yang et al. 1990) Huang Tingjian described the sailing situation, noting that "rich merchants' 10,000-Dan boats could lift huge sails which could touch the constellations of Qianniu and Beidou in the sky." (T. Huang 2011: 1018) This is not a groundless literary exaggeration. Zhang Shunmin saw a 10,000-Dan boat at the Port of Dongting Lake in the water course of the Yangtze River. "The boat looked like an oval large house as wide as three rooms placed together, with windows at its back and elegant interior decorations. You need to go up and down via stairs and could not sail it without a strong wind. It could carry 20 million strings of 1000 coins and 12,000 Dan of rice." (S. Zhang 1990: 475)[12] This is a typical 10,000-Dan boat. Zhang's description suggests that it was difficult to sail in the Yangtze River in the absence of strong wind. This boat was an exception among the boats in the Yangtze River.

Historical records also provide evidence for the large boats with load capacities of 1000 or 2000 Liao. In his voyage, Lu You changed his boat to the Jiazhou-made Zhaoqing Boat at Shashi, which was a large boat with a load capacity of 1600 Hu (Y. Lu 2012a, b: 206). In the 15th year of the Jiading Reign (AD 1222), the horse-carrying boats built by the Military Headquarters of Branch Troops in Ezhou Prefecture could carry 1000 Liao or even 1500 Liao (S. Xu et al. 2014: 7140). The large boats which were used as cargo transportation ships and had a load capacity of 2000 Dan could not sail in the canal of Huainan East and West provinces as the water was too shallow to carry them. Smaller boats had to be used to transfer goods to and from the larger canal boats, in the previously-described process of "panjian" (S. Hong, n.d.; S. Xu et al. 2014: 7066).[13] This process was referred to as "Panjian" (distributing goods from large boats to smaller ones). In the third year of the Jianyan Reign (AD 1129), the royal court summoned private grain ships from Jiangnan East and West provinces, and Hubei Province. Those who could recruit seven' boats with a load capacity of 13,000 Dan each would be conferred the post of Chengxinlang (the ninth-level official); those who could recruit five boats with a load capacity of 10,000 Dan each would be conferred a military post of Bujinwuxiaowei (a military alternate officer below the ninth-level official); those who could recruit two boats with

[12] "Two hundred thousand strings of 1000 coins" was incorrectly written as "20 million strings of 1,000 coins". If each string of 1000 copper coins weighs 5 Jin, then 20 million strings of 1,000 coins weighs up to 64,000 tons, which is impossible. If the fact is the boat could carry two hundred thousand strings of coins, whose weight is 640 tons, and it is close to the weight of 12,000 Dan of rice (710 tons).

[13] Based on the records of *Panzhou Anthology and The Anthology of Laws and Regulations of the Song Dynasty,* the boats with the load capacity from 200 and 300 Liao only served as transporting the taxes paid by the local governments in Liangzhe East and West provinces to the imperial court. The standard is that a transporting fleet consists of 30 boats.

a load capacity of 4000 Dan would be conferred a military post of Bujinyixiaowei (lower than Bujinwuxiaowei) (S. Xu et al. 2014: 9253). Obviously, some boats with a load capacity of 2000 Dan were also recruited for commercial purposes. Merchant boats, for instance, had a load capacity of 2000 Dan. For example, when Lu You went to Sichuan Province from the canal connection at Zhenjiang in Liangzhe West Province, he boarded the Wang Zhiyi Boat, which had a load capacity of 2000 Dan. In his voyage in Shishou County, Lu You once saw "an anchored large boat with a load capacity of 2500 Dan." (Y. Lu 2012a, b: 204)

Among the battleships, the Pedal-wheeled ships with a load capacity of over 1000 Liao were put into use. The Haihu warships with a load capacity of 1000 Liao built by Qin Shifu in Chizhou Prefecture was "33 m long, containing 11 cabins. Its beam was 6 m long, its middle cabin was 4.8 m deep and its bottom plank was 1.3 m wide." (S. Xu et al. 2014: 7139) In the Southern Song Dynasty, when the royal court tried to defeat the rebel Yang Yao, both sides built huge pedal-wheeled ships for battles. Their ships were 66–99 m long (S. Xu et al. 2014: 7129), with two- or three-story cabins seating over 1000 soldiers." (K. Xiong 1985: 171) Based on the calculation standard in the General Record of Military Affairs, one person equals 2 Dan, and thus a boat large enough for 100 people may have the cubage of 2000 Dan. If we include the space for weapons and the soldiers' living quarters, the deadweight tonnage would be larger. In the fifth year of the Shaoxing Reign (AD 1135), Wu Shen mentioned that pedal-wheeled ships, "were over 70 m long, nearly 70 m wide, and 13 m high." Obviously, he was mistaken in his assertion that the proportion of length and width was 1:1. More likely, its width was 7 m (S. Yang et al. 1990). Its shape and structure were also larger than the passenger boat recorded by Xu Jing, which was 33 m long, 10 m high and 8.2 m wide, with a load capacity of over 2000 Hu. Lu You had seen quite a few "large boats in Ezhou Prefecture which were over 70 m long." (Y. Lu 2012a, b: 197) They were longer than passenger boats. Lu You once recorded the three dimensions of large pedal-wheeled boats which were 119 m long, 13.5 m wide and 24 m high (Y. Lu 2012a, b: 6). These were much larger than the 2000-Hu passenger boats recorded by Xu Jing. The height of pedal-wheeled boats most likely refers to the structure above the deck. However, the passenger boats could not have high structures built above the deck, in order to maintain balance when encountering in strong winds. Even if so, the pedal-wheeled boats described by Lu You would probably have the load capacity of 3000 or 4000 Liao or above.

From the above discussions, the long voyage boats along the Yangtze River were much larger boats with a load capacity of over 1000 Liao than those sailing in canals. When Fan Chengda went to take his post to Lin'an (the Southern Song Dynasty's capital city) from Sichuan, at the port of Zhenjiang Prefecture, he boarded a canal boat to sail in the Grand Canal in Liangzhe West Province. As he was accustomed to large boats and not used to taking smaller boats, he lamented, "I frequently went to Jiangnan East and West provinces and Liangzhe East and West provinces on business, hurrying to and from Sichuan and Guangnan East and West provinces. When I took a small boat, I had the imagination of boarding on a fishing boat as usual, I had never thought of my long journey returning from afar." (C. Fan 2012a, b, c: 90) But the cargo transportation boats in the Yangtze River and its branches were mostly medium-sized boats with a load capacity of 300 Liao to 800 Liao. Wang Shipeng, the famous politician and poet in the Southern Song Dynasty, mentioned his experience of sailing in Hubei Province, when he got a letter written by Cao Zimeng, submitted to the royal court that the boat could carry 800 Liao (S. Wang 2012: 341). The beating heart of the shipbuilding industry in Jiangnan West Province mainly produced grain boats with a load capacity of 500 Liao or 300 Liao. In our previous discussions, it was noted that 600 boats undertook the task of transporting 370,000 Dan of grain in the ninth year of the Qiandao Reign (AD 1173). Every year, Jizhou Prefecture had to carry 370,000 Dan of rice on boats with a load capacity of 500 Liao. In the twelfth year of the Jiading Reign (AD 1219), the department of grain shipping in Jiangnan West Province built 108 boats with a load capacity of 300 Dan grains on each boat for Jiangnan East Province (S. Xu et al. 2014: 7139). Also, the boats that Tongchuan Prefecture built and recruited had a load capacity of 300 Dan to carry grains for troops (X. Li 2013: 1413).

The size of battleships in the Yangtze River decreased in the Southern Song Dynasty, most of which had a capacity of less than 1000 Liao. During the Qiandao Reign, the load capacity of batch horse carrying boats was either 700 Liao or 500 Liao (S. Xu et al. 2014: 9107). In the 3rd year of the Jiatai Reign (AD 1203), the Palace Administration built 4 horse-carrying boats with a load capacity of 800 Liao, and 6 horse-carrying boats with a load capacity of 500 Liao (S. Xu et al. 2014: 7138). In the same year, Qin Shifu built the Iron Gunwheel Warship. Its load capacity was 400 Liao, and its cabin was 4.9 m wide at the beam, 1.65 m deep, and 3.35 m wide at the bottom (S. Xu et al. 2014: 7139). From the 9th year of the Chunyou Reign (AD 1249) to the first year of the Xianchun Reign (AD 1265), the navy of the Jiankang Prefecture built 2287 boats, including patrol boats, multi-paddle boats, four-mast seagoing ships, horse-carrying boats, and others. Among them, patrol boats account for 63% of the total, pedal boats 11%, and Fuyang-made warships 8% (Y. Zhou 1990: 1983). The patrol boat is a swift warship with 30 people on board (Songji Sanchao Zhenngyao 2010: 349). In terms of load capacity, the Fuyang-made boats built by Jiankang Prefecture were divided into four categories based on load capacity: 200 Liao, 250 Liao, 300 Liao and 500 Liao (Y. Zhou 1990: 1983). The number of pedal boats was much less. According to *A Historical Account About Shouchang*, pedal boats were swift and much smaller, with a load capacity of only 50 Liao to 70 Liao. In the 15th year of the Jianding Reign (AD 1222), the Military Headquarters of Branch Troops in Ezhou Prefecture built some pedal boats with a load capacity of 50 Liao (S. Xu et al. 2014: 7140). Most of the boats in the Yellow River had a load capacity of 300 Liao to 800 Liao, while most of the ferries built by River and Bridge Department had a load capacity of 300–800 Liao. Generally speaking, the boats with a load capacity of 200 Liao were considered to be small ones (Shakeshi 1990). Additionally, some painted pleasure boats in West Lake had a load capacity of 1000 Liao for carrying 100 people, and were over 60 m long. Some others had a capacity of 500 Liao for carrying 30–50 people, and were over 30 m long. Some smaller ones had a load capacity of 200–300 Liao for carrying twenty to thirty people, and were about 15 m long (Z. Wu 1980: 110). Most of their load capacities were under 1000 Liao.

Some sharp-bottomed ships were often seen in the Yangtze River. The Haihu Warship built by Qin Shifu in Chizhou Prefecture was an example as discussed above. "Its beam was about 6 m long, the middle cabin was 2.8 m deep, and its bottom plank was 1.3 m long." The proportion of depth and width was 2.1:1 and the proportion of its surface width and bottom width was 4.5:1. This was the shape and structure of a typical sharp-bottomed boat. As common boats in the Yangtze River had a deeper draught line than that of a canal boat, they could not sail in the shallow section of the canal. This is attested in the historical records, where it is indicated that, "as the water was very shallow in the section between the west gate of the capital city in Bianhe River and the Port Luokou, most of the cargo transportation boats from the southeast provinces could not sail in the canal," and that people had to "use flat-bottomed boats to carry grains to and from the capital city." (S. Xu et al. 2014: 6964) In fact, most of the boats sailing in the Yangtze River were flat-bottomed boats. The Iron Gunwheel Warship as discussed in the previous section was about 5 m long in its beam, 1.7 m deep, and 2.8 m wide at its bottom. The proportion of depth and width was 2.3:1, and the proportion of its surface width and bottom width was 1.35:1, so it belongs to the category of flat-bottomed boats. The boats passing through the Three Gorges were also flat-bottomed boats as they had to sail and resist the rocks on the riverbed. "The shape of broad-bottomed boats was good for sailing through the sand bars or over rocks on the river bed." (Y. Lu 2012a, b: 216) Few records, however, were made about the proportion of length and width. In March 1960, a wooden boat was found and towed out of water in a narrow course at Shiqiao Town of Yangzhou. The remaining part of the flat-bottomed boat was 18.4 m long. The original length was calculated as 24 m, the middle cabin was 4.3 m wide, its bottom was 2.4 m wide, and it was 1.3 m deep (Jiangsu Heritage Working Team 1961: 53). Thus, the proportion of length and width was 5.6:1, the proportion of surface width and bottom width was 1.8:1, but it was only 1.3 m deep below the deck. Therefore, this vessel belongs to the category of shallow-bottomed boats, suitable for sailing in shallow rivers or sand bars of the Yangtze River. Based on the standard of Huai ruler (Z. Guo 1993: 251), its middle width was 4.3 m wide, which was equivalent to 13 feet, wider than the 8.5-foot-wide sluices in the Huainan East and West provinces. Thus, such boats could sail in the Grand Canal.

Shallow-bottomed boats and flat-bottomed boats were also seen in other canals. In the fourth year of the Zhenghe Reign (AD 1114), the local authority built 1300 boats for transportation in Guangji River, including passenger boats, shallow-bottomed house-shaped boats, and cargo-passenger boats. They had planned to build boats with a load capacity of 300 Liao, but later they changed their mind, instead building 100-Liao passenger boats, 250-Liao house-shaped boats, and cargo-passenger boats (S. Xu et al. 2014: 7124). According to the description in *The General Summary of River-flood Prevention Work*, the 100-Liao boats in the Yellow River were "13.2 m long, 3.96 m wide at the beam, and 2.8 m wide at the bottom, with a cabin 1 m high." The proportion of surface width and bottom width was 1.5:1. Such boats were small shallow-bottomed ones (Shakeshi 1990). The shipwreck which was discovered at Mengyuankou Village of Jinghai County, Tianjin Municipality in 1978, was a flat-bottomed wooden boat built in the Song Dynasty. The function of this privately built boat was to transport goods in inland rivers (Tianjin Municipal Office of Cultural Relics 1983: 53, 58). The wooden boat found at Fengbang of Jiading County, Shanghai Municipality in 1978, was a 10-m-long sand-proof flat-bottomed boat with a load capacity of 5 tons (W. Ni 1979: 33). Such boats could be used in the tranquil waters like West Lake. The small flat-bottomed Wulong boats in West Lake were built with a simple design, and were dedicated to tourists (Sishuiqianfu 1981: 39).

In contrast, the warships in inland rivers were comparatively larger in size. As discussed above, Lu You described the proportion of length and width of large paddle wheel ships as being 8.8:1 (118 m long and 13.5 m wide). The proportion of length and width of the Haihu Warship built by Qin Shifu was 5.6:1, and the proportion of length and width of the Iron Gunwheel Warship was 8:1. Apart from warships, other kinds of ship had a proportion of length and width below 5.6:1, with most of them having a proportion of 3.6:1. As discussed above, the proportion of length and width of the boat found at Yuanmengkou of Jinghai County, Tianjin Municipality was 3.6:1 (its body was 14.62 m long, and the maximum width was 4.05 m). The Pontoon Bridge in Minjiang River of Fujian Province adopted the boats which were 15.2 m long and 5 m wide to structure its bridge gate. The second boat in the structure of the Pontoon Bridge and the third dwarf boat were 14.5 m long and 3.6 m wide. The rest were 12.9 m long and 3.3 m wide (K. Lang 1990: 7830). Their proportion of length and width were 3.1:1, 4:1, and 3.9:1 respectively. According to the notes in The General Summary of River-flood Prevention Work, the boats in the Yellow River with a load capacity of 100 Liao, were 13.2 m long and 3.96 m wide, with a proportion of length and width of 33:1. The boats with a load capacity of 300 Liao, were 14.9 m long and 3.3 m wide, with a proportion of length and width of 4.5:1. The boats with a load capacity of 800 Liao, were 23.1 m long and 5.94 m wide, with a proportion of length and width of 3.9:1 (Shakeshi 1990).

1.3.4 The Deadweight Tonnage, Shapes and Structures of the Seagoing Boats in the Song Dynasty

Accounts About the Capital City recorded the fact that "seagoing vessels had different load capacities, from 5000 Liao holding 500–600 people, to middle boats of 1000–2000 Liao carrying 200–300 people. The rest were called Zhuanfeng Boats (a kind of small swift boat), and they were 6-oar or 8-oar boats carrying some one hundred people." (Z. Wu 1980:111) This quotation mentioned the sizes and categories of seagoing boats, but it did not describe the structures of the vessels in the Song Dynasty. We can set up the standard of medium seagoing vessels based on the three dimensions of privately-owned boats requisitioned by the authority in Fujian Province, which were 3.96 m wide. The large seagoing vessels could be judged by the standard of surface width of 6.93 m. The deadweight tonnage of a medium boat whose surface width was 3.96 m had a load capacity of 300 Liao, providing room for 50 people on board. Those Saury-shaped Warships, also called Fishing Boats, could hold 50 people on board. These vessels were 16.5 m long and 3.96 m wide at the beam. At the standard of costs by private manufacturers, each one may cost 400 strings of 1000 coins (S. Xu et al. 2014: 7125). An 8-oar 26.4-m-long warship with a load capacity of 400 Liao would cost 1159 strings of 1000 coins. The expenditures of a 4-oar 14.8-m-long Haihu Boat with a load capacity of would be 329 strings of 1000 coins." (S. Xu et al. 2014: 7126) As both of them were warships, we can consider them to be built at the same proportion of length and width. The Saury-shaped Warship was 16.5 m long and 3.96 m wide, which was a little bit larger than the 4-oar warship, but smaller than the 8-oar 26.4-m-long warship with a load capacity of 400 Liao. The 4-oar warship built by the Jiankang Prefecture had a load capacity of 300 Liao (Y. Zhou 1990: 1983). Obviously, the surface width of 3.96 m must correspond with the deadweight tonnage of medium seagoing warships, whose deadweight tonnage could have been 300 Liao.

The deadweight tonnage of a seagoing warship with surface width of 6.6 m had a load capacity of 800 Liao. In the fifth year of the Qiandao Reign (AD 1169), Feng Zhan, the general commander of the navy, built a multiple-oar boat which "was 27.4 m long and 6.6 m wide. Judging from the Huai Ruler then, the load capacity of the boat must be 800 Liao" (S. Xu et al. 2014: 7133). The width of 6.9 m can be used to judge whether or not a boat can be classified as a large seagoing boat with a load capacity of 1000 Liao or above. The passenger boat for Xu Jing's missionary voyage was a large seagoing boat with a load capacity of 2000 Dan, "which was over 33 m long, 10 m deep and 8.25 m wide at the beam, large enough to hold 2000 Dan of grain." As a royal missionary expedition, a large seagoing boat was needed to showcase the prosperity of the Song Dynasty. In the third year of the Jianyan Reign (AD 1129), the coastal provinces, such as Fujian and Guangnan East, hired seagoing ships, which can be classified into 3 categories. "The upper-class boats were 7.9 m wide at the beam, the middle were 6.6 m wide at the beam, and the lower-class ones were 5.9 m wide at the beam." (S. Xu et al. 2014: 9253) Taking the surface width of 7.9 m as the width of a large boat, we must conclude that the boat taken by Xu Jing and his delegation was likely an extra-large seagoing boat. The warships adopted by the navy of Guangnan West Province were 7.9-m-wide large warships (S. Xu et al. 2014: 9625). The patrol boats built by Fumenzhai of Pingyang in Wenzhou also fall into this category, as their surface width was 9.2 m (X. Li 2013: 3703). In the Southern Song Dynasty, one of the boats adopted by the Left Wing Navy of Fujian Province would be "9.9 m wide at the beam and 1 m wide at the bottom, with a load capacity of 2000 Liao." (S. Xu et al. 2014: 7130) We did find some evidence regarding the 5000-Liao boats and Xu Jing's Missionary Boat used by the Song Dynasty in Accounts About the Capital City. It is obvious that these were extra-large seagoing boats. Such magic boats were high and broad; the utensils for daily use and people on board were three times than ordinary passenger boats (J. Xu 2006: 129). Such boats must have had a load capacity of 6000 Liao. Only four boats of this type were built for Korean missionary purposes during the respective reigns of Emperors Shenzong and Huizong.

Because of the huge waves and deep water in the sea, the seagoing boats required a sharp-bottomed structure. In 1974, a missing seagoing boat of the Song Dynasty was found in Quanzhou Bay. It was sharp-bottomed, with a flat and broad cabin conducive to sailing in the ocean (Editorial Committee of Excavation Report of the Quanzhou Bay Song Dynasty Shipwreck Excavation 1975: 5). The offshore Saury-shaped Warship was also a kind of sharp-bottomed boat. Its head was small and narrow, its flat deck was suitable to carry soldiers, and its bottom was as sharp as a knife, cleaving waves in the ocean (S. Xu et al. 2014: 7125). The missionary passenger boats had flat decks to carry officials and soldiers and their bottoms were as sharp as a huge knife suitable to cleave waves (J. Xu 2006). Thus, the best boats for traveling in the deep ocean were sharp-bottomed boats. The major warships adopted by the Left Wing Navy of Fujian Province were sharp-bottomed seagoing boats in the Southern Song Dynasty. "Every boat was 9.9 m wide at the beam, and 1 m wide at the bottom, with a load capacity of 2000 Liao." (S. Xu et al. 2014: 7130) The proportion of length and width was 10:1. Compared with the boat of the Song Dynasty found in Shiqiao Town of Yangzhou Prefecture (the proportion of length and width was 1.8:1), such seagoing boats were much sharper at the bottom than those in the canal.

In contrast, flat-bottomed boats were used for offshore voyages in the oceanic areas of Liangzhe East and West provinces, Fujian Province, and Guangnan East and West provinces. One boat, which was built in the Song Dynasty and found in Dazhi River running through Nanhui of Shanghai, was a single-mast flat-bottomed grain boat, also called "flat-bottomed boat in the canal" (S. Ji 1987: 176). The local governments in Wenzhou were ordered to build grain boats for hinterland shipping. However, in the course of transferring grain boats, quite a few "sank in the whirling water near the Sea of Japan." (Y. Lou 1990) The deep ocean was hazardous for such flat-bottomed boats. As they faced the danger of sinking in the offshore areas, it was impossible for them to go further into the huge sea. In the first year of the Xinglong Reign (AD 1163), the royal court ordered Minghzou Prefecture and Wenzhou Prefecture to build flat-bottomed seagoing boats, but Mingzhou replied that "their boats would go into the sea." (S. Xu et al. 2014: 71,331) As waves were bigger and waters were deeper in the offshore areas of Fujian and Guangnan East and West provinces, flat-bottomed boats could not sail safely in such areas. Even boats sailing in the offshore areas of Liangzhe East and West provinces could not sail in the waters of Fujian and Guangnan East and West provinces. For example, "the saury-shaped warships could go into the shallow waters near Mingzhou as waves were small there. On the other hand, the waters in Fujian and Guangnan East and West provinces were deep and broad, and not as calm as the waters in Mingzhou." Thus, the boats that could sail in the offshore waters of Mingzhou could sail smoothly in the sea areas of Fujian (S. Xu et al. 2014: 7130). For these reasons, the local governments set the standard of 3.96-m-width to requisition privately owned boats in Fujian Province, but the standard was reduced to 3.3-m-width by Liangzhe East Province.

Due to multiple rivers running into the sea, including the Yellow River, Huaihe River, the Yangtze River, and others, the coastal areas were clogged with sand sedimentation. For example, in the section from Haizhou of Lianyungang to Tongzhou of Nantong, there were quite a few sandbars like Nansha, Beisha, Miaosha, Yesha,

Waisha, Yaosha and Liuzhusha (J. Luo et al. 1990: 5207; Y. Mei et al. 1990: 5989). A safe voyage along the offshore sea route required experienced sailors who were expert navigators and who could observe the tide. Experienced sailors could seize an opportunity to sail in rising tide and anchor in falling tide. "They would make use of rising tide at the fourth water level or above, but stop sailing at the ninth water level. Boatmen would drive their boats off deep water to anchor them by the shore before the tide reached the tenth level because they need half a day to avoid rocks in the shallow water in their way back to the shore before the tide falls." If they fell off course, the boat would likely be doomed to sink. Thus, experienced sailors were necessary to navigate among the sandbars and remain on the correct route (Y. Mei et al. 1990: 5990; X. Li 2013: 1116). An alternative route could also have been utilized, taking the exterior sea routes to avoid the sandbars. This route would have required boats to sail along the exterior sea routes from Jiaoxi of Shandong Province and bypass the Liaojiao Port in Huainan East Province. In this way they could avoid sailing between sandbars, and directly reach Jinshan of Jiaxing Prefecture by taking a shortcut passing by Hongdao." (Y. Mei et al. 1990: 5983) Flat-bottomed boats were suitable for sailing in this coastal region, and as such, they were built for the purpose of transporting salt and other commodities in this area. As described by people in the Song Dynasty, "flat-bottomed boats could be used in Dengzhou and Tongzhou sea areas, but passing by Liaojiao required sharp-bottomed boats to carry commodities" (Z. Dai 1990). This suggests that flat-bottomed boats were required to carry goods in the sea areas north to Liaojiao of Tongzhou (present-day Nantong), and sharp-bottomed boats were required in the sea areas south to Liaojiao. Some people said that "the large boats built by the Jin Kingdom were flat-bottomed pine-wooden boats, not suitable for seagoing." (X. Li 2013: 3727) Such boats could not sail in the deep sea south to Liaojiao. In the third year of the Shaoxing Reign (AD 1133), Xu Wen, the navy general, defected to Qi Kingdom, and ordered his sailors to give up their flat-bottomed boats and take privately-owned boats at Haimen County. They then took exterior routes to foreign countries." The coastal military commissioner Qui Yu, along with other generals, "chased the rebels by putting their troops together, but failed to reach them." The navy of the Southern Song Dynasty, taking the sharp-bottomed boats to chase the rebels, had to let out sighs seeing them running away (X. Li 2013: 1275), as they could not find enough flat-bottomed boats to catch up with the rebels at Liaojiao.

The proportion of length and width was bigger than 4:1 in the Song Dynasty. The above-mentioned ambassadorial ships to Goryeo had a proportion greater than 4:1, and their proportion of depth and width was 1.2:1 (which was over 33 m long and 9.9 m deep and 8.25 m wide). The proportion of length and width of the multiple-oar boats built by Feng Zhan was 4.15:1 (which was 27.4 m long and 6.5 m wide), while grain boats in the offshore sea had proportions of 4.17:1 (16.5 m long and 3.96 m wide). The Song Dynasty boat discovered in Dazhi River of Nanhui County of Shanghai was 4.2–4.7:1 in the proportion of length and width (the remaining body was 16.2 m long and 3.86 m wide, but originally it was 18 m long). The Haihu Warship built by Qin Shifu to sail in the Yangtze River was 5.6:1 in the proportion of length and width. Such boats were narrow and long, suitable for rapid navigation.

The remains of a vessel found in Quanzhou Bay had a body which was 24.2 m long and 9.15 m wide, with a proportion of length and width was 2.64:1 (Editorial Committee of Excavation Report of the Quanzhou Bay Song Dynasty Shipwreck Excavation 1975: 2). This boat was short and oval. Zhuang Weizu and his colleagues believed that this boat was good in keeping balance in the sea and more capable in load capacity, although its shape may have prevented it from achieving higher sailing speeds (W. Zhuang and J. Zhuang 1977: 81). Xi Longfei claimed that the narrow shape of the boats in the Song Dynasty was good for maintaining standards of rapid navigation, compared to most of the older wooden boats, which sailed more slowly (L. Fei and G. He 1978: 71).[14] The existence of boats with smaller proportions of length and width shows how important such considerations were in the Song Dynasty shipbuilding industry. In fact, boats with such small proportions were common, as evidenced by the seagoing boat found in Ningbo in November 1979. It was 15.5 m long after restoration, and 4.8 m wide, with a proportion of 2.7:1 (L. Xi 1981: 27). Another such seagoing boat was lifted out of the water in 2007, dubbed "South China Sea Boat 1". It was 31 m long, 10 m wide, and 4 m deep in the cabin (Guangdong Institute of Cultural Relics and Archaeology 2011: 7). The proportion of length and depth was 3.1:1 and the proportion of length and width was 2.5:1, smaller than the proportion of boats in historical records.

1.3.5 Summary

In the Song Dynasty, the deadweight tonnage of a boat refers to its effective volume on board, that is its net tonnage, which was used to calculate its taxation for the loaded commodities. The deadweight tonnage adopted the "Liao" as a unit to evaluate the volume of a boat. One Liao is equivalent in volume to one Dan of rice. When people in the Song Dynasty wanted to state the deadweight tonnage of a boat, the terms Liao, Dan, and Hu were used interchangeably. As different substances vary in density, the load capacity of each Liao varies depending upon the commodities on board. The deadweight tonnage is equivalent to the net tonnage minus the weight of non-effective loads. The maximum tonnage of a boat could not be determined based only on its deadweight tonnage.

The shapes and structures of ships in the Song Dynasty varied depending on deadweight tonnage and the proportion of length and width. Different shapes of ships were used for different purposes, and on different routes, depending at least in part on the waters they were meant to travel. The canals were comparatively shallow, with water ranging from 1 to 1.65 m deep. As the water in some sections of the canals was prone to stagnation, the boats built for the canal were often restricted to carrying between 200 and 500 Liao. The Bianhe River was the safest waterway for

[14] In this essay, the size of the remains of a vessel found in Quanzhou Bay was reverted to the actual one, and it turned out to be that the boat is 30 m long, 10.5 m wide with a proportion of length and width 2.86:1.

canal boats in terms of water conditions, as some sections of this river could carry 600-Liao grain boats or even commercial boats and passenger boats of 1,000 Liao. However, traversing the Bianhe River was impossible for the 10,000 Liao boats. After the Bianhe River, the Grand Canal in Liangzhe West Province was the next suitable canal for grain ships with a load capacity of 400–500 Liao. Most of the canal sections in Huainan East and West provinces were favorable for the grain boats with a load capacity of 200–300 Liao. Due to the shallow water, the boats in these canal sections were flat-bottomed. The restrictions of water and sluice width, and the proportion of length and width in the canal reached 4.8:1, or even to 7.6:1, compared to the boats in other similar rivers.

The inland rivers were different from canals. The largest boats in the Yangtze river were 10,000-Dan boats, but boats with a load capacity of 1000-Dan, 2000-Dan and 2500-Dan were also frequently seen by boatmen in the river. The load capacity of the largest paddle-wheeled ship built in the Southern Song Dynasty could reach 3000 or even 4000 Liao. In comparison, the load capacity of most grain boats and warships ranged from 300 to 800 Liao. The boats in the Yellow River had similar load capacities. The boats in the Yangtze River were shallow-bottomed except some seagoing boats sailing from the river into the sea, but they were comparatively sharper-bottomed than those in the canal. The proportion of length and width of inland river boats was larger, reaching 5.6:1 or even 8:1. Other boats' proportions were below 5.6:1, with most of them being approximately 3:1.

The boats with a surface width of 3.96 m were categorized as medium boats, with a deadweight tonnage of about 300 Liao. Those with a surface width of 6.93 m were categorized as large boats, having a deadweight tonnage or 1000 or even 2000 Liao. According to the records of the Song Dynasty, the large boats built at that time may have a load capacity of 5000 or even 6000 Liao, and could only be found during the reigns of Emperor Shenzong and Emperor Huizong. There were only four such boats. The sharp-bottomed boats were usually used as seafaring vessels, but flat-bottomed boats were also used in the offshore areas of Shandong Province and Huainan East and West provinces. The proportion of length and width was a bit larger than 4:1, but they did build some boats at a proportion of about 2:1 or 3:1.

1.4 Estimated Number of Ships in the Song Dynasty

The boom of inland shipping and maritime trade ushered in a prosperous era in the shipbuilding industry, with the construction of a large number of boats necessary to satisfy shipping and trade demands. But what was the scale of the shipbuilding industry in the Song Dynasty? What were the shares of private and official boats, and what were the composition of inland river boats and seagoing boats? Although some researchers have made some preliminary studies on the shares of seagoing warships and private seagoing ships, the general picture of shipbuilding has not been definitively drawn. Furthermore, we consider these studies to be flawed, as they were not as rigorously based on the historical records (F. He 2005; J. Ge 2008: 153). The existing data could not help us to figure out the total number of boats in the entire country. Among all the boats, cargo transportation boats were required as quotas for some provinces. Although the exact quotas changed over time and not all the quotas for shipbuilding in prefectures and counties were given, we could still find some clear records which provided clues regarding the number of cargo transportation boats. As river and maritime defense became an important task in the Southern Song Dynasty, the need for inland river boats and seagoing warships greatly increased. Additionally, the central government set strict rules for ships built by the private sector, with a ship registration book and requisition system. This may have left some records about the number of boats. This provides us the evidence to estimate the number of boats in some areas and in some ages.

1.4.1 The Number of Cargo Transportation Ships in the Song Dynasty

The clues for statistics about the number of inland river boats come from two sources: the records about the quotas set by the royal court for prefectures in building grain ships in the Northern Song Dynasty, and those about river defense and warships in the battles along the Yangtze River in the Southern Song Dynasty. The number of seagoing boats could be calculated by the official registration of boats and their requisition in Liangzhe East and West provinces and Fujian Province. Some of the data were not useful in these calculations; for example, no comprehensive accounts were available of privately owned boats sailing inland rivers. This section offers a preliminary inference about the numbers of the grain vessels in the Northern Song Dynasty, as well as the inland river warships and seagoing warships in Fujian, Liangzhe East and West provinces in the Southern Song Dynasty.

The cargo transportation from southeastern provinces to Kaifeng was important in regular state governance. In the sixth year of the Yuanfeng Reign (AD 1083), Jiang Zhiqi, the deputy supply commissioner, said, "the annual quota for ship building was 1700 Bianhe cargo transportation boats to be made. Prior to this, an imperial edict ordered the production to be reduced to 748, and the money that was saved was sealed in the national treasury for later emergency use. My supply commission needs to transport 6.2 million Dan of grains and fodder for military use, but the boats available were only just over 700. I worried very much about the insufficient quantity of boats as some of them might be ruined in the bad weather and turbulent waters." (T. Li 2004: 8016) These numbers refer to the quotas of cargo transportation boats to be made in the official shipyards of each prefecture for supply commission, not the total boats owned by the agency. If we calculate the total load capacity of 748 boats or 1700 boats by 400 Liao on each boat, then accomplishing the task of transporting 6.2 million Dan of grains would require over twenty trips (with the smaller quantity of boats) or nine trips (with a greater number of boats). This would have been inefficient, as it was the routine for only three round trips to be made each year. In fact, the supply commission set the task of 6000 boats to ship grains in 200 batches with given serial numbers, and 30 boats made up of a transportation batch (S. Xu et al. 2014: 4098). Thus, the grain boats sailing in the Grand Canal and Bianhe River were charged by supply commission. The deadweight tonnage of the boats was between 300 and 400 Liao, with 20% of the load capacity spared for private purposes, and 80% used to carry grain on business. The aforementioned 6000 boats were grain boats, not those used for cargo transportation purposes. They also did not include the cargo transportation boats in the canal sections of Huainan East Province and Huainan West Province or the inland river boats. Judging from the observation that the Bianhe River boats never went into the Yangtze River, the cargo transportation boats must have been large in number. This number would include those sailing the Yangtze River, transferring commodities to Zhenzhou in the section of the Grand Canal in Liangzhe East and West provinces.

The central government of the Northern Song Dynasty also set quotas for shipbuilders. "The quota of 3337 boats required to be built in the late years of the Zhidao Reign was cut down by 421 boats to be built in the late Tianxi Reign." (D. Ma 2011: 743) The total was 2916. This figure was the total number of boats sailing in the Grand Canal, the Yellow River, and the Yangtze River as cargo transportation ships. If we take into consideration of the routine of small maintenance every three years and a comprehensive repair every five years, those boats could be used at least five years. If we calculate the total by the quotas set in the late years of the Tianxi Reign, the inventory of grain boats may be over 15,000. If the quota for building ships was changed in the period of the Tianxi Reign, then the quota of grain vessels changed accordingly. In the second year of the Zhiping Reign (AD 1065), "the boats built by all the relevant provinces numbered 2540" (Toqta 1977: 4253), which was less than the quota of the later years of the Tianxi Reign. In the fifth year of the Yuanyou Reign (AD 1090), "the imperial edict set 600 boats as the quotas of Wenzhou and Mingzhou" (T. Li 2004: 10,525), but prior to this period, the quota of the two prefectures was 302 boats, which means that the quota nearly doubled in the later years of the Tianxi Reign. In the third year of the Daguan Reign (AD 1109), Lü Yuan mentioned the imperial edict that the royal court ordered Jiangxi Province and Jinghu South and North provinces to build over 2700 grain boats (S. Xu et al. 2014: 4088). The number of grain boats built in this period was greater than the total number of boats built by Jiangnan West Province and Jinghu North Province in the late years of the Tianxi Reign (1651 boats, accounting 56.9%). Adding together the boats built by Liangzhe East and West provinces, Shaanxi Province, Sichuan Province, and Huainan Province, the total may also be greater than those built in the later years of the Tianxi Reign. In the fourth year of the Zhenghe Reign (AD 1114), the Supply Commission of Liangzhe East and West provinces submitted a proposal to the royal court mentioning "the quotas of 600 boats each year" set for Mingzhou and Wenzhou (S. Xu et al. 2014: 7124). The quotation indicated the routine quotas initiated in the fifth year of the Yuanyou Reign (AD 1090). In the second year of the Jianyan Reign (AD 1128), Lü Zong, the deputy supply commissioner said, "based on the established regulation, Qianzhou, Jizhou, Tanzhou and Hengzhou prefectures were required to undertake the task of constructing 723 boats." The quota of shipbuilding in the four prefectures is not equal to the amount of Qianzhou and Jizhou (S. Xu et al. 2014: 4098) Such must be the quotas in the late period of the Northern Song Dynasty.

The number of grain ships to be built each year was not fixed in number due to the changes by the temporary imperial edicts and unfinished boats in each prefecture. In September of the fourth year of the Zhenghe Reign (AD 1114), Emperor Huizong laid down an edict to the supply commission of Liangzhe East and West provinces requiring them to build 300 boats with a load capacity of 300 Liao in each province, and set a quota of 300 boats with a load capacity of 500 Liao for Jiangnan East and West provinces, as well as Jinghu South and North provinces, totaling 1800 boats for Kaifeng (S. Xu et al. 2014: 7124). This seems to be the extra boats required by the royal court for Kaifeng in particular. As an additional example, the court ordered 1300 boats to be built for traveling the recently repaired the Jihe River. This figure includes 100 passenger boats, 200 shallow-bottomed house-shaped boats, and 1000 cargo-passenger boats (S. Xu et al. 2014: 7124). After Cai Jing, the prime minister of the Northern Song Dynasty, adopted a direct transfer method of shipping to the central government, quotas were also set for each prefecture. For example, it was noted that "Wenzhou must build 340 cargo transportation boats for provincial use each year." (S. Xu et al. 2014: 7127) The total number of boats ordered to be built across all prefectures reached 2000. When Jia Weijie served as the deputy supply commissioner of Jianghua region, he required the shipyards in those provinces "to build 2400 large boats to carry the tributes submitted to the royal court directly to the capital city." (Toqta 1977: 11,212) In the first year of the Xuanhe Reign (AD 1119), another imperial edict mentioned the fact that "many boats could not be built by prefectures and military prefectures according to the standard, and such boats were easily broken down." (S. Xu et al. 2014: 7124)

In the Southern Song Dynasty, "the provincial supply commissions built grain boats for submitting tributes to the royal court every year, and each shipyard had to accept the quota of shipbuilding." (S. Xu et al. 2014: 7114) For example, "the shipyards of Ganzhou and Jizhou were consigned the task of building 500 boats every year." (S. Xu et al. 2014: 7132) However, with a decrease in the shipping of grain, the number of grain ships was greatly reduced. In the second year of the Jianyan Reign (AD 1128), Tanzhou, Hengzhou, Qianzhou and Jizhou were assigned a quota of 123 boats each year. "Four provinces in the lower reaches of the Yangtze River were given the task of building 1000 grain boats, together with the 839 boats in arrears by the four prefectures of Tanzhou, Hengzhou, Qianzhou and Jizhou, and the 205 boats to be finished by Jiangnan East Province." With the annual quotas of the four prefectures, the total number was 2767 (S. Xu et al. 2014: 7125). This number was calculated by adding together regular annual quotas to the number of boats without any quotas which were consigned to prefectures and counties but required by the temporary imperial edicts. In fact, the boats built in a regular year could not reach such a high number. In the first year of the Shaoxing Reign (AD 1131), Xu Kangguo pointed out that the quotas set for the shipyards of different prefectures were not fully met (S. Xu et al. 2014: 7127). In the seventh year of the Shaoxing Reign

(AD 1137), the Secretariat of Royal Court and Chancellery stated "each province had a designated task of building grain ships each year, but the ships were put into use in arrears." (S. Xu et al. 2014: 7130) Having arrears in shipbuilding became a normal in those years. In the first year of the Qiandao Reign (AD 1165), an amnesty order was issued by the emperor to require Wenzhou, Mingzhoiu, Xiuzhou, Jizhou to build grain boats each year, while Zhenzhou was to build small boats. The number of the boats in arrears before the thirty-second year of the Shaoxing Reign was a large number, but they were exempted from the unfinished task later (S. Xu et al. 2014:7617).

After Emperor Xiaozong was crowned, he greatly reduced the quotas of grain boats for each province. Submitting their proposal to the emperor, Jiangnan West Province suggested that "the court should permit the decree issued on September 27th of the 5th year of the Qiandao Reign, which required to reduce one hundred each year since that year. And the court should require the shipyards of Jiangnan East Province and Jiangnan West Province to build 400 boats." Jinghu South Province submitted a proposal to the court that "the court should reduce the pine grain boats from 168 to 100, by reducing 68 each year." In the first year of the Chunxi Reign (AD 1174), "the annual quotas set for the shipyards of Liangzhe East and West provinces were cut down, and new quotas should be set. The quota of 120 boats for Wenzhou should be reduced by 50." (S. Xu et al. 2014: 7135–36) The quotas for shipyards of different provinces were once again cut down in the first year of the Chunxi Reign, and later the quotas of grain boats set in the second year to sixth year of the Chunxi Reign were remitted. The unfinished boats which were required by the court between the seventh and ninth years of the Chunxi Reign were also set as the following year's quotas after the tenth year of the Chunxi Reign." (S. Xu et al. 2014: 7136) If we calculate the total quotas set for the five prefectures of Tanzhou, Hengzhou, Qianzhou, Jizhou and Wenzhou reduced by Emperor Xiaozong, we arrive at a total of 845 boats, a figure much smaller than the quotas set for different prefectures in the Northern Song Dynasty. After quota reduction by Emperor Xiaozong, the real number of completed boats was only 550. The amount of ships built by Jiagnan West Province, Hunan Province, and Wenzhou accounts for 60% of the state's total. If we calculate the figures based on this approach, the number of grain boats completed annually during Emperor Xiaozong's Reign was less than 1000. Only one third of the boats were built in the Northern Song Dynasty.

Grain boats, however, were not the only ships built by official shipyards. Before the ninth year of the Xi'ning Reign (AD 1076), the department of dredging and deepening of the Yellow River was in charge of 205 boats. However, by the ninth year of the Xi'ning Reign (AD 1076), only 20 were left (S. Xu et al. 2014: 3143). It is difficult to ascertain the total number of official boats owned by other institutions. In the sixth year of Emperor Taizong's Reign (AD 981), Zhang Qixian mentioned the fact that "every year when river water rose, the sandbars and islets were submerged under water, and about 10,000 boats owned by the military prefectures of Qianzhou, Jizhou, Fuzhou, Junzhou, and Hongzhou would prepare to sail downstream." (X. Zhu 2010: 911) That is to say, about 10,000 ships in Jiangnan West Province could be maneuvered to carry grains. In August of the third year of the Tianxi Reign (AD 1019), the Shipping Division in Baibo purchased 3 million tail parts, and dispatched 3000 boats from the north region of Sizhou for official use (T. Li 2004: 2164). As August was the busiest season for grain shipping, the number of 3000 boats dispatched from the Bianhe River was a piece of evidence that official boats in the river numbered more than 6000. A similar situation obtains in the Southern Song Dynasty. In addition to the grain boats in Jinghu South Province, Jiangnan West Province and Lingzhe East and West provinces, Sichuan Province also produced some official boats. For example, in the eleventh year of the Shaoxing Reign (AD 1161), Wang Zhiwang, the general governor of taxation and revenue in Sichuan Province, used 270 300-Liao grain boats to carry over 10,000 soldiers and family members for Wu Gong, the famous general in the Southern Song Dynasty from Xingzhou (Z. Wang 1990a, b, c). The precise number of cargo transportation boats could not be determined.

1.4.2 The Number of Inland River Warships

For the sake of attacking the Southern Tang Kingdom, the Northern Song Dynasty built many inland river warships. This trend was restricted to the Southern Song Dynasty, when more such boats were built for military use. In the seventh year of the Kaibao Reign (AD 974), the Song Dynasty built several thousand large warships and Yellow Dragon Boats to strike the Southern Tang Kingdom. In May of the eighth year of the Kaibao Reign (AD 975), the Song troops defeated the navy of the Southern Tang Kingdom and captured 500 boats as spoils of war. In June of the same year, the Song troops captured an additional several thousand boats outside the castle town of Jiankang. Zhu Lingbin, the general of the Southern Tang Kingdom, dispatched 150,000 soldiers to reinforce the besieged troops there. They quickly took rafts and boats downstream (R. Zhang 1990), likely in great numbers. General Li Fu was entrusted to conquer the Southern Tang Kingdom from Jinghu Province, and in order to supply the grains and fodders he used several thousand boats down the river (Toqta 1977: 9275). Counting the boats sailing in the Yangtze River, it is likely that they must have been over 10,000 in number. After the Southern Song Dynasty conquered other kingdoms in the south, the Yangtze River lost its strategical significance, and the number of inland river boats was therefore greatly reduced.

When the lower reaches of the Yangtze and Huaihe Rivers became military fronts, there was a great demand for warship building. In the fourth year of the Jianyan Reign (AD 1130), the troops of Jin Kingdom crossed the Yangtze River and controlled this great river, noting that "the boats carrying the supplies and gears of the army were connected one by one from Guabu to Luhe in the Yangtze River." (X. Li 2013: 759) Although the exact number of these boats remains unknown, it certainly must have been quite large. In contrast, in the early years of the Southern Song Dynasty, warships in use were quite limited in number. In the third year of the Shaoxing Reign (AD 1133), the royal court ordered General Liu Guangshi "to quickly select 500 boats which could be interconnected so as to conquer Yang Yao and his rebellion". However, as most of the boats were heavily damaged, he could only find a dozen usable ones. In the same year, Yue Fei, the famous loyal marshal of the Song Dynasty, submitted a proposal to the court, stating, "as our troops are lacking boats, in time of emergent military affairs, we wish to borrow official boats or privately-owned boats and hire their boatmen from the prefectures and counties along the rivers. When the military operations end, we would return them in time." At that time, only the general "Han Shizhong could capture 3000–4000 boats thanks to their victory in maritime wars in the Yangtze River." (S. Xu et al. 2014: 7128) In the period of the Shaoxing Reign, Yuan Zhen, the mayor of Hongzhou Prefecture, submitted his proposal to the court that the troops in Xingguo of Jiangzhou Prefecture and the navy of Nankang Military Prefecture and Yue Fei's troops were in urgent need of warships, and he had received the imperial edict "to order the Supply Commission of Jiangnan West Province to hire boatmen and purchase 200 boats for military use." But as quite a few boats were ruined due to continuous battle fires in the Jiangnan East and West provinces, few boats in good conditions could be found. So, "they planned to build 200 warships." (S. Yang et al. 1990)

After Yang Yao and his men were conquered, a rapid development of the Yangtze River Navy was seen in the Southern Song Dynasty with the growing numbers of warships. In the later years of the Chunyou Reign, Wang Ye served as the coastal military commissioner and later the military commissioner of Jiangnan East Province. He inspected Hezhou, Wuwei Military Prefecture and the riverside navy of Anqing Prefecture. "He saw the boats interconnected to each other and piled in the river for almost 15 km. He set up a movable navy with 12,000 soldiers and 10,000 swift warships." (Toqta 1977: 12,576) These were the forces deployed in the middle section of Jiangnan East Province. In the decisive battle along the Yangtze River between the Song troops and the Yuan troops, the number of boats in the Yangtze River reached a peak. In the eleventh year of the Zhiyuan Reign (AD 1274), when the troops of the Yuan Dynasty sailed down Hanjiang River from Xiangyang to attack Ezhou, an important city along the Yangtze River, about 10,000 boats were gathered at the bay mouth of the Lunhe River. However, the garrison soldiers there had "about 10,000 warships occupying crucial strategic points." (L. Song 1976: 3101) Both sides sent 20,000 into the battle. In this battle, 3000 Hanyang-made warships were ruined by the Yuan troops (L. Song 1976: 3103). In the river battles at Dingjiazhou, Jia Sidao, the marshal of the troops, "built the headquarters for the commander-in-chief so as to keep 2500 boats stationed in Dingjiazhou." "At Xiagui, 2500 warships were found in the Yangtze River." (L. Song 1976: 3122; T. Su n.d.) Thus, the boats of the Song Dynasty must have numbered nearly 10,000. In the last battle at Jiaoshan, Zhang Shijie, the general of the Song Dynasty, clustered "10,000 boats to garrison Jiaoshan East Province." The troops of the Yuan Dynasty "shot arrows from both sides of the huge boats. To to burn the covering and sails of boats, they used fire arrows, and the smog rose wildly to the sky." (L. Song 1976: 3123) The reason why they could defeat troops of the Song Dynasty, lies in the fact that the troops of the Yuan Dynasty had a sufficient number of boats in use. After this battle, the Yuan Dynasty controlled the Yangtze River completely. Wen Tianxiang fled upstream from Zhenjiang to Zhenzhou. The scene was depicted thusly: "the banks were lined up with the boats of the Yuan Dynasty, which extended several kilometers." (T. Wen 1987: 498–499) This proves the large number of the warships in the Yangtze River in another aspect. Judging from records and accounts of battles there, it is likely that boats in this section of Ezhou, and downstream, numbered over 30,000.

1.4.3 The Number of the Seagoing Ships in the Song Dynasty

The number of the warships in the Northern Song Dynasty could not be easily determined. As there were quite a few records about the registration and requisition of the boats, especially those in Liangzhe East Province and Fujian Province, we could, however, determine the number of boats in the Southern Song Dynasty. In the period of the Chunxi Reign, when Fan Chengda served as the mayor of Mingzhou Municipality, to ensure the security of the boats, "he separated 5887 boats into different units and put them into the boat registration book (Z. Huang 1990). If someone committed a crime, people in the same unit would be punished for the crime." Thus, there were 5887 privately-owned boats that were registered in Mingzhou. During the Jiaxi Reign, Mingzhou Municipality had 7916 boats listed into the registration book, an increase compared to the period of the Chunxi Reign. "The total number of privately-owned boats in Mingzhou, Wenzhou and Taizhou with a head beam greater than 3.3 m long was 3833, and 15,454 with a head beam below this length." The total number was 19,287. These figures were obtained by examining official notices, which required a thorough accounting of boats, from all areas within 1500 km of the three prefectures which were prolific in shipbuilding. Villages were required to report all boats, regardless of size. The boats whose head beam was longer than 3.3 m in Liangzhe East Province were counted as medium or big and put into the registration book of sea defense for later requisition. Based on this metric, privately-owned boats were classified as being big or small. The ratio of big to small boats in Mingzhou, Taizhou, and Wenzhou was 25:100 in number. The share in Mingzhou was 28:100 (1728 boats above the standard, and 6188 boats below the standard), and it was the same with Wenzhou (1099 boats above the standard, 3984 boats below the standard). However, the share between big and small ones was 19:100 (1006 boats above the standard, 5282 boats below the standard) (Y. Mei et al. 1990: 5991). Of the seagoing ships built in Yuezhou, only Liangzhe East Province had over 20,000 boats in total.

In Fujian Province, the first group of boats which were registered for sea defense and requisition were those whose head beam was 3.96 m long. In the twenty-ninth year of the Shaoxing Reign (AD 1159), because "the boats whose head beam were longer than 3.96 m were quite small in number, the officials adjusted the standard of big boats to 3.3 m, and requested such boats to be registered for sea defense." Later, in the thirty-first year of the Shaoxing Reign (AD 1161), they found that such boats whose head beam was 3.3 m long were not good for sea battles when facing huge waves in the seas," and they could not be used for navy ships. In the next year, the standard of 3.96 m was reinstated and those below the standard were exempted for rotation in the navy. As the sea trade was prosperous in Fujian Province, the seagoing boats in use were large in number. Most of the large boats had a head beam less than 3.3 m. As attested, there were "few commercial boats whose head beam was longer than 3.3 m." The share between the requisitioned boats and the non-requisitioned boats for the navy in Fujian Province was less than Liangzhe East Province (whose share was 1:4).

For the sake of sea defense, cargo transportation requisition, and to combat smuggling by boatmen, Fujian Province introduced strict policies on boat registration. For example, after taking his post as the mayor of Zhangzhou Prefecture, Liao Gang asked his subordinates to make a thorough registration of the boats in the prefecture and established an award mechanism to prevent people from committing fraud. The purpose of this registration was to curtail theft and to ensure that boats were deployed efficiently. He also required seagoing ships to travel in groups of five, further noting that "they were not allowed to go to sea without a permit." (G. Liao 1990) However, the exact number of boats in Zhangzhou Prefecture remains unknown, even after such surveys and registrations were undertaken. Moreover, the specific figures about the number of warships were not known in the four prefectures of Fujian Province, in contrast to the detailed record about seagoing boats in Liangzhe East Province. On the other hand, a rough estimate of the number of seagoing ships in Fujiang Province is possible. In *the Registration Book V* of *Chunxi Period Chronicles of Fuzhou* (Vol. 14), the royal court collected 2434 boats from Fuqing County in the 19th year of the Shaoxing Reign (AD 1149), and 373 boats from nine counties of Fuzhou Prefecture, among which 125 boats were from Fuqing County in the Chunxi Reign. If the 2434 boats requisitioned from Fuqing County could be kept stable from the nineteenth year of Shaoxing Reign (AD 1149) to the period of the Chunxi Reign, then the boats whose head beam was 3.96 m accounted for 5% of the total in Fuqing County. As the cost of building a large boat whose head beam was 3.96 m long was substantial, in the three years' requisition, only one year's service of such boats was put into seagoing trade, especially the requisitioned seagoing boats in the Southern Song Dynasty, "which were required to be recruited in consecutive years to guard crucial passes without being used for commercial purposes." The requisitioned boats were divided three groups, to ensure that crucial passes were garrisoned year-round. However, during emergencies, the three groups of boats were occasionally required to patrol together (S. Xu et al. 2014: 7128; B. Zhou 1990), which disrupted people's enthusiasm for making large boats. "In the worst cases, the boatmen sold their own boats at a very low price to ease such a heavy burden, or went overseas without returning home, or even broke their own boats." (S. Xu et al. 2014: 7128) For this reason, the share of big and small boats in these prefectures may be small, meaning the boats above the standard were less than those below the standard. The rule of sea defense requisition would increase the gap between the number of large and small boats. The share of boats whose head beam was longer than 3.96 m accounted for only 25% of the total in the three coastal prefectures in Liangzhe East Province. Thus, it is not surprising that the share of such large boats in Fujian Province was reduced to only 5%.

If we apply this proportion to calculate the boats in the nine counties of Fuzhou Prefecture, the total must be 7460 (which is the number of boats produced in the preceding 20 years by building 373 boats each year). In terms of the requisition of boats above the standard, 452 boats were requisitioned in the second year of the Qiandao Reign (AD 1166), 560 boats in the 4th year of the Qiandao Reign, and 492 boats in the first year of the Chunxi Reign (K. Lang 1990: 7902), which were more than the average of 373 boats in the period of the Chuanxi Reign. Thus, the quantity of boats in Fuzhou Prefecture must have been substantial, possibly even exceeding 10,000. Several thousand seagoing boats were registered in Changxi County alone. This figure was reported by Song Jinzhi, the deputy county mayor of Changxi County. He ordered his subordinates to register all the seagoing boats, telling Chen Junqing, then the mayor of Fuzhou, and later prime minister, that "the commercial advantages and disadvantages of coastal counties lie in their geographical location." (Y. Lou 1990) When Chen Junqing served as the mayor of Fuzhou Prefecture during the late years of the Qiandao Reign to the early years of the Chunxi Reign (Toqta 1977: 1789), his deeds were recorded in the 14th volume of *Chunxi Period Chronicles of Fuzhou.* There was a detailed description about the number of boats in Changxi County in Category V of *Boats Registration,* which listed the number of boats requisitioned from the nine counties of Fuzhou Prefecture. Among the 373 boats requisitioned from the nine counties, there were 79 boats from Changxi County, 125 from Fuqing County and 80 from Minxian County, so the number from Changxi County was less than those from Fuqing and Minxian counties. From the statistics of Changxi County, we can infer that the estimate of 2434 boats produced in Fuqing County during the the Chunxi Reign was well grounded. We can further infer that there were about 7400 boats in Fuzhou (or possibly even over 10,000), which might be a conservative estimate.

In terms of geographical location, Quanzhou was more important than Fuzhou although they owned equivalent seagoing boats. In the coastal areas of Fujian Province, Xinghua Military Prefecture, and Zhangzhou Prefecture a large quantity of seagoing boats was deployed. In the Southern Song Dynasty, the four coastal areas of Fujian Province were economically more prosperous than the three prefectures of Mingzhou, Taizhou, and Wenzhou of Liangzhe East Province, especially in maritime trade with foreigners. Moreover, Fujian Province sent several hundred boats to Mingzhou and Liangzhe West Province for business purposes every year. Based on these figures, it is clear that the number of boats in Fujian Province was not less than that of the three coastal prefectures in Liangzhe East Province. Fujian's prosperous coastal trade required "the use of several thousand huge commercial boats, but it also attracted thousands of pirates." (H. Bao 1990) It can thus be estimated that at least 20,000 seagoing boats were used in these coastal areas. Considering these figures, it must be the case that the total number of boats in the Liangzhe East and Fujian provinces of the Southern Song Dynasty exceeded 40,000. The above discussions concern privately-owned seagoing boats. Liangzhe East Province, Mingzhou in particular, was garrisoned by several thousand navy soldiers. Considering the total number of Left Wing navy soldiers, local sailors in water villages, and water patrol agencies, the warships must have been great in number. He Feng believes that the number of warships in the coastal areas of the Southern Song was likely to total 18,000 in the 1160s (F. He 2005: 27–43). If the boats in Guangnan East and West provinces, Liangzhe West and Huainan East provinces were counted together, both private and official, their number must be 70,000–80,000, estimated by Ge Jinfang regarding the boats deployed in the Southern Song Dynasty (J. Ge 2008: 153).

1.4.4 Summary

In the Song Dynasty, an economic boom, and an increase in prosperity of inland river shipping and maritime trade, together with the official cargo transportation, resulted in a burgeoning shipbuilding industry, both for private and official ships. The available historical records did not contain sufficient information to offer an authoritative estimate of the total number of boats in the Song Dynasty, but the number of grain boats, warships, and seagoing boats in a certain period could be inferred, based on registration and requisition requirements. From the quotas set for different provinces in the early period of the Southern Song Dynasty, and the service life of boats, we estimate the number of boats must as being in excess of 15,000, with grain boats in the Bianhe River possibly reaching 6000. Since the Southern Song Dynasty, grain boats were greatly reduced, but warships were added for the purposes of sea defense. In the later period of the Southern Song Dynasty, when the troops of the Southern Song Dynasty clashed with the Yuan Dynasty troops, the boats deployed in the inland rivers may have exceeded 30,000. In the later period of the Southern Song Dynasty, Liangzhe East Province owned 20,000 seagoing boats, and Fujian Province also had at least 20,000 seagoing boats. Some scholars estimate a total of 70,000–80,000 seagoing boats in the whole country, which is in accordance with the historical facts.

References

Bao, Hui 包恢. 1990. *Bizhou Gao Lüe* 敝帚稿略 [Anthology of Bao Hui]. Collected in Complete Library in the Four Branches of Literature. Shanghai: Shanghai Chinese Classics Publishing House.

Bao, Zheng 包拯. 1999. *Baozheng Ji Jiaozhu* 包拯集校注 [Selected Works of Baozheng Annotated Version]. Collated by Yang Guoyi. Hefei: Huangshan Publishing House.

Cai, Xiang 蔡襄. 1996. *Caixiang Ji* 蔡襄集 [Works of Cai Xiang]. Punctuated and collated by Wu Yining. Shanghai: Shanghai Chinese Classics Publishing House.

Cai, Tao 蔡絛. 2008. *Tieweishan Congtan* 铁围山丛谈 [Tieweishan Notes]. Sorted by Li Guoqiang. Collected in Complete Song Notes. Elephant Press.

Chang, Tang 常棠. 1990. *Ganshui Zhi* 澉水志 [Chronicles of Ganshui]. Collected in the Series of Chorography of the Song and Yuan Dynasties. Beijing: Zhonghua Book Company.

Chen, Chun 陈淳. 1990a. *Beixi Da Heji* 北溪大全集 [The Complete Works of Chen Chun]. Collected in Complete Library in the Four Branches of Literature. Shanghai: Shanghai Chinese Classics Publishing House.

Chen, Cisheng 陈次升. 1990b. *Danglun Ji* 谠论集 [Political Commentary of Chen Cisheng].Collected in Complete Library in the Four Branches of Literature. Shanghai: Shanghai Chinese Classics Publishing House.

Chen, Dazhen 陈大震. 1990. *Dade Nanhai Zhi* 大德南海志 [Dade Period Chronicles of Nanhai]. Collected in The Series of Chorography of the Song and Yuan Dynasties. Beijing: Zhonghua Book Company.

Chen, Qiqing 陈耆卿. 1990. *Jiading Chicheng Zhi* 嘉定赤城志 [Jiading Period Chronicles of Chicheng]. Collected in The Series of Chorography of the Song and Yuan Dynasties. Beijing: Zhonghua Book Company.

Chen, Xiyu 陈希育. 1991. "Songdai Daxing Shangchuan Jiqi 'Liao' De Jisuan Faze" 宋代大型商船及其"料"的计算法则 [Large Merchant Ships and Computational Rules of Their Load Capacity of 'Liao']. *Journal of Maritime History Studies* 1.

Dai, Zhi 戴植. 1990. *Shupu* 鼠璞 [Waxed Mouse]. Collected in Complete Library in the Four Branches of Literature. Shanghai: Shanghai Chinese Classics Publishing House.

Editorial Committee of Excavation Report of the Quanzhou Bay Song Dynasty Shipwreck Excavation泉州湾宋代海船发掘报告编写组. 1975. "Quanzhouwan Songdai Haichuan Fajue Jianbao 泉州湾宋代海船发掘简报 [Report of the Quanzhou Bay Song Dynasty Shipwrecks]". *Cultural Relics* 10.

Fan, Chengda 范成大. 2012a. *Guihai Yuheng Zhi* 桂海虞衡志 [Records of the Ranger in Guihai]. Collected in Complete Song Notes. Elephant Press.

Fan, Chengda 范成大. 2012b. *Can Luan Lu* 骖鸾录 [The Trip to Guilin]. Collected in Complete Song Notes. Elephant Press.

Fan, Chengda 范成大. 2012c. *Wu Chuan Lu* 吴船录 [Travelogues in Wu Area by Ship]. Collected in Complete Song Notes. Elephant Press.

Feng, Fujing 冯福京, et al. 1990. *Dade Chaoguozhou Tuzhi* 大德昌国州图志[Dade Period Chronicles of Changzhouguo]. Collected in The Series of Chorography of the Song and Yuan Dynasties. Beijing: Zhonghua Book Company.

Ge, Jinfang 葛金芳. 2008. *Nansong Shougongyeshi* 南宋手工业史 [The Handicraft Industry of the Southern Song Dynasty]. Shanghai: Shanghai Chinese Classics Publishing House.

Guo, Zhengzhong 郭正忠. 1993. *Sanzhi shisi Shiji Zhongguo De Quanheng Duliang* 三至十四世纪中国的权衡 [Weights and Measures of China from the Third to Fourteenth Centuries]. Beijing: China Social Sciences Press.

Han, Zhenhua 韩振华. 1988. "Lun Zhonggu Chuan De Chuanliao Jiqi Jisuan Faze 论中国船的船料及其计算法则 [The Computational Rules of Load Capacity of 'Liao' of Chinese Ships]". *Journal of Maritime History Studies* 1.

He, Feng何锋. 2005. "Shier Shiji Nansong Yanhai Diqu Jianchuan Shuliang Kaocha 12世纪南宋沿海地区舰船数量考察[Studies on the Quantity of Ships in the Coastal Areas of the Southern Song Dynasty in the 12th century]". *Journal of Chinese Social and Economic History* 3.

He, Yuan 何薳. 2008. *Chunzhu Jiwen* 春渚纪闻 [Anecdotage of the Song Dynasty]. Collected in Complete Song Notes. Elephant Press.

Huang, Tingjian 黄庭坚. 2011. *Huang Tingjian Quanji* 黄庭坚全集 [The Complete Works of Huang Tingjian]. Nanchang: Jiangxi People's Publishing House.

Huang, Yansun 黄岩孙. 1990. *Xianxi Zhi* 仙溪志 [Chronicles of Xianxi]. Collected in The Series of Chorography of Song and Yuan Dynasty. Beijing: Zhonghua Book Company.

Huang, Zhen. 1990. *Huang Shi Richao* 黄氏日抄 [Notes of Huang]. Collected in Complete Library in the Four Branches of Literature. Shanghai: Shanghai Chinese Classics Publishing House.

Ji, Shuxing 季曙行. 1987. "Shanghai Nanhuixian Dazhihe Guchuan Fajune Jianbao 上海南汇县大治河古船发掘简报 [A Briefing on the Excavation of an Ancient Boat in the Dazhi River of Nanhui County in Shanghai]". *Anthology of Shanghai Museum* 4.

Jiang, Shaoyu 江少虞. 1990. *Song Chao Shishi Leiyuan* 宋朝事实类苑 [Collection of the Song Dynasty's Historical Records]. Collected in Complete Library in the Four Branches of Literature. Shanghai: Shanghai Chinese Classics Publishing House.

Jiangsu Heritage Working Team 江苏省文物工作队. 1961. "Yangzhou Shiqiao Faxian Le Gudai Muchuan扬州施桥发现了古代木船 [Ancient Wooden Boats Found in Shiqiao of Yangzhou]". *Cultural Relics* 6.

Jojin 成寻. 2009. *Xin Jiao Cantiantai Wutaishan Ji* 新校参天台五台山记 [Revised Edition of Travelogues of Jojin]. Edited by Wang Liping. Shanghai: Shanghai Chinese Classics Publishing House.

Li, Fu 李复. 1990. *Yushui Ji* 潏水集 [Selected Works of Li Fu]. Collected in Complete Library in the Four Branches of Literature. Shanghai: Shanghai Chinese Classics Publishing House.

Li, Xinchuan 李心传. 2000. *Jianyan Yilai Chaoye Zaji* 建炎以来朝野杂记 [Laws and Institutions Since the Jianyan Reign]. Edited by Xu Gui. Beijing: Zhonghua Book Company.

Li, Xinchuan 李心传. 2013. *Jianyan Yilai Xinian Yaolu* 建炎以来系年要录 [Chronological Record of Major Events Since 1127]. Beijing: Zhonghua Book Company.

Li, Tao 李焘. 2004. *Xu Zizhi Tongjian Changbian* 续资治通鉴长编 [Continuation to The Comprehensive Mirror for Aid in Government]. Beijing: Zhonghua Book Company.

Liao, Gang 廖刚. 1990. *Gaofeng Wenji* 高峰文集 [Selected Works of Liao Gang]. Collected in Complete Library in the Four Branches of Literature. Shanghai: Shanghai Chinese Classics Publishing House.

Liu, Chang 刘敞. 1990. *Gongshi Ji* 公是集 [Selected Works of Liu Chang]. Collected in Complete Library in the Four Branches of Literature. Shanghai: Shanghai Chinese Classics Publishing House.

Lou, Yao 楼钥. 1990. *Gonggui Ji* 攻媿集 [Selected Works of Lou Yao]. Collected in Complete Library in the Four Branches of Literature. Shanghai: Shanghai Chinese Classics Publishing House.

Lu, Xian 卢宪. 1990. *Jiading Zhenjiang Zhi* 嘉定镇江志 [Jiading Period Chronicles of Zhenjiang]. Collected in The Series of Chorography of the Song and Yuan Dynasties. Beijing: Zhonghua Book Company.

Lu, You 陆游. 2012. *Laoxuean Biji* 老学庵笔记 [The Notes of an Old Pedant]. Sorted by Li Changxian. Collected in Complete Song Notes. Elephant Press.

Lu, You 陆游. 2011. *Lu You Quanji Jiaozhu* 陆游全集校注 [Annotations to Lu You's Works]. Collated by Qian Zhonglian. Hangzhou: Zhejiang Education Publishing House.

Lu, You 陆游. 2012. *Ru Shu Ji* 入蜀记 [Essays about My Journey to Sichuan]. Sorted by Li Changxian. Collected in Complete Song Notes. Elephant Press.

Luo, Jun 罗浚, et al. 1990. *Baoqing Siming Zhi* 宝庆四明志 [Baoqing Period Chronicles of Siming]. Collected in The Series of Chorography of the Song and Yuan Dynasties. Beijing: Zhonghua Book Company.

Luo, Yuan 罗愿. 1990. *Xinan Zhi* 新安志 [Chronicles of Xin'an]. Collected in The Series of Chorography of the Song and Yuan Dynasties. Beijing: Zhonghua Book Company.

Ma, Duanlin 马端临. 2011. Wenxian Tongkao 文献通考 [A Full-Scale Textual Criticism on Ancient Systems and Regulations]. Beijing: Zhonghua Book Company.

Mei, Yingfa 梅应发, et al. 1990. *Kaiqing Siming Zhi* 开庆四明续志 [Sequels to Kaiming Period Chronicles of Siming]. Collected in The Series of Chorography of the Song and Yuan Dynasties. Beijing: Zhonghua Book Company.

Nanhi I hao De Kaogu Shijue "南海I号"的考古试掘 [Archaeological Excavation of "Nanhai I"]. 2011. Edited by Guangdong Institute of Cultural Relics and Archaeology广东省文物考古研究所编. Beijing: Science Press.

Ni, Wenjun 倪文俊. 1979. "Jiading Fengbang Songchuan Fajue Jianbao 嘉定封浜宋船发掘简报 [A Briefing on the Excavation of the Song Boat in the Fengbang River of Jiading County]". *Cultural Relics* 12.

Ouyang, Xiu 欧阳修. 2001. *Ouyang Xiu Quanji* 欧阳修全集 [Selected Works of Ouyang Xiu]. Beijing: Zhonghua Book Company.

Qian, Shuoyou 潜说友. 1990. *Xianchu Linan Zhi* 咸淳临安志 [Xianchun Period Chronicles of Lin'an]. Collected in in The Series of Chorography of the Song and Yuan Dynasties. Beijing: Zhonghua Book Company.

Shakeshi 沙克什. 1990. *Hefang Tongyi* 河防通议 [Summary of River Flood Prevention Works]. Collected in Complete Library in the Four Branches of Literature. Shanghai: Shanghai Chinese Classics Publishing House.

Shen, Kuo 沈括. 2006. *Mengxi Bitan* 梦溪笔谈 [Mengxi Bitan (Dream Pool Essays)]. Sorted by Hu Jingyi. Collected in Complete Song Notes. Elephant Press.

Shi, Juefan 释觉范. 1990. 石门文字禅 [Shi Juefan's Works on Buddhist Service]. Collected in Complete Library in the Four Branches of Literature. Shanghai: Shanghai Chinese Classics Publishing House.

Shi, Su 施宿, et al. 1990. *Jiatai Kuaiji Zhi* 嘉泰会稽志 [Jiatai Period Chronicles of Kuaiji]. Collected in The Series of Chorography of the Song and Yuan Dynasties. Beijing: Zhonghua Book Company.

Shi, Yanzhi 施彦执. 2008. *Beichuang Zhiguo Lu*北窗炙輠录 [Talks and Notes of Song Dynasty]. Sorted by Yu Yunguo and et al. Collected in Complete Song Notes. Elephant Press.

Shiba, Yoshinobu 斯波义信. 1985. "Song Yuan Shidai De Chuanbo 宋元时代的船舶 [Vessels in the Song and Yuan Dynasties]". Translated by Jing Hui. *Marine History Studies* 1.

Shiba, Yoshinobu 斯波义信. 1997. *Songdai Shangyeshi Yanjiu* 宋代商业史研究 [A Study on the Business History of the Song Dynasty]. Translated by Zhuang Jinghui. Daoxiang Press.

Sishuiqianfu 四水潜夫. 1981. *Wulin Jiu Shi* 武林旧事 [Tales of Martial Arts]. Hangzhou: Xihu Publishing House.

Song, Lian 宋濂. 1976. *Yuan Shi* 元史 [History of the Yuan Dynasty]. Beijing: Zhonghua Book Company.

Songji Sanchao Zhwngyao Jianzheng 宋季三朝政要笺证 [Compilations and Revisions on The Chronicle of the Late Southern Song Dynasty]. 2010. Edited by Ruilai Wang 王瑞来. Beijing: Zhonghua Book Company.

Su, Tianjue 苏天爵.n.d. *Guochao Wenlei* 国朝文类 [Poems and Articles of the Yuan Dynasty]. Collected in Collectanea of the Four Categories 1st edn.

Sun, Yi 孙奕. 1990a. *Shier Bian* 示儿编 [Works For Instructing My Children]. Collected in Complete Library in the Four Branches of Literature. Shanghai: Shanghai Chinese Classics Publishing House.

Sun, Yingshi 孙应时. 1990b. *Zhuhu Ji* 烛湖集 [Selected Works of Sun Yingshi]. Collected in Complete Library in the Four Branches of Literature. Shanghai: Shanghai Chinese Classics Publishing House.

Tang, Shenwei 唐慎微. 1990. *Zhenglei Beicao* 证类本草 [The Testament of Herbal Plants]. Collected in Complete Library in the Four Branches of Literature. Shanghai: Shanghai Chinese Classics Publishing House.

Tang, Yong 唐勇, et al. 2008. "Songdai Ningbo Diqu De Zaochuanye 宋代宁波地区的造船业[Shipbuilding of Ningbo Area in Song Dynasty]". *Journal of Ningbo Institute of Education* 1.

Tianjin Municipal Office of Cultural Relics 天津市文物管理处. 1983. "Tianjin Jinghai Yuanmengkou Songchuan De Fajue 天津静海元蒙口宋船的发掘 [The Excavation of the Song Ship at Yuanmengkou Village, Jinghai County, Tianjin]". *Cultural Relics* 7.

Toqta 脱脱. 1977. *Song Shi* 宋史 [History of the Song Dynasty]. Beijing: Zhonghua Book Company.

Wang, Shipeng王十朋. 2012. *Wang Shipeng Quanji* 王十朋全集 [Complete Works of Wang Shipeng]. Edited by Meixi Collection Republication Committee. Shanghai: Shanghai Chinese Classics Publishing House.

Wang, Zengyu 王曾瑜. 1975. "Tan Songdai De Zaochuanye 谈宋代的造船业 [On Shipbuilding in the Song Dynasty]". *Cultural Relics* 10.

Wang, Zhidao 王之道. 1990a. *Xiangshan Ji* 相山集 [Selected Works of Wang Zhidao]. Collected in Complete Library in the Four Branches of Literature. Shanghai: Shanghai Chinese Classics Publishing House.

Wang, Zhiwang 王之望. 1990b. *Hanbin Ji* 汉滨集 [Selected Works of Wang Zhiwang]. Collected in Complete Library in the Four Branches of Literature. Shanghai: Shanghai Chinese Classics Publishing House.

Wang, Zongji王宗稷. 1990c. *Dongpo Xiansheng Nianpu* 东坡先生年谱 [Chronology of Su Dongpo]. Collected in Complete Library in the Four Branches of Literature. Shanghai: Shanghai Chinese Classics Publishing House.

Wen, Tianxiang 文天祥. 1987. *Weng Tianxiang Quanji* 文天祥全集 [Selected Works of Wen Tianxiang]. Collated by Xiong Fei, et al. Nanchang: Jiangxi People's Publishing House.

Wen, Yanbo 文彦博. 1990. *Wenlugong Ji* 文潞公集 [Selected Works of Wen Yanbo]. Collected in Complete Library in the Four Branches of Literature. Shanghai: Shanghai Chinese Classics Publishing House.

Wu, Jingshan 吴景山. 1999. "Song Jin Yuan Shiqi Xibei De Zaochuanye Ji Hangyun Guanli 宋金元时期西北的造船业及航运管理 [Boat making and water transport System in the Northwest Area During the Song, Jin and Yuan Dynasties]". *Journal of Lanzhou University* 1.

Wu, Zeng 吴曾. 2012. *Nenggaizhai Manlu* 能改斋漫录 [Nenggaizhai Notes]. Sorted by Liu Yu. Collected in Complete Song Notes. Elephant Press.

Wu, Zimu 吴自牧. 1980. *Mengliao Lu* 梦粱录 [Accounts About the Capital]. Hangzhou: Zhejiang People's Publishing House.

Xi, Longfei 席龙飞, et al. 1981. "Dui Ninbo Guchuan De Yanjiu 对宁波古船的研究 [A Study on Ningbo Junk of Song Dynasty]". *Journal of Wuhan University of Water Transportation Engineering* 2.

Xi, Longfei 席龙飞. 2000. *Zhongguo Zaochuanshi*中国造船史 [A History of China Shipbuilding]. Wuhan: Hubei Education Press.

Xiong, Ke 熊克. 1985. *Zhongxing Xiaoji* 中兴小纪 [Unofficial Histories in Emperor Gaozong's Reign]. Fuzhou: Fujian People's Publishing House.

Xu, Dongsheng 徐东升. 2006. "Songdai Guanying Zaochuanchang De YunZuo 宋代官营造船场的运作 [Operation of Government-Running Shipyards in the Song Dynasty]". *Journal of Southwest China Normal University*, No.5, 2006

Xu, Jing 徐兢. 2006. *Xuanhe Fengshi Gaoli Tujing* 宣和奉使高丽图经 [Xuanhe Period Maps and Records About Goryeo]. Sorted by Yu Yunguo. Collected in Complete Song Notes. Elephant Press.

Yang, Shiqi 杨士奇, et al. 1990. *Lidai Mingchen Zouyi* 历代名臣奏议 [Memorials to the Thrones in History]. Collected in Complete Library in the Four Branches of Literature. Shanghai: Shanghai Chinese Classics Publishing House.

Yang, Wanli杨万里. 2007. *Yang Wanli Ji Jianjiao* 杨万里集笺校 [Annotations to Selected Works of Yang Wanli]. Collated by Xin Gengru. Beijing: Zhonghua Book Company.

Ye, Mengde 叶梦得. 2002. *Shilin Zouyi* 石林奏议 [Ye Mengde's Memorials to the Emperor]. Collected in Continuation to Complete Library in the Four Branches of Literature. Shanghai: Shanghai Chinese Classics Publishing House.

Ye, Mengde 叶梦得. 2013. *Bishu Luhua* 避暑录话 [Records of the Northern Song Dynasty While Away from the Court]. Sorted by Xu Shiyi. Collected in Complete Song Notes. Elephant Press.

Yu, Xilu 俞希鲁. 1990. *Zhishun Zhenjiang Zhi* 至顺镇江志 [Zhishun Period Chronicles of Zhenjiang]. Collected in The Series of Chorography of the Song and Yuan Dynasties. Beijing: Zhonghua Book Company.

Yue, Ke 岳珂. 1989. *Eguo Jintuo Xubian Jiaozhu* 鄂国金佗续编校注 [Annotation on the Historical Records about Yue Fei]. Collated by Wang Zengyu. Beijing: Zhonghua Book Company.

Zeng, Gong 曾巩. 1990. *Yuanfen Leigao* 元丰类稿 [Selected Works of Zeng Gu]. Collected in Complete Library in the Four Branches of Literature. Shanghai: Shanghai Chinese Classics Publishing House.

Zhang, Hao 张淏. 1990. *Baoqing Kuaiji Xuzhi* 宝庆会稽续志 [Baoqing Period Continuation of the Chronicles of Kuaiji]. Collected in The Series of Chorography of the Song and Yuan Dynasties. Beijing: Zhonghua Book Company.

Zhang, Jiaju 张家驹. 2010. *Zhang Jiaju Shixue Wencun* 张家驹史学文存 [A Collection of Zhang Jiaju's Historical Researches]. Shanghai: Shanghai People's Publishing House.

Zhang, Ruyu 章如愚. 1990. *Qun Shu Kaosuo* 群书考索[Research and Quest on Books of All Sorts]. Collected in Complete Library in the Four Branches of Literature. Shanghai: Shanghai Chinese Classics Publishing House.

Zhang, Shunmin 张舜民. 1990. *Hua Man Ji* 画墁集 [Selected Works of Zhang Shunmin]. Collected in Complete Library in the Four Branches of Literature. Shanghai: Shanghai Chinese Classics Publishing House.

Zhang, Yong 张咏. 1990. *Guaiya Ji* 乖崖集 [Selected Works of Zhang Yong]. Collected in Complete Library in the Four Branches of Literature. Shanghai: Shanghai Chinese Classics Publishing House.

Zhang, Zi 张镃. 1990. *Shi Xue Guifan* 仕学规范 [Norms of Learning and Being an Official]. Collected in Complete Library in the Four Branches of Literature. Shanghai: Shanghai Chinese Classics Publishing House.

Zhao, Rushi 赵汝适. 1996. "Shanhu Shu 珊瑚树 [Coral Tree]". *Zhufan Zhi Jiaoshi* 诸蕃志校释 [Notes on Records of Foreign Countries]. Beijing: Zhonghua Book Company.

Zhao, Shankuo 赵善括. 1990. *Yingzhai Zazhu* 应斋杂著 [Selected Works of Zhao Shankuo]. Collected in Complete Library in the Four Branches of Literature. Shanghai: Shanghai Chinese Classics Publishing House.

Zhao, Yanwei 赵彦卫. 2013. *Yunlu Manchao* 云麓漫钞 [Zhao Yanwei's Notes on Historical Records]. Sorted by Zhu, Xuqiang. Collected in Complete Song Notes. Elephant Press.

Zhou, Yinggu 周应谷. 1990. Jingding Jiankang Zhi 景定建康志 [Jingding Period Chronicles of Jiankang]. Collected in The Series of Chorography of the Song and Yuan Dynasties. Beijing: Zhonghua Book Company.

Zhou, Baozhu 周宝珠. 1997. *Qingmingshanghetu Yu Qingmingshanghexue* 〈清明上河图〉与清明上河学 [Riverside Scene at Qingming Festival and the Studies on the Scroll]. Kaifeng:Henan University Press.

Zhou, Bida 周必大. 1990. *Wenzhong Ji* 文忠集 [Selected Works of Wenzhong]. Collected in Complete Library in the Four Branches of Literature. Shanghai: Shanghai Chinese Classics Publishing House.

Zhou, Cong 周淙. 1990. *Qiandao Linan Zhi* 乾道临安志 [Qiandao Period Chronicles of Lin'an]. Collected in The Series of Chorography of the Song and Yuan Dynasties. Beijing: Zhonghua Book Company.

Zhou, Mi 周密. 1988. *Guixin Zashi* 癸辛杂识 [Miscellaneous Records from Guixin Street]. Punctuated and collated by Wu Qiming. Beijing: Zhonghua Book Company.

Zhou, Qüfei 周去非. 1999. *Lingwai Daida Jiaozhu* 岭外代答校注 [Notes from the Land Beyond the Passes]. Collated by Yang Wuquan. Beijing: Zhonghua Book Company.

Zhou, Yinggu 周应谷. 1990. *Jingding Jiankang Zhi* 景定建康志 [Jingding Period Chronicles of Jiankang]. Collected in The Series of Chorography of the Song and Yuan Dynasties. Beijing: Zhonghua Book Company.

Zhu, Changwen 朱长文. 1990. *Wujun TujingXuji* 吴郡图经续记 [Continuation of the Chronicles of Wu County]. Collected in The Series of Chorography of the Song and Yuan Dynasties. Beijing: Zhonghua Book Company.

Zhu, Xi 朱熹. 2010. *Hui'an Xiansheng Zhuwengong Ji* 晦庵先生朱文公文集 [Selected Works of Zhu Xi]. Punctuated and collated by Liu Yongxiang, et al. Shanghai: Shanghai Chinese Classics Publishing House. Heifei: Anhui Education Publishing House.

Zhuang, Chuo 庄绰. 2008. *Jilei Bian* 鸡肋编 [Complementary Notes to Official Records]. Sorted by Xia Guangxing. Collected in Complete Song Notes. Elephant Press.

Zhuang, Weiji 庄为玑, and Jinghui Zhuang 庄景辉. 1977. "Quanzhou Songchuan Jiegou Fenxi 泉州宋船结构的历史分析 [An Analysis on the Structure of the Song Boat Unearthed in Quanzhou]". *Journal of Xiamen University* 4.

Xu, Song 徐松, et al. 2014. *Song Huiyao Jigao*宋会要辑稿 [The Anthology of Laws and Regulations of the Song Dynasty]. Shanghai: Shanghai Chinese Classics Publishing House.

Zhu, Yu 朱昱. 1990. *Chongxiu Piling Zhi* 重修毗陵志 [Revised Chronicles of Piling]. Collected in The Series of Chorography of the Song and Yuan Dynasties. Beijing: Zhonghua Book Company.

Chapter 2
Hydrological Conditions and Navigation of Inland Rivers in the Song Dynasty

2.1 Navigation Modes and the System of Ports Along the Yangtze River in the Song Dynasty

In the Song Dynasty, the boom of the commodity economy, along with the southward shifts of the taxation and economic centers contributed to the growth of navigation along the Yangtze River. The most economically developed regions, namely Sichuan Province and Southeastern China, had strong ties in commodity exchanges, making Sichuan and Shaanxi provinces crucial for national security during war times in the Southern Song Dynasty. Consequently, this led to a bustling waterway connecting Sichuan with East China via the Yangtze River. Despite several previous studies on navigation along the busy Yangtze River course, little attention has been given to navigation methods (J. Cao 2005; J. Zhang 2008; W. Lin 1992; C. Yu 2007; C. Luo 1991), and only a few studies have examined the actual conditions (Y. Shiba 1985).[1] Navigation methods can provide an essential perspective for the study of shipbuilding and water navigation development in the Song Dynasty by helping to understand the features and technical functions of boats on the Yangtze River course. This section focuses on a series of boats for long journeys on the Yangtze River to investigate navigation methods in the river course.

2.1.1 Sails and Boat Trackers in the Yangtze River Navigation

The Yangtze River course is conventionally divided into three sections by Yichang and Hukou. The course before Yichang is referred to as upstream, the one between Yichang and Hukou is known as midstream, and the section after Hukou is referred

[1] Yoshinobu Shiba holds that river boats in the Song and Yuan Dynasties were mainly powered by sails and the paddlers' strokes.

C. Huang, *A Panoramic View of the Song Dynasty Through the Lens of Shipbuilding Industry*, https://doi.org/10.1007/978-981-97-6128-9_2

to as downstream. However, in the Song Dynasty, the shipping course of the Yangtze River was divided into three sections at Shashi and Ezhou. During this period, boats sailing westward into the Chuanjiang Section (between Chongqing and Yichang) would need to change boats or supplement their life supplies at Shashi. Likewise, when boats sailed eastward into the Chuanjing Section, they would also stop at Shashi. The section from Shashi to Ezhou was generally safe for boats with little ripples, except for the gusts and great waves at the connection of Dongting Lake and the Yangtze River. However, the section from Ezhou downstream contained many sandbars, islets, and flowing-in branches of rivers. Moreover, the section from Jiangzhou (now Jiujiang) going downstream was hazardous due to the uncertain waves on the broad river. Therefore, different methods were required for sailing boats in different sections of the river course.

Lifting sails in a tailwind is a common practice for sailing boats in all river courses. Downstream sailing in the Yangtze River is particularly advantageous for boatmen, as it can significantly reduce journey time, just like riding a swift horse. One example of such swift sailing is described by Yue Ke, who sailed eastward and encountered a tailwind at Chizhou, allowing him to sail 200 km within a day, starting from Yancha and reaching Ditang Port at night. Describing his good fortune, he noted that "thousands of ships gathered at the banks, and sleeping boatmen had their broad fronts of garments unbuttoned all the night. Once boats started sailing, clouds and waves were ploughed through in the long voyage, and winds were driving boats swiftly in the clear sky on the River." (K. Yue 1990) However, due to the broad surface of the Yangtze River, gusts are strong and waves are high, making it difficult for boatmen to utilize a tailwind in some sections. In fact, sometimes the wind can be too strong for boatmen to lift sails or even force them to anchor their boats. In Zhou Bida's eastward voyage we see examples of various wind conditions encountered on the Yangtze River. In May of the sixth year of the Qiandao Reign (AD 1170), Zhou encountered a strong tailwind, but his boatmen could not lift sails due to its strength, causing them to take up a berth at a small bay. Later that month, when the south wind was suitable to lift sails, they travelled 20 km until they saw rare clouds overhead, which suggested the wind would turn to a north wind. As two boats were sailing to each other, their skilled punters were panicked, and they were ordered to change direction immediately. They had to head 5 km in a headwind until they reached the Tonglingjia Mouth of a branch, where they evaded collision and calmed down. In this case, they had no other option but to sail adversely. If their boat was in the port, they could have stayed there for safety. On May 5th, Zhou Bida encountered a headwind, and his boat had to wait until the wind became gentle. If they had no tailwind to utilize, they could also sail boats by making full use of the wind to go slantly. On May 29th, when Zhou Bida travelled in Chizhou, "he had to make use of a north wind to cross the river to the south bank as there was only a north wind to be utilized in the morning." (B. Zhou 1990) Therefore, only in a tailwind could they lift sails going downstream on the Yangtze River. Whenever they met with headwinds, they had to change directions of sailing based on the situation of wind directions.

Amidst the strong gusts that swept over the Yangtze River, boats sailing upstream were able to employ the technique of lifting sails to propel themselves forward. In the sixth year of the Qiandao Reign (AD 1170), Zhou Bida, while travelling downstream in Fanchang County, witnessed a procession of boats going upstream, each lifting its sails (B. Zhou 1990). Similarly, in the sixth year of the Qiandao Reign (AD 1170), Lu You, on his westward journey from Hangzhou to Sichuan, described the scene as "sailing on a huge boat with a load capacity of 2000 Hu, which had 26 sails on the 18-m high mast, as it emerged from the Grand Canal." The worn-out sails were promptly replaced by anchoring the boat at Guazhou and procuring new ones from Gusu. The significance of having sturdy sails while navigating upstream on the Yangtze River cannot be overstated, as Lu You himself discovered. Setting out from Guazhou, Lu You was favored with a tailwind. Lifting his sails enabled him to reach Zhenzhou in just one day. When he left Zhenzhou, "he was lucky to sail in a tailwind gain by raising his sails. Numerous boats on the Yangtze River were rushing forward, only dimly discernible in the misty mountainous background. Soon the gust became stronger, and boats were swimming more swiftly". Later, when they left Jiankang City, "a tailwind favoured them again, and the boatmen again hoisted their sails." On July 27th, "when gusts blew from the north in the early hours, the boatmen had to wake up and swiftly unfasten the boat, foregoing their breakfast." However, "after travelling 75 km, the gusts turned stronger, and they had to sail into a small islet to avoid the huge waves." In a strong tailwind, it was necessary to anchor the boat for the sake of safety. When they were in Dongliu County on July 28th, "they were blessed with a tailwind again, spreading their sails to travel more quickly." (Y. Lu 2012a, b: 167, 184) Similar conditions occurred on August 23rd, en route to Ezhou, as well as on August 30th, upon their subsequent departure (Y. Lu 2012a, b: 168, 201). However, in the Taipingzhou section, the river runs northward, prompting Guo Xiangzheng, who was sailing upstream in a tailwind, to capture his experience in several lines of a stanza: "The wind northbound is coming for me to sail, how happy we are to hoist our sails! Boatmen shouts echoed in the depth of river, their courage is pushing mountains backward. In just a moment, we are passing by a big river mouth, thunderous noises could we hear by looking back the passage." (X. Guo 1990a, b) Finally, Yang Wanli, who had set sail from Zhaotun, recalled how a tailwind had carried him 100 km in a single day, describing his experience, as "gusts send you a floating earth, huge waves fall overhead from the sky. Willows brandished happily and wildly, weed catkins shake tirelessly. Mountains by the river are riding a horse, a sail could send a boat a thousand miles back home in a day." (W. Yang 2007: 1837).

Boats can travel upstream in a tailwind faster than they downstream in the absence of wind. Wu Fei's experience traveling downstream against winds resulted in his boat being stranded in the river course, while others passed by swiftly. He wrote, "if god is selfless, he should treat all equally. Why are they shipping swiftly as an arrow? I have to be stuck by the bank with strong backward wind." (F. Wu 1990) Those who sail in a tailwind experience the opposite and view it as a fortunate occurrence. Lu You's description of sailing in a tailwind in the Taipingzhou section is a testament to this. While two boats were stuck on the Puxu River bank due to a headwind, Lu's boat sailed by smoothly, and his crew reacted with joy and smug laughter to the other boats' curses (Y. Lu 2012a, b: 174). In the third year of the Qiandao Reign (AD 1167), Zhou Bida travelled northbound from Lin'an to Jizhou. In Chizhou, he encountered a tailwind, which allowed his boat to move swiftly upstream (B. Zhou 1990). Similarly, when Huang Tingjian travelled eastward and encountered a headwind at Dalei river mouth, he found a swift boat was taking the wind upward, and let out an exclamation, "Who is the lucky dog that could travel downstream, chasing snowy mountains backwards" (T. Huang 2011: 1018). Lu You's westbound navigation was mostly favored by a tailwind. However, he was stuck in Huangzhou from August 14th and could only resume sailing again on August 23rd, with the aid of a tailwind (Y. Lu 2012a, b: 197). In fact, no wind or headwinds are more frequently encountered than tailwinds. Yang Wanli expressed his frustration with the lack of tailwinds in his poem, "Getting Stuck at Changfengsha of Shuzhou by a headwind." He wrote "when unbutton cables of my boat to sail northbound to the Luxi River, only when reached the east of Yancha, did we get stuck. I enjoyed one day's tailwinds, but four days' headwinds." (W. Yang 2007: 1821) This highlights the scarcity of favorable wind conditions along the Yangtze River.

In the Yangtze River course, encountering a tailwind is a rare occurrence due to abrupt changes in wind direction. Historical records provide examples of boatmen valuing the opportunity to sail in a tailwind, such as Zhou Bida who temporarily stopped at Chikou during the third year of the Qiandao Reign (AD 1167) and encountered a sudden wind change to the south, which quickly turned north with abrupt rains after only traveling 10 km (B. Zhou 1990). Similarly, when Wang Shipeng travelled westward to Sichuan Province, they had to wait for twenty days before being able to sail in a tailwind for two days since starting from Ezhu. When they were in Chiyang, hindered by headwinds for ten days, he wrote, "my returned ship had been stuck in Chiyang for ten days, god of wind seemed to hold me on for his treats." (S. Wang 2012: 354, 459) Boatmen cherished the tailwinds, and encountered hindrances from headwinds, such as when Li Gang travelled westward along the Yangtze River and was hindered by a headwind at the islet. "When a tailwind began to blow at dusk, boatmen were asked to unbuttoned and began to sail in the moonlight. Within a night, we could reach Jinling several hundred miles away." As such a weather condition was rare for boatmen, they ventured to sail at night. People defined the term of "avoid sailing" as the prohibition of sailing when there are risks that may endanger boats. At the islets, sailing is not allowed when water levels are significantly reduced (G. Li 2004: 171, 172). Li Liuqian encountered such a situation. He questioned whether he could lift the sails after departing from Wuhu and reaching Yancha Islet, as boatmen preferred to take advantage of favorable tailwinds and continue sailing without interruption. However, sailing at night was considered hazardous. Li Liuqian described the challenging conditions they faced while sailing against strong headwinds, which required the punters to exert tremendous effort for twenty days. The boat trackers were exhausted, and the sun's heat left sweat beads on their faces from morning till night. One day, they were suddenly blessed with a tailwind, and the boat could swiftly move forward like a clipper ship. When they passed by a village, they did not stop to buy chicken and pork for meals in fear of losing the tailwind. The boatmen were elated with the sailing experience, and passengers also cherished such rare moments (L. Li 1990). For instance, Zhou Bida, who travelled westbound along the Yangtze River, described sailing in a tailwind as one of his three pleasures, as he could admire

Jiuhua Mountain and read *Selected Works of Lize* for leisure (B. Zhou 1990). As it was rare and advantageous to sail in a tailwind, it is no wonder that people would find such conditions pleasurable. Sailing in a headwind was more challenging, and boat trackers were mainly relied upon. Su Shi described his experience of sailing in a headwind at Cihu River-Fork of Taipingzhou, where the masts and towlines whistled and pointed to the sky, and even the soft grass towlines had to fight strong winds to overcome the resistance (S. Su 2010: 4349). Towlines were the only effective way to defeat the resistance of strong headwinds. Lu You noted that sailing boats on the Yangtze River made full use of tailwinds to lift sails, but boat trackers were still essential in certain situations. For example, when Zhou Bida encountered unfavorable winds at Dingjia Passage in Tongling County, he had to rely on boat trackers (B. Zhou 1990). At Chikou Town, the boatmen spent an entire day towing the boat, and when the southeast wind blew adversely the next day, it became even more tedious to reach the river mouth of Liwang River. The next day, when the north wind suddenly halted, they had to use boat trackers again from Shangkou to Zhaotun Village (B. Zhou 1990). In the sixth year of the Qiandao Reign (AD 1170), when Lu You travelled in Taipingzhou, his boat was towed on the narrow artificial passage (Y. Lu 2012a, b:178), and in the Xinzhou section, the headwind made sailing even more difficult, forcing them to detour 7 or 8 km from morning till sunset. On the next day, a stronger west wind brought them more difficulty (Y. Lu 2012a, b: 193). They managed to travel 40–50 km a day in headwinds in August 17th–18th. In reality, the big or medium-sized boats like Lu You's needed boat trackers in the absence of wind. On August 20th, the boat "passed by Huangzhou with calm waves and no wind available, so boat trackers had to pull it to pass by the Red Cliff" (Y. Lu 2012a, b: 194, 196).

Upon reaching Shashi City, the use of sails was viable for upstream navigation. However, the river course section extending west to Shashi was characterized by a strong current, thus rendering the use of sails unnecessary. For instance, Lu You once embarked on a large boat with a load capacity of 2000 Hu and journeyed westward along the Sichuan section of the Yangtze River. In that section, they had to change boats due to the shallow water. Shashi was primarily inhabited by people from Sichuan Province and their spouses. Lu You switched to a more suitable Zhaoqing-made boat for sailing in the narrow river course. This type of boat "has a load capacity of 1600 Hu, equipped with six masts for sails and two carts of 300-m towlines" (Y. Lu 2012a, b: 206). The six masts were used for securing the towlines, which were made of bamboo strips and used for dragging the boat in the section between Jinghu and Sichuan. "To navigate the river course between Dongting Lake and the Xiangjiang River, bamboo-made ropes were used to pull the boat upstream, and were referred to as bamboo strip towlines ("Baizhang" in Chinese), which were often used in the river navigation of the Chuanxia region" (Y. Sun 1990a, b). In preparation for sailing in the section between Yibin and Yichang, Lu You described the acquisition of necessary supplies as follows. "The masts were moved to the boat yesterday, and bamboo strip towlines will be bought today. Firewood will be bought for future use during rainy or snowy weather, and rice will also be stored in large containers in advance." Purchasing supplies was not only necessary before sailing, but also entailed the erection of masts and the securing of towlines on the boat.

Due to constantly changing wind directions, sails were not used when traveling westward from Shashi, and instead, boatmen trackers were relied upon, and masts and bamboo strip towlines were used when passing through narrow gorges (Y. Lu 2012a, b: 206). In the Three Gorges, boat trackers served as the driving force. Boatmen either struggled to row paddles or dragged towlines, depending on the specific section of the river. To quote some lines of Lu You's poem, "dozens of boat trackers were happily dragging towlines, no chat was heard between people sitting face to face. In a moment, people scattered quietly, only squeaky noises were made by two wheels for winding towlines. With the squeaky noises, boatmen have already stood on the sandy beach." (Y. Lu 2011: 120) This indicates the boatmen served as both punters and boat trackers. When a towpath was available, the boatmen would disembark and drag the boat forward. However, when no towpath was present, they had to row paddles laboriously. In his *Ode to the Three Gorges*, Lu You wrote, "The autumn moon cast light over the Goddess Temple, old apes' crying came out of the Huangniu Gorge. Despite hazards, boatmen had no time to care about their safety, dragging the bamboo strip towlines to hurry on with their journey at night." (Y. Lu 2011: 230) When approaching Dadong Beach, boatmen had to unload the cargo and drag the boat through shallow and dangerous waters (Y. Lu 2012a, b: 213, 215). Similarly, Yuan Shuoyou recounted the difficulty of sailing through the Three Gorges, with steep gorges and dangerous waters creating a bumpy waterway. Xintan Shoal was regarded as the most dangerous of the twelve dangerous shoals that boatmen encountered, with all having to unload their cargo and change boats to pass it. Boatmen were small and insignificant against the background of the mountains, struggling to drag the boats with towlines. (S. Yuan 1990) The boat trackers and bamboo strip towlines were not sufficient for the dangerous waters and steep gorges. As such, going upstream westward from the Three Gorges relied heavily on boat-towing. Cao Gongsu's journey into Sichuan from Luzhou also relied on boat-towing, as he sailed from Lu'nan to Jianxi, where the huge waves splashed into numerous peach flowers, making sailing extremely difficult. Boatmen had to use bamboo strip towlines to pull the boats in the spring river, while Cao Gongsu travelled peacefully with his sword and enjoyed the prosperity of the state (G. Chao 1990).

As boat-towing was the only effective way to ensure sailing upstream, towpaths were built along the river banks except for spots where the steep terrain restricted their construction. For example, the section between Ezhou and Yueyang in the Zhuanhe River was characterized by the Bailihuang wilderness spanning 50 km, with only reeds visible across the banks. As a result, small boats were used to pull larger boats ahead due to the absence of towpaths. However, towpaths became available again when sailing upstream from the Zhuanhe River. "The road was encroached frequently ferocious beasts like tigers and wolves, and boatmen who towed their boats at night risked being eaten by wild beasts." (Y. Lu 2012a, b: 202) Therefore, the real danger was not the method of small boats drawing larger ones, but rather the risk of boatmen being consumed by wild animals. During Su Zhe's journey from Ruzhou to Junzhou, when he sailed along the Yangtze River, and the water level rose, floods destroyed the towpaths, and headwinds hindered sailing. He lamented, "Floods inundated all sandbars, and boatmen had no towpath to use. My boat had to wait for strong winds. Without any wind force, how could I sail my boat? Dejectedly, we had to remain in deep swamps, mooring my boat and waiting for the wind to pick up." (Z. Su 1987: 1119).

Sails and boat trackers were the main forces for ships on the Yangtze River, while barge poles, oars and sculls were auxiliary tools. In *Preface to Fishing Pictures*, Cao Buzhi described the inland water sailing in the early winter as "two boatmen dragging the towline on the towpath by steep cliffs, while the third struggled to push the boat with a punt-pole." (B. Chao 1990) As the Yangtze River was deep with torrential waves, barge poles, oars, and sculls had little function in upstream sailing. Guo Xiangzheng observed that barge poles could not touch the riverbed in the Taipingzhou section, making it challenging to make full use of towline force (X. Guo 1990a, b). However, downstream sailing benefited from barge poles, oars, and sculls. Particularly, "a boat could sail downstream several hundred miles in a short period, giving people little time to admire the rapidly passing landscape. A petty mistake might cause the boat to collide with huge cliffs, after which it would begin sinking before the wreckage quickly floated away." (X. Ouyang 2001: 564) Li Cengbo noted that big rocks and dangerous shoals were buried in deep water during the rainy season, making boatmen less concerned about rock collisions. In this context, barge poles, oars, and sculls were preferred over lifting sails with the stream to make the boat more controllable (Z. Li 1990). From Li Cengbo's notes, we can ascertain the conditions of the Yangtze River. Even if boats were sailing smoothly, boatmen had to be working very cautiously. The authorities in the South Song Dynasty planned water navigation for carrying batches of horses, and decided to use barge poles to navigate downstream sections. Horse-carrying vessels were equipped with helmsmen, sculls, sculler assistants, soldiers, and horse pullers as boatmen, depending on their load capacity. For instance, a horse-carrying vessel with a load capacity of 700 Liao (229,600 L) had four helmsmen, four sculls, four sculler assistants, five soldiers, and 25 horse pullers. In contrast, a horse-carrying vessel with a load capacity of 500 Liao (164,000 L) was equipped with three helmsmen, two sculls, and two sculler assistants, together with some soldiers and horse pullers, as boatmen. Sailing to and from Shashi on the Yangtze River, only towlines were used as a driving force, but sculls did not work. It was pointed out that in the return journey, 25 horse pullers could join in the paddling team when sailing upstream. Navigating through the Three Gorges, which were famous for their numerous gravel beaches, was particularly challenging (S. Xu et al. 2014: 9106–07). Fan Chengda, sailing through the Three Gorges, reported that "on top of the huge Yanyu Rock, torrential whirls could be seen in the middle of the Yangtze River, making boatmen nervous, their palms sweating and their faces turning pale with terror". "To ensure safe passage, boats were released one at a time, with soldiers shifting flags on nearby hilltops to signal when it was safe to proceed". "Bonuses were awarded to helmsmen and punters who navigated through the Three Gorges" (C. Fan 2012a, b, c: 75, 80). Overall, this description provides a clear understanding that sailing in the Three Gorges mainly relied on sculls and barge poles.

2.1.2 *Sailing Near the Bank or Going Through River Forks or Artificial Waterways*

Due to its broad surface and turbulent waves, the mid-channel of the Yangtze River was only navigable by extremely large boats, while smaller vessels were compelled to sail near the banks. During his travels along the Yangtze River, Lu You encountered a large raft which was over 150 m long, and 30 m wide. The vessel accommodated 30–40 homes, boatmen and their families, livestock, stone rice grinders, and even a temple. According to the boatmen, such a boat was still considered a small one as larger ones could host additional features such as vegetable gardens or pubs. Additionally, a larger ship would not go through small narrow waterways, opting instead to sail only on great rivers (Y. Lu 2012a, 2012b: 193). A vessel with similar dimensions was described by Zhang Shunmin, with a load capacity of 10,000 Dan (670,000 L) in an oval-shaped, three-chamber structure adorned with decorations and doors on its passages. Such vessels required strong winds as a driving force and could safely navigate in the mid-channel while carrying up to 20 million stings of coins and 12,000 Dan of rice (S. Zhang 1990a, b, c).[2] Small boats were limited to sailing near the banks or going through islets in artificial waterways, and only in the absence of wind could they sail in the mid-channel. Zhou Bida's journey in the Fanchang County region, which took place during little wind conditions, was marked by his decision to follow the river instead of the artificial river course (B. Zhou 1990). The constantly changing wind directions made it impossible for boats to consistently choose the mid-channel. In the event of strong winds, "they would have no shelter to evade danger." (Y. Zhou 1990: 1597) Thus, sailing near river forks or banks was the safer alternative.

When Zhang Shunmin went to take office, he left Kaifeng and travelled along the Yangtze River towards Chenzhou. His boat sailed for over two miles near the north bank in the Changlu section of Zhenzhou Municipality, but had to cross the river to the south bank at Xiayang due to the windy conditions. During this leg of the journey, Zhang Shunmin witnessed enormous waves that were as large as houses and heard the cacophony of thousands of running goats. Even crossing the river was a dangerous operation, and preparations had to be made in advance when leaving Zhenzhou. Furthermore, sailing upstream required avoiding the mid-channel of the river. When no towpath was available by the north bank, their boat had to cross the river to find a safe channel and continue along the south bank. The section of Jieshi in Taipingzhou had a rock that projected over the water, and the strong winds caused water to rush out and waves to become torrential. To navigate safely, "they had to travel eastward along the bank for several miles to pass through the rock-hidden waters." When they left Wuhu sailing eastward, they had to cross the river after only several miles to sail along the west bank. When they reached Shangkou Islet

[2] "Two hundred thousand strings of coins" was incorrectly written as "20 million strings of 1000 coins". If each string of 1000 copper coins weighs 5 Jin, and the boat could carry two hundred thousand strings of coins, their weight reaches one million Jin (640 tons), and it is close to the weight of 12,000 Dan of rice (710 tons).

in Chizhou and sailed for five or six kilometers, they left the main channel of the Yangtze River. They sailed for another 2 or 3 km along the south bank in shallow water and crossed the river to the north bank, where they had to use towlines to travel for 20 km. They then crossed back to the south bank for safe sailing. From Meigen Port, they travelled in the artificial course by towlines along the east bank in the headwind (S. Zhang 1990a, b, c). When they left Qikou, they could sail with the tailwind again and travelled over ten kilometers along the east bank before crossing the river and continuing for about fifteen kilometers along the west bank until they reached Xinye Islet (S. Zhang 1990a, b, c). After passing Daoshi Islet in Qizhou, they had to use towlines again to navigate the headwind along the north bank. "They travelled along the zigzagged water course for over ten kilometers by towlines along the bank" and also sailed along the north bank in Dingjiazhou (S. Zhang 1990a, b, c).

The terms "river fork" or "branch of a river" refer to narrow waterways or artificial channels created by sandbars and river banks. These channels offer an advantage of safe sailing compared to the main channel of a river, as the surface is narrow and the waves are small. The small and medium boats could avoid sailing along the midstream line for fear of huge waves. In the section from the connection of the Yangtze River and the Grand Canal to the lake-mouth of Dongting, there were many sandbars. To ensure safe sailing, the Song authorities completed several digging and renovation projects on the artificial water course. The Changlu water course, for example, was built to allow boats to sail in the Qiantang River and avoid the dangerous boat ruins in torrential waters (T. Li 2004: 2383). An artificial fresh river was also built in the section between Zhenjiang Prefecture and Jiangning Prefecture so that boats could evade danger. In the seventh year of the Chunxi Reign (AD 1180), Emperor Xiaozong praised the broadening of Haixing and Xinhe rivers, stating that "artificial watercourses were friendly for sailing. Well done!" (Song Shi Quanwen 2005: 1846) Xinhe River, ten kilometers southwest of the Yangtze River in Bailuzhou (Y. Zhou 1990: 1597), was originally built by Wu Jiefu, serving as the mayor of Jiangning Prefecture. His project aimed to avoid the five-kilometer-long dangerous passage at Luanjiaji Cliff. This was a wonderful project friendly for sailing (S. Zhang 1990a, b, c). The ancient grain-shipping canal was also dug in Jiangning Prefecture. "From Xiaquekou of Jing'an to Yizhen, the fresh water way (Xinhe River) was 40 km long". "It runs through the river fork of Qingsha to reach Tanyue Port, passing by Yaogangwei and connecting with the North Brook. The Xinhe River runs into Yizhen and reaches Xincheng, enabling boatmen to avoid the torrential waters for a smooth voyage of 40 km, successfully avoiding the 75-km-long dangerous section" (Y. Zhou 1990: 1597). In Jiankang Prefecture (now Jiangning), "boats need to travel southeastward through small river forks for 15 km, then enter the main channel of the Yangtze River. Sailing in the river fork along the east bank northward, boats could enjoy a similar broad surface like that of the Yangtze River. Sailing out of the north river fork, boats travelled 2.5 km to Liezhou to enter the Cihu River Fork in Taipingzhou" (S. Zhang 1990a, b, c). The region also has dangerous Sal-Ammoniac, or sand islets. In the Yuan Dynasty, Zhang Xuan pointed out in travelling diary about *Mountains and Rivers (II) of New Historic Book about the Capital City—Jinling City*

(Vol. 5), that “the two sand islets were 35 km away to the southwest of the City.” He further wrote, “Travelling through the river fork, flat fields and beautiful orchards by the banks came into my eyes, and bamboos were lush near farmers’ houses. Most of them belong to Changlusi (High Reed Temple). After going through the river fork, I can see tall reeds and towers.” (Y. Lu 2012a, b: 169) From this quotation, we know that this river fork was located at Changlusi. Historical records provide more accounts of such river forks, including the numerous sandbars that form them, making them good for boats’ sailing.

In Taipingzhou, there were several narrow river forks. In the period of the Qiandao Reign (AD 1165–1173), Zhou Bida embarked on a journey from Hangzhou to Jiangnan West Province. While passing through Taipingzhou, he “encountered morning rain, which soon gave way to clear weather. However, numerous boats faced difficulty moving forward in a small river, and they had to halt in Caishi Town due to foggy weather. After resuming their journey, the boats finally anchored in Cihu River-Fork.” Zhou Bida noted that the small river leading to Caishi Town was referred to as the Caishi River-Fork during his return journey. He mentioned that “starting from the Qinhuai River, the wind was good for boats to spread sails, and at night boats could be anchored at Caishi River-Fork.” After leaving Caishi River-Fork and going northward, the boats entered another small river fork known as the Cihu River-Fork. From there, it took only half a day to reach the artificial water channel in Jiangning Prefecture, referred to as the New River (Xinhe River) (B. Zhou 1990). This water passage was once travelled by Zhou Bida when he left Jiangnian West Province for Hangzhou. Starting from Egang Port, boats also needed to go through some river forks. “As the small river was clogged, water was running slowly, and later it merged into the Yangtze River. Finally, Zhou’s boat anchored at the river mouth of Xinhe River” (B. Zhou 1990). Here, it probably refers to Cihu River-Fork. There was also a small river fork between Daxinkou and Taipingzhou, whose name was unknown. In the present text, it is referred to as Daxin River-Fork. Zhou Bida attempted to pass through this river fork, but the slow-moving water caused the boats to return to the Yangtze River. Additionally, there was a mountain named Yiwu Mountain in Wuhu County of Taipingzhou, where a sluice gate was built for boats. “When Zhou Bida passed Xijia Watergate, they found that several boats were beating drums and waving flags to boost boatman morale to chase the boats. Alas, they were official boats to levy taxes in Hezhou Prefecture.” When Zhou Bida went to Hangzhou to take his office, “his boat brushed past Fanchang County, and as the wind was very small over the Yangtze River, his boat chose to sail in the mid-channel without going through river forks, and went past Wuhu County” (B. Zhou 1990). These quotations prove that Qingdun River-Fork is between Fanchang County and Wuhu County. In a proposal to imperial court of the Qiandao Reign (Gengyin Year) in *Wenzhong’s Selected Essays (Vol. 170),* Zhou Bida provided more details about Qingdun River-Fork, which lies between Sanshan Cliff and Lujiang Watermouth. He wrote that “after passing Sanshan Cliff, we went into Qingdun River-Fork, and could see Lujiang Watermouth in far away places, and finally we reached Wuhu County.” Lu You once made a reverse sailing from Xikou of Gushu in Taipingzhou Prefecture. “After sailing 15 km by towlines, we could anchor our boat at Daxinkou.” (Y. Lu

2012a, b: 178–179) This shows that they did sail in a narrow river. So these records show that the river forks boats had to pass were Cihu, Caishi, Daxin and Qingdun from east to west.

There were more river forks in the section of Chizhou along the Yangtze River. Dingjia River-Fork was the first one in the section of Chizhou between Taipingzhou and Chizhou, which was formed by Dingjia Sandbar and the river bank (B. Zhou 1990). Dingjia Sandbar, which is more than 40 km long and situated to the south of Chizhou in Fanchang County of Taipingzhou, was split into two by the river fork that runs through it (S. Yang et al. 1990), giving rise to Dingjia River-Fork. Hence, Tongling County was also known as Tongling River-Fork (S. Zhang 1990a, b, c), while the next river port south of it was called Meigen River-Fork. Fan Chengda's *Ode to Meigen River-Fork* includes a line which states, "By struggling to pedal the boats, can we reach the river fork safely." (C. Fan 1981: 279) Another river fork, Chikou Town, is described as being embraced by pine trees on both banks. According to Fan Chengda, boats could exit this fork after travelling 2.5 km by towlines, and enter the Yangtze River. Further upstream lies the Yangchi River-Fork, which could be reached after 10 km (S. Zhang 1990a, b, c). Continuing upstream, boats could reach the Changfeng River-Fork, which was formed by the Changfeng Sandbar and the river bank. Fan Chengda's boat once got stranded in this river fork due to the shallow water. Crossing this fork led to the town of Wankou. Lu You also sailed through this area, but stopped inside Changfeng River-Fork due to gusts of wind (B. Zhou 1990). He witnessed a small boat being shaken violently in the Yangtze River, and struggling to enter the Changfeng River-Fork. These descriptions demonstrate the value of river forks in avoiding dangerous waves (Y. Lu 2012a, b: 184). In Dongliu County, sailing in a tailwind along the narrow watercourse for a while, the boats could reach the east bank of the Yangtze River (S. Zhang 1990a, b, c). From there, boats could enter Wangjiang River-Fork (B. Zhou 1990), located in Wangjiang Town of Suzhou. If travelling downstream, boats could enter Chizhou, where they would pass through Yancha River-Fork and Jiangjia River-Fork. Fan Chengda once travelled downstream from Niuzhuji Valley to Yancha of Anhui Province, covering over one hundred kilometers, until he reached Xiakou of Changfengsha (B. Zhou 1990; C. Fan 2012a, b, c: 88). In total, Chizhou has over ten river forks, including Dingjia, Tongling, Meigen, Chikou, Yanchi, Changfeng, Wankou, Shanjia, Wangjiang, Yancha, and Jiangjiahan. In the sixth year of the Xuanhe Reign (AD 1124), Lu Zong, the deputy transit governor of Jiangnan East and West, Huainan East and West, Jinghu South and North, and Zhejiang East and West provinces, proposed an artificial channel using the two-hundred-kilometer-long sandbars, to save boats from sailing in dangerous waves for over one hundred kilometers. With this artificial river fork as an example, boats could avoid over twenty reefs along the east bank of the Chizhou section and avoid sailing into the destructively hazardous bay in the over-one-hundred-kilometer-long watercourse. The proposal was supported by Emperor Huizong (S. Xu 2014: 9619, 1002), but it is unclear from historical records whether the project was completed by the end of the Northern Song Dynasty.

Going westward along the section of Dongliu County in Chizhou, the first river fork encountered by boats was the Bosi River-Fork. According to Fan Chengda's

Travelogues in Wu Area by Ship, the distance between the Bosi River-Fork and Madang was only two or three kilometers. Further west, boats had to cross the Jiaoshi River-Fork, which Fan Chengda noted was 45 km away from Hukou. According to Zhou Bida's "Record on Boat-sailing" in Vol. 167 of *Wenzhong's Selected Essays*, the Jiaoshi River-Fork lay between Hukou County and Pengze County. After passing through Hukou County, boats could reach the entrance of Jiaoshi River-Fork, where they would stay overnight before continuing their journey at dawn the next day. Poet Yang Wanli also described the Jiaoshi River-Fork, noting that it was "narrow in the middle section, and that deep waters ran slowly there."(W. Yang 2007: 1815) There was also another called Madang River-Fork between Bosi River-Fork and Jiaoshi River-Fork. In his poem *Reply to Xusheng Artificial Hill,* Ouyang Xiu recounted his experience as a lower official to Jingchu, during which he sailed to the south-east region and observed Gushan Mount towering over Madang River-Fork. In his preface to *Prevented from Sailing in Madang River-Fork*, Kong Pingzhong correctly identified the wind-stricken area as Madang River-Fork, formed by the convergence of Madang Mount and Xiaogushan Mount (X. Ouyang 2001: 761). Lu You also mentioned his journey to Sichuan, during which his party "had to stop overnight in Susong County at Shajia River-Fork, less than a kilometer away from Mount Xiaogu" (Y. Lu 2012a, b: 186). The location of Shajia River-Fork was equivalent to that of Madang River-Fork described by Ouyang Xiu and Kong Zhongping in their works. From these records, it can be inferred that Jiaoshi, Madang and Bosi river forks were in the section between Jiangzhou and Hukou.

There were several well-known river forks in the section between Jiangzhou and Ezhou, even up to the mouth of Dongting Lake. After 25 km' sailing from Zhankou Town of Zhanzhou, "boats could reach the upper mouth of Xinye River-Fork". Sailing in this fork, "water was flowing by lush forests, autumn warblers were giggling happily and buffaloes were mowing leisurely". "Herds of buffaloes could not be found in Suzhou Prefecture. This town belonged to Dazhi County of Xingguo Millitary Prefecture." (S. Zhang 1990a, b, c; Y. Lu 2012a, b: 196) Located in the Huangzhou section, the Shuangliu River-Fork possessed a wide surface. Lu You once remarked that after leaving Huangzhou, even when sailing in the Shuangliu River-Fork, one could gain a broad perspective across the river. Continuing upstream towards Ezhou, the Baiyang River-Fork was situated along the way, located only fifteen kilometers from Ezhou."(X. Ouyang 2001; Y. Lu 2012a, b: 196).

The biggest river fork in the section between Ezhou and Dongling Lake was Zhuanhe River in Hubei Province. According to Fan Chengda, sailing in the Zhuanhe River could help to avoid the dangers of huge waves and strong gusts at the lake-mouth of Dongting Lake. In his *Preface to Lujiayu Entering Zhuanhe River*, he wrote, "at the connected point of three rivers (Sanjiangkou) in Yueyang, it was difficult to sail, and going through the Zhuanhe River might be a better choice." (C. Fan 1981, 274) The Zhuanhe River was a small water channel in the Yangtze River, which was the most important water course for boats carrying batches of goods and passengers. After the dry season in September, navigation in the Zhuanhe River was not possible, and boats had to take the waterway from Baling County to Jingzhu islets. Sailing downstream to Ezhou against the headwind could take a day's journey, leading to Tongjikou, "a necessary stop for batches of goods and passengers boarding and disembarking boats in Sichuan Province." (S. Xu 2014: 9665) Regardless of whether goods or passengers were being transported, the Zhuanhe River was the most important water course. Lu You lifted sails in a tailwind from Ezhou on August 30th and made a successful stopover at Tongjikou by taking the channel of the Zhuanhe River. They entered the Zhuanhe River on September 1st and left its waterway on September 8th, with a stopover at Jianning Town of Jiangling, which was at the river mouth. The journey took seven days, and they floated to the border of Shishou County, where the mouth of the Zhuanhe River was located (Y. Lu 2012a, b: 203). Wang Shipeng described the journey in a poem: "From Tongjikou, we kept on sailing until we reached Lujiafu. After sailing half a month out of and into the main channel of the Yangtze River, we were exhausted. In the misty rain, fisherman's houses were passing by on both banks. Looking at Mount Shishou on the floating boat, we began to miss our local sea food again."(S. Wang 2012: 352) Both official cargo shipping and merchants prefer sailing in the Zhuanhe River to avoid torrential water in the Yangtze River. When Fan Chengda left Sichuan for Hangzhou, "he had two water ways to choose from at Lujiafu. One involved sailing along the Yangtze River by passing Yueyang, Linxiang and Jiayu Counties. However, the torrential waves were high and violent, even if in a tailwind, making it difficult to travel. For this reason, passenger boats usually avoided this route. The other route ran from Lujiafu into the Zhuanhe River. As it was a small branch of the Yangtze River, its water was comparatively calm, but its narrow surface is just like that of a canal, eliminating the threat of dangerous winds and waves." Thus, Fan Chengda also chose to enter the Zhuanhe River at Lujiafu to avoid sailing in the main channel of the Yangtze River. His journey took half a day to reach Ezhou from the river mouth of the Zhuanhe River (C. Fan 2012a, b, c: 82). Wang Shipeng also preferred sailing in this river but decided not to take this course when leaving Sichuan Province via the lake mouth of Dongting Lake. "He was greedy about viewing the beautiful landscape in the Dongting Lake" (S. Wang 2012: 444).

From these sources, it can be inferred that the middle and lower reaches of the Yangtze River featured a significant number of river forks. These narrow channels were preferred by boatmen over the main channel of the river due to their calm waters and lack of wind. Naturally, there were many additional river forks not mentioned here, and some which were not named as river forks at all. For example, the Yingwu Sandbar in the Ezhou section was navigated by Lu You and his boatmen, who lifted their sails in a tailwind and traveled southward (Y. Lu 2012a, b: 201). This course was a river fork between Yingwu Sandbar and the banks of the Yangtze River. Similarly, when Zhang Shunmin departed from Ezhou and headed southwest, he encountered the Wujia Sandbar. The river surface between the two mountains was very narrow, indicating that they also followed the course of a river fork. The Dingjia Sandbar in Ruichang County of Jiangzhou Prefecture was another example of a narrow channel that was chosen by boatmen, as evidenced by their travel along its north bank for approximately ten kilometers (S. Zhang 1990a, b, c). The Dingjia Sandbar was garrisoned by soldiers (Toqta 1977: 488), with an area large enough to be a military base. The lower reaches of the Yangtze River also contained numerous sandbars, as mentioned in the *Local Chronicle on Mountains and Rivers* of *Jingding Period Chronicles of Jiankang (Vol. 19),* which notes that the Jiankang Prefecture section alone held dozens of sandbars, some with circumferences ranging from five to twelve kilometers. For example, Bailu Sandbar and Ma'ang Sandbar each had a circumference of seven to eight kilometers, while Jiju Sandbar and Mizi Zhou had twice that. The Manli Sandbar had a circumference of 17.5 km, with the Gaizhou Sandbar and Caizhou Sandbar surpassing it with circumferences of 19 km and 22.5 km, respectively. Certain sandbars often made narrow sailing channels, such as the Lizhou Sandbar, which was considered a haunted place by passenger ships attempting to avoid strong winds.

Not all banks were suitable for boat-towing as "some of them were covered with lush reeds and miscanthus sacchariflorus, while others were built near steep cliffs. In sections of the river with torrential waves, sailing was difficult" (Y. Zhou 1990: 1961). To ensure safety, boatmen chose narrow channels or river forks that were accessible to boat towing. As a result, they frequently crossed the Yangtze River banks. During his travels in the Jiangzhou Prefecture, Zhou Bida crossed the Yangtze River three times in a single day. On the Chinese lunar day "Guimaori", his boat had to cross the river to safely sail in Yanchajia Sandbar, and on the lunar day "Dingweiri", when the wind stopped, his boat had to cross the river to anchor in Wangjiang Channel (B. Zhou 1990). When Zhang Shunmin sailed upstream, his boatmen had to cross the river several times in the section of Taipingzhou. They started from Wuhu and sailed along the eastern bank for several kilometers before crossing the river to reach the western bank. "After that, they started from Tongling in a headwind and sailed two or three kilometers, and then they reached the south bank, which was surrounded by mountains. After sailing about five kilometers, they had to cross the river to reach its northern bank. Later, they sailed westward for 20 km and had to cross the river to reach the southern bank and anchored their boat at Meigen Port. One day, in Chizhou, it was drizzling without any wind. They towed the boat for 2 or 3 km. After they sailed out of the river fork, they entered the Yangtze River. After sailing 10 km, they crossed the river to reach its eastern bank at Jiangjunyan (General Weir). In the narrow channel of Yanchi, they had to anchor their boat at Shangkou. In the section of Qizhou, they sailed in a tailwind close to the eastern bank and started from Qikou, where there were small hills along the banks. After travelling about 10 km, they crossed the river to reach the west bank. After sailing about 15 km, they could reach the mouth of the Xinye River-Fork. In the section of Huangzhou, the north bank was flat and vast, and the small bare hills stood on its south bank. It was suitable to tow the boats along the north bank (S. Zhang 1990a, b, c). From the records about Zhou Bida's journey, as well as Zhang Shunmin's, it is evident that the reason for them to cross the river frequently was not due to the utilization of deflected winds but because of the flat bank that was suitable for towing boats. Xu Jing once mentioned that boatmen could lift cloth sails, small sails on the top of masts, and bamboo cloak sails to drive boats in different winds, except for the headwind that could not be used as a driving force for boats (J. Xu 2006: 130). In his *Reflections about Pingzhou* (Vol. 2), Zhu Yu mentioned that "sailing on the sea could make use of winds from three directions, not restricted to tailwinds. Soon after the boats left the bank, boatmen could use different winds except the headwind, as a headwind would backtrack the boat. The other three kinds of winds include a tailwind and winds from two sides of the boat." When boatmen crossed the river, they usually avoided sailing in the dangerous mid-channel, travelling instead in the river forks or using the flat bank for towing. According to Lu You's account, boatmen were hesitant to cross the river in the section from Guazhou to Jingkou on the opposite bank due to violent waves. "It was difficult for them to cross the river directly, so they sailed westward for some time for the sake of security before crossing the river in a zigzagged way" (Y. Lu 2012a, b: 166), as the winds did not blow from the same direction and the river was not wide enough for boats sailing using side winds, especially when going upstream on the Yangtze River.

2.1.3 The Port System of the Yangtze River Navigation

The authorities established a stopover system in the Yangtze River, which included large ports serving as navigation hubs, as well as county-level government seats. These ports were used as stopovers along the Yangtze River, or while navigating through river forks or smaller ports along the branches of the Yangtze River. The ports located along the Yangtze River can be classified into three tiers based on their transportation volume and significance. The first tier comprises important shipping hubs, including ports in Zhenzhou, Zhenjiang, Ezhou, and Shashi. The second tier consists of the seats of local governments, where the offices of local officials at various levels are located. However, their significance varies. For example, the ports in Jiangyin Military Prefecture, Bozhou, Jiangzhou, Gongzhou, and Jiazhou served as distribution ports, while, less importantly, the ports at Huangzhou and other sandbars were only used as stopovers. The third tier comprises small ports in towns and villages or situated in narrow channels, river forks, and reed marshes.

Zhenzhou served as a transportation hub for goods flowing into the Huainan Canal from the Yangtze River. In the first year of the Zhidao Reign (AD 995), the Jianghuai Grain Shipping Administration established a bureau in the Huai'nan Provinces (F. Sun 1988: 839), with its office in Zhenzhou Prefecture. In Ouyang Xiu's essay "Reflections on Eastern Garden in Zhenzhou" of Volume 4 of *Selected Works of Wenzhong,* Zhou Bida explained that the Grain Shipping Administration established an administrative agency in Zhenzhou because it was a key shipping hub for waterways that connected to the Yangtze River. This bureau was responsible for governing the grain shipping of Jiangnan East and West, Huainan East and West, Liangzhe East and West, Jinghu South and Jinghu North provinces. Zhenzhou Grain Shipping Administration functioned as an administrative office for emperors' temporary residence, and was directed by a director and a deputy director in charge of shipping affairs. During the spring, when there were numerous boats shipping grains, this administrative center dispatched officials to supervise the batches of grain shipping in Yangzhou, Chuzhou, and Sizhou (T. Li 2004: 6281). Zhenzhou was an important gateway for cargoes from the Yangtze River, particularly for batches of grains (S. Xu 2014: 9618). It served as a center for grain shipping and salt distribution in Huainan provinces. Cargoes were shipped from Tongzhou, Taizhou, and Chuzhou to Zhenzhou, and from there, they were sent to Jiangnan East and West, Liangzhe East and West, and Jinghu provinces (S. Yang et al. 1990). As a result, many merchants were attracted to Zhenzhou, making it a commercial hub in addition to Huainan East and West, Liangzhe, and Jiangnan East and South provinces. During Emperor Taizong's Reign, when Yang Yungong chaired the office of grain shipping, he ordered the construction of temporary transfer storehouses for grains from six provinces in the lower reaches of the Yangtze River. Boats carried grains to Zhenzhou and then transported salt back to their home provinces (C. Huang and N. Yi 2002). In the Southern Song Dynasty, the grain shipping administrative center issued Salt and Tea Tickets to attract more merchants for trading (S. Xu 2014: 6708). Lu You once described the scene of "boats busily coming to and from the section of the Yangtze River, which created a fairy land with boats and nearby mountains as the background in the mist."

Zhenjiang was a juncture between the Liangzhe West Canal and the Yangtze River. In the Northern Song Dynasty, Liangzhe West Province became economically prosperous due to its active grain shipping and commercial activities. In the Southern Song Dynasty, the section of the Liangzhe West Canal became a primary supply line, enhancing Zhenjiang's status as a transportation hub. However, in the Northern Song Dynasty, Zhenjiang's port conditions were rather unfavorable. In the sixth year of the Zhenghe Reign (AD 1116), Emperor Huizong issued an imperial edict noting that "Zhenjiang's small port had low capacity, and whenever gusts blew, roughly five hundred boats sank within three years" (S. Xu 2014: 9618). Consequently, he ordered the dredging and deepening of the old river course to the west of Zhenjiang City for boat shelter. In the Southern Song Dynasty, Qiantang City was responsible for managing the imperial stopover by the Yangtze River, including good transportation, provisions, and funds for troops. As river transportation was the only viable option, boats traveling to Zhenjiang along the Yangtze River became calm and safe after passing through the sluice at Zhenjiang. Large ships from Sichuan and Guangnan provinces could reach the capital city directly (S. Xu 2014: 9607). Ganlu Port of Zhenjiang near Beigu Mountain could accommodate boats with a loading capacity of 200,000 Dan (13,400,000 L). The stone gates at the sluice were sturdy and steadfast against wild waves (Z. Huang 1990). Numerous boats frequently visited ports in Zhenjiang, and the passage between the entry and exit at Ganlu Port could only accommodate a few boats, but the Beigu Mountain section was vast as a lake, allowing many boats to sail (X. Lu 1990: 2373). In the 6th year of the Chunxi Reign (AD 1179), Sima Ji, the mayor of Zhenjiang, "initiated a rebuilding project of the river to make it more friendly to boats passing through, significantly enhancing the infrastructure of Zhengjiang Port" (S. Xu 2014: 6168). In the sixth year of the Jiading Reign (AD 1213), the central government carried out another dredging and deepening project "as the sluice gates had become shallow and clogged with floating sand, making it difficult for boats to pass through" (S. Xu 2014: 9607).

Ezhou was the largest harbor in the lower reaches of the Yangtze River, serving as a hub for batches of grain shipping from Sichuan section of the Yangtze River in the west, Dongting Lake from Xiangjiang River in the south, and Hanshui River in the north. The boats that went downstream gathered here. Therefore, Ezhou was dubbed the core city of Sichuan, Guangnan, Jingzhou, Huainan and Liangzhe provinces. The high demand for cargo at the port resulted in all arriving cargoes being sold out within a day, indicating the prosperity of business in Ezhou. Fan Chengda, upon reaching the south market of Yingwu Sandbar in Ezhou, observed the thousands of fisherman's homes arrayed along the Yangtze River, with numerous shops and bars decorated with elegant railings (C. Fan 2012a, b, c: 82). Lu You's boat once anchored at the lower place of the Tinghe River for taxation, where a line of numerous passenger boats and commercial ships awaited their turn to call the port, spanning several kilometers. This highlighted the significance of Ezhou as a port city, as no other port city could accommodate such a high number of boats from Jingkou to the western capital. Nanshi of Zhenjiang was also home to numerous towns and shops of different varieties, making it a cosmopolitan city. "Most of the merchants clustered there were from Sichuan Province" (Y. Lu 2012a, b: 197, 201) Thus, Shuiwuting and Nanshi were two important ports within and beyond Ezhou City.

Shashi was another "transportation hub for ships and carts," (Toqta 1977: 13,309) with "major roads and water courses connecting there," making it a necessary stop for merchants (Toqta 1977: 4412). "It connected the eastern and western regions and served as a passage from the Wu Kingdom to the Shu Kingdom." (S. Yuan 1990) "Many merchants and passengers visited Shashi." (S. Su 2010: 124) This description shows the important status of Shashi as a port for connecting the east and the west. The city had a large population of passengers and merchants, and their boats from the Wu Kingdom to the Shu Kingdom mingled together in the Shashi Port (Y. Lu 2011: 118). One could observe a diverse array of styles from individuals from Dongwu and Sichuan. "Half of the houses in a five-kilometer line were made of bamboo."(S. Yuan 1990 "Sichuan-made boats went southward in a hurry, while Dongwu-made boats went by in Shashi port." (L. Li 1990) "Big firms clustered there, and dwellings densely lined the streets." However, in the seventh year of the Chunxi Reign (AD 1180), a fire destroyed thousands of homes and claimed several lives. Consequently, Gao Kui, the governor, ordered water channels to be dug to prevent fire in the streets of Shashi City (B. Zhou 1990; Toqta 1977: 1381). Shashi's prosperity was due to its important status as a transfer port from Sichuan down the Yangtze River. At that time, almost all the commodities in and out of Sichuan had to make a transfer at Shashi Port. In the Northern Song Dynasty, "in Sichuan and Yizhou, cloth being taxed on the markets was shipped to Jingnan via water channel from Jiazhou. From Jingnan, commodities were transferred on large boats and transported to the ancient capital city Bianliang. 660,000 rolls of cloth were sub-categorized into ten batches annually. In previous years, the volume surpassed one million rolls of cloth, but later transported goods were reduced gradually." (S. Xu 2014: 7029) Batches of cloth, silk, and ox furs were unloaded at Shashi Port (S. Xu 2014: 6955), and a boat repair dock was built at the Xinhekou (new river mouth) two or three kilometers away from Shashi (S. Xu 2014: 7043), serving the repair of boats going into and out of Sichuan Province, the well known "Sichuaners' Boats Repair Center" (Y. Lu 2012a, b: 206). Passengers needed to change boats suitable for sailing in the section between Sichuan's Yibin and Hubei's Yichang. Wang Shipeng once wrote a poem to describe the boat changing at Shashi, that "boats have travelled upstream for a month, but they had to change to smaller Sichuan-made boats at Jiangling" (S. Wang 2012:356). Large boats with a heavy load could not safely sail through the Three Gorges. Sailing through them was likely to involve transferring cargoes and passengers to smaller boats. The most suitable boats were called "Chan", light boats with a broad bottom that could sail in torrential waves. Lu You noticed that "about six-tenths of boats were damaged at the bottom by rocks on the riverbed when they went westward." In this passage, "sharp rocks would pierce the bottom of the boat due to the heavy load of ceramics on board." (Y. Lu 2012a, b: 214, 216) In preparation to carry horses on the Yangtze River, Wu Lin raised funds to build boats with load capacities from 400 to 700 Liao. On Lu You's westward journey from Zhenjiang, he took a large boat with a load capacity of 2000 Liao. Due to the water conditions, he had to change to a smaller boat with a load capacity of 1600 Hu, a much more suitable boat for sailing in the Three Gorges (Y. Lu 2012a, b: 206). Before going into the Three Gorges, boatmen needed to raise a mast for boat towing. "After having submitted their sacrifice of beef and liquor, the empty boats could travel like a flying bird." (Y. Lu 2011: 196) Lu You vividly described the difference between going eastward or westward at Shashi Port. He notes that when going eastward, sails must be raised, whereas going westward, bamboo strips are utilized as ropes to tow boats upstream. He also observes that during eastbound sailing along the Yangtze River, "pigs were sacrificed to the god of the dragon at Xiakou Valley, whereas at Shatou, drums were beaten and sails raised." (Y. Lu 2011: 395, 246) Despite being in the Chu Kingdom, Sichuaners were prevalent in the area. "In the three thousand alleys of Shatou, orange flowers bloomed and reached up towards the misty air, while locals, mostly Sichuaners rather than Chu people, served dogwood-flavored tea to entertain guests." (Y. Lu 2011: 246) Moreover, the majority of Shashi locals residing on the dams were either Sichuaners or married to Sichuaners (Y. Lu 2012a, b: 206). This, in turn, highlights the significance of Shashi in shipping and sailing along the Yangtze River. The *Notes of Warehouse on the River* selected from *Records of Prosperous Lin'an* compare Shashi to a significant business town, while Hanzhou was recognized as the Heaven of Rich Merchants on the Baiyang Lake. Other prefectures and municipalities did not display such levels of prosperity. Although many merchants were concentrated in Jingnan, Shashi, and Huangchi of Taipingzhou, no warehouses were constructed on the river to accommodate them. The author's intention was to emphasize that Shashi and Huangchi were of equal importance to Baiyang Lake in Hangzhou.

In the second tier, Jiangyin, Wuhu, Jiankang, Jiangzhou, Gongzhou, Jiazhou, Jiangyin, Wuhu, Jiankang, Jiangzhou, Gongzhou, and Jiazhou were the most important. No matter in the Northern Song Dynasty or in the Southern Song Dynasty, in terms of inner navigation of the Yangtze River, the main course ranged from the Yangtze River to the canals. However, compared to Zhenzhou and Zhenjiang, which were at the mouth of the canal, Jiangyin was considered less critical. Nonetheless, as a vital relay port for seagoing ships entering the Yangtze River, Jiangyin played an irreplaceable role in linking sea navigation to inland river navigation. Merchants from Fujian Province, Guangnan East and West provinces, and Hainan traveled to Jiangyin from the sea, and a large number of passenger ships from these provinces were used for business purposes. Most of these merchants disembarked at the dam of Jiangning Prefecture, while the majority of the resale trade occurred in Zhenjiang Prefecture (S. Xu 2014: 7126). Jiangyin was closely connected with sea navigation, and no other ports could serve the same function (X. Li 2013: 3186). Wang Anshi described the busy sea trading in Jiangyin, stating that "Waters connected the sky from Huangtian Port, commercial boats were competing in a tailwind. Pearls and rhinoceros horns were put on the market, fishes and crabs were cheap enough for common people." (A. Wang 1990) For this reason, in the 15th year of the Shaoxing Reign (AD 1145), a custom was set up, following the example of Wenzhou, and a concurrent post was taken by an official in service (S. Xu 2014: 4216).

Jiangyin Port also functioned as an inland river port. When the Zhenjiang Canal was dry, it was hard for boats to go through the Zhenjiang Sluice to enter the canal. Instead, boatmen likely traveled eastward to reach Jiangyin and then entered the canal by transferring from several rivers. In the 29th year of the Shaoxing Reign (AD 1159), during the dry seasons of spring and winter, the royal decree ordered all grain boats to take the course from Zhenjiang to Jiangyin. In the sixth year of the Jiading Reign (AD 1213), as the sluice gates at Zhenjiang Port were shallow and no boats could pass through, all batches of staple goods were shipped from Jiangyin and entered the canal at Wuhong Weir, also known as Wuxie Weir due to its conveniently full use of Shengang and Ligang ports in Zhenjiang. However, "boats departing from Zhenjiang could pass by Jianbi and Baogang, where the surface was flat and connected with the sea, but there were no ports for their calls. Due to the torrential waves, many boats risked ruin by storms. Among the grain vessels from the lower reaches of the Yangtze River, some were ruined, while others lost their people and goods on board. It was dangerous for boats to shift navigation channels from Zhenjiang to Jiangyin Port" (X. Li 2013: 3053–54; S. Xu 2014: 9607; Toqta 1977: 2408). The boats entering Zhengjiang West province were mostly small flat-bottom boats with a load capacity of 200–300 Liao (65,600–98,400 L) and did not dare to change into the canal at Jiangyin. Therefore, in terms of inland river navigation, Jiangyin was a less important harbor or one of the preparatory ports.

Wuhu, located at the river mouth of Qingyi River in the lower reaches of the Yangtze River, was an important business harbor. Its significance can be attributed to its connection with Taipingzhou, the merging of Wuhu Lake into Gucheng Lake, and the water channel connecting Taihu Lake and the Liangzhe West Canal. This water channel ran through five weirs and merged into Taihu Lake from Yixing County of Changzhou Prefecture (Y. Zhou 1990: 1592), and then ran through Yinlin and four other weirs into Jingxi River, thus linking Taihu Lake and the Liangzhe West Canal. A small river south of Wuhu in Taipingzhou was also connected to the Yangtze River, running to Huangchi Town and Yinlin from east Wuhu. The river runs eastward from the east dam ranging 9 km, going through Liyang, and Yixing, and finally infills into Taihu Lake." "Running through Yinlin Weir, rivers could go through Liyang and Yixing, and merge into Zhenze Lake" (R. Li 1985: 17). In his poem entitled *Passing Through Gucheng Lake at Dawn*, Yue Ke illustrated the journey from Wuhu, sailing through Gucheng Lake and Yinlin Weir, then through Jingxi to Taihu Lake, writing "Once the sluice gates were opened, ten small boats swiftly passed Gucheng Lake by five o'clock. Mountains by mountains far from Jinling in the east, thousands of big ships passed briskly by the Yin Dam at Yinlin Weir." (K. Yue 1990) According to Shan E's *Field Study of Water Regime in Wuxian County*, the water passage was dug and used by Wu Zixu to conquer the Chu Kingdom during the spring and autumn, and since then it was used for grain shipping. Boats with a load capacity of 200 Liao could sail in the spring and winter seasons, connecting Taihu Lake in the east and the Yangtze River in the west. However, the river gradually silted up during the Five Dynasties Period, and two weirs were dug at Yinlin and Fenshui to make waters from Xuancheng, Yixian, Chizhou, Guangde, and Lishui run through Taipingzhou and Wuhu Lake, merging into Taihu Lake at Jingxi. "From Yinlin Weir, the water channel could reach Jianping and Guangde in the south, and Lishui and Jiangning in the north. Later, the royal court ordered the deepening and widening of the water channel, which provided advantageous conditions for passenger boats and commercial boats". Thus, the water channel connecting Taihu Lake and Wuhu Lake at Yinlin was also suitable for navigation.

In the Northern Song Dynasty, Emperor Huizong issued an order to reclaim low-lying paddy fields surrounded by dikes in Danyang, Gucheng, and Shijiu lakes. However, the repairs of the Yinlin channel were deemed unnecessary (S. Xu 2014: 7515). In the Southern Song Dynasty, Hangzhou, the capital city, became the center of grain shipping and business. Nonetheless, during the dry season, the low water level of the Grand Canal posed challenges to boat navigation. As a result, the authorities recognized the significance of the Yinlin Channel, which could connect the Taihu Lake Project. In the period of Emperor Gaozong's Reign, an official proposed the construction of transfer warehouses in Wuhu to facilitate the unloading, uploading, and storage of grains. The official emphasized the need for such warehouses because of the long distance from Sichuan, Guangnan East and West provinces, Jingzhou, and Huzhou to Hangzhou, where the royal temporary residence was located. The proposal also suggested dredging some weirs, sluices, ditches, and harbors between Yinlin and Dengbu to ensure smooth sailing. Although some would have benefited from the proposed landmass transfer, others opposed the plan based on their interests, leading the proposal to be abandoned. Nevertheless, the water course eventually became a busy one in the Southern Song Dynasty (S. Xu 2014: 7583). In the first year of the Qiandao Reign (AD 1165), Zhang Xiaoxiang, the mayor of Jiankang Prefecture, requested to dredge and deepen the five weirs from Yinlin to Dongba, connecting Liyang, Yixing and Taihu Lake in the east. This development allowed goods from Sichuan, Guangnan East and West provinces to reach Hangzhou. However, some sections of the river remained unsuitable for sailing due to hindrances from the locals (S. Xu 2014: 6158). Zhou Bida travelled through the Grand Canal three times, one of which took the route from Yinlin Weir to Gucheng Lake and reached Huangchi Town. From there, he travelled southward via landmass vehicles to Jiangnan West Province (B. Zhou 1990). From the description, we know that some of the water channel was dredged in the Yinlin section in the period of Emperor Xiaozong. In fact, the water channel of Wuhu was not only a passage to the Yangtze River in the prefectures of Jiangnan East Province but also an essential link connecting Liangzhe West Province with the Yangtze River. *Records of Prosperous Lin'an* asserts that Huangchi Town and Shashi Town were equally important regarding commercial affairs, likely due to their geographical advantage of connecting Wuhu Lake and Taihu Lake. Moreover, Wuhu Port was among the six taxation places in Chizhou Prefecture and Jiankang Prefecture, which also included Yancha, Chikou, Shituan, Wuhu, and Caishi. In the lower reaches of the Yangtze River, Wuhu was among the most prominent ports for ships to call and pay taxes (S. Xu 2014: 6381, 6383).

Jiankang was the provincial capital of Jiangnan East Province, and its importance was demonstrated through its frequent use as a stopping point for boats traveling in both the east and west directions. In this regard, various historical figures including Ouyang Xiu, Zhang Shunmin, Lu You, Fan Chengda, and Zhou Bida all made stopovers at Wuhu. The river channel that passed through Lishui in Jiankang connected to Taihu Lake via the Jingxi River. In the third year of the Qiandao Reign (AD 1167), Zhou Bida took the path of traveling through the Jiangjiang and Lishui Rivers before entering the Yangtze River on his way to Jiangnan West Province from Liangzhe West Province. Additionally, the merchants travelling routes from the Jingxi River in Liangzhe West Province to Wuhu Lake would pass through Yinlin and Dongba before proceeding northward to Jiangning Prefecture. Jiangzhou (now Jiujiang) was the most important river hub into the Poyang Lake system. "For buying grains in Hongzhou, it was advisable to establish Official Transfer Warehouses in Jiangzhou to feed Huainan West Province" (X. Li 2013: 1914, 1912). The warehouses served as storage and distribution centers for batches of commodity transportation.

Gongzhou Prefecture, situated at the confluence of the Jiangling River and the Yangtze River, was a crucial transportation hub for northern Sichuan Province. In the Southern Song Dynasty, major forces were deployed in the regions of north Sichuan Province and Shaanxi Province. Consequently, the Jiangling River became the primary waterway for transporting military supplies, thereby elevating the status of Gongzhou (now Chongqing) as an important hub. During this period, carrying horses required taking the water route passing through Gongzhou from Lizhou and Xingyuan (Y. He 2009; C. Huang 2014). Jiazhou, situated along the Yangtze River in the western region of Sichuan Province, was another transportation hub, often referred to as the "merging point of rivers." (C. Fan 2012a, 2012b, 2012c: 60) It served as a distribution center for batches of goods, such as cloth and satin from Tongchuan and Yizhou prefectures, as well as cloth from taxation markets, which were carried and transferred to Jiazhou by carts. Goods were also shipped to Jingnan from Gongzhou (Toqta 1977: 4252). In the seventh year of the Tiansheng Reign (AD 1027), Li Pan, a royal official, was ordered by imperial edict to immediately check the documents of transactions at the Transfer Official Residence in Yizhou Prefecture by riding on courier relay horses. Once the official documents were processed by lower officials, batches of ox fir, cloth, and other textiles were sent to Jingnan (S. Xu 2014: 6955). Fan Chengda's journey from Sichuan Province is also recorded. "After ordering his crew to build a boat in Xuzhou (now Yibin) of Sichuan, he sailed upstream to reach Jiazhou (now Leshan). Once there, he resumed his voyage on a new ship" (C. Fan 2012a, b, c: 60).

In comparison to Jiazhou and other ports previously mentioned, other prefecture sites functioning as ports were deemed inferior. These sites included Taipingzhou, Chizhou, Huangzhou, Xiazhou, Guizhou, Kuizhou, Wanzhou, Zhongzhou, Fuzhou, Luzhou, and Xuzhou. Several representative ports will be discussed in the following passage. Huangzhou was the only riverside city between Jiangzhou and Ezhou and was recognized as a literary city due to Su Shi's works, poems, and legends associated with this location. However, the infrastructure of Huangzhou Port was subpar, prompting Emperor Huizong to issue an imperial edict to repair and renovate the port to prevent boats from sinking in the section of the Yangtze River, saying "harbors on the both banks should be kept." After years of desolation and disrepair, a comprehensive examination of the port was put on the local officials' agenda. Although the royal court ordered to use ten certificates of monastery taxation exemption for the renovation budget (S. Xu 2014: 9617), the extensive project could not be completed until the early years of the Southern Song Dynasty. In contrast to the well-established ports surrounded by solid sandbars in Jiangzhou, Qikou, Wuhu, Chizhou, and Zhenzhou, Huangzhou's port had a reputation for boats "easily wafting in all directions" (S. Xu 2014: 6383) due to its poor condition. In the fifth year of the Qiandao Reign (AD 1169), Yang Yizhi, the mayor of Huangzhou Prefecture, "initiated the dredging of the postponed Huangzhou Port shortly after taking office. Thus the problem of boats "having no place to anchor in the besieged steep cliffs was finally solved." Twenty days later, the project was completed, allowing boats to have a resting place (X. Zhang 1980: 143). However, when Lu You passed through Huangzhou the following year, he observed a quiet port with few boats calling. He suggested that "probably the local officials were tired of passengers, and then they clogged the port." Perhaps the local officials were not available to meet so many guests and deliberately ruined the port. Thus, Lu You's boat had to call the Zhuyuan Dock several kilometers away from Huangzhou Port (Y. Lu 2012a, b: 196). Many docks were named after their local agricultural produce, such as Guabu Dock (for its abundant melons) and Mabu Dock (for its rich linen) (S. Xu 2014: 6350–51). Even in the fourth year of the Chunxi Reign (AD 1177), when Fan Chengda left Chengdu for Zhejiang, he could not find a suitable port to call in Huangzhou. He noted that "as Huanggang was known as a bad harbor, the long-voyage visitors suffered from its bad conditions. My boat had to rest in a small piece of land in the port, which was surrounded by a stripe of water with a red rock projecting over the water." The county intended to dredge the port for the stopover of passenger boats, but the proposal remained unsettled (C. Fan 2012a, b, c: 84). Consequently, Fan Chengda's boat had to rest in a small bay of the Red Cliff. In the eleventh year of the Chunxi Reign (AD 1184), Lu Tai and ten other merchants submitted a proposal for the repair and renovation of Huangzhou Port. They noted that the torrent waves formed in the Red Cliff posed significant dangers to boats due to the clogged waterway in the Huangzhou taxation administrative region. Prior to the port, the broad surface had numerous boats clustered in huge waves, but they had no suitable docks to call. Several boats were destroyed in the huge waves when waiting to pay taxes, resulting in a loss of over 2000 bags of salt as well as roughly 50 additional boats. Fang Tingrui, the Mayor of Huangzhou Prefecture, was removed from his office due to the accidents (S. Xu 2014: 6379). Nevertheless, there is no record that the repairs of Huangzhou Port were completed.

Fan Chengda, Lu You, and Zhou Bida all embarked on journeys through different regions in China. Fan Chengda's voyage started from Sichuan Province and passed Xuzhou, Luzhou, Gongzhou, Fuzhou, Kuizhou, Guizhou, Chizhou, and Taipingzhou, and his boat called the county sites of Jingjin, Jiangyuan and Shishou. Similarly, Lu You covered over 2500 km and passed through 15 prefectures from the East Wu Kingdom to the Chu Kingdom. Along his way, his boat called Taipingzhou, Chizhou, Guizhou and other counties. Zhou Bida travelled multiple times between Hukou County and Zhenjiang, passing through Hukou County, Chizhou, Taipingzhou, and other riverside counties of Jiankang Prefecture. Most of the county seats were poor in infrastructure. For example, Guizhou Town had only 300–400 households, and its total taxes levied in summer and autumn were only 5000 Dan (335,000 L) of grains, which was equivalent to the revenues levied on a small landlord in the Wuzhong region of the lower reaches of the Yangtze River. Similarly, the towns in Badong County were desolate, with only a little over one hundred households, and most of the houses were covered with grass instead of tiles on the roofs. "Even the port in Hukou County could only accept boat's calls, and had to refuse boats when the water subsided." However, Gong'an County was an exception to this trend, as it exhibited prosperity and magnificence with rich towns. Similarly, Wushan County, despite its location in the valley, had more prosperous towns than those in Guizhou and Xiazhou counties (Y. Lu 2012a, b: 204, 216,217; B. Zhou 1990).

Shashi was an exceptional port among the town-level ports. Most of the riverside towns were important ports, such as Zhankou Town of Xinzhou Prefecture, which "was populous and was frequently visited by Sichuan-made boats". "Zhankou Town levied 150 thousand strings of 1000 copper coins on the people every year, while Yanchi Town levied 260 thousand strings of copper coins." The natural conditions of Zhankou Port were equivalent to those of Jiangzhou (now Jiujiang), "whose taxation places were frequently visited by boats in Jiangzhou, Zhankou, Wuhu, Chizhou, and Zhenzhou along the Yangtze River." (Y. Lu 2012a, 2012b: 193; S. Xu 2014: 6383) Yanchi Town, also called Yancha Town, was under the administration of Chizhou Prefecture, which set up a taxation office to levy taxes on the shipping commodities in the Yangtze River." (B. Zhou 1990; S. Xu 2014:6376)Yanchi Town was one of the six revenue places between Chizhou and Jiankang prefectures, namely Yanchi, Chikou, Shituan, Wuhu, Caishi, and Jiankang (S. Xu 2014: 6381). In the range of Yanchi revenue territory, there were "some two hundred households and numerous boats anchored at the nearby banks," (Y. Lu 2012a, b: 184) making it a significant port at that time. Apart from Wuhu and Jiankang, the other four were port towns. Chikou belonged to Chizhou Prefecture, but Shituan belonged to Hezhou, and Caishi Town was one of the two taxation places in Taipingzhou. Furthermore, ports for boats also included Guazhou Town in Yangzhou, Guabu Town and Changlu Town in Zhenzhou, Datong Town, Chikou Town, Jianning Town in Chizhou, and Fanxikou, located opposite from Huangzhou (B. Zhou 1990; Y. Lu 2012a, b:168, 203; S. Zhang 1990a, b, c).

In general, the seats of local governments were good for anchoring ships and doing business, but due to different environmental conditions, wind directions, and flooding, not all administrative seats were suitable for anchoring boats. In some situations, boats were required to utilize non-administrative ports, characterized by the following features: firstly, they possessed narrow water channels suitable for boat anchorage; secondly, small branch streams were available for anchorage; and lastly, certain places were suitable for temporary stopovers.

The stopovers at the river forks prevented boats from sailing in hazardous rivers. During his voyage, Fan Chengda encountered a sudden change in wind direction, which prompted him to steer his boat into the Tongling River-Fork to avoid the violent waves. While at the fork, he observed another boat struggling to navigate the turbulent waters before finally entering the fork with the aid of other boats. Zhaotun, a small port town as well as a garrison town for soldiers, offered a stopping point for boats traveling in Jiangzhou, where they could dock for the night. In the Dazhi County of Xingguo Military Prefecture, boats were required to stop at the Baiyang Port of the river fork, which was known for its abundance of dwellers and boats. Zhou Bida, who had traversed the Yangtze River multiple times, anchored his boat in the river forks of Xinhe River, Cihu Sandbar, Caishi Sandbar, Changfeng Sandbar, Dingjia Sandbar, Tongling Sandbar, Yancha Sandbar, Jiangjia Sandbar, Wangjiang Sandbar, and Jiaoshi Sandbar. Similarly, during his downstream journey from Chengdu, Fan Chengda's boat made stopovers at the Jiaoshi, Bosi, Changfeng, and Madang river forks.

Moreover, the mouths of the Yangtze River's tributaries served as excellent shelter from turbulent waves. Fan Chengda, on his journey from Sichuan, was forced to make a stopover at the Qianjiang River due to the dangerous conditions in the Fuzhou section. In Chizhou, his boat docked at Qingxikou for a stopover. Similarly, Lu You chose to make a stopover in the Gushuxi River of Taipingzhou, and passed Tongling County and stayed at Shuihongkou at night. During his travels in Huangzhou, he stopped at the mouth of the Bahe River, which served as a grain supply center for boats. After leaving Ezhou, his boat stopped at the Tongjikou mouth of the the Zhuanhe River. Zhou Bida's boat encountered strong gusts twice at the mouth of the Liwang River, prompting his crew to tow the boat into the river mouth for shelter. In the Gushuxi and Qingxi Rivers, the boat had to stopover at the river mouths (Y. Lu 2012a, b: 162, 181, 194; B. Zhou 1990; C. Fan 2012a, b, c: 88; C. Fan 1981: 268). Additionally, "there was a small river southwest of Jiankang City in Liezhou, where boats could take shelter in the small branches to avoid strong gusts" (Y. Zhou 1990: 1616).

There were various ports situated along the Yangtze River that served as docking points for boats. For example, the Nankang Military Prefecture constructed dedicated ports for the transportation of goods and commercial vessels. Additionally, stone-built villages and small brooks running into rivers or lakes in the west provided shelter for boats. These ports were used annually by boats carrying taxes from farmland and exclusive goods, such as salt, iron, and liquor. The boats stopped at these ports during adverse weather conditions (X. Zhu 2010). The Lieshan and Zhuxiao Ports were established by the Jiankang Prefecture, (Y. Zhou 1990: 1569; Y. Lu 2012a, b: 170) while ferry boats were abundant by the riverside in Zhenjiang Prefecture. The local tyrants managed the ferry boats in seven ports, including Tanzhu, Tingzi East and West, Dantu East and West, Jianbi, and Dagang Ports. They also established over thirty private ports. Similar to the aforementioned areas, the counties along the Yangtze River had numerous ferry crossing points, with Zhenzhou having 29 crossing points that were either private or official. Neixuanhua Town was an official crossing point, along with six others, such as Guabushanqian, Hejiaxue, Jianshuiting of Zhenzhou suburb, Chaozha tide gate, Taer River, and Jujia Port. Private managers oversaw the warehouses at the crossing points that regulated rice prices, which were entrusted by the local authorities for tax collection. Due to the profitability of building warehouses, an additional 22 private ports were established in Zhenzhou. Yangzhou had 54 official or private ferry crossing points, with Guazhou Ferry Crossing Point being the only official one (S. Xu 2014: 9539). The other crossing points, such as Digang, Sanshan, Daxin, Dingjiazhou, Yangshan, Qingxi, Lihe, Yancha, and Zhaotun, were monitored by officials and soldiers. However, some crossing points were not under the supervision of the local authorities (S. Yang et al. 1990). As there were numerous branching streams in Jinghu North Province (S. Xu 2014: 9665), boats usually stayed in the narrow channels, branch streams, or little bays by the riverside towns and counties for several months. As a result, local officials were unable to check all passing boats.

Compared with the limited county seats or towns, boats spent more time in sailing in the river forks, branch streams, or small ports during their several-month-long voyages. Lu You and Zhou Bida, two notable travelers, visited various ports during their journeys along the Yangtze River. For instance, Lu You's boat stopped at Zhuxiao Port in Jiankang Prefecture, Digang Port in Taipingzhou, Meigen Port in Chizhou, anonymous port in Dongliu County, Madang Port, Luqifu Dock in Jiangzhou, Qiji Port, and Yangluofu Dock in Huangzhou (Y. Lu 2012a, b: 749, 759, 760, 763, 769, 774). Zhou Bida's boat stopped at Qiji Port, Jiyang Dock, Hengfeng Port, Sungong Bay, Meigen Port, Huaijia Ferry Crossing Point, and Yuezi Port located in Taipingzhou and Chizhou prefectures (B. Zhou 1990). Occasionally, they had to stay at ports without services. For example, during one of his travels, Lu You sailed over fifty kilometers in the Zhuanhe River and found only reeds and grass, without any human habitation along the banks. His boat had to stopover in clusters of reeds for the first time, a ten-household village for the second time, and stayed at Taziji Sandbar for the third time. After passing through the Zhuanhe River, they had to stay in a lotus pond. From Shashi, they had stayed at Guilin Bay, Guanzikou, Longwan Bay, and Chiya, even stayed in a cave of Shibei Valley (Y. Lu 2012a, b: 778–79). Similarly, during Fan Chengda's travel in Huangzhou, which was historically difficult for anchoring boats, they had to stopover in a small bay. After sailing another hundred kilometers, they found temporary shelters in Tongmugou, Matou, and Aobeizhou (C. Fan 2012a, b, c: 85).

2.1.4 Summary

Compared with the previous dynasties, the stronger and prosperous navigation of the Yangtze River marked a striking feature of economic growth in the Song Dynasty. The prosperous navigation can be evidenced by the numerous busy ships on the river. Their navigation methods offer an important perspective for discussion. From the above discussions, it is apparent that lifting sails was an optional method for boats sailing downstream or with a tailwind. This was due to the strong and unpredictable winds above the Yangtze River, making it difficult for boatmen to lift sails for a long time, and there were few occasions keep on sailing in a tailwind. For boats sailing upstream, towing was the most viable method. In the section from Shashi to Sichuan in the Yangtze River, boat-towing was the primary method employed, rather than lifting sails. Consequently, boat-towing paths were built for the sake of convenience. In the absence of such paths, they used several small boats to provide driving force through the use of bamboo strip ropes for pulling the boats.

The lower reaches of the Yangtze River had a broad surface, strong winds, and violent waves, which forced ships to sail in midstream for a brief period. They mainly sailed close to the banks or in river forks. On the one hand, there was little wind in the close bank areas and in the narrow channels. On the other hand, towing the boats close to the banks or in narrow channels was also a frequently used method. In addition, navigating through the widely spread sandbars and branch streams, as well as the man-dug narrow channels, became the preferred approach for safe sailing. Boats had to frequently cross the river to select suitable banks or river forks to avoid headwinds.

Along the Yangtze River, a three-tier port system was created so as to provide safe anchoring places. This system consisted of three sub-categories of ports: (1) major shipping hubs, including Zhenjiang, Zhenzhou, Ezhou, and Shashi; (2) ports located in prefectures or county seats along the riverbank, such as Jiangyin, Jiankang, Wuhu, Jiangzhou, Jiazhou, Zhankou, and Yancha; and (3) small harbors located in towns or temporary ports, including the anchoring places in the river forks, river mouths of branch streams, small ports and temporary ports without any facilities.

A study on the navigation methods of the Yangtze River is helpful not only for us to study the technologies and structures of shipping vessels, but also lays a solid foundation for an analysis of the social stratification of individuals residing along the Yangtze River, including boatmen, boat trackers, and travelers. The diverse groups of people created a comparatively distinctive society, while the goods transported along the river formed a comparatively unpredictable market. Enhanced understanding of the navigation methods employed along the river is crucial for advancing research inquiries into these topics.

2.2 Hydrological Conditions and Navigation of Canals in the Song Dynasty

Canals were the main passage connecting the capital city Kaifeng or the temporary capital Lin'an of the Northern and Southern Song dynasties to the external regions. During the Northern Song Dynasty, the central inland river navigation was comprised of the Yangtze River, the Huainan Canal area, and the Bianhe River, which formed a backward L shape " ⅃". During the Southern Song Dynasty, the key inland river navigation routes were the Yangtze River and the Liangzhe West Canal Province, forming an Arabic figure seven "⅂". The Bianhe River, the Huainan Canal, and the Liangzhe West and East provinces constituted the critical canals of the Song Dynasty (Z. An 2006: 670, 672, 674, 676; Q. Chen 2008: 223, 336, 497).[3] Additionally, a section of the Yuhe River (Yongjiqu Channel) and Lingqu Channel were also utilized. Current research has focused on grain transportation, transit systems, and crew (F. Chen 1986: 211; J. Cao 2002; H. Quan 1946; F. Chen 1992: 12–18; F. Chen 1997a, 119–123, b: 78–82; Z. An 2006; Q. Chen 2008: 223, 293, 336, 497),[4] while few systematic studies have examined water sources, water depth and dynamics, and ship navigation. This study will dive into these topics by examining the Bianhe River, the Huainan Canal, the Liangzhe West Canal, and the Liangzhe East Canal.

2.2.1 *An Overlook of the Canals in the Song Dynasty*

2.2.1.1 The Bianhe River

This section presents an assessment of the canals' water sources, water depth, and dynamics. The Song Dynasty relied largely on the Bianhe River. The Song people described it as "flowing across China, connecting the Yellow River and branching out to benefit the south. Almost half of the fiscal income and trade must pass through it."

---

[3] Except the Bianhe River, the Huainan Canal, the Liangzhe West Canal and the Liangzhe East Canal, are named differently by some scholars. For example, Huainan Canal is called Jianghuai Canal or Chuyang Canal, Liangzhe West Canal is called Jiangnan Canal, and the Liangzhe East Canal is called Liangzhe Canals by An Zuozhang in his book *A History of Chinese Canal Culture.* While the Huainan Canal, the Liangzhe West Canal, and the Langzhe East Canal are named Huainan Canal, Jiangnan Canal and Liangzhe East Canal respectively by Chen Qiaoyi in the *A Chinese History on Canal Development.* The name of the Huainan Canal was used in the Song Dynasty, so it is followed in the section of "Hydrological Conditions and Navigation of Canals in the Song Dynasty". The Liangzhe West Canal was once in use, but the name of Jiangnan Canal never, therefore, this section adopts the name of the Liangzhe West Canal. The Liangzhe Canals generally referred to the Liangzhe West Canal and the Liangzhe East Canal, not specifically referring to the Liangzhe East Canal, hence, the name, the Liangzhe East Canal, is employed based on its location in this section.

[4] No systematic discussion was made on the Hydrological Conditions and Navigation of Canals in the Song Dynasty in the researches by Chen Fengzhen, Cao jiaqi, Chen Feng, An Zuozhang, and Chen Qiaoyi, moreover, their studies on the navigability of the canals are relatively sketchy.

(R. Zhang 1990) The water of the Bianhe River mostly came from the Yellow River until the second year of the Yuanfeng Reign (AD 1079), when a water project was undertaken to redirect the Luohe River to the Bianhe River. This was documented as "the Bianhe River originated from the Yellow River, passing through the capital for grain transportation to the southeast," (S. Xu 2014: 9592) or "it was primarily dependent on the Yellow River, with no other rivers able to flow into it." (T. Li 2004: 6040) The confluence of the rivers frequently shifted, as it was said that "river mouths flow with the currents, so changes are unpredictable." In the fourth year of the Xi'ning Reign (AD 1071), the river mouth stabilized at Zijiankou (T. Li 2004: 5535). Additionally, a chief officer was responsible for managing the water flow into the Bianhe River, with the duty to "adjust the water flow to ensure smooth transportation of grain by ships." (Toqta 1977: 9132) If the water level exceeded expectations, the inflow would be cut; if it was too low or impeding transportation, an official would be dispatched to dredge the river mouth (Toqta 1977: 2321–22). In winter, the river mouth was closed as per previous institutional regulations, which prohibited ships from passing through the area after October (D. Lin 1990). As Mei Yaoshen stated, the Bianhe River's transportation was fast, but it was dry during winters (Y. Mei 1980: 259). This measure was implemented to prevent the Yellow River's ice from entering the Bianhe River, which could block the river or even cause a flood. However, the annual reopening and closing of the river mouth was costly and required significant manpower. At times, the cost could reach one million taels, and grain transportation would stop after the closing (T. Li 2004: 6039). In the tenth year of the Xi'ning Reign (AD 1073), the river mouth was opened once during winter, and wooden rafts were built to block floating ice to ensure smooth transportation in winter (S. Xu 2014: 9591). However, because the water depth remained too shallow and sluggish for shipping, dozens of ships with huge mallets had to break the ice to facilitate travel (D. Lin 1990). Even with these measures, it was still common for ice from the Bianhe River to become stuck in the capital, the river to overflow onto the shore, or the stock of ice to breach the dike. Dozens of soldiers were working along the river from the river mouth to Sizhou Prefecture, rescuing and maintaining upstream and downstream day and night. The cost did not decrease; instead, opening the river mouth caused breaching and flooding (T. Li 2004: 6086, 6175–76, 6620, 6813). Consequently, in the eighth year of the Xi'ning Reign (AD 1075), the previous rule of "closing the Bianhe River twenty days before the winter solstice" was reinstated (S. Xu 2014: 9593).

One of the drawbacks of using the Yellow River as a water source is its high sediment concentration, which could lead to the siltation of the riverway. In the eighth year of the Xi'ning Reign (AD 1075), a proposal was made to address this issue by diverting water from Sanshiliubei west of the capital to the Bianhe River for proper transition. The water sources of Guancheng, Xinzheng, and Mixian were utilized for this purpose. If the river mouth were opened in January and the Bianhe River was filled with water from these clear sources, it could be closed immediately. This would allow the water from the Suoshui River, the Jinshui River, and the Caishui River to be drained to clean up the Bianhe River (T. Li 2004: 6347). This measure helped to improve the problem of siltation. In the first year of the Yuanfeng Reign

(AD 1078), a complaint was lodged that "the Bianhe River had to be opened and closed every year, totaling about 200 days of operation". To address this issue, a proposal was made to bring water from the Luoshui River to the Bianhe River. The Song government initiated this project and appointed Song Yongchen as the chief official. The project began on April 11th and lasted 45 days until June 5th. The water of the Luoshui River was diverted to the Xinkou floodgate to clear the Bianhe River. On July 11th, the river mouth of the Bianhe River was closed, and officials and soldiers were sent to the new river mouth of the Luoshui River (Toqta 1977: 2327; T. Li 2004: 7225). The river mouth of the Luoshui River was opened, and the clear water was diverted into the Bianhe River. Consequently, the Bianhe River was called "Qingbian" (clear Bianhe River) (T. Li 2004: 11,588). After this project, the Bianhe River was no longer closed during winter and could operate throughout the year. Even with a frozen stream, soldiers could be summoned to dredge the ice to keep the river flowing (Toqta 1977: 2333). This development allowed the Bianhe River to operate all year and also cleared up the siltation problem caused by the Yellow River's sand and mud. In support of the project to divert the Luoshui River to the Bianhe River, other measures were also taken. For instance, the water from the Gusuo River was drawn upstream of Fangjia, Huangjia, Mengwanbei, and Sanshiliubei to store it in ponds. These ponds were referred to as "water cabinets" and served as a backup plan when the Luoshui River did not have enough water for the diverting project. "Sometimes, the flow of the Luoshui River was insufficient, and the water cabinet could be utilized" (T. Li 2004: 7257) to keep the Bianhe River working.

Subsequently, unimpeded travel on the Bianhe River was documented, as "the stored water in the water cabinets, which had been deployed since the Song dynasty, was not utilized to pour into the Bianhe River, as its water was clear and self-sufficient, and it was no longer closed during winter." Between the second year of the Yuanfeng Reign (AD 1079) and the eighth year of the Yuanyou Reign (AD 1086), "the river was not obstructed for eight consecutive years." However, the popularity of water mill tea in Kaifeng caused the water used for the wheels to "overflow and have nowhere to go," leading to "insufficient water levels in the Bianhe River to meet the transportation needs for both official and private use." At the same time, farmland was occupied by water cabinets. In the first year of the Yuanyou Reign (AD 1086), the water cabinets plan was abandoned, resulting in "insufficient water for travel." Due to insufficient water flow, the Bianhe River had to rely on the Yellow River as its source again. In the second year of the Yuanyou Reign (AD 1087), the water of the Yellow River was diverted into the mouth of the Luoshui River, causing the Bianhe River to be closed and clogged during winter or even dry up. According to Jia Zhongmin, the commanding official in charge of the Bianhe River bank, "during the Yuanfeng Reign from 1078 to 1085, the river mouth of the Bianhe River was diverted to the Luohe River, called 'Qing Bian (clear the Bianhe River),' while clear water was stored to ensure smooth water flow in case of shallow water depth. During the Yuanyou Reign (AD 1086–1094), the turbid water of the Yellow River was led to the mouth of the Bianhe River. Compared with the clear water of Qingbian, this created more difficulties to modulate." In the first year of the Shaosheng Reign (AD 1094), Emperor Zhezong of Song took over the state affairs. Li Wei and Cai Jing presented that "clearing and diverting the Luohe River to the Bianhe River helped to connect the Huaihe River and the Sihe River, which would benefit future generations. However, since the Yuanyou Reign, dangers often occurred at this critical juncture, and this year was more severe than usual." Therefore, Emperor Zhezong commanded that "following the rules of the Yuanfeng Reign, the project of diverting from the Luohe River to the Bianhe River should be carried out again." In the third year of the Shaosheng Reign (AD 1096), the river mouth of the Bianhe River was reused, and water from the Yellow River was obtained, and the mouth of the Luohe River was abandoned. In the following year, the conduct of the Yuanfeng Reign was resumed, and the use of water from the Luohe River and Sanshiliubei was resumed, which was recorded as "fulfilling the water cabinet to help navigation on the Bianhe River." After this, "Qingbian was put into full operation, and the silty water was never used again." This policy was implemented until the end of the Northern Song Dynasty (Toqta 1977: 2329–2334).

The Bianhe River flowed southward and extended further into Huaihe River in Sizhou. Mei Yaochen's poem described the Yellow River being diverted into the Bianhe River, causing the muddy currents to ripple with constant waves. The Bianhe River ended in Sizhou and flowed in the same direction as the Yellow River (Y. Mei 1980: 278). Prior to diverting the Luohe River to the Bianhe River, the use of water from the Yellow River meant that silty water could flow all the way to the river mouth of the Bianhe River, causing dangerous conditions for boats. After the Luohe River was diverted to the Bianhe River, clear water could directly enter the Huaihe River, resulting in slower and safer water flow (S. Xu 2014: 9596). After July of the second year of the Yuanfeng Reign (AD 1079), the Luohe River was able to flow into the Bianhe River. By September of the third year of the Yuanfeng Reign (AD 1080), reported deaths were reduced by 1500, totaling 540. The quieter currents helped to reduce damage in all aspects (T. Li 2004: 7526). The section between Shangqiu (the southern capital) and Sizhou enjoyed the smoothest water flow, with a depth ranging from 95.04 to 158.4 cm, allowing boats to move without hindrance. The north of this branch was wide and quiet, and wooden stakes were constructed to narrow and deepen the riverway (Toqta 1977: 2322, 2324). Multiple sluices were set up along the Bianhe River to adjust water flow as needed. When the water level of the Bianhe River was too high, the sluices would be opened to release water into the Yellow River, the Guangji River, or other rivers (T. Li 2004: 8191–92, 8348).

Before diverting water from the Luohe River, the Bianhe River was closed during winter, and all transportation activities were canceled, resulting in soldiers being sent back to their stations, a process known as "returning because of frozen river". During the summer, there were instances when the water level in the Bianhe River would suddenly drop, resulting in a cut-off of water flow and depths in low-lying areas ranging from 31.68 to 63.36 cm (S. Xu 2014: 9590), which was below the usual depth range of 95.04–158.4 cm. Although the average depth along the river from Shangqiu to Sizhou was approximately 95.04–158.4 cm, not all sections of the river could reach that depth. In the third year of the Yuanyou Reign (AD 1088), there was a plan to transport rice to the Guanzhong area to alleviate the hunger problem. The plan involved transporting grain from the southeast to the river mouth of the

Luohe River. However, the low water levels from the west of the capital to the Luohe River posed a significant challenge tor transporting boats, as the boats were quite deep and incapable of sailing in shallow waters. As a result, the only option was to use boats with shallow drafts to transport the grain (S. Xu 2014: 6964–6965). To transport 375 tons of goods, every 25 boats were formed into one team, while for boats carrying 360 tons of food, every 30 boats were formed into one team (S. Xu 2014: 7038). The load capacities of 12 tons and 15 tons were commonly used, while boats with a capacity of 18 tons were referred to as "heavy duty boats." (S. Xu 2014: 9596) When the water level was over 126.72 cm, heavy boats could travel through, as the deadweight for grain boats in the Bianhe River was typically around 12–15 tons. In the early years of the Yuanfeng Reign, heavy duty boats with a load capacity of 18 tons were able to pass through when the water level was around 158.4 cm. However, if extra goods were loaded onto boats with capacities ranging from 12 to 18 tons, the heavy duty boats could become stranded, and carrying unreported goods exceeding 200 kg could lead to severe punishments (T. Li 2004: 7307). Using non-load-bearing boats to carry goods reaching 300 tons could also hinder travel, as escorts would sometimes purchase boats with a loading weight of about 300 tons and claim them as passenger boats with the grain transporting boats, leading to potential impediments if traveling through the Bianhe River. To address this issue, the Song dynasty introduced a policy stating that "escorting boats should not exceed the load capacity of the freight cargo, and only two boats should be allowed" (S. Xu 2014: 9593, 7060). Therefore, the escorting boat's capacity should be less than 15 tons. The deadweight of Yang Yao's warships, Dadeshan warships, was 75 tons, and their hull was approximately 4.12 m. Therefore, they could not be the Wandan Boats (huge boats with a load capacity of 300 tons). Jojin once described numerous boats being placed along the Bianhe River, with volumes of 351,000 L, 245,000 L, or 280,800 L, and huge and fully loaded boats being present everywhere (Jojin 2009: 275). Zhou Baozhu believed that the Bianhe River could support Wandan Boats based on Jojin's description (B. Zhou 1997: 58). However, it is apparent that Jojin's description was inaccurate.

During the Southern Song Dynasty, the Bianhe River was gradually abandoned. In the ninth year of the Shaoxing Reign (AD 1139), Zheng Gangzhong undertook a business trip to Shanxi. Upon reaching Sizhou, he chose to abandon the riverway and continue his journey via land route. This decision was made due to the poor condition of the Bianhe River, which was described as "sickly wooded" from the west of Hong County. Although the Bianhe River, from the east of Hong County, connected the outfall of Huaihe, Wanan Lake, and Sizhou, it could only accommodate small boats with a carriage volume less than 3500 L (G. Zheng 1990). Furthermore, it was only navigable during high tide. In the sixth year of the Qiandao Reign (AD 1170), Lou Yao was sent on a diplomatic mission to the north. At that time, the Bianhe River was primarily used for growing wheat (Y. Lou 1990), and was no longer operational for transportation purposes.

2.2.1.2 The Canals in Huainan, Liangzhe West and Liangzhe East Provinces

The canals in Huainan, Liangzhe West, and Liangzhe East provinces were not as accessible as the Bianhe River. The Huainan Canal, in particular, had water levels higher than the Yangtze and Huaihe Rivers, making it difficult for artificial projects to maintain water levels, particularly over long distances. As the Yangtze River and the Huaihe River's water sources could not be fully utilized, the water sources of each section were isolated and fragmented into several parts, leading to the use of sluice gates to regulate water levels for normal sailing activities. The Hainan Canal originated from Zhenzhou in the south and connected with the Yangtze River at Guazhou. The Zhenzhou section drew its water from the Yangtze River and was built with "dams every 4.425 km" and was "heavily dependent on waterwheels." In Tongjiang River, the delivery gate was widened to 4.752 m, and its depth was approximately 15.84 m. Soft dams were constructed at 31.68 m from the river mouth to drain water into the canal (S. Xu 2014: 9618). The section from Guazhou to Yangzhou also utilized the Yangtze River as its source. In the third year of the Jianyan Reign (AD 1129), Jurchens attacked the south, causing the whole city of Yangzhou to flee further south. According to the document, "people who fled traveled by water. When Jin's soldiers arrived, nobody opened the gates to release water, causing many boats to get stranded in mud." (X. Li 2013: 455) At low tide, water could not enter the canal.

The Yangtze River could only enter the south of the Huainan Canal. The reach between Zhenzhou and Yangzhou mainly relied on ponds. Specifically, Chengong Pond, 10 km south of Zhenzhou, was surrounded by mountains on three sides and dikes were constructed on the south and east sides to regulate the water levels. This pond was poured into the canal for transportation purposes every year. The county magistrate of Yangtze County also held the post of "director of Chengong Pond" and was responsible for its maintenance (Toqta 1977: 2394–95). Additionally, the water levels between Chuzhou and Gaoyouting were often low, and there was a lack of water sources for the canal. To operate, the canal depended on lakes to pump water into it (S. Xu 2014: 9618). Sheyang Lake was the source for the section from Baoying to Chuzhou, and Mokou was located to the north of Chuzhou and connected to the Huaihe River (Toqta 1977: 2388–89). This part of the canal, including the Yanhe River in the Huaidong coastal area that flowed into the canal, greatly relied on rainfalls. In the eighth year of the Xi'ning Reign (AD 1075), there was no rain since May, and as a result, this section was not available for ships, including the canals in Yangzhou and Chuzhou and the rivers for transporting salt in Tongzhou, Taizhou, and other regions (T. Li 2004: 6523). In the ninth year of the Xi'ning Reign (AD 1076), the salt transporting rivers in Tongzhou and Taizhou were obstructed, and the suggestion of "releasing Chengong Pond's water to the canal" was brought up. However, Zhang Jie, the supply commissioner, refused to do so, resulting in salt shortages in many regions (T. Li 2004: 6702).

The normal route traveling from Chuzhou to Sizhou was by Huaihe River. However, "170 boats were destroyed annually." In the fifth year of the Xi'ning Reign

(AD 1072), an alternate route was created, beginning from Hongze Lake, located in Shepu at the foot of Guishan Mountain, by excavating the left bank of the section and borrowing water from the Huaihe River. No sluice gates were installed, averting the risks of high winds and floods (S. Yang et al. 1990). This action was to avoid the dangers brought by the Huaihe River. The new section was "26.52 km long, 47.52 m wide, and 4.752 m deep." (S. Xu 2014: 9609) Nonetheless, most parts of the Huainan Canal faced a shortage of water sources, and the canal exhibited a flat bottom, low water levels, and insufficient water storage, requiring frequent dredging. Boats could only sail on the canal when the depth was 1.584 m (S. Xu 2014: 7044). The delivery gate of the Yangtze River in Zhenzhou was only 4.752 m wide and 1.584 m deep (S. Xu 2014: 9618). Thus, as noted by Zeng Xiaoguang, the section from the bank of the Yangtze River in Zhenzhou to the dike of the Huaihe River in Chuzhou relied on weirs to store water and was closed to heavy duty boats. Transferring goods required significant labor and financial resources (Toqta 1977: 4258). This involved carrying and transferring goods to small boats, as grain transportation boats typically utilized large and weight-bearing vessels, which were unsuitable for the shallow and obstructed canal. Hence, goods had to be redistributed separately to small boats. The sluice gates of Guazhou could harness the tides of the Yangtze River. Although the Yangtze River could carry huge boats with a load capacity of up to 134,000 L, sometimes the water level was too shallow to support such large boats, and there were no spare boats to reduce the exceeded loads. Consequently, these boats could not enter the next section of the canal. For example, a boat with a load capacity of 134,000 L would get stranded after entering the canal, and would have to hire 21 passenger boats with a total capacity of 1,640,000 L, using 13 of them to transport the 134,000 L of grain. This meant that those 21 boats could carry a total of 1,640,000 L of goods, i.e., 78,720 L per boat. Among them, 13 boats transported the 134,000 L of grain separately, i.e., 49,200 L per boat. The actual load of the grain boat was 80% of its cargo capacity, making its deadweight capacity 65,600 L. Furthermore, Zhang Shou, Zhu Shi, Zhang Qiu, Liang Ping, Qi Shen, and Wu Qi contended that "6 batches of grains on the boats carried up to 22,505,300 L of goods", that was 3,350,000 L per team. Based on an 80% load rate, each team could only carry 2,255,000 L of goods. Each team had 30 boats, so every boat's average capacity was 65,000–98,400 L (S. Hong, n.d.; S. Xu 2014: 6983).[5] Boats with a load capacity of 65,000–98,400 L were the most suitable for sailing on the Huainan Canal.

During the Northern Song dynasty, the Liangzhe West Canal served as the main passage connecting the Yangtze River. During the Southern Song period, it assumed greater significance and was regarded as the lifeline of Lin'an city, which housed the imperial's temporary palace. The canal's importance was attributed to its role in supporting the emperor's short stay at Lin'an by facilitating the transportation of goods and grains, as well as linking the prefectures. Although some accounts of the

[5] Based on the records of *Panzhou Anthology and The Anthology of Laws and Regulations of the Song Dynasty*, the boats with the load capacity from 200 and 300 Liao only served as transporting the taxes paid by the local governments in Liangzhe East and West provinces to the imperial court. The standard is that a transporting fleet consists of 30 boats.

canal have exaggerated its ease of navigation by likening it to travelling on a flat surface (Toqta 1977: 2405–06), it is important to note that the canal's 283.322-km length traversed different terrains and had multiple headwaters. Only the canal's northern endpoint, Jingkou Sluice, was able to draw water from the Yangtze River. Four routes provided access to Jingkou, namely, Jingkou Sluice itself, Haixian River, Shanyu Port, and Ganlu Port, which enabled boats to travel into the canal. Jingkou was situated at the confluence of the Huaihe River and Qiantang River, and Ganlu Port was also at the junction of the Huaihe River and Qiantang River, thereby allowing it to connect the Yangtze River to the Bianhe River through Zhenjiang. The canal featured sluice gates that could be adjusted as needed, such as the Jingkou Sluice, which was positioned 2.21–2.652 km from Zhenjiang City, and the Zeshui Sluice, which was situated in the northeast corner of Zhenjiang. Jingkou Sluice was used to restrict inflow from the Yangtze River, while Zeshui Sluice regulated the outflow into the canal. "The gates were opened or closed in accordance with transportation needs" (Z. Huang 1990).

The Liangzhe West Canal's journey "from Changzhou to Danyang presented sloping topography, with no available lakes or ports to store water, despite the presence of two sluice gates, Benniu and Lücheng. The following reach from Danyang to Zhenjiang presented even higher terrain, and despite the presence of the Lianhu Lake, the water level was insufficient to be transported further. The lake would dry up whenever there was a prolonged period without rainfall (Toqta 1977: 2405–06)." Starting from Zhenjiang, the canal relied on Lianhu Lake as its source. The journey from Jingkou Sluice of Canhe River running through the city to Benniu Weir totaled 61.88 km and relied entirely on the Lianhu Lake for water (X. Lu 1990: 2365). The lake was replenished by many rivers from mountains the canal that flowed into it, with an old saying stating that "if the lake surface was lowered by one inch, the canal water level would be risen by one foot." Historical records indicate that "The Lianhu Lake gradually resumed the function of storing water, which benefited farmland irrigation and kept the river from drying up." (Toqta 1977: 2405) Yang Wanli vividly described the image of water being released from Lianhu Lake and poured into the canal in his poem "Opening the Sluice Gates of the Lianhu Lake". He wrote that "the sound of releasing water was loud like thunders shaking the land; looking out of the window, silver waves were paddling the boat forwards. The Lianhu Lake just released an inch of water, the waves were jumping as high as 10 thousands piles of snow." (W. Yang 2007: 1384) Additionally, small rivers and streams were diverted into the canal to serve as water sources. For instance, rocks were cleared around Changzhou's Benniu gate to make room for water storage (Y. Lu 2011: 497). This section of the canal linked Yixing's rivers, unclogging or discharging them, and "connected Jingxi Brook to the south." The canal's waterline behind the Jiangzhudi Dike of Wusong was "higher than Jingxi brook," but after the Qinglin Reign, "the brook's water began to flood into the canal." (E. Shan 1990: 3–4).

The Wuxi section of the canal was linked with several rivers, which were historically described as follows: "in the past, these rivers were released into the canal, then water was poured into the Yangtze River to the north by sluice gates." (E. Shan 1990: 3–4) This section also received water from Liangxi Brook and utilized Jiangjun Weir to divert water from the brook to the canal. However, in later years, the weir became outdated and was replaced by 42 water wheels to draw water (S. Yang et al. 1990; S. Su 2010:3384). The stretch from Wuxi to Xiuzhou mainly relied on Taihu Lake for its water supply. "From Shanqing in Xiuzhou to Panmen in Jiangfu, all the rivers were interconnected with Taihu Lake," and "with westerly winds, lake water would enter through the port without the need for dredging." (Toqta 1977: 2406)

The Hangzhou to Xiuzhou section of the canal sourced its water from West Lake, the Qiantang River, and other branches, ponds, and brooks. West Lake had the capacity to flow into the canal and irrigate 5760 hectares of farmland, indicating that the canal was sufficient for these needs (S. Qian 1990: 3672). The headwaters of the Hangzhou reach of the canal included the Waisha River, Caishi River, Huantang River, Chi'an River, and others (S. Qian 1990: 3675–76). To store water from the Beiguan gate of Hangzhou to Shanqing of Xiuzhou, there were weirs or sluice gates north of Hangzhou City. The canal reached Changtui Pond, Haiyan Pond, Huating Pond, Liuli Weir, and others. To prevent water from flooding into undesired areas downstream, the Song court ordered the strengthening of channels and ports. In the Yanguan area, there was a pond which was 11.05 km long that extended to the Changan Sluice, connecting Linping in the north and Chongde in the south. This area was heavily utilized for the transportation of grain and passengers (Toqta 1977: 1401, 2406). "The southernmost part of the canal led to the Qiantang River, with the section within Lin'an receiving water every day". "At Tongjiang Bridge, a sluice was constructed. During periods of low water flow, the flashboard would be opened to allow water in and then dropped to maintain the water level. In such instances, boat travel was not permitted. If water levels were sufficient, the flashboard would be closed, allowing all boats to pass through" (Toqta 1977: 2399, 2400).

The Liangzhe West Canal frequently faced navigational challenges due to its low water level, with the stretch from Zhenjiang to Changzhou being particularly difficult. The region west of Wuxi county of Changzhou, including Henglin, Xiaoniu, Benniu, and Lücheng, had high terrain and low waterlines (S. Xu 2014: 9607–08), leading to insufficient water levels even during the rainy season (Y. Lu 2012a, b: 163; Y. Lu 2011: 497). Despite Lu You's observation of rushing water at the Benniu Sluice in Chuzhou, the canal remained dry during the spring and winter dry seasons, as noted by Su Shi. This caused grain boats in Zhenjiang to be transferred to Jiangzhen, traveling to Wuxi along the Wuxie Weir and then returning to the canal (X. Li 2013: 3531). The juncture of the Wuxie Weir and the canal featured a weir and a gate that were only open to large cargo ships or heavy-duty boats, with smaller boats being dragged to avoid excessive water loss (S. Xu 2014: 6169). In case the Song ambassadors traveling between Song and Jin faced such a situation during their northbound journey, they would travel to Changzhou by water first and disembark at Zhenjiang. During their southbound journey, their gifts would be deposited at the Zhenjiang government, and the vice minister would report back to Lin'an, while the ambassador would wait until the end of the dry season (S. Xu 2014: 9623, 3919). The Hangzhou section of the canal also suffered from drying out. In the 16th year of the Shaoxing Reign (AD 1146), "the canal outside the Beiguan was clogged, so the grain boats mostly were unloaded there." (X. Li 2013: 2934) In the second year of the Chunxi Reign (AD 1175), "in the area of Chang'an Sluice to Public Security Bureau at Xucun village in Lin'an, the grain transportation river was quite low." (Toqta 1977: 2400) Although other parts of the Liangzhe West Canal could also be clogged, the section between Xiuzhou and Wuxi had sufficient water storage. In June of the sixth year of the Qiandao Reign (AD 1170), Lu You observed that "the canal's water overflowed and its waterline was about 30 cm higher than its neighbouring land. There, local people used waterwheels to divert the stagnant water out." (Y. Lu 2012a, 2012b: 161) However, some people acted out of their own private interests and caused damage to the canal, with local influencers claiming lakes, ponds, or farmlands along the canal, resulting in "a shallow and clogged canal that was unable to carry boats." (S. Xu 2014: 7502) To address this, the project to dredge a 61.95-km reach along the Liangzhe West Canal was launched during the seventh year of the Chunxi Reign (AD 1180). The project involved dredging "the section from Lin'an to Zhenjiang, totalling 61.95 km. There were sections with a total length of 36.02 km to be dredged. There were some deep-water sections with a total length of 6.93 km, which were suitable for heavy boats and therefore did not need to be dredged. The rest of the project volume was 29.09 km, which needed to be dredged." (S. Xu 2014: 9606).

In the fifth year of the Xuanhe Reign (AD 1123), a dredging project was initiated in the canal between Lücheng gate and Hangzhou. The plan was to dredge the canal to a depth of 1.56 m (S. Xu 2014: 9619), with the section within Hangzhou already at a depth of "1.49–1.56 m". However, the two parts of the section from Gegong Bridge to Yuhangmen were "maintained at 1.4 m", which was the standard depth (S. Xu 2014: 9621). Later, during the Southern Song Dynasty, the project of the Hangzhou section was carried out and the canal was dug to a width of 15.6 m and a depth of 1.248 m from Beixin Bridge to Gouzang (S. Qian 1990: 3676). When Su Shi was the head of Hangzhou Prefecture, the canal was dug to a depth of 2.496 m, which was "the deepest it had been in the past 30 years." (S. Qian 1990: 3673) According to Shan E's book of *Field Study of Water Regime in Wuxian County*, "Liangzhe's grain ships usually carried under 33,500 L of grain. The canal could hold 1.56–1.872 m of water, which was good enough for these grain ships." Therefore, the water level of 1.56 m and the ships carrying 33,500 L of grain were the standard measurements. However, in reality, the grain ships actually carried about 65,600–98,400 L of grain. For instance, in the fifth year of the Shaoxing Reign (AD 1135), all cities, except for Mingzhou, Wenzhou, Taizhou, Lin'an, and Zhenjiang, purchased ships with a load capacity of 65,600–98,400 L in teams of 30 ships to pay their offerings and taxes. This was in accordance with the report of Transfer Agency of Taxation of Liangzhe Provinces, which stated that "within this purview, most ships' load was 98,400 L." (S. Xu 2014: 7110) In the sixth year of the Dazhongxiangfu Reign (AD 1013), the tonnage of the 40 salt carriers traveling from Hangzhou to Yangzhou was only 6700 L (S. Xu 2014: 6941). However, in the period of the Qiandao Reign (between 1165 and 1173), "light and speedy ships were especially made" to prevent the ambassadorial ships "from getting stranded," resulting in the construction of 100 Tengqian, Tietou, or other ships (S. Xu 2014: 7133). When traveling from Zhenjiang to the canal, people had to transfer boats. For instance, when Lu You was traveling from the canal to the

Yangtze River, he transferred to Wang Zhiyi's ship with a capacity of 656,000 L (Y. Lu 2012a, b:165). When Zhou Bida was on a trip from Jiangxi passing the Yangtze River to Hangzhou, he "hired boats to carry the luggage to enter the Zhengjiang Sluice". In this case, transferring to other ships was necessary to move the luggage (B. Zhou 1990).

The Liangzhe East Canal, located within Yuezhou and connecting the Yuyao River to the east and the Qiantang River to the west, served as a critical transportation route linking Mingzhou and Hangzhou. The estuary of the Qiantang River, characterized by strong winds and rushing waves, posed significant challenges for businessmen and ships, leading to the only option of passing through the Yuyao River and transferring goods to smaller boats to reach Hangzhou and Yuezhou (S. Qian 1990: 3643). The Liangzhe East Canal was fed by various water sources, including the Qiantang River, Jianhu Lake (Mirror Lake), Caohe River, Puyang River, and others. The point where the Qiantang, Puyang, and Caohe rivers intersected at the delivery gate was known as "The Three Rivers" by the people of Yuezhou and called "The Delivery Gate of The Three Rivers". From this point, people could travel to the Mirror Lake and the canal to the southeast or the ocean to the north (S. Shi et al.1990: 6785–86). The section of Xixing Town in Xiaoshan County obtained its water from the Qiantang River, but the inconstant waves often led to canal blockages, preventing boats from passing through (Toqta 1977: 2408). In contrast, the section of Yuezhou running east–west obtained its water from Jianhu Lake and had a delivery gate that was opened upon orders when batch transportation ships or inspectors' ships were present (Toqta 1977: 2407). The city river of Yuezhou flowed into the canal or northeast, running through Xiaoshan to the Qiantang River. Tongming River had the Yuyao River as its source and flowed into the Yangtze River from the west. Ruoye Brook entered the Mirror Lake from the north. The section within Shangyu County sourced water from the Yumenpu reach of Qili Lake, moved from Zaoli Lake, intersected in the west of the canal, and arrived at Lianghu Weir (S. Shi et al.1990: 6879–86).

The Liangzhe East Canal had a more challenging shipping environment compared to those in Liangzhe West Province. While boats could travel with ease in Xiuzhou, Changzhou, Huzhou, Jiangyinjun, and Pingjiangfu, the Liangzhe East Canal required waterwheels to drag ships forward (S. Xu 2014: 7066). Different sections of the canal faced varying challenges in floating ships with different load capacities. For instance, the section from Shanyin County to Xiaoshan County could accommodate ships with a load capacity of up to 33,500 L. However, the section from Xiaoshan to Qiantang County of Lin'an, as well as the section from Shangyu County to Kuaiji County, only allowed ships with a load capacity of 13,400 L (S. Shi et al.1990: 6923–25, 6930, 6933, 6938). To pass ships with the load of 33,500 L, the water level had to reach 1.56 m. Nevertheless, the stretch from Xixing gate to Qianqing Weir was the worst affected by silt. In the period of the Jiading Reign (from 1208 to 1224), this section was obstructed by silt and mud, causing its depth to range from 0.624 to 0.936 m (H. Zhang 1990: 7135). About 10 km of this segment was full of sand and silt, prompting the dispatch of an imperial envoy and 50 soldiers to dredge the Xixing sand river and clear the silty river (Toqta 1977: 2408). Apart from the Mirror Lake section, dredging work was also necessary on the eastern part of the Liangzhe

East Canal. In the first year of the Shaoxing Reign (AD 1131), Xu Kangguo, the transportation administrator of the Liangzhe region, reported that the Lianghu Weir of Shangyu County was shallow and obstructed up to 663.75 m. He reported the issue to the prime minister, noting that the section from Yuezhou to Yuyao County faced the same problem, with destroyed dams and gates halting transportation. Emperor Gaozong instructed Xu Kangguo and other officials to dig and dredge the section from Dusi Weir in Kuaiji County to Caoeta Bridge (S. Xu 2014: 9619–20). Consequently, the load capacity of ships traveling on the Liangzhe East Canal ranged between 65,600 and 98,400 L. In the fifth year of the Shaoxing Reign (AD 1135), Emperor Gaozong directed the cities of Liangzhe area to use ships with a load capacity ranging from 65,600 to 98,400 L for transportation to the capital (S. Xu 2014: 7066). This highlighted the size of grain ships traversing the Liangzhe East Canal.

2.2.2 *The Weirs and Gates of Canals During the Song Dynasty*

Each section of the canals, which varied in terrain, required building weirs and sluice gates to ensure normal operation. The canals in Huainan, Liangzhe West, and Liangzhe East had sections with different elevations, necessitating the installation of weirs and sluice gates to connect them. These hydraulic structures were also used to control water inflow and outflow. This section will focus on the weirs and sluice gates which were directly related to sailing, or located within or at the ends of the shipping lanes. Those built on dams or dikes are not included.

2.2.2.1 The Distributions and Functions of the Weirs and Gates

The Bianhe River was unobstructed, hence the absence of weirs or sluice gates. However, Biankou, the Bianhe River's entrance to the Yellow River, was closed in winter and reopened in the spring. Consequently, weirs were built to seal off the river mouth, with specialized personnel referred to as "weir construction soldiers for the Bianhe River" overseeing this task (R. Zhang 1990). After diverting water from the Luohe River to the Bianhe River, "two gates were installed at the north of Sishui Pass to facilitate the passage of ships between the Yellow River and the Bianhe River" (Toqta 1977: 2328). The southern end of the Bianhe River featured the Hongze Sluice in Sizhou, which was operated by soldiers to handle the pound locks. When Jojin traversed this gate, he had to wait for the flood tides. Subsequently, "upon the opening of the sluice gates, approximately 100 ships were able to enter within a span of two hours, starting from 9–11 pm. Nonetheless, the second gate remained closed." The following day, "the sluice gates were opened, and the ships set sail" (Jojin 2009: 239). During the earlier years of the Southern Song Dynasty, following the withdrawal of the Jurchens, approximately 1000 official ships were left at Hongze Sluice in Sizhou (X. Li 2013: 556). The gates facilitated the connection of the Bianhe River to the Yellow River, the Luohe River, and the Hongze Lake.

The Huainan Canal showed sharp differences in terrain heights. Xiang Ziyin reported that the Grand Canal in Huainan was approximately 10–20 m higher than both the Yangtze and Huaihe Rivers. Within the section between the Yangtze River and the Huaihe River, around several hundred kilometers, it was difficult to even out the terrain height using human power (H. Hu 1900). Therefore, the construction of weirs and sluice gates became necessary. Several weirs, including Huangpu, Beishen, and Xihe, were built in Chuzhou, while Xinhe and Fanliang were built in Gaoyou. In Yangzhou, Xinxing, Zhuyu, Daixian, Zhaobo (Tangyan), and Longzhou (Guazhouyan) weirs were constructed, with Zhenyang (Jiangkouyan) Weir being built in Zhenzhou (Y. Wang 2003: 474; T. Li 2004: 2149; S. Xu 2014: 6168; S. Zhang 1990a, b, c). In the early period of the Northern Song Dynasty, there were various transformations between weirs and sluice gates. Local governments gradually replaced weirs with gates, resulting in "the construction of two delivery gates on the Xihe River's third weir in the first year of the Yongxi Reign (AD 984)" (Toqta 1977: 10,118), thereby transforming the Xihe Weir into sluice gates. The Longzhou, Xinxing, and Zhuyu weirs were destroyed to create new channels in the third year of the Tianxi Reign (AD 1019), "making it easier for grain ships to navigate" (T. Li 2004: 2149). Similarly, "Beishen and Jiangkou weirs were transformed into sluice gates" in the fourth year of the Tiansheng Reign (AD 1126), with the Manpu Sluice gates being erected in place of the Beishen weirs (S. Xu 2014: 6168). *Dream Pool Essays* indicated that "Zhaobo, Beishen, Longzhou, and Zhuyu weirs were abolished" (K. Shen 2006: 96), implying that Zhaobo Weir had also been transformed into a gate. Almost all weirs and dams in Yangzhou and Chuzhou, except those in Gaoyou, were transformed into sluice gates.

However, the Huainan Canal mainly depended on ponds for its water supply, which was scarce. After Cai Jing carried out the direct sailing for grain transportation, the traffic on the canal increased even further. However, there was no fixed schedule for the opening or closing of sluice gates, leading to outflow that could not be easily controlled. As a result, the section from Hongze to Zhaobo, spanning several hundred kilometers, was obstructed. Weirs could hold water in each section without unwanted outflow (S. Xu 2014: 6165). In the second year of the Xuanhe Reign (AD 1120), "a dam was built at the estuary of the Guazhouhe River to restore the Longzhou Weir, another dam was built at the river mouth of the Hailing River to reopen the Zhuyu Weir and Daixian Weir, and a third was built at Beishen Weir to close the Manpu Weir and reuse the Chaozong Sluice. The Chaozong Sluice was the gate that led into Hongze Lake in the Chuzhou area" (H. Hu 1900). The Longzhou Weir, Zhuyu Weir, Daixian Weir, and Beishen Weir were transformed back from gates to weirs, while the Zhaobo Weir remained as a floodgate after reconstruction. In the ninth year of the Shaoxing Reign (AD 1139), Zheng Gangzhong passed the Zhaobo Sluice while traveling on the Huainan Canal (G. Zheng 1990). In the third year of the Xuanhe Reign (AD 1121), the Zhenyang (now Jiangkou) Sluice was improved by constructing eight floodgates to divert water from the Yangtze River at high tide. The riverbed by the gate was dug to a width of 4.68 m and a depth of 1.56 m, and dams with soft foundations were constructed to draw water, shut the gate, and store it. Previously, it was a small weir on the south bank that relied heavily on waterwheels to dredge the Huainan Canal, and it could not divert water effectively, which meant that ships often ran aground. The deepening and widening of the soft foundation dam and floodgate could store several times more water than waterwheels (S. Xu 2014: 9618).

The seven weirs on the Liangzhe West Canal were Jingkou Weir and Lücheng Weir in Runzhou (now Zhengjiang), Wangting Weir and Benniu Weir in Changzhou, Shanqing Weir in Xiuzhou, Hanjiang Weir, Qinghe Weir, and Changan Weir in Hangzhou. In the first year of the Chunhua Reign (AD 990), Emperor Taizong issued a decree to abolish Jingkou Weir and Lücheng Weir in Runzhou, Wangting Weir and Benniu Weir in Changzhou, Shanqing Weir in Xiuzhou, and Hanjiang Weir, Qinghe Weir, and Changan Weir in Hangzhou. However, due to variations in terrain height, in addition to water scarcity and seasonal droughts, abandoning these weirs resulted in a loss of the capacity to hold water in each section. Consequently, Changzhou and Runzhou restored the weirs. (Y. Wang 2003: 476; S. Xu 2014: 6165) In response to the challenging terrain, it was proposed that the section from Zhenjiang to Danyang could be dug deeply, diverting water from the Yangtze River to Piling (now Changzhou) and linking the Taihu Lake (X. Lu 1990: 2365), thereby eliminating the need for constructing Lücheng and Benniu Weirs. However, the proposal was called off in the fourth year of the Zhiping Reign (AD 1067) due to concerns of causing a narrower river bed, making it inconvenient for all, and making it impossible for passing vessels (S. Xu 2014: 6165). Instead, transforming weirs into gates was deemed the best option. Wangting Weir was reconstructed into a floodgate, as recorded in historical documents (S. Xu 2014: 6165). In the fourth year of the Yuanyou Reign (AD 1089), Lücheng Weir was fitted with a floodgate that could be turned on or off as needed. In the middle period of the Shaosheng Reign (between 1094 and 1098), Jingkou Weir in Runzhou and the Benniu Weir in Changzhou were restored into sluice gate valves. As of September of the second year of the Yuanfu Reign (AD 1099), the constructions of Jingkou Sluice in Runzhou and Benniu Gate in Changzhou were completed, and rules and policies were implemented to manage these gates (X. Lu 1990: 2365). In the later period of the Northern Song Dynasty, Jingkou, Lüchengr, Wangting, and Benniu Weirs were all converted into floodgates.

The main gate diverting the Yangtze River into the Liangzhe West Canal was Jingkou Sluice. The Yangtze River flew into the canal through the Guazhou Sluice to the north, passing the Huaihe River and the Bianhe River before flowing into the Yellow River and the Luohe River. The Jingkou Sluice, located to the south, directed the Yangtze River to Wuzhong and then to the Qiantang River (Y. Lu 2011: 497). In the sixth year of the Chunxi Reign (AD 1179), the tide gate, which was the external gate of Jingkou Sluice and the most important in Zhenjiang, was restored with rocks (S. Xu 2014: 6168. According to Huang Zhen, there were four ways to enter the Jingkou Sluice from the Yangtze River: the westernmost Jingkou Sluice, the Haixian River, the Shanyu Port, and the Ganlu Port. However, the Ganlu Port was later abandoned due to clogging, leading to the construction of another floodgate called Upper Kaolao Gate (Z. Huang 1990), located further south of the original

Zeshui Sluice. During the Northern Song Dynasty, the number of ships from all directions was limited, and therefore, one delivery gate was sufficient, which was the Jingkou Sluice. However, during the Southern Song Dynasty, Hangzhou became the temporary capital where the emperor worked, and Zhenjiang functioned as the north entrance to this capital. Transportation activities were busy day and night, leading to the addition of Gaolu Gate to share the traffic by turns (X. Lu 1990: 2373–74).

In Hangzhou, "there were two delivery gates for ships leaving the Qiantang River. One handled the transportation from Wenzhou and Taizhou, while the other one worked for ships from Quzhou and Wuzhou. The gate on the north shore was damaged by tides and remained unrepaired for a considerable period, leading to the merging of ships from both directions" (S. Xu 2014: 6172). Upon entering the canal, three gates were constructed, namely the Hunshui Gate, Qingshui Gate, and Baoan Gate (S. Xu 2014: 6168). These gates were arranged from the estuary of the Qiantang River to the Hangzhou section of the canal from south to north. "Southern ships, passing by Kuapu Bridge of Zhejiang, and northern ships, traveling from Hunshui Gate, Xiaogong Bridge, Qingshui Gate, Zhonghui Bridge, Luomu Bridge, or Zhujia Bridge, turned west to Baoan Gate and its water valve to enter the city" (S. Qian 1990: 3675). The Hunshui Gate, Qingshui Gate, and Baoan Gate formed the pound lock system on the canal. Additionally, there were bridges and gates linking the Yangtze River to regulate the inflow to the city. If the water level was low in the city, the gates would be opened to take water, after which they would be closed to store water. During such times, no ships were allowed to travel. However, if the water was sufficient, the flashboards would be removed to maintain the flow of traffic (Toqta 1977: 2400).

On the Liangzhe East Canal, at the crossroad of the estuary of Qiantang River and the Yuyao River, several weirs and gates were constructed to facilitate the transportation of ships. These included Xixing Gate, Qianqing Weir, Dusi Weir, Caoe Weir, Lianghu Weir, and Tongming Weir. The Xixing Weir was located in Xixing Town Xiaoshan County, and marked the confluence of the Liangzhe East Canal and Qiantang River. To reach the prefecture city from Xixing Gate, travelers had to cover a distance of 26.52 km and pass through Qianqing Weir, located in Qianqing Town of Shanyin County (H. Zhang 1990: 7135), which linked the Qiantang River and sent ships downstream by tides. This was described in Chen Yuan's poem "the Travelogue of Qiantang Weir," wherein it is noted that the comings and goings of tides were unpredictable, and "the anchored ships were eager to swiftly travel (H. Zhang 1990: 7123)". Due to the increasing traffic on the canal the first year of the Jiatai Reign (AD 1201), in both up-going and down-going directions, new weirs had to be constructed at Qianqing Town to avoid riverway congestion. After these two weirs were constructed, it was convenient for travelers (S. Shi et al.1990: 6782). During the Xuanhe Reign, the Dusi Weir and Gate were built to provide water for the Liangzhe East Canal from Jianhu Lake and facilitate the movement of ambassadors traveling to and from Goryeo. And it was abolished until the second year of Longxing Reign (1164). It was the water gate converting water from Jianhu Lake to the Liangzhe East Canal. Thus, "among all weirs and gates, the Dusi Weir and Gate were crucial (S. Xu 2014: 6170)". The Weir was 31.824 km southeast of Kuaiji County, was constructed at the crossroad of Caoejiang Road and the canal (B. Li 1990). In the third year of the Jianyan Reign (AD 1129), Emperor Gaozong passed the Cao'e Weir by boat, and ships and boats were stuck there for three days (D. Zhao 2008). The Lianghu Weir, situated 11.063 km west of Shangyu County, and Tongming Weir, located 4.425 km east of Shangyu County, were essential crossings for all kinds of ships and boats traveling between Mingzhou and Yuezhou. Tides flowed from Dinghai County, went by Qingyuan City, and reached Cixi in the south; or could run through Yuyao County, and reached the North Weir in the west. The section from Yuyao River to Bei Weir was open, and during Emperor Gaozong's passage through the weir in the third year of the Jianyan Reign (AD1129), the river became bountiful with water after his prayers. However, many boats often got stuck at this busy channel and could not move for up to ten days. To reduce traffic congestion, the south Tongming Weir was added in the first year of the Jiatai Reign (AD 1201) to take the share of passenger ships, and the north Tongming Weir was built for cargo ships only (Z. Huang 1990; S. Shi et al.1990).

The weirs and gates on the canal were built to address in terrain heights and storage difficulties. Their purpose was to prevent the flow of water from higher to lower ground and to maintain sufficient water depth for sailing. Acting as dikes or dams, these weirs separated the canal into sections and created a closed water system between them, preventing water loss. Ancient Chinese scientist Shen Kuo noted that dams were built in the Huainan Canal to store water, indicating that the function of weirs was to retain water and keep the river open (K. Shen 2006: 96). *The Field Study of Water Regime in Wuxian County*, authored by Shan E, referred to three weirs, namely Chuangwangting Weir, Lücheng Weir, and Benniu Weir, which were constructed to ensure that water currents flowed in the desired direction, keeping traffic moving. These three weirs functioned as water retention and storage. At the estuary of the Yangtze River, the Huainan Canal was equipped with dams on soft ground and small weirs to form a compound system for water diversion, retention, and storage. The delivery gate was 442.5 m away from the Yangtze River, and allowed water to flow in during high tides, while the dams and small weirs stored water for shipping during low tides. The dams with soft soil, built over 30.2 m from the estuary of the Yangtze River, could be turned on or off. During high tides, the dams were opened to take in water or store the flood tide (S. Xu 2014: 9618). Pan Jixun of the Ming Dynasty, in *The Records of Surveying and Dredging Floodgates,* described how movable dams were used to control the Tongji Gate, limiting water flow into the lake during high tides of the Huaihe River. The dams were closed in June and reopened in September when water levels subsided (J. Pan 1990), indicating that movable dams could be opened or closed as necessary. Small weirs, as noted in the *Records of Rivers,* Volume 25 of *Chronicles of Jiangnan* recorded during the Kangxi Reign, were built between the Huaihe River and Hongze Lake, serving to take in water from the lake during low tides and release it when the tide was rising. These weirs were about one meter high (H. Zhao 1990). In the Song Dynasty, Zhenzhou built small weirs by the south shore, using waterwheels to safely transport grain ships on the canal. When the Yangtze River was at high tides, water flowed over the small weirs into the canal, while during low tides, the weirs retained water from the

Yangtze River, with people using waterwheels to replenish the water supply when needed (S. Xu 2014: 9618).

Different weirs on the canal had different functions. For instance, the weir at the estuary of the Yangtze River and Qiantang River could divert water, keep the river open, and mitigate turbidity. A compound lock was also built at Zhenjiang's Jingkou, which incorporated the Jingkou Sluice outside and the Zeshui Gate inside to regulate the flow of water. The function of Jingkou Sluice was to restrict the inflow of the Yangtze River, and the outer floodgate of Ganlu Port served a similar purpose. The muddy tides of the Yangtze River rise during high tides and settle during low tides, which can cause siltation on the riverbed. Consequently, when the tide came in, mud would be deposited in the river, leading to blockages after a few years. Therefore, the outer floodgate served a vital purpose by closing to prevent floodwater from entering. Only when the upstream area was dry could this floodgate be opened to allow water to flow in. In this way, the canal could "keep clear" (Z. Huang 1990). Zhenzhou and Guazhou built tide gates (Z. Liu 1990a, 1990b) at the crossing of the canal and the Yangtze River to block the water from the Yangtze River (S. Xu 2014: 6168). Hunshui Gate was erected at the estuary of the Qiantang River and the canal. The gate was closed during high tide and reopened after the tide receded, ensuring that the section of the city did not face clogging or the need to clear the canal (Toqta 1977: 2399). Delivery gates operated on a regular schedule to prevent muddy water from flowing into the canal during high tide (S. Xu 2014: 6172). Pound locks were also put into use. As Lu You entered the Yangtze River from Zhenjiang, he noted, "the ships passed through the three gates and stopped at the tide gate" (Y. Lu 2012a, 2012b: 164). Zhou Bida mentions entering the Zhenjiang Gate during high tide but being unable to proceed to the third gate due to low water levels. On the next day, he was able to enter the third gate, but had to stop due to rain, unable to proceed for several days as the inner sluice could not be opened (B. Zhou 1990). Guazhou Sluice was a pound lock system with an upper, middle, and tide gate, while Zhenzhou Gate employed upper and lower floodgates to work as a compound system (S. Xu 2014: 6168). Zhenzhou "enclosed the water from the canal to build the outer gate", which meant "the north one was the inner gate" (S. Hu 1990). Hunshui, Qingshui, and Baoan sluice gates were built at the river mouth of Qiantang River. After these, the water could enter Hangzhou City.

Sluice gates are a viable solution for managing different terrain heights to maintain water levels and ensure the river remains open for use in each section. However, the canal within the Yangzhou area was only clogged at Guazhou and Zhenzhou sluice gates, leading to a loss of water. Zhenzhou was therefore requested to repair the upstream and downstream gates promptly to prevent the canal from becoming shallow and unsuitable for ships (S. Xu 2014: 6168). During the Southern Song Dynasty, the section from Lin'an to Zhenjiang experienced natural disasters and was neglected for a long time, resulting in low water levels and clogging, which made shipping challenging (S. Xu 2014: 7074). In the fourth year of the Shaoxing Reign (AD 1134), when Jurchens invaded the south, Emperor Gaozong ordered the opening of gates in the Huainan Canal, Taizhou, Tongzhou, and other locations, causing water to spill out and prevent enemy ships from using the canal (Toqta 1977: 2393)1. This event demonstrated a defensive function of sluice gates' ability to hold and store water. Lu You also mentioned that Jingkou, Lücheng, and Benniu sluice gates were constructed along the Liangzhe West Canal to intercept and hold water, noting, "for the sake of sailing, water would be poured out in the morning and drained in the evening. That's why those gates were built."(Y. Lu 2011: 497)

To maintain river access between two sections with differing heights, the construction of pound locks was a common solution, which could be raised and closed as necessary. Zhou Qufei described the Lingqu Channel as having "36 delivery gates, so after ships entered one gate, the entrance would be closed, then the ships waited for enough water to go to next section. That's why ships could climb up or sail down quickly and pass through freely for both directions." (Q. Zhou 1999: 27) The four canals under discussion here had smaller height differences than the Lingqu Channel, but functioned similarly. In the fourth year of the Yuanyou Reign (AD 1089), Lücheng Weir was transformed into sluice gates and two gates were added in the up and downstream direction to function as a pound lock. In the fifth year of the Qingyuan Reign (AD 1199), another sluice gate was added to Lin'an and Jiaxing Sluices, bringing the total to three sluice gates. However, due to the age of the two gates in Lücheng, they were no longer effective when water levels rose, and a new sluice gate was built to maintain the condition of the dikes and dams (S. Xu 2014: 6169). In June first of the sixth year of the Qiandao Reign (AD 1170), Lu You "passed through all three gates of the Lin'an area in one day". In the Shaosheng Reign (AD 1094–1098), two delivery gates were constructed, but they were destroyed during war. In the second year of the Shaoxi Reign (AD 1191), these three gates were reconstructed. "The lower gate was about 90 steps to the middle one and the middle one was about 80 steps to the upper gate." It was also written that, "traveling west from Hangzhou, the river would flow out. To manage this, sluice gates were built," (Y. Lu 2012a, 2012b: 159;S. Qian 1990: 3715–16) which were used to solve the uneven ground of sections and to keep them open. Five Sluice Gates of Wuxi also worked in a compound way with upper and lower gates (Toqta 1977: 2409).

To reduce water loss and maintain the flow of traffic through the canal gates, bay reservoirs were also built by the floodgates as the water input. For example, Zeng Xiaoyun built backtrack bay reservoirs along the Huainan Canal to replenish the water supply (H. Hu 1900). Lücheng Gate had bay reservoirs as well, "where waterwheels were often used to transfer water from the bay reservoirs to keep smooth official or private transportation activities." In this case, the waterwheels outside the canal delivered water to the bay reservoirs, then into the containment that the floodgates controlled. When the workforce was insufficient, soldiers were called upon to assist with this task (T. Li 2004: 11,740). The Three Gates of Chang'an were each equipped with an upper and lower bay reservoir, which were used to store excess water during times of abundance, or released when water levels were low (S. Qian 1990: 3716). Three additional bay reservoirs, including Guishui Bay Reservoir, Jishui Bay Reservoir, and Xintan Bay Reservoir, were built at Jingkou Sluice to provide mooring space for ships and to store water for the canal (X. Lu 1990: 2367). Similarly, the bay reservoir at Kaokao Sluice was constructed to prevent water loss and facilitate water retention (Toqta 1977: 4258).

To navigate through gates, ships required additional strength from either cattle or human labor (Z. Huang 1990). To reduce friction between ship bottoms and weirs or dams, wood was used to pave a driveway to push the ships. However, this friction could still cause damage. For instance, Huang Zhen observed the Tongming Weir, which was in disrepair and had only old wooden posts scattered under 31.2 m of water. The Huainan Canal, which had five weirs from Zhenzhou to Chuzhou, required ships to traverse up and down ten times, leading to frequent ship damage and loss of grain. The state-owned ships were rapidly deteriorating due to the damage caused by the weirs and traveling through them caused significant damages each year. To mitigate these damages, one option was to transport empty ships and then reload them after passing through the weirs. Another option was to build transit warehouses by the weirs and transfer the goods to other, lighter ships hierarchically (T. Li 2004: 2149, 2424; Toqta 1977: 10,118, 4258). However, both of these options would increase transportation costs and lower transportation efficiency.

The conversion of weirs into sluices has been identified as an effective strategy to reduce transportation costs and improve the efficiency of water grain transportation. This was prompted by the damage incurred by grain carrying boats traveling repeatedly up and down the five weirs. To address this issue, Qiao Weiyue, the fiscal commissioner of Huainan Province, was tasked with overseeing the construction of two delivery gates located 50 steps apart in the third weir of the Xihe River (Toqta 1977: 1018). Therefore, the third weir was changed into pound locks. In the fourth year of the Tiansheng Reign (AD 1026), the Beishen Weir of Chuzhou and the Jiangkou Weir of Zhenzhou were also converted into sluices to reduce damage to hauling boats and expenses related to towing boats. After Beishen and Jiangkou sluice gates were completed, "over one hundred thousand labor forces and garrisoned soldiers on the weirs were saved every year (A. Wang 1990)."[6] Additionally, boats carrying heavier loads were able to pass through the sluice gates, whereas under the old rules of boat transportation, they were restricted to lighter loads. Zhenyan weir only allowed boats with a load capacity less than 300 Dan (20,100 L) grain to pass, but after the sluice was completed, boats with a load of 400 Dan (26,800 L) were permitted to sail through the sluice gates. Later, the ones with much heavier loads, such as the official boats with a load capacity of 700 Dan (46,900 L), civilian boats with 800 bags of grains (each grain bag weighing up to 2 Dan), could also pass. A weir and a sluice were built at Wuxie, and the weir was the access for the big boats and the sluice for the small ones. Weirs were found to be suitable for boats with lighter loads, while sluices were more suitable for those carrying heavier loads. As a result, Emperor Renzong ordered the promotion of transforming weirs into sluices, and the shipping department reported plans for converting other weirs into sluices. Several dams, such as Beishen, Zhaobo, Longzhou, and Zhuyu, were abolished successively (T. Li 2004: 2424; S. Xu 2014: 6169; K. Shen 2006: 96). Proposals to transform other weirs into sluices were also put forth, including Zeng Xiaoyun's proposal to

[6] "Converting Chuzhou weirs into sluices has saved 217,000 labor forces, garrisoning soldiers on the weir, and their daily consumption of 1.3 million strings of 1000 coins and 68,000 Dan of rice every year" was recorded by Wang Anshi in his work, *Selected Works of Wang Anshi.*

transform the Guazhou, Jingkou, and Benniu weirs into sluices during the Shaosheng Reign, and to turn the Jingkou, Lücheng, Wangting, and Benniu weirs into sluices during the later years of the Northern Song Dynasty. The above discussion highlights the benefits of converting weirs into sluices, and the efforts made to implement this strategy throughout various regions in China during the Song Dynasty.

The challenge of storing water and navigating canals could be solved by constructing weirs and sluices; however, this approach restricted the size of boats that can pass through. The use of manual labor and animals to tow boats through weirs had its drawbacks: the smaller the work force, the more difficult it is for boats to pass through, and increasing the number of people and animals would increase the cost of navigation. Therefore, boats passing through could not be too large. Furthermore, heavier boats generate greater friction, which can damage the boats. In addition, the width of the sluice gate was limited, with larger wooden gates being difficult to open and close, and unable to withstand high water pressure and tension. Two gate pillars stood in the sluice gate (S. Hu 1990), and between them were cross-supported timbers. When the gate was opened, boats could pass through, and water was stored when it was closed. Yuan Shuoyou reported that the Hongze sluice, built in the Tang Dynasty, still had two gate posts with a diameter exceeding 3.12 m on the old gate base. These two gate posts, with a circumference of 9.36 m and believed to be a thousand years old, appeared indestructible. They were believed to be protected by gods, and they were still as solid as city walls (S. Yuan 1990). Despite their size, the Hongze sluice was not wide enough for the 2.7-m-wide boat carrying Emperor Gaozong's biological mother Wei's coffin, which was larger than the previous one shipping Emperor Huizong's coffin, to pass through. This led to damage to city gates, bridges, and weirs along the boat's path. This indicates that the canal sluice gate's width was less than 2.65 m (S. Wang 2012: 657). During the Yuan Dynasty, the beam width limit of the Zhenzhou Sluice gate was 2.65 m. According to the History of Yuan Dynasty, the head of the shipbuilding craftsman reported that a ship with a width of 2.65 m and a length of 20.28 m had to be built to navigate through the sluice gate (L. Song 1976: 1613). This illustrates that the sluice gate limited the size of boats running in the canal. Despite many waiting to pass through the gate, they had to follow a queue as the channel was not wide enough for two boats to go side by side (W. Yang 2007: 1433, 1525). The width of the channel in the sluice was insufficient for two boats to travel alongside each other. The situation arose when an empty batch-shipping boat, which was traveling from the north towards the Guazhou sluice gate, obstructed the passage of loaded boats that had been released from the Yangtze's estuary in the Zhenjiang Prefecture. As a result, the smooth sailing of heavy boats was disrupted. Consequently, the empty boats coming from the north were ordered to exit the Yangtze River at the lower mouth of the Guazhou Sluice, while the boats carrying heavy loads from the south entered the lock at the upper entrance. (S. Xu 2014: 7053) This demonstrates that it was not possible for two ships to traverse the sluice in opposite directions simultaneously. Additionally, the navigable capacity and navigation methods of the weir lock further support the conclusion that it was impossible for ships carrying loads of 10,000 Hu (3,280,000 L) or with a load capacity of 7000 or 8000 Hu (2,296,000–2,624,000 L) to navigate the canal.

2.2.2.2 The Management of the Weirs and Sluices Along the Canal

The post of supervisor was set up to manage weirs and sluices along the canal in the Song Dynasty. *Encyclopedia of 21 Categories* recorded that each of the 21 weirs on the grain transport route had one supervisor and the rest which were not along the canal were managed by the county or prefecture where they were located (Y. Wang 2003: 476). However, in some cases, only one official was responsible for several neighboring weirs and sluices (S. Xu 2014: 6168), such as the three sluices at Hunshui, Qingshui, and Baoan Ship Lock. *Encyclopedia of 21 Categories* further notes that in most cases, one official was assigned to each sluice, although occasionally every delivery gate was managed by one supervisor, as was the case for the eight delivery gates of Zhenzhou sluice (S. Xu 2014: 9618). In the first year of the Chongning Reign (AD 1102), one official was assigned to govern all the bay reservoirs on the route from Hangzhou to Guanzhou of Yangzhou, including the new and old ones in Changzhou, Yunzhou, Yangzhou, Xiuzhou, Hangzhou and others. This official's duties involved the management of bay reservoirs for irrigation and drainage, as well as investigating and handling any cheating related to bay reservoir affairs in accordance with regulations that had been previously issued. Bao Chaomao, the county magistrate of Kunshan, was assigned to supervise all the sluices on the route from Hangzhou to Yangzhou. Finally, the Suzhou governmental building was established to take over the weirs and sluice gates along the canals from Hangzhou to Yangzhou. This entity was named the Bay Reservoir Department of Huainan and Liangzhe Provinces (S. Xu 2014: 6166), and was staffed by civilians and minor officials drafted from Changzhou, Runzhou, Suzhou, Hangzhou, and Xiuzhou.

The supervisors and the county magistrates along the canal all took responsibilities for the operating sluice gates. These officials were held accountable for any leakage of sluice water and were rewarded or punished based on the performance of their duties (Toqta 1977: 2383). If the water level did not meet the required standards, and the sluice gate was opened, the supervisor would receive a penalty of one hundred strokes. The county magistrate and his assistant would also be punished with sixty strokes for not adequately monitoring the supervisor's conduct. Supervisors who successfully dredged the sluice three times during their term could be rewarded with a second term. If the canal water did not drain away at the end of the supervisor's term, their place would remain on the reward list for one year. Similarly, the county magistrate and his assistant would be on the list for six months. The mayor, supervisor of municipal financial affairs, and county procurator were responsible for ongoing examination and supervision (T. Li 2004: 11,740). The magistrate of Wuxi county was appointed to take charge of opening and locking the sluice. In general, the sluice age was opened with more than 1.87 m deep sluice water, and passenger boats were permitted to pass (Toqta 1977: 2409). During the Southern Song Dynasty, prefecture and county officials along the route were also legally required to repair and dredge weirs and sluice gates. "Batch grain boats were stuck in the shallow river course from Lin'an Municipality to Zhenjiang Municipality." "The local officials were ordered to be in charge of repairing the weirs and sluices."(X. Lu 1990: 2365) In the sixth year of the Chunxi Reign (AD 1179), Sima Fan was rewarded for dredging the river and repairing the locks. Fiscal commissioners were appointed by imperial edict to oversee canal affairs (S. Xu 2014: 6168). In the fifth year of the Xuanhe Reign (AD 1123), Emperor Huizong of Song issued an order, appointing officials to drain and irrigate the river course with water wheels to ensure smooth sailing. Later, "in the fourth month of the lunar calendar, the fifth year of Xuanhe Reign (AD 1123), Wang Zhonghong, Liu zhongyuan, the inspector, and Meng Yu, the official of water transport of grain, were sent to deal with the affairs of the Changzhou and Yunzhou sections of the canal." (Toqta 1977: 2390) In the 14th year of the Chunxi Reign (AD 1187), Xiong Fei, the mayor of Yangzhou, requested that the Huainan Transfer Agency of Taxation and Huaidong Salt Bureau repair the Guazhou weir immediately (S. Xu 2014: 168).

The management of weirs and sluice gates was entrusted to local errand forces, who used winches to tow the boats passing through the weirs and operated the sluices. These workers were referred to as "paddle soldiers" or "sluice soldiers". Lu You reported that "since the period of Emperor Taizu's Reign, local errand forces were established at four places, and Lücheng and Jingkou were two of them." (Y. Lu 2012a, 2012b: 163) Here, the local errand soldiers really were "sluice soldiers." In the third year of Jianyan Reign (AD 1129), after the troops of the Jin Kingdom retreated, Sun Sheng, the deputy county magistrate, was selected as the acting county magistrate in the absence of the county magistrate in Huaiyin County. Luo Cheng and his Hongze sluice soldiers refused to follow the county's order, and thus, he and Dong Qing, one of his apprentices, led the soldiers to invade Huaiyin. Rebel soldiers were rampant in the towns and cities of Hongze County, and the officer of the sluice soldiers dared not quell the rebellion. They easily occupied the county site and defeated Lianshui Military forces, taking advantage of the one thousand boats available. The task of sluice soldiers was to use winches to tow boats passing through the sluices, so they were also called "pedal soldiers." (X. Li 2013: 556; M. Xu 1987: 934) During the Xianchun Reign, Huang Zhen, the deputy county magistrate of legal affairs, discovered that only civilians managed winches and charged passing boats at the old weirs in Shiyan, 10 km away east to the Yuyao County site, as there were no sluice soldiers present. These civilians took the opportunity to make money and profit, which was inconvenient for official and private boats. In response to some officials' call for winches, "the local government dispatched two soldiers to charge the passing by boats" (Z. Huang 1990). Yang Wanli once described the scene of boats towing by winches in a poem, stating that "as two fishing boats approached face to face, no efforts were needed to relax the cords from the winches. But when the boats stayed motionless at the winch site, soldiers had to turn the winches laboriously." (W. Yang 2007: 1530) Sluice soldiers included pedal soldiers, who were dispatched to Zhenzhou, Chuzhou, and Changzhou to open and close sluices (Toqta 1977: 4663)1. This was the primary task of sluice soldiers.

In the Northern Song Dynasty, the royal court established quotas for each group of sluice soldiers. One regiment of 500 soldiers was set up in Huainan Province, while Liangzhe East and West provinces each had two regiments of sluice and pedal soldiers responsible for managing the the sluices and weirs there (T. Li 2004: 8398). The Dusiyan Battalion in the section of the Liangzhe East Canal included

25 soldiers, and Caoeyan Battalion, Lianghuyan Battalion, South Qianqingyan, and North Qianqingyan had 50 soldiers each. Tongmingyan Battalion had 25 soldiers, and the Defence Battalion at Xixing had 200 soldiers (S. Shi et al.1990: 6776) responsible for lifting and shutting sluices, as well as dredging and deepening the river (S. Xu 2014: 6160). The old quota for Changanzha sluice soldiers was 120 (S. Qian 1990: 3716), while Zhenjiang was originally given a quota of 30 people, but was unable to meet it. When Shi Mijian guarded Zhenjiang, he was ordered to recruit 30 strong men who were proficient swimmers to serve as sluice soldiers (X. Lu 1990: 2394), according to an imperial edict. Scholars have discovered evidence indicating that after the sluice gates were built at Beishen Weir of Chuzhou, and Jiangkou Weir of Zhenzhou, grain transportation was made more convenient, saving the labor of over one hundred thousand people every year (Y. Wang 2003: 474). However, this does not suggest that the quotas for these two weirs were set for over one hundred thousand soldiers; rather, it refers to amount of labor hours required each year for the garrisoning soldiers at the weirs.

Weirs were used to conserve water in different sections of the river, and in winter the sluice soldiers were given leave and reinstated to to their posts in spring, thus eliminating the problem of opening and closing the sluice gates regularly. The function of the weirs was to ensure direct navigation in various segments of the river. Hence, water conservation and direct navigation were closely intertwined, and the rules of opening and closing the sluice gates were based on the water conditions. The management of the sluice gates required the soldiers to open and close the gates promptly and dredge the riverbed occasionally to allow for boats to pass through without delay (S. Xu 2014: 6168). Their routine work was to open and close the gates at a predetermined time. The norm for opening and closing the sluice gates was to open them in spring and close them in winter, and they needed to be opened and closed daily at a specific time. The opening and closing times varied for different canals based on their water conditions. In the Northern Song Dynasty, a winter holiday system was introduced to manage the Huainan Canal and batch transportation in the Bianhe River. This meant that canal shipping workers would be idle in the dry season of winter and return to their posts in the spring (Toqta 1977: 4252). However, in winter, the soldiers had no food to eat and had to survive in the chilly season when the sluice gates were shut down. To address this issue, Chen Yi suggested that soldiers garrisoned in Zhenzhou, Yangzhou, Runzhou, and Chuzhou prefectures, as well as grain boatmen in these prefectures, should be placed in battalion seats and served with food during the winter. This approach led to the quick gathering of two thousand workers when laborers were needed for dredging and deepening canals, which had been ruined by Fang La and his rebel soldiers (Toqta 1977: 13,182). In the Southern Song Dynasty, the money and grains supplied to the troops in Huainan East Province were stored in Zhenjiang, from where they were distributed to branch troops via the Huainan Canal. As food shortages were prevalent in Huainan East Province, Hong Shi suggested that grain shipping should commence before the sluice gates were shut down to avoid shortages of military supplies and grain. All military supplies were calculated based on the standard in the previous year. If the sluice gates were shut down, all military supplies needed to be provided until the arrival of supplies from

Jiangnan East Province and transported to Guazhou and placed in new warehouses (S. Hong, n.d.). This highlights the seasonal opening and closing of the sluice gates.

In the Song Dynasty, the opening and closing of sluice gates in the canal was a crucial factor in controlling the water yield into the gates. Two conditions needed to be met for the opening of sluice gates. Firstly, the gates were required to be opened according to a routine of three times a day. Secondly, the gates were to be opened when the number of waiting boats reached one hundred at the sluice gates. The officers in charge of the gates treasured water as gold and were expected to strictly comply with the rule of opening the gates three times a day (H. Hu 1900).

Yang Wanli wrote a poem that depicted the officials' reluctance to open the sluice gates due to their concern for conserving water. The poem is as follows:

Little rain couldn't make the spring river swell on

As the officers cherish flowing water as gold long

Boats clustered in the lower bay

Waiting for their companions to go through the gates.

Suddenly the clutters of opening gates were heard

From which thunderous waves rushed out like snow drifts.

So many boats couldn't prevent water from running down,

Torrential waves jumping from the bottom of boats.

The river level quickly rose half an oar

Making upper and lower levels on the same level.

24 tower boats in a row noisily hurried to file out,

Like a swamp of fish swimming through the gates swiftly. (W. Yang 2007: 1500–01)

Jojin documented the regulations concerning the operation of sluice gates in the Huainan Canal. In April of the sixth year of the Xi'ning Reign (AD 1073), in his journey back from Kaifeng to Liangzhe East and West provinces, he arrived at Chuzhou on April 23rd, which happened to be the opening day of the sluices. Although several hundred boats were scheduled to pass through, the Supply Commission informed them that the sluice gate would only be opened if at least one hundred boats had gathered. If the number of boats failed to reach one hundred within three days, the sluice gate would still be opened once, however, frequent opening of the gate for numbers less than one hundred would render the system inefficient. It was the third day and the sluice gates were opened at dusk. However, the However, the gates were opened until April 26th for boats to pass through (Jojin 2009:693–95).

The sluice gates on both the Liangzhe West Canal and the Huainan Canal implemented the same routine opening rule. In the second year of the Yuanfu Reign (AD 1099), Zeng Xiaoji was responsible for the construction of the Jingkou and Bengnjiu sluice gates, and he established a permanent regulation of daily opening to facilitate batch transportation boats (T. Li 2004: 12,285). During his journey on the Liangzhe West Canal, Yang Wanli depicted the scene in his poem "*Passing by Lücheng Sluice Gates*", which reads,

> Boats halted on the river till night veil came down,
>
> Because the number of boats could meet the requirement.
>
> When all the required boats were here for sluice opening, they had to sail along to enter Jingxi River at mid night.
>
> When all the boats were there and the gates were to open,
>
> Boatmen had to adjust their boat heads and lift their sails.
>
> However, only one boat was slow in coming,
>
> Nobody knew the reason.
>
> On hearing the news of sluice opening,
>
> The boatmen on the first boat were happy to laugh.
>
> At first, they expected the gate to open before night's curtain sailed,
>
> Later they could accept the sailing at night after the release of boats at the gates.
>
> I heard of the news that even if the boats were in the gates,
>
> They were stopped to wait for other boats coming, Alas, I became a wretched man.
>
> If you want to know the true news of opening sluice,
>
> Remember to ensure the second sound of bell being struck. (W. Yang 2007: 1433)

A ringing bell was the signal to open the sluice gates. However, due to a shortage of boats, Yang Wanli's boat could not pass through the gates during daytime. Lengthy waits were a common occurrence at the time, as evidenced by the experience of Zhou Bida, who had to wait an entire day at the Chang'an Sluice before passing through at dusk (B. Zhou 1990). In times of drought or sudden rises in water levels, the sluice gates could not be opened according to routine. In one instance, when Zhou Bida sailed into the reservoir tide gates in Zhenjiang, the water was too shallow before the third gate, forcing a halt to their journey. The following day, heavy rainfall prevented their passage through the sluice gates. Similarly, when passing through the Lücheng sluice gates, they were again prevented from progressing due to flooding, requiring the gates to be closed (B. Zhou 1990). Due to the necessity of verifying the itinerary and real water conditions, compliance with the rule of mechanically opening sluices during batch transportation was not possible. When closure of sluices caused delays for the batch transportation boats, the escorted officers were required to assess the current conditions and confirm the exact dates of sluice gate operations, which would then exempt the boats from adhering to the original itinerary (S. Xu 2014: 7027).

The operation of sluice gates is crucial in regulating water flow in canals and rivers. Failure to open the gates regularly can result in significant water loss. For example, local officials' irresponsibility in managing the sluice gates on the canal and Wuxie Weir led to the gates' dysfunction. "As the gates were not opened regularly, the canal lost its water severely, which caused the sluice boards to float and prevented them from being interconnected and placed at the river bed. Consequently, the canal water constantly flowed out to fill the Lihe River through cracks in the gates." (S. Xu 2014: 6169) Alternatively, the frequent opening and closing of the sluice gates might have disrupted sailing in the Lihe section of the Grand Canal by not allowing sufficient time for the sluice section to compensate for the lost water (H. Hu 1900). The irregular opening and closing of sluice gates would lead to disorderly competition between boats. For example, at the Longshan Sluice Gates of the Qiantang River, overcrowded boats would disorderly rush forward upon hearing signals of opening gates, resulting in ten times the usual number of boats. However, the boats were concerned about colliding with each other if they rushed forward, while remaining in the original position risked being overturned by huge waves. To address this issue, a regulation was introduced requiring all boats from exterior sluices to follow the sailing regulations set for the canal. All the boatmen agreed that this would be good for everyone (D. Sun 1990). The exterior sluice refers to the sluice gate on the canal into the Qiantang River, and the regulations for opening and closing gates must be strictly adhered to at Longshan sluice gates, with the exception of any temporary orders from the royal court. In the fifth year of the Xuanhe Reign (AD 1123), an imperial edict was issued mandating that "the sluice gates in the six southeast provinces establish a rule on the regular opening and closing of gates. However, there were rumors about the function of special imperial edicts and the officers' private orders to force the gates open at extra times, resulting in significant water loss and disrupted smooth sailing for batch transportation ships, which should be banned." The officials' capricious orders to open the gates were clearly banned by the royal court (Toqta 1977: 2390). Since the implementation of direct transportation approach of revenues and grains to the royal court, the routine opening and closing of gates three times a day was no longer followed (Toqta 1977: 11,639). "There was no fixed opening and closing time for the batch transportation boats dedicated to the royal court." As a result, boats continued to pass through the sluice gates all day, leaving no time to replenish lost water. Ultimately, this resulted in the dry river in the sections of several hundred kilometers from Hongze Lake to Zhaobo, rendering such river sections unavailable for boat sailing (Toqta 1977: 2389).

The regular opening and closing of sluice gates in various waterways, including the Huainan Canal, the Liangzhe West Canal, the Liangzhe East Canal, the Yangtze River, and the Qiantang River, served the purpose of preventing muddy water from flowing back into the canals, rather than solely preserving water resources. This measure was taken because the return of muddy water would obstruct the riverbed. For instance, the sluice gates preventing muddy water from flowing in at the river mouth of the Qiantang River into the Liangzhe West Canal were closed during the rising tide and opened when the clear water calmed down. Similarly, at Jingkou of Zhenjiang and Ganlu Port of Zhenjiang, external sluice gates were utilized to prevent muddy water from the Yangtze River from entering the canal, and they were opened until the slack tides came. At Guazhou, where the canal and the Yangtze River met, tide gates were constructed to prevent the muddy water of the Yangtze River from filling the canal (Toqta 1977: 2399). The opening and closing of sluice gates was regulated according to the ebb and flow of tides. When the Southern Song Dynasty was invaded by the troops of the Jin Kingdom, residents of Huainan East and West provinces wanted to cross the Yangtze River to escape the war. However, due to the closed reservoir tide gates at Zhenjiang and heavy snow in the northern region of the Yangtze River, they suffered from starvation and cold weather (S. Xu 2014: 7982). The opening and closing of the sluice gates depended solely on the natural laws of ebb and flow of tides, and there was a rule that they would only open during the rising tide. Therefore, "when the residents shouted at the officer to open the gates, he made no response, but instead cupped his one hand in the other before his chest. The gates had to wait until the tides rose again at night, as the early tides had already ebbed away and water had already flowed into the Huaihe River" (W. Yang 2007: 1525). The opening and closing of the sluice gates was thus subject to the natural laws of tides.

2.2.3 The Sails Lifting and Boats Towing

In addition to the continuous waterway of the Bianhe River, the Huainan Canal, Liangzhe West Canal, and Liangzhe East Canal were divided into multiple sections by weirs and sluice gates. Water in the canal flowed quietly or even halted. The canals were shallow, and boats frequently became stuck in some sections. To navigate these canals, boatmen used barge poles, oars, or sculls, which was depicted in *Riverside Scene at Qingming Festival* painted by the famous artist Zhang Zeduan. The other three canals were similar to the Bianhe River in terms of water level, but more tranquil, where the use of barge poles, oars, and sculls remained prevalent. For larger boats, such as long-range grain boats, barge poles, oars, and sculls were used as auxiliary tools for navigation.

Boats could move forward by hoisting sails in the tailwind. The Supply Commission of Huainan East and West provinces utilized the north wind to ship salt in batches to Hubei Province in winter, and transport the supplies to the capital city Kaifeng in the south wind in spring. However, the monsoons over land were less robust than those over the sea, and they were changeable, making them not always suitable for sailing. Furthermore, the winding river courses hindered the boats from consistently sailing in the tailwind, and sometimes they had to sail against the headwind. Hence, the monsoons may not be helpful in sailing boats. For example, in the sixth year of the Xi'ning Reign (AD 1073), the customs of Guangzhou, Mingzhou and Hangzhou reported that "only five hundred out of 120 batches of salt shipping were successful, as the capricious winds had caused damages to boats, and several soldiers and boatmen lost their lives due to natural disasters" (T. Li 2004: 5992). Evidently, sailors had to sporadically make use of the rare tailwind to lift their sails. During Lou Shi's diplomatic delegation to the Jin Kingdom, they sailed in the Huainan Canal and were able to sail in the tailwind by lifting sails at Zhaobo Dam. They traveled

15 km before Lujin, and another 15 km to reach Gaoyou (Y. Lou 1990). Similarly, in Lu You's voyage to Sichuan, they could only lift their sails in the tailwind when they sailed in Xiuzhou (Y. Lu 2012a, b: 161). In the Southern Song Dynasty, Zhao Bo encountered a tailwind in winter while passing by Changzhou, and he expressed his delight by stating, "How fortunate we are to embark on a long journey lifting sails in a tailwind as we left hometown." (F. Zhao 1990) Sailing in a tailwind was considered a rare opportunity.

The prevalent approach involved frequent shifts between sailing with a tailwind and towing boats against a headwind. This approach was described by Prime Minister Wang Anshi, who observed his boatmen's laughter at the struggles of those towing boats against a headwind while they sailed smoothly with the tailwind, describing the scene thusly: "My boatmen were happily chanting folk songs, laughing at those laboriously towing a boat nearby. How quickly fortune rotates in our life, sailing in a tailwind or headwind unreasonably." (A. Wang 1990) The shifts between tailwind and headwind sailing were common, as evidenced by the accounts of Xu Lun and Yang Wanli who observed the changing conditions of the Huainan Canal, noting "yesterday, the strong gusts whistled by, while birds were chirping high, and tow-men could not move a step forward; However, today they could reclaim ropes and lifted sails, the moon wax and wane was just natural," (L. Xu 1990a, b) and, "Duliang Mountain had its huts obscured after snowing for three consecutive days, little boats moved as if running on land. Strong winds blew in Shanyang in the morning, large boats moved as if flying in the sky. Yesterday, the boat trackers nearly wept out of frustration with the cold weather, and reeds were burned to dry their wet clothes. In the morning trackers boarded on the boat, reclaimed ropes and rest their head on headcloth. The tower boat was swiftly sailing as if wings were installed, which split waves at full speed as if riding on waves." (W. Yang 2007: 1421) The unpredictability of the winds made it difficult to rely solely on tailwind sailing, so the normal practice of sailing boats was not lifting sails. In the eighth year of the Qiandao (AD 1172), during Zhou Bida's journey along the Grand Canal's Wangting section, the boat initially sailed effortlessly with the tailwind and rain. However, the winds suddenly shifted northward ten kilometers later, rendering the boat immobile even with the aid of trackers. Eventually, they had to halt the boat several kilometers away from Wangting (B. Zhou 1990). These difficulties in navigating the canal waters made towing by trackers the most common and stable method of propulsion for heavy boats in the shallow canals.

When boats passed through the weirs or sluice gates, boat trackers were the most frequently seen people on the banks. In the fifth year of the Dazhongxiangfu Reign (AD 1012), Emperor Zhenzong laid down an edict, stipulating that they should have a good rest during the winter (S. Xu 2014: 6941). In the early period of the Northern Song Dynasty, passing through the five weirs required boatmen to repeatedly unload and upload grains, which made them exhausted (Toqta 1977: 2380). Chen Zao once described the weariness of the boatmen when passing through Benjiu Weirs, explicitly noting that "towing the boat to pass through Benniu Weirs made the boatmen exhausted." (Z. Chen 1990) In case of labor shortage when passing through Lücheng Sluice Gates, a small number of soldiers could work alongside boat trackers (Toqta

1977: 2383). Retrieving ropes when passing through weirs could be done either by boat trackers or winches, as described by Lu You, who wrote that exhausted winch runners needed to rest all night after towing a boat through a clogged dam (Y. Lu 2011: 14). However, in most cases, oxen were used to tow boats. For example, Jojin's boat used oxen to pass through Qianqing Weir, while a dozen oxen were yoked to tow a boat through Caoe Weir. Sixteen oxen were employed to tow a boat through Yuyao Weir, eight oxen were positioned on both banks to tow a boat through Benjiu Weir, and seven oxen were positioned on both banks to tow a boat through Jingkou Weir. Passing through Guazhou Weir, 11 oxen were put on both banks, but only five oxen on each bank were required on the way back (Jojin 2009: 40, 724–25, 223, 231, 701). *Stories of the Strange* recounted a story of Langjian passing by Benniu Weir at night when he heard a voice saying, "My son will pass by the weir, and I hope you try your utmost efforts to tow the boat." Although he did not find anyone around, he saw some oxen ruminating beneath a hut. The next day, a young man passed the weir, and the flock of oxen automatically towed the boats, the winches rotated quickly, and in a moment they passed the weir (S. Zhang 1990a, b, c). Although this was a fairy tale, it demonstrates that oxen were the primary driving force for boats to pass through weirs. Mei Yaochen described the scene of boat-towing by oxen, stating that "if Zhuyu Weir were put into use, the oxen in Wu Kingdom would be tired to death. If Zhuyu Weir were desolate, the oxen in the East Wu Kingdom would be laid idle." (Y. Mei 1980: 457).

The navigation of sections beyond the weirs was also reliant on the use of towing boats to advance. In the Bianhe River waterway flowing into the Huaihe River via the Yellow River or the Luohe River, oars served as the driving force to sail boats downstream, while towing ropes were necessary for upstream travel. Mei Yaochen described this, stating that "boats busily come and go by either oars or towing ropes." (Y. Mei 1980: 278) During Li Pu's tenure as governor of the Jianghuai Supply Commission, "he transported precious goods by large boats from the southeastern provinces to flatter the important ministers of the court." These boats formed a long queue in the river and were towed into the capital city through the city gates (K. Shen 2006: 170). In his 7-character quatrain *the Ode to the Icy River Again*, Su Zhe wrote that "in the morning, the county magistrate in the name of managing boats, ordered thousands of boat trackers to tow the boats forward." (Z. Su 1987: 340) Jojin made a detailed description of sailing approaches in the section between Sizhou and Nanjing of the Bianhe River, where boat trackers were necessary on specific dates, and towing ropes and lifting sails were needed on others (Jojin 2009: 253–255, 263).[7] In the third year of the Jingde Reign (AD 1006), "as there was a high official's boat anchored near the bank, tall masts were erected, causing other boats to be blocked from passing and resulting in many boats being clogged in the river." Although a regulation was introduced requiring anchored boats by the bank to lay down all masts (S. Xu 2014: 6940), the erected masts of the high official's boat prevented

[7] Towing boats were used on Jojin's voyage in the Liangzhe East Cannal, the Liangzhe West Canal, the Huaihe River and the Bianhe River, which was recorded in the book of *Revised Edition of Travelogues of Jojin*, and will not be listed them all.

boat trackers from towing boats forward along the towpath. Zhang Zeduan's famous painting, *Riverside Scene at Qingming Festival,* depicts boats being towed forward with their masts laid down and towing ropes tied to the top of the mast, parallel to the boat trackers' path. Moreover, the boats anchored near the banks had their masts laid down. This shows that the regulation introduced in the third year of the Jingde Reign (AD 1006) was strictly applied, and towing ropes were frequently used in the navigation on the Bianhe River.

Boat towing was the primary mode of transportation for boats sailing in the Huainan Canal, the Liangzhe West Canal, and the Liangzhe East Canal. In the 9th year of the Xi'ning Reign (AD 1076), while serving as governor of the Supply Commission, Zhang Jie disregarded the shallow and insufficient water levels in the canal section between Zhenzhou and Yangzhou. Despite accepting two imperial edicts to dredge the canal, he offered the excuse that boat towing was sufficient to enable boats to navigate smoothly in the shallow waters, and that boat trackers were necessary in that section regardless, making dredging unnecessary (T. Li 2004: 6702). In the fifth year of the Xuanhe Reign (AD 1123), "in order to transport heavy Taihu Rocks to the capital city, Zhu Li shipped them on large boats being towed by hundreds of people." This required navigating the Liangzhe West Canal, the Huainan Canal, and the Bianhe River, and sometimes necessitated deepening the riverbed, breaking bridges, or enlarging weirs to ensure safe passage, adding several months to the shipping process (Toqta 1977: 2102). Su Zhe's poem, *Farewell to Li Jun,* recounts his journey to the Liangzhe West Province, during which he emphasizes the necessity of boat trackers, even when traveling on small boats in shallow riverbeds (Z. Su 1987: 189). Lou Yao's trip to the canal section of Liangzhe West Province in November of the fifth year of the Qiandao Reign (AD 1169) illustrates the clogged state of the Grand Canal, where boat towing was a necessary propulsive force. Although fortunate enough to sail in deep water, Lou Yao still needed boat trackers in shallower areas. On November 10th, he left Hangzhou on an ambassadorial boat, and then he had to employ boat trackers due to the shallow water on November 11th, until November 15th could they sail smoothly, after travelling 18 km they reached Benniu Weir, and then they travelled 9 km to reach Lücheng Weir, where the river was deep with a bright moon shining overhead and boat trackers were also needed (Y. Lou 1990). In the period of the Qiandao Reign, when Zhou Bida and his family entered Liangzhe provinces by boat, they suffered from the headwind from the south in Danyang, as noted by the quotation, "in Wuxi County, the south wind was blowing strongly and boat trackers had to advance it inch by inch with their shanks half buried in the mud." (B. Zhou 1990) When he traveled from Lin'an to Yixing on the Grand Canal, wild winds and low water levels slowed his progress to less than one kilometer per day, and in the Wangting section, the wind changed direction, making it impossible for boat trackers to move the boat at all (B. Zhou 1990). As the section between Xixing and Qianqing of the Liangzhe East Canal was clogged and its water was less than one meter deep, boat towing was the only viable mode of transportation, although this was often difficult for people to endure, necessitating the redistribution of goods to other boats (H. Zhang 1990: 7135).

Boat trackers were a popular method of sailing and were in great demand. In the Northern Song Dynasty, the load capacity of a grain batch transportation boat was evaluated based on the weight of 50 Dan for each boatman onboard. This standard was also applied to batch transportation boats used for salt, iron, and other commodities (Tianyige Cang Ming Chaoben Jiaozheng 2004: 375). The load capacity of 50 Dan refers to the deadweight tonnage of the boat. For indirect transportation boats, 20% of the load capacity was reserved for the boat owner's private goods, while the remaining 80% was used for carrying grains. To comply with this rule, boat owners needed to hire one boatman for every 40 Dan of rice on the boat (S. Xu 2014: 6979). The deadweight tonnage of a boat was calculated by loading 40 Dan of rice for every 50 Dan of space, configured with a boatman. For fine goods with a deadweight tonnage of 50 Dan, only 40 Dan and one boat tracker were needed (S. Xu 2014: 6948). The Huainan Canal and the Bianhe River were used for shipping grain, with a total volume of 6 million Dan each year. If we calculate the number of boatmen needed for every 40 Dan, we arrive at a total of 150,000. If this volume of grain transportation was completed in three seasons (S. Xu 2014: 4098) and the same group of boatmen were used for batch transportation, then 50,000 boat trackers would be needed. Adding the number of boat trackers used in other batch transportation boats would yield an even greater figure. In addition to boat trackers, oxen were also commonly used as a driving force for boats. In the 4th year of the Jingde Reign (AD 1007), Emperor Zhenzong issued an imperial edict stating that the local government should not ban the use of oxen or donkeys as a driving force for commercial boats (S. Xu 2014: 9588). According to the *Anecdotage of the Song Dynasty*, in the 9th year of the Shaoxing Reign (AD 1139), the famous monk, Mr. Shen, contributed the Huayan Sutra to the Pans in Wujiang County from Pu'an Town of Huzhou Prefecture. The book mentioned that during a dry year, sailing was difficult, so the Pans had to borrow an ox to pull the boat forward (Y. He 2008: 214). However, when the boat was heavy and the river was dry, even oxen could not move the boat. "From May till June, no raindrops were seen, the river was left only 30–40 cm of muddy water. The boatmen were striking drums to drive oxen forward, but the boat remained motionless." (X. Zheng 1990).

Boat towing was the dominant method for sailing boats, and paths for boat trackers were built along the banks of rivers. The famous painting, *Riverside Scene at Qingming Festival,* depicts boat trackers struggling on the dedicated path for boat trackers on the banks. In the fourth year of the Shaosheng Reign (AD 1097), an imperial order was issued mandating that a space of 5 m breadth of the banks be reserved for boat tracker's paths, which were prohibited from being privately or officially occupied. Those who violated the order would be prosecuted at the Kaifeng Prefecture, and whistle-blowers would be rewarded from the reserved fund of salt taxation. As cases of banks being invaded and occupied by families living on both banks of the Bianhe River were reported from time to time, witnesses were encouraged to lodge accusations against the offenders to the Bianhe River Administration via lower officials (T. Li 2004: 11,716). In his collection of essays, *Walk on the Bank of the Bianhe River*, Kong Pingzhong described the elm trees planted on the banks of the Bianhe River,

Long dikes were long as a thread,

As if hidden in the shade of elms stamped by hammers.

Who planted such elms in those years?

They have grown into large shade for passengers. (P. Kong 1990)

This scene can also be found in the painting of *Riverside Scene at Qingming Festival.* The repair of dikes along the Huainan Canal was also of great importance, and elm and willow trees were planted on the dikes. In the fifth year of the Tiansheng Reign (AD 1027), the emperor ordered prefectures and counties along the canal to add officials to manage the dikes and banks of the Grand Canal and to repair the desolate banks by planting elm trees. Failure to comply would result in penalties or lowered official posts (S. Xu 2014: 9613).

In the Southern Song Dynasty, willow trees were planted on the track path of the Liangzhe West Canal. Yang Wanli described the scene in a poem, saying, "Tonight I stayed at Jingxi hostel, but I could not sleep long before the daybreak. In the morning, I, wrapped in a quilt, witnessed boats passing by my window, with hundreds of green willows dangling on both banks." Boat trackers were a common sight on these paths, as they guided the boats through the canal. The boat trackers were often seen "struggling forward like lines of black ants," while burning torches illuminated their path at night (W. Yang 2007: 1497). Huang Luo, a compassionate official, observed the plight of the boat trackers who stumbled down in heavy snow, prompting him to think of ways to help them. When he later served as the deputy governor of the supply commission, he ordered the purchase of thick cotton clothes and straw raincoats for the boat trackers and allocated more food to them. In addition, he directed the prefectures and counties from Jingdu to Jingkou route to pave the path with stone bricks, to ensure that the boat trackers were not exposed to slippery and muddy terrain. The paving of the tow path with bricks was a magnificent project that drew admiration from the ambassadors of the Jin Kingdom (X. Yuan 1990). During the Jiading Reign, the central government repaired and dredged the canal section of Zhenjiang Prefecture, and subsequently paved the tow paths with stone bricks. "The path was paved with stone from the south of Yaocheng in Zhenjiang to Lücheng, ensuring safe passage for boat trackers without the need to navigate slippery and muddy roads (X. Lu 1990: 2367)."

There are some records that describe the collapse or occupation of boat tracker paths. In the later period of the Southern Song Dynasty, the Hangzhou section of the canal had been obsolete for several years due to a lack of repair, which had led to encroachment by the 500 households adjacent to the banks (S. Qian 1990: 3675). As a result, the banks and dikes had become collapsed and ruined, causing the boat tracker's path to become narrower and more difficult to navigate. The damage to the paths was rooted in both the overriding by boat trackers and occupation by farmers. In the fourteenth year of the Jiading Reign, Wang Gang, the local mayor, repaired the paths, making them less muddy, and eliminating the need for boat trackers to tuck up their trouser legs when towing boats (H. Zhang 1990: 7136). Regarding occupation by farmers, the width of the path was recorded on a stone tablet on the Yanqiao Bridge across the canal in the fourth year of the Zhiping Reign, erected by the administrator of criminal affairs, which mentioned the width of the path after being occupied by farmers, which was estimated to be around 3–4 m wide.Twenty years later, farmers living in nearby areas began to encroach the banks by building thousands of houses, which left a very narrow space for the tow path, leading to the gradual narrowing of the river courses. The negotiation resulted in the illegal constructions not being demolished, but owners had to spare the equivalent space from their courtyard to compensate for the encroached areas. The space would be used as wooden railing areas to protect the banks, and some fines were collected by the local government as a fund for repairing the wooden railings (S. Su 2010: 3298). In reality, this simply legalized the encroachment, albeit in a disguised form, leading to further damage to the boat tracker path.

2.2.4 Summary

In the Northern Song Dynasty, the Bianhe River was the only one among the four major canals that could be used as a completely navigable river course. Although the Yellow River served as the primary waterway for shipping during the same period, navigation in winter was restricted due to the presence of sand and ice. In the early years of the Yuanfeng Reign, the section between Luoyang and Kaifeng was available for year-round navigation. However, when the strategy of guiding water from Luoyang to Kaifeng was implemented, the river's water level was reduced to a depth of only 1–1.6 m. This depth was suitable only for grain vessels with a load capacity of 300 Liao (98,400 L) to 400 Liao (131,200 L). Vessels with a load capacity of 1000 Liao (328,000 L) or larger, including large boats with a load capacity of 10 thousand Dan (670,000 L), were difficult to sail.

Compared to the Bianhe River, the Huainan Canal, the Liangzhe West Canal, and the Liangzhe East Canal had relatively limited water advantages due to their different topographical features. Most canals experienced water scarcity, with the exception of the Liangzhe West Canal, which utilized Taihu Lake as its water source, and the Liangzhe East Canal, which drew its water from Jianhu Lake. Typically, the depth of these three canals was around 1.7 m, with some sections having a depth of approximately one meter. Only the southern section of the Liangzhe West Canal boasted a depth of 2.6 m. Almost all the canals had a drought period or some shallow-water sections. These three canals were suitable for grain vessels with a load capacity of 500 Liao or less, which generally accommodated boats with a load capacity of 200 or 300 Liao. They were not suitable for boats with a load capacity of one thousand Liao or 10 thousand Dan.

The mechanism of weirs and sluice gates was established to resolve the connectivity issue between different sections of the Huainan, the Liangzhe West and the Liangzhe East canals, which were at varying water levels. The conventional approach was to convert weirs into sluice gates, and appoint supervisors and sluice soldiers responsible for operating the sluice gates, which had been introduced as a rule. In the

Northern Song Dynasty, the Bianhe River and the Huainan Canal had implemented a routine practice of a winter break. Generally, the sluice gates were opened and closed three times a day, while another rule was set to open when one hundred boats were gathered. The reservoir tide gates were opened and closed once a day, in accordance with the ebb and flow of tides, governing the gates in the canals whose source was the Yangtze River, the Huaihe River, or the Qiantang River. The weir and sluice gates enabled river voyages between different topographies and established a standard for the sizes and shapes of boats.

The canals were characterized by their shallow depth and gentle flow, which made them navigable for small boats using barge poles, oars, and sculls as their driving forces. However, medium and large boats, which had longer ranges to cover, relied mainly on sails and boat towing. While sailing was possible in tailwinds by hoisting sails, such occurrences were infrequent. More common were variable wind directions and headwinds, which made sails one of the frequently used methods in inland river sailing. Both passing through the weirs or sluice gates, or sailing in the middle way, boat trackers were the most effective driving force. Paths for boat trackers, which were made of bricks or stone tablets, were built on both banks of the rivers or canals, to prevent them from treading on the muddy road. Additionally, the central government issued regulations for the maintenance and protection of these tow paths.

The research on the grain shipping system of the Song dynasty offers a major perspective for analyzing the canal studies of that era. However, it is imperative to also direct attention to the basic questions relating to water management and inland river navigation. From the detailed discussions on water management and navigation methods, clear descriptions can be made of the forms of navigation, technical features of canal boats and their shapes, sizes, and structures, as well their functions. At the same time, such studies can lay the groundwork and serve as a point of reference for research on the roles and activities of boatmen, boat trackers, merchants, and passengers.

2.3 The Navigation Methods of Other Inland Rivers

In the Song Dynasty, the shipping industry thrived on all inland rivers, including the Yangtze River, canals, and other inland rivers. Among the commonly used modes of transportation on inland rivers, including the Yangtze River and the Grand Canal, the method of hoisting sails was the most prevalent. However, in shallow watercourses, oars, yulohs, and boat trackers were necessary to propel boats, and towing was the preferred method. Prior research focused primarily on navigation methods on the Yangtze River, with little attention given to other inland rivers. Therefore, this section will particularly examine the use of towing boats.

2.3.1 *Punt-Poles, Oars, Yulohs and Sails in Inland River Navigation*

Punt-poles rely on the reaction force of a bamboo pole against the riverbed to push ships, generating significant propulsive force, but are limited to use in shallow rivers. Oars use the reaction force of a blade to propel boats, while yulohs function similarly to oars, but can continuously produce propulsive force underwater without the virtual work produced by oars in the air. Sails harness wind power to generate driving force for boats. Punt-poles, oars, yulohs and sails are all ship propellers whose technical characteristics, structures and functions have been fully discussed in *The Shipbuilding History of China* by Xi Longfei, as well as others' works (L. Xi 2000; L. Xi 2004). This section will examine the application of punt-poles, oars, yulohs, and sails on inland rivers with varying flow regimes in the Song Dynasty.

2.3.1.1 Punt-Poles, Oars, and Yulohs in Inland River Navigation

Unlike the Yangtze River, which boasts a wide surface and turbulent, fast-moving waters, other inland rivers have narrower surfaces and thus, rougher and swifter flows. The water regimes of inland rivers in China are also diverse and complex, with numerous wide rivers such as the Yellow River, the downstream portion of the Qiantang River, and the Pearl River, as well as smaller rivers such as the Xiangjiang River, the Ganjiang River, and major branches of the Hanshui River, alongside countless narrow, shallow brooks that present their own complexities and diversities. Punt-poles and yulohs were commonly employed for navigation on small and medium-sized inland waterways, particularly in small boats requiring less propulsive force.

In the regions south of the Yangtze River, a vast network of rivers with varying depths existed, which were navigable by boats with a limited load capacity ranging from 300 to 400 Dan. As a result, punt-poles and yulohs became the preferred navigation tools. For instance, Jiangnan East Province had several such rivers. For example, the Xinlinpu river, outside the city of Jiankang, was dry in spring and winter but abundant in summer and autumn. Boats carrying a load of 50 Dan could sail on it. Similarly, Jiangningpu was deep enough for boats carrying a load of 300 Dan in autumn and summer, but only half that in spring and winter. The Molingpu was also navigable by boats carrying a load of 300 Dan in autumn and summer, but only 150 Dan in spring and winter (Y. Zhou 1990: 1619–20). The Jingdu River, located between Changtang Lake and Liyang County, Jiangning Prefecture, was only 15 m wide, and boats on the river could carry a load of 50 Dan in 3 m deep water in spring and summer, or carry only 20 Dan in 0.33 m deep water in autumn and winter (Y. Zhou 1990: 1551). In Shexian County of Huizhou, the Yangzhi, Bushe, and Fengle rivers were navigable only in spring and summer (Y. Luo 1990: 7367), while the East Asian rainy season, also known as the plum-rain season, caused the rivers in Huizhou to rise and become deep enough for boats to move. Travelling traders usually made rafts in advance for the next year's navigation. After the rainy season, the rivers were prone to low levels with significant sand and gravel deposits, which posed a danger to cargo boats (J. Xu 1990). In Xinzhou, surrounded by mountains on two sides, only the west river led to Xigang of Poyang County, and it easily rose or dried up during the rainy season, making it difficult for large ships to sail. Hence, it was believed that small boats marginally wider than fishing boats were the best choice for grain batch vessels (S. Yang et al. 1990).

The mountainous regions of Liangzhe East Province contained a multitude of small rivers. During Fang Dacong's boat journey through Yanzhou, with a load capacity of 50 Liao, passing by Dalang Beach in Liangzhe East Province, he was advised that "the boat was unsuitable for navigation in that area". Instead, he was suggested "to split the original order of hiring one boat into two boats with a load capacity of 20 Liao each." (D. Fang 1990) Fang Dacong found it remarkable that the Tianmu River, originating from Tianmu Mountain and "running southward to converge with the rivers in Liangzhe provinces, could accommodate big boats with a load capacity of over 100 Dan, but only small boats were suitable for the navigation of Dalang Beach. If grain boats from Zhanghua to Qiantang River could use the underflow waterways, then the Tianmu River would become a gathering place for grain boats in Fenshui County." (Y. Zheng et al. 1990: 4407) In Huiji County, the Caoe River and Roye River could accommodate boats with a load capacity of 500 Dan and 50 Dan, respectively. Similarly, Xixiao River in Shanyin County could carry boats with a load capacity of 500 Dan. Shanxi Brook in Shengxian County could carry boats with a load capacity of 100 Dan in spring and summer, while Huanjiang River in Zhuji County could carry boats with a load capacity of 200 Dan. Puyang River and the Canal in Xiaoshan County could carry boats with a load capacity of 200 Dan, while Yuyao River in Yuyao County could carry boats with a load capacity of 500 Dan. Shangyu River in Shangyu County could accommodate boats with a load capacity of 500 Dan during the spring tide and boats with a load capacity of 200 Dan during the neap tide (S. Shi et al.1990: 6938). The upstream of the Guanhe River could only accommodate boats with a load capacity of 10 Dan. The upstream of Yongan Brook in Xianjü County of Taizhou could only carry small boats, while the downstream of Yongan River in Xianjü County of Taizhou could carry boats with a load capacity of 20 Dan (Q. Chen 1990: 7460, 7466). Such small rivers are abundant in Jiangnan West Province, Guangnan Province, Fujian Province, and Jinghu Province, but their enumeration is beyond the scope of this discussion.

As mentioned above, boats navigating shallow rivers are often propelled by punt-poles or oars and yulohs, which is the most efficient method. In Zhao Yanwei's *Notes on Historical Records* (Vol. 9), it is mentioned that "the rivers in the southeast of Liangzhe East Province are shallow and about 16–22 cm deep with gravel deposits on the riverbed," with sandbars present "here and there." Punt-poles used in this region were made of bamboo with an iron drill at one end, while other types of poles, such as those with a shoulder and a head made of wood with an angle at one end, were also available. Punt-poles were a common method for sailing boats in the river branches on the Taihu Plain, as pointed out by Su Shi, who noted that, "in the past, punt-poles were used on both official and privately-owned boats to sail eastward from Suzhou without the need for boat trackers. However, since the Qingli Reign (AD 10,410–1048), boat-tracker paths have been built." (Toqta 1977: 10,814) When Yang Wanli traveled from Liangzhe provinces to Guangnan East Province, on his way from Nanxiong to Shaozhou, his boat was propelled by punt-poles on the North River, as described in the following lines from one of his poems:

> Last night spring thunders were blowing over the land,
>
> This morning punt poles lifted up clear water from the rising river. (W. Yang 2007: 761)

When boats passed through sandbars, they were directed by punt-poles. During Yang Wanli's journey through the Lianyu Sandbars of the North River, the punters wearing yellow hats (punters were often referred to as "yellow-hat men" due to the belief that yellow soil could block water) could keep the boat in the correct direction by making two or three punting maneuvers, even though it was dangerous to sail by too quickly (*Jinxiu Wanhua Gu* 1900). He wrote, "the punters' sudden shouts of passing by the sandbars startled me out of my dream, and I was awakened up to witness the challenging operation." (W. Yang 2007: 840) According to Liu Zihui, when boats traveled on the clear raging waters with jagged rows of stone on the riverbed and thunder roaring in the sky, it is necessary to trust the punters' poles with one's precious life. For example, going through the Qidan Sandbar of South Jianzhou required the use of punt-poles. Therefore, these accounts show that when a boat goes upstream through sandbars, its boatmen needed to use punt-poles. (Z. Liu 1990a, b) During Yang Wanli's journey upstream through the sandbars of the North River, they encountered a headwind that was comparable to "sailing a heavy iron boat in the Milky Way." (W. Yang 2007: 822) In another poem, he described the scene when they sailed with punt-poles on the Qiantang River. "The stagnating water created four or five sandbars in the wide but not deep section of the river. The shipmaster requested the boatmen to pass through them one by one. Several people joined hands to control the boat, but they unexpectedly broke a dozen punt poles. The mast was shaky and insecure in the turbulent water, and boatmen dare not compete with the banks. So, the boatmen began to replace their broken poles as if enemies were approaching." "Sailing in the upstream and shallow water, the giant tower ship got stuck and kept motionlessly even if many oars and punt-poles were used to drive it forward." (W. Yang 2007: 1263) When Lou Yao returned from abroad in the sixth year of the Qiandao Reign (AD 1170) and passed by Wushidalang and Shiwulang sandbars in the south section of the Qiantang River to Chuzhou, locals zealously came to help push boats in groups of five or ten people. As the boat was small, one punter was enough to sail it. However, when the boat rolled on the rough water, the punter suddenly fell into the water with his pole, which frightened observers. Fortunately, he possessed excellent swimming skills and could swim back to the boat easily, as if walking on the ground, and successfully controlled the boat again. (Y. Lou 2013: 42)

Oars and yulohs are traditional means of navigation in wide and deep waterways, where they remain effective even when sailing downstream through sandbars. A historical account by Fan Chengda on his return journey from Guangnan West

Province illustrates the use of a multi-oar boat on the Xiangjiang River. "Six oars were employed to drive the boat through the sandbars, blazing its way in snow-like waves," (C. Fan 1990) demonstrating the efficiency of oars in navigating through difficult waters. When Lou Yao's large boat sailed downstream in the lower reaches of the Qiantang River to the ferry of Yupu Town, "they got stranded due to the lower tides" and "had to be towed and moved forward slowly. When they approached Mountain Miao, they resumed to using yulohs. After the tides came in, the boatman planed to drive fast with oars and yulohs, but the boat advanced inch by inch, which horrified the boatmen. After a short break, the boatmen continued to row the boat forward. It took them a long time to pass the sandbar. Later, the boat was towed forward for more than five kilometers." (Y. Lou 2013: 7) The above quotations highlight the conventional navigation methods adopted on the lower reaches of the Qiantang River, where towing boats was a common method when the tide was falling and the river shallow, while yulohs were used when the tide was rising and the water deepened. On lakes with no wind, yulohs were the most popular propellers, as Xu Xi's voyage from Jiangnan West Province to Bianliang, the capital city, demonstrates. Upon reaching Poyang Lake, he saw scullers rowing the boat silently, and flags fluttering in two huge red ships with a load capacity of ten thousand Hu (300,000 kg) (S. Zhang 1990a, b, c), proving the widespread use of yulohs for propelling boats. Similarly, boats on the Huaihe River were towed upstream by trackers and propelled downstream by yulohs day and night (Y. Mei 1980: 278). Hence, it is evident that yulohs were common in the navigation of the Yangtze River.

2.3.1.2 Lifting Sails in Inland Navigation

In wide rivers like the Yangtze, boats had only limited opportunity to make use of the tailwind by lifting sails. Boats sailing in narrower rivers enjoyed even fewer such opportunities, as it was more difficult to leverage side winds, which would be necessary along the zigzag course of narrow rivers. Only when the wind was blowing in the same direction as the boat's navigation, or when the angle between them was relatively small, was it efficient to advance boats by employing sails. Despite these limitations, sails were still utilized in inland river navigation, as evidenced by Yang Wanli's descriptions of boats with raised sails in his poems, including *Passing by Wangting in a Boat, Passing by Anren City by Lifting Sails, Leaving for Shikou in a Tailwind on the Fifteenth Morning of the Journey* and others, which portray boats swiftly traveling upstream southward in Yanzhou of Liangzhe East Province. Some quotations from these poems follow:

> At sunset, the sails were lowered at Wushi beach, and next morning the boat started out by the bank of Zhaixi Brook.
>
> Good news from punters came that a boat travelled twice journey in the tailwind than one day without wind.

> If ten sails were hung up, the boat took us short time to reach Sanqu afar.

> Our worry was that the wind was still blowing at the end of our journey.

We had to donate our sails and wind to other boatmen.

The power generated by wind is superior to that of oars and yulohs. Moreover, boats with lifted sails in a tailwind could travel faster than smaller ones without lifted sails. This is exemplified by the following lines written by Yang Wanli. "Waves were roaring at daybreak from night, and to overturn the sky the north wind tried. Before sails were lifted, our boat passed Qingni by. In an instant, we are embracing Yusi by our side. Leaving countless small boats behind, we were acclaimed as immortals who can fly." Yang Wanli also recounts how "the sails were lifted because the wind began to blow," with "the boatmen drumming and shouting aloud." However, "one of them sat idly watching the goose feathers floating on the water after he spread the sails on the tall mast." Additionally, Yang Wanli observed that small boats made full use of the tailwind by changing pieces of cloth and umbrellas into sails, and how the fishers sat idly on the stem while the green bamboo punt-pole was erected as a mast with a piece of cloth hung on it as sails. Yang Wanli's journey began in Xuancheng of Jiangnan East Province, passing by Ningguo, Jixi, and Fuliang, and finally reaching Leping, where he changed his land travel into boat sailing. During his voyage, he witnessed "two kids in a small fishing boat putting their oars and punt-poles aside, and opening an umbrella in fine weather. To his surprise, they knew how to use the umbrella as a sail rather than merely as shelter from the rain." (W. Yang 2007: 666, 66, 816, 1263, 1500, 1796)

In the sixth year of the Qiandao Reign (AD 1170), Lou Yao was journeying from the region south of the Yangtze River back to Chuzhou of Liangzhe East Province. He left Liuhe Pogoda and boarded a boat at Mountain Miao. On the 26th day of the second lunar month, he passed by Fuyang. While sailing, a headwind slowed the boat's progress until it arrived at Sanjiangkou where an east wind began to blow gently. The sails were to be lifted in response to this. However, a sudden west wind blew wildly, causing the boat to be towed forward until it reached Tonglu. The following day, the sails were again lifted, this time in an east wind. However, the east wind soon died down. (Y. Lou 2013: 42) Zhao Fan recorded a journey going upstream on the the Tongjiang River in a tailwind with the sail lifted. He noted that the current of Tongjiang River typically flowed fast, making it laborious for boat trackers. However, the journey was relatively easy with the sail lifted in a gentle southwest wind (F. Zhao 1990). Zhou Bida also described sailing experiences. When he traveled along Jingxi Brook from Yixing to Liyang, a headwind shifted into a tailwind, allowing the boat to travel quickly once its sails were lifted. In contrast, when he sailed on the Panjiang River in Raozhou, a tailwind only allowed the boat to move 10–15 km a day due to the broken sails and the river's zigzagged watercourse (B. Zhou 1990). These historical records suggest that navigating inland waterways with sails was challenging due to the unpredictable wind directions and the zigzagged watercourse.

Zhou Bida's diary mentioned the use of sails during river navigation in Jiangnan West Province. In the third year of the Qiandao Reign (AD 1167), he described his travels upstream along the Ganjiang River to Ji'an, setting sail from Nankang County in a gentle north wind, which soon changed to a south wind. After passing by Zuoli and Yanglan, the boat was anchored in the harbor of Zhuxi Brook, where the north wind began to blow again. This change in wind direction occurred twice during his 40-km voyage. On the second day of November in the Chinese Sexagenary Cycle Calendar, "the boat travelled 65 km in a tailwind," demonstrating the use of sails in favorable wind conditions. On the 22nd day of November, sails were also used in a tailwind despite the rain, and the boat moved 20 km. On the 28th day day of November in the Chinese Sexagenary Cycle Calendar, the boat arrived at Xinlang County at nine to eleven o'clock. In the sixth year of the Qiandao Reign (AD 1170), Zhou Bida and his family left Jizhou of Jiangnan West Province, and entered Qiantang River via the Yangtze River. On the 31st day in the Chinese Sexagenary Cycle Calendar, they departed from Xingan County with a strong south wind and reached Linjiang Military Prefecture in the afternoon, indicating the use of sails in downstream river navigation. In the eighth year of the Qiandao Reign (AD 1172), on his way from Lin'an to Ji'an, Zhou Bida's boat travelled up the Ganjing River in Jishui County. The north wind blew gently, and after a divination ceremony, the boatmen hoisted the sails. However, after traveling only a short distance, the north wind changed to the south, which was unusual for the season. (B. Zhou 1990) Zhou Bida's diary indicates that sails were rarely lifted in the navigation of inland rivers in a tailwind. According to the records in *The Trip to Guilin* written by Fan Chengda during his voyage to Guilin of Guangnan West Province to take office, "Wuzi port of Poyang Lake was rampant with burglars. So only by going in the tailwind by lifting sails dare one boat with other companies go through this area." During Fan Chengda's journey upstream the Ganjiang River, the boat sailed in a tailwind at full speed with the sails as propellers, and anchored in the Linjiang Military Prefecture." In other inland rivers, sails were intermittently used in tailwind navigation. During Su Zhe's voyage on the Sishui River, his boat got stranded when approaching Taoyuan in a headwind. After furling the sails, the boat was pushed to the ferry by oars. However, when the river rose overnight, Su Zhe's boat traveled 50 km in a tailwind with the help of the sail (Z. Su 1987: 140).

2.3.2 Boat Trackers and Towpaths in the Inland River Navigation

Boat trackers served as one of the main driving forces for inland river transportation, especially for shipping passengers and grains. Boat tracking was the most important and effective method for sailing upstream in inland rivers. Water transportation was the most important mode of transport during that period, with the main inland rivers serving as the fundamental transportation network, thereby necessitating the construction of towpaths along these heavily trafficked waterways.

2.3.2.1 Boat Trackers on Inland Rivers

Boat towing was the most important navigation method, particularly when navigating upstream or during periods of low water. Boat trackers emerged as the most effective driving force for this purpose. Mei Yaochen's poem cited in the previous section attests to the utilization of boat trackers in sailing upstream on the Huai River, as he notes that "the boats were towed forward upstream by trackers and were propelled downstream by yulohs, day and night." Yang Wanli also provides a description of boats sailing on the Huai River, stating that "boats sailing by both banks of the Huai River headed in opposite directions, but the ripples could make communications easy though in the same river." (W. Yang 2007: 1403) This implies that on the busy sections of the river, boats needed to be towed, and it that it was impossible for boats sailing upstream and downstream to navigate the same course. Therefore, conventional rules were followed, and boats sailed along different courses.

However, many inland river banks were unfit for boat-towing. Consequently, boats had to cross the river, then chose to sail along the river bank with towpaths, like the ones on the Yangtze River. During Zhang Shunmin's journey to Chenzhou, his boat traveled upstream on the Xiangjiang River in Tanzhou and was towed along the west bank against a headwind until it arrived at the mouth where the Liuyang River joins the Xiangjiang River. On the first day of the Chinese Sexagenary Cycle Calendar, when Zhang Shunmin departed from Tanzhou, his boat was towed along the west bank of the river on a windless day. On the fourth day of the Chinese Sexagenary Cycle Calendar, as there was no wind, his boat crossed the river to be towed along the east bank (S. Zhang 1990a, b, c). On Zhang Shunmin's return journey to Chuzhou, his boat sailed southward upstream the Qiantang River. While passing Fuyang, "the boat moved slowly in a headwind. However, when it got to Sanjiangkou, the east wind began to blow, and the sails were lifted. Later, a strong west wind blew again, and the boat had to be towed forward against a headwind until it reached Tonglu." When the boat reached Yanzhou, "it rained heavily and at noon, the west wind blew up, causing the river to rise sharply. The boatmen were exhausted from towing the boat and stopped to rest several times." (Y. Lou 2013: 42) Zhao Fan also recorded towing a boat upstream on the Qiantang River (the section in Yangzhou called Tongjiang River or Tonglu River). "In most cases, the currents of the Tongjiang River were strong, making it difficult to tow a boat upstream." (F. Zhao 1990) On Su Song's journey to take office in Wuzhou, "the boat needed to travel upstream on the fast-flowing Tongjiang River, making it too difficult for the boat trackers to pull it forward. Eventually, the boat was pushed off course by the strong currents, and the mast was broken." (H. Zou 1990).

Boat trackers also served as the driving force for sailing upstream along other rivers. In particular, the fleet of grain ships traveling via the Yellow River was equipped with water troops who acted as boat trackers when sailing upstream along the river. However, in the seventh year of the Tiansheng Reign (AD 1209), the supply commissioner of the Threefold State Finance Administration in Charge of Salt, Iron and Taxation noted that "the boat trackers on the Yellow River were insufficiently informed of the dangers of the roaring waters, resulting in many cases of drowning."

In response, Emperor Renzong ordered the recruitment of two thousand people from the south bank of the Yellow River to establish a water force to serve as boat trackers (T. Li 2004: 2506). During the Tang Dynasty, towing boats was the primary means of transporting grain to Changan via the Yellow River (Y. Wang 2003: 3347). In the thirty-first year of the Shaoxing Reign (AD 1161), Liu Qi fought against the Jin Kingdom's invasion on the Qinghe River. "Jin's grain boats, covered with hair felt, were pulled by boat trackers. Liu Qi responded by recruiting skilled divers to chisel the ships and sink them." (X. Zhang 1990: 5672) Furthermore, in the poem *Droughts in Chenzhou and Caizhou,* Zheng Xie described the severe drought in the two prefectures. He noted that "boats as heavy as mountains were difficult to tow out of the mire," (X. Zheng 1990) indicating that the method of towing boats was also used for navigation on the Yinghe River and Ruhe River in Chenzhou and Caizhou. In the Northern Song Dynasty, sacrifices of grains and annual taxation from Guangnan West Province to the central government were delivered to the capital via small boats. These sacrifices were then reorganized into large batches of different groups in Guizhou and assigned a convoy chief and boatmen for successive transportation. However, many difficulties arose in sailing and towing the boat, resulting in several days being required to deliver the sacrifices to Quanzhou and Yongzhou (S. Xu 2014: 6810–11). In addition, boat trackers were necessary for grain shipping during this period. Finally, in the Southern Song Dynasty, army provisions from Fuzhou, Qianzhou, Kaizhou, and Nanping Military Prefecture were shipped upstream to the north of Sichuan Province and Shanxi Province via towing boats (S. Xu 2014: 6986).

Sailing upstream often required the use of boat trackers to tow boats, especially in areas with dangerous shoals. On Yang Wanli's voyage on the North River of Guangnan East Province, his boat sailed out of Zhenyang Gorge, where he noted that "it was hard to tow a boat upstream on the shoal in the gorge." (W. Yang 2007: 926) During the Southern Song Dynasty, Xiangyang served as a major garrison town, and much of the grain needed by troops stationed in Jingzhou and Ezhou was shipped upstream on the Hanjiang River. Similarly, the transportation of grain and military supplies for the Guangnan and Jinghu provinces relied heavily on the Hanshui River, where boats often lined up stem to stem on a daily basis. "The Haijiang River from Bozhong Mountain, Canglang River, to Dabie Mountain was fast flowing; and on the route upstream from Hankou to Yingzhou, there were comparatively few shoals with sand and gravel, while the course from Yingzhou and Xiangyang to the upper reaches of the river, there were 36 dangerous shoals." There is a saying that the section of the Hanshui River from Yingzhou to Xiangyang was full of shoals with sand and gravel. After frost's descent in winter, water levels fell, which resulted in boats being stranded easily. Therefore, passing through shoals required the aid of boat trackers. In order for large boats to pass through shoals, it was necessary to unload bulk cargoes and transport them by smaller boats, a practice referred to as "Pantan" in Chinese. Bamboo strip towlines, known as "Baizhang" in Chinese, were used to tow boats upstream. If a boat's destination was Xiangyang, new bamboo strip towlines were required at Ezhou on the Hanjiang River. However, if the destination was Junzhou or Guanghua Military Prefecture, new towlines were replaced at Xiangyang, a process called "Huanzhu" in Chinese (S. Xu 2014: 6996, 7005, 7006, 7678). This replacement of towlines indicated that the ropes were excessively worn out. The practice of using bamboo strip towlines originated in Dongting Lake and Xiangjiang River, and was later popularized in Chuanxia Province. This is indicated by the following quote: "To travel in the river course between Dongting Lake and Xiangjiang River, long bamboo-made ropes were used to pull the boat upstream, so they were called bamboo strip towlines ("Baizhang" in Chinese), which was often used in the river navigation of Chuanxia region." (Y. Sun 1990a, b) *Travelogues in Wu Area by Ship,* Volume 1, written by Fan Chengda, documented that when Fan's boat arrived at Xintan Shoal, the most treacherous shoal in the Three Gorges, it was necessary to unload all the cargoes on board and deliver them on small boats in order to survive. The residents on both sides of Xintan Shoal, who were professional cargo porters known as "Tanzi" in Chinese, also towed the empty boat through the shoal. The goods were subsequently reloaded onto the original boat. Professional cargo porters were also present on other inland river shoals. On Zhang Shunmin's journey to Chenzhou, when his boat was passing through Zhaoling Shoal and three other shoals, drums were sounded as a signal to locals for assistance in "Pantan". The locals guided the boat with flags in their hands from Sanmen. The boatmen did not need to do anything during the emptying of the boat to go through the shoal. When official boats passed through these shoals, locals were assembled to unload and reload cargoes, as well as tow boats. Similarly, navigating the Yangtze River required "Pantan" when boats needed to pass shoals (S. Zhang 1990a, b, c). Local porters and boat trackers, or "Tanzi", were employed for this purpose.

When heavy boats navigated shallow rivers, oars and yulohs proved ineffective, and the only viable alternative was to tow the boat forward. In the Northern Song Dynasty, a large troop was stationed in Hebei Province, and the annual transportation of grain supply for the army was conducted via the Jijü Spring waterway in Baozhou. It was laborious for soldiers on duty to tow boats in the shallow and dangerous waters (S. Xu 2014: 9612). Lou Yao's voyage from Chuzhou to Hangzhou on the Qiantang River encountered difficulties when his boat became stranded in the Yupu Town section, and had to be moved slowly by boat trackers (Y. Lou 2013: 7). In the Southern Song Dynasty, the Qiantang River and the Hanshui River served as key channels for the transportation of grain and passengers. Even in sections with lower water levels or during the drought season, these channels were used by heavily loaded boats, which were moved forward by boat trackers. The Lanxi River, on the upper reaches of the Qiantang River, was a vital connector between Hangzhou and the two other prefectures, Yanzhou and Quzhou. Despite its shallow water level, boats with heavy loads always needed to travel on it. Yang Wanli's poem, *Sailing on Lanxi River,* describes the scene as follows: "the sound of water hitting the gravels on its riverbed below suggest it being shallow, the bamboo hats shadows depict the boat trackers struggling to move the boat slow." (W. Yang 2007: 1248)

2.3.2.2 Towpaths of Inland Rivers

Several larger inland rivers played a critical role in the transportation of both passengers and grain, with many heavily-loaded boats regularly traversing these waterways. Such rivers include the North River, the Xiangjiang River, the Ganjiang River, the Qiantang River, the Wusong River, the Yellow River, the Hanshui River, and the Jialing River. The North River served as an important connector between Guangnan Province and the inland regions, while the Xiangjiang and Ganjiang Rivers were key channels linking Jingnan and Jiangxi provinces with the inland and also connecting Guangnan Province with the inland regions. The Qiantang River served as the primary channel both inside and outside the economically prosperous Liangzhe provinces, and the Wusong River connected Taihu Lake and the sea routes. During the Northern Song Dynasty, the Yellow River was a major channel for passenger and grain transport from the central Shangxi plain to the capital of Bianliang and the south. Additionally, the Huaihe River, particularly the section from Sizhou to Haikou, saw heavy passenger and grain traffic. During the Southern Song Dynasty, the Hanshui River transported military supplies to major frontier counties such as Xiangyang, while the Jiangling River undertook the task of delivering military materials to Sichuan and Shangxi provinces. Towing boats along these rivers was a popular and important navigation method, with towpaths constructed for this purpose.

Su Shi gave a description of the extensive construction of towpaths along the the Wusong River during the Qingli Reign (AD 1041–1048). He stated that "since the Qingli Reign, more towpaths have been constructed on both sides of the Wusong River. Long bridges were built along the river, and thousands of timber piles were placed in the water." Su Shi further observed that "after the long bridge was built, public and private grain transportation became much easier than before." (S. Su 2010: 3384) It is worth noting that the long bridge mentioned in Su Shi's account referred to a towpath along the river bank rather than a bridge across the river. In the Ming Dynasty, Zhou Dashao also documented the construction of towpaths along the Wusong River in the Song Dynasty. He wrote that "they built a 500-m-long bridge (as a towpath) consisting of sixty-one bridge arches and thirty-six bridges on the man-made 4500-m-long stone dike." The bridge mentioned by Zhou Dashao referred to a towpath constructed along the river bank, while the stone dike was a dam built on both sides of the river. The thirty-six bridges were built to prevent sediment and sand from blocking the watercourse. Zhou Dashao also noted that "in terms of floods, the Wusong River flooding ranks first throughout China's history, partly caused by its long towpath. But evidence collected from the Song and Yuan dynasties has proven that the long towpath should not be blamed for the floods." During the Ming Dynasty, it was observed that, "out of the three rivers drawing the Taihu Lake water into the sea, only the Wusong River was available. During the Song and Yuan Dynasties, although the long towpath along the Wusong River had become clogged with silt, the riverbank itself remained in good condition." (D. Zhou 1990) "Although the towpath, built with stones and mud and spanning several dozen kilometers, was good for boat trackers, it went against the natural flow of silt in the river," leading to its accumulation with the rising tide. As a result, during the rainy season in summer and autumn, the water level often rose to around 33 cm above the towpath (S. Su 2010: 3384).

This long towpath was also dubbed "Thousand Bridge". The Wusong River was a major course for grain transportation and trading activities. The sediment problem was solved by retaining the old towpath, building a new one nearby, and transforming the stone bank into bridges. One thousand bridges were built on the original towpath, each featuring a 6.6-m-wide arch. This design allowed sediment to flow through the 6600-m-long passage, preventing the main watercourse from becoming obstructed by sand (S. Su 2010: 3384). In essence, the fundamental solution was to keep the original towpath and create a new one. The 6600-m-long "Thousand Bridge" served as a lengthy towpath along the riverbank. Despite the construction of a thousand bridges across the Wusong River, the task of discharging water would not be achievable even by the addition of a 6600-m-long passage, as documented in *Field Study of Water Regime in Wuxian County* by Shan E. Alternative proposals suggested that the dike be cut off and replaced with wooden bridges to increase its function of water discharging. The proposal stated that "in order to make the river discharge water smoothly, the bank should be turned into bridges." Specifically, it recommended breaking down the Wusong River's dike and building a thousand bridges for grain transportation. Each bridge would be made of two 8-m-long waterproof wooden sticks, three 1.92-m-long crossbeams, and six 6.6-m-long pillars. An arch road with a width of 6.6 m could be constructed, excluding the piers at the beginning and end. In ancient China, one Chinese mile consisted of 360 steps (the term "step" is a traditional unit of distance in ancient China), and if ten bridges were constructed every Chinese mile, a total of 6336-m-wide arch roads and a 4696-m-long towpath would be created. The Ming Dynasty also received a similar proposal, suggesting "cutting the dike of the Wusong River into segments to build one thousand wooden bridges." (D. Zhou 1990) More specifically, the old stone dike along the river was to be segmented and converted into one thousand wooden bridges connected to serve as a new towpath.

The Wusong River, which flows through the flat Yangtze River delta, had banks of soft tidal mudflats that were affected by the ebb and flow of the tide. Therefore, stone dikes or long bridges were necessary to create towpaths for boat trackers. Similar towpaths were constructed along other rivers in the plain area, such as the Guangji River and the Yellow River that run through the North China Plain. In June of the seventh year of the Tiansheng Reign (AD 1029), under the instructions of an imperial edict, the Transfer Agency of Taxation of Jingdong provinces assigned workers to excavate river channels along the riverbank of the Guangji River and the Yellow river. The soil excavated from the river was used to reinforce the embankment, and elms and willows were planted outside the track road (S. Xu 2014: 9544). The embankment of the Jinshui River also served as a towpath, "outside which willows were planted by the soldiers stationed there every spring". (S. Xu 2014: 9612) Towpaths were also built along the Yuhe Canal (also named the Yongji Canal) in Hebei Province. Ouyang Xiu once stated, "The towpath along the Yuhe Canal wasn't repaired any more, so the post of the grain transportation escort had been abolished for a long time." (X. Ouyang 2001: 1809) The towpath mentioned by Ouyang Xiu must have also been a dike built on the riverbank.

In mountainous regions, towpaths along rivers were drilled into the side of the mountain. For instance, in the Tang Dynasty, the Yellow River flowed through Sanmen Gorge, where the chief of Shanjun prefecture, Li Qiwu, had the Dizhu Hill excavated and shaped like a door to create a passage for grain boats. A towpath was then cut into the top of the hill by burning the rock and pouring vinegar (Y. Wang 2003: 3347). Thus, the towpath was built in the gorge. In the early Qing Dynasty, a towpath was constructed on the mountain wall in Sanmen Gorge. During Emperor Kangxi's Reign of the Qing Dynasty, an official stated in his memorial to the throne that boats were towed upstream from the Wohu sandbar for one kilometer from the foot of the mountain, carrying 30 Dan of grains and hauled by 30 boat trackers. It should be noted that towpaths were not submerged in water during river overflows (Henan Tongzhi 1990). Similarly, during the Song Dynasty, towpaths were built at the foot of the mountain along the river in Three Gorges. Yuan Shuoyou described the scene of boats being towed through the Three Gorges as "seen from afar, the trackers looked like busy ants and the huge sails of hundred meters high looked like the kites fluttering in the wind." (S. Yuan 1990)

Some towpaths were formed naturally along the river banks, as described in Deng Shen's *Six Seven-character Chinese Quatrains* on *the Current Situation,* which depicts boat trackers struggling to tow the boat forward on the bank filled with reed flowers, with bamboo strip towlines ("Baizhang" in Chinese) on their shoulders while their oars lay idle (S. Deng 1990). These types of towpaths are different from high built dike towpaths and are prone to being buried in water during flood season. In the sixth year of the Qiandao Reign (AD 1170), on Zhou Bida's trip from Lin'an to Ji'an, his boat had to stop running on Panjiang River (Le'an River) 10 km away from Yong'an imperial office (the administration of minting coins) because the river water buried the towpath (B. Zhou 1990). Towpaths along the Panjiang River were also naturally formed banks. Yang Wanli recorded in his work *Boats Stopped Running on the Rising River in Passing through Xukou,* that the towpaths along the North River in Guangnan East Province were overflowed with water, writing that "the two rivers, Beijiang and Xishui joined at Xukou. the roaring waves made a splendid spectacle. The boat hastened to run up the river, but the news from the noisy crowd came that the towpaths were overflowed." (W. Yang 2007: 810) To build towpaths for such rivers, they had to be built on their physical banks.

2.3.3 Summary

Most of the shallow rivers in the regions south of the Yangtze River were suitable for boats with a load capacity of over 10 Dan (670 L), up to a maximum of 200 Dan (13,400 L). Punt-poles, oars and yulohs were economical and practical methods on such rivers. Punt poles were particularly efficient when the boats encountered sandbars, while oars and yulohs were effective tools for deep watercourses. Sails were also used as propellers in the tailwind. However, due to the limited width of inland rivers, side winds could not be efficiently utilized. Furthermore, changeable wind directions or the absence of wind altogether made the likelihood of lifting sails in the tailwind minimal.

Therefore, the most stable driving force for inland river boats was the act of towing, especially for boats traversing the Yellow River, the Huai River, the Hanshui River, the Xiangjiang River, the Zhejiang River, the Ganjiang River, the North River and other crucial transportation channels. These rivers facilitated the navigation of numerous heavily-laden vessels, which predominantly travelled upstream by means of boat trackers. As for the rivers in the plain area, most towpaths were built on the dikes or utilizing long bridges as towpaths along their banks. For the rivers flowing through the gorge, their towpaths were usually cut onto the foot of the mountain by the water. Additionally, some rivers utilized their natural banks as towpaths.

The study of the navigation methods utilized on inland rivers yields not only insights into the distribution of ships on rivers of different water regiments, the shipping technology and its application in the Song Dynasty, but also lays a solid foundation for diving deeper into the lifestyles of boatmen, travelers, and boat trackers who relied on sailing and towing for their livelihood.

2.4 The Regulations on the Transportation of Horses in the Southern Song Dynasty—Discussions on the Costs of Water Transportation

The procurement of horses from Sichuan Province, Shaanxi Province, and Guangnan West Province played a crucial role in the Southern Song Dynasty. Previous research has explored the war horse trade (Y. Feng 1986; W. Du 1990; F. Liu 1995; F. Liu 2008; T. Wei 2007; D. Jia and Y. Chen 1989); C. Huang 2002) and the associated transportation routes in Sichuan and Shaanxi provinces (Z. Liang 1996; P. Shang 2010). The Southern Song Dynasty transported over ten thousand war horses annually from Sichuan Province and Guangnan West Province, covering thousands of miles to the capital city of Lin'an (now Hangzhou) and military prefectures along the Yangtze River. This complicated and critical process was essential for national defense. However, there is a need for further investigation into the Southern Song Dynasty's approach to batch horse transportation, management of transportation costs and efficiency, and the establishment of an incentive mechanism to mobilize all sectors. This section addresses these issues by comparing the costs of water transportation with those of land transportation.

2.4.1 *The Methods and Routes of Horse Batch Transportation in Sichuan and Guangnan West Provinces*

The adversary of the Southern Song Dynasty was the Jin Kingdom, established by the Jurchens, an ancient nationality in China known for their expertise in horsemanship and archery. Therefore, the Southern Song Dynasty had to maintain a certain size of cavalry for national defense. In the face of the powerful cavalry of the Jin Kingdom, the Song Dynasty could not defend itself without war horses. As it was written, "there are millions of soldiers, but no horses to strengthen the military force. Without war horses, if they need to follow up their victory by chasing fleeing enemies, it is equivalent to having no soldiers at all." The situation was such that "the enemy was equipped with enough strong stallions while we were in urgent need of war horses." During the later years of the Jingkang Reign, the Jin troops were ordered to loot horses upon capturing the capital, resulting in fewer than five thousand horses in the capital city where Emperor Gaozong lived and worked. Only a few of the remaining horses could be fitted with armor. As a result, only officials of high rank were allowed to ride horses (S. Yang et al. 1990). The Southern Song Dynasty always needed war horses. Although a general of the middle troops of cavalry in Jinzhou (now Ankang) adjacent to Xingyuan Prefecture was supposed to be allocated one thousand war horses, in the fourth year of the Shaoxi Reign (AD 1193), the cavalry still lacked 487 horses. The supplemental number of horses every year could not offset the number of horses that died or were returned as unqualified the previous year. In the first year of the Qingyuan Reign (AD 1195), the Inspection Bureau reported that military prefectures lacked horses (S. Xu 2014: 9164). Even when the rated number of war horses of the Palace Administration troops was 10,700, in the fourth year of the Jiatai Reign (AD 1204), they lacked over 2000 horses (S. Xu 2014: 9102). Therefore, it was of great significance for the Song to procure horses and transport them in batches for economic growth and national defense.

In the Southern Song Dynasty, previous research by scholars such as Liu Fusheng, Wei Tianan, Jia Daquan, and Huang Chunyan has extensively discussed the procurement of horses in Sichuan Province and Guangnan West Province, including the number of horses obtained. However, this section of the book provides additional information on the methods of grouping horses in batches and their transportation destinations. The Southern Song Dynasty "relied on Sichuan Province, Shaanxi Province and Guangnan West Province to purchase war horses"(Y. Wang 2003: 2740) and established a Tea-horse department (an institution whose function was to exchange tea for horses) in each of these provinces. The Tea-horse Department in Sichuan Province originally had five horse-purchasing venues: Lizhou (now Hanyuan County of Ya'an), Xuzhou, Wenzhou, Changning Military Prefecture, and Nanping Military Prefecture. The Tea-horse Department of Xingyuan Prefecture originally had two horse-purchasing venues: Dangchang Stockade Village in Xihe Prefecture, and Fengtiexia Stockade Village in Jiezhou (now Wudu District of Longnan). Wenzhou was later affiliated with the Tea-horse Department of Xingyuan Prefecture, and Zhenzhou was added as a horse-purchasing venue for the Tea-horse Department in Sichuan Province. The horses procured by the Tea-horse Department of Xingyuan Prefecture were gathered in Xingyuan Prefecture, while those purchased by the Tea-horse Department of Sichuan Province were gathered in Chengdu (X. Li 2000: 425). Horse procurement in Guangnan West Province was mainly carried out in Yongzhou (now Nanning)(Q. Zhou 1999: 187).The annual target number of horse procurement for Sichuan Province and Shaanxi Province was 11,900 during the Qiandao Reign, with 6000 horses for the Tea-horse Department of Sichuan Province and 5900 horses for the Tea-horse Department of Xingyuan Prefecture. In the early years of the Qingyuan Reign, the annual target number of horse procurement was specified to be 11,016, which was later changed to 12,994 in the later years of the Jiatai Reign. The specified annual number of horse procurement in Guangnan West Province was 1500 (X. Li 2000: 425–26). However, there existed a discrepancy between the actual number of horses procured and the annual targets.

Horses were transported in batches to the three Capital Guard Agencies (the Palace Administration, Metropolitan Cavalry Command, and Metropolitan Infantry Commission) in the capital and military prefectures along the Yangtze River. Horses from Sichuan Province were grouped in batches at Chengdu, while horses from Shaanxi Province were grouped in batches at Xingyuan Prefecture. Horses from Guangnan West Province were initially grouped in batches at Yongzhou, but they were regrouped in batches at Guizhou (Jingjiang Prefecture) during transportation. War horses were steadily supplied to the three Capital Guard Agencies and military prefectures and accounted for the majority of batch horse transportation, which was referred to as regular batches. Additionally, there was batch horse transportation dedicated to the emperor, including batches for the emperor's birthday, batches for paying tribute, extra batches, irregular batches, and other batches. The number of horses and convoys varied in different batches. Sichuan Province and Shaanxi Province typically grouped 50 horses in one regular batch. Hong Zun pointed out that Xihezhou, Jiezhou, and Wenzhou procured 3750 horses annually, which were grouped in 75 batches of 50 horses per batch (S. Yang et al. 1990). Sichuan Province grouped 55 horses in a batch, including 5 standby horses (S. Xu 2014: 9143), for the use of the emperor. In the early years of the Southern Song Dynasty, each batch in Yongzhou included 100 horses (S. Xu 2014: 9128). As a standard practice, regular batches consisted of 50 horses per batch. Therefore, the specified annual number of horse procurement was 1500 grouped in 30 batches. Batches dedicated to the emperor contained 30 horses per batch (Q. Zhou 1999: 187, 192).

Horses from Sichuan and Shaanxi provinces were mainly supplied to military prefectures along the Yangtze River and the capital, with the exception of troops on the Sichuan-Shaanxi fronts. According to court officials, "the Tea-Horse Department of Sichuan purchased 10,000 horses annually, with 2000 going to General Wu Lin and 8000 being apportioned to the three Capital Guard Agencies and military prefectures along the Yangtze River." (S. Xu 2014: 9137) Specifically, 750 horses each were apportioned to Zhenjiang, Jiankang, Jingzhou, and Ezhou military prefectures, while Jiangzhou and Chizhou military prefectures received 500 horses each. The Palace Administration received 2500 horses, and the Metropolitan Cavalry Command and

Metropolitan Infantry Commission each received 1000 horses. Additionally, 200 horses from Sichuan Province were presented respectfully to the emperor (D. Ma 2011: 4793). Regarding the horses from Sichuan and Shaanxi provinces, Sichuan was the primary supplier of horses for military prefectures along the Yangtze River, while horses procured by the Tea-Horse Department from the western regions (Tibetan, Huihe, and Dangxiang) were mainly supplied to the three Capital Guard Agencies in the capital. Specifically, "the Trading Horses Agency of Chengdu Prefecture delivered 58 batches to military prefectures along the Yangtze River each year, while the Trading Horses Agency of Xingyuan Prefecture delivered 112 batches to the three Capital Guard Agencies each year (X. Li 2000: 425–26)." Horses from the western regions procured by Xihezhou and Jiezhou were delivered to the Bureau of Military Affairs in batches every year. In the 25th year of the Shaoxing Reign (AD 1155), these horses were delivered to the three Capital Guard Agencies, and this delivery was repeated every three years thereafter. However, horses from the western regions were usually not delivered to military prefectures along the Yangtze River. Military institutions in Zhenjiang were supposed to receive 24 batches from Sichuan and Guangnan West provinces each year, but there were 61 batches in total that were in arrears. In the third year of the Shaoxi Reign (AD 1192), they requested a quota of 20 batches from the western regions, but later reduced this to 10 batches. However, they only received two batches (S. Xu 2014: 9130). Of the eight horse-purchasing venues in Sichuan, five, including Lizhou, Xuzhou, Zhenzhou, Nanping Military Prefecture, and Changning Military Prefecture, were requested to supply military prefectures along the Yangtze River (S. Xu 2014:9169–70). In the 27th year of the Shaoxing Reign (AD 1157), it was ordered that horses procured by Chengdu Prefecture should not be delivered to the capital. Since then, these horses have been delivered to troops in Ezhou (now Wuchang), Jiankang Prefecture, Zhenjiang Prefecture, and Chizhou (now Guichi).

Guangnan West Province originally delivered all of its annual quota of 1500 horses to the capital. In the fifth year of the Shaoxing Reign (AD 1135), it was stipulated that horses from Guangnan West Province should be allocated proportionately to military prefectures along the Yangtze River. The official annual quota of horses was set at 1400, but the author notes that the number was likely to have been 1500. The horses were to be distributed according to a certain ratio, with thirty percent (450 horses) allocated to Jiankang, Zhenjiang, and Ezhou each, and ten percent (150 horses) allocated to Chizhou, transported in three batches. In the first year of the Longxing Reign (AD 1163), it was stipulated that "extraordinary fine horses selected should be delivered to the capital in 10 batches, with 30 horses in each batch." In the second year of the Longxing Reign (AD 1164), six additional batches were procured beyond the annual quota and delivered to Xiangyang Prefecture. Subsequently, horses were procured many times beyond the annual quotas and delivered to Jiankang, Zhenjiang, Chizhou, and the capital (R. Ma 2004: 2857). According to *Laws and Institutions Since the Jianyan Reign*, "fine horses from Guangnan West Province were delivered to the three Capital Guard Agencies, while other horses were delivered to Jiankang, Zhenjiang Prefecture, Chizhou, Ezhou, and Taiping Military Prefecture." (X. Li 2000: 432) The horses from the western regions were considered the best among the war horses procured, with those from Sichuan and Guangnan West provinces following closely behind. Therefore, the horses procured from Xihezhou, Jiezhou and Wenzhou were called war horses. The horses purchased from southern nationalities in ancient China were called horses for appeasement, as they were small and unsuitable for warfare. They were primarily traded to appease the southern nationalities in ancient China (W. Lin 1989). The distribution of batch horse transportation reflects that the Southern Song government attached priorities to the capital and the three Capital Guard Agencies.

The horses belonging to the Tea-Horse Department of Xingyuan Prefecture were organized into batches at the Horse Trading Agency of Xingyuan Prefecture, and then transported overland to military prefectures along the Yangtze River and the capital Lin'an. The main route went through Jinzhou, Junzhou (now Jun County of Shiyan) or Fangzhou (now Fang County of Shiyan), Guanghua Military Prefecture, Xiangyang Prefecture, Yingzhou (now Zhongxiang), Hanyang Military Prefecture, Xingguo Military Prefecture, Jiangzhou (now Jiujiang), Chizhou, Huzhou, and Linan. Liang Zhongxiao regarded this route as a major channel linking the northwest with the southeast (Z. Liang 1996). Another transportation route went through Jinzhou, Fangzhou, and Jiangling. The first route originally went from Jinzhou to Fangzhou, but later was changed to a new route from Jinzhou to Junzhou due to the rugged terrain and steep valleys on the route from Jinzhou to Fangzhou. The new route from Jinzhou to Junzhou was characterized as having "hills and dirt roads without any precipitous terrains." In the third year of the Qiandao Reign (AD 1167), Yu Yunwen suggested shipping horses from Jinzhou and transporting them by the Han River to avoid the mountains between Jinzhou and Fangzhou. Waterways were available for transportation as in the sixth year of the Qiandao Reign (AD 1170), the Transfer Agency of Taxation of Lizhou Province mentioned that Juling, Mipu, Lixi, Shiziwei, and other courier stations en route "were all courier stations in the jurisdiction of Xunyang County in Jinzhou along new waterways." (S. Xu 2014: 9138, 9148) The horses of Sichuan Province were grouped into batches at Chengdu. Initially, the batch horse transportation was directly "delivered via Xingyuan Prefecture, Xiangyang Prefecture to the Directorate of Affairs of Horses of Hanyang Military Prefecture." The route was over 1750 km long and the round trip took them over 120 days (S. Xu 2014: 9149). This shows that the batch transportation route of Sichuan Province's horses by land was the same as that of Xingyuan Prefecture's after the horses were carried from Chengdu to Xingyuan Prefecture.

In the first year of the Qiandao Reign (AD 1165), a proposal was made "to group the horses of the western regions purchased by Dangchang Stockaded Village in batches and transport them by land to Lizhou (now Guangyuan) for further shipment downstream, reaching Jingnan within a month for land carriage to the capital. Similarly, the horses of Sichuan Province purchased by Chengdu Prefecture Province were suggested to be shipped from Hezhou (now Hechuan District of Chongqing) and transported downstream to Jingnan within 20 days for land transportation". The imperial decree assigned Wu Lin to carry out the procurement, and the proposal was implemented accordingly. Subsequently, it was advised that the military prefectures should take the horses during their transportation by land to Ezhou and then proceed down the Yangtze River. However, Emperor Xiaozong expressed concerns that batch horse transportation on the river would be delayed by winds, and thus ordered that the land route from Ezhou should still be taken (S. Xu 2014: 9104). In December of the first year of the Qiandao Reign (AD 1165), the emperor ordered that batch horse transportation should be transported to Jingnan and take the land route there according to the previous imperial decree. Finally, in November of the third year of the Qiandao Reign (AD 1167), the transportation of batch horse transportation by water was abolished (X. Li 2000: 431).

In Guangnan West Province, the trade of horses was primarily conducted in Yongzhou, with horses then being transported to Guizhou (now Jingjiang Prefecture), where the Provincial Military Commission of Guangnan West Province was located. The original transportation route was through Guizhou, Jinghu South Province, and Jiangnan West Province to the capital. However, in the fourth year of the Jianyan Reign (AD 1130), due to disruptions on the roads of Jiangnan West Province, the route was redirected to include Guangnan East Province, Fujian Province, and Liangzhe Province before reaching the capital. After the situation was settled, the route was reinstated via Guangnan West Province, Jinghu South Province, Jiangnan West Province, Jiangnan East Province, and Liangzhe Province to the capital. Specifically, the route followed was Yongzhou—Guizhou (Jingjiang Prefecture)—Yongzhou—Tanzhou (now Changsha)—Fengcheng—Raozhou (now Boyang County of Shangrao)—Chizhou—Zhenjiang—Linan (S. Xu 2014: 9128, 9138–39). When delivering horses from Guangnan West Province to military prefectures along the Yangtze River, the same route was taken up to Tanzhou, after which they were transported northward to Ezhou and then to Xiangyang or eastward to Chizhou, Jiankang, Zhenjiang, and other regions.

2.4.2 *The Supportive Policies on the Composition and Assessment of Convoys of Horse Batch Transportation*

The convoys consisted mainly of soldiers. According to Wang Yingchen, the Tea-Horse Department required palace guards to escort the batch horse transportation and report to the Palace Administration. If understaffed, the Department had the authority to appoint commanders-in-chief and junior military officers. During the busy season of batch horse transportation, if there was a lack of transportation supervisors, the Tea-Horse Department could temporarily send incumbent military officers or local taxation officials to work for them. Additionally, junior military officers escorting horses were required to rank above the minor military official (Chengxinlang, the 52nd tier of Sub-Ninth Rank). The Tea-Horse Department gave priority to allocate staff, and officials ranking below the minor military official (Chengjielang, the 51st tier of Sub-Ninth Rank) could have five subordinates according to the standard of staffs attached to the minor military official (Chengjielang, the 51st tier of Sub-Ninth Rank). Officials ranking between the military official (Baoyilang, the 50th tier of Ninth Rank) and the military official (Eighth Rank) followed the same standard as mentioned above (Y. Wang 1990a, b). The number of horses per batch varied for regular, imperial, and other batches, and their convoys differed as well. The Tea-Horse Department of Sichuan delivered imperial batch horse transportation to the capital with "two junior military officers, one high-ranking official, one veterinarian, and 50 soldiers pulling horses" per batch, totaling 54 convoys. A regular batch of horses from Sichuan had 25 officials and soldiers in total, with each soldier pulling two horses, one convoy chief, one vice supervisor, one veterinarian, one military recorder, two army cooks, and one shield-wielding soldier. There were 32 convoys in total for regular batches. For imperial batch horse transportation of Sichuan, one soldier pulled one horse, while for regular batches, the normal practice was one soldier pulling two horses (S. Xu 2014: 9137, 9146, 9160).

The number of convoys of a batch of horses in Guangnan West Province underwent several changes. In the third year of the Shaoxing Reign (AD 1133), a batch of horses acquired in Yongzhou consisted of 100 horses and 57 convoys, which included two convoy chiefs, one high-ranking official, two inferior military officers, 50 soldiers who pulled horses, one veterinarian, and one military recorder. The number of horses and horse-pullers in this batch was twice that of a regular batch from Sichuan, while seven officials, including convoy chiefs, high-ranking officials, and veterinarians, were equipped for this batch. Based on the number of horses per batch, the actual number of convoys decreased by seven (S. Xu 2014: 8128). In the seventh year of the Qiandao Reign (AD 1171), the Ministry of National Defence stated that the batch horse transportation in Guangnan West Province lacked soldiers. Consequently, for imperial batch horse transportation, one soldier was assigned to pull six horses, while for regular batches, one soldier pulled ten horses. Emperor Xiaozong issued an imperial decree to Guangnan West Province that stipulated that henceforth, during horse transportation, one soldier would pull two horses for imperial batch horse transportation, and one soldier would pull four horses for regular batch horse transportation. A regular batch of horses was only equipped with 12 soldiers who pulled 48 horses. The remaining two horses were pulled by one high-ranking official (S. Xu 2014: 9146–47). *The Land Beyond the Passes* referred to a standard practice in which 25 soldiers pulled horses in a regular batch and 15 soldiers pulled horses in an imperial batch. Each batch had one convoy chief, five high-ranking officials, and one veterinarian. This means that a regular batch had a total of 32 convoys, and an imperial batch had a total of 22 convoys (Q. Zhou 1999: 192), similar to a batch of horses from Sichuan and Shaanxi provinces. As stated in the methods of rewards and penalties in the ninth year of the Qiandao Reign (AD 1173), for regular batch horse transportation in Guangnan West Province, one soldier also pulled two horses. This reward policy applied to normal circumstances.

The personnel involved in batch horse transportation can be categorized into two distinct types. The first category comprises the convoy chiefs, who are accountable for the entire batch, the high-ranking officials, and the veterinarians. The second category consists of the horse-pullers who are accountable for the horses they pull.

The authority of the Southern Song Dynasty established two distinct methods for assessing and rewarding or penalizing the two types of personnel involved in batch horse transportation. Zhou Qüfei, in his summary of the rewards and penalties for personnel involved in batch horse transportation in Guangnan West Province, states that "if all the horses of the batch transportation are delivered safely, the convoy chiefs will be promoted to one-rank higher official, and their tenure before promotion assessment will be reduced by three years. In case 30% of horses are dead or lost, demotion will be enforced as a punishment. Rewards and penalties for other personnel will vary based on the condition of the horses they are responsible for. High-ranking officials and soldiers will be rewarded or penalized based on the state of the horses they pull. Rewards may include promotion to higher ranks, and monetary payment will be made to those who do not wish to be promoted. Penalties may include flogging with a stick and dismissal of the convoy." (Q. Zhou 1999: 192)However, it should be noted that rewards and penalties may differ based on the type of horse batch being delivered.

The Southern Song Dynasty enacted and revised regulations on rewards and penalties for batch horse transportation on multiple occasions. The earliest extant regulation dates back to the second year of the Shaoxing Reign (AD 1132), when an imperial decree stipulated that rewards and penalties for batch horse transportation from Guangnan West Province were to be given in accordance with the practices of Sichuan and Shaanxi provinces. While no detailed regulations were recorded at that time, in the third year of the Shaoxing Reign (AD 1133), rewards and penalties for convoys of batch horse transportation of Guangnan West Province were introduced. If the loss rate during transportation was below 10%, convoy chiefs, high-ranking officials, inferior military officers, and soldiers were to be promoted one tier higher. In contrast, if the loss rate reached 20%, they would be demoted one rank lower. Similar to the earlier decree, these regulations were to be in line with the practices of Sichuan and Shaanxi provinces (S. Xu 2014: 9128). In the 18th year of the Shaoxing Reign (AD 1148), rewards and penalties for supervisors responsible for the postal stations of batch horse transportation of Guangnan West Province were introduced. During their tenure, their performance would be evaluated based on the delivery of over 3000 horses. If the death or illness rate of the horses was below 0.5%, one year would be reduced from their tenure evaluation period before they could be promoted to a higher rank. Conversely, if the rate exceeded 3%, four years would be added to their tenure evaluation period before promotion (S. Xu 2014: 9129–30). In the 26th year of the Shaoxing Reign (AD 1156), rewards and penalties for soldiers who pulled horses were explicitly stipulated, with bounties given or cut based on the number of lost horses. For instance, "if two horses were infected with scabies, no bounty would be given; if one horse was infected with scabies, the bounties would be cut down a half." The stipulations also applied to batch horse transportation delivered from tea-horse departments and Guangnan West Province. In the 27th year of the Shaoxing Reign (AD 1157), the regulations for convoy chiefs were revised, and the assessment of their performance was changed from the proportion to the concrete number of lost horses: "Henceforth, convoy chiefs responsible for 55 horses with the arrival of 54 horses will be promoted one-rank higher official plus 2-year reduction from their tenure evaluation before promotion assessment. With the arrival of 53 horses, convoy chiefs will be promoted one-rank higher official plus 1.5-year reduction from their tenure evaluation before promotion assessment. With the arrival of 52 horses, they will be promoted one-rank higher official plus 1-year reduction from their tenure evaluation before promotion assessment. With the arrival of 51 horses, they will be promoted one-rank higher official plus 0.5-year reduction from their tenure evaluation before promotion assessment." (S. Xu 2014: 9130–31)

The preceding text pertains to the rewards and penalties associated with regular batch horse transportation. In the fourth year of the Qiandao Reign (AD 1168), regulations regarding the rewards and penalties for imperial batch horse transportation were introduced. These regulations were based on the number of horses transported and varied depending on whether one soldier pulled one or two horses. Soldiers pulling one horse would be promoted by one rank upon arrival of the horse they pulled, or demoted by one rank if no horse arrived. For soldiers pulling two horses, arrival of two horses would result in a promotion by one rank, arrival of one horse would not result in any extra rewards, and arrival of no horse would lead to a demotion by one rank (S. Xu 2014: 9143). Around September of the seventh year of the Qiandao Reign (AD 1171), the average number of horses pulled by one soldier in the batch transportation of Guangnan West Province was higher than that of Sichuan and Shaanxi provinces. Prior to this, one soldier would pull six horses in an imperial batch or even ten horses in a regular batch. The regulation reduces the number of horses pulled to two by one person in an imperial batch transportation, or four horses by one person in a regular batch transportation, resulting in naturally different rewards and penalties from those of the Tea-Horse Department of Sichuan. Detailed regulations concerning rewards and penalties were also made for imperial and regular batch horse transportation of Guangnan West Province. Soldiers pulling horses of imperial batches receive rewards and penalties based on the arrival of two horses pulled by one soldier, or the arrival of one dead or one left at the postal station, or whether the horses are infected with scabies. Similarly, soldiers pulling horses of regular batches receive rewards and penalties depending on whether four horses arrive, or if one of the four horses is dead or deposited, and whether the horses are infected with scabies. High-ranking officials and veterinarians are rewarded with a promotion by one rank upon the arrival of all 30 horses of an imperial batch or all 50 horses of a regular batch. However, if 20% of the imperial horses (six horses) or regular batch horses (ten horses) are dead or left at the postal stations due to illness, they are penalized with a demotion by one rank (S. Xu 2014: 9146–47)

Following the transfer station's move to Hanyang Military Prefecture, regulations concerning the rewards and penalties for the Palace Administration, Metropolitan Cavalry Command, and Metropolitan Infantry Commission's departure from Lin'an Prefecture and acquisition of horses from Hanyang Military Prefecture were established. These regulations were based on the practices of batch horse transportation from Xingyuan Prefecture to Jingnan, and were determined according to the arrival of two horses, the absence of horses, and the presence of scabies in the horses. Convoy chiefs were also subject to rewards and penalties based on the number of lost horses. In the event that all horses in a batch arrived without incident, the tenure period before promotion assessment for junior military officers, high-ranking officials, veterinarians, and other personnel would be reduced by three years. Conversely, if 15 horses from a batch were found to be dead and left at the postal stations, junior military officers, high-ranking officials, veterinarians, and others would be demoted by one rank (S. Xu 2014: 9144–45)

In the ninth year of the Qiandao Reign (AD 1173), a systematic set of regulations was introduced to govern rewards and penalties for convoy chiefs (junior military officers), high-ranking officials, veterinarians, and soldiers involved in various batch horse transportation activities. These activities include regular batch horse transportation from the Tea-Horse Department (of Xingyuan Prefecture) to the three Capital Guard Agencies and military prefectures along the Yangtze River, imperial batch horse transportation from tea-horse departments to the capital, batch horse transportation of taking horses from tea-horse departments and being delivered to military prefectures of Jiankang, Zhenjiang Prefecture, and Wufeng of Chizhou, batch horse transportation of Guangnan West Province to the capital and military institutions of Jiankang, Zhenjiang Prefecture, and Chizhou, batch horse transportation of Guangnan West Province to military institutions of Ezhou and Jiangnan, irregular batch horse transportation delivered from military institutions of Jinzhou, Xingzhou, and Xingyuan Prefecture and the Pacification Commission of Sichuan, annual batch horse transportation from tea-horse departments for the birthday of Emperor Gaozong, 20 annual batch horse transportation from horse-tea departments for the imperial carriage as well as batch horse transportation from Wenzhou for the birthday of Emperor Gaozong and for the birthday of Emperor Xiaozong, batch horse transportation from the Provincial Military Commission of Guangnan West Province to military institutions of Xiangyang Prefecture, and batch horse transportation of Wenzhou and Sichuan taken by soldiers of military institutions of Jingnan every year from tea-horse departments to Xiangyang Prefecture. These regulations applied to all personnel involved in batch horse transportation, including generals, soldiers, veterinarians, and horse-pullers.

For instance, let us consider the regular batches of horses transported from Sichuan and Guangnan West provinces. When the three Capital Guard Agencies received their regular batches of horses in Xingyuan Prefecture, junior military officers could receive promotions based on the number of horses that arrived and the number that died or were left at the postal station due to illness. Specifically, if all horses arrived, the junior military officer would receive a two-rank promotion. If one horse was dead or left at the postal station, the officer would receive a one-rank promotion and a reduction of four years from their tenure period before promotion assessment. If two horses were lost, the officer would be promoted by one rank and their tenure period before promotion assessment would be reduced by three years. If three horses were lost, the officer would receive a promotion of one rank and a reduction of two years from their tenure period before promotion assessment. However, if ten or more horses were lost, no rewards or penalties would be given. In the case of 11 or more lost horses, one year would be added to the officer's tenure period before promotion assessment. If the number of lost horses reached 20, the officer would be demoted by two ranks. For more than 20 lost horses, further increases in tenure before promotion assessment and demotions would be imposed. High-ranking officials and veterinarians would also receive rewards and penalties based on the number of lost horses. In the regular batch transportation of horses from Guangnan West Province to the capital and military institutions of Jiankang, Zhenjiang Prefecture, and Chizhou, a system of promotion and reduction in tenure before promotion assessment was in place. Upon the arrival of all horses, junior military officers would be promoted by one rank and their tenure before promotion assessment reduced by three years. In the case of one horse being dead or left at the postal station due to illness, officers would be promoted by one rank and their tenure before promotion assessment reduced by two years. The extent of promotion and reduction in tenure before promotion assessment would decrease in proportion to the number of lost horses. However, if the number of lost horses reached eight, no rewards or penalties would be given. When more than nine horses had died or were left at the postal station due to illness, penalties were imposed. These penalties included a one-year increase in service tenure before promotion assessment and a two-rank demotion if the number of horses that had died or were left at the postal station for illness was 18 or more. If the number exceeded 18, additional service years in the tenure period before promotion assessment and demotion were imposed. High-ranking officials, veterinarians, and others were promoted by one rank and rewarded ten strings of copper coins upon the arrival of all horses. The ranks of promotion and bounties decreased as the number of lost horses increased. When there were 8–12 horses dead or left at the postal station for illness, no rewards or penalties were given. If the number of horses that had died or were left at the postal station was between 13 and 17, a one-rank demotion was imposed. When there were 18 horses dead or left at the postal station for illness, a two-rank demotion was imposed. If the number of lost horses exceeded 18, a one-rank demotion was imposed for every five additional horses that had died or were left at the postal station.

When the three Capital Guard Agencies and military prefectures along the Yangtze River dispatched their own soldiers to acquire horses from tea-horse departments, a promotion of one rank would be granted to a soldier upon delivery of two horses without scabies. Alternatively, for those who decline the promotion, a reward of 30 strings of copper coins would be given. If two horses were delivered, but one of them had scabies, the reward would be reduced to 15 strings of copper coins. For those who refuse the reward, an official credential of a half-rank promotion would be given. If a soldier obtained such an official credential twice, they could be promoted by one rank. If two horses with scabies or one dead or deposited horse were delivered, no reward would be given. If no horse was delivered, a demotion of one rank would be imposed. Those without a rank to be demoted would be subjected to 80 lashings with a stick. Compared to the rewards and penalties of the batch horse transportation of Guangnan West Province, the rewards and penalties of the Sichuan convoys were only half. Upon the delivery of two horses, a reward of 15 strings of copper coins would be given. If two horses were delivered, but one had scabies, the reward would be reduced to 7.5 strings of copper coins. If a soldier is awarded twice at the same standard, they would be promoted one rank. However, if both horses delivered were infected with scabies or if one horse was dead and the other was left at the postal station for illness, no rewards would be given. If both horses were dead, the convoy would be demoted one rank. If the convoy had no rank to be demoted, they would be subjected to 80 lashings with a stick (S. Xu 2014: 9155–59).

In order to ensure a sufficient supply of war horses to the capital and military prefectures, the Southern Song government offered generous rewards for horse transportation. It was even said that "horse transportation was a quick means of promotion for military officers and assistant military officers, with many being promoted from vice military officers to principal military officers (Q. Zhou 1999: 192). Sichuan, in comparison to Guangnan West Province, had more batch horse transportation with longer transportation distances, resulting in even greater rewards for those undertaking batch horse transportation in Sichuan. "Successful delivery of eight horses intact to the capital resulted in a one rank promotion. After completing five or six cargo transportation trips, one could be promoted to the rank of 'Dutou' (now company commander) or even 'Zhihuishi' (now battalion commander in charge of 500 soldiers). With over 300 batches of horses requiring transportation annually, more than 1000 soldiers were needed, providing ample opportunity for military officers to be promoted." However, the rapid promotion through horse transportation resulted in a surplus of high-ranking officials and excessive selection of high-ranking officials in prefectures and counties of Sichuan. The higher the rank, the higher the salary, and several soldiers' salaries could only support one high-ranking official (S. Xu 2014: 9141–42). In an effort to reduce the number of lost horses, the Southern Song government imposed severe penalties. In the seventh year of the Qiandao Reign (AD 1171), the Palace Administration took the 32nd batch of horses with 48 horses, but only 29 arrived intact, resulting in severe punishments for the convoy chiefs, veterinarians, and others of the batch. Those with no ranks for demotion were flogged 100 times with a stick. Convoys were punished to the highest degree beyond the regulations (S. Xu 2014: 9150–51). In the fifth year of the Qiandao Reign (AD 1169), a junior military official named Zhang Heng of Guangnan West Province delivered 50 horses, but all horses were dead. No existing regulations covered the scenario where all horses were dead, and the severest penalty, a one-rank demotion plus a four-year increase in service tenure period before promotion assessment, was insufficient to make up for such a loss. As a result, beyond the system, the official documents of the three-rank promotions awarded to Zhang Heng were taken back and annulled. The army he served in was ordered to punish him and downgrade him to a common soldier (S. Xu 2014: 9145).

The officials of prefectures and counties, as well as the personnel of the postal stations en route, played a critical role in safeguarding batch horse transportation. When the batch horse transportation reached the capital and military prefectures, the trading horse agencies of prefectures and counties en route provided convoys with accommodation, food vouchers, and fodder for horses (Q. Zhou 1999: 192). The main duties of the officials of prefectures and counties en route were as follows: Firstly, they were responsible for ensuring food for the convoys and fodder for the horses. To this end, they prepared postal certificates for officials and soldiers, as well as fodder for horses. They built warehouses near the postal stations in advance with sufficient fodder, money, and grains, and kept ample supplies in the warehouses. They approved the arrival of materials in real-time, which streamlined the procedures of batch horse transportation in their jurisdiction regions. Furthermore, all prefectures and counties en route had to provide guard services in turn to ensure the transportation passed through their areas smoothly (S. Xu 2014: 9127, 9138). Secondly, the officials had to take over sick horses and give them medical treatment. The regulations allowed for all sick horses to be left at the postal station for treatment (S. Xu 2014: 9142). Thirdly, the officials were responsible for ensuring that all facilities were in good condition and that the postal stations were easily accessible. This included building and renovating houses, preparing enough mangers and utensils for daily use, and ensuring that batches of horses had shelters and fodder when they arrived at the postal stations. The royal court issued blueprints of postal stations and colored paintings of postal stations to all provinces, detailing site selection, houses, structure sizes, mangers, and the number of utensils for daily use. Prefectures and counties en route also had to ensure that postal stations were accessible. In the tenth year of the Chunxi Reign (AD 1183), the authority ordered Jiangzhou and Chizhou to rebuild the route of batch horse transportation, making them flat and wide on high terrain free from muddy surfaces (S. Xu 2014: 9098).

Officials at all levels of government were involved in the management of batch horse transportation, from fiscal commissioners to county magistrates, secretaries-general, and supervisors of postal stations. In each province, officials responsible for grain shipping were also responsible for batch horse transportation within their own jurisdiction. These officials were required to inspect the postal stations in their jurisdiction in person and ensure that they were built in accordance with the blueprints issued by the royal court. They were also responsible for dispatching high-ranking officers to guard the postal stations. The supervisors of financial affairs of prefectures and military prefectures directly administered the postal stations and provided provisions and fodder for batch horse transportation. In the absence of supervisors of financial affairs, superintendents of trial affairs or senior assistants were authorized to administer the postal stations. County magistrates were responsible for managing the postal stations in their jurisdiction, while county criminal inspectors supervised the allocation of fodder and ensured that the batch horse transportation left without delay. Mayors were responsible for dealing with affairs beyond the right limit of officials below county magistrates. The tenure assessment of officials of prefectures and counties as well as supervisors of postal stations was closely linked to batch horse transportation. The assessment of mayors was based on the number of sick horses cured within a year. If 50 or more horses were cured, the mayor's tenure before promotion assessment would be reduced by two years. If fewer than 50 horses were cured, rewards were given on the basis of the number of cured horses. Each postal station in the prefecture appointed one junior military official as the supervisor, and a group leader out of six soldiers was required to supervise and clean the postal station for the arrival of batch horse transportation (S. Xu 2014: 9139, 9142, 9154, 9160). The assessments of officials in prefectures and counties, as well as the supervisors of postal stations, had a close connection with batch horse transportation. In addition to the assessment of mayors mentioned above, if supervisors of municipal financial affairs and county magistrates ensured the passage of batch horse transportation through their own jurisdiction, "in the year-end assessment, if without mistakes reported by supervisors to the authority, they were rewarded. If with mistakes or delays, they were punished according to imperial decrees," either "one-year or two-year reduction in tenure before promotion assessment as a reward" or "their tenure period before promotion assessment extended for those who made mistakes." In the sixth year of the Qiandao Reign (AD 1170), the guard leader of Jinzhou and the magistrate of Xunyang County were demoted by one rank because the postal stations in the jurisdiction of Xunyang County of Jinzhou along the new waterway such as Juling and Mipu "were provided with grass but no fodder, or with fodder but no food for people." If the supervisor of the postal station made no mistake, he could "be entrusted such a task once again, and the prefecture was ordered to give him 10 strings of 1000 coins every month as extra pay." (S. Xu 2014: 9129, 9143, 9148, 9160) Convoy chiefs had the right to check fodder preparation. "If there was something against regulations, supervisors and generals were reported to military institutions. Official documents were sent to the prefectures and counties. Unqualified officials involved were punished on the basis of their irresponsibility." The case could even be directly reported to the imperial court (S. Xu 2014: 9099).

In order to ensure the smooth transportation of batches of horses, two systems were established. The first system involves the transportation of horses in batches under the guidance of convoys composed of convoy chiefs, high-ranking officials, veterinarians, and soldiers who were responsible for holding the horses. The second is a supportive system composed of county officials and junior military officers at the postal stations. The duties of personnel in both systems were clearly defined, and a system of rewards and penalties was implemented. Liang Zhongxiao proposed that the postal routes of the Southern Song Dynasty were the main channels that were jointly administered by the central government and local authorities, and were jointly managed by the troops and local authorities. This idea is substantiated by the evidence. This system serves as an important guarantee for the efficiency of batch horse transportation (Z. Liang 1996), as it ensures timely delivery and reduces the incidence of dead or sick horses.

2.4.3 Cost Sharing and Efficiency Guarantee of the Batch Horse Transportation

Efficient batch horse transportation is reliant upon the support system of prefectures and counties through which the transportation passes. However, relying solely on performance evaluations to encourage the initiative of these local entities is insufficient. This is due to the centralized management of fiscal affairs during the Southern Song Dynasty, which resulted in impoverished local governments. Regions such as Guangnan West Province, Kuizhou (now Fengjie County of Chongqing), Lizhou, and other areas through which batch horse transportation passes were typically poor and unable to afford the costs associated with this transportation. As a result, it is necessary to share the costs in order to maintain transportation capacity and stimulate the initiative of prefectures and counties.

2.4.3.1 Segmented Horse Transport and the Mechanism of Reception and Sending Horses

As a standard, the extra pay for a convoy chief in Sichuan was 666 copper coins. For soldiers, 2.5 L of rice and 150 copper coins were given per day, while veterinarians received 170 copper coins and 2.5 L of rice per day. In the Southern Song Dynasty, grain prices in Sichuan varied by region and time. Typically, it cost 5 strings of copper coins to purchase one Dan (60 kg) of grain, but prices could rise as high as 10 strings of coins per Dan during periods of high demand (S. Xu 2014: 164–68). The standard commission for employees of prefectures and counties was calculated based on the rates set for helmsmen and sailors of the batch horse shipping of Sichuan in the early years of the Qiandao Reign, which was 500 copper coins per person per day (see below). A regular batch consisting of 32 people cost 16 strings of 1000 coins per day. A batch of 50 horses consumed 240 kg of fodder per day (8 L per horse per day), costing 8 strings of copper coins per day with an additional 2 strings of 1000 coins for every 60 kg of fodder. Additionally, each batch consumed 325 kg of grass per day (6.5 kg per horse per day). The total daily expenditure on convoys and horses for a single batch, excluding grass, was 24 strings of copper coins (S. Xu 2014: 9106–07, 9131, 9160). According to the Volumes of Army from 23 to 29 of *The Anthology of Laws and Regulations of the Song Dynasty,* Sichuan delivered 11,750 horses in 235 batches in a year at a daily cost of 5640 strings of 1000 coins for convoys and horses, not including the cost of animal feed. When factoring in the daily expenditure of 16 strings of 1000 coins for convoys on their return trips, 3760 strings of 1000 coins were paid per day. Therefore, the total daily expenditure on the 235 batches for round trips was 9400 strings of 1000 coins. It took 40 days to travel from Xingyuan Prefecture to Hanyang Military Prefecture, with the round trip taking more than 80 days. The total expenditure between Xingyuan Prefecture and Hanyang Military Prefecture was 752,000 strings of 1000 coins. Furthermore, transportation costs between Chengdu and Xingyuan Prefecture (a 50-day round trip), between Dangchang and Xingyuan Prefecture (a 40-day round trip), and between Hanyang Military Prefecture and the capital or military prefectures along the Yangtze River exceeded one million strings of copper coins, excluding expenditures on grass, facilities, and personnel of postal stations. The mayor of Kuizhou, Zhang Zhen, once stated that the expenditure on batch horse shipping from Lizhou to Guizhou (now Zigui County of Yichang) was up to 2 million strings of 1000 coins. The transportation costs of batch horse transportation were not affordable for any prefecture and were even a huge burden on a province.

The batch horse transportation of Sichuan was originally carried out by the Tea-Horse Department of Sichuan throughout the entire process. Every year, "prefectures and counties of Sichuan lacked more than 4000 soldiers pulling horses and borrowed over 300,000 copper coins to employ soldiers." (S. Xu 2014: 9148) In December of the first year of the Longxing Reign (AD 1163), Hanyang Military Prefecture established the Directorate of Affairs of Horses to take over and send horses. "The emperor ordered the tea-horse departments to transport the specified annual quotas of horses purchased from Sichuan and Shaanxi provinces under convoys to Hanyang Military Prefecture, where the convoys and horses rest at the postal station. The three Capital Guard Agencies and military prefectures along the Yangtze River were ordered to dispatch soldiers to take horses at Hanyang Military Prefecture. Tea-horse departments were prohibited from following the old practices of employing previous soldiers to pull horses." (S. Xu 2014: 9137) Only "horses purchased from Jingnan and Ezhou were not sent to directorates of affairs of horses but directly delivered to military prefectures." (S. Xu 2014: 9144) The Tea-Horse Department of Sichuan only needed to send horses under convoys to Hanyang Military Prefecture where the three Capital Guard Agencies and military prefectures dispatched soldiers to take horses at the Directorate of Affairs of Horses, which was mentioned by Hong Mai in "*Batch Horse Transportation of Ezhou*," Vol. 7 of the third set of *Strange Tales of the Miraculous by Yijian* that Sichuan arranges for soldiers and high-ranking officials to send batch horse transportation to Hanyang Military Prefecture, "they stayed there for 5 days, waiting for the three Capital Guard Agencies and military prefectures along the Yangtze River to take over horses." The heavy burden on Sichuan is therefore "slightly relieved. However, over 200,000 copper coins borrowed is a large sum beyond description." (S. Xu 2014: 9148)

Later, "horse-raising branches were established in Chengdu, Xingyuan, and Xiangyang prefectures," and the transportation burden was shared by different local governments. For example, in Chengdu Prefecture, 60 batches of horses were shipped, out of which 15 batches were taken by officials and soldiers of military institutions of Ezhou, and the remaining 45 batches were sent by officials of Chengdu Prefecture. The horses were initially sent via Xingyuan and Xiangyang prefectures to the Directorate of Affairs of Horses of Hanyang Military Prefecture, covering a distance of over 1750 km, and taking more than 120 days for the round trip. 1170 soldiers, along with junior military officers and veterinarians, were involved in this task. After the establishment of horse-raising branches in Xingyuan and Xiangyang prefectures, Chengdu Prefecture only delivered batch horse transportation to Xingyuan Prefecture. This reduced the total journey to around 600 km, and the round trip took only 50 days. The number of soldiers involved was reduced to 780, who worked in a circular manner. In Xingyuan Prefecture, among the 101 batches of horse transportation, 20 batches were taken by officials and soldiers of military institutions of Jingnan, while the remaining 81 batches were sent by officials of Xingyuan Prefecture. Initially, the journey of batch horse transportation directly delivered to Hanyang Military Prefecture covered a distance of over 1150 km, and the round trip took over 80 days, involving 2106 soldiers, along with junior military officers and veterinarians. However, after the establishment of horse-raising branches, the journey was shortened to 700 km for sending the horses to Xiangyang Prefecture, and the round trip was reduced to only 60 days. The number of soldiers working in a circular manner was reduced to 1638. In this way, Xiangyang Prefecture needed to transport 126 batches from Xingyuan Prefecture to Hanyang Military

Prefecture, involving 3276 soldiers. The entire journey was over 420 km, and the round trip took 24 days. The soldiers involved were assigned by provincial military commissions of Jingxi South and North and Jinghu North provinces from the Imperial Armies and garrison troops. Xiangyang Prefecture dispatched 1092 soldiers and was allowed to muster deserters of Sichuan Province. If still understaffed, the three Capital Guard Agencies and military prefectures would be ordered to go to the Directorate of Affairs of Horses of Hanyang Military Prefecture to lead its horse-raising officials and then went to Xiangyang Prefecture to take horses. In this manner, the transportation burden was shared, and prefectures and counties were relieved of the heavy burden of batch transportation by inputting soldiers to undertake the tasks of batch horse transportation (S. Xu 2014: 9148–50).

After the implementation of segmented transportation, certain troops were required to dispatch officials and soldiers to take over horses in Sichuan. This involved sending officials and soldiers of military institutions of Ezhou to Chengdu and officials and soldiers of military institutions of Jingnan to Xingyuan Prefecture. Additionally, the military institutions of Chizhou dispatched officials and soldiers to tea-horse departments to take over the annual quota of five batches of horses transported from Sichuan every year (S. Xu 2014: 9168). With regards to horses procured from the western regions by Dangchang, the three Capital Guard Agencies still sent soldiers to Sichuan to take over them. The Tea-Horse Department of Sichuan delivered 3800 horses from the western regions to the Bureau of Military Affairs every year. Initially, these horses were sent independently by Sichuan. However, in the 24th year of the Shaoxing Reign (AD 1154), one commander of the three Capital Guard Agencies was ordered to take away horses by inputting 4400 elite soldiers, who returned in the following year (X. Li 2013: 2735). This was done in Xingyuan Prefecture and the horses were transported in batches because convoys made profit from provisions and fodder, resulting in the deaths of many horses en route. In the second year of the Qiandao Reign (AD 1166), the transportation of batches of horses was shifted to water transport, eliminating the need for convoys from the three Capital Guard Agencies to take over the horses. However, the tea-horse departments continued to dispatch convoys as per prior practice (X. Li 2000: 429). When water transport ceased, the previous practice was restored, and the three Capital Guard Agencies resumed their role in taking horses from Xingyuan Prefecture. In the second year of the Kaixi Reign (AD 1206), the Palace Administration continued to send soldiers to take over 36 batches of horses annually from the Tea-Horse Department of Sichuan (S. Xu 2014: 9170). Initially, convoys were employed to transport horses from the horse-trading place of Dangchang to Xingyuan Prefecture. However, as Dangchang only had just over 100 households, and half of its employees were children aged 14 or 15, the convoy chief sent two soldiers and a veterinarian to supervise the convoys dispatched by the three Capital Guard Agencies. Subsequently, the three Capital Guard Agencies dispatched their own junior military officers and soldiers to transport horses from Dangchang to the Tea-Horse Department of Xingyuan Prefecture, taking full responsibility for the entire process. After the second year of the Shaoxi Reign (AD 1191), horses were primarily dispatched by officials of the tea-horse departments to Xingyuan Prefecture in batches. Subsequently, officials and soldiers of the three Capital Guard Agencies transported the horses to the capital (S. Xu 2014: 9160). In case of delay by the officials and soldiers of the three Capital Guard Agencies, the Pacification Commission of Sichuan "would send officials and soldiers to take over the horses. If the horses were not taken away in time, the Commission would request the Directorate of Affairs of Horses of Hanyang Military Prefecture to temporarily take over the horses. The three Capital Guard Agencies were requested to place the horses at the Directorate of Affairs of Horses temporarily" (S. Xu 2014: 9160).

Originally, each batch of horses from Guangnan West Province was controlled by officials and soldiers assigned by the province. Later, Guangnan West Province only assigned 5 high-ranking officials and a veterinarian, and the prefectures and counties en route needed to assign 11 soldiers to the task when the batches passed through their jurisdictional areas. They worked in turn to share the transportation costs. However, some prefectures did not meet the required number of soldiers. For example, Raozhou only arranged for 5 or 6 soldiers, and from Chizhou to Zhenjiang Prefecture, no soldier was assigned (S. Xu 2014: 9139). Nonetheless, the horses from Guangnan West Province were mainly transported to military prefectures along the Yangtze River, which involved a shorter journey compared to those from Sichuan.

Segmented transportation was helpful for sharing responsibilities and costs with other local governments in areas en route, especially reducing the pressure on the Tea-Horse Department of Sichuan, and stimulating the initiative of different regions to ensure war horses were transported with quality and quantity. Convoys were mainly composed of selected soldiers instead of civilians recruited in service. Expenses were primarily undertaken by the central government, including the expenditures paid by the general supply institutions. The establishment of the Directorate of Affairs of Horses of Hanyang Military Prefecture and horse-raising branches of Xiangyang Prefecture and others increased the costs of postal stations and personnel, but these costs were all undertaken by the royal court. "During transportation, junior military officers and soldiers are all given money and rice." "In addition, official credentials for monks were allocated to the prefectures en route for sale to get their expenditures reimbursed." "Every year, the quantity of cash and rice paid for junior military officers and soldiers was truly reported to the Transfer Agency of Taxation of the province and then reported to the Administration of State Affairs. Then, official credentials for monks are allocated to the provinces en route accordingly. Prefectures could get their expenditures reimbursed for batch horse shipping." If batch horse transportation was conducted during the autumn and winter seasons when grass withered, the imperial court would reimburse taxes on fodder to the prefectures and counties along the route. In addition, the Left National Treasury and the General Supply Administration of Ezhou would provide postal certificates for officials and soldiers from Sichuan on their return trip. The necessary funds for constructing postal stations, preparing items and utensils, and other requirements en route, along with the province's retained earnings, were expected to be appropriated from central government allocations. Lower governments were not allowed to apportion any excuses for cost sharing (S. Xu 2014: 9136, 9138, 9159). The Southern Song government accorded top priority to the effectiveness of war horses for national defense. Cost-sharing and cost increases were implemented with the goal of achieving high efficiency in transporting horses. The reason why the three Capital Guard Agencies dispatched officials and soldiers to Sichuan to acquire horses from the western regions was due to the lack of commitment from convoys employed by tea-horse departments, resulting in dead horses. As a result, the three Capital Guard Agencies directly sent officials and soldiers to obtain horses over long distances. Despite the increased expenditure on money and rice, the high cost ensured the horses intactness and the transportation of fine horses to the three Capital Guard Agencies (S. Xu 2014: 9139).

2.4.3.2 The Costs and Efficiency of the Changeable Batch Horse Shipping of Sichuan

Batch horse transportation is distinct from that of grains and similar commodities, which can be transported over long distances by shipping, providing incomparable advantages over land transport. Canals could transport large batch-shipping boats with a capacity of 600 Liao (196,800 L) or smaller ones with a capacity of 200 Liao (65,600 L) to 300 Liao (98,400 L), while the Yangtze River could accommodate even larger vessels. One Liao contains 92 Song Jin, approximately 60 kg. However, land carriage, on the other hand, required a daily person workload to carry a load of 60 Jin (30 kg) traveling 30 km. The load capacity of a boat, which could carry up to 18,000 kg (Shakeshi 1990), was roughly equivalent to 900 people workloads, while the load capacity of a cart was much less. For instance, boats sailing on the Bianhe River could transport a load equivalent to dozens of Chinese carts (B. Chao 1990). In cases where no waterways were available for transporting feudal land taxes levied in summer and autumn, they would be converted to cash and transported to the imperial court by land. For example, in areas like Wenzhou, Taizhou (now Linhai), Chuzhou (now Lishui), and Huizhou (now Shexian County of Huangshan), which lacked waterways, their taxes, grains, and cloth would be exchanged for an equivalent amount of cash (Toqta 1977: 4217).

In terms of the above-mentioned load capacity, the cost of shipping was cheaper than land transportation. In the Southern Song Dynasty, Wang Shiyu noted that transporting 60 kg of rice from Xinzhou to Chizhou costed over 500 copper coins, while transporting the same amount to Jiankang costed over 700 copper coins, and to Zhenjiang over 900 copper coins. Transporting to Huainan East and West provinces costed more than 900 copper coins, but transporting to the granary of the capital would cost over 1200 copper coins by land transportation (S. Yang et al. 1990). In the Northern Song Dynasty, transportation costs were lower. From the southeast to the capital (Bianliang, now Kaifeng), transporting 30 kg of rice costed about 300 copper coins (T. Li 2004: 679), which was considered a high price at that time. In the eighth year of the Xining Reign (AD 1075), shipping 6 kg of grain traveling 50 km on the Yuhe River costed 3 copper coins, while 60 kg of grain would cost 30 copper coins. If batch grain shipping was done on the Yuhe River, "70 copper coins were needed for labor costs of carrying every 6 kg of grain". In other words, 60 kg of grain would cost 700 copper coins (T. Li 2004: 7219), roughly the same as the cost of transportation on the river from Xinzhou to Jiankang.

In the Southern Song Dynasty, Wu Jie, the pacification commissioner of Sichuan and Shaanxi provinces, "dispatched hired civilians from Sichuan Province to transport 4,500,000 kg of rice to Lizhou at a cost of over 40 strings of copper coins for every 30 kg." During the Jiading Reign, in the midst of war, the transportation fee for a civilian carrying 48 kg of grain for the army by land from Dingzhou (now Changde), Lizhou (now Li County of Changde), or other areas to Zaoyang was even higher, ranging from 40 to 50 strings of copper coins (Toqta 1977: 4260). Additionally, in the Southern Song Dynasty, transporting grain for the army by land from Hechi (now Hui County of Longnan) to Chengzhou (now Cheng County of Longnan) and Minzhou, a journey of 450 km, cost 30,000 strings of copper coins if patrol soldiers carried 126,000 kg of grains. This resulted in an average cost of 14 strings of copper coins for every 60 kg. If civilians were hired to transport grains, the cost was 630,000 strings of copper coins, equivalent to 300 strings of copper coins for every 60 kg (S. Yang et al. 1990). Rice-carrying boats were adopted to transport grains to Linan Prefecture through the Xiatang River. However, due to flow cutoff in the channel, dozens of strings of copper coins were paid for every 60 kg of rice carried on foot (E. Shi 1990: 3328). For short journeys of grain transportation, the cost was over ten strings of copper coins for every 60 kg.

Several scholars have conducted comparative studies on the costs of water transport and land carriage between the same two locations. In general, water transport costs are significantly lower than those of land carriage. However, in the transportation of feudal land taxes levied in summer and autumn, as well as other goods, the land carriage costs in He'nan, Hebei, Hedong provinces, and the eastern regions of Shanhaiguan Pass were found to be less than those of downstream river transportation but higher than those of upstream river transportation. The cost of land carriage on the back of donkeys was found to be 100 copper coins for carrying 50 kg every 50 km, 120 copper coins for carrying 50 kg while walking on mountain slopes, and 900 copper coins for carts carrying 500 kg. As for water transport, on the Yellow River, the cost was 16 copper coins for 5 kg when sailing upstream and 6 copper coins when sailing downstream. On other rivers, the cost was 15 copper coins for carrying 5 kg upstream and 5 copper coins for sailing downstream. In the section of the canal from Lizhou or Jingzhou to Yangzhou, the cost was 4 copper coins when sailing downstream. In the dangerous areas of steep mountain slopes where few donkeys were available, it would cost no more than 150 copper coins for carrying 50 kg. Even when traveling on flat terrain, it would cost more than 80 copper coins. When laborers were available, two employees shared the payment of carrying 50 kg (R. Zhang 1990). During the Northern Song Dynasty, when transporting spices from areas south of the Five Ridges to the capital, tens of thousands of soldiers were arranged in postal stations with 200 soldiers in one postal station to convoy the spices. This was a heavy burden as it required a lot of labor. To address this issue, Ling Ce, the fiscal commissioner of Guangnan West Province, was ordered to make a plan. He suggested that spices should be transported by land to Nan'an and then transported northward by water, requiring only 800 soldiers. This plan could save a significant amount of transportation costs (Toqta 1977: 10,128). Furthermore, the normal practice of salt transportation was to carry salt for 50 km at a cost of 4 copper coins for land carriage and 1 copper coin for water transport, which was taken as the standard (K. Shen 2006: 94).

The Song people lamented that "land carriage posed the most significant difficulty" (S. Su 2003: 278), and "wise individuals opted for water transport to increase profits" (Z. Huang 1990). Emperor Huizong once inquired, "which is convenient in Sichuan Province, land carriage or water transport?" Sun Daofu responded by acknowledging the slow but cost-effective nature of water transport, and the quick yet labor-intensive nature of land carriage, which relied heavily on civilian workers. Initially, the pacification commissions selected water transport, which cost ten strings of copper coins for 60 kg. However, due to their perception of it being slow, they recruited tens of thousands of civilians to provide land carriage services at a cost of over 50 strings of copper coins for 60 kg. "If water transport is more convenient," the emperor said, "then you are suggested to adopt it." (Toqta 1977: 11,766).

The passage above mainly focuses on large-scale long-distance transportation. In terms of lightweight transportation, land carriage costs less. For instance, during the Southern Song Dynasty, when troops from Shouchun County and Haozhou (now Fengyang County of Chuzhou) of Huainan West Province transported grains by water, "they went across a sluice gate from Zhenzhou (now Yizheng) and Yangzhou and entered the Huaihe River via Yangzhou, Gaoyou, and Chuzhou (now Huai'an). After passing through the west of Xuyi, they sailed 90 km to Haozhou," and "235 km to Shouchun." Later, the number of troops in Shouchun decreased, and for the 100-km journey between Luzhou (now Hefei) and Shouchun, the cost of carrying 60 kg of grain (by land) was about one string of copper coins. If there were 1000 garrison soldiers, then 540,000 kg of grains would need to be transported in a year. If the spending on fodder for horses was added, the total cost would be over ten thousand strings of copper coins to transport over 6000 kg of rice. Compared with water transport, land carriage is more convenient and cost-effective (Z. Wang 1990a, b, c).

Horses are capable of walking on their own hooves, but rugged mountain roads can pose a hazard to them. Water transport, on the other hand, requires boats and human labor to use special vessels, resulting in a different cost logic for batch horse transportation by water and by land. Batch horse transportation out of Sichuan, in particular, was challenging and dangerous due to the difficult terrain, especially around Kui Gorge. Batch horse transportation by land from Chengdu had to travel northward to Xingyuan Prefecture before heading east out of Jinzhou and Fangzhou, which also featured numerous massive mountains. "As Jinzhou and Fangzhou are mountainous and rocky, most horses died with damaged hooves." In May of the first year of the Qiandao Reign (AD 1165), Wu Lin, the pacification commissioner of Sichuan, proposed "shipping horses northward" and opening waterways along the Yangtze River to address the issue of horse deaths during transportation. Emperor Xiaozong was receptive to Wu Lin's advice, particularly Ren Xu's proposal that 5000 soldiers from the Imperial Army and garrison troops be dispatched as a navy in the ten prefectures along the river. They would "receive and send boats when batch horse transportation arrives" and "practice navy skills on the river when horse-carrying boats depart," which strengthened Emperor Xiaozong's determination to open waterways for transporting batch horse transportation. The emperor also ordered the dispatch of 3500 soldiers from the Imperial Army and garrison troops for the batch horse shipping (D. Ma 2011: 4793).

The usual method of transporting horses in batches was to gather them in Dangchang Stockaded Village in the western regions, where they were then transported by land to Lizhou for shipment. From there, they were sent downstream to Jingnan within a month and then transported by land to the capital. Horses procured from Sichuan by Chengdu Prefecture were shipped from Hezhou and also sent downstream to Jingnan within 20 days for land carriage. Along the route, 11 prefectures, including Lizhou, Langzhou (now Langzhong), Guozhou (now Northern Nanchong), Hezhou, Gongzhou, Fuzhou (now Fuling District of Chongqing), Zhongzhou, Wanzhou, Kuizhou, Guizhou, and Xiazhou, provided relay transportation (S. Xu 2014: 9104–05). The cost of batch horse shipping was higher than that of land carriage. One-way downstream water transport was quicker than land carriage. Horses from the western regions that were shipped in Lizhou were transported downstream to Jingnan in less than one month. This voyage was only equivalent to the distance transported by land (28 days) from Xingyuan Prefecture to Xiangyang Prefecture. Horses of Sichuan shipped from Hezhou were transported to Jingnan in less than 20 days, which was less than the land carriage time from Chengdu to Xingyuan Prefecture (24 days) (S. Xu 2014: 9104–05). One-way land carriage from Chengdu Prefecture to Hanyang Military Prefecture took 64 days, and the round trip took 120 days. However, upstream transportation in the Chuanjiang River took around three times longer than downstream transportation. For example, "transporting horses downstream relayed by prefectures took 2 or 3 days, while going back upstream took 8 or 9 days." (S. Xu 2014: 9106) The round trip from Hezhou to Jingnan took 80 days. When including the time of transportation from Chengdu to Hezhou and from Jingnan to Hanyang Military Prefecture, water transport took almost the same amount of time as land carriage, but the land carriage of horses from the western regions from Xingyuan Prefecture obviously took less time than water transport.

However, water carriage cost more than land carriage in two aspects: the cost of building boats and the cost of employing helmsmen and sailors. According to Zhang Zhen, each prefecture was ordered to build 15 batches of boats, totaling 45 boats, at an average cost of about 800 strings of copper coins per boat. This amounted to a total cost of 35,000 strings of copper coins. Therefore, the 11 prefectures needed 396,000 strings of 1000 coins to build the necessary boats. Calculating in a similar manner, Wang Shipeng estimated that the total cost of Kuizhou for carrying batches of horses from Sichuan and Shaanxi provinces was 26,000 strings of 1000 coins for more than 30 boats, or over 800 strings of 1000 coins per boat (S. Wang 2012: 635). However, horse-carrying boats were easily damaged and had to be rebuilt annually. Therefore, the 11 prefectures needed 286,000 strings of 1000 coins for boats. Zhang Zhen and Wang Shipeng's estimates were based on all transported horses from Sichuan and Shaanxi provinces. Zhang Zhen calculated the total cost based on 235 batches, while

Wang Shipeng calculated the total cost based on 216 batches. Wu Lin noted that the trial shipping of 50 batches of horses from the western regions required 200 horse-carrying boats, which costed 440 strings of 1000 coins each, totaling 75,000 strings of 1000 coins. The Pacification Commission covered this cost (S. Xu 2014: 9106).

A regular batch transported by land was staffed with 32 convoys, 25 of whom were soldiers pulling horses. Zhang Zhen calculated the cost of employees involved in water transport: three boats for a batch, 40 employees for a boat (36 sailors and 4 helmsmen), 120 employees in total for a batch. As 500 copper coins were paid for an employee a day and the round trip took 15 days, a total of 900 strings of 1000 coins were paid for each batch, and 211,500 strings of copper coins were needed for 235 batches. This was only the cost of one prefecture. Ten prefectures needed over 2 million strings of 1000 coins, but the expenditure of building postal stations and the expenditure on money, grain, and fodder allocated to officials and soldiers were not included (S. Xu 2014: 9104). Compared to the cost of transporting batches by land, the cost of 32 employees should be subtracted from the cost of a batch transported by water, resulting in a lower cost. However, horse transportation still requires covering the cost of 88 employees more than land transportation. Wu Lin calculated the cost of employees for a batch given that two horse-carrying boats, each with a load capacity of 21,000 kg, could undertake the task of carrying one batch of horses. The batch transportation required a total of 38 employees, including 8 helmsmen and minor boatmen, 5 soldiers on the way back, and 25 horse-pullers for one boat carrying 25 horses. Thus, one batch transportation required 76 people. Although he only calculated the cost of 16 helmsmen and minor boatmen who were additionally paid apart from soldiers, ten prefectures along the route needed to pay 20,000 strings of 1000 coins for 50 batches (S. Xu 2014: 9107), which required the cost of 44 employees more than land transportation. For the batch shipping of Kuizhou, Wang Shipeng calculated that about 90 sailors were hired, which was 58 more than a batch transported by land. Wang Shipeng believed that 18,000 employees were needed in a year for Kuizhou to undertake all transportation tasks. Calculated at the cost of 500 copper coins for one employee a day and the 15-day round trip, a total of 120,000 strings of 1000 coins were paid for employees in a year (S. Wang 2012: 635–36). Wang Shipeng emphasized that "the cost of one prefecture Kuizhou calculated above was based on my witness of the passing-by batches of horses." (S. Wang 2012: 638)

As noted by Wang Shipeng, the transportation of horses in Kuizhou required the payment of 150,000–160,000 strings of 1000 coins, which covered the expenses of shipbuilding, employees, fodder for horses, and other costs. In contrast, the tax revenue collected by Kuizhou in a year was less than 200,000 strings of 1000 coins, which included the share given to the imperial court, taxes levied on salt and liquor, sundry tax, and salaries for officials and soldiers. The cost of batch horse transportation was thus nearly equivalent to the tax revenues collected by Kuizhou. Though Wu Lin was responsible for managing the matter, he could not compensate for one-tenth to two-tenths of the costs. Additionally, the labor in Kuizhou was insufficient for transportation. The number of helmsmen and sailors in the three counties administered by Kuizhou was less than 4 or 5 hundred. If helmsmen and sailors did not work by turns, a half more would be needed, and peasants would be employed for transportation (S. Wang 2012: 635). The saying that "the elderly vent their grievances when meeting with each other because most of their sons are employed for the horse-carrying boats" was used as an allegory to demonstrate that local governments extensively recruited civilians for horse-carrying boats (S. Wang 2012: 377). Zhang Zhen also mentioned that prefectures en route, including Lizhou, Xiazhou, and nine other prefectures, paid about 2 million strings of 1000 coins in a year. It was challenging for them to undertake transportation tasks because their tax revenue was not sufficient (X. Li 2000: 430). If all costs were imposed on the prefectures along the route, they surely could not afford it. Despite the efforts of Wang Shipeng and others to report the troubles of batch horse shipping, they received no support from Emperor Xiaozong (X. Li 2000: 431). One of the primary reasons was that the imperial court and the General Supply Commission covered most of the expenses. Zhang Zhen and Wang Shipeng's comments pertained to the trial of transporting 50 batches of horses from the western regions by water, which was implemented by Wu Lin (P. Shang 2010).[8] They inferred that the total number of batches shipped from Sichuan and Shaanxi provinces was 235 or 216. As Wu Lin stated, the cost of batch horse transportation from the western regions was primarily borne by the imperial court. "Fifty batches of horses of the western regions were first transported by water. The costs of all boats, employees and fodder needed by prefectures were all paid in Jiaozi (a kind of paper currency in the Song Dynasty)." Pacification commissions allocated vouchers worth 75,000 strings of 1000 coins to ten prefectures along the route to build 200 horse-carrying boats. Vouchers worth 12,200 strings of 1000 coins for fodder and 20,000 strings of 1000 coins for preparing and employing helmsmen and minor boatmen were also allocated to prefectures. Finally, vouchers worth 107,200 strings of 1000 coins were allocated for shipbuilding, fodder, employing helmsmen and minor boatmen, and other costs. If these funds were insufficient, concrete applications for money could be submitted to the Pacification Commission, with no right to levy on the public (S. Xu 2014: 9106–07). Wang Shipeng's comment that the expenses allocated by Wu Lin could not compensate for one-tenth to two-tenths of the expenditures did not win the support of Emperor Xiaozong.

The idea of transporting batches of horses by water was first proposed at the beginning of the Qiandao Reign (AD 1165), and in October of that year, Kuizhou Province was ordered to build boats for this purpose. By February of the following year, 50 batches of horses from the western regions had been formally transported by water, and this continued until November two years later. While three years were spent on batch horse transportation by water, it was actually implemented for only one and a half years (Y. Wang 2003: 2740). The tea-horse departments and pacification commissions emphasized that water transport costs were allocated by tea-horse departments, so prefectures and counties along the route need not worry about the costs, and water transport should not bother the public, as soldiers were dispatched

[8] By quoting Shang Ping's research work, the foregoing passage argues that transporting batches of horses by water is only a trial, and the frequency of horse shipping and the number of transported horses are both limited.

for the transportation, with helmsmen and coolies being civilians. However, Shang Ping pointed out that batch horse transportation by water had four disadvantages: lack of funds, lack of soldiers, risks of rivers, and trouble in purchasing grains (P. Shang 2010). The main reason for abolishing batch horse shipping was the disruption of water transport on grain-purchasing venues, and the number of horses transported by water was about the same as that transported by land. Provisions and funds for troops were supported by Lizhou and Langzhou, and the purchased provisions were transported on the Jialing River to the front line, which was considered the lifeline of war zones in Sichuan and Shaanxi (Y. He 2009). After Wu Lin's death, Yu Yunwen served as the pacification commissioner of Sichuan, and in October of the third year of the Qiandao Reign (AD 1167), he proposed a new plan for transporting horses. Under this plan, horses in batches were shipped at Jinzhou and transported to Jingkou, finally reaching Waikou for land carriage after passing by five postal stations. After passing by four postal stations on land, horse transportation followed the old route of batch horse transportation via Fangzhou. Horses were carried only through Junzhou and Fangzhou, with a journey of over 250 km, avoiding dozens of huge mountains in Jinzhou and Fangzhou. This method cost nine-tenths less than the cost of water transport from Lizhou. In the sixth year of the Qiandao Reign (AD 1170), the postal stations in the jurisdiction of Xunyang County of Jinzhou along new waterways connecting Juling, Mipu, Lixi, and Shizixian were provided with either grass but no fodder or fodder but no grain, indicating that the imperial court had adopted Yu Yunwen's plan after abolishing water transport on the Yangtze River.

Emperor Xiaozong's imperial decree to abolish water transport only highlighted the disruption caused by batch horse shipping on grain purchase. Specifically, the decree stated that the purpose of the abolition was to ensure the smooth sailing of grain-carrying boats (S. Xu 2014: 9180). Despite this concern, efficiency remained the top priority for the Southern Song Dynasty with respect to batch horse transportation by water, and cost was given less consideration. In terms of system design, the central government, including the General Supply Commission, assumed nearly all the costs and shared some of them with local governments through relay transportation among prefectures along the route, in order to ease their burden and stimulate their initiative. Nevertheless, the primary reason for the abolition of water transport remained the fact that it did not reduce horse losses and hindered the grain purchasing relied upon by the troops. Furthermore, water transport inevitably increased the burden on local authorities, particularly with respect to labor recruitment.

2.4.4 Summary

The transportation of war horses in batches was a crucial matter for the national defense of the Southern Song Dynasty, and was given significant importance by the central government. However, it was a complex and challenging task to transport war horses procured by the Sichuan and Guangnan West provinces to the capital of Lin'an and troops in the middle and lower reaches of the Yangtze River each year. The

Southern Song Dynasty needed to ensure the efficiency of transporting batches of war horses while also considering the affordability of local governments, in order to establish a sustainable and stable mechanism for transporting war horses in batches. To achieve this, the Southern Song Dynasty established two systems to guarantee the transportation of horses in batches. The first system was a transportation system that included convoy chiefs, veterinarians, and horse-pullers. The second was a support system that comprised directorates, bureaus, prefectures, counties along the route, and officials of the postal stations. Additionally, systems of quantitative assessment, rewards, and penalties were established. Rewards with high intensity made batch horse transportation an attractive way for relevant personnel to obtain significant promotions.

The financial situation of local authorities in the Southern Song Dynasty was poor, with limited resources available to support transportation of war horses. Consequently, expenses for convoys, fodder for horses, facilities of postal stations, and other requirements for transportation were primarily funded by the central government, specifically the authority and the General Supply Commission. Soldiers comprised the primary personnel in charge of transporting batches of horses, and expenses related to hiring helmsmen and sailors for water transport, shipbuilding, and other associated costs were also paid from central finance. In terms of system design, transportation burdens were not transferred to local authorities. Instead, measures such as sectional transportation and relay transportation among prefectures were implemented to distribute the transportation burdens among local authorities.

When it comes to transporting grain and other similar commodities on a large scale over long distances, water transport has an incomparable advantage over land carriage. From a load capacity perspective, water carriage surpasses land carriage by carriers and animals. In terms of comparing the costs of water transport and land carriage for the same two destinations, land carriage costs less than water transport against the flow, but costs more than water transport down the current. Generally, land carriage is more challenging than water transport. Horses have to walk on their own, and rugged mountain roads may harm them, while water transport requires special boats with associated boat and labor costs. As a result, the cost comparison of water transport and land carriage follows a different logic.

In the case of batch horse transportation, the Southern Song Dynasty applied the principle of efficiency first, as evidenced by measures such as giving rewards generously, with central governments covering almost all the costs and adopting water transport at higher costs than land carriage. Even though water transport was eventually abandoned, the main reason was not the costs but its inability to reduce the deaths and illnesses of horses and its disruption to grain procurement. In any case, prefectures along the route needed to provide labor and materials. Batch horse transportation still relied on postal stations, with the preparation of grain for convoys and fodder for horses, recruitment of civilians, and other work increasing the burdens on local governments along the route.

References

An, Zuozhang 安作璋. 2006. *Zhonguo Yunhe Wenhui* 中国运河文化史 [A History of Chinese Canal Culture]. Jinan: Shandong Education Press.

Cao, Jiaqi 曹家齐. 2002. *Songdai Jiaotong Guanli Zhidu Yanjiu* 宋代交通管理制度研究 [A Study on Traffic Management System in the Song Dynasty]. Kaifeng: Henan University Press.

Cao, Jiaqi 曹家齐. 2005. *Tang Song Shiqi Nanfang Diqu Jiaotong Yanjiu* 唐宋时期南方地区交通研究 [A Study on the Transportation in the South China During the Tang and Song Dynasties]. Hong Kong: Huaxia Literature and Art Publishing House.

Chao, Buzhi 晁补之. 1990. *Jilei Ji* 鸡肋集 [Works of Chao Buzhi]. Collected in Complete Library in the Four Branches of Literature. Shanghai: Shanghai Chinese Classics Publishing House.

Chao, Gongsu 晁公遡. 1990. *Songshan Ji* 嵩山集 [Works of Chao Gongsu]. Collected in Complete Library in the Four Branches of Literature. Shanghai: Shanghai Chinese Classics Publishing House.

Chen, Feng 陈峰. 1997a. "Beisong De Caoyun Shuidao Jiqi Zhili 北宋的漕运水道及其治理 [The Waterways of the Northern Song Dynasty and their Governance]". *Journal of Xiaogan University* 3.

Chen, Feng 陈峰. 1997b. "Songdai Caoyun Yagang Renyuan Kaoshu 宋代漕运押纲人员考述 [Studies on the Grain Transportation Escorts in the Song Dynasty] ". *Journal of Chinese Historical Studies* 1.

Chen, Qiqing 陈耆卿. 1990. *Jiading Chicheng Zhi* 嘉定赤城志 [Jiading Period Chronicles of Chicheng]. Collected in The Series of Chorography of the Song and Yuan Dynasties. Beijing: Zhonghua Book Company.

Chen, Zao 陈造. 1990. *Jianghuchangweng Ji* 江湖长翁集 [Selected Works of Chen Zao].Collected in Complete Library in the Four Branches of Literature. Shanghai: Shanghai Chinese Classics Publishing House.

Deng, Shen 邓深. 1990. *Dayin Jushi Shiji* 大隐居士诗集 [Poetry Collection of the Great Hermit]. Collected in Complete Library in the Four Branches of Literature. Shanghai: Shanghai Chinese Classics Publishing House.

Du, Wenyu 杜文玉. 1990. "Songdai Mazheng Yanjiu宋代马政研究 [Studies on Horse Administration in the Song dynasty]". *Journal of Chinese Historical Studies* 2.

Fan, Chengda 范成大. 2012a. *Guihai Yuheng Zhi* 桂海虞衡志 [Records of the Ranger in Guihai]. Collected in Complete Song Notes. Elephant Press.

Fan, Chengda 范成大. 2012b. *Can Luan Lu* 骖鸾录 [The Trip to Guilin]. Collected in Complete Song Notes. Elephant Press.

Fan, Chengda 范成大. 2012c. *Wu Chuan Lu* 吴船录 [Travelogues in Wu Area by Ship]. Collected in Complete Song Notes. Elephant Press.

Fan, Zhiming 范致明. 1990. *Yueyang Fengtu Ji* 岳阳风土记 [Geography and Customs of Yueyang]. Collected in Complete Library in the Four Branches of Literature. Shanghai: Shanghai Chinese Classics Publishing House.

Fan, Zhongyan 范仲淹. 1981. *Fan Wenzheng Gong Zhengfu Zouyi* 范文正公政府奏议 [Proposals Submitted by Fan Zhongyan].Collected in Collectanea of the Four Categories 1st edn.

Fang, Dacong 方大琮. 1990. *Tiean Ji* 铁庵集 [Collection of Fang Dacong]. Collected in Complete Library in the Four Branches of Literature. Shanghai: Shanghai Chinese Classics Publishing House.

Feng, Yonglin 冯永林. 1986. " Songdai De Cha Ma Maoyi 宋代的茶马贸易 [The Tea-Horse Trade in the Song Dynasty]". *Journal of Chinese Historical Studies* 2.

Guo, Xiang 郭象. 1990a. *Zhuangzi Zhu* 庄子注 [Annotations to Chuang Tzu's Theory]. Collected in Complete Library in the Four Branches of Literature. Shanghai: Shanghai Chinese Classics Publishing House.

Guo, Xiangzheng 郭祥正. 1990b. *Qingshan Xu Ji* 青山续集 [Continuation to Qingshan Collection]. Collected in Complete Library in the Four Branches of Literature. Shanghai: Shanghai Chinese Classics Publishing House.

He, Yuan 何薳. 2008. *Chunzhu Jiwen* 春渚纪闻 [Anecdotage of the Song Dynasty]. Collected in Complete Song Notes. Elephant Press.

He, Yuhong 何玉红. 2009. "Nansong Chuanshan Zhanqu Junliang De Dimai Yu Zhuanyun—Jianlun Nansong Shiqi Jialingjiang Shuiyun 南宋川陕战区军粮的籴买与转运—兼论南宋时期嘉陵江水运 [Purchase and Transportation of Army Provisions in the War Zones of Sichuan and Shannxi in the Southern Song Dynasty—A Concurrent Discussion of the Transportation on the Jialing River in the Southern Song Dynasty]". *Journal of Southwest University* 5.

Henan Tongzhi 河南通志 [Chronicles of Henan]. 1990. Edited by Yongzheng. Collected in Complete Library in the Four Branches of Literature. Shanghai: Shanghai Chinese Classics Publishing House.

Huang, Chunyan 黄纯艳. 2002. *Sonhdai Chafa Yanjiu* 宋代茶法研究 [A Study on Tea Policy of the Song Dynasty]. Kunming: Yunnan University Press.

Huang, Chunyan 黄纯艳and Na Yin 尹娜. 2002. "Lun Yang Yungong Yanfa Gaige 论杨允恭盐法改革 [YANG Yun-gong's Reform on Salt Policy]". *Social Sciences in Yunnan* 5.

Huang, Tingjian 黄庭坚. 2011. *Huang Tingjian Quanji* 黄庭坚全集 [The Complete Works of Huang Tingjian]. Nanchang: Jiangxi People's Publishing House.

Huang, Zhen. 1990. *Huang Shi Richao* 黄氏日抄 [Notes of Huang]. Collected in Complete Library in the Four Branches of Literature. Shanghai: Shanghai Chinese Classics Publishing House.

Jia, Daquan 贾大泉 and Yishi Chen 陈一石. 1989. *Sichuan Chayeshi* 四川茶业史 [A History of Sichuan Tea Industry]. Chengdu: Bashu Press.

Jojin 成寻. 2009. *Xin Jiao Cantiantai Wutaishan Ji* 新校参天台五台山记 [Revised Edition of Travelogues of Jojin]. Edited by Wang Liping. Shanghai: Shanghai Chinese Classics Publishing House.

Kong, Pingzhong 孔平仲. 1990. *Qingjiang San Kong Ji* 清江三孔集 [Selected Works of Three Kong Brothers]. Collected in Complete Library in the Four Branches of Literature. Shanghai: Shanghai Chinese Classics Publishing House.

Li, Bi 李壁. 1990. *Wangjinggong Shi Zhu* 王荆公诗注 [Annotations to Wangjinggong's Poems]. Collected in Complete Library in the Four Branches of Literature. Shanghai: Shanghai Chinese Classics Publishing House.

Li, Liuqian 李流谦. 1990. *Danzhai Ji* 澹斋集 [Selected Works of Li Liuqian]. Collected in Complete Library in the Four Branches of Literature. Shanghai: Shanghai Chinese Classics Publishing House.

Li, Tao 李焘. 2004. *Xu Zizhi Tongjian Changbian* 续资治通鉴长编 [Continuation to The Comprehensive Mirror for Aid in Government]. Beijing: Zhonghua Book Company.

Li, Xinchuan 李心传. 2000. *Jianyan Yilai Chaoye Zaji* 建炎以来朝野杂记 [Laws and Institutions Since the Jianyan Reign]. Edited by Xu Gui. Beijing: Zhonghua Book Company.

Li, Xinchuan 李心传. 2013. *Jianyan Yilai Xinian Yaolu* 建炎以来系年要录 [Chronological Record of Major Events Since 1127]. Beijing: Zhonghua Book Company.

Li, Zhiyi 李之仪. 1990. *Guxijushi Qian Ji* 姑溪居士前集 [Prequel to Selected Works of Guxijushi]. Collected in Complete Library in the Four Branches of Literature. Shanghai: Shanghai Chinese Classics Publishing House.

Liang, Zhongxiao 梁中效. 1996. "Nansong Dongxi Jiaotong Dadongmai—Magang Yilu Chutan 南宋东西交通大动脉——马纲驿路初探 [The East-west Main Traffic Channel of the Southern Song Dynasty—A Study on Horse Batch Transportation Route,]". *Journal of Chengdu University* 1.

Lin, Dong 林駧. 1990. *Gujin Yuanliu Zhi Lun* 古今源流至论 [The Theories of Historical Origins]. Collected in Complete Library in the Four Branches of Literature. Shanghai: Shanghai Chinese Classics Publishing House.

Lin, Wenxun 林文勋. 1989. "Songdai Xinan Diqu De Shima Yu Minzu Guanxi 宋代西南地区的市马与民族关系 [Horse Trading and the Relations Among Ethnic Groups in the Southwest of the Song Dynasty]". *Thinking* 2.

Lin, Wenxun 林文勋. 1992. “Tang Song Shiqi Changjiang Hangyun Maoyi De Fazhan 唐宋时期长江航运贸易的发展 [The Development of Shipping Trade of the Yangtze River in the Tang and Song Dynasties]”. *Jiangsu Social Sciences* 6.

Liu, Fusheng 刘复生. 1995. “Songdai Guangma Ji Xiangguan Wenti 宋代广马及相关问题 [Studies on Horse Trading in Guangnan Provinces During the Song Dynasty]”. *Journal of Chinese Historical Studies* 3.

Liu, Fusheng 刘复生. 2008. “Songdai Xinan De Yanma Maoyi, 宋代西南的盐马贸易 [Salt-horse Trade in the Southwest During the Song Dynasty]”. *Anthology of the Studies on the History of Song 9*. Baoding: Hebei University Press

Liu, Zai 刘宰. 1990a. *Mantang Ji* 漫塘集 [Anthology of Liu Zai]. Collected in Complete Library in the Four Branches of Literature. Shanghai: Shanghai Chinese Classics Publishing House.

Liu, Zihui 刘子翚. 1990b. *Pingshan Ji* 屏山集 [Selected Works of Liu Zihui]. Collected in Complete Library in the Four Branches of Literature. Shanghai: Shanghai Chinese Classics Publishing House.

Lou, Yao 楼钥. 1990. *Gonggui Ji* 攻媿集 [Selected Works of Lou Yao]. Collected in Complete Library in the Four Branches of Literature. Shanghai: Shanghai Chinese Classics Publishing House.

Lu, Xian 卢宪. 1990. *Jiading Zhenjiang Zhi* 嘉定镇江志 [Jiading Period Chronicles of Zhenjiang]. Collected in The Series of Chorography of the Song and Yuan Dynasties. Beijing: Zhonghua Book Company.

Lu, You 陆游. 2011. *Lu You Quanji Jiaozhu* 陆游全集校注 [Annotations to Lu You’s Works]. Collated by Qian Zhonglian. Hangzhou: Zhejiang Education Publishing House.

Lu, You 陆游. 2012a. *Laoxuean Biji* 老学庵笔记 [The Notes of an Old Pedant]. Sorted by Li Changxian. Collected in Complete Song Notes. Elephant Press.

Lu, You 陆游. 2012b. *Ru Shu Ji* 入蜀记 [Essays about My Journey to Sichuan]. Sorted by Li Changxian. Collected in Complete Song Notes. Elephant Press.

Luo, Chuandong 罗传栋. 1991. *Changjiang Hangyunshi (Gudai Bufen)* 长江航运史 [A History of Shipping in the Yangtze River (Ancient Section)]. Beijing: China Communications Press.

Luo, Yuan 罗愿. 1990. *Xinan Zhi* 新安志 [Chronicles of Xin’an]. Collected in The Series of Chorography of the Song and Yuan Dynasties. Beijing: Zhonghua Book Company.

Ma, Huamin 马华民. 1990. “ ‘Qingmingshanghetu’ Suo Fanying De Songdai Zaochuan Jishu〈清明上河图〉所反映的宋代造船技术 [Shipbuilding techniques of the Song Dynasty Presented in Riverside Scene at Qingming Festival]”. *Cultural Relics of Central China* 4.

Ma, Rong 马蓉. 2004. *Yongle Dadian Fangzhi Jiyi* 永乐大典方志辑佚 [Compilation of Local Chronicles from Yongle Encyclopedia]. Beijing: Zhonghua Book Company.

Mei, Yaochen 梅尧臣. 1980. *Mei Yaochen Ji Biannian Jiaozhu* 梅尧臣集编年校注 [Chronological Annotations to Mei Yaochen’s Anthology]. Collated by by Zhu Dongrun. Shanghai: Shanghai Chinese Classics Publishing House.

Ouyang, Xiu 欧阳修. 2001. *Ouyang Xiu Quanji* 欧阳修全集 [Selected Works of Ouyang Xiu]. Beijing: Zhonghua Book Company.

Qian, Shuoyou 潜说友. 1990. *Xianchu Linan Zhi* 咸淳临安志 [Xianchun Period Chronicles of Lin’an]. Collected in in The Series of Chorography of the Song and Yuan Dynasties. Beijing: Zhonghua Book Company.

Quan, Hansheng 全汉升. 1946. *Tang Song Diguo Yu Yunhe* 唐宋帝国与运河 [The Song and Tang Empires and their Canals]. Beijing: The Commercial Press.

Shakeshi 沙克什. 1990. *Hefang Tongyi* 河防通议 [Summary of River Flood Prevention Works]. Collected in Complete Library in the Four Branches of Literature. Shanghai: Shanghai Chinese Classics Publishing House.

Shang, Ping 尚平. 2010. “Nansong Magang Shuiyun Kaoshu 南宋马纲水运考述 [Batch Horse Shipping in the Southern Song]”. *Journal of Capital Normal University* 1.

Shen, Kuo 沈括. 2006. *Mengxi Bitan* 梦溪笔谈 [Mengxi Bitan (Dream Pool Essays)]. Sorted by Hu Jingyi. Collected in Complete Song Notes. Elephant Press.

Shi, E 施谔. 1990. *Chunyou Linan Zhi*淳祐临安志 [Chunyou Period Chronicles of Lin'an]. Collected in The Series of Chorography of the Song and Yuan Dynasties. Beijing: Zhonghua Book Company.

Shi, Su 施宿, et al. 1990. *Jiatai Kuaiji Zhi* 嘉泰会稽志 [Jiatai Period Chronicles of Kuaiji]. Collected in The Series of Chorography of the Song and Yuan Dynasties. Beijing: Zhonghua Book Company.

Shiba, Yoshinobu 斯波义信. 1985. "Song Yuan Shidai De Chuanbo 宋元时代的船舶 [Vessels in the Song and Yuan Dynasties]". Translated by Jing Hui. *Marine History Studies* 1.

Song Shi Quanwen 宋史全文 [History of the Song Dynasty in Full Scale]. 2005. Edited by Zhiliang Li. Haerbin: Heilongjiang People's Publishing House.

Song, Lian 宋濂. 1976. *Yuan Shi* 元史 [History of the Yuan Dynasty]. Beijing: Zhonghua Book Company.

Su, Shi 苏轼. 2010. *Su Shi Quanji Jiaozhu* 苏轼全集校注 [Annotations to the Selected Works of Su Shi]. Punctuated and collated by Zhang Zhilie, et al. Shijieazhuang: Hebei People's Publishing House.

Su, Zhe 苏辙. 1987. *Luancheng Ji* 栾城集 [Selected Works of Su Zhe]. Shanghai: Shanghai Chinese Classics Publishing House.

Sun, Di 孙觌. 1990. *Hongqingjushi Ji*鸿庆居士集 [Selected Works of Sun Di]. Collected in Complete Library in the Four Branches of Literature. Shanghai: Shanghai Chinese Classics Publishing House.

Sun, Fengji 孙逢吉. 1988. *Zhiguan Fenji* 职官分纪 [Records of Historical Official Systems]. Beijing: Zhonghua Book Company.

Sun, Yi 孙奕. 1990a. *Shier Bian* 示儿编 [Works For Instructing My Children]. Collected in Complete Library in the Four Branches of Literature. Shanghai: Shanghai Chinese Classics Publishing House.

Sun, Yingshi 孙应时. 1990b. *Zhuhu Ji* 烛湖集 [Selected Works of Sun Yingshi]. Collected in Complete Library in the Four Branches of Literature. Shanghai: Shanghai Chinese Classics Publishing House.

Tianyige Cang Mingchao Ben⟨Tiansheng Ling⟩Jiaozheng 天一阁藏明钞本⟨天圣令⟩校证 [Proof-reading of Laws and Regulations During the Tiansheng Period — the Ming hand copied version stored in Tianyi Pavilion]. 2004. Beijing: Zhonghua Book Company.

Toqta 脱脱. 1977. *Song Shi* 宋史 [History of the Song Dynasty]. Beijing: Zhonghua Book Company.

Wang, Anshi 王安石. 1990. *Linchuan Wenji* 临川文集 [Selected Works of Wang Anshi]. Collected in Complete Library in the Four Branches of Literature. Shanghai: Shanghai Chinese Classics Publishing House.

Wang, Shipeng 王十朋. 2012. *Wang Shipeng Quanji* 王十朋全集 [Complete Works of Wang Shipeng]. Edited by Meixi Collection Republication Committee. Shanghai: Shanghai Chinese Classics Publishing House.

Wang, Yan 王炎. 1990a. *Shuangxi Leigao* 双溪类稿 [Selected Works of Wang Yan]. Collected in Complete Library in the Four Branches of Literature. Shanghai: Shanghai Chinese Classics Publishing House.

Wang, Yingchen 汪应辰. 1990b. *Wending Ji* 文定集 [Selected Works of Wang Yingchen]. Collected in Complete Library in the Four Branches of Literature. Shanghai: Shanghai Chinese Classics Publishing House.

Wang, Yinglin 王应麟. 2003. *Yuhai* 玉海 [Encyclopedia of 21 Categories]. Yangzhou: Guangling Publishing House.

Wang, Zhidao 王之道. 1990a. *Xiangshan Ji* 相山集 [Selected Works of Wang Zhidao]. Collected in Complete Library in the Four Branches of Literature. Shanghai: Shanghai Chinese Classics Publishing House.

Wang, Zhiwang 王之望. 1990b. *Hanbin Ji* 汉滨集 [Selected Works of Wang Zhiwang]. Collected in Complete Library in the Four Branches of Literature. Shanghai: Shanghai Chinese Classics Publishing House.

Wang, Zongji 王宗稷. 1990c. *Dongpo Xiansheng Nianpu* 东坡先生年谱 [Chronology of Su Dongpo]. Collected in Complete Library in the Four Branches of Literature. Shanghai: Shanghai Chinese Classics Publishing House.

Wei, Tian'an 魏天安. 2007. "Nansong Guangxi Maima Zhidu南宋广西买马制度 [Guangxi Horse-Procurement System in the Southern Song Dynasty]". *Guangxi Social Sciences* 4.

Wu, Fei 吴芾. 1990. *Hushan Ji* 湖山集 [Selected Works of Wu Fei]. Collected in Complete Library in the Four Branches of Literature. Shanghai: Shanghai Chinese Classics Publishing House.

Xi, Longfei 席龙飞. 2000. *Zhongguo Zaochuanshi*中国造船史 [A History of China Shipbuilding]. Wuhan: Hubei Education Press.

Xi, Longfei 席龙飞. 2004. *Zhongguo Kexue Jishushi (Jiaotong Juan)* 中国科学技术史(交通卷)[The History of Science and Technology in China (Traffic Volume)]. Beijing: Science Press.

Xu, Jing 徐兢. 2006. *Xuanhe Fengshi Gaoli Tujing* 宣和奉使高丽图经 [Xuanhe Period Maps and Records About Goryeo]. Sorted by Yu Yunguo. Collected in Complete Song Notes. Elephant Press.

Xu, Jingheng 许景衡. 1990. *Hengtang Ji* 横塘集 [Selected Works of Xu Jingheng]. Collected in Complete Library in the Four Branches of Literature. Shanghai: Shanghai Chinese Classics Publishing House.

Xu, Lun 许纶. 1990a. *She Zhai Ji* 涉斋集 [Selected Works of Xu Lun]. Collected in Complete Library in the Four Branches of Literature. Shanghai: Shanghai Chinese Classics Publishing House.

Xu, Luqing 徐鹿卿. 1990b. Qingzheng Cungao 清正存稿 [Extant Manucripts of Xu Luqing]. Collected in Complete Library in the Four Branches of Literature. Shanghai: Shanghai Chinese Classics Publishing House.

Xu, Mengshen 徐梦莘. 1987. *Sanchao Beimeng Huibian* 三朝北盟会编 [Records of Wars and Actions between the Song and Jin in Three Song Emperors' Reigns]. Shanghai: Shanghai Chinese Classics Publishing House.

Xu, Song 徐松, et al. 2014. *Song Huiyao Jigao*宋会要辑稿 [The Anthology of Laws and Regulations of the Song Dynasty]. Shanghai: Shanghai Chinese Classics Publishing House.

Yang, Shiqi 杨士奇, et al. 1990. *Lidai Mingchen Zouyi* 历代名臣奏议 [Memorials to the Thrones in History]. Collected in Complete Library in the Four Branches of Literature. Shanghai: Shanghai Chinese Classics Publishing House.

Yang, Wanli 杨万里. 2007. *Yang Wanli Ji Jianjiao* 杨万里集笺校 [Annotations to Selected Works of Yang Wanli]. Collated by Xin Gengru. Beijing: Zhonghua Book Company.

Yu, Chunyan 余春燕. 2007. "Songdai Sanxia Shuiyun Chutan 宋代三峡水运初探 [A Tentative Study on Three Gorges Shipping in the Song Dynasty]". *Chongqing Social Sciences* 10.

Yuan, Shuoyou 袁说友. 1990. *Dongtang Ji* 东塘集 [Selected Works of Yuan Shuoyou]. Collected in Complete Library in the Four Branches of Literature. Shanghai: Shanghai Chinese Classics Publishing House.

Yue, Ke 岳珂. 1990. *Yuchu Ji*玉楮集 [Selected Works of Yue Ke]. Collected in Complete Library in the Four Branches of Literature. Shanghai: Shanghai Chinese Classics Publishing House.

Zhang, Hao 张淏. 1990. *Baoqing Kuaiji Xuzhi* 宝庆会稽续志 [Baoqing Period Continuation of the Chronicles of Kuaiji]. Collected in The Series of Chorography of the Song and Yuan Dynasties. Beijing: Zhonghua Book Company.

Zhang, Jinpeng 张锦鹏. 2008. *Nansong Jiaotongshi* 南宋交通史 [The History of Transportation in the Southern Song Dynasty]. Beijing: People's Publishing House.

Zhang, Ruyu 章如愚. 1990. *Qun Shu Kaosuo* 群书考索[Research and Quest on Books of All Sorts]. Collected in Complete Library in the Four Branches of Literature. Shanghai: Shanghai Chinese Classics Publishing House.

Zhang, Shizheng 张师正. 1990a. *Kuo Yi Zhi* 括异志 [Stories of the Strange]. Collected in Complete Library in the Four Branches of Literature. Shanghai: Shanghai Chinese Classics Publishing House.

Zhang, Shou 张守. 1990b. *Piling Ji* 毘陵集 [Selected Works of Zhang Shou]. Collected in Complete Library in the Four Branches of Literature. Shanghai: Shanghai Chinese Classics Publishing House.

Zhang, Shunmin 张舜民. 1990c. *Hua Man Ji* 画墁集 [Selected Works of Zhang Shunmin]. Collected in Complete Library in the Four Branches of Literature. Shanghai: Shanghai Chinese Classics Publishing House.

Zhang, Xiaoxiang 张孝祥. 1980. *Yuhujushi Wenji* 于湖居士文集 [Selected Works of Zhang Xiaoxiang]. Shanghai: Shanghai Chinese Classics Publishing House.

Zhang, Xuan 张铉. 1990. *Zhida Jinling Zhi* 至大金陵新志 [Zhida Period Chronicles of Jinling]. Collected in The Series of Chorography of the Song and Yuan Dynasties. Beijing: Zhonghua Book Company.

Zhao, Ding 赵鼎. 2008. *Jianyan Bilu* 建炎笔录 [Chronicles of Jianyan Period]. Sorted by Lai Kehong and Liu Qiang. Collected in Complete Song Notes. Elephant Press.

Zhao, Fan 赵蕃. 1990. *Chunxi Gao* 淳熙稿 [Chunxi Period Selected Works of Zhao Fan]. Collected in Complete Library in the Four Branches of Literature. Shanghai: Shanghai Chinese Classics Publishing House.

Zheng, Gangzhong 郑刚中. 1990. *Beishan Ji* 北山集 [Selected Works of Zheng Gangzhong]. Collected in Complete Library in the Four Branches of Literature. Shanghai: Shanghai Chinese Classics Publishing House.

Zheng, Xie 郑獬. 1990. *Yunxi Ji* 郧溪集 [Selected Works of Zheng Xie]. Collected in Complete Library in the Four Branches of Literature. Shanghai: Shanghai Chinese Classics Publishing House.

Zheng, Yao 郑瑶, et al. 1990. *Jingding Yanzhou Xu Zhi* 景定严州续志 [Jingding Period Continuation of the Chronicles of Yanzhou]. Collected in The Series of Chorography of the Song and Yuan Dynasties. Beijing: Zhonghua Book Company.

Zhou, Baozhu 周宝珠. 1997. *Qingmingshanghetu Yu Qingmingshanghexue* 〈清明上河图〉与清明上河学 [Riverside Scene at Qingming Festival and the Studies on the Scroll]. Kaifeng:Henan University Press.

Zhou, Bida 周必大. 1990. *Wenzhong Ji* 文忠集 [Selected Works of Wenzhong]. Collected in Complete Library in the Four Branches of Literature. Shanghai: Shanghai Chinese Classics Publishing House.

Zhou, Qüfei 周去非. 1999. *Lingwai Daida Jiaozhu* 岭外代答校注 [Notes from the Land Beyond the Passes]. Collated by Yang Wuquan. Beijing: Zhonghua Book Company.

Zhou, Yinggu 周应谷. 1990. *Jingding Jiankang Zhi* 景定建康志 [Jingding Period Chronicles of Jiankang]. Collected in The Series of Chorography of the Song and Yuan Dynasties. Beijing: Zhonghua Book Company.

Zhu, Xi 朱熹. 2010. *Hui'an Xiansheng Zhuwengong Ji* 晦庵先生朱文公文集 [Selected Works of Zhu Xi]. Punctuated and collated by Liu Yongxiang, et al. Shanghai: Shanghai Chinese Classics Publishing House. Heifei: Anhui Education Publishing House.

Zou, Hao 邹浩. 1990. *Daoxiang Ji* 道乡集 [Selected Works of Zou Hao]. Collected in Complete Library in the Four Branches of Literature. Shanghai: Shanghai Chinese Classics Publishing House.

Chapter 3
Seagoing Vessels and Voyages in the Song Dynasty

3.1 Crew Composition and Modes of Navigation

The Song Dynasty was an Age of Discovery in ancient China. Previous scholars have made rich contributions to the study of its system of maritime trade, its inventory of commodities, and the construction and types of its seagoing vessels. Many insights were gained due to these studies regarding marine trade, commodities, finances, composition of vessels, division of labor, the various ways in which navigation differed depending on weather and other concerns, sizes of various fleets, *et cetera.* Nevertheless, these topics have not been explored as rigorously and systematically as they deserve.[1] This section offers an attempt to do so.

3.1.1 Crew Composition

In the Song Dynasty, a seagoing vessel could carry at least a hundred people, with some boats large enough to carry hundreds. According to *Reflections about Pingzhou,* written by the ancient geologist Zhu Yu, a sea merchant ship could carry "a few hundred to several hundred people" (Y. Zhu 2006: 149). *Accounts About the Capital* written by Wu Zimu noted that "sea merchant ships differed in size. The bigger ones

[1] Much attention has early been attached to the study of maritime trade in the Song Dynasty, the fruitful findings will not be listed here. The study on the seagoing vessels are as follows *A History of China Shipbuilding* written by Xi Longfei, *Editorial Committee of Excavation Report of the Quanzhou Bay Song Dynasty Shipwreck Excavation, A Preliminary Study on Restoration of the Song Dynasty's Shipwreck Found in Quanzhou Bay, An Analysis on the Structure of the Song Boat Unearthed in Quanzhou* by Zhuang Weij and He Guowei, and *A Study on Ningbo Junk of Song Dynasty* by Xi Longfei. The above are mainly discussed from the perspective of technological history. *A History of Chinese Maritime Science and Technology* by Zhang Xun discusses navigation modes, but lacks the exploration of crew composition and the organization of the fleet. In addition, the study of sailing power and navigation can also be supplemented.

C. Huang, *A Panoramic View of the Song Dynasty Through the Lens of Shipbuilding Industry*, https://doi.org/10.1007/978-981-97-6128-9_3

with a load capacity of 5000 Liao could carry five to six hundred people, while the smaller with a load capacity of two thousand Liao could carry two to three hundred people. Other smaller flat-bottomed boats were called 'wind sailing ships' installed with six or eight oars, and each could carry over one hundred people." (Z. Wu 1980: 111) Both books mentioned above refer to commercial seagoing vessels with a load capacity of over 100 people, including boatmen and passengers on board. This was considered to be the boat's deadweight tonnage. However, counting individuals one at a time would likely yield much smaller numbers. Large ships over 650 tons were capable of carrying hundreds of people, but in practice likely carried dozens, or no more than a hundred. *Xuanhe Period Maps and Records About Goryeo* recorded that a 650-ton merchant ship involved a total of 60 helmsmen and sailors, with the rest being envoys on board. "Shenzhou" (meaning Magic Boat) was recorded as the largest passenger ship built for the mission to Goryeo in the reign of Emperor Huizong. It was "three times the size of a civilian passenger ship, so were its number of decorations, and carrying capacity" (J. Xu 2006: 130) Its full capacity was enough for five to six hundred people, including about one hundred operators. This section places its focus on operators and passengers on board.

The operation of a seagoing ship required an efficiency of organization with a clear division of work among crew members. Such divisions of labor are widely referred in ancient works. Zhen Dexiu, a Neo-Confucianist in the Song dynasty, said that the ship must be equipped with helmsmen, anchor droppers, and sailors. (D. Zhen, n.d.) These three types of work are necessary for ensuring smooth navigation. In the Southern Song Dynasty, penalties for smuggling "lacha", a kind of early spring tea in milk color, are as follows: "any trafficker, ship owner, or helmsman shall be all beheaded; sailors and minor boatmen shall be exiled to remote places 1500 km away," (S. Xu et al. 2014: 6681) providing a record of the inclusion of minor boatmen. The ancient Customs in Mingzhou levied tax in kind on merchant ships coming from Hainan, Champa Kingdom, Xiping (present-day Quanzhou), and Guangzhou: 10% on costs of labors, including captain, mates, helmsmen, paddlers and sailors, 4% on the value of iron-shipping business (J. Luo et al. 1990: 5057). Captain, mates, and paddlers are quoted. Each year when the ships depart, the government granted the authorities a feast. Shipowners home and abroad, head technicians, and helmsmen were all qualified to be invited to join in the feast in accordance with the imperial edict (S. Xu et al. 2014: 4210). *Chunxi Period Chronicles of Fuzhou* mentions that there were four types of crew members recruited from Fujian for passenger boats: helmsmen, head technicians, anchor droppers, and sailors (K. Lang 1990: 7900). This was in addition to other crew members and individuals, including shipmasters, helmsmen, head technicians, boatswains, anchor droppers, handymen, peddlers, sailors, minor boatmen and so on.

In the Song Dynasty, the shipmaster or captain of the ship was referred to as "Gangshou." The court introduced a rule that "those who could drum up ships and levy taxation on the goods at a cumulative value of fifty thousand strings of 1000 coins or more would be granted a position as a lower military officer". The foreign captain Cai Jingfang was such an example (D. Ma 2011: 592; X. Li 2013: 2013). In the fifth year of the Yuanfeng Reign (AD 1082), a foreign captain delivered a letter from the princess of Sri Vijaya to Sun Jiong, the Governor of Ancient Customs (Toqta 1977: 14,090). There was no doubt that both Cai Jingfang and Nan Fan were shipmasters. The shipmaster was often the richest person on the ship, serving as captain, deputy captain, or shipmate (Y. Zhu 2006: 149). Shipowners could also serve as shipmasters, such as Li Chong, a merchant from Quanzhou, In the fourth year of the Chongning Reign (AD 1105), Li Chong recruited some sailors for a trading expedition to Japan. Evidence for this comes from the fact that his name was listed on the trading license as captain (Chaoye Qun Zai 1938: 452–53). Rich merchants could also serve in other managerial staff positions, such as deputy captain or shipmate. According to the regulations of Ancient Customs, those who evaded acquisitions were sentenced to two years of imprisonment, and were sent to local authorities as lower class workers (Chaoye Qun Zai 1938: 452). The goods they were carrying would also be confiscated. The penalty for key members was heavier than that of ordinary sailors. Therefore, the mate and boatswain were also managers, while the helmsman was the highest-ranking technician.

Authorized by the government, the ship-master or captain was responsible for crews and sailing affairs, and had the right to punish crew members. The Ancient Customs granted him a red official seal, allowing the offender to be whipped with a bamboo pole. Criminals sentenced to death were also confiscated of property (Y. Zhu 2006: 149). If a foreigner crew erred, his punishment was decided by his own ship-master. In the Southern Song Dynasty, in the second year of the Chunxi Reign (AD 1175), a Japanese minor boatman, Teng Taiming, beat Chinese sailor Zheng Zuo to death. As a result, he was restrained and handed over to the ship-master, and punished by Japanese law (Toqta 1977: 14,137).The captain also had a right to decide whether to take on additional passengers. In one instance, the Japanese monk Jojin wished to board a seagoing Tang Dynasty ship, managed by Zeng Ju, Wu Zhu, and Zheng Qing. After some discussions, "all of them agreed to give Jojin a ride, allowing him to board on their boat." Each of the three administrators came from different places: Nanjianzhou (present-day Nanping in Fujian Province), Fuzhou and Quanzhou respectively (Jojin 2009: 1). Their job titles were equivalent to captain, deputy captain, and mate as mentioned in *Reflections about Pingzhou.*

The helmsman, head technician and boatswain were major technicians in navigation. Helmsmen were also known as boat technicians, barge pole masters, and rudder masters. Some ships have more than one rudder, so several rudder masters are needed. For instance, Xu Jing mentioned a passenger boat for Goryeo (present-day Korea) which was equipped with two kinds of rudders at the stern. The main rudder is classified into two sizes so as to make timely adjustments as the depth of water varies, while the secondary is equipped with an additional two oars into the form of three helms, and facilitating travel in the ocean (J. Xu 2006: 130). The helmsman was an experienced navigator and could recognize the ship's location simply by observing the stars at night, the sun during the day, and the compass in cloudy weather. Otherwise, sniffing seabed sediments lifted by long rope (33.3 m) would also do. Usually, there was no rain on the sea, if it rained, then the ship was not far from the mountains (Y. Zhu 2006: 149). As for the passenger ship mentioned by Xu Jing, smooth navigation required an experienced captain or ship master who was familiar with seagoing routes, good at dealing with adverse weather conditions, and could successfully manage a crew. A well-managed crew can quickly handle an emergency, following the directions of the helmsman to handle the situation. The helmsman was also responsible for navigation security. Key Banyang, in the vicinity of Penglai Mountain, imposed hazards to boats en route to Goryeo. This was said to be the helmsman's greatest fear (J. Xu 2006: 130, 134), as it was his responsibility to ensure a safe journey. During a war between Song and Yuan troops, a ship-master of the Song Boat named after General Zhang Shijie fled the battle in a lifeboat, and his vessel, suffering due to strong winds and waves, sank to the bottom of the sea (M. Zhou 1988: 182), providing an illustration of what can happen without an experienced helmsman. The Head technician and the boatswain were tasked with navigation operation, second in importance to helmsman. Lu You argued that the head technician was the leader of the three technicians (Y. Lu 2012a, 2012b: 207). This is supported by historical records which note that the head technician was the headman of sailors, craftsmen, and carpenters.

Anchor droppers were in charge of hoisting and the anchor. Larger ships may often have multiple anchors. The passenger boat mentioned by Xu Jing had three anchors: a large one at the stem, and two auxiliary ones. A wheel was installed between two columns at the stem, on which rattan ropes were wound to hang the anchor, a heavy stone which held by wooden hooks. In case of wind and waves, two auxiliary stones were fastened at the sides of the ship. Such a seagoing vessel definitely need more than one anchor dropper.

Sailors were responsible for paddling yulohs, operating sails, and maintaining the ship. They were usually recruited by the owner before departure. "Before the departing on a seagoing voyage, shipowners usually need to spend several months to prepare, including calculating cargo, selecting sailors, and making necessary repairs." Only when these preparations were complete would shipowners dare to set sail (G. Liao 1990). The passenger boat noted by Xu Jing, was equipped with ten yulohs, two masts which were 33 or 26 m high, 50 cloth sails, two of which were made of plants, and ten auxiliary sails (J. Xu 2006: 130). Sailors were in charge of operating these yulohs and sails, and also repairing the ship. "If the ship leaked suddenly, and it could not be repaired from the outside, then the sailors from Southeastern Asian countries were ordered to repair it from outside with a knife and cotton wool, as they were good at swimming, and could even open their eyes in water." The Southeastern Asian sailors were at the lowest rank of crew. But they "were extremely strong and able to carry the burden of several hundred kilograms while keeping their eyes open in the water." Therefore, they were bought and deployed by some seagoing vessels as porters (Y. Zhu 2006: 149). Coolies were also lower-status sailors. According to *Stories in the Jiayou Reign,* written by Jiang Xiufu, a lady was discernible from a simple maidservant, due to her auspicious air and the way maidservants looked at her. Helmsmen could also be distinguished from other crew members in a similar way. Additionally, the wage a helmsman got was twice as much as the wage for a coolie (X. Li 2000: 431), indicating that the status of the coolie was lower than that of the rudder master or helmsman.

The operators on board were of different social strata. The ship owner enjoyed the highest status, and often worked as the captain. If there was no owner on the ship, the captain acted as the ship master, followed by the helmsman. The anchor dropper was lower than the helmsman, and the sailor was lower than the anchor dropper. In the second year of the Jianyan Reign (AD 1128), many people were recruited to safeguard the sea routes. The government covered the starting cost of requisition supplies and drafted personnel, classifying them into three tiers: 50, 40, and 30 strings respectively. And one helmsman was given 10 strings, and two anchor droppers were given 7 strings each, and the courageous who were preparing for battles were given 5 strings each. In the sixth year of Chunxi Reign (AD 1179), the government deployed more soldiers to consolidate the security of the Northwest Territories. Officials distributed coupons that could be exchanged for the same number of coins: 250 coins for an ordinary soldier per day, 150 coins for the helmsman, and 100 coins for a head technician, an anchor dropper and a sailor per day, and an average of 58.63 oz of rice. The requisition benefits on recruiting seamen are as follows: 15 strings for a helmsman, 10 strings for a head technician and an anchor dropper, and 5 strings for a boatman (K. Lang 1990: 7902). The boatmen's benefits were the least, despite earning the same wage as the head technician and anchor dropper, indicating them to be the lowest-status group aboard. The passengers of sea ships vary according to the type of ship, but they were also organized and managed in a certain form. The soldiers on the warship had their own military organization, and the envoys also had their own hierarchical structure from the ambassador to deputy envoys to minor officials. As mentioned in *Reflections about Pingzhou*, even small ships could carry over a hundred passengers, while large seagoing ships could carry hundreds. Most of these passengers were merchants and each of them had a few feet to store their own goods. Dozens or even hundreds of businessmen from different places crowded the ship, temporarily forming a miniature society on board, and thus needed to be organized in an ordered manner. In the third year of Chongning Reign (AD 1104), the Quanzhou merchant Li Chong applied for a trading license in Mingzhou (present-day Ningbo in Zhejiang Province) to go to the sea. He owned a ship of his own, planned to gather some sailors, and left for Japan to purchase some goods for rental. There were a total of 69 members on the ship, including one captain, one helmsman and one mate. Li Chong went as the ship owner. Judging from the fact that the ship did not carry much cargo (a total of 70 silks of various kinds, 300 beds of porcelain) and only one helmsman (as mentioned below, a ship with a 6.6-m-width beam requires two helmsmen), it was likely a medium-sized seagoing vessel, with about 20 or 30 helmsmen and sailors. In addition to the sailors gathered by Li Chong, there were merchants on board as well. The entire ship was divided into three classes: 23 people in the first unit, 25 people in the second, and 18 people in the third (Chaoye Qun Zai 1938: 452–53). This gave rise to a clear hierarchy ranging from the shipowner, captain, mates, sailors to passengers.

The number of crew like helmsmen and sailors was decided on the basis of ship size. Fujian Province conscripted civilian seagoing ships with a beam width of 4–4.33 m, recruiting 1 helmsman, 1 head technician, 1 anchor dropper, 13 sailors, a total of 16 people; 4.66 m, 1 helmsman, 1 head technician, 1 anchor dropper, and

15 sailors, a total of 18 people; 5–5.33 m, 1 helmsman, 1 head technician, 2 anchor droppers, 17 sailors, a total of 21 people; 5.66–6 m, 1 helmsman, 1 head technician, 2 anchor droppers, 20 sailors, a total of 24 people; 6.33 m, 2 helmsmen, 1 head technician, 3 anchor droppers, 23 sailors, a total of 29 people; 6.66 m, 2 helmsmen, 1 head technician, 3 anchor droppers, 27 sailors, a total of 33 people; 7 m and wider, 2 helmsmen, 2 head technicians, 3 anchor droppers, 33 sailors, a total of 40 people (K. Lang 1990: 7902). The beam of the 60-ton "passenger boat" that served as an envoy to Goryeo was 8.33 m wide, with a total of 60 boat masters and sailors while the "Magic Boat" required 180 of them, three times as many as the passenger boat.

More historical records about "the passenger boat" as Xu Jing mentioned classified both anchor droppers and coolies into the category of sailors. According to *The Anthology of Laws and Regulations of the Song Dynasty*, the ship with the maximum width of the middle beam of over 8 m, needs 2 helmsmen and 40 sailors, a total of 42 people; the maximum width of the middle beam of more than 6.6 m requires 1 helmsman, and 35 sailors, a total of 36 people; the maximum width of the middle beam of more than 5.7 m requires 1 helmsman, and 25 sailors, a total of 26 people. (S. Xu et al. 2014: 9253) The number of people allocated stays basically the same as in *Chunxi Period Chronicles of Fuzhou*. In the eighth year of Shaoxing Reign (AD 1138), "peddlers who trafficked goods in Guangzhou and the officials who managed the shipment, totaling 28 people, took a boat together. The number of punters and helmsmen on board were almost the same", totaling 26 (M. Hong 1981: 480). According to this record, the size of the ship beam should be about 6 m wide. In the second year of the Chunxi Reign (AD 1175), Chen Junqing, the mayor of Fuzhou, discusses Fujian Province's practice of requisitioning civilian passenger boats for sea defense, estimating that "570 ships and 14,000 helmsmen and seamen were gathered in total." (X. Zhu 2010: 4474) Each ship needed 25 helmsmen and sailors on average, which was equivalent to the operators of a 6-m ship, and could be used as the average crew of boats above 4 m.

The above-mentioned were all merchant ships or passenger boats that had been requisitioned. The number of sailors in the pure warship configuration was for certainly greater than the figures mentioned above. In the Southern Song Dynasty, the subdued pirate Wang Xian contributed two seagoing boats, which were 5.66 m long at the middle beam, and equipped with 85 helmsmen and seamen in total (S. Hong, n.d.), which was above the standard of 24 crew members. In the thirtieth year of the Shaoxing Reign (AD 1130), the counties of Fujian Province "recruited 130 ships and 5360 sailors". Each ship was equipped with 41 sailors (K. Lang 1990: 7902). The large ships requisitioned by Qingyuan Municipality were equipped with 50 sailors each (Y. Mei et al. 1990: 5995). The pirates looted Zhangzhou native Chen Shitou's goods and abducted a total of 91 sailors and the ship-master." (D. Zhen, n.d.) The crew sizes mentioned above were larger than the maximum standard of large boats. The number of configured sailors was mainly related to the power mode of the ship. For example, Feng Zhan's multi-purpose 6.6-m-wide ship, which was used in rivers, seas and lakes, required the installation of 42 oars. Therefore, there must have been more than 30 sailors, which was above the standard. Many ships, from pirate ships to official warships, place a much higher emphasis on speed and strength than an average merchant ship. Such ships required more oars and yulohs to be installed so as to make full use of wind power.

The Song Dynasty boasted a huge number of seagoing vessels, leading to an ocean of people who sailed and earned their living on navigation. During Emperor Xiaozong's Reign (AD 1174–1189), the number of registered civilian seagoing ships in Mingzhou (present-day Ningbo) was 5887 (Z. Huang 1990). Later, 7916 maritime ships were put into the registration book during Emperor Lizong's Reign (1237–1240), a significant growth. In Mingzhou, Wenzhou, and Taizhou prefectures, there were 3833 registered boats above 3.3 m and 15,454 below it, totaling 19,287 (Y. Mei et al. 1990: 5992). Counting the ships in Yuezhou (present-day Shaoxing), the number of ships in Zhejiang Province likely exceeded 20,000. The number of ships in Fujian Province was greater than that of Zhejiang Province. A saying goes in the Song Dynasty that, "Fujian Province ranked the top in seagoing shipbuilding, followed by Guangdong Province, Changming (present-day abolished) bringing up the rear." (Y. Lü 1990) So, Fujian Province was the most important player of seagoing shipbuilding. Every year in the Southern Song Dynasty, a large number of Fujian naval ships were deployed to Liangzhe East and West provinces, sailing in the waters of Jiangyin, Xupu (present-day Changzhou), Dinghai (present-day Zhenhai, Zhejiang Province) and other places. All of these indicated that Fujian boasted a large number of seagoing vessels, possibly equaling that of Liangzhe East Province. There were more than 40,000 civilian seagoing ships in Fujian and Liangzhe East provinces in the Southern Song Dynasty. Coupled with the coastal provinces of Liangzhe West, Guangnan East, Guangnan West, Huainan and others, there were far more than 40,000 civilian seagoing ships. Including seagoing warships in this figure would result in an even higher number, probably more than 100,000 (F. He 2005). The people on these ships formed huge social groups.

3.1.2 Ocean Shipping Routes and Navigation Modes

3.1.2.1 Ocean-Going Routes

The marine routes in the Song Dynasty consist of two categories: routes through the ocean connecting China's ports to overseas countries, and offshore routes connecting domestic ports. This section mainly focuses on ocean routes, with offshore routes discussed in the subsequent section. The routes to the countries of the South China Sea have been studied in Feng Chengjun's *History of South China Sea Traffic*, *Notes on Records of Foreign Countries*, Kuwahara Zongzo's Researches on *Pu Shougeng*, Han Zhenhua's *Supplementary Notes on Records of Foreign Countries*, Yang Quanwu's *Notes from the Land Beyond the Passes* and so on. These monographs discuss the location of foreign countries mentioned in historical books as *Records of Foreign Countries* and *The Land Beyond the Passes*, presenting the overseas trade routes and scopes. The studies, however, paid no attention to China's domestic ocean-going routes and shipping characteristics. In view of this, this section discusses the routes and characteristics of the ocean-going routes of the Song Dynasty.

The Overseas Trade Administration Law formulated by Ancient Customs of the Song Dynasty pointed out that only the harbors with an existing Ancient Customs had the authority to issue trade licenses and serve as legal departure ports for ocean-going trade. In the fourth year of the Kaibao Reign (AD 971), the fist Ancient Customs was established in Guangzhou. Before the first year of the Yuanyou Reign (AD 1086), three Ancient Customs had been set up by the Song court in Guangzhou, Hangzhou and Mingzhou. In the second year (AD 1087) and the third year (AD 1088) of the Yuanyou Reign, Ancient Customs were established in Mizhou (present-day Jiaozhou, Shandong Province) and Quanzhou. Mizhou Ancient Customs did not last long, dealing mostly with the Entrepot Trade from Guangzhou, Quanzhou, and Mingzhou. The main departure harbors in the Southern Song Dynasty were Guangzhou, Quanzhou and Mingzhou, where the Ancient Customs were established. In the third year of the Yuanfeng Reign (AD 1080), "according to the provisions of the Overseas Trade Administration Law, all seagoing ships to Southern Asian countries must be licensed only by Guangzhou Ancient Customs, and those to Japan and Goryeo (present-day North Korea) must be dispatched exclusively by Mingzhou Ancient Customs, otherwise, they shall be punished in accordance with the regulations." This law clarified the different divisions and responsibilities of Guangzhou and Mingzhou Ancient Customs, and also made it clear that no other customs could issue trade licenses. In the eighth year of the Yuanfeng (AD 1085), the Overseas Trade Administration Law added Hangzhou as a new departure port for maritime ships, emphasizing that merchant ships could only depart from the harbors at Hangzhou, Mingzhou, or Guangzhou Ancient Customs harbors, otherwise they would be punished (S. Su 2010: 3332). Merchants were expected to apply for a trade license and fill in trade declaration at the Ancient Customs. In the fifth year of the Yuanyou Reign (AD 1090), Hangzhou Ancient Custom reported that "a merchant called Wang Yingsheng and his accomplices applied for a Goryeo trade license, with the intention of setting out to trade not in Goryeo, but rather in the Liao Kingdom" [the Liao Dynasty (907–1125), a dynasty established by the Khitan clan in Chinese history, passed down nine emperors, and enjoyed the country for 218 years] (S. Su 2010: 3330). This act was in clear violation of a law that was widely recognized in many overseas countries at that time. According to *Reflections about Pingzhou,* "many pirates overseas looted ships and left for other countries to avoid weakening their domestic trade. If the merchant got a trade license to go to Champa (present-day Vietnam), but unluckily got lost in Zhenla (present-day Cambodia), then the cargo would be robbed away and the crews be tied up and sold as slaves. Finally, the pirates said that you shouldn't have come here".

In order to prevent smuggling and tax evasion, ships went to the departure port to register cargo and personnel before departing to their destination. Returning ships went back to the original port for inspection and taxation. *Compilation of Emperor Zhezong's Orders* stipulates that merchants to overseas countries must apply for a trade license, and "the crews, cargo quantity, and destination country should be recorded, and the license must be handed over to the domestic Ancient Customs upon returning." (S. Su 2010: 3330) In the fourth year of Chongning Reign (AD 1105), the trade certificate granted to Quanzhou businessman Li Chong wrote clearly that "Li Chong purchased some goods for rental in Japan and went to Mingzhou Ancient Customs for ship taxation." It was stipulated that "the ship-master Li Chong must not hide or evade taxation. He should obey the command of the imperial decree, go to Japan with the license for trade, and return to Mingzhou Ancient Customs for paying taxes. Otherwise, he shall be punished strictly in accordance with the law." (Chaoye Qun Zai 1938: 452, 455) In the seventh year of the Shaoxing Reign (AD 1137), a Fuzhou merchant's ship sank, stranding him on an island. Thirteen years later (AD 1150), he eventually returned to his hometown at Gantang Port with thousands of kilos of precious sandalwood. "The patrolling agency escorted the seagoing ship to Min County to prevent it from evading tax. Min County sent them to Quanzhou Ancient Customs to pay tax." (M. Hong 1981: 251–52) This case tells us it was illegal for returning ships to arrive at other ports without paying tax first at Ancient Customs. In the second year of the Longxing Reign (AD 1164), Chinese ministers emphasized the in-kind taxes levied on import and export trade at the departure ports. The Ancient Customs of Guangdong, Fujian and Liangzhe East and West provinces were in charge of issuing trade licenses. Per existing law, the ships were required to pay their taxes at the departure port. Before departure, the maritime merchant was expected to find a guarantor before being granted a license. Upon return, maritime ships went to the departure port to pay the in-kind tax levied by the government. The law was breached when Liangzhe East and West provinces applied for ships to be allowed to sell goods at all ports. The law should be restored in the three provinces (D. Ma 2011: 591)." The late Southern Song Dynasty still kept the regulation that only Mingzhou Ancient Custom could grant trade licenses to Goryeo and Japan. "As for the merchants trading with Goryeo or transporting goods from Japan to China, only Qingyuan Municipality could issue a license for their ships at the departure port." (J. Luo et al. 1990: 5054) From this, it can be inferred that only Quanzhou and Guangzhou Ancient Customs still remained the authority to deal with trade from the South China Sea countries.

These policies that only the ports with an Ancient Customs could issue overseas trade licenses and that merchant ships must return to pay taxes, were established in the mid-Northern Song Dynasty, and were maintained throughout the period of the Southern Song Dynasty, indicating that the legal ocean-going routes were connected by the ports with an established Ancient Customs with overseas countries. The Mingzhou-Goryeo route departed from Dinghai, crossed the eastern waters of the Zhoushan Islands and led directly to Goryeo. On the way to Goryeo, passing by Zhaobao Mountain (at Yongjiangkou, Zhenhai District, Ningbo), Hutou Mountain, Family Shen County (present-day Shenjia Town, Putuo District, Zhoushan City, Zhejiang Province), Meicen (present-day Putuo Mountain), Langgang Mountain, then the ship sailed out of the sea and reached the destination. Returning to Mingzhou, the ship went by Langgang Mountain (present-day Langgang Mountain Archipelago, Zhoushan Islands, Zhejiang), Tantou, Suzhou Ocean (present-day the East China Sea), Ligang Harbor (in Zhejiang) and Jiaomen (present-day Outer Zhumen Island, Yongjiangkou, northeast of Ningbo), Zhaobao Mountain (Yongjiangkou, Zhenhai

District, Ningbo City, Zhejiang Province), then arrived successfully at Dinghai (ancient county name, Zhenhai, Zhejiang). (J. Xu 2006: 19, 148–49) From Japan to Mingzhou, the merchant ships made use of the northeast wind (J. Luo et al. 1990: 5057), going straight out of the ocean east of the Zhoushan Islands. Jojin, a Japanese monk, came to the Song Dynasty passing by T'amlado Island (South Korea), Shifan Mountain in Suzhou Ocean (present-day the East China Sea), Xuweng Mountain, Li Harbor (in Zhoushan, Zhejiang), Hutou Mountain, Zhaobao Mountain, and reached Mingzhou (Jojin 2009: 6, 10, 11). The above was the northern route between Japan and China in the Song Dynasty.

The ocean-going routes to the Southeastern Asian countries had two departure ports: Quanzhou and Guangzhou. The merchant ships heaved up the anchor from Quanzhou and went straight to Qizhou Ocean in the eastern part of the Hainan Island. *Accounts About the Capital* (written by Wu Zimu in the Song Dynasty) mentions that the businessman who wants to trade in foreign countries should "set sail from Quanzhou and he would go abroad through Daiyumen (50 miles southeast of present-day Jinjiang, Fujian)." The ships "zigzagged across the Qizhou Ocean, and the water depth was about 212 m. Ships passed through Kunlun Ocean (the waters between Cambodia and Thailand), Shamo Ocean (the water region west to China's Nansha Islands), Shelong Ocean (the water region close to Indonesia's Natuna Islands), and Wuzhu Ocean (the water region close to China's Shangchuan Island)." (Z. Wu 1980: 112) According to *Chronicles of Maritime Kingdoms* written by Chen Lunjiong in 1730, Qizhou Ocean is in the southeast of Wanzhou (present-day Wanning in Haian Province), and the Kunlun Ocean is in the south of the Qizhou Ocean. *The Customs of Cambodia* written by Zhou Daguan recorded that the Kunlun Ocean is in the open seas of Zhenla (present-day Cambodia). The Wenzhou-Southeast route was through the Qizhou Ocean, Cochin Ocean (present-day Beibu Gulf), Champa (present-day Vietnam), Kunlun Ocean and into Zhenla Harbor. It can be seen that the Cochin Ocean is located between the south of Hainan Island and Champa, and the Kunlun Ocean is in the south of Cambodia and Thailand. The merchant ships bound for the Southeastern Asian countries from Quanzhou "departed in November of the Lunar calendar. With the help of the north wind, they could arrive at Poshe (referring to Java Island) in one month downwind" (R. Zhao 1996: 54), without the need to stop at the coastal ports of Fujian and Guangdong.

The route from Guangzhou to the Southeast Asian countries went through Pearl River Estuary, passing by the eastern part of Hainan Island to Southeast Asia. Guangzhou was 350 km from Xiaohai (a part of Pearl River flows through Guangzhou) to Ruzhou (an island). There was an inspection gate called the first lookout on Ruzhou Island, and a little further north the second and third lookout. Beyond Ruzhou Island was the vast sea. When the merchant ship arrived at Ruzhou Island, it was time to bid farewell to its hometown. The Guangzhou Ancient Customs was built above Xiaohai river. There was a famous Haishan Building in front of Wuzhou Island (Jiangdao Island in the Pearl River Delta outside Guangzhou), below is Xiaohai (Y. Zhu 2006: 148)." *The General Record of Military Affairs,* written by Zeng Gongliang and Ding Du, describes the route from Guangzhou to Southeastern Asian countries as "sailing 107 miles southeast to Tuen Mun Mountain, among which 5.3 miles of water is shallow. Sailing 13.5 miles a day, totaling 54 miles. From Tuen Mun Mountain, traveling southwest with the east wind, 7 days to Jiuruluo (around the Xisha Islands), another 3 days to CulaoCham Mountain (on the border of Luozhou), and 81 miles further south to the east of Lingshan Mountain (present-day Quy Nhon, Vietnam). The distances from Lingshan Mountain Southwest to Abbassides, Buddha, Tianzhu (Tintu, ancient India) and other countries cannot be calculated" (G. Zeng 1990). Ruzhou functions similar to Tuen Mun for the Pearl River Delta. The Guangzhou Ocean Route started from the Pearl River Delta and "boats traveled southwest with the aid of the east wind", passing by Qizhou Ocean from Tuen Mun before reaching Southeast Asia.

There were two junctions on the route from Quanzhou and Guangzhou to the Southeast Asian countries, one was the Cochin Ocean (present-day the Beibu Gulf) in the south of Hainan Island, and the other was the Samboja Country. *The Land Beyond the Passes* recorded that "the ships of the Samboja Kingdom were heading due north, passing Pulo Aor and the Cochin Ocean, before reaching. Ships heading to Guangzhou entered Tuen Mun, while those bound for Quanzhou entered Jiazimen." From Java Kingdom to China, ships sailed northwest and "merged at Pulo Aor with the sea route to the Samboja." Pulo Aor is in the South China Sea between Campa and Samboja, which serves as a transportation hub for the countries west of Samboja and China. "In the South China Sea, Samboja is the traffic fort of the Southeast Asian countries. Ranging from Java in the east, Kulam in the west, all must pass by Samboja into China." "Ships from the Arab Empire first took a small boat south to Kulam, then changed into a large ship and headed east to Samboja Kingdom (the capital is in Palembang, Sumatra, Indonesia), and then transferred from Samboja kingdom to China" (Q. Zhou 1999: 86, 126).

Not all the ocean-going routes through Mingzhou (present-day Ningbo), Quanzhou and Guangzhou were offshore routes along the coastal lines, but they did meet with offshore routes at three points: Mingzhou Port, Quanzhou Port and Guangzhou Port, which was in line with the Overseas Trade Management Law. When maritime ships were ready to leave the port, they were inspected by government staff and escorted from the port (D. Ma 2011: 244). "Any inspector who left before the ship's departure was to be detained to serve one year's hard labor." (S. Xu et al. 2014: 4215) Ships departing for overseas trade were to sail directly along the route from the departure port to the trading country under official supervision, and were not allowed to moor offshore. However, some smuggling still occurred at this time. "After the inspection was completed, merchants would carry the smuggled goods into the ship one by one, having previously hidden them away elsewhere." (H. Bao 1990) This was against the law of the Song Dynasty.

3.1.2.2 Marine Mode in the Song Dynasty

In the Song Dynasty, paddles and yulohs were mainly employed on boats sailing downstream in inland rivers, while tow ropes were used in adverse currents or the canals. Sails were also used downwind in the inland river. However, as the direction of the wind was variable, sails could not serve as the major driving force. Seagoing shipping depended heavily upon sails that could adjust with the changing direction of the wind. Ocean-going navigation particularly relied on seasonal trade winds. While sailing in the ocean, the power was all about the wind; the paddles and yulohs were mostly auxiliary. "If traveling downwind, the ship could travel hundreds of miles with a blink of an eye, otherwise, it would be difficult to move an inch." (Y. Wang 1990a, 1990b) Sailing along the coasts of Fujian, Huainan, and Liangzhe provinces "must make use of the trade winds, making use of the north wind in winter, and sailing northbound in summer (G. Liao 1990). Ships also sailed northward during the summer months along the route from Mingzhou to Goryeo. Lu Yihao proceeded north by the south wind in April and arrived directly in Donglai (present-day Yantai, Shandong)." (X. Li 2013: 1198) "In May and June, when the south wind prevails and the tide rises to four-tenths, it is good time for boat sailing."(Y. Mei et al. 1990: 5990) Xu Jing's Mission sailed in May from Mingzhou to Goryeo "by the south wind." The date registered on the license when Li Chong went to Japan was June in the fourth year of the Chongning Reign (AD 1105). The normal practice for sailing boats was departing from Mingzhou to Goryeo and Japan in May and June by the south wind. Xu Jing's Mission had to make use of the north wind as they "went back to China from Goryeo in mid-July" (J. Xu 2006: 148). But the ship hitched by Jojin, a Japanese monk, left Japan for Mingzhou in mid-March, and could sail in the east and northeast winds (Jojin 2009: 3–10). Between the Southeast Asian countries and China, the ship sailing followed the norm of going to the south by the northeast trade wind in winter and returning to the north by the southwest trade wind in summer. "The southbound boats exploit the driving force of the north wind in November and December, and going to the north need the power of the south wind in May and June. Like a wooden bucket, the ship can't sail without wind on the sea". Therefore, the military commissioner of Guangzhou would pray to the God of Wind in May every year (Y. Zhu 2006: 149). Local officials in Quanzhou also held ceremonies twice a year to pray for the winds during the departure and returning period at the King Tongyuan Temple, noted in the following quotations: "the local governors prayed for wind twice each year," and "paid sacrifices to the God of wind at the King Tongyuan Temple twice." (*A Compilation of Studies on Maritime History in Quanzhou 1*983: 25)

Seagoing boats primarily depended on sails. The merchant ship hitched by Jojin relied on lifting sails in the ocean, but used yulohs only in offshore and inland river navigation. In the fifth year of the Xi'ning Reign (AD 1072), a crew was unable to set sail on March 15th, "as on that day the west wind was blowing." "The following day, the east wind came, so the ship sailed out. Soon, there was a westerly wind, and the ship had to return to the harbor." It was not until March 19th that the northeast wind began to soar, allowing the ship to finally set out. In the tailwind, the ship sailed rapidly like a bullet. By noon of March 23rd, "the wind stopped, leaving the boat in the sea only expecting the wind. At Wu Hours (7:00 to 9:00 p.m.), the ship sailed out again." "The noon of March 24th witnessed another stop again." The wind at night blew the ship northward, and "the crews couldn't help sighing and stayed up all night." On the 25th, the ship was blessed with downwind and entered the Suzhou

Ocean (present-day the East China Sea) (Jojin 2009: 2–4, 6–7, 9–10). Sailing in the deep sea, there was nothing the crews can do but to wait for the downwind. On Xu Jing's boat, fifty cloth sails were in the tailwind, and a sail made of plants was used if the wind was biased." "With the sails open widely, the wind could be utilized to its fullest extent." "The ship could keep sailing with winds from all directions except the headwind." "Under real circumstances, there was hardly a tailwind, so it was better to apply plant sails to keep the boat sailing." Using a variety of sails could give the ship access to winds from different angles apart from the headwind. Furthermore, there was a wild-fox sail, a small auxiliary sail at the top of a mast (J. Xu 2006: 130, 134), which helped to maintain balance and stabilize the ship against the surging waves. According to *Reflections about Pingzhou (Vol. II),* "the ship was driven not only by the tailwind, but by the winds from other directions. Only when the wind was straight against it, the ship would go backwards, unable to sail, and anchor stones must be cast to moor the ship." Winds from any direction except the headwind could be utilized as a driving force.

Some large seagoing ships employed sails exclusively, without oars or sculls. For instance, Han Shizhong (a famous General of the Southern Song Dynasty) deployed more than 100 seagoing ships to battle with the Jin army in Zhenjiang. "After raining, the sunlight glimmers and no wind stirs. The Jin soldiers took advantage of it and sneaked away in small boats. In comparison, the sea ships of the Song army could not sail at all, having suffered the loss of their of oars and sculls." (Y. Zhou 1990: 1959) However, paddles and sculls were frequently used by sea ships while sailing offshore, entering and leaving the harbor. Merchant ships "were equipped with ten sculls each. When sailing offshore or entering the port, the helmsmen rowed the ship with all their might, but could still not reach speeds as high as those the wind could provide (J. Xu 2006: 148). The ship hitched by Jojin had entered Suzhou Ocean (present-day the East China Sea) in the area of Mingzhou on March 26th, rowing the boat due to lack of a downwind; on March 27th, sculling the ship with the north wind; and on April 2nd, still propelling the boat by oar and scull as the tide rose to the highest level (Jojin 2009: 10–11, 14). Nevertheless, when the ship hitched by Jojin and Xu Jing's Mission Ship were sailing in the deep sea, they did not need to scull whether there was no wind or headwind. Many marine ships in Jiangsu, Zhejiang, Fujian and Guangzhou, especially warships, would use paddles and sculls inshore. In the first year of the Jianyuan Reign (AD 1127), Guo Ning, the mayor of Tongzhou (present-day Nantong) said that "all ships going out to sea should employ a canopy made of indocalamus leaf to get full use of the wind, and gain speed by using long oars when chasing enemy troops." (X. Li 2013: 224)A lack of wind could be dangerous in an emergency. In such situations, the use of oars was necessary. Wen Tianxiang, a famous anti-Yuan national hero, found himself in such an emergency, encountering "more than a dozen pirate ships moored to the bay in the East China Sea. His helmsmen hurriedly turned the ship to Lingshan Mountain to avoid the pirates, rowing the ship overnight. At dawn, they were fortunate to shaken off the pirates." (T. Wen 1987: 526) Some small naval warships primarily used oars and sculls, empowering ships to be fast and overcome headwinds. In the third year of the Shaoxi Reign (AD 1192), Chuzhou (present-day Huaian) was given approval to build

100 marine ships which were equipped with 4 ~ 4.3 m maximum beam width, several oars and two masts, valuing 5000 strings of coins each (S. Xu et al. 2014: 7138). Both kinds of ships were multi-paddle seagoing vessels that were easy to operate along the coast of Huaihai East Province. Inferior Officer charging multi-paddle boat was below the Coastal Military Commission (B. Zhou 1990). Fujian Province once forced pirates to surrender and "got 53 multi-paddle boats" (Y. Han 1990), which could sail along offshore routes. Gong Yin, the Yancheng County magistrate, built more than 20 multi-paddle boats during his term (S. Hong, n.d.). Guangdong pirates also used multi-paddle seagoing vessels, named "Long Oar Pirate Ships", mainly sailing in coastal waters. "The big pirate ship was equipped with 30 long oars each and the small one at least 10 oars." (S. Xu et al. 2014: 6568) Most of them sailed along the offshore routes.

In the early years of shipping navigation in the Song Dynasty, boatmen mainly relied on landscape targets, star-drawing operation, and water situations. These methods were mainly learned through experience. In the later period, the compass was employed. In the fifth year of the Xi'ning Reign (AD 1072), the boat hitched by Jojin was navigated using the stars. However, on March 20th, "the night was cloudy and no stars could be seen. The wind blew the ship around in the cloudy night, telling no direction." In the starless night, the boat sailed blindly. However, Chenshi (7:00–9:00 a.m.) of March 21st, "the sun rose, and the navigation could continue." It can be drawn that the star-drawing operation acted as the main navigation method in the deep seas with no islands, not to mention the mainland. The compass had not been put into use, therefore, the islands and mountains along the route serve as landmarks for navigation. On March 23rd the crew on Jojin's Ship climbed on the mast to see if there were any mountains or islands around, but in vain. The next day, they tried again and saw the mountains. Another way to discern location is by throwing lead rope. On March 22nd, "the rope was lowered to the bottom of the sea. The Japan Sea is about 125 m deep with sandstone while the China Sea is about 75 m with dirt but no sandstone." (Jojin 2009: 6, 9) The water depth and bottom sediments could help boatmen to identify the water area.

No later than the period of Emperor Huizong's Reign (AD 1100–1126), the Song Dynasty had begun using the compass to guide navigation. Xu Jing's fleet followed three navigation methods which were applied by Jojin's Ship: star-drawing operation, visible landmarks, and inspection through lead rope. At night, as the ship had no island at which to anchor, so Xu Jing had to keep his ship moving forward while observing the stars. Xu Jing also recorded the main islands along the route, which were the important signs of the route. "The water in Shawei Ocean (present-day the Yellow Sea) was muddy and shallow, so it was quite dangerous for ships to pass through it. The depth of the sea water should be measured with a plumb hammer from time to time, for purposes of safety." However, the advent of the compass proved to be a major change in navigation. If the sky was cloudy and the stars could not be seen, the compass would be used to identify the direction (J. Xu 2006: 134). Still, the compass was only an auxiliary means of navigation at that time, and it was used primarily on cloudy nights when the stars were invisible. The records in *Reflections about Pingzhou* (Vol. II) also mentioned that "the helmsman could identify the geographical location according to the stars at night, the sun during the day, and the compass in cloudy days," reflecting Guangzhou's navigation in the years between 1085 and 1126. The compass had been widely used by merchant ships in the Southern Song Dynasty, mostly at night, but enjoyed more active use over time. *Accounts About the Capital* noted that while the merchant ships "sailed the vast and boundless sea, the compass was all they could depend upon in cloudy, windy or rainy weather. The helmsman was responsible for identifying direction, which concerned everyone on board, so avoiding mistakes was crucial." "The ship would be destroyed if it hit the reef and everyone would end up with being buried in the belly of the fishes." (Z. Wu 1980: 111) Compasses were mainly used in deep-sea navigation. If the ship encountered a cloudy night offshore, the lighthouse on the route could act as a guide, such as the Luhe Pagoda at the Qiantang Estuary. "As the cloudy day and the dim light took place by turn, the stars were invisible, and the boatmen were led by the light of the pagoda. As a result, rich merchants in particular relied on the lighthouses, and were willing to generously donate money to Luhe Pagoda." (X. Cao 1990).

Those navigation methods depended greatly on extensive experience. *Accounts About the Capital* notes that "the helmsman knew whether it was sunny or cloudy, and that by observing the sunrise and sunset, he knew whether it would be tailwind or headwind. Observing the waves, he could ascertain the direction of the wind; when huge waves hit the coast, he knew that there would be a south wind the next day; when there was lightning, he knew the summer would be windy. Few mistakes were made in his judgment. He could determine the distances to the mountain according to the turbidity. In the deep ocean, the water was black like coal but green and clear near the mountains. Closer to the reefs, the water was muddy and whitish. Where there were many reefs, there were schools of fish because many algae and moss grow on the reef, which was what the fish lived on. The 14th and 28th days of the month were seen as the 'Great Day'. If the wind and rain came abnormally in these two days, then it was speculated that there would be more wind and rain in ten days. They also observed the sediment at the bottom of the sea to infer whether there may be a harbor at the foot of a mountain." (Z. Wu 1980: 111–12) These abilities were highly necessary in shipping.

Ships often sailed on the sea in fleets. As discussed above, Xu Jing's Missionary fleet was composed of two "Magic Boats" and six passenger boats (J. Xu 2006: 129). A total of 1000 seagoing ships, including 200 huge vessels, were collected, some of which remained in Mingzhou to defend against Jin troops (X. Li 2013: 685), and still hundreds of which carried Emperor Gaozong in his flight to Wenzhou from Mingzhou (present-day Ningbo). In the thirty-first year of the Shaoxing Reign (AD 1161), Li Bao led a large group of ships totaling 120 seagoing ships and 3000 soldiers to fight against the Jin troops in Jiaoxi County (present-day Jiaozhou, Shandong Province) from Pingjiang Prefecture (present-day Suzhou, Jiangsu Province). (Toqta 1977: 11,499) However, the pirates were organized. For example, the pirates in Fujian coordinated over 10 ships with five or six hundred people armed for robbery (D. Zhen, n.d.). Wang Ziqing and Zhao Lang, the pirate chiefs, sailed 18 ships on the ocean (K. Liu, n.d.). In order to fight against the pirates, merchant ships also sailed in groups. "The ship masters from Hainan who were trading with Guangdong and Fujian Provinces had a number of companion ships sailing together." The captain's ship was known as East Ship and such teams of ships caused dismay for the pirates (X. Li 2013: 1668). Pirates bubbled up not only in the offshore areas but also in deep sea areas, as recorded in *Reflections about Pingzhou.* Merchants could only sail on the sea if the ships were large enough and they had enough boatmen. Additionally, navy patrols along the coastal areas of the Southern Song Dynasty often consisted of multiple ships sailing in teams. Therefore, this had given risen to the need of marine organization and liaison.

The main methods of marine liaison were carried out by flags, torches, and musical instruments like gongs and drums. The Xu Jing Missionary fleet used the three methods as mentioned above. The fleet combined with "eight ships beat drums, hoisted flags, and sailed officially the next day at Zhaobaoshan in Mingzhou orderly." "If the fire was raised as a signal at night, all eight ships responded by lighting torches." As Xu Jing's fleet returned from Goryeo and "passed by Zhudao (present-day Lianyungang, Jiangsu Province), a strong southeast wind almost turned over the ships. Everyone on board was overwhelmed by panic. The drum was beat to summon the fleet back to Zhudao." (J. Xu 2006: 131, 148) Beacon towers were set up along the coast of Mingzhou (present-day Ningbo). "In good weather, smoke, flags, torches or horns could impart messages between ships. But at night, only beacons and horns were effective." "In smoggy days, flags and torches could not transmit messages effectively, but lighting the cannon functioned well." These methods of liaison were also applied to seagoing vessels. "Commercial ships were unexpectedly mixed with pirate boats which moored at night to light a beacon as a signal to get in touch with each other." However, the Beacon Station regulated that "the torch should be raised 5 times and lowered 5 times, which was different from those civil ships, to avoid causing confusion with the merchant ship's torch signals. Only after the ships get in touch with one another can the beacon signal be extinguished." (Y. Mei et al. 1990: 5986) Emperor Gaozong's fleet formed an orderly mechanism, mainly using the sound of flutes and musical yelling to transmit information. The fleet set off from Mingzhou, and "each ship set out together the moment they heard the sound of the imperial boat flute. The royal boat used red silk tassels as a signal, and other ships used one word as a signal. For example, the ship taken by Vice Prime Minister of State Affairs used the word "can", and the ship taken by Administrator of Bureau of Military Affairs used the word "shu", etc. The word was written on a yellow flag which was inserted in the stern, rendering it easy for recognition and liaison." The fleet returned to Mingzhou from Wenzhou, and "the ships directly reached Zhang'an (present-day Zhang'an Town, Taizhou, Zhejiang). Sometimes, the ships could not be seen while sailing. In the evening, the imperial boat taken by the emperor did not arrive, and the ship of the important minister entered the port and then left to check, but the officials on the other ships did not know it. Only the singing for delivering orders and information could be heard, telling that the emperor boat was in front, however, without knowing that it actually hadn't arrived." (D. Zhao 2008: 107, 111) The musical yelling served as a command for the fleet. As the sea was vast and boundless, it was easy for ships to get lost. Li Bao's fleet "set off to Suzhou Ocean (present-day the East China Sea) and had sailed for three days in extremely strong wind, so the ships were scattered over the vast ocean. The crews were panic-stricken and poured liquor on board for praying, gradually, the wind stopped. The scattered ships gathered together again the next day." (Toqta 1977: 11,500) It is because of these effective liaison methods that the fleet could avoid being separated from each other, or to be able to regroup.

3.1.3 Summary

Marine navigation encompasses a diverse range of technical operations such as steering, hoisting sails, sculling, anchoring, assessing wind and water conditions, and ship maintaining the vessel, all of which require the cooperation of personnel with various technical expertise. In the Song Dynasty, a temporary society was formed on sea vessels, consisting of operators ranging from the owner, captain, mate, helmsman, head technician, anchor dropper, paddler, sailor, minor boatman, and passengers. The ship master, likely the wealthiest of the traders and merchants on board, or the owner of the vessel, is the head of the ship. He is responsible for the managing the vessel's affairs, as well as possessing the authority to discipline the crew and to determine whether to allow others to hitch a ride on board. The mate assists the captain in managing the ship, while the helmsman and head technicians hold important roles in navigation, with the helmsman being responsible for the ship's safety The anchor dropper is responsible for raising and lowering the anchor stones while the sailor is tasked with paddling, operating the sails, and maintaining the ship. The coolie is the lowest-ranking sailor, resulting in a hierarchical structure. The number of passengers and crew on sea vessels varies depending on the type and size of the ship, with the total number of operators, including helmsmen, head technicians, and anchor droppers, on large and medium-sized marine ships with a wider beam over three meters ranging from 16 to over 100. There are typically more operators on warships than civilian and merchant ships.

In the Song Dynasty, maritime transportation consisted of two kinds of routes: ocean-going routes from Chinese ports to overseas countries, and inshore lanes sailing the domestic near-sea areas. The Overseas Administration Law, formulated by Ancient Customs of the Song Dynasty, stipulated that only the harbors who established Ancient Customs were authorized to issue trade licenses, and that ships had to return to their departure port for taxation. These policies were established in the mid-Northern Song Dynasty, and continued to the Southern Song Dynasty, indicating that the legal ocean-going routes were those connecting several Ancient Customs ports with overseas countries.

The Mingzhou-Goryeo route departed from Dinghai, crossed the eastern waters of the Zhoushan Islands, and led directly to Goryeo. The Japan–China route in the Song Dynasty passed through T'amlado Island (South Korea), Shifan Mountain in Suzhou Ocean (present-day the East China Sea), Xuweng Mountain, Li Harbor (in Zhoushan, Zhejiang), Hutou Mountain, Zhaobao Mountain, and arrived at Mingzhou.

The ocean-going routes to Southeastern Asian countries had two departure ports: Quanzhou and Guangzhou. Merchant ships departed from Quanzhou and sailed directly to the deep sea Qizhou Ocean in the eastern part of the Hannan Island, passing Cochin Ocean (present-day Beibu Gulf), Champa (present-day Vietnam), Kunlun Ocean, and then arriving in Southeastern Asian countries. The route from Guangzhou to Southeast Asian countries started at Pearl River Estuary, going through Qizhou Ocean and Cochin Ocean in the eastern part of Hainan Island, before arriving in Southeast Asia. The ocean-going routes through Mingzhou, Quanzhou and Guangzhou did not follow the shoreline, but rather intersected, offshore routes at three ports: Mingzhou Port, Quanzhou Port and Guangzhou Port.

In the Song Dynasty, seagoing transportation primarily relied on sails to adapt to the wind conditions. Ocean-going navigation particularly depended on seasonal trade winds. While sailing the ocean, the wind provided the primary source of power, while paddles and yulohs were mostly auxiliary. Between the Southeast Asian countries and China, ships sailed southward with the northeast trade wind in winter and returned north with the southwest trade wind in summer. Officials in Guangzhou and Quanzhou held ceremonies twice a year to pray for favorable winds during departure and return. Sailing from Mingzhou to Goryeo required a south wind in May, while returning southbound in mid-July required the aid of the north wind. Leaving Japan for Mingzhou required the use of the east wind and northeast wind in March. Maine ships used a variety of sails, including major sails and sails made of plant leaves, to make full use of winds from different directions except the headwind. Some large seagoing ships relied entirely on sails, without any oars and sculls, while others used paddles and sculls while sailing inshore, entering, or leaving the harbor.

Prior to the period of Emperor Huizong's Reign, shipping navigation mainly relied on landscape targets, star-drawing operation, and water situations. During the period of Emperor Huizong's Reign, compasses were used on cloudy days and nights for navigation. Additionally, there were beacons providing directional guidance for ships. Experienced crew members were necessary for these navigation methods. Ships often sailed in teams, and the Song Dynasty introduced the marine liaison mechanism to transmit messages by flags, torches, and musical instruments like gongs and drums. There were also special liaison personnel. These liaison approaches ensured the fleet to regroup after being dispersed.

3.2 An Examination of Offshore Routes in the Song Dynasty

This section discusses offshore routes connecting the coastal regions of China during the Song Dynasty. Maritime trade during this time was not only limited to overseas trade, but also included huge-scale offshore trade, forming a relatively independent offshore market. Offshore routes connected all the coastal areas of Guangnan East and West provinces, Fujian Province and Liangzhe Province in the south, and Jingdong

East and West provinces, as well as Hebei East and West provinces in the north. These routes formed the basis of offshore trade in the Song Dynasty, and were integrated with offshore, domestic, and overseas markets through connections with oceangoing routes and inland waterways. While scholars have extensively researched oceangoing trade routes in the Song Dynasty,[2] Feng Hanyong and Cao Jiaqi have done preliminary research on the offshore routes in the Song Dynasty, using the concept of "domestic sea routes". In this section, the author uses the term "offshore routes" to more accurately cover different reigns and distinguish them from the inbound part of oceangoing routes. Compared to previous research, this section provides a more accurate and segmented discussion of the features of offshore routes, examining the connection among offshore routes, oceangoing routes, and inland waterways. The material in this section is more substantial than previous studies,[3] thus promoting further research in this area.

3.2.1 *The Offshore Routes North of Mingzhou*

Based on the inter-regional transportation links and transit conditions during the Song Dynasty, the offshore routes can be divided into several sections from north to south. These sections include the area north of Dengzhou (present-day Penglai); the region from Mizhou (present-day Zhucheng and Jiaozhou) to Mingzhou (including the provinces at the estuary of the Yangtze River), the region from Mingzhou to Quanzhou (including Wenzhou and Fuzhou), the region from Fuzhou and Quanzhou to Guangzhou, and Hainan Island to the mainland. These routes were also interconnected, such as the direct routes from Guangzhou to Mingzhou and from Quanzhou to Hainan Island. The three major trading ports, Guangzhou, Quanzhou, and Mingzhou, played crucial roles as hubs in the offshore routes. Among them, Mingzhou was of

---

[2] *A Study on the Transportation in the South China During the Tang and Song Dynasties* written by Cao Jiaqi and *The History of Transportation in the Southern Song Dynasty* by Zhang Jinpeng, both discussed the Offshore Routes to Goryeo, Japan and the countries in the South China Sea. In addition, the routes to overseas countries during the Song Dynasty are briefly studied in *A History of Navigation in Ancient China* written by Sun Guangqi and in *A History of Foreign Trade in Ancient China* written by Sun Guangyao

[3] Feng Hanyong and Cao Jiaqi have not provided detailed discussions according to the segmental features of offshore routes, and only done preliminary researches on the offshore routes north of the Shandong Peninsula. They could have conducted much detailed study on the routes at the mouth of river (in Liangzhe West Province), in Fujian Province, Liangzhe Province and Guangnan East and West provinces, and could have examined the connection among offshore routes, oceangoing routes, and inland waterways. In addition, The ferry at Xiangshan Port in Xiangshan County was misinterpreted as the navigation route between Xiangshan and Mingzhou, and the location of "Three Convergence" where the ocean currents were divided into three directions in Cochin Ocean (now Beibu Gulf) was mistaken for Qiongzhou Strait in Cao Jiaqi's work, *A Study on the Transportation in the South China During the Tang and Song Dynasties*. In fact, the ferry at Xiangshan Port in Xiangshan County and "Three Convergence" have nothing to do with offshore routes.

particular importance. This was because it was located in the economically developed Jiangnan region and connected to the inland shipping network through the canal in Liangzhe East Province, Qiantang River, and the Yangtze River. As a result, Mingzhou was a vital hub for offshore shipping and trade.

During the early Northern Song Dynasty, Dengzhou served as the starting point for envoys and trade with Goryeo. However, due to tensions between the Song Dynasty and Liao Kingdom, Dengzhou later became a fortress for coastal defense, and communication with Goryeo was transferred to Mingzhou. Apart from contacts with Goryeo, Dengzhou also had offshore routes to Suzhou on the Liaodong Peninsula, which was the territory of the Liao and the Jin kingdoms. In the Northern Song Dynasty, horses were often sold by people from Jurchen sailing from Suzhou to Dengzhou, and after the war in the Yongxi reign, the Liao Kingdom blocked the passage between the Jurchen region and the Song Dynasty, causing the shipping route to be interrupted. Although Emperor Shenzong of Song wished to restore the route and reopen "the horse market", he was unsuccessful (M. Xu 1987: 20). However, this shipping route "still existed" until the reign of Emperor Huizong of Song. Emperor Huizong formed a maritime alliance with the Jin Kingdom and dispatched Guo Yaoshi and Ma Zheng to the Jin Kingdom, planning to attack the Liao Kingdom from both sides. They "sailed from Dengzhou to Suzhou by sea". The Jin Kingdom sent Li Shanqing and others to serve as envoys to the Song Dynasty, following the shipping route from Suzhou to Dengzhou as well (*History of the Jin Kingdom* 1986: 14). At that time, Suzhou was an important town for border defense of the Jin Kingdom. In the seventh year of the Zhenghe Reign (1117 AD), Gao Yaoshi and others of the Song Dynasty were appointed to send an envoy to the Jin Kingdom. They sailed from Dengzhou "to the border of Suzhou, but did not approach when they saw many Jurchen soldiers on the shore who were there for sea patrol" (M. Xu 1987: 3). The route from Dengzhou to Suzhou passed through the Miaodao Archipelago, "starting from Dengzhou and passing through Key Xiaoxietuo, Jimo Island, Shoal Qizi, Dongchenghuikou and Pitun Island", and finally arriving at the border of Suzhou. In the first year of Xuanhe Reign (AD 1119), Zhao Liangsi set off from Dengzhou on March 26th, and arrived in Suzhou on April 14th (M. Xu 1987: 25), sailing for nineteen days. Even after the Jin Kingdom overthrew the Northern Song Dynasty, this route remained in use. The Jin Kingdom used it to "transport grain in Liaodong (present-day Liaoning) to Shandong through sea routes for people's livelihood", and "collected grain from people at a high price and recruited sea merchants' boats for transport" (Toqta 1975: 2772). This route was also a trade route for merchants.

In the Northern Song Dynasty, the central government implemented strict regulations on the trade of civilian boats from the south to Dengzhou due to its proximity to the Liao Kingdom. Official edicts before the Xi'ning Reign stated that "those merchants and passengers engaging in trade by sea were not prohibited from entering Goryeo, Silla, Dengzhou and Laizhou. Violators faced imprisonment for two years, and the government would confiscate their boats and commodities". This provision was reiterated in the reigns of Qingli and Jiayou, with similar stipulations in the

Xi'ning, Yuanfeng and Yuanyou reigns (S. Su 2010: 3331). Coastal areas in Jingdong East Province were designated as "a restricted zone for trade, where boats were not allowed to travel". The law on selling sea salt was temporarily implemented before the fifth year of the Chongning Reign (AD 1106), "enabling merchants to pass through the sea to Huainan Province and other locations to sell salt goods". However, "the official edicts stipulated that, according to the current situations, civilian boats were forbidden from travelling in the coastal areas as before" (S. Xu et al. 2014: 8308). "In the coastal areas of Shandong, including Dengzhou, Laizhou, Yizhou (present-day Linyi), Mizhou (present-day Zhucheng), Weizhou (present-day Weifang), Binzhou, Cangzhou (present-day Tianjin), Bazhou, and other prefectures, many seagoing vessels came to trade from the southeast", but all these were smuggling routes (S. Xu et al. 2014: 8387). Sometimes, the official grain-carrying boats used sea routes, such as in the first year of the Tianxi Reign (AD 1017), when "the Shipping Department of Jianghuai region was ordered to transport 30 thousand Dan of grain to Dengzhou, Weizhou, and Mizhou by sea" (S. Xu et al. 2014: 6943). In the fourth year of the Dazhongxiangfu Reign (AD 1011), "the Shipping Department of Jianghuai region was ordered to hire merchants' boats to transport grain to Dengzhou and Laizhou due to their grain shortage" (S. Xu et al. 2014: 7329). During the Mingdao Reign, there was a famine in Jingdong Province, and the Song Dynasty "transported grain through sea routes" to solve the problem (F. Zhang 1998), taking the routes from the coast of Huainan East Province to the north of Jiaodong Peninsula. Prime Minister Bao Zheng mentioned that the Song Dynasty once transported 350 thousand Dan of grain from Jingdong Proxince, "to Cangzhou by sea", hiring merchants' boats to transport grain twice a year" (Z. Bao 1989: 114,-15).

In the early years of the Southern Song Dynasty, Lü Yihao provided an account of the coastal routes of Jingdong Province and Hebei East Province and Hebei West Province, mentioning that many prefectures in Jingdong Province, including "Weizhou, Mizhou, Dengzhou, Laizhou, and Qingzhou, had offshore offshore routes where passengers and merchants carried commodities from the south on their boats to Banqiao Town in Mizhou to be unloaded". Many prefectures in Hebei Province, such as "Binzhou and Cangzhou also had established sea routes, where merchants had been selling salt for a long time". He suggested assembling seagoing vessels from Fujian and other provinces in Mingzhou, "and sending them to Yizhou and Mizhou", saying that "the border of Jingdong and Hebei provinces was similar to the coast of Liangzhe East and West provinces, with residents and marketplaces", and where people could buy grain (Y. Lü 2012: 22). Thus, towns and marketplaces along the sea routes supported themselves. The excavation of relics in Haifeng Town, Huanghua Prefecture, Hebei Province, has revealed a substantial amount of porcelain, with 90% originating from the Ding Kilns and the Cizhou Kilns. Additionally, products of the Longquan Kilns and the Jingdezhen Kilns in the south were also discovered (C. Zhang 2014). Haifeng Town was governed by Cangzhou in the Song Dynasty, and the existence of offshore smuggling between the south and the north provides evidence supporting Lü Yihao's account. Therefore, it is evident that the offshore routes from Mingzhou and Mizhou to the north of Jiaodong Peninsula were never disrupted.

Due to restrictions placed on Dengzhou, Mizhou, south of Shandong Peninsula, became the most important hub port along the coast of Shandong. It "was adjacent to Guangnan East and West provinces, Fujian Province, Huainan East and West provinces and Liangzhe East and West provinces in the east, and to three provinces in the west, including Jingdong Province, Hebei Province and Hedong Province" (Toqta 1977: 4560). As a result, "it served as a gathering place for merchants from both the north and south". "Mizhou was contiguous to Dengzhou and Laizhou" (S. Xu et al. 2014: 8316), so the offshore routes connecting the north required ships to bypass the Shandong Peninsula, arriving at Dengzhou and Laizhou, then passing through several provinces from north to south, including Huainan Province, Zhejiang Province, and Fujian Province, before finally connecting to Guangnan Provinces. Lü Yihao divided the offshore routes from Mizhou to Liangzhe East and West provinces into two, one passing through Liangzhe East Province and the other through Liangzhe West Province. The former involved "bypassing the sea by passing through Yangshan, Sangu, Yishan Mountain, Daishan Mountain, Lie Port, and the Cenjiang River, and then arriving at Dinghai Town (present-day Zhenhai District in Ningbo)". The latter involved "travelling from Tongzhou (present-day Nantong), Taizhou, Nansha (present-day Chongming in Shanghai) and Beisha to Dongqian sandspit and Huangniu buttress head, going towards Yangshan by sea, then sailing along the coast to the south, arriving at Qinglong Port, then sailing from Paihuaitou to Jinshan along the coast, arriving at Huangwantou, Ganpu Town, Haiyan County, and lastly to the river bank of Lin'an Prefecture" (J. Luo et al. 1990: 5207). It was also possible to arrive at Mingzhou along the route of Liangzhe West Province. "Sea boats travelling from Jingdong Province to Zhejiang Province had to come from Shi Port in Taizhou, Chongming Town (the sandspit of Tongzhou) and other places", "then to the river bank in Pingjiang (present-day Suzhou), then to Jinshan in Xiuzhou (present-day Jiaxing), then to Xiangtou" (Toqta 1977: 11,542). Xiangtou was in Dinghai County which was on the south side of the Qiantang River's estuary.

Liangzhe East Province and Liangzhe West Province were distinguished by their different sea routes. Liangzhe East Province was known for its pelagic routes, whereas Liangzhe West Province was famous for its mouth-of-the-river routes. Three routes were available from the new and original Haizhou to the sea. The first one "went directly to Yangjia Stockaded Village in Gankou, then wound around the sandspit, and then to the Qinglong River and the Yangtze River, which was the estuary"; the second one was "sailed from the original Haizhou and directly to the sea, along Dongdu, Miaosha, Yesha, Waisha, and Yaoliusha in Gankou, then to Paihuaitou, Jinshan, and Ganpu, which was the pelagic route". Although the second one was different from the southern route in Liangzhe West Province, they were both direct routes to the estuary of Qiantang River. The third route sailed "from the original Haizhou, going through the territory of new Haizhou, and going away from the outskirts of Mountain East Corner, heading east then turning south, arriving at Shitong and Guan'ao in Changguo County, then arriving at Dinghai Town by way of Daishan Mountain, the Cenjiang River and Sangu, which was the ocean route" (Y. Mei et al. 1990: 5989).

The two primary destinations of these three routes were Mingzhou and Mizhou. In the Southern Song Dynasty, Dengzhou and Mizhou were part of the territory of the Jin Kingdom, and the above-mentioned routes were predominately intended for coastal defense. However, the routes to Shandong persisted in the form of smuggling, with "merchants from Fujian Province and Yuezhou (present-day Shaoxing) often carrying valuables and selling them to Shandong Province". Despite the Southern Song Dynasty's efforts to deter the coastal troops from peddling goods to Shandong through "punishment and rewards," some traders "continued selling goods openly" (X. Li 2013: 796; S. Xu et al. 2014: 8386). Lü Yihao noted that when cargoes from Liangzhe East Province, Fujian Province, and Guangnan East and West provinces were destined for Jingdong Province and Hebei Province, they were often gathered in Mingzhou first. When the Southern Song Dynasty planned to invade several cities in Jingdong and Heibei provinces, it formulated a strategy to first "assemble seagoing vessels in Fujian and other provinces at Mingzhou Port". Once adequately prepared, they would proceed "to Yizhou and Mizhou", "in order to invade Jingdong Province, Hebei Province, Pingzhou and Yingzhou Prefecture in the Qi State" (S. Yang et al. 1990; X. Li 2013: 1676). When Liu Yu, Emperor of the Qi Kingdom, planned to attack Dinghai County, he "called upon nearly 20,000 soldiers in Dengzhou, Laizhou, Yizhou, Mizhou, and Haizhou, and stationed them in Jiaoxi county in Mizhou" (X. Li 2013: 1484), and made Mizhou their gathering port.

All three of these routes can be classified as southbound routes originating from Mizhou. Both pelagic and ocean routes are both deep-sea routes, which take advantage of monsoons, and "rely on the south wind to go and north wind to come back" (S. Yang et al. 1990). Despite "the risks posed by unpredictable winds and waves", both routes were fast and direct. Wu Qian suggests that in the event that the Jin Kingdom were to march southward, the pelagic routes would be the most likely option, as routes at the mouth of river were "time-costing and circuitous with low speed, and would be avoided by knowledgeable navigators. In my opinion, the Jin army would definitely not choose to pass by the sandspit to the inland waterway of the Yangtze River", and as such, "the pelagic sea route was of higher significance geographically" (Y. Mei et al. 1990: 5989, 5990). In the thirty-first year of the Shaoxing Reign (AD 1161), Emperor Hailing of the Jin Kingdom ordered Su Baoheng to attack the Song Dynasty by sea, and he assembled his army in Jiaoxi County, Mizhou. Li Bao's raid on the Jin army in Mizhou followed the pelagic routes. On the Jia-Yin Day of August, Li Bao's fleet "departed from Jiangyin, and then sailed towards the East China Sea". However, the fleet was scattered against northwest wind and forced to "go back to the Mingzhou Port to anchor and chase the lost boats back". On the Ren-Chen Day of September, the fleet set off from the Mingzhou Port and arrived in Donghai County in Haizhou on the Geng-Zi Day of October, taking a total of nine days' sailing (X. Li 2013: 3725, 3736, 3749). Pelagic routes were fraught with danger, and Li Bao's fleet "suffered from the hurricane and over half of people were drowned to death" (X. Yuan 1990a, 1990b). However, routes at the mouth of river were not insurmountable for the Jin army. In the first year of the Shaoxing Reign (AD 1131), over 50 boats from the Jin Kingdom attacked Tongzhou and Taizhou, and occupied Haimen County, appointing county magistrates, secretaries-general, and other officials (S. Xu et al. 2014: 8891).

The routes at the mouth of river, which followed the shore and passed through several prefectures, were complex. "The water at sandspit was turbulent and dangerous" in the north of the estuary of the Yangtze River, while in the south of the estuary, "the south sea routes of the East China Sea provided fast and direct routes to the Qiantang River", making it convenient to sail on (Y. Wang 2003: 296). However, sailing in the north of Chuzhou (present-day Huai'an) was easier, and boats could be recruited in Chuzhou to sail towards Banqiau Town in Mizhoua in "only two or three days" (T. Li 2004: 8201). The route from Chuzhou to Tongzhou was difficult to due to the accumulation of sediments such as sand in the estuaries of the Shuhe River, the Yellow River, the Huaihe River, and the Yangtze River. Thus, flat-bottomed boats were the most efficient means of transportation due to the low volume of water and large amount of sand. In the third year of the Shaoxing Reign (AD 1133), a Song Dynasty general named Xu Wen betrayed the Song Dynasty and fled to the Qi Kingdom. "He abandoned his sharp-bottomed seagoing boat and instead stole a flat-bottomed boat, and went through Qinglong Town, then to Haimen County" (X. Li 2013: 1275). This choice indicates that he used the routes at the mouth of the river. If he took the pelagic or ocean routes, the sharp-bottomed seagoing boat had more advantages over the other two. Sailing on these routes required a knowledge of water levels and tidal patterns, and it was common to use "channels with high water along the northwest bank. In May and June, south wind could cause rising tides. When the tide rose by four centimeters, the boat could sail. When it rose by nine centimeters, the boat had to anchor and berth immediately, leaving one centimetre for egre to avoid running aground. This route was only feasible for half the time of egre every day" (Y. Mei et al. 1990: 5990). Shen Yuqiu noted that "the water at the sandspit was often turbulent. If control of the boat was lost, it could capsize. Only with help of the sailors on the bank of epeiric sea could the boat be turned around" (X. Li 2013: 1116). However, despite the difficulties, this route was less risky than the pelagic and ocean routes. Therefore, it was the common route for merchants to take. "Sea merchants, with their huge ships, were worried about the risk of unexpected wind and storms on pelagic and ocean routes". As long as the timing of tide egre and ebb was well-mastered, "the wealth and goods could be well-preserved" (Y. Mei et al. 1990: 5989, 5990). Offshore trade was particularly frequent on the south part of the routes at the mouth of river. In the first year of the Zhidao Reign (AD 995), Wang Han noted that, "hawkers traded via illegal routes, with dried fish as their staple goods, while larger merchants used the sea routes via Suzhou and Hangzhou, taking the advantage of wind to reach the regions between the Huaihe River and Chuzhou. Since these merchants carried an array of goods, the tax was several times of that of the hawkers." (S. Xu et al. 2014: 4204) These merchants devoted themselves to offshore trade, and they often sailed directly from Mingzhou to Goryeo and Japan. In the Southern Song Dynasty, it was predicted that if the Jin people marched southwards, they were likely to choose the routes at the river mouth to avoid the risky ocean routes to Dinghai County: "If the Jin people in Shandong attempted to seek their doom in tempestuous storms on sea, they could sail from Jiaoxi County, and pass by several sandbars of the sandspit area in Huainan East Province, directly taking the convenient waterway to arrive at Jinshan in Jiaxing." (Y. Mei et al. 1990: 5983).

It was noted that "sea passages, despite spanning thousands of miles, only have a few key strategic points" (Y. Han 1990). Several strategic points were located at the river mouth. The route started from Mizhou in the south, passing through Haizhou, where Donghai County located. It then entered Chuzhou, which was the estuary of the Huaihe River and the Yellow River, facing the sea to the east, and "connected to the Huaihe River and the coast of Shandong Province to the north", with access to domestic canals. In the Southern Song Dynasty, the government of Chuzhou ordered over two hundred seagoing vessels to transport army provisions in Haizhou, and spy on military movements" (Song Shi Quanwen 2005: 1711). In the Southern Song Dynasty, Yancheng County in Chuzhou was essential for salt production, as well as an important place for anchoring boats on this route. As the general supply administrator of the Huainan East Province, Hong Shi oversaw rice collection in Zhenjiang, transporting it through the canal, by way of Yangzhou and Sizhou (present-day Xuyi) to "Yancheng County in Chuzhou, and then ordered Gong Tao to transport it to Haizhou via sea passages" (S. Hong, n.d.). The Song Dynasty appointed someone to recruit seagoing boats in Yancheng County, and the county magistrate Gong Yi "had over twenty multi-paddle boats and over ten seagoing boats in Yangjia Stockaded Village in Yu Kou" (S. Hong, n.d.). In the late Southern Song Dynasty, Li Quanyi unlawfully occupied Shandong Province, attempted to attack the Southern Song Dynasty by establishing bases in Haizhou and Chuzhou. He trained soldiers for naval warfare in Haizhou, where he also reviewed warships in July of the first year of the Shaoding Reign (AD 1228), In August, Li Quan travelled to Qingzhou, and returned to Haizhou in September, urging the "rapid construction of boats and forcing people to practice swimming". In the following year year, Li Quan inspected troops and warships in Lianshui and Haizhou. Chuzhou was the base for his attack on the Southern Song Dynasty. It is recorded that "he occupied Yangzhou to cross the Yangtze River, and ordered his troops to occupy Tongzhou and Taizhou which were access points to the sea". He built many boats in Chuzhou to enhance maritime strength. At the same time, "he sent seagoing boats from Chuzhou to Pingjiang and Jiaxing through Suzhou Ocean (present-day the East China Sea), asking to purchase grain, but his real intention was to inspect the sea routes and pry about the capital area". These grain-carrying boats, used by Li Quan during during the second year of the Shaoding Reign (AD 1229), followed the routes at the mouth of the river by Yancheng County. At this time, he occupied the county town of Yancheng, as well as Chuzhou (Toqta 1977: 13,840–41). When Xu Wen betrayed the Song Dynasty to the Qi Kingdom, he just "sailed directly to Yancheng County from the estuary of the Yangtze River" (X. Li 2013: 1314)In the third year of the Jianyan Reign (AD 1129), the Song army experienced a major defeat and was forced to retreat on all fronts. In response, the famous general Han Shizhong "went to Yancheng County and rallied thousands of defeated soldiers to his cause", and "took sea boats to Yancheng on a mission to save country and nation from danger", eventually arriving in Changshu (X. Li 2013: 506). This demonstrates that Yancheng held significant importance as a port situated at the mouth of a river. Then he entered Taizhou, including the above-mentioned Shigang. The south end of this route was Tongzhou, "which had a crucial location with its northeast situated at estuary and the south connected to the Yangtze River" (X. Li 2013: 223). Tongzhou possessed strategic locations such as the sandspit and Chongming, whereas Suzhou's (Pingjiang Prefecture) strategic points were Huangniu buttress head and Xupu (Y. Han 1990). Additionally, Jinshan in Xiuzhou and Xiangtou in Mingzhou were also key points (Y. Wang 2003: 296). Han Shizhong further emphasized the importance of "Dinghai County in Mingzhou, Huating County (present-day Songjiang District in Shanghai) in Xiuzhou, Xupu in Suzhou, and the sandspit in Tongzhou, all of which were crucial junctures." (S. Xu et al. 2014: 9254) These locations held vital significance along the routes from Mingzhou to Mizhou.

3.2.2 The Offshore Routes South of Mingzhou

In the south of Hangzhou and Mingzhou, there were occasions where merchants opted for offshore routes as long as they did not trade abroad. Specifically, "if they conducted business solely in Taizhou (present-day Linhai), Wenzhou, Quanzhou and Fuzhou, they were not authorized to go to the Qizhou Sea, the Kunlun Sea or other seas" (Z. Wu 1980: 117). Offshore routes south of Mingzhou can be divided into three: Mingzhou to Quanzhou, Fuzhou (Quanzhou) to Guangzhou, and Hainan Island to the mainland. During the Song Dynasty, Ancient Customs stipulated that trading boats bound for Japan and Goryeo could only depart from Mingzhou, whereas and Ancient Customs of Guangzhou and Quanzhou provided official documentation only for sailing on the South China Sea. Hence, the routes between Mingzhou and Quanzhou, as well as Quanzhou and Guangzhou, were considered offshore routes. Wenzhou served as a vital transfer port on the offshore routes between Mingzhou and Quanzhou. In Wenzhou, "merchants transferred more marine products for sale than land-based ones", and it was said that "the coast of Wenzhou was prosperous" for which "it was always called small Hangzhou" (M. Zhu 2003: 149, 154). Taizhou was another important port. In the fourth year of the Jianyan Reign (AD 1130), "the West Zhejiang Province bought grain stored in Huating County with 100 thousand silver taels and 100 thousand strings of 1000 coins. Zhejiang East Province also bought grain with 100 thousand strings of 1000 coins and stored it in Yuezhou, Wenzhou and Taizhou" (X. Li 2013: 790), as emergency reserves. When Emperor Gaozong took refuge in Zhang'an Town of Taizhou, Song Hui, the deputy supply commissioner of Jianghuai "transported 2.4 million kilograms of grain and 100 thousand strings of 1000 coins and thin silk fabric by sea to the Jinshan Village of Xiuzhou, where the emperor's temporary residence was situated" (X. Li 2013: 705).

Baoqing Period Chronicles of Siming documents the southward route from Mingzhou to Wenzhou as follows: "when boats arrive at Changguo County, they took advantage of southwest wind to sail directly to Zhoushan Port without waiting for the tide. If the wind was against the wind, the boat would be moored at the port of Daxie and Xiaoxie Mountain, or Damao and Xiaomao Mountain, waiting for the tide to rise before setting sail." In the south of Changguo County, Jieqi Town and the bazaar of its affiliated Yuancun Village "gradually formed trade markets due to the coming and going of commercial boats". Continuing southward, "boats would reach Xiangshan County, in a northeast wind, and berth at Wuqitou, Fangmen, and Dutoubu of Chenshan Mountain successively, with the northeast wind. Boats would then travel 7.5 km on land to the office of Fenghua County". Dongmen Stockaded Village, 50 km south of Xiangshan County, "was an artery of sea passages, with boats gathering here" (J. Luo et al. 1990: 5040, 5264). Then sailing southwards, the boat would enter Taizhou and Wenzhou. The route from Taizhou to Wenzhou was recorded in detail when Emperor Gaozong fled to Wenzhou from Mingzhou by sea after being chased by the Jin army by the Jin army and then fled to Wenzhou from Mingzhou by sea, in the period from the end of the third year to the beginning of the fourth year of the Jianyan Reign (1129–1130). He went directly from Changguo County to Zhang'an Town, the port of Taizhou. Then from Zhang'an Town, he berthed at Songmen, Qing'aomen one after another, finally arriving at Wenzhou Port. When he returned to Mingzhou from Wenzhou, he berthed at Guantou and Haimen in Wenzhou, at Songmen and Zhang'an Town in Taizhou, then arrived at Dinghai County from Zhang'an Town. The journey from Mingzhou to Wenzhou took fourteen days each way, not including the time spent at Zhang'an Town. Although factors such as wind-blocking, stranding, and heavy fog sometimes caused delays, such factors were common during the voyage. This suggests that fourteen days was the standard travel time for light transportation (D. Zhao 2008: 101–12; M. Wang 2013: 239–45; J. Luo et al. 1990: 5134–37). However, the schedule for freight transportation was much longer. Before November in the fourth year of the Tiansheng Reign (AD 1026), it was stipulated that freight transportation from Wenzhou to Mingzhou should be completed within 45 days. Although "soldiers and helmsmen tried their best to tow and steer the boat", there were times when the boat encountered tailwinds and ran smoothly", so "no deadline was set henceforth". (S. Xu et al. 2014: 6946)

Fuzhou was the first important port on the southbound route from Wenzhou. As the site of the Fujian provincial government, it held greater importance than Quanzhou, a major port for foreign trade on offshore routes. Cai Xiang commented on Fuzhou's impact on waterway transport in Fujian Province, stating that "the army stationed in Fujian Province, for instance in Jianzhou (present-day Jian'ou), Jianzhou in the southern Song Dynasty (present-day Nanping), Tingzhou (present-day Changting), and Shaowu, connected Liangzhe East and West provinces and Jiangnan East and West provinces. It took a few days to reach Fuzhou, which connected Wenzhou in the east and Xinghua City, Quanzhou, and Zhangzhou in the south. As these cities were near the sea, boats surrounding them could gain easy access. Fuzhou was thus considered the transfer station for all cities in Fujian." (X. Cai 1996: 368) Furthermore, Fuzhou served as the the offshore trade hub, connecting Fujian Province with Liangzhe and Guangdong provinces, and was "linked with Yongjia (present-day Wenzhou) in the north, and Jiao Perfecture and Guangnan East and West provinces in the south". "Fuzhou was diagonally opposite from the East and West Huainan Province and the East and West Zhejiang Province in the north, which were far away. However, if boats turned the rudder with the wind, it would take only a few days to reach these places. During a year of bad harvests when the price of grain surged rapidly, boats from north and south loaded with grain arrived quickly at their destinations" (M. Zhu 2003: 164). In the early years of the Shaoxing Reign, Zhou Gang, transportation officer of Guangdong Province, transported 4.5 million kilograms of grain from Guangnan East and West provinces "to the middle part of the Fujian Province through sea passages, and repeatedly recruited passenger boats to where the emperor was located" (X. Li 2013: 1746), indicating that Fuzhou was a transfer station for transporting grain in Guangnan East and West provinces to Liangzhe East and West provinces. *Chunxi Period Chronicles of Fuzhou* documented a total of fifteen high tides on the sea passage from Yingxian Port, south of Fuqing County in Fuzhou, northbound to Wenzhou. During the first high tide, boats arrived at Libitou when the tide receded halfway from Yingxian Port. By the second high tide, boats passed by Luohua Ocean and Ox-head Men to berth at Jisha. By the third one, boats arrived at Yanxi and berthed at Ponong Bay. The fourth high tide saw boats arrive at Haikou Town, while the fifth resulted in boats arriving and berthing at Dalian and Xiaolian Island. During the sixth high tide, boats set off from Lianmen to the island of Dongxiluo. By the seventh one, boats berthed at Ci Bay, and by the eighth high tide, boats arrived at Liuqi. The ninth high tide saw boats arrive at Jiaocheng and Dilu, while the tenth one resulted in boats arriving Luoyuan Port. By the eleventh high tide, boats arrived at Guanjing Ocean Port, and by the twelfth one, boats berthed at Doumi. During the thirteenth high tide, boats berthed Songshan Port, while the fourteenth one saw boats berthing at Yuantang. By the fifteenth and final high tide, boats passed by Shacheng Port and berthed at Pumen Stockaded Village (K. Lang 1990: 7835–7839). *Chronological Record of Major Events Since 1127* recorded that Wang Xian, who was in charge of seagoing vessels in Wenzhou, once "suggested to build boats according to the style of patrol boats in Pingyang and Pumen Stockaded Village" (X. Li 2013: 3803). It is evident that berthing at Pumen Stockaded Village was within the boundary of Wenzhou.

Boats arriving in Fuzhou from the north followed the Tongpan Mountain and Banyangdui route in Wenzhou, while those coming from the south passed through Nanxiao Mountain and Nanni Stockaded Village in Xinghua. Within Fuzhou's sea passages, several points were of great significance, including "Hantou, Yingxian, Jiangkou, Yanxun, Shangyu, Bolang Bay, and Xiaolian Island, where commercial boats were frequently robbed. Among them, Xiaolian Mountain in the west and Dilutou in the east were strategic passes for north–south routes". Dilu Stockaded Village was particularly important for controlling the route from Wenzhou to Fuzhou; "if it were seized, boats would not be able to sail from north and south" (H. Bao 1990). In order to ensure smooth sailing, the Song Dynasty appointed inspectors of border security at many strategic points along the Fuzhou section of the route. Fuqing County had an inspector of border security at Haikou, namely the inspector of border security of Zhongmen in the early Song Dynasty. He was "in charge of auxiliary boats, ordering his subordinates to patrol the sea", "inspecting the smuggling of spices and medicines", "arresting those smuggling tea, salt, and vitriol, and monitoring foreign boats on guard". Inspectors of border security were also stationed in estuaries, "lying in traffic main arteries, where the boats returning from abroad smuggled without taxation by Ancient Customs," and soldiers were stationed there in order to arrest those smuggling tea and salt. Fuqing County was also equipped with inspectors of Nanni and Songlin security, whose responsibilities included "expediting ship-loading activities and apprehending individuals engaged in smuggling tea, salt, and vitriol". In Changxi County, inspectors of border security of beacon were appointed, including the inspector of border security of six coastal counties: Changxi, Luoyuan, Ningde, Lianjiang, Changle and Fuqing. Their duty was to "capture individuals involved in smuggling activities at sea". Luoyuan County had an inspector of border security of South Bay, and Ningde County had two county inspectors of border security. Huai'an County had five inspectors of border security of stockaded village. Liu Qi held the position of inspector of border security in Min County and was responsible for overseeing Min'an County "which was close to the estuary, and served as a major transportation route for boats". His duties included "supervising the payment of commercial taxes and working as a sub-inspector of border security in coastal counties" to apprehend individuals engaged in smuggling salt (K. Lang 1990: 7939–43, 7995).

Quanzhou and Zhangzhou, located in Fujian Province, were significant transfer stations for connecting the Guangnan provinces with the Liangzhe provinces via offshore routes. In the fourth year of the Jianyan Reign (AD 1130), Emperor Gaozong of Song ordered Guangnan East Province to purchase 4.5 million kilograms of grain, and the Fujian Province 3 million, "storing it in Zhangzhou, Quanzhou, and Fuzhou" (X. Li 2013: 790). Quanzhou established Ancient Customs in the second year of the Yuanyou Reign (AD 1087), which became an important hub for imports and exports and offshore trade in the Fujian Province. According to Zhen Dexiu, "the crackdown on pirates in Quanzhou and Zhangzhou led to their disappearance, allowing foreign boats to pass through." (D. Zhen, n.d.). This includes both oceangoing trade boats and offshore ones. Shijing Port outside Quanzhou, known as "the Anhai City in the Song Dynasty, was divided into the old town in the east, and the new town in the west. For the passenger boats travelling here by sea, the prefecture would appoint local officials to levy on these boats, thus the place was called Shijing Port. In the fourth year of the Jianyan Reign, Shijing Town was founded" (Chronicles of Fujian 1990). Weitou Bay "served as a strategic position for boats to berth at" (D. Zhen, n.d.). Zhangzhou, "located between Quanzhou and Chaozhou, controlled areas south of Five Ridges" (M. Zhu 2003: 224), making it an important player in offshore routes. "In the past, Zhangzhou had an inspector of border security of Huangdantou, which attracted maritime merchants". (X. Cai 1996: 370).

Prior to the establishment of the Ancient Customs, commercial boats in the Fujian Province were required to acquire trading licenses from Guangzhou to conduct foreign trade. Quanzhou was a hub for sea merchants, who "sea merchants visited twice a year, each with twenty boats, and an abundance of foreign goods and prohibited items." (B. Chao 1990). This indicates a significant exchange of commercial boats on offshore routes between Quanzhou and Guangzhou. The coastal areas of Fujian Province, as well as the Guangnan East and West provinces, were notorious for piracy, with "Shanmen in Fuzhou, Shawei in Chaozhou, Congluo in Huizhou, Daxi Mountain in Guangzhou, Gaozhou, and Gangzhou" being infamous pirate gathering places (S. Xu et al. 2014: 8862–63). The flourishing transportation between the East and West Guangnan Provinces and the Fujian Province laid a foundation for the pirates' survival. Chaozhou, due to its developed agriculture and abundant grain production, played a crucial role as a transfer port on offshore routes from Guangzhou to Fujian. In Chaozhou, "rice could get double crops in one year, and silkworm cocoons could be harvested five times a year" (M. Zhu 2003: 644). In the fourth year of Jianyan Reign (AD 1130), officials were appointed by the Song Dynasty to purchase grain in Chaozhou. One part of the grain "filled three groups of boats, with 600 thousand kilograms of grain in each group. Transported by sea, it was discharged in Fuzhou by the first lunar month of the following year (the first year of the Shaoxing Reign, AD 1131)". The other part of the grain "was loaded in Chaozhou in groups, and discharged in Wenzhou" (S. Xu et al. 2014: 6980). Additionally, Chaozhou and Huizhou were ordered by the local government in Fujian Province to buy grain in fields at harvest time (X. Zhu 2010: 1117). In the Song Dynasty, Chaozhou was a prominent exporter of porcelain. Fengling Port, in the downstream of the Hanjiang River, was an important commercial port, where many ancient shipwrecks from the Song Dynasty were discovered, including ship plates, masts, and towropes. Jieyang Port, on the other hand, was a significant port for grain export and foreign trade (T. Huang and J. Du 1994: 53–68).

The offshore routes west of Guangzhou were capable of connecting several cities in Guangnan West Province, including Leizhou, Lianzhou, and Qinzhou, with Qinzhou and Lianzhou being the primary ports in offshore trade west of the East Guangnan Province. During the Yuanfeng Reign, Zeng Bu suggested that, "Qinzhou and Lianzhou should build inns to accommodate traders, and establish trading markets" (S. Xu et al. 2014: 6844). Ship merchants during the Song Dynasty described this route as "easy to sail east from Guangzhou, but difficult to sail west from it, particularly westwards of Qinzhou and Lianzhou, due to the fact that while there were numerous ports in coastal areas of Fujian and Liangzhe East and West Provinces, boats had nowhere to hide in the sandy coastal areas of Guangnan West Province during storms. Furthermore, the southwest sea areas of Qinzhou and Lianzhou were riddled with large rocks which made sailing difficult." Trunk-like sand beaches with a length of hundreds of miles and a depth of a few feet were present in the sea areas between Qinzhou and Lianzhou, which were hidden in sea waves and could potentially shatter boats upon encountering them. Offshore routes west of Qinzhou could reach Cochin, where "people only used small boats to sail along the coast when out of the harbor" (Q. Zhou 1999: 37, 53). Setting off from Qinzhou and sailing westwards, "it cost one day to reach the southwest coast, namely Chaoyang Town in Jiaozhou". There were several strategic passes on this route to reach Chaoyang Town in Cochin, such as Duobu Stockaded Village, Didiao Military post station and Ruhong Town, which served as mooring points and military towns for coastal defense." Sailing westwards from Lianzhou, boats could reach Cochin by way of Qinzhou, with several strategic passes, including "Tanjia Pass, Huangbiao Pass, Zangyong Pass, Xiyang Pass, Great Bay Pass, and Dating Pass, serving as mooring points to the sea". Lujing Stockaded Village was the most important of these, "located in the southwest of Lianzhou, for controlling the trunk-like sand beach, entering the sea by Great Pass, then connecting waterways of Jiaozhou".

Sailing eastwards from Lianzhou, boats could reach Leizhou via "Sancun Stockaded Village, located in the southeast of Lianzhou, for the sake of controlling Baoge Bay, then to waterways in Haikou, sailing southeast to Dijiao Field in Leizhou". "Dijiao Field in Leizhou was close to the South China Sea, namely the opposite of Qiongzhou, to which sailing by sea could arrive quickly", and could quickly connect to Wan'an, Changhua, and Jiyang Military Prefecture on Hainan Island. Heading eastwards from Leizhou, "Tanyuan sailed to Luo Field and Wuzhou County, going against the stream of the Yangtze River, before arriving in Huazhou." Travelling eastwards from Huazhou, boats would arrive in "Ru'en (present-day Yangjiang) and Guangzhou, and reach Jiangnan East and West provinces, Liangzhe East and West provinces, and the Fujian Province" (G. Zeng 1990).

Hainan Island maintained contact with the mainland through sea passages, and it was recorded that was recorded that "official documents and exchanges between merchants were conducted through these channels" (G. Su 1935). In his work, *Overseas Trade of the Song Dynasty,* the author identified three main routes connecting Hainan Island with the mainland (C. Huang 2003: 282). The first route was from coastal prefectures in the Guangnan West Province to Hainan Island. It was recorded that "Dijiao Field of Xuwen County in Leizhou went straight to Qiongzhou Prefecture, and travelling between these two places only cost half a day". "Waterways in Leizhou, Huazhou, Gaozhou, and Taiping Zhou were near" Dijiao Field in Leizhou, and "the journey to Qiongzhou only cost one day to reach by tailwind (Q. Zhou 1999: 45)." The second route was from Guangzhou to Hainan, which served as a pathway for commercial boats entering and leaving Guangzhou to trade in the South China Sea. Guangzhou was known as a "gathering place for foreign spices, passengers, and merchants from Hainan."(T. Li 2004: 7522) It was recorded in *Chapter of Zhang Jian* of *History of the Song Dynasty* that when Zhang Jian worked as mayor of Guangzhou, "some of his relatives were expelled to Qiongzhou, to whom he often sent his salaries and grain via commercial boats". This obviously shows frequent exchanges of commercial boats between Guangzhou and Qiongzhou. The third route was from Quanzhou to Hainan, with merchants in the Fujian and Liangzhe Provinces regularly traveling to and from Hainan according to the monsoon pattern. "They set off at the end or beginning of the lunar year, and returned in May or June. If they shipped fresh areca nuts, they would return to Quanzhou in April." (R. Zhao 1996: 217). Every year, "sea merchants in the Fujian Province and the Zhejiang Province would purchase spices by Yuhang boat, and in the winter, the Li villagers collected agilawood in mountains when the Yuhang boat arrived. The people of Qiongzhou would then buy them and sell them to sea merchants" (J. Chen 1990).

3.2.3 Connections Among Offshore Routes, Oceangoing Routes, and Inland Waterways

The term "oceangoing routes" refers to direct trading routes between trade ports and foreign countries. It is essential to identify the specific trade ports that allow boats to engage in foreign trade. In the fourth year of the Kaibao Reign (AD 971), the first Ancient Customs was established in Guangzhou, and subsequently in Hangzhou and Mingzhou. To be more precise, the Ancient Customs in Hangzhou and Mingzhou were under the supervision of the Ancient Customs in Liangzhe Province. The official office of Ancient Customs in Liangzhe Province shifted its jurisdiction among Hangzhou, Mingzhou and Huating County. In the second year of the Duangong Reign (AD 989), Emperor Taizong issued an edict mandating that, "from then on, merchants and passengers must obtain official documents from the Ancient Customs in Liangzhe East and West Provinces to trade abroad. Violators faced the confiscation of their goods." This limited trade permits to ports with Ancient Customs and related agencies. In the second year of the Xianping Reign (AD 999), Emperor Zhenzong announced an edict that "Hangzhou and Mingzhou respectively set up Ancient Customs (Author's note: actually the official office of Ancient Customs), for the convenience of foreign merchants" (S. Xu et al. 2014: 4204). Guangzhou, which established Ancient Customs earlier and had the largest trading scale, was also authorized to issue trade permits. In the third year of the Yuanfeng Reign (AD 1079), the law on overseas trade mentioned Guangzhou: "any boats engaged in trade activities with southeast Asian countries without the permit issued by Ancient Customs in Guangzhou, or any boats trading with Japan and Goryeo without the permit issued by Ancient Customs in Mingzhou, should be punished". In the eighth year of the Yuanfeng Reign (AD 1084), the law on overseas trade stipulated that "any boats engaging in trade without the permit granted by Ancient Customs in Hangzhou, Mingzhou or Guangzhou, should be punished." (S. Su 2010: 3331–32). Therefore, references to Mingzhou alone, or to Hangzhou and Mingzhou together, actually pertained to the Ancient Customs in Liangzhe East and West provinces.

During the second and third year of the Yuanyou Reign (AD 1087, 1088), Ancient Customs in Mizhou and Quanzhou were established. The Ancient Customs in Mizhou only existed for a brief period and primarily facilitated entrepot trade from ports in Guangzhou, Quanzhou, and Mingzhou. On the other hand, the Ancient Customs in Quanzhou issued trade permits for trade with countries in the South China Sea. In the fourth year of the Yuanyou Reign (AD 1089), the Ancient Customs in Hangzhou handled a case involving "Xu Jian, a resident of Quanzhou, who transported over 2900 scripture boards undisguisedly to Goryeo, and in return received renumeration of three strings of cash". In the fourth year of the Yuanyou Reign (AD 1089), a merchant called Li Qiu "applied for a trade permit from the Ancient Customs in Hangzhou to trade in Goryeo". In the fifth year of the Yuanyou Reign (AD 1090), Xu Cheng, a captain from Quanzhou, reported to the Ancient Customs in Hangzhou that "Wang Yingsheng and other merchants pretended to have trade permits for Goryeo, but instead traded with the Liao Kingdom." (S. Su 2010: 3329–30). In the fourth year of the Chongning Reign (AD 1105), Li Chong, a merchant from Quanzhou, applied for trade permits "from the Ancient Customs in Liangzhe Province," which required him to "pay taxes upon his return to the office of Ancient Customs in Mingzhou" (Chaoye Qun Zai 1938: 453). Jojin, a Japanese monk, sailed to the Song Dynasty and arrived in Mingzhou by boarding a Chinese-style boat owned by Zeng Ju, Wu Zhu, and Zheng Qing. They came from south of Xiongzhou, Fuzhou, and Quanzhou (Jojin 2009: 1). This boat was likely made in the Fujian Province. The boat's journey to and from Mingzhou was essential to expand trade with Japan. The above-mentioned cases demonstrate that Quanzhou merchants who desired to trade in Goryeo and Japan had to acquire trade permits from the official office of Ancient Customs in Hangzhou and Mingzhou under the leadership of Ancient Customs in Liangzhe provinces, as recorded in *Records of Foreign Countries*: "(Merchants from Quanzhou to Goryeo) must first reach Siming and then proceed to trade in Goryeo." (R. Zhao 1996: 151).

Boats engaged in overseas trade were required to the port from which they obtained trade permits to pay taxes and submit their permits. These boats were "permitted to berth at the Ancient Customs of the prefecture which granted them trade permits." (S. Xu et al. 2014: 4207) However, since "the Ancient Customs in the Fujian, Guangnan, and Liangzhe provinces were far apart and lacked unified laws and regulations", there were cases where "boats berthed at ports other than those that granted them trade permits, and some Ancient Customs prohibited boats without trade permits from berthing at their ports". The law on overseas trade management, attached to Li Chong's trade permits, stipulated that "when boats for overseas trade returned to a port that did not granting them trade permits, they must first deliver goods purchased by the government, and then report to the prefecture where they originally applied for trade permits to confirm the authenticity, thus erasing the record". However, Li Chong's permit was still highlighted as "(Li Chong) went to Japan and returned here to get taxed. No deception of his taxation in other prefectures" (Chaoye Qun Zai 1938: 452). Ancient Customs in both Guangzhou and Liangzhe provinces faced situations in which boats were taxed in ports other than ones from which they originally departed. In the fifth year of Chongning Teign (AD 1106), Emperor Huizong of Song announced that "boats were only allowed to return to Guangzhou to pay taxes, as they were granted trade permits by the Ancient Customs in Guangzhou, according to regulations issued in the third year of the Yuanfeng Reign (AD 1080). The emperor ordered a strict implementation of these regulations due to numerous cases of fraud and deception, which resulted in a significant loss of taxation revenue (S. Xu et al. 2014: 4207). In the early Southern Song Dynasty, the administration pattern of Ancient Customs changed, and except for Hangzhou and Mingzhou in the Liangzhe Province, three official offices of Ancient Customs were added in Wenzhou, Huating, and Jiangyin. In the Fujian Province and Guangnan Province, there were still two Ancient Customs in Quanzhou and Guangzhou, respectively, forming a pattern of "two official offices of Ancient Customs in Quanzhou and Guangzhou, and five in Hangzhou, Mingzhou, Wenzhou, Huating, and Jiangyin, respectively" (S.

Xu et al. 2014: 4216; J. Luo et al. 1990: 5054).[4] However, the rule that only the ports with Ancient Customs agencies could directly grant trade permits to boats for overseas trade was reiterated. Officials in the period of Emperor Xiaozong's Reign wrote to the emperor that, "The provinces of Fujian, Guangnan, and Liangzhe had their Ancient Customs agencies respectively. According to previous laws, sea merchants should look for a guarantor so that they could be granted with trade permits to sail and return to the port where it set off to get taxed. However, the existing regulations were undermined since Ancient Customs in Liangzhe Province applied for a free berth for the sale of goods". In the second year of the Longxing Reign (AD 1164), the previous laws and regulations were emphasized again, ordering "Fujian, Guangnam, and Liangzhe Provinces to act according to previous laws." (D. Ma 2011: 591) It was also prohibited to pay taxes in ports which were not the original place where boats set off, although these ports may be set up with Ancient Customs agencies: "If boats granted with trade permits by Ancient Customs in other places come to Quanzhou, they should not be detained and levied taxes. However, they should be sent under escort by officials to leave the port and return to the place in which they got trade permits to get taxed." In the ninth year of the Qiandao Reign (AD 1173), Emperor Xiaozong of Song rejected the proposal to set up Ancient Customs in Qiongzhou to tax goods: "The order was as followed. It was not approved that Governor of Ancient Customs in Guangnan East and West provinces applied for setting up supervisors in Qiongzhou." (S. Xu et al. 2014: 4218–19) Emperor Xiaozong of Song also noted that "when boats granted with trade permits by Ancient Customs in Guangnan and Liangzhe provinces returned, some of them may have returned to non-departure ports on the pretext of wind and rain, leaked hull, damaged mast and rudder". "In such circumstances, they were not to be detained but still required to pay taxes". In general, the provisions of boats returning to the departure ports and paying taxes were still implemented.

To prevent the outflow of copper cash and other prohibited items, boats granted with oceangoing trade permits were required to undergo inspections before leaving port, specifically referred to as "checking the empty boat". Under the supervision of relevant officials, they could sail on oceangoing routes, rather than doing business in offshore areas: "when boats set off, officials from the Transfer Agency of Taxation of Guangnan East Province and Fujian Province would appoint one of their subordinates to temporarily check the boats, and an official without any beneficial links would also perform an inspection. When boats arrived at the estuary, officials would wait for their departure from the port before leaving." "Officials who left before the boat left the port would be put into one-year's servitude." "The official

[4] After the official offices of Ancient Customs in Hangzhou, Jiangyin Prefecture, Wenzhou and Xiuzhou was successively closed in Emperor Guangzhong's Reign and Emperor Ningzong's Reign, "only the official office of Ancient Customs in the Qingyuan municipality (Mingzhou) can issue oceangoing trade permits to the Chinese boats joining trade activities with Goryeo, or those from Janpan and other foreign countries trading to China."(S. Xu 2014: 4216; J. Luo et al. 1990: 5054) The rule was restored that only the official office of Ancient Customs in the Qingyuan municipality(Mingzhou) had the right to issue the permit. The above shows that the other four official offices of Ancient Customs could also grant oceangoing trade permits.

without any beneficial links" referred to "those officials who had no personal gain associated with Ancient Customs affairs, or an independent and upright official", (S. Xu et al. 2014: 4215) namely officials having no vested interests in Ancient Customs affairs. Their role was to ensure that the boats would sail directly to trade countries abroad, rather than berthing at offshore coastlines. In the Northern Song Dynasty, Guangzhou, Hangzhou, Mingzhou, and Quanzhou became trade ports which could directly contact foreign countries and served as starting points for oceangoing routes. Thus, the routes among these ports were offshore routes as well. These offshore routes were connected to oceangoing routes at these ports, enabling the gathering and dispersal of imported and exported goods, as well as the linkage of overseas and offshore markets.

Foreign merchants coming to China were not subject to strict regulations on trade with Goryeo, Japan, and countries in the South China Sea that were under the administration of ports in the Liangzhe provinces, Quanzhou, and Guangzhou. However, ports without Ancient Customs agencies were unable to impose taxes on foreign merchants. For instance, Qiongzhou was banned from setting up supervisors to impose taxes on foreign merchants. Therefore, foreign merchants had to go to ports with Ancient Customs agencies to get taxed. For example, in the first year of the Tianxi Reign (AD 1017), Ma Sili and other Arab merchants "carried purchased pearls and other goods to Mingzhou, where they got taxed by Ancient Customs" (S. Xu et al. 2014: 4204). Ma Sili and other merchants sailed by the South China Sea, and got taxed in Mingzhou. Japanese merchants were taxed in Qingyuan Prefecture (Mingzhou), but they illegally smuggled copper cash along the coast of Liangzhe East Province, leading to an outflow of copper cash not only in Qingyuan Prefecture but also in other places. These Japanese merchants would cross Wenzhou and Taizhou before reaching Qingyuan Prefecture, and berth at the coast", or "after departing from Siming, they didn't return to Japan with goods left. Then they went back again to Wenzhou and Taizhou and sold their goods at low prices" (H. Bao 1990). There was no Ancient Customs agency in Taizhou, and the official office of Ancient Customs in Wenzhou had also been abolished in reign of Emperor Ningzong of Song. Thus, Japanese merchants could only be taxed in Qingyuan Prefecture with Ancient Customs agencies. It was necessary for the Song Dynasty to ensure taxes were appropriately imposed by Ancient Customs. Additionally, ports with Ancient Customs agencies were the starting point of oceangoing routes connecting to overseas countries. Offshore routes connected ports for overseas trade, ports used for other purposes, and inland waterways. On offshore routes, especially those south of Mizhou, trade was frequent, forming a prosperous offshore market. The market extended from Guangnan East and West provinces in the south to Fujian Province, Liangzhe East and West provinces, Huainan East and West provinces, and coastal areas of Jingdong Province in the north. Offshore routes and markets facilitated economic complementation and communication, the transition of oceangoing imported goods to domestic market, and the sale of domestic goods to overseas countries.

Offshore routes were closely associated with inland waterways, specifically with the Yangtze River, the Qiantang River, the Zhedong Canal, and the Pearl River, which were the most extensive and important channels. Additionally, ports in Wenzhou, Fuzhou, Quanzhou, Chaozhou, and Lianzhou were linked to the hinterland via inland waterways. In the north, the estuary of the Yangtze River was linked to the river mouth routes and entered the canal via the estuary of the Huaihe (the Yellow) River in the Huainan Province, reaching Yangzhou in the south, Kaifeng in the north, thereby connecting to inland waterways. The estuary of the Huaihe River contained "a trench from the city (Lianshui Military Prefecture) extending into the East China Sea, with the lower reaches belonging to the Huaihe River." The government controlled the sale of salt and tea in this region, while people transported rice and fish, "with a long queue of boats" (S. Su 1991: 524). Furthermore, there was a salt river from Yancheng to Gaoyou that connected offshore routes and the canal: This route began in Gaoyou and extended to Xinghua before going eastward to Yancheng and finally reaching the sea. It was the access point for passenger boats." (Z. Chen 1990; Toqta 1977: 2395; S. Xu et al. 2014: 9608). The salt river was named because it was a busy transportation route for salt produced in the Huainan Province. The salt was transported from Tongzhou, Taizhou, and Chuzhou to Zhenzhou (present-day Yizheng) and then moved from Zhenzhou to Jiangnan East and West Provinces, Liangzhe East and West Provinces, and Jinghu South and North Provinces (T. Li 2004: 2654–55).

The estuary of the Yangtze River facilitated the connection between the north-bound route at the mouth of the river and the sea passage in the Liangzhe East and West provinces, Fujian Province, and Guangnan East and West provinces. Boats sailing south from Mizhou followed the coast and steered by sandspit and Chongming, from which they sailed west to the Yangtze River. Alternatively, boats could "start from the east of Xupu, which was between Haimen and sandpit. The route direction was opposite to Jiaoxi." (*Chongxiu Qinchuan Zhi* 1990: 1163) Steering by sandspit meant connecting the route in Mizhou. During the Southern Song Dynasty, the sandpit, which was under the management of Tongzhou, was deemed the most important place to control in terms of maritime defense when enemy boats arrived (S. Xu et al. 2014: 3992), highlighting the strategic importance of the sandspit in holding the routes at the mouth of the river. In the south, the estuary of the Yangtze River was linked to the coast of Liangzhe West Province and Mingzhou. Huangyao Town at the estuary of the Yangtze River was a gathering place for large commercial boats from Guangnan East and West provinces, Fujian Province, Wenzhou, Taizhou, Mingzhou, Yuezhou, and other prefectures. These boats took advantage of middlemen to facilitate trade in Ganpu, Huating, Qinglong, and Jiangwan Bay in the south. There were also Gujing, Shuangbang, Wangjiaqiao, Nandachang, Sanchapu, Shajing, Shatou, Juepu, Xiaojing, Xintang, Xue Port, and Tao Port in the north to impose taxes. The monthly commercial tax levied on goods from the south often exceeded ten thousand strings of 1000 coins." (S. Xu et al. 2014: 6387–88) Merchants from Fujian Province and Guangnan East Province could also go to Jiangyin, Zhenjiang, and Jiangning. "Jiangyin Port connected the Yangtze River and the sea, which was convenient for sending boats to sea. No other ports could function the same as Jiangyin Port." (X. Li 2013: 3694). "Many commercial boats from the Fujian Province and Guangnan East and West provinces, together with foreign boats from the Hainan Province, sailed to Zhenjiang Prefecture and conducted trade there. Merchants also disembarked at the river bank of Jiangning Prefecture." (S. Xu et al. 2014: 7126). Offshore routes also connected Suzhou with Xiuzhou by Wusong River. "Merchants and passengers from sea routes sold goods along Jiangwanpu, which was near the estuary of the Wusong River. Most of the commercial boats first entered the Wusong River, and reached Qinglong Town in Xiuzhou by way of Jiangwanpu." (S. Xu et al. 2014: 6365). Sea merchants could reach Suzhou by way of Wusong River and then by the canal. "Merchants from the Fujian Province and Guangnan East and West provinces had no concerns about the danger of sailing on the sea by the wind. Therefore, precious goods produced afar were all gathered at Suzhou for trade." (C. Zhu 1990).

In Mingzhou (Qingyuan Prefecture), seagoing boats gathered by sea routes, with three of them being connected to inland rivers, including the Qiantang River, the Zhedong Canal, and the Yangtze River. Wu Zimu, in the first two volumes of his work, *Accounts About the Capital*, entitled *Boats in Rivers and on Seas,* noted that the "Qiantang River served as a strategic point connecting the river and the sea. Although many seagoing boats berthed at the ferry of Qiantang River, seafood such as fish, crabs, salted or dried fish, and other marine products in Mingzhou, Yuezhou, Wenzhou, and Taizhou were still transported to Jiangnan East and West provinces and Liangzhe East and West provinces." Seagoing boats and large warships, in addition to various boats of different sizes, "all berthed at the bank of Qiantang River." To sail along the coast, one would follow the Qiantang River and enter the hinterland to Wuzhou (present-day Jinhua) and Quzhou. For example, "seagoing boats entered the Qiantang River to smuggle salt and sold it directly in Wuzhou and Quzhou." (S. Xu et al. 2014: 6559) During Emperor Gaozong of Song's temporary stay in Lin'an (present-day Hangzhou), money and goods from the Fujian Province, Guangzhou, Wenzhou, Taizhou, and other places were transported to Mingzhou, then to the Qiantang River via Dinghai County, and finally to Hangzhou. However, many seagoing boats were discharged in Mingzhou due to "the sharp bottom that made them unsuitable for the sand beach on the sea passage from Dinghai County to Lin'an." "Empty flat-bottom boats were recruited to load goods and were sent by officials to the river bank of Lin'an by sea routes". Additionally, many merchants transported goods from Mingzhou to the hinterland via the Zhedong Canal. When Emperor Gaozong of Song stayed temporarily at Shaoxing during his journey, goods and supplies were transported by the canal in Liangzhe East Province, with the record "in the recent two years, grain, money, and goods were transported from the Fujian Province, Guangzhou, Wenzhou, Taizhou to Shaoxing Prefecture by sea, discharged in Yuyao County," and then transported to Shaoxing by river boats on the Zhedong Canal (S. Xu et al. 2014: 6981). When Chengxun, a Japanese monk, came to the Song Dynasty, he "directly went to Yuezhou rather than Mingzhou" when he reached Mingzhou. Then he reached Xiaoshan and Hangzhou via the Zhedong Canal (Jojin 2009: 652–53). Mingzhou could also be connected to the Yangtze River through routes on the East China Sea. Chensheng, an intellectual from Mingzhou, once went to Dongjing (present-day Kaifeng) to take the imperial examinations. He "asked to take a merchant boat in Dinghai County and wanted to reach Tongzhou by sea, then go west by himself, when more than a dozen boats sailed on this route with his one" (B. Zhang 1985: 83). This indicates that many boats were sailing on this route.

Offshore routes and inland waterways were connected through three rivers in Guangzhou. These were the West River, which connected Duanzhou and West Guangnan Province, the East River, which connected Huizhou and Chaozhou, and the North River, which was linked to Shaozhou (present-day Shaoguan). According to Li Cengbo, "cities such as Rongzhou, Liuzhou, Xiangzhou, Xunzhou, Tengzhou, and others, were situated along the banks of the West River, which directly crossed the South China Sea." (Z. Li 1990). Salt produced in Guangnan East Province was transported through the West River and sold in Guangnan West Province. It was noted that while Guangnan East Province was rich in salt production, its inhabitants consumed less salt. Conversely, Guangnan West Province was the opposite. It was convenient to transport salt produced in the former to the latter via the West River and sell it to several prefectures in the latter." (Q. Zhou 1999: 183).During the Southern Song Dynasty, when Ming Tuo spoke of salt smuggling on the coast of Guangnan East Province, it was recorded that "large boats smuggled salt by sea and hid along the coast. Small ones smuggled salt via the East and West Rivers. The involved part of the East River covered from Guangzhou to Chaozhou and Huizhou, while the involved part of the West River was from Guangzhou to Wuzhou and Hengzhou." (S. Xu et al. 2014: 6568). The North River waterway could reach Nanxiong, and the landway was over the Five Ridges and went to the Ganjiang River, then connected to the Yangtze River, which was the main route for freight transportation in Guangzhou. The first volume "Five Ridges" of *The Land Beyond the Passes* documented that "the five routes into the Five Ridges regions might not require climbing up and down the mountains all the way. For example, the first route was reaching Xunzhou and Meizhou in Guangnan East Province from Tingzhou in Fujian Province; the second one was reaching Nanxiong from Nan'an Prefecture in Jiangnan West Province and by climbing over Dageng Ridge; the third one was reaching Lian County from Chenzhou in Jinghu South Province; the fourth one was reaching He County in Guangnan West Province from Dao County, the fifth one was reaching Jingjiang Prefecture from Quanzhou." The second route was the main route from Guangzhou Port to the hinterland, by which exported goods in Guangzhou were transported to the hinterland. Before the eighth year of the Jiayou Reign (AD 1063), freight transportation or land transportation by governments in the East Guangnan Province referred to "transporting spices and medicines produced in Five Ridges by land to the capital city." In the eighth year of the Jiayou Reign (AD 1063), Liu Mengzheng was appointed to adjust the old mode of transportation to "sailing from Guangzhou and Shaojiang to Nanxiong by adverse current, then transporting to Nan'an Prefecture from Dayu Ridge by land, among which had three courier station altogether, each with thirty couriers, and then turned to waterways." (Toqta 1977: 9101) From Guangzhou, it was transported by water along the North River, with only a section of land transport from Dayu Ridge to Nan'an Prefecture, and then transferred to waterways of the Ganjiang River. The third route was for transporting goods from Guangnan East and West provinces to South Jinghu Province. It began in Chenzhou in Jinghu South Province and proceeded to Lianzhou in Guangnan East Province, then into the North

River by the Huangshui River, a tributary of the North River, and finally reaching Guangzhou.

In addition to the main waterways that connect inland rivers, several offshore ports were linked to the hinterland by rivers. The ports of Qinzhou, Lianzhou, and Chaozhou in Guangnan East and West provinces were all connected to the hinterland. Qinzhou, located in the west of Guangzhou, was an important port. The third volume of *the Local Record of Qinzhou*, written during the Jiajing Reign, recorded that in Qinzhou, "Qinjiang River reached Lingshan County in the north and Fangcheng County in the south. Travelling over Lingshan Mountain was necessary to reach Hengzhou, and from there, to arrive in Guizhou along the Luoqing River, cross the Ling Canal, and enter the Xiangjiang River. "Four military prefectures in Hainan, along with Qinzhou, Lianzhou, Leizhou, Huazhou, and Gaozhou, produced salt." The salt fields were all "at the coast, and salt was transported by boats to the Shikang Granary in Lianzhou. Merchants selling salt produced in Guangnan West Province transported salt by land from Lianzhou to Yulin Prefecture, and then switched to water transport" (Q. Zhou 1999: 179). The first volume, "Five Ridges" of *The Land Beyond the Passes*, recorded that the first route "into the Five Ridges" was "from Tingzhou in Fujian Province to Xunzhou and Meizhou in Guangnan East Province," which was a primary route from Chaozhou to the hinterland. Tingzhou was situated upstream of the Hanjiang River, "which connected to Jiaozhou Prefecture and Guangnan East and West provinces in the south, Ganjiang River in the west, and the coast of Chaozhou." (M. Zhu 2003: 229). Sailing south along the Hanjiang River would reach Chaozhou. "Every autumn and winter, when farm work was all finished, dozens or hundreds of men carrying weapons, flags, and drums often travelled from and to eight prefectures to smuggle salt and sell it, including Qianzhou, Tingzhou, Zhangzhou, Chaozhou, Xunzhou, Meizhou, Huizhou, and Guangzhou" (T. Li 2004: 4739). Chaozhou was abundant with porcelain, which was exported to countries in the South China Sea via the Hanjiang River (C. Huang 2003: 258).

The ports of Fuzhou, Quanzhou, and other cities in Fujian Province were linked to the hinterland via sea routes to Mingzhou. In the Northern Song Dynasty, a delivery station was established along the way from Fujian Province to Xinzhou in Jiangnan West Province. However, "freight transportation in Fujian Province was primarily conducted by sea", resulting in delivery personnel "not functioning as expected" (S. Xu et al. 2014: 9488). Prefectures in the northern region of Fujian Province transported goods and supplies to Quanzhou and Fuzhou via river transport, which were then either transferred to freight transport heading north or exported to countries in the South China Sea. Dehua, Yongchun, and Anxi were all centers for porcelain production, which was transported to Quanzhou via the East and West rivers and the Jinjiang River (Z. Lin et al. 1987). In Fuzhou, the Minjiang River was linked to Shaowu, Jianning, and Nanjian in the north of Fujian Province. Zhu Xi once proposed to collect grain sold by merchants in the coastal counties of Fuzhou and transport it to Jianning Prefecture and other disaster-stricken prefectures and towns by flat-bottomed boats (X. Zhu 2010: 1117). Porcelain produced in Shaowu, Jianning, and Nanjian was also transported to Fuzhou by the Minjiang River for export (Z. Lin et al. 1987). At the same time, other supplies in Northern Fujian Province were also transported to Fuzhou via the Minjiang River.

Similarly, Wenzhou mainly connected with the hinterland via sea routes. In the Southern Song Dynasty, prefectures in Liangzhe Province were said to have access to Hangzhou via waterways, except for "Wenzhou, Taizhou, and Chuzhou (present-day Lishui) (S. Xu et al. 2014: 7066)," which had no direct access to inland rivers that linked to Hangzhou. Nonetheless, porcelain produced at the Longquan Kiln situated in the upstream of Yongjia River was transported to Wenzhou by the Yongjia River (W. Ye 1987). The porcelain unearthed from the shank boat "Naihai 1" included many products made by the Longquan Kiln, as well as the Yi Kiln of Minqing County in Fujian Province, Dehua Kiln, Cizao Kiln, and Jingdezhen Kiln in West Jiangnan Province (Guangdong Institute of Cultural Relics and Archaeology 2011: 48–87). Hence, ports in Quanzhou, Fuzhou, and Wenzhou that connected with the hinterland through inland rivers were of great significance.

3.2.4 Summary

In the Song Dynasty, offshore routes could be divided into two major sections: the north section and the south section, with Mingzhou serving as the midpoint. The north section was further segmented into two parts, namely from Mizhou to the north of Shandong Peninsula and from Mizhou to Mingzhou. The former section was primarily influenced by the political climate, as only official shipping was allowed during the Northern Song Dynasty, while civilian shipping was restricted. The latter section was divided into three parts, including routes at the mouth of the river, pelagic routes, and ocean routes, and was also influenced by political conditions. The routes at the mouth of the river were sandy and shallow, requiring boats to sail with the tide. Routes south of Mingzhou could be divided into two subsections: from Mingzhou to Fuzhou (Quanzhou) and from Fuzhou (Quanzhou) to Guangzhou, with Fuzhou and Quanzhou as vital transfer stations. West of Guangzhou and Hainan Island, fixed routes connected the mainland. Routes south of Mingzhou were less impacted by political situations and boasted prosperous communication and multiple stop stations.

Oceangoing routes were connected to offshore routes through several critical ports with Ancient Customs, enabling seagoing trade to access offshore and domestic markets through planned offshore routes. Offshore routes could be linked to the domestic canal system via the Yangtze River, the Qiantang River, the Liangzhe East Canal, and the Pearl River. Ports in Wenzhou, Fuzhou, Quanzhou, and Chaozhou, which were not directly connected to the mainland's river system, were linked to their provinces and prefectures by river, serving as a gateway to the sea for goods and supplies from their provinces and prefectures. Offshore routes connected offshore markets, domestic markets, and overseas markets. The economic interdependence in the coastal regions of the Song Dynasty, the expansion of the commodity economy in coastal regions such as Liangzhe, Fujian, and Guangnan provinces, as well as the flourishing overseas trade, were all intimately connected to the bustling offshore routes.

3.3 Offshore Trade in the Song Dynasty

Offshore trade refers to the maritime trade between coastal areas during the Song Dynasty, as well as the transportation and sale of overseas imports between domestic ports after taxation and procurement from the government. The extensive scale of offshore trade not only perpetuated seagoing trade, but also played a significant role in economic complementation and the development of the commodity economy in coastal regions. This role is no less important than that of seagoing trade. The unprecedented boom of maritime trade during the Song Dynasty attracted substantial attention from academia. Most scholars have focused on the study of seagoing trade with foreign countries during the Song Dynasty and conducted profound investigations on various aspects of trade with foreign countries, including the system of overseas trade, commodity structure, trade ports, trade routes, and others.[5] However, there has been no specific examination of offshore trade and its impact on the dynasty. This section provides a tentative study on this subject.

3.3.1 The Commodity Mix of Offshore Trade

The coastal regions of China, spanning from Guangnan and Fujian provinces in the south to Jingdong provinces and Hebei Province in the north, displayed distinct economic features. Fujian Province and Liangzhe East Province, characterized by hilly terrain and limited arable land, experienced a flourishing commodity economy but a shortage of grain. Conversely, the vast expanse of Guangnan East and West provinces, particularly Guangnan East Province, with a sparse population and a surplus of grain, served as the main frontier of foreign trade. Meanwhile, Liangzhe West Province led the country in both commodity economy and food production. The demand for food and textiles in Jingdong Province and Hebei Province necessitated imports from the south, providing fertile ground for the smuggling of these products between the eastern and southern regions in the Southern Song Dynasty. The mix

[5] Fruitful achievements have been made in the field of the overseas trade research, such as Fujita Toyohachi's research on the system of overseas trade, Kuwabara Jistuzo's study on the merchant of Pu Shougeng, Chen Gaohua and Huang Chunyan's research on the overall situation of trade in the Song Dynasty; Ge Jinfang's discussion on the overseas trade in the Southern Song Dynasty; Cao Jiaqi and Zhang Jinpeng's research on maritime transportation in the Song Dynasty, Lin Tianwei's research on the Song spices and medicines trade; Guan Lüquan's study on Guangzhou's foreign trade in the Song Dynasty, and Sen Keji and Yang Weisheng's research on the Song's trade with Japan and Gorye. There are too many to list.

of commodities in offshore trade revealed the distinct economic characteristics and complementary relationships in the coastal areas.

3.3.1.1 Grain Trade in the Coastal Areas

The coastal regions south of the Yangtze River were characterized by the grain trade, which supplied the middle region from both sides of the river. The provinces of Guangnan East in the south and Liangzhe West in the north exported their grain by sea to Fujian Province and Liangzhe East Province. The land in the coastal area of Fujian Province was sparse, with a large population, and mainly used to produce cash crops such as sugar cane, lychee, sorghum, and sticky rice (raw materials for brewing). In addition, porcelain kilns were established (Z. Fu 1989: 22–29). The grain supply for the region relied on imports from Guangnan East Province and Liangzhe West Province throughout the year. "The four prefectures of Fuzhou, Xingzhou (present-day Lueyang, Shaanxi Province), Zhangzhou, and Quanzhou all relied on these provinces to improve their food supply, even during years without drought or flood. They particularly relied on transported food from Liangzhe provinces and Guangnan provinces to cover food shortages." "Even during good harvest years, they still relied on purchasing grain from these provinces." "If the grain purchased from Guangnan and Liangzhe was insufficient, there would be a severe grain shortage." (B. Zhou 1990; S. Yang et al. 1990; D. Zhen, n.d.) "Despite a grain harvest being collected in the coastal regions, it was inadequate to satisfy the populace's needs for more than half a year. There were also no "large grain households in Jiangnan East and West provinces, or Liangzhe East and West provinces possessing hundreds of thousands of tons of grain. Even households which normally made significant contributions of several thousand or several tens of thousands of kilograms of grain, only had ten or twenty thousand kilograms in their warehouses. Half of the grain was chaff and shriveled" (D. Fang 1990: 247), indicating a severe scarcity of grain. Bao Weimin pointed out that the four prefectures of Jianning (Jianou), Nanjianzhou, Tingzhou, and Shaowu Military Prefecture in Fujian Province were not short of food (W. Bao 1991: 41–56). They made every effort to ensure grain production. "They banned planting sorghum, brewing wine, planting citrus, or digging a pond for fish, wishing to claim every inch of land for grain yield increase." (D. Fang 1990: 248) However, they were only self-sufficient. The four prefectures of Zhangzhou, Quanzhou, Xinghua, and Fuzhou in the north generally could not solve the food shortage by importing from the four prefectures above, who also relied on grain input from Guangnan East and West provinces and Liangzhe East and West provinces in famine years. If Jianning Prefecture (Jianou) suffered from famine, especially if the crop harvest was poor, then purchasing food from Guangnan East and West provinces, Taizhou (present-day Linhai, Zhejiang Province), and Wenzhou became urgent." (X. Zhu 2010: 1187)

Guangnan East Province, with vast territory, low population density, and abundant grain, was the largest producer of grain in the area, where maritime merchants conducted trade throughout the year (X. Zhu 2010: 1117). As the main grain exporter, Liangzhe West Province was famous for the proverb which says "the harvest in

Suzhou and Huzhou prefectures is enough to feed the whole nation". Both Guangnan East Province and Liangzhe West Province were the primary sources of food support for coastal areas in Fujian Province. In addition to the grain produced in Guangnan and Liangzhe provinces, grain shortages were common in the coastal areas of Fujian Province. Grain imports were an important responsibility of the local governments. Five measures were taken to encourage merchants to transport grains, including lending and collecting money from merchants shortly after selling grains (B. Zhou 1990), and combating piracy to ensure smooth sailing. When commercial ships returned, they would fight against pirates, ensuring smooth navigation. Otherwise, pirate ships would loot the grain vessels, causing food shortages in Fujian Province (D. Zhen, n.d.). The third measure was rewarding rice traders who bought more grains. The fourth was setting a bottom price line for grains, which was enforced by the local governments at a protective price (X. Zhu 2010: 1117), and the fifth was exempting grain merchants from taxes on purchasing and shipping from Liangzhe provinces to Fujian Province. "Merchants were allowed to trade grain from the Liangzhe provinces to Fujian Province, with all grain vessels receiving trade licenses in the prefectures and counties of their departure. Additionally, they were exempt from taxes when they passed through these regions." (S. Yang et al. 1990) In times of disaster, the Liangzhe provinces became a significant source of rice for Fujian Province, particularly during the severe drought that occurred in Guangnan East Province during Emperor Xiaozong's Reign (AD 1162–1189). During this period, "the sale of food was halted in Guangnan East Province, causing rice purchasing ships from Fujian Province to return empty." To address this issue, the emperor requested 6000 tons of grain from Pingjiang Prefecture (Suzhou), Zhenjiang, and other coastal areas in Liangzhe West Province be transferred to the coastal areas of Fujian Province as disaster food relief. (S. Yang et al. 1990) Fujian Province also petitioned the imperial court to lift sailing restrictions on seagoing boats from the Liangzhe provinces to sell grains and alleviate the grain shortages there". (S. Xu et al. 2014: 8019) According to Fang Dacong, people "can live without drinking (sugar) for a year, but not without food for a day." It was the stability of the offshore grain market that allowed the coastal areas of Fujian Province to develop an economic structure dominated by commercial agriculture and handicraft production of marine trade products. This market enabled them to exchange their commodities with rice, a daily necessity, and prevent themselves from going hungry.

Bao Weimin, quoted above, said that the Ningshao Plain in Liangzhe East Province was self-sufficient in grain, while the mountainous and densely populated coastal terrain depended on grain imports. It was common for grains from Liangzhe West Province to be imported into coastal counties in Liangzhe East Province. In the early years of the Southern Song Dynasty, a stipulation on grains in Liangzhe West Province was issued, stating that "the frequent arrivals of sharp-bottomed seagoing boats should not reduce the soaring grain prices in coastal areas. This was due to grain brokers who bought the grain in large quantities at a low price, measured it using large volume measuring devices, and sold it at a much higher price. To address this issue, Wenzhou, Taizhou (present-day Linhai), Mingzhou (present-day Ningbo), and Yuezhou (present-day Shaoxing) were instructed to strictly restrain such brokers." (S. Xu et al. 2014: 8338) This was a routine decree targeting the sale of rice from Liangzhe West Province to the coastal area of Liangzhe East Province. In the twelfth year of the Chunyou Reign (AD 1252), Changguo County (present-day Dinghai, Zhejiang) ordered Fei Xu to build granaries and raise funds. This was "a customary practice that was conducted every year to keep prices stable during the period of food shortage between two harvests. The stored grains were then sold at a normal price." (F. Feng et al. 1990: 6073) Such practices were conducted to solve food shortages in uncommon seasons and ensure frequent visits of rice boats from Liangzhe West Province to Changguo County. Grains from Guangnan East Province were often sold to the coastal area of Liangzhe East Province. Li Zengbo noted that "Fujian Province and Liangzhe East Province often bought grains from Guangnan East Province and Guangnan West Province, mostly by sea." (Z. Li 1990) The term "Zhe" referred to Liangze East Province, while the term "Fujian brokers" mainly referred to merchants who bought grains from Guangnan East Province and transferred them to Liangzhe West Province, bypassing Fujian Province. As the largest port in Liangzhe East Province and "the hub of grain boats", "all grain boats from Guangnan East Province and Guangnan West Province gathered in areas under the jurisdiction of Siming Prefecture (Ningbo) (X. Zhu 2010: 793, 1177). Mingzhou (Ningbo) was the major distribution center for grain trade in the coastal areas.

In the event of famine, the coastal prefectures of Liangzhe East Province were more reliant on external sources of food. "When crop failures occurred in Wenzhou and Taizhou of Liangzhe East Province, they relied on sea transportation of grain from Liangzhe West Province to maintain supply." (Song Shi Quanwen 2005: 1766) Despite being adjacent, importing grains from Guangnan East Province and Guangnan West Province was also easy. Wenzhou's sea routes ran through Liangzhe West Province and Guangnan East Province, making securing food supply easier. As Ma Guangzu observed, "Wenzhou had seaways and commercial boats to transport, so it could basically raise money to attract business, and grain carriers should not worry." (Y. Wu 1990) In times of widespread disaster, grains were bought from "Jinghu South Province, Guangnan East Province, Guangnan West Province, and two or three prefectures with a harvest in Liangzhe West Province". "The sea route in Guangnan East Province was a shortcut to Liangzhe East Province", and "the cost of rice is generally low and stable" in Guangnan East Province. Local governments "sent staff to the coastal areas of Fujian Province and Guangnan East Province to recruit merchants for grain trading". Additionally, local governments introduced preferential policies such as exempting taxes levied on the basis of deadweight tonnage of grain boats and "purchasing the rice which couldn't be sold according to the price" to protect the merchants' interests (X. Zhu 2010: 647). The fall of rice imports from Guangnan East and West provinces would lead to the rise of rice prices in Taizhou (present-day Linhai), where "the two disasters of drought and flood made farmers cry for the poor harvest. In autumn, the price of grain was very expensive, and there were few grain boats transporting in and out of Guangnan East and West provinces." (F. Dai 1990 When disasters occurred in places which were self-sufficient in grain, such as Shaoxing Prefecture and Wuzhou, the local governments also "attracted grain traders in the coastal areas of Liangzhe West Province, Fujian Province and Guangnan East

Province", "raised money to recruit seagoing ships, purchased grains from Guangnan East and West provinces, and continuously provided food relief" (X. Zhu 2010: 940). The coastal areas of Mingzhou (present-day Ningbo), Taizhou (present-day Linhai), and Wenzhou in Liangzhe East Province were relatively developed in maritime trade and commodity economy, whose basis was stable and mature offshore grain trade markets.

In the past, there existed a trade in grain from Guangnan West Province to Guangnan East Province, as documented in *the Adjusting Method of Rice Prices*, Volume IV of *The Land Beyond the Passes*. According to this source, "the low rice prices in Guangnan West Province, as low as 50 copper coins per Dou (approximately 6 kg), attracted wealthy merchants who bought the grain at these low prices and transported it by ship to Panyu County, where they sold it for a profit." However, in the Southern Song Dynasty, the increased number of garrisons stationed in Guangnan West Province led to a greater demand for food, which "had to be transported from Guangnan East Province" to Qinzhou Prefecture by sea. This food was intended not only for the garrison in Qinzhou Prefecture but also "for the troops based in Yongzhou (present-day Nanning, Guangxi), which required three-day land transportation." The four prefectures on Hainan Island, namely Qiongzhou (present-day Haikou), Yazhou (present-day Yaxian), Danzhou (present-day Danxian), and Wan'an Prefecture, which fell under the jurisdiction of Guangnan West Province, were all dependent on food imports from China's mainland. The food required for the garrison soldiers on Hainan Island had to be transported every year by dedicated soldiers from Leizhou (present-day Haikang, Guangdong), Huazhou, Gaozhou (present-day Maomingbei, Guangdong), Tengzhou (present-day Tnegxian, Guangxi), Rongzhou (present-day Rongxian, Guangxi), and Baizhou prefectures, who escorted and carried the military food to Qiongzhou (present-day Haikou) by sea." Alternatively, the local people in Leizhou (present-day Haikang, Guangdong), Huazhou, Gaozhou (present-day Maomingbei, Guangdong), and Taipingzhou (present-day Dangtu, Anhui) were ordered "to pay taxes in the form of physical grains to Dijiaochang in Leizhou (Haikang), and soldiers from ethnic groups in Qiongzhou (Haikou) were ordered to transport the grains themselves." (Toqta 1977: 9584–85) Hainan Island was highly dependent on China's mainland for its food supply, and "passenger boats in the north of the island were used to transport grain" for the locals (T. Li 2004: 7521). "The absence of merchants from Gaozhou (present-day North Maoming, Guangdong) and Huazhou meant that Hainan Island lacked sufficient supplies of cattle, rice, and other goods." (S. Xu et al. 2014: 6360). In times of famine, the island had to rely on the merchants from Guangnan East Province to purchase grains (Z. Li 1990).

Shandong Province and the coastal regions of Huainan Province, north of the Yangtze River, relied on maritime transportation to import grains. During the Jianyan Reign (AD 1127–1130) of the Southern Song Dynasty, many individuals from Shandong Province sold rice in the coastal areas of Liangzhe provinces. Those without a fixed occupation in the coastal villages of Mingzhou (present-day Ningbo) and Yuezhou (present-day Shaoxing) primarily originated from Shandong Province and supported themselves by participating in grain trade. Similarly, residents of Huainan East Province and Liangzhe West Province traveled to Shandong Province to conduct profitable transactions. "The price of rice and wheat in Haizhou (present-day Lianyungang), Mizhou (present-day Zhucheng, Shandong), and other prefectures increased significantly, leading sea boat households in Tongzhou (present-day Nantong), Taizhou, Suzhou, and Xiuzhou (present-day Jiaxing, Zhejiang) to transport grains to Banqiao County (present-day Jiaoxian, Shandong), Caoqiao County, and other regions of Mizhou (present-day Zhucheng) for trading. Some individuals from Liangzhe East Province and Fujian Province also engaged in grain trade in Shandong Province. In Mingzhou (present-day Ningbo) and its neighbouring regions, "people with grains in their storehouses aimed to profit from high prices by selling all their grain." The Song Dynasty court issued an order banning such practices in Wenzhou, Taizhou (present-day Linhai), Mingzhou (present-day Ningbo), and Yuezhou (present-day Shaoxing) in Fujian Province. Violators faced punishment under military law, which applied to both the ship owner and helmsman (S. Xu et al. 2014: 9242; X. Li 2013). In certain cases, such as during floods in Huainan Province, it was necessary to import rice from Guangnan provinces. Liu Zai, for example, asked Li Jun, the commander of Fujian Provincial Garrison Troops, who had purchased the most food in Guangnan provinces, to "let traders sell grains in Huainan Province in the event of a poor harvest." (Z. Liu 1990) Thus, offshore grain trade played an important role in supporting the economic development of coastal areas in Fujian Province and Liangzhe East Province under normal circumstances.

3.3.1.2 Imports, Exports and Other Commodities Trade in Offshore Areas

Imports such as spices and medicines played a significant role in offshore trade during the Song Dynasty. The Law on Overseas Trade stipulated that only Mingzhou (Ningbo, Zhejiang) could issue trade licenses to trade with Korea and Japan. However, after the Yuanyou Reign (AD 1086–1094), only Guangzhou and Quanzhou could issue trade licenses for trade with countries in the South China Sea. Prior to this period, only Guangzhou had the authority to issue trade licenses for trade with countries in the South China Sea, and returning seagoing ships were required to pay taxes at the port where the certificate was issued. The second volume of *Reflections about Pingzhou* recorded that "the court had attempted to transfer the administration of ships in Quanzhou to Guangzhou Ancient Customs, which was inconvenient for Quanzhou's merchants". Consequently, without a customs office in Quanzhou, its merchants were required to apply for overseas trade licenses from Guangzhou Ancient Customs. In the seventh year of the Xi'ning Reign (AD 1074), Emperor Shenzong issued an imperial edict stating that "if a boat was blown off course by unexpected winds or storms to other coastal prefectures, the ships owner should immediately report to the local government of the anchoring port. The local government was required to report to the mayor of the prefecture, and then a deputy mayor in charge of financial affairs would work with the county magistrate and officials to check the goods on the spot. Common commercial goods could be sold between individuals after taxation, but prohibited goods would be sealed and sent to the nearest customs for taxation, escorted by dedicated officials." Therefore, the responsibilities of taxation and official procurement of commercial ships blown off course fell upon officials of coastal prefectures and counties. The imperial edict of Emperor Shenzong highlighted Quanzhou and Fuzhou, which lacked customs, stating that commercial ships from southern countries and Hainan Island berthing in the coastal areas of Quanzhou and Fuzhou must submit their trade licenses for verification. Goods could only be put on the market after payment of taxes and receipt of tax receipts from the tax authorities. If merchants could not present trade licenses, receipts after taxation, or documents for the government's share purchased at customs, their goods would be sent to the nearest customs for check and taxation (S. Xu et al. 2014: 4205). This highlights the need for seagoing merchants returning from foreign countries to follow customs procedures at departure ports, distribute goods to other coastal ports after paying taxes, and finally put them on the domestic market. Such trade activities are classified as offshore trade. During the middle of the Northern Song Dynasty, Quanzhou became a busy seaport, with a multitude of foreign seagoing boats calling at its port, and an abundance of goods piled up like hills (Toqta 1977: 10,632). An ancient customs was established at Banqiao Town (present-day Jiaoxian, Shandong), located near the sea in Mizhou (present-day Zhucheng). Before the customs' founding, merchants and rich families gathered there to benefit from seagoing ships. The town enjoyed geographical advantages, with Guangnan East Province, Guangnan West Province, Fujian Province, East Huainan Province, West Huainan Province, and Zhejiang Province as its eastern neighbors and Jingdong Province, Hebei Province, and Hedong Province as its western neighbors. However, franchise regulation was difficult to implement for precious goods like ivory, rhinoceros horn, and frankincense, leading to inevitable underground trading (Toqta 1977: 4560–61).These foreign goods were transported offshore from Guangzhou and Mingzhou.

In the Song Dynasty, merchants were authorized to purchase imported goods which had been taxed at customs ports and sell them in other prefectures and counties. In the seventh year of the Xi'ning Reign (AD 1074), it was stipulated that "all merchants bought goods instead of taxes under customs sampling inspection, applied for trade licenses at the customs, and were allowed to sell them in other prefectures" (S. Xu et al. 2014: 4205–06). Every year, after being levied taxes and the official purchased share being taken away at overseas trading ports, a large amount of imports were officially transported to the capital in the Song Dynasty. In the Northern Song Dynasty, it was stipulated that "valuable spices and medicines should be transported to the capital city by land" and "general goods could be transported by sea" (S. Xu et al. 2014: 7004), which were referred to as "valuable goods transported in batches by land" and "general goods transported in batches by sea" (S. Xu et al. 2014: 4221). In the second year of the Chunxi Reign (AD 1175), general goods and valuable goods were combined for batch transportation, and "fifty thousand kilograms of general goods and valuable goods as a batch" were transported by sea (S. Xu et al. 2014: 4219). Some of the goods were also sold locally at ports for overseas trade. For example, in the Southern Song Dynasty, it was stipulated that "according to the requirements of Lin'an Prefecture, customs in Guangnan purchased frankincense transported by sea, matched it with complete sets according to the grade, and recruited merchants to pay taxes and apply for selling" (Toqta 1977: 4537). After the official purchased share was taken away, the remaining imports were allowed to be sold freely on the market. For instance, after the official purchased share was taken away at Quanzhou Ancient Customs, "the foreign trader should make a guarantee, and apply for a trade license. The customs checked and registered the goods and then issued a trade license." "Then the owner of the goods was allowed to sell in the prefectures of Fujian Province" (S. Xu et al. 2014: 4219). Meanwhile, "the ports in Zhongmen and Haikou (Fuzhou), were frequently called by merchant boats, local officials of prefectures and counties required merchants to buy pearls, rhinoceros horn, ivory, spices, and medicines with money, gold, and silver on their way back" (S. Xu et al. 2014: 4205). Merchants from Liangzhe East Province and other regions traded in Guangnan East Province. "Sometimes, a dozen large ships coming from Wenzhou, Taizhou (present-day Linhai), Mingzhou (present-day Ningbo), Yuezhou (present-day Shaoxing), and other places formed a fleet to trade in Guangzhou". Apart from salt, rice, and paint produced by Guangnan East Province, "there were imports from abroad" (D. Fang 1990). The main domestic markets for imported products were the capital city, Southeast China, and Sichuan (C. Huang 1999: 29–35). Many of these products were transported and sold by offshore routes. The Northern Song Dynasty specified that "after taxation, the pearls imported from the Guangnan East and West provinces should be sold in the capital city and Sichuan Province, and two or three rich people or officials were needed as guarantee. After the letter of guarantee was signed at the taxation office, the taxation office would issue the trade license to permit the goods to be sold in the designated place" (S. Xu et al. 2014: 6934).There were commercial ships transporting pearls and jewelries imported from overseas to Jiangyin. Huangtian Port, which had the Yangtze River as its neighbor, was described by Wang Anshi as a booming market where merchant ships traded in jewelries like overseas pearls and rhinoceros horn. The abundance of fish and crabs in these places made it easy to negotiate prices." (A. Wang 1990) Other imports also applied the same policy. In the Southern Song Dynasty, "merchants in the Lin'an Prefecture Customs bought pepper, Jiangzhen fragrance, shrunk sand, cardamom, wrinkled giant hyssop, and other goods paid taxes at the Lin'an customs, and then the goods were issued trade licenses of Quanzhou and Guangzhou, with the deadline set for selling in Lin'an Prefecture." (S. Xu et al. 2014: 4221) A businessman from Quanzhou, surnamed Yang, transported tambac, borneol, pearl strings, and supang totaling a value of 400,000 strings of 1000 to Lin'an (M. Hong 1981: 589). Many ships in the river running through Hangzhou "carried spices, medicines and other sundries" and redistributed them to other places (Z. Wu 1980: 113). These imports were all transported to Hangzhou by sea.

The continuous influx of commodities from overseas ports required redistribution through offshore trade to other areas. It is evident that the grain boats from Liangzhe East Province and Fujian Province did not sail empty to Guangnan East Province every year. Rather, they transported bulk commodities, such as porcelain and other goods, which were exported to overseas countries through Guangzhou. This is supported by the commodity composition recovered from the sunken ship "Nanhai 1" in the Yangjiang sea area of Guangnan East Province during the Southern Song

Dynasty. The ship likely departed from Guangzhou Port and followed the "southeast seagoing route from Guangzhou, 200 km away, to Tun Mun Mountain. There were 10 km of shallow water, which made ships sail only 25 km a day. The distance was 100 km in total. From Tun Mun Mountain, it took 7 days to sail southwestward to reach Jiuruluozhou (around the Xisha Islands), and 3 days to arrive at Cham Islands, then the boats sailed southbound 300 miles to reach the east of Lingshan (near Guiren in Vietnam today). The distance from the southwest of Lingshan to Arab Empire, Foshizi, Tintu, Sindhub and other countries could not be calculated clearly." (G. Zeng 1990) Although the normal route from Tun Mun was through the sea around Qizhou Archipelago in the east of Hainan Island to Campa and then to countries in the South China Sea, Yangjiang is farther west or southwest of this route. Ships in Guangzhou sailing in the east wind may be blown to the Yangjiang Sea in a storm. However, trade licenses were only issued to Japan and Goryeo by Mingzhou (present-day Ningbo), while licenses for trading with countries in the South China Sea were only available from Quanzhou or Guangzhou. Furthermore, returned ships were only taxed at the port where their licenses were issued, which was strictly enforced in both the Northern and Southern Song Dynasties. Therefore, if "Nanhai 1" sailed from Quanzhou to Southeast Asia, it could directly sail out of the deep-sea route in the east of Hainan Island, as recorded in *Accounts About the Capital* saying "if merchants wanted to go abroad to trade by ship, they could sail overseas from Quanzhou Port". The ship "zigzagged passing by Qizhou Archipelago, and the sea water measured from the ship was more than 200 m. If it passed Kunlun Ocean (the waters between Cambodia and Thailand), Shamo Ocean (the water region west to China's Nansha Islands), Shelong Ocean(the water region close to Indonesia's Natuna Islands), and Wuzhu Ocean (the water region close to China's Shangchuan Island)." (Z. Wu 1980: 112; D. Zhou n.d.; L. Chen 1999)[6] As Qizhou Archipelago situated to the east of Hainan Island, and Kunlun Ocean (the waters between Cambodia and Thailand) and other oceans were located to the south of Hainan Island, it was impossible for "Nanhai 1" to get sank in the Yangjiang Sea. To prevent merchant ships from smuggling contraband such as copper coins, the Song Dynasty troops supervised the deep-sea waterways when the ships docked along the coast after "checking on empty boat". It is therefore likely that "Nanhai 1" sailed from Guangzhou Port, as evidenced by the 120 cultural relics acquired from the ship's first trial excavation, including 108 pieces of porcelain from Dehua Kiln, Cizao Kiln, Jingdezhen Kiln, Longquan Kiln, and Guangzhou Folk Kiln in Fujian Province, as well as Liangzhe East Province, Fujian Province, Jiangnan West Province, Guangnan East Province, and other regions (Guangdong Institute of Cultural Relics and Archaeology 2011: 48–87). For a ship with a load of about 200 tons, centralized purchasing at Guangzhou Port was the most effective means of procurement, rather than purchasing exported goods southward from the

[6] *The Customs of Cambodia* written by Zhou Daguan recorded that the Kunlun Ocean is in the open seas of Zhenla (now Cambodia). The Wenzhou-Southeast route was through the Qizhou Ocean, Cochin Ocean (now Beibu Gulf), Champa (now Vietnam), Kunlun Ocean and sailed into Zhenla Harbor. According to *Chronicles of Maritime Kingdoms* written by Chen Lunjiong, Qizhou Ocean is in the southeast of Wanzhou (present-day Wanning in Haian Province), and the Kunlun Ocean is in the south of the Qizhou Ocean.

coast of Liangzhe East Province, which would have been too expensive (Guangdong Institute of Cultural Relics and Archaeology 2011: 6; Editorial Committee of Excavation Report of the Quanzhou Bay Song Dynasty Shipwreck Excavation 1975; Quanzhou Bay Song Dynasty Shipwreck Restoration Group and Fujian Quanzhou Shipyard 1974: 1–18, 28–35).[7] Therefore, the distribution of exports from different regions at various ports was primarily achieved through offshore trade. Offshore trade was also the foundation of seagoing trade in terms of the distribution of imports and exports.

Offshore trade commodities also included textiles, tea, salt, wood, cattle, sea food and other living products, production and military supplies. Merchants often "sailed to Jingdong Province, Hebei Province, Hedong Province, and other regions (Toqta 1977: 4561). The trade of textiles in Shandong Province proved to be especially lucrative, with a single piece of silk being valued at 30,000 coppers (X. Li 2013: 919).Salt production was widespread in provinces such as Huainan, Liangzhe, Fujian, and Guangnan, while tea was mainly produced in Fujian and Liangzhe provinces. Some tea was transported and sold via sea routes, as Emperor Gaozong "permitted merchants to sell tea and salt by sea" (X. Li 2013: 900–01). During the Southern Song Dynasty, tea franchises were regulated by a strict system, whereas a co-working system with governments was applied to salt franchises. Merchants were required to purchase certificates before initiating maritime trade in tea and salt, and Tongzhou (present-day Nantong) served as a gathering place for salt merchants. "Tongzhou was a coastal city, where the ships of salt merchants gathered" (D. Sun 1990). The sea route was also used by merchants to smuggle tea and salt, and various checkpoints were set up along the coast of Fuzhou to "patrol and search for smuggled spices," "supervise the taxation of Haikou Town," and "capture smugglers of tea, salt, and alum." (K. Lang 1990: 7995) The provinces of Liangzhe East and Guangnan East and West were known for their salt smuggling operations, with groups of approximately 100 people trafficking salt on large ships. County officials often struggled to capture the smugglers and investigate the prefectures' irresponsibility (X. Zhu 2010: 821–22). Tea and salt, especially salt, were popular bulk commodities in both legal and illegal offshore trade (T. Li 2004: 11,167).

The advancement of shipbuilding led to the increased importance of timber in offshore trade. In Chuzhou (present-day Lishui, Zhejiang), the highest quality timber for shipbuilding was transported by sea to Wenzhou. At the time, there were already numerous timber traders, resulting in an excess of timber being transported by sea. The government collected excessive amounts of timber that could not be used by the shipyards in Wenzhou. The surplus was sold to Mingzhou (present-day Ningbo) and Huating (present-day Songjiang, Shanghai) through sea transportation (Y. Lou 1990). In Qinzhou, Guangxi, "Wulan wood was deemed the ideal material for rudders of large boats" and was sold for a much higher price in Panyu County and Quanzhou (Q.

[7] *The Archaeological Excavation of "Nanhai I"* shows that the ship is 30.4 meters long, 9.8 meters wide and 4.2 meters high, the size of the Quanzhou ships of Southern Song. It is estimated that Quanzhou ship could carry more than 200 tons loads and need 50 sailors to operate it.The Quanzhou ship purchased exported goods on its way, which took much time and money.

Zhou 1999: 219, 220). Cattle played a significant role in the trading activities of mainland merchants on Hainan Island. The "residents of Hainan Island traded cattle for spices." (Q. Zhou 1999: 71). The merchant ships "from Gaozhou (present-day north of Maoming), and Huazhou transported grain, pottery, cattle, livestock, and other goods" to Hainan Island. If these merchant ships did not arrive, Hainan Island would face a shortage of cattle and rice" (S. Xu et al. 2014: 6360; Toqta 1977: 4544). The ships of Quanzhou, known as "Quanbo", carried wine, rice, flour, thin silk, lacquer, porcelain, and other goods to Hainan Island (R. Zhao 1996: 217). In the Southern Song Dynasty, "the coastal areas of East and West Shandong Province, Dengzhou (present-day Penglai), Laizhou, Yizhou (present-day Linyi), Mizhou (present-day Zhucheng), Weizhou (present-day Weifang, Shandong), Binzhou, Cangzhou, Bazhou (present-day Baxian,Tianjin) and other prefectures often had copper, iron, buffalo hides, isinglass and other products sold by southeastern sea ships. The Mongols relied on southeastern sea ships to transport raw materials for producing seagoing ships, weapons, and armor." (S. Xu et al. 2014: 8387). Buffalo hides, bamboo arrow shafts, and lacquer goods were considered military materials and were typically traded through smuggling. Seafood was another commodity regularly traded in daily commerce. "Ships that berthed at the ferry port of Qiantang River transported seafood, fish, crabs, pickled fish, and meat food from Mingzhou (present-day Ningbo), Yuezhou (present-day Shaoxing), Wenzhou and Taizhou (present-day Linhai) to Jiangnan East and West provinces and Liangzhe East and West provinces." (Z. Wu 1980: 112) Small offshore merchants mostly sold dried fish and other seafood due to their low costs and profits, making it a popular commodity for smugglers. "These illicit trades occurred primarily on private maritime routes, which were not designated by the government for trade." (S. Xu et al. 2014: 4204).

Offshore trade involved various types of commodities, including specialties from coastal regions. Farmers in the coastal areas of Fujian Province were skilled in growing lychee, sugar cane, and other cash crops instead of grains. Lychee was a highly sought-after commodity that was trafficked to Liangzhe East and West provinces every year. This fruit was paid as tributes to the emperor and sent to high officials at the court, sold in the market, and transported to Hangzhou either by sea or carried on foot, where it was sold until August (*Life in Lin'an During the Southern Song Dynasty* 1996: 652). Jojin met "Fuzhou merchants selling lychee" on the sea from Japan to Mingzhou (present-day Ningbo) (Jojin 2009: 15). Some merchants transported lychee to the capital via waterways, and it was transported to the north of the Mongolian highlands desert and Xixia Kingdom", as well as overseas to places like Korea, Japan, and the Arab Empire. The lucrative trade in lychee benefited local farmers, with approximately one thousand trillion kilograms of lychee sold each year (X. Cai 1985: 2), and even more sugar produced in the region transported to Liangzhe East and Liangzhe West Province annually" (D. Fang 1990). The mining industry in Fujian Province was relatively developed in the Song Dynasty, leading to the export of iron. Iron was not produced by the prefectures of the Liangzhe East and West Provinces, but was transported by sea from Quanzhou and Fuzhou. Rare flowers also grew in Fujian Province and Guangnan East and West provinces, which were planted in pottery and shipped to Liangzhe provinces by sea. People in the local regions bought them for appreciation (B. Zhang 1985: 77). In the early Northern Song Dynasty, Nüzhen crossed the sea from Suzhou (present-day Jinxian, Liaoning Province), and "often went to Dengzhou (present-day Penglai, Shandong Province) to sell horses." (M. Xu 1987: 20) They imported their local specialties and horses into the mainland of the Song Dynasty. The main commodities sold to the mainland from Hainan Island were spices and medicines. Every year, Guangnan West Province asked "four prefectures and the army to buy spices." "The government procured the spices at low prices from farmers according to different price levels, and then sold them to other residents in the city at high prices" (T. Li 2004: 7521). These spices and medicines were shipped to Guizhou and sold at high prices. In addition, merchants from Hainan Island shipped specialties such as betel nut and Ceiba to the mainland. "Because of the unique quality and abundant production of betel nut and Ceiba on Hainan Island, most merchants from Quanzhou and Xinghua prefectures went to Hainan Island for these goods." "Hainan Island also produced valuable commodities such as spices, areca-nut, coconut, ponies, kingfisher feathers, beeswax, supang, Ceiba, and so on. The four prefectures levied commercial taxes to balance their official annual incomes and expenditures" (Q. Zhou 1999: 71). The Li people "traded with Chinese eagle-wood, coarse cloth, hemp skin, and other products," while the provincial people "resold and exchanged with the merchants" (R. Zhao 1996: 217, 220) and sold these products outside the island. Every year in March, there were regular Sanjiang shipments from Taizhou (present-day Linhai, Zhejiang Province) to Tongzhou (present-day Nantong, Jiangsu Province). During his escape from southern Tongzhou, Wen Tianxiang boarded a southbound ship carrying ginger (T. Wen 1987: 521).

3.3.2 Offshore Traders

The Northern Song government authorized merchants to trade in all coastal prefectures, except for Dengzhou (present-day Penglai) and Laizhou of Shandong Province, the border areas close to the Liao Kingdom, and those places within the Liao Kingdom. The imperial edicts on customs regulations, as documented in both the *Compilation of Orders in the Qingli Reign* and the *Compilation of Orders in the Jiayou Reign*, regulated offshore trade in prefectures other than Dengzhou and Laizhou. According to the edicts, "traders involved in overseas trade were prohibited from entering the territories of Goryeo or Shilla, or conducting business in Dengzhou and Laizhou. If they wished to travel to other prefectures, they had to apply for a trade license beforehand, by providing a list of the name and quantity of the goods to be traded, as well as the name of the business destination. Additionally, they needed to find three wealthy locals to guarantee that they would not transport prohibited items or goods that could be used to produce weapons, and that they would not cross the prohibited boundaries. After these formalities were completed, the government would issue a trade license." Many merchants engaged in offshore trade after receiving official licenses to conduct business overseas. "The merchants from Fujian

Province and Liangzhe provinces often exploited this opportunity to travel to Korea and collude with the Khitan," using their trade license to Goryeo to sail their ships to the Liao Kingdom for higher profits." (S. Su 1986: 889–90) The above discussion demonstrates that during the Song Dynasty, customs not only regulated trade with foreign countries but also managed domestic offshore trade. This was confirmed by a proposal made by Guangnan West Province in the fifth year of the Yuanfeng Reign (AD 1082), which stated that "indigenous merchants in the coastal areas who traded on Hainan Island, carrying untaxed goods such as grain, beef, wine, and yellow-fin tuna, did not need to apply for a trade license in Guangzhou." However, this proposal was not approved by the court (T. Li 2004: 7989; Toqta 1977: 4560), indicating that goods involved in offshore trade also needed to be declared at customs and trade licenses obtained.

The offshore trade served as a link between domestic and overseas markets, and it involved not only domestic professional merchants and foreign maritime merchants, but also a significant number of coastal residents and seafaring households. The professional merchants, primarily from coastal provinces, were the most active participants in this trade due to their familiarity with the market and offshore routes. The merchant surnamed Yang, who transported imported goods worth 400,000 strings of coins from Quanzhou to Lin'an, was one such professional. The *Sea Route* in the volume of *Continuation of the Chronicles of Wu County* recorded that Suzhou was a preferred destination for merchants from Fujian Province, and Guangnan East and West provinces. Although most of the business journey from Qinglong in the south to Fushan in the north occurred via sea routes, "maritime merchants from Fujian Province, and Guangnan East and West provinces were not deterred by the risks associated with sailing in windy conditions, thereby enabling the availability of precious goods from remote areas in Suzhou markets." Merchants from Fujian Province, and Guangnan East and West provinces accessed the Yangtze River via the sea route. "There were lots of ships from Fujian Province, Guangnan East and West provinces and foreign ships from Hainan Island trading in Zhenjiang Prefecture by sea", and "there were merchants got off their ships on the river bank of Jiangning Prefecture (present-day Nanjing, Jiangsu)"(S. Xu et al. 2014: 7126). *Financial Affairs* (Article 18) in *The Anthology of Laws and Regulations of the Song Dynasty* indicated that Huangyao Town in Kunshan County was "a crucial hub for large commercial ships from various prefectures, including Fujian Province, Guangnan East, and West provinces, Wenzhou, Taizhou (present-day Linhai), Mingzhou (present-day Ningbo), Yuezhou (present-day Shaoxing), and others. Intermediary merchants in the south of the town facilitated trading in Ganpu (present-day Haiyan, Zhejiang Province), Huating (present-day Songjiang, Shanghai), Qinglong, and Jiangwan, whereas the north was suitable for merchants to pay taxes along the coasts in Gujing, Shuangbang, Wangjiaqiao, Nandachang, Sanchapu, Shajing, Shatou, Daopu, Xiaojing, Xintang, Xuegang, and Taogang. It was remarkable that the taxes imposed on imported goods from the south could amount to 10,000 strings of 1000 coins within a month." (S. Xu et al. 2014: 6387–88) Overall, it is evident that maritime trade occurred at numerous ports in the coastal areas of Liangzhe West Province.

The merchants in Shandong came from various provinces, including Huainan, Liangzhe East and West, Fujian, and Guangnan East provinces. As documented in *The History of the Song Dynasty - Financial Affairs* VIII, "merchants from Guangnan East and West provinces, Fujian Province, Huainan Province, East and Liangzhe West Province imported goods Jingdong Province, Hebei Province, and Hedong Province." In the fourth year of the Zhenghe Reign (AD 1114), the Song government imposed a ban on seagoing ships from abroad or from Hainan Island arriving at Mizhou, which was located near the border regions of Dengzhou (present-day Penglai) and Laizhou." (S. Xu et al. 2014: 6316) The purpose of this ban was to safeguard sovereignty and security. For the same reason, merchant ships were also prohibited from traveling to Mizhou (present-day Zhucheng), Dengzhou, and Laizhou. However, the smuggling trade to Shandong remained prevalent.In the Southern Song Dynasty, Dengzhou (present-day Penglai), and Mizhou (present-day Zhucheng) were returned to the territory of the Jin Kingdom. However, "merchants from Fujian Province and Yuezhou (present-day Shaoxing) continued to trade expensive commodities in Shandong." For example, Wang Juchang, a Wenzhou native, "was arrested by the Qi Kingdom (a puppet regime supported by the Jin Kingdom) for selling goods to Shandong East and West Provinces by sea." (M. Hong 1981: 62) Emperor Gaozong subsequently forbade "people without fixed occupations in Mingzhou (present-day Ningbo), Yuezhou (present-day Shaoxing), and Shandong from selling grains." He also stipulated that "merchant ships carrying grains and silk from Jiangnan East Province, Jiangnan West Province, Liangzhe East Province, and Liangzhe West Province to Jingdong East Province should be intercepted and forbidden to pass. A reward of 3000 strings of 1000 coins would be given to those who capture and deliver the violators to the government. The common people would be entitled to a minor military officer position, while those who already had an official position would receive the emperor's gift or award. Anyone who violated the regulations would be punished according to the military law." Additionally, the Emperor introduced "the regulations on merchant ships trade in Shandong by sea", emphasizing the prohibition of merchants from Fujian Province and Guangnan East Province to trade in Shandong. "Merchants from Fujian Province, Guangnan East and West provinces often transport valuable goods to Shandong, and the governments deployed officials along the coastal areas of Guangnan Province, Fujian Province, and Liangzhe provinces to ban seagoing trade." However, some individuals continued to violate the law and engage in the smuggling trade from the southern coast to the coast of Shandong, which was very rampant (X. Li 2013: 674; S. Xu et al. 2014: 8340, 8386).

As professional merchants began to converge on Hainan Island for the purposes of trade, "a large population of merchants gathered in coastal prefectures and counties on the island. This allowed for the establishment of governmental institutions there, and the taxes levied from the merchants were of sufficient magnitude to support the feeding and training of soldiers". The consequences of reduced trade in this region would have been dire, as the resulting reduction in tax revenue would have caused shortages in soldiers' food supply, as well as in the provision of essential goods for the population at large." (G. Su 1935: 84) In terms of the commodities traded between the coastal prefectures and counties of Guangnan West Province and Hainan

Island, the majority of these were grain, beef, wine, and yellow-fin tuna. These goods were transported by both native inhabitants and merchants". "The native merchants transported grains, beef, wine, yellow fish and others which were exempted from taxes and trade licenses applied by the Ancient Customs of Guangzhou". *The History of the Song Dynasty* calls these people "native merchants" (T. Li 2004: 7989; Toqta 1977: 4560), and some of them were also shipowners who occasionally encountered difficulties when their cargo ships were caught in storms and drifted to other regions, such as the Wusong River in Jiaxing Prefecture, where the officials in charge of supervision would register the cargo ship. The total value of the obtained goods was several thousand strings of coins. Shipowners wishing to reclaim their cargo were refused by the local officials. The shipowners then sued the Ministry of Civil Affairs to claim back their cargoes (L. Wei, n.d.). There were also offshore traders who leased other ships. An incident that occurred during the eighth year of the Shaoxing Reign (AD 1138) involved "a total of 28 people, including itinerant traders and the manager of a bulk cargo transport, who departed from the port of Guangzhou with a large quantity of rich and abundant goods." All of these people were robbed and killed by the punters and helmsman of the ship (M. Hong 1981: 480). These merchants from Guangnan East Province were travelling with the individuals responsible for the bulk cargo transport, and were bound for Fujian or Liangzhe provinces.

The Song government allowed foreign merchants who had already paid their taxes and fulfilled the necessary requirements for official procurement to transport and sell spices and medicines in domestic markets. In the third year of the Chongning Reign (AD 1104), merchants from the Arab Empire and other countries "requested to trade in every prefecture and Bianliang (present-day Kaifeng)", so the Song government implemented a policy requiring foreign merchants to apply for a trade license at Ancient Customs if they intended to trade in other prefectures or the capital city. The foreign merchant ships were checked by customs at the entry port and issued trade licenses. Furthermore, government authorities were to strictly check the destination prefectures of foreign ships (S. Xu et al. 2014: 4207). In addition, "if foreign ships intended to trade in Fujian Province and Liangzhe provinces, the customs of Guangnan provinces dispatched soldiers and weapons to protect offshore navigation." (Toqta 1977: 4561) During Emperor Xiaozong's Reign, foreign merchants were allowed to sell goods only at their arrival ports and were not permitted to leave the port. When this order was issued, merchants feared that there might be something wrong with the rule. In the second year of the Chunxi Reign (AD 1175), the official in charge of foreign trade and taxation in Fujian Province suggested that foreign merchants should apply for a trade license at customs, guaranteeing the imported goods to be sold in other prefectures after taxation. The customs would then check and register the goods and issue trade licenses, allowing the goods to be sold in the prefectures and armies of Fujian Province (S. Xu et al. 2014: 4219), Guangzhou Province, and Liangzhe provinces. Japanese merchants usually traded in the coastal areas of Liangzhe East Province, but they were mainly engaged in illegal smuggling along the coast. "Japanese ships left their country and sailed across the sea, perhaps passing through the boundary of Wenzhou and Taizhou (present-day Linhai) in advance and anchoring at the seashore before they arrived at Qingyuan Prefecture (present-day Ningbo). After leaving Qingyuan Prefecture, they might not immediately return to Japan, as some goods had not been sold out. They returned to Wenzhou and Taizhou, selling goods at low prices, and business continued as usual." Japanese merchants favored copper coins, buying them in such large quantities in the coastal area that they were hardly used in trade in Taizhou. In offshore trade, ships engaged in smuggling copper coins could reach "Qingyuan Prefecture in the north, Fujian Province, or even as far as Guangzhou in the south, in the coastal areas thousands of miles away. Their numbers were countless." (H. Bao 1990) After noticing the secret trading of Japanese merchant ships in the coastal areas, the Southern Song government "introduced a strict ban policy on the entry of Japanese ships. The emperor ordered a strict inspection of Japanese ships' entry in the branching stream." (Song Shi Quanwen 2005: 2345) Overseas foreign trade depended on monsoons in summer or winter. The northbound route was "to leave in the south wind and return in the north wind" (S. Yang et al. 1990). To import from the south, ships needed to follow the rule of "going to the south in winter and returning to the north in summer." (G. Liao 1990) Whether overseas merchants came from Korea, Japan, or the South China Sea, they had to wait for monsoons for at least half a year. After their stay was permitted by the Song government, many of them actively engaged in offshore trade, selling imported goods and buying exported goods for returning home.

Some coastal residents participated in offshore trade as part of a group of non-professional merchants. According to Bao Hui, "maritime merchants were either farmers or fishermen residing in coastal areas." (H. Bao 1990) Not all of these individuals were necessarily professional businessmen. For example, "some delinquent youths in Yunxian County sold fish and salt in the coastal area" and engaged in offshore trade. These individuals were considered to be the "rascals" of the coastal community (Toqta 1977: 10,085).Another instance involved Zhang Duanque, a native of Chuzhou (present-day Lishui, Zhejiang), who "crossed the sea to Quanzhou with a fellow villager from Chuzhou. The boatman intended to avoid taxes and continued to sail southward on the sea until they reached Panyu county of Guangnan East Province." (M. Hong 1981: 96) Zhang Duanque was not a professional merchant but made a temporary decision to engage in trade in Quanzhou. Such non-professional merchants, mostly coastal farmers or fishermen, participated in offshore trade during agricultural slack seasons. The number of individuals who earned subsidies for their livelihood in this manner was significant.

A substantial cohort of individuals who engaged in offshore trade were the coastal boatmen. These individuals were "familiar with the dangerous sea routes and relied on the sale of seafood to generate profits." (X. Li 2013: 3099) They earned their living through three principal avenues: fishing and salt trading in coastal areas, offshore trade, and seagoing trade. Historical records document that "coastal farmers considered trading fish and salt to be a profitable business", and that "they predominantly resided on the riverside or seashore in Liangzhe provinces for fishing." For instance, "a villager in Changxi, Fuzhou, became a son-in-law of a seafaring family and began to make a living from fishing." Emperor Xiaozong adopted measures to ban Yangjiazhai seagoing ships in Gaoyou Prefecture because "he was afraid that such seagoing ships may disrupt the region's fishery development." Prime Minister Zhu Xi recommended granting foreign ships "permission to trade seafood only in Gaoyou Prefecture, at their convenience of shipping." (S. Xu et al. 2014: 9486, 7134; K. Lang 1990: 7939; M. Hong 1981: 474; X. Zhu 2010: 1238) Fishery was a highly commercial industry, especially in coastal areas with open sea routes. Fishermen were required to exchange individual fishing products for general living necessities, thereby necessitating offshore trade as a complement to offshore fishery. This demonstrates that trade was an integral component of the shipowners' lives. "In Zhangzhou, Quanzhou, Fuzhou, and Xinghua Prefectures, boats constructed by coastal residents using their own funds were utilized for business and profit." (S. Xu et al. 2014: 8365) "The shipowners in Tongzhou (present-day Nantong), Taizhou, Suzhou, and Xiuzhou (present-day Jiaxing) were inclined towards trading grains with high profits and transporting grains to Banqiao County (present-day Jiaoxian) and Caoqiao County in Mizhou (present-day Zhucheng) for sale." (S. Xu et al. 2014: 9242) Consequently, their businesses included both ocean-going and offshore trade.

The number of shipowners in the Song Dynasty was substantial. According to *Narrow Ships in Three Cities*, the sixth volume of *Kaiming Period Chronicles of Siming,* during the Jiaxi Reign (AD 1237–1240), there were a total of 19,287 privately owned boats in Mingzhou (present-day Ningbo), Wenzhou, and Taizhou (present-day Linhai), with "3833 boats above 3.3 m in length and 15,454 boats below 3.3 m in length." Only boats with a length greater than 3.3 m were eligible for government requisition and ocean-going navigation, indicating that only a small fraction of ships were used for ocean-going trade, while most ships were used for offshore fishery or offshore trade. The count of ships was limited to the three prefectures of the Liangzhe East Province. If ships in other provinces such as Fujian, Hebei, Jingdong, Liangzhe West, Huainan, Guangnan East, and West were added, the number of seagoing ships would be more substantial. He Feng believed that the governmental naval forces in the coastal areas at the end of the Northern Song Dynasty owned 10,000 seagoing vessels while 7000 were built in the early years of the Jianyan Reign (AD 1127–1130), and 18,000 were built in the 1160s (F. He 2005: 27–43). This was only the number of navy ships. Changxi County in Fuzhou had "thousands of seagoing ships," despite being a remote county (Y. Lou 1990). Ge Jinfang estimated that there were 70,000–80,000 ships in 13 coastal prefectures in the middle and late Southern Song Dynasty (J. Ge 2008: 153). This estimate, which, combined with official and civilian ships, should bring the estimated number of ships closer to the actual number. The large number of ships also meant that more people were engaged in offshore and ocean-going trade. Ge Jinfang estimated that nearly 100,000 people were involved in foreign trade all year round in the southeastern coastal areas of the Southern Song Dynasty (J. Ge 2013: 179–200). Furthermore, large ships used in ocean-going trade as mentioned above, could also be used for offshore trade.

3.3.3 *The Policies on Offshore Trade Administration in the Song Dynasty*

3.3.3.1 Invitation, Guarantee and Taxation in Offshore Trade

The Song government allowed people to participate in maritime trade, including offshore trade. However, once a merchant ship ventured into the vast sea, it was easy to elude government regulation. The administration of offshore trade was similar to that of overseas trade in several ways. Yet, due to the absence of customs at numerous ports and regions, it featured distinct characteristics. Policies governing offshore trade included several aspects:

First, there was the application for a trade license. In the period of Emperor Renzong's Reign, two edicts on offshore trade were issued, namely the *Compilation of Imperial Orders in the Qingli Reign* and the *Compilation of Imperial Orders in the Jiayou Reign*, mandating that merchants engaged in offshore trade needed to obtain an overseas trade license. If merchants intended to trade in prefectures other than Dengzhou and Laizhou, they were required to first apply in the departure prefecture, listing the name and quantity of the goods for sale, and the name of the destination prefecture. After these formalities were completed, the government would issue them trade licenses. Initially, the application for a trade license needed to be submitted at the Ancient Customs of the departure prefecture. However, this strict policy was abolished in Guangnan Province during the fifth year of the Yuanfeng Reign (AD 1082). Prior to the abolition of this policy, merchants who wished to trade their goods in Leizhou (present-day Haikang, Guangdong) and Huazhou on Hainan Island, as well as other prefectures, had to travel 2500 km to Guangzhou, their departure port, to apply for a trade license, which was very inconvenient. In the fifth year of the Yuanfeng Reign (AD 1082), an imperial decree clarified that "if the local merchants in coastal cities of Guangnan West Province transported grain, beef, wine, yellow fish and other goods to Hainan Island, they need not pay taxes or be subject to the official procurement share from their goods, and they were not required to apply for a trade license from Guangzhou (S. Xu et al. 2014: 4206). The only existing trade license for maritime trade is the trade license issued to Li Chong, a merchant from Quanzhou, by the customs of the Liangzhe provinces in the fourth year of the Chongning Reign (AD 1105), which is collected in Japan's *Collection of Japanese Historical Records.* This license is divided into four parts: the name list of the identities and names of sixty-nine people on board, including the ship master, helmsmen, handymen, and sailors, as well as the names of the three guarantors; the list of goods; the specific provisions of the overseas trade management law, recording the business purposes in Japan, regulations on the taxation of returning ships and the person liable; and the signatures of the approval officials, which needed to be recorded in the formalities (Chaoye Qun Zai 1938: 452–55). The main contents of a trade license for offshore trade must be similar to this. In *The Compilation of Imperial Orders in the Xi'ning Reign*, the mutual acceptance and verification of trade licenses between the departure prefecture and the destination prefecture were added.

"The official authorities of the departure prefecture issued a trade license, and the goods on board were also registered in detail. After being checked and approved the trade license at the destination prefecture, a document was issued to the prefecture of departure to confirm the merchant boat's arrival." In this way, the whole process of offshore trade was under the control of the government.

The second aspect pertains to the system of guarantees. *The Compilation of Imperial Orders in the Qingli Reign* and *The Compilation of Imperial Orders in the Jiayou Reign* both stipulated that merchants engaged in offshore trade "were permitted to engage three local residents with substantial financial resources as explicit warrantors." While the trade license was issued by the departure prefecture, the warrantors needed to reside in the locality. The warrantors were collectively and individually responsible for ensuring that the merchant did not violate the law, specifically, that no prohibited or forbidden ordnance was carried into the prefecture, that no trade was conducted across prohibited areas, and that no trade was conducted by sea without a trade license. In the event of any violation, "the guarantor shall be punished with a reduction of three levels of prisoner," (S. Xu et al. 2014: 8316–17) which was the same as the regulation on seagoing trade. As an example, Li Chong, a merchant from Quanzhou who sailed from Mingzhou (present-day Ningbo), was guaranteed by Zheng Yu, Zheng Dunren and Chen You in "the local prefecture," namely Quanzhou, and was issued a trade license by the customs of Liangzhe provinces. If the merchant violated the ban and "the warrantors did not find out, they would be sentenced to more than one hundred floggings." Furthermore, if the merchant did not have enough money or goods to pay the reward to the whistle-blower, the warrantors were obliged to provide the reward (S. Su 1986: 889–90).

The third was the taxation system on offshore trade. The revenue from offshore trade taxation mainly came from big merchants, unlike overseas trade, which was taxed by the customs of the departure port. Offshore trade was taxed by taxation agencies. For example, in Emperor Taizong's Reign, "big maritime merchants selected the sea route from Suzhou, Hangzhou, sailing in the tailwind to the reaches of Huaihe River and Chuzhou (Lishui), where they were rich in goods, and taxes levied on them were several times higher than those levied on any other kinds of peddlers." (S. Xu et al. 2014: 4204) As no customs was established in the region of Huaihe River and Chuzhou (present-day Lishui), the taxes on the offshore trades needed to be collected by the local tax agencies. Merchants bought goods like pepper, incense, and others, which had been taxed in the name of overseas merchants in Quanzhou and Guangzhou. They received trade licenses at the customs in Quanzhou and Guangzhou and docked at Lin'an customs for business. After the merchant ships reached Lin'an, the officials needed to check the trade license and inspect the goods, "examine the varieties and amounts of goods according to the original trade license issued by the departure customs, and rush to the taxation office in Lin'an Prefecture, namely, the capital city, to collect taxes, and then the goods could be transacted on the markets. The tax was collected by the taxation agencies in Lin'an Prefecture and released for sale." (S. Xu et al. 2014: 4221) This article indicates that the basis for taxation was the trade license which recorded the name and quantity of goods. The imports traded in the prefecture with a customs, which have already been taxed, could be sold tax-free, and "the goods that have already been taxed on the ships were not allowed to be taxed again". "In accordance with the law, any one who collects double taxes on those goods that have already been taxed, and such goods are sold inside the prefecture where the customs is located, shall be punished for violating the law." However, only two prefectures were exempted from merchant taxes for trading spices and medicines that had been taxed when they were sold to other prefectures: "a merchant is issued a trade license to the taxation place where the sale takes place, and after inspection and verification of the goods according to the provisions on the trade license, the business taxes of the two trading prefectures can be exempted." (S. Xu et al. 2014: 4217–18) In order to prevent the merchants of maritime trade from evading taxes, the Song dynasty would also adjust the setting of commercial tax agencies with the rise and fall of trade. There were merchants trading goods into the Wusong River from the sea routes. "They can sell goods at Jiangwanpu, the estuary of the Wusong River, so that merchants can evade the business tax." The Song government set up "an overseas trade management agency at the estuary of Jiangwanpu to inspect the goods and levy the circulation tax." The following year, the government also "set up an overseas trade administration agency to collect taxes in Jiangwan Town, Kunshan County" (S. Xu et al. 2014: 6365).

The fourth was the trade ban and reward system. *The Compilation of Imperial Orders in the Qingli Reign* established a regulation for merchants involved in offshore trade. This regulation "prohibited travelling merchants and traders engaged in overseas commerce from travelling to the territories of Korea, Shilla, and Dengzhou and Laizhou. Merchants were required to apply in the departure prefecture and list the name and quantity of goods they would carry, preparing to sell them in the prefecture they intended to visit. They were also required to find three local residents with financial resources to guarantee that they would not carry forbidden objects or goods that could be used to make weapons, and that they would not cross the designated boundaries. After these formalities were completed, the government would issue them trade licenses. If the regulations were violated or if merchant ships traded overseas without a trade license, people were encouraged to expose and arrest them, and the ship and its cargo were to be confiscated and forfeited. The cargo should be evaluated, and half of it would be given as a reward to the whistle-blower, and the violator would be punished according to the criminal law." The prohibition consisted of three articles, namely, entrainment of prohibited goods, entry into prohibited areas, and failure to apply for trade license. Those who violated the regulations took out half of the estimated amount of the goods and rewarded the informant. *The Compilation of Imperial Orders in the Qingli Reign* and the *Compilation of Imperial Orders in the Jiayou Reign* recorded the same regulations. Apart from the prohibited goods and military supplies, there were also some others banned in the offshore trade, such as transporting spring white tea by sea and selling oxen hides, tendons, and horns by sea. Spring white tea in various regions was generally loaded on seagoing ships and transported by sea. The merchants trading banned goods, as well as shipowners and helmsmen, were sentenced to death. Sailors and coolies were exiled to remote places 1500 km away, tattooed on their faces, and put into prison in the border prefectures over one thousand kilometers away (S. Xu et al. 2014: 6681). In the second year of the Shaoxing Reign (AD 1132), "merchants in Liangzhe West Province had planned to transport tea and goods to the designated place, and the government clarified the trading place and deadline. However, the canal in Liangzhe West Province was shallow, and boats were easily stranded. The government made a special decision to allow the merchants to take the offshore route only if they obtained the official permit according to the regulations of salt trafficking." Additionally, "a note needed to be written on the back of the trade license, which clearly indicated the port of entry and exit of merchant ships. These ships could be released after the regulators' inspection and verification of the trade license." (S. Xu et al. 2014: 6711) These ships were not allowed to enter the sea without the special permit to trade via the sea route. In the fourth year of the Zhenghe Reign (AD 1114), in addition to emphasizing the prohibition of "all merchants selling by the sea route without applying for a trade license, or travelling by ship from the sea route to cross the boundary river to Dengzhou (present-day Penglai) or Laizhou," the government also stipulated that "if a ship traded in foreign countries and Hainan Province, returned from the prefecture or county in Hainan Province to the border of Mizhou (present-day Zhucheng), the merchants would also be detained for two years to serve hard labor", and the punishment for those who sold goods to the Liao Kingdom would be upgraded by two levels" (S. Xu et al. 2014: 8316). The provision to apply for a trade license and to reward the whistle-blower was emphasized in the three collections of imperial orders cited above and the quotation of the trade license of merchant Li Yun, and reiterated by the regulations made in the fourth year of the Zhenghe Reign (AD 1114). In addition, the practice of trading via private routes to avoid tax collection agencies was prohibited. During the Song Dynasty, Emperor Taizong dispatched individuals to "observe and determine the routes of seagoing ships sailing in Liangzhe provinces" due to the tendency of seagoing merchants to sell goods through private routes (S. Xu et al. 2014: 4204. In the Southern Song Dynasty, the north of Huaikou was designated as a restricted area, and the severity of rewards or punishments increased with the amount of prohibited goods found. "The coastal areas of Shandong East and West provinces, including Dengzhou, Laizhou, Yizhou, Mizhou, Weizhou, Binzhou, Cangzhou, Bazhou, and other prefectures, frequently traded copper, iron, buffalo hides, isinglass, and other goods through southeastern seagoing ships". "The contraband goods were strictly forbidden in the coastal areas of Huaizhou (present-day Huaian, Jiangshu)", and the trading of arrows, rice, and silk was also prohibited in Shandong. "Merchants from Fujian Province, Guangnan East and West provinces transported valuable commodities to Shandong East and West provinces, and officials stationed in the coastal areas of Guangnan province, Fujian Province, and Liangzhe provinces were ordered to deploy personnel to prohibit such trade by checking boats that passed by." "People without a fixed occupation in Mingzhou, Yuezhou, and Shandong were prohibited from selling grains," and the government also stipulated that "if there were merchant ships selling grains and silk from Jiangnan East Province, Jiangnan West Province, Liangzhe East Province, or Liangzhe West Province to Jingdong East Province, the officials who patrolled along the coast should intercept them. The whistle-blower would receive a reward of 3000 strings of 1000 coins, and the common people would be awarded with a minor military officer position." The government also ordered "five coastal households to form one neighborhood" and "reduced the punishment by one grade for the violator's neighbors" (S. Xu et al. 2014: 8340, 8387).

3.3.3.2 The Influence of the Requisition Policy on Seagoing Ships upon Offshore Trade

During the Southern Song Dynasty, Hangzhou was where the Emperor resided and worked. Due to its proximity to the sea, shipping between Guangnan East and West provinces, Fujian Province, and Liangzhe East and West provinces to Hangzhou was frequent, making sea defense a top priority. To achieve this, the Southern Song government developed a special system for requisitioning civilian ships for sea defense and batch shipping. Payment was made according to the status of the personnel on a ship. In the second year of the Jianyan Reign (AD 1128), ships were classified into three tiers for requisition fees: 50, 40, and 30 strings of 1000 coins, respectively. In addition, helmsmen received 10 strings, and anchor droppers received 7 strings. Furthermore, those preparing for battles were given 5 strings each. In the sixth year of Chunxi Reign (AD 1179), the government deployed more soldiers to strengthen the security of the Northwest Territories. To compensate for their services, officials distributed coupons that could be exchanged for the same number of coins: ordinary soldiers received 250 coins per day, helmsmen 150 coins per day, while head technicians, anchor droppers, and sailors each received 100 coins per day. Additionally, the government provided an average of 58.63 oz of rice per day. The requisition benefits on recruiting seamen were as follows: 15 strings for a helmsman, 10 strings for a head technician and an anchor dropper, and 5 strings for a boatman (K. Lang 1990: 7900, 7902). It was difficult to subsidize the trade profits in terms of hired payments. On the other hand, after the requisition the ships could not go overseas for trade, which directly impacted on the offshore and ocean-going trade. In Fujian Province, for example, civilian ships were requisitioned for two purposes. First, some were requisitioned for coastal defense at places such as Dinghai (Zhenhai, Zhejiang Province), Xupu (Changshu, Jiangsu Province), Huainan East and West provinces, and others. Second, others were requisitioned to transport tributes and supplies to the court. Different from the requisitioned ships' standard with a maximum beam of over 3.3 m in Mingzhou, Taizhou, and Wenzhou in Liangzhe East Province for sea defense at the beginning, ships requisitioned in Fujian Province had a maximum width of the middle beam of over 4 m in the early Southern Song Dynasty. After the twenty-ninth year of the Shaoxing Reign (AD 1159), as "there were not many ships with a maximum beam of 4 m, the requisition standard was reduced to over 3.3 m." In the thirty-first year of the Shaoxing Reign (AD 1161), it was found that "ships with a maximum beam of 3.3 m were not suitable for military operations and difficult to sail in torrential waves at wartime." Therefore, from the following year, "ships with a maximum beam of less than 3.97 m were exempt from requisition." (K. Lang 1990: 7901–02) Hence, Fujian Province requisitioned ships with a maximum beam of 3.3 m or more for only four years from the 29th to the 32nd year of the

Shaoxing Reign (AD 1159–1162). Later, only ships with a maximum beam of 4 m were requisitioned, as ships with a maximum beam of 3.3 m or below could not sail smoothly in strong winds and waves, making them suitable only for offshore trade. Ships with a maximum beam exceeding 4 m are considered medium-sized ships with a load capacity of less than 400 Liao (12,000 kg). The coastal Saury-shape Warship had a maximum beam of over 4 m and a length of 16.5 m, and could carry up to 50 people. According to the customary standards for estimating shipbuilding expenses, the construction of such a vessel could cost around 400 strings of 1000 coins (S. Xu et al. 2014: 7125). On the other hand, an eight-masted seagoing warship built in Pingjiang prefecture (present-day Suzhou, Jiangsu) with a load capacity of 400 Liao (12,000 kg) "was 26.4 m long and cost 1159 strings of 1000 coins. A four-masted Hai Hu warship, which was 15 m long, cost 329 strings of 1000 coins" (S. Xu et al. 2014: 7126). Based on the general proportions of the length and width of seagoing boats, a four-masted boat with a length of 15 m and a maximum beam of 3.67 m has the same proportion as that of the Saury-shape Warship. It can be inferred that the building materials standard of the Saury-shape Warship was less than that of the eight-masted warship with a load capacity of 400 Liao (12,000 kg), which was 26.4 m long. The load capacity of the four-masted seagoing boats built by Jiankang prefecture was 300 Liao (9000 kg) (Y. Zhou 1990: 1983). It is evident that a seagoing boat with a maximum beam of 4 m belongs to the category of medium-sized ships with a standard quantity of building materials of less than 400 Liao (12,000 kg), approximately 300 Liao (9000 kg). Prefectures and counties maintained a registration book of all the ships under their jurisdiction, attempting to curtail fraud and concealment. Shipowners were also organized into groups and were not allowed to sail on the sea without authorization (G. Liao 1990). However, requisitioning of seagoing ships for coastal defense purposes had a negative impact on the business of shipowners. They were able to engage in maritime trade for only one out of three years, disrupting their usual business activities. To alleviate the burden on shipowners, a shift system was introduced by dividing ships into three groups and assigning them to take turns serving sea defense duties. However, this arrangement also had drawbacks, as sometimes "all three groups were required to be on duty together" (S. Xu et al. 2014: 7128; B. Zhou 1990), which dampened the enthusiasm of people in building large ships. As a result, some shipowners sold their seagoing ships to officials at a low price, while others went abroad and did not return. Some extremists even broke or sank their ships in the sea, considering them a liability (S. Xu et al. 2014: 7128).

The boats requisitioned for coastal defense were primarily large and medium-sized boats engaged in ocean trade, with a maximum beam exceeding 4 m. However, this requisitioning resulted in a significant loss to maritime trade. Coastal shipowners in Fujian Province were divided into three groups, each on duty for a period of three years, with a rotation system in place. Not all the ships on duty were sent to Mingzhou (present-day Ningbo, Zhejiang) for defense, with only 90 out of 179 requisitioned ships being sent there in the twenty-ninth year of the Shaoxing Reign (AD 1159). In the first half of their turn, shipowners were prohibited from engaging in overseas trade, only being allowed to participate in local offshore trade. This meant that "shipowners rotating in coastal defense were only permitted to engage in simple nearby trade during the first half of their turn." The government "inspected the ships' size, wood materials, decoration of sails and masts, and preparations of ordnance and spars." As a result, "ships were detained and registered in the household registration system for at least half a year, hindering or even stopping the business of the shipowners" (B. Zhou 1990). The ships even had to undergo intensive training during this time. "The ship was detained for half a year before being dismissed, and the merchant must not conduct business" (X. Zhu 2010: 4474). When the shipowner was on duty, the ships that were not called to Mingzhou (Ningbo, Zhejiang) for sea defense could only trade in their own province: "The shipowners can not go out of their own province for business during the year when they are on duty for defense", "those who shall be on duty in the year, but refuse to return by going abroad, shall be punished with heavy penalties, and their ships shall be confiscated." (S. Xu et al. 2014: 7128) After the shipowners' duty was over, it took several months to prepare for overseas trade. As Liao Gang said, "as a normal practice, before going overseas for business, shipowners must calculate the goods to be transported, select sailors, repair all the appliances on the ship. In addition, shipowners "had to take advantage of the monsoon" to go overseas (G. Liao 1990). If the monsoon was not suitable for sailing upon their return, they could possibly be delayed for some time waiting for the monsoon. Therefore, the shipowners shifted once every three years, they were not allowed to engage in ocean trade for two years. However, the Song government recognized the potential damages to overseas and offshore trade due to the three-year shift rule and hoped to minimize the impact of this policy on offshore trade through flexible management methods based on the shift system design. Shipowners were allowed to trade in local markets and engage in offshore trade in their province during the first half of their duty year and the next standing-by year. Foreign trade ships were not affected by the requisition policy. They could wait for the monsoon to return, and their offshore trade was not impacted. Overall, the coastal defense requisition had a significant impact on the overseas trade of local merchants, but had a relatively minor impact on offshore trade.

In the Southern Song Dynasty, batch cargoes were mainly transported on ships in the coastal areas of Guangnan East and West provinces, Fujian Province, and Liangzhe East Province. In addition to "facilitating the transportation of copper coins and goods by land," "precious commodities such as ordnance were also transported by sea." "Annual batch cargo transportation was carried out by sea." (G. Liao 1990) The batch transportation in Quanzhou and Guangzhou was dependent on monsoons. "Ships were dispatched and loaded in April and May, and they waited for the suitable south wind to sail northbound." "Shipping goods in autumn and winter was strictly prohibited" to prevent "officials in charge of batch cargo transportation from cheating on the excuse of being blocked by the wind and anchoring the boats at the harbor." (S. Xu et al. 2014: 7004) The Southern Song Dynasty stipulated that "the deadline for shipping from Fujian Province to the capital city, Lin'an (present-day Hangzhou) was three months, and the deadline for shipping from Guangnan East and West provinces to Lin'an was six months (S. Xu et al. 2014: 4219). Batch transportation only needed to take offshore routes, and the main requisition was limited to small boats with a maximum beam of less than 4 m. Consequently, owners of boats with a maximum beam of less than 4 m were exempted from batch transportation tasks assigned by prefectures or counties (S. Xu et al. 2014: 7128). The impact of these regulations on shipowners in Fujian Province was primarily observed in offshore trade and coastal fishery. Requisitioning of batch cargo transportation continued to pose a significant burden on shipowners. "According to the general statistics of the prefectures where ships were requisitioned for batch cargoes, compensation for each ship was no less than 200 strings of 1000 coins." "Few small and medium ship owners were classified as middle class. To earn a living, many of them had to leave their families." Such shipowners were less able to bear the burden of ship requisition. Therefore, Liao Gang suggested that "the ship for batch cargo transportation be weighed in value for taxation. According to the load capacity, sixty percent of net load capacity needed to be used for official goods, and forty percent would be reserved for private goods sold by the shipowners." This would allow enlisted shipowners to make profits from batch transportation while simultaneously engaging in private trade. Compared to the regulations of batch cargo transportation in the Northern Song Dynasty which allowed two tenths of load capacity to carry private goods, the Southern Song Dynasty regulations were more favorable for traders to offset the loss of requisition. Furthermore, "the cargo transportation to the imperial court was allowed to wait for favorable monsoon winds blowing in summer, after which the requisitioned ships would set out together. Officials would notify the shipowners of the requisition one year in advance to ensure full preparation," thus preventing shipowners from being charged "waiting fees" (G. Liao 1990) due to the delayed arrival of their maritime trade ships. These measures reduced the losses of enlisted shipowners to some extent.

The number of seagoing ships in the coastal areas of Liangzhe East Province and Fujian Province was small. Large boats with a maximum beam of 3.3–4 m or above accounted for a small share. However, the total amount of seagoing ships in the coastal area was substantial. It is further explained that the requisition for sea defense had a significant impact on oceangoing trade, but a relatively minor impact on offshore trade.

3.3.4 Summary

In the Song Dynasty, offshore trade encompassed both trade between coastal areas and imports into the offshore market after customs' official procurement. As a result, the value of offshore trade exceeded that of seagoing trade. Offshore trade mainly involved the exchange of grains, imports, exports, and specialties from different regions. Coastal areas of Fujian Province, Liangzhe East Province, Jingdong provinces, and Hainan Island were the primary destinations for offshore grains, while Liangzhe West Province and Guangnan East Province were the main grain-producing areas. This established a stable market relationship that greatly supported the development of a sound economic structure in which the proportion of industry and commerce exceeded that of agriculture in Fujian Province, the coastal areas of

Liangzhe East Province, and Hainan Island. Grain trade also became the basis for the trade of local specialties in different regions, enabling the coastal areas to achieve economic complementarity and a positive economic cycle. The offshore trade of imports extended the overseas import trade and provided commodity preparation for the export trade. It can be concluded that without a stable and prosperous offshore trade, the development of overseas trade in the Song Dynasty would have lacked a foundation.

The Song government allowed merchants to engage in offshore trade and incorporated it into the customs administration system. The primary participants in offshore trade were domestic professional merchants. In addition, foreign merchants were allowed by the government to enter the domestic market after taxation and official procurement, and they also played a crucial role in offshore trade. Residents of coastal areas and ship owners engaged in offshore trade as well, and the number of ships used for this purpose greatly exceeded those used in ocean-going trade. The number of ships in coastal areas used for offshore trade and offshore fishery far exceeded the number engaged in ocean-going trade. The Southern Song government sacrificed the interests of ocean-going trade for the sake of sea defense, but tried to reduce the impact on offshore trade in sea defense and the requisition of batch cargo transportation.

The offshore trade created a distinct regional market characterized by a stable commodity composition, merchant groups, and market relations. Moreover, it played a crucial role in linking the mainland and overseas markets, thereby serving as a bridge between the two markets. Consequently, it reflected the unique livelihood of coastal residents, offering an area of exploration for researchers in the future.

3.4 Shipwrecks and Salvation in the Song Dynasty

In 1974, the discovery of Song Dynasty shipwrecks in Quanzhou Bay sparked great interest in the academic world regarding shipbuilding and trade during that era. This interest peaked with the excavation of the sunken boats "Huaguangjiao I" and "Nanhai I". However, these three shipwrecks represent only a small fraction of the total number of shipwrecks from the Song Dynasty. Due to the encouragement of overseas trade for domestic merchants and the welcoming of foreign merchants in the Song Dynasty, marine trade and voyages were more prosperous than ever, leading to frequent shipwrecks. Although historical records and archaeological excavations document these shipwrecks, previous research on Song Dynasty marine trade has focused mainly on management systems and prosperity, rather than shipwrecks and maritime aids. Although some attention has been given to the value of cultural relics and trade patterns associated with these shipwrecks, this research aims to investigate the maritime disasters and aids during that time.

3.4.1 Historical Records About Shipwrecks in the Song Dynasty

The term "shipwreck" refers to the occurrence of unpredictable risks or accidents specific to the sea, which surpass the capability of ships to endure under the prevailing conditions (Z. Liu 2007). In this context, all incidents that surpass the endurance capacity of boats and ships are considered as shipwrecks, with the exception of accidental deviations due to unfavorable wind or seasonal floods, such as the incident encountered by Jojin's boat (Jojin 2009: 9).[8]

3.4.1.1 Shipwrecks in the Song Dynasty Recorded in the Accounts of Archaeological Relics and Historical Materials

The Yanshang Temple mural painting, created during the Dading Reign (AD 1161–1189) of the Jin Kingdom, depicts a seagoing vessel encountering a marine disaster. Despite significant corrosion, the painting's characters and vessel shape remain discernible, showcasing the boat rolling in the waves, the broken mast, the drifting sail, the boatmen rushing to rescue, and the passengers' dazed and frightened expressions (J. Pan 1979). This artwork is a valuable source for understanding the Southern Song people's imagination of marine accidents, which were commonplace in the Song Dynasty. Although the mural painting contains imaginative elements, numerous excavated shipwrecks and remains of the Song Dynasty provide more authentic or even more tragic evidence of marine disasters. For example, the sunken ship excavated in Quanzhou Bay in 1974 was a merchant vessel of the Southern Song Dynasty that sank due to a shipwreck. The wreckage included 2350 kg of spice woods, such as Tanarius major, sandalwood, and eaglewood, as well as a small number of copper coins, porcelains, and pegwoods (Editorial Committee of Excavation Report of the Quanzhou Bay Song Dynasty Shipwreck Excavation 1975). This vessel was likely a merchant ship returning from the South China Sea. In 1987, "Nanhai 1" found in 1987 and excavated completely in 2007 is authenticated as a sunk merchant vessel of the Southern Song Dynasty, fully loaded with a large number of porcelains from Jingdezhen Kiln of Jiangxi Province, Longquan Kiln of Zhejiang Province, and Dehua Kiln of Fujian Province (Guangdong Institute of Cultural Relics and Archaeology 2011), particularly for export trade to countries in the South China Sea region. These two seagoing vessels on exhibition provide material evidence of shipwrecks in the Southern Song Dynasty. "Huaguangjiao 1," a seagoing vessel of the Song Dynasty, was discovered in the Xisha Sea area and is well conserved. The discovery of the "Beijiao 1" and "Beijiao 2" shipwrecks revealed relics including porcelains from

[8] On the 24th,the fifth year of the Xi'ning Reign (AD 1072), when the merchant ship hitched by Jojin was approaching the Suzhou Ocean (now the East China Sea), they should have sailed southwestward, but the unfavorable wind forced them to sail northward at night, and "the crews couldn't help sighing and stayed up all night (Jojin 2009: 9). Such things are very common in the navigation at that time.

the Song Dynasty. Cultural relics discovered during a 2009 archaeological survey in the Xisha Islands sea areas include two sites of remains from the Song Dynasty, as well as porcelains and copper coins found around Zhenghe Reefs, Taiping Island, Royal Charlotte Reef, Western or Flora Temple Reef, Daxian Jiao, and Louisa Reef in the Nansha Islands. Porcelains from the Song and Yuan dynasties were salvaged at the site of the "Shiyu 1" shipwreck, which were likely produced in kilns in Guangdong, Fujian, Longquan of Zhejiang Province and Jingdezhen of Jiangxi Province (Y. Fan 2013: 16, 20, 52, 62–66. 70, 78). Additionally, since 1989, archaeologists have conducted a series of investigations, surveys, and excavations at Dinghai Bay in Lianjiang County in Fuzhou Port, where they found many sunken ship sites and over 4000 cultural relics, including porcelains, ironware, and bronze (Center for Underwater Archaeology Studies of National Museum of China et al. 2011). While these archaeological discoveries provide evidence of shipwrecks during the Song Dynasty, many more marine disasters occurred during this period, drowned in the ocean of history.

A copy of the Yanshang Temple mural painting from Pan Jiezi's *Breathtaking Colorful Wall paintings: A Report of the Murals of the Jin Dynasty at Yanshang Temple Cultural Relics No.2*, 1979

While the focus of such archaeological excavations was not on the people involved in these shipwrecks, their accounts have been documented. The historical records, particularly those written in biographical style, and collected works, provide numerous accounts of shipwrecks involving maritime merchants from Japan and Goryeo. Wu Qian, the military commissioner of Qingyuan Prefecture (Mingzhou, present-day Ningbo, Zhejiang Province), discovered that Japanese and Goryeo's boats that were shipwrecked often drifted to China's coasts. It was recorded that Japanese boats were frequently lost and subsequently found in Qingyuan Prefecture, while Goryeo's boats typically floated to Taizhou, Wenzhou, Fujian Province, and Qingyuan Prefecture due to strong winds. During his two-year tenure, Wu Qian repeatedly saw these foreign boats (Q. Wu 2002). The occurrence of multiple shipwrecks in voyages between China and Japan was documented in historical records. The earliest record dates to the fifth year of the Xianping Reign (AD 1002), when a seagoing merchant from Jianzhou (present-day Jian'ou, Fujian Province) named Zhou Shichang drifted to Japan due to a storm. After seven years, he returned with a Japanese individual named Tengmu Ji. They were summoned by Emperor Zhenzong (Toqta 1977: 14,136). In the third year of the Chunxi Reign (AD 1176), some Japanese drifted to Mingzhou due to a storm, and in the tenth year of the Chunxi Reign (AD 1183), 73 Japanese floated to Huating County in Xiuzhou (present-day Songjiang District of Shanghai). Due to storms, similar events occurred in the first year of the Shaoxi Reign (AD 1190), the sixth year of the Qingyuan Reign (AD 1200), and the second year of the Jiatai Reign (AD 1202). The Japanese involved in these shipwrecks floated to Taizhou, Pingjiang, and Dinghai County (present-day Zhenhai, Zhejiang Province), respectively (D. Ma 2011: 8929). In addition, some people from the Song Dynasty also floated to Danzhou, which is believed to be where Japan is currently located, due to storms during their voyage (J. Luo et al. 1990: 5148). The records mentioned above provide accounts of boats which were fortunately rescued from shipwrecks when they floated to the coasts of the Song Dynasty or Japan.

Goryeo, a maritime country, had extensive political and commercial exchanges with the Song government, as evidenced by historical records of marine disasters. Envoys from both sides encountered shipwrecks during their voyages. In the first year of the Qiande Reign (AD 963), Shi Zan and his envoy delegation from Goryeo "encountered a severe storm and their boats were destroyed, resulting in the death of over seventy people. Only Shi Zan survived." (Toqta 1977: 14,036) *History of Goryeo* recorded this marine peril and pointed out that Shi Zan then served as an envoy conferred by the Emperor of the Song Dynasty to Goryeo (I. Jeong n.d.). In fact, he was likely a maritime merchant entrusted by both sides to act as an envoy. In the third year of the Tianxi Reign (AD 1019), a Goryeo official named Cui Yuanxin, serving as an ambassador to pay tributes to the emperor of the Song Dynasty, suffered a shipwreck when their boat overturned due to strong winds at the Qingwang Port. Consequently, the tributes floated away in Dengzhou. In addition, seagoing vessels were often found in Mingzhou and Dengzhou (Toqta 1977: 14,044). In the fourth year of the Xining Reign (AD 1071), Goryeo resumed paying tributes to the Song Dynasty after a forty-year hiatus, and their envoys would have landed at Siming Port. However, before their arrival, they were blown to Xingang Port of Haimen County in Tongzhou (S. Jiang 1990). In the third year of the Yuanfeng Reign (AD

1080), a boat carrying tributes from Goryeo was hit by a sudden hurricane on the sea, causing the boat to almost capsize (T. Li 2004: 7366). Liu Hong, the Minister of Revenues, and others were on board, and upon arriving in the Song Dynasty, they calculated their precious native products for paying tribute. Almost half of the lost tributes and dead people were accounted for. The lost tributes and dead people accounted for nearly one half (I. Jeong n.d.). In the third year of the Jianyan Reign (AD 1129), Goryeo's ambassadors for paying tribute were attacked by fierce winds when reaching Hongzhou (S. Xu et al. 2014: 3686), while some were forced to return to Goryeo during their voyage due to shipwrecks. In the third year of the Jingyou Reign (AD 1036), in July, Jin Chong, an envoy from Goryeo, returned home due to a broken boat when he reached Ongjin while en route to the Song Dynasty. In the third year of the Shaoxing Reign (AD 1133), Goryeo's envoys Han Weizhong and others also encountered strong winds in Hongzhou while en route to the Song Dynasty. Their boat almost capsized and the tributes were wet, forcing them to return before reaching their destination (I. Jeong n.d.). Additionally, many Goryeo folk merchants were driven to the Song Dynasty by windstorms. More details are presented below.

Envoys sent by the Song government to Goryeo also faced numerous shipwrecks. In the first year of the Duangong Reign (AD 988), Lü Duan served as an envoy to Goryeo and "encoutered treacherous waves on his return journey. The sails and mast broke, causing great fear among the boatmen." Nevertheless, Lü Duan "maintained his composure and continued reading as if he had been in his study at home." Lü Youzhi, an entourage of the diplomatic corps, survived the voyage but had to throw into the water all the outfits purchased with 500 thousand strings of 1000 coins borrowed from the national treasury (T. Li 2004: 652; Toqta 1977: 9514; Toqta 1977: 9873). During Emperor Shenzong's Reign, the Song Dynasty sent more envoys to Goryeo than in any other reign, and some of them encountered shipwrecks. For example, when An Tao led a diplomatic mission to Goryeo, they faced strong winds that caused their mast to break and the boat to nearly capsize due to the large waves. The group was in a state of panic and unsure of what to do, except for Feng Ji, who remained calm throughout the ordeal. Fortunately, the boat returned safely (Toqta 1977: 10,423).

According to the *Selected Works of Yuan Xie*, in the thirty-second year of the Shaoxing Reign (AD 1152), Li Bao, a general in charge of Liangzhe West Province, launched an attack on the navy of the Jin Kingdom anchored in Jiaoxi, with soldiers from Pingjiang. Feng Zhan, an inferior officer with 800 soldiers and 20 seagoing vessels, also joined the battle, but they both experienced shipwrecks, leading to the drowning of over half of their soldiers during a hurricane (X. Yuan 1990a, 1990b). This event is an example of an accident during offshore voyages. Such accidents were not uncommon. During Emperor Shenzong's Reign, a Zen master named Yuantong sailed to Mingzhou from Danyang County. However, when the boat turned north to Haimen, a sudden gust of wind hit the boat, driving it to the east coast of Cixi during the night. The boat was broken, and over a hundred people aboard fled, leaving only Yuantong in the water. He would not have survived if his entourage had not returned to save him (G. Qin 1990). Similar accidents occurred frequently in the southern waters. During Shao Ye's tenure as mayor of Guangzhou, he dug a moat for water transport to protect boats from hurricanes. Before that, every time overseas inbound boats pulled into the shore, they were bothered by hurricanes (Toqta 1977: 12,697). Thus, havens for boats were constructed because of frequent shipwrecks. When Hu Ze served as the fiscal commissioner of Guangnan West Province, many overseas inbound boats floated to Qiongzhou (present-day Haikou, Hainan Province) due to windstorms and could not depart due to a lack of food (Toqta 1977: 9941). Many residents on Hainan Island were domestic and foreign people who experienced shipwrecks. Merchants were prohibited from trading with Cochin through seaways in the Song Dynasty, and Cochin was excluded from the marine trade system at that time (C. Huang 2009). However, foreign merchants in Guangzhou often traded in Cochin, as seaways connect Guangzhou with Cochin and Campa. Most of these foreign merchants floated to foreign countries due to fierce winds, arriving at Cochin unintentionally (T. Li 2004: 2129), which demonstrates the frequency of shipwrecks. Therefore, it is evident that historical books written in a biographical style and collected works often record shipwrecks or emphasize the officials' response to maritime salvage. These accounts are generally objective historical facts.

3.4.1.2 Literary Accounts About Shipwrecks in the Song Dynasty

Literary sketches from the Song Dynasty contain numerous accounts of shipwrecks, with some portraying actual incidents. For instance, *Informal Essays of Pang Yuanying* documented the voyage of Qian Xie, who served as an envoy to Goryeo, and set out from Mizhou (present-day Zhucheng and Jiao County, Shangdong Province) across the ocean. Another boat of the diplomatic delegation encountered an east wind when entering the ocean and was pushed back to Dengzhou (present-day Penglai, Shangdong Province). The boat then set sail again, but by the time it arrived in Goryeo, Qian Xie was already there (Y. Pang 2013: 175). This event was an authentic marine peril. Similarly, Xu Jing recorded his real-life experience as an envoy to Goryeo during the Xuanhe reign. On their way back from Goryeo, when they passed Daeheuksando and the boundary between China and Goryeo, they lowered their sails to reduce the damage caused by the north wind. The next day at noon three auxiliary rudders of the second boat broke and the main rudder also broke during the period from 1 a.m. to 3 a.m. This put the envoys' boat and others in varying degrees of danger (J. Xu 2006: 149). In addition, *Records of the Ranger in Guihai* by Fan Chengda and *Night Talks in Lengzhai* by Shi Huihong provide realistic accounts of survivors' experiences during shipwrecks off the coast of Hainan. Many merchants fell victim to stormy waves, losing their cargo and ending up on Hainan Island. For instance, Fujian maritime merchants encountered a sea storm that washed away their goods, which mostly ended up in the area where the Li ethnic group dwelt (C. Fan 2012a, 2012b, 2012c: 175). Wan'an Military Prefecture (present-day Wanning County) on Hainan Island was home to "Taoists from Cochin, one of whom claimed to have come from Cochin and become a Taoist at the temple on the cliff due to a shipwreck." (H. Shi 1988: 63) *Notes from Mozhuang* documents the harrowing experience of scholar, Chen Sheng, an ancient Chinese scholar who took the imperial examinations at Bianliang (present-day Kaifeng, Henan Province) from

Mingzhou. Chen Sheng sought "a ride on a wealthy merchant's boat from Dinghai County (present-day Zhenhai District, Ningbo, Zhejiang Province), which was part of a fleet of ten boats. However, a sudden storm caused the boats to capsize one after another, except for Chen Sheng's boat, which managed to navigate through the wind and waves with the help of skilled sailors. The boat drifted eastward for several days, losing its way to the ferry (B. Zhang 1985: 83). Finally, during the Xuanhe Reign, Emperor Huizong ordered the transportation of a large juniper tree in the shape of a flying dragon and phoenix to the capital city, which was planted in Anguo Temple of Yanguan County. The juniper was shipped by sea but was destroyed by stormy waves, along with the boat carrying it (S. Fang 2006: 179). These incidents represent genuine shipwrecks that were recorded Song Dynasty.

In the literary sketches of the Song Dynasty, numerous stories of shipwrecks were recorded, often blending with human imagination about marine disasters and the sea. Some of these accounts were written subjectively with the aim of disseminating religion. For example, *Zhang Zhifu's Essays* describe a seagoing vessel in Guangzhou that was originally bound for Mingzhou but was blown off course and drifted to the foot of a mountain. Two people went ashore, one of whom was killed by a tall man from the island, while the other was rescued by a passing seagoing ship. *Strange Tales of the Miraculous by Yijian* also recorded several accounts of shipwrecks. *Tall Men Island* in *t*he third set (Vol. 6) of *Strange Tales of the Miraculous by Yijian* described a similar story to *Zhang Zhifu's Essays,* in which a man from Banqiao Town in Mizhou sailed to Guangzhou and, after over ten days, got stranded on Tall Men Island due to gales and dense fog. The man survived an attempted hunt, but fortunately survived. *Women on the Island* in *The First Set (Vol. 7)* of *Strange Tales of the Miraculous by Yijian* tells the story of a maritime merchant of Quanzhou who sailed to Samboja Kingdom but crashed into rocks and reefs, causing the boat to sink. The merchant, holding onto a plank of wood, floated to an island and was marooned for seven to eight years and had three children with a woman on the island before being rescued by a passing boat from Quanzhou. *Zhao Shizao* in the second set *(Vol. 4)* of *Strange Tales of the Miraculous by Yijian* recorded an account of a marine peril in which six people, including Zhao Shizao's wife, died. Only Zhao Shizao survived. *Seamless Boats* in *the second set (Vol. 8)* of *Strange Tales of the Miraculous by Yijian* describes a man from Fuzhou who suffered a shipwreck and was stranded on an island for thirteen years before sailing back with three men, one woman, and thousands of sandalwood. *Mysterious Bamboos on An Island* in the fourth set *(Vol. 3)* of *Strange Tales of the Miraculous by Yijian* recorded the story of a wealthy businessman named Zhang Yuanshi, who had engaged in marine trade for decades without any accidents. However, in the seventh year of the the Shaoxing Reign (AD 1137), he was caught in a storm and drifted to an unknown place. These literary sketches often contained fictional and bizarre elements while reflecting the realities of frequent shipwrecks to some extent. Some of these accounts were subjective and may have been based on the frequency of shipwrecks.

Seagoing voyages were often fraught with unpredictable stormy waves. Voyagers often relied on divine intervention to protect them from disasters. As a result, tales about shipwrecks, which implied retribution for sin, became a means of disseminating faith. Such stories often feature divine inspirations that warn people to avoid disasters. For example, on July 13th in the 32nd year of the Shaoxing Reign (AD 1162), "Wenzhou was struck by a gale that caused numerous residents, houses, and boats near the Songjiang River to be swept away by the water". A wealthy merchant had berthed his boat outside the Mid River Temple and was spiritually advised in a dream, "You should quickly move your belongings somewhere else. I will participate in the Buddhist ceremony at Maxing tonight. After the ceremony, I will return to guard the pagoda in the temple's backyard." The merchant followed this advice and was spared from the disaster (M. Hong 1981: 1133–34). Thus, voyagers were encouraged to worship deities with piety. The tale of the landlord Jiang in Dinghai County of Mingzhou exemplified the idea of "good begets good." Jiang's belief was that righteousness and benevolence were more important than wealth. During one of his voyages, he was blown into the water by the wind, and the boatman failed to save him. As the boat moved quickly away, the boatman noticed a person being blown towards the boat on the water by the wind. It turned out to be landlord Jiang, who was rescued. People believed that his virtuous conduct had earned him a second chance at life, illustrating the concept of "good begets good." (Z. Zhang 1990) Similarly, Lin Wengyao requested the old statue of Buddha that was to be destroyed by Nantai Temple after being replaced by a new one. He took the statue home and worshipped it there. Later, when he was sailing on the sea, his boat was destroyed, and he nearly drowned. In his distress, he cried out to the Buddha, "I once saved you. Won't you save me without any pessimism?" Miraculously, he was able to float on the surface of the water and catch hold of a plank of wood. He also retrieved a box full of valuables and was able to return home safely. Many people believed he was helped by the Buddha (M. Hong 1981: 1296–97). This tale also conveyed the idea of divine intervention and rewarding for good deeds.

Those who were protected by divinities without making offerings were believed to be susceptible to sea perils. For instance, a maritime merchant named Yang Ke, who had "engaged in marine trade for over a decade and accumulated significant wealth, frequently called upon divinities during stormy weather. He made promises to renovate Buddhist pagodas and temples and sponsor a Buddhist ceremony but failed to fulfill them." In the tenth year of the Shaoxing Reign (AD 1140), while sailing on the sea, he had a dream in which deities urged him to keep his promises. The deities conveyed that his prosperity was due to their protection, but his failure to keep his word required a form of repayment. As a result, Yang Ke's spices and jewelry worth four hundred thousand strings of coins were destroyed in a fire (M. Hong 1981: 1584–85). Those who disregarded divinities or had committed evil acts tended to get retribution in sea perils. In the tale *Zhao Shizao* mentioned above, Liu Ling and Sun Wei died while Zhao Shizao survived a perilous journey because they refused to offer sacrifices and wine to the Guangli Temple. Zhao Shizao was to do so but Liu Ling and Sun Wei considered it to be unnecessary. Namely, Liu Ling and Sun Wei opposed offering a sacrifice to Guangli without paying a visit and were punished by Guangli. Zhao Shizao survived because of his idea to pay a tribute at the beginning. However, he did not offer the sacrifice directly, so his wife and others died (M. Hong 1981: 577–78). Another tale involves a Taoist from Shandong, who, due to his love for beef, was forced to walk on ox horns and brambles, causing excruciating pain. He was criticized for his fondness for beef and repented, but was ordered to share his experience as a warning to others (M. Hong 1981: 797–98). The severity and nature of one's wrongdoing determine the magnitude and form of the disaster that they encounter.

Several stories of sea perils in *Anecdotage of the Song Dynasty* highlight the belief that sutras can placate sea monsters and prevent shipwrecks. According to the book, in the early years of the Yuanfeng Reign, An Tao, acting as an envoy to Goryeo, "prepared sutras and some scruffy and fragmentary scrolls for discarding. On the second day of his voyage, boats lost contact with each other due to appalling winds and surging waves. However, people on board An Tao's boat witnessed sea monsters climbing onto the vessel for sutras and scrolls. After giving the books to the monsters, the winds and waves calmed down, and all boats were able to pull through the turbulent area" (Y. He 2008: 193). Such tales of sea perils strengthened the belief that worshiping divinities could avert disasters, even worshiping regardless of shipwrecks. For instance, Zhu Xi observed the popularity of Buddha worship among civilians in the Zhangquan area of Zhangzhou. Similarly, shamman witches in Quanzhou enticed civilians to rebuild temples and statues, and despite encountering sea perils, some individuals donated money from afar and transported soil and stones by sea (X. Zhu 1986: 2646). Stories about shipwrecks with religious with religious undertones were prevalent not only in literary sketches but also in biographical-style historical books. For instance, *History of the Song Dynasty* documented an incident in which a voyager nearly drowned due to stormy waves. The voyager saw a monk named Zhi Yan approaching on a boat with a rope. The voyager recognized Zhi Yan, who was a boat tracker in the capital city (Toqta 1977: 13,519). This tale reflects the widespread concern for seagoing safety among people from all walks of life during a period of increased voyages.

3.4.2 Official Aid in Response to Shipwrecks

In the context of unprecedented prosperous maritime commerce in the Song Dynasty, shipwrecks were common. The dynasty's policies encouraged both domestic and foreign merchants to engage in marine trade, which was deemed important. Consequently, the emperor recognized the significance of addressing marine accidents, whether for the purpose of promoting a peaceful coexistence between the minority and the majority, propagating the image of a benevolent and wise emperor, or deriving tangible trade benefits. During this period, officials were frequently urged to or volunteered to provide maritime aid, and certain relief methods gradually became customary. Official maritime aid during the Song Dynasty included the following methods.

The first method was to offer accommodation and food to survivors. Historical records indicate that this method was first adopted in the ninth year of the Dazhongxiangfu Reign (AD 1060) when Emperor Zhenzong "instructed Mingzhou municipality to distribute grain rations, to comfort those floating from Silla, and to send them back when the winds were favorable." (T. Li 2004: 1974) This imperial decree was subsequently regarded "as a regulation, rather than a one-off aid, as it was repeatedly implemented." Zeng Gong once "consulted imperial orders issued by Emperor Renzong" and he found an order providing grain ration (G. Zeng 1990), which showed that "the imperial edict of Emperor Zhenzong had been implemented as a normal practice." Other officials also provided grain rations to those shipwrecked survivors they encountered. In the Jiayou Reign (AD 1956–1063), over thirty people coming from Goryeo were treated with wine and food by county magistrate Han Zhengyan after their boat was blown by the wind to the shore of Kunshan County and its mast broke on the sea. As the mast was originally erected on the boat fixedly, workers had to make a revolving shaft as a solution and taught them how to erect and put down the mast (C. Fan 1990: 174). In the ninth year of the Xi'ning Reign (AD 1076), Xing Zhong and others from Goryeo, after meeting strong winds and drifting to the coast of Huating County, were instructed to be accommodated and given food by the Xiuzhou government if investigations determined they were not spies (T. Li 2004: 6781). In the Yuanfeng Reign (AD 1078–1085), Cui Ju and others from who were hit by fierce winds and floated to Quanzhou, were treated with liquor and food, and given vouchers for grain ration and escorts to travel. Mingzhou also accommodated shipwreck survivors in temples, providing daily food, liquor, and meals every five days, and even giving them clothes and inviting them to join in celebrations. Emperor Shenzong also ordered that shipwreck survivors be accommodated in official residences with considerate hospitality. Zeng Gong suggested compiling these provisions into decrees to regulate the treatment of those who floated to coastal prefectures and counties from Goryeo and other countries due to unfavorable winds (G. Zeng 1990). Therefore, the aforementioned evidence indicates that grain ration, accommodation, and clothes were provided to survivors of shipwrecks.

The Southern Song government maintained a practice of providing grain rations to those who were shipwrecked, and gradually established specific criteria for such assistance. In the fourth year of the Shaoxing Reign (AD 1134), "Guang Jin and his entourage of over ten sailed from Luozhou Island in Goryeo to Quanzhou. Due to a strong wind that broke their mast, they floated to Taizhou and Chuzhou (present-day Huai'an, Jiangsu Province)." In response, the emperor ordered "the coastal military commissioner Guo Zhongxun to offer them basic necessities." (X. Li 2013: 1479) In one instance, Zhou Hui saw "a Japanese boat floated to Taizhou with a large crowd of more than twenty people. They were provided food and accommodation in Taizhou." (H. Zhou 1994: 174) In the third year of the Chunxi Reign (AD 1176), a Japanese boat was blown to Mingzhou. "Without food, hundreds of people begged all the way to Lin'an Prefecture. The emperor ordered that they be given 50 coins and 2 L of rice per capita every day." This was the first recorded standard for the provision of assistance. In the tenth year of the Chunxi Reign (AD 1183), seventy-three Japanese floated to Huating County of Xiuzhou. They were aided with money and grain from Changpingyi Barn. In the fourth year of the Shaoxing Reign (AD 1193) and the second year of the Jiading Reign (AD 1202), some Japanese who floated to Taizhou, Huating County, and Dinghai County "were also helped with grain from Changping Barn and subsequently sent back." The emperor "ordered that they be given both money and grain." (Toqta 1977: 14,137) In the Baoyou Reign (AD 1252–1258), Wu Qian observed shipwrecked Japanese in Qingyuan Prefecture who were unable to maintain daily food as their belongings had been lost and they were overcharged by brokers. As a result, they borrowed from those Japanese with cargoes to repay brokers, but they still suffered from a lack of food." Wu Qian "provided these individuals with 2 L of rice per capita every day" using grain and money from the coastal military commission. However, he noted that the commission could not sustain supplies and requested a decree from the emperor establishing a regular practice based on Ancient Customs, which provided 2 L of rice and 1500 coins in the form of 17th-generation huizi (a kind of paper currency) every day to meet the basic needs of shipwrecked Japanese until they returned to Japan. In addition, for people from Goryeo who floated to Liangzhe East Province, Liangzhe West Province, and Fujian Province, the prefectures involved sent money and grain to the coastal military commission. Ancient Customs provided 1500 coins, and the coastal military commission supplied 2 L of grain every day until they returned to Goryeo. Qingyuan Prefecture was designated as a fixed place to aid shipwrecked people from Goryeo. The coastal military commission and Ancient Customs of Qingyuan Prefecture were responsible for distributing grain and money (Q. Wu 2002). According to *Sequels to Kaiming Period Chronicles of Siming*, for shipwrecked Japanese, Wu Qian "received the official document of approval and carried out the aid method that the coastal military commission provided 2 L of grain and Ancient Customs 1500 cash every day until they returned to Japan the following year." (Y. Mei et al. 1990: 6011) In the sixth year of the Baoyou reign (AD 1258), a boat carrying six people from Goryeo floated to Qingyuan Prefecture, and "the coastal military commission provided 2 L of grain and a string of 1000 cash per capita every day. Upon their return, they were given 600 strings of 1000 coins and 12 Dan of grain (Y. Mei et al. 1990: 6012), consistent with the standard for shipwrecked Japanese.

The second method involves repatriating survivors to their homeland. Repatriation has become commonplace since Emperor Zhenzong's Reign. In the third year of the Tianxi Reign (AD 1019), "reports from Mingzhou and Dengzhou indicated frequent sightings of Goryeo's boats. Upon receiving this news, Emperor Zhenzong issued an order expressing sympathy for the shipwrecked and arranging for their repatriation with adequate food for the journey." (D. Ma 2011: 8955) This order was recorded as a regulation and subsequently became a regular institution. In the fourth year of the Tianxi Reign (AD 1020), a similar incident occurred when the islanders of Jiagu Island in Goryeo floated to the coast of Dinghai County, prompting Emperor Zhenzong to issue another order for their repatriation with sufficient food for the voyage back (T. Li 2004: 2183). Local officials were familiar with the regulation of repatriation for such cases and accordingly repatriated the shipwrecked while reporting to the emperor. This serves as evidence that the regulation of repatriation was established and implemented before AD1020.

During the Song Dynasty, the repatriation of shipwreck survivors became a final step in aiding such individuals, with the Goryeo people being the most frequently repatriated. In the ninth year of the Xining Reign (AD 1076), the Song Dynasty repatriated 20 individuals, including Xing Zhong, who had drifted to Huating County of Xiuzhou when Goryeo envoys payed tribute to the imperial court. "They returned with cotton and silk bestowed from the Song emperor." (T. Li 2004: 6781) Zeng Gong reported that Cui Ju and others floated to Quanzhou due to strong winds, and, after being sent to Mingzhou, were repatriated to Goryeo. *The History of Goryeo* also recorded the repatriation in the third year of the Yuanyou Reign (AD 1088) and the later ten repatriations of the shipwrecked Goryeo people, with later repatriations taking place in May of the third year of the Yuanyou Reign (AD 1088) (23 individuals, including Yang Fu), July of the same year (10 individuals, including Yong Ye), the fourth year of the Yuanyou Reign (AD 1081) (24 individuals, including Li Qinfu), the fifth year of the Shaosheng Reign (AD 1098) (3 individuals, including Zi Xin), the second year of the Yuanfu Reign (AD 1099) (6 individuals, including Zhao Xian), August of the 25th year of the Shaoxing Reign (AD 1155) (5 individuals, including Zhi Lixian), December of the same year (over 30 individuals), the first year of the Chunxi Reign (AD 1174) (5 individuals, including Zhang He), the 13th year of the Chunxi Reign (AD 1186) (6 individuals, including Li Han), and the second year of the Shaoding Reign (AD 1229) (28 individuals, including Liang Yongcai) (I. Jeong, n.d.). Additionally, the history of the Song Dynasty records two repatriations of Goryeo shipwreck survivors. In the fourth year of the Shaoxing Reign (AD 1134), the coastal military commissioner Guo Zhongxun assisted in repatriating Goryeo survivors, providing a boat for their return (X. Li 2013: 1479). Similarly, Zhou Hui noted that officials in Taizhou helped Japanese shipwreck survivors, sending them to Mingzhou by water and repatriating them when favorable winds arose in accordance with the imperial decree (H. Zhou 1994: 174).

Apart from the inhabitants of Goryeo, the Song Dynasty repatriated shipwrecked Japanese individuals on multiple occasions. In the 15th year of the Shaoxing Reign (AD 1145), 19 Japanese merchants selling sulphur and cloth were caught in a storm and floated to Xiankou Harbor of Pingyang County in Wenzhou. Emperor Gaozong ordered Liang Rujia to repatriate the Japanese merchants (X. Li 2013: 2918). In the third year of the Chunxi Reign (AD 1176) and the second year of the Jiatai Reign (AD 1202), two separate groups of shipwrecked Japanese who had floated to Mingzhou were repatriated to Japan by water when suitable boats and favorable winds were available (D. Ma 2011: 8929). In the Baoyou Reign (AD 1253–1258), Wu Qian repatriated both the shipwrecked Japanese and inhabitants of Goryeo in Mingzhou. The shipwrecked Japanese waited for a group of boats to take them back to Japan, while the inhabitants of Goryeo waited for merchants from Goryeo to take them back with payment of sufficient money and grain (Q. Wu 2002). These examples demonstrate that, at the very least, a stable repatriation system for shipwrecked Japanese and inhabitants of Goryeo had already been established in the Song Dynasty.

The third method was to protect property of shipwrecked shipowners and merchants. In the Song Dynasty, the earliest law regarding the protection of property of shipwrecked shipowners and merchants was issued in the second year of the

Yuanfu Reign (AD 1099). This law required officials to provide assistance to foreign boats that had drifted to China's coastal areas in a damaged state due to strong winds or had lost their shipowners. The officials required to document the cargo, permit the shipwrecked individuals' relatives to claim their property with guarantors, and formulate rules for situations where individuals made false claims (S. Xu et al. 2014: 4207). By doing so, the inheritance rights of the shipowners' relatives could be secured. In the fourth year of the Zhenghe Reign (AD 1114), "maritime merchant ships were stranded by the Qiantang River and capsized by the river tide, resulting in cargo being lost and people dying. In the chaos, residents along the river and fishermen took the opportunity to steal property. Meanwhile, helmsmen and sailors discussed ways to misappropriate the property and ignored the thievery." In response, Emperor Huizong "ordered the Hangzhou government to carry out a thorough investigation and forbade any carelessness or casualness. An official notice was also put up immediately, offering a reward of 300 strings of 1000 coins for thieves whose names were unknown, with no possibility of forgiveness. The Administration of State Affairs was ordered to prepare a decree for the emperor." As a result, a special decree was issued the following year, stating that "when shipwrecked boats are stranded in prefectures, people who steal their property during official aid shall be convicted of the same crime as that of openly robbing others' property in a fire or flood. In the event that helmsmen and sailors connive with others to steal property and ignore the thievery without prevention, except for places on the sea where salvage is out of reach, they shall be sentenced to two years in prison. If they intentionally connive with the thieves and the thieves commit a major crime, they will be convicted of the same crime as the thieves. If helmsmen and sailors excessively misappropriate property, they will additionally be convicted of openly robbing others' property." (S. Xu et al. 2014: 7123).

There were also many records about protecting the shipwrecked property in the Southern Song Dynasty. "The shipwrecked boats were often found in the coast areas of Wujiang in Liangzhe West Province. Ombudsmen were responsible for recording and estimating the value of all cargoes, which was often worth tens of thousands of strings of 1000 coins. Despite the shipowners' attempts to reclaim their property, local authorities often refused and instead sought to confiscate it. However, the shipowners did not accept this and sued the local officials." In response to these actions, the Minister of Revenues, Xu Xuan, instructed "local authorities to return the properties to their owners" (L. Wei, n.d.) and prohibited them from misappropriating any property of the shipwrecked. In Emperor Xiaozong's Reign, when Zhao Bogui acted as the mayor of Mingzhou and the coastal military commissioner, a foreign merchant died in Mingzhou, leaving behind a considerable amount of wealth. Although inferior officials requested to confiscate the wealth, Zhao Bogui disagreed and ordered the merchant's apprentices to retrieve his body and properties (Toqta 1977: 8687). In the fourth year of the Shaoxi Reign (AD 1193), an imperial decree was issued prohibiting the local authorities of Taizhou and Xiuzhou from taking any property of the shipwrecked Japanese (Toqta 1977: 14,137). This demonstrates that the Southern Song government upheld the traditional principles of protecting the property of shipwrecked merchants, which had been established during the Northern Song Dynasty.

The fourth method entails providing additional rewards, exemptions, loans, and other forms of assistance to the shipwrecked. In the Song Dynasty, offering extra rewards was mainly reserved for foreign envoys. For example, in the third year of the Tianxi Reign (AD 1019), Emperor Zhenzong not only dispatched eunuchs to express sympathy and solicitude to the envoy Cui Yuanxin who came to pay tribute from Goryeo but floated to Dengzhou due to a storm, "but also granted him clothes and colorful silk as a result of his boats capsizing and supplies running low." (Toqta 1977: 14,044) In essence, Cui Yuanxin received extra rewards. The emperor "also ordered Dengzhou authorities to transport all supplies for envoys to the capital Bianliang (present-day Kaifeng, Henan Province)." (T. Li 2004: 2167) Similarly, in the third year of the Yuanfeng Reign (AD 1088), the envoy Liu Hong from Goryeo encountered maritime peril en route to the Song Dynasty. Emperor Shenzong of Song issued an imperial decree to King Wang Hui of Goryeo, requesting forgiveness for the envoys. The decree stated that "envoys should be pardoned because the reason their boats carrying tributes failed in a storm was due to the poor performance of the boatmen (T. Li 2004: 7366–67), not the fault of the envoys." *History of Goryeo* conserves the original imperial decree, which reads "the cause of the shipwreck was the fault of the unskilled boatmen rather than the disrespect of envoys towards their mission. You should countermand the order convicting envoys and forgive them." (I. Jeong, n.d.) At the request of the Emperor of the Song Dynasty, King Wang Hui of Goryeo absolved the envoys. It was a remarkable act of benevolence in the political climate of that era for the Song emperor to intercede on behalf of an envoy.

The Ancient Customs of the Song Dynasty granted exemption from tariffs to shipwrecked ships, meaning that they were duty-free. "Ships that arrived at prefectures due to windstorms" and remained intact "were sent by local officials to nearby Ancient Customs for tariffs." (S. Xu et al. 2014: 4205) However, "tariffs were not to be imposed on boats released by Ancient Customs in Guangnan East Province, Guangnan West Province, and Liangzhe provinces that were broken and had their masts destroyed due to windstorms upon their return." (Toqta 1977: 4566) In such cases, merchants might use shipwreck as an excuse to avoid tariffs. Therefore, regulations were enacted in the Song Dynasty stating that "in the case of boats released by Ancient Customs in Guangnan East Province, Guangnan West Province, and Liangzhe provinces on their return, on which people attempted to avoid tariffs on the pretext of windstorms, broken boats, and destroyed masts and rudders, the local authorities that were not authorized to intercept them for tariffs should appoint officials to send boats back to their port of departure for tariffs." This implies that boats should be returned to their port of departure for tariffs and requisition by purchase (S. Xu et al. 2014: 4218).

Officials attempted to aid the shipwrecked with the method of lending upon consideration. In Emperor Zhenzong's Reign, Hu Ze, the fiscal commissioner of Guangnan West Province, helped foreign boats that had floated to Qiongzhou (present-day Haikou, Hainan Province) due to windstorms and a shortage of food. He ordered that they be lent 3 million strings of 1000 coins. Despite the warnings of inferior officials, who cautioned him that foreigners were cunning and that their return could not be guaranteed due to violent storms and waves at sea, Hu Ze replied that he could not refuse to help them during their time of need. "Later, the foreigners repaid the loan as scheduled." (Toqta 1977: 9941) Lending upon consideration was an individual behavior of officials that was not universally adopted or endorsed by the imperial court. Nonetheless, officials were encouraged to offer assistance to the shipwrecked in the Song Dynasty. For example, in the third year of the Yuanfeng Reign (AD 1080), boats carrying envoys from Goryeo drifted to Xiangshan County in Mingzhou. Zhang Zhongjiu, the deputy county magistrate, received them and composed poems in response to their poems, which "violated the regulation that officials were not permitted to affiliate with foreign envoys." Although Zhang Zhongjiu should have been punished, he was absolved due to his assistance to the Goryeo envoys (T. Li 2004: 7379). Furthermore, in the fourth year of the Tiansheng Reign (AD 1026), Zhang Zhongjiu accepted an invitation from Xia Song "to arrange yachts respectively in Jinshan Village, Great and Small Gu Mountains, Yanglan, Zuoli Town, Madang Mountain, and the estuary of Changlu River, and recruited sailors to save the drowned". Man-powered boats were utilized to provide assistance to passenger boats in the coastal areas of Liangzhe Province and the lower reaches of the Yangtze River (T. Li 2004: 2406).

3.4.3 Summary

The marine trade boom in the Song Dynasty ushered in an unprecedented prosperity in sea navigation. Correspondingly, shipwrecks frequently occurred. Both archaeological materials and historical records from the Song Dynasty provide evidence of numerous shipwrecks. These records are characterized by distinct features. Archaeological relics, history books in biographical style, and collected works are mostly realistic and commend officials for their good performance. Literary sketches also recount real shipwrecks, but there are more subjective writings that combine frequent shipwrecks with imaginings of the sea in literary sketches. One of the important purposes of these writings was to disseminate Buddhism and other religious beliefs, specifically the idea of karma, which resonated with people's mentality of avoiding shipwrecks through worship during the prevalent voyages of the time. Frequent shipwrecks drew the attention of officials in the Song Dynasty, leading to the implementation of measures such as accommodations and grain ration supplies, repatriations, protection of the property of shipwrecked shipowners and merchants, extra rewards for the shipwrecked, exemptions, lending upon consideration, and other aids. Among these measures, grain ration supplies, repatriations, and the protection of the property of the shipwrecked became explicit institutions of the Song Dynasty.

The assistance provided by the Song government to maritime travelers had significant implications for various aspects of their society. On the one hand, the Song government considered itself as the orthodox Huaxia nation and claimed that the majority and the minority were ruled by one emperor. The provision of maritime aid enabled the Song emperor to project a wise and benevolent political image. For example, Wu Qian and Zeng Gong contended that offering assistance to the shipwrecked was an effective means of "spreading the kindheartedness of the Song government to foreigners, thereby demonstrating its goodwill and conciliatory approach towards foreign countries." (Q. Wu 2002) Moreover, Song people believed that foreign traders who encountered sea perils far from their homeland should be assisted, as China, being a nation of etiquette, should help them if they became destitute and homeless (G. Zeng 1990). In contrast, many accounts record that overseas barbarians harmed Chinese merchants. For example, an individual from Mingzhou who drifted to Tall Men Island had a hole bored on his shoulder by the islander's fingers, and was threaded with a huge cane, narrowly escaping death by boiling. Similarly, a maritime merchant from Changguo County in Mingzhou was held captive by islanders with iron fetters and handcuffs, forced to plough fields, and subjected to further physical abuse at a wine party, where the islanders "made fun of him by burning his thighs with iron chopsticks and looking at him stamping his feet and shouting due to intolerable pain." (M. Hong 1981: 671; M. Hong 1981: 229) Such accounts not only appeared in literary sketches but also in official historical records. According to *The History of Goryeo,* "twenty islanders from T'amlado Island floated to a country where people were naked and were subsequently killed, with only three escaping to the Song Dynasty and eventually returning home." (I. Jeong n.d.) *Chunxi Period Chronicles of Fuzhou* similarly documents how Liuqiu fettered shipwrecked people from the Song Dynasty and forced them to labor in the mountains (K. Lang 1990: 7836). According to *Records of Foreign Countries*, the shipwrecked who drifted to ancient Andaman were eaten by the local populace (R. Zhao 1996: 125). These records reinforce the gracious and compassionate image of the Song Dynasty in assisting those who encountered misfortune at sea.

The provision of aid to the shipwrecked in the Song Dynasty holds significance in economics and national defense. The Song government encouraged marine trade and valued the interests of seaborne commerce. Emperor Shenzong noted that marine trade was the most profitable sector in the southeastern regions, while Emperor Gaozong acknowledged the substantial contribution of marine trade to national development, with potential tax revenues in the millions if managed effectively (Toqta 1977: 4560). Maritime aid was instrumental in encouraging marine trade, as exemplified by the case mentioned above of Hu Ze, who lent money to a foreign merchant who promptly repaid the loan. Moreover, as Wu Qian noted, maritime aid played a crucial role in bolstering the Song Dynasty's relations with foreign countries and enhancing national defense. In other words, the provision of aid to shipwrecked foreigners had a close connection with seaway defense (Q. Wu 2002). Wu Qian also proposed the exemption of Japan and Jin from tariffs and requisition by purchase, which was approved based on the rationale that Japan's proximity to Goryeo made it susceptible to the nomadic minority (Mongolia), and that had Japan been enticed by the nomadic minority, "the border of the Song Dynasty would have faced immeasurable security concerns. Such exemptions were seen as acts of kindness that fostered positive relationships between China and foreign countries, thus earning the recognition of foreigners in the Song Dynasty" (Y. Mei et al. 1990: 6011).

3.5 Ocean Knowledge and Imagery in the Song Dynasty

In the Song Dynasty, the state adopted preferential policies to incentivize open maritime trade, leading to unprecedented growth in maritime trade and marine activities. At the same time, the Song people's knowledge of the ocean increased significantly, and their understanding of the sea continued to evolve. Therefore, the Song Dynasty marked a new chapter in the history of ocean exploration in ancient China. However, previous studies have given little consideration to the means by which the Song people acquired their knowledge of the ocean and how they disseminated it. Furthermore, little attention has been paid to the Song people's perceptions of the oceanic world and the imagery they constructed around it. This section will address these neglected questions.

3.5.1 Sources and Dissemination of Ocean Sciences in the Song Dynasty

3.5.1.1 Sources of Ocean Knowledge in the Song Dynasty

This section encompasses ocean knowledge, which comprises understanding of natural phenomena such as tides, wind signals, ocean currents, and geography, as well as knowledge of techniques including sailing and navigation techniques, sea routes, and so forth. Additionally, it includes knowledge of humanity such as customs, beliefs, political and commercial conditions, and other sociocultural factors. The term "ocean world" refers to the realm of water as a geological space, as well as the human inhabitants and their residence within it. For the Song people, ocean knowledge was primarily acquired through three sources: the merchant group, seafaring envoys and monks, and traditional ocean knowledge recorded in historical documents.

The main source of firsthand ocean knowledge was the merchant group, including helmsmen and sailors, who engaged in regular and direct maritime activities. Technical knowledge required long-term practice to acquire. In the early years of the Southern Song Dynasty, Emperor Gaozong sought information on the conditions of the Jin people through Goryeo, and summoned two prominent merchants, Liu Yue and Huang Shishun, who frequently conducted business in Goryeo and even "visited twice a year." Both possessed extensive knowledge regarding the geological features, mountain ranges, and rivers of Goryeo, as well as the distance from China. They could also develop seagoing routes, and produce a comprehensive account of overseas conditions, including maps depicting seagoing routes and situations in Goryeo and the Jin Kingdom (S. Yang et al. 1990). Their extensive ocean knowledge was accumulated through repeated practice, and as such, they were consulted by the government as a reliable source of information.

Helmsmen must possess a wide range of knowledge and skills. Methods helmsmen used to determine geographical location included star-gazing at night, sun-gazing during the day, and watching the compass on cloudy days. Helmsmen would also sometimes use a 33-m rope to collect mud from the bottom of the sea and determine the boat's location based on its smell. Rain is uncommon on the sea, and if it does occur, it likely indicates proximity to a mountain (Y. Zhu 2006: 149). Helmsmen are could also predict weather conditions, such as whether the next day will be sunny or overcast by observing sunrise and sunset. They could also anticipate whether winds will be tailwind or headwind by observing the clouds. Additionally, they knew where the sea breeze came from based on the sight of waves from afar. They knew that waves crashing on the shore indicate that the south wind will blow the next day, and lightning indicates that the wind will blow in summer. Helmsmen were skilled in the judgment of similar conditions. They could also determine the distance from the mountain by observing the clarity of the water. Deep water in the sea is as dark as it is precipitated, and the water around mountains under the sea is turquoise, while the seawater near the reef is turbid and white. Fish are more likely to gather near reefs, where algae is plentiful. The 14th and 28th day of each lunar month are called the great equinox, and if it is rainy and windy on those days, there will be more storms in the following 10 days. Helmsmen also observed the mud and sand on the sea floor to figure out whether there was a port nearby (Z. Wu 1980: 111–12). These techniques were widely applied in the Song Dynasty and included compass navigation, star navigation, surface targeting, and water positioning. These methods were utilized by navigators such as Jojin and Xu Jing. The Song boat that transported the Japanese monk Jojin relied on various navigation techniques to traverse the seas. The crew observed the stars to "determine the azimuth and angle," and "sailors climbed up the mast to scan for nearby mountains and islands." Orientation by these landforms on the route and measuring water depth with a lead rope, according to submarine materials, were other important techniques for boat positioning. For instance, while the "Sea of Japan was 50 Xuns deep (133.5 m) with stones and sand at the bottom, the China Sea was 30 Xuns (80.1 m) deep with mud at the bottom." (Jojin 2009: 6, 9) When serving as an envoy to Goryeo, Xu Jing used a compass to determine directions on overcast nights. He also used the three above-mentioned navigation methods: star navigation, surface targeting (recording the main islands along the marked route), and measurement by a lead hammer to determine the depth of seawater. Additionally, Xu Jing positioned the boat according to the the seawater color, such as white, yellow, or black (J. Xu 2006: 134–35). This knowledge was acquired through oral transmission by the merchant group over generations and verified through rich seafaring practices. Maritime merchant groups were the main providers of first-hand ocean knowledge, including sailing techniques, knowledge of nature, and knowledge of humanities.

To some extent, maritime envoys and monks played a role in conveying first-hand information about the oceans, although most of this knowledge comes from the merchant group on the same boat. One of the duties of protocol officers was to gather information about the envoys' country upon their arrival. This involved creating depictions of their clothing, customs, and geography (Toqta 1977: 3854). The Courts of State Ceremonial undertook the same duty and were tasked with inquiring about foreign countries' capital, customs, and distance from China, and to draw two picture books of their appearance and attire to be sent to the palace and the national archives, respectively (S. Xu et al. 2014: 9951). When the emperor received the envoys, he would also request information about their country. For example, Emperor Taizong of Song inquired about the Arab Empire's location and the products found in its mountains (Toqta 1977: 14,120). Ancient Customs, as well as military and political institutions in related provinces, such as the "Provincial Military Commission, Provincial Military Agency, and Transfer Agency of Taxation, also had the duty of collecting information from foreign envoys. These institutions would inquire about the area of the tributary country, and which countries were similar to its now tributaries." (S. Xu et al. 2014: 9962) when receiving foreign envoys. For example, when Java sent envoys to the Song Dynasty in the third year of the Chunhua Reign (AD 992), Zhang Suxian, the Administrator of Ancient Customs in Mingzhou, conveyed information about the envoys' clothing to the imperial court via courier horses." (Toqta 1977: 14,092) Additionally, in the fifth year of the Zhenghe Reign (AD 1115), it was recorded that the "Lopburi Kingdom had never paid tribute to the Song Dynasty. According to *the Decree of the Zhenghe Reign*, this prompted Ancient Customs to request information about its proximity, area, power, and which country it would pay tribute to." (S. Xu et al. 2014: 9814) The main information provided by foreign envoys to the Song Dynasty included the location of their country, its distance from the Song Dynasty, political systems, customs, clothes, climate, products, and observations made along the way (C. Huang 2011). Consequently, knowledge about the people of maritime countries was recorded and disseminated.

The envoys of the Song Dynasty and inbound monks were also sources of knowledge about the ocean. Although the Song Dynasty sent few envoys to foreign countries, they did send "eight eunuchs with imperial edicts, money, and goods on four groups of batch transportation vessels in the fourth year of the Yongxi Reign (AD 987) to several vassal states in southern coastal regions to invite them to pay tribute to the Song government, bringing along spices, medicines, rhino teeth, pearls, and borneol. Each group also brought three nominal import licenses, encouraging trade with these countries." (S. Xu et al. 2014: 4204) However, there is no evidence to suggest that the Song Dynasty had sent envoys to other countries in the South China Sea, except Cochin and Campa, and quite a few times to Goryeo. Upon their return, these envoys were required to report to the imperial court about what they had seen and heard during their voyages, documenting their experiences in the form of voyage logs (C. Huang 2011). Some pages of *Chronicles of Jilin*, written by Wang Yun, who accompanied the mission to Goryeo in the Chongning Reign, and the *Xuanhe Period Maps and Records About Goryeo*, written by Xu Jing, who accompanied the mission to Goryeo in the Xuanhe Reign, still exist. *Chronicles of Jilin* recorded the fact that the Song Dynasty had sent envoys to Goryeo after the Yuanfeng Reign, as well as the rituals of meeting and words of visiting (D. Ma 2011: 5743). Xu Jing's *Xuanhe Period Maps and Records About Goryeo* were accounts of Goryeo "that were seen and heard by him from multiple sources, leaving out details familiar to the Chinese people. Unfamiliar details were left in the accounts." The book recorded the political situations, customs, and cities of Goryeo, as well as the knowledge of the sea route between Mingzhou to Goryeo and related sailing and navigation techniques. However, what they saw and experienced was quite limited. Xu Jing, who sailed for the first time, was unlikely to have much knowledge about the sea route, sailing, and navigation techniques. The mission from the Song Dynasty to Goryeo primarily relied on the lease of merchant boats. "According to previous regulations, when the imperial court sent envoys to Goryeo, it would first appoint county procurators in Fujian Province and Liangzhe West and East provinces to hire passenger boats and order Mingzhou Prefecture to decorate the boats." (J. Xu 2006: 8, 129) What Xu Jing recorded was mostly from merchants and helmsmen on the boats. It was up to the helmsmen whether Xu Jing's fleet could set sail by judging wind signals. For example, the names of islands like Wuyu Island, Paidao Island, Key Binglang, and others were given by punters and boatmen (J. Xu 2006: 133, 136–37, 139). Monks also took merchant boats to China during the Song Dynasty. For example, a Japanese monk named Jojin took a merchant boat to China. In the *Travelogues of Jojin,* he recorded ocean knowledge, including the route, sea conditions, monsoon, and navigation methods from Japan to Mingzhou, which he likely learned from the merchants and helmsmen on the same boat.

Ocean knowledge was accumulated and passed down for generations through historical records. The traditional knowledge of the ocean was documented in historical records ranging from ancient books and records from the Pre-Qin Dynasty to those of the Han and Tang Dynasties. This method of documenting ocean knowledge was evident in the *Taiping Imperial Encyclopaedia,* where the "Sea" entry of *25 Historical Records in the Category of Di* (Vol. 60) collected accounts about the sea in *Interpretation of Names, Analytical Dictionary of Chinese Characters, Book of History, Book of Rites, Analects of Confucius, Annotation of Chunqiu written by Gongyang, God-Sensing Symbols in the Spring and Autumn Annals, A Study of Different Mail in the Spring and Autumn Annals, Record of the Grand Historian, Book of Han, Book of Later Han, Book of Jin, Anecdotes on the Book of Songs, Lao Tse's Tao Te Ching, Liezi, Chuang Tzu, Tongxuan True Sultra, Mencius, Accounts of Saints, Garden of Anecdote, Model Sayings, Book of Mountains and Seas,* Accounts of Filial Piety, *Accounts of Immortals, Accounts of Gaoshi, Record of the Nether World,* Accounts *of Ten continents, Heart of Mysteries, Records of Strange Things,* and *The Spring and Autumn Annals of the Sixteen Kingdoms,* and other historical records. The "Sea" entry of *Historical Records of Numerous Categories* (Vol. 7) written by Pan Zimu, and the "Sea" entry of *Category of Geography* (Vol. 15) in the prequel of *Collection of Historical Records* written by Zhu Mu, also collected descriptions of the sea in *Category Records, Book of Songs, Guan Zi, Xun Zi, Yang Zi, Tribute of Yu, Records of Foreign Goods in Lingnan Region, Records of Sea,* and *Zuo Zhuan,* among others. Some of these historical records were not included in the *Taiping Imperial Encyclopaedia.* The Song people also acquired ocean knowledge from books such as *Fa Xian's Travels,* which recorded his voyage from India to his homeland, and *Record of Overseas Envoy Cheng Guang* written by Zhang Liao in the Southern Tang Dynasty. The latter provided "detailed information about sea routes in Goryeo, including its mountains, rivers, goods, and products." (Toqta 1977: 5188; Z. Chen 1937: 259) Traditional ocean knowledge documented in historical records was not limited to personal observations, but also included subjective descriptions and imaginings of the sea by ancient people. In summary, both subjective imaginings and firsthand experiences were important components of accumulating ocean knowledge by the Song people.

3.5.1.2 Ways of Disseminating Ocean Knowledge in the Song Dynasty

Knowledge about the ocean was disseminated in the following ways in the Song Dynasty. One method was oral transmission by merchants, who mainly shared their knowledge by word of mouth within their group. Although these merchants were not well-educated, they possessed invaluable expertise in sea routes and navigation techniques. It is unclear whether nautical charts or other texts about ocean knowledge were passed down among this group during the Song Dynasty, but it is known that the knowledge was transmitted orally from generation to generation. This mode of knowledge transmission was not unique to the Song Dynasty. In the Western Han Dynasty, for example, merchants relied on sea routes and navigation techniques to sail from Xuwen County and Hepu County, following the coastline of Indochinese Peninsula, and turning south and west, ultimately reaching the southern part of India (Kancipura) (G. Ban et al.1962: 1671).This navigation knowledge was exclusive to the merchant group and passed down for generations in the group. Zhou Qufei and Zhao Rushi collected extensive nautical knowledge, including information on sea routes, commercial conditions, customs, and political situations of maritime countries. This was acquired through the continuous accumulation of knowledge by oral transmission among the merchant group. Not only did Chinese officials need to collect knowledge from merchants orally, but the maritime countries also required information from merchants. For example, Chanthaburi sought interaction with the Song Dynasty and ways to reach it, writing "we pay attention on the Song's information with respect in our hearts. Since we knew the Song Dynasty is an orthodox imperial court, we have been looking forward to it every day. Xinzhou in Champa is close to the Song Dynasty, and we want to send a bugler near Anian Regnum to ask for information from the ship master of Song. The official reply has been sent to Xinzhou, and we have already known the decree of the Song Dynasty." (S. Xu et al. 2014: 9832) Merchants shuttling between maritime countries established an information network, and exchanged various details related to the sea and maritime markets, such as sea routes, sea conditions, wind signals, navigation methods, and business conditions. While some of this knowledge was lost over time, envoys, officials, monks, and scholars collected and recorded some of it, preserving it for future generations.

The second method was dissemination of writings of ocean experience written by seafaring envoys. These writings included their own personal experiences, as well as the experiences of fellow merchants and helmsmen. The ocean knowledge recorded in these writings was disseminated upon their publication. One of the most typical examples of these writings is the *Xuanhe Period Maps and Records About Goryeo*, written by Xu Jing. This book was disseminated in the last year of the Xuanhe Reign and published in the Southern Song Dynasty. Although the drawings in the book were lost, the written descriptions were preserved. Volume 7 of *Collected Works from Qingbo* written by Zhou Hui recorded that, "in the last years of the Xuanhe Reign, although my father had a chance to see *Xuanhe Period Maps and Records About Goryeo,* he could only copy the text of the book, and omit its paintings. The version published in the study of Jiangyin Prefecture in the Qiandao Reign was the one passed down in my family (namely the one copied by my father), with only the texts but no paintings left. It was likely that Xu Chan had also lost the original handwritten one after the war." This book was widely circulated in the Song Dynasty and was used as a reference for various historical texts, including the revision of *History of Song* in the Yuan Dynasty, *Collection of Historical Records* written by Zhu Mu, *Records of Sea Abyss* written by Pan Zimu, and *Notes on the Combination of Ancient and Modern Matters* written by Xie Weixin (J. Yuan 1990). It was recorded in the *Booklist of Suichu Hall* written by You Mao, *Zhizhai Content Explanation* written by Chen Zhensun, *A Full-Scale Textual Criticism on Ancient Systems and Regulations* written by Ma Duanlin, and *History of Song* written by Toqta. Additionally, it was quoted in the part of sea tides in *Collection of Historical Records* written by Zhu Mu, *Records of Sea Abyss* written by Pan Zimu, and *Notes on the Combination of Ancient and Modern Matters* written by Xie Weixin (M. Zhu 1990; Z. Pan 1990; W. Xie 1990). By reading the book, the Song people were able to learn about ocean knowledge such as sea routes, sea conditions, wind signals, and sailing methods from the Song to Goryeo.

The third method involved disseminating writings of ocean knowledge by government officials. Officials in Ancient Customs, the Provincial Military Commission, and the Transfer Agency of Taxation in related provinces were responsible for gathering information from incoming envoys. Some officials also took the initiative to collect overseas knowledge from merchant groups, documenting their findings in books. Volume 5 of *Zhao Yanwei's Notes on Historical Records,* written by Zhao Yanwei, records that "Ancient Customs of Fujian Province often berthed their boats in various countries," including over 30 countries such as the Arab Empire and Samboja Kingdom. It was also said that "the above countries were mostly not mentioned in history, only Ancient Customs had related recordation," indicating that Ancient Customs was the official institution with the most comprehensive overseas knowledge at that time. Zhao Yanwei likely obtained this information from Ancient Customs in Fujian Province. *Records of Foreign Countries*, written by Zhao Rushi of the Southern Song Dynasty during his tenure as supervisor of Ancient Customs in Fujian Province, is the only extant work written by Song's officials of Ancient Customs to collect overseas knowledge. The book contained information on the distance, locations, natural conditions and social customs, products, and trade with over 70 overseas countries, mainly coming from the collection of merchants. Foreign merchants listed their countries' names, natural conditions and social customs, the routes to, and products of their countries, which were translated into Chinese (R. Zhao 1996: 1). In addition, this book also quoted ancient books and historical records, including the record of Samboja Kingdom and other countries paying tribute to the imperial court (R. Zhao 1996: 34), which could not be provided by merchants. Additionally, the book recorded information about the Chola Dynasty, which "had no trade relations with other countries since ancient times." (R. Zhao 1996: 74) The record dated back to the eighth year of the Dazhongxiangfu Reign (AD 1015), when the Chola Dynasty sent envoys to pay tribute to the Song Dynasty. The interpreter said that the country "had no access to China in the past. And its envoys traveled by water for 1150 days to reach Guangzhou, and the estimated distance was about 205,700 km." (T. Li 2004: 1948) This record was later accepted as an entry in *Tales of Chola Dynasty in History of the Song Dynasty Dynasty* and also as an entry about Chola Dynasty in Vol. 332 of *A Full-Scale Textual Criticism on Ancient Systems and Regulations. Records of Foreign Countries,* written by Zhao Rushi, copied the related record in national history, only changing Guangzhou to Quanzhou. This book was also recorded in *Zhizhai Content Explanation* written by Chen Zhensun and *Studies of Historical Records* in *A Full-Scale Textual Criticism on Ancient Systems and Regulations* written by Ma Duanlin. The 4th Volume of *Notes in the Study of Mizhai* written by Xie Caibo quoted the record of Mirhat and Murabit contained in *Records of Foreign Countries.* This suggests its wide circulation in the Song Dynasty.

Protocol officials and officials of the coastal areas collected overseas information from merchants and envoys and kept a large number of texts and illustrations, resulting in a vast collection of historical records. *History of the Song Dynasty* notes several books that cover such overseas information, including the *Records of Ancient Customs in Guangnan West and East Provinces* by Zhao Xie, *Records of Sea Routes* by Feng Zhongjia, and *Rules on Foreign Countries Paying Tribute,* which included various maritime countries such as Java, the Champa Kingdom, al-Sultān, the Arab Empire, Sohar, the Chola Dynasty, the Samboja Kingdom, and Tambralinga (Toqta 1977: 5107, 5123, 5136–37). The existing writings about the officials who recorded this overseas information include the *Informal Essays of Pang Yuanying* and *Reflections about Pingzhou,* both written in the Northern Song Dynasty, and *The Land Beyond the Passes* written in the Southern Song Dynasty. *Informal Essays of Pang Yuanying* recorded what its author, Pang Yuanying, "had seen and heard" when he served as the chief of protocol in the Yuanfeng Reign, covering the locations of countries in the South China Sea (Y. Pang 2013: 115–16). It was published in Jiankang Prefecture in the Qiandao Reign, which was also recorded in Volume 33 of *Jingding Period Chronicles of Jiankang* written by Zhou Yinghe. In *Reflections about Pingzhou,* the author Zhu Yu recorded what his father Zhu Fu had seen and heard while serving as a local official of Guangzhou, including information on Ancient Customs, residence for foreign merchants, sea merchants, and overseas countries. Both books were widely distributed in the Song Dynasty and were recorded in *Booklist of Suichu Hall* written by You Mao, *Zhizhai Content Explanation* written by Chen Zhensun, and *A Full-Scale Textual Criticism on Ancient Systems and Regulations* written by Ma Duanlin. Li Tao once quoted *Reflections about Pingzhou* in his *Continuation to The Comprehensive Mirror for Aid in Government* (T. Li 2004: 11,637), and Zhu Xi once quoted *Informal Essays of Pang Yuanying* when discussing with his disciples (X. Zhu 2002: 2921, 4155). *The Land Beyond the Passes* recorded information on the locations, natural conditions, and social customs of maritime countries, as well as sea routes, which may have been obtained from merchants' accounts recorded by others or from historical records. Its preface was "what the author had heard and seen and what he had got from the discussion with literati" while serving as an official in Jingjiang Prefecture (present-day Guilin) of Guangnan West Province and at Qinzhou, although it may have also been directly obtained from seagoing merchants (Q. Zhou 1999: 1, 37). Seagoing merchants did business in Qinzhou of Guangnan West Province and four prefectures of Hainan Province during this time, so it is possible that the information in the book about countries other than Cochin came partly from this. The information about the tribute paid by various countries since the Jianlong Reign was obviously from the records of official institutions like Ancient Customs, rather than obtained through visiting private merchants a century later. This book was widespread in the Southern Song Dynasty. *Records of Foreign Countries* quoted a large number of texts in *The Land Beyond the Passes*, which were also mentioned in Feng Chengjun, Rou Keyi, and Han Zhenhua's commentaries on *Records of Foreign Countries* and Yang Wuquan's commentary on *The Land Beyond the Passes* (Q. Zhou 1999: 10; R. Zhao 1996: 7). *The Land Beyond the Passes* was recorded in the *Booklist of Suichu Hall* written by You Mao, *Compendium of Historical Records (the Second Edition)* written by Zhao Xibian, *Zhizhai Content Explanation* written by Chen Zhensun, *A Full-Scale Textual Criticism on Ancient Systems and Regulations* written by Ma Duanlin, and *History of Song* written by Toqta. *A Chronicles of Lin'an*, written by Zhu Mu, quotes this book many times, with its item on "Tide" quoting the difference among tides in Jiangnan East and West provinces, Liangzhe East and West provinces, Qinzhou, Lianzhou, and Qiongzhou (M. Zhu 2003: 770).

The Protocol Department and officials in coastal areas produced pictures of overseas countries that served as a valuable source of ocean knowledge for the Song people. These pictures recorded important facts, including *Maps of Overseas Countries* presented by Li Fu, mayor of Guangzhou, in the third year of the Taipingxingguo Reign (AD 978); *Maps of Overseas Minority Groups* drawn by a merchant from the South China Sea in the fifth year of the Chunhua Reign (994 AD); *Atlas of Overseas Countries* presented by Ling Ce, mayor of Guangzhou, in the sixth year of the Xianping Reign (AD 1003); and "the map from Champa Kingdom to Cochin drawn by" Luo Changhao in the first year of the Yuanfeng Reign (AD 1078). Additionally, the "paintings in the secret study" included images of countries paying tribute to the imperial court, such as the Champa Kingdom, Samboja Kingdom, Lopburi Kingdom, Cochin, Kampoja, and various other foreign countries (Y. Wang 2003: 303, 2817, 2829, 2835). In the ninth year of the Dazhongxiangfu Reign (AD 1016), the Champa Kingdom and other countries paid tribute to the Song Dynasty. The Protocol Department "drew pictures depicting sea routes, customs, people, and clothing, for astronomy and calendar purposes." Emperor Zhenzong ordered the Ritual Academy to retouch *Painting on Four Foreign Countries to Report on Their Work* (Z. Lü 1990), while Zhao Rushi, in the preface of *Records of Foreign Countries*, mentioned that he had read *Maps of Foreign Countries* in his spare time. These paintings all had the information about overseas countries in various aspects. The *Map of the Han and Other Ethnic Groups* drawn in the Song Dynasty contained information about overseas countries. In the second part of Volume 24 of *The Full Text of Song Dynasty History*, it was recorded that during Emperor Xiaozong's Reign, there was a large screen with gold lacquer behind the throne in the Hall of Xuande, "with *Map of the Han and Other Ethnic Groups* as the background screen." Volume 24 of Li Gang's *Staying at Leizhou of Liangxi Collection* expressed "looking at Leizhou on *Map of the Han and Other Ethnic Groups*," and the Forest of Stone Steles Museum had a collection of a stone inscription of *Map of the Han and Other Ethnic Groups*. Finally, the *General Map of Ancient and Modern Chinese and Other Barbarian Regions*, drawn in the Southern Song Dynasty, best reflects the description of sea and maritime countries in *Map of the Han and Other Ethnic Groups* (A. Shui 2013: 473–74).

The fourth method of dissemination was through documentary records and literary works. Officials from Ancient Customs, the Protocol Department, and other relevant officials along the coast collected ocean knowledge mainly from envoys and merchants. In addition, some literati wrote about ocean knowledge based on their indirect hearing or reading, and even created fictional stories about the sea. The Song Dynasty encyclopedias not only collected historical documents but also contemporary ones. *The Collection of Historical Records* and *Records of Sea Abyss* specifically focused on the entries of "sea" and "tide" by quoting ancient records and classics. These encyclopedias were widely read by test-taking candidates. For example, the "synopsis" in *Complete Works of Chinese Classics* and *Yu Hai* said that "this book is designed for the application of Lexicon Exam at Imperial Examination," providing evidence for its widespread use. Local chronicles from coastal areas, such as *Chronicles of Lin'an in Chunyou Reign* and *Chronicles of Lin'an in Xianchun Reign*, also had detailed records of tides and tidal patterns at estuaries (E. Shi 1990: 3315–18; S. Qian 1990: 3642–45). *Baoqing Period Chronicles of Siming* recorded the trade of overseas countries in Mingzhou and tidal patterns of open seas near Mingzhou (J. Luo et al. 1990: 5033, 5054–59). Literary sketches mostly included accounts heard by the author, but some were fictional. Yue Ke's *History of Ting* documented the life of merchants from the South China Sea (K. Yue 1981: 125–27), whereas fictional stories like *Sea Ship Hair, Sea Gods to Raise the Sun, Sea Wells, Sea Maggots, Huoshan Mountain Theophany,* and others in the sequel volume of *Miscellaneous Records in the year of Kuixin* were all about ocean stories, except for *Sea Maggots*, which presented a documentary story (M. Hong 1981: 54, 59, 86, 249, 251–52, 415–16). These fictional ocean stories served as entertainment and conveyed beliefs of dangerous oceans, reverence for the ocean, and punitive justice, but were not a record of real ocean knowledge.

3.5.2 Construction of Oceanic Imagery in the Song Dynasty

Considering the extensive ocean knowledge disseminated through various channels during the Song Dynasty, what type of oceanic imagery was present in the subjective world of the Song people? Specifically, how did their existing ocean knowledge shape their conception of the oceanic world?

3.5.2.1 The Ocean as a Dynamic World Composed of Injected Rivers, Currents, Tides and Monsoons

In the pre-Qin period, the world was imagined as "China," also known as the Divine Land. It consisted of nine prefectures surrounded by inland lakes, with nine other Divine Land-like places outside of it, surrounded by the vast ocean, referred to as "the edge of heaven and earth." This collectively constituted the concept of the "world." (Q. Sima 1959: 2344) As people acquired more knowledge about the outside world, they relinquished the hypothesis of nine prefectures surrounded by inland lakes. Zhang Hua of the Western Jin Dynasty wrote in his *Records of Natural Science,* that "the surroundings of heaven and earth are all linked to seas, so landmass accounts for a small share in the world. Outside the residence where the neighboring ethnic groups live in are nothing but oceans. The East China Sea was generally called the Bohai Sea, also called the deep blue sea. The South China Sea was also called the Zhanghai Sea, the West China Sea was also called Qinghai Sea, and the North China Sea was also named as inland lakes." The Song people adopted this understanding (M. Zhu 1990), and as "no ancient records of the West or North China Seas were available," (M. Zhu 1990) the Song people primarily discussed the East and South China Seas.

In "Autumn Floods" of *Chuang-tzu*, it was said that the sea had a hundred rivers to receive and lower reaches of rivers to drain its seawater, thus making it "the greatest water area in the world." Despite millions of rivers flowing into it, and the continuous drainage of seawater, the sea never overflows nor turns dry. Guo Xiang of the Jin Dynasty explained that the "lower reaches of a river" was where seawater exits the river (X. Guo 1990). While the concept of lower reaches of a river existed since the pre-Qin period, the Song people had a clearer understanding of their locations. For example, *Strange Tales of the Miraculous by Yijian* mentioned that the east of Ninghai County in Taizhou had one of the lower reaches of the river where "the water rushes into a whirlpool and has several lower places which people refer to as drainage from the lower reaches of the sea." (M. Hong 1981: 318–19) *Jiading Period Chronicles of Chicheng* and *A Chronicles of Lin'an* by Zhu Mu referenced *Strange Tales of the Miraculous by Yijian*, indicating that the east of Ninghai County had lower reaches of a river "where the East China Sea drained its water." (Q. Chen 1990: 7472) Others were in the East Pacific Ocean east of Beibu Bay and east of Java, "where seawater drains into the ground and does not return to the human world." (Q. Zhou 1999: 36, 74) Additionally, Gui Xu (meaning "huge abyss"), as recorded in *Liezi*, was a huge pit located to the east of the Bohai Sea, where water flows from the eight directions of the earth, the fields of the nine prefectures, and even the Milky Way, without any increase or decrease in water levels (M. Zhu 1990). This was also what Zhuangzi called the seawater gathering place. These descriptions, together with Japan's concept of the east of the earth being closest to the sun (J. Luo et al. 1990: 5057) and the west of Murabit being where the sun goes down (Q. Zhou 1999: 75), contribute to the Song people's understanding of the sea.

The Song people's perception of drainage from the lower reaches of a river as an extension of the sea was based on limited traditional knowledge and navigation practices, and was ultimately inaccurate. However, their knowledge of ocean currents, tides, and monsoons was grounded in objective observations. For instance, during his voyage to Goryeo, Xu Jing used the color of water currents to determine his location and categorized oceans into white-water, yellow-water, and black-water oceans. The Song people also had some knowledge of the ocean currents in other sea areas. For instance, sailing eastward from Fuzhou would lead to the Ryukyu Kingdom, where "the water flows eastward and returns," (K. Lang 1990: 7836) a phenomenon that merchant boats avoided. Beibu Bay, southwest of Hainan Island, was a place where ocean currents diverged, known as "Three Convergence," with currents flowing in three directions. "One flowed southward to foreign sea areas, another northward to the sea areas of Guangnan East Province, Fujian Province, Jiangnan East and West provinces, and Liangzhe East and West provinces, while the third flowed eastward to the East Pacific Ocean. Merchant boats could take advantage of these currents once they understood their laws. However, boats from southern maritime countries had to be cautious when crossing the area where the currents converged. They had to wait for a slight breeze before sailing, or risk being destroyed at the diversion of the currents in the Beibu Bay (Q. Zhou 1999: 36). So merchants' knowledge of ocean currents was utilised in their voyages.

The Song people had a profound understanding of ocean tides. Xu Jing asserted that previous interpretations of tides were "subjective and baseless narrations with prejudice." According to Xu Jing, tides were a result of the interactions between heaven, earth, water, and air. He argued that "heaven envelops water, water holds the earth below, and air lifts and falls in space." He believed that the earth was controlled by water, with air rising and falling in opposition, and that morning tides are formed when air rises and earth sinks, causing the sea to rise. Conversely, night tides were believed to be formed when air falls and earth floats, causing the sea to recede. Xu Jing said that cold and warm air rise and fall once a day, resulting in tidal waves. The orbit of the sun, he wrote, creates the alternation of day and night, and the number of times the air rises and falls depends on the orbit of the moon. Consequently, the tide changes with the sun and the moon, forming a tidal pattern of day tide and night tide (J. Xu 2006: 127–28). This is similar to Yan Su's view that tides are generated by the rising and falling of air, the sun and the moon, and alternating interaction of yin and yang (E. Shi 1990: 3315–16). Historical records such as *Xianchun Period Chronicles of Lin'an, Chunxi Period Chronicles of Fuzhou,* and *Baoqing Period Chronicles of Siming* documented the day-by-day tidal patterns, including the time and size of tides, for four seasons outside the Qiantang River, in Fuzhou, and in the pelagic sea in Mingzhou (S. Qian 1990: 3644–3645). The semi-monthly change in size and hourly pattern was similar to that recorded in *Xianchun Period Chronicles of Lin'an,* with some minor differences (K. Lang 1990: 7835; J. Luo et al. 1990: 5033). The Song people recognized that tides were regular, rising and falling in accordance with the orbit of the moon. Consequently, offshore routes were measured by tides, not miles, and "boats anchored according to the number of tides, much like courier stations." For example, *Chunxi Period Chronicles of Fuzhou* recorded 15 tides on the route from Yingxianmen to Pumen (K. Lang 1990: 7835–39), while the *Complete*

Chronicles of Changguo County in the *Baoqing Period Chronicles of Siming* recorded the tidal distance from Changguo County to its neighboring counties.

Fa Xian, a renowned monk of the Jin Dynasty, emphasized the importance of utilizing the monsoon winds on the seaway back from Sindhu. Fa Xian, who took a merchant boat sailing eastward from Sindhu (present-day India), explicitly mentioned the assistance provided by the trade winds (X. Fa 2008: 142, 145). The Song people, however, were already skilled in exploiting the monsoon winds for sailing purposes. Merchants trading between the Song Dynasty and the countries in the South China Sea took advantage of the monsoon, sailing southward by the northeast monsoon in winter and northward by the southwest monsoon in summer (G. Liao 1990). Additionally, the Song Dynasty dispatched boats during November and December of the lunar calendar using the north wind, and brought them back in May and June of the lunar calendar using the south wind (Y. Zhu 2006: 149). Sailing northward from Mingzhou also entailed exploiting the south wind for setting off and the north wind for returning (S. Yang et al. 1990). Xu Jing's mission to Goryeo, for instance, departed in May of the lunar calendar, exploiting the south wind on the day of departure, and returned in the middle of July of the lunar calendar by using the north wind (J. Xu 2006: 148). From Japan to Mingzhou, "merchant boats returned by the northeast wind." (J. Luo et al. 1990: 5057) Furthermore, Li Chong, a merchant, sailed from Mingzhou to Japan in June of the lunar calendar, riding on the southwest monsoon (Chaoye Qun Zai 1938: 455). The Song people also mastered the regular patterns of monsoon winds between Southeast Asia and the Indian Ocean, with merchants trading to the west of Southeast Asia staying in Lamuri in winter and waiting for the monsoon (R. Zhao 1996: 70, 89).

In the view of the Song people, the ocean was a dynamic and orderly world composed of the lower reaches of rivers, as well as currents, tides, and monsoons. This understanding enabled the Song people to engage in unprecedented maritime activity, as they utilized this knowledge in a more precise manner than any previous era.

3.5.2.2 The Ocean as a Dangerous and Bizarre World

Due to limited navigation techniques and shipbuilding conditions during the Song dynasty, the ocean posed a significant hazard for the Song people. Xu Jing, who had first-hand experience with the perils of sailing, noted that traversing the sea was exceedingly difficult, requiring a single boat to brave the dangerous sea. He identified three primary risks: the northeast wind that blew in July and August of the lunar calendar, stormy winds, and surging waves. Xu Jing observed that continuous northeast winds made it impossible to distinguish between east and west or north and south, as the dark wind blew rapidly, and the sky turned dark, making it difficult to distinguish day from night. The sea's violent movements produced torrential waves, akin to fire cooking soup, with few surviving such treacherous voyages. Xu Jing's fleet faced varying degrees of danger, with the boat he took encountering stormy waves in the yellow-water ocean, resulting in all three rudders breaking. Despite replacing the rudder, the boat remained unstable, causing the people on board to arrive at Mingzhou, emaciated, haggard, and with pale faces, attesting to their worry and fear (J. Xu 2006: 148–49). In addition to strong winds and waves, boats at sea also faced the danger of aquatic animals, such as saw sharks recorded as being over 330 m long with a nasal bone like a saw that could break boats as if biting rotten timber. Dragons as large as hills were also reported to inhabit the sea (Y. Zhu 2006: 150). Records of maritime accidents were frequently found in historical records of the Song Dynasty, with History of the Song Dynasty, *A Full-Scale Textual Criticism on Ancient Systems and Regulations,* and other historical records documenting six China-Japan maritime accidents and nine China-Goryeo maritime accidents in the Song Dynasty (Toqta 1977: 14,136, 14,036, 14,044, 9514, 10,423; D. Ma 2011: 8929; S. Jiang 1990; T. Li 2004: 7366; S. Xu et al. 2014: 3686). However, the actual number of maritime accidents was likely much higher than recorded. Wu Qian, who served as coastal military commissioner, saw Japanese boats drifting away intermittently and boats from Goryeo suddenly encountering wild winds, leading to their drifting to various locations such as Taizhou, Wenzhou, Fujian Province and Qingyuan Prefecture (Q. Wu 2002). Similarly, during Hu Ze's tenure as fiscal commissioner in Guangnan West Province, foreign boats disrupted by storms would drift to Qiongzhou, reporting food shortages and an inability to depart (Toqta 1977: 9941). Mingzhou and Dengzhou reported many instances of Goryeo seagoing boats encountering storms and drifting into their territories (Toqta 1977: 14,036). Countless other maritime accidents likely occurred but went unrecorded.

The dangerous ocean was portrayed as a bizarre world in literary sketches. For example, *Anecdotage of the Song Dynasty* written by He Yuan, tells the story of An Tao who was sent on a mission to Goryeo. "On the boat, he carried scriptures, worn-out sutras, and scrolls that he had collected before, in preparation for his delivery." However, when the boat encountered wind and waves, "sea gods and monsters climbed up the boat and asked for sutras and scrolls." The boat's crew gave them all the sutras, and "in a moment the wind and waves calmed down." (Y. He 2008: 193) Several other bizarre sea stories were recorded in *Strange Tales of the Miraculous by Yijian.* For example, a sea merchant from Changgguo County was caught by islanders and "made to wear iron shackles and handcuffs, and forced to plow the fields for them," in addition to having his thighs burned with red-hot chopsticks and being generally humiliated. Another example involves Zhao Shizao and his group, who were shipwrecked because they did not go to Guangli King Temple to contribute to the sacrifice in time. The merchants from Mingzhou sailed to the Land of Giants, where they were caught and tortured by the Giants. A merchant from Banqiao Town drifted to the Island of Giants, while another sea merchant from Quanzhou drifted to an island and was confined by a woman in a stone room for 7 or 8 years before escaping. A man from Mingzhou called Landlord Jiang, who had been doing a lot of good deeds, was saved from drowning by a thing that held him up (M. Hong 1981: 54, 59, 86, 217–18, 249, 415–16). *Miscellaneous Records in the Kuixin Reign*, written by Zhou Mi, recorded that Yang Shiliang had met a green-faced ghost and a beautiful woman who came to ask for hair. Zhao Dutong saw "a god of the sea with an entirely red body, blue-green eyes, and a red sun overhead" during his voyage. Another sea merchant bought a treasure in Huating County, a sea well that could turn seawater into sweet spring water (M. Zhou 1988: 122–23, 125). The *Records of the Zhang Family* also recorded that a seagoing boat encountered a wild wind and drifted to the Land of Giants, where the boatman was "caught with two feet, split into two pieces, with each Giant eating one of them."

The Land Beyond the Passes and *Records of Foreign Countries* have also documented accounts of some unusual and hard-to-reach areas for Chinese merchant boats. One example is the southeastern island of Java, where a cannibal tribe called Andaman resided. They were described as "having black-lacquered bodies and eating people alive. As a result, boatmen dared not moor to the shore, and merchants who drifted there by wind were reportedly all eaten by the barbarians". Similarly, the ethnic group of Malano, located southeast of Java, was reported to have captured people from merchant boats that were caught in storms, roasting them with thick bamboo sticks. Another area known as the Land of Women was said to be deadly for visitors as numerous women brought back people on board, and within a few days, all of them died." "The lotus pulp more than one foot long, and the peach pit two feet long are occasionally seen floating in the sea of Land of Women (R. Zhao 1996: 125, 128, 130). Murabit produced wheat grains that were two feet in length, melons around six feet, and foreign sheep that were several Chi tall. The island of Zanzibar was home to a large bird called the roc, and once the tube under its wing feathers was cut off, it could be used as a bucket. The ostrich, with a body and neck length of 6 or 7 feet, had wings but was unable to fly very high. The indigenous people on the islands were often depicted as being painted in black lacquer (Q. Zhou 1999: 107, 113). However, records suggest that most people from maritime countries were barbarians with different customs and practices. In the Song Dynasty, merchants had direct contact with overseas people, and even those who did not sail were able to interact with overseas merchants at their residence. For example, Yue Ke recorded that "overseas merchants" who resided in Guangzhou believed in Islam and had different customs from the Chinese. They were rich and extravagant in their spending habits but remained devoted to their faith. They would worship and pray together in a special hall. Every year in April and May of the lunar calendar, when the merchant boats came, "crowds of foreigners" would pray for a south wind in the high tower (K. Yue 1981: 125–26). Similarly, Zhu Yu recorded that foreign merchants living in Guangzhou "dressed differently from the Chinese but ate the same food, excluding pork." They also refrained from eating the six domestic animals that were not killed by their own hands. However, they consumed both live and dead fish and turtles (Y. Zhu 2006: 150). This provides a contrasting view of the overseas world from the odd descriptions of ordinary people.

3.5.2.3 The Ocean as a World Full of Wealth and Business Opportunities

In Volume 7 of *Historical Records of Numerous Categories,* the entry for "sea" stated that "the ocean had 3 virtues: firstly, it was vast and deep; secondly, it was free from impurities; and thirdly, it contained an infinite collection of treasures." Other books documented that the ocean had either five or eight virtues, with both including its vast collection of treasures. As overseas trade thrived in the Song Dynasty, the awareness of the ocean as a source of wealth and business opportunities grew stronger. *The Land Beyond the Passes* recorded that "the Arab Empire holds the most abundant treasures among foreign countries, followed by Java, the Samboja Kingdom, and others." (Q. Zhou 1999: 126) Staple commodities imported during the Song Dynasty were jewelry, spices, and medicines, among others. *The Land Beyond the Passes* and *Records of Foreign Countries* provided detailed accounts of the types of treasures, spices, and medicines produced by foreign countries. In particular, the second volume of *Records of Foreign Countries* recorded the names, origins, and characteristics of 47 different types of jewelry, spices, and medicines. For common people, maritime trade was lucrative. "Every string of 1000 coins could be exchanged for goods worth a hundred strings, and a hundred strings of 1000 coins could be exchanged for goods worth a thousand strings." (H. Bao 1990)This exchange was based on copper cash. Trading in other commodities also yielded significant returns. A merchant named Peng from Luling (present-day Ji'an) purchased jaggery worth thousands of strings of coins to trade overseas. He encountered young adults of the Dan ethnic group who asked to exchange jaggery for pearls. Another man transported porcelain dogs, chickens, and children's toys to trade overseas, and foreign children exchanged the toys for pearls (M. Zeng 2008: 204). Both individuals were small businessmen engaged in overseas trade. While "those engaged in maritime trade were rich and powerful, and such businessmen were found throughout the Jiangnan East and West provinces, Huainan East and West provinces, Fujian Province, and Liangzhe East and West provinces," (H. Bao 1990) the larger merchants made even greater profits.

In terms of the state revenue, "foreign countries were taxed on their products traded in China," (H. Bao 1990) which enabled the Song government to generate a significant amount of tax revenue from overseas trade. Consequently, maritime trade was viewed as an economic opportunity. An official remarked that "tax revenue from overseas trade ranked first among all taxes collected by the country." Ancient Customs was "fundamental to the country's wealth and prosperity" and "a great complement to the country's economic growth." (X. Li 2013: 3614) Emperor Gaozong of Song fully recognized the potential for seagoing trade to bring fortune to the country and noted that "the profit from seagoing trade is the most, and if appropriately managed, the tax revenue could be calculated in millions"; "the profit from seagoing trade is quite helpful for the country." (X. Li 2013: 2158; Z. Pan 1990) The system of Ancient Customs established in the Northern Song Dynasty encouraged Chinese and foreign merchants to engage in trade, pay taxes, and purchase goods, which reflected the concept of making money from the sea. This idea was novel and had not been seen in the Han and Tang dynasties.

Records of Foreign Countries recorded information about overseas countries with great emphasis on market information such as national products and commodities used by seagoing merchants, fully reflecting the current situation and concept of economic trade as the focus of maritime interactions. For example, the national history of the Champa Kingdom recorded business information in four areas, namely, local products (including ivory, writing paper, Santalum album, yellow wax, pine, rattan, and Ceiba pentandra), trade policies (which involved registration and taxation of foreign merchant goods), commodities carried by sea merchants to the country (such as extract, musk, white sandalwood, grass mat, parasol, tough silk, fans, lacquer-ware, porcelain, lead, tin, wine, and sugar), and the domestic trade and currency situation. Similarly, the national history of Java also recorded business information on native pepper, ivory, rhinoceros horns, pearls, borneol, hawksbill turtles, white sandalwood, fennel, clove, and others, as well as foreign merchants' accommodation, and currency system (where cash was coined from melted alloy of copper, silver, brass, and tin). Foreign merchants traded various goods with China, including mixed gold and silver, vessels of gold and silver, five-color figured silk, black silk, lacquerware, iron tripod, bluish white porcelain, and others. These records served as a comprehensive guide to commercial knowledge and covered not only the Champa Kingdom and Java, but also other main countries and regions where the Song merchants traded, such as the Samboja Kingdom, Lamuri, the Arab Empire, Borneo, Mait, and Sanyu (R. Zhao 1996: 9, 34–43, 51, 55, 89–98, 135–41, 141–43, 143–47). The information collected by Zhao Rushi was largely from sea merchants, and his selection of data objectively reflected the Song people's commercial concept of profiting from the ocean.

In contrast to *Records of Foreign Countries*, which primarily focused on business information, official history books written in biographical style in the Song Dynasty focused particularly on the tribute activities of overseas countries. For example, "Foreign Merchants" in *The Anthology of Laws and Regulations of the Song Dynasty* mainly recorded political information like the tribute and enfeoffment of various countries. While the *Records of Foreign Countries* provided detailed information about Java's business, *The Anthology of Laws and Regulations of the Song Dynasty* recorded only Java's tribute activities over nine years without any business information (S. Xu et al. 2014: 9830). Similarly, *Continuation to The Comprehensive Mirror for Aid in Government, Chronological Record of Major Events Since 1127* and others recorded limited business information, but focused on political exchanges such as tribute activities and enfeoffment. *The History of the Song Dynasty,* revised by the Yuan Dynasty, collected various historical materials from books such as *Records of Foreign Countries,* including products and currency, but did not include information on merchants' trading activities. Nevertheless, it enriched the content related to tribute and enfeoffment. These historical records served as notes to ancient rulers' political pursuit of Sino-centrism, aimed at establishing a world order in which foreign countries paid tribute to the Song imperial court.

3.5.2.4 Awareness of the Geographical Location of Maritime Countries

The extant maps from the Song Dynasty that clearly indicate the geographical location of maritime countries include *The General Map of Ancient and Modern Residences of Chinese and Other Ethnic Groups*, drawn in the Southern Song Dynasty. This map shows that the Japanese islands are located in the sea due east of Suzhou, and the Ryukyu Kingdom (Taiwan Island) is due east of Changguo County in Mingzhou. Additionally, the Samboja Kingdom, Champa Kingdom, and Java are located due east of Zhangzhou, Quanzhou, and Chaozhou, respectively, with all these countries located east of Hainan Island.The inquiry then arises as to whether this represents the objective facts of ocean knowledge in the Song Dynasty. If not, what is the relationship between the oceanic imagery reflected in the maps and the actual knowledge of the Song people regarding maritime locations? Therefore, an examination of the Song people's actual understanding of the locations of maritime countries is necessary.

The *Xuanhe Period Maps and Records About Goryeo* written by Xu Jing provides evidence the Song people had a clear understanding of Goryeo's location. Specifically, the journey is depicted from Mingzhou's Dinghai County to Goryeo by sea (J. Xu 2006: 19), passing through various locations including Mount Zhaobao in Dinghai County, Mount Hutou, Shenjiamen Town in Changguo County, Mount Putuo, Hailü Island, Mount Penglai, Banyang Island, then advanced into the ocean, and passed through white-water ocean, yellow-water river, black-water ocean, Mount Jiajie, Wuyu Island, Pai Island, Mount White, Mount Black, Yueyu Island, Lanshan Island, Baiyi Island, Gui Thatch, Chuncao Thatch, Areca Island, Bodhisattva Thatch, Bamboo Island, Ku Thatch, Qunshan Island, Heng Island, Ziyunshan, Mount Fuyong, Mount Hongzhou, Yazi Thatch, Horse Island, Mount Jiutou, Tang people Island, Shuangwen Island, Daqing Island, Monk Island, Niuxin Island, Niegong Island, Xiaoqing Island, Ziyan Island, Jishui Gate, Toad Cave and watershed, and finally reaching Port Licheng in Goryeo (J. Xu 2006: 130–47). These 40 sea surface targets constituted the route from Mingzhou to Goryeo. The lost "pictures" from Xu Jing's book included pictures of objects things witnessed in Goryeo, maps of "sea routes", namely "the maps of all the continents, islands and keys the Song's ambassadorial fleet passed by" (J. Xu 2006: 129), and four navigation methods, including compass, surface targets, astronomical navigation, and detection by lead hammers. The route map likely included past islands, sea routes, distance travelled, and charts for star navigation, including several key elements of *Zheng He's Nautical Chart.* Chengxun's account described the route from Japan to Mingzhou, which connected Goryeo and Tamna, then Mount Shifan in the East China Sea, Mount Xuweng in Mingzhou, Lie Port, Mount Hutou, Mount Zhaobao, and finally, Mingzhou. This demonstrates the Song people's clear understanding of the location of Japan and the route, schedule, and sea conditions between Japan and the Song Dynasty (Jojin 2009: 6, 10, 11). *Baoqing Period Chronicles of Siming* indicated that boats returned from Goryeo to Mingzhou on south wind and traveled from Japan to Mingzhou on northeast wind (J. Luo et al. 1990: 5057), providing clear understanding of the direction.

The Song people also had a relatively clear understanding of the geographical location of the countries in the South China Sea. According to Zhao Rushi, the *Maps of Foreign Countries* he had examined contained information on the hazardous areas consisting of reefs and sand islets, and identified Beibu Bay and Pulau Aur as the boundaries beyond which countries in the South China Sea could not access China. When he failed to locate relevant information in Chinese classics (R. Zhao 1996: 1), he wrote *Records of Foreign Countries.* While the original map no longer exists, it can be surmised that it would have been "a world map" of Southeast Asia and the countries to its west, with information on surface targets (i.e., the periphery of reefs and sand islets, and the boundaries of Beibu Bay and Pulau Aur), sea routes (*Records of Foreign Countries* indicated that Java was "30 degrees southeast of Quanzhou" on the sea route), and distances. The original map is lost, but *The Land Beyond the Passes* and other books indicate that the Song people had a relatively clear understanding of the geographical location of maritime countries.

The Song dynasty possessed a detailed knowledge of the geographic location of countries within the South China Sea, as evidenced by the use of multiple reference points. These reference points included Cochin, the South China Sea, Beibu Bay, the Samboja Kingdom, Java, Kulam and the Arab Empire. When the Tang people revised *Book of Liang* and *History of Southern Dynasties*, Jiaozhou was utilized as the main reference point to orient countries in the South China Sea (C. Yao and Si. Yao et al.1973: 783; Y. Yan 1975: 1947). Ma Duanlin followed this approach in his revision of *A Full-Scale Textual Criticism on Ancient Systems and Regulations*, stating that the South China Sea countries were located roughly to the south and southwest of Jiaozhou on islets in the middle of the sea, which had been frequently traversed by boats since the Han dynasty (D. Ma 2011: 9123). Zhou Qufei's *The Land Beyond the Passes* also used Cochin as an important reference point, stating that many countries are in the Indian Ocean and that Cochin can be used as a reference point to locate them. To the south of Cochin were the Champa Kingdom, Kampoja, and Beranang, while to the northwest were the Kingdom of Dali, Heishui, and the Tibetan regimes in ancient China. West of Cochin was Silan Sea, with Silan in the middle, Kulam to the south, Rajagriha of Roma and Singhu to the north, and the East Abbassides Sea to the west, beyond which lay the Arab Empire. To the west of the Arab Empire was the Abbassides Sea, which led to Murabit and over one thousand other countries. The further west was where the Sun set, of which the details were unknown (Q. Zhou 1999: 75, 60, 76, 77, 82, 91, 107).[9] The center of the Arab Empire was Malabar, which was in the northwest of Lamuri and could be reached in the favorable northeast wind within sixty days. (Q. Zhou 1999: 91, 99, 101). Cochin was also used as a reference point to locate Zanzibar and the Persian Kingdom in Africa (Q. Zhou 1999: 113–15). The Song people basically had an accurate understanding of the geographical locations of the Champa Kingdom, Kampoja, Silan, Kulam, Roma, Singhu, the Arab Empire, Murabit, Zanzibar, the Persian Kingdom, and others.

The term "southwestern countries" refers to the countries on the Southeast Asian Peninsula, the Indian Ocean coast, and the countries of West Asia and North Africa. The Southeast Asian island countries were commonly known as the "countries in due south" and "countries in southeast." The economic center for countries due south of Cochin was the Samboja Kingdom, while Java was the economic center for countries southeast of Cochin (Q. Zhou 1999: 74). The Samboja Kingdom was due south of

---

[9] The kingdoms recorded in *Notes from the Land Beyond the Passes* are located in the following present-day areas, they are Cochin (northern Vietnam), the kingdom of Silan (Sri Lanka), Roma and Singhu (India), Champa (south-central Vietnam), Kampoja (Cambodia and parts of Vietnam, Thailand and Laos), Kulam (Quelung in southwest India), Murabit (North Africa) and Beranang (the western part of the Malay Peninsula).

Beibu Bay, and its boats traveled northward through Pulau Aur and Beibu Bay to reach China (Q. Zhou 1999: 36, 126). This kingdom was situated in the South China Sea, which was the main waterway for countries in the region. The countries to its east, such as Java, and the ones to its west, such as the Arab Empire and Kulam, all had to pass through its territory to enter China. Java was in the southeast of the South China Sea, and the Samboja Kingdom was northwest of Java (Q. Zhou 1999: 86; R. Zhao 2000: 88). East of Java were "many countries in the southeast sea", such as Suvarna gotra, Sawaku and others, which were rarely visited by sea merchants (Q. Zhou 1999: 111). According to the *Records of Foreign Countries*, it took 15 days to sail from Java to Borneo and another 10 days to reach the Samboja Kingdom (R. Zhao 2000: 88).[10] In fact, Borneo was due north of Java, and one had to sail northwest towards the Samboja Kingdom to reach China. North of Borneo were Mait and Sanyu on the Philippine Islands. Mait was situated to the north of Borneo, and Sanyu, Babuyan, Pollilo, Lingayan, Durorui, and Lubang were all dependencies of Mait. North of Sanyu was Ryukyu (Taiwan Island). The Ryukyu Kingdom was to the east of Quanzhou, and the boat trip was about 5 or 6. The original inhabitants of Ryukyu sometimes sold yellow wax, local gold, yak tails, and slices of dried leopard meat to Sanyu, indicating a connection between the two regions. South of Taiwan Island was Visaya, so close to Penghu in Jinjiang County that smoke from kitchen chimneys could be seen from each other (R. Zhao 1996: 141–43, 143–47; 147–49).[11]

In summary, it is evident that the Song people's assessments of the geographical locations of maritime countries were generally consistent with their actual positions, albeit with some minor errors. Specifically, they exhibited a correct understanding of the island chains surrounding the East and South China Seas, including Goryeo, Japan, Ryukyu, Visaya, Sanyu, Mait, Borneo, Java, the Samboja Kingdom, and Lamuri, as well as the geographical locations of the Champa Kingdom, Kampoja, Chanthaburi, and Tambralinga. Additionally, their estimates of the positions of Silan Island, and India, as well as West Asian and North and East African countries situated west of Malacca, were roughly accurate. If the ocean knowledge acquired by the Song people had been fully utilized, it might have been possible to draw a map similar to *The Selden Map of China,* drawn in the mid-Ming Dynasty and housed in the Bodleian Library (J. Qian 2011; Y. Guo and Y. Liu 2011).[12] This map provided a reasonably clear and accurate depiction of the South China Sea. Thus, *The General Map of Ancient and Modern Residences of Chinese and Other Ethnic Groups* drawn in the Southern Song Dynasty did not accurately represent the Song people's ocean

[10] According to the entry of Borneo in *Supplementary Notes on Records of Foreign Countries,* the statement that Borneo lies in the southeast of Quanzhou is correct, but the record of "it takes 45 days to Java, and 40 to Samboja Kingdom" is in conflict with the entry of Java. Based on the actual locations of the three kingdoms, the record of entry Java makes more sense.

[11] The kingdoms recorded in *Notes on Records of Foreign Countries* are located in the following present-day area, they are Mait (the Mindo Island of the Philippine Archipelago), Sanyu (several islands of the Philippine Archipelago), and Ryukyu (Taiwan).

[12] *The Selden Map of China* collected in Bodleian Library was named *Fujian Navigation Map in the Mid-Ming* by Qian Jiang, and *Nautical Char of the Eastern and Western Oceans* by Guo Yusheng et.al.

knowledge. This map's purpose was not to provide an accurate representation of the oceanic world, but rather to highlight the concept of a China-centric world that emphasized China over foreign countries.

3.5.3 Summary

The Song Dynasty witnessed a significant shift in the perception and understanding of the ocean, in contrast to the immortal world envisaged by the people during the Qin and Han dynasties. The Song people's imagery of the ocean was more realistic and clearer, marking a great change in their growing knowledge of the ocean. This change was driven by the policy of relatively open maritime trade and the gradual southward shift of China's economic center, leading to unprecedented growth in maritime trade and opening a new stage for the accumulation and spread of ocean knowledge. The main source of first-hand ocean knowledge in the Song Dynasty was the group of sea merchants who had been involved in seafaring practice for a considerable period. Additionally, envoys and monks who participated in sailing also contributed to the first-hand ocean knowledge. The records about the sea in ancient classics were also another source of ocean knowledge for the Song people. The knowledge was spread through various means, including oral transmission from generation to generation, circulation of books written by seafaring envoys and monks, and collection of records by the Protocol Department and officials in the coastal areas.

Such increasing ocean knowledge was disseminated through various channels. As a result, the Song people developed a new understanding of the ocean that differed from previous beliefs. They followed the traditional theory of the lower reaches of a river in the sea, providing a clearer view of their location. They envisaged a dynamic ocean world consisting of the lower reaches of a river, tides, monsoons, and currents. Although the concept of the immortal world related to the ocean in the Qin and Han dynasties was not emphasized during the Song Dynasty, the ocean remained a hazardous and mysterious world filled with objective dangers and bizarre images. This contributed significantly to the development of maritime beliefs in the Song Dynasty. Both officials and common people benefited from the growing maritime trade, and the ocean was considered a world full of wealth and business opportunities. Unlike in the Han and Tang dynasties, officials and common people alike viewed the ocean as a means of making money. The Song people acquired ocean knowledge that allowed them to accurately judge the geographical position of the Korean Peninsula, Japanese islands, Taiwan Island, Philippine Islands, Indonesian Islands, and the coastal areas of the Indochinese Peninsula in the East and South China Seas, as well as the geographical position of the countries along the coasts of the Indian Ocean, West Asia, and North Africa, which closely reflected reality.

The Song people approached ocean knowledge and imagery from different perspectives and for different purposes, resulting in differences in their selection and construction of ocean knowledge. The merchant group and coastal officials aimed to uncover the actual patterns of the sea world, such as sea routes, conditions, geographical locations, market information, and so on. On the other hand, officials from the Protocol Department, historians, painters, and foreign maps, focused on exploiting ocean knowledge for political purposes. They intentionally selected political information such as records of tribute and enfeoffment to construct a world order with foreign countries reconciling to China. Additionally, common literati entertained and enlightened audiences with sea stories while incorporated with religious beliefs.

References

Ban, Gu 班固, et al. 1962. *Han Shu* 汉书 [Book of Han]. Beijing: Zhonghua Book Company.

Bao, Hui 包恢. 1990. *Bizhou Gao Lüe* 敝帚稿略 [Anthology of Bao Hui]. Collected in Complete Library in the Four Branches of Literature. Shanghai: Shanghai Chinese Classics Publishing House.

Bao, Weimin 包伟民. 1991. "Songdai De Liangshi Maoyi 宋代的粮食贸易 [Grain Trade in the Song Dynasty]". *Social Sciences in China* 2.

Bao, Zheng 包拯. 1989. *Baozheng Ji Biannian Jiaobu* 包拯集编年校补 [Selected Works of Baozheng in Chronological Order Annotated ersion]. Collated by Yang Guoyi. Hefei: Huangshan Publishing House.

Cai, Xiang 蔡襄. 1996. *Caixiang Ji* 蔡襄集 [Works of Cai Xiang]. Punctuated and collated by Wu Yining. Shanghai: Shanghai Chinese Classics Publishing House.

Cao, Xun 曹勋. 1990. *Songyin Ji* 松隐集 [Selected Works of Cao Xun].Collected in Complete Library in the Four Branches of Literature. Shanghai: Shanghai Chinese Classics Publishing House.

Center for Underwater Archaeology Studies of National Museum of China 中国博物馆水下考古学研究中心, et al. 2011. *Fujian Lianjiang Dinghaiwan Chenchuan Kaogu* 福建连江定海湾沉船考古 [The Archaeological Studies on the Shipwrecks in Dinghai Bay of Lianjiang County of Fujian]. Beijing: Science Press.

Chao, Buzhi 晁补之. 1990. *Jilei Ji* 鸡肋集 [Works of Chao Buzhi]. Collected in Complete Library in the Four Branches of Literature. Shanghai: Shanghai Chinese Classics Publishing House.

Chaoye Qun Zai 朝野群载 [Edited by Kuroita Katsumi]. 1938. Edited by Kuroita Katsumi. Collected in the Revised Edition of Collection of Japanese Historical Records. Tokyo: Yoshikawa Koubunkan.

Chen, Fuliang 陈傅良. 1999. *Chen Fuliang Xiansheng Wenji* 陈傅良先生文集 [Selected Works of Chen Fuliang]. Hangzhou: Zhejiang University Press.

Chen, Qiqing 陈耆卿. 1990. *Jiading Chicheng Zhi* 嘉定赤城志 [Jiading Period Chronicles of Chicheng]. Collected in The Series of Chorography of the Song and Yuan Dynasties. Beijing: Zhonghua Book Company.

Chen, Zao 陈造. 1990. *Jianghuchangweng Ji* 江湖长翁集 [Selected Works of Chen Zao].Collected in Complete Library in the Four Branches of Literature. Shanghai: Shanghai Chinese Classics Publishing House.

Dai, Fugu 戴复古. 1990. *Shiping Shiji* 石屏诗集 [Anthology of Dai Fugu]. Collected in Complete Library in the Four Branches of Literature. Shanghai: Shanghai Chinese Classics Publishing House.

Editorial Committee of Excavation Report of the Quanzhou Bay Song Dynasty Shipwreck Excavation泉州湾宋代海船发掘报告编写组. 1975. "Quanzhouwan Songdai Haichuan Fajue Jianbao 泉州湾宋代海船发掘简报 [Report of the Quanzhou Bay Song Dynasty Shipwrecks]". *Cultural Relics* 10.

Fa, Xian 法显. 2008. *Faxian Zhuan Jiaozhu* 法显传校注 [Annotation of Fa Xian's Travels]. Edited by Zhang Xun. Beijing: Zhonghua Book Company.

Fan, Chengda 范成大. 2012a. *Guihai Yuheng Zhi* 桂海虞衡志 [Records of the Ranger in Guihai]. Collected in Complete Song Notes. Elephant Press.

Fan, Chengda 范成大. 2012b. *Can Luan Lu* 骖鸾录 [The Trip to Guilin]. Collected in Complete Song Notes. Elephant Press.

Fan, Chengda 范成大. 2012c. *Wu Chuan Lu* 吴船录 [Travelogues in Wu Area by Ship]. Collected in Complete Song Notes. Elephant Press.

Fan, Yiran 范伊然. 2013. *Nanhai Kaoku Ziliao Zhengli Yu Shuping* 南海考古资料整理与述评 [A Compilation and Review on Archaeological Materials of the South China Sea]. Beijing: Science Press

Fan, Zhiming 范致明. 1990. *Yueyang Fengtu Ji* 岳阳风土记 [Geography and Customs of Yueyang]. Collected in Complete Library in the Four Branches of Literature. Shanghai: Shanghai Chinese Classics Publishing House.

Fang, Dacong 方大琮. 1990. *Tiean Ji* 铁庵集 [Collection of Fang Dacong]. Collected in Complete Library in the Four Branches of Literature. Shanghai: Shanghai Chinese Classics Publishing House.

Feng, Fujing 冯福京, et al. 1990. *Dade Chaoguozhou Tuzhi* 大德昌国州图志[Dade Period Chronicles of Changzhouguo]. Collected in The Series of Chorography of the Song and Yuan Dynasties. Beijing: Zhonghua Book Company.

Fu, Zongwen 傅宗文. 1989. "Songdai Fujian Yanhai De Shangyehua Langchao 宋代福建沿海的商业化浪潮 [Business Surges in the Coastal Area of Fujian Province During the Song Dynasty]". *Journal of Chinese Social and Economic History* 3.

Fujian Tongzhi 福建通志 [Chronicles of Fujian]. 1990. Edited by Qianlong. Collected in Complete Library in the Four Branches of Literature. Shanghai: Shanghai Chinese Classics Publishing House.

Ge, Jinfang 葛金芳. 2008. *Nansong Shougongyeshi* 南宋手工业史 [The Handicraft Industry of the Southern Song Dynasty]. Shanghai: Shanghai Chinese Classics Publishing House.

Ge, Jinfang 葛金芳. 2013. "Songdai Haishang Qunti De Goucheng, Guimo Jiqi Minyingxingzhi Kaoshu 南宋海商群体的构成、规模及其民营性质考述 [The Research on the Formation, Scale, and Private Nature of the Maritime Merchants in the Southern Song Dynasty]". *Journal of Chinese Literature and History* 4.

Guo, Xiangzheng 郭祥正. 1990. *Qingshan Xu Ji* 青山续集 [Continuation to Qingshan Collection]. Collected in Complete Library in the Four Branches of Literature. Shanghai: Shanghai Chinese Classics Publishing House.

Han, Wei 韩维. 1990. *Nanyang Ji* 南阳集 [Anthology of Han Wei]. Collected in Complete Library in the Four Branches of Literature. Shanghai: Shanghai Chinese Classics Publishing House.

He, Feng 何锋. 2005. "Shier Shiji Nansong Yanhai Diqu Jianchuan Shuliang Kaocha 12世纪南宋沿海地区舰船数量考察[Studies on the Quantity of Ships in the Coastal Areas of the Southern Song Dynasty in the 12th century]". *Journal of Chinese Social and Economic History* 3.

He, Yuan 何薳. 2008. *Chunzhu Jiwen* 春渚纪闻 [Anecdotage of the Song Dynasty]. Collected in Complete Song Notes. Elephant Press.

Hong, Mai 洪迈撰. 1981. *Yijian Zhi* 夷坚志 [Strange Tales of the Miraculous by Yijian]. Edited by He Zhuo. Beijing: Zhonghua Book Company.

Hong, Shi 洪适. n.d. *Panzhou Wenji* 盘洲文集 [Panzhou Anthology]. Collected in Collectanea of the Four Categories 1st edn.

Huang, Chunyan 黄纯艳. 2003. *Songdai Haiwai Maoyi* 宋代海外贸易[Overseas Trade of the Song Dynasty]. Beijing: Social Sciences Academic Press.

Huang, Chunyan 黄纯艳. 1999. "Lun Songdai Jinkoupin De Yingxiao 论宋代进口品的营销 [The Marketing of Imports in the Song Dynasty]". *Journal of Yunnan Education College* 5.

Huang, Kuan-chung 黄宽重. 2009. *Nansong Difang Wuli: Difangjun Yu Mingjian Ziwei Wuli De Tanto* 南宋地方武力:地方军与民间自卫武力的探讨 [Local Forces of the Southern Song—A Study on Local Armies and Civil Self-defence Forces]. Beijing: National Library of China Publishing House.
Huang, Ting 黄挺 and Jingguo Du 杜经国. 1994. "Chaoshan Gudai Shangyi Gangkou Yanjiu 潮汕古代商易港口研究 [Studies on the Ancient Trading Port at Chaoshan]". *Chaozhou-Shantou Culture Research* 1. Shantou: Shantou University Press.
Huang, Tingjian 黄庭坚. 2011. *Huang Tingjian Quanji* 黄庭坚全集 [The Complete Works of Huang Tingjian]. Nanchang: Jiangxi People's Publishing House.
Huang, Yansun 黄岩孙. 1990. *Xianxi Zhi* 仙溪志 [Chronicles of Xianxi]. Collected in The Series of Chorography of Song and Yuan Dynasty. Beijing: Zhonghua Book Company.
Huang, Zhen. 1990. *Huang Shi Richao* 黄氏日抄 [Notes of Huang]. Collected in Complete Library in the Four Branches of Literature. Shanghai: Shanghai Chinese Classics Publishing House.
Jiang, Shaoyu 江少虞. 1990. *Song Chao Shishi Leiyuan* 宋朝事实类苑 [Collection of the Song Dynasty's Historical Records]. Collected in Complete Library in the Four Branches of Literature. Shanghai: Shanghai Chinese Classics Publishing House.
Jojin 成寻. 2009. *Xin Jiao Cantiantai Wutaishan Ji* 新校参天台五台山记 [Revised Edition of Travelogues of Jojin]. Edited by Wang Liping. Shanghai: Shanghai Chinese Classics Publishing House.
Li, Tao 李焘. 2004. *Xu Zizhi Tongjian Changbian* 续资治通鉴长编 [Continuation to The Comprehensive Mirror for Aid in Government]. Beijing: Zhonghua Book Company.
Li, Xinchuan 李心传. 2000. *Jianyan Yilai Chaoye Zaji* 建炎以来朝野杂记 [Laws and Institutions Since the Jianyan Reign]. Edited by Xu Gui. Beijing: Zhonghua Book Company.
Li, Xinchuan 李心传. 2013. *Jianyan Yilai Xinian Yaolu* 建炎以来系年要录 [Chronological Record of Major Events Since 1127]. Beijing: Zhonghua Book Company.
Li, Zhiyi 李之仪. 1990. *Guxijushi Qian Ji* 姑溪居士前集 [Prequel to Selected Works of Guxijushi]. Collected in Complete Library in the Four Branches of Literature. Shanghai: Shanghai Chinese Classics Publishing House.
Liao, Gang 廖刚. 1990. *Gaofeng Wenji* 高峰文集 [Selected Works of Liao Gang]. Collected in Complete Library in the Four Branches of Literature. Shanghai: Shanghai Chinese Classics Publishing House.
Lin, Zhonggan 林忠干, et al. 1987. "Minbei Song Yuan Ciqi De Shengchan Yu Waixiao 闽北宋元瓷器的生产与外销 [The Production and Export of Song and Yuan Porcelain in the North of Fujian Province]". *Journal of Maritime History Studies* 2.
Liu, Ziwen 刘孜文. 2007. "Lun Hainan De Dingyi He Chengli Yaojian 论海难的定义和成立要件[The Definition to Sea Wrecks and Their Necessary Conditions]". *China Water Transport* 11.
Liu, Zihui 刘子翚. 1990. *Pingshan Ji* 屏山集 [Selected Works of Liu Zihui]. Collected in Complete Library in the Four Branches of Literature. Shanghai: Shanghai Chinese Classics Publishing House.
Lou, Yao 楼钥. 1990. *Gonggui Ji* 攻媿集 [Selected Works of Lou Yao]. Collected in Complete Library in the Four Branches of Literature. Shanghai: Shanghai Chinese Classics Publishing House.
Luo, Jun 罗浚, et al. 1990. *Baoqing Siming Zhi* 宝庆四明志 [Baoqing Period Chronicles of Siming]. Collected in The Series of Chorography of the Song and Yuan Dynasties. Beijing: Zhonghua Book Company.
Lu, You 陆游. 2012a. *Laoxuean Biji* 老学庵笔记 [The Notes of an Old Pedant]. Sorted by Li Changxian. Collected in Complete Song Notes. Elephant Press.
Lu, You 陆游. 2012b. *Ru Shu Ji* 入蜀记 [Essays about My Journey to Sichuan]. Sorted by Li Changxian. Collected in Complete Song Notes. Elephant Press.
Lü, Yihao 吕颐浩. 2012. *Lü Yihao Ji* 吕颐浩集 [Selected Works of Lü Yihao]. Hangzhou: Zhejiang Classics Publishing House.

Lü, Zuqian 吕祖谦. 1990. *Donglai Waiji* 东莱外集 [Selected Works of Lü Zuqian]. Collected in Complete Library in the Four Branches of Literature. Shanghai: Shanghai Chinese Classics Publishing House.

Ma, Duanlin 马端临. 2011. Wenxian Tongkao 文献通考 [A Full-Scale Textual Criticism on Ancient Systems and Regulations]. Beijing: Zhonghua Book Company.

Mei, Yingfa 梅应发, et al. 1990. *Kaiqing Siming Zhi* 开庆四明续志 [Sequels to Kaiming Period Chronicles of Siming]. Collected in The Series of Chorography of the Song and Yuan Dynasties. Beijing: Zhonghua Book Company.

Nanhi I hao De Kaogu Shijue "南海I号"的考古试掘 [Archaeological Excavation of "Nanhai I"]. 2011. Edited by Guangdong Institute of Cultural Relics and Archaeology广东省文物考古研究所编. Beijing: Science Press.

Pan, Jiezi 潘絜兹. 1979. "Lingyan Caibi Dongxinpo —Yanshangsi Jindai Bihua Xiaoji 灵岩彩壁动心魄——岩上寺金代壁画小记 [Breathtaking Colorful Wall paintings: A Report of the Murals of the Jin Dynasty at Yanshang Temple]". *Cultural Relics* 2.

Pan, Zimu 潘自牧. 1990. *Jizhuan Yuanhai* 记纂渊海 [Historical Records of Numerous Categories]. Collected in Complete Library in the Four Branches of Literature. Shanghai: Shanghai Chinese Classics Publishing House.

Qian, Shuoyou 潜说友. 1990. *Xianchu Linan Zhi* 咸淳临安志 [Xianchun Period Chronicles of Lin'an]. Collected in in The Series of Chorography of the Song and Yuan Dynasties. Beijing: Zhonghua Book Company.

Qin, Guan 秦观. 1990. *Huaihai Ji* 淮海集 [Selected Works of Qin Guan]. Collected in Complete Library in the Four Branches of Literature. Shanghai: Shanghai Chinese Classics Publishing House.

Shi, Huihong 释惠洪. 1988. *Lengzhai Yehua* 冷斋夜话 [Night Talks in Lengzhai]. Beijing: Zhonghua Book Company.

Shi, Juefan 释觉范. 1990. 石门文字禅 [Shi Juefan's Works on Buddhist Service]. Collected in Complete Library in the Four Branches of Literature. Shanghai: Shanghai Chinese Classics Publishing House.

Shui, Anli 税安礼. 2013. *Lidai Dili Zhizhangtu* 历代地理指掌图 [Historical Atlas of Dynasties]. Collected in the Continuation to Comprehensive Mirror for Aid in Government. Shanghai: Shanghai Chinese Classics Publishing House.

Song Shi Quanwen 宋史全文 [History of the Song Dynasty in Full Scale]. 2005. Edited by Zhiliang Li. Haerbin: Heilongjiang People's Publishing House.

Su, Shi 苏轼. 1986. *Su Shi Wenji* 苏轼文集 [Selected Works of Su Shi]. Punctuated and collated by Kong Fanli. Beijing: Zhonghua Book Company.

Su, Shi 苏轼. 2010. *Su Shi Quanji Jiaozhu* 苏轼全集校注 [Annotations to the Selected Works of Su Shi]. Punctuated and collated by Zhang Zhilie, et al. Shijieazhuang: Hebei People's Publishing House.

Su, Shunqin苏舜钦. 1991. *Su Shunqin Ji Biannian Jiaozhu* 苏舜钦集编年校注 [Chronological Annotations to Su Shunqin's Works]. Collated by Fu Pingji and Hu Wentao. Chengdu: Bashu Publishing House.

Sun, Di 孙觌. 1990. *Hongqingjushi Ji*鸿庆居士集 [Selected Works of Sun Di]. Collected in Complete Library in the Four Branches of Literature. Shanghai: Shanghai Chinese Classics Publishing House.

Toqta 脱脱. 1975. *Jin Shi* 金史 [History of the Jin Dynasty]. Beijing: Zhonghua Book Company.

Toqta 脱脱. 1977. *Song Shi* 宋史 [History of the Song Dynasty]. Beijing: Zhonghua Book Company.

Wang, Anshi 王安石. 1990. *Linchuan Wenji* 临川文集 [Selected Works of Wang Anshi]. Collected in Complete Library in the Four Branches of Literature. Shanghai: Shanghai Chinese Classics Publishing House.

Wang, Mingqing 王明清. 2013. *Huizhu Houlu* 挥麈后录 [Records of the Intermediate Period of the Northern and Southern Song Dynasties]. Sorted by Yan Yongcheng. Collected in Complete Song Notes. Elephant Press.

Wang, Qingsong 王庆松. 2004. "Ershi Shiji Songdai Haiwai Maoyi Yanjiu Zongshu 20世纪宋代海外贸易研究综述 [Review on 20th Century Overseas Trade Researches in the Song Dynasty]". *Journal of Maritime History Studies* 2.

Wang, Yan 王炎. 1990a. *Shuangxi Leigao* 双溪类稿 [Selected Works of Wang Yan]. Collected in Complete Library in the Four Branches of Literature. Shanghai: Shanghai Chinese Classics Publishing House.

Wang, Yingchen 汪应辰. 1990b. *Wending Ji* 文定集 [Selected Works of Wang Yingchen]. Collected in Complete Library in the Four Branches of Literature. Shanghai: Shanghai Chinese Classics Publishing House.

Wang, Yinglin 王应麟. 2003. *Yuhai* 玉海 [Encyclopedia of 21 Categories]. Yangzhou: Guangling Publishing House.

Wen, Tianxiang 文天祥. 1987. *Weng Tianxiang Quanji* 文天祥全集 [Selected Works of Wen Tianxiang]. Collated by Xiong Fei, et al. Nanchang: Jiangxi People's Publishing House.

Wu, Qian 吴潜. 2002. *Song Tejin Zuochengxiang Xuguogong Zouyi* 宋特进左丞相许国公奏议 [Wu Qian's Proposals to the Emperor in the Southern Song Dynasty]. Collected in Continuation to Complete Library in the Four Branches of Literature. Shanghai: Shanghai Chinese Classics Publishing House.

Wu, Yong 吴泳. 1990. *Helin Ji* 鹤林集 [Selected Works of Wu Yong]. Collected in Complete Library in the Four Branches of Literature. Shanghai: Shanghai Chinese Classics Publishing House.

Wu, Zimu 吴自牧. 1980. *Mengliao Lu* 梦粱录 [Accounts About the Capital]. Hangzhou: Zhejiang People's Publishing House.

Xie, Weixin 谢维新. 1990. *Gujin Hebi Shilei Beiyao* 古今合璧事类备要 [Compilation of Natural Phenomena and Institutions in History]. Collected in Complete Library in the Four Branches of Literature. Shanghai: Shanghai Chinese Classics Publishing House.

Xihulaoren Fansheng Lu《西湖老人繁胜录》[Life in Lin'an During the Southern Song Dynasty]. 1996. Collected in Complete Library in the Four Branches of Literature. Jinan: Shandong Qilu Press.

Xu, Jing 徐兢. 2006. *Xuanhe Fengshi Gaoli Tujing* 宣和奉使高丽图经 [Xuanhe Period Maps and Records About Goryeo]. Sorted by Yu Yunguo. Collected in Complete Song Notes. Elephant Press.

Xu, Mengshen 徐梦莘. 1987. *Sanchao Beimeng Huibian* 三朝北盟会编 [Records of Wars and Actions between the Song and Jin in Three Song Emperors' Reigns]. Shanghai: Shanghai Chinese Classics Publishing House.

Xu, Song 徐松, et al. 2014. *Song Huiyao Jigao*宋会要辑稿 [The Anthology of Laws and Regulations of the Song Dynasty]. Shanghai: Shanghai Chinese Classics Publishing House.

Yang, Shiqi 杨士奇, et al. 1990. *Lidai Mingchen Zouyi* 历代名臣奏议 [Memorials to the Thrones in History]. Collected in Complete Library in the Four Branches of Literature. Shanghai: Shanghai Chinese Classics Publishing House.

Yao, Cha and Silian Yao 姚察, 姚思廉. 1973. *Liang Shu* 梁书 [Book of Liang]. Beijing: Zhonghua Book Company.

Ye, Wencheng 叶文程. 1987. "Song Yuan Shiqi Longquan Qingci De Waixiao Jiqi Youguan Wenti Tantao 宋元时期龙泉青瓷的外销及其有关问题的探讨 [A Study on the International Marketing of Longquan Celadon in the Song and Yuan Dynasties]". *Journal of Maritime History Studies* 2.

Yuan, Jue 袁桷. 1990. *Qingrong Jushi Ji* 清容居士集 [Selected Works of Yuan Jue]. Collected in Complete Library in the Four Branches of Literature. Shanghai: Shanghai Chinese Classics Publishing House.

Yuan, Xie 袁燮. 1990a. *Jiezhai Ji* 絜斋集 [Selected works of Yuan Xie]. Collected in Complete Library in the Four Branches of Literature. Shanghai: Shanghai Chinese Classics Publishing House.

Yuan, Xingzong 员兴宗. 1990b. *Jiuhua Ji* 九华集 [Selected Works of Yuan Xingzong]. Collected in Complete Library in the Four Branches of Literature. Shanghai: Shanghai Chinese Classics Publishing House.

Yuwen, MaoZhao 宇文懋昭. 1986. *Da Jin Guozhi Jiaozheng* 大金国志校证 [Revision of History of the Jin Kingdom]. Beijing: Zhonghua Book Company.

Zeng, Gong 曾巩. 1990. *Yuanfen Leigao* 元丰类稿 [Selected Works of Zeng Gu]. Collected in Complete Library in the Four Branches of Literature. Shanghai: Shanghai Chinese Classics Publishing House.

Zhang, Bangji 张邦基. 1985. *Mozhuang Manlu* 墨庄漫录 [Notes from Mozhuang]. Punctuated and Collated by Kong Fanli. Beijing: Zhonghua Book Company.

Zhang, Chunhai 张春海. 2014. "Haifengzhen Yizhi; Song Jin ' Haishang Silu' Beiqidian? 海丰镇遗址:宋金"海上丝路"北起点?[The Site of Haifeng Town: the Northern Start of the "Maritime Silk Road"in the Song and Jin Periods]". *Chinese Social Sciences Today, 4 August 2014.*

Zhang, Fangping 张方平. 1998. *Lequan Xiansheng Wenji* 乐全先生文集 [Selected Works of Zhang Fangping]. Beijing: Bibliography and Document Publishing House.

Zhang, Zi 张镃. 1990. *Shi Xue Guifan* 仕学规范 [Norms of Learning and Being an Official]. Collected in Complete Library in the Four Branches of Literature. Shanghai: Shanghai Chinese Classics Publishing House.

Zhao, Ding 赵鼎. 2008. *Jianyan Bilu* 建炎笔录 [Chronicles of Jianyan Period]. Sorted by Lai Kehong and Liu Qiang. Collected in Complete Song Notes. Elephant Press.

Zhao, Rushi 赵汝适. 2000. *Zhufan Zhi Buzhu* 诸蕃志补注 [Supplementary Notes on Records of Foreign Countries]. Collated by Han Zhenhua. Hong Kong: Asia Case Research Centre at HKU.

Zhao, Rushi 赵汝适. 1996. "Shanhu Shu 珊瑚树 [Coral Tree]". *Zhufan Zhi Jiaoshi* 诸蕃志校释 [Notes on Records of Foreign Countries]. Beijing: Zhonghua Book Company.

Zhou, Bida 周必大. 1990. *Wenzhong Ji* 文忠集 [Selected Works of Wenzhong]. Collected in Complete Library in the Four Branches of Literature. Shanghai: Shanghai Chinese Classics Publishing House.

Zhou, Hui 周辉撰. 1994. *Qingbo Zazhi Jiaozhu* 清波杂志校注 [Collected Works from Qingbo Annotated Version]. Beijing: Zhonghua Book Company.

Zhou, Mi 周密. 1988. *Guixin Zashi* 癸辛杂识 [Miscellaneous Records from Guixin Street]. Punctuated and collated by Wu Qiming. Beijing: Zhonghua Book Company.

Zhou, Qüfei 周去非. 1999. *Lingwai Daida Jiaozhu* 岭外代答校注 [Notes from the Land Beyond the Passes]. Collated by Yang Wuquan. Beijing: Zhonghua Book Company.

Zhou, Yinggu 周应谷. 1990. *Jingding Jiankang Zhi* 景定建康志 [Jingding Period Chronicles of Jiankang]. Collected in The Series of Chorography of the Song and Yuan Dynasties. Beijing: Zhonghua Book Company.

Zhu, Changwen 朱长文. 1990. *Wujun TujingXuji* 吴郡图经续记 [Continuation of the Chronicles of Wu County]. Collected in The Series of Chorography of the Song and Yuan Dynasties. Beijing: Zhonghua Book Company.

Zhu, Mu 祝穆. 1990. *Gujin Shiwen Leiju* 古今事文类聚 [Collection of Historical Records]. Collected in Complete Library in the Four Branches of Literature. Shanghai: Shanghai Chinese Classics Publishing House.

Zhu, Mu 祝穆. 2003. *Fangyu Shenglan* 方舆胜览 [Chronicles of Lin'an]. Edited by Shi Hejin. Beijing: Zhonghua Book Company.

Zhu, Xi 朱熹. 2010. *Hui'an Xiansheng Zhuwengong Ji* 晦庵先生朱文公文集 [Selected Works of Zhu Xi]. Punctuated and collated by Liu Yongxiang, et al. Shanghai: Shanghai Chinese Classics Publishing House. Heifei: Anhui Education Publishing House.

Chapter 4
Warships and Defense on the Yangtze River and the Sea in the Song Dynasty

4.1 Types of Warships and Ways of Battles on the Rivers and the Sea in the Song Dynasty

The Northern Song conquered the Southern Tang by breaking through its river defenses, which proved decisive in the victory of the Yangtze River battle. Later, the Southern Song focused on national defense on rivers and seas, placing great importance on shipbuilding. As a result, the number and variety of warships reached new heights. During this time, especially in the Southern Song Dynasty, warships of different shapes and structures were built for different purposes, including the widely deployed pedal wheel ships that made their debut in battles, as well as light and swift boats. The Song people even developed a preliminary plan for fleet composition. Sophisticated naval deployment and technologies were formed and demonstrated in battles, including those with Yang Yao in the Southern Tang, with Jin Wuzhu in Zhenjiang, with Wanyan Liang in Caishi county and Jiaoxi county, and with the ancient Mongolian navy. This study is significant in revealing the manufacturing level of warships, the power, and the new developments of sea defense in the Song Dynasty. In recent years, studies have been conducted on the classification of boats and warships, as well as discussions on pedal wheel ships in the Song Song Dynasty (Y. Shiba 1985; F. Xi 2000; J. Ge 2008; C. Huang 2013).[1] However, a dedicated and systematic examination of warships and sea battles in the Song Dynasty is yet to be thoroughly undertaken, which is the focus of this chapter.

[1] Warships are discussed in the classification of ships in the researches of Yoshinobu Shiba, Xi Longfei and Ge Jinfang. In addition, Fei Hanyong, Joseph Needham, Wang Zengyu and other scholars have done further studies on the pedal wheel ships in the Southern Song Dynasty.

C. Huang, *A Panoramic View of the Song Dynasty Through the Lens of Shipbuilding Industry*, https://doi.org/10.1007/978-981-97-6128-9_4

4.1.1 Shape, Structure and Function of Warships

The main differences between warships and common official or civilian ships, especially on inland rivers, were their driving force and function. Official and civilian ships, whether large or medium-sized, were usually powered by towlines, with the assistance of sails, barge poles, and paddles. In contrast, sea ships mainly relied on their sails, prioritizing cost and comfort over speed. However, warships relied on two factors to achieve victory. One factor was their combat function, and the other was their swiftness and flexibility. The former was related to their shape, structure, and function, while their power system determined the latter. Warships are also classified according to these two factors.

According to records from the Song Dynasty, more than 40 types of warships were named for their shapes, structures, and functions, including tower ships, Haihu warships, sea loach ships, Saury-shaped warships, Doujian warships, Zouge swift warships, warships covered with cowhide, Youting scouting boats, grasshopper boats, dagger-installed boats, groove boats, yellow dragon warships, black dragon warships, Shuangli warships, Pingcheng boats, victory warships, big swift boats, flagship boats, sand-proof boats, flat-bottomed boats, Feihu paddle wheel warships, iron gunwheel warships, horse-carrying boats, patrol boats, swift horse-carrying boats, Fuyang-made warships, pedal boats, passenger boats, cart-head boats, swift patrol boats, oar boats, board boats, iron-head boats, Luokuang boats, iron-hawk boats, firewood carrying boats, wave-reducing boats, scaling ladder boats, lion boats, Louzi boats, leather-made boats, small boats, and sheepskin rafts. In this section, the warships that were most commonly seen in documents and had the greatest influence, such as tower ships, Haihu warships, Saury-shaped warships, horse-carrying boats, patrol boats, dagger-installed boats, warships protected with cowhide, and sheepskin rafts will be introduced (G. Zeng 1990; Y. Lü 1990; Tianyige Cang Ming Chaoben Jiaozheng 2004; Toqta 1977: 4583; X. Lu 1990: 2396; Y. Zhou 1990: 1983; M. Xu 1987: 1747; S. Xu et al. 2014: 7127).

Tower ships were known for their large size and watch towers on board. According to historical records, the tower ship could carry three levels of towers surrounded by parapets and fences, with many holes left for soldiers inside to use weapons against outside aggression. The tower ship appeared like a 156-m-long castle, large enough for carriages to drive and horses to ride on. Flags were planted, fire-proof leather was used to protect the hull, and gun carriages, giant rocks, and liquid iron were installed (G. Zeng 1990). Tower ships were essential for sea battles in the Song Dynasty because they created a grand and magnificent figure. Tower ships were put into use in the Song Dynasty. In the first year of the Qiande Reign (AD 963), Jiaochuan Lake, also known as Jiangwu Lake, was dug in Kaifeng for military exercises. About a hundred tower ships were built and a navy called "Shuihujie" was organized to conduct combat drills in Jiangwu Lake (Y. Wang 2003: 2706). In the early years of the Jianyan Reign, the Southern Song built up a navy and named it Lingbo Tower Ship Navy (Toqta 1977: 4583). Indeed, tower ships could be seen in the Southern Song army. According to the records of Wang Zhiwang, the deployment of warships in the Southern Song Jiankang Navy was special but rational, with a few tower ships and many sea loach ships. People in the Southern Song Dynasty also built tower ships for the military defense of the Yangtze River (Z. Wang 1990).

The Haihu warship derived its name from its striking resemblance to a sea bird. *The General Record of Military Affairs* describes the ship's design as having a low stem and high stern, mimicking the form of a bird. To enhance stability and prevent capsizing during storms, floating plates were installed beneath the hull, mimicking the function of wings. Rawhide protected the hull, serving as ramparts, while flags, gongs, and battle drums were standard on board (G. Zeng 1990). The Haihu warship first appeared in the Tang Dynasty (Q. Li 1990), and remained in use during the Song Dynasty. In the third year of the Jianyan Reign (AD 1129), a 15-m-long Haihu warship with four sculls on each side was constructed at Pingjiang Prefecture Shipyard for 329 strings of 1000 coins and given to the Jiangning Prefecture Navy (S. Xu et al. 2014: 7126). The application of Haihu warship in battles on the Yangtze River is supported by Lu You's poem, which describes the ship sailing like a flying bird while under attack (Y. Lu 2011: 211).

The sea loach ship, also known as the loach-head ship, derives its name from its unique shape, and is mentioned in records from the Song Dynasty. The ship was over 33.3 m in length, and was described as "a black giant with stretching fins and swinging finlets." It sprayed water into the air, creating a hazy and misty effect, resembling the entrance of a dragon (Q. Chen 1990: 7587). Thus, it was also referred to as the "Hunjiang Dragon" ship. Among Yang Yao's navy, the main forces were pedal wheel ships, oar boats, and sea loach ships (Y. Lu 2012: 5). The number of pedal wheel ships and sea loach ships alone numbered in the hundreds (X. Li 2013: 1190). The loach-head ship was also used as a passenger boat in his navy (R. Zhang 1990). Even officers and army members in the Song Dynasty traveled by sea loach ship. As the record about Wang Zhiwang mentioned before, a few tower ships and many sea loach ships could be seen deployed in Jiankang Navy, providing evidence for the large amount of sea loach ships. For instance, prior to the battle of pacifying Yang Yao, no records of the deployment of such ships among the Song officers and army could be found. However, they became the major force in the Song navy in the last few years of the Shaoxing Reign. Records of river battles between the Song and Jin dynasties in Caishi county during the 31st year of the Shaoxing Reign (AD 1161) revealed that "the Song navy deployed sea loach ships to combat the Jin invaders" (Y. Wang 2003: 2709). This provides evidence for the significance of such ships in naval warfare during the Song Dynasty.

The Saury-shaped warship derives its name from its resemblance to the saury fish, and was first recorded in Song documents. It is a light and swift vessel, described in Guo Xiagzheng's poem as "sailing swiftly, rowed jointly by ten boatmen in fitting clothes, who were yelling happily as if they were coming ashore" (X. Guo 1990). The need for ten boatmen to row the vessel suggests that it is a relatively large craft. The Saury-shaped warship varies in shape and structure to suit local water conditions. Such vessels, used for patrolling coastal and river areas, were also referred to as fishing boats, distinct in shape and size from those used in the Qiantang River and the Yangtze River. The vessel features a small square stem, also known as the "dustpan on waves", a broad tern that separates waters, a large deck for carrying people, and a sharp and narrow bilge, resembling a razor blazing a trail through waves. Food supplies and arms were stored under the yellow board, and flags, arrows, and stones on the two sides. The Saury-shaped warship could carry up to 50 people and was around four meters wide and 16.6 m long, costing over 400 strings of 1000 coins each according to the price of civilian work material (S. Xu et al. 2014: 7125). However, vessels used in inland rivers like the Qiantang River and the Yangtze River were much smaller. Lu You described such a vessel in his poem, "sailing in broad waters, the boat was not even three meters long" (Y. Lu 2011: 163). The Northern and Southern Song dynasties deployed these vessels extensively in river battles, with Emperor Taizu of Song observing "the training of flying-fish sailors on such warships in the Bianhe River" (T. Li 2004: 338). The boundary river between the Song and Liao kingdoms also witnessed the flags of such warships. They were also used for inspection of river security in Bazhou, Hebei province (T. Li 2004: 1080, 1167). Five prefectures, including Qingzhou, Mizhou, Dengzhou, Laizhou and Weizhou, along Jingdong Province, were equipped with inspection commissions that sent out Saury-shaped warships to fight thieves (C. Chen 1990). Officers in coastal Guangnan East Province and Fujian Province also had these vessels. Cai Xiang wrote to the emperor that all Saury-shaped warships in the possession of Fuzhou, Quanzhou, Zhangzhou, and Xinghua Navy, and all ships belonging to the Inspection Commission, were required to be maintained (X. Cai 1996: 371). Additionally, these vessels were used by patrols in the West Sea in Gaungzhou and coastal army in Chaozhou (T. Li 2004: 1485; D. Ma 2011: 8306), indicating their widespread use in inland rivers and seas.

Horse-carrying boats were a type of large or medium-sized ship commonly used as warships for transporting horses. The Song people said that "no ship in the navy is bigger or tougher than horse-carrying boats. Forty officers make up a squad. A horse-carrying boat can hardly carry eight squads" (M. Xu 1987: 1716). Thus, its capacity was less than 400 people. The Song people also stated that only large boats could cross vast rivers. To cross one such a river, two horse-carrying boats were borrowed from the Jiangzhou and Chizhou Military Prefectures, along with experienced boatmen to transport people back and forth (G. Huang 1990). Wu Lin used boats with a load capacity of either 21 or 15 tons, costing 440 strings of 1000 coins each. The two ships with a load capacity of 21 tons could carry 25 horses and 38 people, helmsmen and sailors included. The ships with a load capacity of 15 tons could carry 18 horses and 28 people including helmsmen and sailors (S. Xu et al. 2014: 9107; X. Li 2000: 429; S. Wang 2012: 635–36).[2] According to *The General Record of Military Affairs*, the warships were sorted by size, using rice as the reference object of capacity. The weight of a person was equivalent to 60 kg of rice (G. Zeng 1990), which meant that a horse-carrying boat with a load capacity of 21 tons could carry 350 people.

---

[2] Zhang Zhen and Wang Shipeng believed that each horse-carrying boat costs more than 800 strings of 1000 coins. Zhang Zhen calculated that each ship could carry eighteen horses and 40 people, and Wang Shipeng's calculating result is that each boat could be loaded with 45 people. However, Zhang Zhen and Wang Shipeng' ideas about horse-carrying boats are only based on the personal calculation, so the discussion of this part depends on Wu Lin's remarks because he was the person in charge oāāf the batch transportation of horses.

However, it was not the largest boat. In the third year of the Jiatai Reign (AD 1203), as was recorded, four ships with a load capacity of 24 tons and six horse-carrying boats with a load capacity of 15 tons were built by the Palace Administration (S. Xu et al. 2014). A ship with a load capacity of 24 tons could accommodate 400 people. In the 15th year of the Jiading Reign (AD 1222), the manufacture commission-in-chief of Ezhou city built horse-carrying boats with load capacities of 45, 30, and 9 tons.

Horse-carrying boats showed strength in transporting soldiers, so they were extensively used as warships in areas ranging from Sichuan Province to Zhenjiang, alongside the Yangtze River. From October of the first year of the Qiandao Reign (AD 1165), horse-carrying boats were built to carry battle horses in Kuilu, Sichuan province, which stopped in November of the third year of the Qiandao Reign (AD 1167) (Y. Wang 2003: 2740). However, Sichuan did not quit producing horse-carrying boats. In the sixth year of the Qiandao Reign (AD 1170), about 117 horse-carrying boats had been built in Luzhou, Xuzhou, and other locations in Sichuan, and were sent to Jiangzhou and Chizhou commissioners-in-chief (S. Xu et al. 2014: 7133). According to the document, the commander-in-chief of Zhenjiang Navy went to Hubei province to buy logs with 50 thousand strings of 1000 coins, but he had not been seen back for years until he appeared with masses of bamboo rafts and horse-carrying boats, beating drums and gongs, causing a jam on the river (S. Hong, n.d.). This incident shows that horse-carrying boats existed in Xiazhou. In the 15th year of the Jiading Reign, the commissioner-in-chief of Ezhou city received an order from the emperor to build horse-carrying boats for military use (S. Xu et al. 2014: 7139). Besides Ezhou, Jiangzhou, and Chizhou, Jiankangfu Navy and Zhenjiang commissioners-in-chief also had horse-carrying boats. In the sixth year of the Chunxi Reign (AD 1179), 30 horse-carrying boats were produced by Zhenjiang Prefecture (X. Lu 1990: 2388; Y. Zhou 1990; S. Xu et al. 2014: 7133).

As patrol boats were light and swift, they were able to swiftly break through the Yuan troops' siege and provide aid to the Song troops in Xiangyang city. The Song navy built these boats, which were capable of carrying 30 soldiers, one bag of salt, and 200 bolts of cloth, in Junzhou. Under the leadership of Zhang Shun and Zhang Gui, the Song navy broke through the siege and arrived in Xiangyang. Based on their load capacity of people on board, patrol boats were small warships, boasting flexibility and speed (Songji Sanchao Zhwngyao Jianzheng 2010: 349). They were widely built and deployed by the Jiankang Military Prefecture in the late Southern Song Dynasty. In addition to their deployment in the Yangtze River area, Yongzhou and Wuzhou of Guangnan West Province built and deployed 100 patrol boats at a time, highlighting their popularity (Z. Li 1990).

The history of dagger-installed boats can be traced back to the Western Han Dynasty. According to some scholars, these boats derived their name from the weapons installed at the bilge (Q. Sima 1959: 2975). Others contend that a watch-tower was built on the boat and daggers were installed on it (Y. Wang 2003: 2702). During the Southern Song Dynasty, dagger-installed boats were used for coastal and river defense. Fujian Province constructed the Cuan boat, a kind of swift boat, which was later renamed as a dagger-installed boat due to their similar shapes and structures. Eight coastal counties in Fujian Province built 60 dagger-installed boats at a cost of over 50 thousand strings of 1000 coins, with each boat costing 833 strings of 1000 coins (K. Lang 1990: 7901).

In the first year of the Jianyan Reign (AD 1127), the Song people built dagger-installed boats and watchtowers to guard against Jin aggression, following rumors that the Jin Kingdom was building warships in Yanshan and about to attack (X. Li 2013: 201). During the Caishi River battle between Song and Jin in the 31st year of the Shaoxing Reign (AD 1161), dagger-installed boats were one of the main forces in the Song navy, along with warships covered with cowhide, sea loach ships, lion boats, and Louzi boats. Yu Yunwen deployed dagger-installed boats into five fleets, with two fleets sailing along the banks, one fleet in the middle carrying elite soldiers, and two on standby for emergencies. Although hundreds of the Jin warships covered the river, with 70 reaching the southern bank, the Song navy repelled the attack with the front dagger-installed boats, severed the enemy rear fleets with the hidden fleets in the bay, captured over 2000 enemy warships, and set fire to other enemy ships using light boats. During the battle, the Song also lined up small boats to safeguard the bank and charged at the enemy fleets with dagger-installed boats (M. Xu 1987: 1733–34, 1747; Toqta 1977: 11793; Y. Wang 2003: 2709). Based on the cost and function of dagger-installed boats in the Caishi battle, it can be inferred that they were not light or small boats but rather medium-sized ones.

Mengchong, a type of warship covered with cowhide, was so named due to its distinctive appearance. According to *The General Record of Military Affairs,* "such warships were protected by cowhide with paddle holes on both sides, rendering them impervious to attacks by arrows or stones. Windows and holes were opened in different directions to allow for crossbows and lances to be employed in close combat. It was said that warships covered with cowhide were built into small boats to enable rapid attacks on enemies" (G. Zeng 1990). However, in reality, they were constructed in both small and large sizes. As Liu Zihui noted, "large warships, such as Wuya ships and warships covered with cowhide, were easy to control, while small boats, such as gold-wing boats and tank boats, were more easily gathered" (Z. Liu 1990). Historical records indicate that during the Caishi battle, the Jin only used small ships, while the Song navy deployed warships covered with cowhide, all of which were large vessels. The Song soldiers charged ahead, breaking the enemy ships into pieces (M. Xu 1987: 1733–34, 1747; Toqta 1977: 11793; Y. Wang 2003: 2709). This suggests that warships covered with cowhide must have been of significant size. They were also utilized as sea-faring vessels, with Gong Rong receiving an order to construct 20 warships covered with cowhide to bolster coastal defense while serving as the mayor of Wenzhou (Z. Hong 1990). Generally, warships used at sea were of medium or large size.

The sheepskin raft was "a type of bladder, commonly made from sheepskin, which was inflated and able to float on water" (Toqta 1977: 14110). This type of raft was widely used in northern regions, where it played a vital role in military operations. It was recorded that "when the army ran across a river, but no other ships were available, then sheepskin rafts would help" (Toqta 1977: 10827). Moreover, the use of sheepskin rafts was a necessity on the northwest battlefields. During the Song dynasty's campaigns against the West Xia Kingdom, ropes and sheepskin rafts were a standard part of the army's equipment, as no other boats were available (T. Li 2004: 7643). The West Xia army also regarded sheepskin rafts as a military necessity, and allocated them to officers above the commissioner of the self-defense group, along with other supplies such as tents, bows, ropes, shovels, axes, shields, and wire strainers (Toqta 1977: 14028). Sheepskin rafts were also used as a military supply, as evidenced by Xu Huiyan's request for seamen skilled in sailing dagger-installed boats to embark on sheepskin rafts and attack enemies in swift currents (Toqta 1977: 13192). In the battles between the Song and Yuan dynasties, the Yuan navy used cowhide to construct sheepskin rafts and hide rafts. These rafts were instrumental in the Yuan's victory at Xuzhou, where they were used in fierce battles against the Song navy. Additionally, during combat at Chuzhou, Gong Yanhui led a Yuan army unit on sheepskin rafts to cross the river at night and launch a surprise attack on the Song camps, highlighting the strategic importance of these rafts (L. Song 1976: 3641, 3899). To handle various water situations, warships were designed to be versatile, with different shapes and structures to suit different needs.

4.1.2 Power Systems of Warships in the Song Dynasty

In the Song Dynasty, whether it was for grain shipping or long distance voyages, the most reliable method for towing large or medium-sized civilian ships was human labor. However, this method was not suitable for warships. The effectiveness of a battleship's power depended on either manpower or wind power, and in the case of warships, power had to come from the vessel itself. The Southern Song warships employed two types of manpower: wheel fans and paddles. The use of wind and sails as a driving force was also common in inland ships, but this was not always possible due to the changeable wind directions. The sea warships, on the other hand, frequently utilized wind and sails as a source of power.

During the Southern Song Dynasty, warships propelled by pedal wheels were known as pedal wheel ships. These ships were equipped with wheels on both sides, each wheel having an axle positioned in the middle. Referred to as "a wheel," it served as the power source. By having sailors use their feet to drive the wheels, which would roll in the water, the warships were able to obtain the necessary propulsion. A pedal wheel ship could feature multiple wheels, ranging from a dozen or two, to as many as 30 or 40. The larger pedal wheel ships could reach impressive heights. It is reported that the largest pedal wheel ship measured 120 m in length, 14.6 m in width, and stood 24.2 m tall, with 40 wheels providing its power. During the conflict between the Song navy and Yang Yao's navy, both sides deployed pedal wheel ships, ranging from those equipped with 8 wheels to those with over 20 wheels, capable of carrying 200 to 300 soldiers. Some ships, boasting two or three levels of towers, could accommodate over one thousand soldiers (K. Yue 1989: 1568; K. Xiong 1985: 171). The large pedal wheel ships even surpassed the size of traditional sea warships. In battle, the Song navy faced the eight-wheel pedal ships of Yang Yao's navy. Due to their lower position, soldiers aboard the river ships and sea warships of the Song navy had to ascend ladders to engage in combat. Exploiting the advantages presented by the magnificent pedal wheel ships, Yang Yao's fleet wrecked and overwhelmed the Song sea warships, driving them into the water. The production, maintenance, and operational costs of pedal wheel ships far exceeded those of ordinary vessels. According to reports, the construction of a pedal wheel ship incurred significant expenses (G. Li 2004: 960).

Pedal wheel ships referred to various types of warships equipped with wheels. In *A Tale of Warships Covered with Cowhide,* Zhou Zizhi described how "sailors played the drums and waved flags on the stem, but nothing could be heard or seen on the stern" (Z. Zhou 1990). These warships covered with cowhide were examples of pedal wheel ships. Emperor Xiaozong further affirmed this connection by stating that "the pedal wheel ships were the once called warships covered with cowhide" (R. Zhang 1990). Yang Wanli commented on the warships in the Caishi battle, stating that "the warships covered with cowhide were large and magnificent, while the sea loach ships were small and speedy. Battlements were constructed on these ships" (D. Ma 2011: 4743). According to his account, the warships covered with cowhide were also pedal wheel ships. Another example was the Feihu pedal wheel warship created by Wang Yanhui. It was described as having "four wheels installed on each side, with eight oars on each wheel, and four people operating these wheels" (Y. Zhou 1990: 1960). In the second year of the Duanping Reign (AD 1235), Wei Liaoweng advised the emperor to allocate funds to Hu'nan, Jiangnan West Province, and the military commissions along the river, allowing them to order subordinate counties to produce wood and assemble armies to build sea loach ships with four wheels and various-sized multi-paddle ships (L. Wei, n.d.; D. Peng 2003: 407, 412). This demonstrates that sea loach ships were also modified into wheel-powered ships, showcasing smaller versions of pedal wheel ships.

Multi-paddle ships relied on the motion generated by numerous paddles. Wei Liaoweng advised the emperor to construct sea loach ships with four wheels and multi-paddle ships of various sizes in Hu'nan, Jiangnan West Provinces, as well as in counties and armies along the river. This indicates that wheels and paddles were the primary sources of power for warships in the Song Dynasty. Multi-paddle ships, propelled by multiple paddles, possessed the advantages of flexibility and speed, and were extensively utilized on both the sea and inland rivers. The term "multi-paddle boat" served as a general designation for ships of diverse shapes and structures that operated with multiple paddles. One type of multi-paddle ship documented in *Shouchang Record: Warships* was the Caodi Boat, equipped with 18 paddles, two masts, two sails, 18 canopies, and 10 barge poles. Wind power and barge poles could also serve as alternative means of propulsion when necessary. These boats had load capacities of 6, 7.5, 9, and 10.5 tons. According to illustrations found in *The General Record of Military Affairs*, Haihu warships were also multi-paddle ships (G. Zeng 1990). In the early Southern Song Dynasty, Li Gang advised the prefectures along the rivers, such as the Yellow River, the Yangtze River, and the Huaihe River, to construct warships based on ancient standards, which were multi-paddle ships. These ships featured watch towers that facilitated archery and utilized the stem and long oars to navigate through waves (G. Li 2004: 666). The majority of Yang Yao's warships were pedal wheel ships, sea loach ships and multi-paddle ships (Y. Lu 2012: 5). Prior to their transformation into wheel-powered pedal wheel ships, sea loach ships also utilized multiple paddles for propulsion. Various types of multi-paddle ships were extensively deployed in the Southern Song navy. In the fifth year of the Qiandao Reign (AD 1169), Feng Zhan, the navy commissioner-in-chief, built a multi-paddle ship suitable for different water conditions. It incorporated the bilge of a lake ship, the cover of a warship, and the stem and stern of a seagoing ship. It was 27.6 m long and 6.6 m with a load capacity of 24 tons in the Huai ruler. It sailed with 42 paddles and performed exceptionally well in all water conditions, be it sea, rivers, or lakes. Despite carrying 200 armed soldiers, it maintained impressive speed due to its flat bilge, enabling it to navigate even in water depths as shallow as 0.3 m. Emperor Xiaozong of Song ordered the construction of 50 similar multi-paddle ships (S. Xu et al. 2014: 7133).

In the third year of the Chunxi Reign (AD 1176), Guo Gang, commander-in-chief of Jiankang, advised the construction of more multi-paddle ships by replicating sea warships. Emperor Xiaozong agreed to increase the production of multi-paddle ships, with the condition that there would be no reduction in pedal wheel ships or the conversion of pedal wheel ships into multi-paddle ships. It was documented that "multi-paddle ships could only be built by military prefectures themselves and could not replace pedal wheel ships" (Y. Wang 2003: 2710). During Emperor Lizong's Reign, the Jiankang Navy continued to construct new multi-paddle ships. Between April of the first year of the Kaiqing Reign (AD 1259) and March of the second year of the Jingding Reign (AD 1261), the Jiankang Navy built five light multi-paddle ships. From November of the second year of the Jingding Reign (AD 1261) to April of the third year of the Jingding Reign (AD 1262), they constructed 34 multi-paddle ships (Y. Zhou 1990: 1984). Zhou Bida requested in his proposal submitted to Emperor Xiaozong that the court should provide funds and grain to Zhenjiang for the construction of multi-paddle ships (B. Zhou 1990).

Compared to the high cost of building a pedal wheel ship, multi-paddle ships were significantly cheaper while still maintaining their swiftness. Consequently, there was an increase in the construction of not only multi-paddle ships, but also ships with paddles or wheels. In the fifth year of the Shaoxing Reign (AD 1135), shipbuilders in the Jiangnan and Liangzhe provinces were instructed to imitate the Hu'nan-style ships, which were equipped with five wheels and ten paddles. Subsequently, the court allocated ship quotas to different provinces: fourteen each for Liangzhe East and West provinces, twelve for Jiangnan East Province, and sixteen for Jiangnan West Province, at a cost of 1000 strings of 1000 coins. These ships served as supplementary vessels to the larger pedal wheel ships due to their higher speeds. Each ship had a cost of 1000 strings of 1000 coins. In the fourth year of the Qiandao Reign (AD 1168), 100 thousand strings of 1000 coins were allocated to Jiankang prefecture to construct additional 400-Liao warships with one wheel and twelve paddles (S. Xu et al. 2014: 7130, 7132). In the 3rd year of the Jiatai Reign (AD 1203), the 400-Liao iron gunwheel warship built by Qin Shifu in Chizhou was also equipped with both wheels and paddles. According to historical documents, two wheels and three paddles were installed on each side. The ship measured 30.6 m in length, 5 m in width, and 1.6 m in height, with a bilge width of 2.8 m. It could accommodate 70 soldiers and 20 boatmen (S. Xu et al. 2014: 7138). In comparison to the large pedal wheel ships that could accommodate hundreds to a thousand people, ships with both wheels and paddles required less space.

Multi-oar ships were also common warships in the Southern Song Dynasty. The placement of oars made them less flexible than paddle-ships, resulting in them being less popular than multi-paddle ships. However, unlike paddles, the oars did not need to leave the water when the boat was sailing, allowing them to work continuously. In contrast, half of the paddle was above the water when it was in use, resulting in a waste of power. Therefore, oars were more effective than paddles. In the third year of the Jianyan Reign (AD 1129), Pingjiang Prefecture built 400-Liao warships with eight oars, as well as Haihu warships with four oars, which were later transferred to Jiangning Prefecture (S. Xu et al. 2014: 7126). During the Qiandao Reign, multi-oar ships such as the 700-Liao horse-carrying ships equipped with four oars and the 500-Liao ships with two oars were used in Sichuan (S. Xu et al. 2014: 9104). These examples demonstrate the prevalence of multi-oar ships during that period. Additionally, during the Baoyou Reign, the Jiankang Navy constructed warships in Jizhou, Jiangnan West Province, including fifty 300-Liao sea ships with four oars and fifty 250-Liao Fuyang ships with four oars (Y. Zhou 1990: 1983). This further indicates that multi-oar ships were used not only as inland ships but also as sea ships.

Sea ships were the representative warships in the Song Dynasty, but they were not the only ones powered by wind. This included sea ships used in inland rivers. The previously mentioned Caodi ships and flat-bottomed boats were equipped with barge poles and wind canopies. Ships used for civilian and official purposes primarily relied on towing, paddles, and oars, with sails providing assistance. Due to the changeable presence, strength, and directions of wind in inland rivers, coupled with swift currents, it was not feasible for warships to rely solely on wind power. They needed timely and continuous propulsion. Therefore, warships used in inland rivers primarily relied on wheels, paddles, and oars for propulsion. As mentioned earlier, sea ships could be multi-paddle ships or multi-oar ships. However, large sea ships, such as pedal wheel ships, were not suitable for paddles and oars as their primary source of power. Instead, they relied on wind power. Thus, sea ships were the main force in naval battles at sea. Therefore, this discussion will focus solely on the use of ships in inland rivers.

Sea ships were renowned for their large size and capacity to carry a substantial number of soldiers. The presence of a tailwind significantly enhanced their sailing capabilities. It is documented that "sea ships had eight wind canopies, rendering them flexible and fast, surpassing even the helmsman" (S. Ye 1961: 14). Due to the Southern Song navy's limited development of shipbuilding techniques and scales, sea ships were primarily utilized as the main warships in inland battles. In the third year of the Jianyan Reign (AD 1129), Emperor Gaozong conducted an inspection tour in Yangzhou and issued an order to "dock the sea ships along the banks of Zhenjiang." These ships were exclusively managed by Commander-in-Chief Wang Yuan for river defense, transportation, and emergencies (X. Li 2013: 446–47; Toqta 1977: 11486). A year later, during Han Shizhong's retreat from Huainan East Province to

Liangzhe West Province, his troops sailed on sea ships, carrying soldiers, horses, family members, and essential supplies. Han also employed sea ships as the primary warships in the battle against the Jin army in Zhenjiang. "In the battle, the sea ships promptly opened their canopies to take advantage of the favorable wind, sailing swiftly as if flying" (X. Li 2013: 747–48). In the conquest of Yang Yao and his forces, the Song Navy deployed sea ships, which were smaller than Yang Yao's pedal wheel ships. This necessitated Song soldiers to "climb ladders from their ships to board the enemy's vessels" (X. Li 2013: 1356, 1364). During the Caishi battle, Yu Yunwen ordered the navy to utilize sea ships when a tailwind was present and pedal wheel ships when wind was unavailable, demonstrating their deployment under different water conditions (Toqta 1977: 11794).

After the establishment of the river defense system, sea ships assumed a prominent role in garrisoning strategic downstream defensive locations, particularly in Zhenjiang, Jiangying, and Xupu. By the fourth year of the Jianyan Reign (AD 1130), over 400 sea ships had been assembled in Zhenjiang (S. Yang et al. 1990). In the fifth year of the Shaoxing Reign (AD 1135), Fujian received orders to construct 700 sea ships, which were to be dispersed throughout Jiangzhou city during normal periods and consolidated and utilized when necessary (Toqta 1977: 11608). In the second year of the Kaixi Reign (AD 1206), a mobilization effort was undertaken from Xupu Military Agency, Wenzhou, and Fuzhou, involving 45 sea ships, 27 passenger ships, over 800 sailors, as well as seamen, totaling more than 2480 individuals. Their purpose was to support river defense in the areas of Jiaoshan and Jinshan in Zhenjiang (X. Lu 1990: 2390). The sea ships and Danan ships originating from Fujian Province typically berthed at the Gujing Navy Camps (S. Xu et al. 2014: 7137). In the second year of the Duanping Reign (AD 1235), Wei Liaoweng proposed the consolidation of sea ships from regions such as Zhenjiang, Jiangying, and Pingjiang to upstream areas like Gong'an County and Shishou County to establish standby fleets for emergency situations (L. Wei, n.d.).

4.1.3 The Function and Deployment of the Song Warships

The variety of warships in the Song Dynasty demonstrated the advancement in technical capabilities for river and sea warfare. Each warship possessed its own strengths and weaknesses when engaged in actual combat. People endeavored to develop a versatile warship that could adapt to various situations. For example, the Liao Kingdom designed an amphibious ship described as follows: "As a large boat, it was recorded that it was usually installed with four wheels which enabled it to run on the ground carrying military supplies and soldiers. But when sailing on the ponds and the Yangtze River, its wheels would be removed, it could sail on the river to carrying people and horses across the river. It was expected to come from the east of Cangzhou on the water, severing the reinforcements of enemies" (S. Fang 2006: 215). However, this concept was never implemented. In the sixth year of the Chunxi Reign (AD 1179), Emperor Xiaozong ordered Jiangnan West Province to build 100 horse-carrying ships, equipped with detachable wheel propellers, serving both transportation and combat purposes (S. Xu et al. 2014: 7136). They were intended to be dual-function ships. However, these versatile ships could not fully replace specialized warships. In reality, effective battles necessitated the coordination and supplementation of various types of warships.

Large warships played a significant role in naval deployments, exhibiting a sense of grandeur and serving as essential assets. Wang Zhiwang observed that the composition of the Jiankang navy deviated from conventional warship deployments, with only a few tower ships and a larger number of sea loach ships in use, failing to exert substantial pressure on the enemy (Z. Wang 1990). He deemed the construction of tower ships necessary (G. Zeng 1990). The advantage of large warships lay in their imposing stature. For example, Yang Yao's navy consistently triumphed over the Song navy due to the deployment of numerous large warships such as "Wangsanzhou", "Hezhouzai", "Five Towers", "Nine Towers", "Dade Mountain", and "Xiaode Mountain", totaling 3000 (K. Yue n.d.; K. Yue 1989: 321, 1599). His pedal wheel ships were extremely large, with Hezhouzai and Dade Mountain featuring 24 and 22 pairs of wheels, respectively (K. Yue 1989: 1568). In contrast, the majority of the Song soldiers were originally sailors mobilized from Huainan, whose primary warships consisted of smaller sea ships and lake ships compared to Yang's pedal wheel ships (X. Li 2013: 1356). This discrepancy in vessel size proved crucial in Yang's repeated victories.

The disadvantage of large warships lies in their heaviness, lack of swiftness, and difficulty in control. "In times of storms, they were too difficult to control, and very inconvenient for sailing" (G. Zeng 1990). Wind power has limitations and a potentially fatal flaw when it comes to large sea ships engaged in inland river battles. This was evident in the Zhenjiang battle between Han Shizhong and the Jin navy. Due to the large size of their ships and the advantage of a tailwind, Han's sea ships displayed exceptional maneuverability, resulting in the defeat of the Jin navy. However, when the wind ceased, the sea ships became immobile, providing an opportunity for the Jin troops to launch fire arrows. Consequently, Han's troops had to abandon the sea ships and escape in light boats, experiencing a devastating defeat. If the one thousand reinforcements, led by Pu Lun, who saved Han, had been strategically positioned alongside the sea ships from the outset, the Han forces would have likely avoided failure (Y. Zhou 1990: 1959; M. Xu 1987: 1003). Numerous instances occurred during the Song Dynasty where sea ships were outmatched by pedal wheel ships and multi-paddle ships in inland river battles. In the battles to conquer Yang Yao, the Song navy relied solely on small boats with pointed stems and sterns, as well as sea ships, which were inconvenient for combat on lakes. The Yang forces utilized pedal wheel ships to their advantage by rolling the wheels and overwhelming the Song troops (K. Yue 1989: 1573). In the late Southern Song Dynasty, Zhang Shijie confronted the Yuan navy in Zhenjiang. In the absence of wind, the sea ships of Zhang's navy remained motionless, while the patrol boats of the Yuan navy swiftly glided across the water like fish. Without reinforcements, Zhang's forces suffered defeat, resulting in the sinking of all seamen and ships to the river floor (Songji Sanchao Zhwngyao Jianzheng 2010: 378). Consequently, sea ships were deemed less valuable in inland river battles compared to pedal wheel ships, multi-paddle ships, and multi-oar ships, despite occasional usage.

Medium-sized warships possessed the advantages of being light and swift of being light and swift. In the fifth year of the Shaoxing Reign (AD 1135), large pedal wheel ships with nine or 13 pairs of wheels, were constructed in Jiangnan East and West, as well as Liangzhe East and West provinces. Emperor Gaozong issued an order to build and utilize medium-sized warships with five pairs of wheels and 10 paddles as an equal alternative. These warships were lightweight, fast, and complementary to their larger counterparts (S. Xu et al. 2014: 7130). The aforementioned types, such as Haihu ships, horse-carrying ships, dagger-installed ships, Caodi ships (ranging from 200 to 300 Liao), as recorded in *The Chronicle of Shouchang Military Prefecture,* along with flat-bottomed boats (250 Liao), were all categorized as medium-sized warships. They possessed unique qualities that made them indispensable when compared to large warships. For instance, the saury-shaped ship was flexible and well-suited for navigating inland rivers and shallow seas. It performed admirably in small rivers, such as the boundary river between the Song and Liao states (T. Li 2004: 1070). It was most frequently used for capturing pirates. In the Northern Song Dynasty, officers in Dengzhou ensured an abundant supply of saury-shaped ships as a deterrent against pirate invasions (Toqta 1977: 10493). Similarly, in Liangzhe provinces, riverside and coastal prefectures and counties relied on saury-shaped ships to defeat rampant pirates (S. Xu et al. 2014: 8842). The Coastal Inspection Commissions of Qingzhou, Mizhou, Dengzhou, Laizhou, and Weizhou in Jingdong Province even bestowed upon it the honorary title of "saury-shaped warship, the pirate killer on the sea" (C. Chen 1990). This type of ship was also utilized in Fuzhou, Quanzhou, Zhangzhou of Fujian, as well as the Xinghua Navy, for pirate suppression in the Northern Song Dynasty (K. Lang 1990: 7942). However, it could only sail on shallow seas, restricting its function in sea battles. In the 28th year of the Shaoxing Reign (AD 1158), Fujian Province was ordered to build saury-shaped ships for Chen Min, the left-wing commander. The Fujian officers considered that the original design of saury-shaped ships was suitable for sailing in the shallow seas of Mingzhou, but the deep and expansive waters of Fujian and Guangnan presented different conditions. Consequently, they modified the design into a pointy-bottomed ship with a one-meter-long bilge and 10-m-wide hull (K. Yue 1989: 1573).

Small boats also played a crucial role in battles. Their primary function was to transmit information and relay orders among warships. In the third year of the Jianyan Reign (AD 1129), when the Song officers were consolidating river defenses, they selected two small boats along with skilled seamen, assigning three seamen to each boat. These seamen were rewarded with 300 coins each. The two small boats were specifically designated for conveying confidential military orders and the latest information about the enemies (S. Xu et al. 2014: 9486). During battles, such small boats were utilized for issuing orders since it was challenging for the navy to discern instructions solely through flag signals or drum beats. In the Song Dynasty, regulations prohibited civilians from constructing warships while allowing the construction of common ships. However, a kind of small boat called Diezi (Tianyige Cang Ming Chaoben Jiaozheng 2004: 347) was in the forbidden list. "Diezi" refers to small boats in Chinese and is described as being "as light as a leaf" (Z. Wu 2012: 137). *The General Record of Military Affairs* used the term "Zouge" to describe these small boats. It was written that Zouge were propelled by multiple boatmen, primarily strong and courageous soldiers, enabling them to swiftly maneuver like a seagull, delivering unexpected attacks on enemy ships. Drums and flags were installed on Zouge boats (G. Zeng 1990). *The Record of Loyal Generals* documented an incident during the Yashan battle, where the Song navy established military camps on the river, deploying thousands of large ships. In response, the Yuan navy amassed their own large ships to disrupt the supply lines to the Song camps. However, the Yuan side predominantly relied on sea ships for this purpose. It was the absence of small patrol ships from the Yuan side that allowed the Song's light boats to easily retrieve wood and water supplies. Later, the Yuan troops dispatched patrol boats to block the waterway, preventing the Song troops from obtaining sufficient supplies. This episode underscores the significance of small boats in battles.

Taking into consideration the differences and complementarity of various ships, the Song people put forward a blueprint for fleet composition. According to *The General Record of Military Affairs*, each ship had its specific usage. The tower ships were indispensable in battles as they showcased the majesty of the fleet. However, large ships, such as tower ships and warships, lacked flexibility and speed. Therefore, they were used to enhance the magnificence of the fleet and serve as storage for tools and weapons. In contrast, Zouge boats and Haihu boats were designed to meet the demands of high speed and efficiency. Within the fleet, tower ships, Doujian warships, Zouge boats, and Haihu ships would engage in combat with the enemy on the water. Warships covered with cowhide and Youting scouting boats would carry out attacks on the water (G. Zeng 1990). As Ye Mengde stated, "some ships were deployed for the advantages of their shapes and structures, while others were used for their strong combat capabilities" (M. Ye 2002). With the establishment of a river and coastal defense system in the Southern Song Dynasty, the construction of warships rapidly developed. The Song people learned from their experiences in battles on water, and their ideas regarding fleet composition were successfully applied in real battles.

More people discussed the functions and usages of different warships during the Southern Song Dynasty. Liu Zihui proposed that ships, regardless of their size, had distinct functions. He believed that "large ships, such as Wuya ships and warships covered with cowhide, could take the lead in battles, while small boats, like Jinchi boats and tank boats, were advantageous in terms of mobility. The large warships featured high watchtowers, throwing tools as weapons, and long oars as propulsion, providing ample space to accommodate soldiers and horses. Elite soldiers from the northwest regions could be stationed at crucial positions on these warships. To maximize the effectiveness of such boats, sailors from the Wuyue regions were the preferred choice as soldiers on board due to their agility, bravery, and expertise in diving. Upon diving into the water, they could skillfully break the ship's hull in huge swells like performing a magic show, scaring the enemy to death" (Z. Liu 1990). The aforementioned analysis supports Liu's idea that different ships should be manned by sailors with distinct skills. Lü Yihao stated that "warships covered with cowhide and Doujian warships should be constructed and deployed along the Yangtze River, and their roles in the ancient Battle of the Red Cliffs were also analyzed. Additionally, the significance of small ships like Zouge boats could not be ignored." He further added, "currently, it is possible to create the kind of giant warships that are composed of multiple ships. From ancient times to the present, ships such as tower ships, Haihu ships, Youting scouting boats, and others have all been essential in naval battles. I have witnessed warship drills in Xiongzhou and Bazhou, where saury-shaped ships and scaling ladder boats were crucial to the fleet" (Y. Lü 1990). Wang Yingchen pointed out that during battles, boats required coordinated efforts to approach the shore. He emphasized that "when the battlefield shifted from the sea to the land, only large ships could safely navigate the sea, only tide boats could transport sailors to the river branches, and only small boats could be used for landing" (Y. Wang 1990).

Zhang Yi conducted further research and asserted that a fleet should consist of warships with distinct functions. "Ships would be categorized into three types: large ships serving as front-line vessels, medium-sized warships, and small boats functioning as order transmission vessels. A battle fleet valued stability and solidarity, which is why large ships were utilized as battle ships. Additionally, a fleet required flexibility and high speed, making medium-sized ships crucial. Since traditional communication methods like beating drums and waving flags were ineffective in torrents, small boats sailed back and forth to deliver messages. This demonstrates that there is no universal requirement for large ships, and vessels of all sizes can be strategically deployed in a battle fleet to secure victory." Emperor Gaozong embraced Zhang Yi's proposal and "directed the relevant departments in Huainan provinces to address shipbuilding matters" (X. Li 2013: 968), which had a significant impact on the construction of the navy and actual naval battles during the Southern Song dynasty.

In the conquest of Yang Yao and his men, more concrete ideas about fleet composition were developed. For example, Li Gang pointed out that pedal wheel ships should be accompanied by medium-sized sea loach ships in battles. He believed that due to their heaviness and size, pedal wheel ships were well-suited for navigating large rivers and lakes and overcoming stormy waves, making them pivotal in a fleet. A pedal wheel ship would be accompanied by a dozen sea loach ships, much like the cooperation between light chariots with pointed tree branches and Wugang heavy chariots in ground battles (G. Li 2004: 1165). The third year of the Shaoxing Reing (AD 1133) marked the most challenging period in the conquest of Yang Yao and his rebel forces. Zhe Zhiyan recommended the formation of a mixed fleet consisting of pedal wheel ships and sea loach ships because he believed that pedal wheel ships acted as soldiers in a fixed formation, while sea loach ships provided the ability to respond rapidly. He also determined the number of warships to be constructed and the proportions of pedal wheel ships and sea loach ships in the navy. According to his plan, a navy of 10,000 soldiers would be divided into five branches. Each branch would be allocated two pedal wheel ships, carrying 250 soldiers and over a hundred boatmen each, and 30 sea loach ships, carrying 50 soldiers and 82 boatmen each (X. Li 2013: 1293). "Sea loach ships would cooperate with pedal wheel ships, strategically charging or retreating. When they advanced, enemy ships would be attacked, and when they retreated, the enemies would be lured" (S. Xu et al. 2014: 8813). She

Yanzhi had served as the Xuanfu Commissioner to Hu'nan from the second year to the fourth year of the Shaoxing Reign (AD 1132–1134), during which he was responsible for combating Yang Yao. His advice was based on his own experiences. In battle, the vanguard of the Song navy consisted of a "Dade Mountain ship, three pedal wheel ships equipped with 18 pedals, and 30 sea loach ships, sailing at the rear of the fleet to safeguard the front troops." Such fleet composition followed She Yanzhi's strategy. "The enemy pursued the Song navy with numerous ships until they met and engaged in a fierce fight in the broadest area of the Fengjinkou River. Sensing the danger, Commander Xing Xian immediately dispatched small boats to relay messages to the ships at the front of the formation. General Commander Du Zhan, on a three-storey tower ship, came to assist Mr. Xing and his troops. The tower ship showered the enemy ships with hundreds of arrows, forcing them to retreat slightly. The barrage of arrows continued, and the enemies retreated" (K. Yue 1989: 1575). Pedal wheel ships and sea loach ships were crucial for achieving victory in the battle, but small boats also played a significant role in transmitting information.

The Battle of Caishi provides another example of a mixed fleet composed of pedal wheel ships, sea loach ships, dagger-installed ships, horse-carrying ships, light Zouge boats, and more. In the 31st year of the Shaoxing Reign (AD 1161), Wanyan Liang launched a southward invasion into the Song territory, occupying the Huaihe River and reaching the Yangtze River. Yu Yunwen assumed the perilous task and led the Song navy. The pedal wheel ships left behind by Wang Quan, the former leader of the Song navy, were still stationed there (R. Zhang 1990). Commanders Cai and Han each commanded a large warship and feigned agreement to join the battle but took no action. Yu Yunwen ordered the local militia to board the sea loach ships and pedal the wheels to launch an immediate counterattack (X. Li 2013: 3788). The aforementioned large warships and sea loach ships were all pedal wheel ships. The large pedal wheel ships possessed military power that struck fear into the enemy. On November 19, "when the aggressive Jin army saw the pedal wheel ships, they immediately retreated" (R. Zhang 1990). Sea loach ships played a pivotal role in this battle. On November 18, "the Song navy fought desperately on sea loach ships in the middle of the river, capturing tens of thousands of enemy ships and killing numerous foes." On November 19, "sea loach ships were dispatched to the northern bank to block the Yanglin ferry crossing. Under a barrage of arrows from the Song's ships, the Jin soldiers abandoned their ships and went ashore, only to find themselves sinking in the mud to their deaths" (Y. Zhou 1990: 1960). Therefore, some have attributed the victory in the Battle of Caishi to the sea loach ships (D. Fang 1990). Furthermore, the dagger-installed ships and light Zouge ships deserve credit for the victory on November 18. "The dagger-installed ships charged forward, shooting arrows at enemy boats. The enemies attempted to retreat, but the concealed dagger-installed ships attacked them from behind, capturing over 30 enemy ships. Subsequently, the light Zouge boats were deployed to set fire to the remaining enemy ships" (R. Zhang 1990).

After suffering defeat in the Battle of Caishi, Wanyan Liang attempted to cross the river from Guazhou. Yu Yunwen hurried to Zhenjiang to fortify the river defense.

Following Yu Yunwen's orders, 24 pedal wheel ships were stationed along the riverbank for use by the Song navy, shuttling between Guazhou and the river. The Jin army was astonished to witness the patrol of these massive ships in the middle of the river (Y. Zhou 1990: 1960), demonstrating the intimidation factor of pedal wheel ships. Yu Yunwen also mobilized sea loach ships and dagger-installed ships, as well as transformed horse-carrying ships. At that time, 200,000 soldiers had gathered in Jingkou, with fewer than a hundred sea loach ships and approximately 50 dagger-installed ships available (Toqta 1977: 11794). Yu Yunwen dispatched a hundred dagger-installed ships to Jingkou (X. Yuan 1990). Due to the limited number of warships, he collected wood and forged iron, converting horse-carrying ships into warships (Toqta 1977: 11794). This fleet showcased strength and grandeur on the Yangtze River. The Song sailors shouted and challenged the Jin navy from their ships in the middle of the river. In the sunlight, their weapons and armor gleamed. Warships covered in cowhide, sea ships, sea loach ships, dagger-installed ships, lion boats, Louzi boats, and others were seen sailing swiftly back and forth, striking fear into the enemy (M. Xu 1987: 1747). Wanyan Liang compelled his soldiers to immediately cross the river. However, his troops, already lacking faith in victory, turned against him and killed him. Thus, the Song navy achieved victory without engaging in a battle.

The types of ships deployed at key river defense points in the Song Dynasty reflected their functions, structures, and fleet composition. River defense in Jiankang received top priority. In the second year of the Longxing Reign (AD 1164), Wang Zhiwang witnessed the presence of approximately 1000 ships in Jiankang Prefecture, of which over 470 were pedal wheel ships. Emperor Xiaozong allocated more resources to develop river defense after the Battle of Caishi, leading to an unprecedented flourishing of warships (Z. Wang 1990). Both large and small warships predominantly adopted the structure of pedal wheel ships, which was also the case in other river defense areas, except for Jiankang Prefecture. During a journey to Sichuan, Lu You observed military training in Ezhou, where 700 gigantic warships, ranging from 66.6 to 100 m in length, equipped with watchtowers and ramparts, sailed at incredible speed, breaking through stormy waves, accompanied by waving flags and thundering drums (Y. Lu 2012: 197). These swift giants were undoubtedly pedal wheel ships. In the ninth year of the Chunyou Reign (AD 1249), Jiankang Prefecture continued to employ a variety of warships. Newly built and repaired ships included cart-head boats, swift patrol boats, board boats, iron-head boats, Luokuang boats, pedal boats, iron-hawk boats, firewood-carrying boats, horse-carrying ships, Fuyang-made passenger ships, sea ships with four oars, pedal wheel ships with four wheels, patrol boats, groove boats, paddle ships, multi-oar ships, light multi-paddle ships, and large multi-paddle ships. Around the seventh year of the Jiading Reign (AD 1214), the Zhenjiang General Commission possessed pedal wheel ships, dagger-installed ships, horse-carrying ships, sea ships, light ships, multi-paddle ships, Cuan ships, sea loach ships, and others (X. Lu 1990: 2396).

Later, the structure of warships in river defense during the late Southern Song Dynasty shifted towards lighter and more flexible boats. According to the *Jingding Period Chronicles of Jiankang*, the number of warships newly built and repaired by

Jiankang from the ninth year of the Chunyou Reign (AD 1249) to the first year of the Xianchun Reign (AD 1265) ranged from 500 to 1400, indicating a trend towards lighter structures. In the military exercises in February of the ninth year, 422 ships were built, including 50 cart-head boats, 50 swift patrol boats, 99 paddle boats, 180 board boats, 10 iron-head boats, three Luokuang boats, and 30 pedal boats, showing a decreased share of pedal wheel ships. Between the August of the third year of the Baoyou Reign (AD 1255) and March of the sixth year of the Baoyou Reign (AD 1258), 477 boats were repaired, including 50 cart-head boats, 10 Fuyang boats, 30 pedal wheel ships with four wheels, 20 multi-oar boats, 50 paddle boats, 195 board boats, 20 iron-hawk boats, 20 firewood-carrying boats, 30 swift patrol boats, 10 iron-head boats, and 42 pedal boats. Pedal wheel ships accounted for less than 10% of the total, and they were smaller in size with only four wheels. The overall trend was the construction of lighter and more flexible boats, which became more evident from the ninth year of the Chunyou Reign (AD 1249) to the first year of the Xianchun Reign (AD 1265). In this period, 2287 new warships were built, including 1450 patrol boats, 259 pedal boats, 173 Fuyang boats, 100 multi-oar ships, 100 board boats, 50 iron-hawk boats, 50 sea boats with four oars, 34 large multi-paddle ships, 25 grain-carrying boats, 20 firewood-carrying boats, 10 cart-head boats, 10 horse-carrying boats, five light multi-paddle boats, and one large passenger boat. Notably, no new pedal wheel ships were built, and patrol boats accounted for 63% of the total, followed by pedal boats at 11% and Fuyang boats at 8%. Patrol boats were considered light warships, costing 500 strings of 1000 coins each. The Song people believed that large ships were used extensively in battles but were not agile enough for swift turns or emergency maneuvers. Since the outbreak of war in 1259, the Song navy had achieved victories against enemy forces crossing the river using small patrol boats, earning praise for their swiftness and ease of control. Pedal boats and Fuyang boats were also lightweight vessels. Pedal boats were classified as 500-Liao warships (according to *The Chronicle of Shouchang Military Prefecture*, most of them were 70-Liao or 50-Liao small boats), while Fuyang boats were 250-Liao or 300-Liao multi-oar ships. Fuyang boats were 250-Liao or 300-Liao multi-oar ships. Sea ships with four oars were 300-Liao ships (Y. Zhou 1990: 1983). In the late Southern Song Dynasty, the fleet composition of Changzhou Weicun Camp resembled that of Jiankang. The fleet consisted of 59 warships, including two large ships, seven grain-carrying boats, 20 Fangjiang boats, and 30 patrol boats (Z. Huang 1990). Patrol boats accounted for 51%. According to *The Chronicle of Shouchang Military Prefecture*, the river defense of Wuchang County in the late Southern Song Dynasty deployed 1826 seamen. The fleet of 96 warships, of various sizes, comprised 58 Caodi boats with a load capacity of 350 Liao, 300 Liao, or 250 Liao, as well as flat-bottomed boats with a load capacity of 250 Liao and pedal boats with a load capacity of only 70 Liao or even 50 Liao. The fleet consisted mainly of small and medium-sized warships.

4.1.4 The Fighting Methods of the Navy in the Song Dynasty

In the battles against the Southern Tang, Cochin, Jin and Yuan Kingdoms, as well as in the fight against pirates, the Song Dynasty engaged in unprecedented river and sea battles in terms of quantity and scale. The river battles in Ezhou, Dingjiazhou, and Jiaoshan, fought between the Southern Song and Yuan dynasties, involved over 10,000 ships and over 100,000 soldiers, surpassing any previous battle in history. Similarly, the sea battles in Jiaoxi and Yashan involved over a thousand ships and tens of thousands of soldiers, setting a new record. The methods of warfare on rivers and seas during the Song Dynasty were developed based on the experiences of previous dynasties, reflecting the overall nature of battles in the era of wooden boats and close-quarters combat.

The weapons used in previous dynasties were documented in *The General Record of Military Affairs*. One such weapon was the "Paigan", a throwing tool with a lever that was installed on large warships. During battles, it could be used to hurl stones, boards with nails, and fire, effectively damaging enemy ships. Fire boats were another specialized weapon used to launch fire-based attacks. These makeshift boats, laden with ignited dry grass and wood, would drift downstream with the tailwind, setting enemy ships ablaze. Wood and bamboo shields, as their names suggest, were made from these materials and were utilized to provide protection against fire cannons, fire arrows, and physical confrontations. Hand cannons, which required two people to operate and were armed with 0.25 kg of stone, were used in close-range combat. Gunpowder weapons, such as gunpowder bows, were filled with 250 g of gunpowder in the arrowhead, which would ignite upon launch. Additionally, gunpowder bags containing sulfur, saltpetre, arsenic, pine rosin, edible vegetable oil, and poisonous oil were shot by cannons to create fire or poison attacks (G. Zeng 1990).

In the first year of the Jianyan Reign (AD 1127), Guo Ning, the county mayor of Tongzhou, discussed the preparations for battles on rivers and seas, specifically regarding materials and weapons. He mentioned various tactics such as spreading lime powder to impair the enemies' vision or making the road slippery by pouring mud. Warships covered with cowhide could be utilized to cut the sails of enemy ships using sickles. Skilled swimmers could halt the progress of enemy ships by damaging their bases and ropes with sharp blades. Fire arrows, hand cannons, long oars, bamboo shields, crossbows, daggers, and lances were recommended for battle use. Additionally, preparations should be made for a Great Arm Bow. Emperor Gaozong ordered that the navy in the Yangtze River, Huaihe River, and Haizhou regions should adhere to these standards (X. Li 2013: 224). In the third year of the Jianyan Reign (AD 1129), Lin Zhiping proposed further preparations for river battles, which included observation tools, shields, iron pendulums, hard balls, stone cannons, fire cannons, fire arrows, and other fireproof weapons (S. Xu et al. 2014: 9253). These suggestions encompassed the various methods employed in long-range and close-range battles on water during the Song Dynasty. Observation tools were fixed on the masts of ships to monitor the movements of the enemy. Other weapons served as tools of engagement, illustrating some fundamental techniques of naval battles. First, arrows were used for long-range attacks, with crossbows and the Great Arm Bow employed for offensive purposes, while shields and bamboo shields were utilized for defense. Second, fire-based attacks were employed using fire cannons and fire arrows. However, fireproof materials could counter such weaponry. Fire arrows, fireballs, and fire tribulus, invented by Tang Fu, leader of the Shenwei Navy during the reign of Emperor Zhenzong (Toqta 1977: 4910), were also employed for fire attacks on water. Third, cannons were utilized for attacks, with gun carriers and hand cannons shooting stones and fire at the enemy being a common method. Fourth, close-range battles involved the use of lime powder, iron pendulums, swords, and lances. When boarding enemy ships, individuals primarily relied on swords and spears.

The battle methods of the navy were also exemplified through the division of labor and the proportion of soldiers. According to the *Baoqing Period Chronicles of Siming,* the navy in the Commission in Mingzho consisted of 40,000 soldiers and 11 officers, including a general commander, a commander, three generals, three vice generals, and three third-ranked generals. The main force of 3896 soldiers was divided into 22 platoons responsible for 20 different tasks. These platoons were composed of 20 officers of military exercises, 44 supervisors of military affairs, 44 platoon leaders, 22 military storm-troopers, 132 banner holders, 171 shield-wielding soldiers, 771 swordsmen, 468 lance soldiers, 556 bowman, 860 crossbow men, 22 horners, 23 soldiers with gongs, 61 drummers, 44 third-ranked armoured banner holders, 22 platoon leaders, 22 banner holders in helmsmen and anchor droppers, 66 helmsman, 330 anchor droppers, 22 supervisors of army cooks, and 198 army cooks. Additionally, there were over 600 soldiers not assigned to platoons, over 50 individuals whose names were not recorded, and over 190 classified as poor and solitary soldiers (J. Luo et al. 1990: 5069–70). Within the main forces, there were 638 soldiers who were boatmen, including banner holders in helmsmen and anchor droppers, helmsmen, anchor droppers, supervisors of army cooks, and army cooks. There were 262 platoon-ranked officers, including officers of military exercises, supervisors of military affairs, platoon leaders, military storm troopers, and banner holders. Additionally, there were 172 signalmen and messengers, including horners, soldiers with gongs, drummers, third-ranked armoured banner holders, and platoon leaders. Gongs, drums, flags, and horns were used as signaling tools during battles. Corps moved according to the orders conveyed by generals through flags. When flags leaned forward and drums were struck, the corps would march forward. When flags were held straight and gongs beat, the corps would stand still. When flags were lowered, the corps would withdraw. If the vanguards and patrol boats were besieged by enemies, they should await signals delivered by red flags from the general. Flags pointing towards the enemies indicated a charge. Pointing once at the enemies meant starting a boat. Flags pressed low forward indicated a slow withdrawal. Flags pointing inward once indicated the withdrawal of one boat (G. Zeng 1990). The remaining 2824 soldiers were divided as follows: shield-wielding soldiers, who defended against arrow attacks, accounted for 6%; swordsmen and spearmen, who fought at close range, accounted for 44%; and crossbowmen, who fought at long range, accounted for 50%. She Yanzhi commented on weapons for water battles, ranking bows and arrows as the most important, followed by lances, swords, shields, and cannons. Shields were used to protect the navy and cannons from enemy attacks (S. Xu et al. 2014: 8813). Bao Hui also emphasized the importance of bows and arrows, suggesting their increased preparation. Lances, spears, and swords were also deemed essential weapons in the navy (H. Bao 1990). In conclusion, bows, arrows, swords, and lances were the most critical combat skills during the era of melee weapons, while other methods of combat, such as cannon attacks, should also be valued.

The records also provide insights into water battles during the Song Dynasty, where arrow attacks played a significant role. In the third year of the Jianyan Reign (AD 1129), when the Jin army invaded the southern areas and attempted to cross the river, they were forced to retreat by the Great Arm Bow (Toqta 1977: 13810). During the battle against Yang Yao, the navy led by General Commander Tan was besieged by enemy boats. The Song reinforcements arrived and launched a barrage of arrows at Yang Yao's ships, temporarily causing them to withdraw. The protection boards on General Commander Tan's ship were penetrated, and the sails were hastily used to cover the seamen pedaling the wheels. Over 300 soldiers on the boat were brutally killed, pierced with numerous arrows (K. Yue 1989: 1575). The two sides engaged in fierce arrow exchanges. In the Caishi battle, the Jin navy was defeated by the Song navy, and the fleeing Jin ships were pursued. Yu Yunwen ordered strong arrows to be shot at the enemy ships, inflicting heavy casualties. The Song ships then blocked the Yanglin ferry, preventing the Jin ships from escaping the river. The enemy ships formed a wall-like formation, but under the twang of bowstrings, tens of thousands of enemy soldiers perished (W. Yang 2007: 4609). In the Liaoluo Battle, General Bei Wang of the Fujian navy of the Song Dynasty defeated over 500 pirates who sailed on eight ships, despite having just over 80 soldiers on one ship. The enemy ships were as large as hills and twice the size of Bei's ship. Nevertheless, Bei led his soldiers, intensively shooting arrows with powerful bows, and nearly all pirates on the two ships were killed. In Shen'ao Bay of Chaozhou, when the Guangdong navy pursued the pirates, they used bows and crossbows to shoot at the enemy's large warships. However, they had to retreat when they were outnumbered and besieged by the pirate ships (D. Zhen, n.d.). Arrow attacks were commonly employed in long-range battles.

Cannon attacks were also employed in water battles. During a conflict between Yang Yungong and pirates, the pirates tied their ships together, raised curtains, and launched attacks using powerful bows and short cannons. Yang's soldiers fought back with swords and lances, but their efforts were hindered by the curtains, and Yang himself was hit in the left shoulder by a short cannon (Toqta 1977: 10160). In the Yashan battle, medium cannons and arrows served as the primary long-range weapons. "The roars of cannons were like thunders, and the falling arrows were like a meteor shower" (T. Wen 1987: 535). The Song navy raised curtains to block stones and attached long poles at the sterns of their ships to counter fire boats (Zhao Zhong Lu 1990). Cannonballs filled with lime powder, sulfur, or other substances could also be launched. When besieged by Yang Yao's navy, General Commander Tan Tong, as mentioned earlier, used lime powder cannons to alleviate the situation to some extent. Meanwhile, Yang Yao's navy also attacked with cannons, breaking through the protection boards of Tan's ship (K. Yue 1989: 1575). Lime powder cannons were intended to create a smokescreen to obscure the enemy's vision (Y. Chen 1990). When shot and ignited in the sky, lime powder would generate smoke, hindering the visibility of soldiers and horses. Sulfur cannons were employed for fire attacks. When they exploded in the sky, the sulfur in the cannonballs would scatter over the river, immediately reacting with water and creating an explosive fire, resembling the sound of thunderous booms (W. Yang 2007: 2286).

The warships of that time were primarily constructed from wood, making fire attacks an effective method of warfare. In addition to arrows and stones, bows and cannons were used to launch other flammable materials as fire attacks. During the Huangtiandang Battle, the Jin navy attacked Han Shizhong's navy "with fire arrows that were produced overnight." Taking advantage of Han's ships being becalmed on the windless river, the Jin navy targeted Han's bamboo canopy with fire arrows. The result was chaotic scenes of soldiers screaming amidst raging flames and scorching sun, accompanied by the sounds of horses neighing. Countless soldiers and horses were burned and fell into the river (X. Li 2013: 747–48). In the Jiaoxi Battle, the Jin ships had combustible materials for their sails. Li Bao, recognizing this vulnerability, ordered his navy to shoot fire arrows from all directions. The sails caught fire immediately upon impact, leading to the burning of hundreds of ships (Toqta 1977: 11501). In the Jiaoshan Battle between the Song and Yuan troops, the Yuan forces achieved a decisive victory over Zhang Shijie and his troops by employing fire arrows (Toqta 1977: 13273). Fire boats and fire rafts were also frequently used in addition to fire arrows. The Song navy not only launched fire arrows but also deployed fire boats filled with oiled firewood and grass, taking advantage of tailwinds. These flaming boats would drift to the northern bank and ignite enemy ships, causing a chain reaction of fire and filling the sky with smoke (X. Yuan 1990). During the Caishi Battle, the Song navy attacked the besieged Jin ships on the Yanglin River using drifting fire boats, resulting in the destruction of over 180 enemy ships by fire (X. Yuan 1990). General Zhang Shun reinforced the Song army in Xiangyang by equipping all ships with firelocks, fire cannons, burning charcoals, large axes, and powerful crossbows (Toqta 1977: 13248). Breaking through the defenses of the Mongolian army with fire and arrow attacks, Zhang's army advanced smoothly towards Xiangyang.

Large ships could leverage their size to push smaller boats directly into the river during battles. In Yang Yao's navy, large pedal wheel ships wreaked havoc on hundreds of smaller seagoing and lake ships (K. Yue 1989: 1573). The Song ships, being much larger than the Jin ships, advanced aggressively, causing the opposing soldiers and horses to sink (W. Yang 2007: 2286). Sea loach ships were then deployed to destroy all enemy vessels (Toqta 1977: 11793). Another example is when Han Shizhong fought the Jin navy in Zhenjiang, where he dropped iron chains with huge hooks onto the enemy ships, resulting in the destruction of one ship for each capture (X. Lu 1990: 2342). These large warships were equipped with a throwing tool called Paigan. On Yang Yao's large pedal wheel ships, there was a Paigan resembling a mast, measuring over 33.3 m in length, with giant rocks attached to one end. A rope connected the end of the mast to the turntable bearing below. This arrangement allowed them to shoot rocks when confronted with approaching enemies (R. Zhang 1990), proving to be an effective tactic in close range battles.

Jumping onto enemy ships was the last resort in close range battles when two opposing boats were in very close proximity. Faced with Yang Yao's enormous pedal wheel ships, the Song generals Cui Zeng and Wu Quan ordered their soldiers to climb up Yang's ships using ladders. However, Yang surprised them by attacking from the top and emerged victorious in this battle (X. Li 2013: 1364). In the Jiaoxi Battle, Li Bao set fire to over 600 Jin ships. The remaining enemy ships, which had not been burnt, attempted to retaliate. Li sent brave soldiers to jump onto the enemy ships and killed their occupants with swords and lances (X. Li 2013: 3772). The battle concluded with this tactic of jumping onto enemy ships. In the Liaoluo Battle, the Fujian navy initially attacked the pirates with arrows, but then resorted to jumping onto the third pirate ship, where they killed twenty or thirty pirates (D. Zhen, n.d.). In the third year of the Shaoxi Reign (AD 1192), Zheng Lizhi "encountered rampant pirates while sailing from Panyu to his hometown, Fuzhou. Arrows were shot from his ship, but he quickly ran out of ammunition. Pirate ships closed in on Zheng's boat, and a pirate jumped onto his vessel wielding a spear" (M. Hong 1981: 1058). *The Loyals* recorded that in order to reinforce Xiangyang, Zhang Shun "constructed approximately a hundred light ships, forming teams of three ships each. The middle ship carried supplies, while the other two ships had their bilges removed and were covered to confuse the enemy, sailing on either side." "The Yuan navy sailed closely and jumped onto the side ships as anticipated, resulting in the deaths of tens of thousands of soldiers." This proved to be an effective way to deal with ship jumpers.

In addition, other battle methods were also utilized. One common tactic was diving to break the enemy ships. It is reported that "in the battles against Yang Yao, skilled divers were sent to sabotage the enemy ships, and it proved effective." However, this method was not applicable in all situations. For example, the victory in those battles was attributed to the fact that Yang Yao was sailing on Dongting Lake, where there were no strong undercurrents. The divers could easily hide beneath the ships and use drills to damage them. But in the turbulent waters of Guazhou, where the river flowed rapidly and the undercurrents were as strong as arrows, the divers would struggle to use their tools while also trying to avoid being swept away or drowned (N. Zhou 1990). In the 31st year of the Shaoxing Reign (AD 1161), Liu Qi employed this method in the Huaihe River to combat pirates pirates (X. Li 2013: 3759). The Fujian Navy recruited numerous skilled swimmers and divers and developed more efficient tools for breaking and cutting ships (H. Bao 1990). Additionally, there were wooden crows, heavy stakes over 66 cm long with sharpened ends, that could be affixed with arrows and rocks and shot at the enemy ships. General Wang Xie was struck by arrows and wooden crows from the Yang side (X. Li 2013: 1356). Furthermore, a technique similar to using long giant stakes to crash through parapets on land was also applied in naval battles to ram into enemy ships. Marshal Yue Fei employed this tactic to attack Yang Yao's ships (Toqta 1977: 11384).

Many battle methods were combined in actual combat. For example, tower ships were equipped with various weapons for both offense and defense, and the fortified parapets made them as resilient as fortresses. Additionally, "they featured small windows for shooting arrows and thrusting spears, fire-resistant hides to protect the hull, cannons, stone pendulums, and liquid iron" (G. Zeng 1990). Apart from battle methods, other factors played significant roles. In the Jiaoxi Battle, Liu Bao achieved victory over the Jin navy, which possessed 1000 warships and 100,000 soldiers, using only 120 warships and 3000 soldiers. This victory resulted from six key factors: spies, ships, soldiers, weapons, army ordnance and provisions, and fire attacks. These aspects were detailed components of battle strategies and were consistently valued by military officers. However, despite the well-trained Song navy with skilled combat abilities, they were defeated by the Yuan navy in crucial battles in Ezhou, Dingjiawan, Jiaoshan, Yashan and so on. This demonstrates that battle skills, while important, had limited impact on victory when considered within the broader context of overall strategies and tactics.

4.1.5 Summary

The Northern Song Dynasty placed great importance on water battles and constructed numerous warships prior to the pacification of its southern areas. Water battles played a crucial role in the victory over the Southern Tang dynasty. During the Southern Song Dynasty, river and coastal defenses became a priority for border security, leading to unprecedented development of warships. These warships could be categorized based on their shapes, structures, functions, and propulsion systems. Over 40 types of warships were named according to their shapes, structures, and functions, building upon previous designs while introducing new structures. Inland river warships predominantly relied on wheel propulsion, such as pedal wheel ships, paddle-driven ships, and oar-powered vessels, like multi-paddle ships and multi-oar ships. Wind power was primarily utilized for larger warships at sea and had limited application in inland river vessels. Warships of various shapes and structures could employ the same type of propulsion, and a single warship could utilize multiple types of propulsion simultaneously.

Warships, whether large, medium, or small, served different purposes. Large majestic warships were effective for intimidating enemies and provided advantages with their high hulls during battles. Medium-sized warships were lightweight, fast, and flexible. Small boats were useful for transmitting information and spying on the enemy. Ships of various sizes complemented each other in battle. The Song people developed and enhanced ideas about fleet composition, and their best practices were applied to many coordinated warship scenarios. Even in crucial river defense situations, a mixed fleet approach was adopted. During the reigns of Emperors Gaozong and Xiaozong, there was a significant boost in warship construction, particularly in the construction of large pedal wheel ships. Subsequently, warship construction remained important but tended towards smaller, lighter, and swifter vessels.

After participating in numerous large-scale wars involving thousands of warships on rivers and seas, the Song people extracted valuable insights and techniques from their experiences. Their best practices encompassed a range of strategies employed during battles, including arrow attacks, cannon attacks, fire attacks, boarding enemy ships, immobilizing smaller vessels, Paigan tactics, ship-diving maneuvers, and the use of projectiles like wooden crows. Soldiers were assigned specific roles based on the different battle methods employed. The diversity of warships and battle techniques on rivers and seas drew inspiration from previous dynasties while introducing innovative approaches.

4.2 The Pedal Wheel Ships in the Southern Song Dynasty and Their Historical Fate

Pedal wheel ships are believed to have been first utilized by the Chinese, marking an important invention and a "technical revolution" that preceded Europe by 400 years (Needham 1986: 262; F. Xi 2000; S. Wu 1960). They became widely used following the rebellion led by Yang Yao. Experts consider these ships a significant subject in the study of shipbuilding history and peasant uprisings. However, the question remains unanswered as to why the pedal wheel ship, acknowledged as a "technical revolution", did not contribute to the advancement of social and economic development. Furthermore, there is ambiguity surrounding its initial appearance and the meaning of the term "wheel". These questions remain open, and some opinions lack well-founded explanations. This section aims to analyze the aforementioned questions and explore the historical fate of pedal wheel ships from the perspectives of technological history and economic development.

4.2.1 The Debut of Pedal Wheel Boats and the Connotation of "Wheel"

4.2.1.1 Archaeological Evidence of Pedal Wheel Ships

There have been various opinions regarding the origins of pedal wheel ships. However, aside from some discussions regarding whether the ship was invented by Yang Yao, most of these viewpoints tend to overlook alternative perspectives and remain confined within their own assumptions. Wu Shimo was the first to propose that pedal wheel ships were invented by the Yang Yao army during the Southern Song Dynasty, deeming it a technological revolution. Cai Meibiao shared the same view in *A History of China,* stating that the conspirator army led by Yang Yao constructed the pedal wheel ships, which were considered a remarkable invention (S. Wu and M. Cai 1978: 262). Prior to Wu Shimo's theory, Feng Hanyong suggested that it was invented by Li Gao in the Tang Dynasty, a notion supported by Wang Ruiming and Qi Tao. However, Wang and Qi responded to Wu's article and Cai's book, respectively, without addressing Feng's article. Wu's article also did not discuss Feng's work (H. Feng 1957; D. Wang 1963; T. Qi 1987). The studies mentioned below are mostly individual works that lack dialogue or response to other experts' research. Lin

Lin argued that Li Gao invented pedal wheel ships no later than Emperor Dezong's Reign of Tang, with the "500-km-voyage ship" created by Zu Chongzhi likely being the prototype (L. Lin 1982). Wang Jieyun was convinced that Zu Chongzhi first invented pedal wheel ships during the Jin Dynasty (J. Wang 1983). Joseph Needham also believed that pedal wheel ships appeared first in fifth or sixth-century documents from the Jin Dynasty and certainly existed by the eighth century. The timeline mentioned Zu Chongzhi, Xu Shipu, and Li Gao (Needham 1986: 260), aligning with Wang Jieyun's viewpoint. Xi Longfei asserted that the "500-km-voyage ship" made by Zu Chongzhi was a pedal wheel ship, and earlier warships covered with cowhide in the fifth century were also pedal wheel ships. Additionally, he considered the "water wheel" constructed by Xu Shipu in the sixth century to be an improved version of the pedal wheel ship (F. Xi 2000: 129–30). Lin Sheng believed the invention occurred much earlier, dating back to the Jin, Southern, and Northern Dynasties. The "water wheel" mentioned in *The Master of Preserving Simplicity* referred to a pedal wheel ship, which was clearly recorded in the Tang Dynasty documents (referring to the pedal wheel ship built by Li Gao) (S. Lin 1979). Wang Zengyu posited that the earliest pedal wheel ship was built by Xu Shipu in the Southern Dynasty, referred to as the "water wheel" (Z. Wang 2006).

In conclusion, the origin of pedal wheel ships can be explained through various descriptions, such as the pedal wheel ship developed by Yang Yao or Li Gao in the Tang Dynasty, the Water Wheels by Xu Shipu, the 500-km-voyage ship by Zu Chongzhi, warships covered with cowhide in the fifth century, or the water wheel before the Jin Dynasty. However, a comprehensive literature review of previous studies is needed from historical and theoretical perspectives, along with the establishment of a basic standard for discussing such ships. The fundamental characteristic of pedal wheel ships is that boatmen pedal wheels to generate propulsion (D. Ma 2011: 4741; Toqta 1977: 11384). Yang Yao's warship clearly met the specifications of such boats (see below), but the earlier warships built by Li Gao in the Tang Dynasty also exhibited features resembling those of such boats. As described in historical documents, Li's ship was "equipped with two wheels and pedaled by soldiers. The ship sailed so fast as if it were driven by a strong tailwind" (X. Liu 1975: 3640). However, there is limited ancient documentation, and although the "500-km-voyage ship" built by Zu Chongzhi was tested on the Xinting River and could travel over 50 miles in a day (Y. Li 1975: 1774), no mention of wheels is found in historical records. This discrepancy has been pointed out by Wang Zengyu and Lin Sheng in their articles. Additionally, there is no historical description of water wheels before the Jin Dynasties or the Water Wheel of Xu Shipu. Historical records only mention people racing dabbed water wheels, flying sea birds, or water horses (Y. Zhang and S. Wang et al. 1985). Another record mentions the construction of tower ships, warships with Paigan, fire boats, and water wheels to strengthen the navy (Y. Li 1975: 1639), but does not mention ships equipped with wheels. Therefore, the assumption that water wheels and 500-km-voyage ships are pedal wheel ships cannot be supported by evidence. Discussions regarding pedal wheel ships can only confirm the earliest recorded instances, much like many other inventions in ancient China, but the exact creators cannot be identified.

As we know, Li Gao's ship in the Tang Dynasty has been proven to be a pedal wheel ship, which challenges the viewpoint that it was created by Yang Yao. A related question arises regarding who, between Yang Yao's navy and the Song navy, used the ship in battles first. According to *A History of China* written by Cai Meibiao, Yang Yao was considered the inventor of pedal wheel ships, and the Song navy copied the ships from Yang's navy. While Wang Ruiming disagreed with Yang Yao being the inventor, he agreed that Yang applied such ships in battles first, while the Song navy spied on and learned the techniques of shipbuilding, later copying the ship craftsmanship (D. Wang 1987). Wang Zengyu believed that Yang Yao was unable to build pedal wheel ships until he captured a ship and its builder, Gao Xuan, from the Song navy. This viewpoint is consistent with those of Lin Lin and Li Wenbin (Z. Wang, L. Lin and W. Li 1981). In fact, *The Stories About Yang Yao I* written by secluded individuals, provides clear details. Cheng Changyu, the prefecture mayor of Dingzhou in the Song Dynasty, recruited Gao Xuan to build pedal wheel ships. Yang Yao then captured a pedal wheel ship and the craftsman Gao Xuan. Specifically, "the pirates (referring to Yang Yao) didn't have pedal wheel ships at first." Cheng Changyu had acquired Gao Xuan, who worked for the Baibo Shipping Commission, as the general carpenter for building fascine defenses on the Yangtze River. Gao Xuan presented the draft of a pedal wheel ship and instructed the Song soldiers to build ships with eight, twenty, and even twenty-three wheels. However, Governor Cheng Changyu failed in battle because he ignored the dissuasion and insisted on showcasing those ships. Yang Yao obtained a pedal wheel ship and captured Gao Xuan in the battle. Subsequently, Yang's navy managed to build pedal wheel ships, some of which had 22 or 24 wheels. In summary, Yang Yao had over 10 pedal wheel ships of different sizes, including the initially looted one (K. Yue 1989: 1568–69). From another perspective, if Yang Yao had pedal wheel ships earlier than the Song navy, Cheng Changyu would not have felt the need to showcase such ships. However, Wang Jieyun held the opinion that the story of Gao Xuan is not trustworthy, and there is a possibility that Yang Yao acquired the blueprint of pedal wheel ships from Li Gao in the Tang Dynasty. Moreover, Yang Yao may have built such ships in the third year of the Jianyan Reign (AD 1129) (J. Wang 1983). However, these assumptions have been proven to be unfounded. Zhong Xiang began his revolt in January of the fourth year of the Jianyan Reign (AD 1130), which contradicts the presence of a pedal wheel ship in Yang Yao's arsenal in the third year of the Jianyan Reign (AD 1129).

This kind of ship, made by Gao Xuan, followed the pattern of Li Gao's blueprint. Moreover, Li Gang once built pedal wheel ships in Jinghu Lake, stating that he followed the structure of Li Gao's ship. The document mentions that the Yangtze River and Dongting Lake were strategically and geographically important for Changsha, but no navy or warships were deployed there. Li Gang learned shipbuilding techniques from Li Gao, who was a descendant of Lord Cao in the Qin Dynasty. Li Gang constructed ten warships with three-storey towers on board and installed wheels. The wheels rotated in water to propel the ships forward, even faster than galloping horses. Three thousand navy personnel were recruited to learn and practice battle skills on the water (G. Li 2004: 392). The fact that Li Gang selected

3000 navy personnel in November of the second year of the Jianyan Reign (AD 1132) was recorded in the entry titled "November of the Second Year of the Shaoxing Reign" in Volume 60 of *Chronological Record of Major Events Since 1127.* The entry states that "as there had been no navy in Hu'nan, Li Gang recruited 3,000 navy personnel from the riverside boatmen and stationed them at Tanzhou." By October of the second year of the Shaoxing Reign (AD 1132), Yang Yao's navy had already acquired pedal wheel ships. It was recorded that "pedal wheel ships and sea loach ships numbered in the hundreds" (X. Li 2013: 1026). Cheng Changyu's ship was constructed even earlier than Yang Yao's. As an Imperial Commissioner to Hu'nan and Guangzhou (later demoted to Provincial Military Commissioner to Hu'nan), Li Gang was ordered to instruct Cheng Changyu and other officers in the fight against Yang Yao. Therefore, it is certain that Li Gang was aware of the presence of such ships in Cheng's navy and did not need to build them from scratch. The brief descriptions quoted from *the Old Book of Tang* and *the New Book of Tang* do not provide substantial evidence. The shipbuilding draft attributed to Gao Xuan may be a copy of Li Gao's blueprint. Gao Xuan stated, "the pedal wheel ships sailing on Jinghu Lake were built by Li Gao, a descendant of Lord Cao in the Song Dynasty. The larger ships had thirty to forty wheels, which surpassed the capabilities of the shipbuilders in Dinghu. The new designs and structures of the pedal wheel ships followed the previous ones. With soldiers pedaling the wheels, it sails as if it were flying" (G. Li 2004: 392, 985, 1165).

4.2.2 The Entailment of "Pedal Wheel"

The axle part that powers a pedal wheel ship consists of four elements: axles, wheels, oars, and the people who pedal on it. Pedal wheel ships with one wheel, four wheels, eight wheels, even over 20 wheels, 30 wheels and 40 wheels can be found in the historical records. The question arises as to what exactly the term "wheel" refers to: axles, wheels, oars, or the people? Experts hold different opinions on this matter. Wang Zengyu believes that "a pair of wheels was fixed on both sides of the hull and connected through the hull with an axle, which means a pair of wheels is called a *wheel.*" According to him, the latter "wheel" has been considered a unit of measurement, so a ship with a pair of wheels was called a "pedal wheel ship with one wheel" for simplicity (Z. Wang 2006). Wang Jieyun, on the other hand, argues that "wheel" represents the oars attached to the wheels. He suggests that the number of "wheels" indicates the number of oars on each wheel. For example, "eight wheels" would mean eight oars attached to each wheel (J. Wang 1983). According to Lin Sheng, "eight wheels" means there are eight wheels installed on the ship. He points out that the number of "wheels" must be an even number because the wheels on both sides of the ship need to be balanced. Therefore, the recorded "23 wheels" is considered a mistake and should actually be "22 wheels". Joseph Needham proposes that the pedal wheel ship with "23 wheels" created by Gao Xuan had 11 wheels on both sides and one wheel at the rear end. Both Joseph Needham and Xi Longfei agree that if the number of wheels is even, the ship must have a wheel at the rear end and pairs of wheels on the hull (S. Lin 1979; Needham 1986: 941; L. Xi 2000: 149). The three experts mentioned above concur that the term "wheel" in the ship's name refers to the wheels installed on the ship. However, Li Wenbin presents a different viewpoint, suggesting that "the pedal wheel ship with × × wheels" denotes the power strength, specifically the number of people required to pedal. According to this interpretation, "the pedal wheel ship with 24 wheels" means that 24 people were needed to pedal the wheels. These 24 individuals would pedal one or, at most, two wheels in different positions together, allowing the ship to sail rapidly like an arrow (W. Li 1981). In this opinion, the "wheel" is interpreted as representing the people. The four experts mentioned above present four different perspectives without thoroughly explaining their evidence or engaging in dialogue with other experts. Therefore, further discussions are needed to clarify the matter.

The notion that the number of "wheels" must be an even number has been proven to be unfounded. Historical records provide evidence of ships with odd numbers of wheels. For example, in the fourth year of the Shaoxing Reign (AD 1134), 400-Liao warships with one wheel and twelve paddles were constructed by Shi Zhengzhui (Y. Zhou 1990: 1734). Another example is from the fifth year of the Shaoxing Reign (AD 1135), when orders were issued for the construction of ships with five wheels and ten paddles in the provinces of Jiangnan East and West, and Liangzhe East and West. Additionally, ships with thirteen wheels and nine wheels already existed at that time (X. Li 2013: 1483). In the eighth year of the Chunxi Reign (AD 1181), officers from Ezhou Prefecture altered their construction plans, changing the intended ten pedal wheel ships with eight wheels to five pedal wheel ships with eight wheels and five pedal wheel ships with seven, six, or five wheels, resulting in a total of ten pedal wheel ships (S. Xu et al. 2014: 7136). These examples demonstrate that pedal wheel ships with odd numbers of wheels were indeed present in history, such as those with one wheel, five wheels, seven wheels, nine wheels, and so on.

Li Wenbin's opinion that "wheel" stands for the number of people and "24 wheels", meaning 24 people pedaling one wheel or two wheels at most, is not baseless. People did work by pedaling, and then the wheels rotated with the axle, generating thrust power for the ship. This explains how such ships function. The amount of thrust depended on the size of the water the wheels were beating and the speed of wheel rotation. By adding more people, the limit of individual pedaling frequency could be compensated to some extent, thereby increasing the rotation speed. However, the maximum speed was determined by the maximum reaction rate of human legs. Thus, adding more people could not infinitely increase the speed or thrust if the frequency reached the maximum capacity of people's response.

Although adding more oars to wheels could increase the number of times the water is beaten in a rotation, thereby enhancing the thrust, the limited space available on wooden wheels prevented the installation of additional oars. Consequently, the oars could not be installed at will. The picture titled "wheeled ships" demonstrates that all oars were directly mounted on the axle. Considering the bearing capacity of wood, the oars had to possess a certain thickness. Taking the largest ship with 40 wheels as an example, if each oar measured 10 cm in length, the total thickness of the oars would be four meters long. Assuming a 10-cm gap between every two oars, the axle would need to have a circumference of eight meters and a diameter of 2.55 m. No wood could meet these requirements, rendering the construction of a massive ship like this impractical. Joseph Needham's perspective becomes more justifiable in light of this information. He argued that, prior to the development of iron wheels, the shapes, structures, and sizes of wooden wheels were severely constrained, leaving people with no choice but to add more wheels. As the wheels were constructed from wood, there were limitations on enlarging their diameter and installing additional oars to enhance thrust. The need for a large axle to accommodate more oars consumed excessive space, resulting in a ship being able to bear only one or two at most. Consequently, the thrust could only be increased by adding more wheels. Therefore, the concept of a "wheel" representing an oar is untenable.

The picture of "wheeled Ships" in *Collection of Ancient and Modern Books of Economic Compilation. Military Equipment I of Military Affairs*

How large would a wheel be? How many individuals were required to pedal these wheels? These questions are crucial in debunking the notion that the "wheel" represents the number of people or oars, and in determining its precise meaning. The size of a wheel can be inferred from the records in the sixth volume, *Ship*, of the first half of *The Book of Wubian* written by Tang Shunzhi. According to these records, the "wheeled ships" were 14 m long and 4.3 m wide. The hollow outer frames, where the four wheels were installed, measured 0.3 m in width. At maximum draught, approximately 0.3 m of the wheel would be submerged underwater. The "protection boards" covered the wheels from the top downward on both sides of the ship, with each board measuring about 1.7 m in length and 0.66 m in width, and attached to a spindle at the lower end. As described in *The Stories About Yang Yao*, the wheels were concealed from view by the protective boards. Therefore, a wheel had a diameter of approximately 1.7 m and a width of 0.33 m. Pochuan boats had six wheels on each side, with the axle positioned beneath a five-meter-long cabin. More specifically, three wheels were installed on each side of the five-meter-long cabin, making each wheel around 1.7 m in diameter. The Eight-diagram Flower Ship had a hollow space beneath the cabin and was equipped with eight wheels. A piece of thick nanmu had five grooves carved into it at intervals, with a 0.5-m-wide wheel installed on it. The wheels were secured on both sides of the grooves, where individuals pedaled them. Each wheel had a width of approximately 0.5 m. In conclusion, a wheel had a diameter of about 1.7 m and a width ranging from 0.3 to 0.5 m. Additionally, the installation of wheels on the Eight-diagram Flower Ship provides insight into how ships with an odd number of wheels placed a wheel at the rear.

Within a space of about 1.7 m long and 0.3 to 0.5 m wide, the boat did not require a dozen of people, let alone 40 people, to operate it. According to a document from the Song Dynasty, four people were sufficient to operate a single wheel, rendering additional personnel unnecessary. In the second year of the Shaoxing Reign (AD 1132), Wang Yanhui, the mayor and general of Wuwei Military Prefecture, created the Feihu Pedal Wheel Warship, which had "four wheels on both sides, with each wheel with eight oars operated by four people" (Y. Wang 2003: 2709). Therefore, four individuals were needed to pedal each wheel. Thus, for ships like the Feihu Pedal Wheel Warship, four people were enough to generate maximum thrust power. In the third year of the Jiatai Reign (AD 1203), Qin Shifu created the Iron Gunwheel Warship, a 400-Liao ship with a 5-m-wide stem, which was equipped with two wheels on each side. Each wheel had three oars, and the ship could carry 70 soldiers on board, along with an additional 20 soldiers to pedal the wheels (S. Xu et al. 2014: 7138–39). According to the *Landscape: the Fifth Entry* in the 14th volume of *Chunxi Period Chronicles of Fuzhou*, a ship measuring 4 to 4.3 m in length had a helmsman, a supervisor of seamen, an anchor dropper, and 13 seamen on board. The measurement mentioned here referred to the width of the ship, as clarified in the 32nd entry of the 29th volume: *The Anthology of Laws and Regulations of the Song Dynasty.* It stated that "sea ships in the Song Dynasty were categorized into three levels. First-rank ships were over 8 meters in width, second-rank ships over 6.7 meters, and third-rank ships over 6 meters." It also noted that "only one helmsman was required to sail third-rank ships." The 400-Liao Iron Gunwheel Warship made by Qin Shifu needed to be manned by a helmsman, an anchor dropper, six boatmen, and 12 soldiers to pedal the wheels. Three soldiers pedaled each wheel, which was similar to the arrangement of the Feihu Pedal Wheel Warships.

Based on the size and the number of people pedaling a single wheel, the Feihu Pedal Wheel Warship was equipped with "four wheels on both sides, with each wheel with eight oars operated by four people." This indicates that four individuals rotated one wheel, forming a working unit. The Iron Gunwheel Warship was described as having "two wheels installed on each side," with the term "wheels" referring to these working units. Therefore, in the name of the ship, a "wheel" specifically refers to the wheel on the vessel. In *The Stories About Yang Yao I*, it is mentioned that "the wheels were covered by the protection board and unseen from the outside." It is evident that the term "wheels" in this context refers to the wheels on both sides of the hull, rather than the already "covered" people or axles.

The width of pedal wheel ships also indicated that they worked with the combined effort of three to four people rotating a single wheel and axle, rather than the use of two wheels attached to one axle. In the first volume of *The Notes of an Old Pedant* written by Lu You, there is a record of such a ship which measured "118.6 m long and 13.5 m wide, with a length–width ratio of 8.8:1". In the third year of the Jiatai Reign (AD 1203), Qin Shifu built the Iron Gunwheel Warship, which was 30.36 m long and 3.8 m wide (S. Xu et al. 2014: 7138), resulting in a similar ratio of 8:1. The "13.5 m wide" mentioned by Lu You must refer to the maximum width of the ship.

According to the standards recorded in the 64th volume of the *Canals* in *History of the Yuan Dynasty*, ships with a maximum beam less than 2.8 m could pass through water gates. Therefore, the "width" of a ship should be understood as the maximum width of the cabin. The maximum width of the pedal wheel ship recorded by Lu You and the Iron Gunwheel Warship made by Qin Shifu were 13.5 m and 3.8 m respectively[3] (S. Xu et al. 2014: 7138). As Lu You described, four people pedaled a single wheel together, with each person occupying half a meter of working space. This resulted in a total width of four meters for both sides' working units, leaving a 9.5-m space for people to walk through and for storing weapons. The Iron Gunwheel Warship required three people to pedal its wheels, and the working units on both sides occupied 3 m, leaving a 0.8-m aisle. When Wang Zao was ordered to build pedal wheel ships in Fuzhou, he stated that ships equipped with 26 wheels should not exceed a length of 66 m (Z. Wang, n.d.). Therefore, the 118.6-m-long ship recorded by Lu You was equivalent to the ship described by Li Gang, which was installed with 34 wheels. If the assumption that "wheel" is used as a unit of measurement for every two wheels yoked to one axle is true, it would require a 13.2-m-long piece of wood to make the axles. However, such long pieces of wood could only be found in remote virgin forests (Z. Wang, n.d.). Using spliced wood for such long axles, along with the weight of the support devices, would result in significant waste. Additionally, if 40 long axles pierced through the hull, there would be no room for people to walk through, let alone store weapons.

The length–width ratio of the ship Lu You mentioned and that of the Iron Gunwheel Warship were rare, much larger than the ratio of the excavated Song ships and the ratio in the records of the Ming Dynasty. The length–width ratio of the Northern Song ships excavated in Ningbo is 2.7:1, and that of the Southern Song ships excavated in Quanzhou is 2.5:1. Among the ships documented in *The Ships in the Southern Song Dynasty*, written in the Ming Dynasty, the largest ratio is 5.63:1, and the smallest ratio is 3.4:1, with an average ratio of 4.7:1. The Iron Gunwheel Warship was 5 m in maximum width and 1.3 m wide at the bottom, similar to the sand-proof boat of the Ming Dynasty, whose ratio was 3.85:1 (L. Xi 2004: 176, 205, 188). According to the length- width ratio of 3.85:1, the "100-m long or over 66.7-m long" pedal wheel ship made by Cheng Changyu would be 24.16 m in maximum width and 16.1 m in width at the bottom, further proving the groundlessness of the viewpoint of connecting two wheels across the hull with an axle.

[3] Based on the record of *The Anthology of Laws and Regulations of the Song Dynasty*, in the fifth year of the Qiando Reign (1169 AD), multi-paddle boats made by the navy of the Palace Administration were 83 Chi (26.3 m) long and 20 chi (6.34 m) wide, and their size adopted the the standard of the Huai Ruler (a system for measuring things). That shows the official shipbuilding also adopted the criteria of the Huai Ruler, one of its length units is Chi, and one Chi is about 33 cm. One Chinese Chi is roughly equivalent to one foot.

4.2.3 The Application and Evolution of Pedal Wheel Ships in the Southern Song Dynasty

4.2.3.1 The Fields and Time of the Application of Pedal Wheel Ships

Pedal wheel ships were mainly adopted as warships during the Southern Song Dynasty. However, there is a unique account of a civilian, Jia Sidao, describing a pedal wheel ship used for sightseeing on the West Lake, which was recorded in the 12th Volume of *Lake Boats* of *Accounts About the Capital*. It is mentioned that "nobody used paddles, but rather sailed by pedaling the wheels, resulting in a very fast ship." According to the records, pedal wheel ships were observed in use from the early years of the Shaoxing Reign until the late Southern Song Dynasty.

The pedal wheel ships used by Yang Yao's rebellion army in the early Ming Dynasty to fight against the Song army have been discussed in the previous passages. After conquering Yang Yao and his rebel followers, pedal wheel ships were built in the areas along the Yangtze River as ordered by the Song Dynasty, reaching the peak of pedal shipbuilding. In the bissextile February of the fifth year of the Shaoxing Reign (AD 1135), it was ordered that "Jiangnan East and Liangzhe West provinces build 12 pedal wheel ships with nine wheels respectively, and Liangzhe East Province build eight pedal wheel ships with 13 wheels. Wang Xie captured two giant ships back from the Jinghu battlefield at that time and required the three Shipping Commissions to build ships by replicating the design of such ships." In May of the same year, following the shape and structure of Hu'nan ships, the aforementioned four provinces built 50 small ships with five wheels and ten oars, "using the 50,000 strings of 1000 coins that had been collected as a fine from salt merchants for their delayed delivery as the expenditure for shipbuilding." This kind of ship, compared to those with 13 wheels and 9 wheels, was considered a "light and swift ship"(X. Li 2013: 1425, 1483). The cost of a pedal wheel ship with five wheels and ten oars was 1000 strings of 1000 coins each (S. Xu et al. 2014: 7130). In the fifth year of the Shaoxing Reign (AD 1135), Li Gang suggested "docking the warships and large ships built in previous years along the upstream prefectures and counties in Jiankang, such as Taiping prefecture, Jiangzhou prefecture, Wuhu county, Fanchang county, Hukou county, and so on" (S. Yang et al. 1990). He once mobilized 5000 officers and soldiers with pedal wheel ships to station in Qiyang (G. Li 2004: 894). In the Caishi Battle in the 31st year of the Shaoxing Reign (AD 1161), all the navy along the river was equipped with pedal wheel ships. The Caishi navy had the ships left by Wang Quan. Yu Yunwen led the Song navy to fight against the Jin navy in Guazhou, taking over the 24 pedal wheel ships left by the Zhenjiang navy (Y. Wu 1990; R. Zhang 1990; X. Lu 1990: 2343). After the Caishi Battle, over 6300 soldiers were registered to pedal wheels in Jiankang Prefecture (X. Li 2013: 3854), indicating a considerable number of pedal wheel ships in Jiankang Prefecture. The Jiankang Navy once possessed over 470 pedal wheel ships (Z. Wang 1990).

In the 31st year of the Shaoxing Reign (AD 1161), the impressive performance of the Jin navy in the battles of Caishi and Zhenjiang won the support of Emperor

Xiaozhong for building pedal wheel ships. He subsequently issued orders for the construction of such ships on multiple occasions. In the third year of the Qiandao Reign (AD 1167), Xue Liangpeng, the acting deputy minister of the Ministry of Works, advised the emperor to "recruit soldiers from the riverside boatmen and deploy them in advance." Considering the truce on the frontier, Emperor Xiaozong dismissed his proposal but ordered Jiangkang and Zhenjiang to "make secret preparations for emergencies." In the fourth year of the Qiandao Reign (AD 1168), Shi Zhengzhi, the prefecture mayor of Jiankang, agreed to allocate 100,000 strings of 1000 coins for "building a 400-Liao warship with one wheel and 12 oars." In the third year of the Chunxi Reign (AD 1176), Guo Gang, the commander of the Jiankang navy, informed the emperor that "the pedal wheel ships in our commission were broken but have been repaired and transformed into multi-paddle ships, modeled after sea ships." However, Emperor Xiaozong rejected the proposal to replace the broken pedal wheel ships with multi-paddle ships, stating, "pedal wheel ships were covered by cowhide in ancient times and were used to win the battle in 1611. How can we transform them? Let Guo Gang thoroughly analyze the situation and deliver a message to all navies stationed along the river that the broken pedal wheel ships should be repaired and not transformed. Multi-paddle ships are only allowed to be built exclusively by the navies themselves and should not take the place of pedal wheel ships." In the eighth year of the Chunxi Reign (AD 1181), Yue Jianshou, the commander of the Jingzhou and Ezhou navy, reported that "the construction of ten pedal wheel ships with eight wheels, which appear to be heavy and slow in navigation, as arranged by the former commander, has been completed halfway. I suggest transforming the remaining half." The emperor then responded, "the remaining five ships can be pedal wheel ships with seven wheels, six wheels, or five wheels, totaling ten" (S. Xu et al. 2014: 7132, 7135–36). This evidence demonstrates that Emperor Xiaozong prioritized the repair and construction of pedal wheel ships.

In the third year of the Jiatai Reign (AD 1203), as mentioned earlier, Qin Shifu constructed the Iron Gunwheel Warships in Chizhou prefecture. According to the tenth volume of *The Chorography of Zhenjiang in the Jiading Reign*, "the pedal wheel ships registered as warships in General Commander Commission were docked at Duanyao Port along the bank of Jiangnan" in the regions south of the Yangtze River. In his proposal on *the Ten Affairs Summarized After the Inspection*, Wei Liaoweng advised the emperor to allocate funds to Hu'nan and Jiangnan West provinces, and the military prefectures along the Yangtze River, which supplied wood and were administered by the Military Commissions, for the construction of sea loach ships with four wheels and large and small multi-paddle ships. This proposal likely refers to the failure of Zhao Fan at Xiangyang and must have been written by Weng Liaowong after the third year of Duanping (AD 1236) (L. Wei, n.d.). It is probable that his proposal was accepted, as the 39th volume of *Records of Military Defence II* in *Jingding Period Chronicles of Jiankang* documented the construction of such ships during Emperor Lizong's Reign. According to the records, when Ma Guangzu, the military commissioner, assumed office in August of the third year of the Baoyou Reign (AD 1255), he ordered the construction of "50 Cart-head Ships and 30 pedal wheel ships" within two and a half years. The seventh volume of the *Biography of Emperor Shizu* in the *History of the Yuan Dynasty*, states that Zhang Gui, the Song general in charge of the Xiangyang garrison, "surprisingly sent pedal wheel ships to attack the Yuan navy" in the eighth year of the Xianchun Reign (AD 1272). Furthermore, both Dong Wenbing, the Yuan general, and Zhang Shijie, the Song general, deployed pedal wheel ships in the river battles outside Yangzhou. The records mention that they "sailed on pedal wheel ships, raising the general's flag and beating drums" (L. Song 1976: 3671).

Pedal wheel ships continued to be utilized as warships during the Ming Dynasty. In the 57th volume, *coastal defense,* in the *Book Compilation,* Zhang Huang stated, "pedal wheel ships are crucial for safeguarding against invasions from the sea." In the previously mentioned sixth volume, *Ships* in the *Military Compilation* written by Tang Shunzhi, various shapes and structures of pedal wheel ships were documented. The second volume of *Techniques and Tools* in *the War Tactics* by He Liangchen recorded several types of pedal wheel ships, including "ships with four wheels", "Eight-diagram Flower Ships", "Podi Ships", and more. During the early Qing Dynasty, Lord Lu of the South Ming Dynasty once "constructed over 3,000 pedal wheel ships in Zhoushan, which were sufficiently resilient to withstand fire arrows" (Mingqing Shiliao 2000: 70). Joseph Needham pointed out that passenger ships equipped with wheel propellers emerged during modern navigation between Jiangsu and Shanghai. He mentioned that "three rows of seamen operated together, and the axle was connected with the rear wheel, like the connecting rod of trains. This kind of ship was seen on the Pearl River, too" (Needham 1986: 941). However, these ships only featured a rear wheel, and the rotational motion of the wheels alone could not generate enough propulsive power. Therefore, there was a need to enhance the efficiency, a challenge that the Song people could not overcome when constructing wooden pedal wheel ships with a single axle. Only iron devices could overcome the limitations of wooden axles, such as their bulkiness, limited bearing capacity, and tendency to overheat during high-speed rotation.

4.2.3.2 The Reasons for Pedal Wheel Ships Not Being Used Widely in the Social Economy of the Southern Song Dynasty

During the earlier years of the Shaoxing Reign, the Yang Yao navy and the Song navy extensively deployed pedal wheel ships in battles on Dongting Lake due to two significant advantages they offered: their large size and the ability to launch quick attacks and withdrawals. The application of pedal wheel ships turned the tide of the conflict for Cheng Changyu. Initially, the Yang Yao navy possessed sea loach ships, Zhuolu ships, and others, allowing them to swiftly sail on Dongting Lake and engage in looting with impunity. Cheng Changyu, lacking warships, had no choice but to witness their atrocities and hope for the prompt construction of new warships. Gao Xuan constructed giant pedal wheel ships with eight wheels, and even ships with as many as 22 or 23 wheels for Cheng Changyu. These ships could carry 200 to 300 people and move rapidly on the river, exerting formidable pressure on the smaller ships of Yang Yao's navy. Consequently, Yang Yao refrained from audaciously approaching the Song prefectures (K. Yue 1989: 1568). The sea loach ships of Yang Yao's navy dared not confront the grand and imposing pedal wheel ships of the Song navy. Following the construction of these ships, Cheng Changyu managed to defeat the Song navy. The ships they built were two or three stories tall and could accommodate over 1000 soldiers. They possessed the advantage of easy maneuverability in attacks and withdrawals. "Compared with sea loach ships, which were like the light arm troops on the ground, pedal wheel ships were huge, like the well-arrayed phalanx" (K. Xiong 1985: 171).

Pedal wheel ships demonstrated greater maneuverability on calm rivers and lakes compared to sea ships. This was evident in the battles fought by Han Shizhong against the Jin navy in Zhenjiang during the fourth year of the Jianyan Reign (AD 1130). Sea ships, while capable of carrying a large number of soldiers, revealed their limitations on inland rivers. Han Shizhong deployed the Song navy to block the Yangtze River, hindering the northward movement of the Jin navy. According to records, "sea ships were used to blockade the river. When tailwinds blew, they lifted sails and could travel back and forth as if flying." However, "sea ships were immobile without wind", and the Jin navy, following the strategic advice of Mr. Wang, a native of Fuzhou, defeated the sea ships. The tactic involved attacking the sea ships when the wind subsided and retreating from their range when the wind picked up. Additionally, they launched fire attacks against Han's navy, taking advantage of sunny and windless days when the sea ships were immobilized (X. Li 2013: 635). In the battle against the Yuan navy in Zhenjiang, the sea ships used by Zhang Shijie's troops were "unable to move without wind", while the Yuan's patrol boats "sailed swiftly as if flying". Consequently, the Yuan emerged victorious (Songji Sanchao Zhwngyao Jianzheng 2010: 387). Although sea ships had the advantage of size and the ability to carry hundreds or even thousands of people, they were heavily reliant on wind. The triumph of pedal wheel ships over sea ships is exemplified in Yang Yao's victory against the forces of Cui Zeng and Wu Quanjun, who were defending Dongting Lake. When temporarily stationed at Dongting Lake, they utilized Juetou boats and sea ships, which were unsuitable for navigating the lake. In contrast, Yang Yao dispatched several pedal wheel ships equipped with eight wheels. "By pedaling and freely turning their wheels, Yang's ships forcefully crashed into the Song forces, causing hundreds of ships and soldiers to plunge into the water" (K. Yue 1989: 1573). However, in a later battle against the Jin navy, the Song general Yu Yunwen "ordered pedal wheel ships to shuttle in the middle of the Yangtze River, entering Jinshan three times. This greatly startled the Jin navy, forcing them to draw their bows in anticipation of an attack" (Toqta 1977: 11794).

However, the high costs of building, maintenance, and operation hindered its wide application in the social economy. The 66.7-m-long pedal wheel ships built by Cheng Changyu "cost about 20,000 strings of 1000 coins for board materials, labor, and so on." He also built other ships up to 100 m long (S. Xu et al. 2014: 7129). Ye Mengde talked about those pedal wheel ships managed by Huaixi Imperial Commission that were "mostly large ships with ten wheels or nine wheels, whose length was up to over 100 meters". Wang Zao mentioned that pedal wheel ships of 66.7 and 73.3 m long were ordered to be built in Fuzhou prefecture (M. Ye 2002;

Z. Wang, n.d.). Additionally, Lu You recorded 120-meter-long pedal wheel ships and the ones installed with 30 to 40 wheels, which were more expensive than the 66.7-m-long ship built by Cheng Changyu. In the fifth year of the Shaoxing Reign (AD 1135), after conquering Yang Yao, pedal wheel ships began to be built in large numbers in Jiangnan West Province. Wu Shen, an official in Jiangnan West Province, pointed out its four disadvantages: "First, it costs too much work to build such extra large ships. Second, it drains money, because it won't be used frequently. Third, it will waste soldiers in battles if the conditions needed to operate are not all set. Fourth, it will disrupt farmers' agricultural production." Pedal wheel ships were "over 66.7 m in length, over 66.7 m in width, up to 13.3 m in height, and their planks were about 0.3 m thick. They could not be used to fight in windy days because they were heavy and slow. Confronted with fire or cannon attacks, they would be easily burnt and damaged." "Building a ship costs tens of thousands of strings of 1000 coins, let alone the expenditure of building ten ships like this." "The wheels need to be pedaled by several thousand soldiers in the navy, and fewer than 2500 soldiers would be engaged in battle. Now 20 thousand soldiers are required for ten ships to set sail" (S. Yang et al. 1990). Just as Wu Shen said, large pedal wheel ships had limitations in the battles on the Yangtze River, and cost too much money and labor.

Military and civilian ships of other types were much smaller in size and cost less than large pedal wheel ships. In the third year of the Jianyan Reign (AD 1129), "In Pingjiang Prefecture Shipyard, a 400-Liao 36.7-meter-long warship with eight oars cost 1159 strings of 1000 coins. A 5-meter-long Haihu warship with four oars cost 329 strings of 1000 coins" (S. Xu et al. 2014: 7126). In the fifth year of the Qiandao Reign (AD 1169), the navy of the Palace Administration built multi-paddle ships which "had the bilge of lake ships, the cover of warships, and the stem and stern of sea ships. They were about 27.7 meters long, 6.7 meters wide, according to the measurement of the Southern Tang Dynasty. Each of them was 400 Liao and had 42 paddles. Those ships could sail in all water conditions, including rivers, seas, lakes, and so on". "Every ship cost 1670 strings and over 700 extra coins" (S. Xu et al. 2014: 7133). The ship had a complex structure, so it cost more than others, but much less compared to large paddle wheel ships.

River ships, which cost less than warships, and grain-carrying ships, represented by Bian ships, were primarily seen as inland river vessels. Among the river ships, horse-carrying ships were the most expensive. "No ship is bigger and tougher than horse-carrying ships in the navy" (X. Li 2013: 3268), which usually cost hundreds of strings of 1000 coins each. For instance, a 700-Liao horse-carrying ship with four oars, built by the Sichuan Tea-Horse Trade Commission, "costed 440 strings of 1000 coins, including material costs, labor, food, and so on." Without factoring in the cost of labor, it would be 375 strings of 1000 coins. A horse-carrying ship with six oars "costed 800 strings of 1000 coins each." Usually, a 500-Liao ship was equipped with two oars (S. Xu et al. 2014: 7105, 7107), while a 700-Liao ship had four oars. Therefore, a horse-carrying ship with six oars must be 800-Liao or 1000-Liao. In the first year of the Jianyan Reign (AD 1127), the saury-shaped ships, measuring 16.7 m in length and 4 m in width, "costed over 400 strings of 1000 coins each, calculated based on folk prices" (S. Xu et al. 2014: 7125).

Grain-carrying ships usually cost hundreds of strings of 1000 coins. In the fifth year of the Yuanfeng Reign (AD 1082), the ships used for grain transportation on the Guangji River were exempted from a total tax of 84,000 kg of grains. This exemption resulted in significant savings, as “350 ships, 2700 soldiers and boatmen, 33 supervisors for grain transportation, and 11 officers for arresting criminals were reduced, saving a total of 82,000 strings of 1000 coins.” Based on this, it can be deduced that a 240-kg grain-carrying ship cost 234 strings of 1000 coins in terms of material and labor (T. Li 2004: 7783). During the Tang Dynasty, Liu Yan built 240-kg grain-carrying ships and claimed that “each ship cost 1000 strings of 1000 coins, but in reality, it cost less than 500 strings of 1000 coins… over 500 strings of 1000 coins were used as bribes” (S. Su 2010: 3492), indicating that the actual cost was less than 500 strings of 1000 coins per ship. In the period of the Shaoxing Reign, the Jiangnan West Province Transportation Commission built 200 warships and 100 grain-carrying ships with a budget of 10,000 strings of 1000 coins (S. Yang et al. 1990). This means that each ship cost over 330 strings of 1000 coins on average.

Dagger-installed boats, a type of sea ship, typically cost hundreds of strings of 1000 coins. During the Chunxi Reign, a total of “60 dagger-installed boats were built in Fuzhou, with a cost exceeding 50 thousand strings of 1000 coins” (K. Lang 1990: 7901), averaging over 830 strings of 1000 coins per boat. In the third year of the Shaoxi Reign (AD 1192), “200 sea ships with dual masts and multiple paddles, measuring either 4 m or 4.3 m in maximum width, were constructed at a cost of 10 thousand strings of 1000 coins,” equating to 500 strings per ship (S. Xu et al. 2014: 7138).

Large pedal wheel ships were extremely expensive due to the costs associated with shipbuilding, maintenance, and labor. For example, Yang Yao’s pedal wheel ships were repaired in Huaixi Imperial Commission, and each ship was estimated to cost over 400 strings of 1000 coins. The maintenance expenses alone were equivalent to building a 2000-Liao grain-carrying ship or a 700-Liao horse-carrying ship. Yang Yao’s pedal wheel ship, measuring 91.4 m in length and 16.7 m in height, required the collective effort of over 1000 individuals to operate (M. Ye 2002), resulting in high labor costs. Some individuals claimed that ten large pedal wheel ships, each measuring over 66.7 m in length, over 66.7 m in width, and 13.3 m in height, necessitated the employment of 20 thousand people, with 2000 people assigned to each ship. “Thousands of people were required to work on the wheels” (S. Yang et al. 1990), which was greatly exaggerated. The soldiers on board also served as sailors, as they possessed the necessary skills (X. Li 2013: 1117). Therefore, the aforementioned “thousands of people” included the soldiers who doubled as sailors. In order to optimize the workforce and reduce staff, it was common for individuals to perform multiple tasks. For example, on a horse-carrying ship, aside from helmsmen, “five soldiers and 25 horse-holders sculled together on their way back” (S. Xu et al. 2014: 9107). The soldiers and horse-holders assumed the responsibility of pedaling the wheels. However, during battles, the soldiers did not operate the wheels. Rather, “with swords and lances in hands, the soldiers stood by on the ship, when the strong civilians were pedaling wheels under the deck.”(S. Xu et al. 2014: 7853).

Compared to other civilian ships or grain-carrying ships with the same load capacity, pedal wheel ships required more labor. Navigation on the rivers in Sichuan was particularly challenging and demanded a larger number of helmsmen and sailors. Taking the largest 6-oar horse-carrying ships in Sichuan as an example, "every ship was equipped with six oars, 36 seamen and four helmsmen" (S. Xu et al. 2014: 9104). With a load capacity of approximately 30 tons, these ships carried around 40 helmsmen and seamen, some of whom also served as horse-holders. As Zeng Gongliang mentioned in Volume 1 of *Warships* of Book 1 of *The General Record of Military Affairs*, "In the battles on water, the warships are rated according to their sizes. And their load capacity of carrying people was measured by the standard of rice weight that a person weighs 60 kg of rice." Unlike transporting goods, carrying people did not allow for a full load. The actual number of people on board had to be one-third or less of the ship's load capacity. According to Song Dynasty regulations, "a passenger ship with the load capacity of 97.5 tons was allowed to carry 100 barehanded men, and the 65-ton ship was allowed to carry 60 barehanded men and the 32.5-ton ship 30 barehanded men. If the load capacity is below 32.5 tons, the number of people on board decreases accordingly" (S. Xu et al. 2014: 9104). Tourist ships carried even fewer people, approximately one-tenth of their load capacity. As recorded in the entry of "Ships" in *Records of the Capital*, a tourist ship with a load capacity of 325 tons on the West Lake carried "over 100 tourists", while a ship with a load capacity of 162.5 tons carried "about 30 to 50 tourists". Warships did not require as much living space for the soldiers. If we apply a ratio of 3:1, a warship with a load capacity of 325 tons could accommodate 300 soldiers. According to historical records, "large pedal wheel ships installed with 20 to 30 wheels could carry 200 to 300 people" (K. Yue 1989: 1568). The larger two or three-storey ships mentioned in historical records carried soldiers "with swords and lances in hands on the upper storey", while strong civilians pedaled the wheels beneath the deck. The soldiers on the upper deck, along with the strong civilians pedaling the wheels (including a group of four individuals assigned to pedal the wheel, helmsmen, and anchor droppers), totaled 300 people. Consequently, the load capacity was around 320 tons, comparable to a large horse-carrying ship with a load capacity of 325 tons. However, the labor costs for pedal wheel ships were significantly higher than those for horse-carrying ships. Moreover, horse-carrying ships navigating the rivers in Sichuan required more labor compared to other inland river vessels powered by wind or towing.

As warships prioritized speed, they were powered by paddles or oars instead of wheels. Conversely, grain-carrying ships, commercial vessels, and official ships prioritized endurance for long journeys. Taxes levied on grains were paid in kind once a fiscal year and transported via shipping. Quarterly grain shipping was conducted on the Bianhe River, but the minor officials involved often faced criticism, and the soldiers on these ships had limited time for rest. Overseas trades embarked once a year, following the monsoon season. Given that officials' one-way voyages typically took months (C. Huang 2012), pedal wheel ships were not suitable for carrying passengers due to their high costs. In terms of inland navigation, whether on the mainstream or branches of the Yangtze River, canals, or other watercourses, ships sailed downstream by lifting sails in a tailwind, and upstream by being towed along the banks. In Lu You's trip from Hangzhou to Sichuan, "he took a ship with a load capacity of 60 thousand kilograms". "With 26 sails", the ship left Guazhou in a tailwind with all sails lifted and arrived at Zhenzhou at night... Raising sails in the right wind, lots of ships shoved off from Zhenzhou successively in the mist against the background of countless mountains far away, looming like an impressionistic painting. After a while, the wind blew stronger and the ships became faster... In the morning, the ships set sail from Jiankang. The wind came when they went past Shitou, so they lifted sails". "With the sails lifted in tailwinds, the ships could go very fast". "Encountered with a headwind, the ships need to be towed forward by people." Sailing on the Yangtze River in Sichuan, "it used totally six masts and two wagons of thin bamboo strips". "If there was no space for people trackers on the banks, the large ship would be pulled ahead by small ones with thin bamboo strips" (Y. Lu 2012: 168–69, 173, 184, 193, 202, 206). According to Volume 20 of Zhou Mi's *Explanations of Ship Terms* of *Wild Talks of Eastern Qi*, thin bamboo strips were utilized as tools for towing ships. Zhang Shunmin documented his journey to Chenzhou, where he would assume office. He traveled by water from the Yangtze River to the Xiang River. When encountering headwinds or no wind, and when sailing near the bank, the ship required "boat trackers" to tow it forward. While navigating past a dangerous sandbar, the boatmen were helpless and relied on local people who waved flags to guide the ship. These individuals were known as "sandbar guides". "When the official ships sail through this area, they beat drums to call sandbar guides, who were soon available to help their ships through the dangerous beach" (S. Zhang 1990). "Those sandbar guides did it as a career" (C. Fan 2012: 79). During Zhou Bida's voyage on the Qiantang River and the Canal (B. Zhou 1990), and Fan Chengda's journey on the Gan River (C. Fan 2012: 36, 41), they both obeyed the practice of boat-towing in headwinds and lifting sails in tailwinds. In the Song Dynasty, ships transporting taxes in the form of grains via rivers and lakes were towed by "the men hired by the officials" (Toqta 1977: 10160) or the Song garrison troops. "Some of boat trackers didn't manage to go home in the rest of their lives and died on duty in the watercourse" (T. Li 2004: 4535). Ships undertaking other official tasks were also towed by civilian boat trackers. For example, in the second year of the Mingdao Reign (AD 1033), "30 men towed the new ship from Tanzhou Prefecture to Wuwei Military Prefecture" (T. Li 2004: 2624). It was recorded that civilians were hired as boat trackers for scholar-officials in Huainan East Province during the Song Dynasty (S. Xu et al. 2014: 7134). In the Southern Song Dynasty, to accommodate 35 envoy ships from the Jin Kingdom, Pingjiang Prefecture prepared 100 men for boat towing (S. Xu et al. 2014: 7132). The costs of boat towing could be shared among all the ships in the journey, resulting in reduced operational expenses due to a smaller number of men aboard. Grain-carrying ships on the rivers and lakes even "had just three helmsmen on a ship" (S. Xu et al. 2014: 7126). Therefore, the towing paths were usually built along watercourses. For instance, "bamboo spars were used by both official and private ships in the east of Suzhou in the past. Until the period of the Qingli Reign of Song, towing paths were built widely in the watercourse of the Songjiang River" (Toqta 1977: 10814). Sea ships relied on the power of monsoons, which meant that the number of people on board was minimal. According to the 20th volume of *Records on the Dynasties and Civilians*, a Japanese document, an official voucher issued to a Quanzhou merchant in the fourth year of the Chongning Reign (AD 1105) stated that, apart from the leader Li Chong, there was a helmsman, a steward, sailors, and merchants, totaling 66 people on the ship. Considering the cost, pedal wheel ships were not a practical choice for grain-carrying and merchant ships.

To construct pedal wheel ships in the Song Dynasty, the required wood was typically obtained from the governments of prefectures and counties, which in turn had to seek assistance from civilians (S. Yang et al. 1990). This shifted the burden onto local governments and civilians. During the Caishi Battle, 6346 men were recruited to pedal the wheels (S. Xu et al. 2014: 7853). However, due to the high cost involved, pedal wheel ships often could not be repaired promptly outside of battle. In the tenth year of the Shaoxing Reign (AD 1140), out of the 387 warships managed by the Huaixi Imperial Commission, 154 were deemed beyond repair and scrapped (M. Ye 2002). After the Caishi Battle, "some of the pedal wheel ships' nails, boards, wheels and axles were broken" (S. Yang et al. 1990). As a result, the government gradually abandoned the construction of large pedal wheel ships and instead focused on building smaller pedal wheel ships or ships equipped with both wheels and paddles. In the fifth year of the Shaoxing Reign (AD 1135), the provinces of Liangzhe and Jiangnan produced lightweight and swift ships with five wheels and ten paddles. These ships were used alongside pedal wheel ships with nine or thirteen wheels. After the reign of Emperor Xiaozong of Song, newly built ships were predominantly small pedal wheel ships with less than eight wheels or ships equipped with both wheels and paddles. Guo Gang opted for multi-paddle ships over pedal wheel ships due to their lighter weight and faster speed, albeit with variations in building materials (R. Zhang 1990).

As discussed, multi-paddle ships possessed similar maneuverability to pedal wheel ships but featured smaller structures and lower load capacities. Combining the advantages of both ship types, ships with both wheels and paddles were compact yet powerful. An example of such a ship was the warship built by Shi Zhengzhi, the mayor of Jiankang Prefecture, in the fourth year of the Qiandao Reign (AD 1168). This ship had a single wheel and twelve paddles, with a load capacity of 130 tons. Hence, Joseph Needham's explanation of "12 paddles installed on a wheel" (Needham 1986: 941) was proven incorrect. The Iron Gunwheel Warship, created by Qin Shifu in the third year of the Jiatai Reign (AD 1203), featured four wheels and six paddles. Even when pedal wheel ships without paddles were occasionally built after the reign of Emperor Xiaozong of Song, their sizes and structures were smaller compared to those constructed during the Shaoxing Reign. In the eighth year of the Chunxi Reign (AD 1181), ten pedal wheel ships with eight wheels, which were considered "too heavy and slow", were authorized to be transformed, with five of them redesigned with seven wheels, six wheels, and five wheels. Wei Liaoweng recommended that the sea loach ships with four wheels built in Huainan and Jiangnan West Province should be multi-paddle ships. During the Baoyou Reign, Ma Guangzu built new ships in the Jiankang Commission. Among them, apart from 30 pedal wheel ships with four wheels, the majority were multi-oar ships (Y. Zhou 1990: 1983).

4.2.4 Summary

Pedal wheel ships relied on individuals pedaling on wheels to propel them forward. Based on this characteristic, those constructed by Li Gao are likely the earliest instances documented in historical records. The notion that the "water wheels" in the Jin Dynasty or the "Thousand Mile Ship" created by Zu Chongzhi served as prototypes for pedal wheel ships is purely speculative. In the Southern Song Dynasty, Cheng Changyu commissioned Gao Xuan to construct pedal wheel ships, which were subsequently replicated by Yang Yao's navy. Additionally, the ships built in Jinghu in the Southern Song Dynasty adopted the shape and structure of Li Gao's original design.

The wheels of pedal wheel ships were constructed from wood and operated by manpower, with limitations on their size and rotational speed. Therefore, simply adding more individuals to pedal or increasing the number of paddles could not provide unlimited propulsion. Furthermore, considering the width of large paddle wheel ships and the necessary living space for the crew, it was not feasible to connect two wheels with a single axle. A wheel and an axle together formed a power unit of a pedal wheel ship, referred to as "a wheel". The term "wheel" was used to indicate the number of wheels on the ship, serving as a measurement for the ship's size.

The costs associated with pedal wheel ships were significantly higher than those of regular ships. The expenses for large pedal wheel ships could exceed ten thousand strings of 1000 coins, whereas common ships typically cost less than one thousand strings of 1000 coins. The maintenance costs of large pedal wheel ships alone could equal the price of constructing a new river ship or Bian ship. Additionally, the labor costs, determined by the number of crew members, were higher compared to other ships with similar load capacities. Grain-carrying ships and sea ships in the Song Dynasty were designed for extended voyages, often spanning years or quarters. Unlike warships, these ships relied on wind power and towing by humans, placing little emphasis on speed. Consequently, the sailing costs for these ships were lower compared to pedal wheel ships. The high costs associated with pedal wheel ships limited their application in social and economic activities, leading to their prohibition as commercial or grain-carrying vessels. Furthermore, official warships underwent transformations, becoming smaller pedal wheel ships or ships equipped with both wheels and paddles after the reign of Emperor Xiaozong.

Li Bozhong coined the term "super light structure" (B. Li 2000: 456–69) to describe the characteristics of industrial development in the regions south of the Yangtze River during the Ming and Qing dynasties. This term emphasized the priority given to light industry, the neglect of heavy industry, the limited availability of coal and iron, and the predominant use of wood as the main source of fuel for industrial production. Ge Jinfang further pointed out that the "super light structure" had already emerged during the Southern Song Dynasty, becoming a prominent feature of handicraft development at that time (J. Ge 2012: 238). Even though the shipbuilding industry experienced significant growth during the Southern Song Dynasty, it was also marked by the "super light structure." This applied to pedal wheel ships as well. While numerous wooden ships driven by human power were built during the Southern Song Dynasty, this increase primarily reflected a change in production quantity rather than technological innovation. The speed and carrying capacity of these wooden pedal wheel ships were limited, although the continuous rotation of the wheels by people improved efficiency compared to paddles and oars. To achieve true "technological innovation", pedal wheel ships needed to overcome two factors: the engine and raw materials. This would involve replacing human power with mechanical power and wood with iron. Only through such advancements could technical barriers be overcome. However, ancient China did not possess the economic and technical means to realize these breakthroughs, as they were dependent on the "coal and iron revolution". Consequently, the historical fate of man-powered wooden pedal wheel ships remained unaffected by the emergence of mechanically powered ships in ancient China. Moreover, the absence of a mechanism to encourage technical innovation in ancient China hindered the pedal wheel ships from embarking on a "technological revolution". Consequently, they brought about minimal changes to the shipbuilding industry overall.

4.3 Composition and Functions of the Defense System on the Yangtze River in the Southern Song Dynasty

The focus of frontier defense in the Southern Song Dynasty shifted from the three provinces along the Yangtze River in the Northern Song Dynasty to Sichuan, Shaanxi, the Yangtze River, and the Huaihe River areas. During conflicts with the Jin navy, the Song navy effectively repelled Jin's aggression in the border areas of Sichuan and Shaanxi, resulting in a stalemate at the front-line of the Huaihe River and Dasanguan. While the defense of the Yangtze River was crucial for success, neither side prioritized the Huaihe River as the decisive factor in victory. However, thanks to effective river defense, the Southern Song Dynasty successfully repelled Jin's aggression and maintained peace in the regions south of the Yangtze River. After decades of confrontations, the navy of ancient Mongolia managed to break through the river defense in Ezhou prefecture and ultimately brought down the Southern Song Dynasty within a few years. The river defense system was considered a crucial safeguard for the country. A comprehensive analysis and strategic deployment led to the establishment of a rigorous river defense system. Many experts have studied the river defense in the Sichuan and Shaanxi areas during the Southern Song Dynasty, and further discussions have focused on the mountain and river military camps used in battles against the Jin navy, as well as the river defense system of that time.[4] However, the

[4] The relatively complete research on the defense system of of Sichuan and Shaanxi in the Southern Song Dynasty are as follows: *A History of Military in the Southern Song Dynasty* written by Su pinxiao, *A Study on the Military Defense Mechanism of the Sichuan-Shanxi Frontier Areas in the South Song Dynasty* by He Yuhong, *Local Forces of the Southern Song—A Study on Local Armies*

river defense system in the Southern Song Dynasty has not been studied as a specific topic, which will be addressed in this chapter.

4.3.1 The Situation of the River Defense in the Southern Song Dynasty

The defense of the Yangtze River, the Huaihe River, and the seas held little practical significance for the Northern Song Dynasty. Historical records mention that "the navy in the southeastern regions had strategic advantages in defense. However, in the northwestern regions, the navy was their shortcoming, which could not be dependant on" (R. Zhang 1990). However, for the Southern Song Dynasty, it became a crucial task. A historical account states, "When the emperor's wagons stopped by Lin'an near the Yangtze River and the sea, it was necessary and urgent to ensure the waterway easily accessible to ships" (G. Zhang 1990). By analyzing the national defense of the Southern Song Dynasty from a river defense perspective, we can observe that the defense of Sichuan, Shaanxi, Jingzhou, and Xiangyang in the west, coastal defense in the east, and the Haihe River defense in the north constituted its national defense system. Wei Liaoweng noted that in national defense, priority was given to Jingzhou and Sichuan in the west, the Yangtze River, and the sea. Apart from defending the Yangtze River, "there was defense in Sichuan in the west and coastal defense in the east." "If Sichuan were initially occupied, the enemy could swiftly deploy numerous warships downstream on the Yangtze River. However, with strong winds and rapid currents, even if the Song deployed millions of soldiers armed with bows along the riverbanks, they would struggle to accurately hit their targets." "Additionally, if the enemy's secondary forces launched attacks on coastal areas, putting pressure on our navy and secretly boarding the Shandong-made warships, they could swiftly navigate the waterways from Jiaoxi. With favorable tailwinds, the warships would easily reach Huainan East Province and Liangzhe West Province, threatening the capital city" (L. Wei, n.d.). The common strategy employed by the Jin Kingdom to conquer the Wu Kingdom, by the Sui Dynasty to defeat the Chen Kingdom, and by the Song Dynasty to overthrow the Southern Tang Dynasty was to initially seize control of the upstream portion of the Yangtze River. They would then send warships downstream to attack Jiangnan provinces. This strategy proved to be the most effective way to break through river defense, and ancient Mongolia utilized it to overthrow the Song Dynasty. The Southern Song Dynasty regarded river defense as its frontier, with the defense of Jingzhou and Sichuan and coastal defense serving as its two wings. Among these, Jingzhou, Sichuan and the river defense held significant stakes in national defense.

Avoiding attacks from the upstream was of paramount importance in the two national defense strategies proposed by Chen Yuanjin. It was recorded that "first,

---

and Civil Self-defence Force by Huang Kuanzhong, *A Tentative Study on the Coast Defense of the Southern Song Dynasty* by Wang Qingsong.

the ships and soldiers in the upstream must be abundant. Second, a detailed study on the navy deployment in the upstream must be done". It was also noted that that "if there is a jam in the upstream, the southern part of the Yangtze River won't be safe" (Y. Chen 1990). Li Gang also mentioned the historical fact that "the enemy invaded the southeastern region in the past all from upstream. Those ships sailed in line from the Sichuan branch of the Yangtze River. When the currents and winds were in the right direction, the ships could sail hundreds of miles a day. It took shorter time than three months, even within a month, to reach the Jiangnan and Liangzhe provinces." Consequently, the upstream region was heavily guarded. He emphasized that "the Xianghan region controls Jingzhou and Sichuan, connecting the Yangtze River and the Huaihe River, and facing the capital to the south, which enjoys geographic advantages. As a crucial juncture in defense, it became a place where soldiers must contend. A general together with his populous soldiers should garrison Xiangyang" (G. Li 2004: 983). The key factor in the Song Dynasty's ability to defeat the Jin Dynasty over a span of a hundred years was its effective containment of attacks in the Sichuan and Shaanxi borders, preventing the enemy from occupying Sichuan or capturing Jingzhou and Xiangyang. However, there was a fatal flaw in the upstream defense of the Southern Song Dynasty. Zhang Jun once stated that "the Xiang River and the Hanshui River run through Wuchang, and the grain-carrying ships could reach it" (S. Yang et al. 1990), which had implications for river defense. Ancient Mongolia, however, constructed over ten thousand warships and trained tens of thousands of seamen during the siege of Xiangyang. They then sailed down the Hanshui River, breaching the river defense of the Southern Song Dynasty from Ezhou. Li Chun suggested that "the troops stationed in the south of Jingzhou should be mobilized to the south of the Yangtze River, in case the troops led by Lü Meng use the tactics that Guanyu adopted before" (W. Yang 2007: 4456). After capturing Ezhou, ancient Mongolia employed the same tactics previously used by Lü Meng, sailing upstream and easily seizing Jingzhou, aligning it with Sichuan.

The Yangtze River, the Huaihe River, and the Liangzhe provinces were guarded by strong navies and warships, distracting the Jin military and the puppet Qi Dynasty, and alleviating some pressure on the upstream troops. Hu Songnian submitted his proposal to the emperor, outlining "the following four advantages of warships": First, they would help consolidate the military force of the Southern Song Dynasty. Second, they would reassure the people in Shandong who desired to return to the Song Dynasty. Third, they would deter the enemy and prevent invasions of Jiangnan and the Liangzhe provinces. Fourth, they would divert the attention of Liu Yu, the emperor of the puppet Qi Dynasty, who was plotting to invade Xiangzhou and the Hanshui River (Toqta 1977: 11698). The defense of the river, Sichuan, Shaanxi, Jingzhou, and Xiangyang were interconnected. Leveraging the advantages of their ships, the Song Dynasty defeated the Jin multiple times at sea and established their empire south of the Yangtze River. When ancient Mongolia sailed south from Sichuan, Meng Gong proposed establishing "three barriers upstream of the Yangtze River": First, a related commission should be established, and all military stationed east of Hanguguan should be deployed to Kuizhou to defend a branch of the Yangtze River, extending from the Fu River to the north. Second, defense should be established in Dingzhou and Lizhou. Third, defense should also be established in Chenzhou, Yuanzhou, Jingzhou, and Guizhou (Toqta 1977: 12377). This tactic aimed to resist ancient Mongolia's aggression along the Sichuan section of the Yangtze River and from Dali. Ancient Mongolia bypassed the defenses in the Huaihe River and the Yangtze River, opting to attack the weakly guarded rear of the Southern Song Dynasty by taking a route through Dali and Annan. As a result, Xiangyang, which had been neglected, was occupied by ancient Mongolia, providing them with an opportunity to break through the river defense in Ezhou on the Han River. Since the Wu Kingdom was established alongside the Yangtze River during the Three Kingdoms period, those whose kingdoms were built along the river relied on robust river defense. The protection of soldiers was essential for the Yangtze River to become a solid defense. Only with brilliant tactics and thorough preparations could the Yangtze River serve as a shield against the enemy. Otherwise, it would become a barrier for both sides (Y. Zhou 1990: 1955). This demonstrates that Sichuan, Jingzhou, and Xiangyang were vital for ensuring river defense.

As the temporary residence of the Southern Song court was located in Lin'an, a coastal city, river defense became a top priority. The boundary between river defense and sea defense was established in the third year of the Jianyan Reign (AD 1129). The river defense extended from Chizhou to Jingnan Prefecture, while the sea defense covered Taipingzhou to Hangzhou (X. Li 2013: 464). During Emperor Gaozong's reign, a new boundary was set. In the 30th year of the Shaoxing Reign (AD 1160), Emperor Gaozong issued orders to deploy forces to safeguard Huangyuduo in Kunshan. However, Liu Bao, the General of the imperial army in Zhenjiang, "refused to obey the order". As a result, the court had to send 300 seamen from Mingzhou to Kunshan (X. Li 2013: 3586). Zhenjiang was designated as part of the river defense area, while Kunshan fell under the sea defense area. Therefore, Liu Bao had a valid reason to reject the order, and the court had no choice but to mobilize seamen from Mingzhou, which was also part of the sea defense area. After Emperor Xiaozong's reign, the boundary was mostly settled. The sea defense area stretched from Changzhou in Liangzhe West Province to the east, while the river defense area extended from Zhenjiang Prefecture in Liangzhe West Province to the west (Y. Zhou 1990: 1734; Y. Wang 2003: 2445; Toqta 1977: 641). Along the coastline of Liangzhe West Province, military camps were constructed from Changzhou in the west to Mingzhou in the south, forming a tight network of river defense. A reliable system was established to requisition civilian boatmen and ships from Fujian and Liangzhe East Province to support coastal Liangzhe West Province and Mingzhou.

The defense of the Yangtze River was deemed crucial, with sea defense and the Huaihe River defense providing support. The Song Dynasty believed that the security of the nation relied more on the defense of the Yangtze River than on sea defense. Liao Gang remarked that "taking the battle onto the treacherous sea was an uncommon practice in ancient times" and that "relying solely on sea defense to confront the enemy was a temporary and irresponsible solution, which would disappoint the people and make us inferior to the enemy" (G. Liao 1990). He considered the court's emphasis on sea defense to be a short-term and irresponsible approach, suggesting that a more effective border security policy would involve prioritizing the defense of the Yangtze River and the Huaihe River. Therefore, the river defense navy in the Song Dynasty was not deployed for sea defense, but the sea defense navy could be utilized for river defense. The Xupu Navy, responsible for sea defense, was repeatedly called upon by the court to send troops to Jiankang Prefecture, supporting Jiangzhou, Chizhou, and E'chu in defending the river (C. Fan 1990: 722). In the second year of the Kaixi Reign (AD 1206), 45 sea ships, 27 passenger ships, over 800 anchor droppers and helmsmen, and over 2480 seamen were mobilized from the Xupu Commission, Wenzhou, and Fuzhou to the Jiaoshan and Jinshan areas in Zhenjiang to "protect the river" (X. Lu 1990: 2390). Moreover, the Jin Dynasty was not adept at naval warfare, reducing their chances of defeating the Southern Song troops at sea. The only two naval battles between them were the Mingzhou Sea Battle in the fourth year of the Jianyan Reign (AD 1130) and the Jiaoxi Sea Battle in the 32nd year of the Shaoxing Reign (AD 1162). These battles showcased the overwhelming naval power of the Song Dynasty, leaving no opportunity for the Jin navy to traverse long distances and launch surprise attacks on the Southern Song navy, as described by Weng Lioawong. The primary purpose of the robust sea defense system centered around Lin'an was to combat piracy, while for the Jin navy, it served as strategic protection.

The defense of the Huaihe River was a frontier for the Southern Song Dynasty against the Jin troops. According to Li Chun, eight important locations, including Chuzhou, Xuyi, Zhaoxin, Haozhou, Guokou, Huaye, Zhengyang, and Guangzhou, played a crucial role in protecting the Huaihe River (W. Yang 2007: 4456). Among these locations, Chuzhou held the key to safeguarding the Huaihe River. The branch of the Huaihe River originated from the north, and Chuzhou served as the entrance to the canal. With the exception of the Huainan Canal, no other branches could reach the Yangtze River. As described, "five branches of the Huaihe River, including Qing River, Bian River, Guo River, Ying River, and Cai River, stretch to the north. Only the canal in Chuzhou could run into the Yangtze River in the south. The ships of the Jin sail along the five branches. If they want to reach the Yangtze River, the canal in Chuzhou must be seized." Therefore, Chuzhou acted as the vital link between the south and the north (Toqta 1977: 12183). If Chuzhou was occupied, the Jin navy would sail southward along the canal. There would be a continuous stream of ships threatening the water gate of the Zhenyang Dam. Their goal was to secure transportation convenience provided by the Yangtze River. Once they achieved victory, they could transport grains across the river without further hindrance (Z. Wang 1990). Luzhou (also known as Hefei) held great strategic importance. As Zhang Jun mentioned, "The canal in Chuzhou connects to the Qing River in the north and serves as a vital waterway, ensuring convenient transportation." Additionally, "The Big Lake, which connects to the Yangtze River, can be reached from Hefei areas, and only small ships can navigate this waterway. Hefei is not an ideal location" (S. Yang et al. 1990). This is because none of the rivers in the Huainan West Province flow into the Huaihe River. Sailing north from Jiaohu Lake, Luzhou can be reached. Therefore, it is not suitable for shipbuilding, as the enemy could capture the ships and sail from Jiaohu Lake to the Yangtze River. The enemy typically attacks Chaoxian and Hezhou to gain entry into the Yangtze River, considering them their primary targets. Lyuhe

County and Yangzhou are their secondary choices (Z. Wang 1990). Consequently, there are no waterways in the Huainan West Province that directly connect to the Yangtze River or the Huaihe River. If the enemy broke through the defense of the Huaihe River and seized Luzhou, they could sail into the Yangtze River from Chaohu Lake. To the south of Chaohe Lake, Chaoxian also held military defense significance. As described, "Chaoxian serves as a vital transportation junction with Jiaohu Lake in the north and Hongwu in the south, bordering three prefectures—Hefei, Heyang, and Wuwei" (Y. Zhou 1990: 1962).

The people of the Southern Song Dynasty recognized that "the Huaihe River was relatively shallow and easy to cross, while the Yangtze River was deep, vast, and plain" (M. Ye 2002). "Maybe the defense of the Huaihe River is not enough, but the defense of the Yangtze River is vital and unequivocal" (W. Yang 2007: 4456). In discussions about the capital's location and the emperor's temporary palace, it was suggested that if the military strength was sufficient to defend the southern areas of the Huaihe River, the capital would be set in Jiankang, with the southern Huaihe River serving as protection, gradually reclaiming lost territory (X. Li 2013: 1681). However, if the military strength was lacking, the capital would be established in Wukuai, protected by the Yangtze River, to preserve the court's power. As a result, the palace of the emperor of the Southern Song Dynasty was located in Lin'an (Toqta 1977: 11715). The prevailing understanding among the people of the Southern Song Dynasty was that defending the Huaihe River was challenging, while securing the Yangtze River was crucial. It was recorded that if the Huaihe River was lost, the Yangtze River must be safeguarded. Defending the Yangtze River would undoubtedly require a significant portion of the military forces, but failing to do so would jeopardize the security of the nation (M. Ye 2002). Some people even held that "safeguarding the Huaihe River is hard and protecting the Yangtze River is easy, so the protection of the Yangtze River is better than that of the Huaihe River" (Y. Lü 1990). "The Huaihe River is unreliable as a defense" (Z. Wang 1990). Ni Pu advised Emperor Gaozong that the military forces from the Yangtze River and the Huaihe River should be concentrated on guarding the Yangtze River, leaving the eastern and western provinces of Huainan without garrison soldiers to lure the enemy (P. Ni 1990). He proposed abandoning the defense of the Huaihe River and using it as bait when the Yangtze River was strongly protected. This tendency to neglect the Huaihe River and prioritize the Yangtze River emerged in the late Southern Song Dynasty. Chuzhou was lacking commanding generals, and the Chuzhou Forces were renamed the Huai'an Forces. The defense of Chuzhou was likened to putting a halter on a horse (Toqta 1977: 13837). In Huainan East Province, there used to be around a thousand warships, both new and old, ready for use, preventing the enemy from quickly crossing the Huaihe River. However, in the first year of the Duanping Reign (AD 1234), the warships dispatched from Huainan East Province did not return for a long time. Some speculated that the navy previously stationed on the Huaihe River was called back to protect the Yangtze River (L. Wei, n.d.).

However, there were individuals in the Southern Song Dynasty who fully recognized the importance of defending the Huaihe River. They understood that if Huainan East and West provinces were lost, the defense of the Yangtze River would also fail, and Jiangnan and Liangzhe provinces would not remain peaceful (Q. Hu 1990). They likened the defense of the Yangtze River to a vital door and the defense of the Huaihe River to fences. They believed that the Southern Song Dynasty was established in the southeastern areas, lacking easily defensible locations, with only the Yangtze River functioning as a crucial door to defend against the enemy, and the Huaihe River serving as a fence (B. Cheng 1990). Huainan East Province regarded Chuzhou, Sizhou, and Guangling as its first line of defense, thereby providing shelter to Jingkou and Moling. Similarly, Huainan West Province relied on Luzhou, Shouzhou, and Liyang as its first barrier to better protect Jiankang and Gushu (R. Zhang 1990). They also acknowledged that the Huaihe River was vulnerable to breaches, and therefore, ground defense played a significant role in its defense, while water defense was crucial for the Yangtze River. Historical records described the need to repair warships and train the navy in preparation for river defense. The dispatching of the navy from Huainan East Province to reinforce the Huaihe River defense was emphasized, along with gathering village chiefs and training militia (S. Yang et al. 1990). The function of defense in the Huainan provinces was to safeguard the area, lure the enemy, and collaborate with the Yangtze River defense forces to besiege the enemy. A tactical approach was outlined, involving the establishment of military camps at strategically advantageous locations, patrols led by vice generals, and support from the navy if the enemy launched a direct attack. Generals would provide aid by patrolling back and forth on the Yangtze River, demonstrating a thoughtful approach to defense (Y. Zhou 1990: 1961). Those who prioritized the defense of the Yangtze River while neglecting the Huaihe River were criticized for their lack of foresight. They focused solely on protecting the Yangtze River and left cities along the Huaihe River unguarded, which was deemed inadequate in times of emergency (Toqta 1977: 11935).

The river defense played a crucial role in the front-line security of the Southern Song Dynasty. The defensive system was structured with Jinzhou and Xiangyang serving as barriers in the west, the Huaihe River acting as a northern fence, and sea defense supplementing the eastern side. This comprehensive defensive arrangement effectively countered Jin's aggression and enabled the Southern Song military to protect regions such as Sichuan, Shaanxi, Jingzhou, and Xiangyang. During the conflict, King Hailing of the Jin attempted to breach the Huaihe River with his navy but perished in battle north of the Yangtze River. Thanks to the robust and rigorous defensive system, the Southern Song Dynasty successfully repelled Jin's naval attacks. This strategic blueprint and defensive system proved successful in thwarting frontal assaults by the Jin navy from the Huainan provinces. However, the defensive system faltered when the Mongolian forces advanced eastward along the Yangtze River, breaching the river defense in the process.

4.3.2 *The Navy Deployment and Fortress Layout in the River Defense of the Southern Song Dynasty*

4.3.2.1 The Navy Deployment in the River Defense of the Southern Song Dynasty

A significant number of navies were built beside the Yangtze River during the early Northern Song Dynasty. During Emperor Taizu's Reign, the Shenwei Navy was founded in the capital. Later, Emperor Zhenzong established the Huyi Navy (C. Gao 1990). The formidable strength of the navy in the Song Dynasty was evident in the battles on the Yangtze River aimed at conquering rebellions in the regions south of the river during Emperor Taizu's reign. In the Tongling Battle, Cao Bin captured over 300 warships and more than 800 seamen from the navy of the Southern Tang Kingdom. Subsequently, Li Congshan, a general from Southern Tang stationed in Taining, surrendered to the Song Dynasty along with his subordinates and over 1300 seamen. Li Shu, a commander of the Hanyang Navy of Song, defeated over 3000 enemies from the Jiangnan Ezhou Navy and captured more than 40 warships. Cao Bin defeated thousands of enemies from the Jiangnan Navy at Xinlin Military Camp, capturing 30 warships. Ning Guangzuo, a supervisor of soldiers and horses in the Hanyang Navy of Song, defeated over 3000 enemies from the Ezhou Navy. Cao Bin and other generals also clashed with the Jiangnan Navy at Xinlin Port, resulting in the death of 2000 enemies and the destruction of over 60 warships. Additionally, they defeated over ten thousand enemies from the Jiangnan Navy in Bailuzhou, with more than 5000 enemies killed and over 100 prisoners captured, along with 50 warships. Wang Ming reported the defeat of over ten thousand enemies from the Jiangnan Navy in Wuchang, along with the seizure of 500 warships. Cao Bin mentioned that over 20 thousand enemies were defeated in a city of the Southern Tang, resulting in the capture of thousands of warships. Wang Ming also reported the defeat of over ten thousand enemies from the Jiangnan Navy in Hukou, along with the capture of 500 warships (R. Zhang 1990). Jinming Lake was excavated in the capital city under the orders of Emperor Taizong. The Shenwei Navy and Huyi Navy were instructed to teach sailing skills and engage in water games on Jinming Lake every March. Emperor Taizong frequently attended and observed navy exercises (Y. Wang 2003: 2707). After the southern rebellions were quelled, the Yangtze River became an inland river for the Song Dynasty. "Battling on the water was the strong point of the southern areas. Now that the country is united, the battle skills on the water have no use. People should practice those skills and make sure they won't be forgotten" (R. Zhang 1990). The navy exercises on the lake eventually became mere rituals.

During the early years of the Jianyan Reign, Li Gang submitted a proposal stating that "5,000 seamen should be deployed to the residences of commanders along the Yangtze River, the Huaihe River, and the Yellow River. Another 2,500 seamen should be deployed to important states and prefectures. Prefectures under their command should be governed by military commanders who are skilled in sailing. The navy was named 'Lingbo Navy' and 'Tower Ship Navy'" (Toqta 1977: 4583). The navy responsible for river defense was called the "Jiangshang Navy", along with the Xupu Navy and Yanhai Navy (Toqta 1977: 4870). The number of seamen in the Jiangshang Navy was small. At the beginning of the Jianyan Reign, an order was issued, stating that "people who could dive for a long time should be recruited from Cangzhou, Binzhou, and the military prefectures along the Yangtze River and the Huaihe River. 5,000 eligible individuals are required." In the third year of the Jianyan Reign (AD 1129), Zheng Zizhi, who was in charge of river defense, recruited 5400 seamen (S. Xu et al. 2014: 9253). Initially, Hu'nan had no navy, but Li Gang "gathered 3,000 boatmen near the river to station in Tanzhou" (X. Li 2013: 1202) in the second year of the Shaoxing Reign (AD 1132). Another order was issued in the fourth year of the Shaoxing Reign (AD 1134), stating that "the navy should be recruited along the river, and warships should be prepared. The newly recruited individuals should be capable of diving for extended periods. 500 qualified individuals are needed" (Toqta 1977: 4819). The Provincial Military Commission recruited 500 seamen, and 14 prefectures in Jiangnan East Province, Liangzhe provinces, and Jinghu provinces each recruited 1500 seamen. They were collectively named the Hengjiang Navy (Toqta 1977: 511, 514). A year later, the existing navy in Hu'nan and Zhou Lun's 10 generals, along with their 5000 soldiers, were all marked with "Hengjiang Navy" tattoos on the back of their hands (X. Li 2013: 1777). In the same year, Emperor Gaozong ordered that "7000 seamen and 1500 ships under the command of Zhang Chong and Geng Jin, the general commanders of the Provincial Military Commission in Jiangnan East Province, be temporarily placed under Han Shizhong's command" (X. Li 2013: 1135). During the early years of Emperor Xiaozong's reign, there were over a thousand ships of various sizes and over 470 pedal wheel ships in the Jiankang Navy. The number of ships was "unprecedentedly" large (Z. Wang 1990). This indicates that the number of seamen in the Jiangshang Navy was much higher.

During the later years of Emperor Lizong's Reign, as ancient Mongolia posed a threat, greater attention was given to the construction of the navy, leading to the further development of the Jiangshang Navy. During the Chunyou years, Emperor Lizong ordered that "the construction of navy in the states and prefectures near the river and the sea should adhere to the regulations." The Military Commission, Imperial Commission, Shipping Commission, and Xupu Navy Commission along the Yangtze River, West Jiangnan Road, Hujing Road, Guangnan Road, and Liangzhe Road collectively built 1000 swift and light warships. They dispatched 30,000 strong men as guerrillas to safeguard these areas. The guerrilla army maintained a navy-to-infantry proportion of 50:50. The navy was referred to as the Guerrilla Navy, such as the "Chizhou Guerrilla Navy." An order was issued emphasizing the defense of the Yangtze River and making the repair and training of seamen the criteria for rewards and punishments (Toqta 1977: 833, 843, 845–46). In the later years of the Chunyou Reign, Wang Ye, the coastal military commissioner, inspected the river and reviewed navy exercises. He witnessed "a line of warships extending up to 150 km" and noted that the guerrilla navy had reached a population of 12,000 seamen, with 10,000 cowhide-covered warships deployed for battle (Toqta 1977: 12576). In the fourth year of the Jingding Reign (AD 1263), the New Ningjiang Navy was established, consisting of the Front Ningjiang Navy and the Rear Ningjiang Navy, totaling 6280 soldiers. The Front Ningjiang Navy had 15 camps in Jiankang and Taiping, while the Rear Ningjiang Navy had 14 camps in Chizhou. Within the New Ningjiang Navy, every 1000 soldiers had 200 cavalrymen. The Front Ningjiang Navy stationed 920 soldiers in eight camps in Jiankangfu, 260 soldiers in seven camps in Taipingzhou, and the Rear Ningjiang Navy stationed 3000 soldiers in 14 camps in Chizhou (Y. Zhou 1990: 1964, 1966). The scale of the navy during this period was larger than that of the early Southern Song Dynasty.

Laws and Institutions Since the Jianyan Reign recorded that "the Imperial Military Commissions in Zhenjiang Prefecture, Jiankang Prefecture, Chizhou, and Ezhou had their own navy, with the number of seamen ranging from over a thousand to several thousand" (X. Li 2000: 422). According to historical records, in terms of the number of seamen in the navies along the Yangtze River, Jiangzhou Navy had 1000 seamen in the second year of the Chunxi Reign (AD 1175). The navy in Chizhou Military Commission consisted of 1000 seamen in the first year of the Chunxi Reign (AD 1174) and increased to 3000 during the Jiading Reign. Caishi Navy in Taipingzhou had 5000 seamen in the 14th year of the Jiading Reign (AD 1221). Yancha Navy in Qingxi, Chizhou had 150 seamen in the fourth year of the Jianyan Reign (AD 1130). Hengjiang Navy in Zhenjiang Prefecture had 1000 seamen in the eighth year of the Shaoxing Reign (AD 1138). It recruited an additional 1500 seamen as the Imperial Navy in the fifth year of the Chunxi Reign (AD 1178) (Toqta 1977: 4632–34) and 1600 seamen, including over 800 helmsmen, anchor-droppers, and sailors, for the river defense navy in the second year of the Kaixi Reign (AD 1206). Therefore, the total number of seamen in Hengjiang Navy amounted to 2480. The navy was ordered the following year to recruit no more than 2000 seamen (X. Lu 1990: 2390). The number of seamen stationed in Ezhou, Jiankang, and other places was also around one thousand or several thousand. In terms of the overall deployment of military forces along the Yangtze River in the Southern Song Dynasty, the upstream areas were heavily guarded, while the downstream areas were loosely guarded. In the later years of the Qiandao Reign, the number of seamen in the Military Commission of each state was as follows: 50,000 seamen in Jiankang, 12,000 in Chizhou, 47,000 in Zhenjiang, 49,000 in Ezhou, and 20,000 in Jingnan (Toqta 1977: 4583). The corresponding deployment for the navy was nearly as described.

Apart from the aforementioned prefectures, the Jiangshang Navy was managed by the Coastal Military Commissions. In June of the first year of the Jianyan Reign (AD 1127), a Coastal Military Commission was established in the Song Dynasty. Coastal military commissioners and vice commissioners were assigned the task of "gathering seamen and warships" and "being responsible for river defense and navy affairs in the regions between Jiankang and Ezhou" (Y. Zhou 1990: 1734). The official residence of the Coastal Military Commission changed between Jiankang and Ezhou. Initially, it was located in Jiankang, then moved to Ezhou in the fourth year of the Shaoxing Reign (AD 1134). It was relocated to Jiankang again in the third year of the Qiandao Reign (AD 1167) and back to Ezhou in the 14th year of the Jiading Reign (AD 1221) (Y. Wang 2003: 2445). Wang Ye took office as the Imperial Commissioner and Coastal Military Commissioner in Jiangdong in the later years of the Chunyou Reign (Toqta 1977: 12576) and moved the official residence back to

Jiankang. The Imperial Commissions in the provinces along the Yangtze River also functioned as Coastal Military Commissions. For example, the Jiangdong Imperial Commission was also referred to as the "Jiangdong Imperial and Coastal Military Commission" (S. Xu et al. 2014: 3994). The navies in the provinces were managed by the Imperial Commissions, whose subordinate departments conducted inspections at many crucial locations for river defense. The Shujiang River and the Yanjiang River in Xiazhou were patrolled by two border security inspectors. Guizhou, Xiazhou, and Jingmen were each patrolled by one inspector. In the fourth year of the Qiandao Reign (AD 1168), "an inspector of the Shujiang River was dispatched to Shashi, Jingzhou to build military camps," and "the inspectors in the two counties of Jiangling and Gong'an and the local army were dispatched to Gong'an to build military camps, neighboring the Inspection Commissions of Shishou, Jianli, and Qianjiang." From the Lufu River in Jianli County to the Tongji Ferry in Hanyang, there was a 350-km river called the Zhuanhe River. As described, "it is the river where grain-carrying ships and ships carrying travelers and merchants upstream and downstream of the Yangtze River will pass." Inspection Commissions did not exist until the year 1168 when the first Inspection Commission was established on the Xintan sandbar of the Zhuanhe River (S. Xu et al. 2014: 9665).

In addition to the military defense system, civilians living along the riverside also participated in river defense. The officers of the river defense navy would "unite the militia, who would offer help to station in places where the navy was not available, and cooperate with the navy to safeguard their hometown" (Y. Han 1990). Emperor Gaozong once ordered that conscription should be conducted in the prefectures and military prefectures along the Yangtze River, including Jingnan Prefecture, Yuezhou, Ezhou, Xingguo Military Prefecture, Linjiang Military Prefecture, Jiangzhou, Chizhou, Nankang Military Prefecture, Taipingzhou, Jiangning Prefecture, Zhenjiang Prefecture, Changzhou, Jiangyin Military Prefecture, and Pingjiang Prefecture, with prefecture magistrates, supervisors of municipal financial affairs, county magistrates, and assistants of county magistrates responsible for the conscription. They were to inspect eligible individuals and register land properties one by one, selecting the wealthy and influential individuals as team leaders responsible for designated areas. The stationed places were to be advantageous for defense. Officers were also sent to supervise them. As described, "Chen Yanwen was ordered to choose his designated place for defense from the downstream areas below Chizhou. The upstream places above Jiangzhou can be dispatched a military commissioner" (S. Xu et al. 2014: 9254). Tang Lin assumed the office of Inspection Commissioner and was responsible for inspecting Jiankang Prefecture, Taipingzhou, Chizhou, and Jiangnan West Province. He "warned that local leaders should be friendly to boatmen, tea pickers, salt makers, and those who cut reeds and prepared with tools for cooking on the ships." "Leaders should be selected to lead the ships of the two prefectures to display power to enemies" (Toqta 1977: 12333). Ye Mengde assumed the office of temporary magistrate of the capital and also "cooperated with tens of thousands of riverside militias" and "took over the ferry on the Yangtze River separately" (Toqta 1977: 13135). Wei Liaoweng once advised that "the riverside states and prefectures should gather fish boats to support the navy in defending the river" (L. Wei, n.d.). The river defense was built up through the joint efforts of the navy and the militias.

During the Southern Song Dynasty, the Yangtze River remained relatively free from wars for a long time, resulting in loose management of the navy. Some people commented that "those who safeguarded the Yangtze River were not well-trained navy but rather unruly individuals without proper occupations. They relied on salaries paid by the court and did nothing during times of peace. If enemies were to come, they would flee and loot everything valuable, much like the atrocities committed by Jin soldiers when they insulted the Yellow River during the Jingkang Reign" (D. Sun 1990). When ancient Mongolia invaded the river defense in the upstream of the Yangtze River, the Southern Song Dynasty had no choice but to temporarily conscript civilians into the navy to strengthen river defense. During the Xianchun Reign, "civilians were forcibly enlisted in the navy and had their faces tattooed." Furthermore, "civilians were enticed and captured to become soldiers. Some vendors were tricked into trading on merchant ships, and once they boarded the ships, they would be taken away. Captains were often bribed and sailed rapidly to military camps. Even military prostitutes would entice men on the streets and have their faces tattooed" (Toqta 1977: 4822). Undoubtedly, the situation of river defense did not improve. Although the number of navy personnel and warships was considerable in the late Southern Song Dynasty, "the navy in the upstream neglected their duties. Those who were not registered in the Xupu Navy or Ganpu Navy, along with approximately 3000 seamen downstream, sailed against the current to the Hanshui River, displaying their strength" (Z. Li 1990). The dynasty had to mobilize the sea defense navy from Liangzhe West Province to support the defense of the Yangtze River, but it proved to be a bluff.

4.3.2.2 The Deployment of Crucial River Defense Points

The Song people described the Yangtze River as "dangerous, stretching out thousands of miles. There is more than one way to safeguard rivers. With wise planning, river defense work can yield twofold results with half the effort" (Toqta 1977: 11608). It was crucial to heavily guard vital locations. These vital places included "the delta of the river in the north as the primary station, followed by the islands within the river as secondary importance, and the ports in the south of the Yangtze River as the third most important." The northern delta could repel enemy ships from entering the river, the islands could prevent enemy ships from landing, and the southern ports could house armies and dock ships (Y. Chen 1990). The Southern Song Dynasty stationed troops at strategic points by constructing military camps in riverside areas. "During the Longxing to Baoyou reigns, and later during the Jingding Reign, fortresses and strategic posts were densely built along the banks of the Yangtze River and the Huaihe River, to the extent that people in neighboring fortresses could see each other. The task of protecting the river imposed significant pressure on the people" (Toqta 1977: 4583). This formed the river defense system at vital junctures.

The first tier of vital points in river defense included Jiankang, Zhenjiang, Taipingzhou, Chizhou, Jiujiang (Jiangzhou), Wuchang (Ezhou), and others. Zhang Xiaoxiang listed the vital junctures as Jiankang, Zhenjiang, Jiujiang, and Wuchang (X. Zhang 1980). Wang Zhi argued that "the four vital junctures along the Yangtze River garrisoned by soldiers are Ezhou, Chizhou, Jiankang, and Zhenjiang" (Z. Wang 1990). In his list, Chizhou replaced Jiangzhou. In fact, both were of great significance for river defense. Additionally, the river defense deployment of the Jiangning New Navy indicated that Taipingzhou was as important as Jiankang and Chizhou. Furthermore, Jingzhou was another vital juncture in the upstream region of the Yangtze River.

Jiankang held great significance in river defense during the Southern Song Dynasty as it served as the marshal's residence of Jiangnan East Province. According to records, "Jiankang, being a transportation hub, protects the capital city and controls the border areas of the Huaihe River. Throughout the rise and fall of dynasties, prestigious ministers have been appointed to Jiankang, and high city walls have been constructed. Famous generals and armored navy have been stationed there. Jiankang borders Jingzhou and Ezhou to the north and the sea to the south, making the defense work arduous, with a vital stake in the safety of the dynasty." It was said that "nowhere faces a tougher situation than Jiankang, which is the foundation for the dynasty's revival" (Y. Zhou 1990: 1955–56). Zhenjiang, situated at the intersection of the Yangtze River and the canal in Liangzhe West Province, held undeniable significance for the safety of Liangzhe West Province and Lin'an, where the office of the provincial leader was located. Jiujiang (Jiangzhou) served as the marshal's residence of Jiangnan West Province and was described as a shipping hub, as the Xijiang River from Yuzhang County intersected with the lake from Boyang County at the estuary of the Penshui River. Ezhou was the home of the marshal's residence of the Coastal Military Commission and the leader of Hubei. Numerous rivers, including the Yuanjiang River and the Xiangjiang River, flowed into Dongting Lake, which then ran into the Yangtze River, making Wuchang a shipping hub. Jingzhou also served as a juncture for ships sailing on the Yangtze River through three famous gorges. "Sailing through Kuixia Gorge to Jingzhou, Jiangling is another crucial junction" (R. Zhang 1990). Chizhou and Taipingzhou, bordering Wuwei Military Prefecture and Hezhou to the north and connecting Hefei, Chaohu Lake, and the Yangtze River, served as the most convenient waterway for northern enemies to invade Huainan West Province. Therefore, Chizhou and Taipingzhou played key roles in preventing aggression from Huainan West Province. In the early Southern Song Dynasty, four capable commanders were stationed at strategic points along the riverside. Liu Guangshi, the Imperial Commissioner of Huaixi, stationed at Taipingzhou. Zhang Jun, the Imperial Commissioner of Jiangdong, stationed at Jiankang. Yue Fei, the general commander of Jinghu North Province and Jingxi Province, stationed at Ezhou (Han Shizhong, the Imperial Commissioner of Huainan East Province, stationed at Chuzhou) (R. Zhang 1990). This deployment further emphasizes the importance of Taipingzhou.

The second tier of vital points in the river defense system included key cities and ferries along the Yangtze River. Wu Biaochen listed seven of the most important ferries: "In the southern region of the Yangtze River, from Jingzhou and Ezhou upstream to Changzhou and Runzhou downstream, there are approximately ten prefectures, including seven key ferries. Three important ferries are located upstream in Gong'an and Shishou of Jingnan, and Beijin of Yuezhou. Two important ferries are in the middle stream, namely Wuchang of Ezhou and Caishi of Taipingzhou. Two important ferries are downstream, namely Xuanhua of Jiankangfu and Guazhou of Zhenjiang" (X. Li 2013: 1155). Weng Liaowong pointed out that "considering the defense situation of the Yangtze River, Yidu, Zhijiang, Gong'an, Hanyang, Wuchang, and Xingguo are areas of concern" (L. Wei, n.d.). Yidu, Zhijiang, Hanyang, and Xingguo are places to be concerned about in river defense. Some believe that the river defense from Jiankang to Taipingzhou "includes six vital locations: Jiangning Town, Naosha Sandbar, Caishi, Daxin, as well as Wuhu and Fanchang upstream. All of these locations face Huainan provinces. The remaining places are filled with dense reeds. Some are located on winding banks with swift currents, making it difficult to navigate ships" (Toqta 1977: 11339–40). Ye Mengde emphasized that "there are three places of great significance for river defense," namely, Caishi Ferry, Majia Ferry, and Xuanhua Ferry (M. Ye 2002). Caishi Ferry has always been a crucial point. During the conquest of the Southern Tang, the Song navy crossed the river by constructing pontoon bridges at Caishi Ferry. Jin soldiers also crossed the river from Caishi Ferry during the early Southern Song Dynasty. Some even advised that "the navies in Huainan West Province should be concentrated around Jiankan and Caishi to exert pressure on the enemies" (Z. Wang 1990). Xuanhua Ferry was not within the boundary of Jiankang Prefecture but located in Quanjiao County, Chuzhou, overlooking Jing'an Ferry in Jiankang Prefecture across the river. Jing'an Ferry was also militarily significant. The famous Guazhou Ferry was not situated in Zhenjiang but in Yangzhou, across from Jingkou Ferry in Zhenjiang. Guazhou Ferry played a crucial role in connecting the canal in Huainan provinces, the Yangtze River, and the canal in Liangzhe West Province. Maji Ferry in Jiankang also held importance in river defense. The Jin navy broke through the river defense from this point in the early Southern Song Dynasty. When Ye Mengde was appointed the temporary magistrate of Jiankang, he gathered thousands of civilians to safeguard Maji Ferry (R. Zhang 1990).

The third tier of vital points in the river defense system consisted of secondary ferries and ports. In Taipingzhou, ferries such as Digang Ferry, Sanshan Ferry, and Daxin Ferry, and ports in Chizhou, including Dingjiazhou Port, Yangshan Port, Qingxi Port, Lihe Port, Yancha Port, and Zhaotun Port, were heavily guarded by the Inspection Commissions and protected by militias. Additionally, there were around 20 or 30 other ferries and ports that were not stationed by Inspection Commissions. Inspection Commissions were established only at key ports and ferries (S. Yang et al. 1990). Apart from Digang Ferry and Dingjiazhou port, Cihujia also had an Inspection Commission in Taipingzhou (S. Zhang 1990). Zhaotun Port in Chizhou was also guarded by border soldiers (Y. Lu 2012: 184). An Inspection Commission was set up in Chuishan of Zhenjiang and managed 180 militias. Commissions were also established in Xiaohe Camp of Changzhou, Shipai Camp, and Shen'gang Camp of Jiangyin Military Prefecture (X. Lu 1990: 2394). Along the 535.5-km-long river, "29 military camps of various sizes were built in the prefectures of Jiankang, Taiping, and Chizhou.

Eight military camps were constructed in Jiankang, namely Xiashu, Majiabu, Shahe, Hanqiao, Wangsha, Xinkaihe, Xiasanshan, and Wangcaigang. The seven military camps in Taipingzhou were Pujiawei, Heshan, Caishiji, Bainipu, Shangsanshan, Banziji, and Zhoujiazhuang. The 14 military camps in Chizhou were Changpushan, Datong, Meigen, Ronggang, Qijiagou, Liwanghe, Baosaiji, Huangshiji, Jiyanghu, Zhujiaji, Wushiji, Xiangkou, and Shuanghe" (Y. Zhou 1990: 1964–65). These were different from the aforementioned garrison sites.

These locations were all situated in the southern region of the Yangtze River, reflecting the passive defensive strategy of the Southern Song Dynasty. However, there were also several vital sites in the northern region of the river. Li Chun mentioned that "four places, namely Gaoyou, Liuhe, the Chaohu river-mouth, and Beixia Passage, were used to safeguard the river" in the north. Additionally, Chejia Ferry in Hezhou, which coordinated with Majia Ferry in Jiankang, and Yuxikou in Hezhou, connecting Chaohu Lake and the Yangtze River, were crucial junctures for river defense (W. Yang 2007: 4456). Going down the Chaohu Lake, "sailing from Hezhou to the Yangtze River, there was only one entry point, either through Yanglin River in the north or Caishi River in the south" (S. Yang et al. 1990). Yanglin Ferry served as a vital location for river defense. Ruxu River, which connected Wuwei Military Prefecture to the Yangtze River, was always contested in battles. "The waterway of Chaohu Lake connected Jiaohu Lake in the upstream, and Ruxu River served as the gateway to this waterway. The eastern and western passes supported Ruxu River from both sides." The navies in Jiangzhou, Chizhou, and Taipingzhou had the responsibility to assist Wuwei Military Prefecture. Caishi Navy also had the duty to "sail on Chaohu Lake and timely protect Ruxu River" (Y. Zhou 1990: 1961; X. Zhu 2010: 4329). The significance of Ruxu River was clearly explained. In the middle stream, "Xunyang in Jiangnan West Province played a vital role in river defense. Shuzhou and Qizhou served as the first line of defense for Xunyang. Wuchang in Jinghu North Province was another crucial location for river defense, with Qizhou and Anzhou acting as its outer defense" (R. Zhang 1990). The vital locations in the north of the Yangtze River had the function of protecting the key fortresses in the south.

4.3.3 The Piracy on the Yangtze River and the River Defense in the Southern Song Dynasty

The historical records of pirates on the Yangtze River during the Northern Song Dynasty were quite common. Yang Yungong, the supply commissioner in Emperor Taizong's reign, witnessed "numerous pirates along the Yangtze River" and was assigned the task of overseeing water transportation in the south and capturing pirates. As a result, "cases of robbery or plunder on the Yangtze River waterway became rare" (Toqta 1977: 10160). However, incidents continued to occur in the main waterway from Jingnan upstream to Jiangning downstream. When Li Ruogu assumed office in

Jingnan, he observed pirates committing crimes on the river, with "pirates robbing merchant ships, murdering people, and disposing of their bodies in the river." This situation persisted for a long time. "Li Ruogu apprehended a pirate who was executed by dismemberment on the street. Gradually, pirate activities subsided" (Toqta 1977: 9739). Zhu Shouchang temporarily held office in Yuezhou, "an area near Dongting Lake that was frequently harassed by pirates. Zhu Shouchang registered and marked names on civilian ships, instructing the civilians to discreetly watch one another and report any suspicious activities when entering or leaving. When pirate ships appeared, the navy would determine their direction and apprehend them. Over time, the pirate troubles diminished. Other prefectures adopted similar methods" (Toqta 1977: 13404). During Huang Tingjian's journey on the Yangtze River near Chizhou, he also encountered pirates in Shajia and Daleikou. Accompanying him was Liu San, a skilled archer who killed three pirates with his arrows (T. Huang 2011: 977). On his way to assume the position of Supervisor of Municipal Financial Affairs in Jiangningzhou, Yang Gao witnessed "pirates killing merchants and destroying ships," prompting him to capture those pirates (Toqta 1977: 10073). After pacifying the southern region of the Yangtze River, no comprehensive river defense system was established, leaving local governments to individually address the pirate problem.

The river defense system was established during the Southern Song Dynasty, employing a different approach to address the issue of piracy. While it also served as a strategic defense against the Jin Kingdom, the primary purpose of the Southern Song's river defense system was to combat pirates. There were only two recorded battles on the Yangtze River between the Song and Jin: one occurred from the third to fourth year of the Jianyan Reign (AD 1129–1130), and the other took place in the 32nd year of the Shaoxing Reign (AD 1162). Prior to the direct engagement of the Song Dynasty and ancient Mongolia with the Yangtze River, the river defense system functioned as a strategic defense against external threats and also served as a means to counter pirate activities. This process contributed to the development of the river defense system.

Between the Jianyan Reign and the early years of the Shaoxing Reign, which marked a period of rampant piracy, a small-scale navy for river defense was established. In the first year of the Shaoxing Reign (AD 1131), the traitor Shao Qing sailed from Taipingzhou, passing through Zhenjiang Prefecture and Jiangyin Military Prefecture, and arrived in Changshu County in Pingjiang Prefecture, looting valuable goods along the way. Although Liu Guangshi dispatched strong soldiers, they failed to capture Shao Qing in time due to the specialized sailing skills of Shao Qing's subordinates compared to the ground forces of Liu Guangshi. Shao Qing settled in Chongmingsha of Tongzhou, amassing thousands of ships while the Song Dynasty lacked a navy. The Song court was unable to take action due to the absence of naval forces (X. Li 2013: 989). The activities of Zhong Xiang and Yang Yao during the early period of the Shaoxing Reign were widespread throughout the entire Dongting Lake basin, and even reached the counties in the upper and middle streams of the Yangtze River, such as Zhijiang, Gong'an, and Shishou. During the process of suppressing the Yang Yao rebellion, the weakness of the navy in the early Southern Song Dynasty was exposed, which ultimately led to its improvement. Li Gang (in the second year of the Shaoxing Reign, AD 1132), Cheng Changyu, and Wang Xie (in the third and fourth years of the Shaoxing Reign, AD 1133 and 1134), and Yue Fei (in the fifth year of the Shaoxing Reign, AD 1135) were successively dispatched to fight against Yang Yao. However, they experienced failure in most battles. Eventually, Yue Fei succeeded with the tactic of "using pirates to defeat pirates." Initially, the Song Navy could not match the Yang Yao navy in many aspects. Firstly, the Yang Yao warships were superior to the Song warships. In the battle between Wang Xie and Yang Yao, "the warships of Yang Yao were tall and large, while those of the Song Navy were short and small, with the seamen battling with short weapons like swords and blades. The Song Navy had a hard time winning" (X. Li 2013: 1356). "The Song Dynasty sent low and small ships to fight against the high and huge enemy warships. Arrows and stones were shot by the enemies from above. The Song navy was positioned lower and had to shoot arrows upward, and they could only see the ships but not the enemies" (K. Yue n.d. 321). When Wu Zeng and Wu Quan fought against the Yang Yao navy, they "ordered the Song soldiers to climb up the enemy ships from their lake ships and sea ships using ladders." The ships in Yang Yao's navy were pedal wheel ships with eight wheels, which were so huge that they "destroyed hundreds of ships from the Song navy." Cui Zeng and Wu Quan died in this battle (X. Li 2013: 1363; K. Yue n.d. 1573). Secondly, the sailing skills of the Song navy were not as proficient as those of Yang Yao's navy. After the defeat of Yang Yao's navy, "the shipbuilding technology of Yuzhang in Jiangnan West Province was modeled on the design of Yang Yao's warships, and other provinces adopted the design of Yuzhang" (S. Yang et al. 1990). Prominent officials in the Song Dynasty believed that those pirates "sailed so fast as if they were flying. They were so skilled that our helmsmen were no match for them." Although the Song navy defeated Jin Wuzhu due to their sailing skills, they performed much worse compared to Yang Yao's navy (S. Yang et al. 1990). Additionally, they lacked the experience of Yang Yao's navy in water battles. "The soldiers in his navy all came from the northwest, so they were not accustomed to fighting on water." Yue Fei realized that "this is the enemy's advantage, but the Song's weakness." Therefore, Yue Fei devised the strategy of "using pirates to defeat pirates" (Toqta 1977: 11383–84) and turned the tide.

Yue Fei's victory led to the downfall of Yang Yao's pirate gang, resulting in the capture of over a thousand enemy ships and the establishment of the formidable Ezhu Navy. The defeated enemies were either recruited or new navies were established, such as Li Gang's navy in Hu'nan (Toqta 1977: 11385). As a result, Yue Fei's navy became the strongest, and the Southern Song navy underwent significant upgrades. One notable advancement was the widespread use of pedal wheel ships in the lower and middle reaches of the Yangtze River. During the later years of the Shaoxing Reign, these pedal wheel ships played a crucial role in the Caishi Battle against Wanyan Liang's navy. Unlike the previous Huangtiandang Battle, where the Song navy's sailing ships were immobilized due to lack of wind, they overcame this limitation in the Caishi Battle. Jin Wuzhu took advantage of a narrow opportunity to escape and launched attacks on the Song navy, putting them in a defensive position (C. Huang 2013).

During the early years of the Shaoxing Reign, there were not only large gangs of pirates like Yang Yao's navy, but also instances of robbers murdering people on ships along the Yangtze River. This posed a threat to both merchants and civilians. Bandits were rampant, killing and robbing people. For example, in February of the first year of the Shaoxing Reign (AD 1131), a pirate named Zhang Rong entered Tongzhou. In March of the second year of the Shaoxing Reign (AD 1132), another pirate named Zhai Jin attacked Hanyang Navy and killed the garrison general Zhao Lingkui (Toqta 1977: 486, 496). However, as the Shaoxing Reign progressed, particularly during the reign of Emperor Xiaozong, the power of the navy increased continuously and the river defense system was perfected. This left no space for big pirate gangs like Yang Yao's navy. The days when pirates, such as Shao Qing and his rebels consisting of several thousand people, sailed on the Yangtze River lawlessly were long gone. Big pirate gangs could no longer be found. Nevertheless, in the seventh year of the Chunxi Reign (AD 1180), famine struck Jiankang Prefecture. Xu Wu led pirates to cause trouble and declared himself the General of Jing River. Fan Chengda, the Military Commissioner in Jiangnan East Province, dispatched soldiers to arrest and kill him (Toqta 1977: 11870). However, historical records of such incidents are few. The pirates' aggression on the main waterway of the Yangtze River decreased compared to the situation during the Northern Song Dynasty.

However, despite the efforts to curb piracy, certain river sections and lakes with complex terrains along the Yangtze River were still occupied by pirates. One such area was Dingjiazhou in Fanchang County of Taipingzhou, which was an islet in a river and provided easy access for pirates. "It was a place that pirates always occupied and used as a base for committing crimes. Robberies typically occurred when individuals were resting alone on ships at night or when they were off guard in ports along the Yangtze River. However, in Dingjiazhou, pirates brazenly plundered in broad daylight. They would kill everyone on the ships, rob all the property, and sink the ships, making it difficult for officials to track them down." Although an Inspection Commission was established on the islet, there were no soldiers or ships present, and the pirates operated without fear. To mitigate this, merchants often sailed together in groups. As described, when sailing upstream, merchants would gather and form a team in Wuhu. From there, they would proceed downstream and converge in Hukou of Jiangzhou, sailing together. A fleet needed to consist of at least ten ships, as merchants were reluctant to sail on the river with fewer numbers. Zhang Shou suggested that regulating the Inspection Commission in Dingjiazhou was the most effective solution to combat the rampant piracy. He proposed that generals, accompanied by a hundred to two hundred subordinates and a dozen ships, should be dispatched to station in Dingjiazhou on a rotating basis, changing every month. This approach would contain the pirate bases, preventing them from colluding with each other and sending a clear message that the area was guarded by soldiers, leaving no opportunity for them to continue robbing people. Naturally, the pirates who could not engage in plundering would leave the area (S. Zhang 1990). As the river defense system became more robust, the pirates in the main waterway found it increasingly difficult to gain strength.

Another area plagued by pirates was the Zhuanhe River, which extended from Lufu River in Jianli County to Tongji Ferry in Hanyang Military Prefecture. Initially, "without suppression and management from the Inspection Commission, the pirates had nothing to fear." An Inspection Commission was established on Xintan Sandbar of the Dunhe River in the fourth year of the Qiandao Reign (AD 1168) (S. Xu et al. 2014: 9665). During Lu You's journey to Sichuan, he observed that "the banks were densely covered with reeds, where passing ships were likely to be targeted for robbery. The soldiers in Tongji patrolled the area armed, and Lu You could not sleep all night" (Y. Lu 2012: 187). Despite the soldiers' nighttime patrols and vigilant guarding, Lu You remained awake. When Fan Chengda sailed eastward from Sichuan and passed through the Dunhe River, he noticed "lush reeds lining the banks, interspersed with some houses." "Due to the numerous branches leading to small lakes, it became an attractive spot for pirates. The officials led soldiers to patrol throughout the night, making the pirates afraid to appear in the region." Specifically, the Bailihuang section was described as "covered with water chestnuts and reeds, with no inhabitants, where pirates often appeared." While sailing through this river, Fan Chengda was struck by the fact that "the moonlit sky was as bright as day. The fearless soldiers rowed boats all night, ready to shoot arrows from their bows. They beat drums loudly to display their power, and their vigilance did not waver even at dawn" (C. Fan 2012: 82). However, unlike the Dunhe River, which was plagued by pirates, the main channel of the Yangtze River remained undisturbed by them.

Third, the river mouths of Wuyang and Yugan, located in the southern part of Boyang Lake with numerous branches, provided shelters for pirates. Among them, Wuzikou, situated at the rear of Boyang Lake, remained a haven and operational area for lake pirates. Sailing alone with favorable tailwinds and unfurled sails, only a few ships could successfully navigate this stretch of water during the Qiandao Reign (C. Fan 2012: 36). Boyang Lake had long been plagued by pirates since the Northern Song Dynasty. Rao Huaiying, during the Northern Song Dynasty, "once sailed on Boyang Lake and moored his ship at the estuary, close to what appeared to be a merchant tourist vessel. In the darkness, Rao Huaiying observed suspicious activities and suspected it was a pirate ship." Subsequently, Rao Huaiying set a trap and managed to kill five or six pirates while capturing two of them alive (N. Lü 1990).

The issue of piracy was not limited to the Yangtze River region but also affected other riverside and lakeside areas to some extent. For example, the downstream of Taihu Lake and Qiantang River faced complex water conditions and were severely plagued by pirates. "Liangzhe West Province also had numerous pirates who gathered in Taihu Lake" (Toqta 1977: 13254). During the Jiading Reign, "a man killed people for their belongings and then escaped by sailing away." Eventually, he was apprehended in Taihu Lake along with his ship (Toqta 1977: 12331). Pirates had long been harbored in Taihu Lake, with notable instances of rampant piracy in Dipu of Changxing County. Furthermore, guards stationed at the transportation waterways in the southern shallow lakes colluded with the pirates and provided them with information. When merchant and passenger ships sailed close to the shore, they would be interrogated about the contents of their ships. While passing through critical waterways, pirates would feign ship inspections and then proceed to rob them at will. The Navy was dispatched by the Inspection Commission to arrest the pirates, but whether they were captured or not depended on the border soldiers (F. Fang 1990). These robbers typically operated in groups of hundreds of pirates, using dozens of ships and an arsenal of weapons. They frequently sailed on Taihu Lake, targeting towns and cities for their robberies. In the second year of the Baoyou Reign (AD 1254), the Song Dynasty deployed over 3500 seamen from Xupu, Gujing, Kanpu, and other regions to capture the pirate leaders Chen Chao, Chen You, Shen Wenhai, and Shen Wenhuan alive, along with their 380 subordinates and over 200 ships. The operation involved both land and water attacks (H. Bao 1990). However, after the early years of the Southern Song Dynasty, such large-scale pirate activities were no longer observed on other inland rivers. The downstream area of the Qiantang River also experienced unrest. "The pirates were known to carry out daylight robberies, and passenger ships did not dare to sail westward unless a fleet of at least ten ships traveled together." The pirates were typically local gangsters who engaged in prohibited goods trafficking and stored weapons on their ships. When they encountered passenger ships on the lake, they would pretend to be interested in purchasing goods and board the ships. If the passengers agreed to their demands, they might be spared from being robbed; otherwise, all their belongings would be seized. "Dozens of ships in Yanzhou and Wuzhou fell victim to these robberies" (F. Fang 1990). Nevertheless, starting from the late period of the Shaoxing Reign, no widespread pirate activities like these were reported on the systematically and rigorously defended Yangtze River.

4.3.4 Summary

A significant difference in the national defense situation between the Southern and Northern Song Dynasties was that river defense became a vital task of the Southern Song. River defense was viewed as the final and most important protection against the frontal aggression of the Jin Kingdom. Taking river defense as its foundation, the defense in Sichuan, Shaanxi, Jingzhou, and Xiangyang upstream of the Yangtze River served as barriers, the defense in the Huaihe River served as its fence, and sea defense served as its assistance. This established a defensive system against the Jin aggression. Considerable navies and effective navy management systems were built, establishing a multi-layer river defense system at crucial junctures. The river defense system and its strategies in the Southern Song Dynasty played an active role in battles against the Jin navy, safeguarding the security of the Southern Song Dynasty in the region south of the Yangtze River.

The river defense in the Southern Song had its original purpose as resisting the Jin Kingdom. After the establishment of the river defense system, the Southern Song remained in an overall strategic defensive situation passively, except for two significant victories: the Caishi Battle and the battle in Zhenjiang in the 32nd year of the Shaoxing Reign (AD 1162). Internally, it effectively suppressed pirates, and the growth of the Southern Song Navy was closely related to the suppression of pirates in its early period. By the middle of the Shaoxing Reign, the pirates on the main waterway of the Yangtze River were mainly defeated, but some places with complex water situations still faced pirate threats. It is important to note that suppressing and eradicating pirates was not the primary purpose of the Yangtze River defense but rather a byproduct.

The national defense policy in the Southern Song Dynasty was primarily defense-oriented, focusing on river defense as its foundation. The strategy emphasized strict control and billeting of the ground army and navy along the Yangtze River and the Huaihe River, as vital junctures in the defensive plan (H. Shi 1990). Despite recognizing the significance of upstream defense, the Southern Song Dynasty placed greater emphasis on downstream defense in their overall deployment of river defense. This flaw provided an opportunity for ancient Mongolia to train navies and construct ships in Xiangyang, eventually penetrating the defense system through Ezhou. As a result, they were able to exploit the advantages of the Yangtze River and ships with the Southern Song Dynasty. The two sides confronted each other in the upstream region for decades, but once the river defense was breached, the Southern Song Dynasty was overthrown within a matter of decades.

4.4 The Composition and Functions of Coastal Defense System in the Southern Song Dynasty

During the Northern Song Dynasty, the primary focus of frontier defense was centered around land defense in the three border provinces, with coastal defense playing a secondary role. In contrast, the Southern Song Dynasty relied on land defense of Sichuan Province, Shaanxi Province, Jingzhou, and Xiangzhou for their western frontier defense, while prioritizing military defense along the Yangtze River and the coast in the east, specifically in Ezhou. The Southern Song Dynasty placed great importance on coastal defense and implemented stricter measures than ever before. They emphasized that coastal defense played an essential role in national defense, emphasizing this in their naval institutions, defensive systems, and operations. However, further discussion is needed regarding the regional pattern of coastal defense and its distinctions, including the navy and garrisons, as well as the defensive characteristics of coastal defense (H. Gu 2006; Q. Wang 2004). Additionally, the actual effectiveness of coastal defense remains a question that requires re-evaluation. It is particularly important to objectively assess the strategic design and practical function of the defensive targets of the Southern Song coastal defense, as well as the relationship between river defense and coastal defense.

4.4.1 Stations and Characteristics of the Northern Song's Coastal Defense

According to Dai Zhi, coastal defense originated in the Three Kingdoms period. "Who win the defence of the Yangtze River would win the war. It was in the Jianyan Reign when Prime Minister Zhao Gou moved capital southward to establish the Southern Song that the coastal defense began to be attached importance" (Z. Dai 1990). In other words, coastal defense appeared in the Southern Song Dynasty. From the construction of a coastal defense system and the establishment of the concept of coastal defense, it is safe to say that coastal defense has its origins in the Southern Song Dynasty. The Northern Song Dynasty did not have the best practices in coastal defense. Wang Yingchen stated that "there's no record of how to carry out coastal defense since ancient times" (Y. Wang 1990), even before the Song Dynasty. However, the Northern Song Dynasty did implement coastal defense measures in some areas. The main focus of frontier defense in the Northern Song Dynasty was the land defense of the three border provinces. But contrary to what people in the Song Dynasty said, "after establishing friendly relations with the Liao Kingdom, the maritime border was not completely demarcated." In fact, there was also coastal defense against the Liao in Hebei Province and Jingdong Province. In the eighth year of the Xining Reign (AD 1075), the imperial court decreed that every three months, the Dengzhou Saury-shaped Warship Department must send an inspector to station on Tuoji Island in the North Sea to safeguard the sea with the island as the boundary. In the eighth year of Emperor Zhenghe's Reign (AD 1118), Dengzhou was upgraded to Bianzhou. "Although it was said to be 200 km away from Dengzhou to the Bohai Sea, which was the frontier in the north, it only took one day to reach by following the wind. Now Bianzhou served as the frontier to safeguard territory. A minister asked for enlarging the range of coastal defense, saying, 'Tuoji Island is vast and far away, so I request that Mo Island and Wuhu Island be defined as the border. To the south of Modao Island, there are Qindao Island and Zhudao Island. Please send sentries to make regular patrols. In this way, if there is an enemy invasion, we can strike back in time'" (S. Xu et al. 2014: 9239).

Su Shi provided a detailed description of the coastal defense in the prefectures of Jingdong Province in the Northern Song Dynasty. He noted that "Dengzhou, also known as the remotest border, is located in close proximity to the Liao Kingdom in the northeast. From Dengzhou, one could see the view of the Liao Kingdom, and sailing boats could easily reach Dengzhou with the wind. Since the establishment of the Song Dynasty, an ample number of military forces have been stationed here to practice naval combat and transmit signal fires in the morning and evening to alert for emergencies. Every year in April, soldiers were dispatched to guard Tuoji Island and would return in August to prepare for a sudden attack. From the Jingde Reign onwards, the troop strength has never been less than four or five thousand. Troops were sent from Jingshi, Shangqiu, Jizhou, Yunzhou, Yanzhou, Shanzhou, and other places to garrison, apart from Dengzhou. In the second year of the Qingli Reign (AD 1042), a thousand archers formed the Chenghai Navy, which, together with the thousand personnel from the former Pinghai Navy, were all trained to defend against the Liao Kingdom in the north. Simultaneously, it served as a security guarantee for the route to Jingdong Province. Recognizing the reality, the Liao Kingdom had to restrain itself. In recent years, 60 men from the Pinghai Navy were deployed to Xingyang, Banqiao, and Tao Luo in Mizhou. Last year, a hundred men from the Chenghai Navy were sent to Laizhou, and another hundred were sent to Mizhou. In the future, the 2000 soldiers from Dengzhou, Pinghai and Chenghai are not allowed to be deployed elsewhere" (S. Su 2010: 3005–06). In addition to defending against the Liao Kingdom, they also targeted pirates. There were pirates in Dengzhou in the Northern Song Dynasty as well. During Liu Huan's tenure in Dengzhou, he upgraded the Saury-shaped warships, which deterred pirates from invading the sea (Toqta 1977: 10493). Wang Zhongbao was tasked with traveling to Dengzhou on a post-horse to capture over a hundred pirates, all of whom were apprehended (Toqta 1977: 10513). "The five prefectures, including Qingzhou, Mizhou, Dengzhou, Laizhou, and Weizhou in Jingdong Province were close to the sea, and the coastal Patrol Division from these places to Zhuzhou possessed their saury-shaped warships to capture pirates" (C. Chen 1990). Each coastal prefecture had its own agencies and war ships to defend against pirates.

The coast of Jingdong Province received special attention due to its defense against the Liao Kingdom. In the Northern Song Dynasty, except for Jingdong Province, particularly Dengzhou, where a special mechanism for coastal defense was established, the coastal defense of other provinces lacked clarity and did not receive much attention. Take Fujian Province as an example. Prior to Emperor Renzong's reign, "the coastal military prefectures of Fujian Province were connected to the outside world by the sea, and no special defense had been set up since then" (X. Cai 1996: 369), let alone a coastal defense navy. In the fourth year of Emperor Qingli's reign (AD 1044), the four coastal prefectures of Fujian Province established the inspector of border security. "The inspectors of border security and inner court military officers of Zhangzhou, Quanzhou, Fuzhou, and Xingzhou, as well as 291 officers and soldiers at all levels managed by Lin Keqin pitched their military camp in Huian in Quanzhou. Later, they moved to Guling in Yongtai County. In the second year of the Yuanfeng Reign (AD 1079), the judge Lüqiu Xiaozhi said that "I ask for mobilizing the Patrol Divisions of coastal prefectures and military prefectures", and "the military prefecture of Guling moved to the north shore of Fangshan Du in Min County" (K. Lang 1990: 7932–7933). The Patrol Divisions of the four coastal prefectures were established after the fourth year of the Huangyou Reign (AD 1052). In that year, "the new governor, Cao Mouhou, took office in Fujian Province and diligently handled government affairs. He immediately arranged defense facilities for coastal areas and places vulnerable to foreign invaders." In Quanzhou, Fuzhou, Zhangzhou, Xinghua, and other coastal military prefectures, as well as sea ports, military camps, and Patrol Divisions, were established to "defend and control the sea." During the reigns of Emperors Zhihe and Jiayou, Cai Xiang was in Fujian Province. He observed that in the four prefectures, "the inspector of border security in Bagang and Zhongmen of Min'an, a town in Fuzhou, managed the inspection of imported and exported seagoing vessels at sea; in Quanzhou, the inspector was located 3.5 km away from

Quanzhou city, and performed the same duties as Min'an's inspector every year; in Zhangzhou, there was an inspector of Huangdantou called Zhao Bo previously, who patrolled the sea in summer. In Xinghua Military Prefecture, the inspector was stationed in the mountains, one hundred li away from Xinghua, and there were no other inspectors at sea." Additionally, "because of the fiscal commissioner Gao Yi's submission, the inspector of Huangdantou was moved to Dachiyi, which lay in the mountains of Longyan County. It would take seven days to get to Zhangzhou from here. To prevent thieves, Inviting Sea Merchant was banned" (X. Cai 1996: 370).

Moreover, the sailors from the coastal prefectures lacked training in water battles and were completely inept. "The sailors from the prefectures had no skills in water battles. When they patrolled the sea, they would occasionally catch thieves who stole tea and salt. However, if they encountered a large group of thieves, the thieves would usually prevail as they were adept at water battles. Consequently, the sailors would quickly get injured, and their vessels would be damaged." The sailors did not follow Emperor Renzong's command that "the sailors from the coastal prefectures should acquire the skills of water battles to be prepared for combat." Cai Xiang proposed the reestablishment of the Xinghua military prefecture and the coastal Patrol Division of Zhangzhou. "The Patrol Division within the jurisdiction of Zhangzhou was established and located 2.5 km away from Zhangzhou. The Patrol Division was also tasked with attracting overseas merchants and conducting annual sea patrols. The Patrol Division within the jurisdiction of Xinghua Military Prefecture moved closer to the prefecture, and as it was equipped with ships, patrolling the sea became its responsibility." Furthermore, "the original saury-shaped warships and Patrol Divisions of Fuzhou, Quanzhou, Zhangzhou, and Xinghua military prefecture were reinstated. The number of patrol vessels in the sea was increased, and damaged seagoing vessels were repaired. Additionally, an additional fleet of 35 ships was requested. Among them, Xuanyi Imperial Army soldiers were to be dispatched to the Patrol Division. Moreover, they were required to undergo water battle training and learn to swim" (X. Cai 1996: 371). In this way, the sailors from the coastal prefectures could, to some extent, fulfill their role in coastal defense.

However, the soldiers in the Patrol Division of the four coastal prefectures in Fujian Province primarily consisted of infantry, and their numbers were limited. In the fifth year of the Xi'ning Reign (AD 1072), the headquarters of the Patrol Division in the four coastal prefectures dispatched 200 infantry soldiers from Fuzhou to reinforce coastal defense. In the leap September of the third year of the Yuanfeng Reign (AD 1080), the Patrol Division issued regulations to recruit local soldiers. Due to the remote location of their military camp, only the headquarters of the Patrol Division continued to send grain-supply imperial armies and Song garrison troops on a rotational basis. The law of the Xuanhe Reign stipulated a quota of 175 soldiers. In the sixth year of the Xuanhe Reign (AD 1124), Dong Zhengfeng, the military commissioner of Jingdong Province, assessed the advantages and disadvantages of capturing thieves. He also requested that if the number of soldiers in the Patrol Division exceeded 500, 300 of them should serve as sailors (K. Lang 1990: 7932–7933). It is evident that during the Northern Song Dynasty, Fujian Province had not yet established a dedicated coastal navy. The Patrol Divisions established by the coastal prefectures were even composed of infantry forces. In the later period of Song Renzong's Reign, the camps for the inspector of border security and garrisons were established, but the troops consisted of only 175–300 poorly trained soldiers.

Guangnan provinces faced a similar situation as Fujian Province. In the coastal areas of Guangnan provinces, piracy had been rampant since the Southern Han Dynasty, with some pirate gangs consisting of hundreds of members, causing constant pillaging in prefectures and counties (Toqta 1977: 10160). In the Northern Song Dynasty, apart from the patrol warships of Donghai Sea and Xihai Sea, as well as the inspectors of border security of coastal warships in Lianzhou and Qinzhou, Guangnan Province also had a Warship Department. In the tenth year of the Xi'ning Reign (AD 1077), during the Song Dynasty's conflict with Cangigu, "the warships from the Warship Department only managed to resist the attack by thieves, but many soldiers were injured or killed." Additionally, Guangzhou had a shipyard envoy (T. Li 2004: 1485, 8131, 6882, 4263). These departments were responsible for coastal defense. During the Taipingxingguo Reign, Yang Yungong served as the administrator of ancient customs in Guangzhou and the inspector of border security in Guangzhou and Lianzhou. In the coastal areas of Guangnan provinces, piracy was rampant. "There was a gang of pirates led by a man named Ye. At that time, more than 500 pirates were causing trouble at sea. Yang recruited naval forces to produce light boats and launched a surprise attack, killing the gang's leader. The remaining gang members abandoned their boats and fled, hiding in the valley. Yang cleared a path by cutting wood and wiped them out. When the pirates encountered strong winds and waves, they would anchor among the small islands. Yang led the sailors across the sea and captured almost all of them. They had gained a fearsome reputation for catching pirates. Afterward, Yang and the sailors reached Zhangzhou and Quanzhou, where the pirates had previously stayed, and released the 60 men and women who had been hijacked, sending them back home" (X. Cai 1996: 365–67). These pirates even ravaged Liangzhe East Province and Liangzhe West Province, which included the coastal areas from Fujian Province to Guangnan Province. During Emperor Renzong's reign, a soldier named E Lin turned pirate. "The mishandling of E Lin's gang by the superior officers of the coastal prefectures and military prefectures caused panic among the general population." When such large groups of roaming pirates appeared in the Northern Song Dynasty, the imperial court would send a dedicated envoy for catching them. During Emperor Renzong's Reign, Li Yuanbo was appointed as the envoy from the coast of Liangzhe Province to Guangnan provinces to arrest E Lin (X. Cai 1996: 365–67). However, the Northern Song Dynasty had not yet established a dedicated coastal defense navy. Until the beginning of the Southern Song Dynasty, "there was no warship and navy in the Provincial Military Commissions of Fujian Province and Guangnan provinces. When they encountered pirates, they did not take action to contain but let the pirates do evils at will. The commissions didn't attack actively, and they only sent several soldiers in the coastal areas negatively" (G. Li 2004: 829). In the 32nd year of the Shaoxing Reign (AD 1162), the Provincial Military Commission and the Judicial Department of Guangnan West Province stated that "Qiongzhou, Leizhou, Huazhou, Qinzhou, and Lianzhou of Guangnan West Province had never established a navy. For pirates, invading these places was akin to entering no man's land." That year, 400 sailors were conscripted, and there were six vanguard warships with a maximum beam of 5.28 m in length, along with four large warships with a maximum beam of 7.92 m in length. 200 sailors were stationed at Leizhou, and another 200 were stationed at Qiongzhou (S. Xu et al. 2014: 9625). From that point on, a coastal defense navy was established.

It can be seen that in the Northern Song Dynasty, only Shandong Province had deployed a limited number of sailors for coastal defense. The coastal defense of Liangzhe, Fujian, and Guangnan provinces relied on patrol soldiers. However, when large groups of pirates emerged, the imperial court would dispatch dedicated envoys responsible for apprehending them. In summary, the coastal defense during that period was weak, and the coastal defense system had not yet been fully developed.

4.4.2 The Construction of River and Coastal Defense System in the Southern Song Dynasty

Compared to the Northern Song Dynasty, the Southern Song Dynasty witnessed a qualitative change in coastal defense. At the beginning of the Southern Song Dynasty, a clear division was established between military defense along the Yangtze River and coastal defense. In the third year of the Jianyan Reign (AD 1129), Zheng Zizhi, the deputy director-general, was responsible for building defense along the Yangtze River, while Lin Zhiping, the minister of supervisory censor, oversaw coastal defense. Additionally, talented individuals were recruited as entourages. Lin's administrative region extended from Hangzhou to Taipingzhou, while Zheng's region covered Chizhou to Jingnan Prefecture. Zheng requested the recruitment of two hundred passenger seagoing vessels for transportation and guarding purposes in shifts. Lin Zhiping, on the other hand, requested the recruitment of six hundred seagoing vessels to defend the core region. In the early spring, Lin Zhiping dispatched sailors to Quanzhou and Fuzhou to recruit seagoing vessels from Fujian and Guangdong for defense and deployment. Ultimately, over two hundred large seagoing vessels arrived from the central region of Fujian Province (S. Xu et al. 2014: 9253; X. Li 2013: 464, 685). During Emperor Xiaozong's Reign, the areas below Taipingzhou in the Yangtze River basin to Hangzhou were designated for sea defense. Changzhou in Liangzhe West Province, Jiangyin Military Prefecture, and Pingjiang Prefecture were under coastal defense. Additionally, Zhenjiang Prefecture in Liangzhe West Province and Jiankang Prefecture in Jiangdong Province were responsible for river defense. In the third year of the Qiandao Reign (AD 1167), Shi Zhengzhi, the mayor of Jiankang Prefecture, was appointed as the potamic military commissioner, overseeing the sailors from Jiankang to Ezhou (Y. Zhou 1990: 1734; Y. Wang 2003: 2445; Toqta 1977). The river defense navy was deployed in Zhenjiang Prefecture and directly controlled by the General Command Commission. However, in the Yangtze River Estuary, the division between river defense and coastal defense was not absolute. The primary responsibility of the Xupu navy in Pingjiang Prefecture was coastal defense, but the navy was frequently dispatched to protect the river in Jiankang Prefecture until reinforcements from Jiangzhou, Chizhou, and Ezhou arrived on several occasions (C. Fan 1990: 722).

4.4.2.1 The Distribution and Number of Sailors in the Southern Song Dynasty

In the early Southern Song Dynasty, the imperial court attempted to establish a unified coastal defense system from Huainan East and Liangzhe provinces to Fujian Province. Eventually, an agency was set up to handle the coastal defense of Fujian, Huainan East Province, and Liangzhe provinces. In May of the second year of the Shaoxing Reign (AD 1132), Qiu Yu was appointed as the coastal military commissioner for the coastal areas of Fujian, Liangzhe, and Huainan East provinces. The coastal military commission was established in Xupu Town, Pingjiang Prefecture. In July of the same year, Lü Yihao suggested that the Jin troops could approach from the north of the sea through two routes. The first route involved reaching Dinghai County directly from the deep sea, while the second route involved sailing south along the coastline from Tongzhou and Taizhou to the river bank of Lin'an Prefecture (Liangzhe West Seaway). It was necessary to be on guard and transmit information promptly in case of emergencies. However, one coastal military commission could not manage the defense of both seaways. The imperial court was requested to appoint Qiu Yu to oversee Liangzhe West and Huainan East provinces, while another officer would be assigned to control Liangzhe East and Fujian Province (J. Luo et al. 1990: 5027). Therefore, Qiu Yu served as the coastal military commissioner of Liangzhe West Province, and a coastal military commission was established in Xupu Town. Lü Yuan served as the coastal military commissioner of Liangzhe East and Fujian provinces, and a coastal military commission was established in Dinghai County. These were the two coastal defense systems mentioned above.

After the Jin Kingdom troops withdrew, the coastal military commission became idle. In December of the second year of the Shaoxing Reign (AD 1132), a minister proposed that Qiu Yu, the coastal military commissioner in the coastal area of Liangzhe West Province, had no other duties apart from sending county criminal inspectors to various places. Any local officials from prefectures or counties could handle this task. Similarly, Lü Yuan, the coastal military commissioner of Liangzhe East and Fujian provinces, was left without any responsibilities. As a result, in June of the third year of the Shaoxing Reign (AD 1133), Emperor Gaozong decided to streamline the coastal military commission in the coastal areas of Liangzhe East Province. During the spring of the second year, Lü Yuan was removed from his position as coastal military commissioner, and the sea seagoing vessels under his charge were transferred to the commissioner in Mingzhou. Since the defense of the seaways in Shandong Province could not be suspended, the coastal military commission of Liangzhe West Province was relocated to Dinghai County and merged with the commission in Liangzhe East Province (X. Li 2013: 1213). Qiu Yu was appointed as the mayor and coastal military commissioner of Mingzhou, responsible for overseeing the coastal defense of Huainan East Province, Liangzhe West Province, and Liangzhe East Province. The coastal defense of Fujian Province was no longer under the commissioner's jurisdiction. In July of the third year of the Shaoxing Reign (AD 1133), Guo Zhongxun assumed the position of mayor and coastal military commissioner of Mingzhou (Y. Wang 2003: 2446).

After that, the coastal military commission experienced separation and merger many times. In October of the sixth year of the Shaoxing Reign (AD 1136), under the jurisdiction of Tongzhou, Liaojiao was a fort on the way crowded with pirate ships. To strengthen the coastal defense against the Jin Kingdom, Liang Rujia was appointed as the coastal military commissioner of Liangzhe West Province and Huainan East Province again, and Wang Yan was appointed as the vice commissioner (Y. Wang 2003: 2446). The commission was called the "Liangzhe West Province and Huainan East Province Coastal Military Commission." As a result, the coastal defense was restored to the pattern of being administered by their respective provinces (S. Xu et al. 2014: 3992). However, in the 32nd year of the Shaoxing Reign (AD 1162), when the Southern Song and the Jin were at war, Li Bao was appointed as the coastal military commissioner of Liangzhe East Province, Liangzhe West Province, Tongzhou, Taizhou, and Haizhou Prefecture (S. Xu et al. 2014: 8999). When Qiu Yu served as the mayor and the coastal military commissioner of Mingzhou, the name of the commission was simplified into the Coastal Military Commission, which omitted Liangzhe East Province and Fujian Province. The commission was directly controlled by the Bureau of Military Affairs, and it reported the number of registers, property, weapons, armors, and boats to the Bureau in the last month of each quarter. Regarding the military situation, the commission reported to the Bureau and the Administration of State Affairs every three days (J. Luo et al. 1990: 5069). Shaoxing Prefecture, Wenzhou, Taizhou, and Mingzhou were under the charge of the Commission. In the eighth year of the Shaoxing Reign (AD 1138), the imperial court ordered the military commissioner of Liangzhe East Province to take over Shaoxing Prefecture and the Coastal Military Commission. In the tenth year of the Shaoxing Reign (AD 1140), the mayor of Mingzhou was appointed as the coastal military commissioner as before. In the 11th year of the Shaoxing Reign (AD 1141), the Coastal Military Commission was abolished, and it was reestablished in the first year of the Longxing Reign (AD 1163). Shaoxing Prefecture, Wenzhou, Taizhou, and Mingzhou were governed by the Commission. At the same time, soldiers, generals, county criminal inspectors, and local garrisons in prefectures and counties also took orders from it (J. Luo et al. 1990: 5027; S. Xu et al. 2014: 3992). The Coastal Military Commission of Liangzhe West Province and Huainan East Province was subsequently abolished. In Emperor Xiaozong's Reign, the navy of Liangzhe West Province was subordinate to the Palace Administration and the Imperial Army successively. The Naval General Command in Xupu commanded the navy of coastal areas in Liangzhe West Province, which was called the Imperial Navy (X. Li 2000: 422). The sailors of Jiangyin Military Prefecture, Gu Jing, and Ganpu in Liangzhe West Province were all under the control of Xupu's Naval General Command (X. Li 2000: 422; Toqta 1977: 4633), which was responsible for defense of the coastal area of Liangzhe West Province and the Yangtze River estuary.

The Coastal Military Commission in Mingzhou had three features. First, the mayor and the coastal military commissioner of Mingzhou became a permanent post. In the first year of the Longxing Reign (AD 1163), the officials after Zhao Zixiao, including Zhao Bogui (served twice), Zhang Jin, Zhao Kai (served twice), Zhao Yanyu, Han Yuanli, Zhao Shanxiang and Ye Mengding all served as both mayor and coastal military commissioner of Mingzhou (S. Xu et al. 2014: 399–94, 4684, 5918; Toqta 1977: 8768, 12402, 12434). Second, the Coastal Military Commission was responsible only for the coastal defense of Shaoxing Prefecture, Wenzhou, Taizhou, and Mingzhou, which were part of Liangzhe East Province. Han Yuanli stated that "Wenzhou, Taizhou, Mingzhou, and Yuezhou had extensive seaways, and the presence of pirates was irregular and unpredictable. Due to the lack of unified jurisdictions in the subordinate prefectures and counties, pirates roamed freely across different areas, making it difficult to apprehend them. Consequently, the Coastal Military Commission was established to provide unified jurisdiction and report offenses to the authorities. This way, coastal prefectures and counties could collaborate, preventing them from colluding with pirates and leaving the pirates with no place to hide" (S. Xu et al. 2014: 8876). Qiu Yu and Zhao Bogui also mentioned that "Wenzhou, Taizhou, Mingzhou, and Yuezhou were vast and expansive, with broad seaways. They intended to identify suitable locations for additional beacon towers along the coast, from Yuezhou to Wenzhou, to support one another." As a result, "the pirates appearing in the seaways of Mingzhou and Taizhou were apprehended" (S. Xu et al. 2014: 9255, 5916). When serving as coastal military commissioners, their focus was solely on the coastal defense of Liangzhe East Province. Third, the Coastal Military Commission also oversaw the military forces of coastal prefectures and counties. This means that soldiers, generals, county criminal inspectors, and local officers and troops in prefectures and counties followed its instructions.

In the early Southern Song Dynasty, the number of sailors in the Coastal Military Commission in Liangzhe East Province was unknown. In the 11th year of the Shaoxing Reign (AD 1141), when the Coastal Military Commission was abolished, the sailors of the Commission were also disbanded. However, in the 31st year of the Shaoxing Reign (AD 1161), during the Southern Song Dynasty's war with the Jin Dynasty, two thousand sailors of the Palace Administration were garrisoned at the gate of Mingzhou. In the first year of the Longxing Reign (AD 1163), the Coastal Military Commission was re-established, coinciding with the rise of rampant piracy led by Zhu Baiwu. The two thousand sailors in Mingzhou were under the command of Zhao Zisu, who held the positions of mayor and coastal military commissioner. By the second year of the Longxing Reign (AD 1164), the pirates were suppressed, and Zhao Zisu submitted a request to the imperial court. He requested to retain the 2000 sailors in Mingzhou and recruit an additional 1000 sailors, bringing the total number of garrisoned sailors to 3000. In the seventh year of the Qiandao Reign (AD 1171), Lin Wen, the general commander of the Coastal Military Commission, brought one thousand sailors from Fuzhou, further increasing the total number to four thousand. As the sailors of the reestablished Coastal Military Commission originated from the Palace Administration, the military officers followed the system of the Palace Administration. Thus, "the sailors of the Coastal Military Commission came from the Palace Administration and were under the command of general commanders and commanders" (J. Luo et al. 1990: 5068–69). In the fifth year of the Qiandao Reign (AD 1169), "the navy of Dinghai County in Mingzhou worked as Imperial Navy" (Toqta 1977: 647), but the Coastal Military Commission still existed.

In the thirtieth year of the Shaoxing Reign (AD 1160), there were sea seagoing vessels in Liangzhe West Province and Tongzhou, with a total of 10,000 sailors and helmsmen (X. Li 2013: 3603). However, this number represents the military forces dispatched from various locations before the war, not the specific quota of sailors in Liangzhe West Province. During the Qiandao Reign, the navy of Liangzhe West Province was successively under the authority of the Palace Administration and the Imperial Army. The Naval General Command in Xupu commanded the navy in the coastal areas of Liangzhe West Province, Chuzhou, and other prefectures in Huainan East Province. Initially, the navy's quota was three thousand (X. Li 2000: 422). However, in the third year of the Chunxi Reign (AD 1176), Feng Zhan requested an additional 500 sailors. Subsequently, in the fifth year of the Chunxi Reign (AD 1178), Yu You also requested 500 sailors (C. Fan 1990: 722). As a result, the *Local Chronicles of Qinchuan* recorded a total of 8000 personnel in the navy of Liangzhe West Province (*Qinchuan Zhi* 1163), likely referring to the number in the fifth year of the Chunxi Reign (AD 1178). Since then, the number gradually increased. In the first year of the Shaoxi Reign (AD 1190), 320 helmsmen were recruited in Fuzhou, and an additional 180 sailors were added. In the fourth year of the Jiatai Reign (AD 1204), twenty dealers and boatmen who operated between China and Japan were recruited. Furthermore, in the second year of the Kaixi Reign (AD 1206), another 500 soldiers of three kinds of troops and one hundred Xiaoyong-tier soldiers were recruited. In the fifteenth year of the Jiading Reign (AD 1222), eight hundred and forty helmsmen were recruited. The total number of troops amounted to ten thousand soldiers, including the original troops as part of the quota (C. Fan 1990: 722). In the first year of the Baoqing Reign (AD 1225), the navy's strength in Xupu was increased to fourteen thousand (C. Fan 1990: 722; Y. Ying and L. Yuan n.d.: 1218).

The navy under the General Command in Xupu was garrisoned in Jiangyin, Gujing, and Ganpu. The total number of navy personnel was ten thousand. However, this count needed to exclude those assigned to Gujing, Huangyuduo, Jiangyin prefecture, and Huaihai (which was under the authority of Chuzhou), as well as those sent for pirate-catching or other tasks, and deserters. Consequently, there were not many sailors left in Xupu Prefecture for defense (C. Fan 1990: 722). In the fourth year of the Qiandao Reign (AD 1168), three hundred sailors were initially assigned to station in Jiangyin. Later, two thousand people were dispatched from Quanzhou, and one thousand people were stationed in the Coastal Military Commission. By the end of the Chunxi Reign, the number had increased to four thousand (X. Li 2000: 422; Toqta 1977: 4633). In the Chunxi Reign, the navy of Gujing initially consisted of only five hundred personnel. Subsequently, an additional five hundred people were added, bringing the total to two thousand (C. Fan 1990: 722; Y. Ying and L. Yuan n.d.: 1218). The navy of Ganpu initially deployed one hundred people from the navy of Xupu to Changqiang Mountain in the Chunyou Reign (AD 1241–1252). The team of guard soldiers would be rotated on an annual basis. In the first year of the Kaixi Reign (AD 1205), the garrison of Ganpu Navy was established, with fifteen hundred personnel stationed there (T. Chang 1990: 4633; Toqta 1977: 4633). In the thirtieth year of the Shaoxing Reign (AD 1160), three hundred navy personnel from Mingzhou were sent to guard Huangyuduo in Kunshan and engage in pirate-catching activities with groove boats (Toqta 1977: 959). However, the specific number of Xupu Navy assigned to Huangyuduo is unknown. The navy of Liangzhe West Province also had a garrison in Weicun Village, which was under the jurisdiction of Changzhou. Although the quota was set at five hundred people, the actual count was only three hundred and fifty people (Z. Huang 1990). In the fifth year of the Qiandao Reign (AD 1169), a navy was established in Tongzhou in Huainan East Province (Toqta 1977: 4633) and it was under the control of Xupu's Naval General Command. The number of the navy was unknown.

The Fujian Navy consisted of the Palace Left-wing Navy and the patrol navy of the Provincial Military Commission. The Left Wing Navy was an expansion of the army of the Palace Administration stationed in Fujian during the Shaoxing Reign. In the eighteenth year of the Shaoxing Reign (AD 1148), in response to the requests from the army and the people of Quanzhou, the imperial court ordered Liu Bao's army, which was under the command of the Palace Administration, to garrison in the middle of Fujian Province to combat piracy. The Palace Left-wing Army comprised Liu's army and a portion of the Fujian Provincial Military Commission Army, totaling two thousand seven hundred and seventy-five personnel under Liu Bao's command. In the second year, the Provincial Military Commission selected an additional one thousand five hundred individuals. In the 25th year of the Shaoxing Reign (AD 1155), another one thousand five hundred people from the "Tuhun" army were recruited and stationed in Quanzhou, while 300 people were stationed in Zhangzhou (K. Lang 1990: 7933). Consequently, the Left-wing Navy had a total of 3000 soldiers (X. Li 2000: 422) and the ranks set by the Left-wing Navy were lower than those of Xupu's. Xupu's army was the Imperial Navy, which had a vice general commander, while the Left-wing Army only had general commanders (D. Zhen, n.d.).

In the early Southern Song Dynasty, the number of the Guangnan East Province Navy was unknown. However, in the fifth year of the Qiandao Reign (AD 1170), the navy increased to two thousand. This means that the number of the Cuifeng Army also reached two thousand. Additionally, the Chaozhou Navy, established in the fourth year of the Qiandao Reign (AD 1169), consisted of two hundred people (Toqta 1977: 4633; X. Li 2000: 422). In February of the fourth year of the Chunxi Reign (AD 1177), the emperor issued an imperial edict stating that the Imperial Navy of General Command, the Coastal Military Commission, and the Wefeng Army in Zhenjiang, Jiankang Prefecture, Chizhou, and E'zhou should recommend an officer to the Bureau of Military Affairs from among the generals and vice generals under their jurisdictions. These officers had to be of a higher rank than the commissioner-in-chief and should possess the capability to command soldiers, as well as having made contributions in coastal defense (S. Xu et al. 2014: 3835). Finally, the commander of the Guangzhou Navy would be selected from among these officers. It is evident that the Southern Song Dynasty attached great importance to the construction of the Guangnan East Navy. Qiongzhou, Leizhou, Huazhou, Qinzhou, Lianzhou, and other prefectures in Guangnan West Province had never established sailors. However, in the thirty-second year of the Shaoxing Reign (AD 1162), four hundred people were recruited, with two hundred assigned to the garrison of Qiongzhou and another two hundred to Leizhou respectively (S. Xu et al. 2014: 9625).

In addition to the Palace Administration, the Imperial Navy, the Coastal Military Commission, the Left-wing Army, and the Cuifeng Army, other regular navies played a role in coastal defense. This included the local soldiers under the jurisdiction of the local inspector of border security and the archers under the jurisdiction of the county criminal inspector. There was a Patrol Division for saury-shaped warships involved in river and coastal defense. Another Patrol Division was responsible for capturing pirates in the Yangtze River, the Yellow River, the Huai River, and at sea. When recruiting sailors in the Yangtze River or coastal areas, an inspector of border security would be sent to handle the process. The junction points were controlled by inspectors of border security (Toqta 1977: 3982). Various provinces also had inspectors of border security, who were subordinate to the Provincial Military Commission. Several towns, such as Meishan, Sanshan, and Miaoshan in Yuyao County, Shaoxing Prefecture, and Liangzhe East Province, were strategically located for coastal defense. The officer in charge of Meishan Town, along with two officers each from Sanshan and Miaoshan towns, who were from the navy of the Provincial Military Commission, and three inspection officials dispatched by the Coastal Military Commission of Mingzhou, jointly undertook the task of capturing pirates. There were nine local military camps in Mingzhou responsible for inspection (S. Xu et al. 2014: 4370), with a population of one thousand four hundred and eighty-three soldiers. They collaborated with the Dinghai Navy (Y. Mei et al. 1990: 5985). The number of soldiers in the five barracks of Sangu, Liegang, Hainei, Daishan, and Guanjie was one thousand one hundred and eighteen. Although nominally the Coastal Military Commission could command the local army of the Provincial Military Commission, and the local army was supposed to take orders from the general commander, this was not the case. Each barracks was under the jurisdiction of its own generals, and there were no seagoing vessels or boats to reach the distant Coastal Military Commission from the local military camps. The so-called command was mere empty talk, and regulations were ineffective (J. Luo et al. 1990: 5069). There were also local soldiers in the coastal areas of Liangzhe West Province. The patrol camps of Xupu, Fushan, and Baimao each had 144 local soldiers. In the ninth year of the Chunyou Reign (AD 1249), Fushan Navy and Jiangwan Navy were equipped with 300 people (Y. Ying and L. Yuan n.d.: 1219), and they were responsible for defending the rivers and the sea.

The Left-wing Navy of Fujian Province was not populous. The local patrol soldiers under the jurisdiction of the Provincial Military Commission were responsible for coastal defense. The most important patrol camps under the jurisdiction of Fuzhou were Dilu military camp in Lianjiang County and Yanxiang military camp in Houguan County. In July of the sixth year of the Shaoxing Reign (AD 1136), the Provincial Military Commission of Fujian Province asked the imperial court to dispatch three hundred sailors subordinate to each of the two Patrol Divisions (Dilu and Yanxiang military camps) which controlled Fuzhou, Xingzhou, Zhangzhou, and Quanzhou. One hundred and fifty sailors were dispatched to each of the two military camps separately. The commander of the Provincial Military Commission Navy was appointed as the inspector of border security of Fuzhou and Xingzhou. In April of the ninth year of the Shaoxing Reign (AD 1139), the Patrol Division of Fujian Province was moved to Dilu military camp. Since then, the overall number of the Fujian Navy continued to increase. In the twenty-eighth year of the Shaoxing Reign (AD 1158), the imperial court accepted the request of the Military Commission of Fujian Province and set three hundred as the quotas for the two military camps, Dilu and Yanxiang. In the second year, six hundred and thirty-one local soldiers were selected from sailors led by local chiefs, and one hundred and fifty-four were from Dilu military camp. In the seventh year of the Qiandao Reign (AD 1171), 500 people were added to the navy of Dilu military camp. However, later in the Chunxi Reign, the soldier population was reduced to 445. In the fifteenth year of the Shaoxing Reign (AD 1145), the navy of Yanxiang military camp was staffed with five hundred people. In the twenty-sixth year of the Shaoxing Reign (AD 1156), most of them were merged with Quanzhou, and only 128 people were kept in the camp. In the twenty-eighth year of the Shaoxing Reign (AD 1158), the number of the navy increased to three hundred. In the 30th year of the Shaoxing Reign (AD 1160), two hundred and ninety-seven sailors from Yanxiang military camp, half of which were merged with Mingzhou, leaving only one hundred and forty-nine. In the thirty-first year of the Shaoxing Reign (AD 1161), the population of sailors increased to 450 again. In the seventh year of the Qiandao Reign (AD 1171), the number became six hundred. During the Chunxi Reign, 552 sailors were subordinate to Yanxiang military camp (K. Lang 1990: 7933–34). From all the above discussions, the two military camps, Dilu and Yanxiang, had the largest population of sailors in the seventh year of the Qiandao Reign (AD 1171), with a total number of up to 1150. During the Chunxi Reign, the number was 997. *Laws and Institutions Since the Jianyan Reign* recorded that there were one thousand people in the Yanxiang military camp in Fuzhou (X. Li 2000: 422; Toqta 1977: 4632), which must be the total number of sailors in Dilu and Yanxiang military camps under the jurisdiction of Fuzhou. In the third year of the Chunyou Reign (AD 1243), the imperial court decreed that the Yanxiang and Dilu patrol agencies in Fuzhou should jointly establish the Wuji Navy. Later, soldiers with good water skills from the garrison troops and the imperial guard in Fuzhou were to be organized into the Wuji Navy, with a quota of 1500 people (Toqta 1977: 826). This number was larger than before. In addition to the two patrol agencies, Dilu and Yanxiang, Fuzhou also established patrol divisions in Haikou and Ganzhezhou, as well as other prefectures. The coastal defense barracks garrisoned in the coastal areas of Xinghua military camp, Quanzhou, and Zhangzhou, with sailors from the Left-wing Navy barracks and the local barracks of the Provincial Military Commission. However, the exact number of people was not recorded in detail. In the first year of the Shaoxi Reign (AD 1190), there were six hundred people in the Quanzhou Navy and the Zhangzhou Navy (Toqta 1977: 4633), which must have been local soldiers.

The Left-wing Navy's three barracks in Quanzhou, including Baolin, Fashi, and Yongning, had 576 people stationed there (D. Zhen, n.d.).

The archers managed by the county criminal inspector were responsible for catching pirates, and it was also the duty of the coastal county to search for pirates. Changguo County and Xiangshan County, located outside Mingzhou, were situated along the sea. Whenever pirates appeared on the seaways, the county criminal inspector was authorized to capture them at any time (S. Xu et al. 2014: 4362). Historical records frequently mention cases of pirates being captured by the county criminal inspector. For example, during the Battle of Shataoyang in Zhangzhou, the county criminal inspector of Jinjiang County apprehended a pirate scout named Zhu Shisi. Similarly, in Hui'an County, the county criminal inspector captured a pirate scout named Lin Qinglang (D. Zhen, n.d.). The pirates who fled to Beiyang were later were later apprehended by the county criminal inspector of Yueqing in Wenzhou. Fang Xinru, while serving as the county criminal inspector of Fanyu County, encountered pirates who had robbed maritime merchants. Seizing the opportunity when the pirates were dividing their spoils on the beach, Fang Xinru dispatched troops to apprehend all of them (Toqta 1977: 12059). Wang Nan, during his tenure as the county criminal inspector of Haimen County in Tongzhou, ventured out to sea in a small boat and captured the pirate Xiao Wulang along with seventeen members of his gang (Toqta 1977: 12062). Wang Qingyue, as the county criminal inspector of Yueqing County in Wenzhou, received information about the abundance of pirates in Wenzhou and devised a plan to hunt them down (Y. Lou 1990).

However, there were limitations to the number of archers available. In the thirtieth year of the Shaoxing Reign (AD 1160), Yu Guangyi, the mayor of Xiangshan County in Mingzhou, expressed his concerns about the frequent gathering of pirate ships in the vast sea of Xiangshan County. He pointed out that the archers led by the county criminal inspector numbered only forty-five, whereas each county in Mingzhou required more than eighty archers for their respective county criminal inspectors. In response to his request, the number of archers in Xiangshan County was increased to eighty (S. Xu et al. 2014: 4362). However, even with this increase, they remained ill-equipped to handle a large number of pirates. As Bao Hui once remarked, "It is evident that the small and weak troops of the patrol prefectures and divisions are not capable of defeating pirates. In Fuzhou, only soldiers from Yanxiang and Dilu military camps possess some knowledge of seaways and are familiar with water battles. The patrol divisions and prefectures, which lack expertise in coastal defense, can only serve as assistants" (H. Bao 1990).

Both the local patrol soldiers and the archers under the control of the county criminal inspector constituted the core of the regular navy. Wang Yingchen noted that the Mingzhou Navy consisted of local soldiers recruited from different barracks, including those from the Imperial Armies of the prefecture and archers from various prefectures (Y. Wang 1990). However, the soldiers from the Yanxiang patrol prefectures played a significant role in forming the Left-wing Navy of Fujian. As a result, distinguishing between the regular navy and the local navy was challenging, as they were closely intertwined.

From the aforementioned discussion, it is evident that in terms of sailor numbers in the Southern Song Dynasty, the coastal areas of Liangzhe West Province had the largest number of sailors, followed by Liangzhe East, Fujian, and Guangnan provinces. However, the regular navy of Mingzhou in Liangzhe East Province had once reached four thousand sailors, and this count did not include the local navy. As a prefecture, Mingzhou had a larger troop presence than Xupu, where the General Command of the Liangzhe West Province Navy was located. The number of regular sailors in Liangzhe West Province and Mingzhou in Liangzhe East Province exceeded that of other regions. Despite this, the Song Dynasty still dispatched ships and sailors from Fujian and Guangdong to garrison in Liangzhe West Province and Mingzhou. In the 30th year of the Shaoxing Reign (AD 1160), the imperial court ordered that half of the sailors who were strong enough in the navies of Guangzhou, Quanzhou, and Fuzhou should be selected and sent to Mingzhou (K. Lang 1990: 7934). In the seventh year of the Qiandao Reign (AD 1171), the Bureau of Military Affairs stated that "the navy recruited by the Mingzhou Coastal Military Commission were unfamiliar with swimming", so they transferred five hundred people from the newly recruited sailors. Additionally, all the newly recruited sailors in Fuzhou, the two official ships, weapons, and armors of Guangnan East Province and Fuzhou were dispatched to Mingzhou. In Fuzhou, three ships from Yanxiang Military Camp, two ships from Huolu Military Camp, one ship from Liuqi, and one ship from Nanni Military Camp were also sent. Furthermore, three ships from Baolin Military Camp in Quanzhou, two ships from Chaozhou Navy, and five ships from Guangdong Navy named Tian, Di, Yuan, Huang, and Yu were dispatched to Mingzhou as well (S. Xu et al. 2014: 7134). Part of the requisitioned ships from Fujian and Liangzhe East Province were also sent to the coastal areas of Liangzhe West Province. "Fujian and Liangzhe East Province requisitioned merchant ships every year. Those ships were stationed in eight places such as Gujing and Wujiang, etc., and were controlled by the Fujian General Command for coastal defense" (L. Xu 1990). Particularly, Fujian boatmen were skilled at sailing and were sent every year to Liangzhe East Province and Liangzhe West Province to fight pirates. The reason for sending people and ships from Fujian Province to Xupu was that their ships were sturdy, and the helmsmen were familiar with the situation (B. Zhou 1990). For example, in the eighth year of the Qiandao Reign (AD 1172), the emperor issued an imperial edict ordering the Provincial Military Commission of Fujian to dispatch the five-hundred-man navy that had been recruited. Later, patrol prefectures were asked to dispatch five great ships to carry soldiers to the Coastal Military Commission, which incorporated them (S. Xu et al. 2014: 7134). In the second year of the Chunxi Reign (AD 1175), Fujian Province dispatched five hundred and seventy ships with fourteen thousand helmsmen and sailors (X. Zhu 2010: 4474). Not only sailors but also ordinary boatmen were recruited in turn. "The imperial court had always registered the number of people's boats and ships in the coastal areas of Fujian Province and divided them into A, B, and C groups, which were put on duty in turn" (B. Zhou 1990). "Fujian ships with a maximum beam over 3.96 m were registered and requisitioned in turn" (K. Lang 1990: 7901–02).

The structure of the coastal defense system in the Southern Song Dynasty mostly followed the strategy of "preventing the hazards of seaways" advocated by Li Gang. The imperial court stationed soldiers and generals in Mingzhou and Yuezhou, respectively, to ensure a rapid response to emergencies. While the number of archers and county criminal inspectors in coastal prefectures and counties was considerable, their cooperation made the force strong, while their separation weakened it. An order should be issued to the Provincial Military Commission and the Judicial Department to organize the soldiers they dispatched into a new army and defend key areas. Additionally, wealthy boatmen should be recruited to patrol and defend seaways using their own boats. The imperial court promised them a significant reward after successfully crushing the pirates (G. Li 2004: 982–83). The regular sailors, the county criminal inspectors, and coastal residents collectively formed the coastal defense force. While the regular sailors were primarily responsible for coastal defense, the county criminal inspectors and coastal residents also played a significant role in defending against and apprehending pirates, particularly in the coastal areas of Fujian and Guangnan Province.

4.4.2.2 The Layout of the Coastal Defense Military Camps in the Southern Song Dynasty

From the above-mentioned information, we can deduce that the Southern Song Dynasty assigned different weights to provinces based on factors such as the population of sailors, supplies, and ship maintenance. These provinces had distinct priorities. Liangzhe West Province and Mingzhou in Liangzhe East Province primarily focused on coastal defense, particularly in protecting the northern region and surrounding Lin'an, where the emperor resided. Undoubtedly, this area was crucial for national coastal defense and should have been given priority in deploying sufficient soldiers and ships. Fujian and Guangnan Province, on the other hand, held a secondary position, and their coastal defense primarily revolved around safeguarding maritime trade and coastal areas. This was evident in the layout of their coastal defense military camps.

The layout of coastal defense military camps in Liangzhe West Province had a primary objective of surrounding and protecting Lin'an. The most significant one was the Xupu Navy Prefecture located in Pingjiang Prefecture. "During the Jianyan and Shaoxing Reign, the navy once stationed in Jiangyin, Xupu, and Fushan etc., without definite place" (Y. Ying and L. Yuan n.d.: 1217). However, the Xupu Navy Prefecture was established in the sixth year of the Qiandao Reign (AD 1170) after careful spot reconnaissance. It not only served as the headquarters of the Liangzhe West Province Navy General Command but also held great importance as a navy prefecture. Feng Zhan, the commander of the Imperial Navy, personally visited and inspected the defensive locations along the seaways. Xupu Town in Suzhou (Pingjiang Prefecture) was recognized as a crucial place to defend. The branching stream of Xupu Town provided sufficient depth for mooring, while the surrounding land was high and spacious enough for barracks construction. It was considered superior to Jiangyin in terms of the navy prefecture. Moreover, due to its proximity to the Huaihe River Basin, earth fortresses could be easily built to gather reconnaissance and intelligence. Compared to Dinghai County, the navy stationed in Xupu Town occupied a more advantageous position (C. Fan 1990: 722). When it came to defending the northern coast to the south Yangtze River estuary, Xupu Town was deemed more convenient and important than Jiangyin and Dinghai. In the first year of the Chunxi Reign (AD 1174), Xupu Port underwent extensive renovation. The port stretched for 19 km and had a width of 21.45–26.4 m at the surface, 9.25–11.55 m wide at the bottom, and an entrance width of more than 66 m, spanning 8 km. A flat and sturdy road was built along the shore of the port, measuring fifteen to twenty feet wide (S. Xu et al. 2014: 9607). Xupu Port had already become a high-quality military port.

Gu Jing in Kunshan County served as an important auxiliary military camp for Xupu and played a significant role in coastal defense. The navy stationed at Gu Jing was known as the Xupu Left-wing Army, with a designated commander for the Left-wing Army. Gu Jing was situated over 100 Li (a Chinese length unit, 1 mile $\approx$ 3.2 li) to the east of Xupu. It "faced the Huangyuduo, wound around Liaojiao, ran through Shajiao, and guarded the sea boundary of Shandong Province" (Y. Ying and L. Yuan n.d.: 1219). Wu Ying, the general commander of Xupu Navy, emphasized the strategic importance of Gu Jing, stating that it played a crucial role in the strategic passes within their jurisdiction. Located in the lower reaches of the Yangtze River in Yangzi County, Gu Jing was close to the sea and connected to Shajiao, making it an approachable point to the enemy's territory. Gu Jing's geographical location was highly significant, and at its peak, it had a force numbering over two thousand. Although Xupu Port was known for being a good port, the water depth at Gu Jing Port near the Yangtze River estuary was even deeper. A well-designed dock was constructed at Gu Jing Port to accommodate all warships according to regulations, ensuring convenient and efficient entry and exit (S. Xu et al. 2014: 7137). Therefore, Gu Jing Port served as the port for large deep-water sea warships of the Xupu Town General Command (C. Fan 1990: 722–23). However, prior to the eleventh year of the Chunxi Reign (AD 1184), the Naval General Command of Xupu Town was stationed near Qinglong Town. During that year, the Palace Administration reported that "the navy of the Palace Administration was stationed in Xupu Town, while the sharp-bottom seagoing boats under its jurisdiction were anchored off Qinglong Port. The distance between the barracks and the port was several hundred kilometers. The land route to reach the ships and the waterway to return were tortuous. Additionally, Qinglong Port was narrow with swift currents. Therefore, it was planned to transfer all the sharp-bottom seagoing boats to Gu Jing Port in Kunshan County." After conducting an on-the-spot investigation, the imperial court concluded that "the water in Gu Jing Port was deeper than that in Qinglong Port, and Gu Jing Port was closer to the sea, making it more convenient for berthing the sharp-bottom seagoing boats." As a result, Gu Jing Port became the primary port for mooring the Xupu Navy. In the thirteenth year of the Chunxi Reign (AD 1186), "among the seagoing vessels dispatched by Fujian Province," "twenty-two large sharp-bottom seagoing boats were still anchored at Gujing Port, and a thousand officers and soldiers were deployed to guard the warships with armor and weapons" (S. Xu et al. 2014: 7137).

The region west of Xupu Town served as the primary coastal defense military barrack for the Jiangyin Army. In the second year of the Qiandao Reign (AD 1166), the Palace Administration deployed "two thousand officers and soldiers, along with twenty-six ships recruited from Quanzhou, and appointed Left-wing Army Commander Li Yanchun to temporarily anchor along the coast under the jurisdiction of the Jiangyin Army to suppress pirates" (C. Fan 1990: 7132). Additionally, as mentioned earlier, some sailors were stationed in Weicun Village of Changzhou, which also served as a coastal defense military prefecture. In the southern region of Xupu, there were the coastal defense military prefectures of Ganpu and Jinshan. Ganpu Town, located "2.5 kilometers away from Quanhu, connecting Jiaoguang in the west, facing Kuaiji in the south, and linking with Jiangyin Army and Xupu in the north," played a crucial role. Situated in the middle of the Suzhou Ocean (an ancient name for the East China Sea), it provided access to remote areas. Particularly, to safeguard the Qiantang River estuary, the gateway to Lin'an, Ganpu served as a mooring place for seagoing vessels and was considered a perilous location. Consequently, the Ganpu Navy military prefecture was established (T. Chang 1990: 4662). Among the various sailors stationed in Liangzhe West Province, "Ganpu Navy military prefecture was the closest to the capital." Furthermore, "aside from Ganpu, Jinshan was another significant point for seagoing vessels to pass through or anchor at." Therefore, Wu Qian's suggestion was accepted, resulting in the recruitment of "1000 sailors in Jinshan to serve as an auxiliary military prefecture for the Ganpu Navy" (Y. Mei et al. 1990: 5983).

Regarding the shared responsibility of safeguarding Lin'an Prefecture, the coastal defense forces of Mingzhou and Liangzhe West Province were effectively merged. For instance, "Xupu Navy in Pingjiang Prefecture and Dinghai Navy dispatched generals to conduct monthly sea patrols and exchanged information regarding patrolling the waterways" (J. Luo et al. 1990: 5069). The coastal defense of Mingzhou comprised a system of multiple military camps. Along the coast, there were nine military camps, namely Jieqi, Dasong, Guanjie, Hainei, Baifeng, Daishan, Sangu, Cenjiang, and Luotou (Y. Mei et al. 1990: 5984). Among them, Hainei, Baifeng, Guanjie, and others were part of Dinghai County (S. Xu et al. 2014: 9672). Dinghai Navy dispatched fifty soldiers, one general, one assistant official, and three warships every quarter to patrol the military prefectures (Y. Mei et al. 1990: 5982). Daishan, Sangu Mountain, Liegang, and Cenjiang were under the jurisdiction of Changguo County. Each military camp in Changguo County controlled the Hengjiang River and the local army, with a total of six hundred and thirty-eight personnel stationed there. They oversaw thirty-six patrol boats. Among the garrisons in Changguo County, Sangu Mountain served as the military prefecture. "Cenjiang and Liegang were established as two sub-camps, with troops distributed in different locations to confuse the enemy." This camp did not have a river branch running through it, and only five warships with a total of three hundred sailors could be moored there. However, it held significant geographical importance as "a critical point in Beiyang, where all seagoing vessels heading southward from Shandong Province to Liangzhe East Province and Liangzhe West Province had to diverge." The local armies of the three military camps were under the command of Dinghai County's navy. Every year, two hundred and fifty personnel, along with fifty sailors, totaling three hundred, were stationed at Sangu Mountain. They arrived on the first day of the tenth lunar month and returned on the first day of the third lunar month of the following year. Simultaneously, another one hundred sailors and three warships were dispatched for military intelligence patrols, ensuring that Sangu Mountain was not isolated or vulnerable (J. Luo et al. 1990: 5253; S. Xu et al. 2014: 9671).

Founding a navy in Mingzhou (Qingyuan Prefecture) in the Song Dynasty was one of the important measures taken to safeguard Lin'an Prefecture. "Since southern Qiantang County became the capital, the national power had gradually been restored. The establishment of the Xupu Navy, Ganpu Navy, and Dinghai Navy in Pingjiang Prefecture, Jiaxing Prefecture, and Qingyuan Prefecture provided all-around protection for the capital, Lin'an." These military camps were heavily guarded as they were located along the seaways. If the Jin Dynasty were to advance southward from Shandong Province, they would need "to take a boat from Jiaoxi County to the sea, bypass various islands and reefs in Liujiao of Huainan East Province, and find a convenient route directly to Jinshan in Jiaxing Prefecture. It would be unnecessary for them to enter the Qiantang River via hazardous seaways. In other words, seagoing vessels could potentially enter the Qiantang River directly from offshore or ocean routes. Therefore, Wu Qian pointed out that 'Dinghai Navy was strong enough to resist aggression from Japan and Koryo but unable to shield the capital.' The imperial court accepted his suggestion and established the Xiangtou Military Camp, with five hundred sailors stationed there." Xiangtou Camp was located in Dinghai County, opposite Jinshan. From there, armies could reach Qiantang in the south, Wenzhou and Taizhou in the east, and it also connected Suzhou and Xiuzhou in the west, reaching Qingzhou and Qizhou in the north. It served as the departure port for all seagoing vessels. "Xiangtou Camp was situated on the south bank of the Qiantang River estuary, and a rising tide could send seagoing vessels to the Qiantang River from there." It also "connected with the Jinshan patrol military camp and Ganpu patrol military camp, serving as the second line of defense for the capital city" (Y. Mei et al. 1990: 5982–83).

Beacon towers were established between the military camps to facilitate coordinated efforts. A beacon tower was built between Jinshan and Paihuaitou to maintain communication with the Ganpu patrol military prefecture and provide mutual support. "In cases where coordination was necessary, the navy of Dinghai County could also participate." "Beacon towers were typically erected at critical junctions." The naval beacon towers in Dinghai County had Zhaobao Mountain as their starting point and were divided into three groups. The first group comprised twelve beacon towers from Zhaobao Mountain to Bixia Mountain along the seaway. The second group included nine beacon towers from Zhaobao Mountain to Xiangtouzhai along the coast. The third group consisted of five beacon towers from Zhaobao Mountain to the watchtowers in Qingyuan Prefecture along the Yangtze River. Each beacon tower had a designated person in charge, along with five stationed soldiers. They patrolled the vicinity of the beacon tower back and forth. If they spotted enemies, they would raise flags during the day and light torches at night. "In the event that the signals from the twelve beacon towers at sea were obstructed by clouds and fog, and visibility of flags and torches was hindered for other distant beacon towers, cannons would be fired to relay the signals" (Y. Mei et al. 1990: 5985–86).

From the deployment of troops to the establishment of military camps, the coastal defense of Mingzhou can be considered watertight, and it served as the central defense point for the coastal region of Liangzhe East Province. The other three counties recruited seagoing vessels from the people and brought them to Mingzhou, where they were anchored "from Taizhou, Wenzhou, Mingzhou, and Yuezhou to Daishan, Cenjiang, Sangu Mountain, and Liegang" (Y. Mei et al. 1990: 5988). Dai Xu stated that among the four coastal prefectures in Liangzhe East Province, "Mingzhou and Yuezhou were important military areas. However, in normal times, there were no troops stationed in Wenzhou and Taizhou. The mayors of the two prefectures only focused on coastal defense during tax collection" (X. Dai 1990). The coasts of Yuezhou were encompassed by Hangzhou Bay, and the importance and functions of coastal defense outweighed those of Mingzhou. Furthermore, the coastal defense of Wenzhou and Taizhou was largely inconspicuous.

Tongzhou ranked first among the important coastal defense points in Huainan East Province. "The northeast of Tongzhou was the estuary, and the south of it was connected to the Yangtze River, so its geographical location was particularly important." In the first year of the Jianyan Reign (AD 1127), "the garrison sailors received water battle training, and some people were admitted to prepare warships for sea patrols. They used flags during the day and raised torches at night to send signals." "In particularly important places, large mounds were built for scouting" (X. Li 2013: 223–24). However, the most important military area of Tongzhou was Liaojiao. In the sixth year of the Shaoxing Reign (AD 1136), "eighty ships were assigned to station at Liaojiao in Tongzhou," and the emperor issued an edict ordering Huainan Province to "strengthen coastal defense" (X. Li 2013: 1925). Han Shizhong once said, "Dinghai County in Mingzhou, Huating County in Xiuzhou, Xupu Town in Suzhou, and Liaojiao in Tongzhou are all on important seaways and should be guarded" (S. Xu et al. 2014: 9254). He regarded the importance of Liaojiao on par with that of Dinghai County and Xupu Town. Li Wenyuan also stated, "although the seaway stretches for several hundred miles, there are only a few important places. For example, Liaojiao in Dongqian and Huangniuduo in Pingjiang Prefecture are crucial points on the seaway" (Y. Han 1990). This description even places Liaojiao in the top position. Secondly, Chuzhou reaches the Huaihe River estuary in the east, and there are "places called Fuyugou and Beisha area connecting Huaihe River and the sea, facing Shandong Province across the sea." The military forces in Chuzhou controlled over two hundred seagoing vessels, responsible for carrying military rations for the Haizhou Army and conducting enemy surveillance. In the fifth year of the Qiandao Reign (AD 1169), "two ministers were sent to visit local people who were wealthy and influential, familiar with sea routes, and trusted by the locals. Afterwards, capable individuals would be recommended for official positions to oversee the seagoing vessels and patrol pirates on the seaways from the Huaihe River to the sea" (Song Shi Quanwen 2005: 1711; S. Xu et al. 2014: 9248). It was also an important place for coastal defense.

It is evident that the military camps on the south bank of the Yangtze River estuary extended from Weicun Village in Changzhou, Jiangyin, Xupu in Pingjiang Prefecture, Gujing, Huangyuduo, and Huating County in Xiuzhou in the west. The Yangtze River estuary then proceeded northward to Liaojiao in Tongzhou, Fuyugou in Chuzhou, Beisha, and others. Jinshan and Ganpu on the north bank of the Qiantang River estuary were located to the south of the Yangtze River estuary. Dinghai and Xiangtou, where military camps densely covered the south bank of the Qiantang River estuary, formed a strict coastal defense system surrounding Lin'an Prefecture.

The four coastal prefectures in the south of Fujian had established a coastal defense system. "Fuzhou was at the end, Zhangzhou and Quanzhou were at the head, and Fuzhou and Xinghua Military Camp were in the middle" (H. Bao 1990). The four coastal prefectures had established closely located military camps, with Fuzhou and Quanzhou being the most significant ones. In Fuzhou, the most important coastal defense military camps were Dilu Military Camp and Yanxiang Military Camp. Dilu Military Camp served as the location for the border security inspector, and there were several other military camps as well. In Houguan County, there was a patrol prefecture in Ganzhezhou. In the Northern Song Dynasty, the border security inspectors from Zhangzhou, Quanzhou, Fuzhou, and Xingzhou worked together for border security. The deployed soldiers there numbered one hundred. In Fuqing County, there was a border security inspector at Haikou. In the 30th year of the Shaoxing Reign (AD 1160), there were sixty-three sailors, and in the seventh year of the Qiandao Reign (AD 1171), local soldiers were added with a quota of eighty-four. Changxi County had inspectors of beacon security. In the Northern Song Dynasty, they served as the border security inspectors for the six coastal counties in Fuzhou. 300 soldiers and military officers were deployed there. Later, in the fifth year of the Xining Reign (AD 1072), the number was reduced to 100. In the 30th year of the Shaoxing Reign (AD 1160), fifty-six people were deployed there, and later it was increased to seventy-seven in the seventh year of the Qiandao Reign (AD 1171). Luoyuan County dispatched border security inspectors to Nanwan, which managed the seaways of Lianjiang County and Luoyuan County. In the Northern Song Dynasty, the deployed soldiers numbered seventy. In the ninth year of the Shaoxing Reign (AD 1139), there were fifty-six sailors, and in the seventh year of the Qiandao Reign (AD 1171), the number increased to 108 (K. Lang 1990: 7941). In the second year of the Chunxi Reign (AD 1175), Chen Junqing, the mayor of Fuzhou, stated that "there were a total of 1,900 soldiers in Fuzhou's thirteen patrol camps. More than 1,700 soldiers from the imperial army had been transferred to the regular army. As for the remaining imperial army, they could only send ten soldiers to each patrol camp" (X. Zhu 2010: 4475). This indicates that the number of soldiers in Fuzhou's military camps exceeded those mentioned above.

There were several military camps in Quanzhou. Initially, there were Baolin, Fashi, and Yongning military camps, which were subordinate to the Left-wing Navy. Later, Weitou Military Camp was added. Baolin Military Camp was located just 500 m south of Quanzhou, but it was far from the sea, making its function as a coastal defense point weak. Fashi Military Camp was situated at an important intersection of coastal defense seaways. Yongning Military Camp was positioned on the seaward side, providing a view stretching to the east of Fujian Province. It took a day and a night's ship trip to reach Penghu Island from there. Weitou Military Camp served as the gateway to the south of Quanzhou. Ships traveling between Nanyang and Beiyang had to anchor there, and the nearby branch port led to Shijing Military Camp. Its geographical location was highly significant. Lieyu Island lay south of Weitou Military Camp. Lieyu Island was the first place for control along the seaway from Nanyang to Quanzhou's territory, followed by Weitou Military Camp. Lieyu Military Camp had already mobilized local leaders and militias to safeguard the sea routes. Weitou Military Camp also established a smaller camp with approximately 100 deployed personnel. The seaway of this military camp connected to Yongning County in the north, and Lieyu Island in the south. The military camp also coordinated with nearby places such as Liuluo and Wuyu. Additionally, it controlled and guarded the ports around Shijing in inland areas. Clearly, the local leaders and militias stationed in Lieyu were subordinated to Quanzhou. Additionally, there were four coastal military camps under the jurisdiction of Quanzhou. Among them, Shihu Military Camp in Jinjiang County and Xiaodou Military Camp in Hui'an County held significant roles. Xiaodou Military Camp, in particular, guarded the north of Quanzhou. The seaway connecting Beiyang with Quanzhou's boundary was a primary defense and control point (D. Zhen, n.d.). Moreover, there were Shijing Military Camp and Patrol Divisions under the jurisdiction of Zhangzhou and Quanzhou. In Zhangzhou, the coastal and Zhongshan patrol military camps were located in Zhangpu County. In Xinghua military prefecture, there were Jiliao and Yingqian patrol military camps (S. Xu et al. 2014: 7136). These camps had their own jurisdiction territories. To inspect and patrol the sea routes, each patrol military camp received orders to define their jurisdictions. "The jurisdiction of Shihu Military Camp and Xiaodou Military Camp was defined to control the area north of Daiyu, Xinghua Military Camp, and Liao Military Camp. Similarly, the jurisdiction of Yongning Military Camp and Weitou Military Camp covered the area south to Shuiao Military Camp. Zhongshan Military Camp of Zhangzhou served as the boundary of their patrol. From the area near Daiyu Gateway of Dongyang, Fashi Military Camp's jurisdiction and Yongning Military Camp formed the boundary. Patrolling in that area occurred once a month" (D. Zhen, n.d.).

As mentioned above, the Cuifeng Army deployed specialized coastal defense units. In Guangnan East Province, two thousand sailors were stationed. Additionally, two hundred sailors were stationed in Chaozhou, Leizhou, and Qiongzhou in Guangxi Province, all of whom specialized in coastal defense. In the Northern Song Dynasty, Guangzhou established naval camps at the estuaries of the east and west rivers for the purpose of patrolling seaways. These camps had a width of approximately two hundred and eighty zhang. Located 100 km away from Tunmen Mountain, they controlled saury-shaped warships at sea (G. Zeng 1990). Chaozhou had a military camp called Haimen Military Camp. *The Total Annals of the Ming Dynasty* recorded that Haimen Military Camp was located in Haiyang County and was established during the Song Dynasty. Among the three military camps in the area, one of them was Haimen camp (X. Li et al. 1990). Additionally, in Yangjiang County of Nan'en

Prefecture, there were four military camps, including Haikou, Hailing, Bola, and Suixun, among others.

The defense of the coast in Guangnan West Province was crucial in preventing the invasion of Cangigu. In the coastal areas of Qinzhou, Guangxi Province, there were four patrol military camps and post stations responsible for patrolling and safeguarding the region. These included Duobu Military Camp, Didiao post station, Ruhong Military Camp, and Ruxi post station. Lianzhou housed Lujing Military Camp and Sancun Military Camp (G. Zeng 1990). Furthermore, Guantou Military Camp was situated in Haikang County of Leizhou (Toqta 1977: 2244). At the end of the Southern Song Dynasty, Li Zengbo was concerned about a potential Mongolian invasion by sea from Cangigu. He noted that the people of Cangigu were highly skilled in sailing ships, and although the Mongolians themselves lacked this ability, the Annan Kingdom might assist them. To counter this threat, Li Zengbo requested that the imperial court send one thousand soldiers from Fujian Province and Guangnan East Province to garrison Qinzhou. He emphasized that not only should Qinzhou be guarded, but Leizhou and Lianzhou, which were accessible to ships through seaways, also required attention. In his proposal to the court, Li Zengbo suggested that the warships in Qinzhou had already been transferred to Fujian Province and Guangnan Province by the imperial court, totaling one thousand personnel. On the third day of the seventh lunar month, all the warships from Guangnan East Province set sail, and on the thirteenth day of the seventh lunar month, the warships from Fujian Province passed Guangzhou to reach Leizhou, Lianzhou, and Huazhou. His recommendation to dispatch sailors from Fujian and Guangdong to guard the coast of Guangxi was implemented. Additionally, Guangxi Province sent troops and ships to Qinzhou for defense. Sea-going vessels, troops, and militias from Leizhou, Huazhou, and the neighboring coastal areas were also dispatched, with a total of approximately one thousand people. After the seventh lunar month, these individuals and vessels were ordered to garrison Qinzhou. Qinzhou had already constructed twenty light sea-going vessels, with plans to increase production further (Z. Li 1990). It served as the most critical defense point against the potential invasion from Cangigu.

4.4.3 Functions of the Southern Song Dynasty's Coastal Defense

Bao Hui mentioned in his *Proposal on Capturing Pirates to Secretariat* that the coastal defense system in the Southern Song Dynasty extended from Liangzhe East Province in the north to Guangnan East Province in the south. He stated, "the prefectures of Liangzhe East Province in the north and Guangnan East Province in the south should dispatch troops tightly like a Changshan snake. Generally speaking, Guangnan East Province was at the head, Liangzhe East Province at the end, and Fujian in the middle" (H. Bao 1990). He did not include Liangzhe West and

Huainan East provinces because the coast of Liangzhe West Province, Tongzhou and Chuzhou in Huainan East Province, and Mingzhou in Liangzhe East Province formed another coastal defense system with different goals. Thus, we can divide the coastal defense of the various coastal provinces in the Southern Song Dynasty into two systems: the northern system including Liangzhe West Province, the coast of Huainan East Province, and Mingzhou, which aimed to shield Lin'an, where the emperor lived and worked. It had a strong political mission. Taizhou and Wenzhou of Liangzhe East Province, along with the coast of Fujian, Guangnan East, and Guangnan West provinces, formed the southern system. Its main purpose was to control and contain pirates to safeguard maritime trade and coastal areas. There were significant differences between Taizhou, Wenzhou, and Mingzhou. Among them, the coast of Guangnan West Province focused on defending Cangigu, and the southern coastal defense system was influenced by socio-economic conditions.

During the Song Dynasty, an arc-shaped defensive circle was formed around Lin'an Prefecture, extending from Changzhou and Jiangyin in the west to Mingzhou in the south. Military camps and fortresses were established in various locations, including Weicun Village, Jiangyin Military Prefecture, Xupu, Gujing, Liujiao, Jinshan, Ganpu, Xiangtou, and Dinghai. The regular navy reached its peak at eighteen thousand personnel, with the Liangzhe West Province Coast Navy alone comprising fourteen thousand, which exceeded the combined number of regular sailors from Liangzhe East Province, Fujian, and Guangnan provinces. The navy was under the authority of the Palace Administration or the Imperial Army, ensuring greater security for their warships, weapons, money, and provisions compared to other sailors. In addition, over five thousand individuals were deployed in coastal defense, including regular sailors and local soldiers from Patrol Divisions in Mingzhou. No other prefectures in Fujian and Guangnan provinces could match this force. Furthermore, troops and ships from Fujian, Wenzhou, and Taizhou in Liangzhe East Province, as well as Guangnan provinces, were regularly dispatched to Mingzhou and Liangzhe West Province for garrison duty. Consequently, the number of soldiers in Mingzhou and Liangzhe West Province exceeded the aforementioned count. However, while the number of soldiers was substantial, the number of ships was inadequate for military operations. For example, in Weicun's naval military camps under the jurisdiction of Changzhou, there were five hundred soldiers, but only three hundred and fifty individuals and a total of fifty-nine warships of various sizes. Each warship required twenty soldiers, meaning more than one thousand soldiers were needed. However, the actual number was less than one-third of that, indicating a surplus of warships. Moreover, the shallow sea water posed treacherous sailing conditions. Some claimed that "the armies in Jiangnan Province were concerned about excess warships and insufficient soldiers." Thus, it can be observed that Liangzhe West Province and Mingzhou became the regions with the most abundant supply of warships. Fujian was a significant producer of seagoing vessels, dispatching hundreds of them to Mingzhou and Liangzhe West Province annually. However, despite being referred to as a navy, Fujian's Left-wing Army had no available warships in reality due to the province's shortage (D. Zhen, n.d.). This highlights the prioritization of deploying warships and soldiers to Liangzhe West Province and Mingzhou. Based on the troop deployments and the establishment of military camps, Liangzhe West Province and Mingzhou in the northern coastal defense system held great importance, while Huainan East Province was comparatively less significant. In the southern coastal defense system, Taizhou and Wenzhou in Liangzhe East Province, along with Fujian and Guangnan coastal areas, played secondary roles. Thus, we can summarize the two coastal defense systems as primary and secondary.

At the beginning of the northern coastal defense system, people particularly emphasized the importance of coastal defense against the Jin Kingdom. Dispatching soldiers from various provinces and warships to protect the coastal defense of Liangzhe West Province and Mingzhou was not merely to prevent pirates from invading Lin'an Prefecture. Its main purpose was to form a strong shield around Lin'an, protecting it from the invasion of the Jin Kingdom via the seaways. People in the Song Dynasty analyzed that the Jin would approach from two main routes: the first being from Liangzhe East Province, and the second from Liangzhe West Province. If they took the first route, "sea-going vessels coming from Shandong Province must go through Sangu Mountain by wind." Therefore, a patrol military camp was established on Sangu Mountain (S. Xu et al. 2014: 9671). Various military camps were also established in Dinghai County. If the Jin attempted to invade Dinghai County from the sea, these military camps would safeguard the area. If they attempted to bypass Liaojiao and invade the Yangtze River from an offshore route, the Xupu Navy would block their way. Similarly, if they coveted Zhejiang Province from the seagoing routes, the Minpu Navy and Jinshan Navy would defend against them. Additionally, the newly established Xiangtou camp was connected to Jinshan and Ganpu patrol military camps, creating a second line of defense around the emperor. The navy of Dinghai County had three tasks: first, patrolling and guarding three coastal areas, which involved patrolling from Liegang Port to the Donghai Sea and extending as far as Xupu. The second task was to gather intelligence on enemy movements in the north, from Shenqian and other places to Lüqiao. The third task was to guard the ports, with the navy being in close proximity to the patrol military camps and returning to the camps for meals in turns (Y. Mei et al. 1990: 5989–90). The deployment of the navy could be considered comprehensive and impervious.

The Song envisaged many times that the Jin or the Qi might invade it by sea. In September of the third year of the Jianyan Reign (AD 1129), there was a secret report stating that the people of the Jin were building warships and setting up sailors, and they would invade Jiangnan Province and Liangzhe Province by sea. The emperor issued an edict to order Han Shizhong to guard Chui Mountain and Fu Mountain (Toqta 1977: 468). In the second year of the Shaoxing Reign (AD 1132), intelligence sources reported that the enemy stationed in Huaiyang Military Prefecture and Haizhou respectively. It was worrying that if the enemy sailed south, the Jiangnan provinces, Liangzhe East Province, and Liangzhe West Province would be disturbed. However, Shen Yuqiu considered that building sea-going vessels was the enemy's ruse to scare them (X. Li 2013: 1108, 1116). The result was exactly as he predicted. In the third year of the Shaoxing Reign (AD 1133), General Xu Wen of the Song commanded sixty sea-going vessels and four thousand three hundred officers and soldiers. They sailed and defected to the Qi State and suggested to Emperor Liu Yu that there was no army along the coast and a direct way to invade Liangzhe East and West provinces. They mentioned that Tongzhou, Taizhou, and other nearby prefectures were also on their way. But they failed to reach the coast of Liangzhe East Province and Liangzhe West Province (X. Li 2013: 1314). In 1133, Guo Zhongxun served as the Mayor of Mingzhou. He was worried that people of the Jin Dynasty would invade the south during the monsoon and high tide. Therefore, he sent dinghies into the sea for reconnaissance, stationed troops at the port, and occupied the main seaways to prevent people of the Jin Dynasty from invading (X. Li 2013: 1342). In the following year, the Song Dynasty learned that Liu Yu had mobilized twenty thousand troops and five hundred warships from Dengzhou, Laizhou, Yizhou, Mizhou, and Haizhou. Taking the rebel army led by Xu Wen as the spearhead, "threatened to attack Dinghai County" (X. Li 2013: 1484). As a result, neither the people of the Jin nor the Qi invaded the south. During the Qiandao Reign (AD 1165–1173), when Zhao Bogui served as the mayor of Mingzhou, he learned from prisoners that the Jin intended to invade the border of the Song directly, and there were rumors that they would unite with Goryeo. "Both the emperor and the ministers doubted about the information. The emperor (Zhao Bogui) rectified the warships, and strictly conducted training to spread the prestige of the army." However, Xu Derong, a native of Mingzhou, was sent to investigate and found out that the information was false (Y. Lou 1990). But in fact, there were few water battles along the coast of Liangzhe West Province, except for skirmishes between the Song and Jin Dynasties at the end of the Jianyan Reign, as well as the beginning and end of the Shaoxing Reign in Mingzhou and Zhenjiang. The defense against the Jin Dynasty was primarily strategic in nature. For example, Li Bing analyzed the potential southern invasion by the Jin Dynasty, stating, "The Jin Dynasty is likely to first dispatch an army from the Huaihe River Basin, where they will establish a long-term presence to contain our forces. Subsequently, they will cross the sea from Dengzhou and Laizhou, aiming to seize Wuzhou and Yuezhou, thereby flanking our army on the left. Additionally, they will launch an attack on Jiangzhou and Chizhou from Wuchang, positioning themselves on our army's right side" (Toqta 1977: 11608). However, following Emperor Xiaozong's reign, no water battles against the Jin occurred, and the Jin was unable to pose a maritime threat to the Southern Song. In the thirty-second year of the Shaoxing Reign (AD 1162), the sole attempt at invasion by the Jin Kingdom was completely defeated through the long-distance naval raids conducted by the Southern Song Dynasty in the Jiaoxi Battle. Consequently, it can be concluded that after Song Gaozong's reign, defense against Jin invasions from the south relied solely on strategic measures, and the strict northern coastal defense system did not play a significant role in defending against the Jin Kingdom. Instead, its primary function was to combat piracy.

Then, did a significant number of sailors deployed in Mingzhou and Liangzhe West Province in the Song Dynasty have a plan for a northward sea expedition? This issue was extensively discussed among officials within the Southern Song Dynasty. In the fourth year of the Jianyan Reign (AD 1130), Lü Yihao proposed utilizing the seagoing vessels dispatched from Fujian Province and other provinces to "send troops northward". Consequently, twenty thousand soldiers were sent via the seaway to Wenzhou and Dengzhou to launch an attack on Qingzhou and Qizhou. Another

20,000 soldiers swiftly advanced to Pengcheng through Huaiyang, aiming to attack Yunzhou and Puzhou. In the second year of the Shaoxing Reign (AD 1132), Lü Yihao reiterated the need to "take advantage of summer" and "send troops northward to reclaim the Central Plains, our lost territory." He further proposed leaving three hundred seagoing vessels in Mingzhou and instructed Fan Wen and Yan Gao to sail northward in April, directly occupying Donglai (X. Li 2013: 828, 1198). Lü Yihao believed that they should "leverage the advantages of seagoing vessels to disturb the prefectures of fake Qi Kingdom to the east of Jingdong Province, Hebei Province and the Liao Kingdom." "If we sail by the south wind and return by the north wind, even if the Jin Kingdom had millions of elite cavalry, they would be unable to block us" (Y. Lü 1990). When Zhang Jun assumed leadership of the military administration in the tenth year of the Shaoxing Reign (AD 1140), he "increased the number of seagoing vessels to one thousand for the purpose of attacking Shandong Province." However, he did not receive any combat orders. Towards the end of the Shaoxing Reign, Zhang Jun also devised a plan to "mobilize the seagoing vessels from Fujian Province to launch an attack on Donglai from the East China Sea and occupy Huaiyang from the Qinghe River." Subsequently, Zhang Zigai visited from Zhenjiang Prefecture, and Zhang Jun discussed with him the strategy of reclaiming Shandong Province (W. Yang 2007: 4414). After Emperor Xiaozong ascended the throne, Chen Junqing suggested "directly sending the navy to attack Shandong Province." However, as peace negotiations between the two kingdoms unfolded, the plan was abandoned (Toqta 1977: 11785). Certain civilians also proposed strategies and voluntarily expressed their willingness to join the army. For example, a man named Wang Xian in Wenzhou claimed expertise in seafaring. He boasted of having recruited more than 2000 people and requested the court to provide warships and weapons. His aim was to directly recapture Dengzhou and Qingzhou. However, Wang Yingchen held the view that "the northern expedition plans advocated by civilian groups cannot be implemented. While we may trust their words, their actions will cause minimal damage to the enemy and yield limited benefits for us" (Y. Wang 1990). This perspective reflected a more rational opinion prevalent among Southern Song bureaucrats. In fact, this assessment proved accurate. Apart from Li Bao's successful attack on Jiaoxi in the thirty-first year of the Shaoxing Reign (AD 1161), which resulted in the defeat of the Jin fleet, the Song Dynasty did not embark on a northward sea expedition.

Basically, the defense of the northern coastal defense system against the Jin Kingdom was primarily focused on strategic defense. Apart from the water battles waged by the Jin in the south in the fourth year of the Jianyan Reign (AD 1130) and the 31st year of the Shaoxing Reign (AD 1161), there were almost no other actual water battles. The practical function of the northern coastal defense system was mainly to combat pirates. In terms of dealing with pirates, restoring the regular order of maritime trade was considered more important than eliminating military threats to Lin'an Prefecture. People in the Song Dynasty said that Dinghai County of Mingzhou had a garrison of thousands from the Imperial Navy because it "was connected to the Yangtze River Estuary. For the merchant ships from the South that conducted business in Mingzhou and the merchant ships of Mingzhou, Dinghai

County was like a gate" (J. Luo et al. 1990: 5226). The main role of the Dinghai Navy was to suppress and catch pirates. It is unnecessary to provide specific examples.

The primary function of the southern coastal defense system was to combat pirates, safeguard maritime trade, and ensure coastal social security. The government of the Southern Song Dynasty placed great importance on maritime trade. Emperor Gaozong once emphasized repeatedly that "the income from trade contacts with foreign countries at sea was beneficial to public finance expenditure" and that "merchant ship trade was highly profitable. With proper management, the income tax amounted to tens of thousands" (K. Xiong 1985; X. Li 2013: 2158). Lian Nanfu remarked that "the country earns millions of dollars from overseas trade every year. However, due to rampant pirates this year, the monsoon could not bring foreign merchant ships as it rose. I have heard that some people are riding in imperial chariots and claiming to be vassals. It is not easy for them to surrender" (X. Li 2013: 1702). He pointed out that pirates had severely impacted overseas trade. The emperor and ministers of the Southern Song Dynasty not only recognized that "tax revenue from overseas trade was the highest," but also understood that disrupting maritime trade would harm the country and its merchants. A decline in the number of merchants would result in "four disadvantages for them, and the government would also incur significant losses in two respects." In summary, for businessmen, maritime trade was their livelihood, and for the country, it was "a significant supplement to the country's economic development" (X. Li 2013: 3614). Protecting trade, in addition to preventing pirates from disrupting the normal order of state governance and challenging the state's authority, was a major motivation for national defense and combating pirates in the Southern Song Dynasty.

The significance of offshore trade and ocean trade for Fujian and Guangnan Provinces was even more evident. "The rice produced by Guangnan provinces was the main food source for the people in the four prefectures: Fuzhou, Xingzhou, Zhangzhou, and Quanzhou. The Governor of Ancient Customs in Fujian Province earned profits from foreign merchant seagoing vessels and trading seagoing vessels in the South Sea, collecting tax revenues. However, nowadays, the sea route has been blocked by vicious pirates." Guangnan East Province was also plagued by pirate activities. Li Gang stated, "in Guangnan East and Fujian provinces, many pirates have committed acts of evil in recent years. They have looted and plundered coastal counties, towns, villages, foreign seas, as well as treasures that were supposed to be handed over to higher authorities by Ancient Customs. The total value of these goods amounts to tens of thousands" (G. Li 2004: 829). Pirates in Fujian Province and Guangnan East Province "robbed grain ships for sustenance, looted foreign merchant ships to amass wealth, captured young and middle-aged men, and seized ships to increase their power." They often "went ashore armed to plunder," "stole food from coastal residents, extorted livestock and wine, and lay in wait for foreign merchant ships trading in China, intercepting and robbing them." The robbery of people, ships, and property had a significant impact on maritime navigation and coastal social security. Particularly in April and May each year, when the southwest monsoon began to blow and seagoing vessels returned, "coastal residents and seagoing vessels were inevitably targeted by pirates, causing substantial damage to tax revenues. Additionally, in the three prefectures of Fuzhou, Quanzhou, and Xinghua Military Prefecture, the provisions for the army and common people relied on grain from the Guangnan provinces. With pirate ships rampant at sea, the passage of grain ships was cut off, resulting in food shortages for the army and the people. This led to a rise in grain prices, and the government and the common people detested the piracy" (D. Zhen, n.d.). It is evident that pirates posed a threat to foreign merchant ships engaged in maritime trade and even disrupted offshore trade. "Due to the pirate menace, rice merchants and ship merchants were constantly robbed and plundered" (D. Zhen, n.d.). Simultaneously, pirates also endangered coastal residents. "Pirates, taking advantage of the political unrest, sailed and plundered merchant ships, disturbing the islanders. Allowing these pirates to go unchecked is highly dangerous, and this disaster will grow and expand" (B. Zhou 1990). Chen Chun particularly emphasized that the impact of pirates was a scourge on the livelihood of coastal residents. "The sea routes are treacherous, rice boats and cargo ships are blocked, and the lives of the people are in dire straits" (C. Chen 1990). Maritime merchants united to combat pirates. Yao Zhuo, the Administrator of Ancient Customs in Guangnan, stated that "sometimes merchant ships could trade temporarily, but they were unable to follow the sea route regularly." "Recently, a ship owner engaged in maritime trade together with other ships forming the 'East Fleet,' which terrified the pirates." However, the government was the main force in combating pirates (X. Li 2013: 1668). Therefore, protecting maritime trade, offshore trade, and coastal social security were crucial responsibilities of coastal defense undertaken by the Song Dynasty.

Some scholars argue that the coastal defense strategy of the Southern Song Dynasty was primarily focused on maritime defense (Q. Wang 2004). However, based on the characteristics of the Southern Song Dynasty's coastal defense arrangements, it is clear that shore defense was prioritized to counter the Jin troops and pirates. Han Yuanji once pointed out that the key aspect of the Song's coastal defense against the Jin was not engaging in naval battles, but rather defending the coastline. "The sea is crisscrossed with maritime routes. With the help of favorable winds, a seagoing vessel can travel thousands of miles in a single night. It is impossible to win naval battles on warships. When faced with strong winds and waves, the possibility of warships coordinating with each other diminishes. Deploying soldiers and light boats to guard strategic junctures, patrolling sea routes with light boats to monitor ports, conducting reconnaissance missions, and fortifying city walls were the only effective methods of resisting the enemy. Even if the enemy managed to breach the city walls, they would be unable to find a way back. That is the most effective combat strategy" (Y. Han 1990). This perspective aligns with Wu Qian's opinion. He believed that naval warfare differed from land warfare. Although the enemy might possess thousands of warships, they would be unable to mount a coordinated attack due to the influence of wind and waves at sea. "By stationing three thousand elite soldiers and thirty formidable warships at key points where pirates must pass, all the pirates aboard their ships can be killed. In this way, pirate ships can be eradicated once and for all" (Y. Mei et al. 1990: 5983). Furthermore, since the regular navies in Fujian and Guangnan in the Southern Song Dynasty were limited, coastal defense mainly relied on local soldiers from the Patrol Division, county criminal inspectors, archers, and the general public. It is evident that the defense strategy relied heavily on passive defense. As mentioned earlier, the number of local soldiers in the Patrol Division, county criminal inspectors, and archers was limited. The sailors recruited by local leaders "could be used to defend against small groups of pirates but would be unable to resist a large enemy force" (Y. Han 1990). Despite the Southern Song Dynasty's advancements in shipbuilding technology and naval power, opinions such as Wang Yingchen's perspective on a northern expedition by sea argued that it would cause minimal damage to the enemy and yield little benefit. Wang Yingchen even proposed abandoning maritime defense and focusing solely on shore defense. He stated that throughout history, "we have never heard of the enemy invading from the north by sea." "Even if the Jin Kingdom was not defeated in the Jiaoxi Battle and their seagoing vessels were able to enter the port, they would only come to their demise. All seagoing vessels had to wait for the tide before entering the port, as only the tidal current could carry the seagoing vessels to invade Song's ports. They could disembark only after switching boats. Even if the enemy was well-equipped with weapons, if we occupied high ground and controlled the main roads to await the enemy's attack, they would be completely defeated. Without these warships, military expenditures could be reduced by one million silver units" (Y. Wang 1990). This reveals the Southern Song Dynasty's inclination towards passive defense and the absence of intentions for overseas military expansion.

4.4.4 Summary

The focus of frontier defense in the Northern Song was placed on three border provinces: Shaanxi, Hedong, and Hebei. As there was no threat from the sea, a systematic coastal defense had not been established. Only in the coastal areas of Jingdong Province, such as Dengzhou, a limited number of sailors were deployed to contain the aggression of the Liao Kingdom. However, their duties were limited to patrolling the borders and resisting pirates. Coastal defense in the south mainly relied on patrol soldiers, and in the event of large groups of pirates appearing, the imperial court would send envoys responsible for apprehending thieves. In summary, the coastal defense during that time was weak, and a proper coastal defense system had not yet been developed.

The Southern Song Dynasty was content with the retreated border lines in Jiangnan Province, while the territories north of the coastline and the estuary of the Huaihe River were occupied by the Jin Kingdom. Additionally, in the Southern Song Dynasty, Lin'an, located at the mouth of the Qiantang River, was chosen as the emperor's temporary residence. Concerns about maritime security arose among both the emperor and the ministers of the Southern Song Dynasty. Simultaneously, the Southern Song experienced a significant increase in maritime trade, but its ability to enforce social control was weak. This led to an escalation in piracy, which disrupted social stability and maritime trade in coastal areas. Consequently, the Southern Song Dynasty developed separate coastal defenses for the northern and southern regions.

The northern coastal defense system played a crucial role, primarily aimed at protecting Lin'an. It extended from Weicun Village in Changzhou to the east, covering the southern area of the Yangtze River estuary, Jinshan Village, Ganpu on the north bank of the Qiantang River, the prefecture and patrol division Dinghai County on the south bank, and the Huainan provinces north of the Yangtze River estuary. Strict coastal defenses and garrisons were established in these areas. The number of sailors in the northern coastal defense system surpassed those in Fujian Province, Guangnan Province, and Wenzhou and Taizhou of Liangzhe East Province. The emperor of the Southern Song Dynasty envisioned the northern coastal defense system as a means to defend against Jin attacks from the sea, and vice versa, for the Southern Song to launch assaults on Jin territories via the sea. However, apart from the naval battles of Mingzhou at the end of the Jianyan Reign and Jiaoxi at the end of the Shaoxing Reign, neither side had engaged in direct naval attacks. Therefore, the practical role of the northern coastal defense system was primarily to combat piracy.

The southern coastal defense system was primarily designed to contain pirates and safeguard the security of the coastal areas and maritime trade. As a secondary area of coastal defense, it had fewer garrison soldiers compared to the northern coastal defense. In the Southern Song Dynasty, sailors and seagoing vessels from the southern coastal defense system were consistently deployed to the main defensive positions of the northern coastal defense system each year. This reflects that the main focus in the Southern Song Dynasty was on the northern coastal defense system.

Although the emperor of the Southern Song Dynasty attached importance to a comprehensive coastal defense system, it still played a secondary role in comparison to river defense. It actively cracked down on pirates and safeguarded the security and maritime trade of coastal areas, but it was largely ineffective in terms of external defense.

4.5 Piracy and Measures for Eradicating Pirates in the Southern Song Dynasty

Pirates were a persistent problem throughout the coastal provinces of the Southern Song Dynasty, particularly in Fujian Province, as well as Guangnan East and West provinces. The source and activities of these pirates were closely connected to the residents living along the coast, including officials and soldiers. They traveled between multiple coastal provinces and moved around, which made it challenging for the Southern Song Dynasty to eradicate them completely. The Southern Song employed various methods, including military suppression, conciliation, and mobilization of the people, but their damages persisted despite these efforts.

4.5.1 Distribution and Composition of the Pirates in the Song Dynasty

The growth of piracy was influenced by several factors, including the development of shipbuilding and seafaring industries, the thriving maritime trade, the weakening of military coastal defense and social control, the presence of corrupt governance, and the deterioration of living conditions. These factors combined, particularly in the Southern Song Dynasty, making piracy a significant problem for socio-economic development and military defense in the coastal regions of Song. Throughout the Song Dynasty, piracy affected the coastal areas from Shandong Province in the north to Guangnan East and West provinces in the south. The southern regions, especially those with prosperous maritime trade such as Fujian Province, Liangzhe East Province, and Guangnan East and West provinces, experienced more severe piracy issues than the northern areas.

Fujian Province developed a prosperous maritime trade and was strategically located between Guangnan East and West provinces and Liangzhe East and West provinces. Sea passages in Fujian Province connected it to Liangzhe East and West provinces in the north and Guangnan East and West provinces in the south. In the past, pirates mostly targeted remote and desolate areas, but as they acquired more boats, they began to launch attacks on Fujian Province as well (K. Lang 1990: 7933). Fujian Province not only faced threats from its own native pirates but also from pirates originating in Liangzhe and Guangnan provinces, where piracy was particularly rampant. Fuzhou, being situated close to the sea, was a gathering place for pirates, resulting in rampant piracy in the area (Toqta 1977: 12164, 13586). Pirate ships from the north operated from Mount Tongpan and Banyang Dui on the boundary of Wenzhou, while those from the south were based in Mount Nanxiao and Nanni Mountain Village on the boundary of Xinghua Prefecture. Consequently, Hantou, Yingxian Port, Jiangkou, Yanxun, Shangyu Islet, Bolang Bay, Xiaolian Island, and other locations were frequent targets for pirate attacks on merchant boats (H. Bao 1990). Fuzhou had a significant presence of pirates, including Zheng Guang, who was notorious for plundering money and goods from boats in the terrestrial islands between Pujia Long and Fuzhou. Zheng Guang's ships were swift and armed with sharp weapons, and his group of desperadoes were skilled and courageous in battle, posing a challenge for the official army. Zheng Guang referred to himself as the Rolling Sea Dragon (K. Yue 1981: 41). On the Yihai Day of October in the lunar calendar of the first year of the Shaoxing Reign (AD 1131), Li Yuanyu, acting as vice director of the Ministry of Personnel, was sailing from Jinghu South Province to supervise goods for the imperial court when he was killed upon reaching Dajin Bay in Fuzhou (X. Li 2013: 101). In the first year of the Qiandao Reign (AD 1165), Wang Zhiwang, the mayor of Fuzhou, set out to apprehend a pirate known as Wang Dalao (Toqta 1977: 11539). In the third year of the Shaoxi Reign (AD 1192), a man named Zheng Lizhi from Fuzhou was sailing from Panyu County back to his home. When he arrived at Fuxi Bay in Putian, he learned that there were six pirate ships in the nearby sea, causing him to delay his departure from the port (M. Hong 1981: 1058).

Lin Jizhong had purchased some local products and sent his servants to Zhangzhou and Quanzhou on a passenger boat. However, upon hearing reports that multi-paddle boats in the sea had turned to piracy, the passenger boat hesitated to depart due to fear of pirates (J. Lin 1990).

Quanzhou was prosperous in trade, but piracy was also rampant. When Zhen Dexiu served as the mayor of Quanzhou, "sea pirates staged an insurrection there and were about to occupy the city. The soldiers were defeated, and he paid tribute to those killed in battle. Then he taught stratagems himself and captured the pirates" (Toqta 1977: 12960). In the middle of the Chunxi Reign, it was said that "a pirate named Jiang Daliao invaded southern Quanzhou" (Toqta 1977: 13695). In the fifth year of the Shaoding Reign (AD 1232), "a pirate named Wang Ziqing invaded Weitou Mountain Village" and killed the general-in-chief of the Song troops named Wang Dashou (Toqta 1977: 13338). Pirates from Wenzhou and Mingzhou even ventured southward to invade Quanzhou. After the Northern Expedition in the Kaixi Reign, in Quanzhou, "few defending soldiers returned alive, and boats were damaged with no stock reserves. Then the weapons and equipment for battle were depleted, and military training weakened", and "groups of pirates from Wenzhou and Mingzhou were aware of the weakness of Quanzhou's coastal defense, so they intended to invade there" (D. Zhen, n.d.). Wang Ziqing and other pirates once "set fire and killed people on Wuyu Islet in the sea surrounding Zhangzhou". The Song soldiers and villagers fought together with them and captured the pirate leader and his bandits, totaling 136, in the Shaotao Ocean surrounding Zhangzhou (D. Zhen, n.d.). This evidenced that Fujian Province, from north to Fuzhou and south to Zhangzhou, suffered from piracy with a large number of pirates. In the ninth year of the Shaoxing Reign (AD 1139), when serving as the military commissioner of Fujian Province, Zhang Jun "summoned the sea pirates to surrender and presented 53 multi-paddle boats and 2500 soldiers and generals to the imperial court" (Y. Han 1990). Zhang Jun stayed in Fuzhou for only 2 years but managed to summon such a large number of pirates. When Ye Mengde served as the mayor of Fuzhou and the military commissioner of Fujian Province, "a pirate named Zhu Ming went on a rampage, and Mengde was ordered to lead the imperial generals to suppress them, either by summoning them to surrender or capturing them, or by enticing them to kill each other, and finally pacifying more than 50 groups of pirates" (Toqta 1977: 13135–36). Surprisingly, there were more than 50 pirate groups operating at the same time.

Liangzhe East and West provinces were the most economically prosperous regions, whether it was through ocean trade or offshore trade. Both provinces served as crucial markets for consumption and the transfer of shipments, but they were also severely affected by piracy. Piracy was prevalent in Liangzhe West Province, south to the estuary of the Qiantang River and north to Zhenjiang Prefecture. Pirates operating on the Qiantang River ventured out to the sea, making them a menace both on the river and at sea. They were highly detrimental and posed a significant threat. They moved southward and were active in the lower reaches of the Qiantang River before venturing out to the sea. There were reports of "an evil practice of looting and plundering in broad daylight outside the defending gates in the suburban areas in all four directions. Passenger boats would only dare to travel westward in groups of 30 to 50 boats together. The pirates' location was directly opposite Mount Dragon and Mount Temple. They were based in an area known as Tongjia Hui and later Houhang. The government did not register any individuals within several miles of the pirates' residence. The pirates frequently smuggled prohibited goods between rivers and the sea, and their ships were equipped with a large number of weapons. Nowadays, they specifically targeted passenger boats… some would seize goods from the boats and throw people into the river, while others sailed out to sea with the stolen goods" (F. Fang 1990). Piracy also plagued the coastal regions from Ganpu to Xupu. During Bao Hui's leadership of the Judicial Commission in Liangzhe West Province, "the pirates launched a rebellion, prompting Bao Hui to personally dispatch troops to Xupu and Ganpu and station them in several prefectures. One morning, he gathered all the troops to suppress the pirates" (Toqta 1977: 12592). Pingjiang Prefecture "was close to the sea and haunted by pirates" (Toqta 1977: 8767). When Shen Zuobin served as the mayor there, "the prefecture had an envoy who had previously been a pirate." The envoy was instructed to entice his former pirate comrades, and as a result, "Shen Zuobin assembled several thousand strong and brave men, appointed a general to lead them, and named them righteous men." He declared that "from now on, the sea passage does not need to be guarded" (Toqta 1977: 11962). Pirate activities disrupted Zhenjiang Prefecture. In the third year of the Jiading Reign (AD 1210), Fu Bocheng served as the mayor and discovered that "soldiers from the Tuanshan Mountain Camp were often colluding with the pirates. He investigated their names and arrested and interrogated them during his review of troops in various prefectures, ensuring that none of them escaped" (K. Liu, n.d.).

In several prefectures of Liangzhe East Province, Mingzhou suffered greatly from piracy. In the sixth year of the Qiandao Reign (AD 1170), Zhao Boyao served as the mayor of Mingzhou and observed that piracy was rampant in the area. There were pirates known as Ge Ming and Zhang Shen, and a particularly troublesome individual named Ni De, also known as Ni Lang (Toqta 1977: 8688; Y. Lou 1990). The people of Mingzhou were fierce and brutal. Wealthy individuals formed militias to patrol the seas, harbored the chairwarmers, and forcibly recruited vendors. The poor engaged in robbery and inter-group conflicts, resulting in frequent injuries and deaths (J. Luo et al. 1990: 5180). Many pirates operated at sea, including Wang Xian, a pirate in Mingzhou who commanded ten boats and had over 800 fellow pirates active in Mingzhou and the East China Sea. Upon seeing the notice issued by the Song Dynasty calling for their surrender, Wang Xian convinced all the boat captains to join him, leading two boats and over 160 companions in surrendering. The remaining pirates, pursued by the Song army, fled back to Mingzhou. When they reached the sea within Mingzhou's territory, they sank their ships and escaped (S. Hong, n.d.). Taizhou and Wenzhou also suffered greatly from piracy. In the eleventh year of the Chunxi Reign (AD 1184), Taizhou reported capturing 57 pirates, including their leader Mao Da, while Wenzhou reported capturing 96 pirates, including the vice leader Xu Da. Wang Zhiwang, the mayor of Taizhou, and Chen Yanxiao, the mayor of Wenzhou, both achieved notable success in apprehending pirates (Z. Wang 1990). During his tenure as the mayor of Taizhou, Xiao Zhen made significant efforts to suppress and capture pirates, effectively curbing their activities (Toqta 1977: 11726). In the second year of the Baoyou Reign (AD 1254), pirates plagued Taizhou for many years, causing great suffering for the local residents (Toqta 1977: 852). Wenzhou not only faced domestic piracy but also fell victim to pirates from the sea (Y. Lou 1990; Toqta 1977: 13254). Furthermore, pirates from Wenzhou also ventured southward, launching attacks on Fujian Province. In Fujian, pirates from Wenzhou and Mingzhou, originating from the North Ocean, engaged in widespread piracy and plunder, endangering voyagers (D. Zhen, n.d.). The pirates from Wenzhou were often referred to as "thieves on boats in Wenzhou" and frequently clashed with officials and residents in Lieyu of Tong'an County (D. Zhen, n.d.). Additionally, Shaoxing Prefecture in Liangzhe East Province, being in close proximity to the sea, also faced pirate activities. When Huang Zhen served as the supervisor of municipal financial affairs in Shaoxing Prefecture, he apprehended and eliminated some pirates (Toqta 1977: 12993).

Guangzhou was a prominent hub for foreign trade and offshore trade between Guangnan East and West provinces and Fujian Province. The focus of this trade was the transportation of rice from Guangnan East and West provinces to Fujian Province, which laid the groundwork for the rise of piracy. The region south of the Five Ridges was infested with land and water thieves. Liu Xuan attacked Jieyang from Ganzhou, while Zheng Guang and Zhou Cong plundered sea passages. Zeng Gun established his stronghold in Mount Fuzeng for seven years. There were other pirate groups that called themselves Dawang, Taiwei, Tiezhu, Huoxing, Feidao, and Datian, totaling thousands of pirates in 18 groups (Y. Han 1990). Li Gang once remarked that Panyu County, as the metropolis of Guangnan East Province, was home to many wealthy merchants and foreign traders. It boasted abundant resources and a large population. For the royal court, it was the gathering place for overseas salt trade, and the country's tax revenue relied on the South China Sea trade. Consequently, it became a coveted target for pirates. In order to protect Guangnan East Province, the safeguarding of Panyu County was paramount (G. Li 2004: 1119). In the coastal regions of Guangnan East and West provinces, the descendants of pirates had thrived for generations since the Southern Han Dynasty. Large pirate groups with hundreds of members plagued numerous prefectures and counties. During the Taipingxingguo Reign, Yang Yungong held the positions of Administrator of Ancient Customs in Guangzhou and inspector of border security in Guanglian Prefecture. Despite his efforts, piracy still ran rampant in the coastal regions of Guangnan East and West provinces. One notable pirate, Ye, commanded over 500 fellow pirates and operated at sea. Yang Yungong mobilized the naval force, constructed rafts, and launched a surprise attack on Ye, successfully eliminating him. The remaining pirates abandoned their ships and sought refuge in the valley. Whenever they encountered adverse weather, the pirates took shelter among the islets. Undeterred, Yang Yungong led his men across the sea, capturing almost all of them. The mere sight of the approaching force caused the pirates to flee. Yang Yungong then proceeded to Zhangzhou and Quanzhou, where the pirates had resided, and rescued over 60 kidnapped individuals, returning them safely to their homes (Toqta 1977: 10160). Pirates from Guangnan East and West provinces even made their presence felt in the coastal regions of Fujian Province. The uprising of pirates on the South China Sea caused concern for the Song Dynasty (Toqta 1977: 12671). The authorities in Guangzhou were deeply troubled by pirates and local officials were dedicated to their capture. Fang Xinru, while serving as the commissioner of Panyu County, apprehended pirates who had robbed sea merchants. He captured them while they were dividing their spoils on the beach. The pirates, frightened and seeking to flee to their ships, found that Fang Xinru had already ordered the ships to be removed. As a result, all the pirates were apprehended, and none were able to escape (Toqta 1977: 12059).

The region most heavily affected by piracy in Guangnan East and West provinces, aside from the coast of Guangzhou, was Chaozhou and the border area between Chaozhou and Zhangzhou. Zhu Cong, a prominent pirate during the early Southern Song Dynasty, led naval forces into Guangnan East Province from Chaozhou, causing destruction and looting in various counties (X. Li 2013: 1599). The *Selected Works of Zhang Nie* documented that pirate ships plagued the sea border of Chaozhou in Guangnan East Province, and the imperial envoy Lin Jing led warships in pursuit and capture (N. Zhang 1990). The area between Zhangzhou and Chaozhou was a frequent anchorage and raiding spot for pirates. Year after year, pirate ships traveled to and from the territories of Zhangzhou, Chaozhou, Huizhou, and the crucial estuary to the sea. They pillaged grain from coastal inhabitants, extorted livestock and wine, and specifically targeted foreign merchant ships. Chen Shitou from Zhangzhou fell victim to a robbery in the Dadi Sea, with nine people, including sailors and the captain, being abducted. Notably, Zhelin Bay in Chaozhou and other locations served as pirate hideouts, where 22 pirate ships were anchored and a large number of pirates operated. They plundered grain boats for sustenance, foreign vessels for wealth, and kidnapped young adults to expand their influence. They lay in wait for foreign ships, intercepting and robbing them. On occasion, the pirates even ventured ashore, carrying weapons and utilizing 11 pirate ships carrying 500 to 600 pirates for land-based plundering (D. Zhen, n.d.). Additionally, piracy also plagued the coast of Guangnan West Province. For example, in the fifth year of the Shaoxing Reign (AD 1135), "a pirate named Chen Gan attacked Leizhou and repeatedly defeated the troops" (Toqta 1977: 519). In the 30th year of the Shaoxing Reign (AD 1160), "another pirate named Chen Yantian staged an armed rebellion, attacking Gaozhou and Leizhou. He was eventually captured and killed by Lin Guan, a resident of Nan'en Prefecture" (Toqta 1977: 595).

Piracy also existed on the coast of Jingdong Province, as well as in Huainan East and West provinces. "Qingzhou, Mizhou, Dengzhou, Yuanzhou, and Weizhou in Jingdong Province were located near East China Sea. During times of war, pirates from the coastal region of Jingdong Province would venture out to sea to engage in robbery or assist foreign invaders" (C. Chen 1990). When Liu Huan served as the mayor of Dengzhou, precautions were taken against pirates by improving saury-shaped warships, which deterred them from launching attacks (Toqta 1977: 10493). Wang Zhongbao, on a special order, rode as a courier to Dengzhou and successfully captured over a hundred pirates there (Toqta 1977: 10513). In the Southern Song Dynasty, Jingdong Province was part of the Jin Kingdom's territory, and there are no records in *the History of Jin* regarding piracy, hence the details remain unknown. During Wang Nan's tenure as the commissioner of Haimen County in Tongzhou of Huainan East Province, he embarked on a sea voyage and apprehended a notorious pirate named Little Wulang, along with 17 of his accomplices (Toqta 1977: 12062). However, the sandy coastline of Huainan East and West provinces made sailing difficult, and their level of trade was not comparable to that of Liangzhe East and West provinces, Fujian Province, and Guangnan East and West provinces. As a result, pirate activities were relatively limited in those areas.

Overseas pirates once attacked the Song Dynasty. During Emperor Taizong's Reign, those fleeing from the territory under Le Hoan's control sought shelter in Song territory and, as they were not sent back, they began launching annual attacks. The Song Dynasty eventually caught the pirates and returned them to Le Hoan, who expressed gratitude by capturing the pirates himself (Toqta 1977: 9584). These pirates were believed to be from Cochin. Additionally, the coast of Quanzhou faced invasions from Visayan raiders. In the Qiandao Reign, invaders from Visaya infiltrated the area and killed local residents (D. Zhen, n.d.). Visaya was located south of Ryukyu (Taiwan Island), and the raiders would travel by tying bamboo together as rafts. In case of emergencies, the people would lift the raft and swim to safety (Toqta 1977: 14127). Quanzhou took measures to defend its coastal residents from abductions by Visayan pirates, deploying soldiers annually at a significant cost (Toqta 1977: 12145). However, these instances were occasional and occurred during a short period, as the piracy problem mainly originated domestically.

However, pirates, unlike land invaders, utilized boats as their primary tool and operated at sea. They did not need to traverse prefectures or counties, but instead sailed the open waters. This allowed their activities to extend beyond local areas, often causing trouble for coastal provinces. For example, in Emperor Renzong's Reign, a defector in the army called E Lin fled by sea and became a pirate. The mismanagement of the officials and troops in coastal prefectures led to panic among the people (X. Cai 1996: 365). In response, troops from Fujian Province were dispatched to raid and suppress the pirates. The mere sight of the approaching force prompted the pirates to flee, either to the North Ocean or southward to Guangnan East Province, resulting in some captures. Although the rebellion was quickly suppressed, the potential for similar incidents remained (D. Zhen, n.d.). Another notable event involved pirates Wang Ziqing and Zhao Lang, who led a fleet of 18 boats to plunder Weitou Bay in Jinjiang County. Zhen Dexiu, the mayor of Quanzhou, mobilized the Left-Wing army to pursue and capture them. During the Battle of Shatao Ocean in Zhangzhou, Zhao Lang was captured, while Wang Ziqing managed to escape, only to be later apprehended by the inspector of border security of Dumen in Taizhou (K. Liu, n.d.). In the *Eulogy of the Holy Queen Temple,* written by Zhen Dexiu, it was described how fierce and cunning pirates would sail southward on two ships, plundering wherever they arrived and posing a threat to maritime voyages (D. Zhen, n.d.). This account referred to pirates from Liangzhe East Province attacking Fujian Province. Another example mentioned in Zhen Dexiu's book documented that pirates from Wenzhou and Mingzhou came from the North Ocean. The pirates operating in Wenzhou frequently sailed southward to attack Fujian Province. To counter these threats, the Song Dynasty deployed naval forces from the Left-Wing army in Fujian Province, alongside village troops and local residents. They sent 45 boats and 940 people to encircle and suppress the pirates. Successively, 136 pirates were captured in the sea areas of Jinjiang County, Tong'an County, Shatao Ocean in Zhangzhou, and Shezhou Ocean in Chaozhou. The remaining 14 ships managed to flee to the North Ocean. Among them, those who fled to Wenzhou looted the merchant boat of Chen Batai, a merchant from Fuzhou, but were ultimately captured by the commissioner of Leqing County in Wenzhou (D. Zhen, n.d.). Here, the so-called North Ocean was divided by Fujian Province. The north sea area of Fuzhou was called the North Ocean, the south sea area of Zhangzhou was called the South Ocean, and the east sea area of Fujian Province was called the East Ocean. When Zhen Dexiu mentioned several coastal villages in Quanzhou, he was referring to their strategic locations. For example, Xiaodou Mountain Village was the first line of defense and control as the sea passage entered Quanzhou from the North Ocean. Weitou Mountain Village faced the sea and served as a temporary berth for passenger boats and pirate ships traveling from the South and North Ocean. Lieyu Island was crucial in defending against ships sailing from the South Ocean to Quanzhou. Yongning Mountain Village, close to the sea, provided a vantage point to observe the East Ocean, and it took one day and night to reach the Penghu Islands from there. During the Jiading Reign, the naval army in Fujian Province sent soldiers and boats to explore the Laiwu Ocean, where they encountered a boat sailing from the East Ocean (D. Zhen, n.d.; T. Wen 1987: 523).

Pirates posed a significant threat in various sea areas in the Song Dynasty, necessitating coordinated efforts from multiple provinces to combat them. Fujian Province dispatched troops to confront pirates who had crossed into Guangnan East Province (D. Zhen, n.d.). In the fifth year of the Shaoxing Reign (AD 1135), a pirate named Zhu Cong attacked Guangzhou and Quanzhou, operating in both Fujian Province and Guangnan East Province (Toqta 1977: 518). Emperor Gaozong of Song, in March of the fifth year of the Shaoxing Reign (AD 1135), ordered Guangnan East Province and Fujian Province to demand Zhu Cong's surrender, indicating his connection to Fujian Province (X. Li 2013: 1668). Zhu Cong, in January of the fifth year of the Shaoxing Reign (AD 1135), gathered over 30 ships and more than 200 people to commit acts of violence in several counties of Guangnan East Province. He eventually surrendered in August of the same year, pursued jointly by Fujian Province and Guangnan East and West provinces (S. Xu et al. 2014: 8860). At the time of his surrender, Zhu Cong had hundreds of accomplices and possessed 30 sea ships (X. Li 2013: 1800). In the first year of the Longxing Reign (AD 1163), another pirate named Zhu Baiwu wreaked havoc in Fujian Province, as well as Liangzhe East and West provinces. The Left-Wing army, Military Administration, and naval forces in Wenzhou, Mingzhou, and Fujian Province were unable to apprehend him (X. Yuan 1990). Similarly, in the sixth year of the Shaoxing Reign (AD 1136), a pirate named Zheng Guang gained considerable influence and conducted raids in Fujian Province and Guangnan East and West provinces. In response, Emperor Gaozong of Song commanded the Provincial Military Commission of Fujian to deploy naval forces to suppress the pirate Zheng Qing. Zhang Zhiyuan, the mayor of Fuzhou, was specially appointed to oversee the suppression efforts (Toqta 1977: 525; Toqta 1977: 11628). That same year, the Song Dynasty dispatched another naval force to confront Zheng Guang at Mount Sanzao in Xinhui County (X. Li 2013: 1928). In the third year of the Jiading Reign (AD 1210), the imperial court once again ordered several coastal prefectures' commissioners to capture pirates (Toqta 1977: 755). The campaign to conquer pirates, mentioned in *The Report to Administration of State Affairs on Striking the Pirates* written by Zhen Dexiu, pointed to "the pirate ships travelling to and from Zhangzhou, Chaozhou and Huizhou every year", namely those fleeing to the coastal regions of Fujian Province and Guangnan East and West provinces throughout the year. The Song government did not restrict Fujian Province and Guangnan East and West provinces from individually combating the pirates. Zhangzhou and Chaozhou collaborated in the search and capture efforts, while the Cuifeng Navy in Guangnan East Province and the Left-Wing Navy in Fujian Province worked together, launching attacks against the pirates (D. Zhen, n.d.). Lian Nanfu served as the military commissioner of Guangnan East Province, and was responsible for combating pirates in Qianzhou and Fujian Province (Y. Han 1990), ensuring unified command of the military forces.

Pirates along the southeast coast were numerous and had a significant impact, as evidenced by the numerous names recorded in historical records. One notable pirate during the beginning of the Shaoxing Reign was Liu Cong, who operated in Guangnan East Province. Liu Cong "had been a pirate for a long time, commanding dozens of boats and hundreds of followers who traveled between various cities such as Guangzhou, Fuzhou, Leizhou, Qiongzhou, Qinzhou, Gaozhou, Nanzhou, and Enzhou". According to Zhen Dexiu, the Song Dynasty's soldiers, along with local villagers, managed to capture 136 pirates in the Shatao Ocean near Zhangzhou. Although the number may not have been significant, it is worth noting that after Zheng Guang surrendered to the Song Dynasty, the court selected 400 individuals from his group and placed them in barracks outside Fuzhou city (Toqta 1977: 11628). The remaining members of Zheng Guang's group were allowed to continue their original occupations, indicating that his pirate group comprised far more than just 400 people. Another notable pirate, Wang Xian, commanded a group of 800 individuals, while Zhu Baiwu gathered an even larger force of 2000 people (X. Yuan 1990). When Zhang Jun called for the pirates to surrender, 2500 pirate soldiers surrendered to the imperial court. After Zheng Guang surrendered and became the commander of the navy, he led 300 soldiers in an attack against the pirates. During this encounter, a pirate named Chen Xiaosan sent 60 ships to fight, but Zheng Guang's army managed to overcome them despite being outnumbered (J. Xue 1990). Considering these accounts, it is estimated that this particular group of pirates consisted of approximately 3000 people. During Emperor Lizong's Reign, Bao Hui noted that although pirates had always been present, their activities had become increasingly rampant in recent years. Bao Hui also observed that while pirates used to operate with small boats and few followers, they now had over a few thousand individuals and a thousand large ships (H. Bao 1990). These pirates frequently defeated government troops in battles. For instance, in June of lunar calendar in the sixth year of the Shaoxing Reign (AD 1136), Yan Anya, leading the navy of the coastal military commission, joined forces with Fan Dechong's navy from Guangzhou to confront Zheng Guang on Mount Sanzao in Xinhui County. During this encounter, the pirates capitalized on the wind to launch a surprise attack, resulting in significant casualties for both sides (X. Li 2013: 1928). In the fourteenth year of the Shaoxing Reign (AD 1144), Fujian Province dispatched armed forces to suppress the pirate Zhu Ming, and Zhang Shen, a Song Dynasty general renowned for his Kungfu skills, lost his life in combat with the pirates (X. Li 2013: 2856). The navy of Guangnan East Province went to Chaozhou to search for and capture pirates but encountered them on the Laiwu Ocean. Unfortunately, the naval forces were greatly outnumbered by the pirates, who besieged their ships. As a result, the naval forces were forced to retreat and guard Chaozhou Port. The pirates, displaying their audacity, then berthed their ships at Wutian Bay and confronted the navy of Guangnan East Province, further intensifying the conflict (D. Zhen, n.d.). The pirates demonstrated their aggression by actively pursuing and besieging the official army with unwavering confidence.

The social composition of pirates was quite diverse, consisting of local tyrants, young troublemakers, and boatmen seeking financial gain. For example, in the Kaibao Reign, Pan Mei, the mayor of Guangzhou, had to suppress a rebellion led by local tyrant Zhou Siqiong near the sea (Toqta 1977: 8992). In the coast of Yinxian County, groups of young troublemakers engaged in fishing and salt trading lived on the islands, occasionally resorting to robbery and looting against merchants. This posed a challenge for authorities to investigate and address these crimes (Toqta 1977: 10085). In the second year of the Yuanfu Reign (AD 1099), three residents of Houguan County named Xie Zi, Zhou Zi, and Xi Zi rented a boat from a boat dweller named Lin Lü. However, Lin Lü drowned these three individuals in the remote areas of Sanjiangkou at night. Additionally, there were numerous cases where boats carrying merchants and travelers would be taken to secluded beaches to intimidate and rob them. Tragically, in some instances, these pirates would also commit acts of violence, including rape and murder (K. Lang 1990: 8244). In the eighth year of the Shaoxing Reign (AD 1138), "a group of 28 itinerant traders from Guangzhou, as well as captains transporting official goods", boarded a boat along with 26 helmsmen and punters. "Observing the valuable cargo carried by the passengers, the pirates were enticed to seize the goods". They employed cunning tactics "to make the merchants intoxicated and then threw them into the sea with their hands tied behind their backs, sparing only two servants to cook and serve them". When the boat arrived in Changle County in Fuzhou, the pirates "continued to come ashore periodically to carry out plundering activities and abduct women onto their boat". The county magistrate, Su Wenguan, dispatched patrol soldiers to capture the pirates and apprehend them, revealing the true nature of these villains who willingly engaged in robbery (M. Hong 1981: 480).

However, there were also a large number of unemployed people or individuals who had been driven to piracy due to circumstances beyond their control. Li Chun pointed out that the root cause of piracy lay in poverty and the misconduct of government officials, who imposed heavy taxes on the common people. The burden of these taxes forced the poor to resort to piracy as a last option (S. Yang et al. 1990). Consequently, many individuals turned to piracy as a result of poverty. The government implemented a boat registration system for coastal shipowners, which included the imposition of taxes and a 20-year ownership requirement. However, some of the registered boats were damaged or lost in storms, others were robbed, and some sank due to lack of funds for repairs. Despite these difficulties, the government did not remove the registered boats from the list and continued to demand service from the shipowners each year. As a result, shipowners resorted to mortgaging their land, selling their wives, and leaving their hometowns. Those who had no other means of support ultimately became pirates (Y. Mei et al. 1990: 5991). In Wenzhou, pirates were predominantly a product of unemployment (Y. Lou 1990). Wang Xian, the leader of the pirates in Mingzhou, had previously served as a voluntary soldier in Youyi Mountain Village of the Palace Administration. He stated that due to extreme poverty and unequal pay, he had fled to the countryside and resorted to trade for survival. Seeing the dire situation of the government, he took to the sea with others. His subordinates turned to piracy primarily because they had lost their livelihoods in business and had no other means to sustain themselves. When Wang Xian surrendered to the Song court, more than 160 individuals followed suit. Among them, 147 were under his command, including five former soldiers, while the rest were common people from Wenzhou and Taizhou, most of whom had been abducted and forced into piracy (S. Hong, n.d.). Within the pirate group, many were helmsmen and sailors who had been abducted to serve as pirates. "The scum in the army now entered the sea, abducting helmsmen and sailors from official boats and either robbing or hiring them" (X. Cai 1996: 366). During their raids on merchant vessels, the pirates would burn the smaller ships and claim the larger ones as their own. They would kill those who resisted and release or drown those who were weak and unable to serve them. They also abducted capable individuals who could operate the boats for their own purposes. Disobeying the pirates' orders meant certain death, leaving the abductees with no choice but to comply. Initially, the pirates ventured out to sea with only two or three boats, but their fleet grew to 20 or 30 vessels over time. The size of their group also increased from 30 or 50 members to hundreds or even thousands (D. Zhen, n.d.). This is how the pirate group expanded, through the abduction of merchants and other individuals. Even the leaders of the pirates, Zheng Guang and Zheng Qing, "were initially law-abiding individuals. However, their capture of Zheng Jiu, an official, led to suspicions of disloyalty to the government, ultimately driving them to become pirates" (S. Xu et al. 2014: 8860).

No matter if the pirates were considered good or evil, active or passive, they originated from coastal residents. They formed alliances with residents on the shore, including petty officials in coastal prefectures and counties. Bao Hui noted that while the pirates made their living at sea, they relied on the coast for their daily needs, food, and drink. Coastal dwellers, driven by the desire for wealth and treasures, actively sought to profit from the pirates. The wealthy provided hiding places for the pirates, while the poor followed their orders. Restaurants and brothels were even established to attract pirates, ensuring their cooperation. Fishing boats, operating under the pretense of fishing, served as scouts and guides for the pirates. The pirates were so rampant and fierce that ordinary people felt compelled to join them (H. Bao 1990). Zhen Dexiu described the situation in Quanzhou, stating that pirate ships often interacted with residents on the shore, effectively turning them into pirates as well. Local residents engaged in extensive trade with pirates, encompassing goods such as wine, food, shops, and hotels (D. Zhen, n.d.). The coastal residents formed an association of mutual interest with the pirates, and it was not uncommon for petty officials to collude with them. Pirates in Guangnan East Province, equipped with oared boats, and those in Fujian Province with multi-paddle boats "colluded with officials in the prefecture, who often informed the pirates in advance of official and military actions." A wealthy family in the city even provided a hiding place for the pirates (Y. Wang 1990). In Mingzhou, pirates bribed petty officials in the prefecture, while the grassroots staff was exploited by the pirates to cover their tracks. The pirates became so rampant that they disrupted the smooth sailing of merchant vessels. Cunning local tyrants were also known to harbor the pirates (Toqta 1977: 8747–48). Even the official army of the Song Dynasty colluded with the pirates. For example, in Zhenjiang Prefecture, "soldiers in Tuanshan Mountain Village usually colluded with the pirates" (Toqta 1977: 12443). In the tenth year of the Jiading Reign (AD 1217), some court officials expressed concerns about the pirates' activities, stating that the pirates repeatedly plundered civilians. For example, in terms of multi-paddle boats in Guangzhou and fishing boats in Wenzhou and Taizhou, residents were suffered from these boats. Coastal officials and soldiers colluded with each other, showing little effort to capture the pirates. While they occasionally captured a few pirates, more often than not, they deliberately let them go (S. Xu et al. 2014: 8370). When Zheng Guang surrendered and became an official, his fellow officials discriminated against him and even refused to engage with him. In response, Zheng Guang composed a poem on the spot to satirize them, stating, "I have a poem to share with all the officials who seem to be inept with both the pen and the sword. You officials colluded with pirates, while I, once a pirate, am now an official." During that time, officials were complicit with the pirates, and they were too ashamed to discriminate against pirates (K. Yue 1981: 41). The pirates also utilized their alliances to strategically position scouts ashore. When Fujian Province launched a punitive expedition against Zhao Xique, Lin Tian'er, and other pirate groups, "the Left-Wing army captured two pirate scouts named Zheng Jiuqi and Gao Yan. The commissioner of Jinjiang County captured a scout named Zhu Shisi, while Huian County captured a scout named Lin Qinglang" (D. Zhen, n.d.). This indicates that the pirate group had scouts stationed in multiple locations.

Pirates had been operating in the seas for years, and they possessed expertise in boat handling and sailing. They targeted large, high-quality merchant vessels for their robberies. The boats used by the Song Dynasty soldiers were often inferior to the pirate ships. At the start of the Southern Song Dynasty, the Provincial Military Commission of Fujian and Guangnan Province lacked warships and a navy. When pirates emerged, the officials allowed them to freely wreak havoc since there were no armed forces to suppress them. They simply stationed a few soldiers on the coast as a way to maintain the status quo. While the pirates continued to rob many boats, numerous coastal residents followed suit (G. Li 2004: 829). Even after the establishment of the Left-Wing army in Fujian Province, the situation did not fundamentally change. Although it was referred to as a navy, it lacked proper boat equipment. When there were reports of pirate rebellions, they would temporarily hire boats and boatmen, but their actions were slow, preventing them from timely capturing the pirates. Additionally, the shipowners and boatmen were unfamiliar with one another, making it difficult for them to navigate against the wind and waves and fight for their lives against the audacious pirates. Furthermore, they lacked an adequate number of boats. Fashi Mountain Village had three large warships, one Ninghai boat, and one Pinghai boat, which were roughly sufficient. However, Yongning and Baogai Mountain Village each had only one Pinghai boat, capable of carrying just over 40 warriors (D. Zhen, n.d.). Yanxiang and Dilu Mountain Village in Fuzhou possessed few Chima boats and Baiou boats. When compared to pirate ships at close range, the official boats were small, while pirate ships were significantly larger. The recruited private boats were also small in size and inadequate for engaging the enemy (H. Bao 1990). This inferiority of the official boats was evident in the battles between the Song army and pirates in the sea area of Liaoluo Bay, which was under the administration of Tong'an County in Fuzhou. In the Battle of Liaoluo, General Bei Wang of the Left-Wing army confronted eight pirate ships with over 500 pirates using a boat carrying more than 80 soldiers. The pirate ships towered like mountains, while General Bei Wang's boat was less than half the size of the pirates' vessels. "Although the Song army fought valiantly, they could not achieve a complete victory due to the limitations of their small boats. When private boats from Jinjiang and Tong'an County arrived to provide support, the pirates quickly fled, making it too late to capture them" (D. Zhen, n.d.). The number of pirate ships ranged from 10 to 30, and sometimes even reached 60. The Song Dynasty often had to recruit villagers for the troops and private boats to combat these large pirate groups.

4.5.2 Suppression of Pirates and Offering Amnesty and Enlistment to Pirates in the Southern Song Dynasty

Strike by force was an important method used to suppress pirates in the Song Dynasty. Local officials in coastal prefectures and counties had the duty of containing pirates, and many of these officials actively carried out their duties. Dong Xun, the fiscal commissioner of Guangnan East Province, was commended for his efforts in "capturing pirates" and "deploying troops to fight against and capture or them" (G. Wang n.d.). Zhao Zipu, while serving as the mayor of Mingzhou and military commissioner of the coast, ordered local tyrants and officials colluding with pirates to "set sail on different routes", while soldiers "raided pirate hideouts and apprehended them all". Similarly, Zhao Shanyu, who held the position of secretary-general of Changguo County and oversaw county affairs, was tasked with "apprehending all pirates" (Toqta 1977: 8747–48, 8762). Chen Junqing, serving as the mayor of Fuzhou, was "promoted to a higher rank for capturing the pirate Ni Lang" (B. Zhou 1990). In Quanzhou, when Zhen Dexiu served as the mayor, "the pirates wreaked havoc and approached the city. The generals and soldiers suffered defeat, but Zhen Dexiu paid tribute to those who died in battle and personally trained soldiers in tactics to capture the pirates" (Toqta 1977: 12960). Since the establishment of the navy in the Southern Song Dynasty, capturing pirates had been a crucial duty of the coastal navy. In the fifth year of the Qiandao Reign (AD 1169), "Xia Ju, the navy commander of the Palace Administration, led troops and boats to sea and captured pirates. As a result, he was specially promoted to a higher rank, with a two-year exemption from performance assessments" (S. Xu et al. 2014: 9010). Feng Zhan, the general commander of the Xupu navy, and others embarked on a search for the pirate group led by Wang Xian. "Along their sea route, they encountered 10 pirate ships, captured three of them, and pursued the other five towards the ocean in Mingzhou. The pirates sank these five ships and managed to escape, while the whereabouts of the remaining two were unknown" (S. Hong, n.d.).

Regarding influential pirate gangs, several prefectures and provinces needed to collaborate and mobilize government troops, local forces from prefectures and counties, and coastal residents to launch joint military sieges. As previously mentioned, the Song army encircled and suppressed two pirate groups led by Zhu Cong and Zhu Baiwan, respectively. These operations involved joint efforts between Fujian and Guangnan provinces, as well as between Fujian and Liangzhe provinces. During the Jiading Reign, while Zhen Dexiu served as the mayor of Quanzhou, he documented several pirate suppressions along the coast of Fujian Province. In one instance, in an unspecified year during May of the lunar calendar, the Song Dynasty assembled the navy in Fujian and Guangnan East and West provinces to encircle and suppress a group of approximately one thousand pirates entrenched in deep-water bays in Chaozhou. "22 pirate ships were detected mooring in the deep-water bays," with around one thousand individuals. The Song court was concerned that sending Fujian and Guangnan provinces individually would not solve the problem, so they requested the assistance of Quanzhou's Left-Wing navy, Guangnan Province's Cuifeng navy, as well as forces from Zhangzhou, Chaozhou, Fuzhou, and Xinghua Prefecture to jointly strike the pirates. They also convinced private boats to assemble with warships sent by coastal county criminal inspectors at the junction of Zhangzhou and Chaozhou, cooperating and launching coordinated attacks on the pirates (D. Zhen, n.d.). This operation involved a joint military siege conducted by Fujian and Guangnan provinces, as well as a collaborative effort between the government and the people. Another method involved capturing "pirates on boats from Wenzhou" heading southward to Fujian Province. The Left-Wing army dispatched troops and persuaded several privately owned striking boats in the bays administered by Jinjiang and Tong'an counties to assemble with official troops and capture pirates together. The Left-Wing army deployed a total of five large warships and auxiliary boats, along with 418 navy soldiers. Generals Fang Zhigang, Lin Fang, and other generals garrisoned on Lieyu Island assembled 36 private boats and 462 village soldiers. Wang Xingji, the village chief of Lingdou, assembled four boats and 60 village soldiers. Although there were 14 pirate ships, the official and private boats faced an overwhelming numerical disadvantage. Nevertheless, they pursued the pirates who sailed from Huian and Jinjiang counties in Quanzhou to the Shatao Ocean in Zhangzhou. Over 160 individuals were captured, and the remaining pirates were apprehended in the sea areas of Wenzhou and Chaozhou. This particular pirate group led by Lin Tian'er had been causing havoc, even attacking Quanzhou and killing Song soldiers, including Wang Dashou, in Weitou Bay. Another eight pirate ships, carrying over 500 pirates, engaged in a battle with the Song army in the sea area of Liaoluo in Tong'an County (D. Zhen, n.d.).

Offering amnesty and enlistment to pirates was the most common way of dealing with them, and it was used to eliminate many influential pirates in the Southern Song Dynasty. Liu Cong, Zhu Cong, Zheng Guang, Wang Xian, and others were among those who were granted official positions after surrendering. For instance, Liu Cong was given a minor military officer role and worked for the Provincial Military Commission to catch pirates at sea (X. Li 2013: 1210). Zheng Guang and Zheng Qing were also given junior military officer positions, and "their 19 comrades were granted various official positions" (X. Li 2013: 1958). When Lian Nanfu, serving as the mayor of Quanzhou, summoned the pirate chief Zhu Cong to surrender, Zhu Cong initially expressed dissatisfaction with being offered a minor military officer position (Chengxinlang, the 52nd tier of officers). Concerned that Zhu Cong might escape, Lian Nanfu then promised him a junior military officer position (Wujielang, the 38th tier of officers). This made Zhu Cong satisfied, and he eventually surrendered. Later, Zhu Cong was granted a senior military officer position and served as the navy commander of the Military Governor's Office, stationed in Zhenjiang Prefecture. His subordinate minor chiefs were respectively given senior military officer (Baoyilang, the 50th tier of officers), minor military officer (Chengxinlang, the 52nd tier of officers), and military officer (Jinwuxiaowei, the 53rd tier of officers) roles (X. Li 2013: 1800; S. Xu et al. 2014: 8860). Zhu Cong's initial dissatisfaction with the minor official position offered to him when he surrendered indicates the Song central government's approach toward pirates when providing amnesty and enlistment.

The Song Court employed a strategy of recruiting surrendered pirates into the army to combat other pirates. In the 13th year of the Shaoxing Reign (AD 1143), Chen Kangbo, serving as the mayor of Quanzhou, dealt with the frequent troubles caused by pirates. With the emperor's approval, Chen Kangbo summoned the pirates to surrender, resulting in many of them coming forward and being registered as soldiers in the government troops (Toqta 1977: 11808). In the 19th year of the Shaoxing Reign (AD 1149), the pirates in Liangzhe East Province, who were supposed to be banished, were given a tattoo and incorporated into the coastal army (Toqta 1977: 570). After Zhu Cong, Zheng Guang, Wang Xian, and their followers surrendered, these strong men were recruited into the army. Zhu Cong, the former pirate chief in Fujian, was stationed in Zhenjiang Prefecture and commanded 30 boats as the navy commander of the Military Governor's Office. After Zheng Guang and Zheng Qing surrendered, the strong men from their group were recruited into the navy. Out of the 170 strong men, 50 were assigned to serve in the navy at Qiulu Mountain Village, while the remaining 120 men were assigned to the Imperial Armies and stationed at Temple Yanxiang. They were even dispatched to suppress the pirate chief Chen Xiaosan and his 3000 followers on board 60 pirate ships (K. Lang 1990: 7933). The surrendered pirates played a vital role in the Left-Wing navy, as many of the laborers assigned to the Left-Wing Army were former pirates who had committed robberies at sea. The young and strong men who could swim and operate boats efficiently were selected from the surrendered pirates, given tattoos, and recruited into the Left-Wing army to serve as helmsmen, anchor droppers, and sailors (D. Zhen, n.d.). On Mount Yangshan, the pirate chief Wang Xian from Mingzhou came across an official notice posted in front of the house of the local tyrant Chen Li. The notice, issued by the military commander of Huainan Province, urged pirates to surrender and assured them that their crimes committed at sea would no longer be prosecuted. Wang Xian took the notice back to his pirate ship and persuaded the other ship chiefs to surrender. He led two ships and over 160 pirates to surrender, submitting their surrender document to the governor's office and working for the navy during wartime. In addition to the 33 pirate chiefs, 85 helmsmen and sailors were also willing to serve in the navy (S. Hong, n.d.). Another approach used by the Song Court was to release pirates back to their hometowns. After Wang Xian's group of over 100 pirates surrendered, the government selected and released those who were indeed from Wenzhou and Taizhou. "Through individual interrogations, 27 people, including Sun Yuan, were allowed to return to their respective hometowns. Wang Xian was instructed to exercise caution and ensure that these individuals were recently abducted and not his original crew members. They were provided with responsible written pledges, monetary support, food, and official credentials, after which they were permitted to leave according to the imperial order (S. Hong, n.d.)."

The Song Court's lenient approach of offering amnesty and enlistment to pirates not only failed to eliminate piracy but sometimes even contributed to its proliferation. Li Gang once remarked that "the government should not search for and capture pirates but instead summon them to surrender. Many pirates were given official positions, which created envy among the common people and led to the emulation of pirates" (G. Li 2004: 829). People began to view piracy as a shortcut to obtaining an official post. Zheng Gangzhong strongly believed that offering amnesty and enlistment to pirates could not solve the piracy problem. He pointed out that the Song Court only used this approach to suppress piracy and believed that once the pirates were persuaded to surrender, there would be no more robberies at sea. However, in reality, piracy could not be eradicated through persuasion alone. Often, the pirate chief would receive an official post while the other associates, unable to achieve the same, would resume piracy. Those who were denied official positions would use it as a benchmark, gather in larger groups of pirates, and aim to become the chief of another pirate group, seeing it as a means to obtain an official post. Therefore, shortly after the Court surrendered Zhu Cong, others would gather and become subordinates of another pirate group led by Liu Guang. After the Court surrendered Liu Guang, Liu's subordinates would join the pirate group led by Li Yuan. Each time one pirate group was eliminated, a new one would emerge, creating a vicious cycle. At the same time, Zheng Gangzhong also noted that when pirates faced a strong military force, they would raise their arms to resist when official troops were weak, and escape across the sea by wind when official troops were strong and powerful. In emergencies, pirates would discard their oars and disguise themselves as passenger boats, making it difficult for soldiers to identify the pirate ships. Offering amnesty and enlistment alone could not eliminate all pirates, nor was it possible to eradicate them completely. The best approach was to rely on local tyrants and recruit common people into the army to enhance social control. Coastal prefectures had their own local tyrants who were familiar with individuals capable of finding pirates. Those who were fierce and cunning on the coast usually benefited from the local tyrants, who had extensive knowledge of pirate movements. The proposed solution involved sending gifts to all prefectures and requesting them to defend their areas. Additionally, coastal residents were encouraged to form defense units consisting of five families, ensuring that piracy would not exist in any prefecture. Individuals who devised strategies to fight and capture pirates would be granted official positions based on their contributions (S. Yang et al. 1990). The Song Court attached great importance to the conquest and suppression of piracy while also seeking solutions to eliminate piracy through mobilizing social forces and enhancing social control.

4.5.3 Household Registration and Social Control of Coastal Residents

Zheng Xingyi once said that it was difficult to eliminate piracy with the regular army of the Song Dynasty. The sea was vast, spanning millions and millions of square kilometers. The wrongdoers would suddenly arrive with the wind and stealthily assess the unguarded coast. They would then destroy people's homes and steal food. Coastal prefectures and counties were repeatedly plundered. The Court would mobilize troops to suppress them, but the troops were stationed in the hinterland, making it difficult for them to reach the trouble spots at night when orders were given in the morning. By the time the soldiers gathered from all directions, the pirates had already quickly set sail and fled. Even if the soldiers wanted to pursue the pirates, they could only stand on warships amidst torrential waves, making it impossible to engage in combat. The solution was to order coastal residents to defend themselves. Each coastal prefecture and county had islands and bays, with a selected chief who was a local Kungfu practitioner. Units of five families were formed for coastal defense, and they underwent training in the morning and evening. When the pirates arrived, the chief would lead the group to fight against them. Those who successfully killed pirates would be rewarded by the prefecture and county based on their contributions, while those who harbored pirates or remained passive would not be forgiven. This approach allowed the country to avoid the need to constantly deploy troops and military supplies, gradually reducing pirate rebellions (Toqta 1977: 13594; X. Zheng 1990). In summary, completely eradicating piracy through strikes, amnesty, and enlistment proved difficult. The most effective approach was to mobilize social forces, rely on local leaders, and establish household registration of residents to enhance social control. This was the prevailing view among officials in the Southern Song Dynasty.

Firstly, they proposed to take advantage of village heads, known as tyrants, who were familiar with the local geography and could mobilize the general public effectively. The villagers "were not afraid of officials from the Court, but of the local tyrants. They disobeyed the officials but followed the local tyrants. The three reasons why local tyrants were respected were their intelligence, bravery, and abundance of food supplies. As a result, the unruly people had no choice but to submit to the local tyrants and follow their lead" (S. Yang et al. 1990). Therefore, "capturing pirates only required the assistance of local tyrants in coastal bays and the military commander" (H. Bao 1990). This approach also allowed them to command shipowners in coastal areas, "enabling them to supervise the boats under their command, ensuring that the weapons were well-maintained, and training the soldiers daily for naval combat" (C. Chen 1990). Zheng Gangzhong stated that "local tyrants in coastal prefectures were knowledgeable about village paths and were well-informed about pirate movements since the unruly people benefited from them. The current solution is to visit the local tyrants in the prefectures with gifts and request their assistance in defending themselves against the pirates" (S. Yang et al. 1990). During the Shaoxing Reign, Ye Yiwen also proposed that "local tyrants on the coast were familiar with the dangers of the sea and could dispatch shipowners who benefited from seafood. I suggest stationing troops at key points along the coast, with local tyrants acting as chiefs to administer the troops, in cooperation with the official authorities, to deter pirate activities. If the local army was provided with certain rewards, they might resist the pirates, which could be an effective method to eliminate piracy" (L. Xu 1990). In Fujian Province, sea ships were "levied and reward standards were established, appointing local tyrants who recruited 1000 sailors as minor military officers" (Y. Han 1990), thus mobilizing local tyrants to independently recruit troops. Therefore, the annual prevention efforts in the sea passages involved "recruiting sailors, repairing sea loach ships, forming alliances with mending private boats, and selecting a head of the port. This period was dedicated to defending against pirates on the sea routes" (S. Yang et al. 1990). Among these measures, forming alliances with civilian boats and appointing a head of the port were particularly significant.

The second proposal was to establish a household registration system for coastal residents. Pirates relied on these residents, as "they knew pirates' movements well" (X. Li 2013: 1702). If household registration of coastal residents was implemented for the purpose of coastal defense, no prefecture would suffer from piracy. Alternatively, the court could grant minor posts to those who provided plans to contain and capture pirates based on their contributions (S. Yang et al. 1990). The proposal emphasized the importance of collective action by coastal residents to combat piracy. By preventing pirates from disembarking, through collaboration, coastal residents could effectively starve them. Bao Hui's solution involved categorizing every five families into a unit at each port, overseen by the head of the port. If a family harbored or aided pirates, the entire unit of five families would face punishment. When a pirate ship approached, the militia of the unit, along with the head of the port, were responsible for guarding and defending the coast to prevent the pirates from approaching. If the pirates did approach, people would gather to chase and capture them, with the official troops attacking them later. Bao Hui further advocated for the implementation of the neighborhood administrative system in not only Fujian Province but also all coastal provinces. He argued that strict household registration should be enforced in the few dozen prefectures along the coast, spanning thousands of miles, including the inferior prefectures and counties. Bao Hui proposed that every ten families should form an administrative group, monitoring and reporting on each other. If a family violated the rules, the other nine families would be obligated to report it. Depending on the severity of the case, violators would be exiled or punished with death. Individuals who reported violations would be exonerated, and those who reported multiple times would be rewarded and promoted. If a family violated the rules and the other nine remained silent and concealed the fact, all ten families would be jointly punished without forgiveness. Bao Hui suggested that ten administrative groups would form a larger group, and if any administrative group divulged information or violated the rules, the other nine groups should report it, resulting in the same punishment as mentioned above. Additionally, administrative groups should not include treacherous businessmen such as heads of businesses and agents. Any instance of including such individuals would be treated as a breach of information security and rules. Bao Hui proposed that the military commander should govern the administrative groups (H. Bao 1990). The household registration system not only aimed to isolate pirates from coastal residents but also recognized the potential of recruiting these residents as militia. Since they were familiar with the geographical conditions and skilled in water-related activities, under the guidance of the military commander, they could serve as soldiers, either pinning down or launching attacks against pirates during critical moments of coastal defense (H. Bao 1990).

The above discussion was not just an idea; it had been gradually implemented as early as Emperor Gaozong's reign. In the fifth year of the Shaoxing Reign (AD 1135), Emperor Gaozong of Song ordered the prefecture military commander of Fujian and Guangnan East provinces to organize coastal residents into communities to catch pirates. Local governments were required to authorize prefectures and counties to organize coastal residents, with each community consisting of 500 people and those with fewer than 300 people attached to neighboring communities. They were also instructed to select talented, brave individuals with family property as heads of the communities, followed by deputy heads (X. Li 2013: 1702). Sailors among the coastal residents were registered and trained as well. In the thirtieth year of the Shaoxing Reign (AD 1160), Emperor Gaozong of Song ordered the Provincial Military Commission of Fujian Province to recruit and register local tyrants and sailors. Zhangzhou, Quanzhou, Fuzhou, and Xingzhou recruited and registered 360 boats and 14,000 sailors. However, these sailors did not directly join the army; instead, the local soldiers, who were under the administration of the inspector of border security on the coast, were ordered to train together with local tyrants and sailors once a month. This approach not only regarded the local tyrants and sailors as a reserve fighting force to capture pirates but also helped train the patrol soldiers. Additionally, 631 strong men were selected from the local tyrants and sailors to join the local army (K. Lang 1990: 7933).

The Report to Administration of State Affairs on Striking the Pirates, written by Zhen Dexiu, reflected the situation in which the regular army, local army, and common people joined forces to strike pirates. In Quanzhou, the Left-Wing army was ordered to dispatch warships, and an official document was issued to Jin'an and Tong'an counties, persuading private ships to join the warships dispatched by the coastal county criminal inspector to catch pirates and assemble at the junction of Zhangzhou and Chaozhou. The document also requested the assignment of an official document to the general office of Guangnan East Province to mobilize the Cuifeng navy to assemble with the local Left-Wing army and private boats at several bays to surprise the pirates. Furthermore, official documents were sent to Fuzhou and Xinghua Prefecture to request naval forces to cooperate (D. Zhen, n.d.). The mechanism of joint striking and capturing pirates by the governments and the people played a positive role in the actual battle to catch pirates in Fujian Province. In the naval battle for capturing "the pirates on boats from Wenzhou" recorded by Zhen Dexiu, the Left-Wing navy sent 5 boats with 418 people, and they were joined by 522 village soldiers and 40 boats. This surpassed the Left-Wing navy in terms of the number of boats and people. Fang Zhigang and Lin Hang, who were heads of Lieyu Island governed by Tong'an County in Quanzhou, came from prominent families and were able to convince the public through their credibility and morality. A chief from Tong'an County led the local people to be cautious of pirates. Previously, Wang Ziqing and others had set fire to kill people on Wuyu Islet in the sea of Zhangzhou. Fang Zhigang and others stopped at Lieyu Islet to check the situation and immediately rallied the young adults to prepare arrows and use rocks to defend the coast. When the pirate ships reached Lieyu Islet, they saw that the coast was guarded and did not dare to attack immediately, thus saving the lives of the residents there. Additionally, the pirates from Wenzhou had become enemies of Lieyu Islet, and the local militia was familiar with the boats, which could be used as auxiliary forces for the official army. Wang Xingji, the chief of Lingdou governed by Jinjiang County, led soldiers and boats, brought food and equipment themselves, and followed the Left-Wing army to the sea, capturing 7 pirates, including Zhong Songsan (D. Zhen, n.d.).

Coastal prefectures and counties also registered shipowners and mobilized sea vessels to participate in coastal defense. The practice involved registering the shipowners in coastal ports and counting the total number of ships, which were then divided into several battlefields. The prefecture appointed talented individuals selected from each port as chiefs to command each defensive battlefield (C. Chen 1990). In Liangzhe East Province, a yearly investigation and calculation of sea vessels in Mingzhou, Taizhou, and Wenzhou took place. At the beginning of each summer, inspections and reports were carried out on the ownership of sea vessels. A comprehensive survey was conducted annually, regardless of the size or presence of boats in the village. Official documents pertaining to this survey were posted throughout the village, and even the possessions of common people, including chickens and dogs, were accounted for by the government. The coastal defense tasks placed a heavy burden on the people residing along the coast, spanning one or two thousand kilometers in Mingzhou, Taizhou, and Wenzhou. In these three prefectures, thousands of private boats with a surface width of over 3.3 m were confiscated and divided into 10 groups for duty rotations. Every year, "over 300 boats were confiscated in Dinghai County for coastal defense and assigned to Huainan East Province and Zhenjiang Prefecture" (Y. Mei et al. 1990: 5991). Boats from Dinghai County in Mingzhou served exclusively for local coastal defense. A total of 428 fishermen's boats were assembled from Mingzhou, with 5 boats patrolling each night on a rotational basis. Five tokens for patrol were created, and official offices for managing coastal defense were established in Zhangting and Xianchi. When the tide rose at night, the boat would apply for a patrol token from the Bureau of Zhangting and set off, returning it to the Bureau of Xianchi the next morning. When the tide fell at night, a patrol token was obtained from the Bureau of Xianchi and handed over to the Bureau of Zhangting the following morning (Y. Mei et al. 1990: 5982).

4.6 The Great Convenience of Water Transportation and the Rise and Fall of the Southern Song—A Study from the Perspective of Military History

In the history of the regime standoff between the south and the north in China, many southern regimes in the regions south of the Yangtze River and the Huaihe River relied on the natural barrier provided by these great rivers. They utilized the convenient water transportation to combat the cavalry forces from the northern empires. The water transportation network of inland waterways and seas played a crucial role in official grain transportation, people's travel, trade, and defense of rivers and seas, as boats were heavily relied upon. Thus, the development of the Southern Song Dynasty was heavily dependent on water transportation. In terms of military strategy, the Southern Song Dynasty effectively utilized its advantages in water transportation. They achieved victories in several critical water combats against the Jin Kingdom, suppressing the attacks of the Jin's cavalry forces and safeguarding the unoccupied parts of the country. However, the Southern Song Dynasty missed opportunities to win the war against the Yuan troops as the enemies also established their own navy and occupied regions along the Yangtze River. Previous studies have focused on the history of war between the Song Dynasty and the Jin Kingdom, examining specific battles and the overall process (P. Su et al. 2008; Y. Zhao 2005; Z. Hu 1992; T. Li 1988; Z. He et al. 1999). This section aims to explore the relationship between the significant role of water transportation and the rise and fall of the Southern Song Dynasty.

4.6.1 The Standoff Between the Song Navy and the Jin Cavalry Forces

In the Northern Song Dynasty, the highest priority for national defense was given to the three key border provinces, which limited the deployment of the navy. As one person in the Song Dynasty remarked, "It is well-known that our country has a powerful navy. However, it was never sent to fight the enemy. Why? Because its advantage cannot be fully utilized in defending the northwestern frontier. Therefore, relying on the navy to fight against enemy invasions in the northwestern border is unreliable and risky." After pacifying the rebellion in the south, the Song Dynasty briefly focused on the development of its navy. However, historical records indicate that "little development in the navy occurred after the rebellions in the Yangtze River and the Huaihe River were brought under control" (D. Lin 1990). The Yangtze River and the Huaihe River served as the frontier in the fight against the enemy. Fang Dacong stated, "Defending our country relies on the fact that the Yangtze River is difficult to cross, and the safety of the Yangtze River depends on well-equipped warships" (D. Fang 1990). Consequently, to safeguard the unoccupied region south of the Yangtze River, the Song Dynasty mainly relied on its navy to counter the aggressive attacks from the Jin's cavalry forces.

Nomads were known for their expertise in horse riding, while the people in the southern regions of the Yangtze River excelled in sailing ships. As Yang Wanli pointed out, "people in different regions have their own advantageous skills: northerners are skilled in riding horses and shooting arrows, while southerners are adept at sailing boats" (Toqta 1977: 12865). These distinct advantages were shaped by the natural environment. This is evidenced by Hong Mai's remarks that "southerners don't believe a tent can hold 1,000 people in the north, and northerners don't believe a ship can carry ten thousand Hu of grains" (M. Hong 2005: 737). People's beliefs were influenced by their natural surroundings. Comments made by the people of the Song Dynasty regarding the shortcomings of the Jin Kingdom's army reveal that "the Jin army would not have won the battle without their strong cavalry forces, as they were unskilled in sailing ships and unfamiliar with swimming" (P. Ni 1990; T. Wen 1987: 49; X. Li 2013: 1116). These comments highlight the weaknesses of the Jin troops. The people of the Southern Song, who lived in riverside or lakeside regions, were skilled in sailing boats. Water transportation provided them with convenience (D. Nai 1993: 10). The locals of the Wu Kingdom, who lived by the river, made sailing boats their occupation. They possessed sailing skills and extensive knowledge about water conditions. They believed that different regions favored different modes of transportation, with the northerners preferring horse riding "As the water towns of the Chu Kingdom are lower-lying and easily standing in water, boats weigh more heavily than horses in people's daily travel, where horses are as thin as dogs" (*Quan Song Shi* 1999: 3901, 13354, 13132, 2229). Horse riding held little importance for them as boats played a significant role in their daily travel. The advantage of the Song Dynasty's troops lay in their ability to fight on water. *The History of the Song Dynasty* states, "the Jin troops are good at riding horses, but the Song troops are skilled at sailing boats" (Toqta 1977: 11361). The navy of the Song Dynasty was accustomed to navigating through challenging conditions, and the soldiers displayed exceptional balance and skill during battles (C. Chen 1990). Therefore, the Song's troops needed to fully utilize their strengths. "The Jin troops usually win battles with their cavalry forces, so when our emperor's temporary residence is close to the South China Sea, the navy should leverage their advantages in sailing to prevent the Jin Kingdom from invading" (Y. Lü 1990). During the Shaoxing Reign (AD 1131–1162), Zhang Yi, Minister of Revenue, described the foundation of the Southern Song Dynasty, stating that "the violently flowing Yangtze River and seas form a barrier against the Jin's cavalry forces. The huge waves of the river and sea can be compared to the Great Wall; tower ships serve as watchtowers of the Great Wall; soldiers of the navy, drillers, and divers act as guards on the Great Wall; fire ships, fire rafts, strong soldiers, and poisoned arrows resemble the defense works of the Great Wall." The Southern Song Dynasty made full use of their military advantage to combat the enemy. They strategically stationed the navy in the midstream of the river, beyond the range of cannon fire, stones, and arrows used by the Jin's cavalry. Additionally, the horses of the Jin soldiers were unable to cross the river, rendering their skills ineffective in water battles (S. Yang et al. 1990).

As Zhang Yi, the Minister of Revenue, emphasized, the border security of the Song Dynasty relied on the great convenience of water transportation, which resisted attacks from the Jin's cavalry forces, as well as the natural barriers provided by the Yangtze River, the Huaihe River, and the seas, which shielded the Southern Song. Apart from the battles in Sichuan Province and Shanxi Province, two key battles played a decisive role in the survival of the Southern Song. One of them occurred when Jin Wuzhu invaded the south in the third and fourth years of the Jianyan Reign (AD 1129–1130), and the other when Wanyan Liang invaded the south in the 31st year of the Shaoxing Reign (AD 1161). The Southern Song Dynasty turned the tide of the war by utilizing its navy and laid the foundation for victory. "Fighting in the southeast area depends on naval forces. It was our naval forces that defeated Jin Wuzhu in the Jinshan Battle and snatched victory from Wanyan Liang in the Caishi Battle" (T. Wen 1987: 49). In the third year of the Jianyan Reign (AD 1129), to cope with the pursuing armies of the Jin, Lü Yihao, an official of the Southern Song Dynasty, proposed a strategy where the emperor and officials would evade Jin's attacks by taking ships. This would prevent the enemy cavalry from attacking their offshore ships. The hot climate in Jiangnan and Liangzhe provinces would also limit the enemy's ability to stay in those areas for an extended period. Lü Yihao suggested that when the enemy withdrew their troops, the Southern Song could return to Liangzhe provinces. By employing this time-wasting tactic, the Southern Song Dynasty could synchronize their movements with the Jin forces (X. Li 2013: 676–77). Emperor Gaozong of the Song Dynasty adopted this advice and took the sea route to evade the enemy's pursuit. Early in the third year of the Jianyan Reign (AD 1129), Emperor Gaozong appointed Lin Zhiping to manage the sea defense works and sent officials to recruit ships from Quanzhou and Fuzhou in preparation for possible enemy attacks. Many ships had been gathered by the time Emperor Gaozong fled to Mingzhou, including those from central Fujian Province, ships owned by Zhao Yi, the fiscal commissioner of Guangnan East Province, and 1000 ships provided by Zhang Gongyu, the Secretary of Commerce of the Marshall's Office (X. Li 2013: 685). With these ships, Emperor Gaozong of the Song Dynasty and his entourage successfully escaped by sea. In January of the fourth year of the Jianyan Reign (AD 1130), shortly after the ships carried Emperor Gaozong and his men out to sea, Mingzhou fell to the Jin's forces. Taking advantage of heavy rain, thunder, and lightning, the Jin's navy launched an attack on the ship carrying Emperor Gaozong. However, they were repelled by Zhang Gongyu, a Song officer commanding huge warships (Toqta 1977: 475). The Jin forces had no choice but to witness the ship sailing away with Emperor Gaozong on board. In April of the fourth year of the Jianyan Reign (AD 1130), the Jin's 10,000 soldiers were intercepted by an 8000-strong navy led by Han Shizhong, stationed at sea. They were trapped in Huangtiandang for 48 days, and the majority of their ships were sunk (X. Li 2013: 747; Y. Zhou 1990: 1959). At that moment, Han Shizhong commanded the Song's navy, consisting of over 100 ships, to combat the Jin's forces along the banks of the Yangtze River (X. Lu 1990: 2342–43). The Jin troops managed to fight their way out of the siege during a windless period when Han Shizhong's navy could not sail. Although the Jin's attack dealt a heavy blow to the Song's navy, they were aware of the significant disparities between their forces. Following the battle in 1130, there were smaller skirmishes between the Southern Song's navy and the Jin Kingdom. For instance, in November of the fourth year of the Jianyan Reign (AD 1130), the Jin's navy, consisting of fifty ships, invaded Tongzhou and Taizhou but was defeated by the fierce defense of the Song troops (S. Xu et al. 2014: 8891). During Wanyan Liang's invasion of the southern region of the Song, major battles occurred mostly in the north of the Yangtze River.

The third key water battle and the fourth took place in the 31st year of the Shaoxing Reign (AD 1161). During Wanyan Liang's invasion of the south, the battlefields were at Caishi along the Yangtze River and Jiaoxi in Shandong Province. As Yang Wanli said, "The victories at Caishi along the Yangtze River and Jiaoxi in Shandong Province should not be attributed to cavalrymen, archers, or infantrymen, but rather to the navy" (Toqta 1977: 12865). In the 31st year of the Shaoxing Reign (AD 1161), Wanyan Liang set an ambitious goal to station his troops on the first peak of Mountain Wu and planned to occupy the southern area of the Southern Song (X. Li 2013: 3545). The Jin troops easily crossed the Huaihe River and advanced to the north bank of the Yangtze River. In the Caishi battle, the Southern Song's navy trapped the Jin warships at the Yanglin ferry, attacked them with flying arrows, and set their ships on fire. They ultimately defeated the Jin's troops using sea loach ships and dagger-installed boats (Y. Zhou 1990: 1960). In this battle, the Southern Song's soldier population was significantly smaller than that of the Jin Kingdom. "The Jin's troops had 400,000 soldiers, and the number of their horses was several times that of the Song Dynasty." However, the Southern Song "had 80,000 soldiers and only a few hundred horses" (X. Yuan 1990). It is evident that the Jin's troops would have been victorious if the battle were fought on land. The Southern Song achieved victory solely through its navy. After a severe defeat in the Caishi battle, the troops led by Wanyan Liang escaped to Guazhou Ferry and attempted to cross the Yangtze River. Yu Yunwen deployed soldiers and pedal wheel ships to fight against Wanyan Liang's troops in the midstream of the Yangtze River in Zhenjiang. Their speedy sailing and easy maneuverability shocked the Jin soldiers, greatly alarming them (Y. Zhou 1990: 1960), and causing them to lose confidence in battle. However, Wanyan Liang had commanded his officers to cross the river by a specific deadline, leading to his own demise at the hands of his subordinates. As a result, the Song's troops won the war without engaging in combat. During Wanyan Liang's invasion of the southern region of the Song Dynasty, his plan involved not only a head-on attack on the Yangtze River and the Huaihe River but also a flank from the sea. To execute this plan, he assembled over 1000 warships and recruited 70,000 sailors from the Jurchens (X. Yuan 1990), Bohai ethnic minorities, and the Han ethnic group. However, the troops led by Song general Li Bao embarked on a long march from Suzhou. They "burnt, captured over 600 warships, killed the Jin invaders, captured about 300 Jurchen soldiers, including their leader, and forced more than 3000 Dhan soldiers to surrender" (S. Xu et al. 2014: 8900). Li Bao's troops achieved a great victory with only 120 warships and 3000 soldiers. Furthermore, "these soldiers were not regular forces but all crossbowmen from Fujian Province and Liangzhe Province" (Toqta 1977: 11499). After this battle, the troops of the Jin Kingdom did not launch any invasive battles from the sea.

The victories in the four water battles described above were crucial for the survival of the Southern Song Dynasty and ensuring its safety in the south of the Yangtze River. The success of the small sea battle in Mingzhou in the fourth year of the Jianyan Reign (AD 1130) allowed Emperor Gaozong of Song to break through the Jin attackers, ensuring the survival of the Southern Song Dynasty. The water battle in Zhenjiang played a significant role in demonstrating the advantages of the Song navy and highlighting the difficulties the Jin Kingdom faced in engaging in battles on the Yangtze River. Consequently, the Southern Song Dynasty began attaching great importance to the defense works along the Yangtze River as a means of safeguarding the country and pushing forward with these projects. Wanyan Liang's plan to occupy the Southern Song Dynasty was foiled after the sea battles in Caishi and Jiaoxi. Subsequently, there were no major battles on the Yangtze River and sea. Instead, there was a surge in constructing defense works along the Yangtze River and sea, emphasizing the importance placed on fortifying these areas.

The Southern Song relied heavily on its convenient water transportation to secure victories against the Jin in battles. In contrast to the Southern Song, the Jin lacked shipbuilding techniques, materials, and sailor training. Firstly, the Jin suffered from a lack of high-quality wood resources for shipbuilding, which the Southern Song possessed. The wood produced in the south was ideal for use in sea water, resulting in the construction of top-ranking ships in Fujian Province, followed by Guangnan East Province, and Wenzhou and Mingzhou. Conversely, the wood produced in the north was unsuitable for sea use due to its vulnerability to damage from the saltwater. Therefore, ships built in the north were unable to endure long voyages and were not sufficiently robust to withstand waves, making them prone to sinking (Y. Lü 1990). The south had an abundance of excellent shipbuilding wood, including pine trees, fir trees, camphor trees, and phoebe zhennan, while the north had limited wood supply. Farmers in the north even had to resort to burning wheat straws in their kitchens due to the scarcity of firewood. This is because trees like willows and elms were all used to reinforce the riverbanks (S. Yang et al. 1990). In contrast, shipyards in the north constructed vessels using various local timbers like jujube, which made them prone to getting stranded in shallow, salty waters due to the excessive weight of such planks (Z. Dai 1990). These natural limitations confined the shipbuilding capabilities of the Jin and provided an advantage to the Southern Song. As the people of the Song expressed, "during the fight against the Jin Kingdom's invasion, God blessed us with the great convenience of water transportation, leading to the great rejuvenation of our nation" (Y. Lü 1990).

The second disadvantage of Jin's shipbuilding lies in its undeveloped techniques compared to those of the Southern Song. Wanyan Liang made fewer preparations for invading the Southern Song in warship building compared to the preparations made for invading the following dynasty changes: from the Chen to the Sui, from the Southern Tang to the Song, and from the Song to the Yuan. Prior to the aforementioned dynasty changes, the upper and middle reaches of the Yangtze River had been occupied, numerous warships had been constructed, and intensive training had been conducted. However, Wanyan Liang's troops hastily launched attacks on the Yangtze River and the Huaihe River without addressing the weaknesses in shipbuilding. After occupying the region of the Huaihe River, "Wanyan Liang's troops actively constructed warships in Hezhou day and night, and Yu Yunwen, an officer of the Southern Song Dynasty, believed that the newly-built Jin warships must be larger than those of the Song." It turned out, however, that "the Jin built about one hundred common ships without any matting cover, similar to those found at the ferries in the counties and provinces" (S. Yang et al. 1990). Moreover, "the ships, capable of carrying 20 people, were made of planks taken from private houses, and the use of wood lathing and nails did not follow any shipbuilding rules." These ships were small in size and performed poorly. "The cone-shaped bottom of Jin's ships was as wide as that of a large box, making the ships unstable and inflexible in sailing" (R. Zhang 1990). Some of the canal boats from the Jin kingdom were transformed into multi-paddled boats. "They were flat-bottomed grain boats with raised bows and sterns commonly seen in Shandong Province, capable of carrying over 50 people" (M. Xu 1987: 1717). Yu Yunwen, the renowned general of the Southern Song Dynasty, remarked that "the Jin Kingdom planned to use such ships to attack our dagger-installed boats, which demonstrates their inability to compete with us in shipbuilding despite their efforts" (S. Yang et al. 1990). In the Southern Song Dynasty, "both sides of the warships covered with cowhide and sea loach ships were heavily plated with guard boards. Sailors sat behind these boards and operated pedal wheels to propel the ships, but they were not visible from the outside. Sailing around Jinshan three times, these ships resembled strong and majestic white dragons soaring over the tides." During the war between Jin and Song, "Jin's warships were small and overcrowded with soldiers. Additionally, the ships jostled against each other, weapons obstructed one another, and oars were difficult to maneuver. In contrast, our warships covered with cowhide effortlessly pushed through the enemy's ships" (W. Yang 2007: 4609). "When the Song's warships collided with Jin's, the Jin's ships were broken in half and sank into the sea" (M. Xu 1987: 1717).

Before Wanyan Liang invaded the Southern Song Dynasty, he ordered Su Baoheng to build seagoing vessels on the Luhe River, employing craftsmen from the Song Dynasty. "The traitors Ni Xun and Liang Jian from Huinan and Liangzhe provinces taught the Jin's craftsmen how to build ships" "Su Baoheng led his troops to attack the region along the Qiantang River" (Toqta 1977: 11499). The 600 large flat-bottom boats constructed by the Jin Kingdom in Shandong Province could not be utilized for seagoing transportation as they were made of pine (X. Li 2013: 3727). Only flat-bottomed boats could navigate the river section in Dengzhou and Laizhou, but once they passed Liaojiao, they needed to be replaced with sharp-bottom seagoing boats. While warships could reach their destination with a single tide, they had to anchor multiple times. The Jin Kingdom navy faced a dilemma. In sea battles, a small number of warships could not ensure victory, while assembling a large number of warships proved challenging (Z. Dai 1990). The flat-bottomed boats could sail on the waters south of Dengzhou, Laizhou, and the coastal areas with a sandy floor south of Huainan East Province. However, these ships were not suitable for the deep ocean south of Liaojiao. Therefore, the Jin Kingdom, with its 600 warships, had little chance of posing a threat to the Song troops.

Furthermore, the Jin were far inferior to the Song in terms of soldiers' fighting skills and sailing abilities. The Jin employed many Han people "as punters and sailors from the southeastern areas of the Song" (S. Yang et al. 1990). Specifically, the regions along the river and sea with complex water conditions required experienced and skilled sailors to keep the ships on course and navigate through the treacherous waters of Liaojiao. If the ships deviated from their course, they would sink (X. Li 2013: 1116). In the fourth year of the Jianyan Reign (AD 1130), during the Zhenjiang water battle, the Jin soldiers had difficulty adjusting to the rocking motion of their warships in the river, so they were instructed to load soil onto the ships to reduce the shaking (Toqta 1977: 11361). The Battle of Caishi also revealed the weaknesses of the Jin troops. Due to their lack of training on water, only a dozen soldiers were able to shoot arrows, while the rest struggled to move freely due to seasickness, which weakened their forces (M. Xu 1987: 1713). The Jin's inadequate sailing skills prevented their troops from fully utilizing their fighting capabilities on the rough sea. "Even if the fishermen in Jiangnan and Liangzhe provinces feared traveling on the dangerous sea, how could the enemy launch an invasion without proper preparations?" (L. Chen 1987: 16). Although during the Jiaoxi sea battle, "the Jin's sailors all came from the central plains" (Toqta 1977: 11457), their Jurchen soldiers were unable to maintain stability and had to sleep on their stomachs (Z. Dai 1990). Furthermore, "most of the Jin's sailors were loyalists to the Southern Song. When they spotted the approaching Song forces in the distance, they either tricked the soldiers into cabins or lied to them, claiming that their own troops were on their way" (Toqta 1977: 11500). "Li Bao's troops launched a surprise attack, setting fire to the Jin's sails coated with red camphor oil, taking advantage of a tailwind. This left the Jin's soldiers with no choice but to either flee to the coast or surrender. The Jin's soldiers were caught off guard and remained motionless on the boat, leading to their capture. Their boats were also seized" (Toqta 1977: 11457). Regarding the sailors recruited by the Jin Kingdom, "they were all loyal to the Song Dynasty. When the two kingdoms began to fight, they would run onto the shore and abandon their military duties" (Toqta 1977: 11501). Some of them deserted the Jin forces, burned the Jin's warships, and fought for their native country (Y. Cao 1990).

In general, during the military confrontation between the Song Dynasty and the Jin Kingdom, the Jin's warships only crossed the Yangtze River in the third and fourth year of the Jianyan Reign (AD 1129–1130). One reason for this was that the Yangtze River defense system had not been established during the early years of the Southern Song Dynasty. Another reason was that the Song's generals and officers, fearing for their lives, had no plans to actively defend the Yangtze River. When Emperor Gaozong fled to the south, he appointed Du Chong as the defense general of the Yangtze River and the Huaihe River. However, when the enemy attacked Jiankang municipality, the forces led by Du Chong were not vigilant and made no preparations for the enemy's aggression. As a result, dozens of Jin's ships approached and occupied the coast, and Du Chong surrendered to the enemy, leading to the complete failure and disorderly collapse of the Song's troops (Toqta 1977: 13810). At the same time, another Jin troop crossed upstream of the Yangtze River from Huangzhou. However, upon hearing of the enemy's approach, Wang Xishu, the Song's general, fled with his fleet. "The Jin's troops managed to capture a few boats near the bank, but these boats were not enough for them to cross the river, so they made rafts using planks taken from civilian houses. All of the Jin's soldiers spent three days crossing the Yangtze River on rafts pulled by boats" (X. Li 2013: 660). If the Song's armed forces had taken effective measures to safeguard the Yangtze River, the Jin troops would not have been able to cross the river so easily without enough boats. After the Shaoxing Reign (AD 1131–1162), Emperor Gaozong's administration attached great importance to the construction of the Yangtze River defense works. Despite the hasty preparations for the Battle of Caishi, the Southern Song forces easily defeated the Jin troops by strengthening their navy. The Song forces effectively utilized their advantage in sailing to counter the Jin's attacks and realized that "the Jin's soldiers are skilled in fighting on horseback, but they know little about sailing, so we can win the war by leveraging our strengths" (G. Li 2004: 1630). In this way, the Southern Song successfully blocked the Jin's attacks from the Yangtze River.

Meanwhile, we also need to realize that the key to the success of water combat on the Yangtze River and the sea lay in the coordinated efforts of frontier defense between different regions. It was only through this cooperation that the Jin's formidable land forces had no advantage on the waters. As Yang Wanli stated, "Priority should be given to the defense of Jingzhou and Xiangzhou, just as important as defending Sichuan Province. Only by doing so can the two provinces support each other. Similarly, the defense of Huainan East Province and Huainan West Province should also be emphasized, as they are connected to the Yangtze River. They should be like the lips and teeth of a mouth, relying on each other in times of emergency. We should not assume that the Yangtze River alone can block enemy invasions. Therefore, it is necessary to stockpile more food supplies and build more warships during critical moments" (Toqta 1977: 12867–68). The Southern Song succeeded in repelling Jin troop attacks in Sichuan Province and Shanxi Province, preventing Jingzhou, Xiangzhou, and the upper-middle reaches of the Yangtze River from being attacked. Due to the lack of time and resources to strengthen its naval forces, the Jin Kingdom had no choice but to launch frontal attacks on the Yangtze River and the Huaihe River. However, their cavalry was ineffective on rivers and lakes, making it difficult for them to achieve victory. However, during the Mongolians' invasion of the south, they relied on their cavalry and naval forces, enabling them to easily cross the Yangtze River, which ultimately led to the downfall of the centuries-old Southern Song Dynasty.

4.6.2 The Rising Water Forces of the Yuan Dynasty and the Collapse of the Southern Song Dynasty

After successfully repelling Wanyan Liang's invasion of the southern Yangtze River and the sea, the Southern Song Dynasty placed greater emphasis on defense along the Yangtze River and the sea, significantly increasing the number of navies and warships. During the protracted war with the Jin Kingdom, the Song Dynasty's sailor population and warship count surpassed those of the fourth year of the Jianyan Reign (AD 1130) and the 31st year of the Shaoxing Reign (AD 1161). In the late years of the Chunyou Reign (AD 1241–1252), during Wang Ye's inspection tour of riverside navies in Hezhou, Wuwei, and Anqing, he observed that "warships lined up for 15 kilometers on the Yangtze River, with a rapid response force of 12,000 soldiers, and more than 10,000 warships coated with cowhide" (Toqta 1977: 12576). These were the navies deployed in the middle section of the Yangtze River in Jiangnan East Province. Subsequent battles in Ezhou and Zhenjiang during the Song and Yuan Dynasties also demonstrated the significance of Ezhou and Zhenjiang, as evidenced by the deployed sailors and warships in those regions. As mentioned earlier, the sailors of the Southern Song Dynasty received thorough training in combat skills. In the Ezhou Battle (in the tenth year of the Xianchun Reign, AD 1274), the Dinghai water forces also participated, but their general commander, Liu Cheng, died in the battle (Toqta 1977: 924). Until the first year of the Xianchun Reign (AD 1265), the standards for recruiting sailors remained stringent, as demonstrated by the following quotation: "Those who could sail and swim were recruited with a salary of 60 strings of 1,000 coins, with the tattoo 'Shengjie' on their body. Those who could swim but not sail were admitted with a salary of 40 strings of 1,000 coins, with the tattoo 'Tuhun' on their body. Those who could sail but not swim were accepted with a salary of 20 strings of 1,000 coins, with the tattoo 'Xiongwei'" (Y. Zhou 1990: 1977). Despite the Southern Song's formidable naval forces, they quickly fell apart and declined after Ezhou was occupied by the Yuan troops.

After four pivotal water battles in Ezhou, Dingjiazhou, Mount Jiao, and Mount Ya, the Yuan troops emerged victorious, ultimately leading to the destruction of the Southern Song Dynasty. The Ezhou battle took place in the eleventh year of the Yuan Dynasty. The Yuan forces, both on land and water, smoothly advanced along the Hanshui River, encountering only minor obstacles in Yingzhou. Once they bypassed Yingzhou on their boats, the Yuan troops had an unhindered path until they reached Hankou. "Tens of thousands of warships sailed one after another, with thousands of ships anchored at the Lunhe River Bay, while hundreds of thousands of Mongolian and Han soldiers stationed on the north bank of the Yangtze River." Meanwhile, the Song's 10,000 warships were strategically deployed in the critical area of Ezhou, where Marshal Xia Gui planned to engage in a decisive battle with the Yuan forces at Yangluobao (L. Song 1976: 3101). The spectacle of thousands of warships sailing on the Yangtze River presented an intimidating sight from the Song's military buildups. However, instead of directly engaging with the main forces of the Song Dynasty, the Yuan's naval forces marched upstream, crossed the Yangtze

River at Qingshanji, and launched a surprise attack on Yangluobao. "The Song's troops suffered a heavy defeat at the hands of tens of thousands of Yuan troops, resulting in numerous casualties. Marshal Xia Gui abandoned his ship and fled" (M. Liu 1939: 4). In this battle, 30,000 Hanyang-made warships were burned, and Hanyang and Ezhou, crucial military strongholds along the middle Yangtze River, were swiftly occupied by the Yuan troops (L. Song 1976: 3103). Following the defeat at Yangluobao, the morale and determination of the Song's soldiers, including their marshal Xia Gui, were shattered, dampening their resolve to defend their homeland (T. Wen 1987: 398). The Yuan troops continued their eastward advance with ease, conquering Huangzhou, Qizhou, Jiangzhou, Nankang Military Prefecture, Anqing, and Chizhou (L. Song 1976: 3122).

Another significant water battle occurred at Dingjiazhou. When the Yuan troops reached Taipingzhou, Jia Sidao, the Prime Minister of the Song Dynasty, sent a negotiator to the Yuan camp, proposing the return of the occupied prefectures through annual tribute to the Yuan Dynasty. The Yuan's marshal responded, "If these terms had been presented before we crossed the Yangtze River, they might have been accepted. But now, we need to negotiate face to face." He also insisted that the conquered territories must become subordinate states and submit their cities to the conqueror, or else the matter would be decided through battle. Jia Sidao's reply revealed that the Yuan's occupation of the Yangtze River had deprived the Southern Song of its leverage in negotiating with the Yuan. Unwilling to surrender, Jia Sidao and the Yuan forces went to war in the 12th year of the Yuan Dynasty (AD 1275). "The Southern Song Dynasty established a Military Commandery responsible for 5000 warships in Dingjiazhou, and more than ten thousand soldiers, later inflated to a million soldiers, were stationed there." Additionally, "2500 warships led by Xia Gui, the Song's marshal, were stationed across the Yangtze River, while the remaining troops under Jia Sidao's command fought against the Yuan troops led by Bo Yan." However, in the end, the Song's forces were defeated and fled approximately 80 km (L. Song 1976: 3122; T. Su n.d.: 292–93). The Yuan troops proceeded to occupy Wuwei Military Prefecture, Zhenchao Military Prefecture, and Hezhou on the north bank of the Yangtze River, with Zhenjiang and other prefectures in Jiangnan East Province following suit.

The Battle of Mount Jiao was the decisive conflict in which the Song's naval forces were completely annihilated and the Yuan Dynasty gained full control of the Yangtze River. In the first year of the Deyou Reign (AD 1275), Zhang Shijie and Sun Huchen, the Song's generals responsible for safeguarding Huainan East and Huainan West provinces, gathered and positioned ten thousand warships east of Mount Jiao, linking them together in groups of ten with iron chains, demonstrating their unwavering dedication to their country. Simultaneously, the Yuan's naval forces, led by Azhu's troops in the center and archers on large ships flanking from the left and right sides, countered the Song's forces by igniting their sails with fire arrows, causing thick smoke and flames to fill the sky. Under these circumstances, most of the Song's warships were engulfed in flames, and due to being anchored with large stones, they were unable to escape (L. Song 1976: 3123). Amidst the waving battle flags, thundering drums, and soldiers' shouts, the pedal wheel ships, commanded by Dong Wenbing, charged at the Song's warships, with Dong Shixuan and Dong Shibiao providing support on the left and right flanks, while others followed suit. Simultaneously, the Song's soldiers fought fiercely, leading to a close-quarters encounter between the two sides. The air resonated with their shouts, and the river became filled with the bodies of the fallen and discarded weapons. The battle raged from 3 a.m. to 1 p.m., and ultimately, the Song's forces were defeated, and their generals, including Zhang Shijie, fled eastward. Over ten thousand of the Song's soldiers and seven hundred warships were seized, marking the decline of the Song's naval forces (L. Song 1976: 3671).

It was at Mount Ya that the Southern Song forces were completely destroyed. After escorting Emperor Xiangxing (Zhao Bing) to Mount Ya in Xinhui County, the remaining forces, led by Zhang Shijie, constructed a temporary wooden palace at the foot of the mountain. Around the coast near the palace, one thousand warships were positioned, connected by large ropes, with their bows inward and their sterns outward. Fences resembling city walls were built around the ships, enabling them to withstand the attacks of the Yuan's navy. In response, the Yuan's troops deployed fire ships loaded with thatch and grease to burn the ships in the wind. As a result, the Song's emperor, Zhao Bing, was forced to retreat to the sea since the Yuan's navy had occupied the island and set the temporary palace ablaze. From that point on, the Song's soldiers had to sail small boats attached to Dou Jian Warships every day to collect wood and water on the island. However, they were consistently hindered by the Yuan's troops along the way. Furthermore, the warship carrying Emperor Zhao Bing was targeted by the Yuan's cannons. Around one thousand civilian ships from Guangzhou came to his rescue, but unfortunately, they were almost destroyed. Additionally, the Yuan's troops planned to burn Emperor Zhao Bing's warship using their fire ships. However, they failed as the Song's ships were coated with mud, and countless buckets were hung from them. When the fire ships approached, the buckets were hooked and water was poured down, extinguishing the flames. Towards the end of the battle, one team of the Yuan's navy attacked from the north during low tide, while another team fought from the south during high tide. Despite the strength of most of the Song's soldiers, who hailed from the regions of the Yangtze River and the Huaihe River, and the valiant efforts of both their generals and soldiers as they shot arrows and stones (T. Su n.d.: 292–93), they lost the battle within half a day, with tens of thousands of soldiers drowning (T. Wen 1987: 404). In the end, Zhang Shijie and other officers fought their way through and escaped on 16 warships. Lu Xiufu, the prime minister of the Southern Song Dynasty, tragically drowned himself while holding Emperor Zhao Bing in his arms, symbolizing the demise of the Southern Song Dynasty.

The Yuan troops learned from the mistakes made by the Jin Kingdom in their invasion of the Southern Song, and their successful occupation of the South Song can be attributed to three reasons. First, the Yuan Dynasty established a powerful water force. Liu Zheng, a Song general who surrendered to the Yuan troops, provided advice that emphasized the importance of water forces in conquering the Southern Song. Kublai Khan, the Yuan Emperor, heeded this advice (L. Song 1976: 3787). When Xiangyang and Fancheng were besieged by the Yuan troops, Liu Zheng ordered the construction of five thousand warships and daily training of water forces, even during rainy days, using ship models drawn on the floor of houses. This resulted in the Yuan troops having a well-trained force of seventy thousand soldiers (L. Song 1976: 3787). As one Song official noted, "the enemy captured our ships, recruited our ship makers, cleared our forests, and never stopped building ships in Xiangyang and Fancheng" (D. Fang 1990). During the several years of siege on Xiangyang and Fancheng, the Yuan troops established a powerful water force with tens of thousands of soldiers and ten thousand ships. Furthermore, their water force was well-trained, with soldiers standing firm on the ships, in contrast to the Jin troops. The Yuan troops built warships, trained soldiers, and constructed a ring-shaped fortification to attack Xiangyang. Their strong fortresses on the Hanshui River prevented the Song from providing military aid to Xiangyang and Fancheng. Although water troops led by Xia Gui came to support, they were defeated by the Yuan troops, and over one hundred ships were captured. The troops led by Zhang Shun and Zhang Gui faced a similar fate, despite their advanced pedal wheel ships that had demoralized the Jin troops (L. Song 1976: 3120). The advanced Song ships proved ineffective against the Yuan troops. The Yuan's strategy for capturing Xiangyang and Fancheng involved breaking into the city of Xiangyang to force the troops stationed there to surrender. Once Xiangyang was taken, the Yuan troops faced no obstacles in marching along the Hanshui River and reaching the Yangtze River. Liu Zheng, the Yuan general, emphasized the importance of occupying Xiangyang and Fancheng, stating that "if Xiangyang is occupied, the capital city, Lin'an, would face collapse. Then, our water forces will sail into the Yangtze River, and the area along the river will be taken over by our troops" (L. Song 1976: 3788). As Liu Zheng predicted, the Yuan warships sailed from the Hanshui River into the Yangtze River and successfully broke through the defense works in Ezhou.

In the tenth year of the Xianchun Reign (or the 11th year of the Zhiyuan Reign of the Yuan Dynasty, AD 1274), the Yuan troops had ten thousand warships when they sailed down the Hanshui River. After that, they looted lots of warships from the Southern Song in the following battles. First, in Qingshanji, over one thousand warships were acquired (L. Song 1976: 3102). Second, in Ezhou, the number of warships must have been significant because the Song's water troops deployed about ten thousand warships, excluding those that were broken or burned. Third, in the summoning of Huangzhou, Qizhou, Nankang Military Prefecture, Anqing, and Chizhou to surrender, plenty of warships were looted. Fourth, during the surrender of Qinzhou and Huangzhou, all the warships in Xiangyang, Qizhou, Xinzhou and Huangzhou were taken over (T. Wen 1987: 398). Fifth, in Dingjiazhou, two thousand warships were acquired (L. Song 1976: 3105). Lastly, at Mount Jiao, seven hundred of the Song's ten thousand warships were taken over, excluding those that were burned (L. Song 1976: 3122). When Wen Tianxiang, the Song's general, fled from Zhenjiang to Zhenzhou, he witnessed the Yangtze River and its banks teeming with warships stretching for miles. The resounding toll of striking sticks filled the air, creating a formidable and overwhelming atmosphere (T. Wen 1987: 324). Following the battle at Mount Jiao, the Song's defense projects along the Yangtze River and the sea were completely destroyed. As Bo Yan stated, "the Song Dynasty relied on the

Yangtze River and seas to repel enemy attacks, like wild animals occupying advantageous positions. However, these advantages were lost." Consequently, the Yuan Dynasty's superior naval forces played a decisive role in the war. In October of the first year of the Deyou Reign (or the 12th year of the Zhiyuan Reign of the Yuan Dynasty, AD 1275), Lin'an was besieged by three Yuan troops. One of these troops, under the command of Dong Wenbing, departed from Jiangyin Military Prefecture to attack Ganpu and Huating from the left side. Despite strong resistance from the civil troops led by Zhang Xuan on the sea, Dong Wenbing's forces ultimately compelled the militia to surrender and plundered 500 warships (L. Song 1976: 3107). Following this, Ganpu, Gujing, Shanghaim, and Huating were occupied, and the Zhejiang River Estuary was locked down according to Dong Wenbing's strategic plan. This led to the collapse of sea defenses in Liangzhe West Province and Mingzhou, all without engaging in battles. As a result, the Song government's plan to retreat from the Zhejiang River Estuary failed, and Emperor Gong of Song, Empress Dowager Xie, King Ji (Zhao Shi), King Guang (Zhao Bing), and General Zhang Shijie fled southward to Taizhou (L. Song 1976: 3672). In general, the Yuan Dynasty's pursuit of the disheveled soldiers of the Southern Song proceeded smoothly with little resistance. Firstly, when Zhang Shijie's troops were chased to Taizhou and Wenzhou by Dong Wenbing's forces, they managed to escape without engaging in combat. Additionally, Zhangzhou, Quanzhou, Jianning, and Shaowu Military Prefecture all surrendered, offering gold and silver as tribute (L. Song 1976: 3673). Fuzhou and Xinghua Military Prefecture were also lost despite their mayor's attempts at resistance. Eventually, Emperor Jingyan fled to Guangzhou (X. Zhang 1990).

Another reason lies in the Yuan Dynasty's strategic approach. Li Gang once commented on the historical pattern of war between the southern and northern states in China, stating, "One way to invade the southeast from upstream is by traveling downstream for several hundred miles along the Sichuan section of the Yangtze River. It would take no more than three months to reach Jiangnan and Liangzhe provinces, and even one month would be enough to reach these regions. Another way is to occupy the Xiang River and the Hanshui River, as this area serves as a barrier to Jingzhou and Sichuan Province, overlooking the capital city from the south" (G. Li 2004: 983). During the Mongolian (Yuan) invasion of the southern region, they first attacked Sichuan Province and then captured the upper reaches of the Yangtze River. Additionally, they prioritized the establishment of water forces and achieved victories in multiple battles. For instance, in the Mount Diaoyu battle, the Yuan's water troops, led by Mongolian General Li Jin, defeated the Song's forces with 300 warships using their own fleet of over 70 warships (L. Song 1976: 3639). In another battle in Luzhou, Mongolian General Shimoanzhi's 70 warships destroyed 500 Song warships on the Mahu River in 1258. The following year, the Song's water troops lost another battle in Xuzhou (L. Song 1976: 3640). Xiangyang and Fancheng were under siege for a long time, famously known as "many years witnessing the siege of Xiangyang with one million soldiers attacking a city" (T. Wen 1987: 398). On one hand, "Jinzhou and Xiangzhou connect Qin and Shu prefectures in the west, Pingjiang Municipality in the east, and lie to the south of the Han River and Mian River." "Jinzhou and Xiangzhou play a crucial role in connecting the upper and lower parts of the Yangtze

River," which is vital for the safety of the Southern Song Dynasty. Thus, "for the time being, the strategic pass east of the Yangtze River should be defended. Jingzhou and Xiangzhou may seem ordinary but are actually urgent to defend" (Z. Liu 1990: 84). On the other hand, during the occupation of Sichuan Province and the prolonged siege of Xiangyang and Fancheng, unlike the Jin Dynasty's sudden frontal attacks on the Yangtze River and the Huaihe River without powerful naval forces, the Yuan Dynasty possessed a formidable navy that had sufficient time for training before engaging in battles. Before the Yuan troops advanced onto the Yangtze River, they did not target the heavily fortified lower reaches of the river. Instead, they aimed for Ezhou, which had fewer defense works, and successfully shifted the balance of naval power between the Song and Yuan Dynasties.

After destroying the defense works of the Yangtze River in Ezhou, Boyan and the other generals held a meeting there to discuss further military actions and develop a strategic plan. They all agreed that Ezhou, nestled under a mountain and near a river, was a key location in the south of the Yangtze River with sufficient troops and supplies. They realized that if Ezhou were not guarded and pacified, the Song's troops in the upper reaches of the river could defend it and prevent occupation (L. Song 1976: 3126). Therefore, forty thousand soldiers were deployed to sail west along the river. After occupying Yuezhou, Shashi, and Jiangling Municipality, another group of soldiers was stationed in Xiazhou. Emperor Shizu of the Yuan Dynasty commented that now that the Jingnan Kingdom area had been pacified, there would be no worries about troops marching east (D. Chu 1990). The Yuan army's successful countercurrent attack on Jiangling Municipality fully demonstrated the weak defense of the upper reaches of the Yangtze River in the Southern Song Dynasty. Wen Tianxiang pointed out, "There are two strongholds, Jiangling Municipality and Ezhou, in the upper reaches of the Yangtze River, one upriver and the other downriver, with no defense in between. When the Yuan army enters the unfortified territory of the upper river in the west, our state may be on the verge of collapse" (T. Wen 1987: 399). Furthermore, after capturing Ezhou, the Yuan troops were deployed on its east and west banks to cross the Yangtze River, cutting off military assistance between Huainan Province and the regions south of the river. The Song's main forces were stationed in Yangzhou to protect the capital city, Lin'an (L. Song 1976: 3122). However, after battles at Dingjiazhou and Mount Jiao, the Song's naval forces were completely destroyed, and Yangzhou itself was soon isolated and occupied.

The third reason for the Yuan's victory lies in their flexible and effective tactics. They avoided engaging the Song's major forces, targeted weak points, and set priorities in their battles to achieve victory. The Yuan's warships encountered a blockade when sailing along the Hanshui River, which connects to the Yangtze River. The old and new cities of Yingzhou, located on the north and south banks of the Hanshui River respectively, posed a challenge for the Yuan forces. The Song's warships were stationed across the river, connected by iron ropes, and there were obstacles like densely planted stumps in the water. The elite troops of the nine provinces along the Yangtze River were garrisoned in the two cities in the east and west of Yingzhou. Bo Yan, the marshal, believed that capturing Yingzhou was not their top priority. Instead, the Yuan forces sailed from Lake Teng into the Han River, bypassing Yingzhou and heading downstream (L. Song 1976: 3121, 3100). Upon reaching Hankou, the Song's warships were connected by iron chains to control the waters where the Hanshui River flows into the Yangtze River. The Yuan troops circumvented the Song's defense line by opening a dam to allow ships to enter the Lunhe River and then proceed into the Yangtze River from Shawukou. Their attack on the Song's stronghold, Yanngluobao, did not succeed after three days, so the Yuan forces pretended to commit to taking it to lure the Song's main forces into a rescue mission. The Yuan troops strategically targeted the Song's weakest defense points while avoiding their strongholds. They sailed upstream for 20 km, breaking through the Yangtze River defense from Qingshanji to the south bank, allowing their cavalry forces to cross the river. Subsequently, the warships turned back to attack the Song's troops led by Xia Gui, ultimately occupying Yangluobao (L. Song 1976: 3102). In the initial stages of the Ezhou water battle, both sides deployed ten thousand warships, resulting in an evenly matched confrontation. The Song's army had the advantage of years of operating the Yangtze River defense to repel invasions. However, the Yuan forces utilized their cavalry and artillery to attack on both sides of the river. Despite this, the tactics employed by the Southern Song's troops were clearly inferior to those of the Yuan forces, leading to their complete defeat.

One of the tactics employed by the Yuan troops was the coordination of their water, cavalry, and artillery forces. As they marched into Ezhou by land and water, their warships, adorned with banners, sailed down the Hanshui River, spanning hundreds of miles, with cavalry escorts on both sides (Songji Sanchao Zhengyao Jianzheng 2010: 361). Upon reaching Ezhou, the Yuan army possessed ten thousand warships and hundreds of thousands of Mongolian and Han cavalry. After breaching the Yangtze River defense at Qinshanji, the elite cavalry immediately crossed to the south bank. Following the Ezhou Battle, the Yuan's naval forces advanced eastward along the Yangtze River, while their cavalry attacked cities on both sides of the river. Marshal Bo Yan commanded two ten-thousand-soldier units to launch simultaneous attacks from both sides (L. Song 1976: 3104–05). Aju, a general and chancellor of the Mongol Empire, led the naval forces to engage the Song's fleet. Simultaneously, Bo Yan deployed his cavalry along both sides of the Yangtze River, where cannons were positioned to bombard the Song's main forces, plunging the Song army into chaos. Aju personally steered a ship, leading the charge against the Song's warships, with other ships closely following. Ultimately, the Song's soldiers scattered in all directions (L. Song 1976: 3122). In the 31st year of the Shaoxing Reign (AD 1161), during the Jin Kingdom's invasion of the Southern Song, the Song's warships navigated up and down the Yangtze River, leaving Wanyan Liang and his 400,000 troops shocked and powerless on the river's north bank. However, during the Yuan's invasion of the south, not only did they possess powerful naval forces to contend with the Song's fleet, but their cavalry also utilized their advantages effectively. The same held true for the battle on the Huaihe River. Li Zengbo highlighted two reasons for the breach of the Huaihe River defense. First, he noted that "initially, water troops were a strength of our (the Song's) forces, but the enemy also developed their water forces, which entered the battle after training." The second reason was that "the enemy deployed cavalry and infantry on the north and south banks of the Huaihe

River, supported by cannons and crossbows. In each battle, our army faced attacks from the enemy's water, cavalry, and infantry forces from three different directions. The battles on the Huaihe River demonstrated that the river was no longer a natural barrier impeding the enemy's invasion, as the Yuan had also built a formidable naval force. Both the Yuan and the Song could leverage the several hundred kilometers of the Huaihe River to gain an advantage over the other side" (Z. Li 1990). In the Battle of Mount Ya, the palace of Emperor Xiangxing (also known as Zhao Bing), located on an island, was set ablaze by the Yuan's covertly loaded cavalry troops, who boarded the warships (T. Su n.d.: 291).

The historical cycle was evidenced by the Yuan's conquering of the Song. The Jin built ships on the upper stream of the Yangtze River before invading the Wu Kingdom, and the Sui built ships in Yong'an before invading the Chen. This shows that the winners were those who could learn from the advantages of their counterparts and use them in battle (D. Fang 1990). When the Yuan invaded the Southern Song, they had already established water forces on the upper reaches of the Yangtze River, particularly on the Hanshui River. They no longer relied solely on cavalry, as the situation had changed to the point where "the enemies were good at riding horses, but even at the bank, they could not cross the river without boats" (X. Li 2013: 3695). The reason the Southern Song Dynasty was able to defeat the Jin Kingdom's invasion was due to its powerful water forces. "Fighting in the southeast region depends on water forces. It was our water forces that defeated Jin Wuzhu in the Jinshan Battle and achieved victory against Wanyan Liang's troops in the Caishi Battle" (S. Yang et al. 1990). However, in the battle against the Yuan troops, the Song's water superiority was replaced by the invaders. Wen Tianxiang believed that there were still possibilities for the Song to win the Battle of Mount Ya. He pointed out that the Song's troops had over 1000 warships, most of which were large, while the Yuan's troops only had 500 ships of all sizes, 200 of which had lost their way. Furthermore, upon boarding the ships, the Yuan troops felt sick and dizzy, unable to wield their bows and arrows. Additionally, the Yuan's sailors were from Fujian and Zhejiang Provinces and still loyal to the Southern Song (T. Wen 1987: 405). However, the Yuan soldiers were more united than the Song's. According to *The Loyals*, Zhang Shijie's decision to make a final stand against the enemy instead of advancing westward was because the Song's troops would flee if sent westward. They had been at sea for a long time and had lost their will to fight. On the other hand, there were many large warships belonging to the Yuan crowded on the sea, with soldiers possessing high morale. They attacked the Song from north to south, their shouts echoing throughout the land. After the Yuan troops gained complete control of the Yangtze River, they captured countless warships, including over 1000 ships in the sea battle, as witnessed by Wen Tianxiang during his escape from Huainan East Province to Mingzhou by sea. He mentioned, "Near the east gate of Mingzhou city, there were hundreds of ships on the Yangtze River, all guarded by Yuan soldiers" (T. Wen 1987: 412). Contrary to Wen Tianxiang's expectations, all the coastal provinces lost their loyalty to the country and surrendered upon witnessing the Yuan's powerful forces with countless warships. Several setbacks in previous battles, including the final one against the Yuan in the Battle of Mount Ya, resulted in the fall of the Southern Song Dynasty.

4.6.3 Summary

Under persistent pursuit and fierce attacks by the Jurchen cavalry, the Song Dynasty was forced to retreat to the south and establish the Southern Song Dynasty in Lin'an. This was primarily due to the region's favorable water transportation and powerful water forces, despite the Jurchen cavalry having already destroyed the Liao Kingdom and the Northern Song. On the battlefields of Sichuan Province, Shaanxi Province, Jingzhou, and Xiangzhou, the Southern Song troops effectively halted the Jin's advances. This safeguarded the middle and lower reaches of the Yangtze River, denying the Jin Kingdom the opportunity to establish its own water forces and move eastward down the river. As a result, the Southern Song successfully repelled attacks from the Jin Kingdom on the Yangtze River and the Huaihe River. In several critical battles that determined the survival of the Southern Song, the Song's troops utilized their warships and water forces to defeat the Jin Kingdom. This allowed them to avoid the fate suffered by the Northern Song. If the Jin Kingdom had been unable to cross the Yangtze River, suppress the advantages of the Southern Song Dynasty's water transportation and water forces, and failed to adequately prepare their own warships and water forces, their short-lived frontal attack would have ultimately ended in defeat. The Jin's military forces were inferior to the Song's in terms of the quantity and quality of their warships, as well as their soldiers' proficiency in water-based combat. Consequently, they struggled to fully utilize their cavalry forces in battle.

The collapse of the Southern Song Dynasty can be attributed to the Yuan Dynasty's construction of a formidable water force consisting of ten thousand warships during the siege of Xiangyang and Fancheng. By occupying the Yangtze River and making correct strategic decisions while employing flexible and effective tactics, the Yuan Dynasty undermined the Song's water advantages. As the Yuan troops destroyed the defensive works of the Yangtze River in Ezhou, they advanced westward up the river, seized control of the Jin Kingdom area, and then proceeded eastward downstream. Their water, cavalry, and artillery forces cooperated seamlessly. Following their victories in the Ezhou Battle, Dingjiazhou Battle, and Mount Jiao Battle, the Yuan troops eliminated the water forces tasked with safeguarding the Yangtze River. They gained dominance on the water, severed all military connections between the north and south sides of the Yangtze River, and paved the way for the eventual occupation of the entire Southern Song territory, including the pursuit of remnants at sea. In this situation, the water forces of the Southern Song Dynasty had no opportunity to mount a counterattack, and their fate of destruction became inevitable. In summary, the collapse of the Southern Song Dynasty can be attributed to various factors, and the control of water transportation played a crucial role in its survival or demise.

References

Bao, Hui 包恢. 1990. *Bizhou Gao Lüe* 敝帚稿略 [Anthology of Bao Hui]. Collected in Complete Library in the Four Branches of Literature. Shanghai: Shanghai Chinese Classics Publishing House.

Cai, Meibiao 蔡美彪. 1978. *Zhongguo Tongshi* 中国通史 [A History of China]. Beijing: People's Publishing House

Cai, Xiang 蔡襄. 1996. *Caixiang Ji* 蔡襄集 [Works of Cai Xiang]. Punctuated and collated by Wu Yining. Shanghai: Shanghai Chinese Classics Publishing House.

Cao, Xun 曹勋. 1990. *Songyin Ji* 松隐集 [Selected Works of Cao Xun]. Collected in Complete Library in the Four Branches of Literature. Shanghai: Shanghai Chinese Classics Publishing House.

Chang, Tang 常棠. 1990. *Ganshui Zhi* 澉水志 [Chronicles of Ganshui]. Collected in the Series of Chorography of the Song and Yuan Dynasties. Beijing: Zhonghua Book Company.

Chen, Chun 陈淳. 1990. *Beixi Da Heji* 北溪大全集 [The Complete Works of Chen Chun]. Collected in Complete Library in the Four Branches of Literature. Shanghai: Shanghai Chinese Classics Publishing House.

Chen, Cisheng 陈次升. 1990. *Danglun Ji* 谠论集 [Political Commentary of Chen Cisheng]. Collected in Complete Library in the Four Branches of Literature. Shanghai: Shanghai Chinese Classics Publishing House.

Chen, Liang 陈亮. 1987. *Chen Liang Ji (Zengding Ben)* 陈亮集(增订本) [Selected Works of Chen Liang Revised Edition]. Beijing: Zhonghua Book Company.

Chen, Qiqing 陈耆卿. 1990. *Jiading Chicheng Zhi* 嘉定赤城志 [Jiading Period Chronicles of Chicheng]. Collected in The Series of Chorography of the Song and Yuan Dynasties. Beijing: Zhonghua Book Company.

Chen, Yuanjin 陈元晋. 1990. *Yushu Lei Gao* 渔墅类稿 [The Anthology of Chen Yuanjin]. Collected in Complete Library in the Four Branches of Literature. Shanghai: Shanghai Chinese Classics Publishing House.

Chu, Dawen 储大文. 1990. *Cunyanlou Wenji* 存研楼文集 [Selected Works of Chu Dawen]. Collected in Complete Library in the Four Branches of Literature. Shanghai: Shanghai Chinese Classics Publishing House. Collected in Complete Library in the Four Branches of Literature. Shanghai: Shanghai Chinese Classics Publishing House.

Dai, Xu 戴栩. 1990. *Huanchuan Ji* 浣川集 [A Collection of Huanchuan]. Collected in Complete Library in the Four Branches of Literature. Shanghai: Shanghai Chinese Classics Publishing House.

Dai, Zhi 戴植. 1990. *Shupu* 鼠璞 [Waxed Mouse]. Collected in Complete Library in the Four Branches of Literature. Shanghai: Shanghai Chinese Classics Publishing House.

Fang, Dacong 方大琮. 1990. *Tiean Ji* 铁庵集 [Collection of Fang Dacong]. Collected in Complete Library in the Four Branches of Literature. Shanghai: Shanghai Chinese Classics Publishing House.

Fang, Fengchen 方逢辰. 1990. *Jiaofeng Wenji* 蛟峰文集 [Selected Works of Fang Fengchen]. Collected in Complete Library in the Four Branches of Literature. Shanghai: Shanghai Chinese Classics Publishing House.

Feng, Hanyong 冯汉镛. 1957. "Chechuan Kao车船考[Studies on Pedal Wheel Ships]". *Journal of Literature, History and Philosophy* 9.

Feng, Hanyong 冯汉镛. 1957. "Tang Song Shidai De Zaochuanye 唐宋时代的造船业[Shipbuilding Industry in the Tang and Song Dynasties]". *History Teaching* 10.

Gao, Cheng 高承. 1990. *Shiwu Jiyuan* 事物纪原 [Origins of Things]. Collected in Complete Library in the Four Branches of Literature. Shanghai: Shanghai Chinese Classics Publishing House.

Ge, Jinfang 葛金芳. 2008. *Nansong Shougongyeshi* 南宋手工业史 [The Handicraft Industry of the Southern Song Dynasty]. Shanghai: Shanghai Chinese Classics Publishing House.

Ge, Jinfang 葛金芳. 2012. *Shehui Jingji Yu Duiwai Maoyi (Juan Xia)* 社会经济与对外贸易(卷下) [Social Economy and Foreign Trade (Vol. 2)]. Collected in The Complete History of the Southern Song Dynasty 6. Shanghai: Shanghai Chinese Classics Publishing House.

Gu, Hongyi 顾宏义. 2006. "Nansong Liangzhe Yanhai De Shuijun 南宋两浙沿海的水军 [The Navy in the Coastal Areas of Liangzhe Provinces in the Southern Song Dynasty]. Edited by Zhu Ruixi. *Songshi Yanjiu Lunwenji* 宋史研究论文集 [Collections of Researches on the History of Song Dynasty]11. Chengdu: Bashu Press.

Han, Wei 韩维. 1990. *Nanyang Ji* 南阳集 [Anthology of Han Wei]. Collected in Complete Library in the Four Branches of Literature. Shanghai: Shanghai Chinese Classics Publishing House.

He, Zhongli 何忠礼, et al. 1999. *Nansong Shigao (Zhengzhi Junshi Wenhua)* 南宋史稿(政治军事文化)[Historical Records of the Southern Song Dynasty]. Hangzhou: Hangzhou University Press.

Hong, Mai 洪迈撰. 1981. *Yijian Zhi* 夷坚志 [Strange Tales of the Miraculous by Yijian]. Edited by He Zhuo. Beijing: Zhonghua Book Company.

Hong, Shi 洪适. n.d. *Panzhou Wenji* 盘洲文集 [Panzhou Anthology]. Collected in Collectanea of the Four Categories, 1st ed.

Hong, Zikui 洪咨夔. 1990. *Pingzhai Ji* 平斋集 [Selected Works of Hong Zikui]. Collected in Complete Library in the Four Branches of Literature. Shanghai: Shanghai Chinese Classics Publishing House.

Hu, Quan 胡铨. 1990. *Danan Wenji* 澹庵文集 [Selected Works of Hu Quan]. Collected in Complete Library in the Four Branches of Literature. Shanghai: Shanghai Chinese Classics Publishing House.

Huang, Chunyan 黄纯艳. 2012. "Songdai Guanyuan De Gongwu Lüxing—Yi Ouyang Xiu Yuyi Zhi Wei Zhouxin 宋代官员的公务旅行——以欧阳修(于役志)为中心 [Officials' Business Trips in the Song Dynasty—with a Focus on *Records of the Trip to the Post* by Ouyang Xiu]". *Journal of Chinese Social and Economic History* 1.

Huang, Gan 黄榦. 1990. *Mianzhai Ji* 勉斋集 [Selected Works of Huang Gan]. Collected in Complete Library in the Four Branches of Literature. Shanghai: Shanghai Chinese Classics Publishing House.

Huang, Tingjian 黄庭坚. 2011. *Huang Tingjian Quanji* 黄庭坚全集 [The Complete Works of Huang Tingjian]. Nanchang: Jiangxi People's Publishing House.

Huang, Zhen. 1990. *Huang Shi Richao* 黄氏日抄 [Notes of Huang]. Collected in Complete Library in the Four Branches of Literature. Shanghai: Shanghai Chinese Classics Publishing House.

Needham, Joseph 李约瑟. 1986. *Liyuese Wenji* 李约瑟文集 [A Collection of Joseph Needham's Essays]. Translated by Pan Jixing. Shenyang: Liaoning Science and Technology Publishing House.

Li, Quan 李筌. 1990. *Taibai Yinjing* 太白阴经 [Meridian of Taibai: A Book on Military Strategy]. Collected in Complete Library in the Four Branches of Literature. Shanghai: Shanghai Chinese Classics Publishing House.

Li, Tao 李焘. 2004. *Xu Zizhi Tongjian Changbian* 续资治通鉴长编 [Continuation to The Comprehensive Mirror for Aid in Government]. Beijing: Zhonghua Book Company.

Li, Tianming李天鸣. 1988. *Song Yuan Zhanshi* 宋元战史 [A History of Wars Between the Song and the Yuan Forces]. Taibei: Foodstuffs Press.

Li, Wenbin 李文彬. 1981. "Chechuan Paigan Mulaoya Kao"车船"、"拍竿"及"木老鸦"考 [Studies on "Pedal wheel ships", "Poles Installed with Arrows and Stones" and "Long Sharp-ended Logs"]. *Journal of Liaoning University* 4.

Li, Xinchuan 李心传. 2000. *Jianyan Yilai Chaoye Zaji* 建炎以来朝野杂记 [Laws and Institutions Since the Jianyan Reign]. Edited by Xu Gui. Beijing: Zhonghua Book Company.

Li, Xinchuan 李心传. 2013. *Jianyan Yilai Xinian Yaolu* 建炎以来系年要录 [Chronological Record of Major Events Since 1127]. Beijing: Zhonghua Book Company.

Li, Yanshou 李延寿. 1975. *Nan Shi* 南史 [History of Southern Song Dynasty]. Beijing Zhonghua Book Company.

Li, Zenngbo 李曾伯. 1990. *Kezhai Za Gao* 可斋杂稿 [Selected Works of Li Zengbo]. Collected in Complete Library in the Four Branches of Literature. Shanghai: Shanghai Chinese Classics Publishing House.

Li, Zhiyi 李之仪. 1990. *Guxijushi Qian Ji* 姑溪居士前集 [Prequel to Selected Works of Guxijushi]. Collected in Complete Library in the Four Branches of Literature. Shanghai: Shanghai Chinese Classics Publishing House.

Liao, Gang 廖刚. 1990. *Gaofeng Wenji* 高峰文集 [Selected Works of Liao Gang]. Collected in Complete Library in the Four Branches of Literature. Shanghai: Shanghai Chinese Classics Publishing House.

Lin, Dong 林駉. 1990. *Gujin Yuanliu Zhi Lun* 古今源流至论 [The Theories of Historical Origins]. Collected in Complete Library in the Four Branches of Literature. Shanghai: Shanghai Chinese Classics Publishing House.

Lin, Jizhong 林季仲. 1990. *Zhuxuan Zazhu* 竹轩杂著 [Selected Works of Lin Jizhong]. Collected in Complete Library in the Four Branches of Literature. Shanghai: Shanghai Chinese Classics Publishing House.

Lin, Lin 林琳. 1982. "Chechuan Daodi Shi Shui Faming De "车船"到底是谁发明的 [Who invented 'Pedal Wheel Ships']". *Academic Forum* 2.

Lin, Sheng 林声. 1979. "Zhonggu Gudai De 'Chechuan': Zhongguo Gudai Zaochuan Shiliao Huikao Zhiyi 中国古代的"车船":(中国古代造船史料汇考)之一 ["Pedal Wheel Ships"of Ancient China: One of the Collections of Historical Materials About Ancient Chinese Shipbuilding]". *Journal of Zhengzhou University* 1.

Liu, Xu 刘昫. 1975. *Jiu Tang Shu* 旧唐书 [Old Book of Tang]. Beijing: Zhonghua Book Company.

Liu, Zai 刘宰. 1990. *Mantang Ji* 漫塘集 [Anthology of Liu Zai]. Collected in Complete Library in the Four Branches of Literature. Shanghai: Shanghai Chinese Classics Publishing House.

Liu, Zihui 刘子翚. 1990. *Pingshan Ji* 屏山集 [Selected Works of Liu Zihui]. Collected in Complete Library in the Four Branches of Literature. Shanghai: Shanghai Chinese Classics Publishing House.

Lou, Yao 楼钥. 1990. *Gonggui Ji* 攻媿集 [Selected Works of Lou Yao]. Collected in Complete Library in the Four Branches of Literature. Shanghai: Shanghai Chinese Classics Publishing House.

Lu, Xian 卢宪. 1990. *Jiading Zhenjiang Zhi* 嘉定镇江志 [Jiading Period Chronicles of Zhenjiang]. Collected in The Series of Chorography of the Song and Yuan Dynasties. Beijing: Zhonghua Book Company.

Lu, You 陆游. 2011. *Lu You Quanji Jiaozhu* 陆游全集校注 [Annotations to Lu You's Works]. Collated by Qian Zhonglian. Hangzhou: Zhejiang Education Publishing House.

Lu, You 陆游. 2012. *Laoxuean Biji* 老学庵笔记 [The Notes of an Old Pedant]. Sorted by Li Changxian. Collected in Complete Song Notes. Elephant Press.

Lu, You 陆游. 2012. *Ru Shu Ji* 入蜀记 [Essays about My Journey to Sichuan]. Sorted by Li Changxian. Collected in Complete Song Notes. Elephant Press.

Luo, Jun 罗浚, et al. 1990. *Baoqing Siming Zhi* 宝庆四明志 [Baoqing Period Chronicles of Siming]. Collected in The Series of Chorography of the Song and Yuan Dynasties. Beijing: Zhonghua Book Company.

Luo, Yuan 罗愿. 1990. *Xinan Zhi* 新安志 [Chronicles of Xin'an]. Collected in The Series of Chorography of the Song and Yuan Dynasties. Beijing: Zhonghua Book Company.

Lü, Nangong 吕南公. 1990. *Guanyuan Ji* 灌园集 [Selected Works of Lü Nangong]. Collected in Complete Library in the Four Branches of Literature. Shanghai: Shanghai Chinese Classics Publishing House.

Ma, Duanlin 马端临. 2011. Wenxian Tongkao 文献通考 [A Full-Scale Textual Criticism on Ancient Systems and Regulations]. Beijing: Zhonghua Book Company.

Mei, Yingfa 梅应发, et al. 1990. *Kaiqing Siming Zhi* 开庆四明续志 [Sequels to Kaiming Period Chronicles of Siming]. Collected in The Series of Chorography of the Song and Yuan Dynasties. Beijing: Zhonghua Book Company.

Mingqing Shiliao 明清史料 [Historical Records of the Ming and Qing Dynasties]. 2000. Edited by Institute of History and Philology at Academia Sinica. Taipei: The Commercial Press.

Ni, Pu 倪朴. 1990. *Ni Shiling Shu*倪石陵书 [Selected Works of Ni Pu]. Collected in Complete Library in the Four Branches of Literature. Shanghai: Shanghai Chinese Classics Publishing House.

Qi, Tao齐涛. 1987. "Chechuan Bingfei Shiyu Yangyao 车船并非始于杨么[Pedal Wheel Ships were Initially not Built by Yang Yao]". *Historical Research in Anhui* 4.

Shi, Hao 史浩. 1990. *Maofeng Zhenyin Manlu* 鄮峰真隐漫录 [Selected Works of Shihao]. Collected in Complete Library in the Four Branches of Literature. Shanghai: Shanghai Chinese Classics Publishing House.

Song Shi Quanwen 宋史全文 [History of the Song Dynasty in Full Scale]. 2005. Edited by Zhiliang Li. Haerbin: Heilongjiang People's Publishing House.

Song, Lian 宋濂. 1976. *Yuan Shi* 元史 [History of the Yuan Dynasty]. Beijing: Zhonghua Book Company.

Songji Sanchao Zhwngyao Jianzheng 宋季三朝政要笺证 [Compilations and Revisions on The Chronicle of the Late Southern Song Dynasty]. 2010. Edited by Ruilai Wang 王瑞来. Beijing: Zhonghua Book Company.

Su, Guo 苏过. n.d. *Xiechuan Ji* 斜川集 [Selected Works of Su Guo]. Collected in the Series of Ancient Classics, 1st ed. Beijing: Zhonghua Book Company.

Su, Pinxiao 粟品孝, et al. 2008. *Nansong Junshishi*南宋军事史 [A History of Military in the Southern Song Dynasty]. Shanghai: Shanghai Chinese Classics Publishing House.

Su, Shi 苏轼. 2010. *Su Shi Quanji Jiaozhu* 苏轼全集校注 [Annotations to the Selected Works of Su Shi]. Punctuated and collated by Zhang Zhilie, et al. Shijieazhuang: Hebei People's Publishing House.

Su, Tianjue 苏天爵. n.d. *Guochao Wenlei* 国朝文类 [Poems and Articles of the Yuan Dynasty]. Collected in Collectanea of the Four Categories, 1st ed.

Sun, Di 孙觌. 1990. *Hongqingjushi Ji*鸿庆居士集 [Selected Works of Sun Di]. Collected in Complete Library in the Four Branches of Literature. Shanghai: Shanghai Chinese Classics Publishing House.

Tianyige Cang Mingchao Ben⟨Tiansheng Ling⟩Jiaozheng 天一阁藏明钞本⟨天圣令⟩校证 [Proof-reading of Laws and Regulations During the Tiansheng Period—the Ming hand copied version stored in Tianyi Pavilion]. 2004. Beijing: Zhonghua Book Company.

Toqta 脱脱. 1977. *Song Shi* 宋史 [History of the Song Dynasty]. Beijing: Zhonghua Book Company.

Wang, Jieyun 王界云. 1983. "Chechuan Zhizao Kaolue 车船制造考略 [Studies on the Making of Pedal Wheel Ships]". *Academic Monthly* 11.

Wang, Qingsong 王庆松. 2004. "Ershi Shiji Songdai Haiwai Maoyi Yanjiu Zongshu 20世纪宋代海外贸易研究综述 [Review on 20th Century Overseas Trade Researches in the Song Dynasty]". *Journal of Maritime History Studies* 2.

Wang, Rui-ming 王瑞明. 1963. "Jiaota Chechuan Bu Shiyu Yangyao 脚踏车船不始自杨么 [Initial Pedal Wheel Ships were not Built by Yang Yao]". *Jianghan Tribune* 4.

Wang, Rui-ming 王瑞明. 1987. "Songdai De Zaochuanye Yu Chuanhu 宋代的造船业与船户[Shipbuilding and Boatmen in the Song Dynasty]". *Academic Monthly* 3.

Wang, Shipeng王十朋. 2012. *Wang Shipeng Quanji* 王十朋全集 [Complete Works of Wang Shipeng]. Edited by Meixi Collection Republication Committee. Shanghai: Shanghai Chinese Classics Publishing House.

Wang, Yan 王炎. 1990. *Shuangxi Leigao* 双溪类稿 [Selected Works of Wang Yan]. Collected in Complete Library in the Four Branches of Literature. Shanghai: Shanghai Chinese Classics Publishing House.

Wang, Yingchen 汪应辰. 1990. *Wending Ji* 文定集 [Selected Works of Wang Yingchen]. Collected in Complete Library in the Four Branches of Literature. Shanghai: Shanghai Chinese Classics Publishing House.

Wang, Yinglin 王应麟. 2003. *Yuhai* 玉海 [Encyclopedia of 21 Categories]. Yangzhou: Guangling Publishing House.

Wang, Zengyu 王曾瑜. 2006a. "Zhonggu gudai De Chechuan 中国古代的车船 [Pedal Wheel Ships in Ancient China]". "*Zizhu Bian* 锱铢编 [A Collection of *Wang Zengyu's Essays*]. Baoding: Hebei University Press.
Wang, Zengyu 王曾瑜. 2006b. *Zizhu Bian* 锱铢编 [A Collection of Wang Zengyu's Essays]. Baoding: Hebei University Press.
Wang, Zhidao 王之道. 1990. *Xiangshan Ji* 相山集 [Selected Works of Wang Zhidao]. Collected in Complete Library in the Four Branches of Literature. Shanghai: Shanghai Chinese Classics Publishing House.
Wang, Zhiwang 王之望. 1990. *Hanbin Ji* 汉滨集 [Selected Works of Wang Zhiwang]. Collected in Complete Library in the Four Branches of Literature. Shanghai: Shanghai Chinese Classics Publishing House.
Wang, Zongji王宗稷. 1990. *Dongpo Xiansheng Nianpu* 东坡先生年谱 [Chronology of Su Dongpo]. Collected in Complete Library in the Four Branches of Literature. Shanghai: Shanghai Chinese Classics Publishing House.
Wen, Tianxiang 文天祥. 1987. *Weng Tianxiang Quanji* 文天祥全集 [Selected Works of Wen Tianxiang]. Collated by Xiong Fei, et al. Nanchang: Jiangxi People's Publishing House.
Wu, Shimo 吴示模. 1960. "Shilun Zhongxiang Yangyao Qiyi Zai Lishishang De Zuoyong试论钟相杨么起义在历史上的作用 [On the Historical Role of the Uprising of Zhong Xiang and Yang Yao]". *Journal of Historical Science* 3.
Wu, Yong 吴泳. 1990. *Helin Ji* 鹤林集 [Selected Works of Wu Yong]. Collected in Complete Library in the Four Branches of Literature. Shanghai: Shanghai Chinese Classics Publishing House.
Wu, Zeng 吴曾. 2012. *Nenggaizhai Manlu* 能改斋漫录 [Nenggaizhai Notes]. Sorted by Liu Yu. Collected in Complete Song Notes. Elephant Press.
Xi, Longfei 席龙飞. 2000. *Zhongguo Zaochuanshi*中国造船史 [A History of China Shipbuilding]. Wuhan: Hubei Education Press.
Xi, Longfei 席龙飞. 2004. *Zhongguo Kexue Jishushi (Jiaotong Juan)* 中国科学技术史(交通卷)[The History of Science and Technology in China (Traffic Volume)]. Beijing: Science Press.
Xiong, Ke 熊克. 1985. *Zhongxing Xiaoji* 中兴小纪 [Unofficial Histories in Emperor Gaozong's Reign]. Fuzhou: Fujian People's Publishing House.
Xu, Lun 许纶. 1990. *She Zhai Ji* 涉斋集 [Selected Works of Xu Lun]. Collected in Complete Library in the Four Branches of Literature. Shanghai: Shanghai Chinese Classics Publishing House.
Xu, Luqing 徐鹿卿. 1990. Qingzheng Cungao 清正存稿 [Extant Manucripts of Xu Luqing]. Collected in Complete Library in the Four Branches of Literature. Shanghai: Shanghai Chinese Classics Publishing House.
Xu, Mengshen 徐梦莘. 1987. *Sanchao Beimeng Huibian* 三朝北盟会编 [Records of Wars and Actions between the Song and Jin in Three Song Emperors' Reigns]. Shanghai: Shanghai Chinese Classics Publishing House.
Xu, Song 徐松, et al. 2014. *Song Huiyao Jigao*宋会要辑稿 [The Anthology of Laws and Regulations of the Song Dynasty]. Shanghai: Shanghai Chinese Classics Publishing House.
Xue, Jixuan 薛季宣. 1990. *Langyu Ji* 浪语集 [Selected Works of Xue Jixuan]. Collected in Complete Library in the Four Branches of Literature. Shanghai: Shanghai Chinese Classics Publishing House.
Yang, Shiqi 杨士奇, et al. 1990. *Lidai Mingchen Zouyi* 历代名臣奏议 [Memorials to the Thrones in History]. Collected in Complete Library in the Four Branches of Literature. Shanghai: Shanghai Chinese Classics Publishing House.
Yang, Wanli杨万里. 2007. *Yang Wanli Ji Jianjiao* 杨万里集笺校 [Annotations to Selected Works of Yang Wanli]. Collated by Xin Gengru. Beijing: Zhonghua Book Company.
Ye, Mengde 叶梦得. 2002. *Shilin Zouyi* 石林奏议 [Ye Mengde's Memorials to the Emperor]. Collected in Continuation to Complete Library in the Four Branches of Literature. Shanghai: Shanghai Chinese Classics Publishing House.

Ye, Shi 叶适. 1961. *Yeshi Ji* 叶适集 [Selected Works of Ye Shi]. Punctuated and collated by Liu Gongchun, et al. Beijing: Zhonghua Book Company.

Shiba, Yoshinobu 斯波义信. 1985. "Song Yuan Shidai De Chuanbo 宋元时代的船舶 [Vessels in the Song and Yuan Dynasties]". Translated by Jing Hui. *Marine History Studies* 1.

Yuan, Xie 袁燮. 1990. *Jiezhai Ji* 絜斋集 [Selected works of Yuan Xie]. Collected in Complete Library in the Four Branches of Literature. Shanghai: Shanghai Chinese Classics Publishing House.

Yuan, Xingzong 员兴宗. 1990. *Jiuhua Ji* 九华集 [Selected Works of Yuan Xingzong]. Collected in Complete Library in the Four Branches of Literature. Shanghai: Shanghai Chinese Classics Publishing House.

Yue, Ke 岳珂. 1989. *Eguo Jintuo Xubian Jiaozhu* 鄂国金佗续编校注 [Annotation on the Historical Records about Yue Fei]. Collated by Wang Zengyu. Beijing: Zhonghua Book Company.

Zeng, Gong曾巩. 1990. *Yuanfen Leigao* 元丰类稿 [Selected Works of Zeng Gu]. Collected in Complete Library in the Four Branches of Literature. Shanghai: Shanghai Chinese Classics Publishing House.

Zhang, Ying 张英, Wang Shizhen王士祯, et al. 1985. *Yuanjian Leihan* 渊鉴类涵 [An Enyclopedia Compiled on Imperial Command]. Beijing: Zhongguo Shudian Publishing House.

Zhang, Gang 张纲. 1990. *Huayang Ji* 华阳集 [Selected Works of Zhang Gang]. Collected in Complete Library in the Four Branches of Literature. Shanghai: Shanghai Chinese Classics Publishing House.

Zhang, Nie 张嵲. 1990. *Ziwei Ji* 紫微集 [Selected Works of Zhang Nie]. Collected in Complete Library in the Four Branches of Literature. Shanghai: Shanghai Chinese Classics Publishing House.

Zhang, Ruyu 章如愚. 1990. *Qun Shu Kaosuo* 群书考索[Research and Quest on Books of All Sorts]. Collected in Complete Library in the Four Branches of Literature. Shanghai: Shanghai Chinese Classics Publishing House.

Zhang, Shizheng 张师正. 1990. *Kuo Yi Zhi* 括异志 [Stories of the Strange]. Collected in Complete Library in the Four Branches of Literature. Shanghai: Shanghai Chinese Classics Publishing House.

Zhang, Shou 张守. 1990. *Piling Ji* 毘陵集 [Selected Works of Zhang Shou]. Collected in Complete Library in the Four Branches of Literature. Shanghai: Shanghai Chinese Classics Publishing House.

Zhang, Shunmin 张舜民. 1990. *Hua Man Ji* 画墁集 [Selected Works of Zhang Shunmin]. Collected in Complete Library in the Four Branches of Literature. Shanghai: Shanghai Chinese Classics Publishing House.

Zhang, Xiaoxiang 张孝祥. 1980. *Yuhujushi Wenji* 于湖居士文集 [Selected Works of Zhang Xiaoxiang]. Shanghai: Shanghai Chinese Classics Publishing House.

Zhang, Xuan 张铉. 1990. *Zhida Jinling Zhi* 至大金陵新志 [Zhida Period Chronicles of Jinling]. Collected in The Series of Chorography of the Song and Yuan Dynasties. Beijing: Zhonghua Book Company.

Zhao Zhong Lu 昭忠录 [The Loyals]. 1990. Collected in Complete Library in the Four Branches of Literature. Shanghai: Shanghai Chinese Classics Publishing House.

Zhao, Yongchun赵永春. 2005. *Song Jin Guanxi* 金宋关系史 [A History of the Relationship between the Song and the Jin]. Beijing: People's Publishing House.

Zheng, Xie郑獬. 1990. *Yunxi Ji* 郧溪集 [Selected Works of Zheng Xie]. Collected in Complete Library in the Four Branches of Literature. Shanghai: Shanghai Chinese Classics Publishing House.

Zhou, Bida 周必大. 1990. *Wenzhong Ji* 文忠集 [Selected Works of Wenzhong]. Collected in Complete Library in the Four Branches of Literature. Shanghai: Shanghai Chinese Classics Publishing House.

Zhou, Nan周南. 1990. *Shanfang Ji* 山房集 [Selected Works of Zhou Nan]. Collected in Complete Library in the Four Branches of Literature. Shanghai: Shanghai Chinese Classics Publishing House.

Zhou, Yinggu 周应谷. 1990. *Jingding Jiankang Zhi* 景定建康志 [Jingding Period Chronicles of Jiankang]. Collected in The Series of Chorography of the Song and Yuan Dynasties. Beijing: Zhonghua Book Company.

Zhou, Zizhi 周紫芝. 1990. *Taicang Timi Ji* 太仓稊米集 [Selected Works of Zhou Zizhi]. Collected in Complete Library in the Four Branches of Literature. Shanghai: Shanghai Chinese Classics Publishing House.

Zhu, Xi 朱熹. 2010. *Hui'an Xiansheng Zhuwengong Ji* 晦庵先生朱文公文集 [Selected Works of Zhu Xi]. Punctuated and collated by Liu Yongxiang, et al. Shanghai: Shanghai Chinese Classics Publishing House. Heifei: Anhui Education Publishing House.

Chapter 5
Shipbuilding Industry and Social Life in the Song Dynasty

5.1 The Composition and Livelihood of Inland River Boatmen in the Song Dynasty with a Focus on Grain Transportation

With the center of economic gravity shifting further south, several factors, such as the prosperity of the commodity economy and the extensive scale of grain transportation, led to an unprecedented boom in inland transportation and a larger population of boatmen. These individuals made their living from the water, navigating through a unique and unpredictable environment, which shaped their distinct mentalities, beliefs, and behavioral patterns. Each ship was like a small society with clear divisions of labor and social strata. When considering the addition of travelers and merchants, the size of the sailing society became even more substantial. While numerous studies have examined the prosperity of inland waterway shipping in the Song Dynasty, only a few have focused on the lifestyle of the populous boatmen who lived in such a society during this flourishing shipping age (Y. Shiba 1997: 85–102; J. Cao 2002: 160; F. Chen 1997: 119–123).[1] This section will primarily discuss the order and livelihood of boatmen, with a particular emphasis on grain transportation.

[1] Yoshinobu Shiba studied the combination and division of labor in the operation of the shipping industry in the Song Dynasty. He classified sailors into two groups: superior boatmen and lower boatmen. His discussion of seagoing ships was more detailed than that of inland river boats, while he made no further research on the social strata of sailors. Cao Jiaqi discussed the employment of soldiers and civilian workers in his research on the cargo transportation system. Chen Feng discussed the sources and duties of the grain transportation escorts.

C. Huang, *A Panoramic View of the Song Dynasty Through the Lens of Shipbuilding Industry*, https://doi.org/10.1007/978-981-97-6128-9_5

5.1.1 *The Quantity of Boatmen in the Song Dynasty*

The members of cargo shipping boats could be divided into two groups. The first group consisted of non-driving escorts, such as supercargoes and transportation officers, while the second group included those who operated the ships, such as helmsmen and boat trackers (sailors). On non-cargo shipping boats and private ships, the crew typically consisted solely of helmsmen and boat trackers. In Mei Yaochen's poem, he wrote that "helmsmen sighed for me while the sailors concerned for me" (Y. Mei 1990). Similarly, for grain transportation on the Hanshui River, it was noted that "from helmsmen to pole-men, they were all selected from people who were familiar with the routes" (S. Xu et al. 2014: 7006), highlighting the distinctions between helmsmen, boat trackers, and pole-men. Pole-men were a type of sailor who could also work as boat trackers.

Lu You once described ships sailing upstream in the Three Gorges, stating, "many sailors were singing a chanty to cautiously navigate through dangerous sections. Even if they were sitting face to face in the boat, they could still hear each other's words. Once they had passed the section, silence filled the boat, and the sounds made by the turning rudders could be heard clearly. With the sounds of operating the ship, the sailors were already able to mount on the sandbar" (Y. Lu 2011: 120). When Wen Tianxiang fled from Jiangnan provinces to Zhenzhou on a private salt ship, he observed that "the boatmen rowed and punted with great efforts and pulled if it was possible to do so along the bank" (T. Wen 1987: 499). These descriptions indicate that sailors would row, punt, or pull based on specific circumstances. However, some boat trackers only worked within certain sections of the river and did not travel with the boat.

Yang Wanli vividly portrayed the bustling scene of the Grand Canal in Liangzhe provinces, stating, "the canal was illuminated by flaming torches, making it as bright as daytime, and numerous boat trackers struggled forward like ants" (W. Yang 2007: 1497). The canal operated continuously, day and night, with a large number of boat trackers. While it is challenging to determine the exact number of inland vessels and boatmen during the Song Dynasty, a rough estimation can be made based on the batch shipping system and regulations of that era. Towing was the primary method of long-distance travel on inland rivers, whether on the canal, Yangtze River, or other rivers. Boat towing was considered the most reliable and efficient means, making boat trackers an essential labor force.

The Song Dynasty established regulations for boat trackers regarding staffing. In *the Laws and Regulations During the Tiansheng Period,* the rules for grain transportation on the Bianhe River stated that "every 1,675 liters of grain should be accompanied by one boatman." If salt, iron, or similar goods were being transported, they would be measured using a grain yardstick. In the case of an empty boat, staff arrangements were based on the boat's tonnage (*Tianyige Cang Ming Chaoben Jiaozheng* 2004: 375; G. Huang 1990).[2] It is important to note that the "every 1675 L" mentioned here

[2] In terms of the crew members equipped to a boat, each boatman was supposed to carry fifty-Hu (a unit to evaluate the volume of a boat) of grains as a normal practice when they sail on the river

refers to the deadweight capacity of the boat, not the actual load.[3] Approximately 80% of cargo ships were loaded with grain, while the remaining 20% were used by boatmen to carry private cargo. The staffing arrangement for boatmen and boat trackers was to assign one staff member for every 1675 L of cargo measured by deadweight capacity, or one personnel for every 1340 L if measured by actual loading. This practice aligns with the records stating, "using 1,675 liters of tonnage as the standard, with actual loads of 1,340 liters of grain, one towing boatman was assigned" (S. Xu et al. 2014: 6948). It is important to clarify that "towing boatmen" refers to boat trackers and does not include the captain, helmsman, or escorts. Consider the canal section from Zhenzhou to Kaifeng. "80% of the ship's capacity, which is 164,000 L, is required for carrying grains, while the remaining 20% is allocated for carrying private goods." In this scenario, 80% of the ship's load capacity needs to be dedicated to carrying 13,400 L of grains. The standard practice for staffing the boat is to hire one boatman for every 1340 L (S. Xu et al. 2014: 6979). Therefore, the boat owner's total expenses on boatmen are calculated based on the ratio of 1340 L per person. Regardless of whether the laborer is a soldier or not, both wages and food are necessary. It is important to note that the term "supposed boatmen" does not refer to the exact number of boatmen hired, but rather indicates the payment of one worker's wage and grain based on this standardized ratio.

When it came to soldiers, boatmen, and escorts, Su Shi stated, "the tax transportation department of Huainan provinces unlawfully collected 10,000 strings of 1000 coins from the grain transportation ships. However, if the local governments could contribute 6 million Dan of grains to the royal court through their levied taxes, this behavior would not be punished as a crime due to the payment made to tens of thousands of soldiers and hundreds of escorts involved in the batch grain shipping" (S. Su 2010: 3490; S. Su n.d.: 3490).[4] The ratio of these three positions was 100:10:1. It should be noted that this ratio was a general concept, and the actual employment of captains, helmsmen, sailors, or boat trackers depended on different circumstances, often involving a one-to-many relationship. For example, when transporting Sichuan horses during the Southern Song Dynasty, the ratio of boatmen to boat trackers was approximately 1:9 (C. Huang 2017). Therefore, the regulation of one personnel for

running through plains, and more boatmen need to be equipped to those on the rivers running through mountainous areas, as stated in *Proofreading of Laws and Regulations During Tiansheng Period—the Ming hand copied version stored in Tianyi Pavilion*. And the record of crew members in *Selected Works of Huang Gan* is that more than one hundred officers, soldiers and sailors were allocated to one grain cargo transportation in Funzhou of Jiannan West province, 38 helmsmen and sailors were equipped to the seven-hundred-Liao horse-carrying boat, and 28 helmsmen and sailors to a five-hundred-Liao boat. The above shows that the staffing ratio of a boat in Huang Gan's record is much higher that that of a fifty-Hu boat transporting grain on the river of plains.

[3] Based on the previous discussion, the deadweight tonnage is the net tonnage minus the weight of non-effective loads, and Dian, Hu, Shu and Liao are all equivalent in volume to one Dan of rice (328 l or 30 kg of rice).

[4] In *Annotations to the Selected Works of Su Shi*, it is recorded that as far as Huainan provinces were concerned, the grain transportation tax revenues of the six prefectures, Zhenzhou, Yangzhou, Gaoyou, Chuzhou, Sizhou and Suzhou, were not more than 10,000 strings of 1000 copper coins.

every 1675 L or the actual deadweight load of 1340 L served as the staffing standard for boat trackers on a boat.

According to the standard used to assess personnel requirements for boat transportation in the Northern Song Dynasty, which was based on allocating 1340 L of grain per person, it can be estimated that a considerable number of boat trackers were needed for grain transportation in the southeast regions. The act mandated by the Northern Song Dynasty required the six southeast provinces to contribute 402,000,000 L of grain as tribute in the fourth year of the Tiansheng Reign (AD 1026). Later, in the first year of the Huangyou Reign (AD 1049), the required grain contribution was increased to 415,400,000 L (C. Huang 2003). Lü Cong, the deputy director-general of transportation during the early years of the Southern Song Dynasty, described the grain transportation process as follows: "The fixed teams of grain ships on the Bianhe River numbered 200, with each fleet composed of 30 ships. In total, 6000 ships made three rounds of trips each year to transport the grain tax" (S. Xu et al. 2014: 4098). The total amount of grain taxes levied here amounted to 415,400,000 L. If all the ships and boat trackers were utilized for three rounds of shipping, it would require 18,000 trips to complete the transportation of 402,000,000 L of grain, with each boat carrying 23,048 L per trip. Considering that 80% of the ship's space was used for carrying grains as the standard load capacity, the most commonly used ships on the Bianhe River would have a load capacity of 141,040 L, which aligns with the typical deadweight of 131,200 L for grain ships (C. Huang 2017). "The ships on the Bianhe River had a load capacity of 500 Liao. One fleet consists of 25 ships with a load capacity of 164,000 L, or 30 ships with a load capacity of 131,200 L" (S. Xu et al. 2014: 7038). Additionally, Su Shi mentioned that "30 ships made a fleet" during his time as the mayor of Yangzhou (S. Su 2010: 3494). Hence, it is evident that ships with a load capacity of 131,200 L were commonly used in these two sections of the canal. If we calculate the staffing based on the regulation of hiring one person for every 1675 L of grain, each ship would need to be equipped with 8–9 boat trackers. With 6000 ships in operation, a total of 48,000–54,000 boat trackers would be required. Considering the actual loading of 415,400,000 L of grain for three rounds of shipping, an estimated 51,000 boat trackers would be needed. Yang Yongde, a eunuch of Emperor Renzong, proposed the construction of courier stations for grain shipping along the Bianhe River, which could save 60,000 laborers each year (Toqta 1977: 9961). This measure would effectively reduce the number of boat trackers required, indicating that the actual number of boatmen exceeded 60,000. In the first year of the Zhihe Reign (AD 1054), the government planned to "build barracks along the Bianhe River and recruit tens of thousands of people to two grain ships" (B. Zhao 1990). This recruitment plan further confirms the significant presence of boatmen. Based on this information, it can be inferred that the Bianhe River required tens of thousands of boat trackers, suggesting that around 50,000 boat trackers were hired for the grain shipping tasks.

These 50,000 boat trackers were boatmen working exclusively for the Grand Canal in Huainan provinces and the Bianhe River. This figure does not include the boat trackers responsible for transporting grain to the warehouses in Zhenzhou, Chuzhou, and Sizhou in China's southeastern region. The transportation of taxed grain formed a routine where ships sailing on the Yangtze River were prohibited from entering the Bianhe River, and vice versa (Z. Lü 2014: 370). In the southeastern provinces, the grain was transported to transfer warehouses, and once a year, salt was shipped back along the main route. The process involved the officers of the transportation department directing ships to transfer grain to the warehouses in Zhenzhou, Chuzhou, and Sizhou. They would then return with salt and send the ships back. Bianzhou Municipality was responsible for temporarily transferring these grains stored in the warehouses to the capital city (Toqta 1977: 4252). The annual amount of taxed grain from the six southeastern provinces was 415,400,000 L. Among these, 100,500,000 L were from Huainan, 66,330,000 L from Jiangnan East, 80,400,000 L from Jiangnan West, 43,550,000 L from Hu'nan, 23,450,000 L from Hubei, and 103,850,000 L from Liangzhe. On their return trips, these six routes transported a total of about 214,400,000 L of salt (B. Zhang 1985: 118). Given this information, it is unclear how many boat trackers were required to transport the grain to the warehouses.

The Grand Canal in Huainan faced a comparatively worse situation because it often experienced water shortages, leading to ships getting stranded. Numerous weirs and gates were needed for navigation. Similarly, the routes in the Bianhe River did not have weirs, resulting in frequent instances of ships being stranded in certain sections. Trips to the capital required sailing upstream, and heavily loaded ships primarily relied on boat trackers throughout their journeys. The cargo shipping boats on the Grand Canal in Liangzhe West and Liangzhe East provinces faced similar conditions. The rice contributed to the court in Liangzhe East and West provinces was primarily transported via canals. According to the standard of hiring one boatman for every 40 Dan (a unit of dry measure for grain), 38,750 people would be required as trackers to ship 1.55 million Dan of grain. Although the five provinces of Jiangnan East, Jiangnan West, Hunan, Hubei, and Huainan differed in distance from the transfer warehouses, which necessitated using the Huainan Canal route, their task was to transport grains to the Huainan Canal via the Yangtze River. Except for the cities near the canals in Huainan East and West provinces, ships from southern regions needed to use the Yangtze River as their route, while those from the northern regions had to take the Huaihe River.

As inland rivers had different water conditions, the number of equipped trackers for each boat varied. During Emperor Shenzong's Reign, to transport tea from Sichuan to Shaanxi via branches of the Yangtze River, the government sent 30 ships with a load capacity of 100 Liao. One general and 60 soldiers were assigned to be in charge of the escort (S. Xu et al. 2014: 6661–62). The staffing standard was that each boatman was designated to carry 50 Liao. However, the Sichuan section of the Yangtze River, including many steep gorges like the Three Gorges, was difficult to navigate. In the early years of the Southern Song Dynasty, the 700-Liao horse-carrying boats in the Sichuan section of the Yangtze River were usually equipped with four helmsmen per boat, with 34 boatmen to operate scull yulohs (S. Xu et al. 2014: 9107), and each boatman was supposed to carry twenty Dan.

Although the lower-middle reaches of the Yangtze River were hazardous due to strong winds and torrential waves, the risks were not comparable to those in the Sichuan section. Therefore, the deadweight tonnage or payload of boats sailing in the

Yangtze River must be greater than in the Sichuan section but less than in the canal. Zhao Shankuo mentioned the transportation of military supplies to the emperor's temporary residence or the riverside military camps via the Yangtze River. He stated, "some people sailed from Jiangnan West province to Yingzhou (now Zhongxiang of Hubei Province), and others from Hu'nan to Huainan. Sometimes they stayed stagnant due to the strong upstream current or incurred expenses due to the long journey." The staffing requirement for a boat was that "if the cargo totaled 20,000 Dan and 50 ships with a load capacity each were adopted, then 300 boatmen needed to be recruited" (S. Zhao 1990). If only 80% of the load capacity was used to carry grains, the average deadweight tonnage was 83 Dan, and each boatman was designated a payload of 67 Dan. In the third year of the Jianyan Reign (AD 1129), civilian boats in Jiangnan East, Jiangnan West, and Hubei provinces were recruited to transport grain. Seven or more ships had a load capacity of 13,000 Dan, five or more could carry 10,000 Dan, and two or more could carry 4000 Dan. "The number of helmsmen, trackers, and head crews was 30 for each site" (S. Xu et al. 2014: 9253). This means that each ship carried 2000 Dan, which was supposed to be done by thirty men, so the average payload of 67 Dan needed to be shipped by a boatman. Although the staff included helmsmen, they accounted for a small proportion. If we calculate the staff needed based on the standard of 67 Dan as the payload designated to a boatman, then the tributes submitted by Huainan, Jiangnan East, Jiangnan West, Hu'nan, and Hubei totaled 4.7 million Dan, requiring more than 62,680 trackers. In summary, to transport the rice of 6.2 million Dan to the court, the boat trackers needed in the canals of Huainan, Liangzhe East and West provinces, and sections of the Yangtze River reached 151,430 trackers.

In addition to the shipment of 6 million Dan of rice from six southeastern provinces to Bianjing (now Kaifeng of He'nan) via the Bianhe River, the Guangji River and the Huimin River provided the court with annual supplies of 620,000 Dan and 600,000 Dan of rice, respectively. By employing the standard payload of 40 Dan per boatman, it can be estimated that approximately 30,500 boat trackers would be required for this task. Furthermore, the Sanmen Baibo Shipping Department transported grain from the counties of Shaanxi downstream from the Three Gate Gorges of the Yellow River to Bianzhou (now Kaifeng of Henan Province) (Toqta 1977: 4254, 4251). However, the actual number of boatmen employed remains unknown. It is possible that the recruitment of a navy consisting of 2000 men on the south bank of the Yellow River to tow boats was part of the necessary staff (T. Li 2004: 2506). Additionally, grains were transported to Hebei via the Imperial River. For example, in the eighth year of the Xi'ning Period (AD 1075), 80,000 Dan of grains were transported using 300 ships on the Imperial River, requiring a minimum of 2000 soldiers (S. Xu et al. 2014: 4222). Moreover, the Bianhe River employed a similar arrangement of boat trackers. Considering the actual load of 80,000 Dan shipped by 2000 soldiers, it can be inferred that there was one boatman per 40 Dan of cargo. In terms of deadweight tonnage, each ship carried approximately 260 Dan of cargo with the assistance of six soldiers. Thus, the deadweight tonnage should exceed 300 Liao, aligning with the standard that one man should be employed for each 50 Hu of deadweight tonnage. Therefore, the estimated number of trackers required for grain transportation was at least 34,500. In total, 185,930 individuals were needed to transport grain from Bianjing (now Kaifeng of He'nan Province), nearly reaching 190,000 people. These figures do not include the trackers needed by the prefectures to transport grains through the canal and the Yangtze River. Consequently, it would have required over 200,000 trackers to transport the contributed grains to the court.

Apart from the aforementioned boat trackers (sailors), helmsmen also played a crucial role in operating the boats. In the Southern Song Dynasty, specifically in the Sichuan section of the Yangtze River, the horse-carrying boats had a load capacity of 700 Liao. These boats employed four helmsmen and 34 boat trackers (sailors), resulting in a helmsman-to-tracker ratio of 1:8.5. According to Zhang Zhen, the prefecture magistrate of Kuizhou (now Fengjie of Sichuan Province), a horse-carrying boat that carried 18 horses required "six yulohs installed on each boat, 36 sailors, and four helmsmen." Thus, the helmsman-to-sailor ratio was 1:9 (S. Xu et al. 2014: 9107). Unfortunately, the specific number of helmsmen and trackers (sailors) assigned to boats in the middle and lower reaches of the Yangtze River and the canals is not clearly documented. However, considering the helmsman-to-tracker ratio of the horse-carrying boats in the Sichuan section, it can be estimated that approximately 20,000 helmsmen would be required for grain transportation.

The aforementioned individuals were primarily responsible for operating the grain-carrying boats. However, in addition to the crew, non-boatmen such as convoy officials and officers also played a role on the boats. Starting from the fifth year of the Yuanfeng Reign (AD 1082), the Chariot Transportation Department of the Guangji River made reductions in grain boats and staff. Consequently, the number of boats decreased by 350, soldiers decreased by 2700, officials decreased by 33, and officers decreased by 11 each year (S. Xu et al. 2014: 7048). As the personnel reductions were made in line with the decrease in ships, the same applied to the escort workers, including boat trackers and helmsmen. A fleet of cargo ships under convoy consisted of thirty ships, with each ship being equipped with one escort official and one chief officer. The overall ratio of boatmen (trackers and helmsmen) to convoy staff (fleet chief and escort official) was 61:1. For instance, in the transportation fleet of tea under convoy in Sichuan province, which comprised 30 boats with a load capacity of 100 Liao each, 60 boatmen were hired to operate the boats along with one fleet chief, resulting in a proportion of 60:1. However, the composition of the crew in a fleet varied based on factors such as water conditions, types of goods being transported, and ship sizes. The ratio of approximately 60:1 was not a constant figure for the boatmen-to-convoy staff proportion. An example can be taken from the convoy transportation of horses in Sichuan. Usually, fifty horses were allocated to one transportation fleet. If there were 700 horse-carrying boats with a load capacity of 700 Liao each, then every two boats would form one fleet under convoy, which would be equipped with one escort official and two officers. However, on the returning boats with helmsmen, minor boatmen, and individuals sculling the yulohs, there were a total of 76 personnel, including soldiers and boat trackers. In this case, the ratio of boatmen to convoy staff was 25:1. The ships used for grain transportation in the middle and lower reaches of the Yangtze River and the canals differed from those used for horse shipping in the Sichuan section. Each cargo shipment of grain under convoy on the Yangtze River typically carried 5500 Dan (S. Hong, n.d.).[5] If a 2000-Dan boat was used, each cargo shipment of grain under convoy would require three boats. Considering the allocation of 67 Dan per boatman as mentioned earlier, a total of 82 boatmen would be needed. If one escort official and three officers were required to oversee each cargo shipment task, the ratio of boatmen to convoy staff would be 40:1. Although the proportion varied, the number of convoy staff could reach several thousand, or possibly approach 10,000.

The above-mentioned individuals were the boatmen needed for shipping grains to the court. Apart from grains, a large number of other supplies also needed to be transported, a practice known as "mixed cargo shipping". "Most of the supplies contributed by provinces were grain, silk, silver and money" (D. Ma 2011: 691). Additionally, gold and silver, spices and medicine, rhinoceros horn and ivory, and general merchandise offered by provinces such as Jinghu, Jiangnan, Huainan, and Liangzhe East and West were transported to the court alongside grain. From the Xianping Period (AD 998–1003) to the Tianxi Period (AD 1017–1021) of Emperor Zhenzong's Reign, tributes included 660,000 pieces of cloth from Sichuan Province, as well as gold and silk, over 230,000 strings of copper coins, incense, and 137,500 kg of jewelry from the southeastern provinces. Only the cargo shipping of spices and medicine from Guangnan East and West provinces required more than 6100 boatmen and escort officials (D. Ma 2011: 743). In the second year of the Zhiping Period (AD 1065), gold, silk, and 11,730,000 strings of 1000 coins were shipped from six southeastern provinces, while 8,565,000 kg of firewood and 500,000 kg of charcoal were delivered from Jiangnan West, Shaanxi, and Hedong provinces to the capital city (Toqta 1977: 4253). Since the second year of the Zhidao Reign (AD 996), the grain contributed from six southeastern provinces was shipped to transfer warehouses, and salt was transported on their way back. For example, in the seventh year of the Jiayou period of the Northern Song Dynasty (AD 1062), to complete the 12 batches of salt cargo shipping conducted by Jiangnan West Province from Huai'nan East and West provinces, each batch required 25 boats (Toqta 1977: 4442). The number of boatmen needed for this operation was difficult to estimate, but it must have been considerable. If we calculate the number of boatmen based on half the number required for shipping grains, the number of boatmen hired for mixed cargo shipping may have exceeded 100,000.

Apart from official cargo shipping, the canals and inland waterways were full of merchant ships, warships, and other government-owned or privately-owned boats, which far outnumbered grain ships. Take grain transportation via rivers as an example: six southeastern provinces offered 6 million Dan of grains every year, which seemed like a large amount, but it was less than the grains produced by Suzhou. Fan Zhongyan pointed out that Suzhou produced more than 7 million Dan of grains, while the six southeastern provinces contributed 6 million Dan to the court every year, equal to Suzhou's annual production (Z. Fan 1981). The total trade volume of grains in the whole country was much larger than that of Suzhou, and their trade mainly depended

[5] Hong Shi claimed that 6 batches of grain cargo transportation on the boats, escorted by Zhang Shou, Zhu Shi, Zhang Qiu, Liang Ping, Qi Shen and Wu Qi, carried up to 2,250,530 liters of goods."

on shipping. In the Fourth Year of the Tiansheng Reign (AD 1026), Chuzhou's Beishen Weir and Zhenzhou's Jiangkou Weir were rebuilt into sluice gates, saving more than 100,000 soldiers in charge of sluice gates every year. (Another record stated that 217,000 soldiers were laid idle annually) (T. Li 2004: 2424). Soldiers were set to tow the official and civilian boats passing through the canal weir sluice gates. Only in Beishen Weir and Jiangkou Weir, over 100,000 or even 200,000 people were needed to tow boats each year. We are sure that the number of boats passing through the two weirs was significant. If we make a conservative estimate, then the number of boat trackers needed by other boats, apart from cargo shipping, may be similar to the number of boatmen involved in cargo shipping, exceeding 300,000 people.

In summary, the boatmen required for official and private shipping during the Northern Song period numbered over 600,000 individuals. Inland waterway shipping was more prosperous in the Southern Song compared to the Northern Song. Grain transportation constituted a significant portion of river shipping. While there was a reduction in long-distance transportation tasks around the capital due to changes in financial supplies, the overall volume of goods transported from Sichuan to Shaanxi, as well as various cargo shipments including Jingzhou, Xiangzhou (Xiangfan of Hubei), Huan'nan West, and Huainan East provinces to designated regions or to Lin'an, remained substantial. The export of grain from southeastern provinces to war zones in Huainan and Jing prefecture, as well as Xiangzhou (Xiangfan of Hubei), amounted to 3 million Dan (S. Zhao 1990). Furthermore, the commodity economy and the movement of individuals in the south experienced significant growth compared to the Northern Song Dynasty.

5.1.2 The Sources of Boatmen in the Song Dynasty

In the Northern Song Dynasty, the major source of boatmen was local soldiers. "More than 6 million Hu of grains were transported from the six southeastern provinces every year, but the residents in the six provinces had no worries about transporting grains. The reason was that the shipping adopted official boats and dispatched soldiers as boatmen" (Toqta 1977: 11593). However, before the Zhidao Period, "although the government spent money on hiring people as boat trackers, the local people were afraid of being recruited as boatmen, so the annual tribute rice was no more than 3 million Hu." After Yang Yungong served as the supply commissioner-in-chief of the capital, he registered all the ships and soldiers in the three provinces and introduced the policy of relay transportation. The goods shipped from Jiangnan and Liangzhe provinces would be transferred from Huainan and Sizhou to the capital. "After this policy was implemented for a year, the total amount of tribute rice reached 6 million Hu" (Toqta 1977: 10161). In the Southern Song Dynasty, local soldiers were also recruited to ship grains, and the helmsmen, punters, and boat trackers needed for each shipping task were selected from those swimmers whose families had a heavy burden, according to the staffing regulations (S. Xu et al. 2014: 7066).

Soldiers were also used to tow boats during official trips. If procurators needed to inspect their subordinate prefectures by boat, they could send local soldiers to tow the boat. If no local soldiers were available, imperial armies might be dispatched (S. Xu et al. 2014: 2375). In the sixth year of the Xuanhe Reign (AD 1124), regulations stipulated that county procurators could not continue using local soldiers once their inspection tour was completed. "When procurators recruited boats along the river for their investigation tour, they usually dispatched local soldiers to tow the boats. If they retained these soldiers after the inspection tour, the court would introduce a law to prohibit such conduct" (S. Xu et al. 2014: 8332). A report from the Transfer Agency of Taxation of Fuzhou province in the sixth year of the Dazhongxiangfu Reign (AD 1013) stated that "if officials under the transfer agency of taxation were found to privately buy salt on their way to take office or requested officers of the passenger boats to carry salt, they would be forced to work as boat trackers to Yangzhou, Zhenzhou, Chuzhou (Huaian, Jiangsu), or Sizhou (Xuyi, Jiangsu) to carry grains if the privately bought salt weighed more than 100 kilograms" (S. Xu et al. 2014: 6506). Officials with certain ranks who assumed new office could also use local soldiers to tow the boat, and soldiers who violated the system would be punished as trackers to ship grains. In the fourth year of the Shaoxing Reign (AD 1134), an edict stated that "officials passing through the region were assigned soldiers to tow the boat and were provided with living expenses by the government without paying any money. Those who dispatched soldiers without a permit would be punished" (S. Xu et al. 2014: 9491), effectively prohibiting officials from using local soldiers as trackers for an extended period. However, in the eleventh year of the Chunxi Reign (AD 1184), a proposal submitted by the Bureau of Military Affairs mentioned that "officials privately sending soldiers to ship private goods still remained a problem" (S. Xu et al. 2014: 9505–06).

The "weir soldiers" and "sluice soldiers" responsible for towing boats in the canal were also local soldiers in service. Due to their task of using winches to pull boats through the weirs, they were also referred to as "winch soldiers" (X. Li 2013: 556; M. Xu 1987: 934). For example, Shiyan (Stone Weir), located 20 miles east of Yuyao County, initially had no weir soldiers. Instead, local people worked as boat trackers from time to time, operating winches to take advantage of the geographical location and earn money. However, this practice hindered the passage of official and private boats. In response to the officials' request, the government installed winches and cables at the weir and stationed two weir soldiers there to tow the boats (Z. Huang 1990). Yang Wanli wrote a poem about the weir soldiers operating the winch to pull the boats: "Two fishing boats are going opposite to each other, and the winches are automatically winding cables by themselves. When the winches stopped rotating and boats halted, then winches were operated by people" (W. Yang 2007: 1530). These local soldiers in service, including "winch soldiers", existed in Zhenzhou (Yizheng, Jiangsu), Chuzhou (Huaian, Jiangsu), and Changzhou (Toqta 1977: 4663). In fact, they were weir and sluice soldiers. Not only were there stationed local soldiers for towing boats at the weirs and sluice gates of the canal, but also at other hazardous sections of major rivers. In the first year of the Jingde Reign (AD 1004), a channel was opened to divert water from Mount Liang to the Huaihe River. "As the channel in Xuzhou was so narrow and dangerous, it was difficult for ships to sail through. Therefore, the government assigned 30 boatmen, 20 of whom were team leaders, to tow the boats" (S. Xu et al. 2014: 9612).

After the peace treaty between the Song and Jin was signed, local soldiers were assigned to tow the ambassadorial ships. "The soldiers who carried supplies were chosen to tow the Jin's envoy boats from Xuyi to Lin'an in their round trips" (X. Cao 1990). In the sixth year of the Qiandao Reign (AD 1170), Emperor Xiaozong issued an imperial edict stating that the soldiers serving as boat trackers in Huai'nan East Province for ambassadorial ships would include custodian guards without a general. "From now on, in order to meet the demand of the ambassadorial ships, the river ice-breaking soldiers and the local boat trackers of Huainan East Province will be used as boat trackers indiscriminately, and the population of custodian guards without a general under the supervision of the provincial military governor reached 1800 people" (S. Xu et al. 2014: 4430).

More of the trackers were civilians instead of soldiers. Local governments often recruited civilians to tow boats. As a prosperous transportation hub, Yongcheng County of Bozhou attracted numerous boats, resulting in a great demand for boat trackers. This situation caused significant hardship for the local people. Emperor Taizong ordered that from that day onwards, the people of Yongcheng County would be exempted from towing boats, saving over ten thousand strings of 1000 coins each year (X. Xu 1990). This exemption demonstrated the populous nature of the trackers in service. However, while Yongcheng enjoyed this special amnesty, other prefectures and counties continued to suffer from forced labor. Numerous people were involved in the service of ship towing, shipbuilding, iron smelting, construction, and civil service in Tanzhou (Changsha, Hu'nan) (S. Xu et al. 2014: 8454). In the seventh year of the Xuanhe Reign (AD 1125), the people of Jingdong Province were exempted from services like towing boats for a year due to turmoil (S. Xu et al. 2014: 8209), which provided evidence for the extensive existence of boat towing.

Both the Northern Song and the Southern Song dynasties enlisted civilian laborers to tow boats and provide diplomatic escort services. During Emperor Huizong's reign, ambassadors made annual visits to Goryeo. Villages situated along the canal in Huainan and Liangzhe provinces were compelled to send physically strong men for boat towing, with several hundred individuals being recruited from each county (*Jingkang Yaolu* 1990). Local inhabitants were burdened by the task of boat towing. Although there was an imperial prohibition, they were still required to tow boats (Toqta 1977: 11742). Whenever Goryeo ambassadors arrived or departed from Lin'an, local residents would assemble ten days prior to make preparations for boat towing (G. Li 2004). On an annual basis, the Southern Song received Jin ambassadors, who came to celebrate the New Year and the emperor's birthday. The Pingjiang Transportation Department arranged a contingent of 5314 individuals to serve as trackers, punters, and lantern-holders. Among them, 2600 individuals served as boat trackers, and an additional 150 were prepared to assist with boat towing in the event of headwinds. Furthermore, 296 trackers were assigned to tow ambassadorial boats, 150 individuals served as guards, attendants, and trackers during the banquet in Xuyi, Zhengjiang, and Pingjiang, and 240 trackers were dispatched to tow vice-ambassador boats (Y. Zhao 2013: 164–65). A total of 6842 individuals were employed for the round trips of ambassadorial boats, with the majority recruited from the local population. In the fifth year of the Qingyuan reign (AD 1199), Mao Xian, the mayor of Wengzhou, reported that commoners were used as boat trackers on the rivers of Liangzhe provinces, while soldiers were responsible for tasks on the Huaihe River. This indicates an overreliance on civilian laborers as boat trackers in Liangzhe West Province. After submitting a proposal to the court, soldiers were also employed for boat towing in the canals of Liangzhe West Province (S. Xu et al. 2014: 4440). In reality, civilians were not the sole source of boat trackers in Liangzhe West Province, whereas soldiers exclusively served as boat trackers in Huainan East Province. It was customary for Huainan East Province to use civilians as boat trackers for passing literati and official boats. In the eighth year of the Qiandao reign (AD 1172), an imperial decree was issued, "prohibiting Huainan provinces from recruiting individuals as boat trackers, except for instances involving the imperial court's dispatch of officials to celebrate the emperor's birthday, the New Year, or receiving and sending ambassadors from the northern kingdoms" (S. Xu et al. 2014: 7135). This demonstrates that civilian trackers were still utilized for ambassadorial boats.

The Song government also recruited strong men as trackers to transport military supplies or perform other tasks. In the first year of the Jingde Reign (AD 1004), Zhao Bin provided soldiers with food for shipping grains in the rivers annually and had to recruit local people as boat trackers (S. Xu et al. 2014: 9612). During Emperor Huizong's Reign, prefectures and counties along the route were required to protect the fleet carrying marbles and tow boats (S. Yang et al. 1990). Using civilians as trackers for private purposes was illegal for officials. For example, when Zhu Yanbo served as the mayor of Qianzhou, he framed the sentencing official, Li Yue, through deception. When Li Yue went to Qianzhou (Ganzhou, Jiangxi Province), Yanbo ordered his subordinate officials to send civilians to tow Li Yue's boat and then reported it to the court, accusing Li Yue of violating the law by employing civilians as trackers (T. Li 2004: 11656). There was another incident where a servant of the minister, Sun Zhongyi, traveled from Changshu to Pingjiang (Suzhou, Jiangsu). On the way, he met an official who told him, "the government wants you to tow the boat." The servant thought that the official had no official document, and was not authorized to issue such an order (M. Hong 1981: 245). These instances demonstrate that officials were not allowed to use civilians as boat trackers without an official document.

Apart from conscription, local people were often hired by local governments to tow boats. During the early period of the Northern Song Dynasty, the official cargo shipping employed many civilians as trackers. Each year, four million Hu of grains were transported from the Yangtze River and the Huaihe River to supply the capital, and the government paid to hire civilian boat trackers. In the 8th year of the Taiping Xingguo Reign (AD 983), the government did not directly recruit trackers; instead, boat owners were entrusted to recruit people based on ship staffing standards and transportation expenditures (T. Li 2004: 551). This meant that for every cargo shipping fleet, the costs of boat trackers needed to be calculated first, and then the money was paid to the officer in charge of transportation so that he could hire people himself without additional recruitment of locals (T. Li 2004: 551). In the Zhidao Reign, local soldiers were used to tow the boats, but this method was costly. Cai Xiang once said that in order to reduce the use of local soldiers as trackers, they needed to first reduce the volume of cargo shipping. It was more cost-effective to pay for recruiting civilians than to cultivate and train soldiers as trackers. Hiring boat trackers only required payment for transportation and labor costs, while training soldiers required year-round support, which would certainly cost several times more (X. Cai 1996: 388–89). Therefore, he suggested hiring more civilian trackers. In the third year of the Zhiping Reign (AD 1066), most grain transportation fleets relied on hiring local people, with each boat having only one or two soldiers on board (S. Xu et al. 2014: 7045). During the early period of the Southern Song Dynasty, boat trackers also depended on hiring civilians. "The boat trackers relied on hiring local people and then making payments to them" (S. Xu et al. 2014: 6977). However, in the fifth year of the Shaoxing Reign (AD 1135), the court changed its approach and began recruiting soldiers as boat trackers, which relieved the local people from the burden of serving as trackers (Toqta 1977: 11593), as soldiers became the primary source of trackers.

A large number of merchants, traveling by boats, could only rely on civilian trackers rather than local soldiers as trackers. Private journeys needed to hitch a lift on merchant ships. For example, when Lu You traveled to Sichuan Province, he took a merchant ship from Jiazhou (Leshan, Sichuan). The ship went upstream on the Yangtze River and mainly relied on boat towing. Zhang Shunmin, Su Zhe, Zhou Bida, and others also did the same when they sailed on the Yangtze River (C. Huang 2017). The boat trackers had to be civilians, and sometimes passengers without enough money served as boat trackers to offset their trip expenditures. In the fifth chapter of *Historical Anecdotes,* an important record about the laws, regulation system, and culture of the Song Dynasty, it is recorded that a man went from Lüliang to Pengmen (Xuzhou, Jiangsu) and gave fifty copper coins to the boatman asking for a lift, but the boatman asked for a hundred copper coins. The man said, "Would you please accept half of the expenses first, and I will tow the boat from here to Pengmen (Xuzhou) to offset the other half?" (Y. Zhao 2013: 70). Sometimes, only the original inhabitants familiar with the water conditions were capable of towing boats in dangerous torrential rivers. As Zhang Sunmin sailed through Zhaoling Sandbar, the most dangerous place in Hu'nan, the men on the boat guided the way with flags in their hands. These people were local inhabitants, also dubbed "Tanzi", who were professional trackers in the dangerous sections nearby. Boatmen could do nothing in these sections, so the locals needed to participate in sailing the boats. When official ships passed by in the rapids, they would beat drums to call the local residents to gather at the beach to aid sailing boats. When the ship sailed to Zhaoling Sandbar, they left (S. Zhang 1990). Fan Chengda sailed in the Xintan (New Sandbar), known for being the most dangerous part of the Three Gorges. Many residents dwelt on both sides of the New Sandbar, who were dubbed Tanzi and specialized in helping boats cross the rapids as their job (C. Fan 2012: 79). The two beaches, Lüliang and Baibu of Xuzhou along the Qinghe River, had local boat trackers who specialized in towing boats across dangerous sections (Toqta 1977: 2383). On the Guangji River, local people made towing boats their job (W. Han 1990). These pieces of evidence indicate that local people acted as boat trackers.

Obviously, the main source of boatmen was soldiers, mainly the local soldiers who acted as boat trackers. The other source was civilians. Helmsmen were fixed members of the boat staff, also serving as technical supervisors. Some of the trackers were fixed staff of a boat, but others were only working in specific locations. The soldier trackers for grain boats travelled on foot with these boats, while the soldiers who towed at the weirs or sluice gates of canals remained stationed there. The soldier trackers for the Jin's ambassadorial boats adopted a relay boat towing system, and the counties along the route assigned fixed soldiers for them. As for civilian trackers, some were fixed staff on the boats, while others settled in specific places, like the Tanzi (local residents who towed the boats in hazardous sections of the river).

5.1.3 The Strata and Composition of Boatmen in the Song Dynasty

In grain transportation, the highest ranking individuals responsible for management and supervision were the escort officials and convoy officers. According to the regulations governing cloth cargo shipping in the Chuan Xia region, if more than 50% of the cloth being shipped was lost, failing to meet the required quantity, severe punishments were imposed. The helmsmen and boatmen would be subjected to sixty lashes, while the convoy officers and lower-ranking officers would receive fifty lashes. Additionally, the escort officials, palace guards, and provincial officials would face fines equivalent to one month's worth of food and salaries (S. Xu et al. 2014: 7040). The helmsmen and punters were the boatmen, while the others comprised the convoy members (Y. Gong 1997: 413, 589, 592).[6] During the early period of the Northern Song Dynasty, cargo shipping was conducted under the escort and supervision of escort officials and generals from the Three Bureaus. These officials and generals were originally responsible for managing separate cargo shipping fleets, which later merged into one, jointly supervised by them (T. Li 2004: 1990). Each fleet was typically assigned an escort official or a general, but due to the higher cost of employing an escort official, the Three Bureaus often opted for one general to save expenses. However, this resulted in a shortage of generals to meet the demand, leading to a decision to replace some generals with escort officials. A new policy was introduced during the second year of the Yuanfeng Reign (AD 1079), specifying that 70% of the escorts should be officials, while generals and palace attendants should comprise

[6] According to *Bureaucracy Song Dictionary* written by Gong Yanming, "Jieji" (low-ranking officers) is a general term for various positions which are inferior to the commander-in-chief and superior to the escort leader in the local forces. The escort official or the junior military attache, is a common name for the escort officials at two different levels (named "Dashichen" and "Xiaoshichen").The palace guards are officers with no ranks.

the remaining 30% (S. Xu et al. 2014: 7047–48; Y. Gong 1997: 129).[7] Following the reform during the Yuanfeng Reign, the Three Bureaus were abolished, and escorted transportation predominantly relied on escort officials. The Southern Song Dynasty also employed junior military officers to escort cargo shipments. During the fifth year of the Qiandao Reign (AD 1069), specific criteria were set for selecting capable and intelligent escort officials when escorting Jin's ambassadorial boats from Liangzhe East and West provinces. Each ship had an assigned officer to manage it, and an additional soldier and personal attendant were appointed to oversee the crew's conduct (S. Xu et al. 2014: 7134).

The convoy people were responsible for goods on ships. Every year, grains were delivered to the imperial court from the Jiangnan and Huainan provinces, as well as other provinces, relying on the escort officials on the Bianhe River to manage, restrain the soldiers and helmsmen, and renovate the boats (T. Li 2004: 11392). The convoy members were expected to prevent the transported goods from being stolen or lost. If the escort officials checked and found any incomplete seals, stolen goods, or damage to official possessions, they could immediately apply and urge the inspectors, along with the fleet chief, to open the seal for inspection and then reseal it (T. Li 2004: 12139). In case of any loss of transported goods, the convoy people needed to compensate using their own money. Wang Anshi's wife, Madam Wu, once bought a concubine for him. She recounted, "My husband was a general in the army. When he was in charge of rice shipping, the boat unfortunately sank. The family assets couldn't offset the loss, so he sold me to pay off the debts" (B. Shao 2013: 187). As the leader of grain transportation, the convoy officials needed to undertake overall responsibility and cover the employees' wages.

The fleet chief needed to hire boatmen and pay their salaries on time (S. Xu et al. 2014: 7015). During voyages, it was common for escort officials to cheat and cut employees' wages (T. Li 2004: 11332). The fleet chief was entitled to control ship owners, helmsmen, and sailors, and to punish those who committed crimes. When the ship owners rampantly stole official properties from the goods they shipped, the fleet chief was blamed "for his blind eyes on boatman's cheating" (S. Xu et al. 2014: 7067; T. Li 2004: 11745). "When a crime was committed by a boatman who needed to be punished with flogging, the fleet chief and officers were entitled to flog him 15 strokes with a small cane." If a boatman offended the convoy official, he would be flogged 100 strokes. Those who cursed the convoy official would be put in prison for one year. The rest of the boatmen would be flogged 80 strokes for joint liability, and the troublemaker would be flogged 100 strokes. Those who fought would be put into prison for two years. Those who beat an official to a light injury would be put into prison for three years and would be exiled 250 km away from their home.

Convoy officers were not the pilots, but rather the major drivers of inland river boats were helmsmen and boat trackers. The Shao propeller was a long oar that

[7] According to *The Anthology of Laws and Regulations of the Song Dynasty* written by Xu Song and et al, generals refer to the post subordinate to the Three Bureaus, and their duties are in charge of convoying cargo transportation and official cargoes. The officers with different ranks in Three Bureaus can be promoted to the general.

functioned as both a rudder and an oar for sailing through the Three Gorges, and its controller was the helmsman, who held the top rank among the crew and was responsible for the safety of the boat. In the fifth year of the Qiandao Reign (AD 1169), Liangzhe East and West provinces continued to use helmsmen for Jin's ambassadorial ships. These helmsmen were recruited as experienced sailors from previous boats (S. Xu et al. 2014: 7134). This evidence indicates that helmsmen clearly ranked higher than the rudder controllers.

The helmsman, as the boat leader on the Sichuan Section of the Yangtze River, held the title of the third senior executive. Lu You explained in the third volume of "*Essays about My Journey to Sichuan,*" "Who were these third senior executives? The answer is the helmsmen." The Shao propeller functioned as a long oar used in fast-flowing rivers, making the Shao controller the actual helmsman. Song Qi stated, "The helmsman was called the third senior by Sichuan locals" (Q. Song 2014: 61). The old boatman was referred to as the senior and held the most influential and authoritative position on a boat, similar to the person in charge of the rudder on a seagoing vessel, namely the Shao controller (Z. Tao 1990). On Lu You's boat to Jiazhou, there was a man named Wang Baiyi. He initially took on the responsibility of recruiting sailors and later became the head of the crew. The head of the crew turned out to be the leader of the helmsmen, though he was paid slightly more than others and received more meat during the sacrifice ceremony. The head of the crew was responsible for the long oar at the bow of the boat. If there were multiple helmsmen on a boat (as mentioned above, there were four helmsmen on a horse-carrying boat with a load capacity of 700 Liao), the head of the crew held a higher social status and enjoyed more benefits than other boatmen. "Soon Zhao Qing, the boat owner, appointed his good friend as the head of the crew. This led to Baiyi losing his job and becoming so despondent that he jumped into the river." Eventually, "a swollen corpse was discovered in the water". This incident illustrated the significance of the head of the crew, whose appointment or dismissal determined the fate of others (Y. Lu 2012: 207). It is evident that the helmsman was employed by the ship owner and held the highest status among the boatmen. The leader of the helmsmen was referred to as the third senior executive or the head of the crew. As such, the helmsman held more authority than the sailors: "The boat trackers were not held responsible for losses", while "the helmsman bore the losses and compensated the government" (S. Xu et al. 2014: 6941). Over time, the term "third senior" gradually extended beyond Sichuan and became used in other regions, including southeast areas. In Zhang Xiaoxiang's work *Shipping Impeded by Wind in Wucheng,* there was a saying that "the third senior fluttered the sails repeatedly and wondered when the north wind would arrive in June" (X. Zhang 1990).

The helmsman guided the ship's voyage. When Fan Chengda's ship encountered trouble from wind at the pond's mouth and lost its way while sailing, "The helmsman shouted slogans and pulled down the iron cables, while the head crew beat the drum amidst the windy waves. The poles snapped, and the setting sun nearly merged with the waves. A considerable effort was required for the boat to cover a short distance. The sailors sometimes sought recognition" (C. Fan 1990). This suggests that the ship's commander was the third senior, while those in yellow hats were sailors responsible for operating the boat. During Fan Chengda's ship passage through the steep sandbars of the Three Gorges, it encountered a large wave and a formidable whirlpool. "The helmsman clung to the pole and shouted, desperately attempting to navigate out of the whirlpool" (C. Fan 2012: 77). It was also the helmsman who directed the ship's sailing. Yang Wanli also described a scene in which the ship, commanded by the third senior, successfully navigated perilous rapids. He pointed out that the boat trackers on the shore should not complain about their laborious efforts. The helmsmen shouted loudly, aware of the treacherous rapids that could trap the boat. They leaned back to brace against the mast and then bent down to punt with great force. In critical moments, the third senior sometimes had to take control himself: "Fear not the roaring currents through each sandbar. Sailing downstream is easier than upstream. The helmsman, lacking skills, still overcomes swift currents with just a pole" (W. Yang 2007: 446, 1350). For instance, when Huang Tingjian passed through Huangniu Gorge, "the boatmen offered pork and wine to the ox god. Two boatmen imbibed too much wine during the god-worshipping ceremony and became intoxicated under the god's blessings. The helmsman instructed them to rest for a while." They also conducted the ship's sacrifice ceremony. As Huang's boat neared Bodao County (in Yibing, Sichuan), "the helmsman prepared hairless, cleaned pigs as an offering to the military marquis" (T. Huang 2011: 440, 1566). During the sacrifice ceremony, the helmsman was responsible for flawlessly managing the ritual process (Y. Lu 2012: 202). Of course, the third senior was also a worker on the ship. If the ship did not belong to them, they remained employees on the vessel and were obliged to follow the boat owners' commands. The aforementioned quote indicated that Lu You boarded a boat owned by Zhao Qing, who had the authority to appoint the head crew.

Among ship crews, boat trackers held a lower status compared to helmsmen. Boat trackers, along with sailors, were responsible for towing the boat. The term "yellow hat" was a nickname for regular boatmen, also referred to as "pole punters". In Zhang Lei's poem, it is mentioned that "The Zhou's daughter, in her twenties, married a punter" (L. Zhang 1990). In the case of small boats, the pole punter was both the punter and the boat owner. Zheng Ta depicted the life of a pole punter's family in his poem: "Night voyages filled punters with worries about direction, the sound of oars startling the old dragon in the water; the tranquil moonlight on the water's surface rippled by the moving boat; the eldest son studying in dim light; while his daughter learned sewing by the window" (X. Zheng 1990). In this context, the pole punter served as both a sailor and the proprietor of the boat, traveling with his family on board.

The lowest status of the trackers was reflected in several aspects. On the one hand, being the lowest ranked, they received no rewards but only punishments. When convoy officials and helmsmen committed a crime, they would be demoted to lower positions. If their ranks could not be further lowered, "they would be compelled to serve as trackers for other ships". As a common practice, "if helmsmen or punters committed a crime, they would be sentenced to serve as trackers in the current fleet" (S. Xu et al. 2014: 7021). While the rewards for cargo shipping did not encompass boat trackers, they were included in the scope of punishments. In the second year of the Tianxi Reign (AD 1018), regulations stipulated that if cargo shipping from Yizhou (now Chengdu) to the southern Jingzhou was executed perfectly without any losses, escort officials would receive an award of 15 strings of 1000 coins for each voyage, and the general of the Three Bureaus would receive 10 strings (S. Xu et al. 2014: 6943). In the first year of the Tiansheng Reign (AD 1023), the regulations stated that in the event of no loss in cargo salt shipping to the capital, escort officials and convoy officers would be awarded two strings of 1000 coins each, and each vice convoy official would receive one string of coins, while helmsmen would receive 200 coins each. In the eighth year of the Tiansheng Reign (AD 1030), the awards were adjusted to 1.2 strings of 1000 coins for each escort official, 1 string of coins for each convoy officer, 800 coins for each vice convoy officer, and 400 coins for each punter (S. Xu et al. 2014: 6946, 6954). However, trackers were excluded from the list of recipients for these rewards. In the case of any loss in cargo shipping, all crew members would be punished accordingly. The Northern Song also mandated that regulations be established and applied to inland rivers. "If the grains on board suffered a complete loss during river transportation, helmsmen would be penalized with three years of military service, punters would be demoted by one rank, soldiers would receive 60 strokes of flogging, and escort officers would be demoted by two ranks." The severity of the punishment would decrease with reduced losses (S. Xu et al. 2014: 7020). In the sixth year of the Dazhongxiangfu Reign (AD 1013), regulations pertaining to mountain and river transportation were introduced (S. Xu et al. 2014: 6941). The policy specified that if cloth transported from Sichuan was completely lost, helmsmen and punters would receive 100 strokes of flogging and be sent to prisons in other provinces for detention. Convoy officials and low-ranking personnel would receive 90 strokes of flogging, while convoy escort officials would receive 80 strokes and would also be prohibited from participating in future transport escorts (S. Xu et al. 2014: 7040). Here, the individuals subject to punishment refer to boat trackers and sailors. Trackers could be beaten at the discretion of higher officials. Ye Luyi, an escort official of the Jin dynasty, urged the boat trackers to increase their speed. "He instructed a soldier to pursue and beat the trackers with a stick to encourage them to exert their utmost efforts in towing the boat" (X. Li 2013: 3548).

On the other hand, boat trackers were the most laborious people. Yang Wanli served as an ambassador to the Jin Kingdom during the frigid winter, which he described by saying, "I worried much about my frozen fingers and ears." Sailing on the canal during such a cold season, "I dared not leave the ship. Even though it was not winter but still deep autumn, I felt a chill outside. When the freezing gusts began to blow, where could I find shelter? I found no refuge and had to turn my face immediately to the shore." "I had to shut the curtain to prevent the cold air from coming in. I had to burn a charcoal furnace on a snowy night to keep warm, and the snow outside the window was already three feet deep." These quotations reveal the terrible working conditions of the boat trackers in a blizzard, where "God knows that my straw hat is leaking, but it still deliberately rains. We have to plod on the muddy road," and "our steps were like white gulls standing in the snow with cold legs, and Phalacrocorax flying away to escape the cold wind." "I felt sympathetic for the boatmen, who struggled to tow the boat wearing only straw rain capes and yellow hats." In the cold night, the boatmen could only resist the wind and snow by yelling songs: "The boatmen and the boat trackers sang songs all night." "The boatmen chanted and yelled songs to encourage themselves." "Their voices were filled with sadness and sighs; when one chanted, others joined the song." "Brother Zhang, Brother Li, let's exert our efforts and drag together." "One, two, one, two, how many states could the crescent moon illuminate?" (W. Yang 2007: 1383, 1415, 1416, 1420, 1422, 1423, 1430).[8] Chanting work songs was the only way for the trackers to relieve themselves of the long night's toil. In his poem, Yuan Shuoyou described the working conditions as follows: "The Shao and the Zha rivers merged into one near my house. Noises made by boatmen splashing water accompanied passing boats at night. The mournful songs from the ships at night were so sorrowful that they made it difficult for listeners to fall asleep. The song sobbed again and again, conveying deep sadness. The songs sounded either fragmented or continuous, all expressing the sorrow of parting… Today, while I am traveling in the Wu Kingdom, I suddenly heard the Wu folk song from the boatmen" (S. Yuan 1990). Li Zengbo once described the shouting and calling of trackers on the Sichuan Section of the Yangtze River, as "beating drums and shouting together to gather strength for propelling boats forward." "They were striving to sail in the upper reaches of the Qiantang River. At night, when the scull noises ceased, the sound of the Wu song faded in" (Z. Li 1990). As Xu Lun stated, passengers on the boat watched the passing scenery but overlooked the hardworking trackers on the bank. "Alas, nothing is perfect in the world; the diligent trackers deserve compassion" (L. Xu 1990).

The trackers had to deal with the situation of "working as trackers on the bank and boat pullers with their shins buried in the mud." "They trudged through rain, snow, and mud, like wild geese with broken feet, moving a few inches forward and then retreating a few feet back" (Y. Mei 1990; S. Li 1990). Or, "for fear of getting their clothes wet, the trackers were completely naked as they towed the boat on the snow-covered beach, enduring the cold" (W. Yang 2007: 1402). "Towing the boat was so exhausting that they worked day and night, unable to sleep until early morning." "They could not even rest at night in order to keep the boat running around the clock" (S. Hu 1990). "From winter to summer, boat trackers were far from home and finally died of old age in a foreign land" (T. Li 2004: 679). They risked their lives to tow the boats on steep banks. "Some fell from banks dozens of feet high and lost their lives instantly" (S. Qian 1990: 3969). Fan Zhongyan "encountered six frail individuals in Huainan Province. They told him that they had formed a working group of thirty people to tow boats from Tanzhou to Wuwei. Only six of them survived; the others were either dead or had fled. They had a 2000-kilometer journey to Hu'nan. The six trackers had just arrived here and were uncertain if they would make it back to their hometown alive" (T. Li 2004: 2624). Over 200 boat trackers died each year under the jurisdiction of the Baibo Shipping Department (T. Li 2004: 2108). In the Southern Song, most of them who worked on the Jin's ambassadorial ships wore shabby clothes, and some even froze to death (S. Xu et al. 2014: 3919).

---

[8] "Yellow-hat Men" discussed in Chap. 2 and mentioned by Yang Wanli in his poems both refer to boat trackers.

5.1.4 Boatmen's Work and Benefits in the Song Dynasty

5.1.4.1 Boatmen's Work and Skills

Navigating various rivers, sailors encountered diverse water conditions and unexpected winds or rains. Consequently, they required specialized experience and skills, along with the ability to coordinate with others in various tasks. As the saying goes, "when sailing boats, it is necessary to have helmsmen, anchor droppers, and sailors." This indicates that a boat requires experts in different divisions of labor (D. Zhen, n.d.).

The first skill required for sailing on various waters is knowing the information of winds and water conditions. Wind is closely related to sailing efficiency and safety. Expert boatmen can make accurate judgments based on their experience. Shen Kuo, the renowned ancient scientist, once stated, "when sailing on rivers and lakes, strong gusts are the greatest challenge. Winter winds follow a gradual evolution process, affording boatmen ample time for thorough preparation. However, in summer, the wind suddenly picks up in an instant, making boat navigation difficult. Boatmen must comprehend the patterns of seasonal winds and observe recent wind trends. Summer winds typically intensify in the afternoon. Those intending to sail must rise around 3:00 am. If the moon and stars appear bright and the sky is clear, they can proceed. However, around 9:00 or 10:00 a.m., sailing should cease to avoid potential storms" (K. Shen 2006: 190). When Mei Yaochen traveled on the Yangtze River, the boatmen shared their wind analysis with him: "A halo around the moon indicates impending wind. The boatmen conferred throughout the night. As dawn breaks, it is advisable to hoist the sails, taking advantage of the calm river to navigate the estuary" (Y. Mei 1990). When Chao Yidao's boat encountered a storm at the estuary of the Huaihe River, he was anxious, yet the boatmen remained composed. They reassured him, stating, "there's no need to fear. This wind won't last long; it will soon subside. We have encountered numerous instances like this" (Y. Chao 1990). Su Zhe's boat became ensnared by strong winds in Zhenzhou (now Yizheng, Jiangsu), and the towpath was inundated. Unable to proceed, Su sought guidance from the helmsman. They turned back with smiles, remarking, "navigating upstream or downstream depends on opportune moments," adding that "storms are fleeting, accompanied by sudden heavy rain. When the storm abates, the wind will also cease, allowing us to sail on tranquil waters" (Z. Su 1987: 1119). Lu You encountered a similar scenario while in Zhenjiang. Despite his desire to depart the Yangtze River, the boatmen declined due to contrary tides, leading them to spend the night at the estuary (Y. Lu 2012: 166). Zhou Bida's vessel encountered adverse winds in Chizhou (Guichi, Anhui). "Subtle changes in the drifting clouds prompted the boatmen to halt sailing." "After 3:00 am, a stronger westerly wind materialized, followed by a thunderstorm that caused the ship to sway violently, rendering it nearly uncontrollable" (B. Zhou 1990). These examples highlight sailors' adeptness at accurately predicting wind patterns based on experience. A direct approach involves monitoring the ship's flag. When the end of the flag points toward the bow, experienced sailors predict a tailwind.

By raising the sails and deftly maneuvering the double sculls, they guide the boat forward like a soaring arrow (L. Zhang 1990). Yang Wanli had his crew anchor the boat against a headwind on Poyang Lake. While he slept, he was roused by boatmen at the onset of a tailwind. Not letting the opportunity slip away, they propelled the boat to the lake's center with several well-aimed pole strokes (W. Yang 2007: 694). Experienced boatmen demonstrated an ability to discern varying water conditions, successfully navigating hazardous and intricate rivers. In the third year of the Xi'ning Reign (AD 1070), the Song government sought to launch grain transportation on the rivers of Shaanxi. They aimed to recruit sailors familiar with the mountainous streams in Quzhou (Qu County, Zhejiang) or those knowledgeable about water conditions in the Qutang Gorge. This was because Quzhou's mountainous streams and the Qutang Gorge of the Yangtze River resembled the Yellow River in terms of water dynamics. "As the water level in the Qutang Gorge rises, hidden sand and rocks become less perilous, but the currents become too turbulent for safe navigation." Only those acquainted with the water conditions could successfully navigate. Similar conditions may prevail along the upper reaches of the Yellow River and the Wuding River (T. Li 2004: 5210). The Hanshui River posed a challenging shipping route due to numerous sandbars threatening boats. Experienced pole punters had to be replaced by individuals familiar with the water conditions (S. Xu et al. 2014: 7006).

The second skill required is knowing how to sail a boat. As sailing is a highly professional endeavor, a novice sailor might struggle to steer a boat smoothly. For example, in the Sichuan section of the Yangtze River, where water conditions were extremely complex, few locals possessed the expertise to sail a boat. Consequently, experienced boatmen had to be recruited for grain cargo shipping, as a significant portion of the local population, four out of ten, met a tragic fate by drowning when ships capsized. To address this issue, the special Weizhao shipping troop was established after specialized training, resulting in a notable decrease in boat sinkings (Toqta 1977: 9996). In treacherous sections of the Yangtze River, such as the Three Gorges, the presence of experienced sailors proved to be of immense importance. Despite the intimidating riverbed rocks, skilled boatmen were able to navigate successfully, ensuring safe passage (Y. Lu 2012: 212). Yang Wanli's navigation of hazardous sandbars in the North River is also noteworthy; "the boatman could effortlessly punt over the riverbed, propelling the boat forward like an arrow" (W. Yang 2007: 840). Highly skilled boatmen consistently demonstrated their ability to handle challenges with ease. Warships demanded even more adept sailors. For the establishment of a formidable navy, it was imperative that soldiers possess experience as proficient boatmen. Following training in the art of combat and navigation, these soldiers would evolve into well-rounded sailors (X. Li 2013: 1293). Boatmen with specialized skills were particularly favored among military units. During the Liu Qi regime, boat construction took place in various locations including Dengzhou (now Penglai, Shandong), Mizhou (now Jiaoxian and Zhucheng, Shandong), and Huaiyang. Fearing potential looting of merchants' boats and the exploitation of boatmen and helmsmen by rivals, the Song rulers took measures to safeguard these valuable assets (X. Li 2013: 1116). In the Southern Song Dynasty, Li Quan, who held control over Shandong Province, recognized the potential of the southeast region for cultivating skilled sailors and honing water-based combat skills. Upon the arrival of rice merchants, he strategically acquired all ships and grains, instructing each helmsman to impart sailing skills to ten individuals (Toqta 1977: 13840). This tactic effectively facilitated the recruitment and training of additional sailors. While boat sailing relied not only on the boat's crew but also on boat trackers, as previously discussed, further elaboration on this topic is unnecessary here.

5.1.4.2 The Welfare of Boatmen

Boatmen employed by merchant ships and other civilian boats were also compensated promptly. As mentioned above, the head of the crew aboard Lu You's Zhaoqing-Type Boat from Jiazhou (Leshan, Sichuan) enjoyed greater benefits than ordinary boatmen. However, there is no definitive record of the benefits afforded to boatmen on civilian vessels. To illustrate, let us consider cargo shipping boats. These crews comprised both soldiers and civilian boatmen. Soldiers received military salaries and allowances, whereas civilian workers were provided with sustenance and permitted to transport private goods for profit. Boat trackers for cargo shipping received compensation from the shipping department in the form of freight, ensuring their livelihoods were secure (B. Zhao 1990). In the early Northern Song Dynasty, only soldiers serving as boat trackers for cargo shipping were given food provisions. If a soldier also acted as a helmsman, assuming responsibility for the entire crew, no additional food allowance was provided. Starting from the seventh year of the Dazhongxiangfu Reign (AD 1014), helmsmen were compensated in proportion to the trackers (S. Xu et al. 2014: 6941). Prior to the second year of the Tianxi Reign (AD 1018), soldiers' rations consisted of levied wheat from the prefectures where ships passed through, which was later replaced with polished round-grained rice (S. Xu et al. 2014: 6943). Alongside rice, funds were allocated for soy sauce and salted vegetables. During the winter, soldiers stationed along the Bianhe River were each granted 100 coins for salted vegetables and a 200 coin bonus for grain shipping (S. Xu et al. 2014: 6939). Furthermore, resources were allocated for recruiting ships and boatmen. In the second year of the Jianyan Reign (AD 1128), Jiangnan and Hu'nan provinces dispatched local soldiers to serve as boatmen. "Each individual's basic salary was augmented by one string of coins, with a 20 coin increase for daily food expenses" (S. Xu et al. 2014: 7126). By considering the aforementioned welfare standards, the expenses for local soldiers at Beishen Weir of Chuzhou and Jiangkou Weir of Zhenzhou could potentially save the labor of 27,000 soldier trackers annually, amounting to 1.3 million strings of 1000 coins in wages and 68,000 Dan of rice after the weirs were replaced by sluice gates. Based on these figures, the estimated annual per capita income of each soldier working on weirs was approximately 6 strings of 1000 coins and 31 L of rice.

The employees were compensated directly with both food and money. In the third year of the Zhenghe Reign (AD 1113), Liangzhe East and West provinces hired three boatmen at the rate of seven strings and 500 coins, along with 2.2 Dan of rice. As a result, each boatman received 2.5 strings of 1000 coins and 0.73 Dou of rice (S.

Xu et al. 2014: 7111). However, the exact duration of work for such remuneration remains unknown. In the third year of the Jianyan Reign (AD 1129), riverside military prefectures engaged helmsmen and boatmen for espionage activities. Each boat was crewed by three men, with a daily wage of 300 coins for each individual (S. Xu et al. 2014: 9486). In the first year of the Shaoxing Reign (AD 1131), the Jiangyin military prefecture recruited 114 men as reconnaissance boatmen for both land and river duties, at a cost of 900 strings of 1000 coins per month, amounting to 263 coins per day for each person (S. Xu et al. 2014: 9487). In the reign of Emperor Xiaozong, the horse-carrying boats operating on the Sichuan Section of the Yangtze River employed boatmen and sailors at elevated rates, with each individual receiving 200 coins per day for work and 300 coins for food, totaling 500 coins (S. Xu et al. 2014: 9104). During the early Northern Song Dynasty, the government initially provided the boat owner with only 20% of the hiring fee in advance. Due to the relatively meager payment, there was a shortage of boatmen, leading to the rampant theft of official goods. By the eighth year of the Yuanyou Reign (AD 1093), the advance payment to boatmen was increased to 30% (S. Xu et al. 2014: 7049). In the early Southern Song Dynasty, 70% of the shipping fees were paid to ship owners in advance, while the remaining 30% was retained by officials to compensate for potential losses of goods. By the fifth year of the Shaoxing Reign (AD 1135), transportation fees were paid in full (S. Xu et al. 2014: 7067). During the same period, the transportation fee for each Dan of grains within a journey of 1500 km was set at 300 coins. However, boat owners were responsible for preparing boats and hiring boatmen themselves. Those who opted not to accept transportation fees could potentially be promoted to higher positions based on their accomplishments in grain transportation (X. Li 2013: 3445, 3446). In the 29th year of the Shaoxing Reign (AD 1159), the boat trackers of Liangzhe West Province received compensation of two liters of rice per day (S. Xu et al. 2014: 3916).

Another benefit for boatmen, including convoy officers, was the permission to transport private goods for personal profit. This policy was established during Emperor Taizong's Reign. He directed that "the avenues for making profits are akin to rats' dens, which cannot be completely sealed off. If punters and helmsmen engage in the limited sale of private goods without obstructing their official duties, they shall be spared from punishment." Consequently, all boatmen "carried some private goods on board to earn profits. This led them to treat the ship as their own abode, promptly mending any damage to the vessel" (S. Yang 1990). This approach proved advantageous for both fulfilling official tasks and securing individual gains. The law pertaining to transfer transportation explicitly dictated that 80% of a boat's load capacity be allocated to carrying grains, with the remaining 20% designated for transporting private goods. The government provided subsidies to boat owners based on the number of sailors, which proved more financially advantageous for them than loading official goods up to 80% of the vessel's deadweight tonnage. "The number of crew members was determined based on the official goods comprising 80% of the deadweight tonnage, requiring one sailor for every 40 Dan. Wages and food expenses were provided accordingly. For the 20% allocated for private load, the crew number was determined by one sailor for every 20 Dan" (S. Xu et al. 2014: 7062). The 20%

capacity for transporting private goods was not covered by the awarding policy. In the Xi'ning Reign, a new awarding system was established. However, in the first year of the Yuanyou Reign (AD 1086), this system was abolished (T. Li 2004: 9505). This means that if additional goods were transported, the government would not inquire about or levy taxes on the private goods onboard. "Boatmen were permitted to transport private goods, and tax collectors were prohibited from causing them trouble." The authorization to use 20% of the deadweight tonnage for private goods pertained to helmsmen, not the boat owner. When Su Shi discussed the profitability of allocating 20% of the deadweight tonnage for private goods, he mentioned that "the resulting profits could meet their needs for sustenance and clothing, allowing everyone to enjoy a comfortable life and consider the boat their home" (S. Su 2010: 3497; Toqta 1977: 10815).

During the later period of the Northern Song Dynasty, 20% of the deadweight tonnage was allocated to official grains, and sailors' wages were paid with goods on board. Starting from the third year of the Zhenghe Reign (AD 1113), the Liangzhe East and West provinces ceased the regulation of reserving 20% space for private goods, making it a requirement to load grain instead. Sailors' wages were determined by the standard of "paying one boatman's wage for every 20 Dan." As the standard load capacity of boats managed by the Liangzhe East and West provinces was 300 Liao, this meant that 20% of the load capacity would amount to 60 Dan. "Consequently, each boat needed to account for the wages of three boatmen, totaling 7.5 strings of 1000 coins and 2.2 Dan of rice. Helmsmen could earn nearly the same income from transporting passengers or carrying private goods, which is why they preferred grain cargo transportation" (S. Xu et al. 2014: 7110, 7111). This practice did not cause harm to the government or individuals. Subsequently, the best practice of the Liangzhe East and West provinces gained popularity. For example, Jiangnan East Province adopted the rule of allocating 20% of the deadweight tonnage for transporting grains, and boatmen were compensated according to the crew standard of passenger boats. However, in the first year of the Jingkang Reign (AD 1126), an order was issued stating that "20% of the load capacity could not be used for carrying private goods," and no subsidies would be provided. Consequently, cargo grain shipping ceased to be profitable, leading to a lack of willingness to engage in grain transportation. In the second year of the Jianyan Reign (AD 1128), the previous practice was reinstated. This meant that 20% of the load capacity was allocated to carrying official goods, and subsidies were provided to helmsmen based on the subsidies given to passenger boats. However, the central government expressed concerns that the subsidies for the additional 20% weight were too low, potentially resulting in a loss of official goods. As a response, the central government issued a regulation that introduced additional subsidies for every ten Dan of the extra weight carried (S. Xu et al. 2014: 6977, 6978), resulting in comparatively higher wages for boatmen. In the fourth year of the Jianyan Reign (AD 1130), another change was implemented. This change stipulated that "80% of the load capacity was reserved for official goods, and one boatman needed to be hired for every 40 Dan. The remaining 20% of the load capacity was allocated for additional goods, requiring one boatman for every 20 Dan" (S. Xu et al. 2014: 6979). In the fifth year of the Shaoxing Reign (AD 1135), the regulation was reverted to the previous edition. This meant that each boat engaged in grain transportation was required to reserve 20% of the space for private goods, excluding prohibited items, and no tax on deadweight tonnage would be imposed (X. Li 2013: 1824). In the 28th year of the Shaoxing Reign (AD 1158), the space for carrying private goods was reduced to 10% of the deadweight tonnage. The regulation allowed only 10% space for private goods, and private goods exceeding 10% would be subject to taxation (X. Li 2013: 3445). Boatmen earned their incomes through wages and profits earned from private goods to support their families. In the 31st year of the Shaoxing Reign (AD 1161), Wang Gui, a boatman serving on Jin's ambassadorial boat in the Liangzhe East and West provinces, passed away due to illness in Chuzhou (now Huai'an, Jiangsu). As he had two sons, his wife implored the boat owner to permit their elder son to inherit the father's job, as they could not survive without the primary breadwinner. In response, envoy Huang Shu drafted a petition on her behalf. The following day, her elder son was enlisted as a soldier to take Wang Gui's position (M. Hong 1981: 203).

Soldiers who navigated boats in the canals of Huainan provinces and the Bianhe River were entitled to a holiday season every year. Starting from the fifth year of the Dazhongxiangfu Reign (AD 1012), the boat trackers serving as soldiers in Huainan provinces were granted a winter vacation. The cargo-shipping boats on the Bianhe River were responsible for transporting rice from transfer warehouses to the capital city. "During the winter, when the rivers were dry and unsuitable for shipping, boatmen would return to their camps, reconvening in the following spring," a period known as the "winter vacation". However, later on, the ships on the Bianhe River were deployed to the Yangtze River in winter to transfer grains to other provinces, depriving the soldiers of a proper rest. After towing cargo shipping boats in Jiangnan, Hu'nan, and other provinces and transporting grains to transfer warehouses in Zhenzhou (Yizheng, Jiangsu), Chuzhou (Huaian, Jiangsu), and Sizhou (Xuyi, Jiangsu), the soldiers would carry salt on their return journey, eventually bringing the boats back to their city, and from there, they could return home (T. Li 2004: 1762, 4534, 4535). The previously mentioned winter vacation was hardly enjoyed by these soldiers. Necessary supplies for the soldiers serving as boat trackers were supposed to be provided by the counties along the shipping route. However, as soon as the ships left their home county, other counties along the route would often refuse to provide them with food, using the excuse that these soldiers came from elsewhere. This situation led to widespread theft of rice from the boats, and the soldiers were left nearly starving to death (S. Xu et al. 2014: 7050). Only a few officials, such as Li Ruogu, showed kindness to passing-by boat trackers as fellow citizens. During his tenure as the mayor of Jiangning Prefecture, if he encountered impoverished boat trackers, he would allow them to stay in his prefecture and send them back only after they had fully recovered by the next warm spring. Such benevolent officials were hard to come by (Toqta 1977: 9739). In contrast to Li's benevolence, other officials responsible for grain transportation embezzled the soldiers' food and supplies, causing them to suffer from hunger and malnutrition (Toqta 1977: 4251). "The majority of soldiers involved in cargo shipping in the Southern Song Dynasty did not receive any subsidies. Sometimes, during snowy weather, many people died due to hunger and the harsh cold" (S. Xu et al. 2014: 3915).

5.1.5 Summary

In the Song Dynasty, the thriving transportation networks of the inland rivers attracted a substantial population of boatmen. While determining the exact total of boatmen during that era is challenging, insights can be gained from regulations governing crew allocations on grain vessels. These regulations suggest that over 150,000 boat trackers were required to transport 6.2 million Dan of rice to the capital city. Additionally, more than 200,000 boatmen were needed to convey grains from other rivers to the capital. Apart from boat trackers, grain transportation also necessitated around 20,000 helmsmen, as well as thousands—potentially even tens of thousands—of escort officials and officers. A rough estimation indicates that a minimum of 100,000 boatmen were engaged in various cargo transportation roles, with an additional requirement of over 300,000 boatmen for functions beyond grain transportation. Consequently, the total number of boatmen involved in official and private shipping in the Northern Song Dynasty could have exceeded 600,000. The population of inland shipping crews in the Southern Song Dynasty was similarly substantial.

The primary sources of boatmen in the Song Dynasty were soldiers and civilians. In the Northern Song Dynasty, boatmen engaged in cargo transportation primarily consisted of soldiers serving as boat trackers, and soldiers were also utilized in other official voyages. The "weir operators" and "sluice-gate operators" on the canals, who towed passing official or civilian boats, were also drawn from the local soldier population. The government frequently enlisted civilians to serve as boat trackers as well. Both the Northern and Southern Song Dynasties recruited and employed civilian servants for tasks such as towing ambassadorial boats, transporting military supplies, and undertaking various other responsibilities. For a significant number of merchant ships traversing the entire country, reliance was placed on civilian boat trackers, rather than local soldiers, to serve as boat trackers.

Within the cargo shipping society, escort members held the highest status, serving as supervisors and managers with comprehensive responsibility for the goods on board. If any damage or theft occurred to the shipped goods, they were required to compensate using their private properties. Additionally, they were responsible for paying wages to civilian boatmen and possessed the authority to discipline individuals who committed crimes or disrespected escort officials. Helmsmen occupied the most esteemed position and enjoyed superior benefits in comparison to other boatmen. They were tasked with steering the boat, recruiting sailors, and overseeing ceremonial rituals on board. Conversely, boat trackers held the lowest status, facing penalties without corresponding rewards. They undertook the demanding labor of boat towing, enduring exposure to harsh elements like wind, snow-covered or muddy paths, and even risking their lives.

When facing various water conditions and unforeseen winds and rains while sailing on rivers, sailors needed to possess specialized expertise, skills, and a sense of division of labor and cooperation among fellow boatmen. The primary duties of boatmen involved interpreting wind signals, understanding the water situation, and assessing wind patterns. Based on these factors, they made accurate decisions about whether to proceed with sailing or anchor the boat. Their secondary duty involved ship control, a task that also demanded professional experience. Both official and civilian ships provided food fees to their boatmen. Boatmen and soldiers on cargo shipping vessels received military salaries and subsidies, while civilian servants were given food fees and were entitled to transport private goods for personal profit. Boatmen and soldiers navigating the canals in Huainan provinces and the Bianhe River were granted a yearly winter vacation, although these benefits might not have been consistently extended to them in most cases.

As discussed above, we have unveiled the fact that the population of boatmen during the Song Dynasty was considerable. When combined with the unprecedented surge in sea trade, the entire maritime community, encompassing both boatmen and merchants, becomes even more substantial. This collective of thousands of individuals engaged in river shipping cannot be overlooked. Their distinctive way of life and psychological world deserve our dedicated study.

5.2 Boats and the Daily Livelihood of Southerners in the Song Dynasty

People on the rivers and lakes area of Jiangnan East and West provinces have been inseparable from boats since ancient times. In the Song Dynasty, the population in the south increased greatly (the south refers to the area south of the Huaihe River in this section), economic development and commercial trade were more prosperous than before, and boats were more closely related to people's livelihood. Previous studies on business, transportation, and overseas trade have all touched this question, but not directly and systematically. In the Song Dynasty, there were not only a considerable number of people who lived on boats, but many livelihoods such as fishing, trade and travel were closely related to boats. It is an important perspective to observe how an industry affects the social and economic operation to investigate the impact of boats, which were the foremost means of transportation then, on people's livelihood. This section will examine the relationship between shipping and the livelihoods of the southerners.

5.2.1 The People Who Lived on Boats in the Song Dynasty

Someone in the Han Dynasty described the life of people in the Wu Kingdom that "people in this region regarded boats as home, fish as food, oars as horses. They went ahead quickly like a whirlwind, but it's hard to order them to back" (G. Ban et al. 1962: 1376; Y. Zhao n.d.). Another quotation made by the Song people stated that "I have made a living on water since I was a child; my work was rowing the boat" (S. Su n.d.). People in the river and lake areas south of the Yangtze River and the coastal area not only lived closely with boats, but those living on a boat was numerous on inland rivers, lakes and coastal areas during the Song Dynasty. Among these people, some were water merchants, some were the fishermen fishing for a living, also some were boat dwellers to make a living by selling pearls.

During the Qiandao Reign, Zhou Bida traveled from Lin'an to his hometown Ji'an by waterway and land. When he arrived in the Gushu (Dangtu, Anhui) on the border of Taipingzhou of Jiangnan East Province, he found that more than a dozen peddlers, all of whom took the boat as their home (B. Zhou 1990). During the Southern Song Dynasty, there were boats for rice sellers on the inland river whose home was the boat in various counties that supplied grain to Hangzhou, including the old and children (Z. Wu 1980: 113). Such merchants also existed in the maritime trade. For example, In *Strange Tales of the Miraculous by Yijian*, a collection of stories from the Southern Song Dynasty by Hong Mai, tells of a merchant in Guangzhou who lived with his wife and children on a boat and kept a monkey. "The monkey was kept for a long time so that it could get along well with his family. The owner's wife had a three or four-year-old child. The monkey often held the child without any worry. One day, the merchant went ashore for business while his wife was sleeping. The monkey suddenly carried the child all the way to the top of the mast" and the child fell to his death. Hong Mai emphasized that the story "was witnessed by Zhang Zhengshu, a native of Xiangzhou, who happened to pass by there" (M. Hong 1981: 1061). Just as Bai Juyi in the Tang Dynasty described tea merchants who went to business with their wives at the head of the Xunyang River, there were also many merchants who lived on boats in the Song Dynasty.

Fishing families "who lived on boats and ate fish" in the Song Dynasty could be widely found in inland rivers, lakes and coastal areas. In Huarong County of the Dongting Lake region, the property of the fishermen was just 50 strings of cooper coins. Most of them lived on boats and traveled around on rivers. People who made a living by fishing accounted for 4/10 or 5/10 of the population (Z. Fan 2006: 90). These fishermen were known as Tanhu. Most of their produce came from lake areas." In the seventh year of the Shaoxing Reign (AD 1137), Li Jingshan, a county magistrate of Yongfeng County in Xinzhou prefecture (Shangrao, Jiangxi), wrote that the government falsely arrested "a group of fishermen who lived on their boats" for robbery, and "confiscated their boats along with all their utensils, clothing, money, food and other belongings" (S. Xu et al. 2014: 8501). These fishermen lived on boats with all their belongings on board. Yang Wanli on the canal in Danyang county region also wrote about families living on fishing boats with chickens and dogs. The fisherman's children could not endure the boredom of the long day so they wove bamboo baskets to kill time. The whole family and even the chickens and dogs were on board (W. Yang 2007: 1384). Gao Zhu's poem *Boatmen* also writes about the life of a whole family who lived on a boat: "They loaded all their possessions into the boat and sailed up and down the river for years with their descendants living at the stern near the rudder. They met acquaintances on the beach. The old man got up in the morning to observe and predict the wind, while the young woman used the flowing water as a mirror. I laughed at my drifting life, devoting my livelihood to traveling leisurely on the water" (Z. Gao 1990). On the Baishui River in Fuzhou, Fujian Province, there was an ethnic family called "Baishuilang," who were also called "Yacht dwellers" because they "lived on the boat and by the sea." It was said that "they were the descendants of Lu Xun and scattered on the sea" (K. Lang 1990: 7839). Cai Xiang also talked about the water living groups in Fuzhou that "on boat near the water of Futang county, the whole family lived on the same boat all the year round, eating, illness, and marriage; they never left there" (X. Cai 1996: 621). Their life was completely on the boat. It can be seen that coastal area also had many people "who lived on their boat as a home".

The most typical population among "people living on boats" in Guangnan provinces were pearl collectors who were called "the Dan people" or "pearl collectors". "Those people in Guangnan East and West provinces lived in valleys that were not affiliated with any prefecture or county were also referred to as Yao people, and those on boats were dabbed as Dan people" (S. Chen 2006: 116). They were a large group. Liu Chang, during the Five Dynasties period, "employed thousands of them a day to collect pearls for the government" (X. Li 2013: 3352). In this quotation, they pearl collectors for the government. To improve their life, Kong Yanzhi, transportation officer of Guangan West Province ordered the dissolution of the master-servant relationships so that "600 pearl collectors could work for themselves in the Qinzhou, Lianzhou and Leizhou Prefectures" (G. Zeng 1990). Huang Juan, transportation officer in Guangnan East Province reportedly "exempted tens of thousands of pearl collectors along the coast from mandatory county service work" (X. Zhu 2010: 4281). It was evidenced that Guangnan East and West provinces had at least tens of thousands of families.

Pearl collectors' life had two basic characteristics. The first was they lived on boats. People during the Song Dynasty referred to "coastal people living on boats as Dan dwellers" (G. Zeng 1990). The living feature was not only living in the bay, but living on the boat. That is why they were called "pearl collectors on the boats" (T. Li 2004: 6744). A quotation says that "the Dan people were those earn their living on the sea" (S. Chen 2006: 116). "The Dan people were an ethnic minority living on the sea, who turned boats into their houses (C. Fan 2012: 128). "For them, the boat was a room and the water was like land. They lead a floating life on waters." Whole families would live on boats for generations. "Their children were born on boats, grew up, worked and lived there for generations" (T. Cai 2008: 240). "A couple would live under the boats canopy would have as many as ten children all the while staying on the boat. Mothers would tie a soft cloth so they could swim freely; they would also tie a long rope attached to a piece of wood to a child who could crawl so that if he fell out of the boat he could be pulled out of the water. Children learned to walk on the deck of the boat. When a child learned to walk, he was taught how to dive into the water. All this was regarded as a common thing" (Q. Zhou 1999: 115).

The second characteristic of the Dan people was to make a living on the water. In *Dan dwellers,* Yang Wanli described "their life as arranged by god as part of his aquatic life. They learned to travel on rivers. They cooked fish and crabs. They did not know what white rice tasted like. They twisted plantain fiber into thread to make cloth and did not use silk or wool" (W. Yang 2007: 813). Their livelihoods came from the sea by fishing (T. Li 2004: 6744). "Fishing was their traditional occupation" (T. Cai 2008: 240). "They earned their living by collecting sea treasures" (C. Fan 2012: 128). Zhou Qufei wrote that "there were three kinds of Dan people in Qinzhou, Guanxi Province. The first were fishermen. The second was the oyster and pearl collectors who were able to dive to the bottom of the sea. The third logged in the mountains" (Q. Zhou 1999: 119). But they mainly earned a living from the sea. In Guangxi, most of them were pearl collectors. "Diving into the sea, they were able to find oysters which only they knew how to find (C. Fan 2012: 128). The most productive place in the sea was called "Zhuchi" (The Pool of Pearls). "They would gather dozens of boats loading with their food supplies at the pearl pool at a given time. A stone, called the fixed stone, would be lowered to the bottom attached to a rope. The pearl collector would use this as a guide. A second rope would be tied to his waist. Then he would dive hundreds of meters to collect the oysters. When he could no longer hold his breath, the pearl collector would pull on his rope so that the people on the boat could pull him up. Due to hypoxia, they often lost consciousness and took a long time to revive. Sometimes they would hemorrhage from "the seven apertures in the head" (T. Cai 2008: 240–41). "More seriously could suffer broken limbs or even death" (Q. Zhou 1999: 259).

As they dwelt on waters and knew little about pearls trading, the Dan people "did not understand the value of the pearls they collected at great risk. Sometimes the pearls would be traded for a few liters of liquor by unscrupulous dealers. After the dealers obtained the pearls, they would be divided into grades and sold in a nearby city. By the time they were traded in the capital the price had increased immeasurably" (Q. Zhou 1999: 116). *Selected Works of Zeng Minxing* tells the story of a sugar importer named Peng who was coming back from overseas. He had stopped his journey on an island. In the scorch summer, most of the local Dan people were drinking water to cool themselves. Peng gave them some sugar. Suddenly, a dozen Dan people came forward reaching out their hands. Peng put sugar into their hands and they rewarded him with pearls. Peng received many pearls that day" (M. Zeng 2008: 204). It is clear that "Dan dwellers lived humble lives. Their wives and children would share a handful of rice. When their boats were docked, their children gathered to play on the beach as naked as otters" (Q. Zhou 1999: 116). Not only the Dan people led such a life, but also those living on the boats did so. "Middle and upper class were rare among those who lived on boats. Their livelihoods were dangerous; fatherless families were common" (G. Liao 1990). They "ate simple meals of shrimp and vegetables unaware of the more elaborate elements of Chinese cuisine. They wore simple, coarse clothes unaware of bright, beautiful silks. The women used thorns for hairpins and were unaware of carmine powder make-up. They used matting for protection against the wind and rain unaware of the comfort of a large house with large and quiet rooms. They had no knowledge about the coziness of spacious houses" (X. Cai 1996: 621). As mentioned above, Tanhu families (fishermen families) on the Dongting Lake were considered middle class with just fifty strings of 1000 coins." There were no rich people making a living on the water.

"People who lived on boats were considered subjects of the emperor" (T. Cai 2008: 240). The Song rulers provided protection and relief to Dan dwellers. In the second year of the Dazhongxiangfu Reign (AD 1009), "bandits raided the Dan dwellers and stole their rice in Haiku, Qinzhou Prefecture. Li Wenzhu, the village chief of Ruhong, led a detachment of soldiers on swift boats to give a surprise attack to the Dan dwellers" (T. Li 2004: 1608–09). In the fourth year of the Yuanfeng Reign (AD 1081), the government "sent grants of grain and money to Yizhou, Anhua and other prefectures following several years of bad harvests and unusually harsh winters to prevent starvation and unrest" (S. Xu et al. 2014: 9841). The Dan dwellers were included in this relief effort although, given their drifting nature, they made the relief difficult to manage. "The Dan dwellers were not affiliated with any town or county. Their life was one of instability that made them difficult to control" (S. Huang 1990). But the Song Dynasty never gave up on the idea of controlling them by seeking to attach them to the land (Q. Zhou 1999: 116). First, they were attached to a local landlord. Emperor Shenzong decreed that "poor people should be under the protection of a local landlord as a way to prevent hunger, poverty and homelessness. The people who lived on boats were covered by this" (S. Xu et al. 2014: 6934). One requirement was that "if the people living on boats needed to travel they had to inform their local lord about their destinations. For pearl-collecting Dan dwellers, pearls could be used to pay for that protection. This conduct was good for preventing the pearl collectors from being cheated by foreigners in trading pearls." "Whenever they went out to the sea, they should inform the local landlord." "And this decree was released to the coastal prefectures" (T. Li 2004: 6744). This indirect method of social control proved not only beneficial to both those living on boats and the local lords also to the central government. This method also allowed the Dan people to collect pearls independently, and "entitled the Dan people in Qinzhou, Lianzhou and other prefectures to build own boats for collecting pearls in the sea" (Toqta 1977: 4583).

Emperor Shenzong "created administrative units of five to ten households along waterways that would oversee people living on boats" (Toqta 1977: 298). At the end of the Xianchun Reign, the imperial court once recruited the Dan dwellers as soldiers from Guangnan East Province (Toqta 1977: 4583). Occasionally, prefecture governments would impose a work-levy on Dan dwellers. In August of the fourth year of the Jiatai Reign (AD 1204), the imperial government ordered county officials "not to impose a work-levy on Dan dwellers" (S. Xu et al. 2014: 8363). Huang Qing, as already noted, canceled the work-levy of tens of thousands of Dan dwellers. Wu Yide also exempted Dan dwellers from "additional taxes" (D. Zhen, n.d.). Dan dwellers had paid tributes in pearls since the beginning of the Song Dynasty. In the 26th year of the Shaoxing Reign (AD 1156), an imperial edict "suspended Lian prefecture's pearl tributes because of reports that pearls had become difficult to obtain and to do so could be life threatening. Whether the pearls should be contributed was decided by the Dan people themselves" (X. Li 2013: 3352). Although they were periodic and local exemptions, these actions convey that the imperial government sought to control the Dan dwellers rather than ignore them.

5.2.2 Boats and Fishing of the Southerners

Many people living on waters depended on fishing for their life, and the same was true across the country. "Fishing boats along the Yellow River in Hebei Province were previously banned. When the imperial court heard that people were mostly supported by subsidies, they lifted the restriction" (T. Li 2004: 1646). The plain of Taihu Lake was crisscrossed by rivers. Residents "dug small pools by riverbanks. And they built houses over the pools and hid boats there." "When they saw flags of official boats coming, the fishing boats were rushing to the reeds. Even in the reed, the boats were still wet with rains. But the ships could keep dry with the shelter of houses" (W. Yang 2007: 1476). *Fisherman's Poem* by Zhang Yunsou described the life of fishing households on the Leijiang River. "My home was on the bank of Leijiang River before which the green rivers connected. The number of small boats was more than that of horses, the fishermen in river were like farmer farming on land" (Y. Lu 2012: 7). On both sides of the Xiangjiang River, there were also fishermen (S. Yang et al. 1990). On Juzizhou in the Xiangjiang River, hundreds of the residents were fishermen (S. Zhang 1990). "There were also fishermen on the Jialing River in Sichuan Province." "Every day, they would tow their boats to Jiangnan provinces, and sit on rocks to fish" (M. Hong 1981: 378). Yang Wanli took a boat to pass through Anren County, and saw "a fishing boat carrying two children, they put away the bamboo rod and oars; then they went into the boat."(W. Yang 2007: 1796). Other poets also described the lives of river fishermen. "Making a living by fishing; they gradually added thatches on the roof when it was leaking rain" (Y. Xue 1990). "When the fisherman fell asleep, and the 3-foot-long fish were put in the boat" (X. Cai 1996: 42). "The mountains and the water stretched boundlessly. Farmers and fishermen shared the same river." "The path runs into a flat plot in the mountain, and a boat was anchored by a rock for the night… Fish and shrimps were ample in the twelfth Lunar month, the chicken and ducks were the most delicious in a harvest year" (R. Peng 1990). It is unknown which place was described by the poet here. But it was a common sight of crisscrossed rivers in the south region of the Yangtze River.

Canals were filled with fish. When Zhang Shunmin sailed in the northern section of the Huainan Canal, he caught fish, shrimp, crabs and clams for his daily meals (S. Zhang 1990). Lu You on the west Zhejiang Canal saw schools of fish and crabs. And people in small boats knocked on the side of his boat to sell fish very cheaply (Y. Lu 2012: 160–62). A large number of people made a living by fishing along the river. When Yang Wanli passed through Gaoyou (now Gaoyou, Jiangsu), he saw "fishermen were weaving silver grass in the houses on both sides. Back to the sun, frost on the boat canopy has not melted. Then my boat passed by Guowang Pavilion and I stayed in the boat for the night. It was so noisy that I couldn't fall asleep. All I could hear was splashing sounds of fishing boats in the water." At night Yang heard the sounds of fishing while during the daytime he saw the fisherman hid his hands in his sleeves on the boat, and the boat was sailing so fast as if it were flying" (W. Yang 2007: 1397, 695, 1500).

The affluent fish resources were evidenced by the records made by the Song historians. At that time, the Yangtze River was full of fish, and people there mainly earned their living from fishing or trading fishes as their secondary incomes. When Lu You went to Sichuan on the Yangtze River, he saw Gushu Stream merging into the Yangtze River in Taipingzhou with abundant fish. "Fishes were so populous in the stream that they kept bursting out of the water sometimes, just like silver knives under the setting sun. Numerous fishermen devalued fish on the market". "The fish can be seen clearly. And the fishermen built houses on the south bank of the river." In the Taipingzhou (Dangtu, Anhui) on the Yangtze River, we can see "fishermen pulling nets on the rocks, as was painted in a beautiful picture." "Schools of fish, silver in color and as big as silvery pomfrets, were seen swimming when the boat docked at Meigen Harbor of the Yangtze River. In Chizhou, "the carps with golden scales and vermilion tails were delicious." When passing through Dongliu County, suddenly a big fish with a green back and a vermilion belly jumped up to the helm, to the height of three feet. In Yangluobo of Huangzhou (Huang'gang, Hubei), populous fishermen devalued fish greatly. A hundred coins worth of fish can satisfy twenty people. Because fish were big, it was difficult to buy small fish to feed a cat." In the Jinjifu of Ezhou (Wuchang, Hubei), the breams could weigh five kilograms. Sturgeons clustered there like a small county of people. The residents there mostly relied on selling preserved fish. In Shishou County, numerous big fish swam in the water. At the place named Gangbu on the branch of the Yangtze River, the Dunhe river, more than twenty families were drying nets on the low fences. The tall willow trees and the setting sun structured a beautiful picture. Small boats were sailing frequently, just as we see in a famous painting. There were more than twenty fishing families in counties below the Dunhe River. So abundant supply made fish very cheap. In Huangzhou (Huang'gang, Hubei) along the Yangtze River, fishermen's house were closely linked (Y. Lu 2012: 176–203). Zhou Bida, in Chizhou (Guichi, Anhui), saw hundreds of fishing boats in the turbulent waves catching puffer fish (B. Zhou 1990). What Lu You and Zhou Bida saw was common for the residents along the river.

The life of lakeside residents also was closely related with fishing. Beyond Qingcao Temple on the Dongting Lake, the inspector of border security and ten other residents became fishermen. In southern Baling Prefecture, the water was covered with nets, stretching as far as fifty to one hundred meters, just like a huge wall" (S. Zhang 1990). On his way to Liangzhe West Province, Cai Jing sailed past Xinkai Lake and saw fishing boats going back and forth. He bought 20 fish with 30 cooper coins (T. Cai 2008: 195). Many people earned their living from fishing on the Dongqian Lake in Mingzhou (Ningbo, Zhejiang), and the local governments categorized five hundred households around the lake into four districts (J. Luo et al. 1990: 5152).

In the Luzhou's Jiaohu Lake district, the government made a regulation that "4500 strings of 1000 coins was set a goal to levy on the fishermen therein the second year of the Chunxi Reign (AD 1175), then one third of revenues was reduced and the other two thirds would be levied on the fishermen there" (S. Xu et al. 2014: 8648). There was a five-kilometer-long lake in north Hongxian County (Sixian county, Jiangsu) with an abundance of toadfish, enough to supply to neighboring areas (S. Zhang 1990). Once, Su Zhe sailed in the Liangshan lake in the evening. "When the moon shed light, the surface of lake was like silver. Laid down, I heard the faint sound of the oars, and fishing song singing in antiphonal style" (Z. Su 1987: 141). Evidently, the residents of the large lakes in the north and south regions were engaged in fishing or made a living by fishing.

Hubei Province was blessed with the most lakes. "When fishing boats were forced to carry cargoes, their owners would hide them among desolate water region to evade the official tasks of carrying grains" (X. Liao 1990). In Hubei, "10–20% of the people relied on lakes for fishing in almost all the prefectures and counties", that is to say, 10–20% of the total population made fishing as one of their important occupations. Some lakes were the ancestral property of fishermen. In the lunar month of November, the lake owners cannot catch fish by themselves. Traders from Jingzhou, Xiangzhou (Xiangfan, Hubei), Huainan West, Jiangnan East, and Hunan provinces came with fishing nets. They had negotiated a contract with the owners, and gave the lake owners an equal share of the profit. Lake owners could earn thousands of strings of 1000 coins at most or hundred strings of 1000 coins at the lower end by selling fish. The government acknowledged that fishing lakes were private property similar to cultivated land. Reeds and fish in the lakes of Hubei Province were officially confirmed to be private properties. The government took less than one tenth of the gain, and the lake owner kept the rest. Since anyone could fish in the lake at their wills, could reeds and crops in the lake areas be harvested and owned by them freely (G. Huang 1990)? Private ownership of lakes and fish was not unique to Hubei. In Jiangnan West Province, a wide lake was called Zhao's Pool, "Zhao, the richest man in the village, owned all the profit of the lake. Hundreds of fishermen were his slaves" (B. Zhou 1990). So if the lake was private, the fish were too.

Fishing also played an important role in the livelihood of coastal residents. Xu Luqing said, "the wealthy coastal dwellers who were familiar with the dangers of sea, could boss the boat owners with the profits from sea" (L. Xu 1990). The "profits of sea" were nothing more than trade, fishing and salt. Of the seven prefectures in Liangzhe East Province, four of them were near the sea, so they are salt-producing areas. Dozens, even hundreds, of people gathered together to sell salt illegally, or to collectively transport salt in large boats" (X. Zhu 2010: 821, 822). More people engaged in fishing. "The residents on banks of crooked rivers in Liangzhe provinces lived by fishing" (K. Lang 1990: 7939). Coastal dwellers in Liangzhe provinces were mostly engaged in fishing, and familiar with the fishing rules for various fish in their seasons. March and April were the season for croakers in Mingzhou (Ningbo, Zhejiang). In March and April every year, professional fishermen competed to catch the fish, which was called Yang Mountain croakers, at high tide. The boatmen went out to fish in an alliance of the seven prefectures. There were millions of boats". Spring was the time for fishing. "Every spring during the three leap tides, fishermen raced to catch the fish, which was called 'spring catch'". Thirty-seven species of fish and more than 20 other kinds of sea creatures were recorded in *Baoqing Period Chronicles of Siming* (J. Luo et al. 1990: 5041). Evidently, the fishery in Mingzhou was flourishing. The boats built in Wenzhou shipyards had to be transferred to the mainland. "The sailors needed for each ship came from coastal counties, whose occupation was fishermen" (Y. Lou 1990). History records states that "Wenzhou and Taizhou had their own fishing boats" (S. Xu et al. 2014: 8370). Coastal ship owners in Fujian also depended on fishing and trade as an important livelihood. During the Northern Song Dynasty, seagoing vessels were pressed into service on three separate occasions. In order to reduce the impact of conscription on fishing, the Southern Song Dynasty ordered the boat owners to fish only within their prefectures (X. Zhu 2010: 1238). Coastal fishermen were also called Cao Dwellers. When those Cao Dwellers were prevented from fishing and couldn't make a living, they tended to become robbers (A. Wang 1990). That became their only means of making a living. In Huai'nan East Province, coastal people also survived by fishing. In the seventh year of the Qiandao Period during the Southern Song Dynasty (AD 1171), the general of the Gaoyou and Wufeng armies requested the complete eradication of sea-going vessels in Yangjia Village, but Emperor Xiaozong denied this because of concerns about obstructing fishing (S. Xu et al. 2014: 7134). Some coastal dwellers both farmed and fished. In Yongjia County, land owning ship owners appointed coastal civilians to serve as sailors on each ship from different counties. Fishermen were unwilling to perform such service (Y. Lou 1990).

5.2.3 Boats and the Trade and Entertainment of the Southerners

Boats were the most effective vehicles for common people and merchants engaged in commercial trade. The East and West Mountains, two islands near Dongting, in Taihu Lake "were impossible to reach without a boat". The local residents' daily life was inseparable from the trade on the water. They "grew citrus, mulberry and crops to be sold off the islands." The highly commercial crops they grew, citrus and mulberry, had to be transported by boat. In the second year of the Shaoxing Reign (AD 1132), as the lake was frozen in winter, "rice boats were not available. Most of the residents on the islands starved to death" (C. Zhuang 2008: 63). Residents there could not survive without trade on the water.

Trade was also an important means of livelihood for coastal residents. During the Southern Song Dynasty, the imperial government pressed civilian ships in Fujian into service in turns for coastal defense especially along the Liangzhe coast. This was done on a three-year rotation with one year for defense and two years for maritime trade. Some minsters suggested that "ship-owners who left their provincial waters to avoid this military service should be punished by having their ships confiscated." During the two-year period when ships were not on duty for coastal defense, ship-owners were restricted to trading in their own province and could not voyage to other areas" (S. Xu et al. 2014: 7128). Zhou Bida called for the requisition of ships from Fujian during three separate periods. They "would be informed six months ahead of time so that they could fully prepare for it." "Only when they were set free from coastal defense, could they do business again" (B. Zhou 1990). This suggests that maritime trade was a common livelihood for people along the coast of Fujian because military service would cause middle or lower class families to lose their source of income." "They should be notified ahead of time and being allowed to make preparations by the coast to offer them convenience for business." It should be noted that "all shipbuilding in Zhangzhou, Quanzhou, Fuzhou and Xinghua Prefectures in Fujian was a strictly civilian affair aimed at trade and all trade was a civilian activity" (S. Xu et al. 2014: 8365). Many scholars have studied the private nature of maritime trade during the Song Dynasty (J. Ge 2013: 179–200; C. Huang 2003) so we will not repeat their efforts here.

Overall, water transportation and trade was essential during the Song Dynasty without which the social economy could not function normally. From the rice-carrying boat trade, we can see the importance of water transportation and best by examining how different regions depended on rice boats. The differences of geographical environment and economic structure in the Song Dynasty resulted in some regions' stable dependence of grain on others, which needed to be offered by trade. For example, Jiankang Prefecture of Jiangnan East Province, "was so populous that more than 2000 D*an* of grains could consumed every day. Without a rice reserve, all relied on trade." "If the rice-carrying boat didn't come for one day, the price of rice soared" (Y. Zhou 1990: 1686–87). In riverside prefectures of Jiangnan East Province, the Jiankang Prefecture was not the only case. With barren land and poor people, the Nankang Military Prefecture's grain harvest could not meet their need for rice. They relied on rice transported from upstream areas (X. Zhu 2010: 925). "Every year, the rice-carrying ships sailed down the river. The supplies for the riverside prefectures in Jiangnan East Province relied on imported from other province", which means the grains in need came from Jiangnan West Province (S. Yang et al. 1990).

Large cities, like Lin'an the capital city in the Southern Song Dynasty, were dependent on importing food and other life necessities from other provinces via shipping and trade. As the saying of the Song people goes, "shipping on the river, boats were the most effective vessels" (D. Nai 1982: 14). Because shipping was the most convenient way of transportation in Lin'an, which gathered so many boats there. Boats on the Xiatang, Guantang, and Zhongtang rivers could make a round trip within a day, which witnessed the busy transportation. Ships shuttled every day as water traffic was the most convenient way in and out of the capital including officials and merchants. Most of the boats anchored in the north of the city (Z. Wu 1980: 113). There was a proverb about Lin'an which said, "Vegetables were carried though the east gate, water from the west gate, firewood from the south gate, and rice from the north gate." This meant that "the area around the city's east gate had been used as vegetable farms. Its west gate was utilized to transport water into the city on small boats. Firewood was shipped to the south gate from Fuyang and Yanzhou Prefectures in Jiangsu; and rice boats entered the city via the north gate from Suzhou and Huzhou prefectures" (B. Zhou 1990).

During the Song Dynasty, the coastal areas of Liangzhe East Province and Fujian Province were part of a commodity trading network that relied on rice from Liangzhe West and Guangnan East provinces. "Guangnan provinces were net importers of rice, which was shipped by merchants all the yea round" (X. Zhu 2010: 1117). And Guangnan West Province was a net exporter of rice to Guangnan East Province for its competitive price. Merchants bought rice at lower price and shipped it to Panyu of Guangnan East Province for profits" (Q. Zhou 1999: 176). Guangnan East Province was also an exporter of rice, but Liangzhe East and Fujian provinces were net importers of rice. Guangnan East and West's rice would be transported to Siming (in Liangzhe East Province) by boat down the river" (X. Zhu 2010: 1177). Mingzhou of Liangzhe East Province relied heavily on this trade, "rice boats crowded there along the river" (X. Zhu 2010: 793). "As the land in Fujian was ill-suited for farming rice, people there relied on imported rice from Liangzhe and Guangnan East provinces, any disruption to this supply chain would result in starvation" (S. Yang et al. 1990). "So in densely populated and less arable Fujian, rice had to be imported from Liangzhe and Guannan East provinces on the boats" (S. Yang et al. 1990). The striking feature of grain supply in the regions south of the Yangtze River was that the importer in the central areas need to import grains from the two sides of the Yangtze River, that is to say, Guangnan East Province and Liangzhe West Province need to supply Fujian and Liangzhe East provinces rice. Hainan Island's four prefectures, which were then under the jurisdiction of Gaungnan West Province, were not food self-sufficient and also depended on rice imports from the mainland (C. Huang 2016).

The water-borne rice trade was even more important in times of famine or war. It often became necessary to encourage an expansion of it. In the first year of the Xuanhe Reign (AD 1119), because of the drought in Huainan, the imperial government encouraged merchants "to ship rice by exempting boats carrying it from the deadweight tonnage tax from adjacent areas and prefectures along rivers" (S. Xu et al. 2014: 8022). This conduct was to attract more rice traders. At the beginning of the Song Dynasty, "refugees in Huainan and Huaibei provinces relied exclusively on rice trade to recover". Emperor Xiaozong ordered that "rice merchants' boats should not be exempted from the deadweight tonnage tax, and they were levied taxes in accordance with the old regulations" (S. Xu et al. 2014: 7132). At the beginning of Emperor Ningzong's Reign, Huainan and Liangzhe suffered from droughts and flooding, while Jiangnan West and Hu'nan provinces had good harvests. The imperial government deemed that direct aid, where they purchased rice and transported it, "would be cost-prohibitive because of the extra expense of transportation." So they sought to encourage the rice imports to those places by limiting rice trade in the afflicted areas along the Yangtze River, and by exempting rice-carrying boats from the dead tonnage tax (S. Yang et al. 1990).

When Zhu Xi acted as the county magistrate in Nankang Military Prefecture, "a drought caused crop failure in Jianchang and Duchang Counties. To deal with the resulting food shortage during the harvest period, Nankang Prefecture requested miscellaneous tax exemptions for its boats and recruiting rice-carrying boats to dock. These measures attracted merchants to meet the demand" (*Huian Xiansheng Zhuwengong Wenji Bieji* 5005, 5006). During Emperor Xiaozong's Reign, a disaster struck Shaoxing, Wuzhou, and Quzhou prefectures. Liangzhe East Province sent officials to buy grain from Liangzhe West Province, while also "sending officials to the coast of Fujian and Guangdong to recruit merchants" (X. Zhu 2010: 940). "Whenever Wenzhou and Taizhou failed to have a good harvest, they all relied on grain transported by ships from the western areas of Zhejiang to roughly meet their demand" (Song Shi Quanwen 2005: 1766). Without merchant ships undertaking the long-distance grain trade, the disaster-stricken areas would have found it difficult to survive.

In addition to fishing and trade, boats were interwoven into many parts of life for those living along the water. "In Autumn when crops were ripe, people from Liangzhe provinces sailed with their families to the upper reaches of the Huaihe River to harvest grain. Then they returned home with the payment in rice" (X. Li 2000: 166). This kind of seasonal labor movement depended on boats. "Some residents living in the field also depended on boats for daily activities. With house and land in the middle of field, they dug small canals in order to ship and dock more conveniently. The Song people called the place where boats docked as a *Bang*, meaning a brook" (S. Yang et al. 1990).

Boats were also important for recreation and culture in South China. In the Song Dynasty, following a custom that dated to the third century, people participated in boat to commemorate the death of Qu Yuan on Dragon Boat Festival on the fifth day of the fifth lunar month (M. Zhu 2003: 479). The boat race was also held in Manye of Xizhou Prefecture in the former Chu Kingdom (F. Zhu 1990). In fact, whole regions, especially in the south, held the boat race. Wenzhou was particularly "fond of rowing competitions. They would race on Huichang Lake" (M. Zhu 2003: 148). Fujian, in addition to the Dragon Boat Festival competition, held boat races on the Shangsi Festival (the third day of the third lunar month) (K. Lang 1990: 8249). Ganshui Town in western Zhejiang Province had a boat race on Yongan Lake to mark the arrival of spring (T. Chang 1990: 4662). During the Northern Song Dynasty, "a boat race was held in Jinming Lake in Kaifeng every year" (S. Xu et al. 2014: 8286). In the Southern Song Dynasty, "West Lake in mid-spring and Zhejiang in the middle of autumn also held boat races. The participants' agile movements deserved to be watched" (D. Nai 1982: 14). Emperors Taizu and Zhenzong repeatedly tried to ban the races to prevent the profit competition among different local powerful groups (T. Li 2004: 88, 194, 289, 1067). During the Southern Song Dynasty, Huang Zhen, Fuzhou Prefecture magistrate, forbade boat racing and burned more than one thousand and three hundred boats (Toqta 1977: 12993). However, the tradition always prevailed. Some officials even encouraged it. "People in the Wu Kingdom preferred to race across the river." When Fan Zhongyan acted as the prefecture mayor in Liangzhe West Province, he permitted boat racing (K. Shen 2006: 91). Some boats were intended strictly for pleasure and travel. On West Lake "there were hundreds of such boats. The boats with load capacity of 1000 Liao, and at the length of over 60 meters, could accommodate 100 people. The boats with a load capacity of 500

Liao, at the length of over 30 meters, could carry nearly 50 people. And some others with a load capacity of 200 - 300 Liao, at the length of less than 30 meters, could accommodate nearly 30 people (Z. Wu 1980: 110)." The emperor's royal boat "Big Dragon Boat", and prime ministers and their attendants' big boat were included" (Sishuiqianfu 1990). These traveling boats had fine names in spite of their sizes, such as "Boat Fairy", "Boat Wind", "Boat Snow", "Boat Smoke. " (H. Zhou 1994: 521–522). There were also many small boats to provide tourists with various services. Boats served passengers with fresh fruit, greeted them with tea ceremony. The boats also carried traders, prostitutes, folk artists and the women conducted god warship ceremony by burning incense for others. On some boats, people could enjoy Guban (popular instrumental ensembles), Shualing (folk entertainment consisting mainly of singing, with dancing), Chanqu (folk singing), Touhu (pot casting) and Dadan (an ancient ball game, hitting the ball into a hole), and other varieties of entertainment. The boats came voluntarily here without being summoned. If a boat was hired, "the master would prepare all. In the early morning, they went out boating, and hired others to work (Z. Wu 1980:110)."

Southerners, especially those in Jiangnan provinces and coastal areas, mainly traveled by boats. People in other areas also relied on them for long-distance travel. Mei Yaochen and Zhang Lei in the Song Dynasty described the Jiangnan people's travel, "I just knew that northerners and southerners had different habits; travelling by carriage can't compare with that by boat." "The Chu kingdom was known for numerous rivers and lakes, as well as low-lying land, so they preferred to travelling by boats. So horses were low in function as humble dogs" (Y. Mei 1990). Not only merchants, civilians earned their living from waters, together with officials, scholars, monks and ordinary people left numerous records from their distinctive perspectives when they travelled on water with their distinctive lifestyle, which enriched the descriptions about the society and will be discussed in other section.

5.2.4 Summary

With the economic development and population growth during the southern Song Dynasty, boats were the most important means of transportation and had a close relationship with people's livelihoods. There existed a considerable number of people who lived on boats in inland rivers, lakes and coastal areas. Their whole families and all their belongings were loaded on the boat. Their living was supported by gains from water. Of such groups, the most typical were the Dan dwellers who were isolated from the land, lacked market sense, and lived in a poor situation. Although the government regarded them as subjects to the emperor, and treated them less strictly with some administrative measures, such as establishment of households and servitudes, there was no systematic and stable direct management.

Many waterfront dwellers made a living by boats. Whether along the Yangtze River and major inland rivers, around major lakes, or in coastal areas, many residents were engaged in fishing. For many it was the only livelihood. According to the records, the Yangtze River, the Dongting Lake and others were blessed with affluent fish, and the large population of fishermen turned fish prices lower. Coastal residents also developed seasonal fishery production rules.

In the Song Dynasty, the commodity economy flourished. From the perspective of whole country, the transportation and trade carried out by boats contributed to the social and economic operation. The livelihood of people in the south during the Song Dynasty was closely related to markets, and boats were the main means of transportation for people engaged in commercial trade. Some islanders and waterfront residents regarded trade as an important source. When food shortages occurred in some regions, the long-distance shipping trade was a must to meet the increased for food. If famine occurred, shipping mattered a lot. In addition to fishing and trade, many aspects of waterfront life, such as production, travel and recreation, were closely related to boats. Ships supported southern people's livelihoods in many fronts.

5.3 Water Travel in the Song Dynasty—From the Perspective of Officials' Business Journeys

In ancient times, when land transportation depended on livestock to ride or pull a cart, or on walking, a boat was undoubtedly the most comfortable and convenient way to travel long distances, especially when carrying the old, the young, and lots of luggage. In the south during the Song Dynasty, maritime commerce and official business activities were more frequent than during previous dynasties. In particular, during the Southern Song Dynasty, the south became the main area for official business and commercial activities, and taking a boat became the main way of long-distance travel. Travelling by boat became a noticeable topic about how travelers on the water obtained a boat, how to start the life on a boat and how to observe the world from the perspective of living on water. Inland and sea trade was very prosperous. Business and other forms of travel were very frequent. However, the most abundant information on travel activities is official travel records. This section focuses on official travel and discusses the long-distance water travel by people then.

5.3.1 Comparison on Speed of Travelling by Boat and by Land

Generally, long-distance official travel was rarely by land. There are two main forms of travel: travelling by land and water and travelling by boat during a whole journey. Travelers mainly considered speed, cost and convenience. The normal water and land speed for water transportation and official business required by the Tang Dynasty was: horse riding need to travel 35 km a day, 25 km for walking and donkey riding, and

15 km traveling in a carriage. By waterway, boats with heavy load going upstream, traveled at the speed of 15 km a day on streams, 20 km on rivers and 22.5 km on other river courses. If the boat was empty, the travelling distance per day were required to reach 20 km, 25 km, and 35 km respectively. If boats went downstream with the same load, then the daily distances were 75 km on streams, 50 km in the Yantze River, and 35 km in other rivers respectively. Travelers would not be bound by these restriction when encountering dangerous shoals and shallow water (P. Wang 1990). Obviously, the fastest way was boat travelling downstream, but the speed of traveling upstream is roughly the same as on land.

The daily travel distances during the Song Dynasty were slightly higher than those. Taking water transportation on the Yellow River as an example, "if traveling upstream, the heavy boat would travel 17.5 km a day and the lighter one would travel 25 km a day; if going downstream, a heavy boat was required to travel 50 km a day, and a light boat 100 km a day" (Shakeshi 1990). The daily travel distances on the canals set by the Song government were as follows: "it takes four days and four hours from Xiuzhou (Jiaxing, Zhejiang Province) to Lin'an, for the total distance of 99 km; it takes eight days from Pingjiang (Suzhou, Jiangsu Province) to Lin'an, for the total distance of 180 km; it takes eleven days and eight hours from Huzhou (Wuxing, Zhejiang Province) to Lin'an, for the total distance of 264 km; it takes sixteen days from Jiangyin to Lin'an, for the total distance of 369 km" (S. Xu et al. 2014: 7069). The average distance per day is about 23 km. This referred to transporting bulk cargo.

The actual daily travel distance varied from the requirement of the normal practice required by the central government. In the Yangtze River, sailing downstream, if not hindered by wind, could often exceed 50 km, and for the fastest boats, it could reach 140 km. This can be proved by Fan Chengda's trip from Chengdu to Suzhou. Fan Chengda started for Suzhou from Chengdu on May 29th in the fourth year of the Chunxi Reign (AD 1177), and arrived in Suzhou on September 27th. He went downstream on the Yangtze River to the Canal of Liangzhe West Province. In the upper reaches of the Yangtze River above Shashi, if he didn't go there for a feast and sightseeing, his daily travel distance would be more than 60 km, and for the fastest travel, it could reach about 140 km (July 5th); there were many days he traveled more than 100 km (110 km on July 4th, 130 km on July 9th, 105 km on July 11th, 100 km on July 13th, 110km on July 30th). While he could also exceed 50 km per day when traveling downstream to the Three Gorges (on July 17th, he travelled 50 km to Qutan; on July 18th, he travelled 87.5 km to Guizhou; on July 28th, he travelled 72.5 km to Pingshan Dam, leaving Three Gorges). When sailing on the middle and lower reaches of the Yangtze River, he was not hindered by wind, so they could also travel 100 km per day (start from Shishou County, Hubei Province on August 6th, travelling 100 km; start from Huangzhou County, Hubei Province on August 20th, travelling 115 km; start from Bosijia in Chizhou Prefecture, Anhui Province on September 1st, travelling more than 100 km) (C. Fan 2012: 53–90). Sun Yingshi said that boats in Sichuan Province "set out from Chengdu and arrived at Qinhuai in less than 50 days" (Y. Sun 1990). Although Fan Chengda spent more than four months on this trip, the time was mainly used for sightseeing and entertainment along the way. It was not impossible to travel from Chengdu to Jiankang (Nanjing) in 50 days or less if one traveled without seeing the sights.

The water regime along the Yangtze River and other inland rivers were complex, and could only be navigated in daytime. If one travels during the day and sleeps at night, one could generally travel about 40 km a day on a canal. This was also faster than travelling on land. Liu Qi's army took nine hundred boats from Lin'an to Yingshang, Anhui Province, along the canals in Liangzhe West Province and Huainan Province, and on the Huaihe River. "From Lin'an to Yingshang, they traveled about 1600 km in forty-one days" (X. Li 2013: 22523). On average, they traveled 39 km a day. This was the rate of travel for a large force without unnecessary stops but also without the ability to accelerate a single boat to make a response to emergencies. So, this can be regarded as a normal speed. However, the waters of canals were still, especially in Liangzhe West Province and Huainan Province. As there were tow-paths on both sides, boats could run day and night, more than 50 km could be sailed in a day and night. In the fifth year of the Qiandao Period (AD 1169), Lou Yue went to the Jin Kingdom as an envoy. On November 10th, he boarded a boat from Lin'an and sailed northward along the canal in Liangzhe West Province. He accelerated his journey traveling the day and night. On November 13th, he started out at 4:00 a.m. and traveled 75 km without stopping for the night. On the 14th, he sailed for 45 km and stopped late at night. On the 15th, he traveled 27 km. On the 16th, he covered the remaining 45 km to Zhenjiang. The rate for the canal in Huainan provinces was about the same as the canal in Liangzhe West Province. On the 19th, he sailed 45 km in a day and night. And on the 20th, he traveled about 70 km in a day and night (Y. Lou 1990).

On the Bianhe River, travelling downstream was faster than walking or riding. During the first battle to safeguard Kaifeng, as the attacking Jin approached Kaifeng, the Song's Emperor Huizong fled south, "leaving Tongjin Gate at night and setting out by boat". "He thought the boat was slow, so he took a sedan chair. Still feeling slow, he boarded a tile-carrying boat docked on the shore". "That night, his boat sailed over one hundred kilometers to Nandu (now Shangqiu)". "Then he bought mules and rode to Fuli, where he boarded the official ship and took a short rest on the north shore of the Sishui River." From Kaifeng to Sizhou (northeast of Xuyi, Jiangsu Province), he first took a boat, then a sedan chair, then a boat, then a mule, and finally a boat. The only purpose of constantly changing the mode of transportation was to go faster. This suggests that taking a boat was faster than walking or riding a mule along the Bianhe River (G. Li 2004: 1590–91).

Walking refers to traveling on foot in the day and sleeping at night. Going downstream on the Yangtze River and traveling day and night on a canal far exceeded the speed of walking. For example, Lü Zuqian traveled from Jinhua to Kuaiji and from Wuzhou to Fujian. His travel speed on land was usually 30 to 35 km per day (Z. Lü 1990). Lou Yue set out from Wenzhou north to Lin'an. In the fifth year of the Qiandao Reign (AD 1169), he left the city on October 18th, and boarded his boat on October 28th. During those ten days, he walked 22.5 to 35 km a day (22.5 km on October 19th and 20th, more than 35 km on the 24th, 28.5 km on the 25th, 32.5 km on the 26th, and 30 km on the 27th) (Y. Lou 1990).

It was also possible to travel day and night by carriage on the northern plain. It was slower than traveling downstream on the Yangtze River or sailing on a canal, but faster than on foot. In Nanjing Province of the Jin Kingdom, Lou Yue traveled 40 km by carriage, and another 40 km by horse on December 2nd, 60 km by carriage on December 3rd, 45 km by carriage on December 4th, 22.5 km by carriage, 28.5 km by donkey, 9km by horse on December 6th, and 60 km by carriage on December 7th. Generally, a carriage could exceed 50 km a day (Y. Lou 1990). When dealing with urgent business, a rider on horseback could travel faster than a boat on roughly the same journey by passing through the post station system and avoiding a river's twists and turns. In the second year of the Daguan Reign (AD 1108), An Song, the supervisory official in Liangzhe West Province, "took forty-three days to get to the imperial palace by passenger boat, while Lu Zhongchang, a supervisory official in Jiangnan East Province, rode to the palace instead of taking a boat, in eleven days". Therefore, Emperor Huizong ordered the southeast supervisory officials to "use the post stations instead of taking a boat when they came to Bianliang to report affairs" (S. Xu et al. 2014: 4064).

It was faster to walk on land than to take a heavy ship upstream. Heavy ships could only travel 17.5 miles a day on the Yellow and Yangtze Rivers. Wei Liaoweng said, "there are about 1390 km from Lin'an to Jingzhou and Ezhou (Wuchang, Hubei Province). If you walk 25 km every day with all your strength, you will arrive in about two months. If the carriage is moving slowly, it will take more than two months. If you take a boat, you may not arrive in three months," because "the boat has to go against the current, and every inch forward need to be towed by boat trackers. Disasters caused by wind and waves are also a matter of worry" (L. Wei, n.d.).

But the advantages and disadvantages of traveling by boat or on land were relative, as they were not entirely determined by speed. If traveling with simple dress and a mid-sized carriage, land travel was often better than water travel which needed to follow the twists and turns of the river. But land travel could often be exhausting and made one want to stop. In the first year of the Longxing Reign (AD 1163), Zhou Bida returned to Luling (Ji'an, Jiangxi Province) from Hangzhou. Since he needed to visit his sister in Ningdu County (Ganzhou, Jiangxi), he started from Guixi (Yingtan, Jiangxi Province), he travelled south to Jinxi County of Fujian Province, Nancheng and Nanfeng Counties of Jiangxi Province, Guangchang of Jiangxi Province, and Ningdu of Jiangxi Province, then travelled north on the Ganshui River, totaled several hundred kilometers. He mainly chose land travel at a faster speed. He first sent his wife and children to his uncle's house in Yixing and then headed south with his servants. He said that the land travel was difficult, so he planned to start from Hangzhou and "took a shortcut to Tonglu County." "As it was the hottest time in summer, the hired servants, too weak to walk, had to rest after only a little while walking. I quickly changed my plan and went to Fuyang to rest in the reception center affiliated to the temple." In Shouchang County, "it's been raining heavy all day, and hired servants said they were tired." In Nanfeng County, "the extremely high temperature and fatigue in summer made it almost impossible to speak" (B. Zhou 1990). Compared with land travel, boats had the great advantage of travelling without tiredness despite the dangers. Wu Fei said, "ever since we boarded the boat, the whole house has been happy to not only to abandon the chariots and servants, but also to not have to enter the post stations. Thus, I can put my head on a high pillow and sleep comfortably in a covered boat, and I forget the weariness of travel" (F. Wu 1990). This showed the comfort and ease of the boat travel. In the seventh year of the Xi'ning Reign (AD 1074), Shen Kuo said that the supervisors of Liangzhe provinces inspected in Liangzhe West Province, where boat travel was convenient, "supervisors only travel by boat in Liangzhe West Province," while in the prefectures of Liangzhe East Province, where boat travel is inconvenient, "supervisors never inspect those prefectures and counties. The government affairs are neglected and idle, and no one inspects them" (T. Li 2004: 6175). It was also because boat travel is comfortable while the land travel is wearying. The supervisors were lazy and afraid of difficulties where they could not travel by boat. Even if the water route was more circuitous than the land trip, it was still the most convenient way to travel long distances with more belongings or carrying the old and children. Besides, not all travel can be completed by boat, or boat travel is more effective.

5.3.2 The Choice of Travelling by Boat During the Whole Journey or Travelling by Both Water and Land

Long-distance travel with more goods or carrying the old and young was generally by water, if it were not possible to travel by boat in a whole journey, people would choose to travel by a combination of both land and water. In the third year of the Jingyou Reign (AD 1036), Ouyang Xiu left Kaifeng for Yiling to work as county magistrate in May. The journey was 1300 km between Kaifeng and Yiling. From Kaifeng to Yiling, the nearest route was to travel southwest from Kaifeng to Tangzhou (Tanghe, Henan Province) via Yingchang, and sail downstream along the tributary of the Hanshui River to Xiangzhou (Xiangyang, Hubei Province) and Yingzhou (Wuchang, Hubei Province), and then traveled on land to Yiling, or directly went to Yiling from Xiangzhou. Yin Zhu, who was demoted to Yingzhou following Ouyang Xiu's suit, took this route. Ouyang Xiu "met his elder brother in Ezhou. His brother was told to witnessed Yin Zhu passing by Xiangzhou, and guessed that Ouyang Xiu must be in Yingzhou." As it was August 27th, Yin Zhu must have stayed in Yingzhou for a long time. Ouyang Xiu "was told by Jingzhou locals that it was only two days' journey from Yingzhou." In addition, people could travel directly from Yingzhou to Yiling. "There is a way to Yiling, and it only takes a few days to reach Yingzhou" (X. Ouyang n.d.: 490, 191). If Ouyang Xiu chose this route, he could travel on the river from Tangzhou. Ouyang Xiu did choose the waterway, "it took him 110 days to sail along the Bianhe River, cross the Huaihe River and the Yangtze River, and he finally reached Jingnan (Jiangxian, Hubei Province). And the journey totaled 2500 km." It's a journey from Kaifeng on May 24th to Gong'an Ferry on September 17th (B. Zhou 1990). Ouyang Xiu "reached Yiling on October 26" (X. Ouyang n.d.: 491). So it took him five months and two days. If he took the waterway to enter the Yangtze

River at Yiling via the canal, sailing downstream for Yiling, it would be a journey more time-consuming than on land. But he need take care of his family members in this journey. In his letter to Yin Zhu, he talked about the reason why he chose the water route: "I had planned to go to Yiling on land, but it was too hot and there were no horses, then I adopted the waterway." He also said that "fortunately, my parents and my child had no disease. My mother did not drink alcohol before, after arriving in Yiling, she could drink seven or five glasses of wine a day and could eat delicious food at any time, which is blessing for us." Here, "my child" refers to his son given birth by his first wife Ms. Xu in the second year of the Mingdao Reign (AD 1033). He was Ouyang Xiu's first son. When Ouyang Xiu went to Yiling, his son was already three years old, but his son died very young in the first year of the Baoyuan Reign (AD 1038). Ms. Xu died within a month after their son's birth. Apart from his mother and his child, he would have also been accompanied by family members who took care of the young and the old. It is impossible for the old and the child to walk on land in the summer heat, without horses. Although the water route was farther, they found sailing to be a better option than walking.

The Japanese monk Jojin arrived in China on a merchant ship from Japan in the fifth year of the Xi'ning Reign (AD 1072), landing in Mingzhou (Ningbo, Zhejiang Province). He then visited Tiantai Guoqing Temple in Taizhou (Linhai, Zhejiang Province), before arriving at Yuezhou (Shaoxing, Zhejiang Province). From Yuezhou to Kaifeng, he traveled by the canal the whole way. The boat sailed from Yuezhou on August 17th, stayed in Hangzhou for two days (arrived in Hangzhou on 21st, set off on 24th, and reached Runzhou on September 9th). He arrived at Kaifeng on October 12th. The whole journey lasted forty-six days (Jojin 2009: 197–275). In the sixth year of the Yuanfeng Reign (AD 1083), Zhang Shunmin went to Chenzhou (Chenxian, Hunan Province) to supervise wine taxes. His route went down the Bianhe Canal to the Huainan Canal, then sailing west along the Yangtze River to the Xiangjiang River, and arrived at Chenzhou. He traveled by boat the whole journey (S. Zhang 1990). In the fourth year of the Xuanhe Reign (AD 1122), Xu Jing and others were sent to Korea as envoys. From Kaifeng to Mingzhou, they traveled by canals. They set off from Kaifeng on March 14th and arrived in Mingzhou on May 3rd. The whole journey took 50 days (J. Xu 2006: 131). In the fourth year of the Chunxi Reign (AD 1177), Fan Chengda, the chief inspector in Sichuan, was recalled to the court. He boarded a boat at Chengdu, and sailed along the Yangtze River, then transferred to the canal in Zhenjiang to travel to Suzhou. The journey lasted more than 4 months, most of which was spent for sightseeing and banquets on the way (C. Fan 2012: 53–90). In the sixth year of the Qiandao Reign (AD 1170), when Zhou Bida went from Luling to Hangzhou, "he traveled to Zhejiang with his family by boat." He chose the waterway along the Ganshui River into Boyang Lake, then into the canal via the Yangtze River (B. Zhou 1990).

All the above-mentioned trips of the celebrities chose water routes because they either had more luggage or were traveling with the old or young. In addition to carrying the old and young and more luggage, waterway may also be a more economical means of transportation. Su Shi said, "I had planned to travel on land and rode day and night to take office quickly, but I fell in illness and could not raise more money to go further, and the soldiers could not reach there in time. Besides, Yingzhou locals who worked for me refused to go further outside their territory. I did not have enough money to hire people or buy horses for my left journey" (S. Su 2010: 3642). Ouyang Xiu chose the waterway, not only because it was easier to carry the old and the young, but also because "before leaving, the censorate soldiers me to leave there many times, which made me nervous and worried." After the order of relegation issued, he was urged to leave there within three days, and there was not enough time to sell his properties, to hire people or buy horses. Ouyang Xiu's family was poor and he was lonely from an early age. In the eighth year of the Tiansheng Reign (AD 1030), he was entitled Jinshi (Scholars) by the provincial government, a successful candidate for supreme imperial examinations, and served as an official in Xijing (Xi'an, Shannxi Province) in the following year. His official career started that year, but soon he was demoted in the third year of the Jingyou Reign (AD 1036). He had been an official for only five years, and his family had suffered many misfortunes. Two wives died in quick succession. As his official rank was low, he might not have had enough money.

However, even if some journeys were more suitable for traveling by boat, the mixed transportation was needed due to the limited conditions of roads and waterways. When envoys from the Southern Song went to the Jin Kingdom, they transported a large number of gifts on the boats within the Song territory. For example, according to the rule, "the Fiscal Commission of Liangzhe provinces, Huainan provinces respectively assign fifteen passenger boats." In the 14th year of the Chunxi Reign (AD 1187), diplomatic missions for celebrating new year and the birthday of Jin's King. They brought, as gifts, "100-km gold, 1000-kg silver, and 2000 horses laden with goods" (S. Xu et al. 2014: 4447). They traveled by water until they entered the territory of the Jin Kingdom. Then they had to use carriages to travel overland, similar to Lou Yue who went to the Jin Kingdom as an envoy as mentioned above, and the same as the missions sent by the Northern Song to the Liao Kingdom. The envoys had to write a memorandum, known as a journal about their trip (Y. Zhao 1995) and submit it to the Bureau of Military Affairs. Diplomatic envoys, especially those traveling to congratulate the emperor's birthday, were on special official trips, with planned routes and schedules. They would be accompanied by envoys from the visited country during the mission. The envoys were responsible for diplomatic missions and collecting foreign intelligence (C. Huang 2011), and the extant records, except for *the Log of Journey to the North* by Lou Yue, record their experiences after leaving the country. Very few of these records included their activities and experiences within their own country.

In the first year of the Shaosheng Reign (AD 1094), Su Shi, at the age of sixty, was demoted to Yingzhou (Lingshui, Hainan Province) from Renshang, Dingzhou (Hebei Province), and on the half way, his demotion was changed to Huizhou, Guangdong Province. "I went there with my family members, and suffered from illness due to anxiety and fear. My eyes were dizzy and could only distinguish the road. My left hand was numb, and my right arm was weak. If I forcibly ignored my weak body, walk more than 2000 km on the hot and desolate road by suffering from the roasted summer, I undoubtedly will be exhausted to death on the road." Only through making plans can you delay for a while on the boat, and then spend the rest of your life in the governance house" (S. Su 2010: 3641–42). However, there was no direct waterway from Dingzhou to Huizhou. The journey could only be accomplished by a combination of water and land routes. He traveled with his wife and children, as well as his eldest son Su Mai, to Yixing. Then he traveled with Su Yi, Su Guo and several others on land from Zhending (Zhengding, Hebei Province) to Sizhou (Xuyi, Jiangsu Province), before changing to a boat at Sizhou on a canal to the Yangtze River to the Ganjiang River until they arrived at Ganzhou. Then they went over land crossing the Five Ridges. When they reached Nanxiongzhou (Nanxiong, Guangdong Province), they took a boat again to Guangzhou, sailing along the Dongjiang River to Dongguan. Then they traveled on land to Huizhou (Z. Yang 2006). In the fourth year of the Jiayou Reign (AD 1059), Su Shi's mother died. After his mourning period expired, he and his father and younger brother went from Sichuan to Kaifeng, "sailing east along the Yangtze River for 60 days from Sichuan Province to Hu'nan and Hubei Province" (S. Su 2010: 5212). They traveled on land from Jingmen (Hubei Province), through Yicheng (Hubei Province), Xiangzhou (Xiangyang, Hubei Province), Dengzhou (Henan Province), Tangzhou (Tanghe, Henan Province), Xuzhou (Xuchang, He'nan Province), and Weishi (He'nan Province) to the capital city of Kaifeng (Z. Wang 1990). Su Shi traveled from south to north, against the Hanshui water, so he mainly took the land route. It was possible to transfer from the Yangtze River to the canal to Kaifeng, but in order to take an official post under the imperial examination system, he wanted to travel fast. The fastest way was to sail downstream on the Yangtze River eastward to Jingzhou, and then the land route from Jingzhou to Kaifeng.

In the eighth year of the Qiandao Reign (AD 1172), Fan Chengda went to take a position at Jingjiang Prefecture in Guangnan West Province. He traveled from Pingjiang by water and on land for "1500 km from the Wu Kingdom to Guilin," in 122 days. He took his family, including his Nannie, and traveled by water from Suzhou, Huzhou (Wuxing, Zhejiang Province), Deqing County to Yuhang County. If he wanted to take a shortcut from Yuhang County into Zhejiang, he could have to travel on land to Fuyang (Hangzhou, Zhejiang Province) in one day, but his mother had been seriously ill since boarding the boat. If they traveled by land, then she would soon die. Fan Chengda stayed in Yuhang for five days, not sleeping at night because he could not think of a way forward. Finally, he left his mother with relatives who were local officials before taking land transportation (C. Fan 2012: 32). This also shows that for long-distance travel with a family, it was difficult to withstand the difficulties of land travel, and traveling by water was a safer choice. When it was impossible to sail on the whole way, one had to leave his family and travel in simple dress to double the speed. Fan Chengda set off from Suzhou to Yuhang. There he transferred to land in Fuyang (Hangzhou, Zhejiang Province). Then he changed on a boat, passing through Tonglu County, Yanzhou (Jiande, Zhejiang Province), Lanxi County, Wuzhou (Jinhua, Zhejiang Province). Once again he changed to land travel to Quzhou (Quxian, Zhejiang Province), Changshan County, Yushan County, arriving at Xinzhou (Shangrao, Jiangxi Province), where he boarded a boat again to pass through Yiyang County, Guixi County, Anren County, Yugan County, and entered Boyang Lake. There he sailed to the Ganjiang River; when arriving at Linjiang Prefecture, he traveled on land again, and entered Hunan (South Jingnan Province) through Yuanzhou and Pingxiang, then took a boat to Chuzhou City; and finally abandoned the boat to walk on land to Hengzhou (Hengyang, Hunan Province), and entered Guilin through Yongzhou (C. Fan 2012: 30–48). Fan Chengda traveled to Guangnan West Province in this way, and so did Su Shi, who went to Huizhou.

Similar to the experience of Su Shi and Fan Chengda, Zhou Bida took a trip to return to Ji'an (Luling) in Jiangnan West Province from south of Lin'an in the first year of the Longxing Reign (AD 1163). He left the customs on the Gengshen Day in March and arrived at Yonghe Town in Ji'an on the Renwu day in June, totaled 82 days. He traveled on a canal to Jingxi Town, and then to Yixing County, where he left his wife at his uncle's house. From there, he took a boat, passing through Huzhou, and arrived at Yuhang County. He originally planned to take an overland shortcut to Tonglu because the water route meant a detour to Hangzhou. But the sedan chair carriers was cowardly and walk too slowly, so Zhou changed his route halfway to sail upstream to Tonglu and Yanzhou. There he again changed to overland travel, passing through Shouchang County, Quzhou, Jiangshan, Xinzhou (Shangrao, Jiangxi Province), to Yongfeng County. With the Yongfeng River running through Yongfeng County, he could go downstream on the Raojiang River. Zhou then switched to a boat to reach Yiyang County and Guixi County. In Guixi County, he again changed to land travel to go through Anren, Jinxi, Nancheng, Nanfeng, Guangchang, to Ningdu. There was no waterway between Guixi, Anren and Nanfeng nor was there one between Guangchang and Ningdu. Because he was anxious get to his sister's house in Ningdu, he went over land which was 280 km from Guixi to Ningdu. To finish the journey, he spent only 11 days at the speed of 25 km a day. If he had sailed from Ningdu and entered the Ganjiang River, it could sail along the river through Lingdu County, Wan'an County in Ganzhou, Taihe County, to Yonghe Town (B. Zhou 1990). Zhou Bida chose his route mainly to take the detour to visit his sister in Ningdu. There was no direct waterway from Lin'an to Ningdu. So he left his family in Yixing because land travel was not suitable for carrying the old and the young.

The mixed transportation of land and water travel as the above mentioned was a passive choice. But sometimes in order travel faster, people would actively choose to travel by combining land and water travel. In the third year of the Qiandao Reign (AD 1167), Zhou Bida went to Yixing to visit his uncle, who was critically ill. He carried his family and luggage, sailed downstream in the Ganjiang River to the Yangtze River sailing with the current. When he arrived in Jiankang (Nanjing, Jiangsu Province), he hired a boat to carry his luggage through the canal to Zhenjiang but he traveled on land because it would be faster. He traveled south from Jiankang and arrived at Shenshui County the next day. There he took a boat again and arrived at Yixing on the third day. Despite his best efforts to reach Yixing by the fastest route possible, his uncle had died before he could arrive (B. Zhou 1990). Fan Chengda once noted that people who were in a rush to travel upstream from the Yangtze River to Chengdu would go ashore at Wanzhou. Then they would go on foot to reach Chengdu in less than two days, while it would take ten days on a boat (C. Fan 2012: 74). Land travel could be five times faster than boat travel.

In the eighth year of the Qiandao Reign (AD 1172), Zhou Bida returned to Ji'an from Lin'an. He chose to travel along the south bank of the Yangtze River by both water and land. He first sailed by boat from the canal through Jingxi to Yixing where he left his wife and children. He had already sent the army of Li Zhen and Zou Qi to escort military supplies to Zhenjiang from Changzhou, and then transported them to Ji'an by a cargo boat down the river. Zhou Bida and his underlings sailed from Yixing to the border of Nanling County. On land, they passed through Qingyang County, Jiande, Shimen City in Raozhou, and Sishilidian village in Raozhou, and then took a boat to pass through Yongpingjian, entered Poyang Lake, and sailed upstream on the Ganjiang River to Ji'an (B. Zhou 1990). Zhou Bida traveled between Lin'an and Ji'an several times like this. Each time he went to his father-in-law's house in Yixing. If he did not choose the Yangtze River waterway to Poyang Lake after arriving in Yixing, he would take the route via the land trip along the south bank of the Yangtze River to Poyang Lake, which was the shortest road to Ji'an. So, he needed to find boats to transport a large amount of military supplies and luggage to Ji'an. Zhou Bida's fellow townsman, Yang Wanli, returned from Changzhou to his hometown, Jishui, in Jiangnan West Province. He also chose to travel by both land and water, but the route chosen was different from Zhou Bida's trips to Jishui, Lin'an and Yixing. He took a boat along the canal from Changzhou, passing by Xuexi, and arriving at Yuhang. Then he took land route to Fuyang. There, he boarded a boat, to pass by Yanzhou, Anren City, Quzhou, and Jiangshan County. There, once again, he resumed land travel to Shangrao after passing by Yongfeng County. From Shangrao, he sailed to Poyang Lake, and headed for the Ganjiang River, and following the water flow downstream to Jishui (W. Yang 2007: 645–734).

5.3.3 The Ways to Go on Boats

There were four main ways for people in the Song Dynasty to travel on boats: government boats, chartering boats, hitching a boat, and private ownership. The first was reserved for government officials going to and from their postings or other official duties. The last other three were open to all people. In the first year of the Zhenghe Reign (AD 1111), the Secretariat of Royal Court stated, that "there are no limits on boats used by the former prime minister and the ministers for business purposes." But, later in that year, a stipulation was introduced that "the prime minister could use less than eight official boats each year, ministers six boats each year, and the number for the former prime minister and former ministers is reduced by half" (S. Xu et al. 2014: 7123). The former prime minister, Chen Shengzhi, who was ordered by Emperor Shenzong to visit Wang Anshi in Jinling, "had unlimited number of boats with one followed by another, covering the river. People on board went on the streets to put up announcements and their shouts echoed continuously" (Z. Wang 2008: 140). In the third year of the Yuanyou Reign (AD 1088), a new stipulation was introduced that "those whose official positions are the fifth-rank and Imperial historians of the court or above and have worked in the capital for three years could have boats for private use" (T. Li 2004: 10037). Cai Xiang also mentioned the situation of officials who left their posts. He said, "in the south, officials who are replaced or dismissed can be sponsored a round trip for private use each year, either from the nearest places, Jiangnan and Liangzhe provinces to the capital city, or from the farthest one, Xiangtan (Tanzhou, Hunan Province) to the capital city. One boat can take 10 to 20 people to Bianliang once a year. The cost of a boat ranges from 500 strings of 1000 coins to 700 strings" (X. Cai 1996: 388). Officials who went to their posts could also take boats. In the second year of the Tianxi Reign (AD 1018), it was ordered that "from now on, officials who go to their posts in the south, such as Zhenzhou (Yangzhou, Jiangsu Province), Chuzhou (Huai'an, Jiangsu Province) and Sizhou (Xuyi, Jiangsu Province), can register the boats borrowed from the capital city, or make an agreement with local officials on the shore to borrow boats available for officials to take their posts" (S. Xu et al. 2014: 7121). Officials from Sichuan Province could also take official boats to go to their posts. "Prefecture magistrates, who are newly appointed, will be provided with all the necessary boats, carriages, daily life wares and tools. They are also prepared with enough money for hiring people and purchasing land, even up to 5000 or 6000 strings of 1000 coins, or at least 3,000 strings of 1000 coins" (S. Xu et al. 2014: 4284). Some officials would leverage the official boats to make profits illegally. "Most of the officials in Jiangnan, Huainan, Hu'nan, Hubei, Liangzhe provinces, Jinghu South and North provinces etc. are not eager to handle official business. They often made full use of official boats to load private goods for earning profits" (S. Xu et al. 2014: 7122). Besides, there were also "eunuchs who were ordered to be inspect the Yangtze River and the Huaihe River. Most of them used official boats to carry private goods for personal gain" (T. Li 2004: 2323). In the fifth year of the Yuanfeng Reign, Zhao Ding, the mayor of Xuzhou, was punished for "carrying personal goods on the official boats for personal gain" (T. Li 2004: 7968).

If an official passed away on duty, government boats could be asked to return his remains to his hometown. In the second year of the Tianxi Reign (AD 1018), Chen Zhiwei passed away. "An official boat carrying his coffin was used to send him back to his hometown" (Toqta 1977: 10136). When Wang Ziyu, the deputy minister in charge of admonition and arbitration, passed away, Emperor Zhenzong agreed with his family "to send the coffin back to his hometown by official boat" (T. Li 2004: 1114). In the first year of the Yuanfeng Reign (AD 1078), Emperor Shenzong ordered "the officials of Sichuan, Guangnan and Fujian provinces who died before they left and were replaced by other officials, even if they had already paid for the boat, they could be offered an official boat for returning hometown" (T. Li 2004: 7014–15). Zhao Bian, the mayor of Qianzhou (Ganzhou, Jiangxi Province) asked for approval "to build a hundred boats for dead officials who had worked in the south of the Five Ridges and could carry them back to their hometown. Zhao Bian dispatched all the boats he built to those officials and also gave their families some traveling expenses" (Toqta 1977: 10323). Emperor Zhezong ordered that "Qianzhou is allowed to give no more than 15 boats with a load capacity of 500 Liao and 400 Liao each year to officials who have left their posts to attend their parent's funeral or to carry their bodies back to their hometown" (S. Xu et al. 2014: 7123). Although the number was limited, official boats were still allowed to be used for the funeral or post transfer purposes.

Prefectures along the waterway were equipped with official boats required for official travel. But in the fifth year of the Zhenghe Reign (AD 1115), Tian Wang, who was responsible for Wuwei Military Prefecture, said "the leaders of this army do not take boats often" (S. Xu et al. 2014: 7124). In the Song Dynasty, it was also stipulated that "all official boats stored in prefectures and towns shall be arranged and covered up at their convenience, and shall be guarded. If they are damaged, they shall be repaired. If they cannot be repaired, they shall be registered in the boat accounts attached. All official boats should be described in details in the registration book each year, about the boat's category, load capacity, whether they are available or not" (*Tianyige Cang Ming Chaoben Jiaozheng* 2004: 348). The prefectures possessing official boats along the way should report the changes of boats every year. However, in fact, official boats were not always available when officials needed to travel. One of the reasons was that there were too few official boats. Since "there were few official boats, people who were not dignitaries could not have access to them." Li Di, a former prime minister, was degraded to Hengzhou (Hengyang, Hunan Province) as a vice deputy mayor and he could only "use public boats to travel in the name of Zhang Chizi" (T. Wei 2006: 101). The second reason was that official boats were overused. Tian Wang said, "Since then, when Wuwei Military Prefecture needed to take boats, they could not find enough boats available and they had to remain at their posts for one year or two" (S. Xu et al. 2014: 7124). This evidenced that the need for official boats could be very serious and made it difficult for officials to leave their old posts. Third, the officials in charge of official boats colluded arbitrarily. When Xu Yuan acted as the minister of Shipping Department on the Yangtze River and the Huaihe River, he was in charge of official boats. "There were dozens of officials and gentry who asked for boats every day. If they were a powerful family or nobleman, Xu Yuan immediately sent a large boat to them. If they were minor officials or lonely and powerless people, they had to wait for a long time before they were dispatched a boat" (Toqta 1977: 9945). Sun Mian was demoted to be the deputy mayor of Xuanzhou for his crimes. "The subordinate of Sun Mian passed by Huaiyang and asked the Huaiyang Prefecture Chief for a boat. He did not agree." Bi Conggu sold his wife, children and properties so as to pay for the fees spent on boats and vehicles for him (Z. Bi n.d.). Su Shi was demoted to Yingzhou and asked for an official boat to "stay in Fenfengpu at midnight, the shipping department got the information that he would be demoted again, and sent 500 people to loot the boat." He begged, "Can you allow me to reach the Xingjiang River overnight so that I could buy a boat by myself at the market?" The official agreed to Su Shi's request (J. Shi 1990). Later, he returned the official boat and bought a boat by himself to resume his journey.

Chartering boats was also a way of traveling along the Yangtze River. Officials may also hire boats for their journey. Of the eight boats used for Xu Jing's mission to Goryeo (now Korea), six were chartered passenger boats while only two large luxury seagoing ships were built by the government (J. Xu 2006: 129). In the seventh year of the Xi'ning Reign (AD 1074), the emperor issued an edict to "let the designated officials take office by horses and allow them to shift to boats when waterways were available in the prefectures and counties, which will be covered by governments" (S.

Xu et al. 2014: 9475). Emperor Zhezong asked Zhao Yanruo to take an official boat to return to Qingzhou (Yidu, Shandong Province). Emperor Zhezong "urged him to take the boat he deserves." But he "hired a passenger boat to leave there freely" (T. Li 2004: 11027). He boarded on a private boat rather than the official boat. Officials taking chartered boats were frequent. Tang Bohu, a great painter, once hired a boat from Meizhou (Meishan, Sichuan Province) to visit his father in Hu'nan (Dayaoxian, Yunnan Province). The river was surging and all the passenger boats were stuck on shore. They had to reluctantly rent a fishing boat at a high cost (Toqta 1977: 13101). Liu Yaoju "rent a boat to travel" from Xupu, Pingjiang Prefecture (Suzhou, Jiangsu Province)" (T. Guo 1990). Outside the south gate of Huzhou, a woman "shouted to rent a boat to go to Yishan village via Heshan Road. She paid 20 strings of 1000 coins for renting a boat" (M. Hong n.d.: 892). When Cui Du was sailing on the Yangtze River, he found "a black ribbon on the stern of an empty boat, with a piece of paper. He found it a contract for renting a boat." "It must be left by the merchant who was killed by the owner of the boat, and after his properties were looted, the owner abandoned his boat" (B. Zhang 1985: 120). It was not rare for boat owners to kill their employers. In the second year of the Yuanfu Reign (1099), there was a boatman named Lin Lü in Fuzhou. Xiezhou Xizi, a woman from Baihu Village, Houguan County, went to Nanjian (Nanping City) to seek medical advice for depression. When the woman returned, she rent Lin Lü's boat to take her family home. Lin Lü waited until night to kill the three people of Xiezhou's family in the desolate waters of Sanjiangkou (K. Lang 1990: 8244). In Lin'an, it was reported that a boat owner had killed a scholar's family. Later, it was discovered that he had killed more than twenty families" (C. Zhuang 2008: 54).

Hitching a boat is also a common way. Officials often took a lift on the grain transportation boats, or they were arranged to do so officially. The Song Dynasty had a rule that when the officials went to meet the emperor at the imperial court, they were not allowed to walk on foot, but to go there "by horse or boat." If the officials lived in the region between Suzhou and Hangzhou, they need to charter a boat in Liangzhe West Province to the capital city (M. Wang 2013: 114). After arriving in Zhenzhou (Zhenzhou County, Jiangsu Province), Ouyang Xiu changed to a commercial passenger boat. In the early Northern Song Dynasty, most ships on the Bianhe river stopped when they reached Zhenzhou (Zhenzhou County, Jiangsu Province). The governmental transportation department required that boats sailing on the Bianhe River cannot enter the Yangtze River, while ships sailing on the Yangtze River cannot travel into the Bianhe River because the two rivers had different conditions that required different boat designs. It seems that officials at Zhenzhou (Zhenzhou County, Jiangsu Province) did not allow Ouyang Xiu to use an official boat. He could only travel westward by a commercial boat. When he sailed to Yuezhou (YueYang, Hunan Province), however, officials from Yiling County came to meet him. He was able to borrow a boat from Shao Ai, who may have been an official in Yuezhou. Ouyang Xiu and his party successfully borrowed an official boat (X. Ouyang 2001: 1903). Fan Zuyu used an official boat of the Fiscal Commission to Bianliang from Luoyang at the call of an imperial edict (T. Li 2004: 11540). When Lu You took office in Sichuan, he traveled from the canal in the Liangzhe West

Province to the Yangtze River. There he needed to change boats. He took Wang Zhiyi's boat, a businessman in Jiazhou (Leshan, Sichuan Province) and then took the boat of Zhao Qing, a Jiazhou native, and entered the Three Gorges in Shashi (Jingsha, Hubei Province) (Y. Lu 2012: 165, 206). In the Song Dynasty, it was stipulated that those officials in the process of handover of power could go with 10 cargo boats carrying cloth and silk from Yizhou and other places to Sichuan, Three Gorges, and Jingnan (Jiangling County, Hubei Province). Later, this stipulation was changed into "to draft in several from the cargo boats and personnel for the power handover ceremony without authorization." For another example, in the sixth year of the Tiansheng Reign (AD 1028), in Jingnan provinces, "the government drafted in four boats from Xie Jin's fleet of grain shipping, together with 30 soldiers, and they were used to send Xue Chu, the newly appointed Prison Executive of Langzhou, to take his post, and they were also used to send Yang Shun and his staffs, which was issued an official permit by the Jingnan municipal government. And then they were used to transport the newly appointed senior assistant Yuanbo to his post" (S. Xu et al. 2014: 6951). Private trips were also common. Chengxun came to China by merchant ship. Yitian, the son of the Goryeo Emperor, also came to China by Linning's merchant ship (I. Jeong n.d.). Sun Yingshi sailed out of Sichuan by commercial boat. "Sichuan boats are often suspected of being overloaded and cannot withstand the wind and rain, so they often stay late. He was worried and afraid when he arrived in Ezhou (Wuchang, Hubei Province), so he took another boat to leave" (Y. Song 1990). That is to say, he changed another boat to sail.

Purchasing boats was another way for people to travel by water. When Yang Jing, an official at Tongguan, ended his term of office, he made a cabinet decorated with patterns of pearls, "bought the boat of Chen Liu, a native. Then he let his son, Shiyilang, go to Bianliang with him" (M. Hong 1981: 156). Yang Jing bought a boat because he wanted to send his son for private affairs. During the Chunxi Reign, Mr. Zhang, Geng Daofu's in-law, was responsible for public security. "When the term of office was coming to an end, he bought a boat, to sail to Bianliang" (K. Yue 1981: 52). These are examples of officials purchasing boats when they left their posts. In the 31st year of the Shaoxing Reign (AD 1161), when Zhang Jun took office in Tanzhou as the supervisor of the municipal financial affairs in Jiankang Prefecture. "When he arrived at Yueyang, he bought a boat to sail in huge waves" (Toqta 1977: 11307). These are examples of officials purchasing boats to take office. Civilians also purchased boats for travel. For example, in the second year of the Shaoding Reign (AD 1229), the father of Hou, the wife of Xie Bi, "bought boats to take his family to Jianchang" from Nanfeng (Toqta 1977: 13488).

5.3.4 Activities on the Journey

Traveling by water lasted a long time, and most of people would have meals and sleep on boats. A market, mainly targeting water travelers, formed on the waterway, where tourists could obtain their daily needs. The travel of officials to take or leave their posts was different from their business trips and missions. The time limit of their travel was relatively loose, and officials had sufficient time to meet friends and go sightseeing. This was also an important opportunity for them to accumulate experience and increase insight. Travelers, like boatmen, were faced with all kinds of dangers of the unknown aquatic world and feared the underwater world. Sacrifices became an important activity of water travel. Sacrifice has been discussed separately. This section only discusses visiting friends, banquets and sightseeing activities.

5.3.4.1 Sources of Daily Necessities

The water travel would pass through the prefectures, cities, counties, and towns. It was also possible to "travel in a boat all day without seeing a family, and only see reed flowers in an endless field of vision," or even "a boat stops beside the reeds, and no household smoke is seen for three days" (S. Wang 2012: 346, 347). However, whether docked at the city port or by the wild water, boat travelers basically took the boat as their home. Besides going ashore for sightseeing, they mainly lived and ate on the boat. When Ouyang Xiu went to Yiling, he was "witnessed to meet the local official Zhang Andao in Chuzhou (Present-day Huai'an), and slept in the boat after drinking with friends" (X. Ouyang 2001: 1899). He met friends, and slept in the boat after dining and wining. When Zheng Shu, Zheng Xie's father, marched with Di Qing to Guangnan provinces, he "left his family on the boat at Yongqiu (Qixian, Henan Province)." After Zheng Xie took the final imperial examination in the capital city, his mother and family remained in the boat for good news (Z. Wang 2008: 149). Zhang Lei one described the life in the boat, "at dawn, noises outside the cover of the boat, together with the cold wind penetrated my quilts" (L. Zhang 1990). Zhang Xun once served as the magistrate of Jinling County, Changzhou. After his term of office ended, he set out east to Mingzhou (Ningbo, Zhejiang Province) with his family. At night, he stayed at Yixing Post and "slept in the main cabin of the boat" with his son. He described that "at about two o'clock in the early morning, the maidservant's yelling from a nightmare woke me up suddenly" (T. Guo 1990). When Yang Wanli was sailing through the canal, he felt "the boat was too hot to sleep, and the sounds of fishing boats troubled me all night". Then he went ashore and took the mountain route in Yuhang, to enjoy the cool temperature in the mountainous area rather than being baked in the boat. "In the previous nights I had to sleep on a mat in the boat, but this morning I needed to add clothes at the foot of the mountain" (W. Yang 2007: 662). This evidenced that they made the boat as their bedroom. Besides, cooking was also done on board. For example, when Yang Wanli was sailing on the canal, "he only cooked wild vegetable soup in the morning and chose to buy two fresh fish" (W. Yang 2007: 645). For another example, when the son of Shen in Wuxing sailed to Pingjiang Prefecture (Suzhou, Jiangsu Province), a monk took the boat with him. On the way, "the monk asked for cooked food in the morning, so he shared with him" (Y. He 2008: 213). This also evidenced that boats were both means of transportation and temporary dwellings.

Therefore, purchasing living materials on board was the most important thing on a journey. A large boat usually carried a smaller boat that was easy to navigate for shopping on the way. If the Emperor ordered the boat to go against the wind, "when big boats could not move forward, they had to be anchored at the shore while the small boat would be used to catch fish" (L. Wang 1990). Lu You was sailing on the Yangtze River. One day, "he encountered heavy wind and rain, which prevented him from sailing smoothly. So, a small boat was sent across the river to buy meat dishes on the other side. They bought half a big fish and a black rooster" (Y. Lu 2012: 203). When Zhou Bida sailed to Tonglu County, "the children lined up to go out, and the boatman came back with vegetables bought from the riverside market" (W. Yang 2007: 1244). The so-called boatman was the person who went shopping by sailing a small boat. Occasionally, free gifts would also be given. For example, Lu You was once "given some bamboo shoots by an old countryside man and refused to be paid back" (Y. Lu 2012: 203). When Zhou Bida, returned to Ji'an from Lin'an along the Yangtze River, he wrote that "his rice was running out, and a man surnamed Zhang from a passenger boat in Tanzhou gave him several kilograms of rice and he repaid him with some fruits" (B. Zhou 1990). When Wang Shipeng crossed Bijiachi by boat, since "people on the river knows him. One man picked oranges from the branches and offered him a plate of oranges to show hospitality." It was "the man surnamed Chen that gave him eight oranges" (S. Wang 2012: 350). However, most of his life necessities need to be purchased.

On the journey, people could buy fresh fishes, shrimps and the specialties of different places. During Cai Jing's trip to Liangzhe West Province from Daguanmo, he saw "fishing boats going back and forth on the Xinkai Lake." He bought 20 fish with 30 coins (T. Cai 2008: 195). Lu You, traveling to Gusu Stream in Taiping, saw "many people fishing or casting nets, which made fish prices very low. The children and servants were fed full every day" (Y. Lu 2012: 176). All the people on the boat could taste the local river food. When Wang Shipeng was sailing on the river, he exclaimed that "I had a wonderful experience of boat travel as I had enough fish and shrimp to eat every day" (S. Wang 2012: 345). Yang Wanli, on the Liangzhe West Canal in Suzhou, tasted the specialty bass in Wuzhong area. "The basses with a small bottom are the best and those with white gills are very delicious; fish slices like snow flakes are falling down one after another on the plate. And gush could blow the white fish slices off the plate." "The Wu people called bass Jade Fish. All gills of bass in Taihu Lake are white, whose meat is delicate and delicious without a fishy smell. The bass in the Songjiang River has three gills and a black back, whose meat is rough and tastes mild and fishy" (W. Yang 2007: 1440). Of course, bass in the Songjiang River was also a famous specialty, and "those of seven or eight inches long tasted "good," which could be bought at a very low price in the local area. "Basses are growing among the reed leaves, the hometown of bass while the bass in the Rainbow Pavilion is not valuable. The fish is as short as a jade ruler and as round as a silver shuttle. There are three or four black stripes on the white fish. Their scales are delicate and the meat tastes delicious" (W. Yang 2007: 1488). In the Huaihe River, Yang Wanli still could enjoy the delicious Huaihe fish boiled by the Huaihe river water. "Huaihe fish must be cooked in the Huaihe river water, as the water of the Jiangnan region could not make fish taste best" (W. Yang 2007: 1401). When Yu Ji, a Lishui native, on his way to take office in Xinghua, Taizhou, "sailed with his family, they noticed many clams in the Huaihe River. The boatman buys them every day as food" (M. Hong 1981: 293). When Wang Shipeng sailed to Ezhou, he said that "the oranges are just ripe. I bought 16 oranges with 100 coins, which taste sour slightly, different from the oranges in the countryside" (S. Wang 2012: 350).

Then the riverside market by the major rivers was developed to serve the boat travelers and the boatmen. These markets included not only urban markets along the waterway, but also water markets on the river. For example, the soldiers who accompanied Fan Chengda from Chengdu to Ezhou needed to replenish supplies when they returned. "The soldiers in Sichuan Province should purchase all the supplies and grain needed for their return trip to Hubei because they could not do it in three days" (C. Fan 2012: 83). They purchased supplies for their return trip in Ezhou, the largest market in the middle reaches of the Yangtze River. During Lu You's journey, the life necessities were purchased in coastal towns. When he arrived at Changheyan, "it was a small market, rich in fish and crabs." Passing Helu Town, "the town was densely populated, and there were many people selling dried fish." In Xinfeng City, there were quite a lot stores in the local market" (Y. Lu 2012: 160, 161, 164). They "sold dried fish in the center" of Wujiang County, and "bought concocted medicine in Qikou Town in Qizhou (Qichun County, Hubei Province)" and "purchased sheep and wine in Shishou County. Because of the Chongyang Festival a sheep was killed in that village, and each boat bought some separately, after a while, it was eaten" (Y. Lu 2012: 162, 193, 203). A small pier in a village became a market. When Sun Di sailed a boat on the Jingxi Brook and entered Yixing County, where "the boatman told him that there was not enough firewood and then we went to the market for firewood. He anchored the boat under the Xiaohou Temple to wait for the boatman. Seeing that the boatman came with firewood on his back, he untied the anchor and left" (D. Sun 1990). It can be seen that there were different forms of waterfront markets for water travelers to shop along the waterway.

Some transactions were done directly on the water, forming various floating markets. Local residents and fishermen would trade from boats. Su Shi's boat was forced to anchor in Cihu Lake due to strong winds, and "there were small boats coming to sell cakes, and they were very happy to hear that the village was in front of the mountain" (Z. Zeng et al. 2001: 139). Li Liuqian witnessed the scene that "salt merchants played the flute at night, and the women sellers of water chestnut sailed in the morning to pick water chestnuts. How can people avoid getting drunk after they buy wine and fish? If it were not here, how could I see such a scene by spending much money?" (L. Li 1990). These women sold water chestnut to passers-by in particular. When Lu You sailed on the Xiuzhou Canal, passing by Pingwang, he saw that "small boats were selling fish, knocking on the side of the boat, and the price was very cheap." When he passed Helu, he found that "the town was densely populated with residents, and many people were selling dried fish." In Daxinkou of Taipingzhou, "there were quite a lot of people selling water chestnuts, gorgon fruits and lotus roots." Since the big boats were blocked in the small harbor by the strong wind, "small boats were braving the waves to sell firewood, vegetables, pork and even wild boar meat" (Y. Lu 2012: 162, 161, 179, 185). Wang Shipeng also saw "small boats selling shrimps" on the Yangtze River. "Our boat dare not move forward in the strong wind and torrents. As we were running out fish, meat, fruits and vegetables, and little rice was left, I felt happy at the noises of a small boat coming at dusk. It was blazing waves against the wind, carrying red salt, fish and dried fish to trade. Immediately, boatmen rushed out to buy some. I successfully bought dishes to go with liquor." The freshly caught fish was already sold out on the water before it was put on the market. "The fishermen all live on a sandbar, and they can catch 200 bream in one net, all of which would be sold before they returned home, and tomorrow morning fish would fill the boat again." Water travelers were also excited at buying fresh fish. "At night, everyone on the boat was very happy. With a bucket of rice (6 kg) newly bought, reed as firewood picked from the water, they could cook bream with river water, for dining and wine at night" (S. Wang 2012: 348). Since officials traveling on the water often robbed residents of their fish. Even if they had fish, they would not sell fish to officials on the boats. Yao Mian wrote in his poems, which said "How can people sail on the river without eating fish? But fishermen always said fish unavailable. Here they do not sell fish to official boats as corrupted officials always encroached on their interests. Hiding fish in the cyan bamboo cage, they rowed away. They refused to sell fish to the official boats, as they had no pity on fishermen. As fish soup is the delicious the locals' favorite, I would anchor my boat under a willow tree to search for it. If I were a fisher, I would rather go home and cook fish for myself than selling to official boats" (M. Yao 1990).

5.3.4.2 Visiting Friends and Feasting

On his trip to Yiling, Ouyang Xiu said "Although I have travelled for a long time, I was often entertained by my friends on the way and could not tear myself away from them. My overstaying there was not prevented by storms, either. My mother quoted the fortune teller that it was really lucky of me on the trip" (X. Ouyang n.d.: 490). Traveling with friends made a long trip enjoyable. In *Records of the Trip to the Post,* Ouyang Xiu was most contented interacting and banqueting with friends and relatives. So, Wang Shenzhong said, "this is an account book of feasts and there are also historical record" (Z. Tao 1990). Ouyang Xiu stopped in most prefectures and counties along the way; he often stayed there for several days including five days in Sizhou (Xuyi, Jiangsu Province), seven days in Yangzhou and Jiangning, seventeen days in Chuzhou (Huai'an, Jiangsu Province), and more than a month in Jingzhou. These were not recorded in *Records of the Trip to the Post*. He drank almost every day, rowing on a moonlit night to play chess, or watching the rain and admiring lotus flowers. He mainly stayed with Tian Kuang (Yuanjun) during the seventeen days in Chuzhou. Tian Kuang and Ouyang Xiu were entitled official candidates in the eighth year of the Tiansheng Reign (AD 1030). Later, in Tian's tenure of the senior assistant in Chuzhou, he made a special trip out of Chuzhou to meet Ouyang Xiu. They were inseparable during Ouyang's visit.

As many as 53 relatives and friends mentioned in *the Records of the Trip to the Post,* were visited by Ouyang Xiu during his journey. They can be classified into four categories: local officials, old friends, new acquaintances, and relatives. Cai Xiang, Wang Gongchen, Ye Qingchen, and others were all colleagues who served as officials in the capital. Within four days of Ouyang Xiu's departure (May 24) after being demoted, these colleagues and old friends came to see him off. On the 24th, Ouyang Xiu drank in Gongqi's home; on the 25th, Ouyang Xiu went east out of Dongshuimen and Sunzhi came to play chess and drink with him; on the 26th, thirteen colleagues, including Junkuang, Gongqi, Daozi, and Junmo, came to meet him, made tea, played music, played chess, and drank. Junmo, Jingchun, Muzhi, and Shouchang stayed overnight there. On the 27th, Ziye, Xiucai, and Hanjie came to the gathering while Junkuang, Gongqi, and Daozi came again to compose poems, play the Fangxiang, a seven-stringed musical instrument, and drank together. Except for Ziye who went home that night, everyone stayed overnight. Some visited by him on the way were his old friends, such as Huang Xiaogong in Hongze, and Tian Kuang in Chuzhou. They both passed the imperial examination in the same year as Ouyang Xiu.

Local officials with a special expense account were originally responsible for welcoming and sending off official visitors (C. Huang 2004). Although Ouyang Xiu had been demoted, he was a renowned poet. Local officials were happy to entertain him. In Nanjing, Shi Jie, a current magistrate, Xie Fu, a magistrate of Yingtian Prefecture, Zhao Gun, a county criminal inspector of the Right Army, and Jiang Anshi, an observatory magistrate of Caozhou (Heze, Shandong Province) went to drink with him. "They had a few drinks under the pavilion near the river while I didn't drink due to my illness, and all the guests went back drunk." In Chuzhou (Huai'an, Jiangsu Province), the mayor, Chen Ya, set up a banquet in Weigongn Pavilion for Ouyang Xiu to appreciate the lotus. In Yangzhou, Wang Junyu, Xu Yuan, Tang Zhao, Su Yifu, who served as officials there, took turns to entertain Ouyang Xiu. In addition, Ouyang Xiu made friends with Zhao Shidao, the Fengyang County major, Fan You, the county mayor of Danling, Guo Gongmei, the secretary-general of Qichun County, and Xia Tuntian, the mayor of Huangzhou. Ouyang Xiu met these new acquaintances, such as Chun Qing in Sizhou (Xuyi, Jiangsu Province), Li Dunyu in Hongze, and Linghu Xiuji in Ezhou. He also met his brother in Ezhou.

Zhang Shunmin, Zhou Bida, Fan Chengda, Lu You and others had all met officials or visited relatives and friends during their journey to take or leave their posts, but we will not list all of them.

5.3.4.3 Tours for Sightseeing and Transit Vehicles

Enjoying beautiful scenery and visiting historic spots were also important activities for Ouyang Xiu on his journey. *The Trip to Chenzhou* by Zhang Shunmin, *The Trip to Guilin, Travelogues in Wu Area by Ship* by Fan Chengda, *Essays about My Journey to Sichuan* by Lu You, and *Proposals to the Emperor in the Qiandao Reign* by Zhou Bida mainly focused on sightseeing along the way. These officials enjoyed the unique scenery, made reflections at historic sites, and experienced the poems of predecessors when they were there. Officials widened their horizon and verified their knowledge in this way during the journey. In *the Records of the Trip to the Post,* Ouyang Xiu made detailed accounts of meetings with friends. He also mentioned his sightseeing in the journey, "I arrived at Chenliu and climbed the Yu Temple at noon" on May 23rd, 1036; "I arrived at Lingbi and visited the Suzhiyuan Garden alone in the evening" of July 27th; on June 12th, "Yin Fu, Gao Jilong, Jiao Zongqing and I were drinking liquor in the East Pavilion of the Water and Land Courtyard, watching rain and seeing the lotus blossom"; "Chen Ya, the mayor, drank wine and watched lotus flowers in the Weigong Pavilion" on June 21st; "I was drinking with Junyu at Shouning Temple (Longevity Temple)" on July 1st. This temple was Xu Zhigao's former residence. Later, it was renamed as Xiaoxian Temple (the Temple of Fililal Piety) as the founding emperor worshiped filial piety in the Taipingxingguo Reign." He must have visited historical sites during his stay in Chuzhou (Huai'an, Jiangsu Province) and Jiangning for many days. Both Ouyang Xiu and Fan Chengda spent more than 100 days on the journey. In fact, most of their time was spent on sightseeing along the way.

On his way to Chenzhou (Chenxian, Hunan Province), Zhang Shunmin would have sightseeing in each place where he stayed. He visited Liu's Garden in the northern suburb of Fuli town in Suzhou, the Guishan Temple in Hongzekou, the Puzhao Temple in Sizhou (Xuyi, Jiangsu Province), the Taiping Xingguo Temple in Huainan Province, the ShanYang Ziji Palace, Zhaobo Dam, Zhaobo Temple, the Ganlu Temple in Runzhou, the Stone Castle in Jiangning Prefecture, the Yueyang Tower in Yuezhou (Yueyang, Hunan Province), the Yuelu Academy in Tanzhou, and Hengshan Mountain in Hengzhou (Hengyang, Hunan Province) and other places of interest (S. Zhang 1990). Fan Chengda traveled from Hangzhou to Guangnan West Province and from Chengdu to Hangzhou. He visited the Tengwang Pavilion, the Hengshan Mountain, the Giant Buddha of Leshan, Emei Mountain, and saw the handwriting of Yellow Mountain Valley in Xuzhou (Yibin, Sichuan), Ouyang Xiu's ancestral hall in Yiling County, and visited Su Shi's Dongpo Snow Hall… (C. Fan 2012: 53–90). *Essays about My Journey to Sichuan* records the activities of land travel to places of interest such as West Lake, Jinshan Temple, Lushan Mountain, Dongpo Snow Hall, Yellow Crane Tower among other places. Most of them are stories of visits.

Traveling by water enabled travelers to enjoy the passing landscapes and form artistic conceptions different from travelling on land. Jiang Kui said that people in a boat "are just like lying on their back on the bed, which was stable and less stressed, so their minds could roam freely" (K. Jiang 1990). People could free their body and mind from the tedious journey and enjoy the beautiful scenery on the water and the banks. Yang Wanli described the scenario of boats sailing on the snow-caped river, with clear water and jade twigs of trees passing by on the banks. "White boats were sailing in the crystal kingdom, and the jade twigs were swaying in the chilly air" (W. Yang 2007: 1415). This scene was similar to Mei Yaochen's description about boating on the river on a starry night. "The raft floats lightly on the water and goes in the star light" (Y. Mei 1990). These artistic conceptions can only be experienced from a special perspective on water. Lu You navigated on the broad surface of the lower reaches of the Yangtze River. "The weather was always warm and sunny, and the river was as calm as matting; white clouds and green mountains were separated from each other, and it was like sailing in a picture all day." The river reflects the white clouds in the sky and the green mountains on both sides, which was a great creation of nature. When he passed by Dongliu County, he described that "Trees in the distant and near places have overlapped, like an unfurled landscape screen, ranging out dozens of miles." It was also like a giant picture roll unfolding gradually. On both sides of the river in Zhuanzhong, he said that "dense bamboo forests, tall trees, clean banks came into my eyes. Chicks and dogs are very roaming leisurely, and ducks are swimming freely on the river. People are walking in the shade of the trees, and some others are calling for boats at the ferry. This scene was attractive, because it's just like a created fantasy" (Y. Lu 2012: 181, 184). On the Fuyang River, Fan Chengda "rested in the bow and enjoyed the passing-by landscapes." He saw that "the mountains were covered with snow and the river was dyed dark blue." The water was "so clear and beautiful" (C. Fan 2012: 33) that he could only experience it when he was on a boat.

Only during a journey can people have the opportunity to appreciate beautiful the scenery depicted in ancient poems. At the Daxinkou Ferry of the Yangtze River, Lu You saw mountains on the both sides of the river, and personally experienced the description in Li Bai's poem, "Dark cliffs stand pointy by my sides, and a sail lonely is approaching from the horizon." At the mouth of Poyang Lake, Lu You witnessed the wild wind blowing and the clouds rolling and changing, and the horizon was endless from all directions, so he exclaimed, "I didn't realize the artistic conception of Li Bai's poem which said 'sailing into the mirror-like Poyang Lake' until now" (Y. Lu 2012: 186). But Fan Chengda failed to find the scenery in Su Shi's poem when he passed Chibi in Huangzhou, "I didn't see the so-called 'huge rocks pointing to the sky,' the 'disorderly erected rocks' and the 'endless stretches of rocks.'. Of course, Su Shi made exaggerated description about the rocks" (C. Fan 2012: 84). Ouyang Xiu once wrote about the Yellow Ox Gorge of the Three Gorges in his poem, "The Yellow Ox Mountain can be seen in several consecutive days, which made travelers worry about how to go through it. It can also be viewed from afar, not because it detains passenger ships, but the circuitous river." The local proverb said that "The Yellow Ox Gorge greets me from morning to night, as an old friend" (X. Ouyang n.d.: 4). Li Bai also wrote a poem about it. However, Fan Chengda did not have the similar experience as Ouyang Xiu when he passed there. He wrote "as the old saying goes, 'if you set sails at the Yellow Ox Gorge in the morning, you need to stay there overnight, and see it for three days and nights in a row. The Yellow Ox Gorge greets you as an old friend.'... which was also quoted by Mr. Ouyang in his poem. However, when I went downstream the river and turned around, the Yellow Ox Mountain could not be seen anymore." He thinks that "the phrase 'as an old friend' is also the words used by affected ones" (C. Fan 2012: 79). Fan Chengda sailed downstream and passed it quickly, while Lu You went upstream and experienced the scene in Ouyang Xiu's poem. He arrived at the foot of the Yellow Ox Mountain on the ninth day, and was still travelling in the mountain on the eleventh so that he deeply agreed with Li Bai and

Ouyang Xiu. Lu You wrote, "Li Bai's poem goes like this. 'Three morns in Yellow Ox I travelled, three nights I stayed there though. Sailing was made for three days in full. My newly added gray hairs made me sorrow.' Mr. Ouyang said that 'the Yellow Ox Mountain can be seen in several days, which made travelers worry about how to cross it. It can also be viewed from afar, not because it detains passenger ships, but the circuitous river.' The proverb goes like this '"The Yellow Ox Gorge greets me from morning to evening, as an old friend does.' So both of them referred to it" (Y. Lu 2012: 213).

The travel diaries kept by officials also recorded many social conditions, which not only enriched their knowledge, but also preserved valuable first-hand information for future generations. In Hubei, Zhang Shunmin saw that "'Wandan Boat' with a load capability of 300 thousand kilograms, is oval shaped, like a three-storey house. Its cabins are built on the back, and its internal structures are gorgeously decorated. Ladders are used to go in and out of the cabins. Only strong winds could move the boat. Such a boat could carry twenty million strings of 1000 coins, or 12,000 Dan (360,000 kg) of rice" (S. Zhang 1990). For another example, Fan Chengda noticed that fir wood from Huizhou was heavily taxed in Yanzhou which greatly increased the price of fir wood shipped to Hangzhou. "The road from Wuzhou (Jinhua) to Quzhou was paved with bricks by two rich locals in the two prefectures as they jointly built this road to facilitate visits because they were tied by marriage." Besides, in Jiangnan West Province, he saw "the cooking smoke from every household gathered along the bank. There were orange orchards here and there along the Yangtze River with trees continuously shading the river. The bamboo fences and tile-roofed houses in the orange orchards were not like villages, but suggested the wealth that came from planting orange trees." Litchi could be found along the Yangtze River in Sichuan Province from Meizhou (Meishan, Sichuan Province), Qianwei County, Jiazhou (Leshan, Sichuan Province), Xuzhou (Yibin, Sichuan Province) to Wanzhou (Wanning County, Hainan Province). He also said that Wuzikou of Poyang Lake, "is a theft-rampant area. People dare not pass it by lifting sails without companion boats." The reach of the Jingjiang River and mouth of the Dongting Lake were also a theft-rampant area. "Passenger boats cannot pass it unless they travel together to strengthen their momentum." He also said that the Leshan Giant Buddha was "thirteen stories tall from head to foot." Chongqing (Gongzhou) is already a furnace, "which makes people difficult to stay cool." The mainstream water of the Yangtze River was "yellow and turbid", similar to that of the Yangtze River from Chengdu downward. To manage the waterway at the Three Gorges, "military commissioners send soldiers to stand on the mountain with flags. When a boat enters the gorge, they wave the flags to signal to boats behind. After each boat enters the Three Gorges, it will travel several miles before the boats behind it dare to continue" (C. Fan 2012: 34; C. Fan 2012: 61, 72, 75). Lu You met a "wooden raft on the Yangtze River with more than 30 meters wide and more than one hundred-fifty meters long. There were thirty or forty families living on the raft, each with a wife, children, and rice pounding equipment. There were cross paths and even small temples for gods among the families. The boatman said, 'this raft is still small. Large rafts are too big to sail into narrow waterways and can only sail in big rivers when they are used as vegetable gardens or taverns.'" (Y. Lu 2012: 193). This was like a village floating on water and there were many such stories.

During their journeys, in addition to enjoying the scenery on the water and along the river banks on larger passenger boats, these officials and poets also used small boats and sedan chairs to enter the tributaries and even go deep into the mountains. Officials often visited scenic spots during trips on water, which required convenient small boats, and sedan chairs for mountain climbing. A small boat was, also, better for short distances. "The small boat has no fixed place, it can be moored at will by the riverside villages. I borrowed a small fishing boat to sail in a small stream and tied it at the mouth of the stream, to a quinoa stem on the shore. "River boats are not narrow enough, and narrow boats navigate streams better" (Z. Su 1987: 313). Even in slippery rainy days and cold snowy days, when horses cannot move, boats can still travel freely. "I do not love the rich child's precious horse, but admire the landlord's white covered boat" (Y. Lu 2011: 34, 327, 314). Some small waterways can only be navigated with small boats. In Dazhou, "there is a salt mine in Xuanhan County, more than 500 kilometers away from Dazhou, that can only be accessed by a small stream and can passed by small boats" (*Wenguo Wenzhenggong Wenji n.d.*). Zhang Shunmin visited Dinglin Temple by boat with Xin Daguan in Hongxian County (Sixian, Anhui Province) and Jinshan Temple by boat in Runzhou (Zhenjiang) (S. Zhang 1990). Lu You once chartered a boat to sail on West Lake. In Guizhou, he took a boat to the south bank of the Yangtze River to climb a mountain to visit South Temple of Jiangdu. One day, he saw "a stream on the other side of the river with green and clear water, so he crossed the river in a small boat" (Y. Lu 2012: 159, 214, 215).

When Zhang Shunmin climbed Hengshan Mountain, he "took a sedan chair on a zigzagged mountain path that went straight up without twisting and folding. More than a dozen people were needed to carry the sedan chair forward" (S. Zhang 1990). In the Three Gorges, When Lu You passed Dadong Sandbar, as the land routes were bad, he and his relatives had to go in sedan chairs (Y. Lu 2012: 213). On the way to Hangzhou, Zhou Bida visited Jianji Abbey by sedan chair (B. Zhou 1990). Officials traveled on land mostly in sedan chairs. Fan Chengda went to Guangnan West Province and arrived in Hangzhou by land. His relatives, who had come to see him off, "were crying and refused to let the sedan chair pass." This shows that he apparently traveled by the sedan chair. Passing by Yichun in Jiangnan West Province, the bearers walked in mud so deep that the road was buried. They staggered on the road. When he arrived at Chuzhou City in Jinghu South Province, he got out of the sedan chair and sailed downstream (C. Fan 2012: 33, 41, 42). When Fan Chengda was returning to Hangzhou after finishing his term of office in Chengdu, he visited Mount Emei on the way. "One man rode a horse to Mount Emei" (C. Fan 2012: 61). He also traveled by horse, but this was not common.

5.3.5 Summary

Water transportation saw unprecedented development during the Song Dynasty and people traveling on water created prosperity. The downstream speed of inland river and the speed of canal travel was significantly faster than land travel. In particular, people could travel downstream more than 100 km a day on the fast-flowing Yangtze River. Canals, with their calm water and towpath, could be navigated day and night making them much faster than land travel. The speed of sailing upstream on inland rivers was generally slower than land travel. But there were many other factors that influenced travel choices besides speed. Long distance trips with children and heavy luggage were obviously more suitable for boat travel rather than land travel. However, land travel was more advantageous for journeys with little luggage and fewer people that required a faster rate.

There were generally two forms in the long distance travel. One was to travel by boat the whole way. Fan Chengda sailed downstream from Chengdu to Suzhou on the Yangtze River and canals. Travelers would chose to travel entirely by boat when possible especially if they were traveling with the old or young. Ouyang Xiu, traveling from Kaifeng to Yiling, Zhang Shunmin, going from Kaifeng to Chenzhou (Chenxian, Hunan province), and Lu You, traveling from Lin'an to Kui Zhou (Fengjie County, Chongqing City) chose this option. The other way was to travel both by water and land. When a journey did not have a water route, travelers had to use this method. Zhou Bida, making round trips between Jishui and Lin'an or Yixing, Yang Wanli, going from Changzhou to Jishui, and Fan Chengda going from Pingjiang Prefecture (Suzhou, Jiangsu Province) to Jingjiang Prefecture were all forced to do so. Sometimes, in order to pursue speed, they would also choose to travel by water and land. Su Shi and his son went from Meizhou to Kaifeng by sailing down the river to Jingzhou and then overland the rest of the way. And those who went upstream the river to Sichuan in Wanzhou would also choose to travel by land to save time.

Water travelers acquired boats in four main ways: official dispatch, rental, passenger boat, and chartering a boat. The first was mainly for officials when they went to or left from their postings or traveled on official business. The last three were commonly used by both officials and civilians. Water travel could last a long time, so people treated the boat as their home during the journey. Their daily needs came from coastal and floating markets. The main activities of the officials during these trips were meeting friends, enjoying banquets and sightseeing. Much of their time was spent on socializing with friends. Sacrifices were also important activities on the journey. During these activities, officials visited old friends, made new friends, went sightseeing and observe social conditions. Official travel had also become an important way for officials to accumulate experience, verify knowledge and increase insight. A saying in the Song Dynasty said, "You can't read poems by Du Fu unless you travel thousands of miles and read thousands of books" (M. Wang 1990). It was in this process that the scholar-officials of the Song Dynasty developed their style of knowledge and deeds.

5.4 Sacrificing Ceremonies of the Song People for Smooth Sailing

Under the conditions of shipbuilding and navigation technology in the Song Dynasty, water navigation was fraught with risks. Navigators placed their hopes of eliminating risks on the blessings of gods. Numerous ancestral temples were dotted along the inland river and ocean routes. Rituals were frequently held before and during the navigation, and navigators would hold a snap one in face of danger. Worshiping God was an important part of boatman's daily life in Song Dynasty.

5.4.1 The Risks of Navigation in the Song Dynasty

Navigation on the water often involves a variety of risks, from delayed journeys to financial and life-threatening consequences, and the most common one is being blocked by the wind. The wind direction on the river is unpredictable, not only can you not set sail when the wind is strong, but you can't tow the boat forward. So it is often necessary for boatmen to stop and wait for the favorable wind. When Wang Shipeng went westward into Sichuan, he said "it took us almost twenty days after getting on board from Ezhu (Wuhan, Hubei), before we had two-day smooth sailing in a tailwind." He was even blocked for ten days in Chiyang (now northwest of Jing Yang County, Shaanxi), "The returned boat was stopped by the wind in Chiyang, and the god of wind had good intentions to keep us here" (S. Wang 2012: 354, 495). When Li Liuqian was sailing on the Yangtze River, "since departure from Wuhu, his ship had to sail against the wind" (L. Li 1990). On the way from Guangzhou to Shaozhou (now Shaoguan, Guangdong), Yang Wanli lamented that "the boat was moored in Zhongjia village, three days after leaving Yingzhou, and we travelled only 10 km, as if we were rowing up the boat to the sky in an iron boat" (W. Yang 2007: 822). When they were blocked by the wind, either waited patiently as Wang Shipeng did, and comforted themselves at the excuse of wind, or prayed for divine help. For example, Zhang Lei "sailed against the wind in Guiling Bay for three days and prayed to the god of Gushan Mountain before the wind ceased." "Since we left Fuchi Town, we prayed to the Dragon King for favorite winds three times a day, and all of our wishes were satisfied. As a result, the weather was clear, and our boat could travel peacefully and go anywhere at our wishes." The favorite wind is considered to be the protection of the Dragon King. "I have heard that the Dragon King of the West River is all mighty in the whole world. Anyone who prays would be satisfied in time" (L. Zhang 1990).

The greater risk of sailing is capsizing, rather than being blocked by the wind. In the voyage of the Yangtze River, the section of the Three Gorges is the most dangerous. As the boats sailed through the gorges, "the scullers had pale faces and sweaty hands, giving up the thought of life." "The people nearby were horrified" (C. Fan 2012: 75). A person in the Song Dynasty depicted the thrilling path through

Xintan sandbar at Three Gorges as the following: "In the distance, I saw a ship approaching, riding the wind and waves, with noises louder than deafening drums … With their wives and children sitting securely in the boat, boatmen celebrated their success in going through the dangerous sections as if they had been reborn" (S. Yuan 1990). "The awnings were dancing in the wind and cables were used to tie the awnings. All the people in the boat with me looked at each other with horror" (Z. Li 1990). Lu You was in danger at Xintan sandbar when he entered Sichuan. "His boat was going through Xintan from the south bank, and about eight-tenth of the boats had their bottom damaged by rocks and were halted there. Before they got sunk, they were repaired by locals in time. The reason was probably that they were carrying a lot of potteries, which made them close to the riverbed." So that the local people repaired the leaking boats. As the locals need to earn a living from repairing boats, they objected the government to dredge the water course and clear the rocks on the riverbed. "The government had planned to remove the sharp stones on the riverbed when water fell in winter and spring and the stones became visible. As the local inhabitants benefited from the damaged boats by selling broken slabs, and traders may have the opportunity to trade there, they were undoubtedly reluctant to clear the riverbed. And the local inhabitants bribed the stonemasons to prove that these stones could not be removed. Only if the government was determined to clear the riverbed, could such projects be completed" (Y. Lu 2012: 214–15). So it was common for boats to run into trouble there. When Fan Chengda traveled to Dongben sandbar of the Three Gorges, "In the torrents, the boat was floating like a dead leaf. It fell into the whirlpool as if it entered a grinder. Pulling on the bamboo pole, the helmsman shouted and tried desperately to steer it out of the whirlpool (C. Fan 2012: 77). The Yanyu sandbar of Qutang Gorge was very dangerous, "the scullers' hands were so sweaty that they even gave up the thought of life when passing by. Only when the previous boat was a few miles away, could the rear boats be released. The local official sent soldiers to wave flags on the hill in turn, signifying the safe distance from the previous one (C. Fan 2012: 75). Lu You also said "many boats did not dare to go through Qutang Gorge, and the boatmen who sailed there were terrified" (Y. Lu 2011: 134). The Three Gorges is not the only dangerous part of the Yangtze River. "The most dangerous section is known as Zhangqisantan (three Jiliang sandbars) near Luzhou, where water runs so violently that boats have already sailed through three sandbars before flag signals are given" (C. Fan 1990). "Yuzhou (now Chongqing) section is dangerous at the junction of the two rivers, so the cargo boats were prone to be overturned by wind and waves" (T. Li 2004: 2503). So this quotation evidences that boats would be easily overturned at the confluence of the Jialing River and the Yangtze River.

Every section of the Yangtze has its hazardous places. For example, "boatmen avoid sailing in the section between Yueyang and the Dongting Lake as the waves are huge, even if there is a tailwind" (C. Fan 2012: 82). In June of the 25th year of the Shaoxing Reign (AD 1155), "it was said when a red dragon was crossing the water like a mountain in Hukou County (now Hukou County, Jiangxi Province), it brought chilly winds and aroused huge waves. Dozens of boats were overturned and scores of soldiers got drowned" (Toqta 1977: 1364). This was also true of the Chizhou section, "there are more than twenty hidden rocks near the east bank. To the west bank there is a sandbar, dabbed the ship-breaking bay, which is more than 100 km wide, causing numerous boats broken" (S. Xu et al. 2014: 9619). Travelling by boat in Dongliu County, Lu You felt that the vast river with huge waves like mountains tossed the 2000-Dan boat like a leaf. The boat was suddenly caught in "a gust, and the boatmen were so frightened that they hurriedly lowered his sails and went to the small harbour." With the aid of four or five moored boats, it could enter the harbour successfully (Y. Lu 2012: 184–85). When Zhou Bida was sailing in Datong section, he encountered "a big thunderstorm, which forced their boat to enter a small harbor for safety. And the distance between ships was several feet, resulting in the sinking" (B. Zhou 1990). The ship went through Dagu and "met a salt boat that broke down near the shore. In the previous day, both boats arrived at Jiaoshi Clamp. But as the merchants on the other boat hurried on their journey, they were unfortunately caught in a gale at night and their boat collided on the rocks there" (B. Zhou 1990). The Zhenjiang section of the lower reach of the Yangtze River is so vast and windy that if viewed from the top of Jinshan Mountain, "huge waves rolled up by the wind are like thousands of running sheep" (S. Zhang 1990), which often incurred more shipwrecks. In the sixth year of the Zhenghe Reign (AD 1116), it is said that as Zhenjiang "had not enough ports to anchor boats, if they encountered a storm there, they would have no shelter. So, over 500 boats were sunk there in the past three years" (S. Xu et al. 2014: 9618). In the Southern Song Dynasty, it was said, "in the dangerous section of the Yangtze River near Nanjing, ships should not berth there". "The Zhenjiang section was densely populated with boats in a narrow channel, so quite a few passenger boats got sank when storm came" (Song Shi Quanwen 2005). And the wind became even more fierce if boats went eastward from Zhenjiang. In the Southern Song Dynasty, if the canal was dry in spring and winter, all the grain boats would take the route from Zhenjiang to Jiangyin and then enter the canal. However, "If the grain boats entered the Yangtze River from Zhenjiang, the shipwrecks were frequently witnessed resulting in total loss of people and cargo on board" (X. Li 2013: 3531). Such cases can also be found in other rivers. For example, the Huaihe River, "has seen countless public and private sunk vessels in recent years"," with one hundred and seventy ships lost every year" (S. Yang et al. 1990). The strong winds and huge waves along Huaihe River from Chuzhou (Huai'an, Jiangsu province) to Lianzhou incurred many sunk ships (Toqta 1977: 10636). This is true even for the canals compared to be "calm rivers". In the early years of the Jianlong Reign, shortly after conquering Li Chongjin and his rebels, Wang Zan was ordered to administrate Yangzhou, and "after setting out, his boat was capsized under the Gate Bridge and three of his relatives and attendants got drowned" (Toqta 1977: 9350). And Jojin saw "more than 20 sunken boats" in Nanjing section of the Bianhe River (Jojin 2009: 264).

It is more dangerous for sea voyages. Xu Jing once experienced the dangers of sea navigation, being tossed up and down between the waves. At that time, he had the only thought of "escaping from death". As a matter of fact, maritime navigation means "life and death in an instant." He summed up the three biggest risks on the sea: "It's called Chifeng (northeast wind), Heifeng (storm) and Haidong (swell). If the northeast wind keeps blowing for days, it is howling with anger and making people loss in directions. Storm blows violently without fix directions, and the sky turns so dark that it is impossible to tell day from night. Few people can be spared from such dangers in the ocean. Swells, like boiling water, can push a ship more than a dozen of miles away, few people can survive. A dozen-meter-wide ship sinking between the waves is like a hair falling from a horse." He lamented that ships, big or small, were only a drop in the ocean in the boundless sea. "So what is important for boatmen is not the size of ship, but their right operation in time of emergency." For maritime navigation, the most important to the seafarer does not rely on the size of boat, but the devotion to the gods. For example, "to venture out on the sea in a small boat, relying on the blessing of the court may help the ship to sail safely, if not, how can people ensure their safety only by their strength". "If in times of great danger, they prayed and pleaded with the gods, all their wishes were satisfied." Their fleet was caught in a storm in the Yellow Sea, "three oars were all broken". "All the boatmen cut their hair and begged piteously to the gods. Then, an auspicious light appeared and the god of Fuzhou Yanyu appeared." "Their faces turned pale on horror, so one can imagine their worry and horror at that time" (J. Xu 2006: 148). There is also the danger posed by large marine life in the sea. According to *Pingzhou Notes*, "A sea sawshark about 100 feet long, has a saw snout and it can break a ship easily" (Y. Zhu 2006: 150). As Zhao Ding was relegated to Zhuya (now Haikou, Hainan Province), he made a southbound journey from Leizhou (now Haikang, Guangdong Province) when he came across a "giant loach" in the sea. "The boatmen shook their hands in terror and required everyone to freeze, then hurriedly stood up in the boat, with their hair draped and sharp swords in hands, and with their backs to the sails, cut their tongues and dripped blood into the water, and told the missionary official to sit down in the cabin and close their eyes. After two hours, the boatmen were heard to say to each other in excitement, 'We are spared. We are spared.'" (M. Zhu 1990).

Apart from the natural disaster, the boatmen also encountered threats of evil people during the voyage, namely the risks imposed by thieves. Along the Yangtze River, Poyang Lake and Zhuan River between Ezhou (Wuchang, Hubei) and Gong'an (Gong'an County, Hubei Province) are known as "pirate areas" because pirates were rampant there in normal years. The Wuzikou of Poyang Lake "was notorious as a piracy area and can only be sailed through in a tailwind and in the company of other boats." The banks were covered with reeds and there were many branches of the harbour, "as it was a pirate area, passenger boats dare not go through it unless they were courageous with companies" (C. Fan 2012: 36; C. Fan 2012: 82). In his voyage along the Yangtze River at night, Wang Shipeng found that "dogs began to bark, and it was supposed to be a thief. Then the boatmen were startled and stayed awake all night" (S. Wang 2012: 444). It is clear that anti-theft is also a normal practice in the voyage. The risk of thieves there is even greater when sailing at sea. "Pirates robbed rice boats to feed themselves, trade ships to enrich themselves and captured men and boats to increase their maritime power." During the season when traders are in and out of town, "they waited for foreign ships, intercepted and robbed them" (D. Zhen, n.d.). "Whenever the pirates plundered a passenger ship, they burned it if it was small, and took it for their own use if it was large. If anyone wanted to fight with the pirates, they would be killed, and if they were too weak, they would be released or thrown into the water, while those who were strong enough to steer the ships were taken for their own use. If they wanted to rebel, they would be killed by pirates" (D. Zhen, n.d.).

In the face of unpredictable events, people often view strange phenomena as omens. On a boat at the port of the Yugan River, Zhou Bida saw "a small snake pulling the boat with its head up to the shore and then back". This was often considered to be the guidance and blessing of the river god. "The silver lake, as smooth as a bronze mirror, guided boats forward in a zigzagged way. Any official's career is full of ups and downs, how many people could have such a calm lake to sail in the voyage like me" (B. Zhou 1990). When Lu You navigated the Madang section of the Yangtze River, he ran into a dangerous situation. He saw that "a large green-backed fish, with a belly as bright red as a pearl, suddenly jumped up more than two feet high near the oars, which startled people. At night, all the masts and the sails were broken, which astonished them" (Y. Lu 2012: 185). In times of great danger, people naturally asked gods for help. In the face of all the risks, the passengers on board exclaimed, "My boat is as small as a blade of grass, and my life is as light as a strand of hair" (F. Zhao 1990). As Liu Zihui said, "I have always cherished my life. Can I trust my life to the boatmen?" (Z. Liu 1990). In times of great danger, people could only pray to the god. When Zhang Yi administrated Qingshen County, "there was a pine beach in the southeast of the county. In summer and autumn the torrential river capsized many boats. Zhang Yi prayed to the river god, and then in less than a month water retreated nearly three kilometers from the beach, which surprised the locals" (Z. Liu 1990: 12699). It was their hope that the river god could ensure their boat sailing smoothly. As Xu Jing said above, once deep at sea, people's psychological dependence is not on the size of the ship, but on their worship of god. There was a temple on Furong Island in Laizhou, "There were less than 100 kilograms of rice in the temple. Whenever a fisherman was stopped by wind, he could stay and eat the rice there. After he managed to go home, he could return to the temple with more rice than he had eaten, dare not deceive the god" (Y. Zhu 2006: 159). Such is the honesty and reverence that people have for the gods.

5.4.2 *Belief in Gods in Inland River Navigation*

People on the water believed that "if they prayed cordially, the gods could divide the wind into two directions to suit their boats" (Y. Lu 2012: 192). They frequently presented sacrifices to the gods during their voyage for smooth sailing. This is why many gods were imagined for people to worship in the inland waterways, where there were a lot of navigation operations.

5.4.2.1 God Worship in the Yangtze River Navigation

As the busiest inland waterway in the Song Dynasty, the Yangtze River served as water course for grain transportation, passenger travel and circulation of goods connecting economically prosperous Sichuan with the southeast and south provinces, and Kaifeng in the Norther Song Dynasty, as well as the transportation from the provinces along the Yangtze River to Hangzhou. The highest-ranking deity on the Yangtze River is River God, one of the four gods, whose original temple was built in Chengdu. When the Sichuan-made Boat "left Chengdu, they could stop at the Jiangdu Temple. Before dawn, people entered the temple to pray" (M. Hong 1981: 398). Sailing on the Yangtze River, the river god was omnipresent. Both upwind and downwind are considered to be controlled by gods. As Wang Shipeng put it, "if the river god did not help the boatmen, the boat could move inch by inch in the swift currents" (S. Wang 2012: 344). Wu Fu encountered a headwind in the Yangtze River and considered it to be anger of the river god. "It was not easy to meet with pleasure, but the wind was against the current. The boatmen knew that the river god was angry, and immediately rowed back to the small river" (F. Wu 1990). Wang Zhidao also considered the tailwind to be a gift from the river god. "Our boat can ride downstream in the tailwind, and it turns out that the river god is also affectionate" (Z. Wang 1990). The river god worship was included the middle rite category of national rituals, organized regularly by the imperial court. Officials for business trip on the Yangtze also often worshiped the river god before departure. In his journey from Kaifeng to Yiling, when Ouyang Xiu "arrived at Xinye County, he prayed to the river god". "At Zhaohua port, a strong wind began to blow at night and the ships could not anchor, so he prayed to the river god" (X. Ouyang 2001: 1902, 1903). Zheng Gangzhong was ordered to pacify the people of Guanshan region (now Shaanxi). Before he crossed the river, he presented sacrifice to him at Zhenjiang, praying that "the wind and waves would stop so that the ships could sail safely." Later, he was ordered to inspect the Sichuan-Shaanxi war region and traveled westward via the Yangtze River, where he sacrificed to the river god in the hope that the ships could sail smoothly. And it is also the duty of the river god to help him fulfil the mission given by the emperor. "Missions entrusted by the emperor must be fulfilled not only openly but also secretly. The affairs of the imperial court are undertaken not only by hundreds of officials, but the hundreds of gods. It is now your duty to calm the river and make it smooth for the ships to cross" (G. Zheng 1990). Zhou Zizhi also worshiped the river god for his own reasons, firstly to thank the gods for "ensuring him sailing safety four times in crossing the river without fear of great winds and waves;" and secondly to pray that this time the gods would "bless him calm currents while he crossed it." In the next year, he prayed to the river god in June to thank them "for he blessed him with smooth water flow in last summer, and on the river-crossing day, the wind calmed down, the demons were hidden and the river was like a flat mirror. This was the great gift of the river god" (Z. Zhou 1990). Wang Zhiwang once paid a formal visit to the Jiangdu Temple in Chengdu, saying that he had "been travelling along the Yangtze River for over forty years since he was a child, but he had no worry about winds and waves, which was actually a blessing from the river god. Therefore, he must pay a formal visit to the temple" (Z. Wang 1990). Although he worked in Chengdu, he actually worshiped for personal reasons. The Temple of River God was originally built in Chengdu, and later some temporary temples to worship the river god were built in the Three Gorges, Shashi (now Jing Sha in Hubei) and Jiankang (now Nanjing, Jiangsu). But boatmen could pay tributes to the river god anywhere when they sailed on the Yangtze River. When traveling in Hukou, Dong Cigao wrote a poem, saying that "The ashes of paper as an offering to the dead were floating in the air, carnivores' appearance was seen on the river god's face. He stopped in calling back the dead's soul, leaving the river without looking back any more. Then I was startled to wake up from my imagination for fear that my life would be claimed by him" (S. Dong 1990).

Apart from the river god, people on the boat also worshiped many other deities associated with navigation along the Yangtze River. The section between Zhenjiang and Jiangzhou (now Jiujiang in Jiangxi) had the largest number of deities on the water, and the most famous is God of Sanyuan Shuifu (the God of Water Kingdom). The Xiashuifu Temple (the Lower Water Kingdom Temple) was built in Zhenjiang and was originally attached to the Jinshan Longyou Temple (Dragon King Temple). In the early years of the Yuanfeng Reign, it was relocated to Xijindu on the south bank of the river (X. Yu 1990: 2725). From Guazhou in the north of the river you can see the Water Kingdom Temple. When Lu You travelled in Zhenjiang by boat, he "presented a pig and a jug of wine to the Temple of Good-Luck King, also known as lower water kingdom. It was affiliated to the Jinshan Temple, where two monks were often assigned to guard it, and no other monks in it. However, it was recorded in the sacrifice book that the pig's head, which was used to pay tribute to the god, was considered to be the belongings of this temple. Everyone laughed at the record" (Y. Lu 2012: 165). When Zhou Bidai, travelled in Zhenjiang, he "visited the Lower Water Kingdom Temple" (B. Zhou 1990). The Middle Water Kingdom Temple was built on Niuzhu Cliff, Caishi Town, Taiping Zhou (now Dangtu, Anhui Province), namely Caishi Cliff (B. Zhou 1990). "The cliffs are precipitous and dangerous, and there the river water is turbulent. Boats suffer greatly from it." When boatmen passed the Water Kingdom Temple, they "must first disembark their boat, and present the sacrificial animals and money to the temple", and "cook the animals as the sacrifice and submit elegy for the god before they pray". In the early years of the Qingli Reign, after the new fork river was dug by Niuzhu Cliff, all boats travelled here, the sacrificers reduced in number, and the ancestral temple became dilapidated later (J. Yang 1990). In the middle of the Jiayou Reign, a man rode on a horse to Jiangnan, but when he turned back to cross Caishi Cliff, the wind and waves became so strong that he could not halted there for three days. He tried again but the wind became even stronger. So he held a dedicated ritual to pray at the Middle Water Kingdom Temple. That night, he dreamed that the water god said that he could only cross the river by leaving his horse behind. The next day he did so, and the wind stopped and he crossed the river without any trouble" (Z. Tao 1990). The Upper Water Kingdom Temple was built on Madang Mountain on the south bank of the Yangtze River in Pengze County of Jiangzhou (now Jiujiang, Jiangxi). "In Madang, they can pray at the Lower Water Kingdom Temple" (Y. Lu 2012: 184–85). Voyagers passing through this area also worshiped the god of Water Kingdom. "Livestock meat and tasty liquor were offered to the god for his blessing of sailing in a tailwind." Only after sacrifice contributed to the god can one be blessed. "People said it was difficult for boats to go through Madang section, but I made it. I rowed the oars, sailing down the river, as if commanding thousands of horsemen" (Z. Zhang 1990). When Lu You came here, he also paid a visit to the Upper Water Kingdom Temple, stating that "this is the best temple along the river" (Y. Lu 2012: 185).

In addition to the gods of Xia Shui Fu, Zhenjiang also has the god of Jiao Shan, who also has the duty of protecting navigation because "Jiaoshan is in the Yangtze River waterway", "the prayers of the people on board were mostly answered" (*Song Da Zhaoling Ji,* 485), Emperor Zhenzong made the mountain god a duke (D. Ma 2011: 2769). It also became the god of navigational protection. Across the river in Yangzi County, Yangzhou, on the other side of Zhenjiang, there is the Temple of Zixu, which is dedicated to Wu Zixu for his ability to guide the tides (S. Zhang 1990). The Zixu Temple at Yangzhou has been in existence since the Tang Dynasty. "It is used for worshiping the river god, but Wu Zixu, the military strategist was invited to share sacrifice with god" (M. Ouyang 2003: 574). The navigators of the Zhenjiang River section also worshiped Master Lei Haiqing. When Wen Tianxiang's boat was below the Ganlu Temple in Zhenjiang, they "asked for a favorite wind, they prayed to 'Master Lei Haiqing in Jiangnan'. Soon, they were blessed with a tailwind and they knelt down to thank him" (T. Wen 1987: 698). The Lei Haiqing Worship was developed in Jizhou, Jiangxi (now Jixian, Shanxi) (M. Xie et al. 1990), which must be a water-based belief popular among boatmen in the lower reach of the Yangtze River. When Yuan Shuoyou's boat went past Sanshan Cliff, on which a goddess temple was set up to worship Madam Li. He paid a formal visit and wrote a poem, stating "I am chanting at the Goddess Temple who patrols and safeguards the river. Ancients and the past events have gone, leaving us reflecting over the past. I handle affairs by faithfulness in my life, I beg the emperor to think over my promotion request" (S. Yuan 1990). The God Zhaoming of Guichi (now Guichi District, Chizhou, Anhui) had the function of administrating navigation. "The people of Guichi worshiped the God Zhaoming also dabbed 'the Ninth God of the West City'. When a big boat capsized and twelve people were drowned, they thought it was the god's power" (T. Huang 2011: 976). This quotation is about the deity who is in charge of the bliss and woe of navigation. A temple dedicated to the god Huiji and Madam Anji is located at Xiaogu Mountain in Susong County, Shuzhou (now Qianshan, Anhui). When Zhang Lei "sailed against the wind in Guiling Bay for three days, he prayed to the gods of the Xiaogu Mountain before the wind stopped" (L. Zhang 1990). Once before he crossed Xiaogu Mountain, Ouyang Xiu "prayed to the god of Xiaogu Moutain" (X. Ouyang 2001: 1902). "When Lü Yuanzhong sailed past Xiaogu Mountain, he entered the temple to pay his respects" (M. Hong 1981: 547). There was also a branch of Xiaogu Temple and the Penglang Temple on Penglang Cliff in Pengze County (Pengze, Jiangxi), which can be visited by boat, "when boats pass here, even if there is no wind, the waves swell up". As was described in an ancient poem, "Merchants in the boat should not be frivolous to customers, Xiaogu married to Penglang in the year before (This allusion means that the Xiaogu Mountain was wedded to the Panglang

Cliff)" (Y. Lu 2012: 186). So it is clear that when merchants on boats passed by, they were sure to pay respectful homage to the Penglang Temple.

The belief in Dragon King Shunji had a great influence in Poyang Lake area. As that time, people believed that "the prestige of Dragon King Shunji has benefited countless people in the water regions". Su Shi stayed in the Nankang Military Prefecture at night, silently praying for the help of King Shunji, "before his words were finished, the wind began to sweep past his ears, the punters lifted the sails. Before the meal was ready, they had passed Yanglan and could anchor their boat at Yuzhang at midday" (J. Shi 1990). In the Jianzhong Jingguo Reign, Su Shi returned from Dan'er in the north, "anchored below the Dragon King Shunji Temple in Wucheng Mountain, he paid homage to the Dragon King and returned to the ship" (S. Su 2010: 1279). The Dragon King Shunji, also known as the "Divine Snake". The emperor named him the Marquis of Shunji in the eighth year of the Dazhongxiangfu Reign (AD 1015) and the King of Shunji in July of the ninth year of the Xi'ning Reign (AD 1076), after which he was repeatedly ennobled by the emperor, until the second year of the Xuanhe Reign (AD 1120), when he was ennobled as the King of Smooth Navigation, Peace and Benevolence, whose duty was to ensure smooth navigation. In the period of the Xi'ning Reign, when the Northern Song conquered Cochin, its fleet was escorted by Divine Snake, who was conferred a royal title and worshiped by people (S. Xu et al. 2014: 1087). The area under the jurisdiction of King Shunji "extended from the Dongting Lake in the south to Huaihe and Sishui Rivers in the north" (S. Su 2010: 1280). After Divine Snake, who escorted the Song army fleet, arrived at the Dongting Lake, "it returned to Nankang with a merchant ship. The legend has it that the Pengli Divine Snake was active up to Dongting and never went further south". Returning north from Hainan Island, when Su Shi passed by the Dragon King Shunji Temple, he "paid a formal visit to it and returned to his boat" (S. Su 2010: 1280). When Fan Chengda's boat moored in Bosi River Fork, "a divine snake appeared on the river and people scrambled to see it" (C. Fan 2012: 88). Another time he stayed at Wuzikou in Poyang Lake, "the wind and snow were raging, his boat was moored at the Dragon King Temple. The next day, the wind became even stronger, (so) he prayed to the river god" (C. Fan 2012: 36–37). Zhao Qi, the general commander of the Southern Song Dynasty, moored his boats below the Shunji Temple in Hongzhou (now Nanchang, Jiangxi). "After the sacrifice ceremony, Zhao took the prostitute to the temple for a drink", which was disrespectful to the Dragon King. As a result, "dozens of boats were capsized and soldiers were lost. Most of the tycoons were drowned" (M. Hong 1981: 266). We can see that the officials and the people were very respectful to the divine snake and believed in its power.

On the way upstream from Jiangzhou, the sacrificial rites to the Dragon King Shunji at Fuchikou of the Xingguo Military Prefecture were also done frequently. Zhang Lei said, "all travelers prayed to the temple". When his ship passed through Fuchikou, Zhang Lei "prayed to the Dragon King to bless his boat with a tailwind, and all were answered" (L. Zhang 1990). The greatest benefit of the Xingguo Military Prefecture was given by the God of Fuchi Zhaoyong, or God Gan Ning, who was the great general of the Wu Kingdom in the period of the three Kingdoms. "None of passing-by travelers dared not worship, and livestock meat were sacrificed every day"

(M. Hong 1981: 547). In the fifth year of the Kaibao Reign (AD 972), the imperial court entitled him Duke of Protecting Nation, in the fifth year of Xuanhe Reign (AD 1123) he was crowned King Wuhui, and King Wuhui Zhaoyi in the second year of the Jianyan Reign (AD 1128), King Zhaoyi Wuhui Xianling two years later (AD 1130), and King Zhaoyi Wuhui Yiai Lingxian in the twenty-first year of the reign of Shaoxing (AD 1151). In the second year of the Zhenghe Reign (AD 1112), the temple was granted the title of Zhaoyong Temple. His two wives were named by the emperor Lady Shunyou and Lady Rouyi, and two sons were named Duke Shaowei and Duke Shaoling (Y. Lu 2012: 192). After the temple was repaired by Yue Fei, the marshal of the state army, "none of the temples along the Yangtze were as good as it. It overlooked the river and stop for boats." People on the water believed that "if they prayed, the gods could change the wind into two directions to suit the boat." This is why boats were often stationed to pay homage, so that "the sacrifice ceremonies were held day and night". Then the believers' donated money was great. "This temple's contribution to the local government was considerable as the believers paid 1200 strings of 1000 coins to the government every year." This is much different from the Youlong Temple in Digang, Fanchang County, which had no travelers to worship, leaving only one old Taoist there, "with only two bundles of firewood cut by himself to trade in life necessities. And he begged for help when it rained or snowed." When Lu You passed by the temple on his boat, "he brought a jug of wine and a pig with him to pay homage to the god of King Zhaoyi Wuhui Yiai Lingxian" (Y. Lu 2012: 192). The main building of Zhaoyong Temple was called Building Juanxue. According to *The Catalogue and Notes of the Cao's Library*, there were two volumes of *Building Xuelou Collections*, dedicated to collecting the preface and poems of the Zhaoyong Temple of Fuchi (X. Zhao 1990). This shows the grand rituals held there. Yuan Shuoyou also paid tributes to the temple when he passed by it. He said that it "was very important in its rituals and the reputation of the deity was known far and wide. The sacrifice meat was a pig, and the wrapped meal drew flocks of birds". (S. Yuan 1990). When Zhang Lei's boat "crossed Fuchi, he begged for a tailwind by offering yellow wine to the Master Wu Gan Temple." He said that "there is an ancestral temple built for Master Wu Gan by the river, and the sacrificial prayers are solemn and respectful in it" (L. Zhang 1990).

Entering the Zhuanhe River from Ezhou (Wuchang, Hubei Province) in the west, boat trackers working at dawn were subject to tigers and wolves on the steep hills or deep swamps. Lu You's boatmen burned incense and asked for blessings, "the red-haired and red-bearded helmsmen should avoid the mistake of praying to the wrong god." But I don't know what gods were worshiped by them (Y. Lu 2012: 202). There was a Houtu Shrine in Shishou County, which was once visited by Lu You (Y. Lu 2012: 203). On the river bank of Gong'an County, "there is the Two Saints Temple, where boatmen must go to pray" (S. Wang 2012: 443). Wang Yan said in *Stay Overnight at the Temple of Two Saints* that it was located in a town inhabited by ten thousand people, with a good harbor, "tens thousand residents gathered in Mengcheng, which was sheltered by the pier." "The boats lined up one by one, and those passing by were surprised at the scene" (Y. Wang 1990). There were many worshipers. Fan Chengda and Lu You both visited the Two Saints Temple when their boats traveled through Gong'an (C. Fan 2012: 81; Y. Lu 2012: 205). "Boatmen must pray" here (S. Wang 2012: 443). Boats revered it, as Wang Yan mentioned that "boats were lining up one by one to pay tribute, and those passing by revered it" (Y. Wang 1990). When Wang Shipeng's boat "left Shashi, the sky changed and the boatmen were afraid, so he took a short break in Gong'an before marching, praying that his would be answered by gods" (S. Wang 2012: 443). But he didn't know to pray to whom. Shashi was a large port where people to and from the Three Gorges needed to change boats, anchor boat and worship the gods. Before Lu You's boat entered the Three Gorges, "the boatmen sacrificed a pig to the god of the gorge" at Shashi. "The next day another sacrifice was made to River God Temple, with a jug of wine and a pig" (Y. Lu 2012: 206, 207).

There were no other places that were more hazardous than the Three Gorges for sailing boats along the Yangtze River, and as a result more gods and deities were worshiped by boatmen and travelers to pray for safety. The Huangniu Gorge had the Huangniu Temple, also known as Linggan Temple, "where the Huangniu God resides", "boats are very respectful of it" (C. Fan 1990). Lu You "sacrificed a pig and a jug of wine to the Linggan Temple" (Y. Lu 2012: 213). "Prayers from Wu-made boats and Sichuan-made ones were all answered" (Y. Lu 2011: 125). When Su Shi and Fan Chengda passed by, they also paid homage to the Huangniu Temple, and it "had a trail of yellow bulls on top of the peak, which was greatly respected by the guest boats" (C. Fan 1990). Quite a few temples of Wu Zixu were built in the Three Gorges, and "from Jingmen to the west, there were many such temples." In the Wuxia Gorge, there was the Ningzhen Taosit Temple, or the Shrine of Magical Goddess, "Here the goddess refers to the so-called Goddess of Wushan Mountain", which was visited by Lu You once. And the Baidi Temple situated in Qutang Gorge, and Lu You paid homage to the god in a sedan chair (Y. Lu 2012: 217, 218). To the west to Guizhou (Zigui, Hubei), five miles away from the east city gate was the Duke Qinglie's Ancestral Hall, namely Quping Temple, and two miles away from the south gate was Mingfei Temple. There was Xiandu Daoist Temple in Fengdu County, Zhongzhou. In Fuzhou (Fuling, Sichuan), the temple of Zhang Yide was built in Lewen County, who was given the title Xiongwei in the Daguan Reign by the emperor, and the title King Faith in the Shaoxing Reign. On the river bank in Hejiang County, Luzhou (now Luzhou, Sichuan), the Temple of King Dengtian was said to be the Temple of Lüguang Temple, where "boatmen would go to the temple when they arrived in Hejiang County to make sacrifices, using fresh fish or fish as a substitute. The famous monk Kumarajiva was also offered as a companion, and cakes were used as offerings" (C. Fan 2012: 72).

5.4.2.2 God Worship in Canals and Other Inland River Navigation

The numerous ancestral temples along the canal for ships served the needs of people's worship in river navigation. And two temples were built along the Nanjing section of the canal, namely Zhangxun Temple and Xuyuan Temple. The Song people added Nan Jiyun, Yao He and Lei Wanchun as their deities, together with the above tow, they were named the Temple of Five Kings. Zhang Shunmin paid a visit to the five temples when his boat passed by (S. Zhang 1990). During the period of the Xifeng Reformation, the Sinong Temple ordered the purchase of the Nanjing Yanbo Temple, the Weizi Temple and the Double Temple for profit, but was stopped due to the strong opposition by Zhang Fangping and other officials (Toqta 1977: 10853), which showed the lucrative nature of the temples. Pagodas were built in the Sizhou (northeast of Xuyi, Jiangsu) section of the Bianhe River. Su Shi wrote in his poem, "I once took a boat sailing southward, but had to stop when I reached Bianliang because of the headwind for three days and the dust pounded on my face. People on the boat advised me to pray at the efficacious monk's pagoda, but before the incense could be put away, the wind direction had already changed" (Z. Zeng et al. 2001: 517). There was Duke Changyuan Temple in the south of Hongzekou Canal, Huaiyin Temple at the north end of Huainan Canal, and Zhaobo Temple in Zhaoboyan of Yangzhou (S. Zhang 1990). The Lingyou Temple was set up in the Suzhou section of the Western Zhejiang Canal, that is, the Temple of Madam Huiseng Xianyou Shanli, who was is the daughter of Minister Seng Zan. "Seng Zan used his former residence as a temple (Chongxuan Temple), where his wife once lived". "The temple was dedicated to God Galan, the Saint Lady". Before the Song Dynasty, no record was found about the gods' protection of voyage. In the middle of the Kaibao Reign, Qian Chu made a pilgrimage to Kaifeng from Hangzhou. "From the Wusong River, the ship was almost capsized in a gale. He witnessed a women being rescued, who claimed to be a deity from Chongxuan Temple," and it had the function of safeguarding voyages. In the Song Dynasty, it was titled Effective Goddess by the emperor. The Lingji Temple of Yangshan in Suzhou, the Madam Bailong Temple, were related to the navigation deities. Legend has it that the White Dragon, disguised as an old man with a white beard, bought a boat from the ferry of Zhenjiang to Yangshan in Suzhou, "made all the punters sleep", and the boat travelled 360 miles in a short time to the bottom of Yangshan Mountain (C. Fan 1990: 784). In Kuaiji County of the East Zhejiang Canal, there was the Lady Zhaoshun Lingxiao Temple, dedicated to Cao'e, a filial daughter of the Han Dynasty, because the temple was located at the intersection of the Cao'e River and the East Zhejiang Canal, it was an important meeting place for official and private shipping between Mingzhou (Ningbo, Zhejiang) and Hangzhou. During the period of Emperor Huizong's Reign, Cao'e was given the duty of protecting canal navigation and she was the goddess of Eastern Zhejiang Canal and the Cao'e River (D. Shen 1959: 357).

God worships were also prevalent in the busiest branches of the Yangtze River, including the Xiangjiang River and the Ganjiang River. Many deities were worshiped in the region of the Dongting Lake. Qin Guan, the 8-class official, paid tributes to the gods of the Dongting Lake, including "King Zhaoling of the Dongting Lake, King Calm Currents, Duke Morality, Duke of Smooth Sailing, Duke Loyalty, Queen Chastity and Piety, and Duke Piety" (G. Qin 1990). Among them, Queen Chastity and Piety was also named Queen Piety, known as the goddess of Xianghu Lake. A story narrates that she was Luo's daughter, and "her father was drowned by a cruel official of the Qin Kingdom and his body could not be found. Then she dived into the water to search for her father. As a result, both father and daughter were missing in the lake. To admire her piety, villagers began to worship her". She was worshiped as a deity responsible for blessing the area with enough water (T. Li 2004: 7792). Villagers built a temple in her name on the eastern hill of the Dongting Lake (S. Zhang 1990). As for the identity of King Calm Currents, "not knowing who he was," the local people guessed that he was probably Master Grass of the Dongting Lake, as was recorded in *Xianchun Period Chronicles of Lin'an* that "the three Dragon Kings of Qiantang Lake, Dongting and Green Grass were brothers and all were bestowed with the Emperor's favors." The temple is located on Green Grass Oasis, which is the juncture of the Dongting Lake and the Xiangjiang river, built by Ma Yin in Kaiping, in the Liang Dynasty. And Master of Benevolence (Great Saint of Sizhou) and King of Soul Returning (Master Mayuan), were also worshiped in the same temple for both of whom are related to navigation. God worship was a normal practice for the ships going into and from the Dongting Lake from the Yangtze River. "Generally, when boatmen traveled in the area of the Dongting Lake in the south and Luzhou in the north, they would pray for the river gods' blessing to safely sail in the rivers and lakes. They worshiped gods with wine and meat". An iron pot on a black dragon boat in the west hall of Lizhou was used to contain the sacrifices, which "flew upstream to the temple from the lake by passing through the Chuanxia Gorges" (S. Zhang 1990; S. Qian 1990: 1999). Four sandbars at Zhaoling Sandbar on the Xiangjiang River posed threats to the passing-by boats, "so boatmen had no other choice", but to hire local residents to go through the four sandbars. This is why a temple of Zhaoling was built at the exit of the sandbar for passing-by travelers to worship (S. Zhang 1990).

The Ganjiang River was shallow, with several dangerous sections extending hundreds of miles. "The Xianqing Temple situated in the east of Qianzhou Water. Sometimes when prayers offered sacrifices to the god, the water would rise several feet overnight and the boats could travel safely. The scholar prayers were always answered, so many of them marked the temple with inscriptions on stones" (S. Fang 2006: 180). The Master Xiao Temple was created for worshipers in Xinjiang County. Master Xiao Boxuan, a native of the same county, died as a god during the period of the Xianchun Reign, and the locals set up a temple for him. In the Ming Dynasty, he was conferred the title of Almighty God of Water Kingdom by the emperor (X. Li et al. 1990). The Song Dynasty must have worshiped Master Xiao as a deity on the water. The Temple of Duke of Smooth Sailing, also known as Divine Snake, was worshiped by travelers for their southbound safe voyages, to protect their tents and arms, which was easily found and worshiped. Emperor Shenzong sent an official to pay tributes, "Divine Snake fell on the historian official, Ouyang Jun's shoulders, coiling in the incense heap, poking its head out during the rituals. When the ritual was over, Divine Snake swam out of the incense heap, coiled among the vessels on the case and slowly swam into the tent. Its colour, length and size keeps changing. Hundreds of officials at the ceremony found witnessed the divine snake" (T. Li 2004: 6770). Then it was crowned King of Smooth Sailing. Xingzi County had established another Divine Snake Temple. When Lu You made a shift to new post from Jingkou to Yuzhang, in strong winds and waves, he set off by boat from Xingzi County, and arrived at the Little Dragon Temple on Wucheng Mountain in less than half a day" (Y. Lu 2011: 93). Fan Chengda stayed at Wuzikou in Poyang Lake because "the wind and snow were raging, and his boat had to be moored at the Temple of the Dragon King. The next day, the wind became even stronger, so he prayed to the river god. His boat did not start until the snow stopped in the afternoon" (C. Fan 2012: 37). It can be seen that the Dragon King worship was very popular along the Ganjiang River. In the Jialing River, the largest tributary of the upper reaches of the Yangtze River, the worship of Jialing River God became widespread among boatmen, who was named Duke of Shanji by the emperor in the early southern Song Dynasty, "Wu Lingyan, the deputy pacification commissioner of Sichuan and Shaanxi Provinces, shipped food to the army via waterway and should be knighted for his great contribution" (X. Li 2013: 2000).

As a busy inland river course, the Qiantang River had quite a few gods to be worshiped by people on the boats. They said that "the gods of Zhejiang are numerous", and "various river gods are worshiped", including Wu Zixu, the god worshiped at the Zhongqing Temple, who had the function of stabilizing waves and suppressing tides. The god Wu Wang Fuchai was worshiped at Zhaoji Temple. A god worshiped at the Shunji Temple was dedicated to the Feng Clan of Zhejiang. They also had gods worshiped at the Master Yingxian Tongying Temple. The Tang Village Dragon King Hall could calm tides of the river. And the God of Shanshun Temple could ensure ships safe, so it was called "Smooth-Sailing Shrine". The Fuying Temple was designated to worship the Dragon King of Water Kingdom. The Guangshun Temple was for worshiping Zhenjiang Dragon King. The Huishun Temple was for worshiping the tide god. The Dragon King Shunji Temple was to worship Qiantang Dragon King Shunji; and the Jiaze Temple to worship the Dragon King of Qiantang Lake (S. Qian 1990: 3995–99). The Duke Smoothness Temple was titled the Zhejiang Tide God by the emperor, for "satisfying prayers' wishes", the temple was added the word "Faith" later (F. Chen 1990). The Wushan Temple God of Hangzhou was "in charge of the torrent" and is the god of Tao, whose function is to prevent "sudden outbreaks of turbulence" (*Song Da Zhaoling Ji*, 485).

Other inland rivers also have many water gods being worshiped, such as the Xin'an River God, namely Dragon King, who was bestowed Duke Lingji by the emperor in the sixth year of the Qingyuan Reign. And the god of Dongyang River was bestowed the title of Duke Guangrun (Y. Zheng et al. 1990: 4387). There was a Deji Temple in Jiaohu of Luzhou dedicated to Queen of Confidence and Help. "The entire 200-kilometer region of the Jiaohu Lake was safe for boat sailing blessed by the gods there." And the Song army was credited with defeating the Jin's aggression on the water during the Wanyan Liang invasion southward. "In normal years, winds and waves were peaceful for smooth navigation of merchant ships, but in case of turmoil and war, the huge waves were raised to block the rebel boats" (B. Zhou 1990). The Black Dragon God, dwelling under Zhaozhou Bridge, "assisted boats crossing the Stone Bridge by raising waves when the river was shallow. And the boat need to go through three sandbars before crossing the bridge. After the boat went through the bridge, the river was as shallow as it had been". So the imperial court sent officials to submit sacrifices (T. Li 2004: 1828). There was Queen of Smoothness and Help on the Imperial River who secretly assisted the navigation and repair of the river (*Song Da* Zhaoling *Ji*, 486). The two major water systems of the Yellow River and Huaihe

River had many gods apart from the Yellow River God and Huaihe River God in the past, which are not listed here.

There are not only prayers but also offerings. The most common sacrifice is a pig head. When Huang Tingjian went through the Huangniu Gorge, "the boatmen sacrificed the Huangniu God with pork and wine", his boat traveled to Bodao County in western Sichuan, "where the boatmen prepared scalded pigs to sacrifice to Duke Zhuge Liang" (T. Huang 2011: 440, 1566). Mei Yaochen worshiped the Dragon Princess Temple at Changlukou, "boat masters and helmsmen dressed each other and came to slaughter pigs in the temple" (Y. Mei 1990). Chen Hui, the fiscal commissioner of Jiangnan West Province, sacrificed a pig to the temple of the Dragon King when his boat traveled through Wucheng, and then another pig to the temple in Nankang. When the boat arrived at Daguo Mountain, the boatmen asked for another sacrifice, Chen Hui said angrily, "After eating my pigs for days, the dragon should have eaten its fill" (M. Hong 1981: 313, 314, 315). When Lu You went through Zhenjiang by boat, he "presented a pig and a jug of wine to the Temple of Good-Luck King, also known as lower water kingdom. It was affiliated to the Jinshan Temple, where two monks were often assigned to guard it, and no other monks in it. However, it was recorded in the sacrifice book that the pig's head, which was used to pay tribute to the god, was considered to be the belongings of this temple. Everyone laughed at the record". The worshipper expressed devotion, but the monks had the pig head in mind. "The boatmen sacrificed a pig to the gods of the gorge" in Shashi. After repairing the boat, a new one would be introduced, "another sacrifice was presented to the River God Temple, with a jug of wine and a pig." Before a boat entered the Three Gorges, it anchored in Guilin Bay to make some preparations. "The boatmen killed more than a dozen pigs to worship God for a good start." In the Three Gorges, boatmen slaughtered sheep and poured wine in honour of Huangniu God. In the Huangniu Gorge (Linggan Temple) "they sacrificed a pig and a jug of wine to the Inspiration Temple" (Y. Lu 2012: 165, 192, 206–08, 213). Although the pigs were slaughtered for the ritual, the pork from the ritual was later distributed to the ship's crew according to their rank, of which "the head of the boat, as the head crew, was paid more, and after the god worship ceremony was completed, he received more than twice as much meat as the others" (Y. Lu 2012: 207).

Apart from the pig head, other offerings were submitted. For example, there is the King Heaven-Ascending Temple in Hejiang County, Luzhou, which was said to be the Lü Guang Temple, where "boatmen would go to the temple when they arrived in Hejiang County to make offerings, presenting fresh fish or fish as a substitute. The famous monk Kumorajiva was respected as a god to share the sacrifice, and cakes were used as offerings to him" (C. Fan 2012: 72). Wang Ronglao, an official, once went to Guanzhou and needed to cross the Guanjiang River. He successively offered a Fuchen Fly Whisk, a Duanzhou Inkstone, a soft package, and a tiger tent to the god, but no god replied to them. Later, the cursive script of Wei Yingwu's poem written by Huang Tingjian was used as sacrifices. "The south wind began to blow, after the sails were lifted for a moment, the boat crossed the river". He speculated that "the god of the river must have been a degraded official during the Yuanyou Reign, otherwise how could he have had such a deep preference for the fan written by Huang Tingjian" (H. Shi 1990). Rituals thus became a major cost and even a burden during the voyage. When Wang Yan passed through the Two Saints Temple in Gong'an County and had no money to offer as a sacrifice, "Two hundred people in the monastery were striking wooden fish, bells and drums, and I was too poor to give alms. Tomorrow I would step on frost to leave the river bank and support the boat with my will" (Y. Wang 1990). Zhang Lei also had no sacrifice to offer and pleaded, "what can I rely on? I can offer nothing. Do the gods of the river take pity on me for being poor and waver my sacrifices? People know that I am poor and have been banished from my post" (L. Zhang 1990). Wang Shipeng burned paper money to worship God for the wind, "the boatmen burned paper money and I made fun of the river gods who were also corrupt officials" (S. Wang 2012: 354). But people were worried about that the absence of sacrifices may offend the gods of the river. Su Zhe said "the river God bullied me into poverty and repeatedly used winds and rains to anneal me" (Z. Su 1987: 138). When Li Yan returned from Guangzhou, "the boat need to cross Xiaogu Mountain. Although the wind was in my favour, oars did not work, so I decided to pay a visit to the Dragon Temple and offer sacrifices of wine and cattle, but they still did not work." Only after Buddhist relics were cast into the water, could oars work effectively to aid the boat going forward. In the early period of the Yuanfeng Reign, when An Tao went as an ambassador to Goryeo, he also cast sutras into the sea to save himself from the storm (Y. He 2008: 192).

5.4.3 Deity Beliefs in Seafaring Activities in the Song Dynasty

5.4.3.1 Distribution of Escort Deities in Coastal Areas

In the nautical conditions and knowledge system of the Song Dynasty, the navigators contributed their safety to gods' protection. Coastal deities associated with seafaring were large in number, and varied in different regions. Liangzhe provinces left the most records about deities, Fujian and Guangnan provinces were second after them. But the north left comparatively less records about them. The northernmost seafaring-related deity recorded in the Song Dynasty was the God of the Eastern Sea, whose temple was located in Laizhou. "Less than 10 kilometers outside the eastern gate of Laizhou Prefecture, it overlooked the sea at a stone's throw". The Jin's fleet, led by Li Bao from Suzhou to Jiaoxi, was said to have been blessed by the gods of the Eastern Sea. There was also a temple on Furong Island, twenty kilometers away going eastward from the East China Sea, where fishermen only discreetly believe in the god, not knowing which god was worshiped there (Y. Zhu 2006: 159; J. Luo et al. 1990: 5238).

The Saint Queen Temple in Jingkou, Zhenjiang, Zhejiang Province (called Queen Heaven Temple in the *Zhishun Period Chronicles of Zhenjiang* in the Yuan Dynasty), was founded during the period of the Chunyou Reign to worship Ma Zu (Goddess Lin), who originated from Putian, Fujian Province, and was titled Saint Queen by the Song emperor. The purpose of building the temple in Zhenjiang was to protect

Zhenjiang as it was like "coastal provinces of Zhejiang, Fujian and Guangnan East provinces, where ships could sail on the wind and waves" (X. Yu 1990: 2730). Hangzhou also had built the Saint Queen Temple, also known as the Shunji Shengfei Temple, outside the Genshan Gate, and others at Xiaogong Bridge, outside the Houchao Gate (S. Qian 1990: 4014). The Saint Queen worship originated in Fujian and spread to Zhejiang due to the beliefs of sea merchants. There was a Yiling Temple at Kanpu outside Hangzhou, to worship Master Wu Zhen of Fujian, "who crossed the sea by boat to the shore, he settled here." "The Fujian merchants painted and sculpted his portrait to worship him. Later, as more and more people gathered here, the temples were built to meet worshipers' need." He was widely worshiped by the merchants. The Duke Epiphany Temple was famous, where "if guests on the sea prayed for help, their wishes could be satisfied by him. He was considered to be a wise and upright man from Shifan village, and everyone in the coastal region in the south respected him" (T. Chang 1990: 4665).

The temple was located in Xixing Town, Xiaoshan County, Yuezhou (Shaoxing, Zhejiang Province), Liangzhe East Province. In the sixth year of the Zhenghe Reign (AD 1116), "when an emissary from Goryeo was about to arrive and no tide carried their ship forward." Then, the god helped them out of difficulty, and he was bestowed the title of Duke of Sea Assistance (S. Shi et al. 1990: 6809–10). The most important god of navigation in Mingzhou (Ningbo, Zhejiang) was the God of the East Sea, who was built a separate temple in Dinghai after the period of the Yuanfeng Reign. In the fourth year of the Daguan Reign (AD 1110), the halls of Wind God and Rain God were built on both sides of the Temple of the God of the East Sea. And in the third year of the Xuanhe Reign (AD 1121), the god of wind was named Duke of Peace and Smoothness and the god of rain was named Duke of Peace and Assistance (J. Luo et al. 1990: 5238). In the Southern Song Dynasty, Laizhou, where the Temple of the Eastern Sea was located, was included in the territory of the Jin Kingdom, and the Song people proposed that "our should locate our capital in southeast China, and include the East China Sea and the South China Sea into our real boundaries". "The East China Sea made Tongzhou, Taizhou, Mingzhou, Yuezhou, Wenzhou, Haizou, Quanzhou and Fuzhou as its divide line". The East Sea God Temple of Dinghai was used as the main venue to hold grand rituals (Toqta 1977: 2488). In Meicen, Dinghai, Mingzhou (Ningbo, Zhejiang Province), there was the Baotuo Courtyard, built by Xiao Liang, with a statue of the Buddha of Wutai Mountain donated by a Silla merchant. "The seagoing ships coming or leaving there are sure to pray for blessings and the god is very responsive to their wishes". "The messengers to Goryeo were sure to pray here" (J. Xu 2006: 132). And the Duke Assistance Temple was dedicated to a wicked man surnamed Kong in Xiangshan County. In his lifetime, "the villagers were afraid of him and did not dare to call him". But, after his death, he was worshiped for blessing General Qian of Wuyue Kingdom at Jinghai Town who survived out of the stormy sea. In the fourth year of the Jianyan Reign (AD 1130), he was ennobled for helping Emperor Gaozong escape from the sea. Other temples granted by Emperor Gaozong during his voyage included the Yangshan Temple at Dinghai of Mingzhou (Ningbo, Zhejiang), the Imposing Maritime Duke's Temple and the Loyal Duke Temple at Chenshan. The Zhaoli Temple had a god to bless maritime voyages. As ambassadors to Goryeo, Lu Yundi and others went to pray at the temple (J. Luo et al. 1990: 5239). The Yangshan Temple was set up in the sea of Changguo County, Mingzhou. "Some of the seafarers witnessed the guards lining up in the air", they claimed that Emperor Yang of the Sui Dynasty visited this mountain and built a shrine. In the fourth year of the Jianyan Reign (AD 1130), the emperor managed to survive on the sea. Because Emperor Yang could not be ennobled by himself, he named his two concubines as Concubine Hui and Concubine Shun, and his wife Lady Mingde. "Those who live by the sea depend on him". The Daishan Temple was dedicated to worship God Chen Leng of the Sui Dynasty, who "sailed and defeated Liuqiu Kingdom". The temple of General Chen was built in the second year of the Duangong Reign (AD 989) and had been worshiped for generations. The Liegang Temple was also called "Guanghui Temple of Guangde Military Prefecture" (J. Luo et al. 1990: 5253). The Shrine of Master Chongying in Xiangshan County, Mingzhou (Ningbo, Zhejiang), was used to worship Master Tao Hongjing, who also served as the navigation god. "The people who lived next to it must get up to see the sacrifices there. Some people traded in Tiantai County. Once, when they were crossing the sea, the boat was almost capsized in a hurricane before they reached Xianbu. About seventy people on board were saved by Master Tao". In the first year of the Dazhongxiangfu Reign (AD 1008), when the ship was transporting timbers from Wenzhou to Kaifeng to repair Zhaoying Palace, it "encountered the wind and waves and was almost overturned". Master Tao appeared and said to them, "I am Master Tao of Penglai Taoist Monastery in Xiangshan, and I will save you". There was a sacred temple of Zuosheng, whose deity is called Tianmen Commander, who protected the ships sailing to the South China Sea and "the ships are sure to pray here". "Once there was a boatman who took the sacrificial meat by mistake and left, the boat traveled more than ten miles, and then a wind suddenly blew against him and he was sent back and unable to proceed. He was so frightened that he realized he had taken the meat by mistake and immediately returned it to the temple, praying and apologizing for his evil. By the time he returned, the wind stopped, and he could have a smooth sailing" (J. Luo et al. 1990: 5273). These legends reinforced the reverence of the merchants for the god.

The Daishi Temple situated in Huangyan County, Taizhou (now Linhai of Zhejiang Province). The god worshiped was a Wuzhou local and died while travelling to Taizhou. The locals worshiped him as he "competed with the god of the Qiantang River and divided three the tides into three parts" to control the tides there. The temple of Marshal Zhang in Taizhou, who was welcomed there by "a Merchant Chen of Kangding people from Mount Tai with sacrificial meat". He was a sea merchant from Shandong. There was a Chuanshi Temple by the sea, "as an old legend said that a merchant ship hit a rock because of the wind and waves. The situation was very dangerous, so he tried to climb up the rock but the water was torrential. The merchant was angry and hit the rock hard, trying to use it to stable his boat, which was eventually capsized. The people then considered it to be the god's deeds." As for the Huangshan Temple, "a stone there ran across the temple like a bull's nose, and the residents considered it to be the place for fixing sea vessels." At the mouth of the Yongning River was the Jiangting Temple, where "people on boats would turn to the gods for help, especially when there were so many sea traders" (Q. Chen 1990: 7522–23). Wenzhou Prefecture had built the Temple of Benevolence and Kindness, dedicated to the god of the sea, King Smoothness and Adaptation, who was crowned as King Smoothness, Adaptation and Benevolence in the second year of the Jiatai Reign (S. Xu et al. 2014: 1089). Sun Zusou, an official of the Song Dynasty, said that "there are now people in Liangzhe East Province who killed and worshiped the sea gods" and requested that "the ancestral temples set up by the people themselves be abolished" (D. Ma 2011: 2773). It can be seen that there are a number of other sea gods that are excluded in the ritual canon.

The most famous seafaring deity in Fujian is Mazu. The Fujian Xinghua Military Prefecture was the birthplace of Mazu faith, with the Saint Queen Temple, and "on the island, boatmen all served her politely" (M. Zhu 2003: 220). During the Song dynasty, the Mazu was favored by the emperors for fifteen times (Y. Wang 2006: 183–196). In addition, there was a god at Longtan in Changle, Fuzhou, who had scared off the pirate Zhu Cong during the Shaoxing Reign and was bestowed the temple name "Xianying" by the imperial court. It was granted the title of Duke Yuansu by the emperor in the middle of the Longxing Reign, then Fuji in the middle of the Chunxi Reign, and Guangyou in the middle of the Jiading Reign (L. Liu 1990). There was a temple of Lady Chongfu in Putian. When Zheng Lizhi, a Fuzhou native, returned home from Panyu and encountered pirates in Putian, he "prayed from afar to the temple" and was rescued by Lady Chongfu (M. Hong 1981: 1058). The Weiji Temple was built in Zhangpu County, Zhangzhou, dedicated to the gods Chen Dazhong, Chen Dajie, Chen Dazhi and Chen Dayong, who were named Duke of Lingyou, Duke of Xianyou, Duke of Shanyou and Duke of Zhaoyou in the 11th year of the Chunxi Reign (AD 1184) (S. Xu et al. 2014: 1089).

The most important nautical god in Guangnan provinces was the Nanhai God, whose temple was located in Guangzhou. The worship of the Sea God also reached a climax during the Song Dynasty, when it was repeatedly ennobled by the court. After the Song Dynasty pacified Guangnan provinces, they "sent Deputy Agriculture Minister, Li Jifang, to pay homage to the South China Sea". In the first year of the Kangding Reign (AD 1040), Nanhai was crowned King Broadness and Smoothness, and in the fifth year of the Huangyou Reign (AD 1053), it was crowned King of Broadness, Benefits and Smoothness (Toqta 1977: 2485, 2488). The King Loyalty Temple in Qiongzhou, Hainan Island, Guangnan West Province was to worship General Fubo of the Han Dynasty, Lu Bode, who was crowned this title in the middle of the Xuanhe Reign. The King Junling Temple in Changhua Military Prefecture, formerly known as King of Sea and Morality, was granted the title of Junling in the fifth year of the Yuanfeng Reign (AD 1082) (S. Xu et al. 2014: 1087). There was a "Temple of Duke Loyalty and Smoothness, where merchants prayed for wind". The Dugang Temple, situated in the east of the city, was respected and trusted by the people. There prayers are answered immediately, and the ships come to pay their respects before departure" (R. Zhao 1996: 219).

5.4.3.2 Deity Worship in the Song People's Seafaring Activities

Xu Jing said that "the waves can push a ship more than several kilometers away, and a ten-meter-long ship is floating on the waves like a hair on a horse. So those who sail in the sea do not give priority to the size of boat, but to safe sailing. When in urgent distress, they prayed and pleaded with the gods, and all wishes were satisfied" (J. Xu 2006: 148). In the face of a violent and strange sea, devotion to the gods is the only way to pray for peace. It is believed that shipwrecks are often incurred by a lack of faith in the gods. For example, Zhao Shizao was deposed from his post in Guangnan East Province, crossing the sea to return to Lin'an. When he passed the King Guangli Temple without paying homage, eventually the boat sank in the waves, but only Zhao Shizao was saved from death. All the others got drowned (M. Hong 1981: 217–18). Although no dragons were ever seen on sea voyages, merchants believed that they did exist, once it appeared, "they would bring huge waves, turn the sun and the moon upside down, break sails and bend helms, capsize ships like a leaf. And the dragon would salivate and hold the men on board, tasting their blood to fill their bellies, so boatmen dare not neglect god worship." Therefore, whenever "old captains and merchants passed by, they would organize rituals, present meat and wine and money to the temple, hoping that the dragon would bless them" (P. Mao 1990). So mariners would conduct routine and temporary rituals, which accompanied the voyage for almost its entire duration.

The rituals began before departure. The local officials of Quanzhou and Guangzhou held wind praying ceremonies at the time when sea merchants went to sea, while folk prayed for wind all over Mingzhou (now Ningbo, Zhejiang) and south to Hainan Island (C. Huang 2003: 81–84). Civilian seafarers also performed their own rituals for safety before departure. For example, the merchant Wang Yingsheng, who went to trade in the Liao Kingdom with a license to Goryeo, was disclosed, and "two prayers were found by officials for safe sailing to the Liao Kingdom" (S. Su 2010: 3330). In the fifth year of the Xuanhe Reign (AD 1123), Lu Yundi and others went on a mission to Goryeo, before leaving Dinghai County, "he dispatched an imperial ambassador, Rong Pengnian, the Wugong minister, to build a temple within seven days at the Zongchi Palace, and to pray at the Temple of King Benevolence, Smoothness, Assistance and Morality, where a divine object shaped like a lizard appeared, which was in fact the Dragon King of the East China Sea". After receiving this auspicious omen, "the Chinese ambassador, Guan Bi, climbed onto Mount Zhaobao, burned the imperial incense and kowtowed to the ocean". The fleet of eight ships "played the drums and raised the flags and set off in order" (J. Xu 2006: 131).

The gods along the maritime route are worshiped, especially in time of distress, they would be worshiped temporarily by water travelers. For example, when Xu Jing's delegation arrived at the Shen's Gate the next day, "the west wind began to blow" and "the boatman said they were hindered by the wind". So "a curtain was hung against the mountain and the site was cleaned up for the ritual, which was called Cisha (imperial ritual sacrifice)". Each boat cast into sea a wooden boat miniature, sutras, dried food, a book with all the prayers' names, as a form of witchcraft to pray for diminishing calamity, bringing good fortune or subduing evils." At the Baotuo Courtyard in Meicen, Lu Yundi also invited "the monks to burn incense and chant sutras, praising the virtues of Buddha, and his officials and soldiers all bowed respectfully and discreetly". On Hailü Reef, he asked "vice commissioners to put on court dress to pay visit to Erdao Monastery, they looked up to the heaven and worshiped again. They cast into the sea the Imperial Token of Heaven Decree and Magic Power, Official Documents of Wind God and Dragon King, Heaven Pass, and Mountain Gods and others, totaled 13 tokens and documents." When the boat arrived at the Yellow River, also dabbed the Yellow Water Ocean, "they offered nice meals including chicken and rice as sacrifices. As many people got drowned incurred by sand damage, their souls needed to be sacrificed by a special Sicha ceremony." In Haku, the boat was moored by the hill, where "there was a dragon shrine at the ridge of the hill, and boatmen must go to pay their respects." When the ship returned to the Yellow Water Ocean in storm, "people on board cut their hair short and begged piteously to the gods". Miraculously, the god of Fuzhou Divine Islands helped them out of difficulty in time. As Xu Jing said "in times of great danger, they prayed and pleaded with the gods, and all were answered" (J. Xu 2006: 132, 133, 134, 148). Other seafarers always prayed in time of emergency or disaster. For example, in the later years of the Shaoxing Reign, the Song army ran against the Jin's navy in Jiaoxi. "The wind did not blow from the south, how could they advance? Burning incense and praying, soon the fierce wind changed to the opposite direction as a south wind. At that time, waves were rough, the fleet advanced in the tailwind and began to run fast, as if propelled by the divine" (X. Yuan 1990). The above papers discussed that Zhao Ding was deposed to Zhuya (now Haikou, Hainan Province) and was travelling south from Leizhou (now Haikang, Guangdong Province) when he came across a "giant loach" in the sea. "The boatmen with steel swords in hands, with hair draped, cut their tongues and dripped blood into the water". This served as a sacrifice ceremony. In order to convince the seafarers that the monks along for the voyage were necessary, merchants asked them to chant prayers. "After the monks prayed in dangerous situation on the sea, the God could be seen in the air, finally all the people on the ship were saved". As a result, "merchants attached great importance to foreign monks". And on their return voyage, they "offered tributes to them, which was called Luohan Zhai (food offered to monks)" (Y. Zhu 2006: 150). The Japanese monk Jojin, under the cover of the merchants, evaded inspection and took a merchant ship to the Song Dynasty because the merchants welcomed monks on board. In return, the owner was blessed with a daily sutra chanting. "They recited *the Saints Guanyin Spell* and *True Words of Wind and Heaven* for 10,000 times a day, praying to the heavens and the earth for safe sailing". On March 15th, the day of embarkation, the sutra was recited and the Rotation Ceremony of Good Luck were made three times, and Worship Ceremony of Manjusri Bodhisattva was made once, as well as on March 16th and 17th. Before the ship set sailing, "the gods were worshiped with ginger wine, paper streamers were burned, and prayers were chanted". On the 21st day, the wind was not favourable, they "prayed to the gods". Jojin even "recited Manjusri Bodhisattva of Wutai Mountain 10,000 times, and recited 500 arhats at Buddha platform tens of thousands of times". The next day, when the favourable wind was blowing, he still kept "chanting sutras thousands of times, not daring to stop" (Jojin 2009: 2, 3, 4, 6).

5.5 The System of the Water Deities and Gods and Their Evolution in the Song Dynasty

Along with the unprecedented prosperous sailing on inland waterways and seaways, the Song Dynasty saw a dramatic increase in the shipping related personnel, who had a very different respect on nature and mentality comparing with the people whose life are mostly land-based. The Deities and gods systems they believed in were separate with their own unique features, also with crossovers. In this section, beliefs of water deities refers to the ones people believe in while practicing activities on water. The studies on gods of seas, the holy goddess, gods of the Yangtze River are well developed, which also can be found in the studies of folk beliefs and system of rites.[9] Therefore, here we will look at it from available researches from a comprehensive perspective of the Song's water activities.

5.5.1 The Constitution of the Song's Water Deities System

In the system of Chinese ancient gods and deities, those who were in charge of the waters formed a separate system. The Song people performed "the rituals of mountains, towns, seas, and rivers" and worshiped the water deities in seas and rivers. Here, "seas" referred to four seas, which were the East Sea, the South Sea, the West Sea and the North Sea; and the "rivers" referred to four rivers—the Yangtze River, the Huaihe River, the Yellow River, and the Jishui River. After pacifying its territory, the Song Dynasty gradually established its rituals for normal water activities, abandoned and re-conferred the titles that were entitled during the separation period, took control over rituals. In this way, "the responsibilities of the emperors are not only shown on the table but also under the rose; national affairs are not only conducted by the government official, but also the gods and goddesses" (G. Zheng 1990). The rituals were held on Lichun (the first day of spring) in Laizhou of the East Sea and Tangzhou of the Huaihe River; Lixia (the first day of summer) in Guangzhou of the South Sea

[9] The following scholars' studies are directly relevant to the topic of this section, they are Gurin Morihiro's research on the belief in the gods of the East Sea and the South Sea and the Yangtze River God Worship (the belief in God of Water Kingdom) during the Song Dynasty, Wang Yuanlin's investigation of the origin and development of the belief in the South Sea God and that in Water Kingdom and Li Bozhong and other scholar's examination of the function and evolution of Mazu belief. In addition, the topic of this section also discussed in Zhu Yi's study of the propitious rituals in the Song Dynasty, Jia Erqiang's research of folk beliefs during the Tang and Song Dynasties and Pi Qingsheng's study on beliefs and believers' sacrifices in the Song Dynasty. The researches of the above scholars will be discussed in this part, and not be listed here.

and Chengdu of the Yangtze River; Liqiu (the first day of autumn) in Hezhong Prefecture for the West Sea and the Yellow River and ritual of West Sea's from afar; and Lidong (the first day of winter) in Mengzhou for the North Sea and the Jishui River and the North Sea from afar. "Rituals were held within each prefecture whose officials acted as dedicatory official respectively" so that "county magistrates and the assistant governed and assist the governance of the temples respectively to take control of the rituals" (Toqta 1977: 2485). These were the supreme water rituals of the state.

Among the four seas, the East Sea and the South Sea referred to actual sea areas, so gods of them were in charge of certain areas. The East Sea here referred to the Bohai Sea, the Yellow Sea and the East China Sea as far south as Fujian coastal waters. In the Northern Song Dynasty, the temple of the god of the East Sea was constructed in Laizhou, that is to say "the temple of the god of the East Sea were 6.64 km away to east gate of Laizhou overlooking the sea" (Y. Zhu 2006: 159). Laizhou was within the area of the Bohai Bay. In the early years of Northern Song Dynasty, the god of the East Sea was conferred as King Guangde and officials were sent to Laizhou for rituals, as prescribed in *The New Rules of Etiquette* during the Zhenghe Reign (D. Ma 2011: 2551). Temples of King Guangde in Dengzhou and Mizhou must be the temporary shrines (S. Su n.d.: 2915, 4113). In the first year of the Kangding Reign (AD 1040), he was made King Yuansheng Guangde. In the first year of the Yuanfeng Reign (AD 1078), An Tao was sent to Goryeo as an ambassador and accomplished his mission successfully. Temporary shrines for god of the East Sea were built between Dinghai and Changguo County in Mingzhou as he suggested, and "and passing-by businessmen helped out." In the fourth year of the Daguan Reign (AD 1110) and the fifth year of the Xuanhe Reign (AD 1123), because of the visits of missioners from Goryeo, it was asked to add "Zhushun" and "Xianling" four characters in his nobility title. In the fourth year of the Jianyan Reign (AD 1130), Emperor Gaozong managed to get out of seaway, so god of the East Sea was made "Zhushun Yousheng Yuande Xianling Wang" (King Smooth Sailing, Assistance, Virtue and Epiphany) (J. Luo et al. 1990: 5239). In the fifth year of the Qiandao Reign (AD 1169), the nobility title was changed to "Zhushun Fusheng Guangde Weiji Wang (King of Assistance, Confidence, Virtue and Smooth Sailing) to avoid two characters in Emperor Qingzong's name (S. Xu et al. 2014: 1085).

In the early years of Southern Song Dynasty, the temple in Laizhou was still the master temple, but Laizhou was occupied by the Jin Kingdom at that time, so in the 13th year of the Shaoxing Reign (AD 1143) rituals were done from afar as this temple "located in the blocked area" out of the Song's administration. The gods of seas and rivers in the "accessible areas" were "Hongsheng Guangli Zhaoshun Weixian Wang" (King of Magnificence, Benefit, Smooth Sailing and Majesty) in Guangzhou of the South Sea and King Guangyuan in Yizhou of the Yangtze River only. Officials were sent to held the rituals (S. Xu et al. 2014: 525). In the fifth year of the Qiandao Reign (AD 1169), Emperor Xiaozong took Lin Li's advice, deputy minister of the imperial rituals, to build a temple in Mingzhou for the god of the East Sea using Guangzhou's as reference (D. Ma 2011: 2560). The next year, the rituals for worshiping the gods of five imperial mountains and four rivers in Mingzhou were considered accessible together with the ones in Guangzhou and Yizhou (B. Zhou 1990). Since then, the one in Mingzhou, located 2.21 km away northeast to Dinghai County, became the master temple and the title of its master god became "Zhushun Fusheng Guangde Weiji Wang" (King of Smooth Sailing, Assistance, Confidence, and Virtue and Majesty). "Taoist priests were invited there to make offerings every year." In the third year of the Baoqing Reign (AD 1227), the temple was refurbished with the state order and donation from civilian merchants (J. Luo et al. 1990: 5239). It meant that god of the East Sea had a great influence on people's life as well as the state.

The god of the South Sea was worshiped in Guangzhou, titled King Guangli in the Tang Dynasty, and his temple was "35.4 km away from the southeast seaway of Guangzhou, the entrance Fuxu and Huangmu Bay" (*Jinxiu Wanhua Gu* 1990). After Emperor Taizu pacified Guangnan East and West Provinces, "Li Jifang, the vice minister of agriculture, was ordered to perform rituals for the South Sea. The god of the South Sea was honored as Emperor Zhaoming by Liu Chang, with Congzheng Palace as his temple, dragons and phoenixes decorated on his clothing. Then, Emperor Taizu commanded to abandon his title and palace name and changed to rank one official uniform" (D. Ma 2011: 2556). His title was demoted in order to match the god of the East Sea. In the first year of the Kangding Reign (AD 1040), the god of South Sea was made "Hongsheng Guangli Wang" (King of Sage and Benefit). In the fifth year of the Huangyou Reign (AD 1053), because the enemy Nungz Cigauh fled, the god of the South Sea was titled "Hongsheng Guangli Zhaoshun Wang" (King of Sage, Benefit and Smooth Sailing) (Toqta 1977: 2488). In the seventh year of the Shaoxing Reign (AD 1137), his title was added as "Hongsheng Guangli Zhaoshun Weixian Wang" (King of Sage, Benefit, Smooth Sailing and Majesty) (X. Li 2013: 2141). Speaking of the area of the South Sea, Hong Mai explained the four seas as "The North Sea covered Qingzhou and Cangzhou. The South Sea referred to Jiaochi and Guangzhou. The East Sea meant Wu Kingdoms and Yue Kingdom. There's no such place as the West Sea" (M. Hong 2012: 41). During the Song Dynasty, the South Sea referred to the sea area beyond Guangnan and Jiaochi, including the whole the South China Sea and others. Sometimes, it even referred to anyplace west of Southeast Asia. Just as Zhou Qufei said "Samboja Kingdom was in the South Sea and the import intersection of many states' river ways" (Q. Zhou 1999: 86).

However, Hong Mai's explanation was not consistent with the other Song people's explanations of the East sea, and did not conform to the rituals from afar for the North Sea. In the fifth year of the Kaibao Reign (AD 972), local officials who were incharge of rituals and their imperial edicts had never mentioned the West Sea nor North Sea, which only had records as "mountains, rivers along with the temples of the East and South Seas were all assigned to local magistrates and heads of security bureaus to take control of the rituals" and "Heads of the prefectures should inspect temple every month" (D. Ma 2011: 2556). The West and North Sea did not refer to any virtual seas just as mentioned above. The Song people explained that "the West and North Sea was as far as the Yimo region, so rituals was done in Fangzhou from afar", which meant that there were no West Sea nor North Sea within the Song's territory. In the third year of the Zhenghe Reign (AD 1113), *The New Rules of Etiquette* stated that "rituals were done in Hezhong Prefecture for the west seas and rivers" and "in

Menzhou for the north seas and rivers" (D. Ma 2011: 2559). The gods of West and North Sea were worshiped from Xidu and Beidu Temples far away, especially during the Southern Song. Since the 13th year of the Shaoxing Reign (AD 1143), rituals for "Tongsheng Guangrun Wang" (King of Power and Smoothness) of the West Sea and "Chongsheng Guangze Wang" (King of Supremacy and Benevolence) of the North Sea were done like that (S. Xu et al. 2014: 525; B. Zhou 1990).

The highest level of inland water deities were gods of the four rivers, which meant the Yangtze River, the Yellow River, the Huaihe River and the Jishui River. During Emperor Taizu's Reign, the regimen of sacrifices and rituals were made: rituals for the Huaihe River (east rivers) should be held in Tangzhou on the first day of spring; the Yangtze River (south rivers) in Chengdu on the first day of summer; the Yellow River (west rivers) in Hezhong Prefecture on the first day of autumn; and the Jishui River (north rivers) in Mengzhou on the first day of winter (Toqta 1977: 2486). In March of the fifth year of the Kaibao Reign (AD 972), commands were given to the temples of four rivers that "local magistrates and heads of security bureaus should be responsible for the rituals" and "heads of each region should inspect every month" (*Song Da* Zhaoling *Ji*, 483). In the first year of the Kangding Reign (AD 1040), the god of the Yangtze River was renowned as King Guangyuan, the Yellow River King Xiansheng Lingyuan, the Huaihe River King Changyuan, and the Jishui River King Qingyuan (Toqta 1977: 2488). The main temple for the Yangtze River's master god was set in Chengdu, whose construction started from the year the second year of Kaihuang Reign (AD 582) of the Sui Dynasty. In the early years of the Qing Dynasty, the temple was in the city and west of the south gate (T. Huang et al. 1990). During the period of Li Shun rebellion, Yang Huaizhong, mayor of Shuzhou Prefecture, led his army against Li Shunjun in Chengdu in front of the temple of the Yangtze River outside the city (T. Li 2004: 989–90). This showed that this temple was still outside of the city in the Song Dynasty. During Five Dynasty Period, Sichuan was divided by Former and Later Shu Kingdom and rituals were performed at the river mouth of the Yangtze River to worship the god of the Yangtze River in Yangzhou by Later Zhou. It was not returned to Chengdu until the sixth year of the Qiande Reign (AD 968) (D. Ma 2011: 2556). Emperor Taizu ordered to renovate it in the sixth year of the Kaibao Reign (AD 973), and again in the seventh year of the Qingli Reign (AD 1047), the third year of the Chunxi Reign (AD 1176), and the fifth year of the Qingyuan Reign (AD 1199).

the Yangtze River was "topped among four rivers" (Y. Lu 2011: 400; S. Yuan 1990). Defense on the Yangtze River became the top priority of border defense of Southern Song and the significance of Yangtze River increased prominently. In the 31st year of the Shaoxing Reign (AD 1161), for the victory of Caishi, six characters were added to the title of the god of the Yangtze River, which became Zhaoling Fuying Weilie Guanyuan Wang (King of Epiphany, Inspiration, majesty, and Resources) and Youde (Virtue and Blessing) was bestowed as the temple name (X. Li 2013: 3810). Based on the Song's rules, "the titles of nobility conferred to gods, temples should be given if no title, title should be given if it had a temple. The order of the rank should be duke, lord and king. If titles were given alive, then the posthumous title comply with them. For women being worshiped, madam should be made first, then

Queen. The first conferral vouchsafed two-character title, then four-character title. For immortals, Master first, then Lord. Following these rules, the rites and rituals would be well regulated" (S. Xu et al. 2014: 1081). Normally, two characters were added to the title each time, so adding six characters was a special case. The Court of Imperial Sacrifices, which asked to confer a title, said that he had the two-character title originally, "adding six characters for this special case to eight characters." This conferral was performed for the temporary shrine in Jiankang (east of Qingliang Temple). "The main temple of King Guangyuan was in Chengdu and "the main temple could use the same as the one in Jiankang" (Y. Zhou 1990). These kind of shrines were not only built in Jiangkang, so as Sanxia and Shashi. When Lu You went through the Three Gorges, to the north temple and south temple of the Yangtze River along the Xintan shore. Going through Shashi, he wrote "liquor and pig were sacrificed to worship the Yangtze River in the temple." Fan Chengda also had "rested by the temple of the Yangtze River" (Y. Lu 2012: 207, 214; C. Fan 2012: 81).

The Huaihe River, the Yellow River, and the Jishui River were all included in the Jin Kingdom territory during the Southern Song Dynasty. In the Northern Song Dynasty, officials were sent to the Huaihe River to pray for rain, and the temples were refurbished and vessels were replenished, and many civilians also offered sacrifices (T. Li 2004: 1904, 10791), whereas in the Southern Song Dynasty, sacrifices could only be made from a distance. In the Northern Song Dynasty, the sacrifice of the Jishui River was just a routine ritual without any special attention. Among the gods of the three rivers, the Yellow River was related to the security of Kaifeng and the water supply of the Bianhe River, in addition to the ritual sacrifice of the temple in Hezhong Prefecture, the Northern Song court also offered sacrifices to the God of the Yellow River at Biankou every year. In the first year (AD 1008) and the fourth year (AD 1011) of the Dazhongxiangfu Reign, Emperor Zhenzong went to offer sacrifices to the Yellow River Temple in Caozhou, which was originally built one in Hezhong Prefecture (Y. Wang 2003: 1879). However, in the Southern Song Dynasty, Hezhong Prefecture had already entered the territory of the Jin Kingdom, and only the original temple and temporary ancestral hall of the god of the Yangtze River were still within the territory of the Song Dynasty, thus the god of the Yangtze River was bestowed the title of the eight-character king, which none of the other three gods were conferred.

The Song Dynasty followed the Three-Tier Worship System of the Sui and Tang dynasties. It was the Sui Dynasty that created such a system, stipulating that "gods of heaven, the emperor of the five sides, the sun, the moon, god of the earth, god of state sovereignty, god of Land and Grain, and their temples should be put at the supreme rituals. Sacrifices to stars, five sacrifices to state fortunes and four sacrifices to rivers and mountains are categorized into middle rituals; sacrifice to God of Heaven, sacrifice to God of Fortune, Wind Master, Rain Master and all stars, mountains and rivers are categorized into minor rituals" (*Sui Shu* 1973: 117). The system inherited by the Tang Dynasty from the Sui Dynasty, and the culted deities were changed slightly, but the four gods of seas and the four gods of rivers were always placed at the middle rituals, while the Wind Master, Rain Master, gods of mountain and forest, river gods, the Five Dragon Shrine, the prefecture's shrines and their gods remained at the minor rituals (Y. Zhu 2014: 57). In the Song Dynasty, the highest status of gods of seas and rivers, were included in the middle rituals in the early Northern Song Dynasty (from Emperor Taizu's Reign to Emperor Yingzong's Reign), and the gods of rivers and lakes were included in the minor rituals. During the period of the Xi'ning Reign, the ceremonies for worshiping gods of seas, rivers, lakes, wind and rain, conducted by the officials of prefectures and counties, had be removed from the middle and minor rituals which should be carried out by the Court of Imperial Sacrifices, only with reference to their standards. And it was only during the Yuanfeng Reign that the middle ritual status of the gods of seas and rivers was restored. The new rituals of the Zhenghe Reign stipulated that the gods of seas and river were elevated to the middle rituals, and the gods of rivers and lakes, and lakes were put at minor rituals. For the gods of wind and rain, those worshiped by the Court of Imperial Sacrifices were classified into the middle rituals, but those worshiped by the prefectures classified into the minor rituals (Q. Pi 2008: 58, 67–84). Ma Duanlin listed a number of "Zaci (miscellaneous ancestral temples) or Yinci (folk ancestral temples)". Among them, miscellaneous ancestral temples were basically put at minor rituals, including worshiping the gods of three branch rivers of the Yangtze River, the wave god of the Wushan Temple in Hangzhou, Li Bing worshiped as the King of Guangji, the god of the Nankang Military Prefecture at Gongting temple, the Dragon King of Shunji, and the god of Jiaoshan Mountain in Zhenjiang, who, in spite of a mountain deity, protected sailing ships in the river. Such water deities were countless. For example, *Xianchun Period Chronicles of Lin'an* recorded that "the gods of the earth, mountains, seas, lakes and rivers, the sages of the past, and those who had died in the service of the people, were all given edicts by the emperor to be honored with titles and posts, and were given offerings on time, and officials were sent to worship them from time to time" (S. Qian 1990: 3994). There were a large number of the above-mentioned deities along the coast and along inland rivers.

And the system of god worship keeps changing. Pi Qingsheng pointed out that only a small number of ancestral deities were officially accepted by the Song court, most of which were Yinci (folk ancestral temples) to be eliminated from the rituals, and ancestral deities in the middle ground between Zhengsi (formal sacrifice) and Yinsi (folk sacrifice). Many of these spontaneous beliefs were initially not included in the official rituals and were even "Yinci" (folk ancestral temples), which gradually gained official recognition and were included into the state rituals (Q. Pi 2008: 294). The Song Dynasty stipulated that "those folk ancestral temples that were not put into the ritual list should be cracked down" and that "military and civilians were forbidden to erect folk temples without official permission". But the number of civilian sacrifices out of the state ritual list was still large. In the first year of the Zhenghe Reign (AD 1111), Kaifeng alone "destroyed 1338 civilian folk ancestral temples". Until the Southern Song Dynasty, officials still believed that the state "should forbid evil folk ancestral temples. Civilians were so ignorant that they even killed people to sacrifice the witchcraft, and were convinced of the witchcraft. Such practices were rampant in Huzhou, Guangzhou, Kuizhou and the Three Gorges, and in recent years have been spread to other places". "There were also people in Liangzhe East Province who killed and sacrificed to the sea gods". In the 23rd year of the Shaoxing Reign (AD

1153), "some folk ancestral temples were cracked down and removed once again" (D. Ma 2011: 2772–73). Lu You saw at the River God Temple in Shashi "more gods were worshiped improperly on both sides of the corridor, a custom was handed down from the ancient the Chu Kingdom" (Y. Lu 2012: 207). In the later period of the Southern Song Dynasty, Chen Chun still believed that "the Southern Song people were fond of folk ancestral temples". "From cities to the countryside, many people knew the name of the witches, so hundreds of temples were built to worship them" (C. Chen 1990). It is clear that not only the folk ancestral temples were not eliminated, but they existed in large numbers. Only a small number of them were cracked down, while the majority existed in marginal regions or may be elevated to the status of formal temples.

Apart from the three-tier system of water deities in the Song Dynasty as mentioned above, there were quite a few subsystems, including the four gods of seas and the four gods of rivers at the top level which were later included in the middle rituals, other gods of the rivers, waves, tides, and Dragon Kings which were categorized into minor rituals, the various miscellaneous rituals, the uncatalogued civilian cults and the folk beliefs in the marginal regions. All these deities within the system and the various ancestral temples formed spatial subsystems, together with the Holy Goddess Cult as discussed below, formed a complex system of god worship. Some deities that were not originally the deities of rivers and lakes were endowed new functions of protecting navigation through the worship of navigators, and thus became a component of the belief system of water deities, as described below in the Cao E Cult. The beliefs in water deities in the Song Dynasty formed an intertwined system of deities.

5.5.2 New Changes to the Original Beliefs in Water Deities in the Song Dynasty

In addition to the above-mentioned changes in the status of the middle rituals during the period of Emperor Shenzong's Reign, the belief in the gods of the four seas underwent significant new changes during the Southern Song Dynasty, when the country grew its economy by relying on the sea. First, the original temple of the East Sea God was moved to Mingzhou (Ningbo, Zhejiang); and second, the sacrifice to the Sea God was elevated to the major grade. Gurin Morihiro's research on the faith of East Sea God and North Sea God mainly focused on the grants and repair of temples and the function of the two Gods, but did not pay attention to the changes of the faith in them in the Southern Song Dynasty. The same was true of Wang Yuanlin's research on the god of the South Sea (M. Gurin 1995: 112–36; Y. Wang 2006). In the fifth year of the Qiandao Reign (AD 1169), Lin Li, the vice minister of the Court of Imperial Sacrifices, submitted a petition that "our country should build its capital in the southeast region to actually control the East China Sea and the South China Sea within its boundaries. According to *Imperial Rituals*, offering sacrifices to the God of the East Sea was conducted in Laizhou on the first day of spring. Rituals for South Sea were held in Guangzhou on the first day of summer, the western and northern seas are far away, and only Fangzhou conducted the rituals two times. After crossing of the Yangtze River, only on the anniversary of the Temple of King Guangli in the South Sea, the imperial court issued an edict of blessing to hold a ritual in Guangzhou every year; and in the seventh year of the Shaoxing Reign (AD 1137), the Temple of King Guangli was even crowned with eight-character title. As for the rituals for the East Sea God, they were not conducted only because of the long distance from Laizhou. They seldom realized that Tongzhou, Taizhou, Mingzhou, Yuezhou, Wenzhou, Taizhou, Quanzhou and Fuzhou were all within the boundaries of the East Sea". In the thirty-first year of the Shaoxing Reign (AD 1161), "the God of the East Sea made contributions to the country" during the Jiaoxi Naval Battle. The temple was already built in Mingzhou (Ningbo, Zhejiang Province) in Dinghai County during the Yuanfeng Reign, so "all the temples dedicated to the East Sea God in this dynasty were in Mingzhou, and there's no need to conduct rituals in Laizhou". According to his proposal, Emperor Xiaozong set up the Temple of East Sea God in Mingzhou to offer sacrifices (D. Ma 2011: 2560–61). This was a new change in the belief in the East Sea God in the Southern Song Dynasty.

On the one hand, coastal defense had a vital stake in the national security of the Southern Song Dynasty. As Lin Li said, the victory of the Jiaoxi War was secured by the blessing of the East Sea God. The Southern Song Dynasty set its capital at Lin'an and established naval strongholds at Jiangyin, Xupu, Jinshan and Dinghai and at the mouth of the Yangtze River north of Tongzhou to establish a sea defence system. The Song people believed that the protection of the East Sea gods was needed within the boundaries of the East Sea. On the other hand, the sacrifices to the East Sea God involved an orthodox dispute with the Jin Kingdom. Five years before Lin Li's proposal submitted, that is, in the fourth year of the Jin Dynasty (AD 1164), the Jin Kingdom developed a specific system for the worship of gods of mountains, towns, seas and rivers, including "those rituals held at this temple in spring, summer, autumn, winter and the 18th day before autumn, and those rituals held at remote locations within the boundaries of other states and counties". On the first day of spring, sacrifices to the East Sea God was offered in Laizhou, and sacrifices to the East River God in Tangzhou; on the first day of summer, the South Sea God and the Yangtze River God were sacrificed in remote Laizhou; on the first day of autumn, the West Sea God and the West River God were sacrificed remotely in Hezhong Prefecture; on the first day of winter, the North Sea God and the Jishui River God were sacrificed in remote Mengzhou. "The bestowed titles of water gods still followed the old practices of the Tang and Song dynasties". And the Jin Dynasty followed the Song Dynasty's *The New Rules of Etiquette* (Toqta 1975: 810; Dajin Ji Li 1990). The worship of the gods of the four seas was of great political significance. The purpose of the rituals was to show that the Song Dynasty was "full of merits and virtues," as it stated in the chapter on the rituals to the gods of the West and North Seas. "We hold the rituals so that the four seas are worshiped equally (Toqta 1977: 3202). The sea has no favorites, so I am very happy." the Southern Song Dynasty moved the Temple of the East Sea God to Mingzhou, and instead of offering "remote sacrifices", the same rituals as those of the South Sea God were practised, which also had the important significance of competing with the Jin Dynasty for orthodoxy. More than forty years after the founding of the Southern Song, and five years after the Jin Dynasty had enacted the ritual system of the gods of mountains, towns, seas and rivers, this change was clearly an important response to the Jin Dynasty.

Since its founding, the Northern Song Dynasty had followed the Tang dynasty, placing the gods of mountains, towns, seas and rivers at the middle rituals, lower than the supreme rituals such as heaven, earth, temples and the five emperors, but higher than the minor rituals such as worshiping the gods of mountains, rivers, wind and rain. This system continued until the middle period of the Southern Song Dynasty. In the twelfth year of the Chunyou Reign (AD 1252), Emperor Lizong decreed that "since the Zhongxing Reign, when the capital was built by the sea, the worship of the sea gods should be lifted at top rituals," he also issued an edict to build an altar dedicated to the gods of the sea in Lin'an, and ordered the Court of Imperial Sacrifices to conduct the ceremonies and ordered Ma Guangzu to build a temple for the implementation of the remote sacrifices, which came into effect in the first year of the Baoyou Reign (AD 1253) (S. Qian 1990: 3379; Toqta 1977: 847). The altar for the gods of the seas was set up in the east of the Taiping Bridge outside the Dongqing Gate in Hangzhou, and "it was an ancestral temple, and officials were dispatched to conduct the ritual from a distance in the middle of spring and autumn" (Z. Wu 1980: 123). The major, middle and minor rituals of the Song Dynasty inherited the Tang's system. The ritual system of the Tang Dynasty stipulated that "there are supreme, middle and minor rituals. Worshiping the god of heaven, the emperor of the five sides, the sun and the moon, god of the earth, god of state sovereignty, god of Land and Grain ware placed at the supreme rituals" (S. Xiao et al. 1990). *The New Rules of Etiquette Issued in the Zhenghe Period* inherited this system and gave more specific instructions (*Zhenghe Wuli Xinyi* 1990). The gods of the seas were lifted to the rank of the supreme rituals, surpassing the four gods of inner rivers and ranking with the gods of heaven and earth, the highest of the water deities in the national ritual system. In addition, we could see that the status of the god of the South Sea weighed more in the Song Dynasty than the previous dynasties. During the Tang Dynasty, the god of the South Sea was named King Guangli, and during the Song Dynasty, he was bestowed the nobility titles four times, in the fourth year of the Kaibao Reign (AD 971), the first year of the Kangding Reign (AD 1040), the fifth year of the Huangyou Reign (AD 1053) and the Shaoxing Reign, as the King of "Eight Characters". In the period of Emperor Huizong's Reign, the wife of the South Sea God was named Queen Xianren (Queen of Kindness), the eldest son was named Duke Fuling (Duke of Country Defender), the second son Duke Zanning (Duke of Peace) and the daughter Madame Huiyou (Madam of Virtue) (S. Xu et al. 2014: 1085).[10]

The elevation of the status of both the East Sea God and the South Sea God was linked to the closer relationship between people and sea during the Song Dynasty, especially in the Southern Song. On the one hand, the gods of seas and rivers, like

---

[10] Wang Yuanlin also explored the God of South Sea being entitled by the court during the Song Dynasty in the book *State Sacrifices and Relics Along the Maritime Silk Road—Researches on the Nanhai God Temple in Guangzhou.*

many other deities, served to protect locals from disasters, and they were also hoped to bless people with favorite weather and rain, and no disasters or illnesses falling on people (D. Zhen, n.d.). This was a function entrusted on many deities, but the gods of the East and South Seas stood out, not only over other local deities, but also over the gods of the West and North Seas, namely because the gods of East and South Seas were more important places for the Song people to engage in maritime activities. The lyrics of a Song ritual to the South Sea God expressed that "waves of the South China Sea are swelling high to the sky, connecting many ethnic groups. Ships with sails can fly fast, and those with precious jade return. People and merchants pray for blessings, hoping that the god could block the invaders out" (Toqta 1977: 3202). The South Sea God is a deity who protects the safety of the merchants' navigation. The Song people also hoped that the god of sea could contain pirates. "The vast and stormy sea are really dangerous. How can we survive safely without the help of gods" (D. Zhen, n.d.). Hong Shi expressed his gratitude for being blessed by the Sea God on behalf of the maritime merchants in the *Prayer on the God's Blessing of a Tailwind:* "Seafarers travelled a thousand kilometers through the sea in a blink of an eye, and if sailing against the wind, the ship would be capsized and passengers got drowned. How could we sail safely and smoothly without the help of gods? Now, the ships returned home with treasures and moored at the docks, people need not worry about being eaten up by fishes. How can people forget to reciprocate the gods when they make the country rich and prosperous?" (S. Hong, n.d.). That evidenced Ye Shi's remarks, hoping for "calm winds and waves on the river and sea" (S. Ye 1961: 534).

The unprecedented boom of beliefs in the original deities on the Yangtze River was also a major change in water beliefs reflecting in the new social and economic development of the Song Dynasty. During the Song Dynasty, the economic prosperity in the south, the southward shift of the economic centre of gravity, and the more close links between the economically developed Sichuan and the southeast regions made the water activities on the Yangtze River more frequent than ever. An example of this is the lifted status of river gods. Another typical change is the rise in the belief in the Dragon King, who dwell in "the Water Kingdom" (Z. Guo 1990). "Palace of Dragon King" is a place where underwater immortals get together in primeval times. Its master is the Dragon King (S. Qian 1990: 3998), and "the Palace of Dragon King situated between Jinshan mountain and Jiaoshan Mountain" (X. Yu 1990: 2731). There was a group of divine bureaucrats, "the palace of the fish and dragons is the house of the gods" (M. Zhu 2003: 57), and there is "a group of immortals gathering in the Palace of Water Kingdom" (Z. Zhang 1990). "Wen Taizhen saw that the clothes and carriages that looked like earthly ones were what the world calls water officials (Z. Huang 1990). Before Qi Jue, a native of Raozhou, died, he "dreamed that a man came with an official document, declaring the Dragon King invitation to him as the judge of Water Kingdom" (M. Hong 1981: 32), which was an official position in Water Kingdom. These officials were enshrined in the canon for administration. In the Tang Dynasty, Mr. Kong, a native of Tongwengpu village, Xiangshan County, entrusted a dream to someone after his death, saying that "the God has recorded my good deeds in life and appointed me as a mirror god, and my name has been registered in the

Water Kingdom" (J. Luo et al. 1990: 5239). It is known that the Palace of Dragon King in people's mind is a system of underwater deities. Gulin Senguang made a systematic discussion on the origin, granting and function of belief in the Palace of Dragon King. Besides, Wang Yuanlin discussed briefly the evolution of the Palace of Dragon King belief after the Song Dynasty, besides the Tang and Song Dynasties (M. Gurin 1995: 86–108; Y. Wang and F. Qian 2014). This section examines the new developments in the Song Dynasty's belief in it related to the Tang and Five Dynasties.

There were many records about the Palace of Dragon King in the Tang Dynasty. For example, Wang Bo met the God of Zhongyuan Water Kingdom in Madang, so the boat arrived at Hongzhou (now Nanchang, Jiangxi) at night and composed *the Preface to Tengwang Pavilion* (M. Zhu 1990). Lei Man dug a pond in his house, stating that "all the water monsters come here. It is an entry to the Water Kingdom" (X. Ouyang 1974: 445). Bai Youqiu, an petty scholar of the Tang Dynasty, as recorded in *the Extensive Records of the Taiping Period*, went under the sea to meet the King of the Water Kingdom on the river. Zhou Han explored the octagonal well in Bianzhou by using southeastern sailors. "This well is where the Dragon King lives, and the venue of the Water Kingdom Temple". The most famous story about Water Kingdom is that Liu Yi went to the Palace of Dragon King to send letters to the Dragon King's daughter (F. Li et al. 1961: 257, 285, 1089, 1780, 3410). The Tang Dynasty also "treated Qutang Gorge as the water world and sacrificed it in the period Spring and Autumn" (G. Sun 2014: 89). In the Tang Dynasty, with the prevalence of Taoism, the Dragon King, King of Heaven, and King of Earth were called the Three Lords in a general term, and the water kingdom, the heaven and the earth were called triple worlds in a general term. And the dragon casting ceremonies were held to pray for rain and blessings (Z. Zhang 2007), but the Water Kingdom God was not bestowed a noble title in the Tang Dynasty.

In the second year of the Qianzhen Reign (AD 928), Emperor Yang Pu of South Wu Kingdom during the Five Dynasties was the first emperor to bestow nobility titles to the Lords of Water Kingdom as King of Peaceful River in the Upper Water Kingdom of Madang, and King of Calm River in the Middle Water Kingdom of Caishi, and then King of Sedated River in Lower Water Kingdom of Jinshan (X. Ouyang 1974: 758). In the Baoda Reign of the South Tang Kingdom, the emperor bestowed nobility titles to make the god of Madang Water Kingdom to be King of Protection and Peaceful River, the god of Caishi Water Kingdom to be King of Expedition and Calm River, the god of Zhenjiang Water Kingdom to be King of Efficiency and Sedated River (S. Xu et al. 2014: 1081). The above titles of nobility bestowed by emperors symbolized the lifted status of the gods, but the South Wu and the Southern Tang kingdoms were just division regimes. And the granting of noble titles to the three water world of the Yangtze River reflected the geographical features of their regimes.

The Song Dynasty still considered the gods of Heaven, Earth and Water to be the Three Lords based on the Taoist concepts, as stated by the Taoist Temple of Chengtian Lingying in Hangzhou (S. Qian 1990: 4030). The Song court also threw dragon bamboo slips every year. During the period of the Tiansheng Reign (AD

1023–1032), the number of venues for casting dragon slips ceremony was reduced to twenty, including the Upper Water World on Madang Mountain in Jiangzhou, the Middle Water Kingdom in Taipingzhou, the Lower Water Kingdom in Jinshan of Runzhou (Zhenjiang), the Water Kingdom on Qiantang River in Hangzhou, the Water Kingdom of the Jidu North Sea in Heyang, the Xianyou Lake of Shengqiu in Fengxiang Prefecture (part of Qinfeng Road in Song Dynasty), the Honglong Lake in Hezhong Prefecture, the Dragon Lake by Tianmu Mountain in Hangzhou, and the Chexiang Lake in Huazhou (H. Zhou 1994: 376). The Song Dynasty saw the lifted boarder restrictions on navigation along the Yangtze River between different regimes, and the need for merchandise trade and official grain shipping made the Yangtze navigation even more important than that in the Five Dynasties. The belief in the triple gods of the water kingdom along the Yangtze River reached its climax. Not only did they grow considerably compared with the previous dynasties, but also the Ming and Qing dynasties also saw a decline in the belief in the water deities compared with the Song Dynasty (Y. Wang and F. Qian 2014).

The locations of the temples were recorded in the history as "the Upper Water Kingdom in Madang of Jiangzhou; the Middle Water Kingdom in Caishi of Taiping; and the Lower Water Kingdom in Jinshan of Runzhou". The Lower Water Kingdom Temple was originally attached to the Longyou Temple in Jinshan. In the early years of the Yuanfeng Reign, the Buddhist monk, Liaoyuan, saw that "civilians pray for good health by means of slaughtering domestic animals as sacrifices. I feel sorrow for their evils". Jingzhou requested the court to relocate the temple to Xijin, an important land and water juncture on the south bank of the Yangtze River (X. Yu 1990: 2731). The Water Kingdom Temple was located at the XiJin Ferry. In the third year of the Jianyan Reign (AD 1129), Emperor Gaozong fled south from Yangzhou, crossed the river and "arrived at Xijin Ferry, and finally stay at the temple of Water Kingdom" (M. Xu 1987: 880). When Wei Liangchen and Wang Hui went on a mission to the Jin Kingdom, they crossed the river from Xijin Ferry to the river mouth. "The wind was so strong that the ships could not cross the river. Wang had to wait at the Water Kingdom Temple" (M. Xu 1987: 1169). The Middle Water Kingdom Temple situated at Caishi Cliff (B. Zhou 1990), Taiping County. "Passing by the Mount Wangfu in Caishiji, we reach the Middle Water Kingdom" (S. Zhang 1990), where situated the Temple of the Middle Water Kingdom (M. Zhu 2003: 264). The Upper Water Kingdom Temple was built on Madang Mountain in Pengze County, Jiangzhou, "with a splendid pavilion" (B. Zhou 1990). It situated at the juncture of Dongliu County of Chizhou and Pengze County of Jiangzhou. After crossing it, "when you reach Madang, you will find the Lower Water Kingdom Temple there" (Y. Lu 2012: 184–85).

In the second year of the Dazhongxiangfu Reign (AD 1009), the title of the Southern Tang Dynasty was abolished and it was re-granted the Three Water Kingdom Temples. The god of the Upper Water Kingdom Temple in Madang, Jiangzhou, was renamed King of Happiness and Peaceful River from King of Protection and Peaceful River King. The god of the Middle Water Kingdom Temple in Caishi, Taipingzhou was renamed King of Smoothness and Peaceful River from King of Protection and Peaceful River. The god of the Lower Water Kingdom Temple in

Jinshan, Runzhou was renamed King of Faithfulness and Sedated River from King of Efficiency and Sedated River. That is, "the nobility titles conferred to the water worlds by the emperors of the Southern Wu and Southern Tang kingdoms were considered to be pseudo-names in the Baoda Reign of the Southern Tang Kingdom, then the Song rulers began to rename them" (S. Xu et al. 2014: 1107). According to the ritual system of the Song Dynasty, the gods were "ennobled as Duke first, then as Lord, and last as King." This time, it changed the original titles of the gods of water worlds, and directly awarded them King with supreme courtesy. At the same time, the Song Dynasty also clarified the status of the gods of the Water Kingdoms under the god of the Yangtze River. At the end of the Shaoxing Reign, the Song army defeated the Jin army in the Caishi battle, and made the it flee without a fight in the Zhenjiang confrontation. Some people consider the battle to be a blessed one by the gods of the Water Kingdoms, so they petitioned for the gods to be given the title of King. After discussion, the Ministry of Rites and the Court of Imperial Sacrifices considered that "the gods of the Yangtze River, the Yellow River, the Huaihe Ruver and the Jishui River were all only crowned Kings, and that the gods of Water Kingdoms should not be ranked above them", so the they should not be crowned "emperor" (Y. Lu 2012: 165). At that time, the title of the god of the Yangtze River was "Zhaoling Fuying Weilie Guangyuan Wang (King of Magic Power, Confidence, Courage and Resources)". Although considered to be of lower status than the god of the Yangtze River, the god of Lower Water Kingdom was bestowed the same eight-character title as him in the 14th year of the Shaoxing Reign (AD 1144), he was awarded the title of Shunji Yinghui Zhaoxin Taijiang Wang (King of Smooth Sailing, Wisdom, Faithfulness and Sedated River), because it was located in the most important section of the Southern Song River defence, as the front line to safeguard Lin'an (X. Yu 1990: 2731).

People wanted the gods of Water Kingdom to "immediately dispel any good luck" (F. Yang 1990). The specific duties entrusted to the gods of Water Kingdoms were firstly, to protect the navigation of ships and secondly, to ensure favorite rain and snow. In the fourth year of the Jianyan Reign (AD 1130), the Song Army defeated the Jin Army in the Yangtze River. "There was no invincible attack, which depended on the blessing of the gods." In the 14th year of the Shaoxing Reign (AD 1144), when people carried the coffin of Emperor Huizong to cross the river "without the threat of huge waves", people believed they were blessed by the god of Water Kingdom (X. Yu 1990: 2731). Because he was in charge of the wind and waves on the river, ships sailing on the boundary of Sanyuan Water Kingdom once visited its Temple. As Li Liuqian described in his poem, "the small and dangerous mountain is under the jurisdiction of the Upper and Middle Water Kingdoms. As the passers-by were so extremely afraid of being extorted for money, they usually paid their respects at the prow of the boat" (L. Li 1990). Lu You and Zhou Bida both worshiped the Lower Water Kingdom when passed by Zhenjiang. They "presented a pig and a jug of wine to the Temple of Good-Luck King, also known as lower water kingdom. It was affiliated to the Jinshan Temple, where two monks were often assigned to guard it, and no more in it. However, it was recorded in the sacrifice book that the pig's head, which was used to pay tribute to the god, was considered to be the belongings of this temple. Everyone laughed at the record" (Y. Lu 2012: 165; B. Zhou 1990). The Middle and Upper Water Kingdoms were the places where passing-by boatmen must perform rituals (J. Yang 1990).

In the fourth year of the Zhiping Reign (AD 1067), "court officials were sent to the temples of five imperial entitled mountains, four rivers and various Water Kingdoms to pray for rain" (S. Xu et al. 2014: 955). The duties of the Water Kingdoms are "to extend God's blessings to the people". "If there was no snow in winter, there is no wheat growth; and if there no rain in spring, there is no grain harvest". When there is no snow or rain, local officials would go to Caishi to pray to the Water Kingdom god (D. Zhen, n.d.). "Among the gods, only the Middle Water Kingdom God is famous for his effective prayer for rain" (G. Zheng 1990), and he "can answer all prayers" (Z. Li 1990). Zheng Gangzhong had "been ordered by the emperor to leave the capital and pray for rain to the god of Middle Water Kingdom at the ancestral temple" (G. Zheng 1990). Li Zengbo was also instructed to pray for rain because of the severe drought in Jiangnan and Liangzhe provinces, where crops were withering and ships could not sail forward. This situation was also presented to the god of the Middle Water Kingdom (Z. Li 1990). The Lower Water Kingdom also served this function. When there was a severe drought in the region of the Yangtze and Huaihe Rivers, Zhen Dexiu was ordered to pray for rain in the Lower Water Kingdom (D. Zhen, n.d.).

As is discussed above, the belief in the Sanyuan Water Kingdom developed greatly and underwent several changes during the Song Dynasty. Not only were they bestowed a unique eight-character title and elevated to the supreme position, but they were also entrusted the mission of blessing navigation and praying for rain and snow, and the rituals performed by officials and people became more frequent. This was the result of an unprecedented increase in the importance of shipping and river defense on the Yangtze River.

Another notable change in beliefs on the Yangtze River during the Song Dynasty was the evolution of snake cult. "Whenever a snake boarded a boat sailing on the river, the boatmen considered it to be the appearance of a deity" (M. Zeng 2008: 153). The Song people worshiped the lizards or the small snakes they saw on the voyage as figurative images of dragons, and called them Little Dragons. In the middle period of the Chongning Reign, a snake appeared on the rope at the stern of a boat at Biankou of the Huaihe River and crawled up the stern. The helmsman's wife didn't know what a lizard meant". It was worshiped as a little dragon and ushered into the palace by Emperor Huizong and they "prepared wine to greet the little dragon, who leaped out of the box at once, grasped the cup of wine in both claws and drank several cups of wine". The small dragon has claws and is clearly not a snake, but a lizard. There were also those who saw the snake as a figurative representation of the little dragon. "This lizard often swam between the oars, similar with normal snakes, but while normal snakes must crawl in a winding path, the Pengli Dragon moved in a straight line, so the boatmen relied on this feature to identify it" (T. Cai 2008: 254). Dozens of boats that transported military staffs for the Song Dynasty's conquest of the Cochin in the middle of the Xi'ning Reign traveled south across the river, "since leaving Zhenzhou, a small snake had crawled onto the boat, and the master on board said it was Pengli Dragon" (K. Shen 2006: 151). The temple where the Little Dragon was sacrificed was located in Hongzhou in Poyang Lake, hence it was bestowed title "Pengli Dragon". And it was repeatedly bestowed with the title. In the sixth year of the Dazhong Xiangfu period (AD 1013), "Pengli Dragon was awarded the title of Duke Shunji" (T. Li 2004: 6770). It was renamed "King Shunji" (King of Smooth Sailing) in the ninth year of the Xi'ning Reign (AD 1076), "Yingling Shunji Wang" (King of Courage and Smooth Sailing) in the third year of the Chongning Reign (AD 1104), "Lingshun Zhaoying Anji Wang" (King of Smooth Sailing, Faithfulness and Peace) the next year (AD 1105), and it was bestowed the 8-character title of "Lingshun Zhaoying Anji Huize Wang" (King of Smooth Sailing, Faithfulness, Peace and Benevolence) in the second year of the Xuanhe Reign (AD 1120) (S. Xu et al. 2014: 1082). It was also known as "Shunji Longwang" (Dragon King of Smooth Sailing).

The area under the jurisdiction of "Pengli Dragon" was considered to extend from Biankou at the juncture of the Huaihe River, the Sishui River and the Grand Canal in the west to the Dongting Lake in the east. Su Shi said, "the prestige of King Shunji was extended to the Dongting Lake in the south and the Huaihe and Sichui Rivers in the north" (S. Su 2010: 1280). A small snake was seen boarding a Song army transport fleet at Zhenzhou during the Xi'ning Reign, suggesting that Pengli Dragon appeared. "Then, the snake returned to Nankang with a merchant boat. Legend has it that the Pengli Dragon never moved further southward beyond the Dongting Lake (K. Shen 2006: 151)". The movement area of the Little Dragon swam "only in the east of Jiangnan East and West provinces, Jinghu South and North provinces, but never appeared in the Liangzhe East and West provinces". But in exceptional cases, it could reach Hangzhou and Jiangling. The Little Dragon in Biankou received the favor of Cai Jing, the prime minister of the Northern Song Dynasty. In the late period of the Daguan Reign, when Cai Jing went to the southeast, he saw the Little Dragon out to welcome him at Biankou. During the period of the Zhenghe Reign, Cai Jing was in Hangzhou and the Dragon appeared at his home. In the early years of the Jingkang Reign, Cai Jing was relegated to the south of the Five Ridges, and when he reached Jiangling, the Dragon reappeared (T. Cai 2008: 254). Normally, the administrative area of the Little Dragon ranged from Biankou of the Huaihe River in the east, along the Huainan Canal and the Yangtze River, to Jiangling in the west, from the north border of Liangzhe Provinces to the south border of the Dongting Lake in the west. In fact, it was the deity who managed the navigation of the middle and lower reaches of the Yangtze River.

The main function of the "Pengli Dragon" was to protect the safety of ships on the Yangtze River. In the middle period of the Xi'ning Reign, the Song fleet "could travel hundreds of kilometers a day from Zhenzhou to the Dongting Lake with the help of wind and waves", just because the Pengli Dragon "protected the military baton". "The chief of worshipers presented a cleaned utensil to the snake, and then it crawled into it," and shielded the army all the way. Lin Xi was ordered by Emperor Shenzong to bestow the title to Pengli Dragon, "a snake fell on the shoulder of the chief official of the ritual, then it was considered to be the presence of the dragon king". When the messenger's boat returned, "the snake saw him off on the stern of the boat, and returned after at the place of Pengli". And "Pengli Dragon showed his power many times, and many people could tell stories about him" (K. Shen 2006: 150–51). Such cases of magic power of the gods were frequently viewed by worshipers.

It was believed that if the boatmen and passengers served him with respect, the Little Dragon would offer his blessing in return. Su Shi, returning northward from Hainan Island, anchored his boat below the Temple of Dragon King Shunji. He said "after visiting the Dragon King, I returned to my boat and sailed safely on the river" (S. Su 2010: 1279). In the third year of the Daguan Reign (AD 1109), Lu Duanzao docked his boat at the Shunji Ancestral Temple in Nankang, and the Dragon King entrusted him to write poems for the temple and promised to bless him with a favorite tail wind. Later, when he acted as the prime minister of Nankang, he saw an unknown animal crawling on the bridge for three consecutive days. It was also known as the Little Dragon (M. Hong n.d.: 968). When Fan Chengda moored his boat in Bosijia, Jiangzhou, "a snake appeared on the river and people rushed to see it" (C. Fan 2012: 88). The belief in snake was prevalent among the boatmen, and it was highly revered. When Zhou Bida sailed in the Poyang Lake, he "arrived at Wuzizhai Military Camp, after paying his respects at the temple, he asked the soldiers to lead the boat forward into the Lake". "Then a small snake led the boat with its head up to the shore and then came back". Zhou Bidai's poem said that "it was because the river god who did not know worldly wise" (B. Zhou 1990). If anyone was disrespectful to him, he would spell disasters over them. "The little dragon curled up on the table" at the Little Dragon Temple in Zhenzhou, "it would shake the pavilion down at the slightest sign of offense and overturn the mountain and the sea before it calm down. That's why there was a constant stream of people praying after the boats are moored there" (*Jinxiu Wanhua Gu* 1990). In the period of the Chongning Reign, the helmsman's wife didn't know what the dragon was and mistook it for a lizard, "she hit the dragon in the head with a firewood. Immediately a loud noise was heard, and the boats in Biankou, whether official or private, or the passenger boats totaled seven hundred, collided with each other and broke into pieces, causing several hundred deaths" (T. Cai 2008: 254). When Master Zhu, a scholar official in charge of examinations, was sailing on the Yangtze River, "the boatmen suddenly reported seeing a little dragon and asked for prayers. But in Zhu's eyes, it was nothing but a a small snake". He "caught the snake in the boiling water with chopsticks, it leaped out and jumped itself into the river". In a few moments, the thunders came loudly, heavy smoke covered the boat, and Master Zhu died in it (M. Zhou 1983: 208).

The middle reaches of the Yangtze River are not the only places where snakes or lizards were worshiped as small dragons. In the palace of Emperor Renzong, "a maid went to carry water from a well, and a small dragon came out by coiling on the rope" (X. Ouyang 2001: 1841). In the fourteenth year of the Chunxi Reign (AD 1187), after Su Guangting went to pray at Caotan Lake in Xianju County, a black dragon and a yellow one leaped out of the lake (Q. Chen 1990: 7466). There's also a small dragon in the sea that showed its power. In the fifth year of the Xuanhe Reign (AD 1123), When Xu Jing led a mission to Goryeo, they offered sacrifices to the gods of the East Sea in Dinghai County, and they saw "the god appearing in the shape of lizards, as a matter of fact, it was the Dragon King of the East Sea" (J. Xu 2006: 131).

But Pengli Dragon was the most important, with the largest number of believers and the most frequent manifestations of its magic power, and such rich record about it was never seen in previous dynasties.

In the Song Dynasty, some gods that had nothing to do with navigation were added to the function of protecting navigation, which was also a new change of water beliefs. For example, the belief in Master Tian was adopted by the Yangtze River voyagers. When General Wen Tianxiang fled from Zhenjiang to Zhenzhou (Yizheng County, Jiangsu Province), warships and patrol ships of the Yuan army were seen along the way. So, he anxiously prayed for a favorable wind. "The boatmen knelt and prayed, saying 'Master Tian of Jiangnan provinces, please bless us' (T. Wen 1987: 698). Then they got a favorable wind and knelt to express their gratitude and celebration". Master Tian must refer to the belief prosperous in Jiangnan West Province. His name was Tian Yang, once served at the governor of Jizhou in the Dazhong Reign of the Tang Dynasty. He "cared much about the people' benefits, but died while still in office". On his deathbed, he said that "I will not forget to protect the people of Jizhou (now Jixian County, Shanxi)". After his death, people built a temple to commemorate him, that is the origin of the Temple of Master Tian (M. Xie et al. 1990). He was originally the local god responsible for protecting people, and the Song Dynasty added him the function of protecting the voyagers. In addition, the eldest son of Chen Yan, an official supervisor of Fujian in the Tang Dynasty, was enshrined in Zhaoli Temple of Lianjiang, Fujian Province, who was treated as a deity in Lianjiang Count, but irrelevant to navigation. In the second year of the Xuanhe Reign (AD 1120), "he descended to Fuzhou and and work for people there, later the local people set up a temple to commemorate him". It was only at the end of the Northern Song Dynasty that it was extended from Lianjiang County to Fuzhou, which was considered to have ties with the beliefs of the Fujian merchants. In the fifth year of the Xuanhe Reign (AD 1123), Lu Yundi was on a mission to Goryeo when he was caught in a storm at sea and prayed for safety. "After his return, the deity's fame was known to all and the temple was bestowed the title plate of Zhaoli Temple by an imperial decree". This belief was transmitted to Mingzhou later. At the request of Lu Yundi, a temple was also built in Mingzhou in the fifth year of the Xuanhe Reign (AD 1123) (K. Lang 1990: 7864; J. Luo et al. 1990: 5239).

"Zhaoshun Lingxiao Furen Miao" (The Temple of Madam of Piety and Smooth Sailing) in Kuaiji County was a representative of the transformation of Cao E from a filial daughter to a god of navigation in the Song Dynasty. Cao E was originally a filial daughter in the Han Dynasty who stepped into the water to save her father from death but finally failed, and her temple was built on the bank of the river running through Cao E Town. According to the story in the Ming Dynasty, "her father got drowned, so Cao E bore hatred to the water kingdom" (D. Shen 1959: 357). Until the middle period of the Northern Song Dynasty, Cao E remained a filial daughter in people's mind. In the second year of the Zhiping Reign (AD 1065), the statue of the filial daughter Zhu E was also worshiped as another filial daughter in the Cao E Temple. Because Cao E town was located at the juncture of Cao E River and the Liangzhe East Canal, it was the shipping hub for official and private shipping between Mingzhou and Hangzhou. During the period of Emperor Huizong's Reign, Cao E

Goddess was entrusted the responsibility of protecting the navigation. In November of the fifth year of the Zhenghe Reign (AD 1115), "when Goryeo sent envoys to pay tribute to the Song emperor, they passed through the area at a time of high water and prayed that they could rely on the tide to cross the river, and received an immediate response". At the request of the Goryeo envoys, Cao E was entitled Madam of Piety and Smooth Sailing. Since then, many people who passed through Cao E Town via the canal worshiped her. In the middle of the Chunxi Reign, when King Wei, the royal son, passed through the Cao E town, "at a time of high water, he prayed to cross the river safely, and received an immediate response" (H. Zhang 1990: 7130; S. Shi et al.1990: 6805). Shi Hao, whose home was in Mingzhou, traveled many times between Mingzhou and Hangzhou, and he also paid homage to Cao E Temple. He said that "it has been nearly fifteen years since I resigned, and every time when I passed by the shrine, I was either a mercenary or urging the delivery of a rune, and the god blessed me with his mighty power" (H. Shi 1990). In fact, since Emperor Huizong's Reign, Cao E had become the god of the canals in Liangzhe East Province and the Cao'e River. The Ming people called Madam Lin of Putian and Madam Cao E of Kuaiji as "the River Goddess and the Sea Goddess" (D. Shen 1959: 358).

5.5.3 Newly Created Deities to Protect Navigation in the Song Dynasty

The Song Dynasty witnessed the creation of many new deities to protect navigation, of which this section gives a brief overview. The most famous was the belief in Mazu Goddess, the highest title conferred by the emperor during the Song Dynasty was Holy Goddess, and this title could be a reference to Mazu cult. Jia Erqiang pointed out that the belief of Heavenly Concubine (Holy Goddess) represented the great transition from the belief of sea God to the personal god in Song Dynasty (E. Jia 2002: 143).[11] The belief in the Holy Goddess first emerged as a folk belief in Putian, Fujian. The Holy Goddess had a specific prototype, who was originally "Lin's daughter from Meizhou in Puyang". Meizhou is an offshore island in Putian. "When the she was young, she was able to foretell people's fortunes and remained unmarried at home. After her death at the age of thirty, she was worshiped in the temple as the "Goddess Tongxian", or "Dragon Princess". And "she came to rescue people many times". The belief of the Holy Goddess originated from the folk belief in Putian, that is, the temple set up by people themselves, and then it was included into the sate sacrificial ceremonies. So, Chen Chun said that "the so-called Holy Goddess was originated from a lady in Putian" (C. Chen 1990), and that "every household in Putian worshiped her, and the ancestral hall were built in every house, and the most famous ones situated in Meizhou, Shengdui, White Lake and Jiangkou". Shengdui

[11] Jia Erqiang called the goddess in charge of the sea "Tian Fei", the name had been used after the Yuan Dynasty when he discussed the Mazu belief in *Folk Beliefs during the Tang and Song Dynasties*", which is not appropriate.

was an island in Putian, and its temple was first built by the locals during the Yuanyou Reign. As stated in *Chronicles of Lin'an*, "the temple of the Holy Goddess was built on the island for the boatmen to worship" (M. Zhu 2003: 220).

The title "Shunji" was given to the temple in the Xuanhe Reign and it was included in the national rituals. In the fifth year of the Xuanhe Reign (AD 1123), on his voyage to Goryeo, Lu Yundi's fleet encountered a strong gust, but they managed to cross the sea safely because "the God was accompanying them". In the following year, he submitted a petition to the court so the temple was bestowed the title of "Shunji". This was closely related to the beliefs of the voyagers in Fujian. As the mission chartered six merchant ships from Fujian and Liangzhe provinces, they "took the merchants from Fujian with them, and in the middle of the voyage, when the wind changed, they followed the merchants' words and trusted the god to save them out of disasters" (J. Qiu 1990). It is believed that the Fujian seafarers prayed to the Lin family when they were facing potential shipwrecks, and the mission was considered to have been blessed by Madam Lin because they were saved from shipwrecks. The worship of the Holy Goddess had been flourished since then. During the Shaoxing Reign, a shrine was set up at Jiangkou in Putian. Later, the Prime Minister, Chen Junqing, set up another temple at White Lake in Putian with a land voucher. And "these temples flourished not only in Putian, but also in Fujian, Guangdong, Jiangsu, Zhejiang and Huaidian (the Huaihe River basin)". In Hangzhou, there was the Shunji Temple of the Holy Goddess, which was built and renovated during the Kaixi and Baoqing periods, outside the Genshan Gate. People constructed another shrine at Xiaogong Bridge outside the Houchao Gate (S. Qian 1990: 4014). Moreover, the Temple of the Holy Goddess was built in Dantu County, Zhenjiang. This is proved by the following quotation: "In the east of the Shushi Mountain, which used to be in the west of the tide lock, and was moved here by Weng Daiyi, a tribute scholar during the Song Dynasty" (X. Yu 1990: 2730). And another Temple of the Holy Goddess between Mount Lulong and Mount Ma'an in Jiankang (Y. Zhou 1990: 1562), and one more built in Guangzhou (the provincial capital of Guangdong Province). Liu Kezhuang saw that "the fervour and devotion of the people along the coast of Guangzhou to the Holy Goddess was no less than that of Putian in Fujian, where the prestige of the Holy Goddess had spread". As a native of Fujian, Liu Kezhuang paid many visits to the Temple of the Holy Goddess in Guangzhou (K. Liu, n.d.). In the Song Dynasty, ten temporary shrines were built in Putian, Mingzhou (Ningbo, Zhejiang), Lin'an, Quanzhou, Nanxiong (belonging to Guangdong Province), Wuzhou, Dantu County in Zhenjiang, Junxianxi County in Xinghua, Zhangzhou and other places (Q. Pi 2008: 352–53), and their titles continued to increase. The title of "Madam Linghui" was bestowed by the emperor at a ritual in the 26th year of the Shaoxing Reign (AD 1156). Later, her temple was bestowed a new title for the achievements in removing epidemics, quelling thefts and drought reliefs. In the third year of Shaoxi Reign (AD 1192), her title was changed into "Linghuifei" (Queen of Cleverness and Kindness), and in the fourth year of the Qingyuan Reign (AD 1198), she was added the Chinese characters "Zhushun" (Assistance and Smoothness). During the Jiaxi Reign, she was ennobled as "Linghui Zhushun Jiaying Yinglie Fei" (Queen of Cleverness, Smoothness, Virtue and Heroine). In the 18th year of the Yuan Dynasty

(1281), she was named "Huguo Mingzhu Tianfei" (Queen of Guardian, Cleverness and Enlightenment) (X. Yu 1990: 2730; S. Qian 1990: 4014). According to the nobility conferring system of the Song Dynasty, "if a woman is made goddess, the first title is conferred as Madam, and the second as Queen. The first title contains two Chinese characters, and the second title six characters; and the top eight characters" (S. Xu et al. 2014: 1081). Here, the eight-character nobility name was already the supreme honour.

The rise and dissemination of the beliefs in the Holy Goddess was largely due to the fervour of seafaring merchants (V. Hansen 1999: 146). One of the functions of the Holy Goddess was to protect navigation. According to Wu Zimu, "the spirituality of the goddess lay in her blessing of smooth sailing in the sea" (Z. Wu 1980: 130). So "whoever sails at sea would rely on her and treat her to be the Goddess of Fortune" (D. Zhen, n.d.). "When merchants entered the sea, they would pray at the temple" (M. Hong n.d.: 950–51), just as stated in *Chronicles of Lin'an*, "the boatmen all served it with respect". It was first conferred by the court for escorting the ships of the Song on their mission to Goryeo in the fifth year of the Xuanhe Reign (AD 1123). In Putian, she was also credited with "the Goddess of Escorting the Ships to Goryeo" (Y. Lou 1990). When the grain vessels from Guangnan Provinces travelled northward, they encountered "a strong northwest wind which kept blowing for ten days, and made the northbound ships impossible to move. then the goddess reversed the direction of wind so that people on board were spared from food scarcity" (S. Qian 1990: 4015). It was the merchants who spread the belief in the Holy Goddess to Zhejiang, Huainan, Guangnan and other provinces. In addition to protecting navigation, she was also a local goddess with many functions. "as Goddess Linghui (Queen of Cleverness and Kindness), she blessed both Fujian and Guangnan East provinces, and was in charge of the White Lake, droughts and floods" (B. Li 1997). When a drought troubled Huai'an County, local people prayed for rain at the Palace of the Holy Goddess. She also helped to contain privacy in the coast areas of Fujian. When the sea pirates of Putian entered the country, "the Goddess Linghui captured them all by exploiting sticky ships" (S. Qian 1990: 4015). When Zhen Dexiu served as an official in Fuzhou, pirates frequently "sailed southward by ship, robbed and looted in all the places they visited, posing great harm to local people and merchants". The government and the army were able to put down many invasions thanks to the blessing of the Holy Goddess (D. Zhen, n.d.). And she also helped to defend the country against foreign enemies. During the period of the Kaixi Reign, the Jin army attacked Huainan, and the Song "dispatched soldiers to the frontier by carrying incense and the statue of the Holy Goddess with them. One battle was fought in Huayan Town first, then in Zijin Mountain, and last in Hefei, where the goddess appeared in the clouds", blessing the Song army with victories one after another. People's expectations for the Holy Goddess increased greatly with more and more worshipers. "Although the Holy Goddess was the goddess of Putian, her blessings extended to every corner of the world. Therefore, people ushered her in and bid farewell to her with the ebbs and flows of tides. When people sailed southward or northward, they worshiped her before departure. When people defended the country or capture the thieves, they followed her orders. Merchants did not care about the prices of life necessities, they followed her instructions" (S. Qian 1990: 4015). The Holy Goddess was in charge of the state sovereignty, community security, floods and droughts, all the affairs on the land and the sea.

Qiu Jun, the Minister of Rituals in the Ming Dynasty, commented on the significance of the Holy Goddess Cult, suggesting that "the gods of the four seas worshiped before the Song Dynasty were conferred titles of nobility as a natural man, but no dedicated goddess like her to be worshiped by boatmen" (J. Qiu 1990). She was a newly emerging sea goddess in the context of great navigation in the Song Dynasty. Due to Fujian merchants' efforts, the sea goddess cult was spread to the coastal areas and included into the state rituals, thus she was sealed by the emperors frequently. Although the Gods of the four seas at state rituals were higher than that of the Holy Goddess, but for seafaring people, the Holy Goddess cult gradually became the most important water-based belief in coastal areas after the Song Dynasty. In the Yuan Dynasty, she was crowned the Princess of Heaven, and in the Qing Dynasty, she was bestowed the title of the Queen of Heaven and this cult was also spread overseas.

In addition to the belief in the Holy Goddess, the Song Dynasty also saw the creation of many new gods to protect navigation. In the Xianying Temple in Tupu, Shengxian County, a completely new belief was created during the Song Dynasty. The deity worshiped was Chen Kuo, a native of Qingxi County, Muzhou, who was once the county mayor of Yong'an (Xianju), Taizhou (now Linhai, Zhejiang). When he passed by Tupu, "his boat was capsized and he got drowned. After that, the gods showed their presence in his spirit. So the people worshiped him" and built the Temple of Master Chen. In the first year of the Qingyuan Reign (AD 1195), the temple was bestowed the title plate by the emperor (H. Zhang 1990: 7130). For another example, the Temple of Duke Xianying in Ganpu, was built in the second year of the Jianyan Reign (AD 1128) and was conferred the title by the emperor. And in the third year of the Baoqing Reign (AD 1227), "at the beginning, Duke Xianying had no name or birthplace unknown to the general public, but later, the villagers commonly called him King of the Yellow Road". And "the god Minister Yang in the temple was particularly magical. All the passenger boats which were crossing the sea, would receive a quick response after they prayed" (T. Chang 1990: 4655). This was a newly emerged regional god of seafaring protection in the Song Dynasty. The Huangshan Temple in Taizhou was built in the eighth year of the Qiandao Reign (AD 1172). "It runs across the temple like a bull's nose, and the inhabitants say it is the place where people anchor their boat to offer sacrifices" (Q. Chen 1990: 7523). Later, it was conferred the title of "Huguo Ganying Xianqing Wang" (King of Guardian, Telepathy and Assistance). The temple was not a temporary temple of the outsider deity, but a cult newly born with mariners stopovers.

Duke Shunji was worshiped at the Shunji Temple in Jinsan, who was also a newly created god of navigation protection during the Song Dynasty. The god was originally a merchant from Fujian, "who was born in a rich family and ranked seventh". "He was born in the Minyue tribe and did business by boat". After his death, he was worshiped in Jinshan. Every year, "on the 21st of June, the birthday of King Yinglie, the coastal people worshiped him at the ancestral temples with great care". "On this day, salt and sea merchants celebrated by beating gongs and drums and offering incense to him". At first, it was just a folk sacrifice, "there was no title, nor did it conform to the national rituals. They lined up with a bow and knife, called Minister Qian. He was worshiped in the desolate temples, whose reputation was low". "In the year of the submission of Shandong, the Jin people were still contending and raising an army in the eastern border, and Duke Qian was able to offer help." He was bestowed the title by the emperor (M. Zhao 1990).

There was also another Shunji Temple in Hangzhou, dedicated to a deity "named Feng Jun, courtesy name Deming, born in Qiantang on the 14th day of the 6th lunar month in the Xi'ning Reign". "He lost his father at a young age and served his mother dutifully. At the age of eighteen, he dreamed that God had sent someone to change his lungs, saying that there would be an order for him. He was able to predict whether his fortune was good or bad". He was worshiped even when he was still alive. He stated that "God appointed me to be in charge of the rivers" and "although my feet had never even stepped out of my family gate, someone could find me at sea in time of emergence. One day, in the period of the Yuanyou Reign, as a boat crossing the river ran into a storm, its boatmen would die for sure, but Feng Jun appeared in time and shouted his name loudly, and in a moment the storm subsided". He died in the third year of the Daguan Reign (AD 1109) at the age of thirty-six. In addition to the merits of protecting navigation, he had the achievements of leveling the sandbars in Zhejiang, which were hazardous to ships. "When the officials offered prayers, the sandbars would be leveled completely by the river god". "Not only did the merchant ships relied on his power, but also the entire country relied on him many times to fight against floods and droughts within a thousand miles". In the 30th year of the Shaoxing Reign (AD 1160), his temple was bestowed the title plate of Shunji, and he was made King Yinglie during the Shaoding Reign (S. Qian 1990: 3998).

Li Deyu, the prime minister of the Tang Dynasty, was worshiped as the Sea God in the Song Dynasty. Lu Weize, a native of Wenzhou in the Song Dynasty, wrote a book entitled *Stories About the Sea Gods*, in which a story goes as follows. "In the period of the Yuanyou Reign, Fan Xun, who was in charge of Wenzhou, had a dream of a deity named "Li Deyu of the Tang Dynasty". There was a temple at Haixian Temple in the northeast corner of the county. At first, he did not know which dynasty this god came from. The next day he went to visit the statue of god, whom had met him in his dream. Since then his prayers were all answered. However, the title was only bestowed to the god of the sea" (D. Ma 2011: 5727). Xue Jixuan, a native of Wenzhou in the Southern Song Dynasty, wrote "Prayer at the Ceremony of Worshiping Master Li Deyu as the Sea God of Loyalty and Hero", stating that Li Deyu answered the prayers of the people "without failure, and satisfied all their requests", claiming that "he was a man of virtue who should be entitle to share the sacrifices with other gods" (J. Xue 1990). All this evidenced that Li Deyu was indeed worshiped as the sea god in Wenzhou during the Song Dynasty.

5.5.4 *Summary*

In terms of state policy, in the Song Dynasty people developed a system of water deities with gods at high or low levels, being worshiped either formally or informally. The gods of the four seas and the gods of four rivers were at the top of the system, and were basically included in the middle rituals in the Northern Song Dynasty, while the Southern Song court elevated the Eastern Sea God to the supreme rituals. The gods of rivers and lakes were included in the minor rituals, while the gods of wind and rain were distinguished between the rituals presided by the Court of Imperial Sacrifices (Middle Rituals) and those offered by the prefectures (Minor Rituals). In addition to the official rituals, there existed a large number of folk beliefs that were not included in the official ones, either as self-established shrines or as a middle ground between self-established rituals and official rituals. In spite of the vertical system as described above, the water gods and their temples also formed a number of sub-systems, and many other non-local gods who were given the responsibility of protecting navigation were included into this water system, which together formed this complex system.

The new changes in the beliefs of water deities during the Song Dynasty were mainly manifested in two ways: first, the new changes occurred in the original system of beliefs. This was reflected, firstly, in the enhancement of the original functions and status of the deities, and then, apart from the safeguarding navigation by original deities, they were added new functions. Secondly, the new beliefs were created by people to meet their needs of safe navigation during the Song Dynasty, reflecting the new features of its historical development. The Song Dynasty was experiencing the great development in water navigation. Due to the growth of commodity economy, flourishing maritime trade, and the huge scale of official shipping, water navigation became more frequent than ever, leading to more and more people travelling on water. So the water god worship got a momentum in development. The close links between water navigation and the state's financial support, economic activities, and people's daily life, as well as the importance attached to water gods by both civilians and the country, were the underlying reasons for the new changes in water beliefs.

5.6 The Ferry Operation and Management in the Song Dynasty

It is extremely difficult to build strong bridges with the ancient technology, especially the bridges across large rivers as the Yangtze River, the Yellow River, and the Qiantang River, except the pontoons. Ferrying with boats served as an important player of transportation in the Song Dynasty which enjoyed business boom and frequent exchanges both politically and militarily between the south and the north regions. Ferries, both public and private, were in urgent need of a huge number of boats. The ferries all over China were large in number, including the public and the private. Of course, the private ferries were banned by the authorities for the sake of border security and tax income. However, the private still had room to survive on a large scale due to some practical needs and the drawbacks of public ferries.

5.6.1 Establishment and Management of the Public Ferry

5.6.1.1 Establishment of the Public Ferry

The transformation of private ferries into the public was the basic tendency in the Song Dynasty, and the public were largely put into the registration book. Sixty-seven ferries of the early North Song Dynasty were recorded in *The Anthology of Laws and Regulations of the Song Dynasty*, which were "Suanzao and Zhangjia in Kaifeng, Wangwu, Changzong and Nanjin in He'nan, Fanshui and Jiuding in Mengzhou (in He'nan), Santing and Qingrun in Hezhong (now Yongji, Shanxi Province), Songjia in Huaizhou (now Qinyang, He'nan Province), Doujin and Santing in Shaanzhou (now Sanmenxia, He'nan Province), Weiqiao in Jingzhao (now Beijing), Dabaojin in Zhende Military Prefecture, and Ronghe in Qingcheng Military Prefecture, Wangjiahe in Qingzhou (Yidu in Shandong Province), Huangdui in Shanzhou (Shanxian County), Heyinkou, Gengjikou and Gaojiakou in Qizhou (now Ji'nan, Shandong Province), Boshui, Fengjiakou, Qinhekou, Yukou, Laosengkou, Litangkou, Ganghekou in south of the Yellow River, Hejin and Jiegou in Yingzhou (in Fuyang, Anhui Province), Heliu and Yancheng in Xuzhou (now Xuchang), Wangqiao and Zoujia in Yunzhou (now Dongping, in Shandong), Ligu and Baigao in Huazhou (now Huaxian County, in He'nan), Guantai in Cizhou (now Cixian County in Hebei), Jinghekou, Nanpikou, Guoqiaokou, Changlukou and Jujiakou in Cangzhou, Lejia and Qili in Lizhou (Huimin in Shandong), Zhangjia, Lijia, Qimenzhen, and Xiaohe in Weizhou (now Weihui in Henan), Yaozikou and Xiejie in Binzhou (in Shandong), Lijia in Beizhou (Qinghe in Hebei), Dongjin in Jingnan (now Jingzhou in Hubei), Beishen, Huaiyin and Hongze in Chuzhou (now Huai'an in Jiangsu), Zhugao in Guangzhou (now Huangchuan in He'nan), Dushu in Qizhou (now Qichun in Hubei), Huangpihe in Huangzhou (now Huanggang in Hubei), Guazhou in Yangzhou, Haokou in Haozhou (now Fengyang in Anhui), Jingshan, Wohe and Tonghai in Suzhou (now Suxian County in Anhui), Linhuai in Caizhou (now Runan in Henan), Chaoxian in Lianshui Military Prefecture (in Jiangsu), Shuiyang in Xuanzhou (now Xuancheng in Anhui), and Zhejiang and Longshanmiao in Hangzhou (in Zhejiang)" (S. Xu et al. 2014: 9534). These ferries ran by the governments were of great importance, but this number was far less than the total of public ferries. According to the imperial edict in the first year of the Jianlong Reign (AD 960), "39 ferries along the Yellow River and the Wenhe River were constructed and charged for fees in consequence of the heavy rain in the border areas of Cangzhou, Dezhou, Lizhou, Zizhou, Qizhou and Yunzhou" (S. Xu et al. 2014: 9534). This was only the number of dry ferries, free of charge, in six prefectures. The above-mentioned records about ferries were more detailed in the north, and less detailed about ferries in the south. However, the south boasted much more ferries in the crisscrossed waterways than the north.

Baoqing Period Chronicles of Siming recorded that Mingzhou (now Ningbo) enjoyed a total of 37 public ferries in its counties, namely, Taohua, Xijiang, Tongpenpanshi, Zhousu, and Yugonglijia ferries in Yinxian County (J. Luo et al. 1990: 5158); Chenshan, Yuancun, Jiangyu, Hutou and Baicha ferries in Xiangshan County; Beidu, Dongsu, Nandu, Huanjiang, and Shijia Ferries in Fenghua County (J. Luo et al. 1990: 5267, 5187); Huangmu, Lixi, Qinglin, Renjia, Guanpu, Zheshan, Shenjia, Zhangting, Wuweng, Shushan, Dongnan, Chengshan, and Chejiu ferries in Cixi County (J. Luo et al. 1990: 5211); Dajia, Xiaojia, Dongjiang, Zhujia, Hujiang, and Lupu ferries in Dinghai County (J. Luo et al. 1990: 5234); as well as Zhoushan, Qianlan and Jintang ferries in Changguo County (*Zhizheng Siming Zhi* 1990: 6495).

According to Chunxi Period Chronicles of Fuzhou, Fuzhou and its Changle County had Hekou, Dayi, Hangtou, Yangmen, Linshui, Baitian, Yangxia, Dongjiang, Yingqian, Yangyu, Chouqi, Fuqi, Wengqi, Wangbu, Shijie, Gaoqi, Yangqi, Dazhang, Yuefeng, Chongguang, Wushikou, Hongmian, Xidong and Fukoucheng ferries. In the other counties of Fuzhou, there were the following ferries: Jiangting, Luolun, Dongan, Qihou, Chuanputou, Panlang and Dilu ferries in Lianjiang County; Xiaoruo, Anren, Xikou and Damu ferries in Houguan County; Yantian, Fanxi, Huangqi Town and Shenpu ferries in Changxi County; Chengtou, Yiqi and Keyu ferries in Fuqing County; Qingtan and Xiaomu ferries in Gutian County; Xidong, Yuefeng, Wushi, Hongmian, Chongguang Temple and Yuefeng ferries in Gutian County; Batatou and Tianwang ferries in Minqing County; Feiquan, Xibi, Chengdang, Xixi, Jinxi, Buxi, Jinchui, Shenpu, Chijianmen and Anle ferries in Ningde County. In lower reaches of the Yangtze River of Jiankang (now Nanjing), six ferries, Lieshan, Nanpu, Longwan, Dongyang, Dachenggang and Anle Ferry, were established under Changping and Jiankang Ministry (K. Lang 1990: 7833–34, 7897–98). In the lower reaches of the Yangtze River in Jiankang (now Nanjing), "along the over 500-kilometer river from Caishi to Guabu (now southeast of Luhe), six ferries were set up", which were Lieshan, Nanpu, Longwan, Dongyang, Dachenggang and Gangsha ferries, under the Supply Commission and Jiankang Prefecture Office (S. Yang et al. 1990). These referred to the most important public ferries. Besides, there were other ferries in Jiangkang, like Shitou, Fangshan, Nanjin, Wuma, Huishan, Wucheng, Majia, Zhuge and Zhanggongtu ferries. These should be also public ferries with official management (Y. Zhou 1990: 1552–53). As discussed above, we can draw that there were a sea of ferries in the south according to the situation in Mingzhou, Fuzhou and Jiankang. The situation in other places would not be repeated here.

Important ferries usually would be accompanied by the city clusters, post offices, and wine shops. Take Fenghua County for example, its South Ferry was developed into a city with South Ferry Post Office and South Ferry Wine Workshop, and the North Ferry set up its own post office and wine workshop. Yuancun Ferry itself was Yuancun City, and Dongsu Ferry developed its own Dongsu Wine Shop (J. Luo et al. 1990: 5180, 5190). The busiest ferry in Mingzhou (now Ningbo) must be East Ferry. It was the transportation hub of Mingzhou, located at the foot of Guoyin County with a town gate named East-ferry Gate close to three-river estuary. When Emperor

Gaozong fled from Mingzhou to Wenzhou, "he ran away through East-ferry Gate by horse and took the tower ship". The East Ferry established Taohua (East-ferry) Post Office and Mingzhou Tax Revenue Office in the fourth year of the Jingde Reign (AD 1007) (J. Luo et al. 1990: 5025, 5135). Xiaomu and Anren ferries in Fuzhou were special post roads with three boatmen on duty. Xiaoruo Ferry was equipped with a post office and a post road. Dayi Ferry set up the Linjin Post Road (K. Lang 1990: 7833).

5.6.1.2 The Establishment of Public Ferry Supervisor and Boatmen

The local prefecture and county-level officials jointly administrated the ferries and they must deploy river staffs randomly to curb tax evasion. The inspectors of border security at Guazhou Ferry in Yangzhou, and Xijin Ferry in Zhenjiang were also part-time ferry supervisors. In the eighth year of the Qiandao Reign (AD 1172), a group of officials were demoted or suspended for "failing to check the illegal tax evasion by the private ferries along the Huaihe River", who were Xia Jun, the military official of Huainan East Province (now Jiangsu Province), Chen Rui, head of Shanyang County in Chuzhou (now Huai'an, Jiangsu), Sun Chun, the would-be Inspector of Maluo, Shanyang County, Zhang Shunchen, Inspector of Chuzhou border security, Yan Zongyan, Inspector of Xialiupu, Shanyang County (S. Xu et al. 2014: 9539). However, ferries were mainly administrated by the dedicated ferry supervisors.

In the Northern Song Dynasty, the posts of ferry supervisor had not been set up, but gradually, it was established in the important public ferries during the Southern Song Dynasty. Zhongdu Ferry and Huaye Ferry over the Huaihe River were not managed by specialized supervisors initially. Important ferries tended to be equipped by two ferry supervisors, such as the Xingdu Ferry, to the west the Qiantang River. Caishi Ferry, "a significant land and water transportation hub", which levied business taxes and checked spies, was also under the charge of two supervisors. In the sixth year of the Qiandao Reign (AD 1170), only one ferry supervisor was there with the other being cut down. The ferry supervisor was at low rank, busy with his work, "as civilian officials had a good opinion of themselves, despising such posts", therefore, the administrator of Bureau of Military Affairs tend to select military officer to work for it. In this way, the ferry supervisor was also called "Ferry Administrator" (S. Xu et al. 2014: 8724). In the second year of the Jiatai Reign (AD 1202), the posts were shifted from military officers to civilian officials to administrate the four ferries: Zhejiang, Longshan ferries of Lin'an (now Hangzhou) Prefecture, Xixing and Yupu ferries of Shaoxing Prefecture at the request of Mr. Chenjingsi, Zhejiang Minister of Water Transportation. However, the benefit did not last long, in the third year of the Kaixi Reign (AD 1207), "the military administrator was again pointed to hold the post" only with "some extra meal subsidies and being promoted in accordance with the regulations on the civilian ministers promotion after the term" (S. Xu et al. 2014: 9541). The term of ferry supervisor in Liangzhe provinces was limited to one year, or "one year term", and the wooden board, carved with large characters of "the Administrator Dispatched by Bureau of Military Affairs, was erected by the river".

In comparison, the term of Ferry Supervisor of the Huaihe River was at least two years. For instance, according to the edict of Emperor Xiaozong in the eighth year of the Qiandao Reign (AD 1172), "the ferry supervisor, only after pledging no illegal acts during his two-year term, could he be promoted by Transfer Agency of Taxation, otherwise, the head of agency would be punished equally as the collaborators of the same crime as the river supervisor" (S. Xu et al. 2014: 9538–39). The terms may vary on the basis of different regions with the Huaihe River as its boundary river.

The duty of the ferry supervisors was, first and foremost, to ensure the safety of both people and boats. In the seventh year of the Shaoxing Reign (AD 1137), Emperor Gaozong's edict required that "if the goods are overloaded, the punishment of 80 lashings with a stick will fall on the helmsman; and if there are death casualties, his penalty would be doubled. If the supervisor connived a crime, he would be put on trial equally for his neglecting the crime, he would be beaten 100 times with a stick" (S. Xu et al. 2014: 9537). Emperor Xiaozong stipulated in the third year of the Qiandao Reign (AD 1267) that in Xixing, Longshan, and Yupu ferries of Zhejiang, etc., "if there are no accidents like ship sinking or loss of life within the supervisor's one-year term, his assessment can be shortened one year before promotion and an additional 6000 coins meal subsidies every month". "Otherwise, if making violations against the decree, like overloading, hiding the oars to interrupt the voyage, forgetting to count the number of personnel, departure delayed, conniving the helmsman and the sailor to intercept the cable halfway, and losing the opportunity of crossing tides", "the ferry supervisor shall be punished according to the law" (S. Xu et al. 2014: 9538). The safety of the ferry ships and people and the safe navigation were important criteria for assessing the supervisors. In the tenth year of the Chunxi Reign (AD 1183), Xu Yuanli, the ferry supervisor of Longshan, ferried to Fushan but sank on the way. Huo Lingxun, the supervisor of Yupu Town, and Guo Xiaozhong, the supervisor of Yudu, rowed a boat rescuing 79 people. As a result, Xu Yuanli was dismissed, Huo Lingxun and Guo Xiaozhong were rewarded with a three-year reduction of promotion assessment (S. Xu et al. 2014: 9540).

The second responsibility of the ferry supervisors was to check forbidden object. "While in office, supervisors who caught tea and salt smugglers will be rewarded and promoted as the same as the county criminal inspector. Otherwise, he would also be punished equally by the regulation on tax dodging cases". Xuyi Military Prefecture stationed at the border area of the Huaihe River Ferry, "whose priority should be given to preventing smuggling forbidden objects like silver as hundreds of merchants and tourists crossed the Huaihe River for business every day". In the first year of the Xinglong Reign (AD 1163), a Zhejiang ferry vessel "was overturned in the mid-stream, and some of the passengers lost their lives. However, Ji Yan, the supervisor and the Administrator of Bureau of Military Affairs, lied absurdly that the ship overturned but the people on board had already come ashore". As a result, Ji Yan, the ferry supervisor, was sacked, and Li Sheng, the helmsman, was expelled 250 km away from home and incorporated into the border household registration, subject to local officials.

The third duty of ferry supervisors was to prevent tax evasion and search for spies. In the seventh year of the Xi'ning Reign (AD 1074), with the border tension growing,

Emperor Shenzong ordered that the ferries along the Yellow River should "detect spies, forbidden objects and check the official documents while soldiers, officers, yamen runners, and officials crossing the river. Only urgent military documents could be delivered at night" (S. Xu et al. 2014: 9535). It was stipulated in the first year of the Yuanfu Reign (AD 1098) that "the ferry supervisor should check the passing-by soldiers, and if there were tax evasion or desertion, all the soldiers and supervisors shall be beaten with a hundred bludgeon even though they know nothing about it. Reporting each illegal case would be rewarded with ten strings of 1000 coins. If there was a covered illegal transaction within the territory, the ferry supervisor was subject to the punishment of flogging with a stick, and will be degraded two ranks" (T. Li 2004: 11906). In the Southern Song Dynasty, spies were probably hidden among the overseas Chinese returning from the north, and the supervisors must "keep an eye on them. The ferry supervisor and the patrol officer would be degraded one rank if tax evasion was found out. Otherwise, they would get promotion after the end of their regular term". Furthermore, "if the supervisor caught and sent the spy to the central government, he would be rewarded with extra 300 strings of 1000 coins" (S. Xu et al. 2014: 9537). The other two duties of the ferry supervisor were to levy ferrying taxes and prevent smuggling, which will be discussed below.

In addition to the ferry supervisor, other management personnel and boatmen for ferries were equipped. For example, Shitou and Fangshan ferries "each set up one ferry supervisor, one ferry clerk, and five sailors" (Y. Zhou 1990: 1552). Ferry supervisor was the top leader, the clerks and boatmen worked under his leadership. In the Southern Song Dynasty, the ferries of the Qiantang River were very busy "as more than a thousand boats crossed the river every day. As for the huge ship, at least 30 skillful sailors were required to keep it moving". "Ordinary boats would be equipped with 10 to 20 sailors according to their sizes" (S. Xu et al. 2014: 9540). In summary, the extra-large ships required 30 sailors and the ordinary with 10–20 sailors. Chenshan Ferry in Xiangshan County, Mingzhou, was equipped with two ships with 2-m-wide beam and 20 boatmen on board (J. Luo et al. 1990: 5267). And the sailor population was in line with the standard of the Qiantang River ferries.

County	Ferry	Xi'ning and Yuanfeng Reigns number	County	Ferry	Xi'ning and Yuanfeng Reigns number
Lianjiang	Jiangting	6	Yongfu	Xidong	1
	Luolun	2		Yuefeng	1
	Dong'an	1		Wushi	1
	Qihou	1		Hongmian	1
	Chuanpu	1		Chongguangsi	2
	Panlang	1		Yuefeng	
	Dilu	1	Minqing	Baitatou	3
Houguan	Xiaoruo	1		Tianwang	2
	Anren	3	Ningde	Feiquan	15

(continued)

(continued)

County	Ferry	Xi'ning and Yuanfeng Reigns number	County	Ferry	Xi'ning and Yuanfeng Reigns number
	Xiaomu			Xibi	1
	Damu	15		Chengdang	1
	Xikou	1		Xixi	1
Changxi	Yantian	11–13		Jinxi	1
	Fanxi	2		Puxi	1
	Huangqizhen	4		Jinchui	1
	Shenpu	2		Shenpu	2
Fuqing	Chengtou	2		Chijianmen	2
	Yiqi	2		Anle	
	Keyu	1	Changle	No official records were found in Emperor Shenzong's Reign	
Gutian	Qingtan	3		In 1091, Linshui Ferry was equipped with 23 sailors	

The sailors were mainly dispatched before the implementation of *Law on Recruiting Inferior Officials* drafted by Wang Anshi, the prime minister of the Northern Song Dynasty. It was ruled in Emperor Renzong Edict that "at the important ferries, the ship transportation should be widely employed", and "the recruited workers should be sent on errand as sailors" (*Tianyige Cang Ming Chaoben Jiaozheng* 2004: 370). In the Northern Song Dynasty, sailors could serve for both part-time and full-time. And "labors on errand whose salary below one string of coins only served as the minor clerks in prefecture office for one year; and lower clerks acted as the village chief in charge of collecting taxes or as boatmen for half a year". Only civilians of upper three classes had the opportunity of being recruited by prefecture office (T. Lü 1990). Some ferries recruited soldiers as boatmen, for instance, two boats were available at the ferry station along the way from Changguo (now Dinghai, Zhejiang) to Yinigyuan Prefecture (Mingzhou), "the soldiers at Jiangdong fortified village were ordered to sail boats in turn". The boatmen either being recruited or temporary on errand were paid salaries. The soldiers of Changuo County "were rewarded with salary and rice" (J. Luo et al. 1990: 5250). For the twenty punters at Chenshan Ferry of Xiangshan County, "each was paid one string and 250 coins per month", that was 42 coins per day (J. Luo et al. 1990: 5267). Xiaomu and Anren ferries of Fuzhou enjoyed three dedicated boatmen, and Gutian Ferry recruited three criminal clerks, at the expense of 70 to 80 strings of 1000 coins per year. If the boatmen and criminal clerks enjoyed equal pay, then a boatmen was paid 36 coins per day (K. Lang 1990: 7834). But in terms of salary, there was a difference between helmsmen and boatmen. "If the boatman earned 100 coins a day, then the helmsman could get 200 coins. So the helmsman's salary was twice than that of the boatman" (S. Xu et al. 2014: 9541). Ye Mengde, a well-known poet in the Song Dynasty, once proposed that "the wage of the boat master and sailor should come from the local government instead of the customers" (M. Ye 2002). In fact, the sailor's salary was part of the ferry money from customers. The six ferries ranging from Caishi to Guabu Ferry along the Yangtze River "initially paid officials and punters no salary", but they enjoyed 10 thousand strings of 1000 coins income per year. It was stipulated in the fifth year of the Jiading Reign (AD 1212) that "apart from the official pre-stored money for money lending, half of the revenue was used for the repair of boats, the other for the salary of officials, helmsman, punters, and sailors" (S. Yang et al. 1990). Ferries in the Qiantang River "distributed the whole daily ferrying income to the sailors" and stipulated that "if the ferry concealed the revenue under all sorts of pretexts, not practically benefiting the sailor and helmsman, once it was confirmed by the helmsman and seamen, it shall be punished with a heavy sentence by the authority" (S. Xu et al. 2014: 9540–41).

5.6.1.3 The Manufacture of Ferry Boats

Generally, the boats for public ferries were provided by the government, and it was the same case in the Northern Song Dynasty. In the seventh year of the Taipingxingguo Reign (AD 982), Lizhou (now Hanyuan, Sichuan Province) authorities "built a boat for the southern tribute-payers to cross the Dadu River (the largest branch of the Minjiang River)" (S. Xu et al. 2014: 9534). In the fourth year of the Tianxi Reign (AD 1020), "the authorities were ordered to provide boats for passengers of Jinghu East, Jingnan West, and Hebei provinces" (T. Li 2004: 2206). In the sixth year of the Yuanyou Reign (AD 1091), Linshui Ferry in Changle County, Fuzhou, built official boats with the load capacity of 15 to one hundred people on board (K. Lang 1990: 7834). In the fifth year of the Shaoxing Reign (AD 1135), the Transfer Agency of Taxation of Liangzhe provinces "was ordered by the emperor to find five 97.5-ton ships within ten days, which were to be put into ferrying and could not be used for other purposes" (S. Xu et al. 2014: 7129). In the 32nd year of the Shaoxing Reign (AD 1162), the central government, Jiankang (now Nanjing), Zhenjiang, Jiangyin Military Prefecture, Taiping, Chizhou, Jiangzhou, Ezhou (now Wuchang, Hubei Province) and Jingnan prefecture spent 230,000 strings of 1000 coins in building boats for the seven ferries along the over 250-mile section of the Songjiang River (S. Xu et al. 2014: 7131). In the second year of the Qingyuan Reign (AD 1196), the four ferries, including Zhejiang and Longshan Ferries of Lin'an (now Hangzhou), Xixing and Yupu Ferries of Shaoxing Prefecture "imitated the Yangtze River ferry boats built by Zhenjiang Command-in-chief Office", and "temporarily gathered 20 master shipbuilders to complete this task" (S. Xu et al. 2014: 7138). The military ferry boats were definitely provided by the government. In the fourth year of the Yuanfeng Reign (AD 1081), Emperor Shenzong ordered the Hedong Transfer Agency of Taxation to prepare a boat "for delivering the papers" for Wubao Fortified Village on the west bank of the Yangtze River (T. Li 2004: 7749). In the fifteenth year of the Jiading Reign (AD 1222), the emperor commanded Ezhou (Wuchang, Hubei) Command-in-chief Office to build 30 passenger ships, 30 horse-carrying boats and 30 pedal boats (light and swift warships), with different deadweight tonnages ranging from 45,000, 30,000, 9000 and 2100 kg (S. Xu et al. 2014: 7139–40).

Some ferries also prepared standby boats and rescue boats. At Xiling Ferry of Zhejiang, "one boat was equipped with another standby boats" (Y. Lu 2011: 374). "Every year a lot of people got drowned" in important ferries, including Jinshan, Yanglan, Zuoli, Dagu, Xiaogu, Madang, Changlukou ferries along the Yangtze River, so "the government prepared some small boats with sailors on board for emergencies" (S. Xu et al. 2014: 9535). They also built pavilions and thatches at the ferry for customers' brief stay. "The government once built dozens of thatches by the river for customers to wait for the boat", to shield "the passengers from the scorch sun" (Y. Lu 2011: 374).

The expenditures of military ferries were funded by national finance. In the fifteenth year of the Jiading Reign (AD 1222), the expenditures of shipbuilding, including 95,600 strings and 175 coins and 98,245 labor costs, were completely covered by the Manufacturing Agency (S. Xu et al. 2014: 7139). Important ferries were also financially supported by governments. For example, in the second year of the Qingyuan Reign (AD 1196), all the expenditures of shipbuilding of the four ferries mentioned above, including raw materials, salaries, and transportation fees, "were all supported by Liangzhe Transfer Agency of Taxation", and "temporarily hired 20 ship craftsmen in Zhenjiang Command-in-chief Office to complete this task" (S. Xu et al. 2014: 7138). The official ferry ship was also repaired and maintained by the government. In the fifth year of the Shaoxi Reign (AD 1194), Transfer Agency of Taxation and Lin'an Prefecture (now Hangzhou) was required to repair the damaged ships of Xixing Ferry at the proposal of ministers (S. Xu et al. 2014: 7138). Some less important ferries usually needed to raise fund from the local authorities or the private sector. In the third year of the Baoqing Reign (AD 1227), the ferry boats running from Changguo County to Mingzhou (now Ningbo) were worn out and Hu Jü, the prefecture magistrate, "donated over 500 strings of 1000 coins to build another two new ones" (J. Luo et al. 1990: 5250). In the second year of the Longxing Reign (AD 1164), Zhao Yan, the deputy county magistrate, built two large ships and recruited sailors for a ferry at the bay on the offshore route from Xiangshan County to Mingzhou. Shipbuilding expenses and sailors' salaries were covered by extra commercial taxes levied on merchants, that was, "for every hundred gold earned by merchants", part of which was used to build boats and recruit sailors (Y. Lou 1990). Xiao Zhen, a native of Pingyang, Wenzhou, "saw that customers quarreling with the ferrymen, yet only to be ended up with being drowned. Therefore, Xiao Zhen built a big ship and hired some sailors to benefit the people. In memory of his noble virtue and kindness, the spot was named Xiao Family Ferry" (Toqta 1977: 11727).

5.6.2 The Privately Contracted Public Ferry and the Management of Private Ferry

5.6.2.1 The Privately Contracted Public Ferries

The important and busy ferries tended to be directly administrated and operated by the government, while the inferior ferries with less customers and poor income were mostly contracted by the private sector. The privately contracted ferries had already been carried out in the early Northern Song Dynasty. In the first year of the Zhidao Reign (AD 995) the edict mentioned that "most of the small ferries on the Jiangnan streams were operated by public servants and civilians, who imposed heavy taxes on customers yet paid little to the government" (Toqta 1977: 4542), which was the privately tax contracted ferry in nature. During the period of Emperor Shenzong's Reign (AD 1068–1077), "Wang Anshi introduced a new law on privately tax contracted system, selling off some public precincts and ferries" (D. Luo 1983: 207). Some people even deemed that "this system in the Song Dynasty stemmed from Wang Anshi's proposal in the Xi'ning Reign" (Z. Wu 2012: 22). The privately contracted ferries was more common in the Southern Song Dynasty. In Mingzhou, Taohua Ferry, Xijiang Ferry, Tongpenfan Shidu Ferry, Zhousu Ferry, and Yugong Lijia Ferry were "contracted with private households" (J. Luo et al. 1990: 5158). "Ferries in Huangchi County had always been administrated by private sector", but it was operated by the Taiping prefecture government since the fourth year of the Chunxi Reign (AD 1177) (S. Xu et al. 2014: 9539). In the 12th year of the Chunxi Reign (AD 1185), "Forty five public ferries like Tingbo in Jiangling Prefecture (now Jingzhou City), were banned from private sector's operation" (S. Xu et al. 2014: 9540). In the Southern Song Dynasty, ferries under the Supply Commission completely implemented the privately tax contracted system, "the Tongjin River Ferry in Jiangnan West Province was under the Supply Commission, looking for private contractors". Therefore, ferries under the Supply Commission were also called "Contracted Supply Commission Ferry". In the sixth year of the Chunxi Reign (AD 1179), six ferries at Zhenzhou (Yizheng County, Jiangsu) along the Yangtze River, Guabushan Ferry, Hejiaxue Ferry, Tax Inspection Pavilion Ferry, Chaozha Ferry, Otter River Ferry, Jujiagang Ferry, and two ferries in Taixing County of Yangzhou, Chuanpo Port and Máozhuang Port, and one ferry in Haimen County of Tongzhou (now Nantong, Jiangsu), Suntuan Ferry, were all privately contracted Supply Commission ferries (S. Xu et al. 2014: 9539). In the first year of the Qingyuan Reign (AD 1195), the Supply Commission was ordered that "the ferries could still be contracted except for the transportation hub" (S. Xu et al. 2014: 9540).

The approach to contract a ferry was bidding, by means of "paper application". "When the prefecture and county posted up selling off the ferry, the appliers scrambled with each other at high prices" (Z. Wang 1990). And even "the officials' relatives vied for the contract" (Y. Xu 1990). The government decided the annual tax volume according to the numbers of competitors. In the second year of the Duangong Reign (AD 989), the Three Bureaus mentioned that "Dongluowan Ferry in Yancheng,

Xuzhou (now Xuchang) was privately contracted with 450 strings of 1000 coins per year" (S. Xu et al. 2014: 9534). Before the fourth year of the Tiansheng Reign (AD 1026), Qiandu Ferry in Tangyang County, Jizhou, "was privately contracted with annual tax over 60 strings of 1000 coins" (S. Xu et al. 2014: 9535). In the Southern Song Dynasty, Taohua Ferry and Dinghai Ferry "were administrated by officials' families for over a decade" at the payment of 1487 strings of 1000 coins per year (J. Luo et al. 1990: 5061). North Ferry in Fenghua County, Mingzhou (now Ningbo), "was also privately contracted by its local natives", Wang Ji, paying annual taxes with his personal gold (J. Luo et al. 1990: 5187).

Privately contracted mainly accounted for laying a heavy burden on customers. "The contractor paid taxes from charging the customers", and "charged increasingly monthly to bribe officials and exploit merchants so as to satisfy their lusts" (Y. Xu 1990). The contractor, after his expensive bidding, "charged doubly for ferrying tolls in the name of paying taxes". "The behavior of raising prices willfully was getting wilder" (Z. Wang 1990). Guanshan Ferry in Fuyang County "was originally a private ferry, during Emperor Gaozong's Reign (AD 1131–1162), a powerful minister Mr. Zhang was the first to contract it. However, the people suffered a lot for that the ship would not sail out until being fully loaded, sometimes the heavy load even caused the shipwreck. The people around Miaoshan Ferry were also oppressed in the same way" (S. Qian 1990: 3717). "Many people even chose to wade across the river in the dry season. Nevertheless, privately contracted ferries would block them in the name of collecting official taxes, or force them to pay so-called dry season toll" (S. Xu et al. 2014: 9535). The objective reason why a contractor overcharged for ferrying was the pressure from the prefecture and county to hand over taxes, "the contractors used to collect fixed ferry money. Sometimes due to the newly built bridge, no more money could be levied, however, the government insisted charging the prescribed taxes without any relief even at the appealing of local prefectures for them" (S. Xu et al. 2014: 9541). Nonetheless, the major reason for overcharging was the contractor's lust for illegal interests. Some were "foxy and cunning, under the guise of contracting ferries, they intercepted customers in high water, and prevented them crossing the low water on foot in the dry season, manipulating the boats behind the scenes. What's more, demolition of wooden bridges, the looting of ferrying money, and the persecution of rich traveller were even more severe" (S. Xu et al. 2014: 9540).

5.6.2.2 The Operation and Management of Private Ferries

Since the beginning of the Northern Song Dynasty, the private ferry had been strictly banned. In the second year of the Qiande Reign (AD 964), the emperor stated that "if anyone dare to cross the river secretly, the boatmen and the violator were punished equally and severely by law". In the fifth year of the Kaibao Reign (AD 972), it was prescribed that "the private ferries were banned from Tongguan to Wuli", which means the Yellow River was banned from the private ferry. In the second year of the Taipingxingguo Reign (AD 977), "though Jiangnan had come back to peace, the private ferry remained forbidden, and those who wanted to privately cross the Yellow River would be punished in accordance with the law". The ban on private crossing had always been there. In the third year of the Xianping Reign (AD 1000), the edict banned private ferries on the Yellow River (S. Xu et al. 2014: 9534). In the first year of the Qingli Reign (AD 1041), "private ferry ships along the Yellow River in Huoshan and Baode Military Prefecture (now in Shanxi Province) were banned" (T. Li 2004: 3192). In the third year of the Daguan Reign (AD 1109), the imperial edict ordered that "anyone who set up the private ferry privately must be flogged with one hundred bludgeons without the kind pardon as before" (S. Xu et al. 2014: 9536). In the Southern Song Dynasty, the prohibition of private ferry was further emphasized. In the 12th year of the Shaoxing Reign (AD 1142), "the officials in charge of grain transportation of Huainan East and West Provinces (now Jiangsu and Anhui Province) strictly prevent the inbound customers from tax evading at the private ferries" (X. Li 2013: 2718). In the 24th year of the Shaoxing Reign (AD 1154), Cao Yong, mayor of Lin'an Prefecture (now Hangzhou), proposed that according to the imperial edict, "private ferries like Qiantang should be banned", and "should be checked by ministers of the central government according to the Private Ferry Regulation". At Cao Yong's request that year, a court official dispatched by Lin'an Prefecture temporarily took over it (S. Xu et al. 2014: 9537). During the Southern Song Dynasty, the Huaihe River was the boundary river, so "private ferries was strictly prohibited". "The reward for disclosing tax evasion had been increased to 1000 strings of 1000 coins, and the magistrate who failed to detect tax evasion should be convicted too". "Patrol troops targeting at private ferries had been set up to supervise this at crucial junctures of Jiangsu and Anhui Province". The responsible organization was named Patrol Administration, and the army "was named Patrol Troop", stationing thousands of soldiers in both Jiangsu and Anhui (L. Zhou 1990).

The officials ranging from military commissioner, judicial commissioner, mayor to supervisor of the municipal financial affairs were all responsible for the private ferry ban. In the 29th year of the Shaoxing Reign (AD 1159), Emperor Gaozong ordered that "the trade of stolen horses and other smuggling business should be completely banned at the private ferries along the Huaihe River. Considering that the violators did business under the guise of the money, power, or army, the Provincial Military Commission, mayor and supervisor of the municipal financial affairs must keep an eye on private ferry passengers" (X. Li 2013: 3536). Within the jurisdiction of the state and county, the officials would be punished for such problems resulted from private ferries. In the third year of the Jiayou Reign (AD 1058), Wangqi, Binzhou Mayor, and Song Dingguo, Superintendent of Trial Affairs, were suspended to be promoted for their serious failings at private ferries, "infringing on the interests of public one" (T. Li 2004: 4533). In the eighth year of the Qiandao Reign (AD 1172), Xia Jun of Huainan East Provincial Military Commissioner, Chen Rui of Chuzhou (now Huaian) Shanyang County Mayor, Sun Chun, the inspector of border security of Shanyang County, Zhang Shunchen, the inspector of Huaihe River patrol office at the Chuzhou border, Yan Zongyan, the inspector of Xialiupu patrol office, they were all demoted or suspended "for neglecting the tax evasion at the private ferries along the Huaihe River" (S. Xu et al. 2014: 9539). In the same year, Xu Yin, the commissioner of tea and salt in Huaidong Province, "was demoted for failings on the check of the private ferry" (Y. Lou 1990). The officials would also be punished for deaths at the private ferries. Liu Xingxing, the Xixing ferry supervisor, and Wang Dewen, the ferry supervisor of Zhejiang, "were both deposed for the sunken boat accident, causing 20 to 30 deaths" (B. Zhou 1990). Officials and supervisors who were unable to check the private ferry or indulged the customers not coming back on time "shall be severely punished and banished in accordance with laws and regulations. Reporting to the government was encouraged with a reward of 500 strings of 1000 coins. Officials with government posts should be exiled, receiving a severer punishment" (X. Li 2013: 3476).

In conclusion, the authority reasoned the ban on private ferries for shipwreck deaths, tax evasion and the smuggling of forbidden objects. However, the same problems would also arise in public ferries. In the early years of Emperor Gaozong's Reign (AD 1131–1162), the greedy boatmen overloaded the boat for more benefits, and stopped in the midstream of the Qiantang River to extort passengers, resulting in "numerous accidents of sunken boat" (Y. Lou 1990). The policy of private ferry ban was sure to keep the order and safety of the ferry, however, it was mainly because "the private ferries stole the cheese of government taxes". In the fifth year of the Jiading Reign (AD 1212), Huang Du said that "apart from the Lieshan Ferry taxes being paid as usual", among the annual incomes of other five ferries, "20% was for ships maintenance, while the rest was used to pay the salaries of officials, helmsman, and sailors. And if there were any surplus, it is required to hand over to the prefecture government. After these measures were adopted, private ferries could be completely banned" (S. Yang et al. 1990). So this conduct was to increase the incomes of the public ferries.

Although the policy of private ferry was implemented strictly, the public ferries could not meet people's needs geographically and quantitatively. Besides, public ones had their disadvantages in operation. In the fifth year of the Jiading Reign (AD 1212), the boats had been left without maintenance for years in Jiankang prefecture (now Nanjing), and the officials and helmsman suffered no salaries. "As a result, some violators set up private ferries". "So few customers crossed river via the public ferry" (Toqta 1977: 2412). Along the border river, the Huaihe River, the private ferries managed to survive even under the strictest check. "The check on private ferries of the Huaihe River was very strict, but the people continued to violate the law as ever" (D. Ma 2011: 514). In the sixth year of the Chunxi Reign (AD 1179), there were more than 40 ferries in Zhenjiang Prefecture including both the private and public, of which Xijinguan and Guazhouan were under the public authorities, seven of them were privately contracted ferries like Tanzhu Port, and over 30 were private ferries. Zhenzhou (Yizheng County, Jiangsu) enjoyed a total of 29 official and private ferries along the river with one in Xuanhua Town under the official supervision, six ferries as Guabushan privately contracted and 22 private ferries. Yangzhou boasted a total of 54 official and private ferries along the river with Guazhou, one official ferry, Chuanpo Port in Taixing County and Maozhuang Port, two privately contracted, and fifty-one private ferries. Among the five ferries in Taizhou, Shizhuang Port was the official one, and the other four were private. Tongzhou (now Nantong, Jiangsu) enjoyed a total of 64 official and private ferries along the river, including one official, one privately contracted, and sixty-two private ones (S. Xu et al. 2014: 9539–40). Statistics showed that the quantity of private ferries was much more than the public and the privately contracted ferry. In the other regions, the private also had existed for a long time. In Changle of Fuzhou, four ferries named Linshui, Yangmen, Yangxia and Baitian, at first "people crossed the river with private boats". During the period of the Jiayou Reign (AD 1056–1063), "three public ferries were established in Linshui" (K. Lang 1990: 7833). In the area of Zhenjiang Prefecture and Yangzhou, "people used small boats to transport people", and "no authority had ever restrained it", that is, private ferries had existed for a long time (S. Xu et al. 2014: 9538). Chenshan Ferry in Xiangshan County (under Ningbo) was "privately dominated by old civilian boats" and it was not transformed into the public ferry until Zhao Yanyu, the deputy county magistrate, built two ships in the first year of the Longxing Reign (AD 1163). Yuancun Ferry "used to be equipped with private boats only, and suffered from robbers and sunken boat accidents frequently. Later the county built its own official boat" and transformed it into a public ferry (J. Luo et al. 1990: 5267).

5.6.3 *Charges of Ferry Boats*

Ferry tolls were levied on passengers at the public ferry in form of ferrying cards, which were handed out to them with a given number on each. "As each ship had limited seats, the cards were made in line with its capacity and in different colors so as to make a distinction for the Chief Official Supervision to check. Passengers should board the designated ship with the relevant card. If the number was different from the ship, the passenger cannot got on board" (D. Sun 1990). "On June 4th 1137 (the seventh year of the Shaoxing Reign), it was stipulated that a 9000-kilogram ferry ship could carry 100 people without goods, 6000-kilogram ship with 60 people, and less than 3000-kilogram with decreasing load capacity as above", the approved capacity was one-third of the total deadweight tonnage of the boat (S. Xu et al. 2014: 9537). This was the same case of the ferry in the Qiantang River: According to "Zhejiang Public Ferry Regulation, each passenger was given a card after paying boat fare in accordance with the regulation" (J. Luo et al. 1990: 5250). "Setting up a ferry boat, a five-color flag and card, and sell them to customers" (S. Xu et al. 2014: 9538). "As each boat capacity was fixed, the colors of the flags and the cards sold by various boats were different. The incomes of selling the cards could be used to cover the costs of helmsman and punters, and the boat maintenance" (Y. Lou 1990).

The charge rate for ferrying varied with time and place. "The width of the river and the weight of the goods were used as the basis of charge". "The charging for people, carriages, cattle, and horses was made clear on bulletin board, and no overcharge was allowed" (S. Yang et al. 1990). Obviously, the livestock as cattle were also charged. For example, in Jingnan (now Jiangling County, Hubei), Gong'an County once "charged fifty coins for each cattle, and levied annual taxes with only nineteen strings of 1000 coins per year", which were abolished in the sixth year of the

Tiansheng Reign (AD 1028). In the eighth year of the Tiansheng Reign (AD 1030), the public ferrying tolls that farmers crossed the Yellow River for farming were canceled (S. Xu et al. 2014: 9535). However, in the fifth year of the Jiading Reign (AD 1212), Huang Du still stated in his memorial to the emperor that "the charges for people, carriages, cattle, and horses were specified", and the charges on livestock had not been completely abolished, mainly charging passengers for transportation fares. Wang Zhiwang witnessed in Hu'nan that "crossing the river alone at a small ferry in the countryside, one person was charged about 10 to 20 coins, and the capacity of the boat and the width of the ferry can be speculated" (Z. Wang 1990). In the first year of the Jiatai Reign (AD 1201), the four ferries of the Qiantang River, Zhejiang, Longshan, Xixing, and Yupu, charged "each passenger 31 coins for a card to board the ship". "If there were goods, carriages, and horses, the load capacity of passengers should be decreased in proportion". "Officials, soldiers, tea and salt merchants, beggars, monks and Taoists were free of charge" (S. Xu et al. 2014: 9540). During the period from the Jiading Reign to the Baoqing Reign, public ferries of Zhejiang charged "each passenger fifty coins", and "checked them one by one, without excessive overload on board" (J. Luo et al. 1990: 5250). During the period of the Jiayou Reign, in Linshui Ferry, Changle County, Fuzhou, "each customer paid five coins", after the fifth year of the Shaoxing Reign (AD 1135), boat fares "were ordered to be collected daily, and the total amount at the end of the year was considered to be the yardstick of political performance". During the period of the Chunxi Reign (AD 1174–1189), "a customer spent only ten coins for ferrying" (K. Lang 1990: 7834). In Fenghua County, North Ferry charged less. "People who transport goods were charged three coins for official transportation, and the scholar-officials, monks and Taoists were free of charge" (J. Luo et al. 1990: 5187). The low ferrying tolls benefited from Wang Ji's kindness for covering the expenditures of private boat manufacture and boatmen salaries by himself, and three-coin was only used to pay the annual fixed taxes. In contrast, if the costs of building ferry boats, salaries of boatmen, and the annual taxes were all paid by passengers, it was impossible to enjoy such a low rate. In the sixth year of the Chunyou Reign (AD 1246), mayor of Qingyuan Prefecture proposed that at Taohua Ferry and Dinghai Ferry, "charges should be exempted to benefit the people and the civilian ships remained to ferry people, charging only two coins" (J. Luo et al. 1990: 5060). Two coins were charged symbolically, which was a special policy approved by the court in advance to carry out good governance.

Like other taxes, boat fares was set an annual amount, which were "household, labor, tax, grip, mining, ferrying, and land annual rental taxes" (Toqta 1977: 4356). Major public ferry taxes were set up an annual rate at ferries. In the second year of the Jingde Reign (AD 1005), "the annual charge rate of four ferries was abolished, indicating that annual fares were charged at the East, West, Qingwu and Jialing Ferries in Sanquan County before". The fixed annual rates of ferries were decided by their shipping volume, the busy ferries would be charged over a thousand coins or several hundred strings of 1000 coins per year while the sluggish one be charged only dozens of coins or several strings of 1000 coins. The two ferries in Mingzhou, Taohua and Dinghai ferries, were quite busy, "as the transportation hub with farmers, shepherds, cattle, horses and shoulder poles coming and going day and night". "Taohua Ferry in Yin County paid more than 3425 strings of 1000 coins for three-year tax volume. Jiangnan Ferry in Dinghai County paid over 1037 strings of 1000 coins for three-year taxes". It was recorded that two ferries above totally handed over a bit more than 1487 strings of 1000 coins a year, half of which were paid in coins and another half in paper currency" (J. Luo et al. 1990: 5060). Lieshan Ferry in the lower reaches of the Yangtze River, "was under the Supply Commission and was charged for annual charges". Five ferries like Nanpu Ferry "administrated by the prefecture government need to pay annual taxes. The annual tax amount levied on the six ferries was over 10,000 strings of 1000 coins in total" (S. Yang et al. 1990). Before the seventh year of the Jiading Reign (AD 1214), Shihong Ferry in Hengyang County, Hengyang City, Hunan, "earned net interest of 560 strings and 196 coins" (S. Xu et al. 2014: 9541). Luowan Ferry in the east of Yancheng, Xuzhou (now Xuchang, Henan Province), "paid 450 strings of 1000 coins per year". Zihu Ferry of Hanyang Military Prefecture "handed over 36 strings of 1000 coins per year" (S. Xu et al. 2014: 9534). "Lanzhou (now Lüliang, Shanxi) was levied annual taxes of over 280 strings of 1000 coins". After Yunlun Fortified Village was abolished, merchant travelers changed their route, passing by Baode, Shagu, Dabao and other ferries. Emperor Zhenzong decreed that "Hehe, Shagu, Dabao and other ferries should not charge boat fares", exempting the fares (T. Li 2004: 1374). Before the Dry Ferry in Tangyang County of Jizhou was abolished, it "was privately contracted with 60 strings of 1000 coins for annual taxes". Changlu Ferry in Lunan County, Xingzhou (now Xingtai, Hebei) paid 56 strings of 1000 coins for annual taxes initially (S. Xu et al. 2014: 9535). And it was exempted boat fares after the newly built bridge was put into use in the first year of the Tianxi Reign (AD 1017) (S. Xu et al. 2014: 9535). Huanggu Ferry in Xianglin was "a crossroad of important roads". "The annual boat fares levied by the government was ten times that of the previous one", and "the monthly ferrying fares totaled 14 strings of 1000 coins" (Y. Xu 1990). North Ferry still need to "pay the annual taxes with personal properties in advance" even after the privately funded operation by Wang Ji (J. Luo et al. 1990: 5187), suggesting that the annual tax still need to be paid even if for the benefit of people. Fenyi County of Yuanzhou (now Yichun, Jiangxi Province), changed the ferry to a pontoon bridge and among the annual fares, "five thousand coins served as the revenue" (F. Chen 1990), indicating that the original ferry amount was five thousand coins. No fixed annual rate was set up for sluggish ferries who suffered from extremely low revenues. In the first year of the Zhidao Reign (AD 995), Emperor Taizong ordered that the ferrying taxes should be exempted if "its annual fares were below 5000 coins" (Toqta 1977: 4542).

The prefecture and county also charged ferrying annual rate. For example, the supervisor of the municipal financial affairs was in charge of boat fare collection for Qingyuan Prefecture at 1858.439 strings of 1000 cash, Yin County, totaled 467.13 strings, Fenghua totaled 230.86 strings, Cixi County totaled 656.799 strings, Dinghai County 223.74 strings, and Xiangshan County 280.8 strings. All the ferrying taxes were paid to the Supply Commission especially (J. Luo et al. 1990: 5060, 5164, 5191, 5216, 5238, 5271). State and county officials were responsible for collecting ferrying fares, and those who failed to reach the quota would be punished. In the sixth year of the Yuanfeng Reign (AD 1083), the emperor announced that in Dengzhou (now in He'nan), Zeng Fu, Nanyang County magistrate, and Chen Zhichun, the Zhirang County mayor, were respectively fined for failing to collect ferrying fares of 50,000 coins and money lending of 800 strings of 1000 coins, and failing to collect ferrying fares of 40,000 coins, money lending of 900 strings of 1000 coins (T. Li 2004: 8043). In order to accomplish the ferrying tax amount, "the privately contracted ferries once levied a fixed amount of taxes, and was unable to collect ferrying fares due to the newly-built bridge. However, the government still insisted that the prescribed taxation should be submitted in full regardless the county's appealing, causing them to levy taxes on other pretexts". Such kinds of ferrying taxes were ordered to be exempted in the third year of the Jiatai Reign (AD 1203), the second year of the Kaixi Reign (AD 1206), the second year of the Kaixi Reign (AD 1209), the fifth year (AD 1212) and the fourteenth year (AD 1221) continuously (S. Xu et al. 2014: 9541). This shows that such cases were very common even under the pressure of the prefecture and county authorities to finish the task of collecting boat fares.

In addition to collecting ferry fares as stipulated by the government, the boatmen usually extorted from customers, which evidenced the remarks that "boatmen had been overcharged passengers since ancient times" (L. Zhu 2008: 90), and "passengers with heavy goods were often charged surplus fares" (J. Luo et al. 1990: 8187). The boatman extortion was done in two ways. The first was overcharging passengers at the ferry. In the Qiantang River, "wherever there were merchant travelers on the ferry boat, the boatmen would extort from them by hook and crook, and the passengers could cross the water only after meeting their desire for money. If the money was less, the boatman would put up obstacles in every possible way, so the passengers suffered greatly". After the emperor set Lin'an (now Hangzhou) as the capital city, then the Qiantang River enjoyed busy ferrying. "Every time when crossing the river, the helmsmen and punters would ask for extra fees, allowing customers to board the boat in the order of the luggage weight first, made passengers competing for space with each other, resulting in an overloaded boat exceeding its deadweight tonnage" (S. Xu et al. 2014: 9536). Their overloading operation was for more boat fares. The second was extorting passengers on the way. On the public ferrying boats, "inferior officials and clerks extorted customers to realize the annual goal of taxation", "pursuing more revenues", "even charging passengers in the midstream" (S. Yang et al. 1990). In the fourth year of the Jingde Reign (AD 1007), as Khitan attacked Hebei Province, "people flooded in Yangliu Ferry in panic, the boat owner, however, did not set sail on time unless he was ensured higher interests". Ding Wei killed the boatman who charged more boat fares randomly on the river, and "the other boatmen were scared so that the people could cross the Yellow River successfully" (Toqta 1977: 9567). In the third year of the Jianyan Reign (AD 1229), as the Jin army attacked and occupied Yangzhou, the officials together with civilians hurried to the ferry, and "the boatmen blackmailed them while parking their boat by the riverbank, even charged each passenger 50-g gold before boarding the ship" (M. Wang 2013: 196). The third was charging fares without services in the dry season. This situation was more common at the privately contracted ferries. "Some people chose to wade across the shallow river in the dry season. However, private contractors would block them in the name of collecting official taxes, or urge them to pay passing-by money" (S. Xu et al. 2014: 9535). The fourth was charging more by aiding smugglers. In the second year of the Longxing Reign (AD 1164), there were smuggling gangs in Guangnan West Province and Jinghu South Province, in the name of selling tea and salt, "when crossing the river, every smuggler must pay a hundred coins and if with an abducted woman, one thousand coins need to be paid for each person". In Guangnan East and West Provinces, "when smugglers came back at important ferries of prefectures and counties, they extorted in the name of replenishing livestock taxes or by the number of people". "The important ferries were ordered to strictly ban it" (S. Xu et al. 2014: 9538). The extortion not only increased burdens on customers but also affected the safety of navigation. At Xixing Ferry of Zhejiang, the boatman's "extortion and allowing more passengers on board resulted in overloading and capsizing hazard." From the first year to the seventh of the Shaoxing Reign (AD 1131–1137), "there were already three sunken boat accidents incurring numerous casualties" (S. Xu et al. 2014: 9537). Ferries, therefore, became a harm to local people and governments. At Taohua Ferry and Dinghai Ferry, "violent, scoundrel, and unreliable helmsmen and punters served the devil together. They tore up the passengers' clothes and smashed their utensils if the customers were lucky enough not to be killed cruelly. If the ship was overturned, the passengers would probably be drowned. They harmed passengers with great arrogance and colluded privately with merchants, fishermen, and traffickers to evade taxes and hide goods, doing harm to the local government". "The public ferries and river banks incurred damages to Qingyuan Prefecture" (J. Luo et al. 1990: 5060).

It was stipulated in the Song Dynasty that boat fares be exempted in the following situations. First, crossing the river in the dry season. "The dried-out waterbed served as the bridge and the dry-ferry boat fares should be exempted". In the early years of the Jianlong Reign (AD 960–963), "the imperial edict abolished dry-ferry boat fares of 39 places such as Cangzhou, Dezhou, Lizhou (now Huimin, Shandong), Qizhou (now Jinan), Yunzhou (now Dongping)", and "allowed civilians to establish ferries freely without paying any taxes in the water season". But, five ferries in Binzhou including Goutai Ferry and Nanbeikou Ferry and others, "were still urged by the minor officials to pay taxes in the dry season". In the second year of the Zhidao Reign (AD 996), the emperor ordered to exempt the taxes. In the fifth year of the Huangyou Reign (AD 1053), the imperial edict emphasized "each ferry should abolish the dry-ferry boat fares. If there were any ferries against it, the chief official need to report" (S. Xu et al. 2014: 9535). The contractor of ferry, for the sake of money, "when encountering people wade to cross the river in the dry season, tend to hold them back in the name of levying taxes". In the tenth year of the Xi'ning Reign (AD 1077), the privately contracted ferries were ordered to mitigate the taxes during the dry season (S. Xu et al. 2014: 9535).

Second, the victims of a natural disaster were exempted from ferry boat fares. In the second year of the Dazhongxiangfu Reign (AD 1009), "the victims of Yuncheng, Zizhou, and Qizhou could be exempted from ferry boat fares" (T. Li 2004: 1627). After the war in the Southern Song Dynasty, a large number of refugees fled the war or returned home after peace, and they were also exempted from ferrying fares. The Southern Song stipulated that in Huainan Provinces (now Anhui and Jiangsu

Provinces) and Jingxi Province, the state armies "should prepare more boats and ships so as to ferry people more conveniently without fares". "People and carriages returned to their hometowns after the war, they could be exempted ferry boat fares". In the fourteenth year of the Jiading Reign (AD 1221), "the local government had deployed rapid relief and pensions to restore agriculture production for the exiled in Huangzhou (now Huanggang, Hubei)". Troops along all waterways "were prohibited from extorting money at the ferries or could not block civilians crossing the river. Otherwise, civilians were encouraged to make straight appeals to the upper governments" (S. Xu et al. 2014: 9542).

Third was taxation. "Those, who had already paid taxes via the ferry, should not be charged ferry boat fares repeatedly. Wherever they crossed the river, they were free of charge to cross the river". In the second year of the Duangong Reign (AD 989), the imperial edict stipulated that no matter whether the ferry was public or private one, "the people who had paid land taxes and those woodmen, fishermen, the poor, the old and orphans were free of charge". In the same year, at Luowan Ferry in the east of Yancheng, Xuzhou (now Xuchang), "the remaining taxes in Caizhou (now Runan, Henan) were sent to Xuzhou and handed over to Kaifeng. Carriages and horses crossing the ferry were charged 75 coins. Considering that it was collected beyond the fixed tax amount, it would not be handed over to the government, and called for special permission to be exempted" (S. Xu et al. 2014: 9534).

Fourth, ferry boat fares were exempted for the purpose of labor. In the third year of the Dazhongxiangfu Reign (AD 1010), "Emperor Zhenzong exempted the poor, fisherman, and woodman all over the country from paying ferry boat fares" (T. Li 2004: 1696). In the ninth year of the Dazhongxiangfu Reign (AD 1016), "the people who made a living by growing grains were exempted from ferrying fares in Hebei (Hebeidong and Hebeixi Province) and Jingdong (Jingdongdong and Jingdongxi Province)" (T. Li 2004: 2031). In the eighth year of the Tiansheng Reign (AD 1030), the farmers along the Yellow River "were allowed to cross the river free of charge" (S. Xu et al. 2014: 9535).

The ferry boat fares levied by the government were to cover the salaries of supervisors, officials, boatmen, shipbuilding and ship maintenance. The ferry boat fares were used to pay "the salary of the boatmen and the rest was left for the ship's maintenance" (K. Lang 1990: 7834).

The ferrying fares were distributed by different organizations. A fixed amount of ferrying fares of Taohua Ferry and Dinghai (Zhenhai, Zhejiang) Ferry in Qingyuan Prefecture went to the Supply Commission, and some people suggested that "ferrying fares should be exempted for the benefit of civilians". But the quota of the Supply Commission should be guaranteed at the same time, then they suggested that "the central government might as well allocate some from national treasury, to meet the boat fares wavered by the Supply Commission for the civilians' benefit" (J. Luo et al. 1990: 5060). Four ferries in Lin'an Prefecture, "Zhejiang, Longshan, Xixing, and Yupu Ferry were in charge of 35 ferry ships in total, of which 19 under the Domestic Transfer Agency of Taxation and 16 under the Lin'an Prefecture authority". The Transfer Agency of Taxation and Lin'an Prefecture were both in charge of ferry boats for the purpose of sharing ferry fares. It was stipulated originally that "among the ferrying fares, one out of ten was used for maintaining the boats", and the Lin'an Prefecture, "after deducting additional taxes, paid the rest of ferrying fares to the boatmen on duty". And "all the damaged ships should be repaired by themselves" (S. Xu et al. 2014: 9540–41). Among the ferries between Changguo County and Qingyuan Prefecture, "their ferrying fares were paid to the Military Supplies Office at the end of month for repair reserves" (J. Luo et al. 1990: 5250). And as for the ferrying fares of Yuancun Ferry in Xiangshan County, "after being paid to the Supply Commission, the rest served as the ship maintenance and granted scores of strings of 1000 coins as scholarships" (J. Luo et al. 1990: 5267), so the money was also used for student subsidies.

After *the Law on Recruiting Inferior Officials* was introduced, the salaries of minor clerks for transportation were paid by the ferrying fares. Emperor Zhezong renewed the law, with only part of the ferry boats fares to cover the salary of minor clerks for shipping, and some of them were dispatched on secondment. In the first year of the Yuanyou Reign (AD 1086), Su Zhe, a well-known essayist, mentioned that "the gross national ferrying revenue of official markets was over 42 million strings of 1000 coins, while the annual salary for the minor clerks for goods transportation and convoy leaders was over 15 million strings of 1000 coins in total", that was only one third using for recruiting the minor clerks for shipping. Su Zhe suggested that the ferrying fares of official markets should be totally used for their salaries (Z. Su 1987: 833–34). In the second year of the Yuanyou Reign (AD 1087), the ferrying fares served for paying the minor clerks of transportation and if there were more, it would benefit other inferior clerks (Toqta 1977: 4316).

5.6.4 Summary

Due to the laggard technology of bridge building and limited shipbuilding costs, boat ferrying served as the major means to cross rivers in the Song Dynasty, especially on large rivers like the Yangtze, the Yellow, and the Qiantang rivers, which were primarily ferried by boats. The ferry directly operated by the government was the public ferry with supervisors and boatmen. The ferry supervisors, principally held by the military officials, were responsible first for safeguarding the safety of people and boats, second for checking forbidden subjects, and third for preventing tax evasion and finding out spies. In addition to the ferry supervisors, operators were set up, named boatmen, which varied according to the size of ferry and the number of boatmen. The boatmen were mainly equipped officially before the implementation of Law on Recruiting Inferior Officials, and soldiers served at some ferries. No matter be officially equipped or recruited, boatmen all enjoyed rewards from the ferrying fares. Ferry ships were generally provided by the local government, not to mention the military ferries. Some ferries also prepared standby boats and rescue boats. The funds for military ferries definitely came from the national finance, and the important ferries were generally funded by the government. The ferry boats were also maintained by the authority.

In addition to the public ferries operated by the government in the Song Dynasty, there were another two kinds of ferries: privately contracted ferries and private ferries. Inferior ferries which suffered few customers and poor income were mostly contracted by the private sector. Privately contracted ferries had already been introduced in the Northern Song Dynasty, in the period of the Xi'ning Reign, privately contracted ferries were greatly developed and more common in the Southern Song Dynasty. In the Southern Song Dynasty, ferries under the Supply Commission gradually implemented the privately tax contracted system in all respects. The approach to contract was bidding, through "paper application". The government decided the annual tax quota according to the business volume there. Privately contracted ferries were the main reason for laying a heavy burden on passengers. The objective reason why contractor overcharged for ferrying was the pressure from the prefecture and county governments to pay taxes. Nonetheless, the major reason for overcharging lies in the contractor's lust for illegal interests.

In the early period of the Northern Song Dynasty, the government had actively banned private ferries, and the prohibition has been strengthened until the Southern Song Dynasty. During the Southern Song Dynasty, the Huaihe River was a boundary river, so private ferries were sternly prohibited under the responsible organization. The Patrol Administration and "the Patrol Private Ferry Army" were equipped with thousands of soldiers in both Huainan East Province and Huainan West Province. The heads ranging from military commissioners, judicial commissioners, mayors to supervisors of the municipal financial affairs were all responsible for private ferry ban. Within the jurisdiction of prefectures and counties, the officials would be punished for any problems caused by the private ferry. The authority accounted the ban on private ferries for shipwreck deaths, tax evasion and smuggling forbidden objects. However, the same problems will also arise in public ferries. Ensuring the safety and order was part of the reason for private ferry ban, however, it was mainly because it stole the cheese of public taxes. Private ferries were strictly banned so as to better protect the interest of the public ferry. In spite of the repeated prohibitions, private ferries still sustained for a long time and on a large scale, as the public ferries could not meet the people's needs geographically and quantitatively. The quantity of the private ferries outnumbered the public and the privately contracted ferries.

The collection of the public ferrying fares from passengers was by selling boarding cards, which were handed out according to the number of people on board. Livestock as cattle were also charged fares. The charge rates on ferry tolls varied with time and place. Ferrying fares, as other taxes, were set with an annual amount, which varied according to the busyness of ferry: the busy ferry with over a thousand or hundreds strings of 1000 coins per year while the sluggish one with only tens or even several strings. In addition to the ferrying fares stipulated by the government, the boatmen usually extorted customers. The first was the ferry overcharging; the second was the extortion on the way; the third was the fees on dry-ferrying tolls; and the fourth was aiding smugglers for money. Ferries, therefore, had done much harm to civilians and authorities. The Song Dynasty exempted the ferrying fares in the following situations: in the dry season, for the victims suffered from natural disasters, people to cross the river after paying official taxes, and farmers crossing the river for laboring.

The ferrying fares levied by the government were mainly used to cover the salaries of supervisors, officials, boatmen, as well as the shipbuilding and maintenance. The ferrying fares were shared by different organizations, including the Supply Commission, the Transfer Agency of Transportation, and Prefecture government, serving for the purpose of the ship maintenance, scholarships, and salaries for minor clerks of water transportation.

5.7 Management, Requisition and Recruitment of the Civilian Boats

In the Song Dynasty, the civilian shipbuilding was driven by three active players: development of commodity economy, economic center shifted southward, and flourishing inland shipping and marine trade. As some scholars had figured out the number of maritime ships and crew members (J. Ge 2008: 153; J. Ge 2013: 179–200; C. Huang 2016), though the detailed holdings of civilian boats were not sure due to the limited history materials, the quantity of both inland and marine civilian boats was definitely huge. Only Liao Dake made a special study on the management of civilian boats, mainly the household registration, neighbourhood administrative system and association of marine ships in the Southern Song Dynasty (D. Liao 2001).[12] Due to few comprehensive studies on the management of civilian boats, both inland and marine, this section intends to make a systematic discussion this topic in the Song Dynasty.

5.7.1 Registration of the Civilian Boats

It was stipulated in the Song Dynasty that any kind of warships were banned being used by civilians, specifically "battle warships, Haihu Warships, warships covered with cowhide, Yellow Dragon Warships, Shuangli Warships, Pingcheng Boats, warships with eight oars, Grasshopper Boats, but other small boats could be possessed and used by civilians" (*Tianyige Cang Ming Chaoben Jiaozheng* 2004: 347), which refers to all the boats but the warship. The registration of the civilian boats was not universally implemented in the Northern Song Dynasty, with only individual regions doing so for different reasons. During the period of Emperor Renzong's Reign, Xiangyi County (now Suixian County, Henan) "suffered from the drought for a long time and the county mayor Fan Chunren told the merchants that

[12] The article "A Review on Ship Registration, Management and Boatman Pre-military Groups" written by Liao Dake explores the ship registration, management and boatmen neighborhood unit, and the historical records and subjects in his study focuses the Southern Song Dynasty. In addition, Cao Jiaqi, Chenfeng and other scholars' study on the use and employment of civilian boats in the transportation and that of grain transportation in the Song Dynasty will not be recounted in this section.

'the people would starve soon. You store grains in the Buddhist temple first, and later I will purchase from you when we need grains.' The merchants followed his suggestion and stored more than 3 million kilograms of grain in advance" (Toqta 1977: 10282). This was the registration policy on the merchant ships in the special period. Emperor Shenzong once ordered Hebei Province "In the regions with Xin'an, Baoding Military Prefecture, Xiongzhou, Bazhou, Mozhou in the east, with Shun'an, Guangxin, Ansu Army, Baozhou (Baoding, Hebei) Tangluo in the west, shipowners were all registered with cards" (T. Li 2004: 6959). During the period of Emperor Huizong's Reign (AD 1100–1126), when Ren Liang, as the warden of Jingdong Jail, "the fishermen in Liangshanluo were not put into the household registration to eradicate the root of earn a living from stealing. Ren Liang grouped five families into one neighborhood carving a signal on their boats. Nobody except the locals could enter the neighborhood" (Toqta 1977: 11220). The registration of the civilian boats there was conducted locally and temporally, not a long-term mechanism covering the whole country.

The registration of inland civilian boats was implemented in more provinces in the Southern Song Dynasty. In the fifth year of the Shaoxing Reign (AD 1135), the imperial edict ruled that "a neighborhood should be formed by five boatman families. If anyone of the neighbourhood unit committed a crime, including tax evasion, spying, stealing and smuggling, all people of the unit would be convicted of the same crime. The reward of 200 strings of 1000 coins would be given to those reporting crimes to the local government. If the criminal confessed his crime, he might be exempted from punishment after paying off the whistle-blower's reward. The military prefectures along the river implemented the same regulations" (S. Xu et al. 2014: 8348). For example, at an important fort by the Yangtze River, "the territory of Hanyang Military Prefecture, boatmen households were scattered on the river", and "all the boat households were clustered to safeguard the river banks" (Y. Cao 1990). This was the river defense of the Song Dynasty, which means that "the fisher households by the river were put into registration book, and the patrolling fishing boats were given a fixed registration number each" (Y. Mei et al. 1990: 5981). As the river defense had become an important player of national security in the Southern Song Dynasty, the military boat owners along the Yangtze River had been grouped, and their ships were also registered. And in the prefectures and counties in Hubei, "the boat owners were registered into the record such as Baowu, the basic household registration system, and the neighborhood shared the weal and woe together" (X. Liao 1990). The civilian boats and their households were all registered in Hubei Province. And in the second year of the Chunxi Reign (AD 1175), in Jiaohu, southeast of Luzhou, Huainan Province, "after the registration of the boats and their households was done, they were issued a number card", and "five households composed a neighborhood unit" (S. Xu et al. 2014: 8648).

The registration of seagoing ships was introduced in the Northern Song Dynasty. In the sixth year of the Yuanyou Reign (AD 1091), "every twenty sea-ship households in Guangzhou, Huizhou, Nanzhou, Enzhou, Duanzhou, Chaozhou and other prefectures composed one neighborhood unit "Jia". Two respectful people with good virtue should be selected as the chief and deputy head, and then they would be registered with names, ages and the number of oars. As for the unregistered people, who have too many oars and carry goods or strangers illegally, if the neighbour chiefs cover them up, they are considered to be equally culpable with the criminal" (S. Xu et al. 2014: 7213). This was the system of registration on the seagoing vessels and households in Guangnan East Province. As the gravity of sea defense was placed in Mingzhou and Liangzhe West Province, Fujian Province ranked first in terms of quality and quantity of seagoing ships, followed by Liangzhe East Province, therefore, a large number of ships need to be requisitioned from Fujian Province and Liangzhe East Province to Mingzhou and Liangzhe West Province for coast defence.

The registration of the civilian boats in the Southern Song Dynasty started from the fourth year of the Jianyan Reign (AD 1130). In order to prevent civilian boats from entering the Jingdong and being leveraged by the Jing Kingdom, Emperor Gaozong ordered that "in Fujian, Wenzhou, Taizhou, Mingzhou, Yuezhou, Tongzhou, Taizhou, Suzhou, Xiuzhou and other prefectures, the maritime ship households and those who wanted to be a sailor need be temporarily registered, furthermore, five families were classified as one neighborhood unit" (X. Li 2013: 811). In the second year of the Shaoxing Reign (AD 1132), it was stipulated that in Guangnan East Province and Fujian Province, "the households with ships, no matter big or small, shall be registered, and every three or five households composed one neighborhood unit called "Bao". When merchants were sailing on the sea, if anyone dared became a robber, all of the neighborhood unit was entitled to arrest and punish him" (S. Xu et al. 2014: 8856). In May of the fifth year of the Shaoxing Reign (AD 1135), the registration system of seagoing-ship households was further extended to the whole country. "As for the sea-ship households, five families were grouped with one neighborhood in the coastal prefectures. No tax evasion was allowed; otherwise, all neighbors would be punished together if anyone within the neighborhood committed a robbery" (X. Li 2013: 1724). In November of the fifth year of the Shaoxing Reign (AD 1135), it was reiterated again that "the households with ships along the coast, five composed one neighborhood unit. If any robbery or theft occurred, all people would be punished" (X. Li 2013: 1823). The system of basic household registration was to prevent people from committing crimes instead of targeting at the requisition of seagoing ships.

The requisition of seagoing ships for coastal defence had already existed in the second year of the Jianyan Reign (AD 1128). In the same year, "Military Office started recruiting military seagoing vessels for sea and coastal defense" (K. Lang 1990: 7900). In the second year of the Shaoxing Reign (AD 1132), "as the seagoing ships in Fujian Province were mostly damaged after the long-time service for coastal defense, and were not suitable for maritime trade, therefore, the shipowners viewed theirs ship as a heavy burden". With the situation of selling and destroying their ships, or not returning from overseas, the size and frequency of the conscripted ships were made clear. "The registered seagoing ships with a maximum beam over 4 meters in length are classified into three groups for sea defense in turns" (S. Xu et al. 2014: 7128). In the tenth year of the Shaoxing Reign (AD 1140), "the seagoing ships with a maximum beam above 4.3 meters in length", "were grouped into one loyal community", within which every ten people were made one Jia (group), and five Jia (groups) were made one Dui (team), every four Dui (teams) one Bu (branch), every five Bu (branches) one She (Community), and every five She (communities) one Du (borough). In the 29th year of the Shaoxing Reign (AD 1159), "the ships with a maximum beam over 3.3 meters in length were also put into the registration book". In the 32nd year of the Shaoxing Reign (AD 1162), the ship with a maximum beam over 4 m in length were resumed to be registered and requisitioned. "The registered and newly built ships should be inspected by the local magistrate and recorded in the registration book. If the ship were damaged, it could be crossed out after the verification and report. If there was a newly built ship, registration was needed" (K. Lang 1990: 7901–02). The cancellation and adding shall be adjusted based on the current condition of ships. The "registration" mentioned above referred to the special one aimed for the requisitioned ships with a certain width, which was "the registered household for fortress defense" as mentioned below. Just as Ye Mengde, Fujian military commissioner, said that "ordinary ships and those vessels with the beam under 4-meter-long took turns to patrol" (X. Li 2013: 2848). Indeed, they need to be registered first, which means that the registration system had been widely implemented.

The seagoing-ships household registration was not only carried out in Fujian, but in the coastal areas as Mingzhou, Wenzhou and Taizhou in Liangzhe East Province. "Zhangzhou, Quanzhou, Fuzhou and Xinghua, and other states banned implemented registration system", "Wenzhou, Taizhou, and Mingzhou wherever boasted the seagoing ships also carried out the household system" (S. Xu et al. 2014: 8365). In the eighth year of the Chunxi Reign (AD 1181), "five coastal ship families were grouped as a neighborhood unit ("Jia"). If one ship committed a crime, punishment would fall on everyone of the neighborhood unit together" (S. Xu et al. 2014: 8869). During the period of the Jiaxi Reign, "the Military Commission Office requisitioned civilian boats from Mingzhou, Wenzhou, and Taizhou to defend Dinghai, Huaidong provinces and Jingkou every year. It had been nearly 20 years since the registration was introduced", whether intact or damaged, "the ships would be conscripted based on the registration information". In the fifth year of the Baoyou Reign (AD 1257), the military commissioner Wu Qian implemented the "Law on Compulsory Services of Civilian Boats" on conscripted naval ships along the coast in Liangzhe East Province, which stated that "if a state government was going to recruit three ships a year among fifty to sixty ship households, all the shipowners should jointly prepare six ships, half of which were for recruitment, and half for their own profits; if they had more ships, the rest should be kept for next years' recruitment" (Y. Mei et al. 1990: 5991). The universal application of Law on Compulsory Services of Civilian Boats was based on the universal registration system.

In the fifth year of the Jiading Reign (AD 1212), the emperor ruled that "the mission of border defense should be maintained all the time, and the registration (of naval ships in Liangzhe East Province and Fujian Province) should be accomplished". "Small boats below the requisition standard cannot be enrolled in the requisitioned books, and they can not be assigned any military task" (S. Xu et al. 2014: 8365). This conduct referred to the fact that ships were not requisitioned, but no ship could be excluded out of the registration book. Actually, the requisitioned ships could only be decided after the comprehensive registration, and the ship with a maximum beam under 4 m in length would also be recruited for cargo shipping. "The ship with the beam below 4-m-long did cargo transportation. If the households had suitable ships for coastal defense, their ship could not be requisitioned by local prefectures" (S. Xu et al. 2014: 7128). This means that local prefecture and county cannot dispatch the requisitioned ships for other purposes out of coastal defense, and ships with the beam under 4-m-long were not requisitioned for coastal defense. In the 19th year of the Shaoxing Reign (AD 1149), a universal registration policy was adopted, stating that "the shipowner's name should be put into the registration book, and every five of them were classified into one Jia (group) so as to prevent them from being used for other purposes." Here, the ships referred to all the maritime ships. When Liao Gang, the prefecture mayor of Zhangzhou came to his post, he ordered to "register all the ships and set up rewards to eradicate deception and concealment", and "to combine the seagoing ships into a neighborhood, and no one could go out without authority permission" (G. Liao 1990). This regulation applied to all kinds of naval ships. The Liangzhe East Province also implemented a census registration system for civilian boats, which stated that "any boats should be registered no matter big or small" (Q. Wu 2002). Along the 1000–1500 km coastal line connected by Mingzhou, Wenzhou, and Taizhou "a complete inventory need be applied to all the households regardless of possessing a boat or not, size of the boat, and type of boats. The notices were put up in every corner of the villages, with no place uncovered by the notices". Thanks to the universal registration system, a survey found out that there were 3833 ships with a maximum beam above 3.3 m, and 15,454 ships below the criteria (Y. Mei et al. 1990: 5991).

5.7.2 The Taxation System on Civilian Boats

In the Song Dynasty, the taxation on civilian boats was categorized into two: ship tax and cargo tax. Ship tax, aimed for the ship itself, or "levying even on empty ship" (Toqta 1977: 4547). In the early years of the Northern Song, the former conventions of the Five Dynasties were followed, "the chains and locks were secretly installed in the ferries for more taxes. The civilian boats with a load capacity of 3000 kg shall be levied one hundred coins as its tax, and those with goods on board would be levied double taxes". This quotation means that two kinds of taxes were levied on civilian boats: the first was the ship tax levied according to the deadweight tonnage, or "the ships with capacity of 3000 kg shall be levied one hundred coins"; the second was the cargo tax levied on the goods, "ships with goods on board would be levied double or more taxes". Emperor Taizong abolished this policy in the third year of the Taipingxingguo Reign (AD 978) because "the merchants and travelers suffered greatly from it" (S. Xu et al. 2014: 9548). Apart from setting up the chains, there were block-boards for levying taxes. For instance, "in Qinzhou, Sima Yan set up private boards and levied taxes to passing merchant ships", which was abolished by the Emperor Taizong in the first year of the Chunhua Reign (AD 990) (S. Xu et al.

2014: 6250). And the next year, Emperor Taizong issued an edict twice that: "the Debarkation Office was established by the military prefectures along the gorges of the rivers, which levied on merchant ships as soon as they boarded, ranging from 100 to 1200 coins each, such offices shall be abolished from now" (S. Xu et al. 2014: 6351). This refers to the ship tax. However, the chains set in the river for revenues lingered on until the Southern Song Dynasty. Fan Chengda saw in the Xuzhou River, the upper reaches of the Yangtze River, that "chains were installed in the midstream for nothing but collecting taxes" (C. Fan 2012: 71). The imperial abolition of chains, boards and Debarkation Office did not mean no taxes levied on boats but to regulate taxation on civilian boats. In the third year of the Tiansheng Reign (AD 1025), Emperor Renzong issued the exemption edict on empty ship taxes of the grain boats for official food in Jinghu Province (S. Xu et al. 2014: 6355), indicating that the empty boat taxes remained all the time. What was exempted was the empty civilian boat taxes carrying grains for the government. In the seventh year of the Xuanhe Reign (AD 1125), the emperor issued an edict that "taxation on the boats of places and temples, together with officials' boats shall be levied in accordance with the previous regulations. But those edicts that particularly reduced and exempted taxes would not be implemented" (S. Xu et al. 2014: 7125). The ships of the palaces, temples and officials which were considered to be private ones, equivalent to civilian boats, were levied taxes till the end of the Northern Song Dynasty. The ordinary civilian boats were impossible to be exempted from taxes, which lingered on to the Southern Song Dynasty. *The Regulations in the Chunxi Reign* recorded "the levy on livestock, boats and contracts" (Toqta 1977: 4993), listing the ship tax as a category of taxes.

The deadweight tonnage tax was another kind of ship taxes, which was a tax relevant to load capacity. During the period of Emperor Gaozong's Reign (AD 1127–1162), some criticized the phenomenon that "empty boats were levied extra tonnage taxes, but the full-loaded boats were deemed as fostering trading activities, and such regulations should be modified" (S. Xu et al. 2014: 6373). The ministers during the period of Emperor Xiaozong's Reign (AD 1162–1189) also complained that "the tonnage taxes levied on the empty boats as they were supposed to be levied a large quantity of taxes, but the heavy loaded boats were not charged heavy taxes, which were unfair to empty boats" (S. Xu et al. 2014: 6375). Obviously, the tonnage tax levied on empty boat did existed. Yoshinobu Shiba argued that "the tonnage tax was a tax on the gross cargo, serving as the parking and service fee in ports, which was a ship tax. Generally speaking, it was a transportation tax", "stemming from the ship tax, but it evolved into a tax on the cargo load capacity". He stressed that "commercial taxes (including circulation and trade tax) were systematically different from the tonnage tax, which was an additional tax to the circulation tax" (Y. Shiba 1997: 504, 507, 509). Yoshinobu Shiba pointed out clearly that the nature of tonnage tax was a ship tax, but it was inappropriate to regard it as an additional tax to the circulation tax, which levied on commodities by a certain proportion (2% in the Song Dynasty), while the tonnage tax was based on the ship's load capacity, aiming for the ship itself, and enjoyed independent taxable objects and calculation methods, rather than an additional tax attached to the circulation tax.

The ship tax in Hainan was levied according to the size of the ship instead of the load capacity: "Hainan levied on the ship by its size, dabbed 'Gena'. It classified ships into three classes, the 17.66-meter-long ships were classified as the second class, but 17.33-meter-long boats were classified the third class. One 0.33-meter shorter than the second class ship, the tax reduced ten times. In addition, the values of cargoes on board were different. The cargoes transported from Quanzhou, Fuzhou, Liangzhe and Huguang was mostly gold, silver and silk, worth tens of thousand strings of 1000 coins. In comparison, those from Gaozhou and Huazhou were mostly rice, potteries, and cattle, valuing only 200 to 300 strings". Therefore, "the merchants from Quanzhou and Fuzhou made great profits but the businessman from Huazhou and Huazhou earned little". In this way we could see that in Hainan, the ship tax was decided on ships' sizes and had nothing to do with the cargo on board; the ship tax was collected and cargo tax was not exempted. In the third year of the Yuanfeng Reign (AD1080), Zhu Chuping, the magistrate of Hainan, suggested that "nowadays, if the legislation was to be established fairly, the cargo tax should be levied and the ship tax be exempted after the merchant ships mooring in Qiongzhou, Yazhou, Danzhou, and Wanzhou. And the cargo could only be traded with a permission granted by the government". In other words, the ship tax was actually canceled, and cargo tax was levied, taxes were levied on the basis of "the value and quantity of the goods", which was approved by Emperor Shenzong (S. Xu et al. 2014: 6359–60; Toqta 1977: 4544).

Apart from Hainan Island, the ship tax was levied in other coastal areas in different names. In the early years of the Southern Song Dynasty, "the seagoing ship tax was collected at Pukou in the bay" (Toqta 1977: 4546). In the fifth year of the Jiading Reign (AD 1212), "the marine ship tax in the coastal states was abolished" (Toqta 1977: 758). But there were other ship taxes in different pretexts. During the period of Emperor Gaozong's Reign (AD 1131–1162), Huangyan County canalized a port in the east and established a lock, "for draining water into the river nominally, but in fact, the county tried to attract boats to pass through it and levied ship taxes for filling the official pocket" (Toqta 1977: 2416), which were actually tolls levied on the ships.

Cargo tax was a commercial tax levied on goods, which was remarkably distinguished from ship tax. In the Northern Song Dynasty, the attribution of cargo and ship tax had already been distinguished. For example, in the Bianhe River, "the Tax Revenue Office levied transaction tax", and "Water Conservancy Bureau was responsible for toll collection" (S. Xu et al. 2014: 3710). In the third year of the Jianyan Reign (AD 1129), for the ships trading the grains to Beijing, "the commercial tax and tonnage tax along the way were exempted" (S. Xu et al. 2014: 6364). The commercial tax (cargo tax) and tonnage tax were differentiated. Moreover, only some goods were to be taxed, and some were tax-free. In the 22nd year the Shaoxing Reign (AD 1152), "when merchants' cargo ships carrying the imperial grains passed by, the supervisor and his colleagues should check the goods and collect taxes in accordance with the regulations. If there were no goods to be taxed on board, the ships should be released immediately" (S. Xu et al. 2014: 6368). Tax-free cargo varied from time to time. In the early years of the Northern Song Dynasty, in the water channel of the Three Gorges, "the rice and wheat were levied taxes by the measure of Chinese Dou, boatmen loaded the rice on a bamboo mat from the merchant ship waiting for being taxed". And the carry-on goods of the boatmen shall be also levied, but these taxes were exempted in the second year of the Chunhua Reign (AD 991) (S. Xu et al. 2014: 6351). In the first year of the Jianyan Reign (AD 1127), Emperor Gaozong ordered "the merchants who trade goods to Kaifeng should be free of tax". The next year, it was stipulated that the trade of forage into Kaifeng, and the sale of bamboo, wood, bricks and tiles in poor prefectures and counties were exempted from taxes. In the third year of the Shaoxing Reign (AD 1133), the transit taxes of bamboo and wood were exempted as Lin'an suffered from a big fire (Toqta 1977: 4546). The exemption of food taxes was the most common. Emperor Gaozong once ordered that "the military prefectures in Jiangnan and Liangzhe Provinces should welcome the merchants who traded rice and grain so as to promote commercial exchanges, which were managed by the local government. If the soldiers dare to stand in the way unreasonably, merchants were given the right to sue them to the Administrative of State Affairs directly, and the officials were to be suspended posts and minor clerks be punished with flogging" (S. Xu et al. 2014: 8337). When Fujian suffered from natural disasters, the prefecture mayor Zhang Shou suggested that "all merchants ships who sold rice into Fujian would be granted with official certificates at departure, and they should be exempted from taxation in the passing-by prefectures and counties" (S. Yang et al. 1990). An ocean of similar examples will not to be illustrated.

Besides, private goods carried by the captain and helmsman of transportation team were free of tax. Since the beginning of the Northern Song Dynasty, "the private goods carried with the cargo shipping had been exempted from taxes", and "the toll gate was prohibited from levying taxes". After the third year of the Yuanyou Reign (AD 1088), the cargo boats to Kaifeng began to be levied taxes at the check points, causing many being stranded there. "Dealing with taxation on a fleet of 30 boats, however, only one official staff was on duty". "When one boat was checked, the other 29 had to wait by the bank". The taxes were mainly levied on the private goods of the captain and helmsman, and the government didn't make a fortune from it. Yangzhou Tax Revenue Office collected grain taxes over 4700 strings of 1000 coins for three years in total, with only 1600 strings or so per year, but the head of the official tax collectors secretly earned ten times more than the government, making "the boatmen in a state of extreme poverty", "struggle to survive only by stealing official rice and demolishing shipboard for sale". The fleet cannot arrive at Kaifeng with full amount of rice, greatly impeding the grain transportation, therefore, the tax was canceled three years later. "The prefectures along the route lost some commercial taxes for sure, the capital, however, acquired abundant supplies" (T. Li 2004: 11327, 11330, 11333). The tax exemption policy on ship captains and helmsmen was an important measure adopted by the court to ensure smooth cargo shipping.

Cargo tax was not influenced by the exemption of ship tax. Sometimes the rice and grain taxes were exempted, but the tonnage tax remained to be levied. In the fifth year of the Xuanhe Reign (AD 1123), Emperor Huizong ordered that "merchant ships from six southeastern provinces trading rice to Kaifeng were still levied tonnage taxes since the beginning of October", while rice was free of tax (S. Xu et al. 2014: 6363). It was the same case in the Southern Song Dynasty. In the 18th year of the Shaoxing

Reign (AD 1148), the Ministry of Revenue in feudal China mentioned that "the grain traded by merchants shall be exempted from taxes in accordance with the imperial edicts issued repeatedly", but prefecture and county authorities "often broke the law and charged shipowners in the name of tonnage tax" (S. Xu et al. 2014: 6367). During the period of Emperor Xiaozong's Reign (AD 1165–1173), as rice prices were soaring in spring and people had little food to eat, then rice was exempted from taxes, but "Chartered Agency for Trading Salt and Iron illegally levied taxes in all sorts of pretexts such as tonnage tax" (S. Xu et al. 2014: 6374). In the 27th year of the Shaoxing Reign (AD 1157), Tax Revenue Office in prefectures "falsely reported the weight of the rice in the name of other grain, obstructed the merchants in every possible way, and collected taxes illegally" (S. Xu et al. 2014: 6370). In the 22nd year of the Shaoxing Reign (AD 1152), Tax Revenue Office along the river "forced the shipowners to pay taxes in the name of tonnage tax regardless of whether there were taxable goods or not, charging them more than one thousand of strings of 1000 coins, but the captain and helmsman had to admit the tough luck" (S. Xu et al. 2014: 6368). In fact, those cargoes should have been exempted taxes, but they were levied taxes in the name of tonnage tax.

Sometimes, commercial and tonnage taxes were exempted by the imperial court at the same time. For instance, "the edict issued by Emperor Renzong" required that "merchants who trade grains and the poor exchanging firewood and charcoal for food shall be exempted from the tonnage taxes" (S. Su 2010: 3523). In the sixth year of the Xi'ning Reign (AD 1073), "Suzhou and Huzhou enjoyed good harvests, and food prices were only half that of Huainan, but merchant ships did not come for grain procurement due to the ship taxes, which therefore were exempted temporarily later" (Toqta 1977: 4544). In the eighth year of the Yuanyou Reign (AD 1093), the emperor ordered that "the merchants of other provinces who were willing to carry grains to Kaifeng that should have been levied tonnage tax, but now they should be exempted" (S. Xu et al. 2014: 6360). In the fifth year of the Shaoxi Reign (AD 1194), "the Tax Revenue Office in prefectures along the river were ordered to exempt tonnage taxes in accordance to the law for merchant ships trading grains" (S. Xu et al. 2014: 6383). These examples evidenced that the ships with tax-free grain were exempted from tonnage tax at the same time.

In addition to ship tax and cargo tax, the Song government also levied ship transaction tax. In the 25th year of the Shaoxing Reign (AD 1155), Emperor Gaozong issued an edict that "when pawning the ships, the contract shall be stamped with an official taxation seal in accordance with the law" (X. Li 2013: 3912), actually means levying the ship transaction tax. But, in the first year of the Daguan Reign (AD 1107), a new regulation made clear that "people who pawn cattle, carriages, and boats, etc. without the official seal on the contract, can be exempted from extra taxes within one hundred days". The extra taxes means additional taxes in addition to the ship transaction tax (Toqta 1977: 4545), which was in fact a kind of property transaction tax.

The Song Dynasty implemented strict management on merchant ships to ensure the collection of ship taxes and cargo taxes. For instance, as a merchant ship "left Guoshikou Port for Hanyang", and Guoshikou should register and note down the distance to Hanyang like 10 km, "one or two days' deadline of transportation. If the ship failed to arrive even after four to five days, it may have already traded goods secretly half way for tax evasion. Then its shipowner should be punished for tax evasion" (G. Huang 1990). In addition, it was stipulated that "if some of the taxable goods were illegally hidden and were found out by official tax-collectors, one-third of them be confiscated, among which half will be given to officials as rewards. The trafficking shipowners who did not follow the official route should be punished" (Toqta 1977: 4541).

In contrast to the tax evasion of merchant ships, the forced and additional taxes were levied by the authorities. One was the multiple tax revenue offices, for instance, "the distance between the closely connected taxation offices was no more than 3 kilometer. From Chizhou (now Guichi, Anhui Province) to Jiankang (now Nanjing), about 350 km, six Chartered Agencies for Trading Salt and Iron stood on the way, namely, Yancha, Chikou, Shituan, Wuhu, Caishi and Jiankang" (S. Xu et al. 2014: 6381). As a result, the merchant ships suffered from being repeatedly taxed. The other was levying illegal extra taxes. "With corrupt officials increasing year by year, they intercepted ships unreasonably for extra taxes and set up private accounts. Merchants and travelers were very worried about them and compared Qiyang in Qichun, Hukou in Jiangzhou, and Yancha in Chizhou (now Guichi) to be the large and small execution grounds" (S. Xu et al. 2014: 6368). Huangzhou (now Huanggang, Hubei) and Ezhou (now Wuchang, Hubei) Tax Revenue Offices were also execution grounds, and "they forced the ship to pay taxes on trumped-up items", and "the tax collectors drove a boat to intercept merchant ships from ten miles away, searching and looting the goods", and "the clerks on patrol all armed with bows and arrows, knives and guns, intercepting the passing-by merchants and forcing them to pay taxes", all of which were illegal means (S. Xu et al. 2014: 6377–78). When Zhou Bida sailed in Hukou County, he encountered "the official tax collectors on a boat, who intercepted him for taxes" (B. Zhou 1990). The official collectors chased him for more taxes.

During the Southern Song Dynasty, the extra ship taxes on the Yangtze River had greatly agonized navigators. On the way to Hangzhou from Sichuan, a scholar for the final imperial examination, had to suffer "the merchant taxes in Zigui, Yiling, Jiyang, and Yancha", in spite of the natural obstacles such as the Three Gorges, the Dongting Lake and the Pengli Lake (another name of the Poyang Lake), so "the poor in Sichuan Province could not finish the journey and dare not to go through the tax check points, only to give up the imperial examinations in other pretexts" (Z. Du 1990). The indiscriminate taxation had a greater negative impact on water trade, market operation and commercial tax collection. "The official expenditures of the prefectures and counties relied on the taxes levied on merchants, and especially on the wealthy one". However, the indiscriminate extra ships taxes greatly reduced merchant ships, and those with close relations with the local officials passed by the check points free of charge. In the fifth year of Jiading Reign (AD 1212), the supervisor, Shi Zongwan pointed out that "nowadays, the business along the river was depressed, and the government revenues reduced by more than 50% over the previous year. The reason lied in the officials' corruption. Nowadays, the giant boats loaded with cargoes were sailing westward one after another, as steadily as a mountain, they were all under the charge of the scholar-bureaucrats". Officials and soldiers traveling between Southeast China and Sichuan traded along with the ships, "for the sake of tax exemption by the Chartered Agency for Trading Salt and Iron along the route". The merchants could only load their goods on the official ships to evade taxes, so they were eager to know that "when some official leave Sichuan, and then they rushed to be his accompanies. Thus, the scholar-bureaucrats civilian merchants high boat fares, and could earn thousands of strings of 1000 coins by a single ship". As a result, it was stipulated that in the Song Dynasty that "the prefecture governments along the river were entitled to take over the tax collection offices and strictly check tax evasion. If there were any violators, the prefecture government can report the violator's position and name to the Administrative of State Affairs and the Watchdog directly to punish him" (S. Xu et al. 2014: 6386).

5.7.3 Requisition and Recruitment of Civilian Boats

5.7.3.1 Requisition of Civilian Boats

In the Song Dynasty, the requisition of civilian boats was mainly completed during the Southern Song Dynasty, and was mostly the institutional requisition for coastal defense. In the second year of the Jianyan Reign (AD 1128), "the Imperial Defense Command began recruiting the army ships along the coastal states for seaway defense", marking the beginning of the coast defense by the civilian boats. However, recruitment served as the major approach. The requisition registration system on civilian boats and the standard of requisitioned ship sizes were gradually developed. In the second year of the Shaoxing Reign (AD 1132), Fujian Province implemented the policy that "the registered seagoing ships with a maximum beam above 4 meters in length, whatever the quantity, should be registered and divided into three groups for coastal defense under the charge of county, and each group was on duty for three years" (S. Xu et al. 2014: 7128), which means each ship would be requisitioned every three years. In the tenth year of the Shaoxing Reign (AD 1140), the requisition standard was changed to the seagoing ship with a maximum beam above 4.3 m in length. "The Transfer Agency for Taxation registered a batch of ships with a maximum beam above 4.3 meters in length". In the 29th year of the Shaoxing Reign (AD 1159), the ship with a maximum beam above 3.7 m in length were requisitioned, but later "as such boats were less than enough, the standard was changed to the ships with a maximum beam above 3.3 meters in length to be registered". In the 32nd year of the Shaoxing Reign (AD 1162), "the Provincial Military Commission though that the ships with a maximum beam less than 3.3 m in length were not easy to survive in the huge waves, almost useless at war. Since then, ships with a maximum beam less than 3.2 meters in length were exempted from requisition". But the ships with a maximum beam above 4 m in length were resumed to be requisitioned (K. Lang 1990: 7900–02). Since then, Fujian Province kept on requisitioning ships with a maximum beam over 4 m in length. Different from Fujian, in the three states of

Liangzhe East Province, the civilian boats which were used to "safeguard Dingha, Huainan East Province and Jingkou every year" adopted the requisition standard of ships with a maximum beam more than 3.3 m in length. But the three prefectures classified civilian maritime ships into three categories: ships with a maximum beam more than or less than 3.3 m in length. And ships in the prefecture and county were all registered in these two categories. The marine ships above the standard of 3.3 m were requisitioned for coastal defense, but the smaller ships were "unable to serve as warships" (Y. Mei et al. 1990: 5991).

After the second year of the Shaoxing Reign (AD 1132), Fujian Province generally implemented the three-shift requisition system for civilian boats along the coast. In the second year of the Qiandao Reign (AD 1166), three categories of ships were named A, B, C groups (in Chinese "Jia", "Yi", "Bing") on duty for sea defense, "but later they were classified into four groups by equally equipped with same number of ships of different qualities." In the fourth year of the Qiandao Reign (AD 1168), "the four-group system was adjusted to three-group system on duty each year". No more changes were made since then. During the period of the Chunxi Reign, nine counties of Fuzhou still implemented three-group requisition policy, of which eight carried out three-group requisition apart from Houguan County classified seven ships into two groups "three for Group B and four for Group C" (K. Lang 1990: 7901–02). Not all the requisitioned marine ships on duty from Fujian Province were dispatched to Liangzhe Province, with "one-third were dispatched for defense, and not all requisitioned ships were dispatched unless there were emergencies" (X. Zhu 2010: 4474). In the 31st year of the Shaoxing Reign (AD 1161), as Jiaoxi (now Jiaozhou, Shandong) War broke out, "257 marine ships were dispatched to Pingjiang (now Suzhou, Jiangsu) in three groups". However, during the period of the Chunxi Reign, the total requisitioned ships in nine counties of Fuzhou were 592, of which 179 were on duty, but only 90 were dispatched to Mingzhou (now Ningbo) (K. Lang 1990: 7902).

The requisition of civilian boats in Liangzhe East Province was divided into ten groups, which means every ship would be put into sea defense once every ten years. In the early years of the Duanping Reign, "civilian boats in Wenzhou and Taizhou were clustered and were classified into ten groups, and 140 ships were dispatched to Zhenjiang for river defense every year" (Q. Wu 2002). During the period of the Jiaxi Reign (AD 1237–1240), "over three hundred ships were requisitioned and classified into ten groups for coastal defense in Dinghai (now Zhenhai, Zhejiang), Huainan East Province and Zhenjiang". In the fifth year of the Baoyou Reign (AD 1257), when Wu Qian introduced the *Law on Compulsory Services of Civilian Boats*, "three ships were requisitioned a year from the community of fifty to sixty shipowner households", which means one ship was requisitioned for sea defense every twenty years (Y. Mei et al. 1990: 5991). The requisition frequency in Liangzhe East Province was far less than that of Fujian Province. As Mingzhou (now Ningbo) served as an important player for safeguarding Lin'an (now Hangzhou), local shipowner households had the mission for Mingzhou coastal defense. Along the coast of Mingzhou, "428 fishing boats were clustered, with five of them patrolling in turn every night, placing five signs at different places, and setting up offices in Zhangting and Xianchi. As the tide rose in the evening, the Zhangting Office asked for the permit of patrolling, the next morning, it returned the permit to the Xianchi Office. With the tide falling in the evening, the Xianchi Office asked for the permit of patrolling, and it returned the permit to the Zhangting Office the next morning" (Y. Mei et al. 1990: 5982). Therefore, the mission for civilian boats for Mingzhou coastal defense was indeed challenging.

The marine ships from Fujian and Liangzhe East Provinces were mainly requisitioned to station in Mingzhou, coastal cities of Zhexi Province and Huaidong Province, which were responsible for safeguarding Li'nan and defending against the Jin Kingdom. As mentioned above, the civilian boats requisitioned from Mingzhou, Wenzhou, and Taizhou in Liangzhe East Province were deployed to Dinghai (now Zhenhai, Zhejiang), Huaidong, and Zhenjiang; and Fujian civilian boats were requisitioned to Pingjiang Prefecture (now Suzhou, Jiangsu) and Mingzhou. In the fifth year of the Chunxi Reign (AD 1178), Emperor Xiaozong ordered that "ships from Fujian were sent to Xupu of Pingjiang Prefecture for temporarily detaining thieves", and "ships from Liangzhe East Province going to Mingzhou Coastal Military Commission were stationed in Dinghai" (S. Xu et al. 2014: 7135). In the 12th year of the Chunxi Reign (AD 1185), the marine ships of Fujian Province followed the orders in July 19th, 1167 (the third year of the Qiandao Reign), "were sent to Xupu, Pingjiang Prefecture to temporarily detain thieves" (S. Xu et al. 2014: 7137). Some maritime ships of Liangzhe East Province were also requisitioned to safeguard Pingjiang Prefecture. "Fujian and Liangzhe East Province dispatched ships respectively guarding eight prefectures like Gujing and Wujiang every year, and together defending Xupu" (L. Xu 1990). When Ji Ji served as the Kunshan County mayor, "he registered over sixty marine ships", and General Dai Kezhong wanted to "pocket them all, and requisition the registered ships from Wenzhou and Taizhou to safeguard the river". Ji Ji refuted that "these ships belonged to our county instead of Wenzhou and Taizhou." And ships served for patrolling Xupu instead of the river" (Z. Liu 1990). This case illustrated that the ships in Wenzhou and Taizhou were not only for coastal defense but for river defense.

The ships requisitioned by the government enjoyed payment, under the items of "departure money and rice for captain and boatmen, rewards and bonus, maintenance cost and blessing money", which "came from the additional taxes and grain storage warehouse" (Y. Wang 1990). For example, the requisitioned ships in Fujian "were paid with money and rice, the money came from additional tax, and rice was allocated from the grain storage warehouse". The standard for departure money and rice was "the official as the captain was given securities that could be exchanged for the same number of coins; an ordinary man was paid 250 coins and 1.8 kg of rice a day; the helmsman with 150 coins and 1.8 kg of rice per day; the head crew, anchorman and sailors with 100 coins and 1.8 kg of rice per day. In addition, other bonuses were given to them, "helmsman, 15 strings of 1000 coins, head crew, anchorman and sailor 7.5 strings of 1000 coins", as well as the maintenance subsidies to the captain (K. Lang 1990: 7902). The requisition payment was substantial. In the second year of the Chunxi Reign (AD 1175), the marine ships of Fujian got requisitioned, "with 570 ships and 40,000 helmsmen and sailors in total. In May, the garrison stationed and applied to the government for rewards at more than 600,000 strings of 1000 coins, and rice about over 1800 tons. Clothing, weapons, prefecture and county expenses were not even included. It can be inferred that the costs of Liangzhe Province should be times of this" (X. Zhu 2010: 4474). In the sixth year of the Baoyou Reign (AD 1258), Wenzhou, Taizhou, Mingzhou, and Yuezhou in Liangzhe East Province requisitioned "24 large ships, classified them into two groups, and recruited 1200 sailors", "patrolling on the sea in turn". "Every ship carried 50 people as a standard, each person was given 50 strings of 1000 coins and 36 kg rice by the prefecture government", which provided them with securities and bonus for 350,000 strings of 1000 coins and rice 180 tons (Y. Mei et al. 1990: 5995). This could not cover all the costs of the seagoing ships requisitioned by Liangzhe East Province.

5.7.3.2 Recruitment of Civilian Boats

In the Northern Song Dynasty, as the revenue center, the economic center, and the political-military center were not converged, long-distance cargo transportation became a state top priority relevant to effective administration of the country. In the Southern Song Dynasty, problems still existed in providing supplies to four major war areas and the capital city, especially more after the river and coastal defense were included in the national defense system. Neither the Northern Song nor the Southern Song could provide all the ships for cargo shipping and national defense, so they had to rely on recruiting and requisitioning civilian boats to undertake these tasks.

In the Northern Song Dynasty, 180,000 tons of grain and other supplies were transported from the southeast provinces to Kaifeng every year. Apart from supplying the capital city, a large part was transported to the border areas where the troops were stationed, such as Shaanxi, Hedong and Hebei provinces. Employing civilian boats for the large-scale transportation was more efficient and cheaper than the official boats. The border prefecture authorities of Hebei deposited grains for military reserve in inland counties, which were shipped on the royal river from inland to border. "It was calculated by shipping 1 Dou (6 kg) of grain at the cost of 70 coins for an official ship. But for a civilian boat, only 13 to 15 coins were need to cover the cost of carrying 1 Dou of grain in the 50-kilometer journey. Assuming the journey of 500 kilometers, half of the expenditures could be spared, therefore, the civilian boats were very economic" (T. Li 2004: 7219). So it was the same case for the grain transportation from the southeast provinces to Kaifeng. "There were totally hundreds of grain transportation boats in various river courses every year, and those employed official boats to transport grains suffered a loss, while those recruited civilian boats sustained. The merchants were honest and kind, cherished their boats a lot. Most of the official boatmen, however, who were supported by the government with no life pressure, suffered a loss of 900 tons of grains a year" (X. Zhu 2010: 4296). Another example, Jiangnan West Province offered rice to the central government, which was transported by official boats, "suffering 900 tons deficit for several years. Only four prefectures, Jiangzhou, Yuanzhou, Xingguo and Jianchang, recruited civilian boats and earned a profit" (B. Zhou 1990).

Therefore, the official cargo transportation was basically secured by the official shipbuilding and local soldiers' protection, with recruiting numerous civilian boats for assistance at the same time. In the early Northern Song Dynasty, "Jiangnan and Huainan provinces had already recruited civilian boats for grain transportation", and Emperor Zhenzong worried that the recruited civilian boats would impede merchants trading activities. "As the businessmen prioritize profits, recruitment may stand in the way of commercial activities, but the soaring rice prices would also be problematic". Therefore, the emperor ordered "not to recruit civilian boats again" (T. Li 2004: 1562). However, the recruitment of civilian boats still existed. In the third year of the Tiansheng Reign (AD 1025), the imperial court stipulated that "the civilian boats in Jingmen, Hubei, carrying the official grains should be exempted from tonnage taxes" (T. Li 2004: 2384). Su Zhe also mentioned that "If the government recruited some businessmen from the six southern provinces, and transported official grain on their boats, wherever they passed by, they should be exempted from commercial taxes" (Z. Su 1987: 473). These merchant ships were hired to transport official grains. For the cargo transportation, the Southern Song governments still preferred to employing a large number of civilian boats, "whenever rice was to be transported to Jiangnan and Huainan provinces from Jizhou (now Ji'an, Jiangxi), the governments hired civilian boats as ever, and avoid using official ships" (B. Zhou 1990). "Many prefectures and counties in Liangzhe provinces embezzled money and food from the army to recruit civilian boats" (S. Xu et al. 2014: 6985), and even for shipping grains to the capital, "most boats were civilian ones". The civilians were so scared of their boat being recruited that "they broke their boats and sank them to avoid service" (X. Li 2013: 1824). In the Southern Song Dynasty, as for the water transportation of military grain from Sichuan to Lizhou and Langzhou, "a Transfer Warehouse was built in Hezhou (now Hechuan, Sichuan)", and "the rice from Jiazhou, Meizhou, Luzhou and Xuzhou was shipped along the river to Chongqing, going with the inland waters to Hezhou", "and then tracing Xihan River to Lizhou and Langzhou", "the boats and boatmen were all recruited by the government" (*Zhijiang Zhi Caoyun* n.d.: 3133). Some shipowners deposited their boats in the family of influential officials which may be exempted from recruitment. For example, in Chunan County, "close to Lin'an, all ships were deposited with the influential officials, and only one boat accepted the official transportation mission" (M. Zeng 2008: 166). The reasons why "the people were panicky as if they were robbed whenever the prefectures started recruiting civilian boats for official transportation", lay in two factors: "one was little payment, and the other was too long journey" (D. Cui 1990). Thus, some people said that "recruitment of civilian boats for transportation would harm the interests of the government and civilians", and they suggested that the authorities should purchase boats and transport on by themselves, benefiting both the government and civilians (S. Xu et al. 2014: 7129). In the ninth year of the Jiading Reign (AD 1216), for cargo transportation, "70% of the money was paid to the shipowner, and 30% was temporarily hypothecated at the unloading place" (S. Xu et al. 2014: 7003). Obviously, the recruitment of civilian boats accounted for a majority in undertaking official shipping tasks.

In the early Southern Song Dynasty, many troops, in the name of army development, at the pretext of recruitment, "directly robbed civilian ships for their urgency", with only tea and salt on the official and merchant boats spared. This rudeness firstly impacted "the big picture of commercial exchanges of good"; secondly, it "harmed taxes in an unknown way"; and thirdly, it "frightened civilian not to build boats". The government recognized that recruiting civilian boats in a normal market manner was beneficial to both civilians and the governments. In the second year of the Shaoxing Reign (AD 1132), the emperor ordered twice in February and March, when the authority recruited civilian boats, that "payment was a must, and no encroachment of civilian boats could be accepted in the name of recruitment", and "no appropriation of the ships be made in all sorts of pretexts". If the government violated the order, "shipowners were allowed to leapfrog for appeal", and the violator official would be "demoted". Another edict issued in April, emphasized to "recruit civilian boats in market value, and no services and extra taxes was permitted" (S. Xu et al. 2014: 7127). But some regions were perplexed by less boats available to undertake heavy transportation tasks, then "competition for recruiting civilian boats" occurred. For example, all the prefectures of Tanzhou (now Changsha, Hu'nan) recruited boats for cargo transportation", about 18,000 tons of rice to Wuchang, Jingnan (now Jingzhou), and Xiangyang for the stationed forces. "If it was going to accomplish the task in time, the shipowners must be satisfied with high rewards, and then the price went higher and higher in bidding". "Assuming that Changsha priced fifty, Shanhua may increase to sixty, Xiangtan raised to seventy, other counties also acted like this, until all of them being satisfied. Each county was to transport 3000 tons of rice, costing one to two thousand strings of 1000 coins" (S. Yang et al. 1990). This was also a price game between private shipowners and the government.

Not only being recruited for grain transportation, civilian boats were also employed for military affairs and other temporary affairs. In the ninth year of the Xi'ning Reign (AD 1076), during the Cochin War, the civilian boats recruited from Guangdong and Fujian Province were used to carry soldiers. "Each province sent 10,000 people to the designated places by the end of autumn. After the war, the shipowners would be paid and rewarded" (T. Li 2004: 6664). "A total of one hundred and thirty certificates issued by the government were given to Fuzhou shipowners as compensation, because they were recruited to conquer the southern ethnic minorities, and some of their ships got damaged" (T. Li 2004: 6995). In the Southern Song Dynasty, the recruited ships were used in coastal defense apart from the requisitioned ships. In the second year of the Shaoxing Reign (AD 1132), "the guiding principle and detail rules of recruitment of ships were established to spread the emperor's kindness", and the coastal military commission employed marine ships. "If a ship with a maximum beam above 6 meters in length was recruited, an ordinary person and a military official, or the officials could be promoted three years earlier after the performance assessment" (S. Xu et al. 2014: 7127). In the third year of the Dazhongxiangfu Reign (AD 1010), at the request of Yangzhou prefecture major, Xu Di, "the imperial edict ordered Liangzhe provinces to abolish the employment of ships, hoping that merchants would be able to transport grains for drought relief" (T. Li 2004: 1688). The next year, due to the famine in Dengzhou (now Penglai, Shandong) and

Laizhou, the Transfer Agency of Taxation of Jiangnan and Huainan provinces was ordered to recruit civilian boats for grain transportation to relieve victims" (S. Xu et al. 2014: 7960). In the early years of the Shaoxing Reign, the transportation officer of Guangnan East Province, Zhou Gang, "purchased 4500 tons of rice with official funds under the imperial order, and transported by the sea courses to the middle of Fujian and then recruited civilian boats sailing forward to the capital". At last, he was promoted to a higher post (X. Li 2013: 1746). These are the cases of temporary recruitment of civilian boats.

5.7.4 Summary

The Song Dynasty boasted a large number of civilian boats, which were important and universal players in national transportation, social and economic growth and people's daily life. The household registration system of civilian boats was implemented in the Song Dynasty. Only several regions implemented it temporarily in the Northern Song Dynasty, and it was further strengthened in the Southern Song Dynasty, especially making a survey and registration of civilian maritime ships in coastal areas. Besides, those ships which met the requisitioned standard were registered in particular.

There were two types of major taxes on civilian boats in the Song Dynasty: ship tax and cargo tax. The ship tax was levied on the empty ship itself, according to its deadweight tonnage, or another measure called "Gena", being taxed on its load capacity, which was taxed on the size of boat. The taxation of goods was mainly commercial tax, and tax exemptions were implemented for grains and private goods carried by captain and helmsman, as well as the relief supplies. When tax exemption was given, cargo tax was not related to ship tax, and ship tax was always charged. Only when special regulations were implemented, cargo tax and ship tax could be exempted at the same time. Due to the corruption of tax officials, more extra taxes and indiscriminate levies were made on ships which greatly discouraged civilian boats in navigation and trade.

The local governments extensively recruited civilian boats for coastal defense and grain transportation. The registration and shift-system were mainly implemented in coastal areas such as Fujian and Liangzhe East Provinces, and requisitioned ships were dispatched mainly to the important coastal defense areas, such as Liangzhe West Province and Mingzhou for defending the capital city Lin'an. Fujian had gradually formed a stable requisition system of classifying the ships with a maximum beam above 4 m in length into three groups, while Liangzhe East Province requisitioned ships with a maximum beam above 3.3 m in length in ten groups or even more. The ships requisitioned by the government received payments. The Northern Song Dynasty employed civilian boats mainly for official cargo transportation, especially the grain transportation to Kaifeng, but the Southern Song Dynasty employed a large number of civilian boats for other purposes, such as official cargo transportation, emergency relief, and military affairs. Employing civilian boats was more economic than the official ones in terms of efficiency and cost. However, the government often paid less and kept them waiting for a long time, which had caused various resistances from civilian boat owners, by means of getting their boats broken, going on strikes, or hiding their ships. Due to the heavy task of shipping in some regions, shipowners had also raised the shipping prices, reflecting the price game between the civilian boat owners and the government.

In general, the management and requisition of the Southern Song Dynasty on civilian boats were more influential than the Northern Song Dynasty. The scope of registration and formation was extended, and the recruitment and requisition of civilian boats were also more extensive. The recruitment of civilian seagoing ships for coastal defense was more regular and common in particular, which was never implemented in the Northern Song Dynasty. This evidences that ships for national defence in the Southern Song Dynasty weighed more than in the Northern Song Dynasty.

References

Ban, Gu 班固, et al. 1962. *Han Shu* 汉书 [Book of Han]. Beijing: Zhonghua Book Company.

Cai, Tao 蔡絛. 2008. *Tieweishan Congtan* 铁围山丛谈 [Tieweishan Notes]. Sorted by Li Guoqiang. Collected in Complete Song Notes. Elephant Press.

Cai, Xiang 蔡襄. 1996. *Caixiang Ji* 蔡襄集 [Works of Cai Xiang]. Punctuated and collated by Wu Yining. Shanghai: Shanghai Chinese Classics Publishing House.

Cao, Jiaqi 曹家齐. 2002. *Songdai Jiaotong Guanli Zhidu Yanjiu* 宋代交通管理制度研究 [A Study on Traffic Management System in the Song Dynasty]. Kaifeng: Henan University Press.

Cao, Xun 曹勋. 1990. *Songyin Ji* 松隐集 [Selected Works of Cao Xun]. Collected in Complete Library in the Four Branches of Literature. Shanghai: Shanghai Chinese Classics Publishing House.

Chang, Tang 常棠. 1990. *Ganshui Zhi* 澉水志 [Chronicles of Ganshui]. Collected in the Series of Chorography of the Song and Yuan Dynasties. Beijing: Zhonghua Book Company.

Chao, Yidao 晁以道. 1990. *Jingyusheng Ji* 景迂生集 [Works of Chao Yidao]. Collected in Complete Library in the Four Branches of Literature. Shanghai: Shanghai Chinese Classics Publishing House.

Chen, Feng 陈峰. 1997. "Beisong De Caoyun Shuidao Jiqi Zhili 北宋的漕运水道及其治理 [The Waterways of the Northern Song Dynasty and their Governance]". *Journal of Xiaogan University* 3.

Chen, Feng 陈峰. 1997. "Songdai Caoyun Yagang Renyuan Kaoshu 宋代漕运押纲人员考述 [Studies on the Grain Transportation Escorts in the Song Dynasty] ". *Journal of Chinese Historical Studies* 1.

Chen, Chun 陈淳. 1990. *Beixi Da Heji* 北溪大全集 [The Complete Works of Chen Chun]. Collected in Complete Library in the Four Branches of Literature. Shanghai: Shanghai Chinese Classics Publishing House.

Chen, Cisheng 陈次升. 1990. *Danglun Ji* 谠论集 [Political Commentary of Chen Cisheng]. Collected in Complete Library in the Four Branches of Literature. Shanghai: Shanghai Chinese Classics Publishing House.

Chen, Qiqing 陈耆卿. 1990. *Jiading Chicheng Zhi* 嘉定赤城志 [Jiading Period Chronicles of Chicheng]. Collected in The Series of Chorography of the Song and Yuan Dynasties. Beijing: Zhonghua Book Company.

Chen, Shidao 陈师道. 2006. *Houshan Tan Cong* 后山谈丛 [Notes of Chen Shidao]. Collected in Complete Song Notes. Elephant Press.

Cui, Dunli 崔敦礼. 1990. *Gongjiao Ji* 宫教集 [Selected Works of Cui Dunli]. Collected in Complete Library in the Four Branches of Literature. Shanghai: Shanghai Chinese Classics Publishing House.

Dajin Ji Li 大金集礼 [Rites of Jin]. 1990. Collected in Complete Library in the Four Branches of Literature. Shanghai: Shanghai Chinese Classics Publishing House.

Dong, Sigao 董嗣杲. 1990. *Lushan Ji* 庐山集 [Selected Works of Dong Sigao in Lushan]. Collected in Complete Library in the Four Branches of Literature. Shanghai: Shanghai Chinese Classics Publishing House.

Du, Zheng 度正. 1990. *Xingshantang Gao* 性善堂稿 [Manuscripts of Good Nature Hall]. Collected in Complete Library in the Four Branches of Literature. Shanghai: Shanghai Chinese Classics Publishing House.

Fan, Chengda 范成大. 2012. *Guihai Yuheng Zhi* 桂海虞衡志 [Records of the Ranger in Guihai]. Collected in Complete Song Notes. Elephant Press.

Fan, Chengda 范成大. 2012. *Can Luan Lu* 骖鸾录 [The Trip to Guilin]. Collected in Complete Song Notes. Elephant Press.

Fan, Chengda 范成大. 2012. *Wu Chuan Lu* 吴船录 [Travelogues in Wu Area by Ship]. Collected in Complete Song Notes. Elephant Press.

Fan, Zhiming 范致明. 1990. *Yueyang Fengtu Ji* 岳阳风土记 [Geography and Customs of Yueyang]. Collected in Complete Library in the Four Branches of Literature. Shanghai: Shanghai Chinese Classics Publishing House.

Fan, Zhongyan 范仲淹. 1981. *Fan Wenzheng Gong Zhengfu Zouyi* 范文正公政府奏议 [Proposals Submitted by Fan Zhongyan]. Collected in Collectanea of the Four Categories, 1st ed.

Gao, Zhu 高翥. 1990. *Jujian Ji* 菊磵集 [Selected Works of Gao Zhu]. Collected in Complete Library in the Four Branches of Literature. Shanghai: Shanghai Chinese Classics Publishing House.

Ge, Jinfang 葛金芳. 2008. *Nansong Shougongyeshi* 南宋手工业史 [The Handicraft Industry of the Southern Song Dynasty]. Shanghai: Shanghai Chinese Classics Publishing House.

Ge, Jinfang 葛金芳. 2013. "Songdai Haishang Qunti De Goucheng, Guimo Jiqi Minyingxingzhi Kaoshu 南宋海商群体的构成、规模及其民营性质考述 [The Research on the Formation, Scale, and Private Nature of the Maritime Merchants in the Southern Song Dynasty]". *Journal of Chinese Literature and History* 4.

Gong, Yanming 龚延明. 1997. *Songdai Guanzhi Cidian* 宋代官制辞典 [Bureaucracy Song Dictionary]. Beijing: Zhonghua Book Company.

Guo, Tuan 郭彖. 1990. *Kuiche Zhi* 睽车志 [Kuiche Zhi: Strange Tales of the Miraculous]. Collected in Complete Library in the Four Branches of Literature. Shanghai: Shanghai Chinese Classics Publishing House.

Gurin, Morihiro 古林森广. 1995. *Zhongguo Songdai De Shehui Yu Jingji*中国宋代的社会与经济[China's Society and economy in the Song Dynasty]. Kokusho Kankokai.

Hansen, Valerie 韩森著. 1999. *Bianqian Zhishen: Nansong Shiqi De Minjian Xinyang* 变迁之神:南宋时期的民间信仰 [Changing Gods in Medieval China, 1127–1276]. Translated by Bao Weimin. Hangzhou: Zhejiang People's Publishing House.

He, Yuan 何薳. 2008. *Chunzhu Jiwen* 春渚纪闻 [Anecdotage of the Song Dynasty]. Collected in Complete Song Notes. Elephant Press.

Hong, Mai 洪迈撰. 1981. *Yijian Zhi* 夷坚志 [Strange Tales of the Miraculous by Yijian]. Edited by He Zhuo. Beijing: Zhonghua Book Company.

Hong, Mai 洪迈撰. 2012. *Rongzhai Suibi* 容斋随笔 [Notes of Hong Mai]. Collected in Complete Song Notes. Elephant Press.

Hong, Shi 洪适. n.d. *Panzhou Wenji* 盘洲文集 [Panzhou Anthology]. Collected in Collectanea of the Four Categories 1st edn.

Huang, Chunyan 黄纯艳. 2003. *Songdai Haiwai Maoyi* 宋代海外贸易[Overseas Trade of the Song Dynasty]. Beijing: Social Sciences Academic Press.

Huang, Chunyan 黄纯艳. 2004. "Lun Songdai De Gongyongqian 论宋代的公用钱[The Administrative Expenses of the Song Dynasty]". *Social Sciences in Yunnan* 2.

Huang, Gan 黄榦. 1990. *Mianzhai Ji* 勉斋集 [Selected Works of Huang Gan]. Collected in Complete Library in the Four Branches of Literature. Shanghai: Shanghai Chinese Classics Publishing House.

Huang, Shu 黄庶. 1990. *Fantan Ji* 伐檀集 [Anthology of Huang Shu]. Collected in Complete Library in the Four Branches of Literature. Shanghai: Shanghai Chinese Classics Publishing House.

Huang, Tingjian 黄庭坚. 2011. *Huang Tingjian Quanji* 黄庭坚全集 [The Complete Works of Huang Tingjian]. Nanchang: Jiangxi People's Publishing House.

Huang, Zhen. 1990. *Huang Shi Richao* 黄氏日抄 [Notes of Huang]. Collected in Complete Library in the Four Branches of Literature. Shanghai: Shanghai Chinese Classics Publishing House.

Jeong Inji 郑麟趾. n.d. *Goryeosa* 고려사 [History of Goryeo]. n. p.

Jia, Erqiang 贾二强. 2002. *Tangsong Mingjian Xinyang* 唐宋民间信仰 [Folk Beliefs during the Tang and Song Dynasties]. Fuzhou: Fujian People's Publishing House.

Jiang, Kui 姜夔. 1990. *Baishidaoren Gequ* 白石道人歌曲 [Music Scores Collection of Baishidaoren]. Collected in Complete Library in the Four Branches of Literature. Shanghai: Shanghai Chinese Classics Publishing House.

Jinxiu Wanhua Gu 锦绣万花谷 [Collection of My Books]. 1990. Collected in Complete Library in the Four Branches of Literature. Shanghai: Shanghai Chinese Classics Publishing House.

Jojin 成寻. 2009. *Xin Jiao Cantiantai Wutaishan Ji* 新校参天台五台山记 [Revised Edition of Travelogues of Jojin]. Edited by Wang Liping. Shanghai: Shanghai Chinese Classics Publishing House.

Li, Bozhong 李伯重. 1997. "'Xiangtu Zhi Shen' 'Gongwu Zhi Shen' 'Haishang Zhi Shen—Jianlun Mazu Xingxiang De Yanbian "乡土之神"、"公务之神"与"海商之神"——简论妈祖形象的演变 ["God of Soil", "God of State" and "God of Ship Merchants"—The Image Changes of Mazu]". *Journal of Chinese Social and Economic History* 2.

Li, Liuqian 李流谦. 1990. *Danzhai Ji* 澹斋集 [Selected Works of Li Liuqian]. Collected in Complete Library in the Four Branches of Literature. Shanghai: Shanghai Chinese Classics Publishing House.

Li, Tao 李焘. 2004. *Xu Zizhi Tongjian Changbian* 续资治通鉴长编 [Continuation to The Comprehensive Mirror for Aid in Government]. Beijing: Zhonghua Book Company.

Li, Xinchuan 李心传. 2000. *Jianyan Yilai Chaoye Zaji* 建炎以来朝野杂记 [Laws and Institutions Since the Jianyan Reign]. Edited by Xu Gui. Beijing: Zhonghua Book Company.

Li, Xinchuan 李心传. 2013. *Jianyan Yilai Xinian Yaolu* 建炎以来系年要录 [Chronological Record of Major Events Since 1127]. Beijing: Zhonghua Book Company.

Li, Zhiyi 李之仪. 1990. *Guxijushi Qian Ji* 姑溪居士前集 [Prequel to Selected Works of Guxijushi]. Collected in Complete Library in the Four Branches of Literature. Shanghai: Shanghai Chinese Classics Publishing House.

Liao, Dake 廖大珂. 2001. "Songdai Haichuan De Zhanji, Baojia He Jieshe Zhidu 宋代海船的占籍、保甲和结社制度述略 [A Review on Ship Registration, Management and Boatman Pre-military Groups]". *Journal of Maritime History Studies* 1.

Liao, Gang 廖刚. 1990. *Gaofeng Wenji* 高峰文集 [Selected Works of Liao Gang]. Collected in Complete Library in the Four Branches of Literature. Shanghai: Shanghai Chinese Classics Publishing House.

Liao, Xingzhi 廖行之. 1990. *Xingzhai Ji* 省斋集 [Selected Works of Liao Xingzhi]. Collected in Complete Library in the Four Branches of Literature. Shanghai: Shanghai Chinese Classics Publishing House.

Lou, Yao 楼钥. 1990. *Gonggui Ji* 攻媿集 [Selected Works of Lou Yao]. Collected in Complete Library in the Four Branches of Literature. Shanghai: Shanghai Chinese Classics Publishing House.

Lu, You 陆游. 2011. *Lu You Quanji Jiaozhu* 陆游全集校注 [Annotations to Lu You's Works]. Collated by Qian Zhonglian. Hangzhou: Zhejiang Education Publishing House.

Lu, You 陆游. 2012. *Laoxuean Biji* 老学庵笔记 [The Notes of an Old Pedant]. Sorted by Li Changxian. Collected in Complete Song Notes. Elephant Press.

Lu, You 陆游. 2012. *Ru Shu Ji* 入蜀记 [Essays about My Journey to Sichuan]. Sorted by Li Changxian. Collected in Complete Song Notes. Elephant Press.

Luo, Jun 罗浚, et al. 1990. *Baoqing Siming Zhi* 宝庆四明志 [Baoqing Period Chronicles of Siming]. Collected in The Series of Chorography of the Song and Yuan Dynasties. Beijing: Zhonghua Book Company.

Lü, Tao 吕陶. 1990. *Jingde Ji* 净德集 [Selected Works of Lü Tao]. Collected in Complete Library in the Four Branches of Literature. Shanghai: Shanghai Chinese Classics Publishing House.

Lü, Zhong 吕中. 2014. *Leibian Huangchao Dashi Ji Jiangyi* 类编皇朝大事记讲义 [Notes on History of the Northern Song Dynasty]. Edited by Zhang Qifan and et al. Shanghai: Shanghai People's Publishing House.

Lü, Zuqian 吕祖谦. 1990. *Donglai Waiji* 东莱外集 [Selected Works of Lü Zuqian]. Collected in Complete Library in the Four Branches of Literature. Shanghai: Shanghai Chinese Classics Publishing House.

Ma, Duanlin 马端临. 2011. Wenxian Tongkao 文献通考 [A Full-Scale Textual Criticism on Ancient Systems and Regulations]. Beijing: Zhonghua Book Company.

Mao, Pang 毛滂. 1990. *Dongtang Ji* 东堂集 [Selected Works of Mao Pang]. Collected in Complete Library in the Four Branches of Literature. Shanghai: Shanghai Chinese Classics Publishing House.

Mei, Yaochen 梅尧臣. 1990. *Wanling Ji* 宛陵集 [Selected Works of Mei Yaochen]. Collected in Complete Library in the Four Branches of Literature. Shanghai: Shanghai Chinese Classics Publishing House.

Mei, Yingfa 梅应发, et al. 1990. *Kaiqing Siming Zhi* 开庆四明续志 [Sequels to Kaiming Period Chronicles of Siming]. Collected in The Series of Chorography of the Song and Yuan Dynasties. Beijing: Zhonghua Book Company.

Ouyang, Min 欧阳忞. 2003. *Yudi Guangji* 舆地广记 [Historical Records of the System of Prefectures and Counties]. Edited by Li YongXian. Chengdu: Sichuan University Press.

Ouyang, Xiu欧阳修. 2001. *Ouyang Xiu Quanji* 欧阳修全集 [Selected Works of Ouyang Xiu]. Beijing: Zhonghua Book Company.

Peng, Ruli 彭汝砺. 1990. *Poyang Ji* 鄱阳集 [Selected Works of Peng Ruli]. Collected in Complete Library in the Four Branches of Literature. Shanghai: Shanghai Chinese Classics Publishing House.

Pi, Qingsheng 皮庆生. 2008. *Songdai Minzhong Sishen Xinyang Yanjiu* 宋代民众祠神信仰研究 [A Study on Beliefs and Believers' Sacrifices in the Song Dynasty]. Shanghai: Shanghai Chinese Classics Publishing House.

Qian, Shuoyou 潜说友. 1990. *Xianchu Linan Zhi* 咸淳临安志 [Xianchun Period Chronicles of Lin'an]. Collected in in The Series of Chorography of the Song and Yuan Dynasties. Beijing: Zhonghua Book Company.

Qin, Guan 秦观. 1990. *Huaihai Ji* 淮海集 [Selected Works of Qin Guan]. Collected in Complete Library in the Four Branches of Literature. Shanghai: Shanghai Chinese Classics Publishing House.

Qiu, Jun 邱濬. 1990. *Chongbian Qiongtai Gao* 重编琼台稿 [Qiu Jun's Works Revised Version]. Collected in Complete Library in the Four Branches of Literature. Shanghai: Shanghai Chinese Classics Publishing House.

Shakeshi 沙克什. 1990. *Hefang Tongyi* 河防通议 [Summary of River Flood Prevention Works]. Collected in Complete Library in the Four Branches of Literature. Shanghai: Shanghai Chinese Classics Publishing House.

Shen, Kuo 沈括. 2006. *Mengxi Bitan* 梦溪笔谈 [Mengxi Bitan (Dream Pool Essays)]. Sorted by Hu Jingyi. Collected in Complete Song Notes. Elephant Press.

Shi, Juefan 释觉范. 1990. 石门文字禅 [Shi Juefan's Works on Buddhist Service]. Collected in Complete Library in the Four Branches of Literature. Shanghai: Shanghai Chinese Classics Publishing House.

Shi, Su 施宿, et al. 1990. *Jiatai Kuaiji Zhi* 嘉泰会稽志 [Jiatai Period Chronicles of Kuaiji]. Collected in The Series of Chorography of the Song and Yuan Dynasties. Beijing: Zhonghua Book Company.

Shiba, Yoshinobu 斯波义信. 1997. *Songdai Shangyeshi Yanjiu* 宋代商业史研究 [A Study on the Business History of the Song Dynasty]. Translated by Zhuang Jinghui. Daoxiang Press.

Song Shi Quanwen 宋史全文 [History of the Song Dynasty in Full Scale]. 2005. Edited by Zhiliang Li. Haerbin: Heilongjiang People's Publishing House.

Song, Qi 宋祁. 2014. *Song Jingwen Gong Biji* 宋景文公笔记 [Notes of Song Qi]. Sorted by Chu Lingling. Collected in Complete Song Notes. Elephant Press.

Su, Guo 苏过. n.d. *Xiechuan Ji* 斜川集 [Selected Works of Su Guo]. Collected in the Series of Ancient Classics, 1st ed. Beijing: Zhonghua Book Company.

Su, Shi 苏轼. 2010. *Su Shi Quanji Jiaozhu* 苏轼全集校注 [Annotations to the Selected Works of Su Shi]. Punctuated and collated by Zhang Zhilie, et al. Shijieazhuang: Hebei People's Publishing House.

Su, Tianjue 苏天爵. n.d. *Guochao Wenlei* 国朝文类 [Poems and Articles of the Yuan Dynasty]. Collected in Collectanea of the Four Categories 1st edn.

Su, Zhe 苏辙. 1987. *Luancheng Ji* 栾城集 [Selected Works of Su Zhe]. Shanghai: Shanghai Chinese Classics Publishing House.

Sun, Di 孙觌. 1990. *Hongqingjushi Ji*鸿庆居士集 [Selected Works of Sun Di]. Collected in Complete Library in the Four Branches of Literature. Shanghai: Shanghai Chinese Classics Publishing House.

Sun, Guangxian 孙光宪. 2014. *Beimeng Suoyan* 北梦琐言 [Anecdotes of Beimeng]. Sorted by Yu Gang. Collected in Complete Song Notes. Elephant Press.

Sun, Yi 孙奕. 1990. *Shier Bian* 示儿编 [Works For Instructing My Children]. Collected in Complete Library in the Four Branches of Literature. Shanghai: Shanghai Chinese Classics Publishing House.

Sun, Yingshi 孙应时. 1990. *Zhuhu Ji* 烛湖集 [Selected Works of Sun Yingshi]. Collected in Complete Library in the Four Branches of Literature. Shanghai: Shanghai Chinese Classics Publishing House.

Tao, Yao 谈钥. 1990. *Jiatai Wuxing Zhi* 嘉泰吴兴志 [Jiatai Period Chronicles of Wuxing], Collected in in The Series of Chorography of the Song and Yuan Dynasties. Beijing: Zhonghua Book Company.

Tianyige Cang Mingchao Ben⟨Tiansheng Ling⟩Jiaozheng 天一阁藏明钞本⟨天圣令⟩校证 [Proofreading of Laws and Regulations During the Tiansheng Period—the Ming hand copied version stored in Tianyi Pavilion]. 2004. Beijing: Zhonghua Book Company.

Toqta 脱脱. 1975. *Jin Shi* 金史 [History of the Jin Dynasty]. Beijing: Zhonghua Book Company.

Toqta 脱脱. 1977. *Song Shi* 宋史 [History of the Song Dynasty]. Beijing: Zhonghua Book Company.

Wang, Anshi 王安石. 1990. *Linchuan Wenji* 临川文集 [Selected Works of Wang Anshi]. Collected in Complete Library in the Four Branches of Literature. Shanghai: Shanghai Chinese Classics Publishing House.

Wang, Ling 王令. 1990. *Guangling Ji* 广陵集 [Selected Works of Wang Ling]. Collected in Complete Library in the Four Branches of Literature. Shanghai: Shanghai Chinese Classics Publishing House.

Wang, Mao 王楙. 1990. *Yeke Congshu* 野客丛书 [Textual Researches by Wang Mao]. Collected in Complete Library in the Four Branches of Literature. Shanghai: Shanghai Chinese Classics Publishing House.

Wang, Mingqing 王明清. 2013. *Huizhu Houlu* 挥麈后录 [Records of the Intermediate Period of the Northern and Southern Song Dynasties]. Sorted by Yan Yongcheng. Collected in Complete Song Notes. Elephant Press.

Wang, Shipeng王十朋. 2012. *Wang Shipeng Quanji* 王十朋全集 [Complete Works of Wang Shipeng]. Edited by Meixi Collection Republication Committee. Shanghai: Shanghai Chinese Classics Publishing House.

Wang, Yan 王炎. 1990. *Shuangxi Leigao* 双溪类稿 [Selected Works of Wang Yan]. Collected in Complete Library in the Four Branches of Literature. Shanghai: Shanghai Chinese Classics Publishing House.

Wang, Yingchen 汪应辰. 1990. *Wending Ji* 文定集 [Selected Works of Wang Yingchen]. Collected in Complete Library in the Four Branches of Literature. Shanghai: Shanghai Chinese Classics Publishing House.

Wang, Yinglin 王应麟. 2003. *Yuhai* 玉海 [Encyclopedia of 21 Categories]. Yangzhou: Guangling Publishing House.

Wang, Yuanlin 王元林, and Fengshun Qian 钱逢顺. 2014. "Changjiang Sanshuifu Xinyang Yuanliu Kao长江三水府信仰源流考 [A Research on the Origin and Change of Yangtze Sanshuifu Belief]". *Historical Research in Anhui* 4.

Wang, Zengyu 王曾瑜. 2006. "Zhonggu gudai De Chechuan 中国古代的车船 [Pedal Wheel Ships in Ancient China]". "*Zizhu Bian* 锱铢编 [A Collection of *Wang Zengyu's Essays*]. Baoding: Hebei University Press.

Wang, Zengyu 王曾瑜. 2006. *Zizhu Bian* 锱铢编 [A Collection of Wang Zengyu's Essays]. Baoding: Hebei University Press.

Wang, Zhi 王铚. 2008. *Moji* 默记 [The Collection in Memory of My Conquered Nation]. Sorted by Tang Fule. Collected in Complete Song Notes. Elephant Press.

Wang, Zhidao 王之道. 1990a. *Xiangshan Ji* 相山集 [Selected Works of Wang Zhidao]. Collected in Complete Library in the Four Branches of Literature. Shanghai: Shanghai Chinese Classics Publishing House.

Wang, Zhiwang 王之望. 1990b. *Hanbin Ji* 汉滨集 [Selected Works of Wang Zhiwang]. Collected in Complete Library in the Four Branches of Literature. Shanghai: Shanghai Chinese Classics Publishing House.

Wang, Zongji 王宗稷. 1990c. *Dongpo Xiansheng Nianpu* 东坡先生年谱 [Chronology of Su Dongpo]. Collected in Complete Library in the Four Branches of Literature. Shanghai: Shanghai Chinese Classics Publishing House.

Wei, Tai 魏泰. 2006. *Dongxuan Bilu* 东轩笔录 [Dongxuan Notes]. Sorted by Yan Yongcheng. Collected in Complete Song Notes. Elephant Press.

Wen, Tianxiang 文天祥. 1987. *Weng Tianxiang Quanji* 文天祥全集 [Selected Works of Wen Tianxiang]. Collated by Xiong Fei, et al. Nanchang: Jiangxi People's Publishing House.

Wu, Fei 吴芾. 1990. *Hushan Ji* 湖山集 [Selected Works of Wu Fei]. Collected in Complete Library in the Four Branches of Literature. Shanghai: Shanghai Chinese Classics Publishing House.

Wu, Qian 吴潜. 2002. *Song Tejin Zuochengxiang Xuguogong Zouyi* 宋特进左丞相许国公奏议 [Wu Qian's Proposals to the Emperor in the Southern Song Dynasty]. Collected in Continuation to Complete Library in the Four Branches of Literature. Shanghai: Shanghai Chinese Classics Publishing House.

Wu, Zeng 吴曾. 2012. *Nenggaizhai Manlu* 能改斋漫录 [Nenggaizhai Notes]. Sorted by Liu Yu. Collected in Complete Song Notes. Elephant Press.

Wu, Zimu 吴自牧. 1980. *Mengliao Lu* 梦粱录 [Accounts About the Capital]. Hangzhou: Zhejiang People's Publishing House.

Xiao, Song 萧嵩, et al. 1990. *Datang Kaiyuan Li* 大唐开元礼 [Book of Tang Dynasty's Etiquette]. Collected in Complete Library in the Four Branches of Literature. Shanghai: Shanghai Chinese Classics Publishing House.

Xie, Weixin 谢维新. 1990. *Gujin Hebi Shilei Beiyao* 古今合璧事类备要 [Compilation of Natural Phenomena and Institutions in History]. Collected in Complete Library in the Four Branches of Literature. Shanghai: Shanghai Chinese Classics Publishing House.

Xu, Yuanjie 徐元杰. 1990. *Meilin Ji* 楳埜集 [Selected Works of Xu Yuanjie]. Collected in Complete Library in the Four Branches of Literature. Shanghai: Shanghai Chinese Classics Publishing House.

Xu, Mengshen 徐梦莘. 1987. *Sanchao Beimeng Huibian* 三朝北盟会编 [Records of Wars and Actions between the Song and Jin in Three Song Emperors' Reigns]. Shanghai: Shanghai Chinese Classics Publishing House.

Xu, Song 徐松, et al. 2014. *Song Huiyao Jigao*宋会要辑稿 [The Anthology of Laws and Regulations of the Song Dynasty]. Shanghai: Shanghai Chinese Classics Publishing House.

Xu, Xuan 徐铉. 1990. *Qisheng Ji* 骑省集 [Selected Works of Xu Xuan]. Collected in Complete Library in the Four Branches of Literature. Shanghai: Shanghai Chinese Classics Publishing House.

Xue, Jixuan 薛季宣. 1990. *Langyu Ji* 浪语集 [Selected Works of Xue Jixuan]. Collected in Complete Library in the Four Branches of Literature. Shanghai: Shanghai Chinese Classics Publishing House.

Xue, Yu 薛嵎. 1990. *Yunquan Shi* 云泉诗 [Collected Poems of Xue Yu]. Collected in Complete Library in the Four Branches of Literature. Shanghai: Shanghai Chinese Classics Publishing House.

Yang, Fang 阳枋. 1990. *Zixi Ji* 字溪集 [Selected Works of Yang Fang]. Collected in Complete Library in the Four Branches of Literature. Shanghai: Shanghai Chinese Classics Publishing House.

Yang, Jie 杨杰. 1990. 无为集 [Selected Works of Yang Jie]. Collected in Complete Library in the Four Branches of Literature. Shanghai: Shanghai Chinese Classics Publishing House.

Yang, Shiqi 杨士奇, et al. 1990. *Lidai Mingchen Zouyi* 历代名臣奏议 [Memorials to the Thrones in History]. Collected in Complete Library in the Four Branches of Literature. Shanghai: Shanghai Chinese Classics Publishing House.

Yang, Wanli杨万里. 2007. *Yang Wanli Ji Jianjiao* 杨万里集笺校 [Annotations to Selected Works of Yang Wanli]. Collated by Xin Gengru. Beijing: Zhonghua Book Company.

Yang, Ziyi 杨子怡. 2006. "Shiren Lie Kuqiong, Qianli Qian Bentao: Sushi Nanbian Ruyue Luxian 诗人例苦穷, 千里遣奔逃:苏轼南贬入粤路线 [The Route of Su Shi's Demotion to Guangnan East Province]". *Journal of Leshan Normal University* 8.

Yao, Mian 姚勉. 1990. *Xuepo Ji* 雪坡集 [Selected Works of Yao Mian]. Collected in Complete Library in the Four Branches of Literature. Shanghai: Shanghai Chinese Classics Publishing House.

Ye, Mengde 叶梦得. 2002. *Shilin Zouyi* 石林奏议 [Ye Mengde's Memorials to the Emperor]. Collected in Continuation to Complete Library in the Four Branches of Literature. Shanghai: Shanghai Chinese Classics Publishing House.

Ye, Shi 叶适. 1961. *Yeshi Ji* 叶适集 [Selected Works of Ye Shi]. Punctuated and collated by Liu Gongchun, et al. Beijing: Zhonghua Book Company.

Yu, Xilu 俞希鲁. 1990. *Zhishun Zhenjiang Zhi* 至顺镇江志 [Zhishun Period Chronicles of Zhenjiang]. Collected in The Series of Chorography of the Song and Yuan Dynasties. Beijing: Zhonghua Book Company.

Yuan, Shuoyou 袁说友. 1990. *Dongtang Ji* 东塘集 [Selected Works of Yuan Shuoyou]. Collected in Complete Library in the Four Branches of Literature. Shanghai: Shanghai Chinese Classics Publishing House.

Zeng, Gong曾巩. 1990. *Yuanfen Leigao* 元丰类稿 [Selected Works of Zeng Gu]. Collected in Complete Library in the Four Branches of Literature. Shanghai: Shanghai Chinese Classics Publishing House.

Zhang, Bangji 张邦基. 1985. *Mozhuang Manlu* 墨庄漫录 [Notes from Mozhuang]. Punctuated and Collated by Kong Fanli. Beijing: Zhonghua Book Company.

Zhang, Hao 张淏. 1990. *Baoqing Kuaiji Xuzhi* 宝庆会稽续志 [Baoqing Period Continuation of the Chronicles of Kuaiji]. Collected in The Series of Chorography of the Song and Yuan Dynasties. Beijing: Zhonghua Book Company.

Zhang, Lei 张耒. 1990. *Keshan Ji* 柯山集 [Selected Works of Zhang Lei]. Collected in Complete Library in the Four Branches of Literature. Shanghai: Shanghai Chinese Classics Publishing House.

Zhang, Xuan 张铉. 1990. *Zhida Jinling Zhi* 至大金陵新志 [Zhida Period Chronicles of Jinling]. Collected in The Series of Chorography of the Song and Yuan Dynasties. Beijing: Zhonghua Book Company.

Zhang, Zehong 张泽洪. 2007. "Tangdai Daojiao De Toulong Yishi 唐代道教的投龙仪式 [The Taoist Sin-exemption Incantation Casting Ceremony in the Tang Dynasty]". *Journal of Shaanxi Normal University* 1.
Zhang, Zi 张镃. 1990. *Shi Xue Guifan* 仕学规范 [Norms of Learning and Being an Official]. Collected in Complete Library in the Four Branches of Literature. Shanghai: Shanghai Chinese Classics Publishing House.
Zhao, Bian 赵抃. 1990. *Qingxian Ji* 清献集 [Selected Works of Zhao Bian]. Collected in Complete Library in the Four Branches of Literature. Shanghai: Shanghai Chinese Classics Publishing House.
Zhao, Fan 赵蕃. 1990. *Chunxi Gao* 淳熙稿 [Chunxi Period Selected Works of Zhao Fan]. Collected in Complete Library in the Four Branches of Literature. Shanghai: Shanghai Chinese Classics Publishing House.
Zhao, Mengjian 赵孟坚. 1990. *Yizhai Wenbian* 彝斋文编 [Selected Works of Zhao Mengjian]. Collected in Complete Library in the Four Branches of Literature. Shanghai: Shanghai Chinese Classics Publishing House.
Zhao, Rushi 赵汝适. 1996. "Shanhu Shu 珊瑚树 [Coral Tree]". *Zhufan Zhi Jiaoshi* 诸蕃志校释 [Notes on Records of Foreign Countries]. Beijing: Zhonghua Book Company.
Zhao, Shankuo 赵善括. 1990. *Yingzhai Zazhu* 应斋杂著 [Selected Works of Zhao Shankuo]. Collected in Complete Library in the Four Branches of Literature. Shanghai: Shanghai Chinese Classics Publishing House.
Zhao, Yanwei 赵彦卫. 2013. *Yunlu Manchao* 云麓漫钞 [Zhao Yanwei's Notes on Historical Records]. Sorted by Zhu, Xuqiang. Collected in Complete Song Notes. Elephant Press.
Zhao, Ye 赵晔. n.d. *Wuyue Chunqiu* 吴越春秋 [History of the Wu and Yue States in the Spring and Autumn Period]. Collected in the First Version of Assembled Printings from the Four Divisions. n.p.
Zhao, Yongchun 赵永春. 1995. *Fengshi Liao Jin Xingchenglu* 奉使辽金行程录 [Travelogue of the Mission to Liao and Jin Kingdoms]. Changchun: Jilin Literature and History Press.
Zheng, Gangzhong 郑刚中. 1990. *Beishan Ji* 北山集 [Selected Works of Zheng Gangzhong]. Collected in Complete Library in the Four Branches of Literature. Shanghai: Shanghai Chinese Classics Publishing House.
Zheng, Xie 郑獬. 1990. *Yunxi Ji* 郧溪集 [Selected Works of Zheng Xie]. Collected in Complete Library in the Four Branches of Literature. Shanghai: Shanghai Chinese Classics Publishing House.
Zheng, Yao 郑瑶, et al. 1990. *Jingding Yanzhou Xu Zhi* 景定严州续志 [Jingding Period Continuation of the Chronicles of Yanzhou]. Collected in The Series of Chorography of the Song and Yuan Dynasties. Beijing: Zhonghua Book Company.
Zhou, Bida 周必大. 1990. *Wenzhong Ji* 文忠集 [Selected Works of Wenzhong]. Collected in Complete Library in the Four Branches of Literature. Shanghai: Shanghai Chinese Classics Publishing House.
Zhou, Hui 周辉撰. 1994. *Qingbo Zazhi Jiaozhu* 清波杂志校注 [Collected Works from Qingbo Annotated Version]. Beijing: Zhonghua Book Company.
Zhou, Linzhi 周麟之. 1990. *Hailing Ji* 海陵集 [Selected Works of Zhou Linzhi]. Collected in Complete Library in the Four Branches of Literature. Shanghai: Shanghai Chinese Classics Publishing House.
Zhou, Mi 周密. 1983. *Qidong Yeyu* 齐东野语 [Wild Talks of Eastern Qi]. Punctuated and collated by Zhang Maopeng. Beijing: Zhonghua Book Company.
Zhou, Qüfei 周去非. 1999. *Lingwai Daida Jiaozhu* 岭外代答校注 [Notes from the Land Beyond the Passes]. Collated by Yang Wuquan. Beijing: Zhonghua Book Company.
Zhou, Yinggu 周应谷. 1990. *Jingding Jiankang Zhi* 景定建康志 [Jingding Period Chronicles of Jiankang]. Collected in The Series of Chorography of the Song and Yuan Dynasties. Beijing: Zhonghua Book Company.

Zhou, Zizhi 周紫芝. 1990. *Taicang Timi Ji* 太仓稊米集 [Selected Works of Zhou Zizhi]. Collected in Complete Library in the Four Branches of Literature. Shanghai: Shanghai Chinese Classics Publishing House.

Zhu, Fu 朱辅. 1990. *Ximan Cong Xiao* 溪蛮丛笑 [Ethnography of Ximan]. Collected in Complete Library in the Four Branches of Literature. Shanghai: Shanghai Chinese Classics Publishing House.

Zhu, Li 朱翌. 2008. *Yijueliao Zaji* 猗觉寮杂记 [Yijueliao Notes]. Sorted by Zhang Kai and Jiang Hanchun. Collected in Complete Song Notes. Elephant Press.

Zhu, Mu 祝穆. 1990. *Gujin Shiwen Leiju* 古今事文类聚 [Collection of Historical Records]. Collected in Complete Library in the Four Branches of Literature. Shanghai: Shanghai Chinese Classics Publishing House.

Zhu, Mu 祝穆. 2003. *Fangyu Shenglan* 方舆胜览 [Chronicles of Lin'an]. Edited by Shi Hejin. Beijing: Zhonghua Book Company.

Zhu, Xi 朱熹. 2010. *Hui'an Xiansheng Zhuwengong Ji* 晦庵先生朱文公文集 [Selected Works of Zhu Xi]. Punctuated and collated by Liu Yongxiang, et al. Shanghai: Shanghai Chinese Classics Publishing House. Heifei: Anhui Education Publishing House.

Zhu, Yi 朱溢. 2014. *Shi Bangguo Zhishenzhi:Tang Zhi Beisong Jili Bianqian Yanjiu* 事邦国之神祇:唐至北宋吉礼变迁研究 [Offerings Sacrifices to the Deities of State: The Propitious Rituals in Tang and Northern Song China]. Shanghai: Shanghai Chinese Classics Publishing House.

Zhuang, Chuo 庄绰. 2008. *Jilei Bian* 鸡肋编 [Complementary Notes to Official Records]. Sorted by Xia Guangxing. Collected in Complete Song Notes. Elephant Press.

Zhuang, Weiji 庄为玑, and Zhuan Jinghui 庄景辉. 1980. "Quanzhou Songchuan Mupai Muqian Kaoshi 泉州宋船木牌木签考释 [The Interpretation of the Wooden Slips in the Song Boat Unearthed in Quanzhou]". *Journal of Xiamen University* 1.

Zou, Hao 邹浩. 1990. *Daoxiang Ji* 道乡集 [Selected Works of Zou Hao]. Collected in Complete Library in the Four Branches of Literature. Shanghai: Shanghai Chinese Classics Publishing House.

Xu, Jing 徐兢. 2006. *Xuanhe Fengshi Gaoli Tujing* 宣和奉使高丽图经 [Xuanhe Period Maps and Records About Goryeo]. Sorted by Yu Yunguo. Collected in Complete Song Notes. Elephant Press.

Xu, Lun 许纶. 1990. *She Zhai Ji* 涉斋集 [Selected Works of Xu Lun]. Collected in Complete Library in the Four Branches of Literature. Shanghai: Shanghai Chinese Classics Publishing House.

Xu, Luqing 徐鹿卿. 1990. Qingzheng Cungao 清正存稿 [Extant Manucripts of Xu Luqing]. Collected in Complete Library in the Four Branches of Literature. Shanghai: Shanghai Chinese Classics Publishing House.

Yuan, Xie 袁燮. 1990. *Jiezhai Ji* 絜斋集 [Selected works of Yuan Xie]. Collected in Complete Library in the Four Branches of Literature. Shanghai: Shanghai Chinese Classics Publishing House.

Yuan, Xingzong 员兴宗. 1990. *Jiuhua Ji* 九华集 [Selected Works of Yuan Xingzong]. Collected in Complete Library in the Four Branches of Literature. Shanghai: Shanghai Chinese Classics Publishing House.

Zhang, Shizheng 张师正. 1990. *Kuo Yi Zhi* 括异志 [Stories of the Strange]. Collected in Complete Library in the Four Branches of Literature. Shanghai: Shanghai Chinese Classics Publishing House.

Zhang, Shou 张守. 1990. *Piling Ji* 毘陵集 [Selected Works of Zhang Shou]. Collected in Complete Library in the Four Branches of Literature. Shanghai: Shanghai Chinese Classics Publishing House.

Zhang, Shunmin 张舜民. 1990. *Hua Man Ji* 画墁集 [Selected Works of Zhang Shunmin]. Collected in Complete Library in the Four Branches of Literature. Shanghai: Shanghai Chinese Classics Publishing House.

Postscript

"Book knowledge, like seawater, is rich and diverse. It is impossible for a person to read all the books in one's limited life. Therefore, you should focus on what you need to know." In his "Reply to Wang Xiang", Su Shi stated "there is no shortcut to learning" and it is better for one to specialize in a particular area of knowledge. In Su Shi's opinion, in the vast ocean of books, one should not dabble at will, nor be greedy for perfection. It is advisable to explore one area at a time without distraction, in order to achieve a comprehensive understanding of the field through multiple explorations. Based on this perspective, I have conducted three projects on the Song Dynasty's overseas trade in the ocean of historical records: my doctoral dissertation "A Research on Overseas Trade in the Song Dynasty", my postdoctoral work report "A Research on Tea Law in the Song Dynasty" and "A Panoramic View of the Song Dynasty through the Lens of Shipbuilding Industry."

The third project on the overseas trade of the Song Dynasty examined three topics: the financial history of the Song Dynasty, the tributary system of the Song Dynasty, and the shipbuilding industry of the Song Dynasty. Data collection on these three topics was almost completed between 2004 and around 2010. As the deadline for the project sponsored by the National Social Science Fund of China in 2010 approached, the paper titled "Research on the Tributary Trade in the Song Dynasty" was written. After revision, it was published as a book titled *Research on the Tributary System of the Song Dynasty* in January 2014. In September 2013, the book *The Financial History of the Song Dynasty* was completed and published.

The paper titled "On the Pedal-Wheel Ship and Its Historical Fate in the Southern Song Dynasty" (published in *Academic Monthly*, Vol. 3, 2013) was my first research report about the shipbuilding industry in the Song Dynasty. In 2014, a contract was signed with Shanghai People's Publishing House for the publication of the book *A Panoramic View of the Song Dynasty through the Lens of the Shipbuilding Industry*, and it was planned to be delivered by the end of that year. The purpose of pre-signing the contract was to put pressure on myself to complete the writing. However, new problems arose during the writing process, such as the need for supplemental materials related to marine knowledge and water belief, among others. Additionally,

C. Huang, *A Panoramic View of the Song Dynasty Through the Lens of Shipbuilding Industry*, https://doi.org/10.1007/978-981-97-6128-9

the writing was intermittent due to job shifts, and the final draft was delayed until May 2016.

My monograph, *A Panoramic View of the Song Dynasty through the Lens of Shipbuilding Industry*, was selected and included in the National Achievements Library of Philosophy and Social Sciences, thanks to the application by Shanghai People's Publishing House. Ms. Zhou Zhen, the editor-in-charge of this book, devoted a significant amount of time to applying for acceptance by the library, editing the manuscript, and overseeing its publication. The reviewers from the library provided valuable suggestions for the modification of the book.

During the final draft phase, I received great assistance from Dr. Tian Xiaozhong and postgraduate students Hu Yan, Xiang Lulin, Dong Shilin, Kou Bowen, Chen Yana, and Li Liangji, who were affiliated with the Institute of Chinese Economic History at Yunnan University. Throughout the research process, I received generous support from Professor Yu Yunguo, Professor Zeng Weihua, Professor Liu Zikui, and others. Certain portions of the book were well-received and published in several academic journals during the writing process (due to limited printing space, I am unable to mention them here).

Towards the end of this project, I was honored to be invited by Professor Ma Jianchun to join his major research project, sponsored by the National Social Science Fund of China, titled "Research on the Ancient Middle-East Merchants Along the 'Maritime Silk Road'" (No. 16ZDA118). This opportunity allowed me to continue my research on marine and shipbuilding aspects of the Song Dynasty. I would like to express my heartfelt gratitude to all those who generously offered their help and support throughout this endeavor.

Huang Chunyan
March 3, 2016

Bibliography

Cao, Yanyue 曹彦约. *Changgu Ji* 昌谷集 [Cangguo Notes]. Collected in Complete Library in the Four Branches of Literature. Shanghai: Shanghai Chinese Classics Publishing House.

Cai, Xiang 蔡襄. 2008. *Lizhi Pu* 荔枝谱 [Book of Litchi]. Punctuated and collated by Huang Chunyan and Zhan Xiumei. Collected in the Economic Records of the Song Dynasty. Lanzhou: Gansu People's Publishing House.

Chaoye Qun Zai 朝野群载 [Edited by Kuroita Katsumi]. 1938. Edited by Kuroita Katsumi. Collected in the Revised Edition of Collection of Japanese Historical Records. Tokyo: Yoshikawa Koubunkan.

Chen, Bixian 陈璧显. 2001. *Zhongguo Dayunheshi* 中国大运河史 [A History of the Grand Canal in China]. Beijing: Zhonghua Book Company.

Chen, Bo 陈波. 2010. "Haiyun Chuanhu Yu Yuanmo Haikou De Shengcheng海运船户与元末海寇的生成 [Boatmen of Sea Transportation and Formation of Pirates in Late Yuan Dynasty]". *Historical Review* 2.

Chen, Chengde 陈承德, and Hong Chengqi 洪成器. 1960. "Fujian Shibazhong Muzhucai Pingheng Hanshuilü De Yanjiu 福建18种木竹材平衡含水率的研究 [The Study on the Equilibrium Moisture Content of 18 kinds of Wood and Bamboo in Fujian]". *Journal of Fujian College of Forestry* 1.

Chen, Gaohua 陈高华 and Wu Tai吴泰. 1978. "Guanyu Quanzhouwan Chutu Haichuan De JigeWenti 关于泉州湾出土海船的几个问题, [Several Views on the sea vessels unearthed in Quanzhou Bay]". *Cultural Relics* 4.

Chen, Jing 陈晶. 1982. "Jiangsu Wujinxian Chutu Haidai Muchuan 江苏武进县出土汉代木船 [The Han Wooden Boat Unearthed in Wujin County of Jiangsu]". *Archaeology* 4.

Chen, Jing 陈敬. 2008. *Chen Shi Xiangpu* 陈氏香谱 [Chen's Incense Divination]. Punctuated and collated by Huang Chunyan and Zhan Xiumei. Collected in the Economic Records of Song Dynasty. Lanzhou: Gansu People's Publishing House.

Chen, Liang 陈亮. 1990. *Longchuan Ji* 龙川集 [Anthology of Chen Liang]. Collected in Complete Library in the Four Branches of Literature. Shanghai: Shanghai Chinese Classics Publishing House.

Chen, Lunjiong 陈伦炯. 1990. *Haiguo Wenjian Lu* 海国闻见录 [My Trips to Foreign Countries]. Collected in Complete Library in the Four Branches of Literature. Shanghai: Shanghai Chinese Classics Publishing House.

C. Huang, *A Panoramic View of the Song Dynasty Through the Lens of Shipbuilding Industry*, https://doi.org/10.1007/978-981-97-6128-9

Chen, Shoucheng 陈守成. 2010. *Songchao Bianhe Qingmingshanghetu Chuanbo Jiegou* 宋朝汴河船:〈清明上河图〉船舶解构 [Boats on the Bianhe River of the Song Dynasty: Deconstruction of Boats on the Scroll of Riverside Scene at Qingming Festival]. Shanghai: Shanghai Bookstore Publishing House.

Chen, Shunyu 陈舜俞. 1990. *Duguan Ji* 都官集 [Selected Works of Chen Shunyu]. Collected in Complete Library in the Four Branches of Literature. Shanghai: Shanghai Chinese Classics Publishing House.

Cheng, Minsheng 程民生. 2008. *Songdai Wujia Yanjiu* 宋代物价研究 [A Study on Prices in the Song Dynasty]. Beijing: People's Publishing House.

Dun, He顿贺and Cheng Wenhui 程雯慧. 2004. "Zhongguo Gudai Chuanbo De Zaoxing Tezheng Yanjiu 中国古代船舶的造型特征研究 [A Study of Shapes and Functions of Ancient Chinese Ships]". *Journal of Wuhan University of Technology* 3.

Fan, Chengda 范成大. 1981. *Fanshihu Ji*范石湖集 [Anthology of Fan Chengda]. Shanghai: Shanghai Chinese Classics Publishing House.

Fan, Chengda 范成大. 1990. *Wujun Zhi* 吴郡志 [Chronicles of Wujun]. Collected in the Series of Chorography of Song and Yuan Dynasty. Beijing: Zhonghua Book Company.

Fang, Shao 方勺. 2013. *Bozhai Bian* 泊宅编 [Selected Works of Fangshao]. Collected in Complete Song Notes. Elephant Press.

Feng, Chengjun 冯承钧. 2005. *Zhongguo Nanyang Jiaotongshi* 中国南洋交通史 [A History of South China Sea Traffic]. Shanghai: Shanghai Chinese Classics Publishing House.

Feng, Hanyong 冯汉镛. 1986. "Songchao Guonei Haidao Kao 宋朝国内海道考 [Studies on Offshore Routes in the Song Dynasty]". *Literature and History* 26.

Gan, Ming-feng 干鸣丰. 2005. "Gudai Hedu Chongsi Zhidu Jiexi 古代河渎崇祀制度解析 [An Analysis on the System of Offering Sacrifices to the God of the Yellow River]". *Journal of Southwest Minzu University* 11.

Ge, Jinfang 葛金芳. 2003. "Liangsong Dongnan Yanhai Diqu Haiyang Fazhan Luxiang Lunlue两宋东南沿海地区海洋发展路向论略 [A Discussion about the Developing Tendency Towards the Southeast Foreland in the Song Dynasty]". *Journal of Hubei University* 5.

Gu, Gengyou 谷更有. 2000. "Shilun Tangdai Chuanshang De Shehui Shenghuo 试论唐代船商的社会生活 [Social Life of the Ship Merchants in Tang Dynasty]". *Thinking* 6.

Han, Yuanji 韩元吉. 1985. *Nanjian Jiayi Gao* 南涧甲乙稿 [Anthology of Han Yuanji]. Collected in Collectanea of the Four Categories 1st edn.

Hu, Hong 胡宏. 1990. *Wufeng Ji* 五峰集 [Selected Works of Hu Hong]. Collected in Complete Library in the Four Branches of Literature. Shanghai: Shanghai Chinese Classics Publishing House.

Hu, Su 胡宿. 1985. *Wengong Ji* 文恭集 [Selected Works of Hu Su]. Collected in the Series of Ancient Classics 1st edn. Beijing: Zhonghua Book Company.

Hu, Yin 胡寅. 1990. *Feiran Ji* 斐然集 [Selected Works of Hu Yin]. Collected in Complete Library in the Four Branches of Literature. Shanghai: Shanghai Chinese Classics Publishing House.

Hu, Zhaoxi 胡昭曦. 1992. *Songmeng(Yuan) Guanxishi* 宋蒙(元)关系史 [A History of the Relationship between Song and Mongol-Yuan]. Chengdu: Sichuan University Press.

Huang, Chunyan 黄纯艳. 2009. "Songchao Yu Jiaozhi De Maoyi 宋朝与交趾的贸易 [Trade with Cochin in the Song Dynasty]". *Journal of Chinese Social and Economic History* 2.

Huang, Chunyan 黄纯艳. 2011. "Songchao Souji Jingwai Xinxi De Tujing 宋朝搜集境外信息的途径 [Channels for Gathering Information abroad in the Song Dynasty]". *Journal of Peking University*.

Jiang, Xidong 姜锡东. 2000. "Songdai Liangshang De Goucheng, Neibu Fenggong Yu Jingying Zhuangkuang 宋代粮商的成分、内部分工与状况经营 [The Composition, Division of Labor and Operation of Grain Merchants During the Song Dynasty]". *Researches In Chinese Economic History* 3.

Jiangnan Tongzhi 江南通志 [Chronicles of Jiangnan]. 1990. Edited by Zhao Hongen and et al. Collected in Complete Library in the Four Branches of Literature. Shanghai: Shanghai Chinese Classics Publishing House.

Jiangxi Neihe Hangyunshi(Gu,Jin Bufen) 江西内河航运史(古、近代部分)[Jiangxi History of Inland Shipping (Ancient and Modern Sections)]. 1991. Edited by Shen, Xingjing. Beijing: China Communications Press.

Jiangxi Tongzhi 江西通志 [Chronicles of Jiangxi]. 1990. Edited by Xie Min and et al. Collected in Complete Library in the Four Branches of Literature. Shanghai: Shanghai Chinese Classics Publishing House.

Jiu Jia Jizhu Du Shi 九家集注杜诗 [Commentaries on Du Fu's Poems]. Edited by Guo Zhida. Collected in Complete Library in the Four Branches of Literature. Shanghai: Shanghai Chinese Classics Publishing House.

Li, Qingxin李庆新. 2012. "Nansong Haiwai Maoyi Zhongzhong De Waixiaoci, Qianbi, Jinshu Zhipin Ji Qitang Wenti—Jiyu 'Nanhai I' Hao Chenchuan Chushui Yiwu De Chubu Kaocha' 南宋海外贸易中的外销瓷、钱币、金属制品及其他问题—基于"南海 I号沉船出水遗物的初步考察[The Export Porcelain, Copper Coins, Metal Artifacts and other Problems in Southern Song's Oversea Trade—A Preliminary Study Based on the Wreckship 'Nanhai I']". *Academic Monthly* 9.

Li, Bozhong 李伯重. 2000. *Jiangnan De Zaoqi Gongyehua* 江南的早期工业化 [Early Industrialization in the South of the Yangtze River]. Beijing: Social Sciences Academic Press (CHINA).

Li, Cheng 李铖. 2010. "Zhongguo Guchuan Jiegou Tedian Jiqi Dianxing Jiegou Ge Qiangdu Fenxi 中国古船结构特点及其典型结构的强度分析 [The Structural Characteristics of Chinese Ancient Ship and Strength Analysis of the Typical Structure]". Master's diss., Wuhan University of Technology.

Li, Gang 李纲. 2004. *Li Gang Quanji* 李纲全集 [The Complete Works of Li Gang]. Changsha: Yuelu Press.

Li, Hongqi 李弘祺. 2013. "Nansong Xihu Shang De Youchuan You Duoda—Lun Songdai Chuanzhi Daxiao De Danwei Yu Fangfa 南宋西湖上的游船有多大——论宋代量度船只大小的单位与方法, 载辛薇主编《南宋史及南宋都城临安研究(续上)[The Size of the Cruise Ships on the West Lake in the Southern Song Dynasty—The Units and Ways of Measuring Ships in the Song Dynasty]". *Sequels to the Researches on the Southern Song Dynasty History and the Capital City Lin'an* 1. Beijing: People's Publishing House.

Li, Ruchi 李如篪. 1990. *Dongyuan* 东园丛说 [Dongyuan Notes]. Collected in Complete Library in the Four Branches of Literature. Shanghai: Shanghai Chinese Classics Publishing House.

Liang, Kejia 梁克家. 1990. *Chunxi Sanshan Zhi* 淳熙三山志 [Chunxi Period Chronicles of Fuzhou]. Collected in The Series of Chorography of the Song and Yuan Dynasties. Beijing: Zhonghua Book Company.

Lin, Kaiming 林开明. 1994. *Fujian Hangyunshi (Gu,Jindai Bufen)* 福建航运史 (古、近代部分) [A History of Shipping in Fujian (Ancient and Modern Sections)]. Beijing: China Communications Press.

Liu, Chang 刘敞. 1990. *Gongshi Ji* 公是集 [Selected Works of Liu Chang]. Collected in Complete Library in the Four Branches of Literature. Shanghai: Shanghai Chinese Classics Publishing House.

Liu, Hongyou 刘宏友 and Cheng Xu 徐诚. 1995. *Hubei Hangyunshi* 湖北航运史 [A History of Shipping in Hubei]. Beijing: China Communications Press.

Liu, Kezhuang 刘克庄. *Houcun Xiansheng Daquanji* 后村先生大全集 [The Complete Works of Liu Kezhuang]. Collected in Collectanea of the Four Categories 1st edn.

Liu, Minzhong 刘敏中. 1990. *Ping Song Lu* 平宋录 [Records of Pacifying the Southern Song]. Collected in Complete Library in the Four Branches of Literature. Shanghai: Shanghai Chinese Classics Publishing House.

Ma, Yi 马依 and Ruiping Shu 舒瑞萍. 1991. *Guangxi Hangyunshi* 广西航运史 [A History of Shipping in Guangxi]. Beijing: China Communications Press.

Ming Yitong Zhi 明一统志 [Chronicles of the Ming Dynasty]. 1990. Edited by Li Xian and et al. Collected in Complete Library in the Four Branches of Literature. Shanghai: Shanghai Chinese Classics Publishing House.

Nai, Deweng 耐得翁. 1990. *Ducheng Jisheng* 都城纪胜 [Records of Prosperous Lin'an]. Collected in Complete Library in the Four Branches of Literature. Shanghai: Shanghai Chinese Classics Publishing House.

Nanjing Museum 南京博物院. 1974. "Rugao Faxian De Tangdai Muchuan 如皋发现的唐代木船 [The Wooden Boat of the Tang Dynasty Unearthed in Rugao]". *Cultural Relics* 5.

Nansong Ji Nansong Ducheng Lin'an Yanjiu (Xiu Shang) [Sequel 1 to the Researches on the Southern Song History and Its Capital City Lin'an]. 2013. Edited by Xin We. Beijing: People's Publishing House.

Ouyang, Xiu 欧阳修. 1975. *Xin Wudai Shi* 新五代史 [Historical Records of the Five Dynasties] Beijing: Zhonghua Book Company.

Pan, Jixun 潘季驯. 1990. *Hefang Yilan* 河防一览 [Records of Flood Control]. Collected in Complete Library in the Four Branches of Literature. Shanghai: Shanghai Chinese Classics Publishing House.

Pang, Yuanying 庞元英. 2014. *Wenchang Zalu* 文昌杂录 [Informal Essays of Pang Yuanying]. Sorted by Jin Yuan. Collected in Complete Song Notes. Elephant Press.

Qi, Jixiang 齐吉祥. 2005. "Zhongguo Gudai Chuanbo De Liangxiang Zhongda Faming—Duo He Shuimigecang 中国古代船舶的两项重大发明——舵和水密隔舱 [Two Major Inventions of Ancient Chinese Ships—Boats and Water-tight Bulkheads]". *History Teaching*, No. 4, 2005.

Qi, Qingfu 祁庆富Changling Zheng 郑长铃, and Yuling Ding 丁毓铃. 2009. "Shuimigecang Haichuan Lishi Wehhua Yichan Yanjiu 水密隔舱海船历史文化遗产研究 [Study of the Historical and Cultural Heritage of Watertight Compartment Sea Crafts]". *Journal of Dalian University* 2.

Quan Song Shi 全宋诗 [Collection of Song Poetry]. 1996. Beijing: Peking University Press.

Quanzhou Haiwai Jiaotong Shiliao Huibian 泉州海外交通史料汇编 [A Compilation of Studies on Maritime History in Quanzhou]. 1983. Edited by Quanzhou Maritime Museum. Quanzhou: China Society for Maritime History Studies.

Shan, E 单锷. *Wuzhong Shuili Shu* 吴中水利书 [Field Study of Water Regime in Wuxian County]. Collected in Complete Library in the Four Branches of Literature. Shanghai: Shanghai Chinese Classics Publishing House.

Shen, Guangyao 沈光耀. 1985. *Zhongguo Gudai Duiwai Maoyishi* 中国古代对外贸易史 [A History of Foreign Trade in Ancient China]. Guangdong People's Publishing House.

Shen, Yushui 沈玉水. 1983. "Cong Chuanzhou Songchuan Yiwu Kan Songdai Haiyuan De Shenghuo 从泉州宋船遗物看宋代海员的生活 [The Life of Sailors Presented by the relics of Song Ships Unearthed in Quanzhou]". *Navigation* 1.

Shi, E 施谔. 1990. *Chunyou Linan Zhi*淳祐临安志 [Chunyou Period Chronicles of Lin'an]. Collected in The Series of Chorography of the Song and Yuan Dynasties. Beijing: Zhonghua Book Company.

Shi, Wenying 释文莹. 2014. *Yuhu Qinghua Shi* 玉壶清话释 [Insights on History Written in Yuhu]. Collected in Complete Song Notes. Elephant Press.

Shi, Yanzhi 施彦执. 2008. *Beichuang Zhiguo Lu*北窗炙輠录 [Talks and Notes of Song Dynasty]. Sorted by Yu Yunguo and et al. Collected in Complete Song Notes. Elephant Press.

Sima, Guang司马光. n.d. *Wenguo Wenzheng Sima Gong Wenji* 温国文正司马公文集 [Selected Works of Sima Guang]. Collected in Collectanea of the Four Categories 1st edn.

*Sichuan Neihe Hangyunshi*四川内河航运史(古、近代部分 [A History of Inland Shipping in Sichuan (Ancient and Modern Sections]. 1989. Edited by Wang Shaoquan. Chengdu: Sichuan People's Publishing House.

Sichuan Tongzhi 四川通志 [Chronicles of Sichuan]. 1990. Edited by Huang Yangui and et al. Collected in Complete Library in the Four Branches of Literature. Shanghai: Shanghai Chinese Classics Publishing House.

Sishuiqianfu 四水潜夫. 1981. *Wulin Jiu Shi* 武林旧事 [Tales of Martial Arts]. Hangzhou: Xihu Publishing House.

Song Da Zhaoling *Ji* 宋大诏令集 [Collections of Song Dynasty's Major Imperial Edicts]. 1962. Beijing: Zhonghua Book Company.

Su, Guo 苏过. 2012. *Suguo Shiwen Bianian Jianzhu* 苏过诗文编年笺注 [Annotations to Su Guo's Anthology]. Beijing: Zhonghua Book Company.

Su, Shunqin苏舜钦. *Sun Xueshi Ji* 苏学士集 [Selected Works of Su Shunqin]. Collected in Collectanea of the Four Categories 1st edn.

Su, Zhe 苏辙. 2013. *Longchuan Lüezhi* 龙川略志 [Works of Su Zhe Written in Longchuan]. Sorted by Sun Fanli. Collected in Complete Song Notes. Elephant Press.

Sun, Guangqi 孙光圻. 1989. *Zhongguo Gudai Hangyun Shi*中国古代航海史 [A History of Navigation in Ancient China]. Beijing: China Ocean Press.

Tang, Chunsheng 唐春生. 2013. "Songdai De Tongyou 宋代的桐油 [Tung oil in the Song Dynasty]". *Agricultural Archaeology* 3.

Tao, Zongyi 陶宗仪. 1985. Chuog*eng Lu* 辍耕录 [Historical Verification of the Yuan and Song Dynasties]. Beijing: Zhonghua Book Company.

Wang, Guanzhuo 王冠倬. 1983. "Cong Wenwu Ziliao Kan Zhonggu Gudai Zaochuan Jishu De Fazhan 从文物资料看中国古代造船技术的发展 [The Development of Shipbuilding Technology in Ancient China Presented by Cultural Relics]". *Bulletin of the National Museum of Chinese History*.

Wang, Guanzhuo 王冠倬. 2000. *Zhongguo Gudai Chuanpu*中国古船图谱 [A Pictorial History of Ancient Chinese Boats]. Beijing: SDX Joint Publishing Company.

Wang, Qingsong 王青松. 2004. "Nansong Haifang Chutan南宋海防初探 [A Tentative Study on the Coast Defense of the Southern Song Dynasty]". *China's Borderland History and Geography Studies* 3.

Wang, Rongguo 王荣国. 2012. " Songdai Haiyangxing Shenling Xinyang De Miaoyu — Fuqing Zhaolingmiao宋代海洋性神灵信仰的庙宇——福清昭灵庙 [A Song Temple Worshiping the Sea-god — Zhaoling Temple in Fuqing]". *Fujian Wenbo* 3.

Wang, Rui-ming 王瑞明. 1987. "Songdai De Zaochuanye Yu Chuanhu 宋代的造船业与船户[Shipbuilding and Boatmen in the Song Dynasty]". *Academic Monthly* 3.

Wang, Shucai 王树才. 1988. *Hebeisheng Hangyunshi* 河北省航运史 [A History of Shipping in Hebei Province]. Beijing: China Communications Press.

Wang, Yuanlin 王元林. 2006. *Guojia Jisi Yu Haishangsilu Yiji — Guangzhou Nanhai Shenmiao Yanjiu* 国家祭祀与海上丝路遗迹——广州南海神庙研究 [State Sacrifices and Relics Along the Maritime Silk Road — Researches on the Nanhai God Temple in Guangzhou]. Beijing: Zhonghua Book Company.

Wang, Zao 汪藻. *Fuxiji* 浮溪集 [Selected Works of Wang Zao]. Collected in Collectanea of the Four Categories, 1st ed.

Wang, Zhengshu 王正书. 1983. "Chuanyanghe Guchuan Fajue Jianbao 川扬河古船发掘简报 [A Briefing on the Excavation of an Ancient Boat in the Chuanyang River]". *Cultural Relics* 7.

Wang, Zhengshu 王正书. 1984. "Chuanyanghe Guchuan Jiegou De Tezheng Ji Lishi Yiyi 川扬河古船结构的特征及历史意义 [Construction Features of the Ancient Boat Excavated in Chuanyang River and Its Historical significance]". *Archaeology* 7.

Wang, Zhi 王质. 1990. *Xueshan Jin* 雪山集 [Selected Works of Wang Zhi]. Collected in Complete Library in the Four Branches of Literature. Shanghai: Shanghai Chinese Classics Publishing House.

Wei, Guofeng 魏国锋, et al. 2013. "Tongyou Huijiang De Wuli Xingneng Yu Xianwei Jiegou 桐油灰浆材料的物理性能与显微结构 [Physical Properties and Microscopic Structure of Tung Oil-Lime Putty]". *Journal of Building Materials* 6.

Wei, Liaoweng 魏了翁. *Heshan Xiansheng Daquan Wenji* 鹤山先生大全文集 [Anthology of Heshan's Literary Works]. Collected in Collectanea of the Four Categories, 1st ed.

Wenzhang Bianti Huixuan 文章辨体汇选 [Selected Works of Various Literary Genres]. 1990. Edited by He Fuzheng. Collected in Complete Library in the Four Branches of Literature. Shanghai: Shanghai Chinese Classics Publishing House.

Xi, Longfei 席龙飞. 1994. "Dui HanguoXin'an Haidi De Chenchuan De Yanjiu 对韩国新安海底沉船的研究 [A Study of the Sunken Ship in Sinan of South Korea]". *Journal of Maritime History Studies* 2.

Xi, Longfei 席龙飞. 2001. “Zhongguo Zaochuan Jishu De Shijiexing Gongxian 中国造船技术的世界性贡献 [The Contribution of Chinese Shipbuilding Technology to the World]”. *Journal of Journal of Maritime History Studies* 2.

Xia, Shihua 夏时华. 2011. “Songdai Xiangyao Zousi Maoyi 宋代香药走私贸易 [Aromatic Drug Smuggling in the Song Dynasty]”. *Social Sciences in Yunnan* 6.

Xu, Hai 徐海. 2012. “Wuzixiu Xinyang Yanjiu 伍子胥信仰研究 [The Study of the Faith of Wu Zixu] ”. Master’s diss., Lanzhou University.

Xu, Sanjian 徐三见. 1989. “Jiangdu, Huaidu Fenghao Kao 江渎、淮渎封号考 [On The Titles Given to the Gods of Yangtze River and Huaihe River]”. *Social Science Front* 2.

Xue, Juzheng 薛居正. 1976. *Jiu Wudai Shi* 旧五代史 [Old History of the Five Dynasties]. Beijing: Zhonghua Book Company.

Yang, Wanli杨万里. 2006. *Yang Wanli Shiwen Ji* 杨万里诗文集 [Collected Poems of Yang Wanli]. Nanchang: Jiangxi People’s Publishing House

Yang, You 杨槱. 2005. *Fanchuan Shi* 帆船史 [A History of Sailing Ships]. Shanghai: Shanghai Jiao Tong University Press.

Ye, Xianen 叶显恩. 1989. *Guangdong Hangyun Shi (Gudai Bufen)* 广东航运史(古代部分)[A History of Shipping in Guangdong (The Ancient Part)]. Beijing: China Communications Press.

Yuan, Xiaochun 袁晓春. 2006. “Penglai Sansou Guchuan Fajue Jiebao 蓬莱3艘古船发掘简报 [A Brief Report on Three Ancient Boats Unearthed in Penglai of Shandong]”. *Journal of Maritime History Studies* 2.

Yue, Ke 岳珂. 1985. *Ting Shi* 桯史 [The History Book Written on a Bedside Table]. Punctuated and collated by Wu Qiming. Beijing: Zhonghua Book Company.

*Yunhe Fanggu*运河访古 [Exploring the Canals in the Tang and Song Dynasties]. 1986. The Exploration Team of the Tang and Song Canals. Shanghai: Shanghai People’s Publishing House.

Zeng, Gongliang 曾公亮, et al. 1990. *Wujing Zongyao* 武经总要 [The General Record of Military Affairs]. Collected in Complete Library in the Four Branches of Literature. Shanghai: Shanghai Chinese Classics Publishing House.

Zeng, Minxing 曾敏行. 1990. *Duxing Zazhi* 独醒杂志 [Selected Works of Zeng Minxing]. Sorted by Zhu Jieren. Collected in Complete Song Notes. Elephant Press.

Zhang, Bincun 张彬村. 2009. “Songdai Minnan Haimao Xisu De Xingcheng宋代闽南海贸习俗的形成 [Maritime Tradition in Minnan during the Song Dynasty]”. *Journal of Maritime History Studies* 1.

Zhang, Cong 张聪. 2015. *Xin Wanli Lu: Songdai De Lüxing Yu Wenhua* 行万里路:宋代的旅行与文化 [Transformative Journeys: Travel and Culture in Song China]. Hangzhou: Zhejiang University Press.

Zhang, Fangping 张方平. 1998. *Lequan Xiansheng Wenji* 乐全先生文集 [Selected Works of Zhang Fangping]. Beijing: Bibliography and Document Publishing House.

Zhang, Shengcheng 张圣城. 1989. *Henan Hangyunshi* 河南航运史 [A History of Shipping in He’nan]. Beijing: China Communications Press.

Zhao, Ding 赵鼎. 1990. *Zhongzheng Dewen Ji* 忠正德文集 [Selected Works of Zhao Ding]. Collected in Complete Library in the Four Branches of Literature. Shanghai: Shanghai Chinese Classics Publishing House.

Zhao, Ruyu. 1999. *Songchao Zhuchen Zouyi* 宋朝诸臣奏议 [Anthology of the Song Dynasty’s Memorials]. Shanghai: Shanghai Chinese Classics Publishing House.

Zhen, Dexiu 真德秀. *Xishan Xiansheng Zhenwenzhonggong Ji* 西山先生真文忠公文集 [Selected Works of Zhen Dexiu]. Collected in Collectanea of the Four Categories, 1st ed.

Zheng, Juzhong 郑居中, et al. 1990. *Zhenghe Wuli Xin Yi* 政和五礼新仪 [The New Rules of Etiquette Issued in the Zhenghe Period]. Collected in Complete Library in the Four Branches of Literature. Shanghai: Shanghai Chinese Classics Publishing House.

Zhongguo Yunhe Kaifashi 中国运河开发史 [A Chinese History on Canal Development]. 2008. Edited by Chen Qiaoyi. Beijing: Zhonghua Book Company.

Zhou, Daguan 周达观. 1981. *Zhenla Fengshi Ji Jiaozhu* 真腊风土记校注 [Customs of Cambodia Collated and Annotated Version]. Collated by Xia Ding. Beijing: Zhonghua Book Company.

Zhou, Dashao 周大韶, et al. 1990. *Sanwu Shui Kao* 三吴水考 [Hydrological Records of Sanwu]. Collected in Complete Library in the Four Branches of Literature. Shanghai: Shanghai Chinese Classics Publishing House.

Zhou, Feng 周峰. 2008. "Jindai De Zaochuan Yu Shuizhan 金代的造船与水战 [Shipbuilding and Naval Warfare of the Jin Kingdom]. *Museum Research* 1.

Zhou, Shide 周世德. 1989. "Zhongguo Guchuan Jiangxi Kaolue 中国古船桨系考略 [A Brief Textual Research on the System of the Oars of Ancient Chinese Boats]". *Studies in the History of Natural Sciences* 2.

Zhu, Jianjun 朱建君. 2007. "Cong Haishen Xinyang Zhongguo Gudai De Haiyang Guannian 从海神信仰看中国古代的海洋观念 [On Ancient Chinese Ocean Conception from the Perspective of Sea-god/goddess]". *Worship, Qilu Journal* 3.

Zhu, Jinsheng 朱金升. 1978. "Hebei Cixian Nankaihecun Yuandai Muchuan Fajue Jianbao 河北磁县南开河村元代木船发掘简报 [A Briefing on the Excavation of Wooden Boats of the Yuan Dynasty at Nankaihe Village of Cixian County in Hebei]". *Archaeology* 6.

Zhu, Shengfei 朱胜非. 1990. *Gan Zhu Ji* 绀珠集 [Excerpts of Masterpieces]. Collected in Complete Library in the Four Branches of Literature. Shanghai: Shanghai Chinese Classics Publishing House.

Zhu, Yu 朱彧. 2008. *Pingzhou Ketan* 萍洲可谈 [Reflections about Pingzhou]. Sorted by Li Guoqiang. Collected in Complete Song Notes. Elephant Press.

Zhuzi Yu Lei. 朱子语类. [The Analects of Zhuzi]. 2002. Edited by Li Jingde. Punctuated and collated by Zheng Ming. Shanghai: Shanghai Chinese Classics Publishing House. Hefei: Anhui Education Publishing House.

SPRINGER NATURE

GPSR Compliance

The European Union's (EU) General Product Safety Regulation (GPSR) is a set of rules that requires consumer products to be safe and our obligations to ensure this.

If you have any concerns about our products, you can contact us on ProductSafety@springernature.com

In case Publisher is established outside the EU, the EU authorized representative is:

Springer Nature Customer Service Center GmbH
Europaplatz 3
69115 Heidelberg, Germany

The manufacturer's authorised representative in the EU is Springer Nature Customer Service Centre GmbH, Europaplatz 3, 69115 Heidelberg, Germany. If you have any concerns regarding our products, please contact ProductSafety@springernature.com

Printed and bound by CPI Group (UK) Ltd, Croydon, CR0 4YY
01/10/2026
02225897-0018